HUM 300

HISTORY AND METHODS OF SCIENCE

2009 Custom Edition

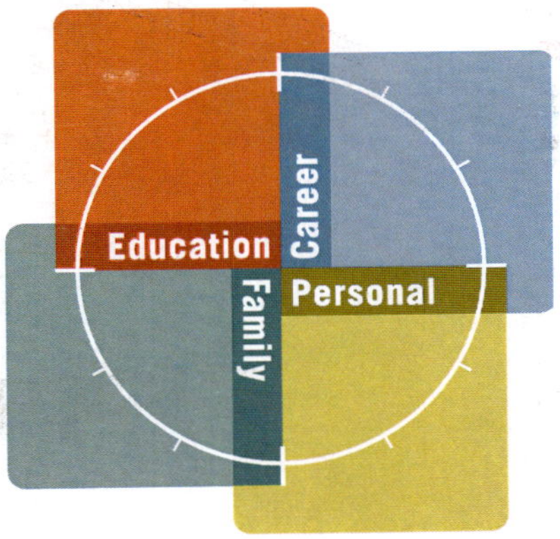

Taken from: The Sciences: An Integrated Approach, Fifth Edition James Trefil and Robert Hazen

STRAYER UNIVERSITY

WILEY
CUSTOM SERVICES

HUM 300: HISTORY AND METHODS OF SCIENCE
2009 Custom Edition

To order books or for customer service, please call 1(800)-CALL-WILEY (225-5945).

Printed in the United States of America.

ISBN 978-0-470-07240-0

Printed and bound by J&M Reproducion Corp.

10 9 8 7 6 5 4 3 2 1

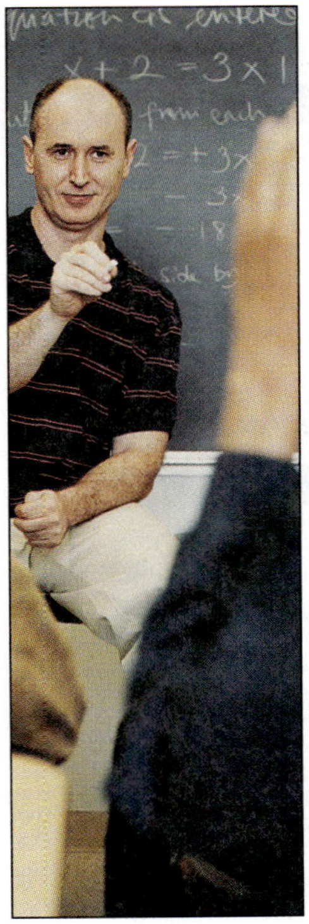

The first person to invent a car that runs on water…

… may be sitting right in your classroom! Every one of your students has the potential to make a difference. And realizing that potential starts right here, in your course.

WILEY PLUS

When students succeed in your course—when they stay on-task and make the breakthrough that turns confusion into confidence—they are empowered to realize the possibilities for greatness that lie within each of them. We know your goal is to create an environment where students reach their full potential and experience the exhilaration of academic success that will last them a lifetime. *WileyPLUS* can help you reach that goal.

Wiley**PLUS** is an online suite of resources—including the complete text—that will help your students:

- come to class better prepared for your lectures
- get immediate feedback and context-sensitive help on assignments and quizzes
- track their progress throughout the course

"I just wanted to say how much this program helped me in studying… I was able to actually see my mistakes and correct them. … I really think that other students should have the chance to use *WileyPLUS*."

Ashlee Krisko, *Oakland University*

---

www.wiley.com/college/wileyplus

80% of students surveyed said it improved their understanding of the material.*

TO THE INSTRUCTOR

WileyPLUS is built around the activities you perform

Prepare & Present

Create outstanding class presentations using a wealth of resources, such as PowerPoint™ slides, image galleries, interactive simulations, and more. Plus you can easily upload any materials you have created into your course, and combine them with the resources Wiley provides you with.

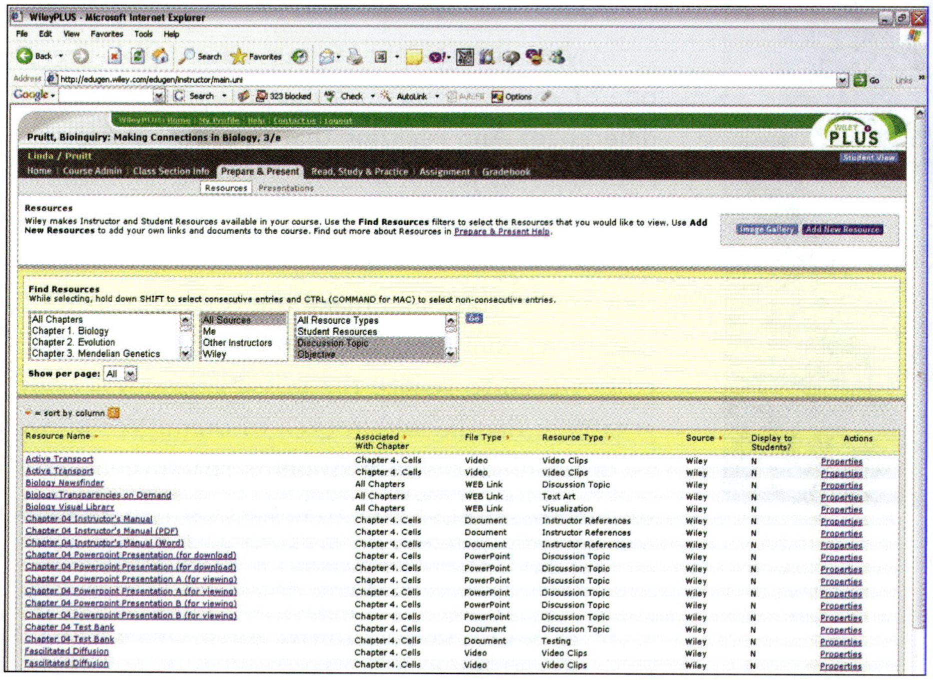

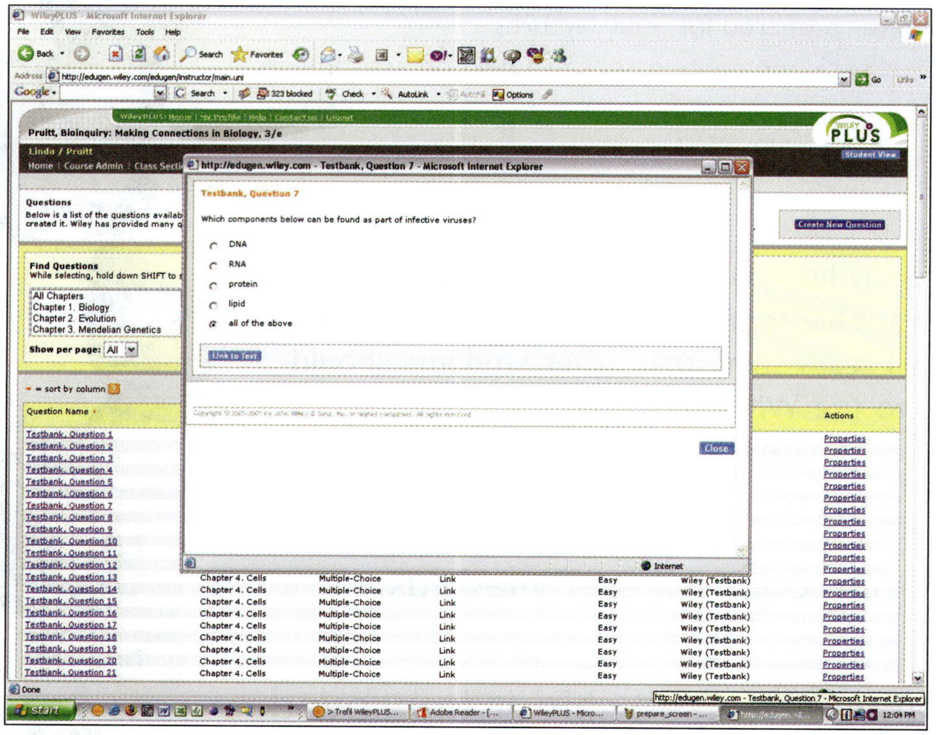

Create Assignments

Automate the assigning and grading of homework or quizzes by using the provided question banks, or by writing your own. Student results will be automatically graded and recorded in your gradebook. *WileyPLUS* also links homework problems to relevant sections of the online text, hints, or solutions— context-sensitive help where students need it most!

*Based on a spring 2005 survey of 972 student users of *WileyPLUS*

in your class each day. With Wiley**PLUS** you can:

Track Student Progress

Keep track of your students' progress via an instructor's gradebook, which allows you to analyze individual and overall class results. This gives you an accurate and realistic assessment of your students' progress and level of understanding.

Now Available with WebCT and Blackboard!

Now you can seamlessly integrate all of the rich content and resources available with *WileyPLUS* with the power and convenience of your WebCT or BlackBoard course. You and your students get the best of both worlds with single sign-on, an integrated gradebook, list of assignments and roster, and more. If your campus is using another course management system, contact your local Wiley Representative.

WebCT

Bb Blackboard

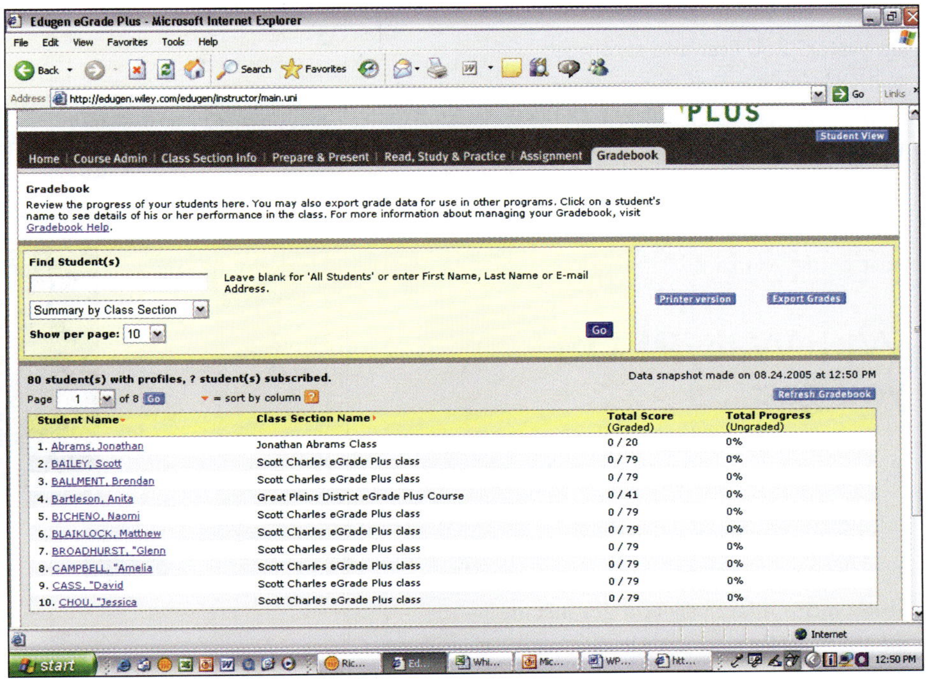

"I studied more for this class than I would have without *WileyPLUS*."

Melissa Lawler, *Western Washington Univ.*

For more information on what *WileyPLUS* can do to help your students reach their potential, please visit

www.wiley.com/college/wileyplus

76% of students surveyed said it made them better prepared for tests. *

TO THE STUDENT

You have the potential to make a difference!

Will you be the first person to land on Mars? Will you invent a car that runs on water? But, first and foremost, will you get through this course?

WileyPLUS is a powerful online system packed with features to help you make the most of your potential, and get the best grade you can!

With WileyPLUS you get:

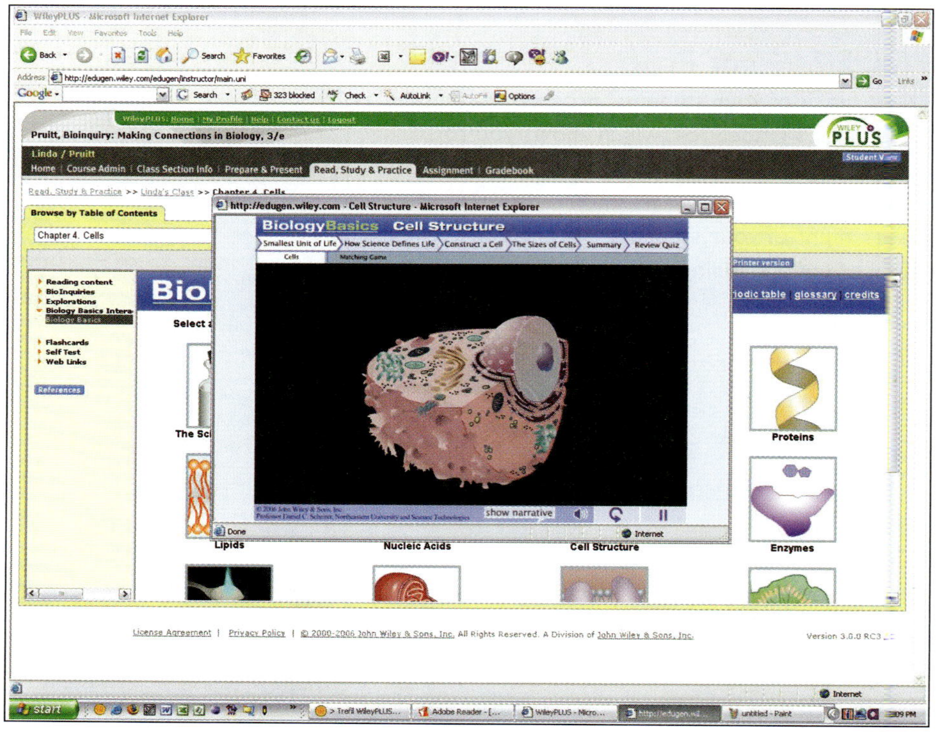

A complete online version of your text and other study resources

Study more effectively and get instant feedback when you practice on your own. Resources like self-assessment quizzes, tutorials, and animations bring the subject matter to life, and help you master the material.

Problem-solving help, instant grading, and feedback on your homework and quizzes

You can keep all of your assigned work in one location, making it easy for you to stay on task. Plus, many homework problems contain direct links to the relevant portion of your text to help you deal with problem-solving obstacles at the moment they come up.

The ability to track your progress and grades throughout the term.

A personal gradebook allows you to monitor your results from past assignments at any time. You'll always know exactly where you stand.

If your instructor uses *WileyPLUS*, you will receive a URL for your class. If not, your instructor can get more information about *WileyPLUS* by visiting www.wiley.com/college/wileyplus

"It has been a great help, and I believe it has helped me to achieve a better grade."

Michael Morris, *Columbia Basin College*

69% of students surveyed said it helped them get a better grade.*

WILEY PLUS

BICENTENNIAL 1807 WILEY 2007 BICENTENNIAL

THE WILEY BICENTENNIAL–KNOWLEDGE FOR GENERATIONS

Each generation has its unique needs and aspirations. When Charles Wiley first opened his small printing shop in lower Manhattan in 1807, it was a generation of boundless potential searching for an identity. And we were there, helping to define a new American literary tradition. Over half a century later, in the midst of the Second Industrial Revolution, it was a generation focused on building the future. Once again, we were there, supplying the critical scientific, technical, and engineering knowledge that helped frame the world. Throughout the 20th Century, and into the new millennium, nations began to reach out beyond their own borders and a new international community was born. Wiley was there, expanding its operations around the world to enable a global exchange of ideas, opinions, and know-how.

For 200 years, Wiley has been an integral part of each generation's journey, enabling the flow of information and understanding necessary to meet their needs and fulfill their aspirations. Today, bold new technologies are changing the way we live and learn. Wiley will be there, providing you the must-have knowledge you need to imagine new worlds, new possibilities, and new opportunities.

Generations come and go, but you can always count on Wiley to provide you the knowledge you need, when and where you need it!

William J. Pesce
PRESIDENT AND CHIEF EXECUTIVE OFFICER

Peter Booth Wiley
CHAIRMAN OF THE BOARD

The Sciences
An Integrated Approach

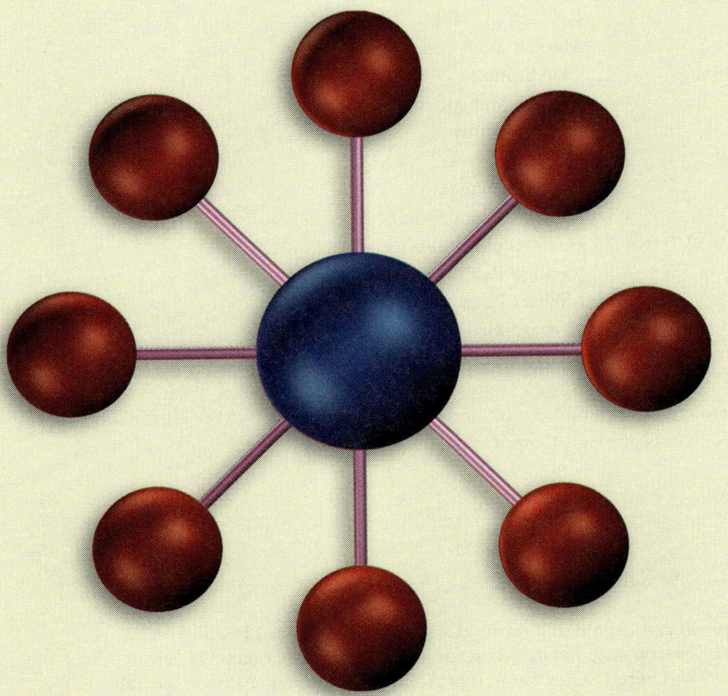

Fifth Edition

JAMES TREFIL
ROBERT M. HAZEN
George Mason University

John Wiley & Sons, Inc.

EXECUTIVE EDITOR	Rebecca H. Hope
ASSOCIATE EDITOR	Merillat Staat
EXECUTIVE MARKETING MANAGER	Clay Stone
SENIOR PRODUCTION EDITOR	Patricia McFadden
SENIOR DESIGNER	Kevin Murphy
SENIOR ILLUSTRATION EDITOR	Anna Melhorn
SENIOR PHOTO EDITOR	Hilary Newman
PHOTO RESEARCHER	Ramon Rivera-Moret
PRODUCTION MANAGEMENT SERVICES	Hermitage Publishing Services
EDITORIAL ASSISTANT	Stephen Reiss
INTERIOR DESIGN	Michael Jung
COVER DESIGN	Howard Grossman
COVER PHOTO	Raif Greiner/Look/Getty Images, Inc.

This book was set in Galliard by Hermitage Publishing Services and printed and bound by Von Hoffmann Corporation. The cover was printed by Von Hoffmann Corporation.

This book is printed on acid free paper.

To order books or for customer service please call 1-800-CALL WILEY (225-5945).

Library of Congress Cataloging in Publication Data

Trefil, James S., 1938–

The sciences : an integrated approach / James Trefil, Robert M. Hazen. 5th ed.

p. cm.

Includes bibliographical references and index.

ISBN 0-471-76992-4 (acid-free paper)

1. Science-Study and teaching (Higher)-United States. I. Hazen, Robert M., 1948. II. Title.

Q161.2T74 2004

500-dc21 2003041129

ISBN-13: 978-0-471-76992-7

ISBN-10: 0-471-76992-4

Printed in the United States of America

10 9 8 7 6 5

Preface

Scientific advances touch our lives every day. We benefit from new materials in the form of cosmetics, appliances, clothing, and sports equipment. We rely on new sources of energy and more efficient ways to use that energy for transportation, communication, heating, and lighting. We call upon science to find new ways to treat disease and to allow people to lead longer, healthier lives. Science represents our best hope in solving the many pressing problems related to a growing global population, limited resources, and sometimes our fragile environment.

In spite of the central role that science plays in modern life, most Americans are poorly equipped to deal with basic scientific principles and methods. Surveys routinely show that large numbers of Americans are unaware that Earth orbits Sun or that human beings and dinosaurs didn't live at the same time. At a time when molecular biology is making breakthrough discoveries almost daily, fewer than a quarter of Americans understand the term "DNA," and only about 10% understand the term "molecule." There can be little doubt that we are faced with a generation of students who complete their education without learning even the most basic concepts about science. They lack the critical knowledge to make informed personal and professional decisions regarding health, safety, resources, and the environment.

Science Education Today

Science education has always been a problem in the United States. As far back as 1983, a widely circulated report titled *A Nation at Risk* issued a stern warning that our system of science education was failing to produce enough scientists and engineers to drive our economy forward. And as recently as 2006, in a report by the National Academy of Sciences titled *A Gathering Storm*, the authors argued that in the years since 1983, not much had been done to rectify this situation.

In fact, we can define two problems with science education. The first is the aspect on which national reports tend to spend most of their time—the need to produce a technologically skilled workforce. For the relatively small number of students pursuing these sorts of careers, specialized courses are vital, as they must learn an appropriate vocabulary and develop skills in experimental method and mathematical manipulations to solve problems.

The second important task of university education, however, is to deal with the fact that most students are not on track to become scientists or engineers. For them, the kind of specialized courses taken by students who major in the sciences tends to divorce science from its familiar day-to-day context. All too often, these courses leave the university setting seeing science as difficult, uninteresting, and irrelevant.

Yet these students will live in a world increasingly dominated by science and technology. The Internet, stem cells, global warming, and cloning are just a few examples of the issues that these students will have to deal with as citizens. Considering how today's students will use science in their lives, it is easy to see that there is another problem with the way the subject is taught in our universities. Science rarely presents itself in neat, compartmentalized form in public discussions. Instead, specific problems arise, and these problems typically cut across the lines set up between science departments at universities. Take global warming as an example: it involves the mining of fossil fuels (geology), burning those fuels (chemistry), and the release of carbon dioxide into the atmosphere where it can affect Earth's heat balance (physics). As a result, there is the possibility that our climate may change (Earth sciences) with serious consequences for living things (biology, ecology).

It is clear that to equip students to deal with these sorts of issues they need to acquire a broad base in all branches of the sciences. The problem with most introductory science courses at the college level, even among those science courses specifically designed for nonscientists, is that they rarely integrate physics, astronomy, chemistry, Earth science, and biology. Such departmentally based courses cannot produce graduates who are broadly literate in science. Those students who take introductory geology learn nothing about lasers or nuclear reactions, while those who take physics courses for nonmajors remain uninformed about the underlying causes of earthquakes and volcanoes. Neither physics nor geology classes touch on such vital modern fields as genetics, environmental chemistry, space exploration, or materials science. Therefore, students would have to take courses in at least four departments to gain the basic overview of the sciences they will need to function as informed citizens.

Perhaps what is most disturbing is that few students, science majors or nonmajors, ever learn how the often arbitrary divisions of specialized knowledge fit into the overall sweep of the sciences. In short, traditional science curricula of most colleges and universities fail to provide the basic science education that is necessary to understand the many scientific and technological issues facing our society.

This situation is slowly changing. Since the preliminary edition of *The Sciences: An Integrated Approach* appeared in 1993, hundreds of colleges and universities have begun the process of instituting new integrated science courses as an option for undergraduates. In the process, we have had the opportunity to interact with hundreds of our colleagues across the country, as well as more than 3000 of our own students at George Mason University, and have received invaluable guidance in preparing this extensively revised edition.

The Need for a New Science Education

In the coming decades, the 1996 publication of the *National Science Education Standards* by the National Research Council may be seen as a pivotal event in American science education. The *Standards*, which represents the collective effort and consensus of more than 20,000 scientists, educators, administrators, and parents, offers a dramatically new vision of science education for all of America. The authors of this book have been part of a small team that put together the final version of the *Standards*, and thus have had a ring-side seat as the standards have been modified and adopted in states throughout the country.

The *National Science Education Standards* calls for reform in both the content and context of science education. The central goal of science education must be to give every student the ability to place important public issues such as the environment, energy, and medical advances in a scientific context.

A central emphasis throughout the *Standards* is the development of a student's understanding of the scientific process, as opposed to just the accumulation of scientific facts. Emphasis is placed on the role of experiments in probing nature and the importance of mathematics in describing its behavior. Rather than developing esoteric vocabulary and specialized knowledge, the *Standards* strives to empower students to read and appreciate popular accounts of major discoveries in physics, astronomy, chemistry, geology, and biology, as well as advances in medicine, information technology, and new materials. Students should develop an understanding that a few universal laws describe the behavior of our physical surroundings—laws that operate every day, in every action of our lives.

Achieving this kind of scientific proficiency requires a curriculum quite different from the traditional, departmentally based requirements for majors. Most societal issues concerning science and technology draw on a broad range of knowledge. For example, to understand the debate over nuclear waste disposal, one needs to know how nuclei decay to produce radiation (physics), how radioactive atoms interact with their environment (chemistry), how radioactive elements from waste can enter the biosphere (Earth science), and how the radiation will affect living things (biology). These scientific principles must be weighed along with other factors such as economics, energy demand, perceptions of risk, and demographics. Other important public issues, such as global warming, space research, alternative energy sources, and AIDS prevention, also depend on a spectrum of scientific concepts as well as other social concerns.

The Goals of This Book

This text, based on our course "Great Ideas in Science," which has been developed at George Mason University, is an attempt to respond to the future needs of today's students. Our approach recognizes that science forms a seamless web of knowledge about the universe. Our integrated course encompasses physics, chemistry, astronomy, Earth sciences, and biology, and emphasizes general principles and their application to real-world situations rather than esoteric detail.

Having set as our goal providing education for people who will not be scientists but who need some knowledge of science to function as citizens, we have to address another issue. There is no question that anyone who actually does science will be required to use high levels of mathematics to carry out his or her work. We would argue, however, that this same level of mathematics is not required by the average person confronting political issues. It has been our experience that many students come into our class with a fear of science that is matched only by their fear of mathematics. We would hope that these students will be able to conquer these fears sometime during their education, but we do not feel that it is appropriate to tackle both at once. In addition, it is our firm belief that any scientific concept at the citizen's level can be understood without mathematics – that most ideas in science are inherently simple and intuitive at their deepest level. For this reason, we have kept the mathematics in this book to a minimum. In this way, instructors who wish to make their courses more mathematically rigorous may do so, while those who wish to teach concepts will not have to skip large sections of the text.

There are two central features of *The Sciences: An Integrated Approach* that allow us to offer a text with the expressed goal of helping students achieve scientific literacy. These features are (1) organization around Great Ideas, and (2) an explicit integration of the sciences, starting with the first chapter.

Great Ideas

One of the best kept secrets in the world is this: the core ideas of the sciences are really quite simple. Furthermore, these core ideas form a framework for our understanding of the universe—they give our ideas structure and form. As we argue in the text, these Great Ideas represent a hierarchy in the sciences that transcend the boundaries of specific disciplines. The conservation of energy, for example, is part of the intellectual framework of sciences from astronomy to zoology.

By organizing our presentation around the central Great Ideas rather than around specific disciplines, students can deal with the universe as it presents itself to them, rather than with disciplinary divisions that have little meaning to the citizen, no matter how important they are to working scientists. The goal, of course, is to give the student the intellectual framework that will allow him or her to deal with the scientific aspects of problems that come into public debate.

No one can predict what the major subjects of public concern will be in twenty years' time—certainly no one twenty years ago would have guessed that we would be arguing about cloning today. What we can guarantee, however, is that whatever those future issues are, they will present themselves in relation to the Great Ideas.

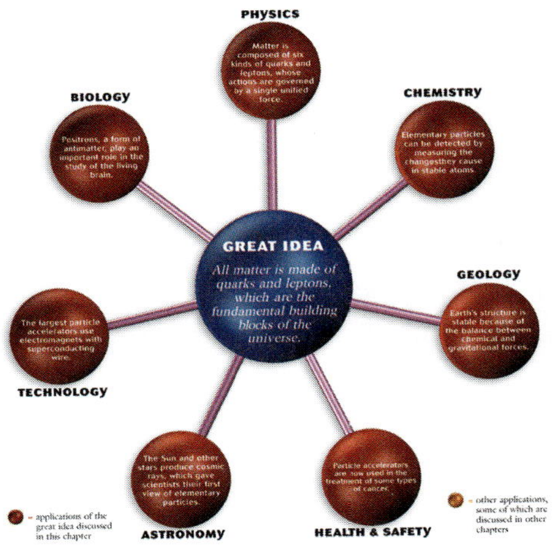

Integration

Every chapter in this book opens with a list of how the concepts to be discussed relate to every area of science. In the chapters themselves, we use the Special Features described below to bring in aspects of science from other areas. Thus, for example, in the chapter on electricity (normally thought of as the domain of physics) we discuss the workings of the nerve cell, while in the chapter on electromagnetic radiation we talk about the design of the human eye and its connection to the evolution of life on Earth.

For us, integration is more than a cosmetic feature—it goes to the very heart of science. The universe presents itself to us as a seamless web of interacting phenomena and our understanding of science should do the same.

The Organization of *The Sciences*

As authors of substantial segments of the *Standards*, we continue to revise *The Sciences: An Integrated Approach* with the *Standards'* mandate in mind. We have increased the emphasis on the scientific process, reorganized and added text to elucidate the historical significance of key principles, and underscored the integrated nature of scientific knowledge and its application to everyday experience.

We were, in fact, the first to adopt a distinctive and innovative approach to science education based on the principle that general science courses are a key to a balanced and effective college-level science education for nonmajors and future elementary and high school teachers, and a broadening experience for science majors. We organize the text around a series of 25 scientific concepts. The most basic principle, the starting point of all science, is the idea that the universe can be studied by observation and experiment (**Chapter 1**). A surprising number of students, even science majors, have no clear idea of how this central concept sets science apart from religion, philosophy, and the arts as a way to understand our place in the cosmos.

Once students understand the nature of science and its practice, they can appreciate some of the basic principles shared by all sciences: Newton's laws governing force and motion (**Chapter 2**); the laws of thermodynamics that govern energy and entropy (**Chapters 3 and 4**); the equivalence of electricity and magnetism (**Chapters 5 and 6**); and the atomic structure of all matter (**Chapters 8–11**). These concepts apply to everyday life explaining, for example, the compelling reasons for wearing seat belts, the circulation of the blood, the dynamics of a pot of soup, the regulation of public airwaves, and the rationale for dieting. In one form or another, all of these ideas appear in virtually every elementary science textbook, but often in abstract form. As educators, we must strive to make them part of every student's day-to-day experience. An optional chapter on the theory of relativity (**Chapter 7**) examines the consequences of a universe in which all observers discern the same laws of nature.

Having established these general principles, we go on to examine specific natural systems such as atoms, Earth, or living things. The realm of the nucleus (**Chapter 12**) and subatomic particles (**Chapter 13**), for example, must follow the basic rules governing all matter and energy.

In sections on astronomy and cosmology (**Chapters 14–16**), students learn that stars and planets form and move as predicted by Newton's laws, that stars eventually burn up according to the laws of thermodynamics, that nuclear reactions fuel stars by the conversion of mass into energy, and that stars produce light as a consequence of electromagnetism.

Plate tectonics (**Chapter 17**) and the cycles of rocks, water, and the atmosphere (**Chapter 18,** substantially revised in this edition), unify the Earth sciences. The laws of thermodynamics, which decree that no feature on Earth's surface is permanent, can be used to explain geological time, gradualism, and the causes of earthquakes and volcanoes. The fact that matter is composed of atoms tells us that individual atoms in

Earth, for example in a grain of sand or a student's most recent breath, have been recycling for billions of years.

Living things (**Chapters 19–25**) are arguably the most complex systems that scientists attempt to understand. We identify seven basic principles that apply to all living systems: interdependent collections of living things (ecosystems) recycle matter while energy flows through them; living things use many strategies to maintain and reproduce life; all living things obey the laws of chemistry and physics; all living things incorporate a few simple molecular building blocks; all living things are made of cells; all living things use the same genetic code; and all living things evolved by natural selection.

The section covering living things has been extensively revised. **Chapter 19** includes new information on ecosystems and their importance to the environment. One chapter (**20**) covers the organization and characteristics of living things. A revised chapter on biotechnology (**24**) explores several recent advances in our molecular understanding of life that helps to cure diseases and to better the human condition. We end the book with a discussion of evolution (**25**) that emphasizes observational evidence first. To improve the book's integration, we have also added more biological coverage to the early chapters on basic scientific principles.

The text has been designed so that four chapters—relativity (**7**), quantum mechanics (**9**), particle physics (**13**), and cosmology (**15**)—may be skipped without loss of continuity.

Major Changes in the Fifth Edition

The fifth edition of *The Sciences* is largely updated to provide the most current scientific coverage and the most useful pedagogical elements to students taking integrated science courses. To reach this goal, numerous revisions and additions were made including completely revised Science News features to reflect only the most recent discoveries and innovations. Additionally, each chapter has new end-of–chapter questions to address new material and to provide students with better study tools.

Some of the most major changes to this edition are:

Chapter 1	**Science: A Way of Knowing,** contains new material on measurements and units of measurement as well as significant changes to the section on hypotheses and theories.
Chapter 3	**Energy,** includes an expanded discussion on heat and thermal energy to include more about atoms and molecules. Additionally, there is a new section entitled "The United States and Its Energy Future."
Chapter 7	**Relativity,** Relativity, features new information on predicting and testing the theory of relativity.
Chapter 9	**Quantum Mechanics,** incorporates a new section on quantum entanglements.
Chapter 10	**Atoms in Combination,** attempts to clarify definitions and connections with a new opening section on electron shells, the periodic table, and chemical bonding.
Chapter 11	**Properties of Materials,** contains a new section on field-effect transistors..
Chapter 13	**The Ultimate Structure of Matter,** includes added material on string theory and new accelerators.
Chapter 14	**The Stars,** contains the updated list of orbiting observatories as well as a major revision of the section on black holes.
Chapter 15	**Cosmology,** now discusses the discovery and implications of dark energy.

Chapter 16 **Earth and Other Planets,** is reorganized to reflect numerous solar system objects and the NASA missions to study them. Two new sections are included in this chapter: "The Formation of the Solar System" and "Exploring the Solar System." Additional new material on "Xena" the "tenth planet" has also been added.

Chapter 19 **Ecology, Ecosystems, and the Environment,** has been updated with the most recent global warming data.

Chapter 20 **Strategies of Life,** incorporates Carl Woese's delineation of the three domains of life to more accurately reflect modern thinking on the subject.

Chapter 21 **The Living Cell,** formerly Chapter 22, has been moved forward in order to make the discussion of cells and their structure a more natural fit before delving into **Chapter 22**, **The Molecules of Life.**

Chapter 23 **Classical and Modern Genetics,** expands the discussion of the Human Genome Project, AIDS, embryonic development, and stem cells.

Chapter 24 **The New Science of Life,** reflects this rapidly evolving area of science with new coverage of genetic engineering, DNA fingerprinting, cloning, stem cells, and cancer.

Chapter 25 **Evolution,** includes significantly updated and enhanced coverage on the origin of life (especially chemical evolution), creationism and intelligent design, and hominid evolution.

Additional changes include:

As the Internet continues to grow more useful in an educational setting, Weblinks for each chapter are included on the book's website (www.wiley.com/college/trefil) to provide students with additional, current resources. Also available with the fifth edition is Wiley PLUS, a course management system that seamlessly integrates both text and media components. You can read more about Wiley PLUS in the **Supplements** section later in this preface or on the Wiley PLUS website (www.wiley.com/college/wileyplus).

We are all too familiar with the challenges associated with engaging the non-science major in these course areas, and with the growing importance of establishing a more active and visual approach to teaching. With this knowledge in mind, we are proud to introduce a significantly expanded support package to accompany The Sciences, Fifth Edition. The enhanced supplements package for the fifth edition, based on extensive suggestions and feedback from text adopters and reviewers, includes:

- An expanded Instructor's Manual, now with a strong emphasis on providing unique, tested in-class activities and teaching strategies.
- A thoroughly revised Test Bank that now reflects an increased emphasis on conceptual and critical thinking items. This Test Bank is available in several formats including a computerized test generator as well as in Microsoft Word and RTF.
- New to this edition are ready-made PowerPoint presentations for each chapter that incorporate key illustrations and text art and maintain an emphasis on visual representation rather than regurgitating text material in a bulleted format (as so many ready-made PowerPoint presentations tend to do).
- Also new to this edition, **all illustrations, tables, and photographs** are available in both JPG and pre-formatted PowerPoint presentations for easy incorporation into classroom lectures, lecture outlines or other instructor-customized materials. These files are supplied on an **Instructor's Resource CD-ROM**.
- Text illustrations in JPG format are also available for download from the text's book companion site (www.wiley.com/college/trefil).
- Also available on the **Instructor's Resource CD-ROM**, as well as on the student's book companion site, are a variety of **flash animations** designed to help instructors illustrate and students visualize key concepts covered in the text.

A more detailed list of all support materials can be found later in this preface, in the **Supplements** section.

Special Features

In an effort to aid student learning and underscore the integration of the sciences, we have attempted to relate scientific principles to each student's everyday life. To this end, we have incorporated several distinctive features throughout the book.

Great Ideas •

Each chapter begins with a statement of a great unifying idea or theme in science, so that students immediately grasp the chief concept of that chapter. These statements are not intended to be recited or memorized, but rather to provide a framework for placing everyday experiences into a broad context.

Great Ideas Across the Sciences •

Our theme of integration is reinforced with a radiating diagram that appears at the beginning of every chapter. The diagram ties together some of the examples discussed in the text and shows how the Great Idea has been applied to different branches of science and to everyday life.

Science Through the Day

Each chapter begins with a "Science Through the Day" section in which we tie the chapter's main theme to common experiences such as eating, driving a car, or sun tanning. These 25 vignettes, taken in sequence, tell the story of one student's day from sunrise, through an excursion to the beach, and then to the day's end. In this way we emphasize that all the great ideas of science are constantly part of our lives.

The Science of Life •

To help show the interdisciplinary nature of the many concepts we introduce, we have included sections on living things in most chapters. Thus, while chapters emphasizing principles specifically related to life are at the end of the book, biological examples appear throughout.

Science in the Making •

These historical episodes trace the progress of scientific discovery and portray the lives of some of the central figures in science. In these episodes, we have tried to illustrate the process of science, examine the interplay of science and society, and reveal the role of serendipity in scientific discovery.

The Ongoing Process of Science •

Science is a never-ending process of asking questions and seeking answers. In these features, we examine some of the most exciting questions currently being addressed by scientists.

Stop and Think!

At various points in each chapter we ask students to pause and think about the implications of a scientific discovery or principle.

TECHNOLOGY •

The application of scientific ideas to commerce, industry, and other modern technological concerns is perhaps the most immediate way in which students encounter science. In most chapters, we include examples of these technologies such as petroleum refining, microwave ovens, and nuclear medicine.

Science News

Scientific breakthroughs are happening every day. In many chapters we include summaries of recent articles taken from the weekly periodical *Science News*. These sections are intended to give students a better understanding of new discoveries that were reported in the popular press.

MATHEMATICAL EQUATIONS AND WORKED EXAMPLES

Unlike the content of many science texts, formulas and mathematical derivations play a subsidiary role in our treatment of the subject matter. We rely much more on real-world experiences and on everyday vocabulary. We believe that every student should understand the role of mathematics in science. Therefore, in many chapters, we have included a few key equations and the appropriate worked examples. *Whenever an equation is introduced, it is presented in three steps*: first as an English sentence, second as a word equation, and finally in its traditional symbolic form. In this way, students can focus on the meaning rather than the abstraction of the mathematics. We also include an appendix on English and SI units.

SCIENCE BY THE NUMBERS •

We also think that students should understand the importance of simple mathematical calculations in areas of magnitude. Thus we have incorporated many nontraditional calculations. These include, for example, how much solid waste is generated in the United States, how long it would take to erode a mountain, and how many people were required to build Stonehenge.

Thinking More About

Each chapter ends with a section that addresses a social or philosophical issue tied to science such as federal funding of the sciences, nuclear waste disposal, the Human Genome Project, and the priorities in medical research,

OTHER FEATURES

Key Words. Most science texts suffer from too complex a vocabulary. We have tried to avoid unnecessary jargon. Because the scientifically literate student must be familiar with many words and concepts that appear regularly in newspaper articles or other material for general readers, each chapter contains key words for the student that appear in boldface type. These words are also listed at the end of each chapter. For example, in **Chapter 12** on nuclear physics, key words include proton, neutron, isotope, radioactivity, half-life, radiometric dating, fission, fusion, and nuclear reactor. These are all terms that are likely to appear in a newspaper. In the back of the book you will find a glossary of all the key words.

There are many other scientific terms that are more specialized but also important. We have highlighted these terms in *italics*. We strongly recommend that students learn the meaning and context of all the key words but not be expected to memorize the words that appear in italics. We encourage all adopters of this text to provide their own lists of key words and other terms, both ones we might have omitted and ones they feel should be eliminated from our list.

Questions. We feature four levels of end-of-chapter questions. "Review Questions" test important factual information covered in the text and are provided to emphasize key points. Many of the Review Questions have been substantially rewritten for this edition. "Discussion Questions" are also based on material in the text, but they also examine student comprehension and explore the application and analysis of the scientific concepts. "Problems" are quantitative questions that require students to use mathematical operations, typically those introduced in worked examples or "Science by the Numbers." Finally, "Investigations" require additional research outside the classroom. Each instructor should decide which level of questions is most appropriate for his or her students. We welcome suggestions for additional questions which we will add to the next edition of this text.

Illustrations. Students come to any science class with years of experience dealing with the physical universe. Everyday life provides an invaluable science laboratory. This includes the physics of sports, the chemistry of cooking, and the biology of just being alive. This book has been extensively illustrated with color images in an effort to help amplify the key ideas and principles. All the diagrams and graphs have been designed for maximum clarity and impact.

Supplements

FOR THE STUDENT

Book Companion Site (**www.wiley.com/college/trefil**). Student Resources on the book companion site include web links related to the topics within the text chapters, self-tests students can use to prepare for exams, and flash cards.

The Study Guide, written by Anthony Gaudin of Ivy Tech Community College, contains many elements to help a student be successful. These elements include chapter reviews, learning objectives, key chapter concepts, and key concept charts. Because of the importance of the individuals who made important scientific discoveries, also included is an exposition of these key individuals that link the scientists with their findings. Since many scientific concepts are linked to math, key formulas and equations are also provided. Self-tests and crossword quizzes allow students to test their knowledge.

FOR THE INSTRUCTOR

Instructor's Resource CD-ROM. Provides all instructor support materials for *The Sciences, 5th Edition* in one convenient and portable tool. The IRCD includes:

Test Bank by Richard Jones, Texas Woman's University and Cynthia Ledbetter, University of Texas at Dallas, contains over 50 multiple choice and essay questions per chapter to test various levels of understanding. The test bank is included on the Instructor's Resource CD-ROM in two formats: MS Word Files and a Computerized Test Bank. The easy-to-use test-generation program fully supports graphics, print tests, student answer sheets, and answer keys. The software's advanced features allow you to create an exam to your exact specifications.

Instructor's Manual by Bambi Bailey, Midwestern State University, and prepared by Sandy Buczynski, San Diego University, contains teaching suggestions, lecture notes, answers to problems from the textbook, additional problems, and over 70 creative ideas for in-class activities.

All Line Art and Photos from *The Sciences, 5th Edition,* in jpeg files and PowerPoint format.

PowerPoint Presentations by Denice Robertson, Northern Kentucky University are tailored to *The Sciences, Fifth Edition's* topical coverage and learning objectives. These presentations are designed to convey key text concepts and are illustrated by embedded text art. An effort has been made to reduce the number of words on each slide and to increase the use of visuals to illustrate concepts.

Animations. Key concepts covered in the text are illustrated using flash animation, specifically designed for use in classroom presentations.

Book Companion Site (**www.wiley.com/college/trefil**). Instructor Resources on the book companion site include a Visual Library containing all of the line illustrations in the textbook in jpeg format; the Instructor's Manual; the Test Bank; PowerPoint Presentations tailored to each chapter of *The Sciences, Fifth Edition*; and select flash animations for use in classroom presentations. Instructor Resources are password protected.

Wiley PLUS

Provides an integrated suite of teaching and learning resources, including an online version of the text, in one easy-to-use website. Organized around the essential activities you perform in class, Wiley Plus helps you:

Prepare and Present. Create class presentations using a wealth of Wiley-provided resources, including an online version of the textbook, PowerPoint slides, animations, and more—making your preparation time more efficient. You may easily adapt, customize, and add to this content to meet the needs of your course.

Create Assignments. Automate the assigning and grading of homework or quizzes by using Wiley-provided question banks or by writing your own. Student results will be automatically graded and recorded in your gradebook. Wiley Plus can link homework problems to the relevant section of the online text, providing students with context-sensitive help.

Track Student Progress. Keep track of your students' progress via an instructor's gradebook, which allows you to analyze individual and overall class results to determine their progress and level of understanding.

Administer Your Course. Wiley Plus can easily be integrated with other course management systems, gradebooks, or other resources you are using in your class, providing you with the flexibility to build your course in your own way.

Acknowledgments

The development of this text has benefited immensely from the help and advice of numerous people. For the Fifth Edition we would particularly like to thank Edward Archer who provided invaluable assistance in reviewing and revising our end-of-chapter questions.

STUDENT INVOLVEMENT

Students in our "Great Ideas in Science" course at George Mason University have played a central role in designing this text. Approximately 3000 students, the majority of whom were nonscience majors, have enrolled in the course over the past 15 years. They represent a diverse cross section of American students: more than half were women, and many minority, foreign-born, and adult learners were enrolled. Their candid assessments of course content and objectives, as well as their constructive suggestions for improvements, have helped shape our text.

FACULTY INPUT

We are also grateful to members of the Core Science Course Committee at George Mason University including Richard Diecchio (Earth Systems Science), Don Kelso and Harold Morowitz (Biology), Minos Kafatos and Jean Toth-Allen (Physics), and Suzanne Slayden (Chemistry), who helped design many aspects of this treatment.

We thank the many teachers across the country who are developing integrated science courses. Their letters to us and responses to our publisher's survey inspired us to write this text. In particular we would like to thank Michael Sable of The Massachusetts College for the Liberal Arts, whose long and thoughtful letter after the first edition was a tremendous help.

We especially thank the professors who used and class-tested the preliminary edition, sharing with us the responses of their students and their own analyses. Their classroom experience continues to help us shape the book.

REVIEWERS OF THE FIFTH EDITION

Marian Elaine Melby Aanerud
University of Michigan – Flint

Bambi L. Bailey
Midwestern State University

Gloria Brown Right
Monmouth University

Randy Criss
Saint Leo University

Jerry Easdon
College of the Ozarks

Jacek K. Furdyna
University of Notre Dame

Harold A. Geller
George Mason University

William Good
Suffolk University

Richard C. Jones
Texas Woman's University

Mark E. Mattson
James Madison University

Jeffrey J. Miller
The Metropolitan State College of Denver

Ashraf Mongroo
New York City College of Technology of CUNY

Dr. Kanchana Mudalige
Monmouth University

E. Herbert Newman
Coastal Carolina University

Steven Perry
Monroe Community College

Barbara T. Reagor
Monmouth University

Denice Robertson
Northern Kentucky University

Susan Rolke
Franklin Pierce College

Stephen Taber
Saginaw Valley State University

Barry J. Vroeginday
Devry University

Laura A. Whitlock
Louisiana State University — Shreveport

Steven Wiles
Montana State University — Billings

REVIWERS OF EARLIER EDITIONS

C. Brannon Andersen
Furman University

Felicia Barbieri
Gwynedd-Mercy College

Debra J. Barnes
Contra Costa College

Sheila K. Bennett
University of Maine at Augusta

Doug Bingham
West Texas State University

Tarun Biswas
State University of New York at New Paltz

Larry Blair
Berea College

Susan Bornstein-Forst
Marian College

J.-Cl. De Bremaeker
Rice University

Linda Brown
Gainesville College

Virginia R. Bryan
Southern Illinois University

Joe C. Burnell
University of Indianapolis

Lauretta Bushar
Beaver College

W. Barkley Butler
Indiana University of Pennsylvania

George Cassiday
University of Utah

Tim Champion
Johnson C. Smith College

Kailash Chandra
Savannah State University

Ben B. Chastain
Samford University

LuAnne Clark
Lansing Community College

John Cobley
University of San Francisco

Stan Cohn
DePaul University

Marjorie Collier
St. Peter's College

Rod Cranson
Lansing Community College

Phillip D. Creighton
Salisbury State University

Randy Criss
University of Saint Leo

Whitman Cross II
Southern Museum of Flight

John Cruzan
Geneva College

E. Alan Dean
University of Texas at El Paso

Richard Deslippe
Texas Tech University

David Dimattio
St. Bonaventure University

Normand A. Dion
Franklin Pierce College

Robert T. Downs
University of Arizona

David Emigh
Quinebaug Valley Community College

Raymond L. Ethington
University of Missouri at Columbia

William Faissler
Northeastern University

Michael F. Farona
University of North Carolina at Greensboro

Paul Fishbane
University of Virginia

Maura Flannery
St. John's University

John Freeman
Rice University

William Fyfe
University of Western Ontario

Robert Gannon
Dowling College

Anthony J. Gaudin
Ivey Tech State College

Biswa Ghosh
Hudson County College
Marvin Goldberg
Syracuse University
Ben Golden
Kennesaw State University
John Graham
Carnegie Institution of Washington
James Grant
St. Peter's College
Benjamin Grinstein
University of California-San Diego
Annette Halpern
California State University at Bakersfield
J. Howard Hargis
Auburn University
David Hedgepeth
Valdosta State University
Michael Held
St Peter's College
Dennis Hibbert
North Seattle Community College
David Hickey
Lansing Community College
Jim Holler
University of Kentucky
Patricia M. Hughey
Lansing Community College
Louis Irwin
University of Texas at El Paso
Anthony Jacob
University of Wisconsin, Madison
Gerry Karp
University of Florida, Gainesville, Emeritus
Robert Kearney
University of Idaho
William Keller
St. Petersburg Junior College
Patricia Kenyon
City College of New York
Larry Kodosky
Oakland Community College
Roger Koeppe
Oklahoma State University
Diona Koerner
Marymount College
Mary H. Korte
Concordia University Wisconsin
Hallie M. Krider
University of Connecticut
Albert Kudo
University of New Mexico
Charles J. Kunert
Concordia College
Kathleen H. Lavoie
University of Michigan-Flint
Joseph E. Ledbetter
Contra Costa College
Jeffrey A. Lee
Texas Tech University
Gary Lewis
Kennesaw State University
Robley J. Light
Florida State University
Robert W. Lind
University of Wisconsin-Plattesville
Sam LittlePage
University of Findlay
Becky Lovato
Lansing Community College
Bruce MacLaren
Eastern Kentucky University
Lynn Maelia
Mount Saint Mary College
Kingshuk Majumdar
Berea College
David E. Marx
University of Scranton
Leigh Mazany
Dalhousie University
Donald Miller
University of Michigan at Dearborn
Jeffrey J. Miller
Metropolitan State College of Denver
Scott Mohr
Boston University
Harold Morowitz
George Mason University
Kevin Morris
Carthage College
Bjorn Mysen
Geophysical Laboratory
Lynn Narasimhan
DePaul University
Michael J. Neilson
University of Alabama
Charlotte Ovechka
University of St. Thomas
Reno Parker
Montana State University
Barry Perlmutter
New Jersey City University
Richard Petriello
St. Peter's College
Patrick Pfaffle
Carthage College
Scott Pinkus
New Jersey City University
Ervin Poduska
Kirkwood Community College
Harry Pylypiw
Quinnipiac University
Joseph Ruchlin
Lehman College of CUNY
Joaquin Ruiz
University of Arizona
Selwyn Sacks
Carnegie Institution of Washington
Rick Saprano
Contra Costa College
Frederick D. Shannon
Houghton College
Paul Simony
Jacksonville University
Gail Steehler
Roanoke College
Howard J. Stein
Grand Valley State University
Herbert H. Stewart
Florida Atlantic University
Neal Sumerlin
Lychburg College
Timothy D. Swindle
University of Arizona
Francis Tam
Frostburg State University
John S. Thompson
Texas A&M University at Kingsville
John Truedson
Bemidji State University
Andrew Wallace
Angelo State University
Barbara E. Warkentine
Lehman College of CUNY
Steven Warren
Andrews University
David Wong
University of California at San Diego
David P. Wright
St. Edward's University
Jim Yoder
Hesston College

PUBLISHER SUPPORT

Finally, as in the previous editions, we gratefully acknowledge the dedicated people at John Wiley and Sons who originally proposed this textbook and have helped us in developing every aspect of its planning and production for all five editions. We thank our Executive Editor, Rebecca Hope for her support and innovative ideas. Associate Editor Merillat Staat managed the project and the supplements package, while Stephen Reiss served with skill and professionalism as editorial assistant. Executive Marketing Manager Clay Stone championed the book in his marketing and sales efforts.

We also thank the production team of the fifth edition. The project was ably managed by Patricia McFadden and meticulously produced by Hermitage Publishing Services who dealt with the countless technical details associated with an integrated science book. Kevin Murphy designed the handsome text while Howard Grossman designed the cover. Hilary Newman and Ramon Rivera-Moret researched the numerous new photos for the Fifth Edition. Anna Melhorn coordinated the development of our new illustrations. To all the staff at John Wiley, we owe a great debt for their enthusiastic support, constant encouragement, and sincere dedication to science education reform.

Contents

23 Classical and Modern Genetics: Why do offspring resemble their parents?

Great Idea: *All living things use the same genetic code to guide the chemical reactions in every cell.*

24 The New Science of Life: Can we cure cancer?

Great Idea: *Our new understanding of genetic mechanisms is leading to enormous technological advances in medicine and other aspects of our lives.*

25 Evolution: How did life emerge on the ancient Earth?

Great Idea: *All life on Earth evolved from single-celled organisms by the process of natural selection.*

Appendices

1

Science: A Way of Knowing

How do you know what you know?

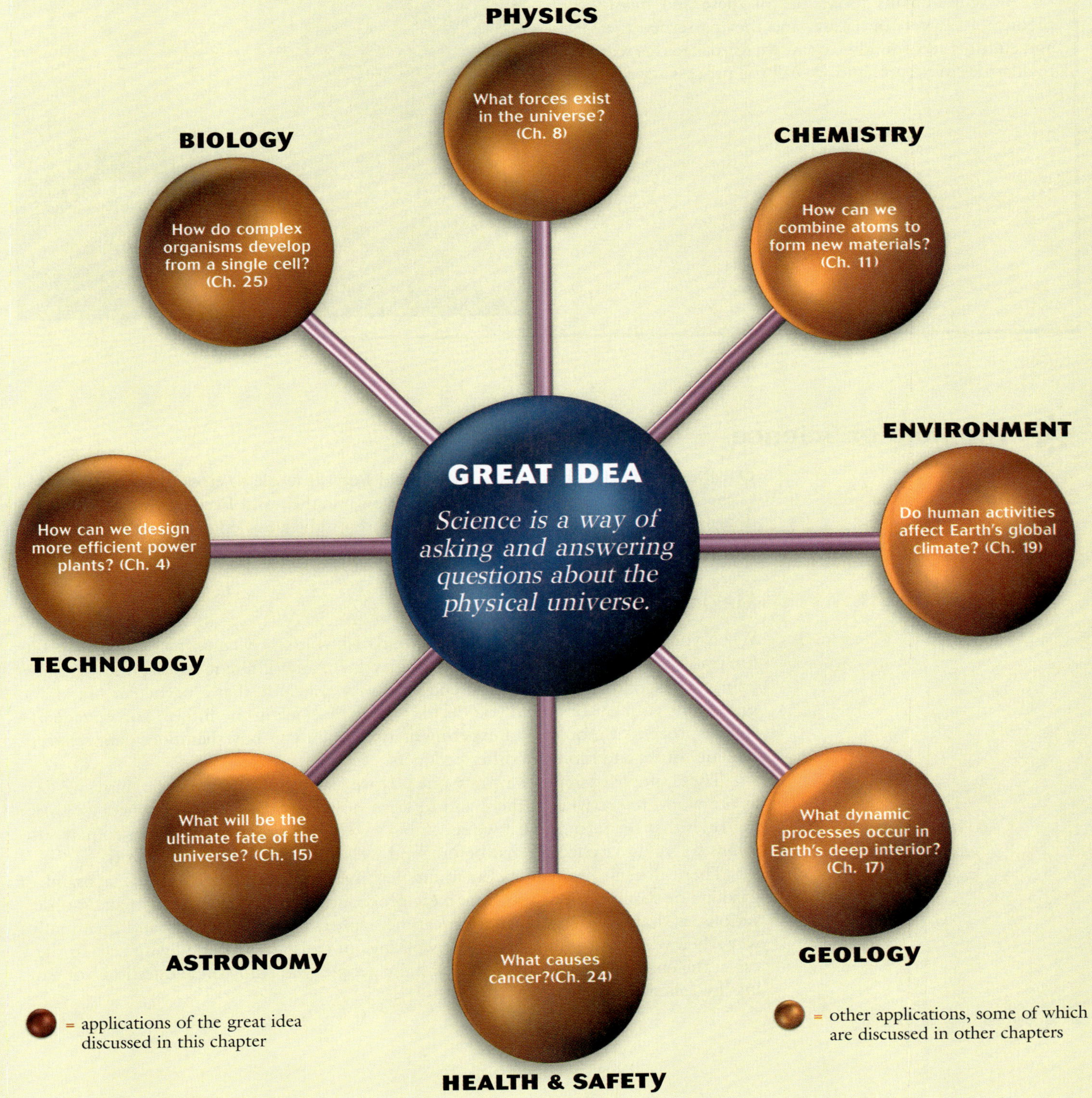

Science Through the Day | Sunrise

Sunlight streams through your East window. As you wake up, you remember it's Saturday. No classes! And you're headed to the beach with friends. It looks like it's going to be a beautiful day, just like the weather forecast promised.

We take so much about the natural world for granted. Every day the Sun rises at a precisely predictable time in the East. Every day the Sun sets in the West. So, too, the phases of the Moon and the seasons of the year follow their familiar repetitive cycles.

Ancient humans took note of these and many other predictable aspects of nature, and they patterned their lives and cultures accordingly. Today, we formalize this search for regularities in nature, and we call the process science.

John Arsenault/Photonica/Getty Images

The Role of Science

Our lives are filled with choices. What should I eat? Is it safe to cross the street? Should I bother to recycle an aluminum can, or just throw it in the trash? Every day we have to make dozens of decisions; each choice is based, in part, on the knowledge that actions in a physical world have predictable consequences. By what process do you make those decisions?

Making Choices

When you pull into a gas station you have to ask yourself what sort of gasoline to buy for your car. Over a period of time you may try many different types, observing how your car responds to each. In the end, you may conclude that a particular brand and grade suits your car best, and you decide to buy that one in the future. You engage in a similar process of inquiry and experimentation when you buy shampoo, pain relievers, athletic shoes, and scores of other products.

These simple examples illustrate one way we learn about the universe. First, we look at the world to see what is there and to learn how it works. Then we generalize, making rules that seem to fit what we see. Finally, we apply those general rules to new situations we've never encountered before, and we fully expect the rules to work.

There doesn't seem to be anything Earth-shattering about choosing a brand of gasoline or shampoo. But the same basic procedure of asking questions, making observations, and arriving at a conclusion can be applied in a more formal and quantitative way when we want to understand the workings of a distant star or a living cell. In these cases, the enterprise is called science, and the people who study these questions for a living are called scientists.

Why Study Science?

Science gives us our most powerful tool to understand how our world works and how we interact with our physical surroundings. Science not only incorporates basic ideas and theories about how our universe behaves, but it also provides a framework for learning more and tackling new questions and concerns that come our way. Science represents our best hope for predicting and coping with natural disasters, curing diseases, and discovering new materials and new technologies with which to shape our world. Science also provides an unparalleled view of the magnificent order and symmetry of the universe and its workings—from the unseen world of the atomic nucleus to the inconceivable vastness of space.

Pick up your local newspaper any morning of the week and glance at the headlines. On a typical day you'll see articles about the weather, environmental concerns, and long-range planning by one of your local utility companies. There might be news about a new treatment for cancer, an earthquake in California, or new advances in biotechnology. The editorial pages might feature comments on cloning humans, arguments for a NASA planetary mission, debates about teaching evolution, or perhaps a trial involving DNA fingerprinting. What do all of these stories have in common? They may affect your life in one way or another, and they all depend, to a significant degree, on science.

We live in a world of matter and energy, forces and motions. The process of science is based on the idea that everything we experience in our lives takes place in an ordered universe with regular and predictable phenomena. You have learned to survive in this universe, so many of these scientific ideas are second nature to you. When you drive a car, cook a meal, or play a pickup game of basketball, you instinctively take advantage of a few simple physical laws. As you eat, sleep, work, or play, you experience the world as a living biological system and must come to terms with the natural laws governing all living things.

So why should you study science? Chances are you aren't going to be a professional scientist. Even so, your job will may well depend on advances in science and technology. New technologies are a driving force in economics, business, and even many aspects of law: new semiconductor technology, agricultural methods, and information processing have altered our world. Biological research and drug development play crucial roles in the medical professions: genetic diseases, AIDS vaccines, and nutritional information appear in the news every day. Even professional athletes must constantly evaluate and use new and improved gear, rely on improved medical treatments and therapies, and weigh the potential risks of performance-enhancing drugs. By studying science you will not only be better able to incorporate these advances into your professional life, but you will also better understand the process by which such advances were made.

Science is no less central to your everyday life away from school or work. As a consumer, you are besieged by new products and processes, not to mention a bewildering variety of warnings about health and safety. As a taxpayer, you must vote on issues that directly affect your community—energy taxes, recycling proposals, government spending on research, and more. As a living being, you must make informed decisions about diet and lifestyle. And as a parent, you will have to nurture and guide your children through an ever-more-complex world. A firm grasp of the principles and methods of science will help you make life's important decisions in a more informed way. As an extra bonus, you will be poised to share in the excitement of the scientific discoveries that, week-by-week, transform our understanding of the universe and our place in it. Science opens up astonishing, unimagined worlds—bizarre life forms in deep oceans, exploding stars in deep space, and aspects of the history of life and our world more wondrous than any fiction.

Chris Martinez/Getty Images News and Sport Services

Even something simple like choosing a brand of gasoline can involve observation and experiment.

The Scientific Method

Science is a way of asking and answering questions about the physical universe. It's not simply a set of facts or a catalog of answers, but rather a process for conducting an ongoing dialogue with our physical surroundings. Like any human activity, science is enormously varied and rich in subtleties. Nevertheless, a few basic steps taken together can be said to comprise the **scientific method.**

Plato argued that humans observing nature were like men watching shadows on the wall of a cave.

(*School of Athens*, detail of the centre showing Plato and Aristotle with students including Michelangelo and Diogenes, 1510-11 by Raphael (Raffaello Sanzio of Urbino) (1483–1520) ©Vatican Museums and Galleries, Vatican City, Italy/ The Bridgeman Art Library

Observation

If our goal is to learn about the world, then the first thing we have to do is look around us and see what's there. This statement may seem obvious to us in our modern technological age, yet throughout much of history, learned men and women rejected the idea that you can understand the world simply by observing it.

Some Greek philosophers living during the Golden Age of Athens argued that one cannot deduce the true nature of the universe by trusting the senses. The senses lie, they would have said. Only the use of reason and the insights of the human mind can lead us to true understanding. In his famous book *The Republic,* Plato compared human beings to people living in a cave, watching shadows on a wall but unable to see the objects causing the shadows. In just the same way, he argued, observing the physical world will never put us in contact with reality, but will doom us to a lifetime of wrestling with shadows. Only with the "eye of the mind" can we break free from illusion and arrive at the truth, Plato argued.

In the Middle Ages in Europe, a similar frame of mind was to be found, but with a devout religious trust in received wisdom replacing the use of human reason as the ultimate tool in the search for truth. A story about an Oxford College debate on the question "How many teeth does a horse have?" underscores this point. One learned scholar got up and quoted the Greek scientist Aristotle on the subject, and another quoted the theologian St. Augustine to put forward a different answer. Finally, a young monk at the back of the hall got up and noted that since there was a horse outside, they could settle the question by looking in its mouth. At this point, the manuscript states, the assembled scholars "fell upon him, smote him hip and thigh, and cast him from the company of educated men."

As these examples illustrate, many distinguished thinkers have attacked the problem of learning about the physical world without actually making observations and measurements. These approaches are perfectly self-consistent and were pursued by people every bit as intelligent as we are. They are not, however, the methods of science, nor did they produce the kinds of advanced technologies and knowledge that we associate with modern societies.

In the remainder of this book, we differentiate between **observations,** in which we observe nature without manipulating it, and **experiments,** in which we manipulate some aspect of nature and observe the outcome. An astronomer, for example, observes distant stars without changing them, while a chemist may experiment by mixing materials together and seeing what happens.

Identifying Patterns and Regularities

When we observe a particular phenomenon over and over again, we begin to get a sense of how nature behaves. We start to recognize patterns in nature. Eventually, we generalize our experience into a synthesis that summarizes what we have learned about the way the world works. We may, for example, notice that whenever we drop something, it falls. This statement represents a summary of the results of many observations.

It often happens that at this stage scientists summarize the results of their observations in mathematical form, particularly if they have been making quantitative **measurements.** Every measurement involves a number that is recorded in some standard *unit of measurement.* In the case of a falling object, for example, you might measure the time (measured in the familiar time unit of seconds) that it takes an object to fall a certain distance (measured in the distance unit of meters, for example). More examples of units of measurement are given in Appendix B.

Quantitative measurements thus provide a more exact description than just noticing that the object falls. The standard scientific procedure is to collect careful measurements in the form of a table of data (see Table 1-1). These data could also be presented in the form of a graph, in which distance of the fall (in meters) is plotted against time of the fall (in seconds; Figure 1-1). As we explore the many different branches of science, from physics to biology, we'll see that most scientific measurements require both a number and a unit of measurement, and we'll encounter many different units in the coming chapters.

After preparing tables and graphs of their data, scientists would notice that the longer something falls, the farther it travels. Furthermore, the distance isn't simply proportional to the time of fall. If one object falls for twice as long as another, it will travel four times as far; if it falls three times longer, it will travel nine times as far; and so on. This statement can be summarized in three ways (a format used throughout this book):

- ▶ **In words:** The distance traveled is proportional to the square of the time of travel.
- ▶ **In equation form:**

$$\text{distance} = \text{constant} \times (\text{time})^2$$

- ▶ **In symbols:**

$$d = k \times t^2$$

The constant, *k,* has to be determined from the measurements. We'll return to the subject of constants in the next chapter.

Table 1-1 Measurements of Falling Objects

Time of Fall (seconds)	Distance of Fall (meters)
1	5
2	20
3	45
4	80
5	125

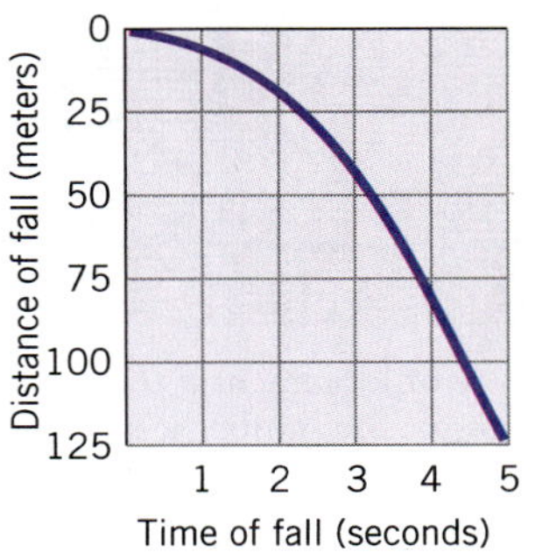

• **Figure 1-1** Measurements of a falling object can be presented visually in the form of a graph. Time of fall in seconds (on the horizontal axis) is plotted versus distance of fall in meters (on the vertical axis).

Mathematics: The Language of Science

To many people science brings to mind obscure equations written in strange, undecipherable symbols. The next time you're in the science area of your college or university, look into an advanced classroom. Chances are you'll see a confusing jumble of formulas on the blackboard. Have you ever wondered why scientists need all those complex mathematical equations? Science is supposed to help us understand the physical world around us, so why can't scientists just use plain English?

Take a stroll outside and look carefully at a favorite tree. Think about how you might describe the tree in as much detail as possible so that a distant friend could envision exactly what you see and distinguish that tree from all others.

A cursory description would note the rough brown bark, branching limbs, and canopy of green leaves, but that description would do little to distinguish your tree from most others. You might use adjectives like lofty, graceful, or stately to convey an overall impression of the tree. Better yet, you could identify the exact kind of tree and specify its stage of growth—a sugar maple at the peak of autumn color, for example—but even then your friend has relatively little to go on.

Your description would be far more accurate by giving exact dimensions of the tree—measurements expressed in units, such as its height, the distance spanned by its branches, or the diameter of the trunk. You could document the shape and size of leaves, the thickness and texture of the bark, the angles and spacing of the branching limbs, and the tree's approximate age. You could approach measuring the tree from other perspectives as well, by calculating the number of board feet of lumber the tree could yield, or how much life-supporting oxygen the tree produces every day. Finally, you could talk about the basic molecular processes that allow the tree to extract energy from sunlight and carry out the other chemical tasks we associate with life.

As we move through these descriptions of the tree, our language becomes more and more quantitative. In some cases, such as supplying a detailed description of the tree's shape or its chemistry, that description could become quite

There are many ways of describing a tree.

Corbis Digital Stock/Corbis Images

One way of looking at a tree is to think about the lumber it might produce.

long and cumbersome. That's why scientists employ **mathematics,** which is a concise language that allows them to communicate their results in compact form and often, as an added benefit, allows them to make very precise predictions about expected outcomes of experiments or observations. But anything that can be said in an equation can also be said (albeit in a less concise way) in a plain English sentence. When you encounter equations in your science courses, you should always ask, "What English sentence does this equation represent?" Learning to "read" equations will keep the mathematics from obscuring the simple ideas that lie behind most equations.

Facts, Hypotheses, Laws, and Theories

Scientific discoveries may be broadly categorized into four groups: facts, hypotheses, laws, and theories, in order of increasing importance. A scientific **fact** is simply a confirmed observation about the natural world. "Earth orbits around the Sun" or "My car keys fall when I drop them" are examples of such facts. Scientific progress is built on such facts, but facts, by themselves, are not where the primary excitement of science lies.

Once we have collected a number of facts and verified experimental and observational results, we can form a **hypothesis**—a tentative educated guess—about how the world works. In the case of our everyday experience with falling objects, this hypothesis could be very simple. We could say, "If I drop any object, then it will fall." In other cases, the formation of the hypothesis may be more complicated, and the hypothesis may be stated in the form of mathematical equations. When confronted with a new phenomenon, scientists often weigh several different hypotheses at once, much as a detective in a murder mystery may consider several different suspects.

A more refined type of scientific statement, called a **law,** arises when many observations or measurements point to a regular, predictable pattern of behavior in nature. After observing and measuring hundreds of dropped objects, for example, we could state a law of falling objects such as, "In the absence of wind resistance, all objects fall a distance proportional to the square of the time of the fall." The law provides a description of nature, often in the form of an equation, without explaining the origin of that behavior.

A **theory** is a well-substantiated explanatory description of the world based on a large number of independently verified observational and experimental tests. A theory often incorporates many seemingly unrelated hypotheses and laws into one grand conceptual framework. It's important to note that a theory in science is not just an educated guess or an inspired hunch; rather, it represents the highest level of scientific discovery and achievement. Thus, for example, Charles Darwin's theory of evolution by natural selection (Chapter 25) is one of the most thoroughly tested ideas in all science, and it provides the essential cornerstone for modern biology.

Prediction and Testing

In science, every hypothesis, law, and theory must be tested by using it to make **predictions** about how a particular system will behave, then observing nature to see if the system behaves as predicted. The theory of evolution, for example, makes countless specific testable predictions about the similarities and differences of modern living organisms, as well as the distribution of extinct fossil organisms.

Think about the hypothesis that all objects fall when they are dropped. That idea can be tested by dropping all sorts of objects. Each drop constitutes a test of our prediction, and the more successful tests we perform, the more confidence we have that the hypothesis is correct. As long as we restrict our tests to solids or liquids on Earth's surface, then the hypothesis is consistently confirmed. Test a helium-filled balloon, however, and we discover a clear exception to the rule. The balloon "falls" up. The original hypothesis, which worked so well for most objects, fails for certain gases. And more tests would show there are other limitations. If you were an astronaut in a space shuttle, every time you held something out and let it go, it would just float in space. Evidently, our hypothesis is invalid in the orbiting space shuttle as well.

This example illustrates an important aspect about testing hypotheses, laws, and theories in science. Tests do not necessarily prove or disprove an idea; instead, they often serve to define the range of situations under which the idea is valid. We may, for example, observe that nature behaves in a certain way only at high temperatures or only at low velocities. In these sorts of situations, it usually happens that the original hypothesis is seen to be a special case of a deeper, more general theory. In the case of the balloon, for example, the simple "things fall down" will be replaced by a much more general theory of gravitation, based on statements called Newton's laws of motion and the law of universal gravitation—laws we'll study in the next chapter. These laws of nature describe and predict the motion of dropped objects both on Earth and in space and, therefore, are a more successful set of statements than the original hypothesis. We will discuss them in more detail in the next chapter.

We will encounter many such laws and theories in this book, all backed by millions of observations and measurements. Remember, however, where these laws and theories come from. They are not written on tablets of stone, nor are they simply good ideas that someone once had. They arise from repeated and rigorous observation and testing. They represent our best understanding of how nature works.

We never stop questioning the validity of our hypotheses, theories, or laws of nature. Scientists constantly think up new, more rigorous experiments to test the limits of our theories. In fact, one of the central tenets of science is this:

Every law and theory of nature is subject to change, based on new observations.

This is an extremely important statement about science, and one that is often ignored in public debates. It means that it must be possible, in principle, that every statement in a scientific model *could* be false. You should, in other words, be able to imagine an experimental outcome that would prove the statement false, even if that outcome never happens in the real world.

Consider the theory of evolution (see Chapter 25), which makes countless predictions about the historical sequence of organisms that have lived on Earth. According to the current model of life's evolution, for example, dinosaurs became extinct millions of years before human beings appeared. Consequently, if a paleontologist found a human leg bone in the same geological formation with a *Tyrannosaurus rex*, then that discovery would call into question the theory of evolution.

Altrendo Images/Getty Images

Equations allow us to describe with precision the behavior of objects in our physical world. One such equation predicts the behavior of falling objects.

The Scientific Method in Operation

These elements—observation, hypothesis, prediction, and testing—together comprise the scientific method. In practice, you can think of the method as working as shown in Figure 1-2. It's a never-ending cycle in which observations lead to hypotheses, which lead to more observations.

If observations confirm a hypothesis, then more tests may be devised. If the hypothesis fails, then the new observations are used to revise it, after which the revised hypothesis is tested again. Scientists continue this process until the limits of existing equipment are reached, in which case researchers often try to develop better instruments to do even more tests. If and when it appears that there's just no point to going further, the

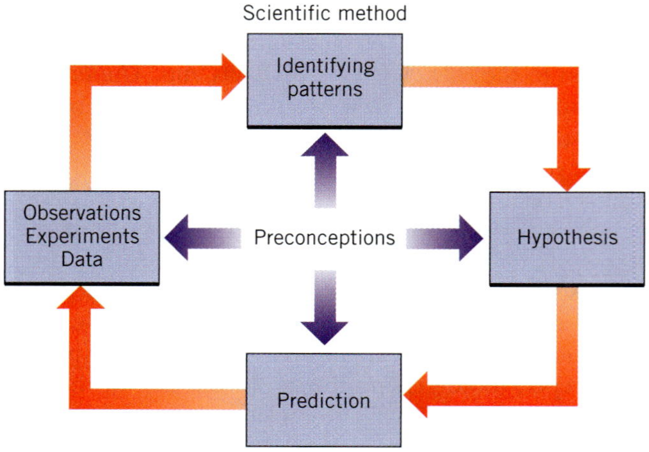

• **Figure 1-2** The scientific method can be illustrated as an endless cycle of collecting observations (data), identifying patterns, and regularities in the data, forming hypotheses, making predictions, and collecting more observations.

hypothesis may be elevated to a law of nature.

It's important to realize, however, that while the orderly cycle shown in Figure 1-2 provides a useful framework to help us think about science, it shouldn't be thought of as a rigid cookbook-style set of steps to follow. Science can be every bit as creative an endeavor as art or music. Because science is done by human beings, it involves occasional bursts of intuition, sudden leaps, a joyful breaking of the rules, and all the other characteristics we associate with other human activities.

Several other important points should be made about the scientific method.

1. Scientists are not required to observe nature with an "open mind," with no preconceptions about what they are going to find. Most experiments and observations are designed and undertaken with a specific hypothesis in mind, and most researchers have preconceptions about whether that hypothesis is right or wrong. Nevertheless, scientists have to believe the results of their experiments and observations, whether or not they fit preconceived notions. Science demands that whatever our preconceptions, we must be ready to change those ideas if the evidence forces us to do so.
2. There is no "right" place to enter the cycle. Scientists can (and have) started their work by making extensive observations, but they can also start with a theory and test it. It makes no difference where you enter the cycle—eventually the scientific process takes you all the way around.
3. Observations and experiments must be reported in such a way that anyone with the proper equipment can verify the results. Scientific results, in other words, must be **reproducible,** and they must be reproducible by anyone with appropriate equipment and training, not just the original experimenters.
4. The cycle is continuous; it has no end. Science does not provide final answers, nor is it a search for ultimate truth. Instead, it is a way of producing successively more detailed and exact descriptions of wider and wider areas of the physical world—descriptions that allow us to predict more of the behavior of that world with higher and higher levels of confidence.

The Ongoing Process of Science •

Biodiversity

The dynamic process of scientific research is illustrated by a recent experiment in *ecology*—the study of communities of interdependent living things. Many current public debates focus on possible adverse effects of human activities on *biodiversity,* which is defined as the number of different species that coexist at a given place. Before we can identify human influences, however, we must first examine the role that biodiversity plays in nature. To answer this question, researchers apply the scientific method and design an experiment to study areas that differ only in the number of species.

Starting in 1982, ecologist David Tilman at the University of Minnesota carried out just such an experiment. He began by choosing four grassy fields in the Cedar Creek Natural History Area. These fields had either never been tilled or had lain fallow for a

David Tilman

These three photos illustrate a nitrogen addition experiment at Cedar Creek Natural History Area near St. Paul, Minnesota. The aerial photo, on the left, shows one of the four fields at Cedar Creek in 1983, the second year of the experiment. The different colors of the plots illustrate visually the changes in plant species composition caused by the different rates of nitrogen (N) addition. The center photo shows a typical control plot at this same field. This plot has high plant diversity, is dominated by native plant species, and did not receive any added nitrogen. The photo on the right shows a plot that received the highest rate of N addition and has become almost totally dominated by the nonnative perennial weedy grass, *Agropyron repens* (quack grass).

minimum of 14 years. First Tilman fenced off the fields, and then he split them into plots about 12 feet on a side—207 plots in all. Different plots were treated in different ways with nutrients that are known to affect plant growth.

1. Some plots, called controls, received no treatment.
2. Some plots were given a group of essential nutrients such as phosphorus and potassium, but no nitrogen.
3. Some plots were given the same set of nutrients, but different amounts of nitrogen.

Think for a moment about this experimental design. All of the plots start with the same soil and receive the same rainfall. The only difference between them is the amount of nitrogen and other nutrients. In the language of experimental science, we say that the amounts of nitrogen and other nutrients are the "independent variables," and results such as biodiversity or the amount of vegetation on each plot are "dependent variables." Thus whatever results we find can be attributed to the presence or absence of nitrogen and other nutrients.

During each of the 11 years that the experiment ran, the experimenters measured two things: (1) the amount of vegetation (or biomass) on each plot and (2) the number of species (or biodiversity). In normal years, there was a clear result: the more nitrogen added, the more biomass produced, while the amounts of other nutrients had little effect. Furthermore, the plots with the highest biomass tended to have fewer species, and hence lower biodiversity, because when a few species flourished they crowded out the others.

By chance, however, the period of the experiment included the years 1987–1988, which contained the third worst drought in the last 150 years. In the year of this drought, adding nitrogen made little difference—all the plots produced very low biomass. But the drought also highlighted the role of biodiversity, because, while the biomass in plots with low biodiversity dropped to as low as one-eighth of its nondrought levels, the biomass of plots with high biodiversity fell by only a half. (Although the percentage drop was bigger for plots with more nitrogen, in fact all plots produced roughly the same biomass in the drought years.)

Thus biodiversity appears to represent a kind of insurance policy for natural ecosystems; it's not too important in normal years, but it carries the system through periods

Courtesy Chemical Club Library

Dimitri Mendeleev recognized regular patterns in the properties of known chemical elements and thereby devised the first periodic table of elements.

of high stress (like droughts). By designing and performing carefully thought-out experiments, scientists are able to arrive at this kind of understanding. •

Science in the Making •

Dimitri Mendeleev and the Periodic Table

Discoveries of previously unrecognized patterns in nature, a key step in the scientific method, provide scientists with some of their most exhilarating moments. Dimitri Mendeleev (1834–1907), a popular chemistry professor at the Technological Institute of St. Petersburg in Russia, experienced such a breakthrough in 1869 as he was tabulating data for a new chemistry textbook.

The mid-nineteenth century was a time of great excitement in chemistry. Almost every year saw the discovery of one or two new chemical elements, and new apparatus and processes were greatly expanding the repertoire of laboratory and industrial chemists. In such a stimulating field, it was no easy job to keep up to date with all the developments and summarize them in a textbook. In an effort to consolidate the current state of knowledge about the most basic chemical building blocks, Mendeleev listed various properties of the 63 known chemical elements (substances that could not be divided by chemical means). He arranged his list in order of increasing atomic weight and then noted the distinctive chemical behavior of each element.

Examining his list, Mendeleev realized an extraordinary pattern: elements with similar chemical properties appeared at regular, or *periodic*, intervals. One group of elements, including lithium, sodium, potassium, and rubidium (he called them group-one elements), all were soft, silvery metals that formed compounds with chlorine in a one-to-one ratio. Immediately following the group-one elements in the list were beryllium, magnesium, calcium, and barium—group-two elements that form compounds with chlorine in a one-to-two ratio, and so on.

As other similar patterns emerged from his list, Mendeleev realized that the elements could be arranged in the form of a table (Figure 1-3). Not only did this so-called

• **Figure 1-3** The periodic table systematizes all known chemical elements.

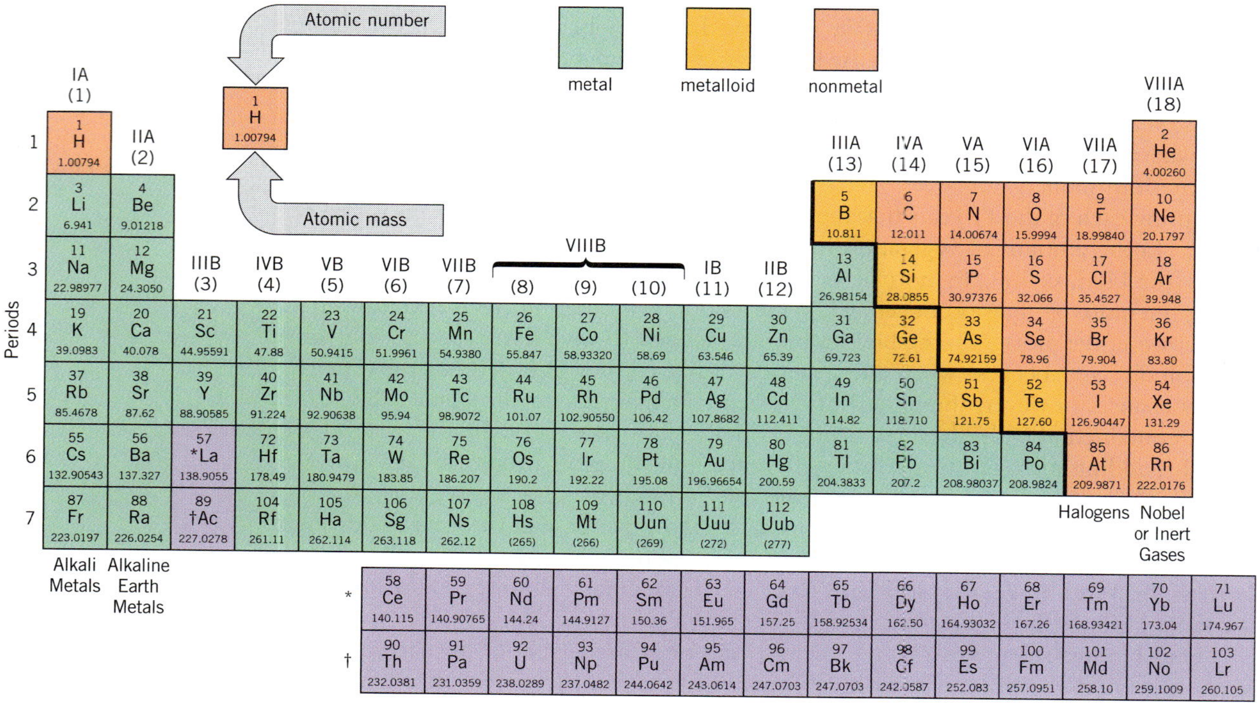

periodic table highlight previously unrecognized relationships among the elements, it also revealed obvious gaps where as-yet undiscovered elements must lie. The power of Mendeleev's periodic table of the elements was underscored when several new elements, with atomic weights and chemical properties just as he had predicted, were discovered in the following years.

The discovery of the periodic table ranks as one of the great achievements of science. It was so important, in fact, that Mendeleev's students carried a large poster of it behind his coffin in his funeral procession. •

The Science of Life •

William Harvey and the Blood's Circulation

It's common knowledge that blood circulates in your body, but stop and think for a moment. How do we know? One of the great puzzles faced by scientists who studied the human body was deducing the role played by the blood. English physician William Harvey (1578–1657) gave us our current picture of the pattern of circulation, in which blood is pumped from the heart to all parts of the body through arteries, and returned to the heart through veins. His experiments reveal the scientific method at work.

Prior to Harvey's work, several competing hypotheses had been proposed. Some scientists had taught that blood didn't move at all, but simply pulsed in response to pumping of the heart. Others taught that the arteries and veins constituted different systems, with blood in the veins flowing from the liver to the various parts of the body, where it was absorbed and its nutrients taken in. Harvey, on the other hand, adopted the hypothesis that blood circulates through a connected system of arteries and veins. When confronted with such conflicting hypotheses, a scientist must devise experiments that test the distinctive predictions of each competing idea.

To establish the circulation of the blood, Harvey first performed careful dissections of animals to trace out the veins and arteries. Second, he undertook studies of live animals, often killing them so that he could observe the veins and arteries as the heart stopped beating. Then, as now, animals were sometimes sacrificed to advance medical science (see Investigation 7). Finally, Harvey performed a series of experiments to establish that blood in the veins did indeed flow back to the heart, rather than simply being absorbed in tissue like a stream of water in the desert. One of those experiments is shown in Figure 1-4. A tourniquet was applied to a subject's arm, and he was asked to squeeze something so that the veins filled with blood and "popped." (You have probably done the same thing when having blood drawn in a doctor's office.) Harvey would then press down on the vein and note that it would subside (indicating that the blood was leaving it) on the side toward the heart. This result is just the opposite of what would occur if blood were flowing from the liver to the extremities. Based on this experiment, and many others like it, Harvey eventually concluded that blood circulates continuously. •

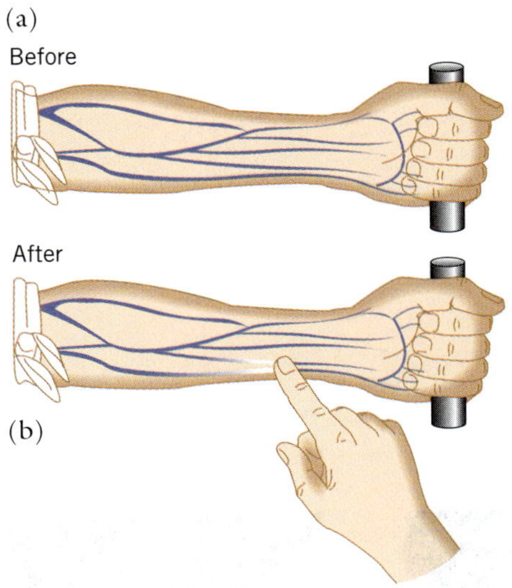

• **Figure 1-4** One of William Harvey's famous experiments on the circulation of the blood tested the hypothesis that blood flows from veins to the heart. Harvey first applied a tourniquet to a subject's arm and had the subject squeeze something to raise the veins *(a)*. Pressing down on the vein caused it to gradually subside *(b)*, indicating that the blood was indeed flowing back to the heart.

Other Ways of Knowing

Scientists discover laws that describe how nature works by performing reproducible observations and measurements. Every idea in science must be subject to this kind of testing. If an idea cannot be tested in a manner that yields reproducible results, even if that idea is correct, then it simply isn't a part of science.

Different Kinds of Questions

The first step in any scientific investigation is to ask a question about the physical world. A scientist can ask, for example, whether a particular painting was completed in the seventeenth century. Various physical and chemical tests can be used to find the age of the paint, study the canvas, X-ray the painting, and so on. The question of whether the painting is old or a modern forgery can indeed be investigated by the scientific method.

But the methods of science cannot answer other equally valid questions. No physical or chemical test will tell us whether the painting is beautiful or how we are to respond to it. These questions are simply outside the realm of science.

The scientific method is not the only way to answer questions that matter in our lives. Science provides us with a powerful way of tackling questions about the physical world—how it works and how we can shape it to our needs. But many questions lie beyond the scope of science and scientific methods. Some of these questions are deeply philosophical: What is the meaning of life? Why does the world hold so much suffering? Is there a God? Other important personal questions also lie outside of science: What career should I choose? Whom should I marry? Should I have children? Scientific information might influence some of our personal choices, but we cannot answer these questions fully by the cycle of observation, hypothesis, and testing. For answers, we turn instead to religion, philosophy, and the arts.

Symphonies, poems, and paintings are created to be enjoyed and are not, in the end, experiences that need to be analyzed scientifically. This is not a criticism. These art forms address different human needs than science, and they use different methods. The same can be said about religious faith. Strictly speaking, there should be no conflict between the questions asked by science and religion, because they deal with different aspects of life. Conflicts arise only when people attempt to apply their methods to questions where those methods aren't applicable.

Pseudoscience

Les Wies/Stone/Getty Images

Fortune telling, astrology, and other activities at this psychic's shop in Hollywood are examples of pseudoscience.

Many claims of natural phenomena, including extrasensory perception (ESP), unidentified flying objects (UFOs), astrology, crystal power, reincarnation, or many other notions you see in the tabloids at supermarket checkout counters, fail the elementary test that defines the sciences. None of these subjects, collectively labeled **pseudoscience,** can be tested in the sense that we are using the term. There is no reproducible test you can imagine that will convince people who believe in these notions that their ideas are incorrect. Yet, as we have seen, the central property of scientific ideas is that they are testable and could be wrong, at least in principle. Pseudoscience lies outside the domain of science and falls instead in the realm of belief or dogma.

In the following "Science by the Numbers" section we examine the nature of one pseudoscience, astrology. When confronted with other kinds of pseudoscience, you can ask a number of questions to come to your own conclusions:

1. Are the "facts" true as stated?

   The first step is to be sure that the facts stated in support of a pseudoscientific claim are actually true. For example, the Great Pyramids of Egypt are frequently the subject of these sorts of arguments. In one version, it is argued that the pyramids must have been built by extraterrestrials because, among other things, their bases are perfect squares and laying out a perfect square was beyond the capability of Egyptian engineers. In fact, according to modern surveys of the pyramids, the longest side of the Pyramid of Cheops is 8 inches longer than the shortest side—it is not a perfect square at all. Digging out the true facts can sometimes be tedious, but it is a necessary first step.

2. Is there an alternative explanation?

   In dealing with UFO sightings, it often happens that you can't prove that the object seen wasn't a UFO, but there exists a "normal" explanation for the same event. For example, a light in the sky could be an extraterrestrial spaceship, but it could also be the planet Venus (the most commonly reported UFO). In this case, it is necessary to invoke a doctrine called the "burden of proof." If someone makes a claim, it is up to that person to establish the claim: it is not up to you to disprove it. Furthermore, the more far-reaching the claim, the higher the standard of proof becomes. In the words of the noted planetary astronomer and public television science educator Carl Sagan (1934–1996), "Extraordinary claims require extraordinary proofs."

3. Is the claim falsifiable?

   As we stated above, a central aspect of the scientific method is that every scientific statement is subject to experimental or observational test, so that it is possible to imagine an experimental result that would prove the statement wrong (although whether that result will ever actually be seen is a separate question). Such statements are said to be falsifiable. Statements that are not falsifiable are simply not part of science. For example, some creationists talk about the doctrine of "created antiquity," by which they mean that the universe was created to look *exactly* as if it were billions of years old, even though it was really created by God a few thousand years ago. This statement is not falsifiable, and therefore this doctrine is not part of science.

> **Stop and Think!** Can any experiment or observation (in principle) show created antiquity to be false?

4. Have the claims been rigorously tested?

   Many pseudoscientific claims are based on anecdotes and stories. An example is provided by the practice known as "dowsing" or "water witching," in which someone walking on the surface (usually holding a forked stick) can detect the presence of underground water. Stories about this practice can be found in almost any rural area of the United States. Yet when the Committee for the Scientific Investigation of Claims for the Paranormal (CSICOP) conducted controlled tests in which water pipes were buried beneath a plowed surface, dowsers did no better than chance at locating the water. Tests like these are difficult to arrange, and often do not get much publicity, but they are worth looking for (see, for example, http://www.csicop.com).

5. Do the claims require unreasonable changes in accepted ideas?

   Often a pseudoscientific claim will seem to explain a small set of facts but at the same time will require that a much wider assortment of facts be ignored. The psychiatrist Immanuel Velikovsky, for example, looked at stories in ancient texts and tried to alter astronomy (violating most of the laws of physics in the process) in order to preserve the texts as literal statements of fact, rather than as allegory or metaphor. From a scientific perspective, it is much more reasonable to accept the well-verified laws of physics and give up the literal reading of the text.

Science by the Numbers •

Astrology

Astrology is a very old system of beliefs that most modern scientists would call a pseudoscience. The central belief of astrology is that the positions of objects in the sky at a given time (a person's birth, for example) influence a person's future. Astrology as it has been practiced in the Western world developed as part of a complex set of omen systems used by the Babylonians, and it was practiced by many famous astronomers well into modern times.

As Earth travels around the Sun, the stars in the night sky change. The band of background stars through which the Sun, the Moon, and the planets appear to move is called the zodiac. The stars of the zodiac are customarily divided into 12 constellations, which are called "signs" or "houses." If you could block out the light of the Sun, these stars would appear (as they do during a total solar eclipse). You would then notice the Sun's position to lie within a certain zodiac constellation, just as the Moon and planets do at night. Furthermore, if you watched the Moon and planets from night to night, you would see them appear to move through these constellations.

Astrology is a pseudoscience that is based on the belief that the positions of astronomical objects influence our personal lives.

At any time, the Sun, the Moon, and the planets all appear in one of these constellations, and a diagram showing these positions is called a horoscope. Astrologers have a complex (and far from unified) system in which each combination of heavenly bodies and signs is believed to signify particular things. The Sun, for example, is thought to indicate the outgoing, expressive aspects of one's character, the Moon the inner-directed ones, and so on. When this system was first introduced, the constellation in which the Sun appeared at the time of your birth was said to be your "Sun sign," or, simply, your "sign." Today, the position of the Sun in the sky has shifted due to the motion of Earth's axis, but the original dates for the "signs" are still used.

Scientists reject astrology for two reasons. First, there is no known way that planets and stars could exert a significant influence on a child at birth. It is true, as we shall learn in Chapter 2, that they exert a miniscule gravitational force on the infant, but the gravitational force exerted by the delivering physician (who is smaller but much closer) is much greater than that exerted by any celestial object.

More importantly, scientists reject astrology because it just doesn't work. Over the millennia, there has been no evidence at all that the stars can predict the future.

You can test the ideas of astrology for yourself, if you like. Try this: Have a member of the class take the horoscopes from yesterday's newspaper and type them on a sheet of paper without indicating which horoscope goes with which sign. Then ask members of your class to indicate the horoscope that best matches the day they actually had. Have them write their birthday (or sign) on the paper as well.

If people just picked horoscopes at random, you would expect about 1 person in 12 to pick the horoscope corresponding to his or her sign. Are the results of your survey any better than that? What does this tell you about the predictive power of astrology? •

The Organization of Science

Scientists investigate all sorts of natural objects and phenomena: the tiniest elementary particles, microscopic living cells, the human body, forests, Earth, stars, and the entire cosmos. Throughout this vast sweep, the same scientific method can be applied. Men and women have been carrying out this task for hundreds of years, and by now we have a pretty good idea about how the many parts of our universe work. In the process, scientists have also developed a social structure that provides unity to the pursuit of scientific knowledge, as well as recognition of important disciplinary differences within the larger scientific framework.

The Divisions of Science

Science is a human endeavor, and humans invariably form themselves into groups with shared interests. When modern science first started in the seventeenth century, it was possible for one person to know almost all there was to know about the physical world and the "three kingdoms" of animals, vegetables, and minerals. In the seventeenth century, Isaac Newton could do forefront research in astronomy, in the physics of moving objects, in the behavior of light, and in mathematics. Thus, for a time prior to the mid-nineteenth century, scholars who studied the workings of the physical universe formed a more-or-less cohesive group, calling themselves "natural philosophers." But as human understanding expanded and knowledge of nature became more detailed and technical, science began to fragment into increasingly specialized disciplines and subdisciplines.

Today, our knowledge and understanding of the world is so much more sophisticated and complex that no one person could possibly be at the frontier in such a wide variety of fields. Today most scientists choose a major field—biology, chemistry, physics, and so on—and study one small part of the subject at great length. Each of these broad disciplines boasts hundreds of different subspecialties. In physics, for example, a student may elect to study the behavior of light, the properties of materials, the nucleus of the atom, elementary particles, or the origin of the universe. The amount of information and expertise required to get to the frontier in any of these fields is so large that most students have to ignore almost everything else to learn their specialty. Even so, many of the most interesting problems in science, from the origin of life to the properties of matter to curing cancer, are interdisciplinary, and they require the collective efforts of many scientists with different specialties.

Science is further divided because scientists within each subspecialty approach problems in different ways. Some scientists are *field researchers,* who go into natural settings to observe nature at work. Other scientists are *experimentalists,* who manipulate nature with controlled experiments. Still other scientists, called *theorists,* spend their time imagining universes that might exist. These different kinds of scientists need to work together to make progress.

The fragmentation of science into disciplines was formalized by a peculiar aspect of the European university system. In Europe, each academic department traditionally had only one "professor." All other teachers, no matter how famous and distinguished, had to settle for less prestigious titles. And so, as the number of outstanding scientists grew in the nineteenth century, universities were forced to create new departments to attract new professors. A number of German universities, for example, supported separate departments of theoretical and experimental physics. And Cambridge University in England at one point had seven different specialized departments of chemistry!

In North America, each academic department generally has many professors. Nevertheless, American science faculties are often divided into several departments, including physics, chemistry, astronomy, geology, and biology—the so-called branches of science.

Gary Buss/Taxi/Getty Images

Scientists work at many different tasks.

The Branches of Science

Several branches of science are distinguished by the scope and content of the questions they address:

Physics is the search for laws that describe the most fundamental aspects of nature: matter, energy, forces, motion, heat, light, and other phenomena. All natural systems, including planets, stars, cells, and people, display these basic phenomena, so physics is the starting point for almost any study of how nature works.

Chemistry is the study of atoms in combination. Chemicals form every material object of our world, while chemical reactions initiate vital changes in our environment and our bodies. Chemistry is thus an immensely practical (and profitable) science.

Astronomy is the study of stars, planets, and other objects in space. We are living in an era of unprecedented astronomical discovery thanks to the development of powerful new telescopes and robotic space exploration.

Geology is the study of the origin, evolution, and present state of our home, planet Earth. Many geology departments also emphasize the study of other planets as a way to understand the unique character of our own world.

Biology is the study of living systems. Biologists document life at many scales, from individual microscopic molecules and cells to expansive ecosystems.

In spite of this practical division of science into separate disciplines, all branches of science are interconnected in a single web of knowledge. Most natural processes can only be studied by resorting to an integrated approach. Understanding such diverse topics as changes in the global climate, the availability of natural resources, the safe storage of nuclear waste, and the discovery of alternative sources of energy requires expertise in physics, chemistry, geology, and biology. All of the sciences are integrated in the natural world.

The Web of Knowledge

The organization of science can be compared to an intricate spider web (Figure 1-5). Around the periphery of the web are all the objects and phenomena examined by scientists, from atoms to fish to comets. Moving toward the web's center, we find the cross-linking hypotheses that scientists have developed to explain how these phenomena work. The farther in we move, the more general these hypotheses become and the more they explain. Radiating out from the center of the web, connecting all the parts and holding the entire structure together, we find a small number of very general principles that have attained the rank of laws of nature.

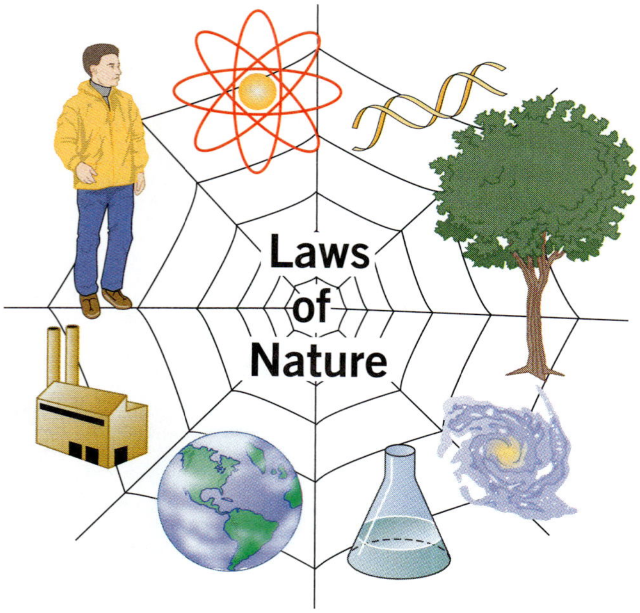

• **Figure 1-5** The interconnected web of scientific knowledge.

No matter where you start on the web, no matter what part of nature you investigate, you will eventually come to one of the fundamental overarching ideas that intersect at the central core. Everything that happens in the universe happens because one or more of these physical laws is operating.

The hierarchical organization of scientific knowledge provides an ideal way to approach the study of science. At the center of any scientific question are a few laws of nature. We begin by looking at those laws that describe everyday forces and motions in the universe. These overarching principles of science are accepted and shared by all scientists, no matter what their field of research. These ideas recur over and over again as we study different parts of the world. You will find that many of these ideas and their consequences seem quite simple—perhaps even obvious—because you are intimately familiar with the physical world in which these laws of nature constantly operate.

After introducing these general principles, we look at how the scientific method is applied to specific physical systems in nature. We examine the nature of materials and the atoms that make them, for example, and look at the chemical reactions that form them. We explore the planet on which we live and discover how mountains and oceans, rivers and plains are formed and evolve over time. And we examine living organisms at the scale of molecules, cells, organisms, and ecosystems.

By the time you have finished this journey, you will have touched on many of the great discoveries about the physical universe that scientists have deduced over the centuries. You will explore how the different parts of our universe operate and how all the parts fit together, and you will know that there are still great unanswered questions that drive scientists today. You will understand some of the great scientific and technological challenges that face our society, and more importantly, you will know enough about how the world works to deal with many of the new problems that will arise in the future.

Basic Research, Applied Research, and Technology

The physical universe can be studied in many ways, and many reasons exist for doing so. Many scientists are simply interested in finding out how the world works—in knowledge for its own sake. They are engaged in **basic research** and may be found studying the behavior of distant stars, obscure life-forms, rare minerals, or subatomic particles. Although discoveries made by basic researchers may have profound effects on society (see the discussion of the discovery of the electric generator in Chapter 5, for example), that is not the primary personal goal of most of these scientists.

Many other scientists approach their work with specific practical goals in mind. They wish to develop **technology,** in which they apply the results of science to specific commercial or industrial goals. These scientists are said to be doing **applied research,** and their ideas are often translated into practical systems by large-scale **research and development (R&D)** projects.

Government laboratories, colleges and universities, and private industries all support both basic and applied research; however, most large-scale R&D (as well as most applied research) is done in government laboratories and private industry (Table 1-2).

Technology •

SETI@HOME

The Search for Extraterrestrial Intelligence (SETI) has had a long and somewhat varied history. Scientists in the early 1960s realized that radio telescopes then in operation could detect signals from other civilizations (provided, of course, that the signals were being sent). Since that time, astronomers have looked for these signals without success. Nevertheless, the importance of finding even one extraterrestrial civilization is so great that the search goes on.

Hunting for a signal is a little like looking for a radio station in an unfamiliar city. You dial across the frequencies, listening for a moment to each station, until you find what you are looking for. In the same way, SETI astronomers point their telescope at a small region of the sky, dial through the frequencies, then move on to the next region. Because there is a lot of sky and many frequencies, the sheer volume of data that has to be analyzed has been the primary roadblock in the search.

Recently, scientists at the University of California at Berkeley have harnessed the Internet to attack this problem. Radio data from the Arecibo Observatory in Puerto Rico are sent to Berkeley, where they are sorted into small chunks. These data chunks are then sent out to participants in the *SETI@home* project—over a million participants in hundreds of countries worldwide. Typically, these participants use downloaded software to let their personal computers analyze the data when the machine isn't doing anything else (a typical setup uses the SETI program as a screen saver). When the chunk of data is analyzed, it is sent back to Berkeley and new data are returned.

Table 1-2 Major Research Laboratories

Facility	Type	Location
Argonne National Laboratory	Govt/Univ	Near Chicago, IL
AT&T Bell Laboratories	Industrial	Murray Hill, NJ
Brookhaven National Laboratory	Government	Long Island, NY
Carnegie Institution	Private	California, Maryland, and DC
Dupont R&D Center	Industrial	Wilmington, DE
Fermi National Accelerator Lab	Govt/Univ	Near Chicago, IL
IBM Watson Research Laboratory	Industrial	Yorktown Hts, NY
Keck Telescope	University	Mauna Kea, HI
Los Alamos National Laboratory	Government	Los Alamos, NM
National Institutes of Health	Government	Bethesda, MD
National Institutes of Standards and Technology	Government	Gaithersburg, MD
Oak Ridge National Laboratory	Government	Oak Ridge, TN
Stanford Linear Accelerator	Govt/Univ	Stanford, CA
Texas Center for Superconductivity	University	Houston, TX
United States Geological Survey	Government	Reston, VA
Woods Hole Oceanographic Institution	University	Woods Hole, MA

The radio telescope at Arecibo, in Puerto Rico, is one instrument used in SETI.

Seth Shostak/Photo Researchers

Several million computers connected in this way form perhaps the largest computing project on Earth. More importantly, they are probably a taste of things to come, when distributed computers, working part time, will help scientists analyze massive data sets that are being developed in all sorts of fields. If you want to join, the address is http://setiathome.ssl.berkeley.edu. •

Funding for Science

An overwhelming proportion of funding for American scientific research comes from various agencies of the federal government—your tax dollars at work (see Table 1-3). In 2005, the U.S. government's total research and development budget was about 130 billion dollars. The *National Science Foundation*, with an annual budget of about 4 billion dollars, supports research and education in all areas of science. Other agencies, includ-

Table 1-3 Your Tax Dollars: 2006 Federal Science Funding

Agency or Department	Funding (in millions of $)
Department of Agriculture	2,394
Department of Defense	73,039
Department of Energy	8,608
Department of the Interior	629
Department of Transportation	841
Environmental Protection Agency	573
Homeland Security	1,281
National Aeronautics and Space Administration	11,367
National Institutes of Health	27,749
National Institutes of Standards and Technology	438
National Oceanographic and Atmospheric Administration	661
National Science Foundation	4,123
Nuclear Regulatory Commission	64
Smithsonian Institution	140

ing the National Institutes of Health, the Department of Energy, the Department of Defense, the Environmental Protection Agency, and the National Aeronautics and Space Administration, fund research and science education in their own particular areas of interest, while Congress may appropriate additional money for special projects.

An individual scientist seeking funding for research will usually submit a grant proposal to the appropriate federal agency. Such a proposal will include an outline of the planned research together with a statement about why the work is important. The agency evaluating the proposals asks panels of independent scientists to rank them in order of importance, and funds as many as it can. Depending on the field, a proposal has anywhere from about a 10 to a 40% chance of being successful. This money from federal grants buys experimental equipment and computer time, pays the salaries of researchers, and supports advanced graduate students. Without this support, much of the scientific research in the United States would come to a halt. The funding of science by the federal government is one place where the opinions and ideas of the citizen, through his or her elected representatives, have a direct effect on the development of science.

As you might expect, scientists and politicians engage in many debates about how this research money should be spent. One constant point of contention, for example, concerns the question of basic versus applied research. How much money should we put into applied research, which can be expected to show a quick payoff, as opposed to basic research, which may not have a payoff for years (if at all)?

Communication Among Scientists

Sometimes it's easier to do your homework with other students than by yourself, and the same is true of the work that scientists do. Working in isolation can be very hard, and scientists often seek out other people with whom to converse and collaborate. The popular stereotype of the lonely genius changing the course of history seldom describes the world of the working scientist. The next time you walk down the hall of a science department at your university, you will probably see faculty and students deep in conversation, talking and scribbling on blackboards. This direct contact between colleagues is the simplest type of scientific communication.

Scientific meetings provide a more formal and structured forum for communication. Every week of the year, at conference retreats and convention centers across the country, groups of scientists gather to trade ideas. You may notice that science stories in your newspapers often originate in the largest of these meetings, where thousands of scientists converge at one time, and a cadre of science reporters with their own special briefing room is poised to publicize exciting results. Scientists often hold off announcing important discoveries until they can make a splash at such a well-attended meeting and press conference.

Finally, scientists communicate with each other in writing. In addition to rapid communications such as letters, fax, and electronic mail, almost all scientific fields have specialized journals to publish the results of research. The system works like this: When a group of scientists finishes a piece of research and wants to communicate their results, they write a concise paper describing exactly what they've done, giving the technical details of their method so that others can reproduce the data, and stating their results and conclusions. The journal editor sends the submitted manuscript to one or more knowledgeable scientists who act as referees. These reviewers, whose identities are not usually revealed to the authors, read the paper carefully, checking for mistakes, misstatements, or shoddy procedures. Each reviewer then sends the editor a list of necessary modifications and corrections. If they tell the editor that the work passes muster, it will probably be published. In many fields papers are published online almost immediately, with archival paper copies following some weeks later. This system, called **peer review,** is one of the cornerstones of modern science.

Peer review provides a clear protocol for entering new results into the scientific literature. Little wonder, then, that scientists get so upset when one of their colleagues tries to bypass the system and announces results at a press conference. Such work has not been subject to the thorough review process, and no one can be sure that it meets established standards. When the results turn out to be irreproducible, overstated, or just plain wrong, it damages the credibility of the entire scientific community. So, if you read about a new discovery in the newspaper or on the Internet and you can't track the story back to a published, peer-reviewed journal article, then you should question the veracity of that finding.

Thinking More About | Research

Stem Cells

When cells in your body divide, they make cells like themselves. Muscle cells produce more muscle cells, skin cells produce more skin cells, and so on. On the other hand, in the very early stages of development, cells in an embryo retain the ability to form into any kind of cell whatsoever. Cells that have this property are called stem cells. Normally, stem cells lose their ability to develop freely after a few generations—in effect they "choose" one type of cell to produce.

In 1998, researchers at a number of institutions succeeded in keeping stem cells proliferating for long periods of time. The medical implications of this development are enormous. If we have cells that can develop into any kind of human tissue, you can imagine being able to treat degenerative diseases like Parkinson's and Alzheimer's, and perhaps even heal crippling spinal cord injuries.

On the other hand, the most reliable source of such stem cells is human embryos, either those grown specifically in the laboratory or those harvested from abortions or miscarriages. In the United States, federal funds cannot be used to develop new cell lines from these sources.

How do you weigh the possible good that could come from research on stem cells against the moral objections to this type of use of human embryos? Should the moral standards of one segment of the population prevent research that would benefit those who do not share those standards? Who should make decisions like this?

Summary

Science is a way of learning about our physical universe. The *scientific method* relies on making *reproducible observations* and *experiments* based on careful *measurements* of the natural world. Once scientists have collected a number of *facts*, which are confirmed observations about the natural world, then they can form a *hypothesis*—a tentative educated guess about how the world works. Hypotheses, in turn, lead to *predictions* that can be tested with more observations and experiments. A scientific *law* arises when numerous measurements point to a regular, predictable pattern of behavior in nature, whereas a scientific *theory* is a well-substantiated explanation of the natural world based on a large number of independently verified observational and experimental tests. Laws and theories, no matter how successful, are always subject to further testing. Experimental analyses and the development of theories are often guided by the language of *mathematics*. Science and the scientific method differ from other ways of knowing, including religion, philosophy, and the arts, and differ from *pseudosciences*.

Science is organized around a hierarchy of fundamental principles. Overarching concepts about forces, motion, matter, and energy apply to all scientific disciplines, including *physics, chemistry, astronomy, geology,* and *biology*. Additional great ideas relate to specific systems—molecules, cells, planets, or stars. This body of scientific knowledge forms a seamless web, in which every detail fits into a larger, integrated picture of our universe.

Scientists engage in *basic research* to acquire fundamental knowledge, as well as *applied research* and *research and development (R&D)*, which are aimed at specific problems. *Technology* is developed by this process. Scientific results are communicated in *peer-reviewed* publications. The federal government plays the important role of funding most scientific research and advanced science education in the United States.

Key Terms

scientific method
observation
experiment
measurement
mathematics
fact
hypothesis
law
theory
prediction
reproducible
pseudoscience
physics
chemistry
astronomy
geology
biology
basic research
technology
applied research
research and development (R&D)
peer review

REVIEW QUESTIONS

1. What is science?

2. How might the ancient Greek philosopher Plato, a medieval scholar at Oxford, and the Italian scientist Galileo have differed in the importance each placed on the role of rational processes, observations, and received wisdom in the study of nature?

3. How is observation different from imagination?

4. Write an equation in words and then in symbols for the following sentence: The price of coffee beans is equal to the weight of the beans times the price of the beans per pound.

5. Write an equation in words and then in symbols for the following sentence: The change in the number of individuals in a population is equal to the difference between the number of births and deaths.

6. Describe the steps of the scientific method.

7. Describe the roles of hypotheses, theories, and predictions in the scientific method.

8. Describe the difference between an observation and an experiment.

9. Why might the term *scientific cycle* be a good substitute for *scientific method?*

10. By what criteria might you determine whether a question might be answered using the scientific method?

11. Describe the difference between basic and applied research. Give examples of basic and applied research that might be undertaken on transportation and on health.

12. In what ways do scientists communicate with their colleagues?

13. Describe the steps a scientist would take to obtain funding for a research project. What sources of funds might be available? What role would peer review play in the process?

DISCUSSION QUESTIONS

1. Why is research in astronomy considered science but studying astrology regarded as psuedoscience? What evidence (i.e., predictions and observations) might change scientists' minds about astrology?

2. Which of the following statements could be tested scientifically to determine whether it is true or false?

a. Women are more intelligent than men.
b. Most of the Sun's energy is in the form of heat energy.
c. Unicorns are now extinct.
d. Beethoven wrote beautiful music.
e. Earth was created over 4 billion years ago.
f. Earth was created in a miraculous event.
g. Diamond is harder than steel.
h. Diamond is more beautiful than ruby.
i. Baseball is a better sport than football.
j. God exists.

3. What role did observation play in the creation of the periodic table by Dimitri Mendeleev?

4. How did competing hypotheses lead William Harvey to his experiments on the circulation of blood?

5. Scientists are currently investigating whether certain microscopic organisms can clean up toxic wastes. How might you set up an experiment to determine that you had found such an organism?

6. Categorize the following examples as basic research or applied research.

a. the discovery of a new species of bird
b. the development of a more fuel-efficient vehicle
c. the breeding of a new variety of disease-resistant wheat
d. a study of the ecological role of grizzly bears in Yellowstone National Park
e. the identification of a new chemical compound
f. the development of a new drug for cancer or AIDS patients
g. the improvement of wind turbines for energy production

7. The claim is sometimes made that the cycle of the scientific method produces closer and closer approximations to "reality." Is this a scientific statement? Why or why not?

8. A recent television commercial claimed that a breakfast cereal "contains 3 grams of soluble fiber" and "promotes healthy arteries." How might you test these statements in the laboratory? As a consumer, what additional questions would you ask before deciding to buy this product? Are all of these questions subject to the scientific method?

9. What are some of the criteria that scientists might use to select which one research grant proposal, among five finalists, to fund? What criteria would you use to decide on funding research projects?

10. With respect to science, what did Isaac Newton mean when he said, "If I have seen further it is by standing on the shoulders of giants."

11. If you were a research scientist, what would you study? Would your research be basic or applied?

PROBLEMS

1. Marcus kept a record of the average daily temperature in his town for one month. He noted that on the 1st of May the average temperature was 20 degrees Celsius; between the 2nd and the 15th, the average for each day was 22 degrees; between the 16th and the 30th, the average was 24 degrees; and on the 31st the average was 25 degrees Celsius. Describe and illustrate some of the ways you might present these data. What additional data or information would you like to obtain to improve your description?

2. Tabulate the hours spent studying and the test scores of 12 classmates from your last exam. Present these data both in a table and in one or more graphs. Is the graph or the table more effective in representing this data? Do you observe any interesting trends?

Why might students and their instructors find such a graph or table useful?

3. Pick a favorite food and write down at least 10 adjectives to describe this food. Then cite at least five ways in which you might use numbers to describe this food, (e.g., weight, temperature, fat content), more precisely than using just words. Make one or more of these measurements on your chosen food. What laboratory equipment will you need to carry out your investigation?

4. Someone says to you, "I was thinking about Aunt Maria the other day, and she called me on the phone. Doesn't that prove ESP exists?" What other information would you need to know to investigate this claim? How would you design an experiment to test this sort of claim?

Investigations

1. What is the closest major government research laboratory to your school? What is the closest industrial laboratory? Describe one research project that is now under way at one of these laboratories.

2. What are the major science departments at your school? How many professors are performing research in each department? Are these professors doing basic or applied research? Describe a program of scientific research carried out by a member of your school's faculty. How is the scientific method employed in this research?

3. Identify a current piece of legislation relating to science or technology (perhaps an environmental or energy bill). How did your representatives in Congress vote on this issue? Did they use scientific knowledge or received wisdom to arrive at their decision?

4. Look at a recent newspaper article about science funding. What is the funding agency? Is the proposed research basic or applied?

5. Find a science story in a newspaper or popular magazine. Who were the scientists who conducted the research? Where did they do the work? How was the research funded?

6. How were scientists depicted in the novel and film versions of *Jurassic Park* by Michael Crichton? Were you convinced by these portrayals? Why? How do these portrayals compare with the faculty doing research at your school?

7. Was Harvey justified in his use of animals in studies of the circulatory system? What limits should scientists accept in research using animals? What organizations (e.g., institutional animal control and review boards) at your school protect animals from unnecessary harm? What are their national standards regarding animal research? What national organizations are involved in this debate? What specific drugs, medicines, and procedures were developed using animal research?

8. Design an experiment to test the relative strengths of three different kinds of aluminum can. What data would you need to collect? What laboratory equipment would you need? How might you present these data in tables and graphically?

9. Malaria, the deadliest infectious disease in the world, kills more than 2 million people (mostly children in poor countries) every year. The annual malaria research budget in the United States is less than a million dollars, a minuscule fraction of spending on cancer, heart disease, and AIDS. Should the United States devote more research funds to this disease, which does not occur in North America? Why or why not? Can we use the scientific method to answer this question?

10. Look at a carefully tended lawn at a golf course or ball field and compare it with a patch of wild ground. Do your observations match those of the Minnesota biodiversity experiment? Why or why not? What hypotheses might you derive from your observations?

11. Does your school recycle? If so, why? What are the benefits of recycling paper, metal, or plastic? Is there a benefit to recycling paper since we can always grow more trees?

12. Think of an idea or a topic in which you are interested. Go to Google Scholar: http://scholar.google.com/ and search peer-reviewed journals to read about how research scientists with your interests have studied the idea.

2

The Ordered Universe

Why do planets appear to wander slowly across the sky?

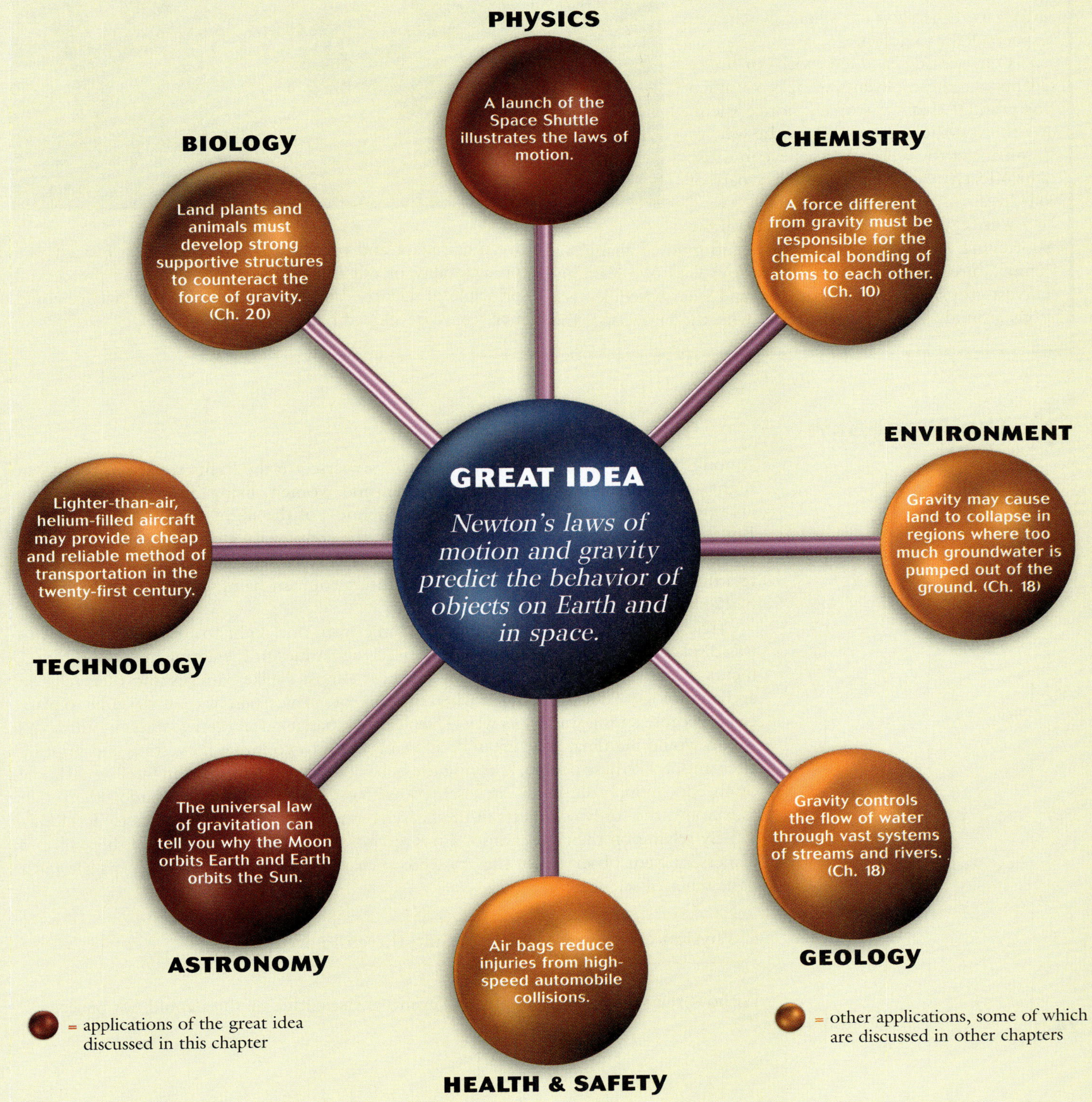

Science Through the Day | Cause and Effect

You jump out of bed, eager to start the day. The air smells fresh and cool, but the Sun's rays already feel warm. It should be perfect beach weather.

When the Sun comes up in the morning you expect temperatures to become warmer; in the evening, as the Sun goes down, you expect temperatures to fall. When you turn the key in the ignition in your car you expect it to start. When you flip a light switch, you expect a light to go on.

Our world is filled with ordinary events like these—events we take so much for granted that we scarcely notice them. Yet they set the background for the way we think about the world. We believe in cause and effect because it's so much a part of our lives.

David Sacks/Photographer's Choice/Getty Images

The regular passage of seasons, with the shortening and lengthening of days and gradual changes in temperature, provides a template for our lives. We plant and harvest crops, purchase wardrobes, and even schedule vacations around this predictable cycle, with the knowledge that we must adapt and prepare for nature's cycles. Indeed, the predictability of our physical world has become the central principle of science—an idea so important that science could never have developed had it not been true.

The Night Sky

Among the most predictable objects in the universe are the lights we see in the sky at night—the stars and planets. Modern men and women, living in large metropolitan areas, are no longer very conscious of the richness of the night sky's shifting patterns. But think about the last time you were out in the country on a clear moonless night, far from the lights of town. There, the stars seem very close, very real. Before the nineteenth-century development of artificial lighting, human beings often experienced jet-black skies filled with brilliant pinpoint stars.

The sky changes; it's never quite the same from one night to the next. Living with this display all the time, our ancestors noticed regularities in the arrangement and movements of stars and planets, and they wove these almost lifelike patterns into their religion and mythology. They learned that when the Sun rose in a certain place, it was time to plant crops because spring was on its way. They learned that at certain times of the month a full Moon would illuminate the ground, allowing them to continue harvesting and hunting after sunset. To these people, knowing the behavior of the sky was not an intellectual game or an educational frill, it was an essential part of their lives. It is no wonder, then, that astronomy, the study of objects in the heavens, was one of the first sciences to develop.

By relying on their observations and records of the regular motions of the stars and planets, ancient observers of the sky were perhaps the first humans to accept the most basic tenet of science:

Physical events are quantifiable and therefore predictable.

Without the predictability of physical events the scientific method could not proceed.

Stonehenge

No symbol of humankind's early preoccupation with astronomy is more dramatic than Stonehenge, the great prehistoric stone monument on Salisbury Plain in southern England. The structure consists of a large circular bank of earth surrounding a ring of single upright stones, which in turn encircle a horseshoe-shaped structure of five giant stone archways. Each arch is constructed from three massive blocks—two vertical supports several meters tall capped by a great stone lintel. The open end of the horseshoe aligns with an avenue that leads northeast to another large stone, called the "heel stone" (see Figure 2-1).

Stonehenge was built in spurts over a long period of time, starting in about 2800 B.C. Despite various legends assigning it to the Druids, Julius Caesar, the magician Merlin (who was supposed to have levitated the stones from Ireland), or other mysterious unknown races, archaeologists have shown that Stonehenge was built by several groups of people, none of whom had a written language and some of whom even lacked metal tools. Why would these people expend such a great effort to erect one of the world's great monuments?

Stonehenge, like many similar structures scattered around the world, was built to mark the passage of time. It served as a giant calendar based on the movement of objects in the sky. The most famous astronomical function of Stonehenge was to mark the passage of the seasons. In an agricultural society, after all, you have to know when it's time to plant the crops, and you can't always tell by looking at the weather. At Stonehenge, this job was done by sighting through the stones. On midsummer's morning, for example, someone standing in the center of the monument will see the Sun rising directly over the heel stone.

Building a structure like Stonehenge required accumulation of a great deal of knowledge about the sky—knowledge that could have been gained only through many years of observation. Without a written language, people would have had to pass complex information about the movements of the Sun, the Moon, and the planets from one generation to the next. How else could they have aligned their stones so perfectly that modern-day Druids in England can still greet the midsummer sunrise over the heel stone?

If the universe was not regular and predictable, if repeated observation could not show us patterns that occur over and over again, the very concept of a monument like Stonehenge would be impossible. And yet, there it stands after almost 5000 years, a testament to human ingenuity and to the possibility of predicting the behavior of the universe we live in.

Jeremy Walker/Getty Images

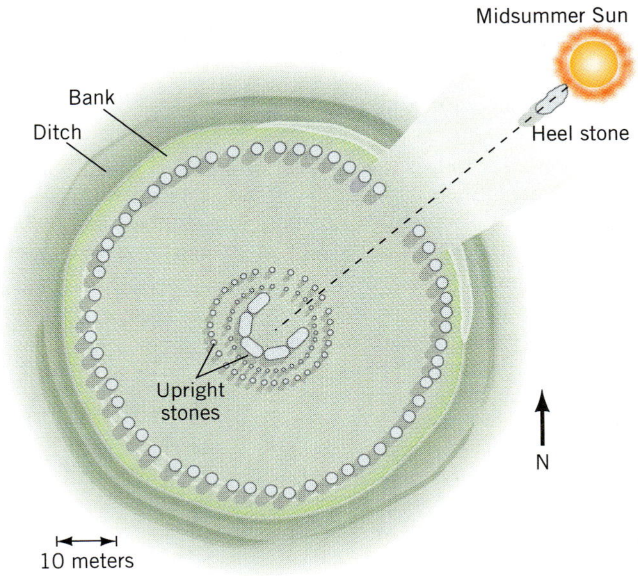

• **Figure 2-1** Stonehenge is built so that someone standing at the center will see the Sun rise over the heel stone on midsummer's morning.

Science in the Making •

The Discovery of the Spread of Disease

Observing nature is a crucial part of the scientific method. During the nineteenth century, for example, Europe experienced an epidemic of cholera, a severe and often fatal intestinal disease. No one knew the cause of the disease (the discovery of the germ theory of disease was still decades in the future), but doctors could record their observations about the illness. A list of cholera outbreaks was chronicled in 1854 by John Snow (1823–1858), a distinguished London physician who pioneered the use of anesthetics

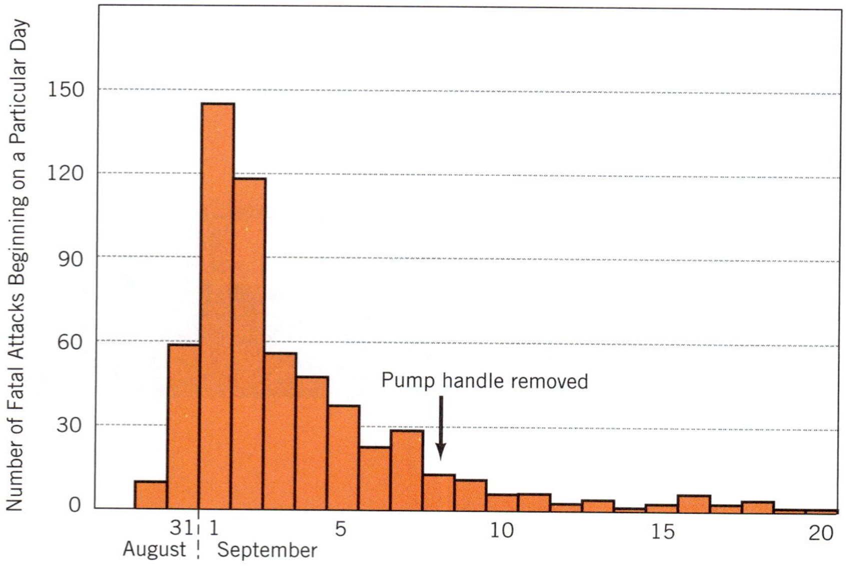

• **Figure 2-2** John Snow plotted the number of cases of cholera versus the date for residents in the vicinity of the Broad Street pump. The number of cases declined in early September because most residents fled the area, but few new cases occurred after the pump handle was removed on September 8.

and assisted at the birth of Queen Victoria's children. He noticed that in London the diseases seemed to be centered around certain public squares. At that time, most people in London got their drinking water from fountains and pumps in those squares. The Broad Street pump, located in a place called Golden Square, seemed to be the focus of a particularly large number of cases. Upon investigation, Snow found that the square was surrounded by a large number of homes where human waste was dumped into backyard pits. He argued that these findings suggested the disease was somehow related to contamination of the water supply (Figure 2-2).

Driven by Snow's findings, the city of London (and soon all major population centers) began to require that human waste be carried away from dwellings into sewers. Thus Snow's discovery of a regularity in nature (in this case between disease and polluted water) was the foundation on which modern sanitation and public health systems are based.

Just as the builders of Stonehenge had no idea of the structure of the solar system or why the heavens behave as they do, Snow had no idea why keeping human waste out of the drinking water supply should eliminate a disease such as cholera. It wasn't until the early 1890s, in fact, that the German scientist Robert Koch first suggested that the disease was caused by a particular bacterium, *Vibrio cholerae,* that is carried in human waste. •

Science by the Numbers •

Ancient Astronauts

Confronted by a monument such as Stonehenge, with its precise orientation and epic proportions, some people refuse to accept the notion that it could have been built by the ingenuity and hard work of ancient peoples. Instead, they evoke some outside intervention, frequently in the form of visitors from other planets whose handiwork survives in the monument today. Many ancient monuments, including the pyramids of Egypt, the Mayan temples of Central America, and the giant statues of Easter Island, have been ascribed to these mysterious aliens.

Such conjecture is unconvincing unless you first show that building the monument was beyond the capabilities of the indigenous people. Suppose, for example, that Columbus had found a glass-and-steel skyscraper when he landed in America. Both the ability to produce the materials (steel, glass, and plastic, for example) and the ability to construct a building dozens of stories tall were beyond the abilities of Native Americans at that time. A reasonable case could have been made for the intervention of ancient astronauts or some other advanced intelligence.

Is Stonehenge a similar case? The material, local stone, was certainly available to anyone who wanted to use it. Working and shaping stone was also a skill, albeit a laborious one, that was available to early civilizations. The key question, then, is whether people without steel tools or wheeled vehicles could have moved the stones from the quarry to the construction site (Figure 2-3).

The largest stone, about 10 meters (more than 30 feet) in length, weighs about 50 metric tons (50,000 kilograms, or about 100,000 pounds) and had to be moved over-

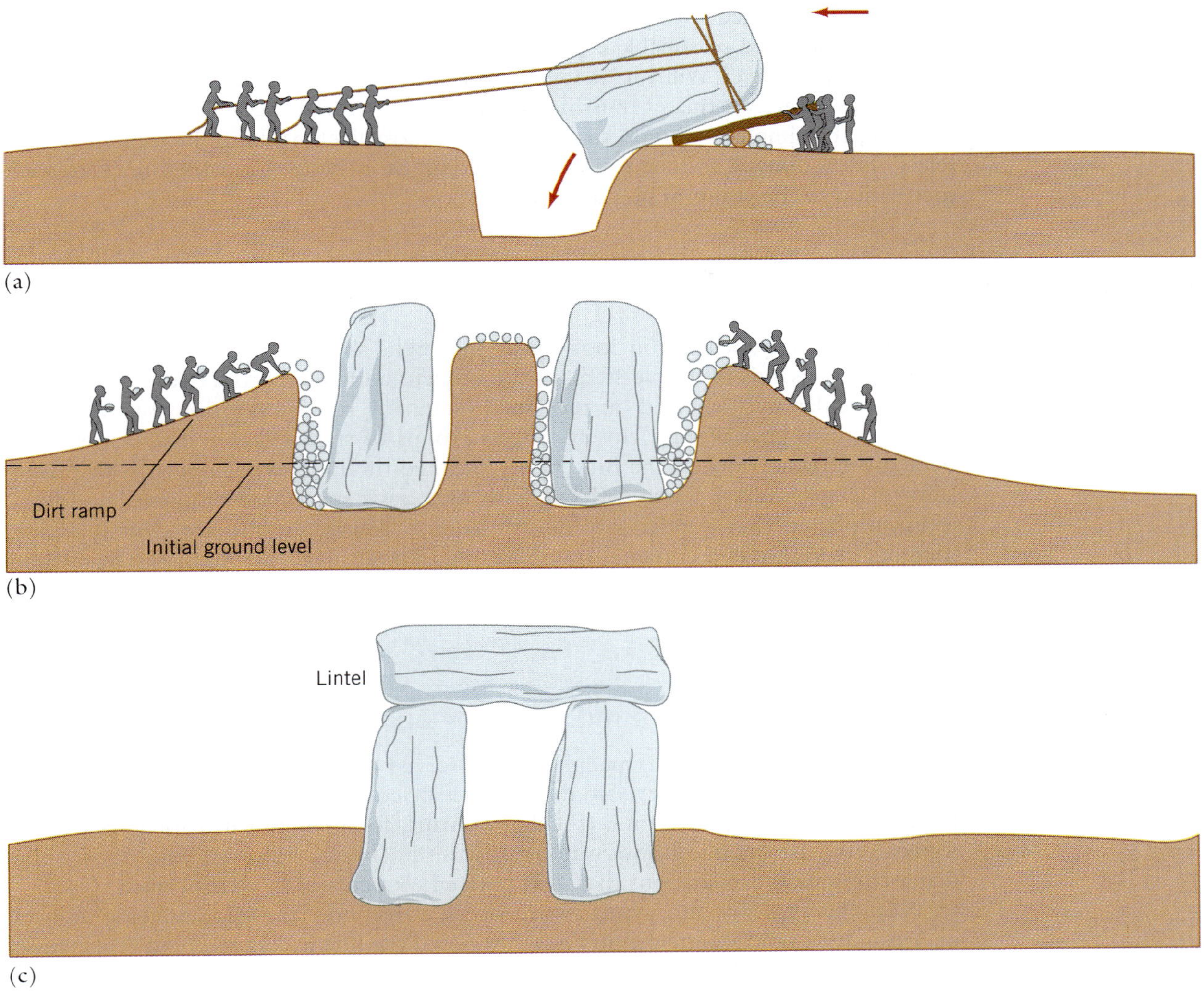

• **Figure 2-3** One puzzling aspect of the construction of Stonehenge is the raising of the giant lintel stones. Three steps in the process were probably *(a)* to dig a pit for each of the upright stones; *(b)* to pile dirt into a long sloping ramp up to the level of the two uprights so that the lintel stones could be rolled into place; and *(c)* to cart away the dirt, thus leaving the stone archway.

land some 30 kilometers (20 miles) from quarries to the north. Could this massive block have been moved by primitive people, equipped only with wood and ropes?

While Stonehenge was being built, it snowed frequently in southern England, so the stones could have been hauled on sleds. A single person can easily haul 100 kilograms on a sled (think of pulling a couple of your friends). How many people would it take to haul a 50,000-kilogram stone?

$$\frac{50{,}000 \text{ kilograms}}{100 \text{ kilograms pulled by each person}} = 500 \text{ people}$$

Organizing 500 people for the job would have been a major social achievement, of course, but there's nothing physically impossible about it. So, while scientists cannot absolutely disprove the possibility that Stonehenge was constructed by some strange, forgotten technology, why should we evoke such alien intervention when the concerted actions of a dedicated, hard-working human society would have sufficed?

When confronted with phenomena in a physical world, we should accept the most straightforward and reasonable explanation as the most likely. This procedure is called *Ockham's razor,* after William of Ockham, a fourteenth-century English philosopher who argued that "postulates must not be multiplied without necessity"—that is, given a choice, the simplest solution to a problem is most likely to be right. Scientists thus reject the notion of ancient astronauts building Stonehenge, and they relegate such speculation to the realm of pseudoscience. •

The Birth of Modern Astronomy

Far from the city, when you look up at the night sky you see a dazzling array of objects. Thousands of visible stars fill the heavens and appear to move each night in stately circular arcs centered on the North Star. The relative positions of these stars never seem to change, and closely spaced groups of stars called constellations have been given names such as the Big Dipper and Leo the Lion. Moving across this fixed starry background are Earth's Moon, with its regular succession of phases, and half-a-dozen planets that wander through the zodiac. You might also see swift streaking meteors or long-tailed comets—transient objects that grace the night sky from time to time.

What causes these objects to move, and what do those motions tell us about the universe in which we live?

The Historical Background: Ptolemy and Copernicus

Since before recorded history people have observed the distinctive motions of objects in the sky and have tried to explain them. Most societies created legends and myths tied to these movements, and some (the Babylonians, for example) had long records of sophisticated astronomical observations. It was the Greeks, however, who devised the first astronomical explanations that incorporated elements of modern science.

Claudius Ptolemy, an Egyptian-born Greek astronomer and geographer who lived in Alexandria in the second century A.D., proposed the first widely accepted explanation for complex celestial motions. Working with the accumulated observations of earlier Babylonian and Greek astronomers, he put together a singularly successful model—a theory, to use the modern term, about how the heavens had to be arranged to produce the display we see every night. In the Ptolemaic description of the universe, Earth sat unmoved at the center. Around it, on a concentric series of rotating spheres, moved the stars and planets. The model was carefully crafted to take account of observations. The planets, for example, were attached to small spheres rolling inside of the larger spheres so that their uneven motion across the sky could be understood.

This system remained the best explanation of the universe for almost 1500 years. It successfully predicted planetary motions, eclipses, and a host of other heavenly phenomena, and was one of the longest-lived scientific theories ever devised.

During the first decades of the sixteenth century, however, a Polish cleric by the name of Nicolas Copernicus (1473–1543) considered a competing hypothesis that was to herald the end of Ptolemy's crystal spheres. His ideas were published in 1543 under the title *On the Revolutions of the Spheres.* Copernicus retained the notions of a spherical universe with circular orbits, and even kept the ideas of spheres rolling within a sphere, but he asked a simple and extraordinary question: "Is it possible to construct a model of the heavens whose predictions are as accurate as Ptolemy's, but in which the Sun, rather than Earth, is at the center?" We do not know how Copernicus, a busy man of affairs in medieval Poland, conceived this question, nor do we know why he devoted his spare time for most of his adult life to answering it. We do know, however, that in 1543, for the first time in over a millennium, the Ptolemaic system was faced by a serious challenger (see Figure 2-4).

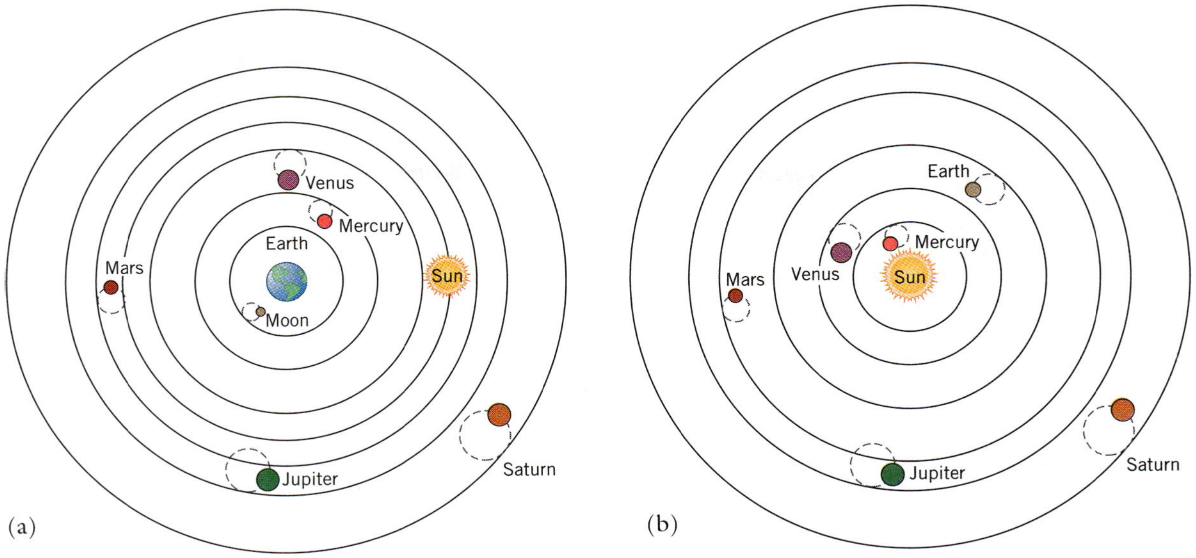

• **Figure 2-4** The Ptolemaic *(a)* and Copernican *(b)* systems both assumed that all orbits are circular. The fundamental difference is that Copernicus placed the Sun at the center.

Observations: Tycho Brahe and Johannes Kepler

With the publication of the Copernican theory, astronomers were confronted by two competing models of the universe. The Ptolemaic and Copernican systems differed in a fundamental way that had far-reaching implications about the place of humanity in the cosmos. They both described possible universes, but in one Earth, and by implication humankind, was no longer at the center. The astronomers' task was to decide which model best describes the universe we actually live in.

To resolve the question, astronomers had to compare the predictions of the two competing hypotheses to the observations of what was actually seen in the sky. When they performed these observations, a fundamental problem became apparent. Although the two models made different predictions about the position of a planet at midnight, for example, or the time of moonrise, the differences were too small to be measured with equipment available at the time. The telescope had not yet been invented, but astronomers were skilled in recording planetary positions by depending entirely on naked-eye measurements with awkward instruments. Until the accuracy of measurement was improved, the question of whether Earth was at the center of the universe couldn't be decided.

The Danish nobleman Tycho Brahe (1546–1601) showed the way out of this impasse. Tycho, as he was known, is one of those people who, in addition to making important contributions to knowledge, led a truly bizarre life. He was, for example, abducted in infancy and raised by his uncle. As a young man he lost the end of his nose in a duel with a fellow student over who was the better mathematician; for the rest of his life he had to wear a silver and gold prosthesis.

Tycho's scientific reputation was firmly established at the age of 25, when he observed and described a new star in the sky (in fact, a supernova—see Chapter 14). This dramatic discovery challenged the prevailing wisdom that the heavens are unchanging. Within the next five years, the Danish king had given him the island of Hveen off the coast of Denmark and funds to construct a royal observatory there.

Tycho built his career on the design and use of vastly improved observational instruments. He determined the position of each star or planet with a "quadrant," a large sloping device something like a gun sight, recording each position as two angles. If you

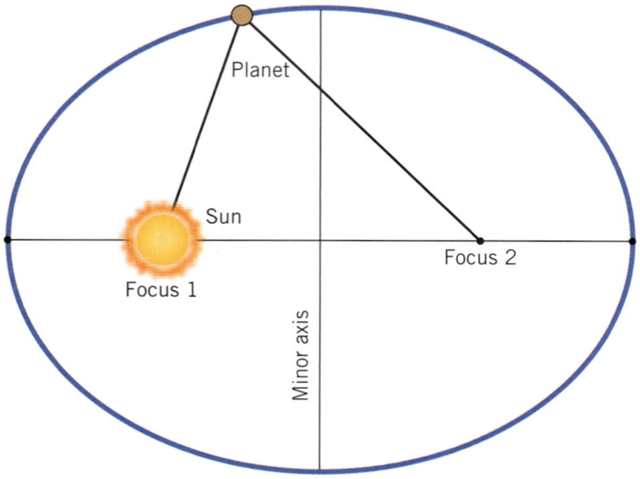

• **Figure 2-5** Kepler's first law, shown schematically, states that the orbit of every planet is an ellipse, a geometrical figure in which the sum of the distances to two fixed points (each of which is called a focus) is always the same. For planetary orbits in the solar system, the Sun is at one focus of the ellipse (greatly exaggerated in this figure).

were to do this today, you might, for example, measure one angle up from the horizon and a second angle around from due north. Tycho constructed his sighting device of carefully selected materials, and he learned to correct his measurements for thermal contraction—the slight shrinkage of brass and iron components that occurred during the cold Danish nights. Over a period of 25 years, he used these instruments to accumulate extremely accurate data on the positions of the planets.

When Tycho died in 1601, his data passed into the hands of his assistant, Johannes Kepler (1571–1630), a skilled German mathematician who had joined Tycho two years before. Kepler analyzed Tycho Brahe's decades of planetary data in new ways, and he found that the data could be summarized in three mathematical statements about the solar system. Kepler's first and most important law (shown in Figure 2-5) states that all planets, including Earth, orbit the Sun in elliptical, not circular, paths. In this picture, the spheres-within-spheres are gone, because ellipses fully account for the observed planetary motions. Not only do Kepler's laws give a better description of what is observed in the sky, but they present a simpler picture of the solar system as well.

Previous astronomers had assumed that planetary orbits must be perfect circles, and many believed on theological or philosophical grounds that Earth had to be the center of a spherical universe. In science, such assumptions of ideality may guide thinking, but they must be replaced when observations prove them wrong.

The work of Tycho Brahe and Johannes Kepler firmly established that Earth is not at the center of the universe, that planetary orbits are not circular, and that the answer to the contest between the Ptolemaic and Copernican universes is "neither of the above." This research also illustrates a recurrent point about scientific progress. The ability to answer scientific questions, even questions dealing with the most fundamental aspects of human existence, often depends on the kinds of instruments scientists have at their disposal, and the ability of scientists to apply advanced mathematical reasoning to their data.

At the end of this historical episode, astronomers had Kepler's laws that describe how the planets in the solar system move, but they had no idea *why* planets behave the way they do. The answer to that question was to come from an unexpected source.

The Birth of Mechanics

Mechanics is an old word for the branch of science that deals with the motions of material objects. A rock rolling down a hill, a ball thrown into the air, and a sailboat skimming over the waves are all fit subjects for this science. Since ancient times, philosophers had speculated on why things move the way they do, but it wasn't until the seventeenth century that our modern understanding of the subject began to emerge.

Galileo Galilei

The Italian physicist and philosopher Galileo Galilei (1564–1642) was, in many ways, a forerunner of the modern scientist. A professor of mathematics at the University of Padua, he quickly became an advisor to the powerful court of the Medici at Florence as well as a consultant at the Arsenal of Venice, the most advanced naval construction center in the world. He invented many practical devices, such as the first thermometer, the

Uffizi, Florence Italy/Scala/Art Resource

Galileo Galilei (1564–1642)

pendulum clock, and the proportional compass that draftsmen still use today. Galileo is also famous as the first person to record observations of the heavens with a telescope, which he built after hearing of the instrument from others (Figure 2-6). His astronomical writings, which supported the Sun-centered Copernican model of the universe, led to his trial, conviction, and eventual imprisonment by the Inquisition.

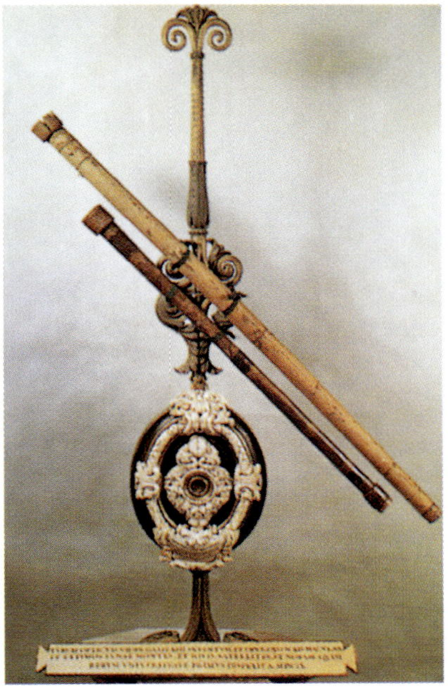
Museo della Scienza, Florence, Italy/Art Resource

• **Figure 2-6** Telescopes used by Galileo Galilei in his astronomical studies.

Science in the Making •

The Heresy Trial of Galileo

In spite of his great scientific advances, Galileo is remembered primarily because of his heresy trial in 1633. In 1610, Galileo had published a summary of his telescopic observations in *The Starry Messenger,* a book written in everyday Italian rather than scholarly Latin. Some readers complained that these ideas violated Catholic Church doctrine, and in 1616 Galileo was called before the College of Cardinals. The Catholic Church supposedly warned Galileo not to discuss Copernican ideas unless he treated them as an unproven hypothesis.

In spite of these instructions, in 1632 Galileo published *A Dialogue Concerning Two World Systems,* which was a long defense of the Copernican system. This action led to the famous trial, at which Galileo purged himself of suspicion of heresy by denying that he held the views in his book. He was already an old man by this time, and he spent his last few years under house arrest in his villa near Florence.

The legend of Galileo's trial, in which an earnest seeker of truth is crushed by a rigid hierarchy, bears little resemblance to the historical events. The Catholic Church had not banned Copernican ideas. Copernicus, after all, was a savvy Church politician who knew how to get his ideas across without ruffling feathers. But Galileo's confrontational tactics—notably putting the Pope's favorite arguments into the mouth of a foolish character in the book—brought the predictable reaction.

A footnote: In 1992, the Catholic Church reopened the case of Galileo and, in effect, issued a retroactive "not guilty." The grounds for the reversal were that the original judges had not separated questions of faith from questions of scientific fact. •

Speed, Velocity, and Acceleration

To lay the groundwork for understanding Galileo's study of moving objects (and ultimately to understand the workings of the solar system), we have to begin with precise definitions of three familiar terms: speed, velocity, and acceleration.

Speed and Velocity

Speed and velocity are everyday words that have precise scientific meanings. **Speed** is the distance an object travels divided by the time it takes to travel that distance. **Velocity** has the same numerical value as speed, but it is a quantity that also includes information on the direction of travel. The speed of a car might be 40 miles per hour, for example, while the velocity is 40 miles per hour due west. Quantities like velocity that involve both a speed and a direction are called *vectors.* Velocity and speed are both measured in units of distance per time, such as meters per second, feet per second, or miles per hour.

▶ **In equation form:**

$$\text{velocity or speed (m/s)} = \frac{\text{distance traveled (m)}}{\text{time of travel (s)}}$$

▶ **In symbols:**

$$v = \frac{d}{t}$$

Thus, if you know the distance traveled and the time elapsed during the travel, you can calculate the speed.

EXAMPLE 2-1

Driving

If your car travels 30 miles per hour, how many miles will you go in 15 minutes?

Reasoning and Solution: This question involves changing units, as well as applying the equation that relates time, speed, and distance. First, we must know the travel time in hours:

$$\frac{15 \text{ minutes}}{(60 \text{ minutes/hour})} = \tfrac{1}{4} \text{ hour}$$

Then, rearranging the relationship between speed, distance, and time given above, we find:

$$\begin{aligned} \text{distance} &= \text{speed} \times \text{time} \\ \text{distance} &= 30 \text{ miles/hour} \times \tfrac{1}{4} \text{ hour} \\ &= 7.5 \text{ miles} \end{aligned}$$

It would take the average person about two hours to walk this far.

A word about units: You may have noticed that in the example we put ¼ hour into the equation for the time instead of 15 minutes. The reason we did this was that we needed to be consistent with the units in which an automobile speedometer measures speed. Since the automobile dial reads in miles per hour, we also put the time in hours to make the equation balance. A useful way to deal with situations like this is to imagine that the units are quantities that can be canceled in fractions, just like numbers. In this case, we would have:

$$\begin{aligned} \text{distance} &= (\text{miles/hour}) \times \text{hour} \\ &= \text{miles} \end{aligned}$$

If, however, we put the time in minutes, we'd have:

$$\text{distance} = (\text{miles/hour}) \times \text{minutes}$$

and there would be no cancellation.

Whenever you do a problem like this, it's a good idea to check to make sure the units come out correctly. This important process is known as *dimensional analysis.*

Acceleration

Acceleration is a measure of the rate of change of velocity. Whenever an object changes speed or direction, it accelerates. When you step on the gas pedal in your car, for example, the car accelerates forward. When you slam on the brakes, the car accelerates backward (what is sometimes called deceleration). When you go around a curve in your car, even if the car's speed stays exactly the same, the car is still accelerating because the direction of motion is changing. The most thrilling amusement park rides combine these different kinds of acceleration—speeding up, slowing down, and changing direction in bumps, tight turns, and rapid spins.

- **In words:** Acceleration is the amount of change in velocity divided by the time it takes that change to occur.
- **In equation form:**

$$\text{acceleration } (\text{m/s}^2) = \frac{\text{final velocity} - \text{initial velocity}}{\text{time}}$$

▶ **In symbols:**

$$a = \frac{(v_f - v_i)}{t}$$

Like velocity, acceleration requires information about the direction, and it is therefore a vector.

When velocity changes, it may be by a certain number of feet per second or meters per second in each second. Consequently, the units of acceleration are meters per second squared, usually described as "meters per second per second" (and abbreviated m/s^2), where the first "meters per second" refers to the velocity, and the last "per second" to the time it takes for the velocity to change.

To understand the difference between acceleration and velocity, think about the last time you were behind the wheel of a car driving down a long straight road. You glance at your speedometer. If the needle is unmoving (at 30 miles per hour, for example), you are moving at a constant speed. Suppose, however, that the needle isn't stationary on the speedometer scale (perhaps because you have your foot on the gas or on the brake). Your speed is changing and, by the definition above, you are accelerating. The higher the acceleration, the faster the needle moves. If the needle doesn't move, however, *this doesn't mean you and the car aren't moving.* As we saw above, an unmoving needle simply means that you are traveling at a constant speed without acceleration. Motion at a constant speed in a single direction is called *uniform motion.*

The Founder of Experimental Science

Galileo devised an ingenious experiment to determine the relationships among distance, time, velocity, and acceleration. Many scientists now view Galileo's greatest achievement as this experimental work on the behavior of objects thrown or dropped on the surface of Earth. Greek philosophers, using pure reason, had taught that heavier objects must fall faster than light ones. In a series of classic experiments, Galileo showed that this was not the case—that at Earth's surface all objects accelerate at the same rate as they fall downward. Ironically, Galileo probably never performed the one experiment for which he is most famous—dropping two different weights from the Leaning Tower of Pisa to see which would land first.

To describe falling objects, it's necessary to make precise measurements of two variables: distance and time. Distance was easily measured by Galileo and his contemporaries using rulers, but their timepieces were not precise enough to measure the brief times it took objects to fall straight down. While previous workers had simply observed the behavior of falling objects, Galileo constructed a special apparatus designed purely to measure acceleration (see Figure 2-7). He slowed down the time of fall by rolling large balls down an inclined plane crafted of brass and hard wood, and measured the time of

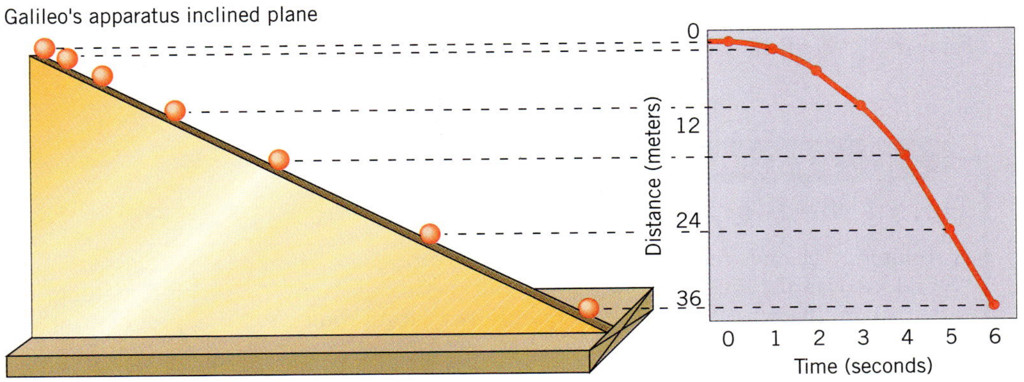

Time	Distance
0	0
1	1
2	4
3	9
4	16
5	25
6	36

• **Figure 2-7** Galileo's falling-ball apparatus with a table of measurements and a graph of distance versus time.

• **Figure 2-8** The accelerated motion of a falling apple is captured by a multiple-exposure photograph. In each successive time interval the apple falls farther.

descent by listening to the "ping" as the ball rolled over wires stretched along its path. (The human ear is quite good at hearing equal time intervals). The balls accelerated as they moved down the plane, and by increasing the angle of elevation of the plane, he could increase that acceleration. At an elevation of 90 degrees, of course, the ball would fall freely.

Galileo's experiments convinced him that any object accelerating toward Earth's surface, no matter how heavy or light, falls with exactly the same constant acceleration. For balls on his plane, his results can be summarized in a simple equation:

► **In words:** The velocity of an accelerating object that starts from rest is proportional to the length of time that it has been falling.

► **In equation form:**

$$\text{velocity (m/s)} = \text{constant } a \text{ (m/s}^2) \times \text{time (s)}$$

► **In symbols:**

$$v = a \times t$$

The velocity of Galileo's objects, of course, was always directed downward.

This equation tells us that an object that falls for 2 seconds achieves a velocity twice that of an object that falls for only 1 second, while one that falls for 3 seconds will be moving three times as fast as one that falls for only 1 second, and so on. The exact value of the velocity depends on the acceleration, which, in Galileo's experiment, depended on the angle of elevation of the plane.

In the special case where the ball is falling freely (i.e., when the plane is at 90 degrees), the acceleration is such an important number that it is given a specific letter of the alphabet, g. This value is the acceleration that all objects experience at Earth's surface. (Note that the Moon and other planets have their own very different surface accelerations; g applies *only* to Earth's surface.) The value of g can be determined by measuring the fall rate of objects in a laboratory (Figure 2-8) and turns out to be

$$g\ 9.8 \text{ m/s}^2 = 32 \text{ feet/s}^2$$

This equation tells us that in the first second a falling object accelerates from a stationary position to a velocity of 9.8 m/s (about 22 miles per hour), straight down. After 2 seconds the velocity doubles to 19.6 m/s, after three seconds it triples to 29.4 m/s, and so on.

Galileo's work also demonstrated that the distance covered by an accelerating object depends on the square of the travel time.

► **In equation form:**

$$\text{distance traveled (m)} = 1/2 \times \text{acceleration (m/s}^2) \times \text{time}^2 \text{ (s}^2)$$

► **In symbols:**

$$d = \frac{1}{2} \times a \times t^2$$

Armed with the several equations that relate distance, velocity, acceleration, and time (Table 2-1), scientists were poised to study motions throughout the cosmos.

Table 2-1 Equations Relating *d*, *v*, *a*, and *t*

$v = \frac{d}{t}$	$d = v \times t$
$t = \frac{d}{v}$	$a = \frac{(v_f - v_i)}{t}$
$v = a \times t$	$d = \frac{1}{2} \times a \times t^2$

EXAMPLE 2-2

Out of the Blocks

A sprinter accelerates from the starting blocks to a speed of 10 meters per second in one second. Answer the following questions about the sprinter's speed, acceleration, time, and distance run. In each case, answer the question by substituting into the appropriate motion equation.

1. What is his acceleration?

$$\text{acceleration} = \frac{(\text{final velocity} - \text{initial velocity})}{\text{time}}$$

In this case, the sprinter starts at rest at the beginning of the race, so his initial velocity is 0.

$$\text{acceleration} = \frac{10 \text{ m/s}}{1\text{s}}$$
$$= 10 \text{ m/s}^2$$

2. How far does the sprinter travel during this 1 second of acceleration?

$$\begin{aligned}\text{distance} &= 1/2 \times \text{acceleration} \times \text{time}^2 \\ &= 1/2 \times (10 \text{ m/s}^2) \times (1 \text{ s})^2 \\ &= 5 \text{ meters}\end{aligned}$$

3. Assuming the sprinter covers the remaining 95 meters at a speed of 10 m/s, what will be his time for the event? We have already calculated that the time to cover the first 5 meters is 1 s. The time required to cover the remaining 95 meters at a constant velocity of 10 m/s is:

$$\text{time} = \frac{\text{distance}}{\text{velocity}}$$
$$= 95 \text{ m}/(10 \text{ m/s})$$
$$= 9.5 \text{ s}$$

Thus,

$$\text{total time} = 1 \text{ s} + 9.5 \text{ s} = 10.5 \text{ seconds}$$

For reference, the world's record for the 100-meter dash, set by Asafa Powell of Jamaica in 2005, is 9.77 seconds.

EXAMPLE 2-3

Dropping a Penny from the Sears Tower

The tallest building in the United States is the Sears Tower in Chicago, with a height of 1454 feet. Ignoring wind resistance, how fast would a penny dropped from the top be moving when it hit the ground?

Reasoning: The penny is dropped with zero initial velocity. We first need to calculate the time it takes to fall 1454 feet. From this time we can calculate the velocity at impact.

Step 1—Time of fall: The distance traveled by an accelerating object is:

$$\begin{aligned}\text{distance} &= 1/2 \times \text{acceleration} \times \text{time}^2 \\ &= 1/2 \times 32 \text{ ft/s}^2 \times t^2 = 16 \text{ ft/s}^2 \times t^2\end{aligned}$$

Recall that distance equals 1454 feet, so rearranging gives:

$$t^2 = \frac{1454 \text{ ft}}{16 \text{ ft/s}^2}$$
$$= 90.88 \text{ s}^2$$

Taking the square root of both sides gives time:

$$t = 9.5 \text{ s}$$

Step 2—Speed at impact: The speed of an accelerating object is:

$$\text{velocity} = \text{acceleration} \times \text{time}$$
$$= 32\ \text{ft/s}^2 \times 9.5\ \text{s} = 304\ \text{ft/s}$$

This high speed, about 200 miles per hour, could easily kill a person, so *don't* try this experiment! In fact, most objects dropped in air will not accelerate indefinitely. Because of air resistance an object will accelerate until it reaches its *terminal velocity;* and it will continue falling at a constant speed after that point. The terminal velocity of a falling penny would be considerably less than 200 miles an hour. In addition, it would depend on whether the penny was falling face down or on edge, because the air resistance would be different in those two cases.

The Science of Life •

Experiencing Extreme Acceleration

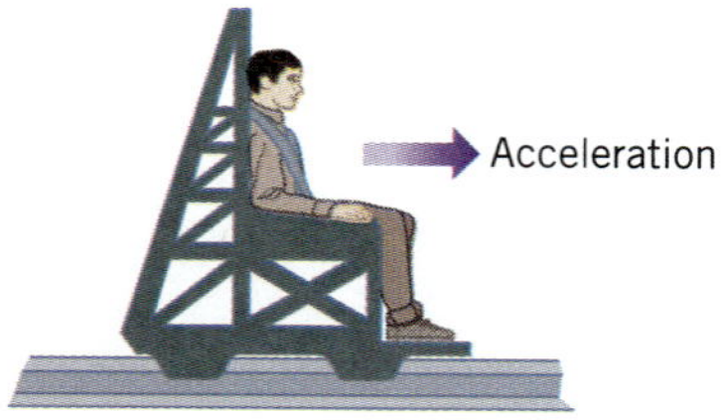

You experience accelerations every day of your life. Just lying in bed you feel acceleration equal to g, due to Earth's gravitational pull. When you travel in a car or plane, ride an elevator, and especially when you enjoy amusement park rides, your body is subjected to additional accelerations, though rarely exceeding 2 g. But jet pilots and astronauts experience accelerations many times that caused by Earth's gravitational pull during takeoffs, sharp turns, and emergency ejections. What happens to the human body under extreme acceleration, and how can equipment be designed to reduce the risk of injury? In the early days of rocket flights and high-speed-jet design, government scientists had to know.

Controlled laboratory accelerations were produced by rocket sleds (Figure 2-9) or centrifuges, which may reach accelerations exceeding 10 g. Researchers quickly discovered that muscles and bones behave as an effectively rigid framework. Sudden extreme acceleration, such as that experienced in a car crash, may cause damage, but these parts can withstand the more gradual changes in acceleration associated with flight.

The body's fluids, on the other hand, shift and flow under sustained acceleration. A pilot in a sharp curve will be pushed down into the seat and experience something like the feeling you get when an elevator starts upward. The blood in the arteries leading up to the brain will also be pushed down, and, if the acceleration is big enough, the net effect will be to drain blood temporarily from the brain. The heart simply can't push the blood upward hard enough to overcome the downward pull. As a result, a pilot may experience a blackout, followed by unconsciousness. Greater accelerations could be tolerated in the prone position adopted by the first astronauts, who had to endure sustained 8 g conditions during takeoffs.

One of the authors (J.T.) once rode in a centrifuge and experienced an 8 g acceleration. The machine itself was a gray, egg-shaped capsule located at the end of a long steel arm. When in operation, the arm moved in a horizontal cir-

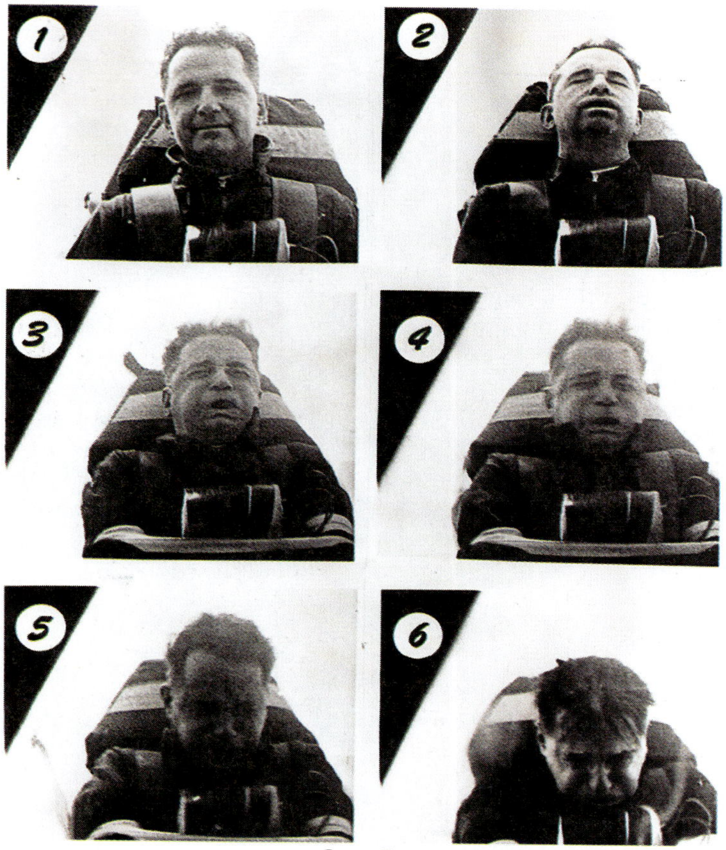

Courtesy Department of Defense/Still Media Record Center

• **Figure 2-9** Colonel John Stapp experienced extreme acceleration in rocket sled experiments. The severe contortion of soft facial tissues was recorded by a movie camera.

cle. Funny things happen at 8 *g*. For example, the skin of your face is pulled down, so that it's hard to keep your mouth open to breathe. The added weight feels like a very heavy person sitting on your chest.

There is, however, one advantage to having had this particular experience. Now, whenever he encounters the question, "What is the most you have ever weighed?" on a medical form, the author can write "1600 pounds." •

Isaac Newton and the Universal Laws of Motion

With Galileo's work, scientists began to isolate and observe the motion of material objects in nature, and to summarize their results into mathematical relationships. As to why bodies should behave this way, however, they had no suggestions. And there was certainly little reason to believe that the measurements of falling objects at Earth's surface had anything at all to do with motions of planets and stars in the heavens.

Isaac Newton (1642–1727)

The English scientist Isaac Newton (1642–1727), one of history's most brilliant scientists, synthesized the work of Galileo and others into a statement of the basic principles that govern the motion of everything in the universe, from stars and planets to clouds, cannonballs, and the muscles in your body. These results, called **Newton's laws of motion,** sound so simple and obvious that it's hard to realize they represent the results of centuries of experiment and observation, and even harder to appreciate what an extraordinary effect they had on the development of science.

The young Newton was interested in mechanical devices and eventually enrolled as a student at Cambridge University. For most of the 1665–1666 school year the University was closed due to the Great Plague that devastated much of Europe. Isaac Newton spent the time at a family farm in Lincolnshire, reading and thinking about the physical world. There he began thinking through his extraordinary discoveries in the nature of motion, as well as pivotal advances in optics and mathematics.

Three laws summarize Newton's description of motions.

The First Law

A moving object will continue moving in a straight line at a constant speed, and a stationary object will remain at rest, unless acted on by an unbalanced force.

Newton's first law seems to state the obvious: if you leave an object alone, it won't change its state of motion. In order to change it, you have to push it or pull it, thus applying a force. Yet virtually all scientists from the Greeks to Copernicus would have argued that the first law is wrong. They believed that because the circle is the most perfect geometrical shape, objects will move in circles unless something interferes. They believed that heavenly objects would keep turning without any outside force acting (indeed, they had to believe this or face the question of why the heavens didn't slow down and stop).

Newton, basing his arguments on observations and the work of his predecessors, turned this notion around. An object left to itself will move in a straight line, and if you want to get it to move in a circle, you have to apply a force (Figure 2-10). You know this is true—if you

Mark A. Leman/Stone/Getty Images

• **Figure 2-10** This hammer thrower is applying a force to keep the weight moving in a circle.

swing something around your head, it will move in a circle only as long as you hold on to it. Let go, and off it goes in a straight line.

This simple observation led Newton to recognize two different kinds of motion. An object is in **uniform motion** if it travels in a straight line at constant speed. *All other motions are called acceleration.* Accelerations can involve changes of speed, changes of direction, or both.

Newton's first law tells us that when we see acceleration, something must have acted to produce that change. We define a **force** as something that produces a change in the state of motion of an object. In fact, we will use the first law of motion extensively in this book to tell us how to recognize when a force, particularly a new kind of force, is acting.

The tendency of an object to remain in uniform motion is called *inertia*. A body at rest tends to stay at rest because of its inertia, while a moving body tends to keep moving because of its inertia. We often use this idea in everyday speech; for example, we may talk about the inertia in a company or government organization that is resistant to change.

The Second Law

The acceleration produced on a body by a force is proportional to the magnitude of the force and inversely proportional to the mass of the object.

If Newton's first law of motion tells you when a force is acting, then the second law of motion tells you what the force does when it acts. This law conforms to our everyday experience: it's easier to lift a child than an adult, and easier to move a ballerina than a defensive tackle.

Newton's second law is often expressed as an equation.

- **In words:** The greater the force, the greater the acceleration; but the more massive the object being acted on by a given force, the smaller the acceleration.
- **In equation form:**

$$\text{force} = \text{mass (kg)} \times \text{acceleration (m/s}^2\text{)}$$

- **In symbols:**

$$F = m \times a$$

This equation, well known to generations of physics majors, tells us that if we know the forces acting on a system of known mass, we can predict its future motion. The equation conforms to our experience that an object's acceleration is a balance between two factors: force and **mass,** which is related to the amount of matter in an object.

A force causes the acceleration. The greater the force, the greater the acceleration. The harder you throw a ball, the faster it goes. Mass measures the amount of matter in any object. The greater the object's mass, the more "stuff" you have to accelerate, the less effect a given force is going to have. A given force will accelerate a golf ball more than a bowling ball, for example. Newton's second law of motion thus defines the balance between force and mass in producing an acceleration.

Newton's first law defines the concept of force as something that causes a mass to accelerate, but the second law goes much further. It tells us the exact magnitude of the force necessary to cause a given mass to achieve a given acceleration. Because force equals mass times acceleration, the units of force must be the same as mass times acceleration. Mass is measured in kilograms (kg) and acceleration in meters per second per second (m/s^2), so the unit of force is the "kilogram-meter-per-second-squared" ($kg\text{-}m/s^2$). One $kg\text{-}m/s^2$ is called the "newton." The symbol for the newton is N.

EXAMPLE 2-4

From Zero to Ten in Less Than a Second

What is the force needed to accelerate a 75-kilogram sprinter from rest to a speed of 10 meters per second (a very fast run) in a half second?

Reasoning and Solution: We must first find the acceleration, and then use Newton's second law to find the force.

$$\text{acceleration (m/s}^2) = \frac{[\text{final velocity} - \text{initial velocity (m/s)}]}{\text{time(s)}}$$

$$= \frac{(10 \text{ m/s} - 0 \text{ m/s})}{0.5\text{s}}$$

$$= 20 \text{ m/s}^2$$

What force is needed to produce this acceleration? From Newton's second law,

$$\text{force (N)} = \text{mass (kg)} \times \text{acceleration (m/s}^2)$$
$$= 75 \text{ kg} \times 20 \text{ m/s}^2$$
$$= 1500 \text{ newtons}$$

The second law of motion does not imply that every time a force acts, motion must result. A book placed on a table still feels the force of gravity, and you can push against a wall without moving it. In these situations, the atoms in the table or the wall shift around and exert their own force that balances the one that acts on them. It is only the net, or unbalanced, force that actually gives rise to acceleration.

Reza Estakhrian/Getty Images, Inc.

• **Figure 2-11** Two automobiles in a collision exert equal and opposite forces on each other.

The Third Law

For every action there is an equal and opposite reaction.

Newton's third law of motion tells us that whenever a force is applied to an object, that object simultaneously exerts an equal and opposite force (Figure 2-11). When you push on a wall, for example, it instantaneously pushes back on you; you can feel the force on the palm of your hand. In fact, the force the wall exerts on you is equal in magnitude (but opposite in direction) to the force you exert on it.

The third law of motion is perhaps the least intuitive of the three. We tend to think of our world in terms of causes and effects, in which big or fast objects exert forces on smaller, slower ones: a car slams into a tree, a batter drives the ball into deep left field, a boxer punches his opponent's eye. But in terms of Newton's third law it is equally valid to think of these events the "other way around." The tree stops the car's motion, the baseball alters the swing of the bat, and the opponent's eye blocks the thrust of the boxer's glove, thus exerting a force and changing the direction and speed of the punch.

Forces always act simultaneously in pairs. You can convince yourself of this fact by thinking about any of your day's myriad activities. As you sit in a chair reading this book, your weight exerts a force on the chair, but the chair exerts an equal and opposite force (called a contact force) on you, preventing you from falling to the floor. The book feels heavy in your hands as it presses down, but your hands hold the book up, exerting an equal and opposite force. You may feel a slight draft from an open window or fan, but as the air exerts that gentle force on you, your skin just as surely exerts an equal and opposite force on the air, causing it to change its path.

Robin Smith/Stone/Getty Images

Newton's laws of motion can be seen in operation in many places, including this roller coaster.

Newton's Laws at Work

Every motion in your life—indeed, every motion in the universe—involves the constant interplay of all three of Newton's laws. The laws of motion never occur in isolation but

Courtesy NASA

The space shuttle *Discovery* rises from its launch pad at Cape Canaveral, Florida. As hot gases accelerate violently out the rocket's engine, the shuttle experiences an equal and opposite acceleration that lifts it into orbit.

rather are interlocking aspects of every object's behavior. The interdependence of Newton's three laws of motion can be envisioned by a simple example. Imagine a boy standing on roller skates holding a stack of baseballs. He throws the balls, one by one. Each time he throws a baseball, the first law tells us that he has to exert a force so that the ball accelerates. The third law tells us that the baseball will exert an equal and opposite force on the boy. This force acting on the boy will, according to the second law, cause him to recoil backward.

While the example of the boy and the baseballs may seem a bit contrived, it exactly illustrates the principle by which fish swim and rockets fly. As a fish moves its tail, it applies a force against the water. The water, in turn, pushes back on the fish and propels it forward. In a rocket motor, forces are exerted on hot gases, accelerating them out the tail end. By the argument just presented, this means that an equal and opposite force must be exerted on the rocket by the gases, propelling it forward. Every rocket, from simple fireworks to a space shuttle, works this way.

Isaac Newton's three laws of motion form a comprehensive description of all possible motions, as well as the forces that lead to them. In and of themselves, however, Newton's laws do not say anything about the nature of those forces. In fact, much of the progress of science since Newton's time has been associated with the discovery and elucidation of the forces of nature.

Momentum

Newton's laws tell us that the only way to change the motion of an object is to apply a force. We all have an intuitive understanding of this tendency. We sense, for example, that a massive object like a large train, even if it is moving slowly, is very hard to stop. This knowledge is often used by people who make science fiction movies. It's almost a cliché now that when a spaceship is huge and bulky, the film-makers supply a deep, rumbling soundtrack that mimics a slowly moving train. (In this case artistic truth conflicts with the laws of nature, because in the vacuum of space there can be no sound waves.)

At the same time, a small object moving very fast—a rifle bullet, for example—is very hard to stop as well. Thus, our everyday experience tells us that the tendency of a moving object to remain in motion depends both on the mass of the object and on its speed. The higher the mass and the higher the speed, the more difficult it is to stop the object or change its direction of motion.

Physicists encapsulate these notions in a quantity called *linear momentum*, which equals the product of an object's mass times its velocity.

▶ **In equation form:**

$$\text{momentum (kg-m/s)} = \text{mass (kg)} \times \text{velocity (m/s)}.$$

▶ **In symbols:**

$$p = m \times v$$

EXAMPLE 2-5

Play Ball

A baseball with mass 0.3 kg moves to the right with a velocity of 30 meters/second (about the speed of a good fastball). What is its momentum?

Solution: The momentum is defined to be

$$p = m \times v$$

If we substitute the numbers for mass and velocity, we find that

$$p = 0.3 \text{ kg} \times 30 \text{ m/s} = 9 \text{ kg-m/s}$$

Conservation of Linear Momentum

We can derive a very important consequence from Newton's laws. If no external forces act on a system, then Newton's second law says that the change in the total momentum of a system is zero. When physicists find a quantity that does not change, they say that the quantity is *conserved*. The conclusion we have just reached, therefore, is called the *law of conservation of linear momentum*.

It's important to keep in mind that the law of conservation of momentum doesn't say that momentum can never change. It just says that it won't change unless an outside force is applied. If a soccer ball is rolling across a field and a player kicks it, a force is applied to the ball as soon as her foot touches it. At that moment, the momentum of the ball changes, and that change is reflected in its change of direction and speed.

You saw the consequences of the conservation of momentum the last time you watched a fireworks display. The rocket arches up and explodes just at the moment that the rocket is stationary at the top of its path, at the instant when its total momentum is zero. After the explosion, brightly colored burning bits of material fly out in all directions. Each of these pieces has a mass and a velocity, so each has some momentum. Conservation of momentum, however, tells us that when we add up all the momenta of the pieces, they should cancel each other out and give a total momentum of zero. Thus, for example, if there is a one-gram piece moving to the right at 10 meters per second, there has to be the equivalent of a one-gram piece moving to the left at the same velocity. Thus conservation of momentum gives fireworks their characteristic symmetric starburst pattern.

Milton Heiberg/Photo Researchers

This symmetrical fireworks display illustrates the law of conservation of linear momentum.

Angular Momentum

Just as an object moving in a straight line will keep moving unless a force acts, an object that is rotating will keep rotating unless a twisting force called a *torque* acts to make it stop. A spinning top will keep spinning until the friction between its point of contact and the floor slows it down. A wheel will keep turning until friction in its bearing stops it. This tendency to keep rotating is called angular momentum.

Think about some common experiences with spinning objects. Two factors increase an object's angular momentum, and thus make it more difficult to slow down and stop the rotating object. The first factor is simply the rate of spin; the faster an object spins, the harder it is to stop. The second, more subtle factor relates to the distribution of mass. Objects with more mass, or with mass located farther away from the central axis of rotation, have greater angular momentum. Thus, a solid metal wheel has more angular momentum than an air-filled tire of the same diameter and rate of spin.

The consequences of the conservation of angular momentum you're most likely to experience occur when something happens to change a spinning object's distribution of mass. A striking illustration of this point can be seen in figure skating competitions. As a skater goes into a spin with her arms spread, she spins slowly. As she pulls her arms in tight to her body, her angular momentum must remain constant, since no outside force acts to affect the spin. Her rate of spin must increase.

When the skater spins faster as she pulls in her arms, she is demonstrating the conservation of angular momentum.

Paul Sutton/Duomo Photography, Inc

Technology •

Inertial Guidance System

The conservation of angular momentum plays an important role in so-called inertial guidance systems for navigation in airplanes and satellites. The idea behind such systems is very simple. A massive object like a sphere or a flat circular disk is set into rotation inside a device in which very little resistance (that is, almost no torque) is exerted by the bearings. Once such an object is set into rotation, its angular momentum continues to point in the same direction, regardless of how the spaceship moves around it. By sensing the constant rotation and seeing how it is related to the orientation of the satellite, engineers can tell which way the satellite is pointed. •

The Universal Force of Gravity

Gravity is the most obvious force in our daily lives. It holds you down in your chair and keeps you from floating off into space. It guarantees that when you drop things they fall. The effects of what we call gravity were known to the ancients, and its quantitative properties were studied by Galileo and many of his contemporaries, but Isaac Newton revealed its universality.

By Newton's account, he experienced his great insight in an apple orchard. He saw an apple fall and, at the same time, saw the Moon in the sky behind it. He wondered whether the gravity that caused the apple to move downward could extend far outward to the Moon, supplying the force that kept it in its orbit.

Look at the problem this way: If the Moon goes around Earth, then it isn't moving in a straight line. From the first law of motion it follows that a force must be acting on it. Newton hypothesized that this was the same force that made the apple fall—the familiar force of gravity (see Figure 2-12).

Eventually, he realized that the orbits of all the planets could be understood if gravity was not restricted to the surface of Earth but was a force found throughout the uni-

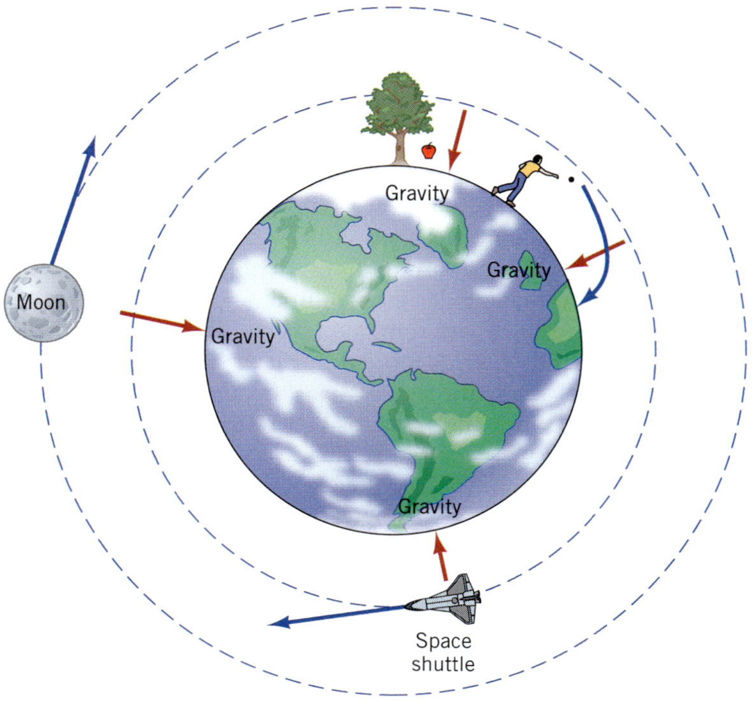

• **Figure 2-12** An apple falling, a ball being thrown, a space shuttle orbiting Earth, and the orbiting Moon, all display the influence of the force of gravity.

verse. He formulated this insight (an insight that has been overwhelmingly confirmed by observations) in what is called **Newton's law of universal gravitation.**

- **In words:** Between any two objects in the universe there is an attractive force (gravity) that is proportional to the masses of the objects and inversely proportional to the square of the distance between them.
- **In equation form:**

$$\text{force of gravity (newtons)} = \frac{[G \times \text{mass}_1\ (\text{kg}) \times \text{mass}_2\ (\text{kg})]}{[\text{distance (m)}]^2}$$

- **In symbols:**

$$F = \frac{(G \times m_1 \times m_2)}{d^2}$$

where G is a number known as the *gravitational constant* (see below).

In everyday words, this law tells us that the more massive two objects are, the greater the force between them will be; the farther apart they are, the less the force will be.

The Gravitational Constant, *G*

When we say that A is *directly proportional to* B, we mean that if A increases, B must increase by the same proportion. If A doubles then B must double as well. We can state this idea in mathematical form by writing

$$A = k \times B$$

where k is a number known as the constant of proportionality between A and B. This equation tells us that if we know the constant k and either A or B, then we can calculate the exact value of the other. Thus the constant of proportionality in a relationship is a useful thing to know.

The gravitational constant, G, is a constant of direct proportionality; it expresses the exact numerical relation between the masses of two objects and their separation, on the one hand, and the force between them on the other.

$$F = \frac{(G \times m_1 \times m_2)}{d_2}$$

Unlike g, however, which applies only to Earth's surface, G is a universal constant that applies to any two masses anywhere in the universe.

Henry Cavendish (1731–1810), a scientist at Oxford University in England, first measured G in 1798 by using the experimental apparatus shown in Figure 2-13. Cavendish suspended a dumbbell made of two small lead balls by a stiff wire and fixed two larger lead spheres near the suspended balls. The gravitational attraction between the hanging lead balls and the fixed spheres caused the wire to twist slightly. By measuring the amount of twisting force, or torque, on the wire, Cavendish could calculate the gravitational force on the dumbbells. This force, together with knowledge of the masses of the dumbbells (m_1 in the equation) and the heavy spheres (m_2), as well as their final separation (d), gave him the numerical value of everything in Newton's law of universal gravitation except G, which he then calculated using simple arithmetic. In metric units, the value of G is 6.67×10^{-11} m^3/s^2-kg, or 6.67×10^{-11} N-m^2/kg^2 (recall that N is the symbol for a newton, the unit of force). This constant appears to be universal, holding true everywhere in our universe.

• **Figure 2-13** The Cavendish balance measures the universal gravitational constant G. This experimental device balances the gravitational attractive force between the suspended balls and fixed spheres, against the force exerted by a twisted wire.

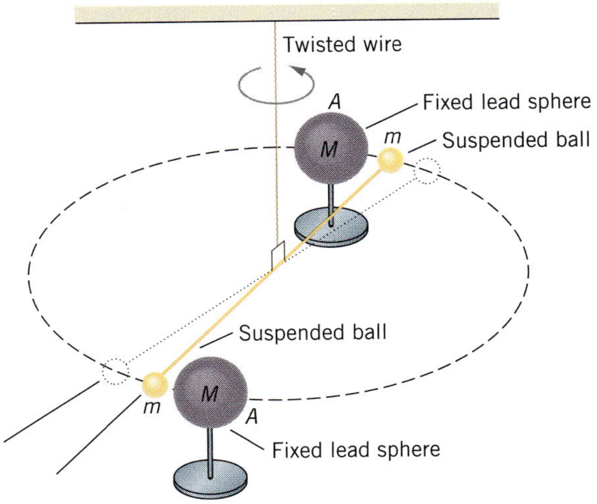

Weight and Gravity

The law of universal gravitation says that there is a force between any two objects in the universe: two dancers, two stars, this book and you—all exert forces on each other. The gravitational attraction between you and Earth would pull you down if you weren't standing on the ground. As it is, the ground exerts a force equal and opposite to that of gravity, a force you can feel in the soles of your feet. If you were standing on a scale, the gravitational pull of Earth would pull you down until a spring or other mechanism in the scale exerted the opposing force. In this case, the size of that counterbalancing force registers on a display and you call it your **weight.**

Weight, in fact, is just the force of gravity on an object located at a particular point. Weight depends on where you are; on the surface of Earth you weigh one thing, on the surface of the Moon another, and in the depths of interstellar space you would weigh next to nothing. You even weigh a little less on a high mountaintop than you do at sea level, because you are farther from Earth's center. Weight contrasts with your mass (the amount of matter), which stays the same no matter where you go.

Big *G* and Little *g*

The law of universal gravitation, coupled with the experimental results on bodies falling near Earth, can be used to reveal a close relationship between the universal constant G and Earth's gravitational acceleration g. According to the law of universal gravitation, the gravitational force on an object of any mass at Earth's surface is

$$\text{force} = \frac{(G \times \text{mass} \times M_E)}{R_E^2}$$

where M_E and R_E are Earth's mass and radius, respectively. On the other hand, Newton's second law says that

$$\text{force} = \text{mass} \times g$$

Equating the right sides of these two equations,

$$\text{mass} \times g = \frac{(G \times \text{mass} \times M_E)}{R_E^2}$$

Dividing both sides by mass,

$$g = \frac{(G \times M_E)}{R_E^2}$$

But the values of G, M_E, and R_E have been measured:

$$g = \frac{[(6.67 \times 10^{-11}\ \text{N-m}^2/\text{kg}^2) \times (6.02 \times 10^{24}\ \text{kg})]}{(6.40 \times 10^6 \text{m})^2}$$

$$= \frac{(4.015 \times 10^{14}\ \text{N-m}^2/\text{kg})}{(4.10 \times 10^{13}\ \text{m}^2)}$$

$$= 9.8\ \text{N-kg} = 9.8\ \text{m/s}^2$$

Thus the value of Earth's gravitational acceleration, g, can be calculated from Newton's universal equation for gravity.

This result is extremely important. For Galileo, g was a number to be measured, but whose value he could not predict. For Newton, on the other hand, g was a number that could be calculated purely from Earth's size and mass. Because we understand where g comes from, we can now predict the appropriate value of gravitational acceleration not only for Earth, but for any body in the universe, provided we know its mass and radius.

Stop and Think! Can the gravitational force between two objects in the universe ever be equal to zero? Why or why not?

EXAMPLE 2-6

Weight on the Moon

The mass of the Moon is $M_M = 7.18 \times 10^{22}$ kg, and its radius R_M is 1738 km. If your mass is 100 kg, what would you weigh on the Moon?

Reasoning: We have to calculate the force exerted on an object at the surface of an astronomical body. This time both the mass and the radius of the body are different from that of Earth, although G is the same.

Solution: From the equation that defines weight, we have

$$\text{weight} = \frac{(G \times \text{mass}_1 \times \text{mass}_2)}{\text{distance}^2}$$

$$= \frac{(G \times 100\text{ kg} \times M_M)}{R_M^2}$$

$$= \frac{[(6.67 \times 10^{-11}\text{ N-m}^2/\text{kg}^2) \times 100\text{ kg} \times (7.18 \times 10^{22}\text{ kg})]}{(1.738 \times 10^6\text{m})^2}$$

$$= \frac{[(6.67 \times 10^{-11}\text{ N-m}^2/\text{kg}^2) \times (7.18 \times 10^{24}\text{ kg}^2)]}{(3.02 \times 10^{12}\text{m}^2)}$$

$$= \frac{(4.79 \times 10^{14}\text{ N-m}^2)}{(3.02 \times 10^{12}\text{m}^2)}$$

$$= 159\text{ newtons}$$

This weight is about one-sixth of the weight that the same object would have on Earth, *even though its mass is the same in both places.*

Newton bequeathed a picture of the universe that is beautiful and ordered. The planets orbit the Sun in stately paths, forever trying to move off in straight lines, forever prevented from doing so by the inward tug of gravity. The same laws that operate in the cosmos operate on Earth, and these laws were discovered by the application of the scientific method. To a Newtonian observer, the universe was like a clock. It had been wound up and was ticking along according to God's laws. Newton and his followers were persuaded that in carrying out their work, they were discovering what was in the mind of God when the universe was created.

Of all celestial phenomena, none seemed more portentous and magical than comets, yet even these chance wanderers were subject to Newton's laws. In 1682, British astronomer Edmond Halley (1656–1742) used Newtonian logic to compute the orbit of the comet that bears his name, and he predicted its return in 1758. The "recovery" of Halley's Comet on Christmas Eve of that year was celebrated around the world as a triumph for the Newtonian system.

Roe, D. Malin/AAO/Photo Researchers

Halley's comet as it appeared on its last visit to Earth, in 1985.

Thinking More About | The Ordered Universe

Predictability

The Newtonian universe seemed regular and predictable in the extreme. Indeed, from the point of view of the Newtonians, if you knew the present state of a system and the forces acting on it, the laws of motion would allow you to predict its entire future. This notion was taken to the extreme by the French mathematician Pierre Simon Laplace (1749–1827), who proposed the notion of the *Divine Calculator.* His argument (in modern language) was this: If we knew the position and velocity of every atom in the universe and we had infinite computational power, then we could predict the position and velocity of every atom in the universe for all future times. There is no distinction in this argument between an atom in a rock and an atom in your hand. Thus Laplace would say that all of your movements are completely determined by the laws of physics to the end of time. You cannot choose your future. What is to be was determined from the very beginning.

This idea has been negated by two modern developments in science. One of these, the Heisenberg uncertainty principle (see Chapter 8), tells us that at the level of the atom it is impossible to know simultaneously and exactly both the position and velocity of any particle. Thus you can never get the information the Divine Calculator needs to begin working.

Furthermore, scientists working with computer models have recently discovered that many systems in nature can be described in simple Newtonian terms, but have futures that are, to all intents and purposes, unpredictable. These situations are called chaotic systems, and their field of study is called chaos.

Whitewater in a mountain stream is a familiar chaotic system. If you put two chips of wood down on the upstream side of the rapids, those chips (and the water on which they ride) will be widely separated by the time they get to the end. This is true no matter how small you make the chips, or how close together they are at the beginning. If you know the exact initial position of a chip and every aspect of the waterway in such a system with complete mathematical precision, you can in principle predict where it will come out downstream. But if there is the slightest error in your initial description, no matter how small, the actual position of the chip and your prediction may differ significantly. Every measurement in the real world has some error associated with it, so it is never possible to determine the exact position of the chip at the start of its trip. Therefore you cannot predict exactly where it will come out *even if you know all the forces acting on it.*

The existence of chaos, then, tells us that the philosophical conclusions drawn from the Newtonian vision of the universe don't apply to some systems in nature. The flow of Earth's atmosphere and the long-term development of weather, for example, appear to be chaotic, and it may turn out that ecosystems (see Chapter 19) behave this way as well. If this is true, what implications might there be when governments have to deal with issues such as global warming (see Chapter 19) and the preservation of endangered species? How confident do you have to be that something bad is going to happen before you start taking steps to avoid it?

Summary

Since before recorded history, people have observed regularities in the heavens and have built monuments such as Stonehenge to help order their lives. Models such as the Earth-centered system of Ptolemy and the Sun-centered system of Copernicus attempted to explain these regular motions of stars and planets. New, more precise astronomical data by Tycho Brahe led mathematician Johannes Kepler to propose his laws of planetary motion, which state that planets orbit the Sun in elliptical orbits, not circular orbits as had been previously assumed.

Meanwhile, Galileo Galilei and other scientists investigated the science of *mechanics*—the way things move near Earth's surface. These investigators recognized two fundamentally different kinds of motion: *uniform motion,* which involves a constant *speed* and direction *(velocity),* and *acceleration,* which entails a change in either speed or direction of travel. Galileo's experiments revealed that all objects fall the same way, at the constant acceleration of 9.8 meters/second^2. Isaac Newton combined the work of Kepler, Galileo, and others in his sweeping *laws of motion* and the *law of universal gravitation.* Newton realized that nothing accelerates without a *force* acting on it, and that the amount of acceleration is proportional to the force applied, but inversely proportional to the *mass.* He also pointed out that forces always act in pairs.

This understanding of forces and motions led Newton to describe *gravity,* the most obvious force in our daily lives. An object's *weight* is the force it exerts due to gravity. He demonstrated that the same force that pulls a falling apple to Earth causes the Moon to curve around Earth in its elliptical orbit. Indeed, the force of gravity operates everywhere, with pairs of forces between every pair of masses in the universe.

Key Terms

mechanics
speed
velocity
acceleration
Newton's laws of motion
uniform motion
force
mass
gravity
Newton's law of universal gravitation
weight

Key Equations and Their Units

$$\text{velocity or speed (m/s)} = \frac{\text{distance (m)}}{\text{time (s)}}$$

$$\text{distance (m)} = \frac{\text{speed or velocity (m/s)}}{\text{time (s)}}$$

$$\text{time (s)} = \frac{\text{distance (m)}}{\text{speed or velocity (m/s)}}$$

$$\text{acceleration (m/s}^2\text{)} = \frac{[\text{final velocity} - \text{initial velocity (m/s)}]}{\text{time (s)}}$$

$$\text{velocity of a falling object (m/s)} = g\ (\text{m/s}^2) \times \text{time (s)}$$

$$\text{velocity (m/s)} = \text{acceleration (m/s}^2\text{)} \times \text{time (s)}$$

$$\text{force (N)} = \text{mass (kg)} \times \text{acceleration (m/s}^2\text{)}$$

$$\text{force (N)} = \frac{[G \times \text{first mass (kg)} \times \text{second mass (kg)}]}{\text{distance}^2\ (\text{m}^2)}$$

$$\text{force (N)} = \text{mass (kg)} \times g = \text{weight}$$

Constants

$g = 9.8\ \text{m/s}^2$ = acceleration due to gravity on Earth

$G = 6.67 \times 10^{-11}\ \text{N-m}^2/\text{kg}^2$ = universal gravitational constant

Review Questions

1. In what ways did Stonehenge serve as a calendar? How did Stonehenge allow ancient people to make predictions?

2. Why do scientists argue that Stonehenge was not built by ancient astronauts?

3. What were Tycho Brahe's principal contributions to science? How did he try to resolve the question of the structure of the universe?

4. What was Kepler's role in interpreting Tycho Brahe's data?

5. How did Galileo apply the scientific method to his study of falling objects?

6. A hockey player hits a puck at one end of an empty skating rink. The puck travels across the ice in a straight line until it is stopped by the goal at the other end. Explain how each of Newton's laws of motion applies to this situation.

7. According to Newton, what are the two kinds of motion in the universe? How did this view differ from those of previous scholars?

8. Why is gravity called a universal force?

9. What is the difference between the constants g and G?

10. What similarities did Newton see between the Moon and an apple?

11. What is the difference between weight and mass?

Discussion Questions

1. What role did the observation of the natural world play in the design and construction of Stonehenge?

2. Can scientists prove that Stonehenge was not built by ancient astronauts?

3. Why was Earth at the center of the universe in Ptolemy's system?

4. Which of the following is in uniform motion, and which is in accelerated motion?

a. a car heading west at 55 mph on a level road
b. a car heading west at 55 mph on a hill
c. a car going around a curve at 55 mph
d. a dolphin leaping out of the water
e. a tennis ball tossed into the air; the same ball as it bounces off the ground
f. an apple sitting on your kitchen table

5. Which, if any, of the following objects does not exert a gravitational force on you?

a. this book
b. the Sun
c. the nearest star
d. a distant galaxy
e. the Atlantic ocean

6. What pairs of forces act in the following situations?

a. a pitcher throws a baseball
b. a batter hits a baseball out of the park
c. a leaf falls to the ground
d. the Moon orbits Earth
e. you sit in a chair

7. What was the role of mathematics in the science of mechanics?

8. In what sense is the Newtonian universe simpler than Ptolemy's? Suppose observations had shown that the two did equally well at explaining the data. Construct an argument to say that Newton's universe should still be preferred.

9. Why don't the planets just fly off into space? What keeps them in their orbits?

10. How did Henry Cavendish's experiment fit into the scientific method?

11. What did Edmund Halley predict? How was his prediction confirmed?

12. Why are observatories built as far away from major cities as possible?

13. Why is it possible for a rocket to travel in space? Which of Newton's laws of motion explain an accelerating rocket?

14. What forces keep a pendulum swinging back and forth?

Problems

1. What do you weigh in pounds? in newtons?

2. If you run 1 mile on an oval track in 10 minutes, what is your average speed in miles per hour? Did you accelerate during the 10 minutes?

3. If your car goes from 0 to 55 miles per hour in 6 seconds, what is your acceleration? If you step on the brake and your car goes from 55 miles per hour to 0 in 3 seconds, what is your acceleration?

4. What is your mass in kilograms?

5. How much force are you exerting when you lift a 20-pound dumbbell? What units will you use to describe this force?

6. What would you weigh on Mars? on Jupiter? (Data on the masses and radii of planets appear in Appendix E.)

7. If a basketball player's mass is 100 kg, how much force must he exert to have his feet leave the ground as he dunks a basketball. Remember, he must overcome Earth's gravitational acceleration of 9.8 m/s^2.

8. In Chapter 1 we discussed why scientists consider astrology to be a pseudoscience. Calculate the gravitational forces on a 3-kg newborn infant exerted by the planets Venus, Mars, and Jupiter at their closest approach to Earth (see Appendix E for the relevant distances and masses). Compare these forces with the gravitational force exerted by a 100-kg physician 0.1 m away. [*Hint:* The closest approach of a planet equals the difference between Earth's distance from the Sun and the other planets' distance from the Sun.]

Investigations

1. Galileo was arrested and imprisoned for his studies and publications. Discuss the dilemma faced by scientists whose discoveries offend conventional ideas. What scientific research does today's society find offensive or immoral? Why?

2. Do you believe in fate? Is there free will? The concept of predestination plays an important role in some kinds of theology. What is it? How does it relate to Laplace? to chaos?

3. What other kinds of models of the universe did old civilizations develop? Look up those of the Mayans, the Chinese, and the Indians of the American Southwest.

4. Investigate the scientific contributions of Galileo. What other experiments did he design? What instrumentation did he use? How was this research funded? Was he engaging in basic or applied research?

5. The gravitational constant is now known to one part in 10,000, yet physicists are still trying to measure this constant. Why?

6. People have claimed that the Great Pyramids of Egypt had to have been built by ancient astronauts because the Egyptians were too primitive to have built them. Look up the weight of the largest stones in the pyramids and estimate the number of people it would take to move them. Then comment on the ancient astronaut argument.

7. Throw a frisbee to a friend. Describe the path that the frisbee takes as it travels from one person to another. What forces cause the frisbee to travel the way it does? Can you describe that path using mathematics as well as words?

8. Galileo was one of the first people to look at the planets through a telescope. He discovered the four largest moons of Jupiter, which are still called the "Galilean" moons. Why did this discovery cast doubt on the Ptolemaic system? What else did Galileo see through his telescope?

9. How does gravity affect the flow of blood in your body? and the flow of sap in trees? How have organisms evolved to counteract the force of gravity?

10. Galileo built his own telescope after learning about it from others. Search the web for links that would help you build your own telescope. What materials will you need? Where did Galileo get his materials?

11. Try to build a sundial. What information do you need for your sundial to work. What observations do you need to make in order for your sundial to be more accurate? How does a sundial make use of the movement of celestial bodies?

12. What role does momentum play in bowling? in billiards or pool?

13. What role does torque play in using a YoYo? What other forces are at work as the YoYo goes up and down the string?

14. Newton made a number of contributions to the field of mathematics. What were they, and why are they important?

15. Find a plastic or paper cup. Drill or punch two holes (approximately one-quarter inch in diameter) on opposite sides of the cup . Fill the cup to the rim with water. The water will flow from the cup through the holes. Now refill the cup, cover the holes with your fingers, and drop the cup from an elevated position. The water won't flow out of the holes during this free fall. Why? What force or forces are keeping the water in the cup?

3

Energy

Why must animals eat to stay alive?

Science Through the Day | Morning Routine

The daily routine begins. You turn on the overhead light, squinting as your eyes adjust to the brightness. Then you take your morning shower; it feels great to just stand there and let the hot water wash over you. Soon you'll boil water for coffee, eat a hearty breakfast, and then drive to the beach.

During every one of these ordinary actions—indeed, every moment of every day—you use energy in its many varied and interchangeable forms.

Vince Streano/Stone/Getty Images

The Great Chain of Energy

Hundreds of millions of years ago, a bit of energy was generated in the core of the Sun. For thousands of years, that energy percolated outward to the Sun's surface; then, in a mere eight minutes, it made the trip through empty space to Earth in the form of sunlight. Unlike other bits of energy that were reflected back into space by clouds or simply served to warm Earth's soil, this particular energy was absorbed by organisms known as algae floating on the warm ocean surface.

This oil pump in Colorado is bringing up solar energy stored millions of years ago.

Lowell Georgia/Photo Researchers

Through the process of photosynthesis (see Chapter 22), these algae transformed the Sun's energy into the chemical energy needed to hold together its complex molecules. Eventually these algae died and sank to the bottom of the ocean, where, over long eons, they were buried deeper and deeper. Under the influence of pressure and heat, the dead algae were eventually transformed into fossil fuel—petroleum.

Then, a short while ago, engineers pumped that petroleum with its stored energy up out of the ground. At a refinery, the large molecules were broken down into gasoline, and the gasoline was shipped to your town. A few days ago you put it into the tank of your car. The last time you drove you burned that gasoline, converting the stored energy into the engine's mechanical energy that moved your car. When you parked the car, the hot engine slowly cooled, and that bit of heat, after having been delayed for a few hundred million years, was radiated out into space to continue its voyage away from the solar system. As you read these words, the energy you freed yesterday has long since left the solar system and is out in the depths of interstellar space.

Scientifically Speaking

At this moment, trillions of cells in your body are hard at work turning the chemical energy of the food you ate yesterday into the chemical energy that will keep you alive today. Energy in the atmosphere generates sweeping winds and powerful storms, while the ocean's energy drives mighty currents and incessant tides. Meanwhile, deep within Earth, energy in the form of heat is moving the continent on which you are standing.

All situations where energy is expended have one thing in common. If you look at the event closely enough, you will find that, in accord with Newton's laws of motion (Chapter 2), a force is being exerted on an object to make it move. When your car burns gasoline, the fuel's energy ultimately turns the wheels of your car, which then exert a force on the road; the road exerts an equal and opposite force on the car, pushing it forward. When you climb the stairs, your muscles exert a force that lifts you upward against gravity. Even in your body's cells, a force is exerted on molecules in chemical reactions. Energy thus is intimately connected with the application of a force.

In everyday conversation we speak of someone having lots of energy, but in science the term *energy* has a precise definition that is somewhat different from the ordinary meaning. To see what scientists mean when they talk about energy, we must first introduce the familiar concept of work.

Jerry Ohlinger's Movie Material Store

Work is done when a force is exerted over a distance.

Work

Scientists say that **work** is done whenever a force is exerted over a distance. Pick up this book and raise it a foot. Your muscles applied a force equal to the weight of the book over a distance of a foot. You did work.

This definition of work differs considerably from everyday usage. From a physicist's point of view, if you accidentally drive into a tree and smash your fender, work has been done because a force deformed the car's metal a measurable distance. On the other hand, a physicist would say that you haven't done any work if you spend an hour in a futile effort to move a large boulder, no matter how tired you get. Even though you have exerted a considerable force, the distance over which you exerted it is negligible.

Physicists provide an exact mathematical definition of their notion of work.

▶ **In words:** Work is equal to the force that is exerted times the distance over which it is exerted.

▶ **In equation form:**

$$\text{work (joules)} = \text{force (newtons)} \times \text{distance (meters)}$$

where a joule is the unit of work, as defined in the following paragraph.

▶ **In symbols:**

$$W = F \times d$$

In practical terms, even a small force can do a lot of work if it is exerted over a long distance.

• **Figure 3-1** A weightlifter applies a force (in Newtons) over a distance (in meters).

As you might expect from this equation, units of work are equal to a force unit times a distance unit (Figure 3-1). In the metric system of units, where force is measured in *newtons* (abbreviated N), work is measured in newton-meters (N-m). For reference, a Newton is roughly equal to the force exerted on your hand by a baseball (or by 7 Fig Newtons!).

This unit is given the special name "joule," after the English scientist James Prescott Joule (1818–1889), one of the first people to understand the properties of energy. One *joule* is defined as the amount of work done when a force of one newton is exerted through a distance of one meter.

$$1 \text{ joule of work} = 1 \text{ N of force} \times 1 \text{ m of distance}$$

In the English system of units (see Appendix B), where force is measured in pounds, work is measured in a unit called the foot-pound (usually abbreviated ft-lb).

EXAMPLE 3-1

Working Against Gravity

How much work do you do when you carry a 20-kg television set up a flight of stairs (about 4 meters)?

Reasoning: We must first calculate the force exerted by a 20-kg mass before we can determine work. From the previous chapter, we know that to lift a 20-kg mass against the acceleration of gravity (9.8 m/s^2) requires a force given by

$$\begin{aligned} \text{force} &= \text{mass} \times g \\ &= 20 \text{ kg} \times 9.8 \text{ m/s}^2 \\ &= 196 \text{ newtons} \end{aligned}$$

Solution: Then, from the equation for work,

$$\begin{aligned} \text{work} &= \text{force} \times \text{distance} \\ &= 196 \text{ N} \times 4\text{m} \\ &= 784 \text{ joules} \end{aligned}$$

Energy

Energy is defined as the ability to do work. If a system is capable of exerting a force over a distance, then that system possesses energy. The amount of a system's energy, which can be recorded in joules or foot-pounds (the same units used for work), is a measure of how much work the system might do. When a system runs out of energy, it simply can't do any more work.

Power

Power provides a measure of both the amount of work done (or, equivalently, the amount of energy expended) and the time it takes to do that work. In order to complete a physical task quickly, you must generate more power than if you do the same task slowly. If you run up a flight of stairs, your muscles need to generate more power than they would if you walked up the same flight, even though you expend the same amount of energy in either case. A power hitter in baseball swings the bat faster, converting the chemical energy in his muscles to kinetic energy more quickly than most other players.

Scientists define power as the rate at which work is done, or the rate at which energy is expended.

▶ **In words:** Power is the amount of work done divided by the time it takes to do that work.

▶ **In equation form:**

$$\text{power (watts)} = \frac{\text{work (joules)}}{\text{time (seconds)}}$$

where the watt is the unit of power, as defined in the following paragraph.

▶ **In symbols:**

$$P = \frac{W}{t}$$

If you do more work in a given span of time, or do a task in a shorter time, you use more power.

In the metric system, power is measured in **watts,** after James Watt (1736–1819), the Scottish inventor who developed the modern steam engine that powered the Industrial Revolution. The watt, a unit of measurement that you probably encounter every day, is defined as the expenditure of 1 joule of energy in 1 second:

$$1 \text{ watt of power} = \frac{(1 \text{ joule of energy})}{(1 \text{ second of time})}$$

The unit of 1000 watts (corresponding to an expenditure of 1000 joules per second) is called a **kilowatt** and is a commonly used measurement of electrical power. The English system, on the other hand, uses the more colorful unit *horsepower,* which is defined as 550 foot-pounds per second.

The familiar rating of a lightbulb (60 watts or 100 watts, for example) is a measure of the rate of energy that the lightbulb consumes when it is operating. As another familiar example, most electric hand tools or appliances in your home will be labeled with a power rating in watts.

The equation we have introduced defining power as energy divided by time may be rewritten as follows:

$$\text{energy (joules)} = \text{power (watts)} \times \text{time (seconds)}$$

This important equation allows you (and the electric company) to calculate how much energy you consume (and how much you have to pay for). Note from this equation that, while the joule is the standard scientific unit for energy, energy can also be measured in units of power × time, such as the familiar kilowatt-hour (often abbreviated kwh) that appears on your electric bill. Table 3-1 summarizes the important terms we've used for force, work, energy, and power.

Athletes must release their energy quickly and with great power to succeed in events such as the javelin throw.

Table 3-1 Important Terms

Quantity	Definition	Units
Force	mass × acceleration	newtons
Work	force × distance	joules
Energy	ability to do work	joules
Energy	power × time	joules
Power	$\frac{\text{work}}{\text{time}} = \frac{\text{energy}}{\text{time}}$	watts

James Watt boiling water in his fireplace.

Science in the Making •

James Watt and the Horsepower

The horsepower, a unit of power with a colorful history, was devised by James Watt so that he could sell his steam engines. Watt knew that the main use of his engines would be in mines, where owners traditionally used horses to drive pumps that removed water. The easiest way to promote his new engines was to tell the mining engineers how many horses each engine would replace. Consequently, he did a series of experiments to determine how much energy a horse could generate over a given amount of time. Watt found that an average, healthy horse can do 550 ft-lb of work every second over an average working day—a unit he defined to be the horsepower, and so he rated his engines accordingly. We still use this unit (the engines of virtually all cars and trucks are rated in horsepower), although we seldom build engines to replace horses these days. •

EXAMPLE 3-2

Paying the Piper

A typical CD system uses 250 watts of electrical power. If you play your system for three hours in an evening, how much energy do you use? If energy costs 12 cents a kilowatt-hour, how much do you owe the electrical company?

Reasoning and Solution: The total amount of energy you use will be given by

$$\begin{aligned} \text{energy} &= \text{power} \times \text{time} \\ &= 250 \text{ W} \times 3 \text{ h} \\ &= 750 \text{ Wh} \end{aligned}$$

Because 750 watts equals 0.75 kilowatt,

$$\text{energy} = 0.75 \text{ Kwh}$$

The cost will be as follows:

$$\begin{aligned} \text{cost} &= 12 \text{ cents per Kwh} \times 0.75 \text{ Kwh} \\ &= 9 \text{ cents} \end{aligned}$$

Forms of Energy

Energy, the ability to do work, appears in all natural systems, and it comes in many forms. The identification of these forms posed a great challenge to scientists in the nineteenth century. Ultimately, they recognized two very broad categories. **Kinetic energy** is energy associated with moving objects, whereas stored or **potential energy** is energy waiting to be released.

Kinetic Energy

Think about a cannonball flying through the air. When it hits a wooden target, the ball exerts a force on the fibers in the wood, splintering and pushing them apart and creating a hole. Work has to be done to make that hole; fibers have to be moved aside, which means that a force must be exerted over the distance they move. When the cannonball hits the wood, it does work, and so a cannonball in flight clearly has the *ability* to do work—that is, it has energy—because of its motion. This energy of motion is what we call kinetic energy.

This breaching humpback whale has kinetic energy because he is moving.

You can find countless examples of kinetic energy in nature. A fish moving through water, a bird flying, and a predator catching its prey all have kinetic energy. So do a speeding car, a flying Frisbee, a falling leaf, and anything else that is moving.

Our intuition tells us that two factors govern the amount of kinetic energy contained in any moving object. First, heavier objects that are moving have more kinetic energy than lighter ones: a bowling ball traveling 10 m/s (a very fast sprint) carries a lot more kinetic energy than a golf ball traveling at the same speed. In fact, kinetic energy is directly proportional to mass: if you double the mass, then you double the kinetic energy.

Second, the faster something is moving, the greater the force it is capable of exerting and the greater energy it possesses. A high-speed collision causes much more damage than a fender bender in a parking lot. It turns out that an object's kinetic energy increases as the square of its speed. A car moving 40 mph has four times as much kinetic energy as one moving 20 mph, while at 60 mph a car carries nine times as much kinetic energy as at 20 mph. Thus a modest increase in speed can cause a large increase in kinetic energy.

These ideas are combined in the equation for kinetic energy.

- ▶ **In words:** Kinetic energy equals the mass of the moving object times the square of that object's speed, times the constant $\frac{1}{2}$.
- ▶ **In equation form:**

$$\text{kinetic energy (joules)} = \frac{1}{2} \times \text{mass (kg)} \times [\text{speed (m/s)}]^2$$

- ▶ **In symbols:**

$$E_K = \frac{1}{2} \times m \times v^2$$

EXAMPLE 3-3

Bowling Balls and Baseballs

What is the kinetic energy of a 4-kg (about 8-lb) bowling ball rolling down a bowling lane at 10 m/s (about 22 mph)? Compare this energy with that of a 250-gram (about half-a-pound) baseball traveling 50 m/s (almost 110 mph). Which object would hurt more if it hit you (i.e., which object has the greater kinetic energy)?

Reasoning: We have to substitute numbers into the equation for kinetic energy.

Solution: For the 4-kg bowling ball traveling at 10 m/s:

$$\begin{aligned}\text{kinetic energy (joules)} &= \frac{1}{2} \times \text{mass (kg)} \times [\text{speed (m/s)}]^2 \\ &= \frac{1}{2} \times 4 \text{ kg} \times (10 \text{ m/s})^2 \\ &= \frac{1}{2} \times 4 \text{ kg} \times 100 \text{ m}^2/\text{s}^2 \\ &= 200 \text{ kg-m}^2/\text{s}^2\end{aligned}$$

Note that

$$\begin{aligned}200 \text{ kg-m}^2/\text{s}^2 &= 200 \text{ (kg-m/s}^2) \times \text{m} \\ &= 200 \text{ N} \times \text{m} \\ &= 200 \text{ joules}\end{aligned}$$

For the 250-g baseball traveling at 50 m/s:

$$\text{kinetic energy (joules)} = \tfrac{1}{2} \times \text{mass (kg)} \times [\text{speed (m/s)}]^2$$
$$= \tfrac{1}{2} \times 250 \text{ g} \times (50 \text{ m/s})^2$$

A gram is a thousandth of a kilogram, so 250 g = 0.25 kg:

$$\text{kinetic energy (joules)} = \tfrac{1}{2} \times 0.25 \text{ kg} \times 2500 \text{ m}^2/\text{s}^2$$
$$= 312.5 \text{ kg-m}^2/\text{s}^2$$
$$= 312.5 \text{ joules}$$

Even though the bowling ball is much more massive than the baseball, a hard-hit baseball carries more kinetic energy than a typical bowling ball because of its high speed.

Potential Energy

Almost every mountain range in the country has a "balancing rock"—a boulder precariously perched on top of a hill so that it looks as if a little push would send it tumbling down the slope. If the balancing rock were to fall, it would clearly acquire kinetic energy, and it would do "work" on anything it smashed. The balancing rock has the ability to do work even though it's not doing work right now, and even though it's not necessarily going to be doing work any time in the near future. The boulder possesses energy just by virtue of its position.

This kind of energy, which could result in the exertion of a force over distance but is not doing so now, is called potential energy. In the case of the balancing rock, it is called *gravitational potential energy* because the force of gravity gives the rock the capability of exerting its own force. An object that has been lifted above Earth's surface possesses an amount of gravitational potential energy exactly equal to the total amount of work you would have to do to lift it from the ground to its present position.

▶ **In words:** The gravitational potential energy of any object equals its weight (the gravitational force exerted downward by the object) times its height above the ground.

▶ **In equation form:**

$$\text{gravitational potential energy (joules)} = \text{mass (kg)} \times g \text{ (m/s}^2) \times \text{height (m)}$$

where g is the acceleration due to gravity at Earth's surface (see Chapter 2).

▶ **In symbols:**

$$E_P = m \times g \times h$$

In Example 3-1 we saw that it requires 784 joules of energy to carry a 20-kg television set 4 meters distance up the stairs. Thus 784 joules is the amount of work that would be done if the television set were allowed to fall, and it is the amount of gravitational potential energy stored in the elevated television set.

We encounter many other kinds of potential energy besides the gravitational kind in our daily lives. *Chemical potential energy* is stored in the gasoline that moves your car, the batteries that power your radio, and the food you eat. All animals depend on the chemical potential energy of food, and all living things rely on molecules that store chemical energy for future use. In each of these situations, potential energy is stored in the chemical bonds between atoms (see Chapter 9).

Dennis Galante/Taxi/Getty Images, Inc.

Jack Hollingsworth/PhotoDisc, Inc./Getty Images

Vladimir Pcholkin/Taxi/Getty Images, Inc.

• **Figure 3-2** Potential energy comes in many forms.

Wall outlets in your home and at work provide a means to tap into *electrical potential energy,* waiting to turn a fan or drive a vacuum cleaner. A tightly coiled spring, a flexed muscle, and a stretched rubber band contain *elastic potential energy,* while a refrigerator magnet carries *magnetic potential energy.* In every case, energy is stored, ready to do work (Figure 3-2).

Heat, or Thermal Energy

Two centuries ago, scientists understood the basic behavior of kinetic and potential energy, but the nature of heat was far more mysterious. It's easy to feel and measure the effects of heat, but what are the physical causes underlying the behavior of hot and cold objects?

We now know that all matter is made of minute objects called *atoms,* which often clump together into discrete collections of two or more atoms called *molecules.* We'll examine details of the structure and behavior of atoms and molecules, which are much too small to be seen with an ordinary microscope, in Chapters 8 through 10. A key discovery regarding these minute particles is that the properties of all the materials in our environment depend on their constituent atoms and how they're linked together. The contrast between solid ice, liquid water, and gaseous steam, all of which are made from molecules of three atoms (two hydrogen atoms linked to one oxygen atom, or H_2O), for example, is a consequence of how strongly adajacent atoms or molecules interact with each other (Chapter 10).

The key to understanding the nature of heat is that all atoms and molecules are in constant random motion. These particles that make up all matter move around and vibrate, and therefore these particles possess kinetic energy. The tiny forces that they exert are experienced only by other atoms and molecules, but the small scale doesn't make the forces any less real. If molecules in a material begin to move more rapidly, then they have more kinetic energy and are capable of exerting greater forces on each other in collisions. If you touch an object whose molecules are moving fast, then the collisions of those molecules with molecules in your hand will exert greater force, and you will perceive the object to be hot. By contrast, if the molecules in your hand are moving faster than those of the object you touch, then you will perceive the object to be cold. What we normally call **heat,** therefore, is simply **thermal energy**—the random kinetic energy of atoms and molecules.

Granger Collection

Benjamin Thompson, Count Rumford, in a Bavarian cannon foundry in 1798, calling attention to the transformation of mechanical energy into heat.

Science in the Making •

Discovering the Nature of Heat

What is heat? How would you apply the scientific method to determine its origins? That was the problem facing scientists 200 years ago.

In many respects, they realized, heat behaves like a fluid. It flows from place to place, and it seems to spread out evenly like water that has been spilled on the floor. Some objects soak up heat faster than others, and many materials seem to swell up when heated, just like waterlogged wood. Thus, in 1800, after years of observations and experiments, many physicists mistakenly accepted the theory that heat is an invisible fluid—they called it "caloric." According to the caloric theory of heat, the best fuels, such as coal, are saturated with caloric, while ice is virtually devoid of the substance.

One of the most influential investigators of heat was the Massachusetts-born Benjamin Thompson (1752–1814), who led a remarkably adventurous life. At the age of 19 he married an extremely wealthy widow, 14 years his senior. He sided with the British during the Revolutionary War, first working as a spy, then as an officer in the British Army of Occupation in New York. After the Americans won the war, Thompson abandoned his wife and infant daughter and fled to Europe, where he was knighted by King George III. Later in his turbulent life he was forced to flee England on suspicion of spying for the French, and he eventually wound up in the employ of the Elector of Bavaria, where his duties included the manufacture and machining of cannons.

If heat is a fluid, then each object must contain a fixed quantity of that substance. But Thompson noted that the increase in temperature that accompanies boring a cannon had nothing at all to do with the quantity of brass to be drilled. Sharp tools, he found, cut brass quickly with minimum heat generation, while dull tools made slow progress and produced prodigious amounts of heat.

Thompson proposed an alternative hypothesis. He suggested that the increase in temperature in his brass was a consequence of the mechanical energy of friction, not some theoretical, invisible fluid. He proved his point by immersing an entire cannon-boring machine in water, turning it on, and watching the heat that was generated turn the water to steam. British chemist and popular science lecturer Sir Humphry Davy (1778–1829) further dramatized Thompson's point when he generated heat by rubbing pieces of ice together on a cold London day.

The work of Thompson, Davy, and others inspired English researcher James Prescott Joule to devise a special experiment to test the predictions of the rival theories. As shown in Figure 3-3, Joule's apparatus employed a weight that was lifted up and attached to a rope. The rope turned a paddle wheel immersed in a tub of water. The weight had gravitational potential energy, and, as it fell, that energy was converted into kinetic energy of the rotating paddle. The paddle wheel's kinetic energy, in turn, was transferred to kinetic energy of water molecules. As Joule suspected, the water heated up by an amount equal to the gravitational potential energy released by the weights. Heat, he declared, is just another form of energy. •

• **Figure 3-3** Joule's experiment demonstrated that heat is another form of energy by showing that the kinetic energy of a paddle wheel is transferred to thermal energy of the agitated water.

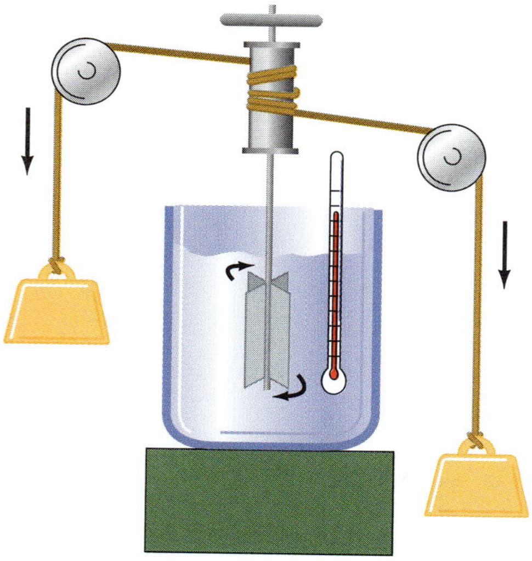

Wave Energy

Anyone who has watched surf battering a seashore has firsthand knowledge of **wave energy.** In the case of water waves, the type of energy involved is obvious. Large amounts of water are in rapid motion and therefore possess kinetic energy. It is this energy that we see released when waves hit the shore.

Other kinds of waves possess energy, as well. For example, when a *sound wave* is generated, molecules in the air are set in motion and the energy of the sound wave is associated with the kinetic energy of those molecules. Similar sound waves traveling through the solid earth, called *seismic waves,* can carry the potentially destructive energy that is unleashed in earthquakes (see Chapter 17). In Chapter 6 we will meet another important kind of wave, the kind associated with electromagnetic radiation, such as the radiant energy (light) that streams from the Sun. This kind of wave stores its energy in changing electrical and magnetic fields.

Mass as Energy

The discovery that certain atoms, such as uranium, spontaneously release energy as they disintegrate—the phenomenon of radioactivity—led to the realization in the early twentieth century that mass is a form of energy. This principle is the focus of Chapter 7, but the main idea is summarized in Albert Einstein's most famous equation.

- **In words:** Every object at rest contains potential energy equivalent to the product of its mass times a constant, which is the speed of light squared.
- **In equation form:**

$$\text{energy (joules)} = \text{mass (kg)} \times [\text{speed of light (m/s)}]^2$$

- **In symbols:**

$$E = mc^2$$

where c is the symbol for the speed of light, a constant equal to 300,000,000 meters per second (3×10^8 m/s).

This equation, which has achieved the rank of a cultural icon, tells us that it is possible to transform mass into energy and to use energy to create mass. (*Note:* This equation does not mean the mass has to be traveling at the speed of light; the mass is assumed to be at rest.) Furthermore, because the speed of light is so great, the energy stored in even a tiny amount of mass is enormous.

EXAMPLE 3-4

Lots of Potential

According to Einstein's equation, how much potential energy is contained in the mass of a grain of sand with a mass of 0.001 gram?

Reasoning and Solution: Substitute the mass, 0.001 gram, into Einstein's famous equation. Remember that 1 gram is a thousandth of a kilogram, so a thousandth of a gram equals a millionth of a kilogram (10^{-6} kg). Also, the speed of light is a constant, 3×10^8 m/s.

$$\begin{aligned} \text{energy (joules)} &= \text{mass (kg)} \times [\text{speed of light (m/s)}]^2 \\ &= 10^{-6}\ \text{kg} \times (3 \times 10^8\ \text{m/s})^2 \\ &= 10^{-6} \times 9 \times (10^{16}\ \text{kg-m}^2/\text{s}^2) \\ &= 9 \times 10^{10}\ \text{joules} \end{aligned}$$

The energy contained in the mass of a single grain of sand is prodigious: almost 100 billion joules, which is 25,000 kilowatt-hours. The average American family uses about 1000 kilowatt-hours of electricity per month, so a sand grain—if we had the means to convert its mass entirely to electrical energy (which we don't)—could satisfy your home's energy needs for the next two years!

In practical terms, Einstein's equation showed that mass could be used to generate electricity in nuclear power plants, in which a few pounds of nuclear fuel is enough to power an entire city.

The Interchangeability of Energy

You know from everyday experience that energy can be changed from one form to another (Table 3-2). Plants absorb light streaming from the Sun and convert that radiant energy into the stored chemical energy of cells and plant tissues. You eat plants and convert the chemical energy into the kinetic energy of your muscles—energy of motion

Table 3-2 Some Forms of Energy

Potential Energy	Kinetic Energy	Other
Gravitational	Moving objects	Mass
Chemical	Heat	
Elastic	Sound and other waves	
Electromagnetic		

A Slinky provides a dramatic example of energy changing from one form to another. Can you identify some of the kinds of energy changes involved?

Andy Washnik

that in turn can be converted into gravitational potential energy when you climb a flight of stairs, elastic potential energy when you stretch a rubber band, or heat when you rub your hands together. The lesson from these examples is clear.

The many different forms of energy are interchangeable.

Energy in one form can be converted into others.

Bungee jumping provides a dramatic illustration of this rule (Figure 3-4). Bungee jumpers climb to a high bridge or platform, where elastic cords are attached to their ankles. Then they launch themselves into space and fall toward the ground until the cords stretch, slow them down, and stop their fall.

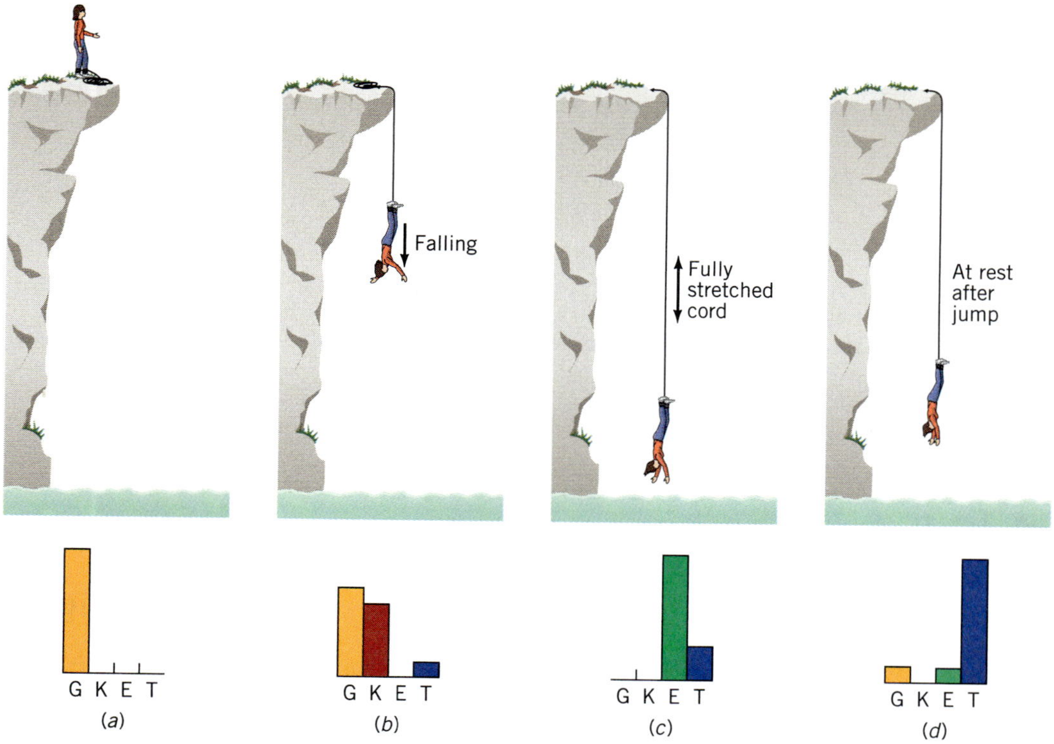

• **Figure 3-4** Energy changes form during a bungee jump, though the total energy is constant. Histograms display the distribution of energy among gravitational potential (G), kinetic (K), elastic potential (E), and thermal (T). Initially *(a)*, all of the energy to be used in the jump is stored as gravitational potential energy. During the descent *(b)*, the gravitational potential energy is converted to kinetic energy. At the bottom of the jump, the bungee cord stretches *(c)*, so that most energy is in the form of elastic potential. At the end of the jump *(d)* most of the energy winds up as heat.

From an energy point of view, a bungee jumper uses the chemical potential energy generated from food to walk up to the launching platform. The work that had been done against gravity provides the jumper with gravitational potential energy. During the long descent, the gravitational potential energy diminishes, while the jumper's kinetic energy simultaneously increases. As the cords begin to stretch, the jumper slows down and kinetic energy gradually is converted to stored elastic potential energy in the cords. Eventually, the gravitational potential energy that the jumper had at the beginning is completely transferred to the stretched elastic cords, which then rebound, converting some of the stored elastic energy back into kinetic energy and gravitational potential energy. All the time, some of the energy is also converted to thermal energy: increased temperature in the stressed cord, on the jumper's ankles, and the air as it is pushed aside.

One of the most fundamental properties of the universe in which we live is that every form of energy on our list can be converted to every other form of energy.

The Science of Life •

Energy for Life and Trophic Levels

All of Earth's systems, both living and nonliving, transform the Sun's radiant energy into other forms. Just how much energy is available, and how is it used by living organisms?

At the top of Earth's atmosphere, the Sun's incoming energy is 1400 watts per square meter. To calculate the total energy of this solar power, we first need to calculate Earth's cross-sectional area in square meters. Earth's radius is 6375 kilometers (6,375,000 meters), and so the cross-sectional area is

$$\begin{aligned}\text{area of a circle} &= \text{pi} \times (\text{radius})^2 \\ &= 3.14 \times (6{,}375{,}000\ \text{m})^2 \\ &= 1.28 \times 10^{14}\ \text{m}^2\end{aligned}$$

Thus the total power received at the top of Earth's atmosphere is

$$\begin{aligned}\text{power} &= \text{solar energy per m}^2 \times \text{Earth's cross-sectional area} \\ &= 1400\ \text{watts/m}^2 \times 1.28 \times 10^{14}\ \text{m}^2 \\ &= 1.79 \times 10^{17}\ \text{watts}\end{aligned}$$

Solar photovoltaic cells, like this array in Albuquerque, New Mexico, convert the energy in sunlight directly into electrical current.

Dave Jacobs/Stone/Getty Images

Each second, the top of Earth's atmosphere receives 1.79×10^{17} joules of energy, but that is more than twice the amount that reaches the ground. When solar radiation encounters the top of the atmosphere, about 25% of it is immediately reflected back into space. Another 25% is absorbed by gases in the atmosphere, and Earth's surface reflects an additional 5% back into space. These processes leave about 45% of the initial amount to be absorbed at Earth's surface.

All living systems take their energy from this 45% but absorb only a small portion of this amount—only about 4% to run photosynthesis and supply the entire food chain. A much larger portion heats the ground or air, or evaporates water from lakes, rivers, and oceans.

The concept of the food chain and its trophic levels is particularly useful when tracking the many changes of energy as it flows through living systems of Earth. A **trophic level** consists of all organisms that get their energy from the same source (Figure 3-5).

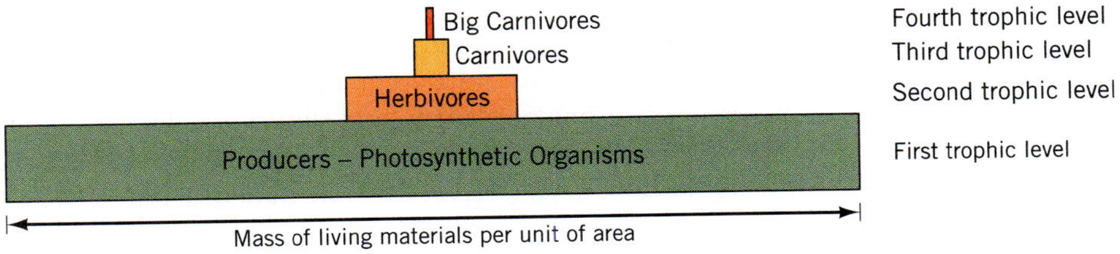

• **Figure 3-5** The food chain. Living organisms are arranged in trophic levels according to how they obtain energy. The first trophic level consists of plants that produce energy from photosynthesis. In the higher trophic levels, animals get their energy by feeding on organisms from the next lowest level.

In this ranking scheme, all plants that produce energy from photosynthesis are in the *first trophic level.* These plants all absorb energy from sunlight and use it to drive chemical reactions that make plant tissues and other complex molecules subsequently used as energy sources by organisms in higher trophic levels.

The *second trophic level* includes all *herbivores*—animals that get their energy by eating plants of the first trophic level. Cows, rabbits, and many insects occupy this level. The *third trophic level,* as you might expect, consists of *carnivores*—animals that get their energy by eating organisms in the second trophic level. This third level includes such familiar animals as wolves, eagles, and lions, as well as insect-eating birds, blood-sucking ticks and mosquitoes, and many other organisms.

A few more groups of organisms fill out the scheme of trophic levels on Earth. Carnivores that eat other carnivores, such as killer whales, occupy the fourth trophic level. Termites, vultures, and a host of bacteria and fungi get their energy from feeding on dead organisms and are generally placed in a trophic level separate from the four we have just described. (The usual convention is that this trophic level is not given a number because the dead organisms can come from any of the other trophic levels.)

A number of animals and plants span the trophic levels. Human beings, raccoons, and bears, for example, are *omnivores* that gain energy from plants and from organisms in other trophic levels, while the Venus flytrap is a green plant that supplements its diet with trapped insects. •

Stop and Think! From which trophic levels did you obtain energy during the past 24 hours?

Although you might expect it to be otherwise, the efficiency with which solar energy is used by Earth's organisms is very low, despite the struggle by all these organisms to use energy efficiently. When sunlight falls, for example, on a cornfield in the middle of Iowa in August—arguably one of the best situations in the world for plant growth—only a small percentage of the solar energy striking the field is actually transformed as chemical energy in the plants. All the rest of the energy is reflected, heats up the soil, evaporates water, or performs some other function. It is a general rule that no plants anywhere transform as much as 10% of solar energy available to them.

The same situation applies to trophic levels above the first. Typically, less than 10% of a plant's chemical potential energy winds up as tissue in the animal of the second trophic level that eats the plants. That is, less than about 1% (10% of 10%) of the original energy in sunlight is transformed into chemical energy of the second trophic level. Continuing with the same pattern, animals in the third trophic level also use less than 10% of the energy available from the second level.

You can do a rough verification of this statement in your supermarket. Whole grains (those that have not been processed heavily) typically cost about one-tenth as much per pound as fresh meat. Examined from an energy point of view, this cost differential is not surprising. It takes 10 times as much energy to make a pound of beef as it does to make a pound of wheat or rice, and this fact is reflected in the price.

One of the most interesting examples of energy flow through trophic levels can be seen in the fossils of dinosaurs. In many museum exhibits, the most dramatic and memorable specimen is a giant carnivore—a *Tyrannosaurus* or *Allosaurus* with 6-inch dagger teeth and powerful claws. So often are these impressive skeletons illustrated that you might get the impression that these finds are common. In fact, fossil carnivores are extremely rare and represent only a small fraction of known dinosaur specimens. Our knowledge of the fearsome *Tyrannosaurus,* for example, is based on only about a dozen skeletons, and most of those are quite fragmentary. By contrast, paleontologists have found hundreds of skeletons of plant-eating dinosaurs. This distribution is hardly chance. Carnivorous dinosaurs, like modern lions and tigers, were relatively scarce compared to their herbivorous victims. In fact, statistical studies of all dinosaur skeletons reveal a roughly 10:1 herbivore-to-carnivore ratio, a value approaching what we find today for the ratio of warm-blooded herbivores to warm-blooded carnivores, and much higher than the herbivore-to-carnivore ratio observed in modern cold-blooded reptiles. This pattern is cited by many paleontologists as evidence that dinosaurs were warm-blooded.

The First Law of Thermodynamics: Energy Is Conserved

Scientists are always on the lookout for attributes of the ever-changing universe that are constant and unchanging. If the total number of atoms, electrons, or electrical charges is constant, then that attribute is said to be conserved. Any statement that an attribute is *conserved* is called a **conservation law.** (Note that these meanings of "conserved" and "conservation" are different from the more common uses of the words associated with modest consumption and recycling.)

Before describing the conservation law that relates to energy, we must first introduce the idea of a system. You can think of a **system** as an imaginary box into which you put some matter and some energy that you would like to study. Scientists might want to study a system containing only a pan of water, or one consisting of a forest, or even the entire planet Earth. Doctors examine your nervous system, astronomers explore the solar system, and biologists observe a variety of ecosystems. In each case, the investigation of nature is simplified by focusing on one small part of the universe.

If the system under study can exchange matter and energy with its surroundings—a pan full of water that is heated on a stove and gradually evaporates, for example—then it is an *open system*. An open system is like an open box where you can take things out and put things back in. Alternatively, if matter and energy in a system do not freely exchange with their surroundings, as in a tightly shut box, then the system is said to be *closed* or isolated. Earth and its primary source of energy, the Sun, together make a system that may be thought of for most purposes as closed, because there are no significant amounts of matter or energy being added from outside sources.

The most important conservation law in the sciences is the law of *conservation of energy*. This law is also called the **first law of thermodynamics.** (*Thermodynamics*—literally the study of the movement of heat—is a term used for the science of heat, energy, and work.) The law can be stated as follows:

In an isolated system the total amount of energy, including heat, is conserved.

This law tells us that, although the kind of energy in a given system can change, the total amount cannot. For example, when a bungee jumper hurls herself into space, the gravitational potential energy she had at the beginning of the fall is converted to an equal amount of other kinds of energy. When she's moving, some of the gravitational potential energy changes into kinetic energy, some into elastic potential energy, and some into the increased temperature of the surroundings. At each point during the fall, however, the sum of kinetic, elastic potential, gravitational potential, and heat energies has to be the same as the gravitational energy at the beginning.

Energy is something like an economy with an absolutely fixed amount of money. You can earn it, store it in a bank or under your pillow, and spend it here and there when you want to. But the total amount of money doesn't change just because it passes through your hands. Likewise, in any physical situation you can shuffle energy from one place to another. You could take it out of the account labeled "kinetic" and put it into the account labeled "potential"; you could spread it around into accounts labeled "chemical potential," "elastic potential," "heat," and so on; but the first law of thermodynamics tells us that, in a closed system, you can never have more or less energy than you started with.

To many scientists of the nineteenth century the first law of thermodynamics represented more than just a useful statement about energy. For them it carried a profound significance about the underlying symmetry—even beauty—of the natural order. Joule described the first law in the following poetic way: "Nothing is destroyed, nothing is ever lost, but the entire machinery, complicated as it is, works smoothly and harmoniously . . . Everything may appear complicated in the apparent confusion and intricacy of an almost endless variety of causes, effects, conversions, and arrangements, yet is the most perfect regularity preserved—the whole being governed by the sovereign will of God." To Joule, the first law was nothing less than proof of the beneficence of the Creator—a natural law analogous to the immortality of the soul.

Science by the Numbers •

Diet and Calories

The first law of thermodynamics has a great deal to say about the American obsession with weight and diet. Human beings take in energy with their food, energy we usually measure in *calories.* (Note that the calorie we talk about in foods is defined as the amount of energy needed to raise the temperature of a kilogram of water 1° Celsius, a unit we will later call a kilocalorie.) When a certain amount of energy is taken in, the first law says that only one of two things can happen to it: It can be converted into work and increased temperature of the surroundings, or it can be stored. If we take in more energy than we expend, the excess is stored in fat. If, on the other hand, we take in less than we expend, energy must be removed from storage to meet the deficit, and the amount of body fat decreases.

William Thomson, Lord Kelvin (1824–1907)

Here are a couple of rough rules you can use to calculate calories in your diet:

1. Under most circumstances, normal body maintenance uses up about 15 calories per day for each pound of body weight.
2. You must consume about 3500 calories to gain a pound of fat.

Suppose you weigh 150 pounds. To keep your weight constant, you have to take in

$$150 \text{ pounds} \times 15 \text{ calories/pound} = 2250 \text{ calories per day}$$

If you wanted to lose one pound (3500 calories) a week (7 days), you would have to reduce your daily calorie intake by

$$\frac{3500 \text{ calories}}{7\text{days}} = 500 \text{ calories per day}$$

Another way of saying this is that you would have to reduce your calorie intake to 1750 calories—the equivalent of skipping dessert every day.

Alternatively, the first law says you can increase your energy use through exercise. Roughly speaking, to burn off 500 calories you would have to run 5 miles, bike 15 miles, or swim for an hour.

It's a whole lot easier to refrain from eating than to burn off the weight by exercise. In fact, most researchers now say that the main benefit of exercise in weight control has to do with its ability to help people control their appetites. •

Science in the Making •

Lord Kelvin and Earth's Age

The first law of thermodynamics provided physicists with a powerful tool for describing and analyzing their universe. Every isolated system, the law tells us, has a fixed amount of energy. Naturally, one of the first systems that scientists considered was the Sun and Earth.

British physicist William Thomson (1824–1907), enobled as Lord Kelvin, asked a simple question: How much energy could be stored inside Earth? And, given the present rate at which energy radiates out into space, how old might Earth be? Though simple, these questions had profound implications for philosophers and theologians who had their own ideas about Earth's relative antiquity. Some biblical scholars believed that Earth could be no more than a few thousand years old. Most geologists, on the other hand, saw evidence in layered rocks to suggest an Earth at least hundreds of millions of years old. Biologists also required vast amounts of time to account for the gradual evolution of life on Earth. Who was correct?

Kelvin assumed, as did most of his contemporaries, that Earth had formed from a contracting cloud of interstellar dust (see Chapter 16). He thought that Earth began as a hot body because impacts of large objects on it early in its history must have converted huge amounts of gravitational potential energy into thermal energy. He used new developments in mathematics to calculate how long it took for a hot Earth to cool to its present temperature. He assumed that there were no sources of energy inside Earth, and found that Earth's age had to be less than about 100 million years. He soundly rejected the geologists' and biologists' claims of an older Earth because these claims seemed to violate the first law of thermodynamics.

Seldom have scientists come to such a bitter impasse. Two competing theories about Earth's age, each supported by seemingly sound observations, were at odds. The calculations of the physicist seemed unassailable, yet the observations of biologists and geologists in the field were equally meticulous. What could possibly resolve the dilemma? Had the scientific method failed? The solution came from a totally unexpected source when scientists discovered in the 1890s that rocks hold a previously unknown source of energy, radioactivity (see Chapter 11), in which thermal energy is generated by the conversion of mass. Lord Kelvin's rigorous age calculations were in error only because he and his contemporaries were unaware of this critical component of Earth's energy budget. Earth's deep interior, we now know, gains approximately half of its thermal energy from radioactive decay. Revised calculations suggest an Earth several billions of years old, in conformity with geological and biological observations. •

The United States and Its Energy Future

The growth of modern technological societies since the Industrial Revolution has been driven by the availability of cheap, high-grade sources of energy. When fuel wood became expensive and scarce at the end of the eighteenth century, men like James Watt figured out how to tap into the solar energy stored in coal. In the early twentieth century, the development of the internal combustion engine and other new technologies made petroleum the fuel of choice. Both of these transitions took about 30 years.

Fuels like *oil (petroleum), coal,* and *natural* gas are called *fossil fuels* because they are the result of processes that happened long ago. As you can see from Figure 3-6, the economy of the United States today depends almost completely on the burning of fossil fuels. This state of affairs leads to two difficult problems. One characteristic of fossil fuels is that they are not replaceable—once you burn a ton of coal or a barrel of oil, it is gone as far as any timescale meaningful to human beings is concerned. Another characteristic, as we shall discuss in Chapter 19, is that an inevitable result of burning fossil fuels is the addition of carbon dioxide to the atmosphere. This, in turn, may well lead to long-term climate change. Thus, the search for alternate energy sources to drive our economy is well under way.

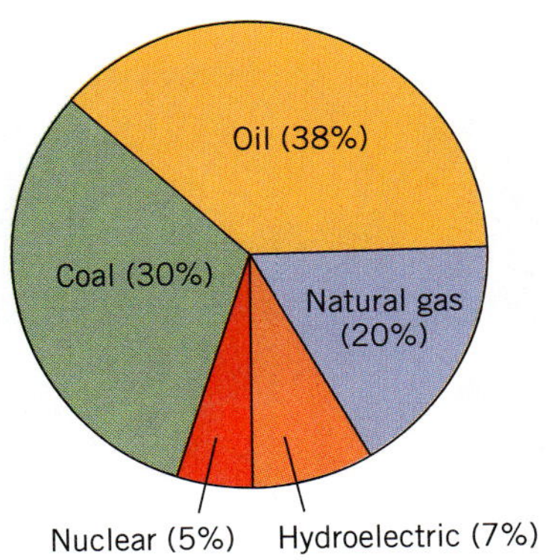

• **Figure 3-6** Sources of energy for the United States and other industrial nations. Note that most of our energy comes from fossil fuels.

The two most important alternate energy sources being considered are solar energy and wind. Because they are constantly being replaced, solar energy and wind are

Lester lefkowitz/Photographer's Choice/Getty Images

Electricity generated from this sort of wind turbine is starting to become economically competitive in the United States.

usually classed as *renewable energy sources*. Neither contributes to global warming, and both are considered to be part of the process of weaning ourselves from fossil fuels.

The question of when these energy sources will be available in commercially useful quantities is a complicated mix of technology and economics. As an example, think about generating electricity from these sources. Commercial electrical generation in the United States can be divided into two types—*base load* and *peak load*. Base load is electricity that has to be delivered day in and day out to run essential services like lighting and manufacturing. Peak load refers to the extra electricity that has to be delivered on, for example, a hot day when everyone turns on his or her air conditioner. Typically, base load power is delivered by large coal or nuclear plants. These plants are expensive to build, but since the construction cost is spread out over a long time period, the net cost per kilowatt-hour is low. Peak load, on the other hand, is typically delivered by systems such as gas turbines. These plants are cheap to build but expensive to operate because they typically use more expensive fuels. Thus, peak load electricity is usually more expensive than base load. (You probably don't see this difference in your electricity bill because the costs are folded together). Thus, the best place for alternate energy sources to enter the economy is in the peak load market.

The United States has enormous solar and wind resources. A "wind belt" runs from the Dakotas to New Mexico, and, of course, the deserts of the American Southwest have sunlight in plenty. Enormous improvements in windmill technology over the past few decades have lowered the cost of wind power to the point where it is competitive with conventional forms of generation. This is why you see windmill "farms" springing up all over the place.

Solar energy is further behind. In 2005, the cost of solar-generated electricity was 24 cents per kilowatt hour versus about 4 cents for coal. Some experts estimate that by 2025, the cost of solar energy will have dropped to 6 cents per kilowatt-hour and that about half of all new electrical generation in the United States will be solar.

> **Stop and Think!** You often see highway signs and traffic counters being powered by solar cells. Given the high cost of solar energy, why do you suppose these devices are used even in areas where it would be easy to hook up to the ordinary electrical power grid?

To understand why this practice makes sense, you have to realize that the cost of electricity is only a small portion of the cost of maintaining something like a traffic counter. Typically, the major expense is the installation itself. As one engineer told the authors, "You can just drop these in place where you want them. You don't have to bring in electricians to connect them, and that makes them a lot cheaper."

Most analysts think that the energy future of the United States will involve some mix of coal, oil, natural gas, nuclear, wind, and solar, with an eventual shift to completely renewable sources. The magnitude of the effort required to accomplish such a transition should not be underestimated, however. To generate all of America's electricity by wind power would require a windmill every quarter mile over the entire states of North and South Dakota. Similarly, to generate the same amount of energy from sunlight would require covering an area four times that of Massachusetts with solar collectors. Neither of these tasks would be a trivial undertaking, and no one as yet has given serious thought to the environmental or social consequences of an engineering project of this scale.

Another area of energy use is in transportation, which consumes about a third of the United States' energy budget. Much of this energy is used to run gasoline-powered internal combustion engines (ICE) in cars and trucks. There is at the moment a tremendous technological ferment as engineers advocating different ways of replacing ICE work hard to make their systems as good as they can be. Some leading contenders are as follows.

Solar photovoltaeic cells, like those shown, are semiconducting diodes that convert the energy in sunlight to electrical current. They are already used in niche markets in the United States, but require more development to become a major source of electrical power.

John McGrail/Taxi/Getty Images

Electric cars Batteries power these cars, so that their energy actually derives from the electrical power grid. There are many small electric vehicles in the United States (think of golf carts) and a number of prototype passenger cars. The problem with electric cars is primarily technological because the best current batteries don't store a lot of energy per pound of weight. It would, for example, take about 800 pounds of ordinary car batteries to store as much energy as is found in a gallon of gasoline. Because of this problem, the distance that electric cars can go (a quantity referred to as "range") is significantly less than cars with ICE. As new, high-efficiency, light-weight batteries are developed, however, you can expect to see electric cars play a bigger role in the country's transportation system.

Hybrids A hybrid vehicle is one in which a small gasoline motor operates a generator that charges a bank of batteries that, in turn, power the electric motor that drives the car. Because the batteries are constantly being recharged, the car can operate with fewer batteries than are required in a fully electric vehicle. Because the drive system can take the energy of motion of the car during deceleration and use it to generate electricity, a hybrid vehicle uses much less gasoline than a conventional ICE. The first hybrid to enter the American market was the Toyota Prius, which was followed by many other models.

EPA/Marijan Murat/Landov/Landov LLC

Hybrid cars, like this one, are starting to become popular in the United States. They use a gasoline engine to charge the batteries that run the electric motor that drives the car. These cars have high gas mileage and ranges comparable to ordinary internal combustion cars.

Fuel Cell Cars A **fuel cell** is a device in which hydrogen combines with oxygen to form water, producing heat energy in the process. This process is very efficient, and since the only exhaust product is water, it's very clean as well. Engineers consider two approaches to a fuel cell transportation system: one in which pure hydrogen is fed into the fuel cell and one in which the hydrogen is carried into the engine as part of a larger molecule like methanol. In both cases, energy has to be expended to provide the hydrogen. In the case of pure hydrogen fuel, this energy is usually in the form of the electricity needed to separate hydrogen from water molecules. In the case of methanol, it's the energy needed to run the farms that grow the plants (often corn) from which the molecule is made. In both cases, a new distribution system would be needed for the new fuel.

Thinking More About | Energy

Fossil Fuels

All life is rich in the element carbon, which plays a key role in virtually all the chemicals that make up our cells. Life uses the Sun's energy, directly through photosynthesis or indirectly through food, to form these carbon-based substances that store chemical potential energy. When living things die, they may collect in layers at the bottoms of ponds, lakes, or oceans. Over time, as the layers become buried, Earth's temperature and pressure may alter the chemicals of life into deposits of fossil fuels.

Geologists estimate that it takes tens of millions of years of gradual burial under layers of sediments, combined with the transforming effects of temperature and pressure, to form a coal seam or petroleum deposit. Coal forms from layer upon layer of plants that thrived in vast ancient swamps, while petroleum represents primarily the organic matter once contained in plankton, microscopic organisms that float near the ocean's surface. While these natural processes continue today, the rate of coal and petroleum formation in Earth's crust is only a small fraction of the fossil fuels being consumed. For this reason, fossil fuels are classified as *nonrenewable resources.*

One consequence of this situation is clear. Humans cannot continue to rely on fossil fuels forever. Reserves of high-grade crude oil and the cleanest-burning varieties of coal may last less than 100 more years. Less efficient forms of fossil fuels, including lower grades of coal and oil shales in which petroleum is dispersed through solid rock, could be depleted within a few centuries. All the energy now locked up in those valuable energy reserves will still exist, but in the form of unusable heat radiating far into space. Given the irreversibility of burning up our fossil fuel reserves, what steps should we take to promote energy conservation? Should energy be taxed at a higher rate? Should we assume that new energy sources will become available as they are needed?

Summary

Work, measured in *joules* (or foot-pounds), is defined as a force applied over a distance. You do work every time you move an object. Every action of our lives requires *energy* (also measured in joules), which is the ability to do work. *Power,* measured in *watts* or *kilowatts,* indicates the rate at which energy is expended.

Energy comes in several forms. *Kinetic energy* is the energy associated with moving objects such as cars or cannonballs. *Potential energy,* on the other hand, is stored, ready-to-use energy, such as the chemical energy of coal, the elastic energy of a coiled spring, the gravitational energy of dammed-up water, or the electrical energy in your wall socket. *Thermal energy* or *heat* is the form of kinetic energy associated with vibrating atoms and molecules. Energy can also take the form of *wave energy,* such as sound waves or light waves. And early in the twentieth century it was discovered that mass is also a form of energy. All around us energy constantly shifts from one form to another, and all of these kinds of energy are interchangeable.

Energy from the Sun is used by photosynthetic plants in the first *trophic level;* these plants provide the energy for animals in higher trophic levels. Roughly speaking, only about 10% of the energy available at one trophic level finds its way to the next.

The most fundamental idea about energy, expressed in the *first law of thermodynamics,* is that it is *conserved:* the total amount of energy in an isolated *system* never changes. Energy can shift back and forth between the different kinds, but the sum of all energy is constant.

At present, most industrialized countries use fossil fuels to run their economies. Alternative sources for the future include solar and wind energy and, for transportation, electric and *fuel cell* cars.

Key Terms

work (measured in joules)
energy (measured in joules)
power (measured in watts or kilowatts)
kinetic energy
potential energy
thermal energy (heat)
wave energy
trophic level
conservation law
system
first law of thermodynamics
fuel cell

Key Equations

work (joules) = force (newtons) × distance (meters)
energy (joules) = power (watts) × time (seconds)
kinetic energy (joules) = ½ mass (kg) × [speed (m/s)]^2
gravitational potential energy (joules) = g × mass (kg) × height (m)
energy associated with mass at rest (joules) × mass (kg) × [speed of light (m/s)]^2

Constant
$c = 3 \times 10^8$ m/s = speed of light

Review Questions

1. What is the scientific definition of work? How does it differ from ordinary English usage?

2. What is the difference between the watt and the horsepower?

3. What is the difference between energy and power?

4. List some different kinds of energy. Explain how they differ from each other.

5. What is the relationship between heat, energy, and motion?

6. Explain why waves carry energy.

7. What does it mean to say that different forms of energy are interchangeable?

8. Give an example of change of energy from potential to kinetic; from kinetic to potential.

9. What is a trophic level? Give some examples.

10. What does it mean to say that energy is conserved?

11. How did the discovery that mass is a form of energy resolve the debate over Earth's age?

12. Explain what it means to say, "Energy flows through Earth."

Discussion Questions

1. How does the scientific meaning of the words "energy" and "power" differ from their common usage.

2. What forms of energy are used in the following sports:
a. surfing
b. Nascar racing
c. hot air ballooning
d. sailing
e. tennis
f. horse racing

3. Does a tablespoon of olive oil have more stored chemical energy than a tablespoon of sugar?

4. Would it be energy efficient to use a solar water heating system in Alaska? Why or why not?

5. Think about your energy intake today. Pick one food and identify the chain of energy that led to it. What trophic level do you eat from most? Where will the energy that you ingest eventually wind up?

6. What forms of energy are you using when you make a piece of toast? When you make ice? When you dry your clothes?

7. Where does geothermal energy come from? Is it a renewable source of energy? Is hydroelectricity a renewable form of energy?

8. What are the potential environmental drawbacks to the use of the following technologies:

a. wind [*Hint:* Think about birds and bats.]

b. solar

c. geothermal

d. nuclear

e. hydro

9. Plants and animals are still dying and falling to the ocean bottom today. Why, then, do we not classify fossil fuels as renewable resources?

10. Some people say that you lose more calories by eating celery than you gain. How could that be? Is it possible to eat your way to thinness?

11. Ancient human societies are described as labor intensive, while modern society is said to be energy intensive. What is meant by these terms?

12. How do "warm-blooded" animals warm their blood? What form of energy do "cold-blooded" animals use to warm their blood and bodies?

Problems

1. How much work against gravity do you do when you bench-press a 75-kg mass a distance of about 1 meter? Compare this work to that done by a 100-watt lightbulb in an hour. How many times would you have to press the 75-kg mass to equal the work of the lightbulb in one hour?

2. Which has more gravitational potential energy: a 200-kg boulder 1 meter off the ground, a 50-kg boulder 4 meters off the ground, or a 1-kg rock 200 meters off the ground? Which of these can do the most work if all the potential energy was converted into kinetic energy?

3. Compared to a car moving at 10 miles per hour, how much kinetic energy does that same car have when it moves at 20 miles per hour? 50? 75? Graph your results. What does your graph suggest to you about the difficulty of stopping a car as its speed increases?

4. According to Einstein's famous equation, $E = mc^2$, how much energy would be released if a pound of feathers was converted entirely into energy? a pound of lead? (*Note:* You will first need to convert pounds into kilograms.)

5. If you eat 500 calories per day (roughly 4 ounces of potato chips) above your energy needs, how long will it take to gain 10 pounds? How long would you have to walk (assuming 80 calories burned per mile walked) to burn off those 10 pounds?

6. Joules and kilowatt-hours are both units of energy. How many joules are equal to 1 kilowatt-hour?

7. If the price of beef is $2.50 per pound, estimate what the price of lion meat might be, and give reasons for your prediction.

Investigations

1. Look at your most recent electric bill and find the cost of one kilowatt-hour in your area. Then,

a. Look at the back of your CD player or an appliance and find the power rating in watts. How much does it cost for you to operate the device for one hour?

b. If you leave a 100-watt lightbulb on all the time, how much will you pay in a year of electric bills?

c. If you had to pay $10 for a high-efficiency bulb that provided the same light as the 100-watt bulb with only 10 watts of power, how much would you save per year of electric bills, assuming you used the light five hours per day? Would it be worth your while to buy the energy-efficient bulb if the ordinary bulb cost $1 and each bulb lasts three years?

2. In this chapter we introduced several energy units: the joule, the foot-pound, the kilowatt-hour, and the calorie. There are other energy units as well, including the BTU, the erg, the electron-volt, and many more. Look in a science reference book for conversion factors between different pairs of energy units; you may find more than a dozen different units. Who uses each of these different units? Why are there so many different units for the same phenomenon—energy?

3. What kind of fuel is used at your local power plant? What are the implications of the first law of thermodynamics regarding our use of fossil fuels? our use of solar energy?

4. Keep a record of the calorie content of the food you eat and the amount of exercise you do for a few days. If you wanted to gain a pound per month for the next year, how might you change your current habits?

5. Check your household's electric bills for the past year and calculate your total electric consumption for the year.

a. How many 50-kg weights would you have to bench-press 1 meter to produce a gravitational potential energy equal to this consumption?

b. How much mass is equal to this consumption ($E = mc^2$)?

c. Identify five ways that you might reduce your energy consumption without drastically changing your lifestyle.

d. Draft a plan by which you reduce your energy consumption by 10%. About how much money might this save you per year?

6. Investigate the history of the controversy between Lord Kelvin and his contemporaries regarding Earth's age. When did the debate begin? How long did it last? What kinds of evidence did biologists, geologists, and physicists use to support their differing

calculations of Earth's age? Is there still a debate as to the age of Earth?

7. Investigate and find out how your household hot water is heated. Do you use oil, natural gas, solar, or electricity? What is the most efficient way to heat water in your area? Why?

8. Rub your hands together. What conversion of energy is occurring?

9. The geyser "Old Faithful" in Yellowstone National Park sprays water and steam hundreds of feet into the air. What form of energy is being used? Will "Old Faithful" ever run out of energy?

10. Why do electric and hybrid cars cost more than other compact cars? What is the environemental impact of disposing of large numbers of batteries? Do you think that the government should offer more incentives for people to buy hybrid and other fuel-efficient vehicles?

11. If you work out on a stationary bike at a power output of 100 watts for 30 minutes, does this energy output compensate for eating a 250-calorie jelly-filled doughnut? (Assume that the body coverts 20% of the energy input to work and the other 80% is lost as heat and extraneous movements.) 1 food "calorie" = 1 kilocalorie; and 1 calorie = 4.2 kilojoules

12. The next time you are in an appliance store, check out the efficiency ratings of major appliances such as dryers and dishwashers. If you were going to buy one of these appliances, would energy consumption be a factor in your purchase. If one machine is cheaper to run but more expensive to buy, how would you calculate which machine is a better buy?

13. Different parts of the United States receive varying amounts of sunshine. How much solar energy reaches the ground in your part of the country on an average summer day and an average winter day? Is solar power a possibility in your area during the summer? During the winter?

4

Heat and the Second Law of Thermodynamics

How do humans control their body temperature?

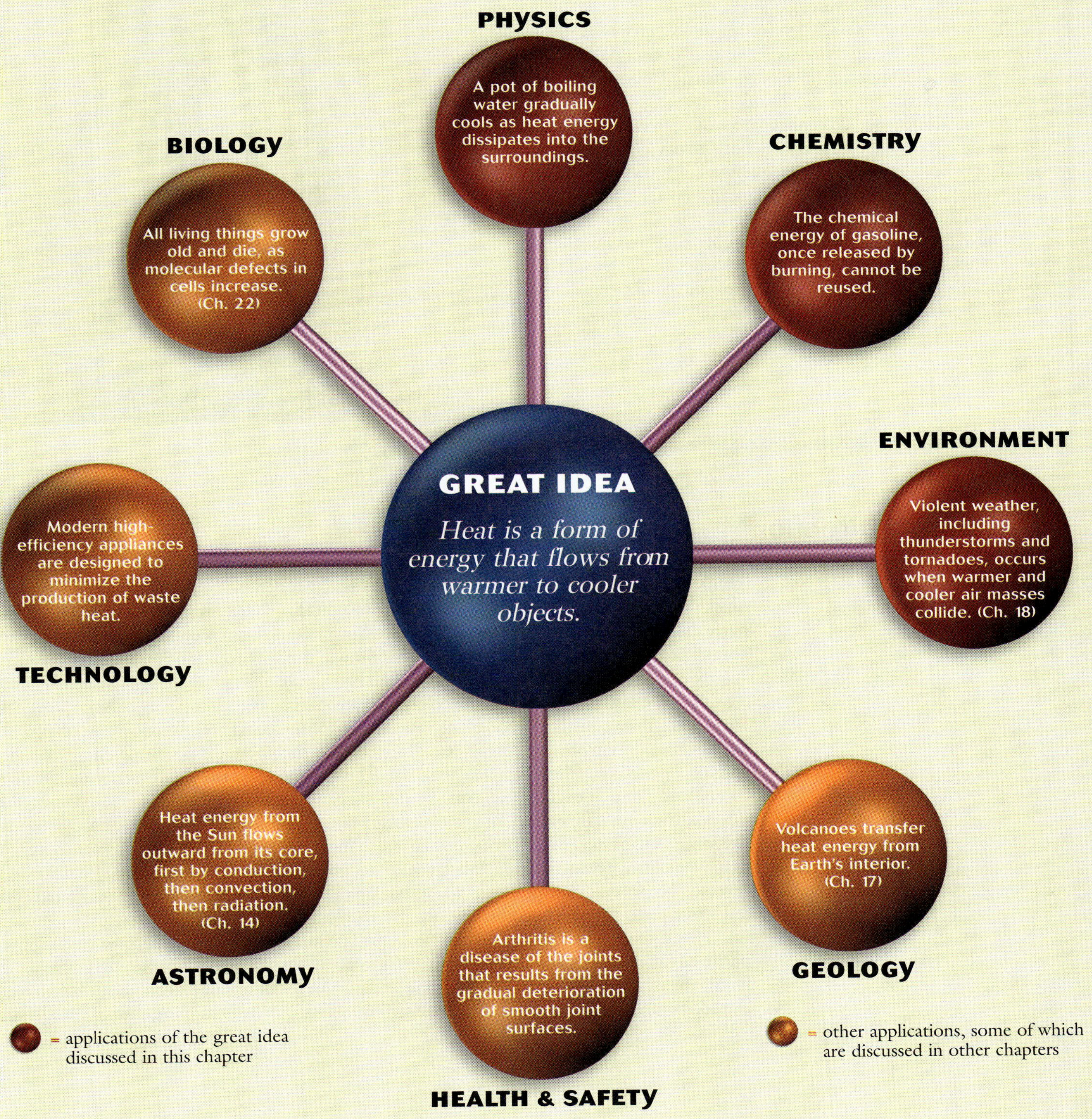

Science Through the Day | A Hot Breakfast

Time for a hearty breakfast. You scramble eggs, squeeze some fresh juice, toast a muffin, and brew a pot of coffee. As you prepare the meal, you notice an obvious but extraordinary fact: nature seems to have a direction. Many events in daily life progress only one way in time. It's easy to scramble eggs but impossible to unscramble them. You can squeeze juice from a piece of fruit, but never unsqueeze it. Toast can't be untoasted and coffee can't be unbrewed.

But why should this be? Nothing in Newton's laws of motion or the law of gravity suggests that events work only in one way. Nothing that we have learned about energy explains the directionality of nature.

As you drink your cold juice and hot coffee, you realize that food and drinks that are very hot or very cold display a similar kind of direction. A glass of ice-cold juice gradually gets warmer, while a cup of steaming hot coffee cools. Heat spreads out uniformly.

These everyday events are so familiar that we take them for granted, yet underlying the scrambling of an egg and the cooling of a hot drink is one of nature's most subtle and fascinating laws: the second law of thermodynamics.

FoodCollection/Age fotostock America, Inc.

Nature's Direction

Think about the dozens of directional events that happen every day. A drop of perfume quickly pervades an entire room with scent, but you'd be hard pressed to collect all those perfume molecules into a single drop again. Your dorm room seems to get messy in the course of the week all by itself, but it takes time and effort to clean it up. And you constantly experience the inevitable, irreversible process of aging.

The first law of thermodynamics, conservation of energy, in no way prohibits events from progressing in the "wrong" direction. For example, when you cook a hard-boiled egg, heat energy from your stove is converted into the chemical potential energy of the cooked egg. According to the first law of thermodynamics, the energy that was added to cook the egg is exactly the same as the energy that would be released if you could uncook the egg. The energy of a room with perfume molecules dispersed throughout is the same as the energy of the room with those molecules tightly bottled. And the energy that went into strewing things about your room is exactly the same energy it takes to reverse the process and put everything back again. Yet there seems to be some natural tendency for things to become less orderly with time.

This directionality in nature can be traced, ultimately, to the behavior of the minute particles called atoms and molecules that form all materials. If you hold an object in your hand, for example, its atoms are moving at more or less the same average speed. If you introduce one more atom into this collection, an atom that is moving much faster than

Alain Denantes/Gamma-Presse, Inc.

• **Figure 4-1** The second law of thermodynamics tells us that it is easier to tear something down than to build it. This law is shown dramatically in this sequence of photos showing the demolition of an apartment building.

any of its neighbors, you will have a situation in which many atoms move slowly and one atom moves rapidly.

Over the course of time, the fast atom will collide again and again with the others. In each collision it will probably lose some of its energy, much as a fast-moving billiard ball slows down after it collides with a couple of other billiard balls. If you wait long enough, the fast-moving atom will share its energy with all the other atoms. Consequently, every atom in the collection will be moving slightly faster than those in the original collection, and there will be no single fast atom.

If you watch this collection of atoms for a long period of time, it's extremely unlikely that the collisions will ever arrange themselves in such a way that one atom moves very fast in a collection of very slow ones. In the language of the physicists, the original state with only one fast atom is highly improbable. Over the course of time, any unlikely initial state will evolve into a more probable state—a situation like the one in which all the atoms have approximately the same energy.

The tendency of all systems to evolve from improbable to more probable states accounts for the directionality that we see in the universe around us (Figure 4-1). There's no reason from the point of view of energy alone that improbable situations can't occur. Fifteen slow-moving billiard balls have enough energy to produce one fast-moving ball. The fact that this situation doesn't occur in nature is an important clue as to how things work at the atomic level.

Nineteenth-century scientists discovered the underlying reasons for nature's directionality by studying heat, the motion of atoms and molecules. Before dealing with the details of these discoveries, as summarized in the second law of thermodynamics, let's consider some properties of heat.

Coming to Terms with Heat

Atoms never sit still. They are always moving, and in the process they distribute their kinetic energy—what we call *thermal energy,* or *internal energy.* If you have ever tried to warm a house during a cold winter day, you have practical experience of this fact. If you turn off the furnace, the energy in the house gradually leaks away to the outside, and the house begins to get cold. The only way you can keep the house warm is to keep adding more thermal energy. Similarly, our bodies constantly produce energy to maintain our core body temperature close to 98.6 degrees Fahrenheit (37°C). Both your furnace and your body produce energy on the inside—energy that will inevitably flow to the outside as heat. You use that heat on the fly, as it were.

In order to understand the nature of heat and its movement, we need to define three closely related terms: heat, temperature, and specific heat capacity.

Heat and Temperature

In everyday conversation we often use the words "temperature" and "heat" interchangeably, but to scientists the words have different meanings. Heat is a form of energy that moves from a warmer object to a cooler object; heat is thus energy in motion. Any object that is hot can transfer its internal energy to the surroundings as heat. A gallon of boiling water contains more internal energy than a pint of boiling water, and it can thus transfer more heat to its surroundings.

Heat is often measured in calories, a common unit of energy defined as the amount of heat required to raise one gram of room-temperature water by one degree Celsius in temperature. (Don't confuse this calorie, abbreviated cal, with the calorie unit commonly used in nutrition discussions. The dietary calorie, abbreviated Cal, equals 1000 calories. See Appendix B.)

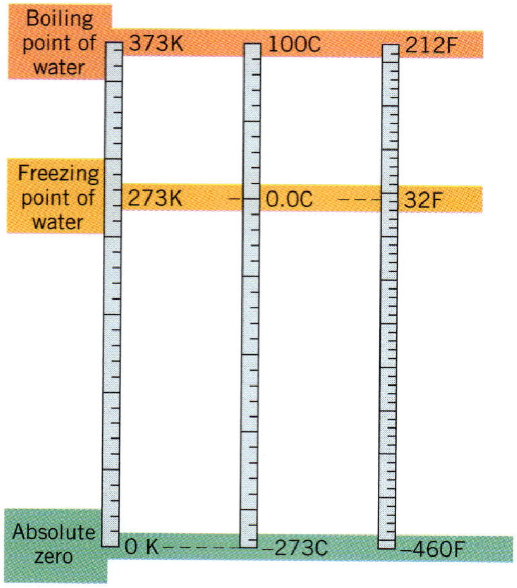

• **Figure 4-2** The Fahrenheit, Celsius, and Kelvin temperature scales compared.

Temperature, on the other hand, is a term that compares how vigorously atoms in a substance are moving and colliding in different substances. Two objects are defined to be at the same temperature if no heat flows spontaneously from one to the other. A gallon of boiling water, therefore, is at the same temperature as a pint of boiling water. The difference in temperature between two objects is one of the factors that determine how quickly heat is transferred between those two objects: the larger the temperature difference, the more rapidly heat is transferred. You may have seen this phenomenon at work in the summertime when violent winds, often accompanied by a line of thunderstorms, precede a cold front. The strong winds are the result of convection (see below), which helps to transfer heat between two air masses at very different temperatures.

Temperature scales provide a convenient way to compare the temperatures of two objects. Many different temperature scales have been proposed; all scales and temperature units are arbitrary, but every scale requires two easily reproduced temperatures for calibration. The freezing and boiling points of pure water are commonly used standards today in the *Fahrenheit scale* (32 and 212 degrees for freezing and boiling, respectively) and the *Celsius scale* (where 0 and 100 degrees correspond to freezing and boiling water, respectively). The Kelvin temperature scale uses the same degree as the Celsius scale, with 100 increments between the freezing and boiling points of water. This scale defines 0 Kelvin (abbreviated K) as **absolute zero,** which is the coldest attainable temperature—the temperature at which it is impossible to extract any heat at all from atoms or molecules. The temperature of absolute zero is approximately –273C, or –460F. It turns out, therefore, that freezing and boiling occur at about 273 and 373 Kelvins, respectively (Figure 4-2).

Temperature Conversions

It's often necessary to convert from one temperature scale to another. American travelers, for example, often have to convert from degrees Celsius (used in most of the rest of the world) to degrees Fahrenheit. This conversion requires the following formula:

$$°F = (1.8 \times °C) + 32$$

The 1.8 in this formula reflects the fact that the Fahrenheit degree is smaller than the Celsius degree, while the 32 reflects the fact that water freezes at 32°F but 0°C. To convert the opposite way, from Fahrenheit to Celsius, the formula is:

$$°C = \frac{(°F - 32)}{1.8}$$

Remember, all temperature scales measure the exact same phenomenon; they just use a different number scale to do so.

EXAMPLE 4-1

What to Wear?

You awake in Paris to a forecast high temperature of 32°C. Should you wear gloves and an overcoat?

Reasoning and Solution: Apply the equation to convert temperature from Celsius to Fahrenheit:

$$
\begin{aligned}
°F &= (1.8 \times °C) + 32 \\
&= (1.8 \times 32) + 32 \\
&= 89.6°F
\end{aligned}
$$

Looks like you won't be needing your overcoat today!

Technology •

Thermometers

A *thermometer* is a device used to measure temperature. Most thermometers display temperature either digitally or on a numbered scale. Thermometers work by incorporating a material whose properties change significantly with temperature. Many materials expand when heated and contract when cooled, and this behavior can be used to gauge temperature. In the old-style mercury thermometer, for example, a bead of mercury expands into a thin glass column with increasing temperature; you read the height of the mercury against a scale marked in degrees. Many other (much safer) thermometers rely on changes in the electrical properties of a temperature sensor. •

Stop and Think! Why are the freezing and boiling points of pure water commonly used as standards for temperature scales? Can you think of other standards that would be useful for everyday measurements?

Specific Heat Capacity

Specific heat capacity is a measure of the ability of a material to absorb heat and is defined as the quantity of heat required to raise the temperature of one gram of that material by 1°C. Water displays the largest heat capacity of any common substance; by definition, one calorie is required to raise the temperature of a gram of water by 1°C. By contrast, you know that metals heat up quickly in a fire, so a small amount of absorbed heat can cause a significant increase in the metal's temperature.

Think about the last time you boiled water in a copper-bottomed pot. It doesn't take long to raise the temperature of a copper pot to above the boiling point of water because copper, like most other metals, heats up rapidly as it absorbs heat. In fact, one calorie will raise the temperature of a gram of copper by about 10°C. But water is a

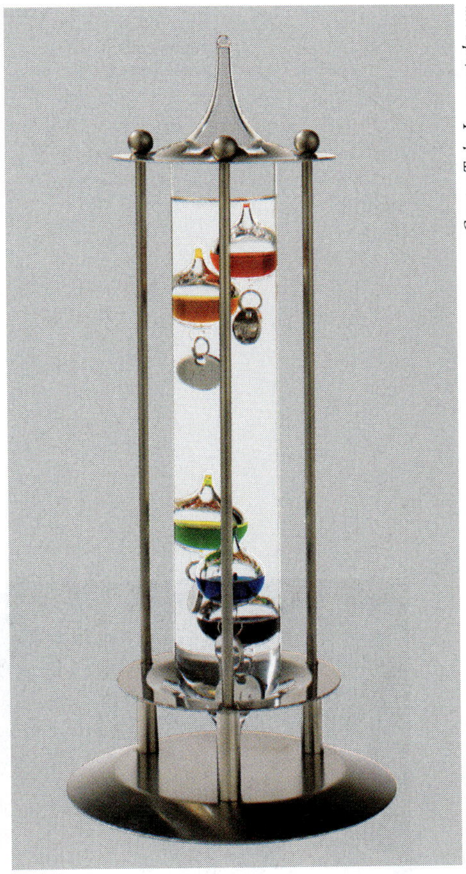

Courtesy Torka Inc. www.torka.com

One of the most visually intriguing types of thermometers, invented by Galileo Galilei in the early 1600s, employs changes in liquid density as a function of temperature. The "Galilean thermometer" consists of a large sealed flask with a liquid that changes density as it is heated. Suspended in this liquid are dozens of small numbered weights, each of a slightly different density. At low temperature, most of the weights rise to the top of the flask. As temperature increases, the denser weights sink one-by-one to the bottom. The temperature is read simply as the lowest number on the weights that remain floating at the top of the thermometer.

different matter; it must absorb 10 times more heat per gram than copper to raise its temperature. Thus, even at the highest stove setting, it can take several minutes to boil a pot of water. This ability of water to store thermal energy plays a critical role in Earth's climate, which is moderated by the relatively steady temperatures of the oceans.

Heat Transfer

You can't prevent heat from moving from an object at high temperature to its cooler surroundings; you can only slow the rate of movement. In fact, scientists and engineers have spent many decades studying the phenomenon known as **heat transfer**—the process by which heat moves from one place to another. Heat transfers by three basic mechanisms—conduction, convection, and radiation—each of which is important to different aspects of everyday experience.

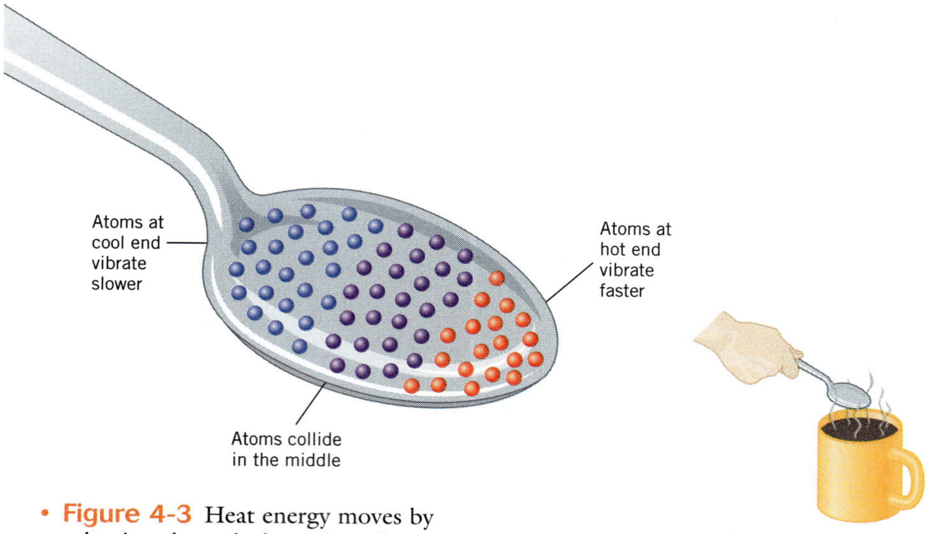

• **Figure 4-3** Heat energy moves by conduction through the action of atoms or molecules that jostle their neighbors.

Conduction

Have you ever reached for a pan on a hot stove, only to have your fingers burned when you grasped the metal handle? If so, you have had firsthand experience of conduction, the movement of heat by atomic-scale collisions.

As shown in Figure 4-3, **conduction** works through the action of individual atoms or molecules that are linked together by chemical bonds. If a piece of metal is heated at one end, the atoms and their electrons at that end begin to move faster. When they vibrate and collide with atoms farther away from the heat source, they are likely to transfer energy to those atoms, so that the molecules farther away will begin to move faster as well. A chain of collisions occurs, with atoms progressively farther and farther away from the heat source moving faster and faster as time goes by.

Conduction of heat is responsible for a large part of the heating bills in homes and office buildings. The process works like this: The air inside a house in winter is kept warmer than the air outside, so that the molecules of the air inside are moving faster than the molecules in the air outside. When the molecules inside collide with materials in the wall (a windowpane, for example), they impart some of their heat to the molecules in those materials. At that point, conduction takes over and heat is transferred to the outside of the wall. There the heat is transferred to the outdoors by convection and radiation, processes that we will describe in a moment. The key point, however, is that you can think about every part of your house as being a kind of conduit carrying heat from the interior to the outside.

One way of slowing down the flow of heat out of a house is to add insulation to the walls or to use special kinds of glass for the windows. These processes work because materials differ in their **thermal conductivity**—

Charles Thatcher/Stone/Getty Images

Steelworkers test a molten sample from the furnace. Why does the worker at the left use thick insulated gloves to hold the cool end of the rod? Heat transfers from the hot end to the cool end by the process of conduction.

their ability to transfer heat from one molecule to the next by conduction. Have you ever noticed that a piece of wood at room temperature feels "normal," while a piece of metal at the same temperature feels cold to the touch? The wood and metal are at exactly the same temperature, but the metal feels cold because it is a good *heat conductor*—it moves heat rapidly away from your skin, which is generally warmer than air temperature. The wood, on the other hand, is a good *heat insulator*—it impedes the flow of heat, and so it feels comparatively warm. The insulation in your home is designed to have especially low thermal conductivity, so that heat transfer is slowed down (but never completely stopped). Thus, when you use special insulated windowpanes or put certain kinds of insulation in your walls, you make it more difficult for heat to flow outside, and thereby allow yourself to use the heat longer before it ultimately leaks away.

Stuart & Michele Westmorland/The Image Bank/Getty Images

Even an unexpected material like ice can provide insulation.

Convection

Let's look carefully at a pot of boiling water on a stove. On the surface of the water you will see a rolling, churning motion as the water moves and mixes. If you put your hand above the water, you feel heat. Heat has been transferred from the water at the bottom of the pot to the top by **convection**, the transfer of heat by the bulk motion of the water itself, as shown in Figure 4-4.

Water near the bottom of the pan expands as it is heated by the flames. Therefore, it weighs less per unit volume than the colder water immediately above it. A situation like this, with colder, denser water above and warmer, less dense water below, is unstable. The denser fluid tends to descend and displace the less dense fluid, which in turn begins to rise. Consequently, the warm water from the bottom rises to the top, while the cool water from the top sinks to the bottom (Figure 4-4). In convection, masses of water move in bulk and carry the fast-moving molecules with them.

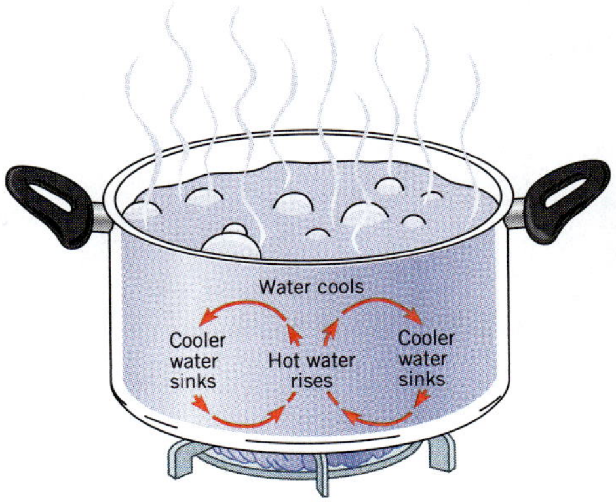

• **Figure 4-4** Convection. Heat is transferred by the bulk motion of a fluid, such as air or water. In the case of a boiling pot, hot water rises as cooler water sinks.

Convection is a continuous, cyclic process as long as heat is added to the water. As cool water from the top of a pot arrives at the bottom, it begins to be heated by the burner. As hot water gets to the top, its heat is sent off into the air. The water on the top cools and contracts, while the water on the bottom heats and expands. The original situation is repeated continuously, with the less dense fluid on the bottom always rising and the more dense fluid on the top always sinking. This transfer of fluids results in a kind of a rolling motion, which you see when you look at the surface of boiling water. Each of these regions of rising and sinking water is called a **convection cell.**

The areas of clear water, which seem to be bubbling up, are the places where warm water is rising. The places where bubbles and scum tend to collect—the places that look rather stagnant—are where the cool water is sinking, leaving behind whatever passengers (such as minerals) it happened to be carrying at the surface. Heat is carried from the burner through the convection of the water and is eventually transferred to the atmosphere. Convection is thus a very efficient way of transferring heat.

You experience many examples of the convection process, from the small-scale circulation of cold water in a glass of iced tea, to air rising above a radiator or toaster, to large-scale motions of Earth's atmosphere. You may even have seen convection cells in operation in large urban areas. When you're in the parking lot of a large shopping mall on a hot summer day, you can probably see the air shimmer. What you are seeing is air, heated by the hot asphalt, rising upward. Some place farther away, perhaps out in the countryside, cooler air is falling. The shopping center is called a "heat island" and is the hot part of a convection cell.

Brenda Tharp/Photo Researchers

Convection cells in the air keep this hang glider in California aloft.

You may also have noticed that the temperature in big cities is usually a few degrees warmer than in outlying suburbs. Cities help create their own weather because they are heat islands where convection cells develop. Rainfall is typically higher in cities than in the surrounding atmosphere because cities set up convection cells that draw in cool moist air from surrounding areas.

Technology •

Home Insulation

Today's homebuilders take heat convection and conduction very seriously. An energy-efficient dwelling has to hold onto its heat in the winter and remain cool in the summer. A variety of materials provide effective solutions to this insulation problem.

Fiberglass, the most widely used insulation, is made of loosely intertwined strands of glass. It works by minimizing the opportunities for conduction and convection of heat out of your home. Solid glass is a rather poor heat insulator, but it takes a long time for heat to move along a thin, twisted glass fiber, and even longer for heat to transfer across the occasional contact points between pairs of crossed fibers. Furthermore, a cloth-like mat of fiberglass disrupts airflow and prevents heat transfer by convection. A thick, continuous layer of fiberglass in your walls and ceiling thus acts as an ideal barrier to the flow of heat.

Windows pose a special insulation problem. Old-style single-pane windows conduct heat rapidly, so how do we let light in without letting heat out? One solution is double-pane windows with sealed, airtight spaces between the panes that greatly restrict heat conduction. In addition, builders employ a variety of caulking and foam insulation to seal any possible leaks around windows and doors.

Recent high-tech materials are providing new types of insulation. Like fiberglass, most of these new materials depend on the insulating properties of trapped air for their effectiveness. Older homes are now routinely insulated by injecting liquid foams between exterior and interior walls, for example. When the foam hardens, tiny bubbles of trapped air slow down the transfer of heat. In new construction, sheets of solid Styrofoam, which contain the same kind of trapped air bubbles, are often used instead of fiberglass, and foams are sprayed onto the inner surface of concrete to increase its insulating power.

Even windows can be made into good insulators by using new experimental window glasses in which microscopic air bubbles are trapped. Although this distorts the incoming light a bit—the effect is roughly like looking through a dirty window—a glass pane made from this material has an insulating power equivalent to 6 inches of fiberglass. •

The Science of Life •

Animal Insulation: Fur and Feathers

Houses aren't the only place where insulation can be seen in our world. Two kinds of animals—birds and mammals—maintain a constant body temperature despite the temperature of their surroundings, and both have evolved methods to control the flow of heat into and out of their bodies. Part of these strategies involves the use of insulating materials—furs, feathers, and fat—that serve to slow down the heat flow. Because most of the time an animal's body is warmer than the environment, the most common situation is one in which the insulation works to keep heat in.

Whales, walruses, and seals are examples of animals that have thick layers of fat to insulate them from the cold arctic waters in which they swim. Fat is a poor conductor of heat and plays much the same role in their bodies as the fiberglass insulation in your attic.

Feathers are another kind of insulation; in fact, many biologists suspect that feathers evolved first as a kind of insulation to help birds maintain their body temperature,

Ray Coleman/Photo Researchers

David E. Meyers/Stone/Getty Images

B & C Alexander/Photo Researchers

Feathers, fur, and fat help animals by providing insulation to keep body heat in.

and only later were adapted for flight. Feathers are made of light, hollow tubes connected to each other by an array of small interlocking spikes. They have some insulating properties themselves, but their main effect comes from the fact that they trap air next to the body, and, as we have pointed out, stationary air is a rather good insulator.

Birds often react to extreme cold by contracting muscles in their skin so that the feathers fluff out. This has the effect of increasing the thickness (and hence the insulating power) of the layer of trapped air. (Incidentally, birds need insulation more than we do because their normal body temperature is 41°C or 106°F.)

Hair (or fur) is actually made up of dead cells similar to those in the outer layer of the skin. Like feathers, hair serves as an insulator in its own right and traps a layer of air near the body. In some animals (for example, polar bears), the insulating power of the hair is increased because each hair contains tiny bubbles of trapped air. The reflection of light from these bubbles makes polar bear fur appear white—the strands of hair are actually translucent.

Hair grows from follicles in the skin, and small muscles allow animals to make their hair stand up to increase its insulating power. Human beings, who evolved in a warm climate, have lost much of their body hair as well as the ability to make most of it stand up. We have a reminder of our mammalian nature, however, in the phenomenon of "goose bumps," which is the attempt by muscles in the skin to make the hair stand up. •

Radiation

Everyone has had the experience of coming inside on a cold day and finding a fire in the fireplace or an electric heater glowing red hot. The normal reaction is to walk up to the source of heat, hold out your hands, and feel the warmth moving into your skin.

How did the heat get from the fire to your hands? It couldn't have done so by conduction; it's too hard to carry heat through the air that way. It couldn't have been convection either because you don't feel a hot breeze.

What you experience is the third kind of heat transfer—**radiation**, or the transfer of heat by electromagnetic radiation, which is a form of wave energy that we will discuss in Chapter 6. A fire or an electric heater radiates energy in the form of *infrared radiation*. This radiation travels from the source of heat to your hand, where it is absorbed and converted into the thermal energy of molecules. You perceive heat because of the energy that the infrared radiation carries to your hand.

Objects throughout the universe radiate energy in this way. Under normal circumstances, as an object gives off radiation to its surroundings, it also receives radiation from those surroundings. Thus a kind of equilibrium is set up, and there is no net loss of energy because the object is at the same temperature as its surroundings. If, however, the object is at a higher temperature than its surroundings, it will radiate more energy than it receives. Your body, for example, constantly radiates energy into its cooler surroundings. You will continue to radiate this energy as long as your body processes the food that keeps you alive (see Chapter 20).

Radiation is the only kind of energy that can travel through the emptiness of space. Conduction requires atoms or molecules that can vibrate and collide with each other. Convection requires atoms or molecules of liquid or gas in bulk, so that they can move. But radiation, remarkably, doesn't require any medium to move heat; radiation can even travel through a vacuum. The energy that falls on Earth in the form of sunlight, which is almost all of the energy that sustains life on Earth, travels through 93 million miles (150 million km) of intervening empty space in the form of radiation.

In the real world, all three types of heat transfer—conduction, convection, and radiation—occur all the time. Any one can occur by itself or in combination with another or all three can occur simultaneously. At this moment, heat is being generated in your body. It travels by conduction through tissues, by convection through blood circulation, and by radiation from the surface of your skin. In fact, everywhere in the natural world heat is constantly being transferred by these three mechanisms.

The Science of Life •

Temperature Regulation

Animals get the energy they need to run their metabolism by "burning" fuels they take in as food, and the laws of thermodynamics tell us that this process must generate waste heat. For small animals, this heat can be dumped into the environment by simple conduction, but the larger an animal is, the more complex the system for disposing waste heat has to be.

By the same token, animals must be able to absorb heat from their environment to maintain their internal temperature. Some animals (reptiles, for example) absorb energy directly from radiation. This is why you often see snakes and lizards "sunning" themselves on warm days and why they are so sluggish on cold mornings. Other animals, such as mammals (a group that includes human beings) and birds, have intricate mechanisms for maintaining a constant body temperature.

Human beings have complex ways of raising and lowering the body's temperature in response to changes in the temperature of the environment. If your body temperature starts to rise, blood vessels near the surface of your skin dilate so that the blood can carry more heat to the surface by convection. There, the excess heat can be radiated away. This response is why you often appear flushed after being in the sun for a while. In addition, you start to sweat. The purpose of sweating is to put water on your skin, then use body heat to evaporate that water.

When the temperature falls, the blood vessels near the surface contract, lowering the ability of the blood to carry heat to the surface. In extreme cases, this situation can lead to frostbite, in which cells die because they are denied oxygen and other substances normally carried to them by the blood. Consequently, your body's metabolism increases and generates more heat in response to cold weather. Shivering, for example, is a response in which the heat generated by involuntary contractions of the muscles is used to counterbalance the falling temperature.

Incidentally, you may recall that you often start shivering at the onset of a fever. This seemingly paradoxical response occurs because, in response to the disease, the body's internal "thermostat" is adjusted to a higher than normal setting. You shiver and feel cold because, when this happens, normal body temperature is below the new setting of the "thermostat" and more heat is needed to raise the body's temperature. •

Stop and Think! The ears of an elephant are believed to function partly to keep the animal from overheating. What properties of the ears would make them well suited to this function? What types of heat transfer would be involved?

The Second Law of Thermodynamics

Throughout the universe the behavior of energy is regular and predictable. According to the first law of thermodynamics, the total amount of energy is constant, though energy may change from one form to another over and over again. Energy in the form of heat can flow from one place to another by conduction, convection, and radiation. But everyday experience tells us that there is more to the behavior of energy—that there is a direction to energy's flow. Hot things tend to cool off, cold things tend to warm up, and an egg, once broken, can never be reassembled. These commonsense ideas are the domain of the **second law of thermodynamics,** which is one of the most fascinating and powerful ideas in science.

The second law of thermodynamics places restrictions on the way heat and other forms of energy can be transferred and used to do work. We will explore three different statements of this law:

1. Heat will not flow spontaneously from a cold to a hot body.
2. You cannot construct an engine that does nothing but convert heat to useful work.
3. Every isolated system becomes more disordered with time.

Although these three statements appear very different, they are actually logically equivalent—given any one statement, you can derive the other two as a consequence. Given the statement that heat flows from hot to cold objects, for example, a physicist could produce a set of mathematical steps that would show that no engine can convert heat to work with 100% efficiency. In this sense, the three statements of the law all say the same thing.

1. Heat Will Not Flow Spontaneously from a Cold to a Hot Body

The first statement of the second law of thermodynamics describes the behavior of two objects at different temperatures. If you take an ice cream cone outside on a hot summer afternoon, it will melt. In the language of energy, heat will flow from the warm atmosphere to the cold ice cream cone and cause its temperature to rise above the melting point. By the same token, if you take a cup of hot chocolate outside on a cold day, it will cool as heat flows from the cup into the surroundings.

From the point of view of energy alone, there is no reason things should work this way. Energy would be conserved if heat stayed put, or even if heat flowed from an ice cream cone into the warm atmosphere, making the ice cream cone grow colder. Our everyday experience (and many experiments) convince us that our universe does not work this way. In our universe heat flows in only one direction, from hot to cold. This everyday observation may seem trivial, but in this statement is hidden all the mystery of those changes that make the future different from the past.

This version of the second law is easy to explain at the molecular level. If two objects collide and one of them is moving faster than the other, chances are that the slower object will be speeded up and the faster object slowed down by the collision. It's unlikely that events will go the other way. Thus, as we saw in the discussion of heat conduction, faster-moving molecules tend to share their energy with slower-moving ones. On the macroscopic scale, this process is seen as heat flowing from warm regions to cold ones by conduction. For the second law to be violated, the molecules in a substance would have to conspire so that collisions would cause slower-moving molecules to slow down even more, giving up their energy to faster molecules so they could go even faster. Experience tells us that this doesn't happen.

The second law does not state that it's impossible for heat to flow from a cold to a hot body. When a refrigerator is operating, heat is removed from the colder interior to the warmer exterior, a fact that you can verify by putting your hand under the refrigerator and feeling the warm air coming off it. The second law merely says that this action cannot take place spontaneously, of its own accord. If you wish to cool something in this way, you must supply energy. In fact, an alternative statement of the second law of thermodynamics could be: A refrigerator won't work unless it's plugged in.

The second law doesn't tell you that you can't make ice cubes, only that you can't make ice cubes without expending energy. Paying the electric bill, of course, is another part of our everyday experience.

2. You Cannot Construct an Engine That Does Nothing but Convert Heat to Useful Work

The second statement of the second law of thermodynamics places a severe restriction on the way we can use energy. At first glance, this statement about heat and work seems to have very little to do with the idea that heat never flows spontaneously from a cold object to a hot object. Yet the two statements are logically equivalent—given the one, the other must follow.

Energy can be defined as the ability to do work. This second statement of the second law tells us that whenever energy is transformed from heat to another type—from heat to an electrical current, for example—some of that heat must be dumped into the environment and is unavailable to do work. This energy is neither lost nor destroyed, but it can't be used to make electricity to play your radio or gasoline to drive your car.

Scientists and engineers have defined a specific term, *efficiency,* to quantify the loss of useful energy. **Efficiency** is the amount of work you get from an engine, divided by the amount of energy you put into it.

In Chapter 3 we discovered that heat and other forms of energy are interchangeable, and the total amount of energy is conserved. From the point of view of the first law of thermodynamics, there is no reason why energy in the form of heat could not be converted to electrical energy with 100% efficiency. But the second law of thermodynamics predicts that such a process is not possible. The flow of energy, like time, has a direction. Another way of stating this law is to say that energy always goes from a more useful to a less useful form.

Your car engine provides a familiar example of this everyday rule of nature. When you turn on the ignition, an exploding mixture of gasoline and air creates a high-temperature, high-pressure gas that pushes down on a piston. The piston's motion is converted into rotational motion of a series of machine parts that eventually turn the car's wheels. Some of the energy is lost because of friction, but the second law of thermodynamics predicts that our use of the energy is restricted even if friction did not exist, and even if every machine in the world was perfectly designed.

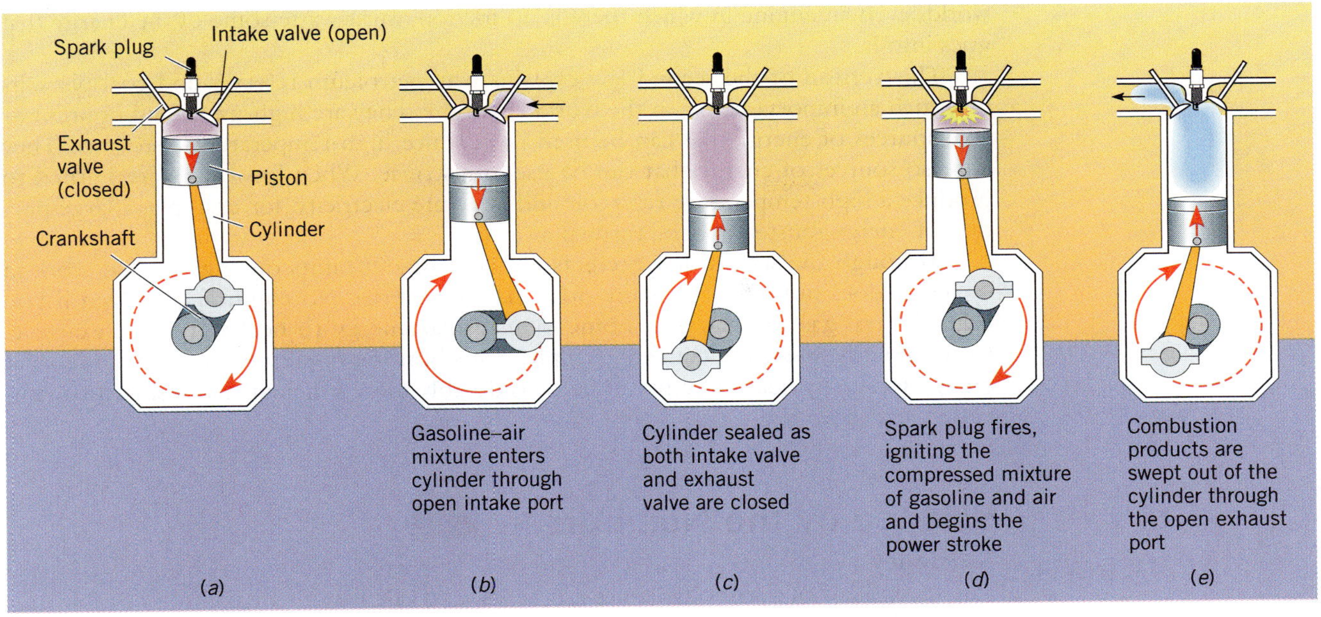

• **Figure 4-5** The cycle of an engine's piston. *(a)* The beginning of the intake stroke. *(b)* The middle of the intake stroke as a gasoline-air mixture enters the cylinder. *(c)* The beginning of the compression stroke. *(d)* At the beginning of the power stroke the spark plug fires, igniting the compressed mixture of gasoline and air. *(e)* At the beginning of the exhaust stroke, combustion products are swept out. Note that each cycle involves two complete rotations of the crankshaft.

Look at the various stages of an engine's operation (Figure 4-5). There seems to be no obvious reason why energy in the form of heat in the exploding air-gas mixture could not be converted with 100% efficiency into energy of motion of the engine's piston, which is translated into the motion of the car. But you can't just think about the downward motion of a piston, what engineers call the *power stroke,* in the operation of your car's engine. If that was all the engine did, then the engine in every car could turn over only once. The problem is that once you have the piston pushed all the way down—once you have extracted useful work from the air-gas mixture—you have to return the piston to the top of the cylinder so that the cycle can be repeated. In other words, in order to reset the engine to its original position so that more useful work can be done, some energy has to be expended to lift the piston back up.

Ignore for a moment the fact that a real engine is more complicated than the one we are discussing. Suppose that all you had to do was to lift the piston up after you had gotten the work from it. The cylinder is full of air, and consequently when you lift the piston up the air will be compressed and heated. In order to return the engine to the precise state it was in before the explosion, the heat from this compressed air has to be taken away. In practice, it is dumped into the atmosphere.

In the language of physics, the exploding hot gas-air mixture is called a *high-temperature reservoir,* and the atmosphere into which the heat of compression is dumped is called a *low-temperature reservoir.* The second law of thermodynamics says that any engine operating between two temperatures must dump some energy in the form of heat into the low-temperature reservoir. In your car's engine, for example, heat produced by moving the piston back up has to be dumped. A similar argument can be made for any conceivable engine you could build.

Some of the chemical potential energy stored in gasoline can be used to run your car, but most of the energy must be dumped into the low-temperature reservoir of the atmosphere. Once that heat has gone into the atmosphere, it can no longer be used to run the engine. Thus this version of the second law tells us that any real engine operating in the world, even an engine in which there is no friction, must waste some of the energy that goes into it.

This version of the second law explains why petroleum reserves and coal deposits play such an important role in the world economy. They are high-grade and nonrenewable sources of energy that can be used to produce high-temperature reservoirs. They are also sources of energy that can be used only once. When fossil fuels are burned to produce a high-temperature reservoir and generate electricity, for example, a large portion of energy must simply be thrown away.

Although the second law predicts rather stringent limits on engines that work in cycles, it does not apply to many other uses of energy. No engine is involved if you burn natural gas to heat your home or use solar energy to heat water, for example. Consequently, these limits needn't apply. Thus burning fossil fuels or employing solar energy to supply heat directly can be considerably more efficient than using it to generate electricity.

Science by the Numbers •

Efficiency

The second law of thermodynamics can be used to calculate the maximum possible efficiency of an engine. Let's say that the high-temperature reservoir is at a temperature T_{hot} and the low-temperature reservoir is at a temperature T_{cold} (temperatures are measured in the Kelvin scale). The maximum theoretical efficiency—the percentage of energy available to do useful work—of any engine in the real world can be calculated as follows:

- **In words:** Efficiency is obtained by comparing the temperature difference between the high-temperature and low-temperature reservoirs with the temperature of the high-temperature reservoir.
- **In equation form:**

$$\text{efficiency (percent)} = \frac{(\text{temperature}_{hot} - \text{temperature}_{cold})}{\text{temperature}_{hot}} \times 100$$

- **In symbols:**

$$\text{efficiency (percent)} = \frac{(T_{hot} - T_{cold})}{T_{hot}} \times 100$$

Any loss of energy due to friction in pulleys or gears or wheels in a real machine will make the actual efficiency less than this theoretical maximum. This maximum is actually a very stringent constraint on real engines.

Consider the efficiency of a normal coal-fired electrical generating plant. The temperature of the high-energy steam (the hot reservoir) is about 500 K, while the temperature of the air into which waste heat must be dumped (the "cold" reservoir) is around room temperature, or 300 K. The maximum possible efficiency of such a plant is given by the second law to be:

$$\begin{aligned}\text{efficiency (percent)} &= \frac{(T_{hot} - T_{cold})}{T_{hot}} \times 100 \\ &= \frac{(500 - 300)}{500} \times 100 \\ &= 40.0\%\end{aligned}$$

In other words, more than half of the energy produced in a typical coal-burning power plant must be dumped into the atmosphere as waste heat. This fundamental limit is independent of the engineers' ability to make the plant operate efficiently. In fact, engineers do very well in this regard—most generating plants operate within a few percentage points of the maximum efficiency allowed by the second law of thermodynamics.

This result has important implications for energy policy. It tells us that there are fundamental limits to the efficiency with which we can convert heat generated by coal or nuclear reactors to electricity. An important question we will have to debate in the future is whether it is better to use our stocks of coal and petroleum to generate electricity, thereby converting most of them to waste heat, or retain them for use in the production of synthetic materials such as plastic (see Chapter 10). •

3. Every Isolated System Becomes More Disordered with Time

The third statement of the second law of thermodynamics, in many ways the most profound, describes the familiar tendency of systems all around us to become increasingly disordered. Your carefully cleaned room gets messy, your brand new car becomes dirty and scratched, and we all age as our bodies gradually wear out. For physicists, however, this statement of the second law has a very precise and special meaning.

To understand this statement of the second law, you need to know what a physicist means by "order" and "disorder" (Figure 4-6). An ordered system is one in which a number of objects, be they atoms or automobiles, are positioned in a completely regular and predictable pattern. Atoms in a perfect crystal or automobiles in a perfect line, for example, form highly ordered systems. A disordered system, on the other hand, contains objects that are randomly situated, without any obvious pattern. Atoms in a gas or automobiles after a multicar pileup on a freeway are examples of disordered systems.

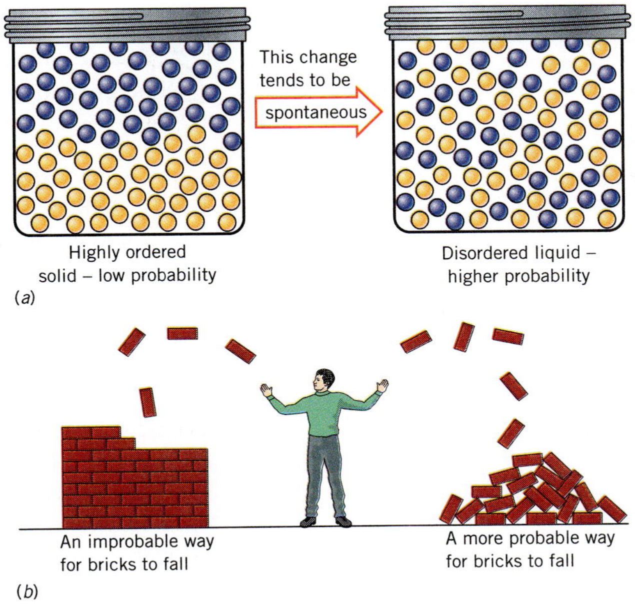

• **Figure 4-6** Highly ordered, regular patterns of objects are less likely to occur than disordered, irregular patterns.

A mathematical definition of order and disorder requires considering the number of different ways a system can be arranged. To get a feel for this idea, consider three orange balls numbered 1, 2, and 3, and three green balls numbered 4, 5 and 6. Ask yourself, how many different ways are there to arrange these six balls in a row (Figure 4-7)? There are six different possibilities for the first ball, then five possibilities for the second, four for the third, and so on. So if you multiply that out:

$$6 \times 5 \times 4 \times 3 \times 2 \times 1 = 720$$

It turns out that there are 720 ways to arrange these six numbered balls in a row—720 different possible configurations.

But how many of those arrangements have the ordered state with three orange balls followed by three green balls? There are exactly six different ways to arrange three orange balls ($3 \times 2 \times 1$), and then six different ways to arrange the three green

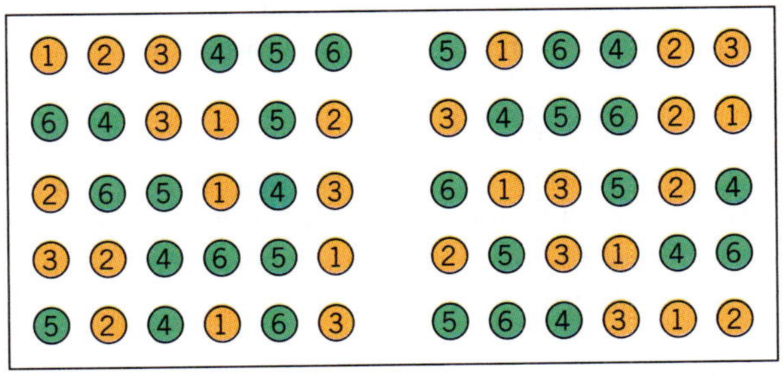

• **Figure 4-7** There are 720 different ways to arrange six numbered balls. If three balls are orange and three are green, then only a small fraction of these arrangements are ordered by color.

balls. Altogether, that's 6 × 6, or 36 different configurations with three orange balls followed by three green balls out of 720 total configurations. Only 5% of all possible arrangements (36/720) are ordered in this way. All of the remaining 684 configurations are different. So, by a 19:1 margin, these other arrangements are much more probable because there are many more ways to achieve a disordered state than an ordered one.

You can repeat this exercise for other numbers of balls (see Problems 4 and 5). For a sequence of 10 balls (five orange and five green), it turns out that there are more than 3.6 million different configurations, but only 120 of those sequences have five orange followed by five green balls. That's only 0.003% of all possible arrangements!

As the number of objects increases from 6 to 10 to trillions of trillions (as we find in even a very small collection of atoms), the fraction of arrangements that is highly ordered becomes infinitesimally small. In other words, highly ordered configurations are improbable because almost every possible configuration is disordered.

This concept of a system's state of disorder is described by the term **entropy.** The second law of thermodynamics can be restated as:

The entropy of an isolated system remains constant or increases.

The word *entropy* was proposed by the German engineer Rudolf Clausius (1822–1888), who played a central role in the formulation of the second law of thermodynamics. In his own words: "I propose to name the [quantity] entropy, . . . from the Greek word for a transformation. I have intentionally formed the word entropy so as to be as similar as possible to the word energy, since both these quantities . . . are so nearly related to each other."

The definition of entropy, as a measure of disorder, may seem a bit fuzzy, but it was placed on a firm quantitative footing in the late nineteenth century by the German physicist, Ludwig Boltzmann (1844–1906). Boltzmann used probability theory to demonstrate that the entropy of any arrangement of atoms is related to the number of possible ways that you can achieve that arrangement. The numerical value of entropy is thus related to the number of ways a system like the numbered balls in a row can be rearranged. If you have a collection of sodium and chlorine atoms, for example, there are many more ways to mix those atoms randomly in a liquid than there are to have them strictly alternating, as they do in a salt crystal. That's why the entropy of sodium and chlorine atoms dissolved in water is much greater than the entropy of those atoms in a salt crystal.

According to the second law of thermodynamics, any system left to itself will evolve toward the most disordered state, the state with the maximum uncertainty in the arrangement of its parts. Without careful chemical and physical controls, atoms and molecules will tend to become more intermixed; without careful driving, collections of automobiles will also tend to become more disordered.

The example we gave at the beginning of the chapter, with the one fast atom in a collection of slow atoms, shows very clearly how such a process works. In the most likely situation, when all of the atoms are in the same low-energy state, the entropy is maximized. A much less probable situation occurs when one of the atoms is in a high-velocity state. Another way of saying this is that systems tend to avoid states of high improbability.

While systems tend to become more disordered, the second law does not require every system to approach a state of lower order. Think about water, a substance of high disorder because water molecules are arranged at random. If you put water into a freezer you get an ice cube, a much more ordered state in which water molecules have formed a regular crystal structure. You have caused a system to evolve to a state of higher order. How can this be reconciled with our statement of the second law?

The answer to this seeming paradox lies in the simple word "isolated." The freezer in which you make the ice cubes is not an isolated system because it has a power cord plugged into the wall and is ultimately connected to the generating plant. The isolated system in this case is the freezer plus the generating plant. The second law of thermodynamics says that the system's total entropy must increase. It does not say that the entropy has to increase in all the different parts of the system.

In this example, one part of the system (the ice cube) becomes more ordered, while another part of the system (the generating plant, its burning fuel, and the surrounding air) becomes more disordered. All that the second law requires is that the increase of disorder at the generating plant be greater than the increase of order at the ice cube. As long as this requirement is met, the second law is not violated. In fact, in this particular example, the disorder at the generating plant greatly exceeds any possible order that could take place inside your refrigerator.

Science in the Making •

The Heat Death of the Universe

The nineteenth-century discovery of the second law of thermodynamics was a gloomy event. The prevailing philosophy of the time was that life, society, and the universe in general were on a never-ending upward spiral of progress. In this optimistic climate, the discovery that the energy in the universe was being steadily and irrevocably degraded was very hard for nineteenth-century scientists and philosophers to accept. The second law seemed to imply that all the energy in the universe would eventually be degraded into waste heat and that everything in the universe would eventually come to the same temperature. This outcome was called the "heat death" of the universe, and some scholars saw it as the ultimate consequence of the laws of thermodynamics.

This notion even affected the literature and music of the time. For example, here is an excerpt from Algernon Swinburne's "The Garden of Proserpine":

From too much love of living
From hope and death set free
We thank with weak thanksgiving
Whatever gods there be
That no man lives forever
That dead men rise up never
That even the weariest river
Flows somewhere safe to sea.

Today, we have a more nuanced view of how the universe will end—a view that will be discussed in Chapter 15. Suffice to say, however, that Swinburne and his colleagues may have been premature in their gloom (although one could argue that poets of that period seemed to grab at any excuse for being gloomy). •

Consequences of the Second Law

The Arrow of Time

We live in a world of four dimensions. Three of these—the dimensions of space—have no obvious directionality. You can go east or west, north or south, and up or down in our universe. But time, the fourth dimension, has direction.

Take one of your favorite home movies or just about any videotape and play it in reverse. Chances are that before too long you'll see something silly—something that couldn't possibly happen, that will make you laugh. Springboard divers fly out of the water and land completely dry on the diving board. From a complete stop golf balls fly off toward the tee. Ocean spray coalesces into smooth waves that recede from shore. Most physical laws, such as Newton's laws of motion or the first law of thermodynamics, say nothing about time. The motions predicted by Newton and the conservation of energy are independent of time. They work just as well if you play a video forward or backward.

The second law of thermodynamics is different. By defining a sequence of events—heat flows from hot to cold; concentrated fuels burn to produce waste heat; the disorder of isolated systems never spontaneously decreases; you get older—we have established a direction to time. We experience the passage of events as dictated by the second law. Scientists cannot answer the deeper philosophical question of why we perceive the arrow of time in only one direction, but through the second law they can describe the effects of that directionality.

Built-in Limitations of the Universe

The second law of thermodynamics has both practical and philosophical consequences. It poses severe limits on the way that human beings can manipulate nature and on the way that nature itself operates. It tells us that some things cannot happen in our universe.

At the practical level, the second law tells us that if we continue to generate electricity by burning fossil fuels or by nuclear fission, we are using up energy that is locked in those concentrated nonrenewable resources. These limitations are not a question of sloppy engineering or poor design; they're simply built into the laws of nature. If you could design an engine or other device that would extract energy from coal and oil with higher efficiency than the second law limits, then you could also design a refrigerator that would work when it wasn't plugged in.

At the philosophical level, the second law tells us that nature has a built-in hierarchy of more useful and less useful forms of energy. The lowest or least useful state of energy is the low-temperature reservoir into which all energy eventually gets dumped. Once the energy is in that lowest-energy reservoir, it can no longer be used to do work. For Earth, energy passes through the region that supports life, the biosphere, but is eventually lost as it is radiated into the black void of space.

The Science of Life •

Does Evolution Violate the Second Law?

Creationists, who argue that life on Earth was created in a single miraculous event, often use the second law of thermodynamics to argue against theories of life's gradual evolution. These arguments reflect a common misunderstanding of the second law.

Creationists point out that because life is a highly ordered system, in which trillions of atoms and molecules must occur in exactly the right sequence, it could not possibly have arisen spontaneously without violating the second law. What they neglect to consider, however, is that the energy that drives living systems is sunlight, so that the "isolated system" that the second law speaks of is Earth's biosphere plus the Sun. All that you need to make the evolution of life consistent with the second law is that the order observed in living things must be offset by a greater amount of disorder in the Sun. Once again, as with the earlier example of the ice cube, this requirement is easily met by the Sun and the biosphere taken together. Science cannot yet give a complete, detailed description of how life arose on our planet, but it can show that this development is in no way inconsistent with the universal laws of thermodynamics. •

Thinking More About | Entropy

Aging

Nothing in our experience better illustrates the directionality of nature than human aging. It's all very well to talk about collisions of atoms and the making of ice cubes, but when we see the inevitable effects of aging in ourselves and those around us, we come to realize that the second law of thermodynamics has a very real meaning for each of us. In fact, there is probably no older dream in human history than that somehow, someday, someone will find out how to reverse the aging process.

Modern biologists approach the problem of aging by noting that the process of evolution (see Chapter 25) acts to preserve those traits that help an organism survive until it has offspring to which those traits can be transmitted. After that, no particular reason exists from the point of view of a species' survival for an individual to live any longer. Indeed, throughout most of the history of the human race, few individuals lived past the age of 40, so aging was not perceived to be a significant problem until recently.

Two general types of theory attempt to explain why aging occurs. The first we can call *planned obsolescence.* It suggests that the human body is actually designed to self-destruct after a certain time, perhaps to ensure that more food and other resources are available for children. The second, which we can call the *accumulated accident* school, holds that the general wear and tear of existence eventually overcomes the body's ability to make repairs, and the system just runs down. In modern language, scientists talk of accumulated damage to DNA (see Chapter 23), the molecule that contains the cell's operating instructions.

At the moment, the evidence seems to support the second of these alternatives. Scientists are starting to identify specific processes that damage DNA and to document the precise sort of damage that occurs. As always, the research must be done on animals before it can be applied to humans. One group at the University of California at Irvine, for example, has produced a strain of fruit fly that lives twice as long as normal, and has identified a substance produced in their cells that seems to explain their enhanced lifetime. Another group at McGill University in Montreal has identified specific changes in the DNA of a microscopic worm that can increase the life expectancy from nine days to two months (although in this case, the changes also cause the worm to move and feed more slowly). It is, of course, a long way from fruit flies to human beings, but it's not too much of a stretch to say that sometime we will understand why our bodies age; and from that point, it's probably only a small step to being able to do something about it.

What sort of problems do you think society would have to face if life expectancy increased to 120 years? What kinds of changes in education, work habits, and government might you expect to see? Do you think this sort of research should be pursued?

Summary

All objects in the universe are at a *temperature* above *absolute zero,* and thus they hold some internal energy—the kinetic energy of moving atoms. *Heat* is energy that moves spontaneously from a warmer to a cooler object. *Specific heat capacity* defines how much energy is required to raise 1 gram of a substance by 1°C.

Heat transfer between two objects that are at different temperatures may occur in three ways. *Conduction* involves the transfer of heat through collisions at the scale of atoms and electrons. *Thermal conductivity* is a measure of how easily this energy transfer occurs. *Convection* involves the motion of a mass of fluid in a *convection cell,* in which warmer atoms are physically transported from one place to another. Heat can also be transferred by *radiation*—infrared energy and other forms of light that travel across a room or across the vastness of space until they are absorbed.

The first law of thermodynamics promises that the amount of energy never changes, no matter how it shifts from one form to another, but the *second law of thermodynamics* restricts how you can shift energy. Three different but equivalent statements of the second law underscore these restrictions.

1. Heat will not flow spontaneously from a colder to a hotter body. This first statement places a restriction on the transfer of heat; for example, you have to supply an external source of energy to a refrigerator before it will work.
2. It is impossible to construct a machine that does nothing but convert heat into useful work. This different but equivalent statement of the second law precludes the construction of an engine that operates with 100% *efficiency.* All engines operate on a cycle, and every engine must expend some of its energy returning to its initial state.
3. The *entropy* of an isolated system always increases. The third statement of the second law of thermodynamics introduces the concept of entropy—the tendency of isolated systems to become more disordered with time. This directionality of energy flow in the universe defines our sense of the direction of time.

Key Terms

temperature
absolute zero
specific heat capacity
heat transfer
conduction
thermal conductivity
convection
convection cell
radiation
second law of thermodynamics
efficiency
entropy

Key Equation

$$\text{Efficiency (percent)} = \frac{(T_{hot} - T_{cold})}{T_{hot}} \times 100$$

Review Questions

1. What are the three different ways by which heat is transferred? How are these three phenomena occurring while you are reading this book?

2. What is the difference between temperature and heat?

3. Why does it take longer to heat a kilogram of water to a given temperature than to heat a kilogram of copper to the same temperature?

4. Describe three common temperature scales. What fixed points are used to calibrate them?

5. State the second law of thermodynamics in three different ways. In what ways are these three statements equivalent?

6. What is the high-temperature reservoir in your car's engine? What is the low-temperature reservoir?

7. What is entropy? Give an example of a situation in which entropy increases.

8. In what way is aging an example of the second law of thermodynamics?

9. What is meant by the "heat death" of the universe?

Discussion Questions

1. Why is it possible to briefly touch a loaf of bread that is baking without being burned but not the metal pan that it is in.

2. Generally, the first thing you see when you approach an electrical generating plant is the big cooling stacks. Given what you know about efficiency, what do you think the function of these stacks might be?

3. Give three examples of the directionality of nature that you have experienced since you woke up this morning. How do these examples relate to the second law of thermodynamics?

4. Imagine lying on a hot beach on a sunny summer day. In what different ways is heat transferred to your body? In each case what was the original source of the energy? What happens to some of that thermal energy if you jump into the ocean?

5. Cogeneration is a term used to describe systems in which waste heat from electrical generating plants is used to heat nearby homes and businesses with efficiencies much greater than 50%. Does cogeneration violate the second law? Why or why not?

6. Why is it not possible to construct a perpetual-motion machine—a machine that runs forever without any energy input? Is the energy loss due to friction the only reason a perpetual-motion machine is impossible?

7. Does a block of ice have thermal energy? Why or why not?

8. Describe at least five examples of heat transfer that occur while you drive an automobile on a cold day. In each instance, state whether the heat transfer is by conduction, convection, or radiation. Where does the energy come from? Where does it end up?

9. Why can penguins, whales, and seals survive in near-freezing water? What role does fat play in the maintenance of body heat?

10. If you were going to heat a brick building so that it would stay warm overnight, would you want to heat the air inside or would you want to heat the bricks and cement that make up the walls and floor? Why?

11. Why does the handle of a metal spoon heat up rapidly when placed in a cup of hot coffee, but a plastic spoon does not?

Problems

1. Calculate the maximum possible efficiency of a power plant that burns natural gas at a temperature of 600 K, with low-temperature surroundings at 300 K. How much more efficient would the plant be if it were built in the Arctic where the low-temperature reservoir is at 250 K? Why don't we build all power plants in the Arctic?

2. The Ocean Thermal Electric Conversion system (OTEC) is a kind of a high-tech electric generator. It takes advantage of the fact that in the tropics, deep ocean water is at a temperature of 4°C, while the surface is at a temperature around 25°C. The idea is to find a material that boils between these temperatures. The material in fluid form is brought up through a large pipe from the depths, and the expansion associated with its boiling is used to drive an electric turbine. The gas is then pumped back to the depths, where it condenses back to a liquid and the whole process repeats itself.

a. What is the maximum efficiency with which OTEC can produce electricity? [*Hint:* Remember to convert all temperatures to the Kelvin scale.]

b. Why do you suppose engineers are willing to pursue the scheme, given your answer in part (a).

c. What is the ultimate source of the energy generated by OTEC?

3. Calculate how much energy would be needed to raise 1 kg of water from 273 to 373 Kelvins. What is the temperature of the water in degrees Fahrenheit and Celsius after the water is heated? What state will the water be in? How much energy would be needed to raise 1 kg of copper from 273 to 373 Kelvins? What state will it be in?

4. You have a collection of eight numbered balls; 1 through 4 are blue and 5 through 8 are green. How many different arrangements of these balls in a line are possible? What percentage of those arrangements have four blue balls followed by four green balls?

5. Repeat Problem 4 for a collection of 12 numbered balls (six blue and six green). What happens to the probability of an ordered configuration as the total number of balls increases?

6. The temperature in New York city is 50 degrees Fahrenheit on Monday, 60 degrees on Tuesday and Wednesday, 55 degrees on Thursday though Saturday, and 65 degrees on Sunday. What is the average temperature for that week in both Kelvin and Celsius? Graph your data and results using both a line graph and a bar graph. Which graph better represents your data?

Investigations

1. Investigate the daily high and low temperatures for the past week in a coastal city like New York or San Diego, a city in the Midwest such as Kansas City or St. Louis, and a city in the desert such as Las Vegas or Tucson. On average, what is the difference in temperature? What causes this difference? What part does the ocean play in the regulation of temperature?

2. How are your home's walls, windows, and doors insulated? What could you do to improve your home's insulation? What form of energy transfer is most important with regard to energy loss in home heating? conduction? convection? or radiation?

3. Fill a glass, an aluminum cup, a coffee mug, and a plastic drinking cup with hot water. Which transfers the heat to your hand the most quickly? Which holds the heat longest? What does this mean in terms of heat capacities and conductivity?

4. Propose an experiment that you could perform at home to measure the relative heat capacities of different substances such as soap, wood, and glass.

5. What does the term *green building* mean? Is energy efficiency a major consideration in new construction?

6. Play a videotape of a favorite movie backward. How many violations of the second law of thermodynamics can you spot?

7. Boil a pan of water on your stove. Can you identify the convection cells in the pan? How hot does the water have to be before convection starts? [*Hint:* A small amount of food coloring can reveal the formation of convection cells.]

8. Research how night vision equipment, including video cameras, works? What forms of energy are used in the production of these images?

9. Draw a line. Now measure that line using a metal ruler. Place that ruler in the freezer for 15 minutes. How are your measurements affected by the temperature of the ruler? What would happen to your measurements if you heated your ruler? Name the scientist mentioned in an earlier chapter who had to understand thermal expansion and contraction for his detailed astronomical observations.

5

Electricity and Magnetism

What is lightning?

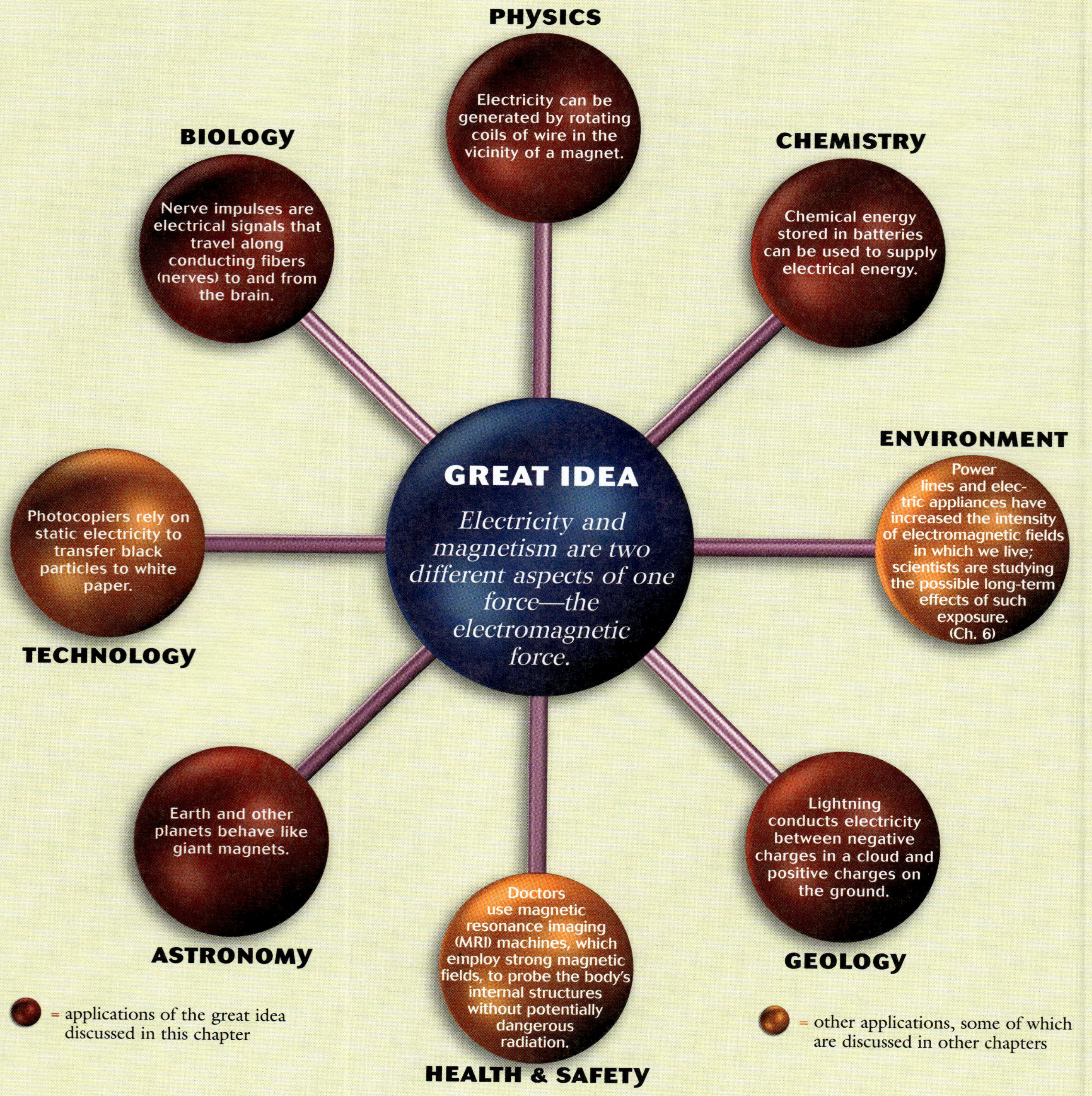

Science Through the Day | The Hidden Force

Time to clean up from breakfast. You rinse off your dishes and turn on the garbage disposal; the powerful motor whirs into action. As you open the refrigerator to put away the milk and butter, the light comes on and the refrigerator's compressor hums. On the refrigerator door you see the magnet that holds the note reminding you to renew your driver's license. Then your digital watch beeps the hour; 8 A.M.—better get moving.

All of these familiar objects—lights, motors, magnets, beepers, and dozens of other essential technologies—owe their existence to the pervasive, invisible force called electromagnetism.

SUPERSTOCK

Nature's Other Forces

According to Newton's laws of motion, nothing happens without a force, but the law of gravity that Newton discussed cannot explain many everyday events. How does a refrigerator magnet cling to metal, defying gravity? How does a compass needle swing around to the north? How can static cling wrinkle your shirt, or lightning shatter an old tree? These phenomena point to the existence of some underlying force that is different from gravity.

Newton may not have known about these forces, but he did give us a method for studying them. First observe natural phenomena and learn how they behave, then organize those observations into a series of natural laws, and finally use those laws to predict future behavior of the physical world. This is the process we have called the scientific method.

In particular, we will find Newton's first law of motion (see Chapter 2) to be very useful in our investigation of nature's other forces. According to this law, whenever we see a change in the state of motion of any material object, we know that a force has acted to produce that change. Thus, whenever we see such a change and can rule out the action of known forces such as gravity, we can conclude that the change must have been caused by a hitherto unknown force. We shall use this line of reasoning to show that electrical and magnetic forces exist in the natural world.

Our understanding of the phenomena associated with static electricity and magnetism began in the eighteenth century with a group of scientists in Europe and North America who called themselves "electricians." These researchers were fascinated by the many curious phenomena associated with nature's unseen forces. Their thoughts were not focused on practical applications, nor could they have imagined how their work would transform the world.

Static Electricity

When the girl touched the electrically charged sphere, her hair became electrically charged as well. Individual hairs repel each other and thus "stand on end."

Will & Deni McIntyre/Photo Researchers

Have you ever noticed how your hair tends to stand on end and your clothes stick together on dry winter days? Such phenomena related to static electricity have been known since ancient times. The Greeks knew that if you rub a piece of amber with cat's fur and then touch other objects with the amber, those other objects are repelled from each other. The same thing happens, they found, if you rub a piece of glass with silk: objects touched with the glass are repelled from each other. On the other hand, if you bring objects that have been touched with the amber near objects touched with the glass, they are attracted toward each other. Objects that behave in this way are said to possess electrical charge, or to be "charged."

The force that moves objects toward and away from each other in these simple demonstrations was named electricity. (from *electro,* the Greek word for amber). In these simple experiments, the electrical charge doesn't move once it has been placed on an object, so the force is also called static electricity.

The electrical force is clearly different from gravity. Unlike the electrical force, gravity can never be repulsive: when a gravitational force acts between two objects, it always pulls them together. The electrical force, on the other hand, can attract some objects toward each other and push other objects apart. Furthermore, the electrical force is vastly more powerful than gravity. A pocket comb charged with static electricity easily lifts a piece of paper against the gravitational pull of the entire Earth.

Today, we understand that the properties of the electrical force arise from the existence of two kinds of electrical charges (Figure 5-1). We say that objects touched with the same source, be it amber or glass, have the same electrical charge and are repelled from each other. On the other hand, one object touched with amber will have a different electrical charge than a second object touched with glass. This difference is reflected in their behavior—they attract each other.

• **Figure 5-1** The two kinds of electrical charges. Opposite charges attract, while like charges repel.

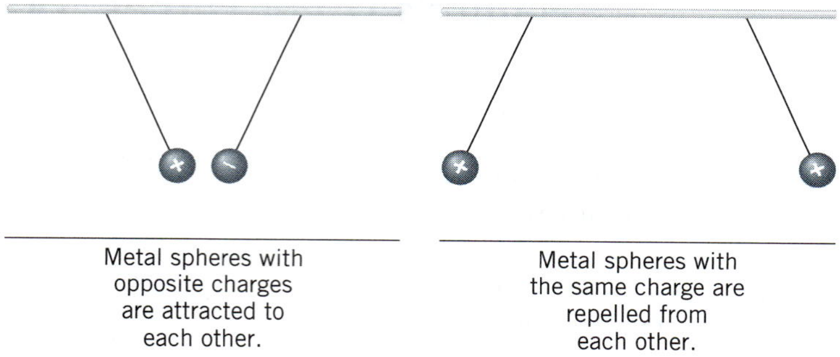

Science in the Making •

Benjamin Franklin and Electrical Charge

The most famous North American "electrician" was Benjamin Franklin (1706–1790), one of the pioneers of electrical science as well as a central figure in the founding of the United States of America. Franklin began his electrical experiments in 1746 with a study of electricity generated by friction. Most scientists of the time thought that electrical effects resulted from the interaction of two different "electrical fluids." Franklin, however, became convinced that all electrical phenomena could be explained by the transfer of a single electrical fluid from one object to another. He realized that objects could have an excess or a deficiency of this fluid, and he applied the names "negative" and "positive" to these two situations.

Following this work, Franklin is said to have demonstrated the electrical nature of lightning in June 1752 with his famous (and extremely dangerous) kite experiment.

A mild lightning strike hit his kite and passed along the wet string to produce sparks and an electrical shock. Not content with acquiring experimental knowledge, Franklin followed his discovery of the electrical nature of lightning with the invention of the lightning rod, a metal rod with one end in the ground and the other end sticking up above the roof of a building. It carries the electrical charge of lightning into Earth's surface, diverting it away from the building. Lightning rods caught on quickly in the wooden cities of North America and Europe, preventing countless deadly fires. They are still widely used. •

Benjamin Franklin engaged in his famous (and potentially lethal) kite experiment.

(Painting by Benjamin West, c. 1805, Mr. and Mrs. Wharton Sinkler Collection, courtesy Philadelphia Museum of Art.)

The Movement of Electrons

We now understand that there are two kinds of electrical charge, so observations of both attractive and repulsive behavior of charged objects are easy to understand. In modern language, we say that all objects are made up of minute building blocks called atoms, and all atoms are made up of still smaller particles that have electrical charge. As we shall see in Chapter 8, negatively charged electrons move around a heavy, positively charged nucleus at the center of every atom. Electrons and the nucleus have opposite electrical charges, so an attractive force exists between them. This force in atoms plays a role similar to that played by gravity in keeping the solar system together. Most atoms are electrically neutral, because the positive charge of the nucleus cancels the negative charge of the electrons.

Electrons, particularly those in outer orbits far from the nucleus, tend to be rather loosely bound to their atoms. These electrons can be removed from the atom (for example, by friction) and, once removed, can move freely in metals or can react with other elements.

When negative electrons are stripped off of a material, they no longer cancel the positive charges in the nucleus. The result is a net excess of positive charge in the object, and we say that the object as a whole has acquired a positive electrical charge. Similarly, an object acquires a negative electrical charge when extra electrons are added to it. This addition of electrons happens when you run a comb through your hair on a dry day; electrons are stripped from your hair and added to the comb, so the comb acquires a negative charge. Simultaneously, your hair loses electrons, so individual strands become positively charged.

During a thunderstorm, the same phenomenon occurs on a much larger scale, as wind and rain disrupt the normal distribution of electrons in clouds. When a charged cloud passes over a tall tree or tower, the violent electrical discharge called lightning may result from the attraction of the positive charges on the ground and negative charges in the cloud (although in the case of lightning, both the positive and negative charges move).

Although historical investigations of electrical charge tended to concentrate on somewhat artificial experiments, we have come to know that electrically charged particles play important roles in many natural systems. Virtually all of the atoms in the Sun, for example, have lost electrons; the Sun is thus made of a turbulent mixture of positive atoms and negative electrons. In all advanced life-forms (including human beings), charged atoms constantly move into and out of cells to maintain the processes of life. As you read these words, for example, positively charged potassium and sodium atoms are moving across the membranes of cells in your optic nerve to carry signals to your brain.

Lightning will be attracted to this metal rod and allowed to run harmlessly into the ground. Lightning rods like this were first introduced by Benjamin Franklin.

Paul Katz/Index Stock/Jupiter Images Corp

Coulomb's Law

The phenomenon of electricity remained something of a mild curiosity until the mid-eighteenth century, when scientists began applying the scientific method to investigate it. One of the first tasks was to develop a precise statement about the nature of the electrical force. The French scientist Charles Augustin de Coulomb (1736–1806) was most responsible for this work. During the 1780s, at the same time the United States

Constitution was being written by Benjamin Franklin and others, Coulomb devised a series of experiments in which he passed different amounts of electrical charge onto objects and then measured the force between them.

After repeated measurements he discovered that the electrical force was in some ways very similar to the gravitational force that Isaac Newton had discovered a century earlier. Coulomb observed that if two electrically charged objects are moved farther away from each other, the force between them gets smaller, just like gravity. In fact, if the distance between two objects is doubled, the force decreases by a factor of four—the familiar 1/distance^2, or inverse-square relationship, that we saw in the law of universal gravitation in Chapter 2. Coulomb also discovered that the size of the force depends on the product of the charges of the two objects—double the charge on one object and the force doubles; double the charge on both objects and the force increases by a factor of four.

Coulomb summarized his discoveries in a simple relationship known as Coulomb's law:

- ▶ In words: The force between any two electrically charged objects is proportional to the product of their charges divided by the square of the distance between them.
- ▶ In equation form:

$$\text{force (newtons)} = k \times \frac{\text{1st charge} \times \text{2nd charge}}{\text{distance}^2}$$

- ▶ In symbols:

$$F = k \times \frac{q_1 \times q_2}{d^2}$$

where distance d is measured in meters, charge q is measured in a unit called the coulomb (see the following explanation), and k is the coulomb constant, a number that plays the same role in electricity that the gravitational constant G plays in gravity. Like G, k is a number (9.00×10^9 newton-meter^2/coulomb^2 in one common system of units) that can be determined experimentally and that turns out to be the same for all charges and all separations of those charges anywhere in the universe.

Coulomb's law is a summary of a large number of experiments done on stationary electrical charges, or static electricity. In order to come to a result like this, scientists had to define a unit of electrical charge, called the *coulomb* (abbreviated C) after the scientist who did so much of this important work. A coulomb equals the charge on 6.3×10^{18} electrons, a very large number. When this many electrons have been added to or subtracted from an object, that object will have one coulomb of electrical charge.

Science by the Numbers •

Two Forces Compared

In Chapter 7 we will examine compelling evidence that the atoms that compose all the materials in our physical surroundings have a definite internal structure. Tiny negatively charged particles called electrons circle in orbits around a positively charged nucleus. Thus, inside an atom, two forces act between the nucleus and an electron: the force of gravity and the electrical force. We can use this fact to get a sense of the relative strength of the two forces.

The simplest atom is hydrogen, in which a single electron circles a single positively charged particle known as a proton (see Chapter 7). The masses of the electron and proton are 9×10^{-31} kg and 1.7×10^{-27} kg, respectively. The charge on the proton is 1.6×10^{-19}C, and the charge on the electron has the same magnitude but is negative. A typical separation of these two particles in an atom is 10^{-10} m.

Given these numbers, what are the values of the electrical and gravitational attractions between these two particles?

- Gravity. The force of gravity between the two particles is given by Newton's law of gravity:

force of gravity (in newtons)

$$= G \times \frac{\text{mass}_1 \text{ (kg)} \times \text{mass}_2 \text{ (kg)}}{\text{distance (m)}^2}$$

$$= (6.7 \times 10^{-11} \text{ m}^3/\text{kg-s}^2) \times \frac{(1.7 \times 10^{-27} \text{ kg}) \times (9 \times 10^{-31} \text{ kg})}{(10^{-10} \text{ m})^2}$$

$$= 1.0 \times 10^{-47} \text{ N}$$

- Electricity. The electrical force, on the other hand, is given by Coulomb's law:

force of static electricity (in newtons)

$$= k \times \frac{\text{charge}_1 \text{ (C)} \times \text{change}_2 \text{ (C)}}{\text{distance (m)}^2}$$

$$= (9 \times 10^9 \text{ N-m}^2/\text{C}^2) \times \frac{(1.6 \times 10^{-19} \text{ C}) \times (1.6 \times 10^{-19} \text{ C})}{(10^{-10} \text{ m})^2}$$

$$= 2.6 \times 10^{-8} \text{ N}$$

From this simple calculation we can see that, in the atom, the electrical force (2.6×10^{-8} N) is many orders of magnitude (factors of 10) larger than the gravitational force (1.0×10^{-47} N). This is why our discussion of the atom in subsequent chapters ignores the effects of gravity completely. •

The Electrical Field

Imagine that you have an electrical charge sitting at a point (Figure 5-2). The charged object could be a piece of lint, an electron, or one of your hairs. If you brought a second charged object to a spot near the first, the second object would feel a force. If you then moved the second object to another spot near the lint, it would still feel a force, but the force would, in general, be a different magnitude and point in a different direction than at the first spot. In fact, the second charged object would feel a force at every point in space around the first.

Every charged object exerts forces on its surroundings to create an electric field. The electric field at a point is defined to be the force that would be felt by a positive 1-coulomb charge if it were brought to that point. The field is usually drawn so that the directions of the arrows correspond to the direction of the force, and the lengths of the arrows correspond to its magnitude. In this way you can make a picture that represents the electric field around the charged object as in Figure 5-2. Notice that the electrical field is defined as the force that would be felt by another charge if that charge were located at a particular point, so that the field is present even if no other charge is in the region.

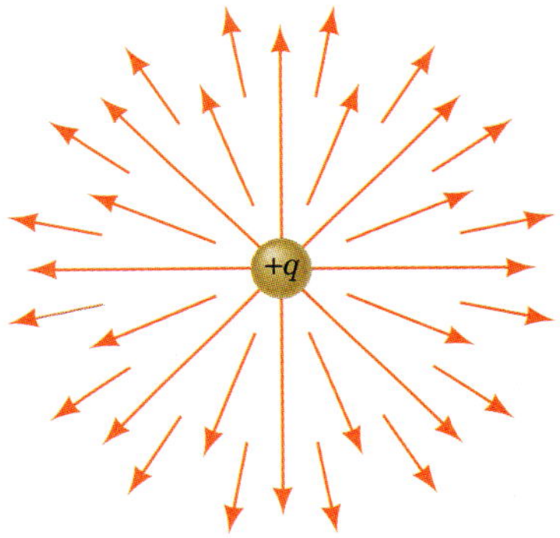

• **Figure 5-2** An electrical field surrounding a positive charge, $+q$, may be represented by lines of force radiating outward. Any charged object that approaches $+q$ experiences a greater and greater electrical force the closer it gets. Positively charged objects will be repelled, while negatively charged objects will be attracted.

Magnetism

Just as electrical phenomena were known to the ancient philosophers, so too were the phenomena we place under the title of magnetism. The first known magnets were naturally occurring iron minerals. If you bring one of these minerals (a common one is magnetite or "lodestone") near a piece of iron, the iron will be attracted to it. You have undoubtedly seen experiments in which magnets were placed near nails, which jumped up and hung from them.

The fact that the nails behave in this way tells you that there must be yet another force in nature, a force seemingly different from both electricity and gravity. Electrical attraction doesn't make the nails move, nor is it gravity that causes the nails to jump up. The simple experiment of picking up a nail with a magnet illustrates beyond a shadow of a doubt that there is a magnetic force in the universe—a force that can be identified and described by the same methods we used to investigate gravity and electricity.

Whereas electricity remained a curiosity until well into modern times, magnetism was put to practical use very early. The compass, invented in China and used by Europeans to navigate the oceans during the age of exploration, is the first magnetic device on record. A sliver of lodestone, left free to rotate, will align itself in a north–south direction. We use compasses so often these days that it's easy to forget how important it was for early travelers to know directions, particularly travelers who ventured out of sight of land in sailing ships.

In the late sixteenth century, the English scientist William Gilbert (1544–1603) conducted the first serious study of magnets. Though revered in his day as a doctor (he was physician to both Queen Elizabeth I and King James I), his most lasting fame came from his discovery that every magnet can be characterized by what he called poles. If you take a piece of naturally occurring magnet and let it rotate, one end of the magnet points north and the other end points south. These two ends of the magnet are called poles. The two poles of a magnet are given the labels north and south, and the resulting magnet is called a *dipole magnet*.

In the course of his research, Gilbert discovered many important properties of magnets. He learned to magnetize iron and steel rods by stroking them with a lodestone. He discovered that hammered iron becomes magnetic and found that iron's magnetism can be destroyed by heating. He realized that planet Earth itself is a giant dipole magnet, a fact that, as we shall see, explains the operation of the compass. Gilbert found that if two magnets are brought near each other so that the north poles are close together, a repulsive force develops between the magnets and they are forced apart. The same thing happens if two south poles are brought together. If, however, the north pole of one magnet is brought near the south pole of another magnet, the resulting force is attractive. In this respect, magnetism seems to mimic the eighteenth-century studies of static electricity. William Gilbert's results can be summarized in two simple statements.

1. **Every magnet has two poles.**
2. **Like magnetic poles repel each other, while unlike poles attract.**

Once you know that a magnet has two poles, you can understand how a compass behaves. Earth itself is a giant dipole magnet, with one pole in Canada and the other pole in Antarctica. If a piece of magnetized iron (for example, a compass needle) is allowed to rotate freely, one of its poles will be attracted to and twist around toward Canada in the north, and the other end will point to Antarctica in the south (see Figure 5-3).

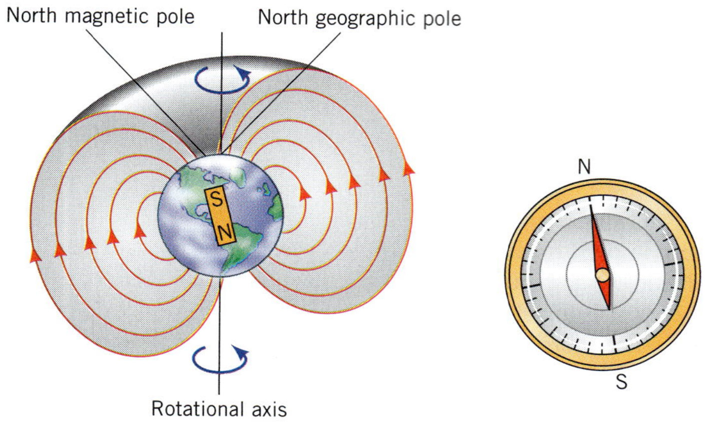

• **Figure 5-3** A compass needle and Earth. Any magnet will twist because of the forces between its poles and those of Earth. Note that Earth's north and south magnetic poles don't quite line up with Earth's axis of rotation.

Recall that an electrical force can be represented by an electric field, with arrows that represent

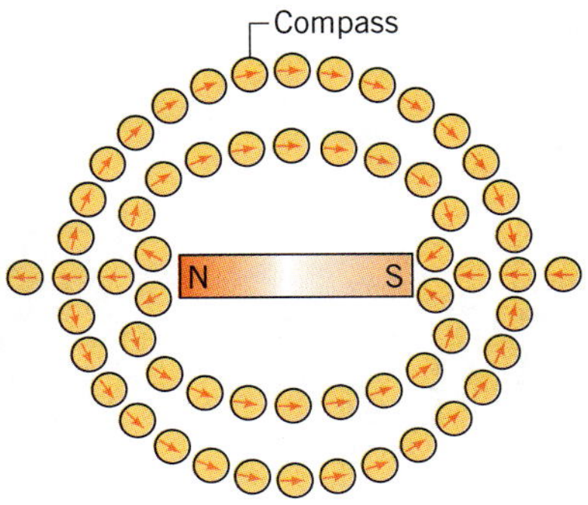

• **Figure 5-4** The curving lines of a magnetic field are revealed by an array of small compass needles that surround a bar magnet.

the direction and strength of the field at every point (Figure 5-2). So, too, can the magnetic force be represented in terms of a magnetic field. Magnets display a curving field pattern, with arrows that indicate the direction and strength of magnetic forces at any point around the magnet. If many small compass needles are brought near the magnet, as shown in Figure 5-4, the forces exerted by the magnet will twist the needles around parallel to the magnetic field at each point. Taken together, these compass needles will follow curving lines that start and end at the north and south poles of the dipole magnet.

Just as we can imagine any collection of electrical charges as being surrounded by the imaginary lines of force of an electric field, we can imagine every magnet as being surrounded by an imaginary set of lines of the magnetic field (Figure 5-5). These lines are drawn so that if a compass were brought to a point in space, the needle would turn and point along the line. The number of lines in a given area is a measure of the strength of the forces exerted on the compass. You can see one consequence of this effect in the northern lights, or aurora borealis. Charged particles streaming from the Sun can emit light when they interact with a magnetic field. The convergence of magnetic field lines near Earth's North and South Poles enhances this effect and produces the colorful display.

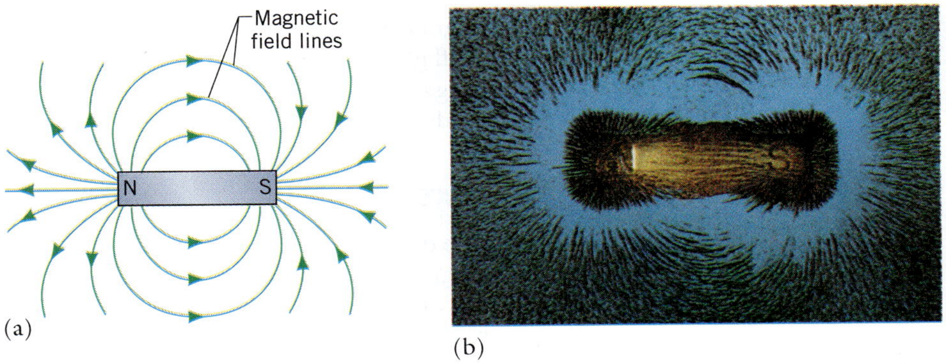

Andy Washnik

• **Figure 5-5** *(a)* A bar magnet and its magnetic dipole field. *(b)* Iron filings placed near a bar magnet align themselves along the field.

A spectacular example of the aurora borealis, caused by particles from the Sun interacting with Earth's magnetic field.

Carson Ganci/Age Fotostock America, Inc.

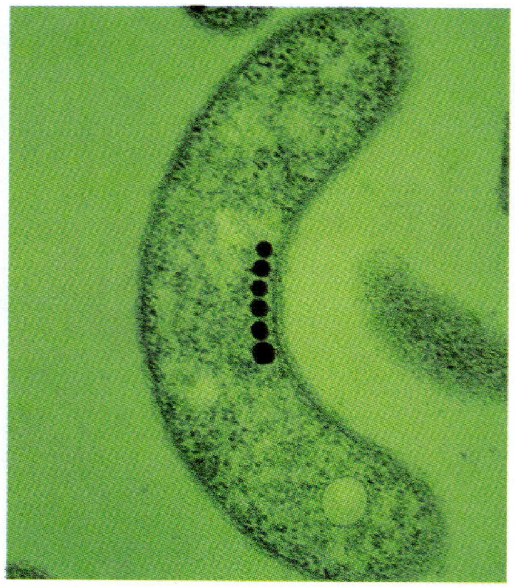

D. Blackwill & D. Maratez/Visuals Unlimited

Grains of iron minerals in this bacterium allow it to tell up from down.

The Science of Life •

Magnetic Navigation

Many living things in addition to humans use Earth's magnetic field for navigation. This ability was demonstrated by scientists at the Massachusetts Institute of Technology in 1975, when they were studying a single-celled bacterium that lived in the ooze at the bottom of nearby swamps. They found that the bacteria incorporate about 20 microscopic crystals of the mineral magnetite into their bodies. These minute crystals are strung out in a line, in effect forming a microscopic compass needle.

Because Earth's magnetic field dips into the surface in the Northern Hemisphere and rises up out of it in the Southern, the Massachusetts bacteria have a built-in "up" and "down" indicator. This internal magnet allows the bacteria to navigate down into the nutrient-rich ooze at the bottom of the pond. Interestingly enough, related bacteria in the Southern Hemisphere follow the field lines in the opposite direction to get to the bottom of their ponds.

Since 1975, similar internal magnets have been discovered in many animals. Some migratory birds, for example, use internal magnets as one of several cues to guide them on flights thousands of miles in length. In the case of the Australian silvereye, evidence suggests that the bird can "see" Earth's magnetic field, through a process involving modification of molecules normally involved in color vision. •

Pairs of Poles

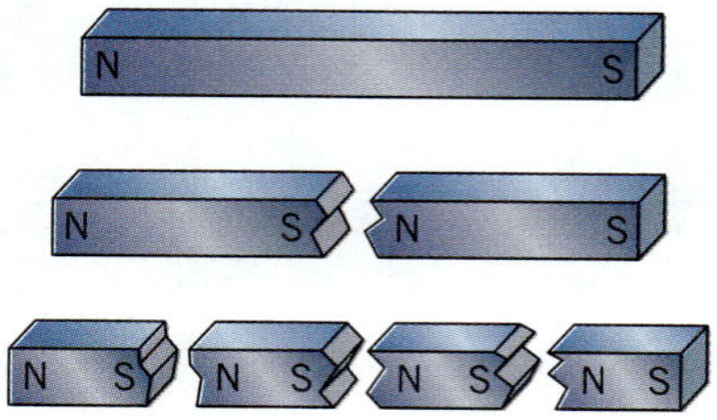

• **Figure 5-6** Cut magnets. If you break a dipole magnet in two, you get two smaller dipole magnets, not an isolated north or south pole.

The dipole magnetic field shown in Figure 5-5 plays a very important role in nature. All magnets found in nature have both north and south poles—you never find one without the other. Even if you take an ordinary bar magnet and cut it in two, you don't get a north and a south pole in isolation, but rather two small magnets each with a north and a south pole (Figure 5-6). If you took each of those halves and cut them in half, you would continue to get smaller and smaller dipole magnets. In fact, it seems to be a general rule of nature that

There are no isolated magnetic poles in nature.

In the language of physicists, a single isolated north or south magnetic pole would be called a *magnetic monopole*. Although physicists have conducted extensive searches for monopoles, no experiment has yet found unequivocal evidence for their existence.

Batteries and Electric Circuits

Discovery of the surprising connection between electricity and magnetism had to await the invention of two familiar devices—the battery and the electric circuit. Remarkably, these commonplace technologies were inspired by the study of frogs.

The Science of Life •

Luigi Galvani and Life's Electrical Force

Scientists of the eighteenth century discovered unexpected links between life and electricity. Of all the phenomena in nature, none fascinated these scientists more than the mysterious "life force," which seemed to allow animals to move and grow. An old doctrine called *vitalism* held that this force was found only in living organisms, and not in the rest of nature. Luigi Galvani (1737–1798), an Italian physician and anatomist, added fuel to the debate about the nature of life with a series of classic experiments demonstrating the effects of electricity on living things.

Galvani's most famous investigations employed an electric spark to induce convulsive twitching in amputated frogs' legs—a phenomenon not unlike a person's involuntary reaction to a jolt of electricity. Later he was able to produce a similar effect simply by poking a frog's leg simultaneously with one fork of copper and one of iron. In modern language, we would say that the electrical charge and the presence of the two metals in the salty fluid in the frog's leg led to a flow of electrical charge in the frog's nerves, a process that caused contractions of the muscles (Figure 5-7). Galvani, however, argued that his experiments showed that there was a vital force in living systems, something he called "animal electricity," which made them different from inanimate matter. This idea gained some acceptance among the scientific community but provoked a long debate between Galvani and the Italian physicist Alessandro Volta (1745–1827). Volta argued that Galvani's effects were caused by chemical reactions between the metals and the salty fluids of the frogs' legs. In retrospect, both of these scientists had part of the truth. Muscle contractions are indeed initiated by electrical signals, even if there is no such thing as animal electricity, and electrical charges can be induced to flow by chemical reactions.

The controversy that surrounded Galvani's experiments had many surprising effects. On the practical side, as we discuss in the text, Volta's work on chemical reactions led to the development of the battery and, indirectly to our modern understanding of electricity. The notion of animal electricity proved a great boon to medical quacks and con men, and for centuries various kinds of electrical devices were palmed off on the public as cures for almost every known disease. Some of these devices can be seen on sale today, in the form of magnets that, when strapped to the body, are supposed to cure various illnesses.

Finally, in a bizarre epilogue to Galvani's research, other researchers used batteries to study the effects of electrical currents on human cadavers. In one famous public demonstration, a corpse was made to sit up and kick its legs by electrical stimulation. Such unorthodox experiments helped to inspire Mary Shelley's famous novel, *Frankenstein*. •

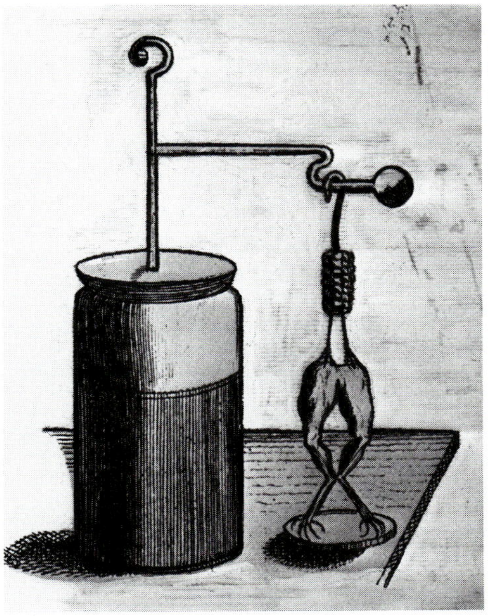

Bettmann/Corbis Images

• **Figure 5-7** Luigi Galvani showed that the frog's legs would twitch when stimulated by electrical current, a phenomenon that eventually led to the invention of the battery (as well as the novel *Frankenstein*).

Jerry Ohlinger's Movie Material Store

The idea behind the legend of Frankenstein may have been suggested by early experiments on animal electricity.

Batteries and Electrical Current

Although we encounter static electricity in our everyday lives, most of our contact with electricity comes from moving charges. In your home, for example, negatively charged electrons move through wires to run all of your electric appliances. A flow of charged particles is called an electrical current.

Until the work of Alessandro Volta, scientists could not produce persistent electrical currents in their laboratories and therefore knew little about them. As a result of his investigations into Galvani's work, Volta developed the first battery, a device that converts stored chemical energy in the battery materials into kinetic energy of electrons running through an outside wire.

The first battery was a crude affair, but we now use its descendants to start our cars and run all sorts of portable electrical equipment. Your car battery, a reliable and beautifully engineered device, routinely performs for years before it needs replacing. It is made of alternating plates of two kinds of material, lead and lead oxide, immersed in a bath of dilute sulfuric acid. When the battery is being discharged, the lead plate interacts with the acid, producing lead sulphate (the white crud that collects around the posts of old batteries) and some free electrons. These electrons run through an external wire to the other plates, where they interact with the lead oxide and sulfuric acid to form lead sulphate. The electrons running through the outside wire are what start your car.

When the battery is completely discharged, it consists of plates of lead sulphate immersed in water, a configuration from which no energy can be obtained. Running a current backward through the battery, however, runs all the chemical reactions in reverse and restores the original configuration. We say that the battery has been recharged. Once recharged, the whole cycle can proceed again. In your car, the generator constantly recharges the battery whenever the engine is running, so that it's always ready to use.

Electric Circuits

Most people come into contact with electrical phenomena through electric circuits in their homes and cars. An electric circuit is an unbroken path of material that carries electricity. Such materials are called *electrical conductors.* Copper wire is an example of a conductor. The electric light that you use to read this book, for example, is part of an electric circuit that begins at a power plant that generates electricity many miles away. That electricity continues through power lines into your town and is distributed on overhead or underground wires until it finally gets to where you live. There, the circuit of which the light is a part is made up of wires that run through the walls of your home. One set of these wires goes first to a circuit breaker (to break the circuit in case of a dangerous overload of too much current), then to a switch, and finally to the lightbulb. When you turn on the switch, you complete an unbroken path that runs all the way from the generating plant to the lightbulb. When electricity flows through the bulb, the electrical current must pass through a very narrow wire called a *filament,* in which electrons are crowded and jostled together to heat up the wire until it glows. When you put the switch in the "off" position, it's like raising a drawbridge: the current is blocked from flowing into this part of the circuit, and none reaches the light. The room becomes dark.

Every circuit consists of three parts: a source of energy like a battery, a closed path usually made of metal wire through which the current can flow, and a device such as a motor or a lightbulb that uses the electrical energy (Figure 5-8).

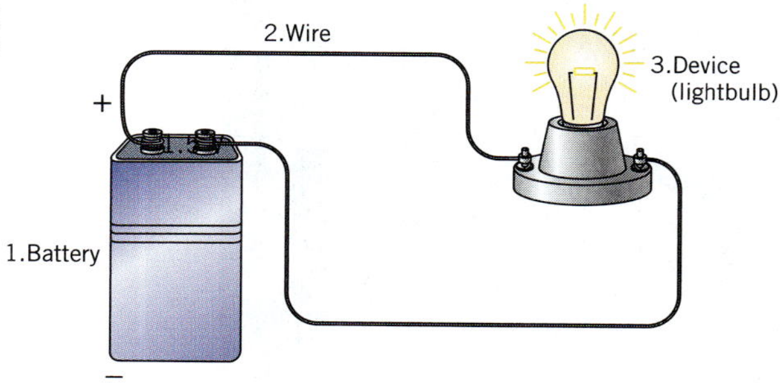

• **Figure 5-8** Every electrical circuit incorporates a source of energy (1), a loop of wire (2), and a device such as a lightbulb (3).

Ohm's Law

One way to think about electric circuits is to draw an analogy between electrons flowing through a wire and water flowing through a pipe. In the case of water, we use two quantities to characterize the flow: the amount of water that passes a point each second, and the pressure behind that water. The numbers we use to describe the flow of electrons in an electric circuit are exactly the same.

The amount of current (the number of electrons) that actually flows in a wire is measured in a unit called the ampere or amp, named after French physicist Andre-Marie Ampere (1775–1836). One amp corresponds to a flow of one coulomb (the unit of electrical charge) per second past a point in the wire:

1 amp of current = 1 coulomb of charge per second

Electrical current, therefore, is analogous to the current of a river or stream. Typical household appliances use anywhere from about 1 amp (100-watt bulb) to 40 amps (an electric range with all burners and the oven blazing away).

We call the pressure produced by the energy source in a circuit the voltage, measured in volts (abbreviated *V*) and named after Alessandro Volta, the Italian scientist who invented the chemical battery. You can think of voltage in circuits much the same way you think of water pressure in your plumbing system. More volts in a circuit mean more "oomph" to the current, just as more water pressure makes the water flow faster. Typically, a new flashlight battery produces 1.5 volts, a fully charged car battery produces about 15 volts (even though they are called 12-volt batteries), and ordinary household circuits operate on either 115 or 230 volts.

Wires through which the current (electrons) flows are analogous to pipes carrying water: the smaller the pipe, the harder it is to push water through it. Similarly, it is harder to push electrons through some wires than others. The quantity that measures how hard it is to push electrons through wires is called electrical resistance, and it is measured in a unit called the ohm. The higher the resistance (i.e., the lower the efficiency), the more electron energy that is converted into heat. Ordinary copper wire, for example, has a low resistance, which explains why we use it to carry electricity around our homes. Toasters and space heaters, on the other hand, employ high-resistance wires so that they will produce large amounts of heat when current flows through them. In transmission lines, it's important that as much energy as possible gets from one end of the line to the other; thus we use very thick low-resistance (high-efficiency) wires.

The relationship between the resistance in a circuit, the current that flows, and the voltage is called *Ohm's law*, after German scientist Georg Ohm (1787–1854). It states:

- In words: The current in circuits is directly proportional to the voltage and inversely proportional to the resistance. The higher the electrical "pressure," the higher the flow of charge. The higher the resistance to flow, the smaller the flow.
- In equation form:

$$\text{voltage (volts)} = \text{current (amps)} \times \text{resistance (ohms)}$$

- In symbols:

$$V = I \times R$$

Every electric circuit can be characterized by its voltage, current, and resistance, so Ohm's law comes into play whenever electricity flows through a circuit. You can understand the behavior of lightning, for example, in terms of Ohm's law. In a thunderstorm, collisions between particles in the clouds produce a buildup of negative charge at the bottom of the cloud and a corresponding buildup of positive charge in objects on the ground underneath the cloud. This buildup creates a voltage between cloud and ground, and the lightning stroke is the electrical current that runs between the two when the voltage is high enough. Lightning, like any other electrical current, will flow along the path of least resistance. Lightning normally strikes tall objects like buildings

These lightning strikes over Seattle are examples of electrical currents in nature.

PhotoDisc, Inc./Getty Images

and trees because the resistance of the building is lower than the resistance of the air. As we mentioned earlier, the lightning rod, invented by Benjamin Franklin, uses this principle by allowing the lightning to flow through a low-resistance bar of metal instead of the building.

Stop and Think! In Franklin's time, some people believed that one way to prevent lightning damage was to climb into church steeples and ring the bells. Was this a good idea?

The *load* in any electric circuit is the "business end"—the place where useful work gets done. The filament of a lightbulb, the heating element in your hair dryer, or an electromagnetic coil of wire in an electric motor are typical loads in household circuits. The power used by the load depends both on how much current flows through it and the size of the voltage. The greater the current or voltage, the more power is used. A simple equation allows us to calculate the amount of electrical power used.

- In words: The power consumed by an electric appliance is equal to the product of the current and the voltage.
- In equation form:

$$\text{power (watts)} = \text{current (amps)} \times \text{voltage (volts)}$$

- In symbols:

$$P = I \times V$$

This equation tells us that both the current and the voltage have to be high for a device to consume high levels of electrical power. Table 5-1 summarizes some key terms about electric circuits.

Table 5-1 Terms Related to Electric Circuits

Term	Definition	Unit	Plumbing Analog
Voltage	Electrical pressure	volt	Water pressure
Resistance	Resistance to electron flow	ohm	Pipe diameter
Current	Flow rate of electrons	amp	Flow rate
Power	Current × voltage	watt	Rate of work done by moving water

EXAMPLE 5-1

Starting Your Car

When you turn on the ignition of your automobile, your 15-volt car battery must turn a 400-amp starter motor. What is the resistance of this circuit, and how much power is required to start your car?

Reasoning and Solution: In order to calculate resistance, we need to rearrange Ohm's law:

$$\text{resistance (ohms)} = \frac{\text{voltage (volts)}}{\text{current (amps)}}$$

$$= \frac{15 \text{ volts}}{400 \text{ amps}}$$

$$= 0.0375 \text{ ohms}$$

That's a very low resistance, less than a thousandth of the resistance of a typical lightbulb.

In order to calculate electrical power, we need to multiply current times voltage:

$$\text{power (watts)} = \text{current (amps)} \times \text{voltage (volts)}$$
$$= 400 \text{ amps} \times 15 \text{ volts}$$
$$= 6000 \text{ watts} = 6 \text{ kilowatts}$$

Most early automobiles were started by a hand crank, which might have required 100 watts of power, a reasonable amount for an adult. Modern, high-compression automobile engines require much more starting power than could be generated by one person.

EXAMPLE 5-2

The Power of Sound

A typical compact disc system has a resistance of 50 ohms. Assuming that this system is plugged into a normal household outlet rated at 115 volts, how much current will flow through the stereo, and what is the power consumption?

Reasoning and Solution: The current can be calculated by rearranging Ohm's law:

$$\text{current (amps)} = \frac{\text{voltage (volts)}}{\text{resistance (ohms)}}$$

$$= \frac{115 \text{ volts}}{50 \text{ ohms}}$$

$$= 2.3 \text{ amps}$$

The power consumption can then be calculated:

$$\text{power (watts)} = \text{current (amps)} \times \text{voltage (volts)}$$
$$= 2.3 \text{ amps} \times 115 \text{ volts}$$
$$= 264.5 \text{ watts}$$

That's similar to the power consumption of three ordinary lightbulbs.

The Science of Life •

The Propagation of Nerve Signals

All of your body's movements, from the beating of your heart to the blinking of your eyes, are controlled by nerve impulses. Although nerve signals in the human body are

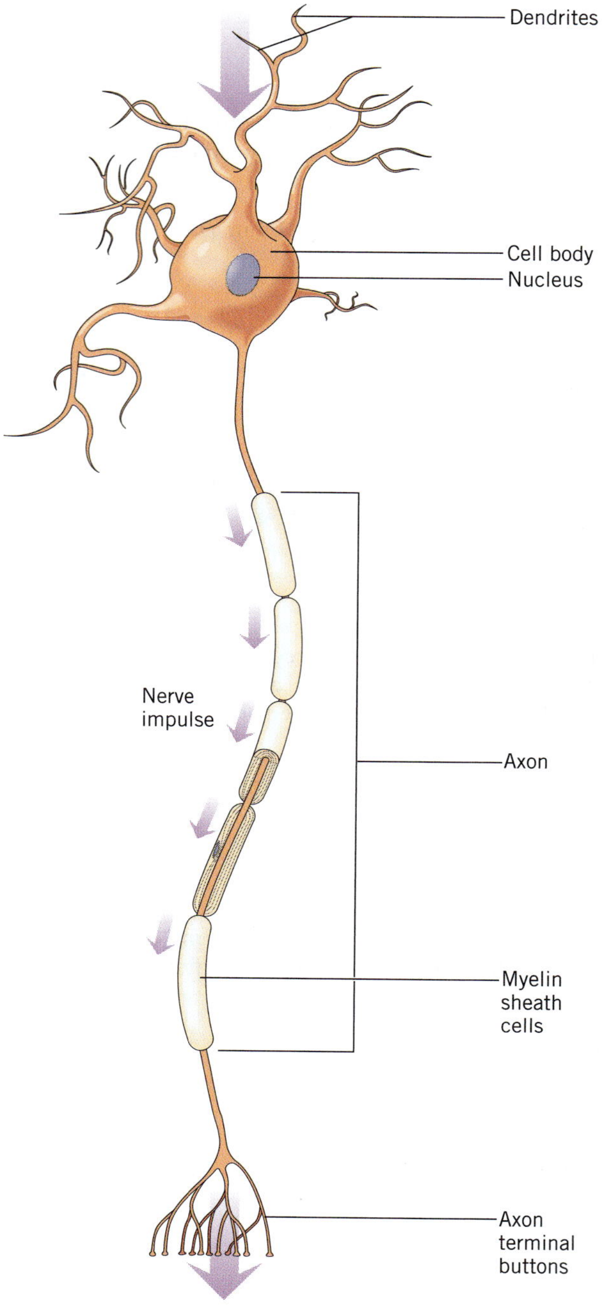

• **Figure 5-9** A nerve cell consists of a central body and a number of filaments. The dendrites receive incoming signals, and the axon conducts outgoing signals away from the cell body. The myelin sheath helps insulate the axon from neighboring electrical interference.

electrical in nature, they bear little resemblance to the movement of electrons through a wire. Nerve cells of the type illustrated in Figure 5-9 form the fundamental element of the nervous system. A nerve cell consists of a central body with a large number of filaments going out from it. These filaments connect one nerve cell to others. The branched filament that carries signals away from the central nerve body and delivers those signals to other cells is called the *axon*.

The membrane surrounding the axon is a complex structure, full of channels through which atoms and molecules can move. When the nerve cell is resting, positively charged objects tend to be outside the membrane, negatively charged ones inside. When an electrical signal triggers the axon, however, the membrane is distorted, and, for a short time, positive charges (mainly sodium atoms) pour into the cell. When the inside becomes more positively charged, the membrane changes again and positive charges (this time mainly potassium) move back outside to restore the original charge. This charge disturbance moves down the filament as a nerve signal. When the signal reaches the end of one of the filaments, it is transferred to the next cell by a group of molecules called *neurotransmitters* that are sprayed out from the end of the "upstream" cell, and received by special structures on the "downstream" cell. The reception of neurotransmitters initiates a complex and poorly understood process by which the nerve cell decides whether to send a signal down its axon to other cells. Thus, although the human nervous system is not an ordinary electric circuit, it does operate by electrical signals. •

Two Kinds of Electric Circuits

Common household circuits come in two different types, depending on the arrangement of wires and loads. In *series circuits* (Figure 5-10*a*), two or more loads are linked along a single loop of wire. In *parallel circuits* (Figure 5-10*b*), by contrast, different loads are situated on different wire loops.

The differences between these two types of circuits can become obvious around Christmastime. Many older strands of Christmas lights were linked by a single series circuit. If any one light burned out, the entire strand went dark because the electric circuit

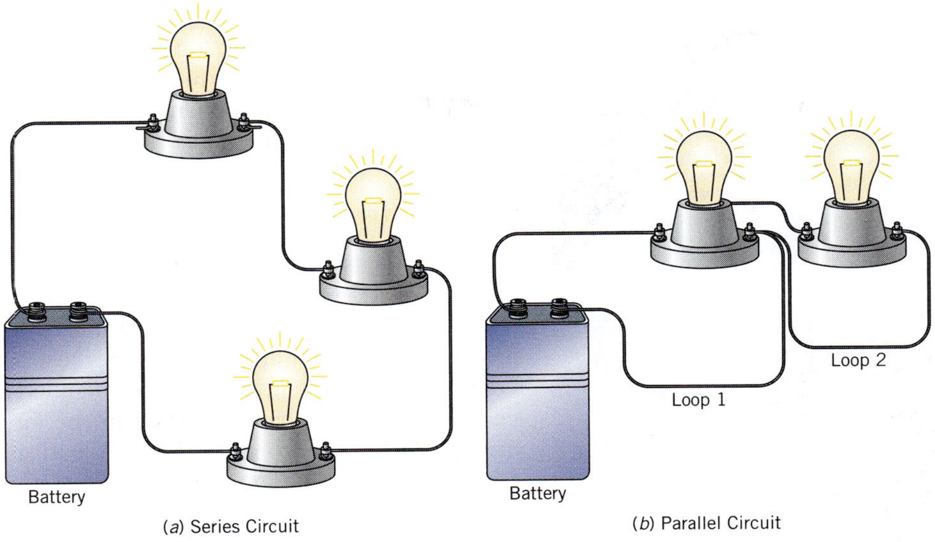

• **Figure 5-10** Two kinds of electric circuits. *(a)* In a series circuit more than one device lies on the same loop of wire. *(b)* In a parallel circuit devices lie on separate loops.

was broken (and it could be a frustrating experience trying to find the one bad bulb). Most modern light strands, on the other hand, feature several parallel loops, each with just a few lights. So today, if one light burns out, only a few bulbs along the strand will go dark.

Connections Between Electricity and Magnetism

In our everyday experience, static electricity and magnetism seem to be two unrelated phenomena. Yet scientists in the nineteenth century, probing deeper into the electrical and magnetic forces, discovered remarkable connections between the two—a discovery that transformed every aspect of technology.

Magnetic Effects from Electricity

In the spring of 1820, a strange thing happened during a physics lecture in Denmark. The lecturer, Professor Hans Christian Oersted (1777–1851), was using a battery to demonstrate some properties of electricity. By chance he noticed that whenever he connected the battery (so that an electrical current began to flow through a circuit), a compass needle on a nearby table began to twitch and move. When he disconnected the battery, the needle went back to pointing north. This accidental discovery led the way to one of the most profound insights in the history of science. Oersted had discovered that electricity and magnetism—two forces that seem as different from each other as night and day—are in fact intimately related to each other. They are two sides of the same coin.

In subsequent studies, Oersted and his colleagues established that whenever electrical charge flows through a wire, a magnetic field will appear around that wire. A compass brought near the wire will twist around until it points along the direction of that field. This leads to an important experimental finding in electricity and magnetism.

Magnetic fields can be created by motions of electrical charges.

Like all fundamental discoveries, the discovery of this law of nature has important practical consequences. Perhaps most importantly, it led to the development of the electromagnet, a device composed of a coil of wire that produces a magnetic field whenever an electrical charge runs through the wire. Almost every electric appliance in modern technology uses this device.

Electromagnets, which can be turned on and off, are ideal for moving scrap iron at a junkyard.

Arthur Hill/Visuals Unlimited

The Electromagnet

Electromagnets work on a simple principle, as illustrated in Figure 5-11. If an electrical current flows in a loop of wire, then a magnetic field will be created around the wire, just as Oersted discovered in 1820. That magnetic field will have the shape sketched in the figure, a shape familiar to you as the dipole magnetic field shown in Figure 5-5.

In other words, we can create the equivalent of a magnetized piece of iron simply by running electrical current around a loop of wire. The stronger the current (i.e., the more electrical charge we push through the wire), the stronger the magnetic field will be. But unlike a bar magnet, an electromagnet can be turned on and off. To differentiate between these two sorts of magnets, we often refer to magnets made from materials such as iron as permanent magnets.

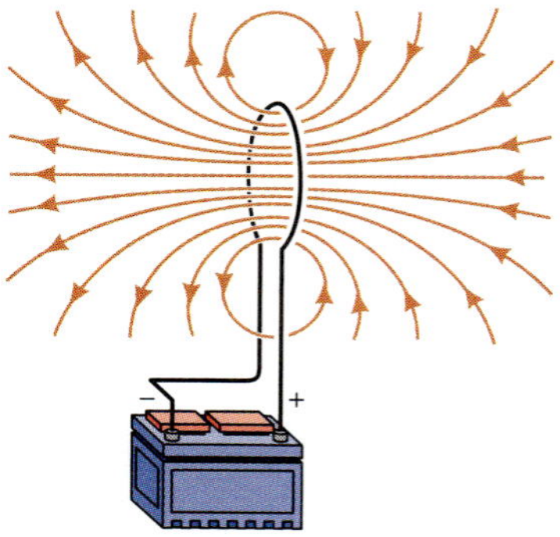

• **Figure 5-11** A schematic drawing of an electromagnet reveals the principal components—a loop of wire and a source of electrical current. When a current flows through the wire loop, a magnetic field is created around it.

The electromagnet can be used in all sorts of practical ways, including buzzers, switches, and electric motors. In each of these devices a piece of iron is placed near the magnet. When a current flows in the loops of wire, the iron is pulled toward the magnet. In some cases, the electromagnet can be used to complete an electrical circuit by pulling a switch closed. As soon as the current is turned off in the electromagnet, a spring pushes the iron back, and the current in the larger circuit also shuts off.

You use electromagnetic switches in many household appliances. For example, your home is probably heated by a furnace that is linked to a thermostat on the wall in your living room or hallway. You set the thermostat to a specific temperature. If the temperature in the room falls below the desired temperature, the thermostat responds by using an electromagnet to close a switch, allowing a small current to flow. While the current flows, the switch is closed and the furnace operates, heating the rooms in your house. When the temperature reaches the level you have set, the thermostat stops the current that flows to the electromagnet, the switch opens, and the furnace shuts off. In this way, you can adjust the temperature of your house without having to run to the basement every time you need to turn on the furnace.

Technology •

The Electric Motor

Look around your room and try to count the number of electric motors that you use every day. They're in fans, clocks, disk drives, CD players, hair dryers, electric razors, and dozens of other familiar objects. Electromagnets are crucial components in every one of those electric motors.

The simplest electric motors, as shown in Figure 5-12, employ a pair of permanent magnets and a rotating loop of wire inside the poles of the magnets. The current in the rotating loop adjusts so that when it is oriented as shown in Figure 5-12*a*, the south pole of the electromagnet lies near the north pole of the permanent magnet, and the north pole of the electromagnet lies near the south pole of the permanent magnet. The attractive forces between north and south poles cause the wire loop to spin. As soon as the loop gets to the position shown in Figure 5-12*b*, the current reverses so that the south pole of the electromagnet lies just past the south pole of the permanent magnet, and the north pole of the electromagnet lies just past the north pole of the permanent magnet. The repulsive forces between like magnetic poles act to continue the rotation. By alternating the current in the loop, a continuous rotational force is kept on the wire, and thus the wire keeps turning.

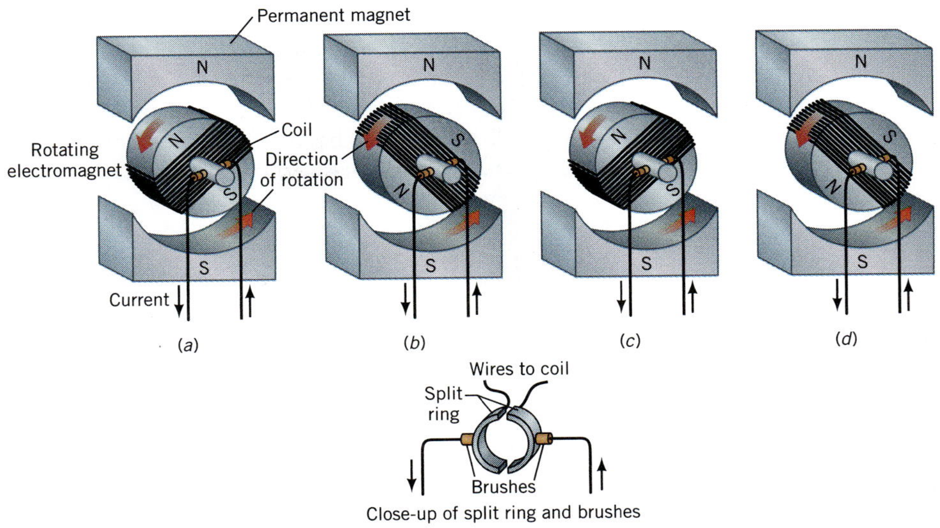

• **Figure 5-12** An electric motor. The simplest motors work by placing an electromagnet that can rotate between two permanent magnets. *(a)* When the current is turned on, the north and south poles of the electromagnet are attracted to the south and north poles of the permanent magnets. *(b)–(d)* As the electromagnet rotates, the current direction is switched, causing the electromagnet to continue rotating.

This simple diagram contains all the essential features of an electric motor, but most electric motors are much more complex. Typically, they have three or more different electromagnets and at least three permanent magnets, and the alternation of the current direction is somewhat more complicated than we have indicated. By artfully juxtaposing electromagnets and permanent magnets, inventors have produced an astonishing variety of electric motors: fixed-speed for your CD player, variable-speed for your food processor, reversible motors for power screwdrivers and drills, and specialized motors for many industrial uses. •

Why Magnetic Monopoles Don't Exist

Earlier we stated that isolated north or south magnetic poles don't exist in nature. Electromagnets provide a basis for understanding where this law comes from. At the atomic scale, an electron in motion around an atom constitutes a "current," analogous to the circle of wire in an electromagnet. As we shall see in Chapter 10, the magnetism in permanent magnets can be traced ultimately to the summation of the behavior of countless electrons, each in motion about an atom's nucleus. This fact explains why ordinary magnets can never be broken down into magnetic monopoles. If you break a magnet down to one last individual atom, you still have a dipole field because of the atomic-scale current loop. If you try to break the atom down further, the dipole field will disappear and there will be no magnetism except that associated with the particles themselves. Thus magnetism in nature is ultimately related to the arrangement of electrical charges rather than to anything intrinsic to matter itself.

The Science of Life •

Magnetic Resonance

Just as the motion of electrons in atoms creates a current that produces a magnetic field, so too does the rotation of the nucleus of the atom. In fact, the nucleus of most atoms can be pictured as a microscopic dipole magnet. This fact gives rise to one of the most useful tools in modern medicine—magnetic resonance imaging (MRI).

In this technique, the patient is placed between the poles of a strong magnet. The magnetic field that permeates the patient's tissue causes the tiny nucleus-scale magnets in those tissues to rotate at frequencies characteristic of each kind of atom. Because of

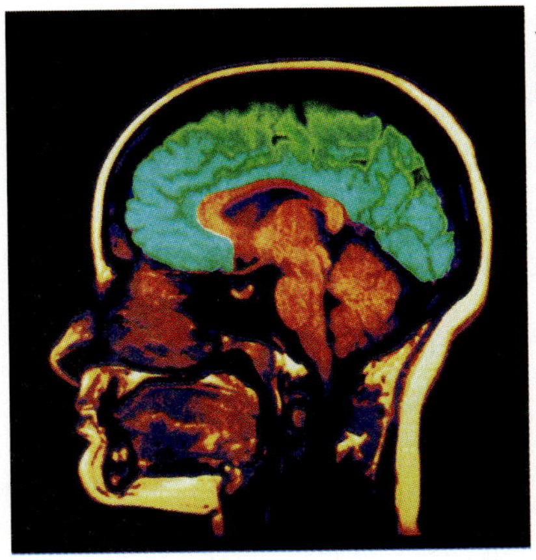

Scott Camazine/Photo Researchers

Magnetic resonance image (MRI) of the human head and shoulders, showing the ability of this technique to produce visualizations of soft tissue.

this effect, the nuclei absorb radio waves whose frequency is timed to coincide with the rotation. By sending radio waves into the patient's tissue and seeing which frequencies are absorbed by rotating nuclei, doctors can determine what sorts of atoms are present at each place in the body, and hence form detailed images of the body's tissues. Unlike X-rays, which have difficulty distinguishing between different kinds of soft tissue, MRI can provide detailed cross-sectional images of any part of the body. •

Electrical Effects from Magnetism

Once Oersted and others demonstrated that magnetic effects arise from electricity, it did not take long for scientists to realize that electrical effects arise from magnetism. Several scientists contributed to this insight, but British physicist Michael Faraday (1791–1867) is most directly associated with this discovery.

Faraday's key experiment took place on August 29, 1831, when he placed two coils of wire—in effect, two electromagnets—side by side in his laboratory. He used a battery to pass an electrical current through one of the coils of wire, and he watched what happened to the other coil. Astonishingly, even though the second coil of wire was not connected to a battery, a strong electrical current developed in it. We now know what happened in Faraday's experiment: the loop of wire through which current was running produced a magnetic field in the neighborhood of the second loop. This changing magnetic field, in turn, produced a current in the second loop by means of a process called *electromagnetic induction* (see Figure 5-13). An identical effect was observed when Faraday waved a permanent magnet in the vicinity of his wire coil. He produced an electrical current without a battery.

Michael Faraday's research can be summarized by a simple law:

Electrical fields and electrical currents can be produced by changing magnetic fields.

Figure 5-14 illustrates the electric generator, or *dynamo,* a vital tool of modern technology that demonstrates this effect. Place a loop of electrical wire with no batteries or other power source between the north and south poles of a strong horseshoe magnet. As long as the loop of wire stands still, no current flows in the wire, but as soon as we begin to rotate the loop, a current flows in the wire. This current flows in spite of the fact that there is no battery or other power source in the wire.

From the point of view of the electrons in the wire, any rotation changes the orientation of the magnetic field. The electrons sense a changing magnetic field and hence, by Faraday's findings, a current flows in the loop. If we spin the loop continuously, then a continuous current flows in it. The current flows in one direction for half of the rotation, then flows in the opposite direction for the other half of the rotation. This vitally

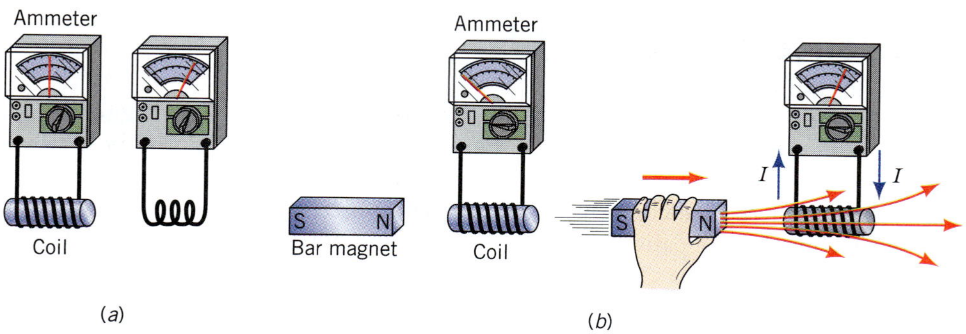

• **Figure 5-13** Electromagnetic induction. *(a)* When a current flows in the circuit on the left, a current is observed to flow in the circuit on the right, *even though there is no battery or power source in that circuit. (b)* Moving a magnet into the region of a coil of wire causes a current to flow in the circuit, even in the absence of a battery or other source of power.

important device, the electric generator, followed immediately from Faraday's discovery of electromagnetic induction.

In an electric generator, some source of energy, such as water passing over a dam, steam produced by a nuclear reactor or coal-burning furnace, or wind-driven propeller blades, turns a shaft. In your car, the energy to turn the coils in a magnetic field comes from the gasoline that is burned in the engine. In every generator the rotating shaft links to coils of wire that spin in a magnetic field. Because of the rotation, electrical current flows in the wire, and that electricity can be tapped off onto external lines. Almost all the electricity used in the United States and elsewhere in the world is generated in this way.

You may have noticed a curious fact about electric motors and generators. In an electric motor, electrical energy is converted into the kinetic energy of the spinning shaft, while in a generator, the kinetic energy of the spinning shaft is converted into electrical energy. Thus motors and generators are, in a sense, exact opposites in the world of electromagnetism.

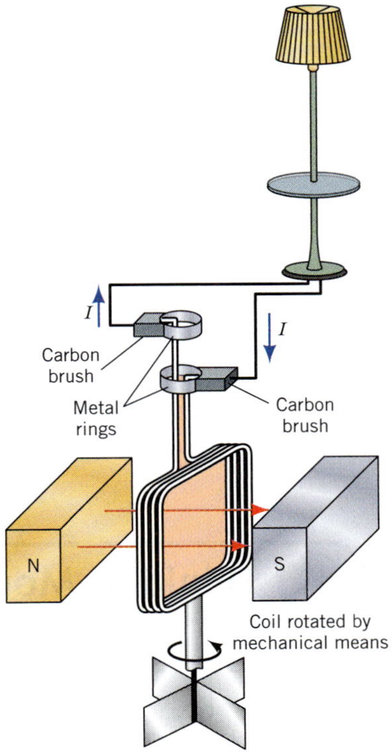

• **Figure 5-14** An electric generator. As long as the loop of wire rotates, there is a changing magnetic field near the loop and a current flows in the wire.

Technology •

AC versus DC

Because the current in the generating coils flows first one way and then the other, it will do the same thing in the wires in your home. This kind of current, the kind used in household appliances and cars, is called alternating current, or AC, because the direction keeps alternating. In contrast, chemical reactions in a battery cause electrons to flow in only one direction and thus produce what is called direct current, or DC.

On a historical note, a major debate raged in the United States in the late nineteenth century about whether to use AC or DC as the commercial standard. Some very famous people—Thomas Edison, for example—were on the losing side. •

Science in the Making •

Michael Faraday

Michael Faraday, one of the most honored scientists of the nineteenth century, did not come easily to his profession. The son of a blacksmith, he received only a rudimentary education as a member of a small Christian sect. Faraday was apprenticed at the age of 14 to a London book merchant, and he became a voracious reader as well as a skilled bookbinder. Chancing upon the *Encyclopedia Britannica,* he was fascinated by scientific articles, and he determined then and there to make science his life.

The young Faraday pursued his scientific career in style. He attended a series of public lectures at the Royal Institution by London's most famous scientist, Sir Humphry Davy, a world leader in physical and chemical research. Then, in a bold and flamboyant move, Faraday transcribed his lecture notes into beautiful script, bound the manuscript in the finest tooled leather, and presented the volume to Davy as his calling card. Michael Faraday soon found himself working as Davy's laboratory assistant.

After a decade of work with Davy, Faraday had developed into a creative scientist in his own right. He discovered many new chemical compounds, including liquid benzene, and enjoyed great success with his own lectures for the general London public at the Royal Institution. But his most lasting claim to fame was a series of classic experiments through which he discovered a central idea that helped link electricity and magnetism. •

Time Life Pictures/Getty Images News and Sprot Services

Michael Faraday (1791–1867)

Maxwell's Equations

Electricity and magnetism are not distinct phenomena at all, but are simply different manifestations of one underlying fundamental entity—the electromagnetic force. In the

1860s, Scottish physicist James Clerk Maxwell (1831–1879) realized that the four very different statements about electricity and magnetism that we have talked about constitute a single coherent description of electricity and magnetism.

The four mathematical statements that he wrote down have come to be known as *Maxwell's equations,* because he was the first to realize their true import. Maxwell manipulated the mathematics to make important predictions, which we will discuss in detail in the next chapter. For reference, the four fundamental laws of electricity and magnetism known as Maxwell's equations (even though we present them here in statement form) are:

1. Coulomb's law: like charges repel, unlike attract.
2. There are no magnetic monopoles in nature.
3. Magnetic phenomena can be produced by electrical effects.
4. Electrical phenomena can be produced by magnetic effects.

Thinking More About | Electromagnetism

Basic Research

It's hard to imagine modern American society without electricity. We use it for transportation, communication, heat, light, and many other necessities and amenities of life. Yet the men who gave us this marvelous gift were not primarily concerned with developing better lamps or modes of transportation. In terms of the categories we introduced in Chapter 1, they were doing basic research. Galvani and Volta, for example, were drawn to the study of electricity by their research on frog muscles that contracted by jolts of electrical charge. Volta's first battery was built to duplicate the organs found in electric fish. Scientific discoveries, even those that bring enormous practical benefit to humanity, can come from unexpected sources.

What does this tell you about the problem of allocating government funds for research? Can you imagine trying to justify funding Galvani's experiments on frogs' legs to a government panel on the grounds that it would lead to something useful? Would a federal research grant designed to produce better lighting systems have produced the battery (and, eventually, the electric light), or would it more likely have led to an improvement in the oil lamp? How much funding do you think should go to offbeat areas (on the chance that they may produce a large payoff) as compared to projects that have a good chance of producing small but immediate improvements in the quality of life?

While you're thinking about these issues, you might want to keep in mind Michael Faraday's response to a question. When asked by a political leader what good his electric motor was, he is supposed to have answered, "What good is it? Why, Mr. Prime Minister, someday you will be able to tax it!"

Summary

The forces of *electricity* and *magnetism* are quite different from the universal gravitational force that Newton described in the seventeenth century. Nevertheless, Newton's laws of motion provided eighteenth- and nineteenth-century scientists with a way to describe and quantify a range of intriguing electromagnetic behavior.

The phenomena of *static electricity,* including lightning and static cling, are caused by *electrical charges,* which arise from the transfer of electrons between objects. An excess of electrons imparts a *negative charge,* while a deficiency causes an object to have a *positive charge.* Objects with like charge experience a repulsive force, while oppositely charged objects attract each other. These observations were quantified in *Coulomb's law,* which states that the magnitude of electrostatic force between any two objects is proportional to the charges of the two objects and inversely proportional to the square of the distance between them.

Scientists investigating the very different phenomenon of magnetism observed that every *magnet* has a *north* and *south pole* and that magnets exert forces on each other. No matter how many times a magnet is divided, each of its pieces will have two poles—there are no isolated magnetic poles. Like magnetic poles repel each other, while opposite poles attract. A compass is a needle-shaped magnet that is designed to point at the poles of Earth's dipole magnetic field. Both *electrical* and *magnetic forces* can be described in terms of force *fields*—imaginary lines that reveal directions of forces that would be experienced in the vicinity of electrically charged or magnetic objects.

Batteries provide a continuous source of electricity. All electrical currents (measured in *amperes* or *amps*) are characterized by an electric "push" or *voltage* (measured in *volts*) and *electrical resistance* (measured in *ohms*). An *electric circuit* is a closed loop of material that carries electricity.

Nineteenth-century scientists discovered that the seemingly unrelated phenomena of electricity and magnetism are actually two aspects of one *electromagnetic force*. Hans Oersted found that an electrical current passing through a coil of wire produces a magnetic field. The *electromagnet* and *electric motor* were direct results of his work. Michael Faraday discovered the opposite effect when he induced an electrical current by placing a wire coil near a magnetic field, thus designing the first *electric generator*, which produced an *alternating current (AC)*. Batteries, on the other hand, develop a *direct current (DC)*.

James Clerk Maxwell realized that the many independent observations about electricity and magnetism constitute a complete description of electromagnetism.

Key Terms

electrical charge
electricity
static electricity
positive electrical charge
negative electrical charge
Coulomb's law
electric field
magnet
magnetic force
poles (north and south)
magnetic field
electrical current (measured in amperes or amps)
battery
electric circuit
voltage (measured in volts)
electrical resistance (measured in ohms)
electromagnet
electric motor
electric generator
alternating current (AC)
direct current (DC)
electromagnetic force

Key Equations

$$\text{electrostatic force (newtons)} = k \times \frac{\text{1st charge (coulombs)} \times \text{2nd charge (coulombs)}}{[\text{mass (kilograms)}]^2}$$

1 coulomb = the charge on 6.3×10^{18} electrons
voltage (volts) = current (amps) × resistance (ohms)
electric power (watts) = current (amps) × voltage (volts)
1 ampere of current = 1 coulomb of charge per second
Universal Electrostatic Constant: $k = 9.00 \times 10^9$newton-meter^2/coulomb^2

Review Questions

1. How might you demonstrate the existence of an electrical force?
2. Compare and contrast the behavior of an electrical force and gravity.
3. How can the movement of negative charges such as the electron produce a material that has a positive charge?
4. How might you demonstrate the existence of a magnetic force?
5. Why do magnets have dipole fields and not monopole fields?
6. Under what circumstances can electrical charges produce a magnetic field?
7. Describe the working and function of an electromagnet.
8. How does an electromagnet differ from a permanent magnet?
9. Explain how electromagnets can be used in the design of an electric motor.
10. Identify two different ways that a single atom might produce a magnetic field.
11. Under what circumstances can a magnetic field produce an electrical current?
12. Explain why electric motors and electric generators are opposites. Under what conditions is each type of device useful?
13. Which of Maxwell's four equations was derived from observations of each the following:
   a. bar magnets
   b. wire loops carrying electrical current
   c. two different materials being rubbed together
   d. the effects of a current-carrying wire coil on a nearby coil
14. What properties of electrical currents are measured by amperes, volts, and ohms? Where do you run across each of these terms in your everyday experience?
15. Identify differences between the diagnostic benefits of medical X-rays and medical magnetic resonance imaging.
16. What is the relation between the power an appliance consumes, the voltage across it, and the current through it?

Discussion Questions

1. Why can you start your car and drive around town many times without draining the battery, but if you leave the lights on when the engine is off, the battery gets drained?

2. If you took an electric motor and turned it by hand, what do you think would happen in the coils of wire?

3. If you rub a balloon on your head, it will adhere to the ceiling. Why? What does this observation tell you about the relative strengths of attraction of electricity and gravity?

4. How did Benjamin Franklin discover that lightning had an electrical nature? How did he apply this understanding? Why did he use a wet string?

5. Identify five things in the room where you are sitting that would not have been possible without the discoveries in electromagnetism discussed in this chapter.

6. How does the first law of thermodynamics apply to electric circuits?

7. How does the second law of thermodynamics apply to electric circuits?

8. There is an old saying that lightning never strikes the same place twice. Given what you know about electrical charge, is this statement likely to be true? Why or why not?

9. Why does a lightning rod work? Why does the electrical energy travel through the rod and not the building? Why should you never seek the shelter of a tree if you get caught out in a thunderstorm?

10. Why should you never operate an electrical appliance (e.g., a hair dryer) while you are in a bathtub filled with water?

11. Why are there signs at gas stations that suggest that you should ground yourself (i.e., touch a metal object) prior to refueling your vehicle? To what hazards and forms of energy are the signs refering?

Problems

1. Many bonds between atoms result from the attraction of positively and negatively charged atoms. Based on electrical charges and separations, which of the following atomic bonds is strongest? [*Hint:* You are interested only in the relative strengths, which depend only on the relative charges and distances.]

a. a + 1 sodium atom separated by 4.0 distance units from a –1 chlorine atom in table salt

b. a + 1 hydrogen atom separated by 2.0 distance unit from a –2 oxygen atom in water

c. a + 4 silicon atom separated by 3 distance units from a –2 oxygen atom in glass

2. A current of 2 amps flows through a wire with a resistance of 10 ohms. What is the voltage of this circuit?

3. A flashlight uses two 1.5-volt batteries to light a 5-watt bulb. What is the current when the flashlight is on? What is the resistance of the circuit?

4. When a video camera's nickel cadmium (Ni-Cad) or nickel metal hydride (Ni-MH) battery runs down, it is recharged by running current through it backward. Typically, you might run 4mAH (Milliampere-hour) at 6 volts for an hour. How much energy does it take to recharge this battery?

5. Most household circuits have fuses or circuit breakers that open a switch when the current in the circuit exceeds 15 amps. Would the lights go off when you plug in an air-conditioner (2 kilowatt), a TV (450 watts), and four 60-watt lightbulbs? Why?

6. Find the energy usage of five electrical appliances in watts, and graph the data using a bar graph. What can you tell from the graph about the energy consumption of these appliances?

7. An energy-efficient water heater draws 12 amps in a standard 115-volt circuit. It costs $75 more than a standard water heater that draws 15 amps. If electricity costs 10 cents per kilowatt-hour, how long would you have to run the efficient water heater to recoup the difference in price?

Investigations

1. Make an inventory of all your electric appliances. Which ones use electromagnets? How many watts does each use?

2. Most household circuits have fuses or circuit breakers that open a switch when the current in the circuit exceeds 15 amps. How many of the appliances in (1) could you run on the same circuit without overloading it?

3. Michael Faraday presented a hand-tooled, leather-bound manuscript to Sir Humphry Davy to obtain a position in his lab. What do you have to do to earn a research assistanship with one of your professors?

4. Imagine that you were stranded on a mineral-rich island. What steps would you take to develop basic electrical devices? What reference books would you want to have with you on the island?

5. Examine carefully your most recent electric bill. How much power did you use? How much did it cost? Is there a discount for electricity used at off-peak hours? Examine your use of electricity and plan a strategy for reducing your electric bill by 10% next month. You can reduce consumption by turning off lights and appliances when not in use, installing lower-wattage bulbs, or using electricity during low-rate times.

6. Find out where your electrical power is generated. Does your local utility buy additional power from some other place? What kind of fuel or energy is used to drive the turbines? Are there pollution controls that restrict the use of certain kinds of fuels at your local power plant? See if you can arrange a tour of the power plant.

7. How many kilowatts of electrical power does a typical commercial power plant generate? How much electricity does the United States use each year? Is this amount going up or down?

8. Take an old appliance with a small electric motor (a razor, coffee grinder, or fan, for example) and dissect the motor. How many permanent magnets are inside? How many electromagnets (i.e., separate coils of wire)?

9. Identify the major electric-circuit components in your automobile. Which require the greatest power?

10. Investigate how electric eels generate electrical shocks. Do any other living things create electrical currents?

11. How does an electroencephalogram (EEG) work? How does it differ from an electrocardiogram (EKG)?

12. Many kinds of living things, from bacteria to vertebrates, incorporate small magnetic particles. Investigate the ways in which living things use magnetism.

13. Read the novel *Frankenstein* (or see the classic 1931 movie with Boris Karloff and Colin Clive, which is admittedly only loosely based on the novel). Discuss the ideas about the nature of life that are implicit in the story. Does it represent a realistic picture of scientific research? Why or why not?

14. How long is the average commute between home and work for people in your area? Might electric cars be of use in the future?

15. If you place the north poles of two magnets next to each other, what happens? Can you explain the result in terms of Newton's laws of motion?

16. Are there any lightning rods on the buildings on your campus? Why does a building need more than one?

17. Look at a camera, watch, or calculator battery. Where are the negative and positive poles?

18. Use the Internet to find out how to make a battery with a potato or a lemon.

6
Waves and Electromagnetic Radiation

What is color?

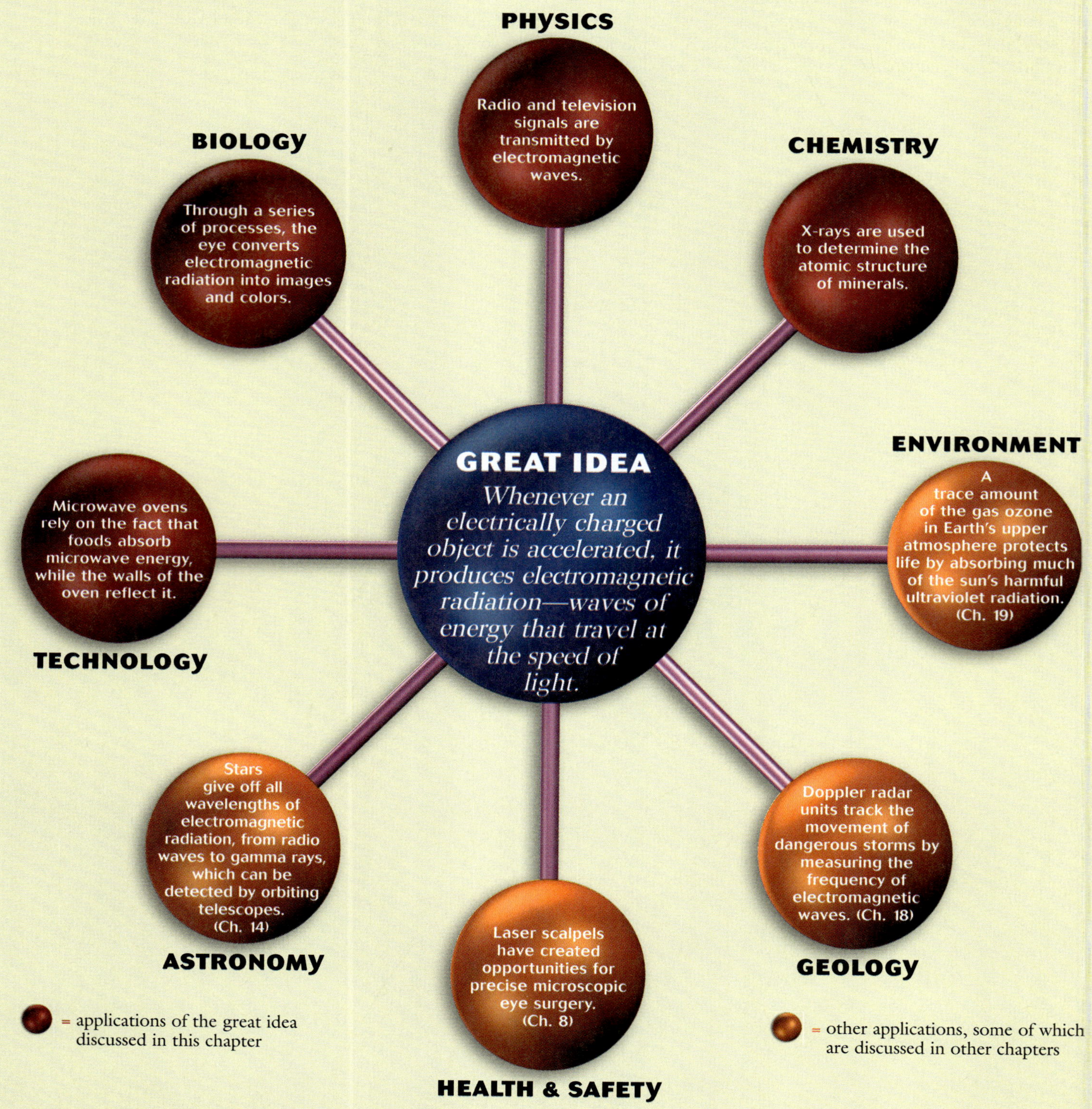

Science Through the Day | The Radio

The car is packed and ready to go. As you begin the 90-minute drive to the beach, you tune the radio to a favorite FM music station and turn up the volume to feel the beat. From time to time, though, you check an AM station that features traffic and weather reports, just to avoid any problems.

The radio is so familiar and essential, yet still it's somewhat magical. How can music and news travel invisibly through air from the radio station? How can so many different stations broadcast at the same time without interfering with each other? The answers, surprisingly, are intimately tied to the behavior of waves and the electromagnetic force.

Digital Vision/Getty Images

The Nature of Waves

Waves are all around us. Waves of water travel across the surface of the ocean and crash against the land. Waves of sound travel through the air when we listen to music. Some parts of the United States suffer from mighty waves of rock and soil called earthquakes. All of these waves must move through matter.

But the most remarkable waves of all can travel through an absolute vacuum at the speed of light. The sunlight that warms you at the beach and provides virtually all of the energy necessary for life on Earth is transmitted through space by just such a wave. The radio waves that carry your favorite music, the microwaves that heat your dinner, and the X-rays your dentist uses to check for cavities are also types of electromagnetic waves—invisible waves that carry energy and travel at the speed of light. In this chapter, we will look at waves in general, then focus on electromagnetic waves, which play an enormous role in our everyday life.

Waves are fascinating, at once familiar and yet somewhat odd. Waves, unlike flying cannonballs or speeding automobiles, have the ability to transfer energy without transferring mass.

Energy Transfer by Waves

Energy can be transferred in two forms in our everyday world: the particle and the wave. Suppose you have a domino sitting on a table and you want to knock it over, a process that requires transferring energy from you to the domino. One way to proceed would be to take another domino and throw it. From the standpoint of energy, you would say that the muscles in your arms impart kinetic energy to the moving domino, which, in turn, would impart enough of that energy to the standing domino to knock it over (Figure 6-1*a*). We say that the energy transfers by the motion of a solid piece of matter.

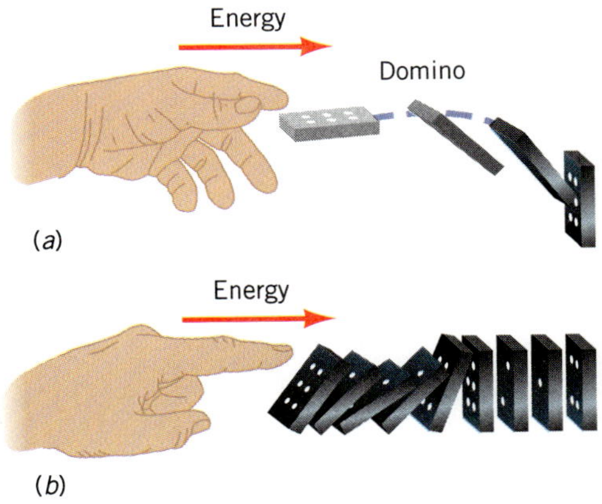

• **Figure 6-1** You can use a domino to knock over other dominoes in two different ways: *(a)* you can throw a domino, or *(b)* you can trigger a wave of dominoes.

Alternatively, you could line up a row of standing dominoes, knock over the first, which would then knock over the second, which in turn would knock over the third, and so on (Figure 6-1*b*). Eventually the falling chain of dominoes would hit the last one, and you would have achieved the same goal. In the case of the lined-up dominoes, however, no single object traveled from you to the most distant domino. In the language of physics, we say that you started a wave of falling dominoes and the wave is what knocked over the final ,domino. A **wave,** then, is a traveling disturbance; it carries energy from place to place without requiring matter to travel across the intervening distance.

Remember in Chapter 4 when we examined the flow of heat from a campfire to your hand by the process of radiation? Radiation now reenters our story as the way that light waves transfer energy from one object to another.

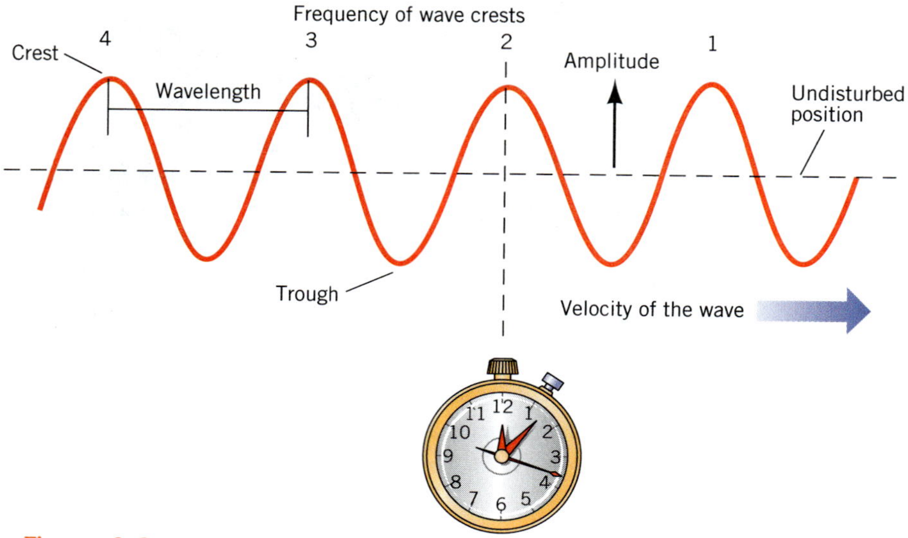

• **Figure 6-2** A cross section of a wave reveals the characteristics of wavelength, velocity, and amplitude. Successive wave crests are numbered 1, 2, 3, and 4. An observer at the position of the clock records the number of crests that pass by in a second. This is the frequency, which is measured in cycles per second, or hertz.

The Properties of Waves

Think about a familiar example of waves. You are standing on the banks of a quiet pond on a crisp autumn afternoon. There's no breeze and the pond in front of you is still and smooth. You pick up a pebble and toss it into the middle of the pond. As soon as the pebble hits the water, a series of ripples moves outward from the point of impact. In cross section, the ripples have the familiar wave shape shown in Figure 6-2. You can use four measurements to characterize the ripples.

1. **Wavelength** is the distance between crests, or the highest points of adjacent waves. On a pond the wavelength might be only a centimeter or two, while ocean waves may be tens or hundreds of meters between crests.
2. **Frequency** is the number of wave crests that go by a given point every second. A wave that sends one crest by every second (completing one cycle) is said to have a frequency of one cycle per second or one **hertz** (abbreviated 1 Hz). Small ripples on a pond might have a frequency of several Hz, while large ocean waves might arrive only once every few seconds.
3. *Velocity* is the speed and direction of the wave crest itself. Water waves typically travel a few meters per second, about the speed of walking or jogging, whereas sound waves in air travel about 340 meters (1100 feet) per second.
4. *Amplitude* is the height of the wave crest above the undisturbed position, for example, the undisturbed water level.

The Relationship Among Wavelength, Frequency, and Velocity

A simple relationship exists among wavelength, frequency, and velocity. In fact, if we know any two of the three, we can calculate the third from a simple equation.

To understand why this is so, think about waves on water. Suppose you are sitting on a sailboat, watching a series of wave crests passing by. You can count the number of wave crests going by every second (the frequency) and measure the distance between the crests (the wavelength). From these two numbers, the speed of the wave can be calculated.

If, for example, one wave arrives every two seconds and the wave crests are 6 meters apart, then the waves must be traveling 6 meters every 2 seconds—a velocity of 3 meters per second. You might look out across the water and see a particularly large wave crest that will arrive at the boat after four intervening smaller waves. You would predict that the big wave is 30 meters away (five times the wavelength) and that it will arrive in 10 seconds. That kind of information can be very helpful if you are plotting the best course for an America's Cup yacht race or estimating the path of potentially destructive ocean waves.

This relationship among wavelength, velocity, and frequency can be written in equation form:

- **In words:** The velocity of a wave is equal to the length of each wave times the number of waves that pass by each second.
- **In equation form:**

$$\text{wave velocity (m/s)} = \text{wavelength (m)} \times \text{frequency (Hz)}$$

- **In symbols:**

$$v = \lambda \times f$$

where λ (the Greek letter lambda) and f are common symbols for wavelength and wave frequency. This simple equation holds for all kinds of waves.

Adrian Dennis/AFP/Getty Images News and Sport Services

Waves passing a sailboat reveal how wavelength, velocity, and frequency are related. If you know the distance between wave crests (the wavelength) and the number of crests that pass each second (the frequency), then you can calculate the wave's velocity.

EXAMPLE 6-1

At the Beach

On a relatively calm day at the beach, ocean waves traveling 2 meters per second hit the shore once every 5 seconds. What is the wavelength of these ocean waves?

Reasoning: We can solve for wavelength, given the wave's velocity (2 meters per second) and frequency (1 wave per 5 seconds, or $\frac{1}{5}$ Hz = 0.2 Hz):

$$\text{wave velocity (m/s)} = \text{wavelength (m)} \times \text{frequency (Hz)}$$

Solution: We can rearrange the equation to solve for wavelength.

$$\text{wavelength (m)} = \frac{\text{velocity (m/s)}}{\text{frequency (Hz)}} = \frac{(2\ \text{m/s})}{0.2\ \text{Hz}} = 10\ \text{m}$$

The Two Kinds of Waves: Transverse and Longitudinal

Imagine that a chip of bark or a piece of grass is lying on the surface of a pond when you throw a rock into the water. When the ripples go by, the floating object and the water around it move up and down; they do not move to a different spot. At the same time, however, the wave crest moves in a direction parallel to the surface of the water. This means that *the motion of the wave is different from the motion of the medium on which the wave moves.* This kind of wave, where the motion is perpendicular to the direction of the wave, is called a *transverse wave* (Figure 6-3*a*).

You can observe (and participate in) this phenomenon if you ever go to a sporting event in a crowded stadium where fans "do the wave." Each individual simply stands up and sits down, but the visual effect is of a giant sweeping motion around the entire stadium. In this way, transverse waves can move great distances, even though individual pieces of the transmitting medium hardly move at all.

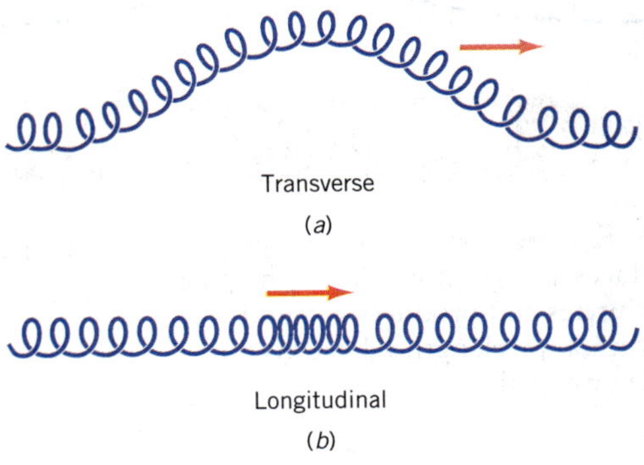

• **Figure 6-3** Transverse *(a)* and longitudinal *(b)* waves differ in the motion of the wave relative to the motion of individual particles.

Not all waves are transverse waves like those on the surface of water—we used the example of a pond simply because it is so familiar and can be visualized. Sound is a form of wave that moves through the air. When you talk, for example, your vocal cords move air molecules back and forth. The vibrations of these air molecules set the adjacent molecules in motion, which sets the next set of molecules in motion and so forth. A wave moves out from your mouth, and that wave looks similar to ripples on a pond. Sound waves differ, however, because in the air the wave crest that is moving out is not a raised portion of a water surface, but a denser region of air molecules. In the language of physics, sound is a *longitudinal wave.* As a wave of sound moves through the air, gas molecules vibrate forward and back *in the same direction as the wave.* This motion is very different from the *transverse wave* of a ripple in water, where the water molecules move *perpendicular to the direction of the waves* (see Figure 6-3). Note that in both longitudinal and transverse waves, the energy always moves in the direction of the wave.

Different-sized instruments in a New Orleans jazz ensemble play in different ranges. The larger tuba on the right plays lower notes, while the trumpet on the left plays a higher range.

Bob Handelman/Photographer's Choice/Getty Images

Stop and Think! How would you do a longitudinal wave in a stadium?

Science by the Numbers •

The Sound of Music

The speed of sound in air is more or less constant for all kinds of sound. The way we perceive a sound wave, therefore, depends on its other properties: wavelength, frequency, and amplitude. For example, what we sense as loudness depends on both the amplitude of a sound and its frequency—the greater the amplitude, for example, the louder the sound. Similarly, we hear higher-frequency sound waves (sound with shorter wavelengths) as higher pitches, while we perceive lower-frequency sound waves (with longer wavelengths) as lower-pitched sounds.

You can experience one consequence of this contrast when you listen to a symphony orchestra. The highest notes are played by small instruments, such as the piccolo and violins, while the lowest notes are the domain of the massive tuba and double basses. Similarly, the size of each of a big pipe organ's thousands of pipes determines which single note it will produce. An organ pipe encloses a column of air in which a sound wave can travel back and forth, down the length of the pipe over and over again. The number of waves completing this circuit every second—the frequency—defines the pitch that you hear (see Figure 6-4).

We can calculate the necessary length of an organ pipe from the desired frequency and the known speed of sound. The note that we hear as "middle A," the pitch to which most orchestras tune, has a frequency of 440 Hz. Sound travels through air at about 340 meters per second. An organ pipe that is open at both ends produces a note with a wavelength twice as long as the pipe. The length of an organ pipe air column that plays middle A, therefore, is given by half the wavelength in the equation:

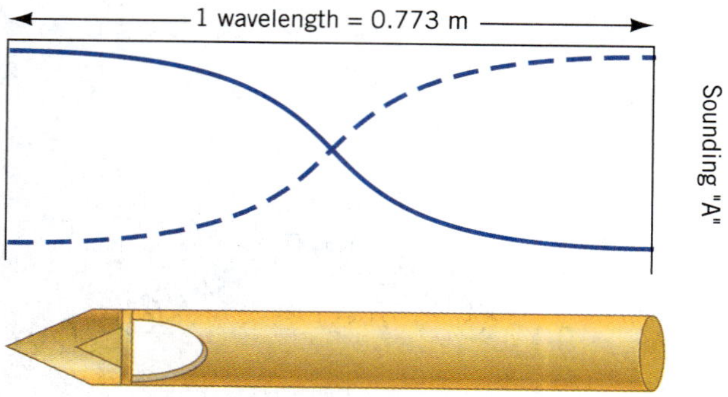

• **Figure 6-4** An organ pipe produces a single note. Air in the pipe vibrates and produces a sound wave with a wavelength related to the length of the pipe.

$$\text{wavelength (m)} = \frac{\text{velocity (m/s)}}{\text{frequency (Hz)}}$$
$$= \frac{(340\ \text{m/s})}{(440\ \text{Hz})}$$
$$= 0.773\ \text{m (about 2 ft)}$$

The length of the organ pipe is half the wavelength:

$$\text{organ pipe length (m)} = \frac{\text{wavelength (m)}}{2} = \frac{0.773\ \text{m}}{2} = 0.387\ \text{m (about 15 in.)}$$

Notes in the middle range on the pipe organ are thus produced by pipes that are about one-half-meter long. •

Stop and Think! At which end of a clarinet would you expect to find the keys for playing low notes? Why?

EXAMPLE 6-2

The Limits of Human Hearing

The human ear can hear sounds at frequencies from about 20 to 20,000 Hz. What are the longest and shortest wavelengths you can hear? What are the longest or shortest organ pipes you are likely to see?

Reasoning: Each organ pipe has a fixed length and produces just one note. We have to calculate the wavelength needed for both the lowest and highest frequency.

Solution: The lowest audible note, at 20 Hz, would require a wavelength as follows:

$$\text{wavelength (m)} = \frac{\text{velocity (m/s)}}{\text{frequency (Hz)}} = \frac{(340\ \text{m/s})}{(20\ \text{Hz})} = 17\ \text{m (about 50 ft)}$$

Similarly, the highest audible note, at 20,000 Hz, is produced by

$$\text{wavelength (m)} = \frac{\text{velocity (m/s)}}{\text{frequency (Hz)}} = \frac{(340\ \text{m/s})}{(20{,}000\ \text{Hz})} = 0.017\ \text{m (about two-thirds of an inch)}$$

Organ pipes producing these notes would be about half the wavelengths or approximately 8.5 and 0.009 meters, respectively. Most large pipe organs have pipes ranging from about 8 meters to less than 0.05 meter in length. Next time you have the chance, visit a church or auditorium with a large pipe organ and look at the variety of pipes. Not only are there many different lengths, but there are also many distinctive shapes, each sounding like a different instrument.

The Science of Life •

Use of Sound by Animals

Humans use sound to communicate, of course, as do many other animals. But some animals have refined the use of sound to a much higher level. In 1793, Italian physiologist

Joe MacDonald/Visuals Unlimited/Getty Images

A bat navigates by emitting high-pitched sounds and listening for their echoes.

Lazzaro Spallanzani did some experiments with bats establishing that they use sound to locate their prey. He took bats that lived in the cathedral tower in Pavia, blinded them, and then turned them loose. Weeks later, those bats had fresh insects in their stomachs, proving that they didn't locate food by sight. Similar experiments with bats that were made deaf, however, showed that they could neither fly nor locate insects.

Today, we understand that bats navigate by emitting high-pitched sound waves and then listening for the reflection of those waves off of other objects. By measuring the time it takes for a pulse of sound waves to go out, be reflected, and come back, the bat can determine the distance to surrounding objects, particularly the flying insects that make up its diet. Typically, a bat can detect the presence of an insect up to 10 meters away.

In an interesting application of the principle of natural selection (see Chapter 25), some species of moths have developed sophisticated sense organs to hear the sound emitted by bats. Using ears on their thorax or abdomen, these moths can hear the high-pitched sounds emitted by bats and thus can tell when they are being "seen." When they hear the sound, the moths take immediate evasive action. In a few cases, moths have developed an even more sophisticated defense. When a bat approaches, they emit a series of high-pitched clicks that "jam" the bat's detection system.

At the opposite end of the sound spectrum, when confronted by very low-frequency sounds, we often don't so much hear sound waves as feel them. We sense the vibrations in our bodies. You may have experienced this sensation when hearing very low notes on an organ. Some animals (elephants, for example) routinely use sound in the 20–40 Hz range to communicate with each other over long distances. The mating call of the female elephant, for example, is experienced as a vibration by humans, but attracts bull elephants from many miles away.

Whales, dolphins, and porpoises use low-frequency sound echoes as a navigation tool in the ocean, much as bats do in air. Sometimes, however, the sounds that they emit are in the audible range for humans. Perhaps the most famous examples of sophisticated use of sound by animals are the songs of humpback whales, which have appeared on a number of commercial recordings. The functions of these songs are not clear. It appears, however, that all of the whales in a wide area of ocean (the South Atlantic, for example) sing the same song, although some individuals may leave out parts. The songs change every year, but the whales in a given area change their songs together. •

Interference

Waves from different sources may overlap and affect each other in the phenomenon called interference. **Interference** describes what happens when waves from two different sources come together at a single point—each wave interferes with the other, and the observed wave amplitude is the sum of the amplitudes of the interfering waves. Consider the common situation shown in Figure 6-5. Suppose

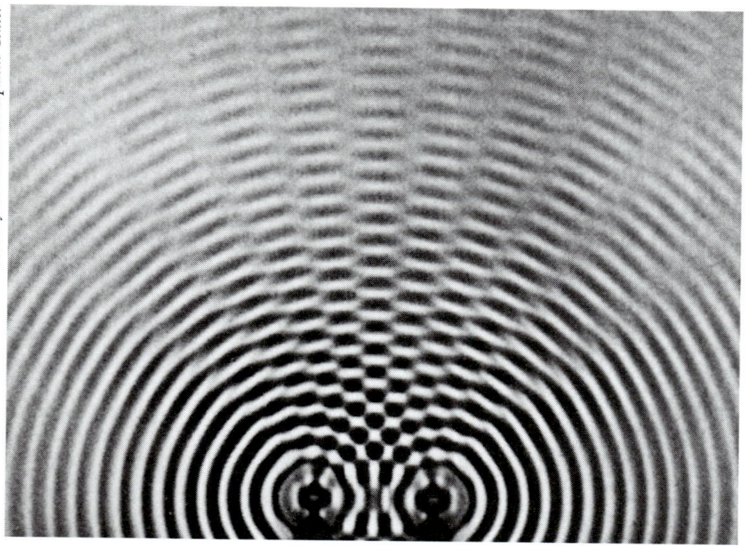

Courtesy Education Development Center

• **Figure 6-5** Two waves originating from different points create an interference pattern. Bright regions correspond to constructive interference, while dark regions correspond to destructive interference.

you and a friend each throw rocks into a pond at two separate points as in the figure. The waves from each of these two points travel outward and eventually will meet. What will happen when the two waves come together?

One easy way to think about what happens is to imagine that each part of each wave carries with it a set of instructions for the water surface—"move down 2 inches," or "move up 1 inch." When two waves arrive simultaneously at a point, the surface responds to both sets of instructions. If one wave says to move down 3 inches and the other to move up 1 inch, the result will be that the water surface will move down 2 inches. Thus each point on the surface of the water moves a different distance up or down depending on the instructions that are brought to it by the two waves.

One possible situation is shown in Figure 6-6*a*. Two waves, each carrying the command "go up 1 inch" arrive at a point together. The two waves act together to lift the water surface to the highest possible height it can have. This effect is called *constructive interference*, or reinforcement. On the other hand, you could have a situation like the one shown in Figure 6-6*b*, where the two waves arrive at a point such that one is giving an instruction to go up 1 inch and the other to go down 1 inch. In this case, the water surface will not move up or down at all. This situation is called *destructive interference*, or cancellation. And, of course, waves can interfere anywhere between these two extremes.

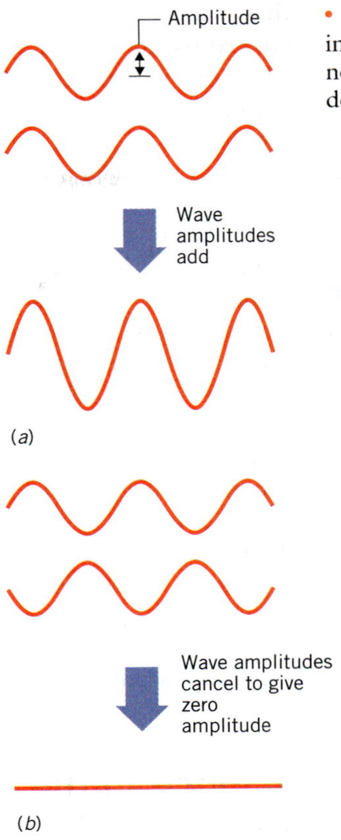

• **Figure 6-6** Cross sections of interfering waves illustrate the phenomena of *(a)* constructive and *(b)* destructive interference.

The most familiar example of destructive interference does not take place with water waves but with sound waves. Occasionally an auditorium may be designed in such a way that almost no sound can be heard in certain seats. This unfortunate situation results when two waves—for example, one directly from the stage and one bouncing off the ceiling—arrive at those seats in such a way as to cause partial or total destructive interference. One of the main goals of acoustical design of auditoriums, a field that relies on complex computer modeling of sound interference patterns, is to avoid such problems.

The Electromagnetic Wave

Have you ever had your teeth X-rayed? cooked a meal in a microwave oven? watched television or listened to radio? If so, then you have firsthand experience with the phenomenon of electromagnetic waves.

Physicists characterize waves by a mathematical expression called a *wave equation*, which describes the movement of the medium for every wave, whether it's a water wave moving through a liquid, a sound wave in air, or a seismic wave (a sound wave traveling through rocks) causing an earthquake. Physicists have learned that whenever an equation of this or some closely related form appears, a corresponding wave should be seen in nature.

Soon after Maxwell wrote down the four equations that describe electricity and magnetism (see Chapter 5), he realized that some rather straightforward mathematical manipulation led to yet another equation, one that describes waves. The waves that Maxwell predicted are rather strange sorts of things, and we'll describe their anatomy in more detail later. The important point, however, is that these are waves in which energy is transferred not through matter, but through electrical and magnetic fields. It appears from the equations that whenever an electrical charge is accelerated, for example, one of

Time Life Pictures/Getty Images news and Sport Services

James Clerk Maxwell (1831–1879)

these waves is emitted. Maxwell called this phenomenon **electromagnetic waves** or **electromagnetic radiation.** An electromagnetic wave is a wave that is made up of electrical and magnetic fields that fluctuate together; once it starts, the wave keeps itself going, even in a vacuum.

Maxwell's equations also predicted exactly how fast the waves could move—the wave velocity depends only on known constants such as the universal electrostatic constant in Coulomb's equation (see Chapter 5). These numbers are known from experiment, and when Maxwell put the numbers into his expression for the velocity of his new waves, he found a very surprising answer. The predicted velocity of the mystery waves turned out to be 300,000 kilometers per second (186,000 miles per second).

If you just had an "aha!" moment, you can imagine how Maxwell felt. The number that he calculated is the speed of light, which means that the waves described by his equation are actually the familiar (but mysterious) waves we call "light."

This result was astonishing. For centuries scientists had puzzled over the origin and nature of light. Newton and others had discovered natural laws that describe the connections between forces and motion, as well as the behavior of matter and energy. But light remained an enigma. How did radiation from the Sun travel to Earth? What caused the light produced by a candle?

There is no obvious reason why static cling, refrigerator magnets, or the workings of an electric generator should be connected in any way to the behavior of visible light. Yet Maxwell discovered that **light** and other kinds of radiation are a type of wave that is generated whenever electrical charges are accelerated.

Science in the Making •

The Ether

When Maxwell first proposed his idea of electromagnetic radiation, he was not prepared to deal with a wave that required no medium whatsoever. Previous scientists who had studied light, including such luminaries as Isaac Newton, assumed that light must travel through a hypothetical substance called "ether" that permeates all space. Ether, they thought, served as the medium for light, and so Maxwell assumed that ether provided the medium for his electromagnetic waves. In Maxwell's picture, the ether was a tenuous transparent substance, perhaps like invisible Jell-O, that filled all of space. An accelerating charge shook the Jell-O at one point, and after that the electromagnetic waves moved outward at the speed of light.

The idea of an ether goes back to the ancient Greeks, and for most of recorded history scholars logically assumed that the vacuum of space was filled with this imaginary substance. It wasn't until 1887 that two U.S. physicists, Albert A. Michelson (1852–1931) and Edward W. Morley (1838–1923), working at what is now Case Western Reserve University in Cleveland, performed experiments that demonstrated that the ether could not be detected. This failure was interpreted to mean that the ether did not exist.

The concept of the experiments was very simple. Michelson and Morley reasoned that if an ether really existed, then the motion of Earth around the Sun and the Sun around the center of our Milky Way Galaxy would produce an apparent ether "wind" at Earth's surface, much as someone riding in a car on a still day feels a wind. They used very sensitive instruments to search for interference effects in light waves, effects that would result from the deflection of light by the ether wind. When their experiment turned up no such deflection, they concluded that ether does not exist.

In 1907, Albert Michelson became the first U.S. scientist to win a Nobel Prize, an honor that recognized his pioneering experimental studies of light. •

The Anatomy of the Electromagnetic Wave

How does an electromagnetic wave move in the absence of any transmitting medium? A typical electromagnetic wave, shown in Figure 6-7, consists of electrical and magnetic fields arranged at right angles to each other and perpendicular to the direction the wave is moving. To understand how the waves form, go back to Maxwell's equations that describe how a changing magnetic field produces an electrical field, and vice versa (Chapter 5). At the point labeled *A* in Figure 6-7, the electrical and magnetic fields associated with the wave are at maximum strength, but these fields are changing slowly, so they both decrease in strength. At point *B*, the fields are at minimum strength, but they are changing rapidly and so begin to increase. Thus at point *A*, the magnetic and electrical fields begin to die out, while at point *B* just the reverse happens. In this way the electromagnetic wave leapfrogs through space, bouncing its energy back and forth between electrical and magnetic fields as it goes.

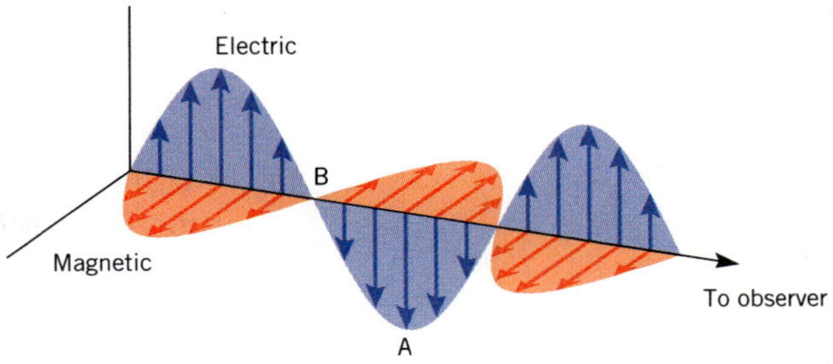

• **Figure 6-7** A diagram of an electromagnetic wave shows the relationship of the electrical field, the magnetic field, and the direction that the wave is moving. A and B indicate points of maximum and minimum field strength.

All of the other kinds of waves we've talked about—those on water or in air, for example—are easy to visualize because the wave moves through a medium. Electromagnetic waves are different, and therefore somewhat mysterious (indeed, many scientists find their behavior difficult to understand). However, once you understand that the electromagnetic wave has this kind of ping-pong arrangement between electricity and magnetism, you can get a sense of how it can travel through a vacuum. The key is that the motion of a wave is not the same as the motion of the medium. The electromagnetic wave is, in a sense, an extension of this idea. It's a wave that has no medium whatsoever, but simply keeps itself going through its own internal mechanisms.

Electromagnetic waves, then, transfer energy—what we have called ***radiation*** (see Chapter 4). These waves are created when electrical charges accelerate, but once they start moving they no longer depend on the source that emitted them.

Light

Once Maxwell understood the connection between electromagnetism and light, his equations allowed him to draw several important conclusions. For one thing, because the velocity of the electromagnetic waves depends entirely on the nature of interactions between electrical charges and magnets, it cannot depend on the properties of the wave itself. Thus, all electromagnetic waves, regardless of their wavelength or frequency, have to move at exactly the same velocity. This velocity—the **speed of light**—turns out to be so important in science that we give it a special letter, *c*. The speed of electromagnetic waves in a vacuum is one of the fundamental constants of nature. (Light moving through solids, liquids, or gases travels at a somewhat slower speed.)

For electromagnetic waves traveling in the vacuum of space, the relation among velocity, wavelength, and frequency takes on a particularly simple form:

$$\text{wavelength} \times \text{frequency} = c$$
$$= 300{,}000 \text{ km/s } (= 186{,}000 \text{ mi/s})$$

In other words, if you know the wavelength of an electromagnetic wave, you can calculate its frequency and vice versa.

The Energy of Electromagnetic Waves

Think about how you might produce an electromagnetic wave with a simple comb. Electromagnetic waves are generated any time a charged object is accelerated, so imagine combing your hair on a dry winter day when the comb picks up a static charge. Each time you move the comb back and forth, an electromagnetic wave traveling 300,000 kilometers per second is sent out from the comb.

If you wave the electrically charged comb up and down slowly, once every second, you create electromagnetic radiation, but you're not putting much energy into it. You produce a low-frequency, low-energy wave with a wavelength of about 300,000 kilometers. (Remember, each wave moves outward 300,000 kilometers in a second, which is the separation between wave crests.)

If, on the other hand, you could vibrate the comb vigorously—say at 300,000 times per second—you would produce a higher-energy, high-frequency wave with a 1-kilometer wavelength. By putting more energy into accelerating the electrical charge, you have more energy in the electromagnetic wave.

Visible light, the first example of an electromagnetic wave known to humans, bears out this kind of reasoning. A glowing ember has a dull red color, corresponding to a relatively low range of energies. Hotter, more energetic fires show a progression of more energetic colors, from the yellow of a candle flame to the blue-white flame of a blowtorch. These colors are merely different ranges of frequencies, and therefore different energies, of light; higher-frequencies of light correspond to a blue color, lower-frequencies to red.

Red light has wavelengths corresponding to a range of distances between about 600 and 700 nanometers (a nanometer is 10^{-9} meter, about 40 billionths of an inch). Red light includes the longest wavelengths that the eye can see and is the least energetic of the visible electromagnetic waves. Violet light, on the other hand, has a range of shorter wavelengths corresponding to about 400 to 440 nanometers, and includes the most energetic of the visible electromagnetic waves. All of the other colors have ranges of wavelengths and energies between those of red and violet.

EXAMPLE 6-3

Figuring Frequency

The average wavelength of yellow light is about 580 nanometers, or 5.8×10^{-7} m. What is the frequency of an average yellow light wave?

Reasoning: We know that for all electromagnetic waves,

$$\text{wavelength} \times \text{frequency} = 300{,}000 \text{ km/s} = 3 \times 10^8 \text{ m/s}$$

We want to determine frequency, so we rearrange this equation:

$$\text{frequency} = \frac{(3 \times 10^8 \text{ m/s})}{\text{wavelength}}$$

Solution: This means that for yellow light with a wavelength of 5.8×10^{-7} m,

$$\text{frequency} = \frac{(3 \times 10^8 \text{ m/s})}{(5.8 \times 10^{-7} \text{ m})} = 0.52 \times 10^{15} \text{ Hz} = 5.2 \times 10^{14} \text{ Hz}$$

(Remember, a hertz equals one cycle per second.) In order to generate yellow light by vibrating a charged comb you would have to wiggle it more than 500 trillion (520,000,000,000,000) times per second.

The Doppler Effect

Once waves have been generated, their motion is independent of the source. It doesn't matter what kind of charged object accelerates to produce an electromagnetic wave; once produced, all such waves behave exactly the same way. This statement has an important consequence that was discovered in 1842 by Austrian physicist Christian Johann Doppler (1803–1853). This consequence is called the **Doppler effect** in his honor. The Doppler effect describes the way the frequency of a wave appears to change if there is relative motion between the wave source and the observer.

Let's take sound as an example. Figure 6-8*a* shows the way a sound wave looks when the source is stationary relative to a listener—when you listen to your radio, for example. In this case everything sounds "normal."

If the source of sound—a racing ambulance, for example—is moving relative to the listener, however, a different situation occurs (Figure 6-8*b*). Periodically the crest of a longitudinal sound wave moves away from the ambulance and travels out in a sphere *centered on the spot where the source was located when that particular crest was emitted*. By the time the ambulance is ready to emit other sound waves, it will have moved, and the second sound-wave sphere emitted will be centered at the new location. As the source continues to move, it will emit sound waves centered farther and farther to the right in the figure, producing a characteristic pattern as shown.

To an observer standing in front of the source, the crests appear to be bunched up. To this observer, the frequency of the wave appears to be higher than it would normally be. In the case of a sound wave, this means that the sound will be higher-pitched than it would have been had the source been stationary. On the other hand, if the observer is standing in back of the source, the distance between crests will be stretched out, and the frequency and pitch of the resulting sound will be lower.

You probably have heard the Doppler effect. Think of standing on a highway while cars go by at high speeds. The engine noise appears to be very high-pitched as a car approaches you and then suddenly drops in pitch as the car passes you. This effect is particularly striking at automobile races where cars are moving at very high velocity.

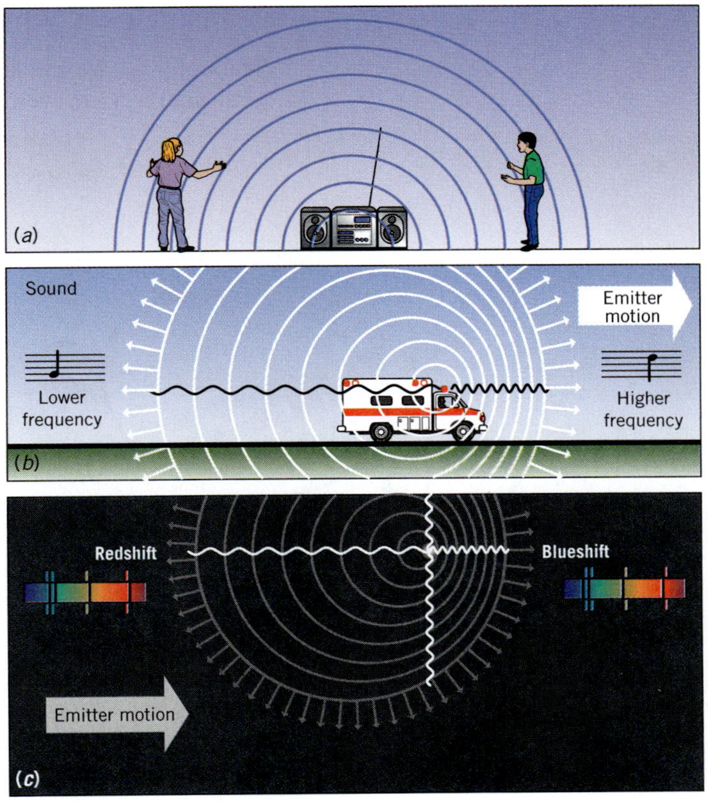

• **Figure 6-8** The Doppler effect occurs whenever a source of waves is moving relative to the observer of the waves. *(a)* Sound waves spread out from a source in all directions; stationary listeners hear the same pitch. *(b)* Sound waves from a moving source seem to increase or decrease in pitch, depending on whether the sound is approaching or receding. *(c)* The Doppler shift for light waves causes a blueshift for approaching sources and a redshift for receding sources.

This sort of change in pitch provided the first example of the Doppler effect to be studied. Scientists hired a band of trumpeters to sit on an open railroad car and blast a single long, loud note as the train whizzed by at a carefully controlled speed. Musicians on the ground determined the pitches they heard as the train approached and as it receded, and they compared those pitches to the actual note the musicians were playing.

The same sort of bunching up and stretching out of crests can happen for any wave, including light. If you are standing in the path of a source of light that is moving toward you, the light you see will be of higher frequency and hence will look bluer than it would ordinarily. (Remember, blue light has a higher frequency than red light.) We say the light is *blueshifted* (Figure 6-8*c*).

If, on the other hand, you are standing in back of the moving source, the distance between crests will be stretched out and it will look to you as if the light had a lower frequency. We say that it is *redshifted*. In Chapter 15 we will see that the redshifting of light from distant moving sources is one of the main clues that we have about the structure of the universe.

The Doppler effect also has practical applications much closer to your home. Police radar units send out a pulse of electromagnetic waves that is absorbed by the metal in your car, then reemitted. The waves that come back will be Doppler shifted, and by comparing the frequency of the wave that went out and the wave that comes back, the speed of your car can be deduced. Similar techniques are used by bats, who rely on the Doppler shift to detect the motion of their insect prey, and by meteorologists, who employ Doppler radar to measure wind speed and direction during the approach of potentially damaging storms (see Chapter 18).

Transmission, Absorption, and Scattering

The only way we can know about electromagnetic radiation is to observe its interaction with matter. Our eyes, for example, interact with visible light and send nerve impulses to our brain—impulses that are interpreted as what we "see." When an electromagnetic wave hits matter, one of three processes takes place:

1. *Transmission*. The wave will often pass right through matter, as does the light that passes through your window. This process is called **transmission.** Transparent materials do not affect the wave other than slowing it down a bit while it is in transit, or perhaps changing its direction slightly as in eyeglasses—a process called **refraction** (Figure 6-9).
2. *Absorption*. Other matter, like an asphalt driveway on a summer day, may soak up the wave and its energy—the process of **absorption.** The energy of absorbed electromagnetic radiation is converted into some other form of energy, usually heat. Black and dark colors, for example, absorb visible light: you've probably noticed how hot black pavement can become on a sunny day.
3. *Scattering*. Alternatively, electromagnetic waves may be absorbed and rapidly reemitted in the process of **diffuse scattering** (Figure 6-10). Most white materials, such as a wall or piece of paper, scatter all wavelengths of visible light in all directions. White objects such as clouds and snow, which scatter light from the Sun back into space, play a major role in controlling Earth's climate (see Chapter 18). Mirrors, on the other hand, scatter visible light at the same angle as the original wave in the process called **reflection** (Figure 6-11). Colored objects, by contrast, scatter only certain ranges of wavelengths. A red sweater, for example, will typically scatter light primarily in the red wavelengths, while absorbing light in the green wavelengths.

Skip Nall/Age Fotostock America, Inc.

• **Figure 6-9** The lenses in eyeglasses use the phenomenon of refraction to focus light.

• **Figure 6-10** Clouds appear white because of diffuse scattering of sunlight.

Adam Jones/Photo Researchers

• **Figure 6-11** Mirrors scatter light through the process of reflection.

Gail Mooney/Masterfile

Jack Hollingsworth/PhotoDisc, Inc./Getty Images

The asphalt on this highway absorbs sunlight and heats up on warm days.

All electromagnetic waves are detectable in some way. For each of them to be useful, researchers must find appropriate materials to transmit, absorb, and scatter the waves. For each wavelength there must be instruments that produce the waves and others that detect their presence. While only a very narrow range of electromagnetic waves can be detected by the human eye, scientists have devised an extraordinary range of transmitters and detectors to produce and measure electromagnetic radiation that we can't see.

The Electromagnetic Spectrum

A profound puzzle accompanied Maxwell's original discovery that light is an electromagnetic wave. Waves can be of almost any length. Water waves on the ocean, for example, range from tiny ripples to globe-spanning tides. Yet visible light spans an extremely narrow range of wavelengths, only about 390 to 710 nanometers. According to the equations that Maxwell derived, electromagnetic waves could exist at any wavelength (and, consequently, any frequency) whatsoever. The only constraint is that the wavelength times the frequency must be equal to the speed of light. Yet when Maxwell looked into the universe, he saw visible light as the only obvious example of electromagnetic waves. It was as if a splendid symphony, ranging from the deep bass of the tuba to the sharp shrill of the piccolo, was playing, but you could hear only a couple of notes.

In such a situation, it would be natural to wonder what had happened to the rest of the waves. Scientists looked at Maxwell's equations, looked at nature, and realized that something was missing. The equations predicted that there ought to be more kinds of electromagnetic waves than light—waves performing the waltz between electricity and magnetism, but with frequencies and wavelengths different from those of visible light. These as-yet unseen waves would have exactly the same structure as the one shown in Figure 6-7, but they could have either longer or shorter wavelengths than visible light depending on the acceleration of the electrical charge that created them. These waves would move at the speed of light, and would be exactly the same as visible light except for the differences in the wavelength and frequency.

Between 1885 and 1889, German physicist Heinrich Rudolf Hertz (1857–1894), after whom the unit of frequency is named, performed the first experiments that

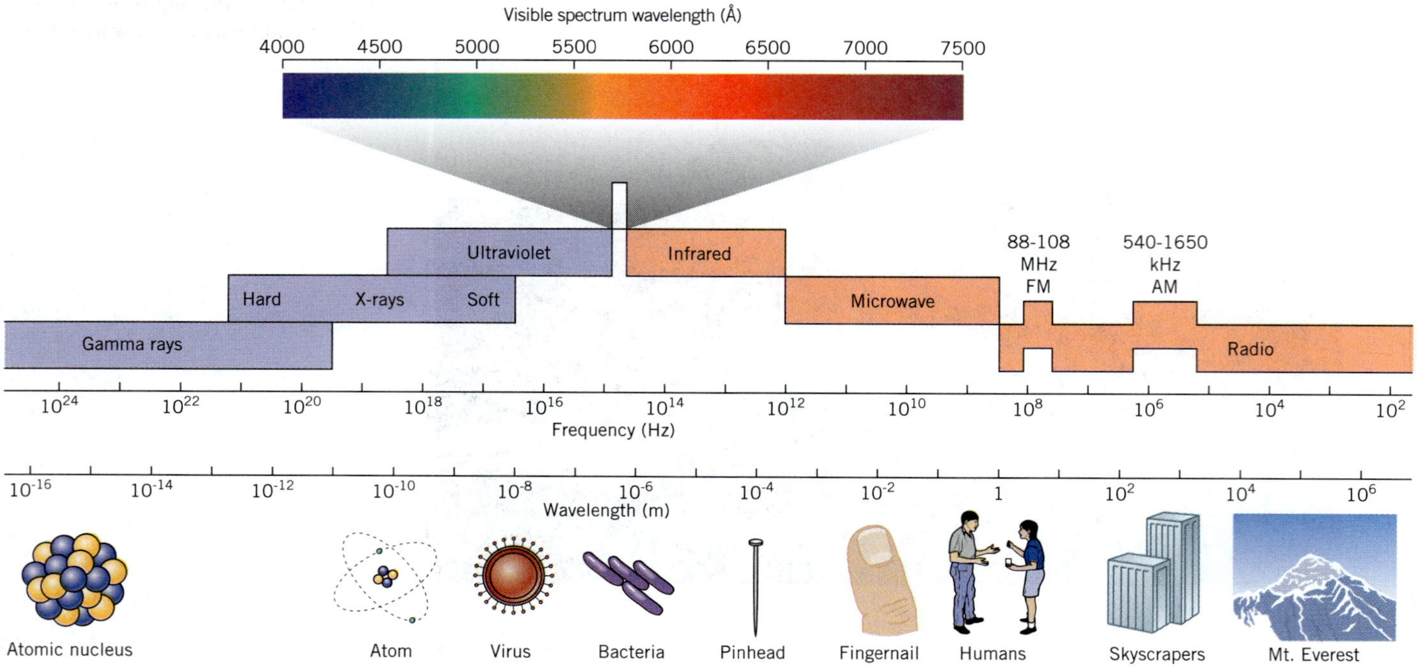

• **Figure 6-12** The electromagnetic spectrum includes all kinds of waves that travel at the speed of light in a vacuum, including radio, microwave, infrared, visible light, ultraviolet, X-rays, and gamma rays. Note that sound waves, water waves, seismic waves, and other kinds of waves that require matter in order to move travel *much* slower than light speed.

confirmed these predictions. He discovered the waves that we now know as radio. Since that time, all manner of electromagnetic waves have been discovered, from those with wavelengths longer than Earth's diameter to those with wavelengths shorter than the size of the nucleus of the atom. They include radio waves, microwaves, infrared, visible light, ultraviolet, X-rays, and gamma rays. This entire symphony of waves is called the **electromagnetic spectrum** (see Figure 6-12). Remember that every one of these waves, no matter what its wavelength or frequency, is the result of an accelerating electrical charge.

Radio Waves

The **radio wave** part of the electromagnetic spectrum ranges from the longest waves, those whose wavelength is longer than the size of Earth, to waves a few meters long. The corresponding frequencies, from roughly a kilohertz (a thousand cycles per second, or kHz) to several hundred megahertz (a million cycles per second, or MHz), correspond to the familiar numbers on your radio dial. There are various rather arbitrary subdivisions of radio waves, but the most important fact about them is that, like light, they can penetrate long distances through the atmosphere. This feature makes radio waves very useful in communication systems.

Have you ever been driving at night and picked up a radio signal from a station a thousand miles away? If so, you have had firsthand experience of the ability of radio waves to travel long distances through the atmosphere. In Chapter 14, we will see how important this fact is for astronomy, where scientists speak of the "radio window" in the atmosphere, which allows Earth-based telescopes to monitor radio waves emitted by objects in the sky.

A typical radio wave used for communication can be produced by pushing electrons back and forth rapidly in a tall metal antenna. This acceleration of electrons produces outgoing radio waves, just as throwing a pebble in a pond produces outgoing ripples. When these waves encounter another piece of metal (for example, the antenna in your radio or TV set), the electrical fields in the waves accelerate electrons in that metal, so that its electrons move back and forth. This electron motion constitutes an electrical current that electronics in your receiver turn into a sound or a picture.

Most construction materials are at least partially transparent to radio waves. Thus you can listen to the radio even in the basement of most buildings. In long tunnels or deep valleys, however, absorption of radio waves by many feet of rock and soil may limit reception.

In the United States, the Federal Communications Commission (FCC) assigns frequencies in the electromagnetic spectrum for various uses. Each commercial radio station is assigned a frequency (which it uses in association with its call letters), as is each television station. All manner of private communication—ship-to-shore radio, civilian band (CB) radio, emergency police and fire channels, and so on—need their share of the spectrum as well. In fact, the right to use a part of the electromagnetic spectrum for communications is very highly prized because only a limited number of frequency slices or "bands" exist, and many more people want to use those frequencies than can do so.

Technology •

AM and FM Radio Transmission

Radio waves carry signals in two ways: AM and FM. Broadcasters can send out their programs at only one narrow range of frequencies, a situation very different from music or speech, which use a wide range of frequencies. Thus radio stations cannot simply transform a range of sound-wave frequencies into a similar range of radio-wave frequencies. Instead, the information to be transmitted must be impressed in some way on the narrow frequency range of your station's radio waves.

This problem is similar to one you might experience if you had to send a message across a lake with a flashlight at night. You could adopt two strategies. You could send a coded message by turning the flashlight on and off, thus varying the brightness (the amplitude) of the light. Alternatively, you could change the color (the frequency) of the light by alternately passing blue and red filters in front of the beam.

Radio stations also adopt these two strategies (see Figure 6-13). All stations begin with a carrier wave of fixed frequency. AM radio stations typically broadcast at frequencies between about 530 and 1600 kHz (thousands of hertz), whereas the carrier frequencies of FM radio stations range from about 88 to 110 MHz (millions of hertz).

The process called *amplitude modulation,* or *AM,* depends on varying the strength (or amplitude) of the radio's carrier wave according to the sound signal to be transmitted (Figure 6-13*a*). Thus the shape of the sound wave is impressed on the radio's carrier wave signal. When this signal is taken into your radio, the electronics are designed so that the original sound signal is recovered and used to run the speakers. The original sound signal is what you hear when you turn on your radio. Because AM frequencies easily scatter off the layers of the atmosphere, they can be heard over great distances.

Alternatively, you can slightly vary the frequency of the radio's wave according to the signal you want to

• **Figure 6-13** AM (amplitude modulation) and FM (frequency modulation) transmission differ in the way that a sound wave (A) is superimposed on a carrier wave of constant amplitude and frequency (B). The carrier wave can be varied, or modulated, to carry information (C) by altering its amplitude or its frequency.

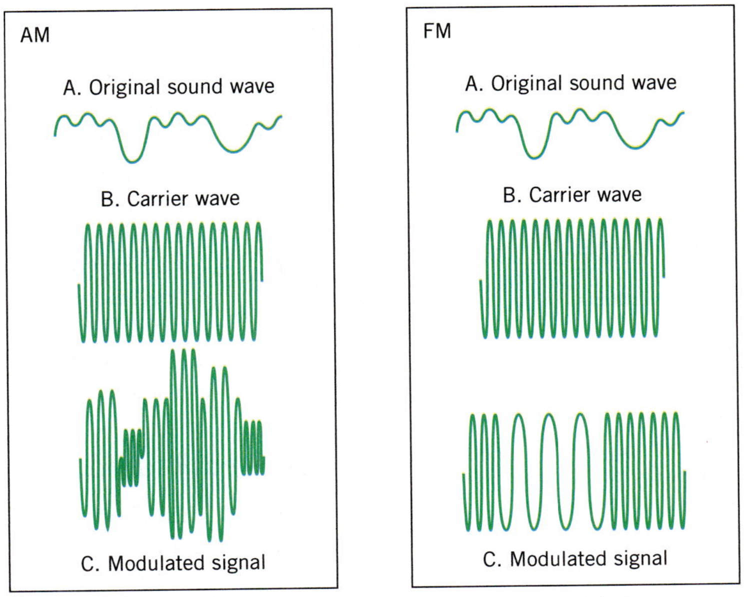

(*a*) Amplitude modulation

(*b*) Frequency modulation

U.S. Air Force Photo by Staff Sgt. Andy Dunaway, Department of Defense

The Stealth fighter has been engineered to reflect and absorb microwave radiation and thus avoid detection by radar.

transmit, a process called *frequency modulation,* or *FM,* as shown in Figure 6-13*b*. A radio that receives this particular signal will unscramble the changes in frequency and convert them into electrical signals that run the speakers so that you can hear the original signal. TV broadcasts, which use carrier frequencies about a thousand times higher than FM radio, typically send the picture on an AM signal, and the sound on an FM signal at a slightly different frequency. •

Microwaves

Microwaves include electromagnetic waves whose wavelengths range from about 1 meter (a few feet) to 1 millimeter (a thousandth of a meter, or about 0.04 inch). The longer wavelengths of microwaves travel easily through the atmosphere, like their cousins in the radio part of the spectrum, though most microwaves are absorbed by rock and building materials. Therefore, microwaves are used extensively for line-of-sight communications. Most satellites broadcast signals to Earth in microwave channels, and these waves also commonly carry long-distance telephone calls and TV broadcasts. The satellite antennas that you see on private homes and businesses are designed primarily to receive microwave transmissions, as are the large cone-shaped receivers attached to the microwave relay towers found on many hills or tall buildings.

The distinctive transmission and absorption properties of microwaves make them ideal for use in aircraft radar. Solid objects, especially those made of metal, reflect most of the microwaves that hit them. By sending out timed pulses of microwaves and listening for the echo, you can judge the direction, distance (from the time it takes the wave to travel out and back), and speed (from the Doppler effect) of a flying object. Modern military radar is so sensitive that it can detect a single fly at a distance of a mile. To counteract this sensitivity, aircraft designers have developed planes with "stealth" technology—combinations of microwave-absorbing materials, angled shapes that reduce the apparent cross section of the plane, and electronic jamming to avoid detection.

Technology •

Microwave Ovens

The same kind of waves used for phone calls, television broadcasts, and radar can be used to cook your dinner in an ordinary microwave oven. In this type of oven (Figure 6-14) a special electronic device accelerates electrons rapidly and produces the microwave radiation, which carries energy. These microwaves are guided into the main cavity of the oven, which is composed of material that scatters microwaves. Thus the wave energy remains inside the box until it is absorbed by something.

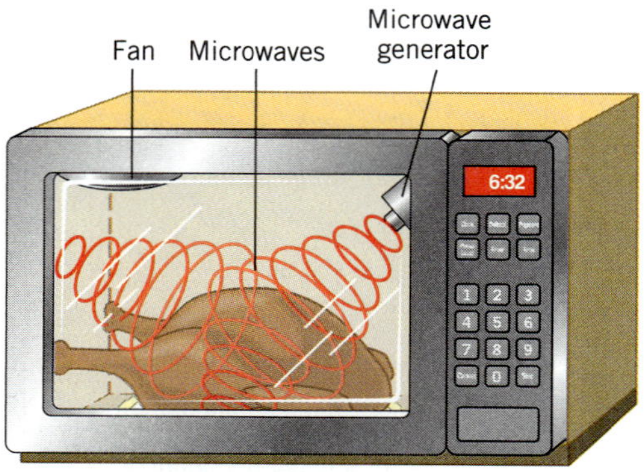

• **Figure 6-14** Every microwave oven contains a device that generates microwaves by accelerating electrons, and walls that scatter the microwaves until they are absorbed, usually by water molecules that get hot from the absorbed energy.

It turns out that microwaves are absorbed quickly by water molecules. This means that the energy used to create microwaves is carried by those waves to food inside the oven, where it is absorbed by water and converted into heat. This absorption of microwave energy results in a very rapid rise in temperature, and rapid cooking. Paper and glass, which don't contain water molecules, are not heated by microwaves. Despite the different applications, from the point of view of the electromagnetic spectrum there is no fundamental difference between the microwaves used for cooking and those used for communication. •

Infrared Radiation

Infrared radiation includes wavelengths of electromagnetic radiation that extend from a millimeter down to about a micron (10^{-6} meter, or less than a ten-thousandth of an inch). Our skin, which absorbs infrared radiation, provides a crude kind of detector. You feel infrared radiation when you reach your hands out to a warm fire or the cooking element of an electric stove. Infrared waves are what we feel as heat radiation (see Chapter 4).

All warm objects emit infrared radiation, and this fact has been used extensively in both civilian and military technology. Infrared detectors are used to guide air-to-air missiles to the exhaust of jet engines in enemy aircraft, and infrared detectors are often used to "see" human beings and warm engines at night. Similarly, many insects (such as mosquitoes and moths) and other nocturnal animals (including opossums and some snakes) have developed sensitivity to infrared radiation; thus they can "see" in the dark.

Infrared detection is also used to find heat leaks in homes and buildings (Figure 6-15). If you take a picture of a house on a cold night using film that is sensitive to infrared radiation, places where heat is leaking out will show up as bright spots on the film. This information can be used to correct the heat loss and thus conserve energy. In a similar way, Earth scientists often monitor volcanoes with infrared detectors. The appearance of a new "hot spot" may signal an impending eruption.

Tony McConnell/Photo Researchers

• **Figure 6-15** A photograph using infrared film reveals heat escaping from people. This "false-color" image is coded so that white is hottest, followed by red, pink, blue, and black.

Stop and Think! We often say that we get heat from the Sun. What actually travels between the Sun and Earth?

Visible Light

What we perceive as the colors of the rainbow are contained in **visible light,** whose wavelengths range from red light at about 700 nanometers down to violet light at about 400 nanometers (Figure 6-16). From the point of view of the larger universe, the visible electromagnetic world in which we live is a very small part of the total picture (see Figure 6-12).

Our eyes distinguish several different *colors,* but these portions of the electromagnetic spectrum have no special significance except in our perceptions. In fact, the distinct colors that we see—red, orange, yellow, green, blue, and violet—represent very different-sized slices of the electromagnetic spectrum. The red and green portions of the spectrum are rather broad, spanning more than 50 nanometers of frequencies; we thus perceive many different wavelengths as red or blue. In contrast, the yellow part of the spectrum is quite narrow, encompassing wavelengths from only about 570 to 590 nanometers.

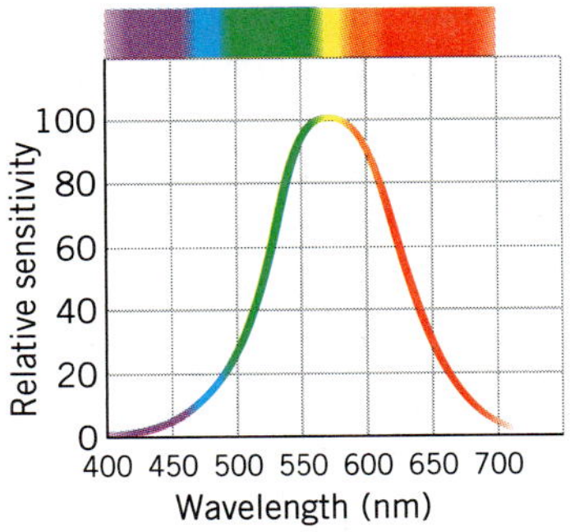

• **Figure 6-16** Humans perceive the visible light spectrum as a sequence of color bands. The relative sensitivity of the human eye differs for different wavelengths. Our perception peaks near wavelengths that we perceive as yellow, though the colors we see have no special physical significance.

Why should our eyes be so sensitive to such a restricted range of the spectrum? The Sun's light is especially intense in this part of the spectrum, so some biologists suggest that our eyes evolved to be especially sensitive to these wavelengths, in order to take maximum advantage of the Sun's light (Figure 6-16). Our eyes are ideally adapted for the light produced by our Sun during daylight hours. Animals that hunt at night, such as owls and cats, have eyes that are more sensitive to infrared wavelengths—radiation that makes warm living things stand out against the cooler background.

A glass prism separates white light into the visible spectrum of colors, because different wavelengths of light bend different amounts.

David Parker/Photo Researchers

The Science of Life •

The Eye

The light detector with which we are most familiar is one we carry around with us all the time—the human eye. Eyes are marvelously complex light-collecting organs that send nerve signals to the brain. Your brain converts these signals into images through a combination of physical and chemical processes (Figure 6-17).

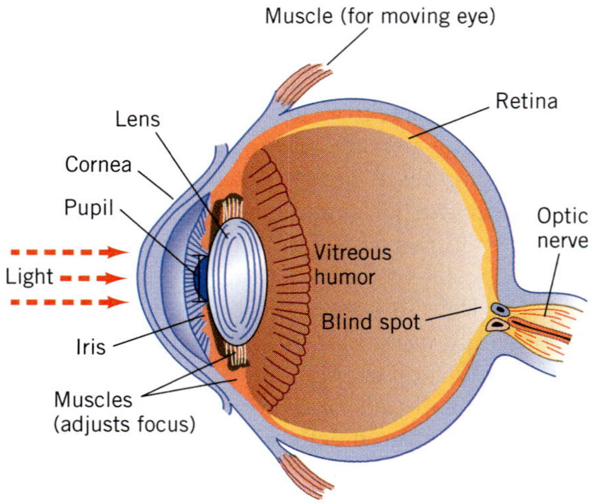

• **Figure 6-17** A cross section of the human eye reveals the path of light, which enters through the protective cornea and travels through the colored iris. The pupil changes the size of the aperture through which light passes, thus controlling the amount of light entering the eye. Muscles move the eye and change the shape of the lens, which focuses light onto the retina, where the light's energy is converted into nerve impulses. These signals are carried to the brain along the optic nerve.

Light waves enter the eye through a clear lens whose thickness can be changed by a sheath of muscles around it. The direction of the waves is changed by refraction in the lens so that they are focused at receptor cells located in the retina at the back of the eye. There the light is absorbed by two different kinds of cells, called rods and cones (the names come from their shape, not their function). The rods are sensitive to light and dark, including low levels of light; they give us night vision. Three kinds of cones, sensitive to red, blue, and green light, allow us to see colors

The energy of incoming light triggers complex changes in molecules in the rods and cones, initiating a series of reactions that eventually leads to a nerve signal that travels along the optic nerve to the brain (see Chapter 5). •

Ultraviolet Radiation

At wavelengths shorter than visible light, we begin to find waves of high frequency and therefore high energy and potential danger. The wavelengths of **ultraviolet radiation** range from 400 nanometers down to about 100 nanometers in length. The energy contained in longer ultraviolet waves can cause a chemical change in skin pigments, a phenomenon known as tanning. This lower-energy portion of the ultraviolet is not particularly harmful by itself.

Shorter-wavelength (higher-energy) ultraviolet radiation, on the other hand, carries more energy—enough energy that this radiation, if absorbed by your skin cells, can cause sunburn and other cellular damage. If the ultraviolet wave's energy alters your cell's DNA, it may increase your risk of developing skin cancer (see Chapter 23). In fact, the ability of ultraviolet radiation to damage living cells is used by hospitals to sterilize equipment and kill unwanted bacteria.

The Sun produces intense ultraviolet radiation in both longer and shorter wavelengths. Fortunately, our atmosphere absorbs much of the harmful short wavelengths and thus shields living things. Nevertheless, if you spend much time outdoors under a bright Sun, you should protect exposed skin with a sunblocking chemical, which is transparent (colorless) to visible light, but reflects or absorbs harmful ultraviolet rays before they can reach your skin.

The energy contained in both long and short ultraviolet wavelengths can be absorbed by atoms, which in special materials may subsequently emit a portion of that absorbed energy as visible light. (Remember, both visible light and ultraviolet light are forms of electromagnetic radiation, but visible light has longer wavelengths, and therefore less energy, than ultraviolet radiation.) This phenomenon, called *fluorescence,* provides the so-called black light effects so popular in stage shows and nightclubs. We'll examine the origins of fluorescence in more detail in Chapter 8.

X-rays

X-rays are electromagnetic waves that range in wavelength from about 100 nanometers down to 0.1 nanometer, smaller than a single atom. These high-frequency (and thus high-energy) waves can penetrate several centimeters into most solid matter but are absorbed to different degrees by all kinds of materials. This fact allows X-rays to be used extensively in medicine to form visual images of bones and organs inside the body. Bones and teeth absorb X-rays much more efficiently than skin or muscle, so a detailed picture of inner structures emerges. X-rays are also used extensively in industry to inspect for defects in welds and manufactured parts.

The X-ray machine in your doctor's or dentist's office is something like a giant lightbulb with a glass vacuum tube. At one end of the tube is a tungsten filament that is heated to a very high temperature by an electrical current, just as in an incandescent lightbulb. At the other end is a polished metal plate. X-rays are produced by applying an extremely high voltage—negative on the filament and positive on the metal plate—so electrons stream off the filament and smash into the metal plate at high velocity. The sudden deceleration of the negatively charged electrons releases a flood of high-energy electromagnetic radiation—the X-rays that travel from the machine to you at light speed.

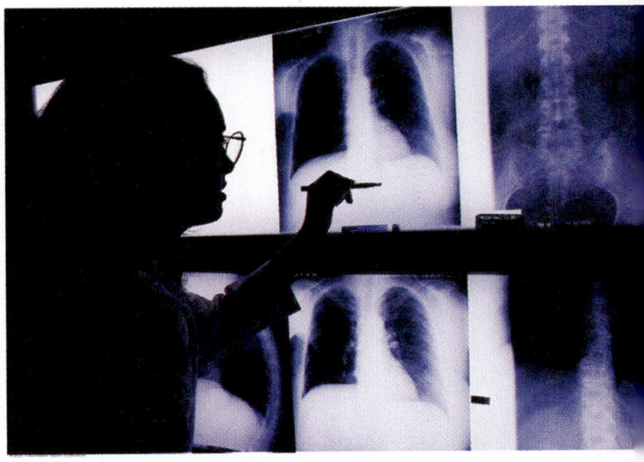

David Mendelsohn/Masterfile

A physician examines medical X-rays. Internal structures are revealed because bones and different tissues absorb X-rays to different degrees.

The Ongoing Process of Science •

Intense X-ray Sources

X-rays have become supremely important in many facets of science and industry. X-ray crystallographers use beams of X-rays to determine the spacing and positions of atoms in a crystal (see Chapter 10), physicians use X-rays to reveal bone fractures and other internal injuries, and many industries use X-rays to scan for defects in manufactured products. However, many potential applications, such as structural studies of very small crystals or scans of unusually large manufactured products, are unrealized because of the relatively low intensity of conventional X-ray sources.

A major effort is now under way to develop new, more powerful X-ray sources. One such facility, the Advanced Photon Source (APS) near Chicago, Illinois, generates intense X-ray beams a billion times stronger than conventional sources by accelerating electrons in a circular path (remember, electromagnetic radiation is emitted when charged particles are accelerated). Scientists converge on the APS from around the world to study the properties of matter. Eventually, even more powerful X-ray beams might be produced by an X-ray laser (see Chapter 8), though such a technology is now only a dream. •

(a) A variety of chemical reactions, including fire, produce light energy. *(b)* One way of producing light is to convert stored chemical energy, as is done in this emergency flare. *(c)* Chemical reactions also produce the light given off by a firefly.

(a)

Photo Disc, Inc.

(b)

Jamie McDonald/Getty Images News and Sport Services

(c)

Darwin Dale/Photo Researchers

Gamma Rays

The highest energies in the electromagnetic spectrum are called **gamma rays.** Their wavelengths range from slightly less than the size of an atom (about 0.1 nanometer, or 10^{-10} meter) to the size of a nucleus (less than a trillionth of a meter, or 10^{-12} meter). Gamma rays are normally emitted on Earth only in very high-energy nuclear and particle reactions (see Chapters 12 and 13), but they are produced abundantly in distant energetic stars (see Chapter 14).

Gamma rays have many uses in medicine. Some types of medical diagnosis involve giving a patient a radioactive chemical that emits gamma rays. If that chemical concentrates at places where bone is actively healing, for example, then doctors can monitor the healing by locating the places where gamma rays are emitted. The gamma ray detectors used in this specialized form of nuclear medicine are both large (to capture the energetic waves) and expensive. Doctors also use gamma rays for the treatment of cancer in humans. In these treatments, high-energy gamma rays are directed at tumors or malignancies that cannot be removed surgically. If the gamma ray energy is absorbed in those tissues, the tissues will die and the patient has a better chance to live.

Gamma rays are also studied extensively in astronomy because many of the interesting processes going on in our universe involve bursts of very high energy and, hence, the emission of gamma rays.

Thinking More About | Electromagnetic Radiation

Is ELF Radiation Dangerous?

Maxwell's equations tell us that any accelerated charge will emit waves of electromagnetic radiation, not just those that are frequencies of millions or billions of hertz. In particular, the electrons that move back and forth in wires to produce the alternating current in household wiring generate electromagnetic radiation. Every object in which electrical power flows, from power lines to toasters, is a source of this weak, *extremely low-frequency (ELF) radiation.*

For more than a century, human beings in industrialized countries have lived in a sea of weak ELF radiation, but until recently no questions were raised about whether that radiation might have an effect on human health. In the late 1980s, however, a series of books and magazine articles created a minor sensation by claiming that exposure to ELF radiation might cause some forms of cancer, most notably childhood leukemia.

Scientists tended to downplay these claims, because the electrical fields most residents experience due to power lines are a thousand times smaller than those due to natural causes (such as electrical activity in nerve and brain cells). They also pointed out that age-corrected cancer rates in the United States (with the exception of lung cancer, which is caused primarily by smoking) have remained constant or dropped over the last 50 years, though exposure to ELF radiation has increased enormously. They also questioned the statistical validity of some studies: more detailed analysis of results did not demonstrate the connection between ELF radiation and disease. In 1995, the prestigious American Institute of Physics reviewed the scientific literature on this subject and concluded that there is no reliable evidence that ELF radiation causes any form of cancer; most funding for research in this area was subsequently cut off.

This situation is typical of encounters at the border between science and public health. Preliminary data indicate a possible health risk but do not prove that the risk is real. Settling the issue by further study takes years, while researchers carefully collect data and weigh the evidence. In the meantime, people have to make decisions about what to do. In addition, as in the case of ELF radiation, the cost of removing the risk is often very high.

Suppose you were a scientist who had shaky evidence that some common food—bread, for example, or a familiar kind of fruit—could be harmful. What responsibility would you have to make your results known to the general public? If you stress the uncertainty of your results and no one listens, should you make sensational (perhaps unsupported) claims to get people's attention?

Summary

Waves provide a way to transfer energy from one place to another through a medium without matter actually traveling across the intervening distance. Every wave can be characterized by a *wavelength,* a velocity, an amplitude, and a *frequency* (measured in cycles per second, or *hertz*). Transverse waves, such as swells on the ocean, occur when the medium moves perpendicular to the direction of the waves. Longitudinal waves, such as sound, occur when the medium moves in the same direction as the wave.

Two waves can interact with each other, causing constructive or destructive *interference*. The observed frequency of a wave depends on the relative motion of the wave's source and the observer—a phenomenon known as the *Doppler effect*. Waves encountering a surface can be *reflected*, or they may enter the medium moving in a different direction, a process called *refraction*.

The motion of every wave can be described by a characteristic wave equation. James Clerk Maxwell recognized that simple manipulation of his equations that describe electricity and magnetism pointed to the existence of *electromagnetic waves* or *electromagnetic radiation*, alternating electrical and magnetic fields that can travel through a vacuum at the *speed of light*. This discovery solved one of the oldest mysteries of science, the nature of *light*. While visible light was the only kind of electromagnetic radiation known to Maxwell, he predicted the existence of other kinds with longer and shorter wavelengths. Soon thereafter a complete *electromagnetic spectrum* of waves, including *radio waves, microwaves, infrared radiation, visible light, ultraviolet radiation, X-rays,* and *gamma rays,* was recognized.

Electromagnetic radiation can interact with matter in three ways: it can be *transmitted, absorbed,* or *scattered*. We use these properties in countless ways every day—radio and TV, heating and lighting, microwave ovens, tanning salons, medical X-rays, and more. Much of science and technology during the past 100 years has been an effort to find new and better ways to produce, manipulate, and detect electromagnetic radiation.

Key Terms

wave
wavelength
frequency (measured in hertz)
interference
electromagnetic wave, or electromagnetic radiation
light
speed of light, *c*
Doppler effect
transmission
refraction
absorption
diffuse scattering
reflection
electromagnetic spectrum
radio wave
microwaves
infrared radiation
visible light
ultraviolet radiation
X-rays
gamma rays

Key Equations

wave velocity (m/s) = wavelength (m) × frequency (Hz)

$$\text{wavelength (m)} = \frac{\text{velocity (m/s)}}{\text{frequency (Hz)}}$$

1 hertz = 1 cycle/second

For light: wavelength (m) × frequency (Hz) = c

Constant: speed of light

c = 300,000 km/s = 3×10^8 m/s

Review Questions

1. Which form of energy transfer occurs when sunlight heats beach sand? when microwaves are used to detect the flight path of an airplane? when radio waves transmit music?

2. Identify three characteristics that can be used to describe a wave. How are these three related?

3. Identify everyday examples of waves that travel through solids, liquids, and gases.

4. Use a Slinky™ toy to illustrate the difference between a longitudinal wave and a transverse wave.

5. What happens when two different waves overlap?

6. Under what circumstances will an electromagnetic wave form? Under what circumstances will no electromagnetic waves be produced?

7. What features are shared by all electromagnetic waves? In what ways might two electromagnetic waves differ?

8. Why did Maxwell think there were kinds of electromagnetic radiation other than visible light?

9. What was meant by the ether? What prompted the assumption that it existed? What proof destroyed the idea of its existence?

10. A vat of molten iron is heated until white hot, then poured into a mold. As it cools, its color changes to yellow and then red. Explain why this occurs.

11. Identify three common uses of microwaves.

12. Why is short-wave ultraviolet light more damaging to the skin than long-wave ultraviolet light?

13. What are some uses of gamma rays?

14. What kinds of electromagnetic radiation can you detect with your body?

15. What are some of the similarities and differences between water waves and light waves?

16. Describe the Doppler effect. Give an example of how you experience this effect.

17. Identify a substance that:

a. absorbs radio waves

b. scatters microwaves

c. transmits visible light

d. absorbs X-rays

e. scatters infrared radiation

Discussion Questions

1. In what ways do ocean waves differ from electromagnetic waves? In what ways are they similar?

2. If a tree falls in a forest, what kinds of waves are created? Where did the energy that produced those waves come from?

3. Why does your body create a shadow? Is your body transparent to the visible spectrum? to X-rays?

4. How do reading glasses work? Describe how the light is interacting with the lens.

5. What is ether? How did Michelson and Morley demonstrate that ether does not exist? What was their hypothesis?

6. Why do people wear light-colored clothing in summer and dark-colored clothing in winter?

7. Why are X-rays used for medical diagnosis? What other wavelengths of electromagnetic radiation are used in medicine?

8. If a painted wall reflects light with wavelengths 600 to 700 nm, but absorbs light with wavelengths 400 to 500 nm, what color is it? What if it reflects light 400 to 500 nm and absorbs light 600 to 700 nm?

9. What causes a rainbow? What is happening to the sunlight to cause us to perceive many individual colors? Why do we not see all the colors all the time?

Problems

1. An organ pipe is 3 meters long. What is the frequency of the sound it produces? *Extra credit:* To what pitch does that frequency correspond?

2. An ocean liner experiences broad waves, called swells, with a frequency of one every 20 seconds (0.05 Hz) and a wavelength of 440 feet. Assume the waves are moving due east. If the liner maintains a speed of 15 miles per hour, will it have a smoother trip going east or west? Why?

3. Radio and TV transmissions are being emitted into space, so new *CSI* episodes are streaming out into the universe. The nearest star is 9.5×10^{17} meters away. If civilized life exists on a planet near this star, how long will they have to wait for the next episode?

4. What is the wavelength of the carrier wave used by your favorite radio station?

5. The FM radio band in most places goes from frequencies of about 88 to 108 MHz. How long are the wavelengths of the radiation at the extreme ends of this range?

6. The AM radio band in most places goes from frequencies of about 535 to 1610 kHz. How long are the wavelengths of the radiation at the extreme ends of this range?

7. Why can we see the moon at night? Calculate the amount of time it takes for light from the Sun to reach Earth after it is reflected from the Moon.

Investigations

1. Visit a local hospital and see how many types of electromagnetic radiation are used on a regular basis. From radio waves to gamma waves, how are the distinctive characteristics of absorption and transmission for each segment of the spectrum used at the facility?

2. What frequencies of electromagnetic radiation are used for emergency communications by police, fire, and medivac in your community? What are the corresponding wavelengths of these signals? What organizations allocate and monitor these frequencies?

3. Examine a microwave oven or, better yet, obtain an old broken oven that you can dissect. Locate the source of microwaves. Which materials in the oven transmit microwaves? Which ones scatter microwaves? Do you think any of the components absorb microwaves? Why?

4. In large metropolitan areas, a license to broadcast electromagnetic waves at an AM frequency may change hands for millions of dollars.

a. Why is electromagnetic "real estate" so valuable? Investigate how frequencies are divided up and who regulates the process. Should individuals or corporations be allowed to "own" portions of the spectrum, or to buy and sell pieces of it?

b. Currently, the only portions of the electromagnetic spectrum that are regulated by national and international law are the longer wavelengths, including radio and microwave. Why are the shorter wavelengths, including infrared, visible light, ultraviolet, and X-ray wavelengths, not similarly regulated?

5. Different colors represent different wavelengths of electromagnetic radiation. Investigate the process by which the human eye detects color, as well as the means by which the brain interprets color. Do all mammals see in color? How do we know?

6. Find out how sonar works. Compare it to the use of sound by bats and the use of radar by police. Discuss the similarities and differences among the defenses of submarines against sonar, moths against bats, and motorists against police radar.

7. What radio frequencies does your favorite local TV station use? your cell phone?

8. Keep an "electromagnetic journal" for one day. What activity makes use of the most electromagnetic energy?

9. When you are at a loud concert, you can actually "feel" the music. What are you feeling? What type of wave is being created?

10. The next time you are driving on a long stretch of road on a hot day, see if you can observe the mirage (i.e., an optical illusion) that is often seen in the distance. Why does it look like water? What causes this illusion?

11. What type of waves can travel through rock? How fast can they travel? Can you outrun an earthquake in a car?

7

Albert Einstein and the Theory of Relativity

Can a human ever travel faster than the speed of light, at "warp speed"?

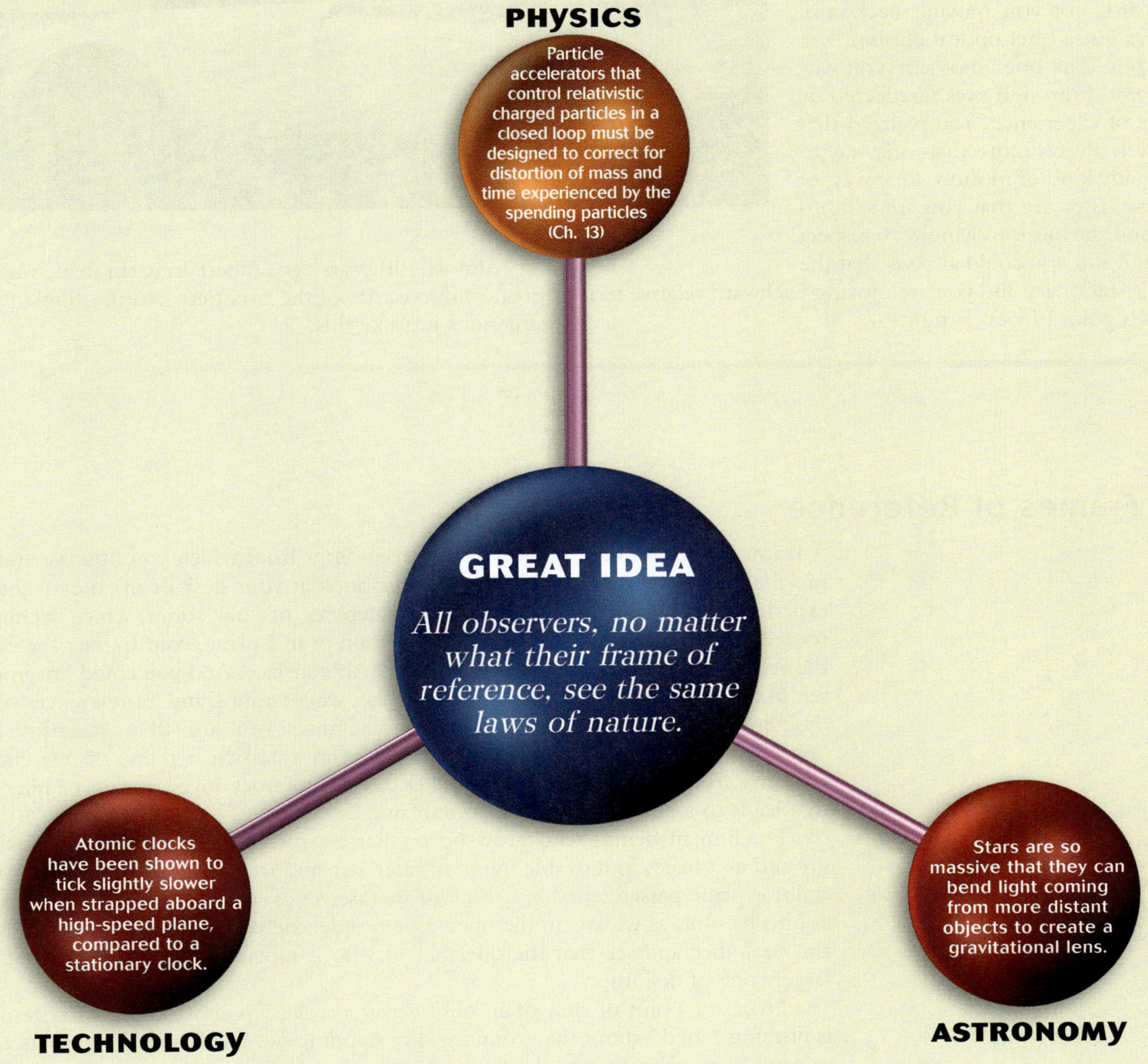

= applications of the great idea discussed in this chapter

= other applications, some of which are discussed in other chapters

Science Through the Day | Waiting at the Stoplight

Waiting in your car at a long stoplight, you daydream about the friends you're going to meet. You don't even notice the large bus in the lane next to you.

Suddenly you have the strange sensation that your car is moving backward. But your foot is on the brake—how can that be? You quickly realize that it's the bus that's moving forward, not you moving backward. It was just a brief optical illusion.

Jeff Titcomb/Photographer's Choice/Getty Images

For that brief moment you saw the world through eyes unaffected by years of experience. You realized that there is always more than one way to view any kind of motion. One way, of course, is to say that you are stationary and the bus is moving with respect to you. But you could also say that the bus is stationary and you are moving backward relative to it. Which point of view is right?

Almost 100 years ago, Albert Einstein made one of the greatest discoveries of the twentieth century thinking about situations just like this.

Frames of Reference

A **frame of reference** is the physical surroundings from which you observe and measure the world around you. If you read this book at your desk or in an easy chair, you experience the world from the frame of reference of your room, which seems firmly rooted to the solid Earth. If you read on a train or in a plane, your frame of reference is the vehicle that moves with respect to the Earth's surface. And you could imagine yourself in an accelerating spaceship in deep space, where your frame of reference would be different still. In each of these reference frames you are what scientists call an "observer." An observer looks at the world from a particular frame of reference with anything from casual interest to a full-fledged laboratory investigation of phenomena that leads to a determination of natural laws.

For human beings who grow up on Earth's surface, it is natural to think of the ground as a fixed, immovable frame of reference and to refer all motion to it. After all, train or plane passengers don't think of themselves as stationary while the countryside zooms by. But, as we saw in the opening example, there are indeed times when we lose this prejudice and see that the question of who is moving and who is standing still is largely one of definition.

From the point of view of an observer in a spaceship above the solar system, there is nothing "solid" about the ground you're standing on. Earth is rotating on its axis and moving in an orbit around the Sun, while the Sun itself is performing a stately rotation around the galaxy. Thus, even though a reference frame fixed in Earth may seem "right" to us, there is nothing special about it.

Descriptions in Different Reference Frames

Different observers in different reference frames may provide very different accounts of the same event. To convince yourself of this idea, think about a simple experiment. While riding on a train, take a coin out of your pocket and flip it. You know what will happen—the coin will go up in the air and fall straight back into your hand, just as it would if you flipped it while sitting in a chair in your room (Figure 7-1*a*). But now ask yourself this question: How would a friend standing near the tracks, watching your train go by, describe the flip of the coin?

To that person it would appear that the coin went up into the air, of course, but by the time it came down the car would have traveled some distance down the tracks. As far as your friend on the ground is concerned, the coin traveled in an arc (Figure 7-1*b*).

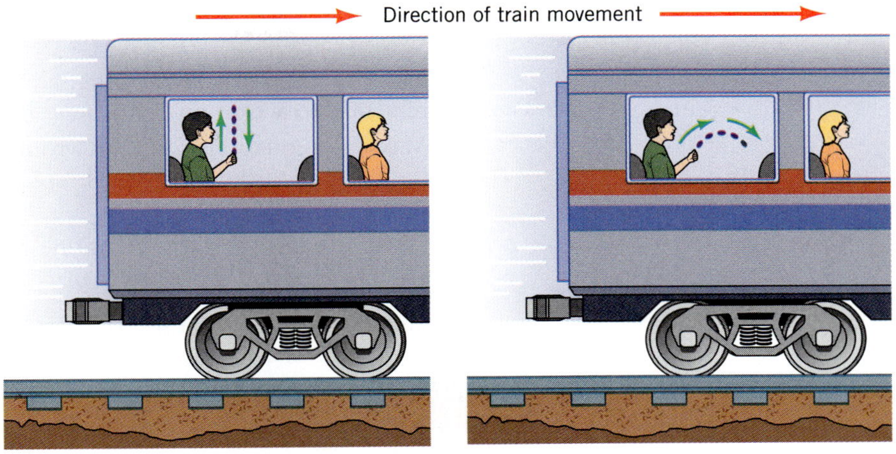

• **Figure 7-1** The path of a coin flipped in the air depends on the observer's frame of reference. *(a)* A rider in the car sees the coin go up and fall straight down. *(b)* An observer on the street sees the coin follow an arching path.

So you, sitting in the train, say the coin went straight up and down, while someone on the ground says it traveled in an arc. You and the ground-based observer would describe the path of the coin quite differently, and you'd both be correct in your respective frames of reference. The universe we live in possesses this general feature—different observers will describe the same event in different terms, depending on their frames of reference.

Does this mean that we are doomed to live in a world where nothing is fixed, where everything depends on the frame of reference of the observer? Not necessarily. The possibility exists that even though different observers give different descriptions of the same event, they will agree on the underlying laws that govern it. Even though the observers disagree on the path followed by the flipped coin, they may very well agree that motion in their frame is governed by Newton's laws of motion and the law of the universal gravitation.

The Principle of Relativity

Albert Einstein came to his theories of relativity by thinking about a fundamental contradiction between Newton's laws and Maxwell's equations. You can see the problem by thinking about a simple example. Imagine you're on a moving railroad car and you throw a baseball. What speed will the baseball have according to an observer on the ground?

If you throw the ball forward at 40 kilometers per hour while on a train traveling 100 kilometers per hour, the ball will appear to a ground-based observer to travel 140 km/h—40 km/h from the ball plus 100 km/h from the train. If, on the other hand, you throw the ball backward, the ground-based observer will see the ball moving at only 60 km/h—the train's 100 km/h minus the ball's 40 km/h. In our everyday world, we just add the two speeds to get the answer, and this notion is reflected in Newton's laws.

Suppose, however, that instead of throwing a ball you turned on a flashlight and measured the speed of the light coming from it. In Chapter 6 we saw that the speed of light is built into Maxwell's equations. If every observer

Time & Life Pictures/Getty Images News and Sport Services

Albert Einstein (1879–1955)

is to see the same laws of nature, they all have to see the same speed of light. In other words, the ground observer would have to see light from the flashlight moving at 300,000 km/s, and *not* 300,000 km/s plus 100 km/h. In this case, velocities wouldn't add, as our intuition tells us they must.

Albert Einstein thought long and hard about this paradox, and he realized that it could be resolved in only three ways:

1. The laws of nature are not the same in all frames of reference (an idea Einstein was reluctant to accept on philosophical grounds); or,
2. Maxwell's equations could be wrong and the speed of light depends on the speed of the source emitting the light (in spite of abundant experimental support for the equations); or,
3. Our intuitions about the addition of velocities could be wrong, in which case the universe might be a very strange place indeed.

Einstein focused on the third of these possibilities.

The idea that the laws of nature are the same in all frames of reference is called the *principle of relativity,* and can be stated as follows:

Every observer must experience the same natural laws.

This statement is the central assumption of Einstein's **theory of relativity.** Hidden beneath this seemingly simple statement lies a view of the universe that is both strange and wonderful. The extraordinary theoretical effort required to understand the consequences of this one simple assumption occupied Einstein during much of the first decades of the twentieth century.

Stop and Think! It may seem obvious that the laws of nature are the same everywhere in the universe, but how can we know for sure? How might you test this statement?

We can begin to understand Einstein's work by recalling what Isaac Newton had demonstrated three centuries earlier, that all motions fall into one of two categories: uniform motion or acceleration (Chapter 2). Einstein therefore divided his theory of relativity into two parts—one dealing with each of these kinds of motion. The easier part, first published by Einstein in 1905, is called **special relativity** and deals with all frames of reference in uniform motion relative to one another—reference frames that do not accelerate. It took Einstein another decade to complete his treatment of **general relativity,** mathematically a much more complex theory, which applies to any reference frame whether or not it is accelerating relative to another.

At first glance, the underlying principle of relativity seems obvious, perhaps almost too simple. Of course the laws of nature are the same everywhere—that's the only way that scientists can explain how the universe behaves in an ordered way. But once you accept that central assumption of relativity, be prepared for some surprises. Relativity forces us to accept the fact that nature doesn't always behave as our intuition says it must. You may find it disturbing that nature sometimes violates our sense of the "way things should be." But you'll have little problem with relativity if you just accept the idea that the universe is what it is, and not necessarily what we think it should be.

Another way of saying this is to note that our intuitions about how the world works are built up from experience with things that are moving at modest speeds—a few hundred, or at most a few thousand, miles per hour. None of us has any experience with things moving near the speed of light, so when we start examining phenomena in that range our intuitions won't necessarily apply. Strictly speaking, we shouldn't be surprised by anything we find.

Relativity and the Speed of Light

As the example of the train and the flashlight shows, one of the most disturbing aspects of the principle of relativity has to do with our everyday notions of speed. According to the principle, any observer, no matter what his or her reference frame, should be able to confirm Maxwell's description of electricity and magnetism. Because the speed of light is built into these equations, it follows that:

The speed of light, *c*, is the same in all reference frames.

Strictly speaking, this statement is only one of many consequences of the principle of relativity. However, so many of the surprising results of relativity follow from it that it is often accorded special status and given special attention in discussions of those theories.

Science in the Making •

Einstein and the Streetcar

Newton and his apple have entered modern folklore as a paradigm of unexpected discovery. A less-well-known incident led Albert Einstein, then an obscure patent clerk in Bern, Switzerland, to relativity.

One day, while riding home in a streetcar, he happened to glance up at a clock on a church steeple (Figure 7-2). In his mind he imagined the streetcar speeding up, moving faster and faster, until it was going at almost the speed of light. Einstein realized that if the streetcar were to travel at the speed of light, it would appear to someone on the streetcar that the clock had stopped. The passenger would be like a surfer on a light-wave crest—a crest that originated at 12 noon, for example—and the same image of the clock would stay with him.

On the other hand, a clock moving with him—his pocket watch, for example—would still tick away the seconds in its usual way. Perhaps, Einstein thought, *time as measured on a clock, just like motion, is relative to one's frame of reference.* •

• **Figure 7-2** Albert Einstein, moving away from a clock tower, imagined how different observers might view the passage of time. If Einstein were traveling at the speed of light, for example, the clock would appear to him to have stopped, even though his own pocket watch would still be ticking.

Special Relativity

Time Dilation

Think about how you measure time. The passage of time can be measured by any kind of regularly repeating phenomenon—a swinging pendulum, a beating heart, or an alternating electrical current. To get at the theory of relativity, though, it's easiest to think of a rather unusual kind of clock. Suppose, as in Figure 7-3, we had a flashbulb, a mirror, and a photon detector. A "tick-tock" of this clock would consist of the flashbulb going off, the light traveling to the mirror, bouncing down to the detector, and then triggering the next flash. By adjusting the distance, *d*, between the light source and mirror, these pluses could correspond to any desired time interval. This unusual "light clock," therefore, serves the same function as any other clock—in fact, you could adjust it to be synchronized with anything from a grandfather clock to a wristwatch.

Now imagine two identical light clocks: one next to you on the ground (Figure 7-3*a*), and the other whizzing by in a spaceship (Figure 7-3*b*). Imagine further that

• **Figure 7-3** A light clock incorporates a flashing light and a mirror. A light pulse bounces off the mirror and returns to trigger the next pulse. Two light clocks, one stationary *(a)* and one moving *(b)*, illustrate the phenomenon of time dilation. Light from the moving clock must travel farther, and so it appears to the stationary observer to tick more slowly.

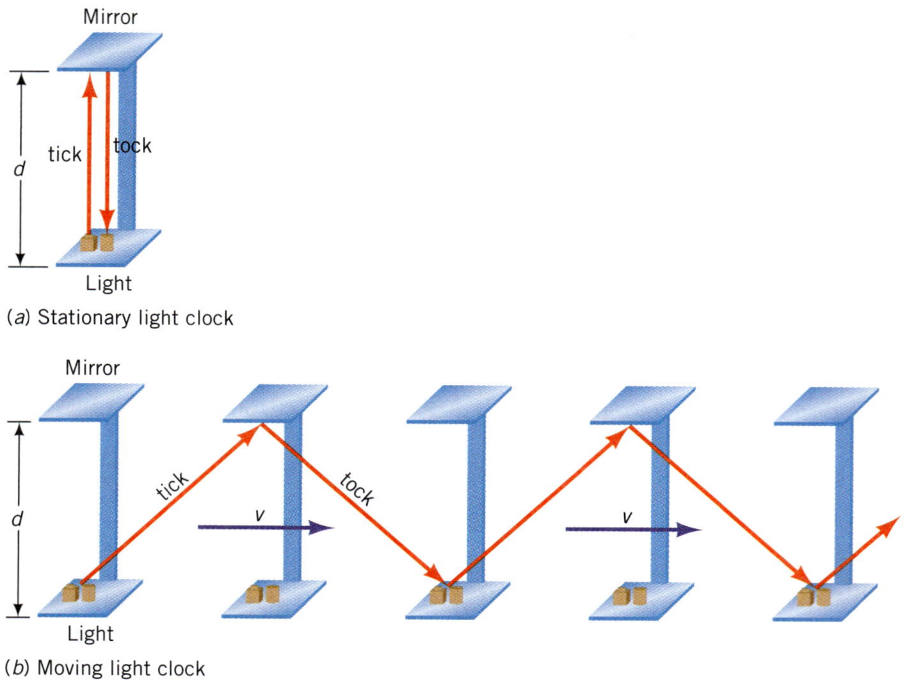

the mirrors are adjusted so that both clocks would tick at the same rate if they were standing next to each other. How would the moving clock look to you?

Standing on the ground, you would see the ground-based clock ticking along as the light pulses bounce back and forth between the mirror and detector. When you looked at the moving clock, though, you would see the light following a longer zig-zag path. If the speed of light is indeed the same in both frames of reference, it should appear to you that the light in the moving frame takes longer to travel the zig-zag path from light to detector than the light on the ground-based clock. Consequently, from your point of view on the ground, the moving clock must tick more slowly. The two clocks are identical, but the moving clock runs slower. This surprising phenomenon is known as **time dilation,** and it is an essential consequence of relativity.

Remember that each observer regards the clocks in his or her own reference frame as completely normal, while all other clocks appear to be running slower. Thus, paradoxically, while we observe the spaceship clock as slow, observers in the speeding spaceship see the Earth-based clock moving and believe that the Earth-based clock is running more slowly than theirs.

Relativity's prediction of time dilation can be tested in a number of ways. Scientists have actually documented relativistic time dilation by comparing two extremely accurate atomic clocks, one on the ground and one strapped into a jet aircraft. Even though jets travel at a paltry hundred-thousandth of the speed of light, the difference in the time recorded by the two clocks can be measured.

Time dilation can also be observed with high-energy particle accelerators that routinely produce unstable subatomic particles (see Chapter 12). The normal half-life of these particles is well known. When accelerated to near the speed of light, however, these particles last much longer because of the relativistic slowdown in their decay rates.

Thus, although the notion that moving clocks run slower than stationary ones violates our intuition, it seems to be well documented by experiment. Why, then, aren't we aware of this effect in everyday life? To answer that question, we have to ask how big an effect time dilation is. How much do moving clocks slow down?

The Size of Time Dilation

We have tried, in general, to talk about science in everyday terms and stay away from formulas in this book. But we have now run into a rather fundamental question that requires some simple mathematics to answer. In this section, you'll be able to follow the kind of thought process used by Einstein when he first formulated his revolutionary theory.

Consider the two identical light clocks in Figure 7-3, one moving at a velocity, v, and one stationary on the ground. Each clock has a light-to-mirror separation distance of d. (The various symbols we are using are summarized in Table 7-1).

Table 7-1 Symbols for Deriving Time Dilation

Symbol	Description
v	Velocity of the moving light clock relative to the ground
d	Distance between the clock's light and mirror
t_{GG}	Time for one tick (ground clock, ground observer)
t_{MG}	Time for one tick (moving clock, ground observer)
t_{GM}	Time for one tick (ground clock, moving observer)
t_{MM}	Time for one tick (moving clock, moving observer)
c	Speed of light, a constant

The notation for the time it takes for light to travel the distance d from the light to its opposite mirror—that is, one "tick" of the stationary clock—is a little trickier, because we have to keep track of which clock we're looking at and from which reference frame we're looking. We will use two subscripts—the first subscript to tell us if the clock is on the ground (G) or moving (M), and the second subscript to indicate if the observer is one the ground or moving. Thus, t_{GG} is the time for one tick of the ground-based clock as observed by an observer on the ground. On the other hand, t_{MG} is the time for one tick of the moving clock from the point of view of this ground-based observer. According to the principle of relativity, all observers see clocks in their own reference frames as normal. Or, in equation form,

$$t_{GG} = t_{MM}$$

As ground-based observers, we are interested in determining the relative values of t_{GG} and t_{MG}—what we see as "ticks" of the stationary versus the moving clocks. In the stationary ground-based frame of reference, one tick is simply the time it takes light to travel the distance d:

$$\text{time} = \frac{\text{distance}}{\text{speed}}$$

Substituting values for the light clock into this equation,

$$\text{time for one tick} = \frac{\text{light-to-mirror distance}}{\text{speed of light}}$$

or,

$$t_{GG} = \frac{d}{c}$$

where c is the standard symbol for the speed of light.

We argued that to the observer on the ground, it appears that the light beam in the moving clock travels on a zig-zag path as shown in Figure 7-3, and that this made the moving clock appear to run more slowly. In what follows, we will show how to take an intuitive statement like this one and convert it into a precise mathematical equation. We begin by labeling the dimensions of our two clocks.

The moving clock travels a horizontal distance of $v \times t_{MG}$ during each of its ticks. In order to determine the value of t_{MG}, we must first determine how far light must travel in the moving clock as seen by the observer on the ground. As illustrated in Figure 7-4, we know the lengths of the two shortest sides of a right triangle. One side has length d, representing the vertical distance between light and mirror (a distance, remember, that is the same in both frames of reference). The other side is $v \times t_{MG}$, which corresponds to the distance traveled by the moving clock as observed in the stationary frame of reference. The distance traveled by the moving light beam in one tick is represented by the hypotenuse of this right triangle and is given by the Pythagorean theorem.

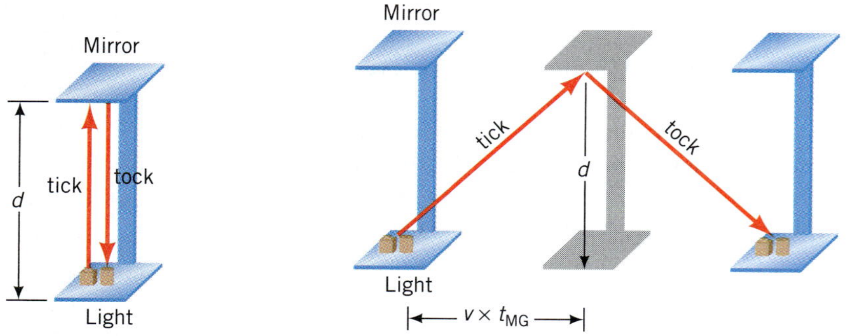

(a) Stationary light clock (b) Moving light clock

• **Figure 7-4** Light clocks with dimensions labeled. Both the stationary clock *(a)* and the moving clock *(b)* have light-to-mirror distance *d*. During one tick the moving clock must travel a horizontal distance $v \times t_{MG}$.

- ▶ **In words:** The square of the length of a right triangle's long side equals the sum of the squares of the lengths of the other two sides.
- ▶ **In words (applied to our light clock):** The square of the distance light travels during one tick equals the sum of the squares of the light-to-mirror distance and the horizontal distance the clock moves during one tick.
- ▶ **In symbols:**

$$(\text{distance light travels})^2 = d^2 + (v \times t_{MG})^2$$

We can begin to simplify this equation by taking the square roots of both sides.

$$\text{distance light travels} = \sqrt{d^2 + (v \times t_{MG})^2}$$

Remember, time equals distance divided by velocity. So the time it takes light to travel this distance, t_{MG}, is given by the distance $\sqrt{d^2 + (v \times t_{MG})^2}$ divided by the velocity of light, *c*:

$$t_{MG} = \frac{\sqrt{d^2 + (v \times t_{MG})^2}}{c}$$

We now must engage in a bit of algebraic manipulation. First, square both sides of this equation.

$$t_{MG2} = \frac{d^2}{c^2} + \frac{v^2 \times t_{MG2}}{c^2}$$

But we saw previously that $t_{GG} = d/c$, so, substituting,

$$t_{MG2} = t_{GG2} + \frac{v^2 \times t_{MG2}}{c^2}$$

Dividing both sides by t_{MG}^2 gives

$$\frac{t_{MG2}}{t_{MG}^2} = \frac{t_{GG2}}{t_{MG}^2} + \frac{[v^2 \times t_{MG}^2/c^2]}{t_{MG}^2}$$

or,

$$1 = \left(\frac{t_{GG}}{t_{MG}}\right)^2 + (v/c)^2$$

Finally, regrouping yields

$$t_{MG} = \frac{t_{GG}}{\sqrt{[1-(v/c)^2]}}$$

This equation expresses in mathematical form what we said earlier in words—that moving clocks appear to run slower. It tells us that t_{MG}, the time it takes for one tick of the moving clock as seen by an observer on the ground, is equal to the time it takes for one tick of an identical clock on the ground *divided by a number less than one*. Thus the time required for a tick of the moving clock will always be greater than that for a stationary one.

The expression $\sqrt{1-(v/c)^2}$ is a number, called the *Lorentz factor*, that appears over and over again in relativistic calculations. In the case of time dilation, the Lorentz factor arises from an application of the Pythagorean theorem.

One important point to notice is that if the velocity of the moving clock is very small compared to the speed of light, the quantity $(v/c)^2$ becomes very small and the Lorentz factor is almost equal to one. In this case, the time on the moving clock is equal to the time on the stationary one, as our intuition demands that it should be. Only when speeds get very high do the effects of relativity become important.

Science by the Numbers •

How Important Is Relativity?

To understand why we aren't aware of relativity in our everyday life, let's calculate the size of the time dilation for a clock in a car moving at 70 km/h (about 50 miles per hour).

The first problem is to convert the familiar speed in km/h to a speed in meters per second so we can compare it to the speed of light. There are 60 × 60 = 3600 seconds in an hour, so a car traveling 70 km/h is moving at a speed of

$$\begin{aligned} 70\ \text{km/h} &= \frac{70{,}000\ \text{m}}{3600\ \text{s}} \\ &= 19.4\ \text{m/s} \end{aligned}$$

For this speed, the Lorentz factor is

$$\sqrt{[1-(19.4/300{,}000{,}000)^2]} = 0.9999999999999999$$

Thus the passage of time for a stationary and speeding car differs by only one part in the sixteenth decimal place.

To get an idea of how small the difference is between the ground clock and the moving one in this case, we can note that if you watched the moving car for a time equal to the age of the universe, you would observe it running *10 seconds slow* compared to your ground clock.

For an object traveling at 99% of the speed of light, however, the Lorentz factor is

$$\begin{aligned} \sqrt{[1-(v/c)^2]} &= \sqrt{[1-(0.99)^2]} \\ &= \sqrt{(0.0199)} \\ &= 0.1411 \end{aligned}$$

In this case, you would observe the stationary clock to be ticking about seven times as fast as the moving one—that is, the ground clock would tick about seven times while the moving clock ticked just once.

This numerical example illustrates a very important point about relativity. Our intuition and experience tell us that the exterior clock on our local bank doesn't suddenly slow down when we view it from a moving car. Consequently, we find the prediction of time dilation to be strange and paradoxical. But all of our intuition is built up from experiences at very low velocities—none of us has ever moved at an appreciable fraction of the speed of light. For the everyday world, the predictions of relativity coincide precisely with our experience. It is only when we get into regions near the speed of light, where that experience isn't relevant, that the "paradoxes" arise. •

The Science of Life •

Space Travel and Aging

While humans presently do not experience the direct effects of time dilation in their day-to-day lives, at some future time they might. If we ever develop interstellar space travel with near-light speed, then time dilation may wreak havoc with family lives (and genealogists' records).

Imagine a spaceship that accelerates to 99% of the speed of light and goes on a long journey. While 15 years seem to pass for the crew of the ship, more than a century goes by on Earth. The space explorers return almost 15 years older than when they left, but biologically younger than their great-grandchildren! Friends and family all would be long-since dead.

If we ever enter an era of extensive high-speed interstellar travel, people may drift in and out of other people's lives in ways we can't easily imagine. Parents and children could repeatedly leapfrog each other in age, and the notion of relatedness could take on complex twists in a society with widespread relativistic travel. •

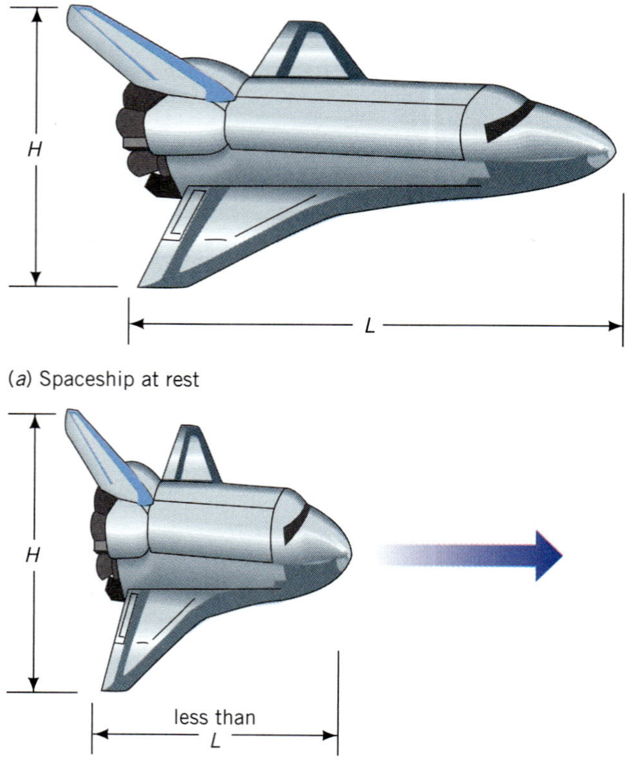

(*a*) Spaceship at rest

(*b*) Spaceship at high speed

• **Figure 7-5** A spaceship in motion appears to contract in length, *L*, along the direction of motion. However, the height, *H*, and width of the ship do not appear to change.

Distance and Relativity

Many results from relativity run counter to our intuition. They can be derived by procedures similar to (but more complicated than) the one we just gave for working out time dilation. In fact, using arguments like those we have presented, Einstein showed that *moving yardsticks must appear to be shorter than stationary ones in the direction of motion* (see Figure 7-5).

The equation that relates the ground-based observer's measurement of a stationary object's length, L_{GG}, to that observer's measurement of the length of an identical moving object, L_{MG}, is

$$L_{MG} = L_{GG} \times \sqrt{[1-(v/c)^2]}$$

The term on the right side of this equation is the familiar Lorentz factor that we derived from our study of light clocks. The equation tells us that the length of the moving ruler can be obtained by multiplying the length of the stationary ruler by a number less than one, and thus must appear shorter. This phenomenon is known as **length contraction.**

Note that the height and width of the moving object do not appear to change—only the length along the direction of motion. A moving basketball, then, takes on the appearance of a pancake at speeds near those of light.

Length contraction is not just an optical illusion. While relativistic shortening doesn't affect most of our daily lives, the effect is real. Physicists who work at particle accelerators inject "bunches" of particles into their machines. As these particles approach light speed, the bunches are observed to contract according to the Lorentz factor, an effect that must be compensated for.

> **Stop and Think!** What does the "spaceship at rest" in Figure 7-5 look like to an observer in the "spaceship at high speed?" Does it appear to be normal length, shorter, or longer?

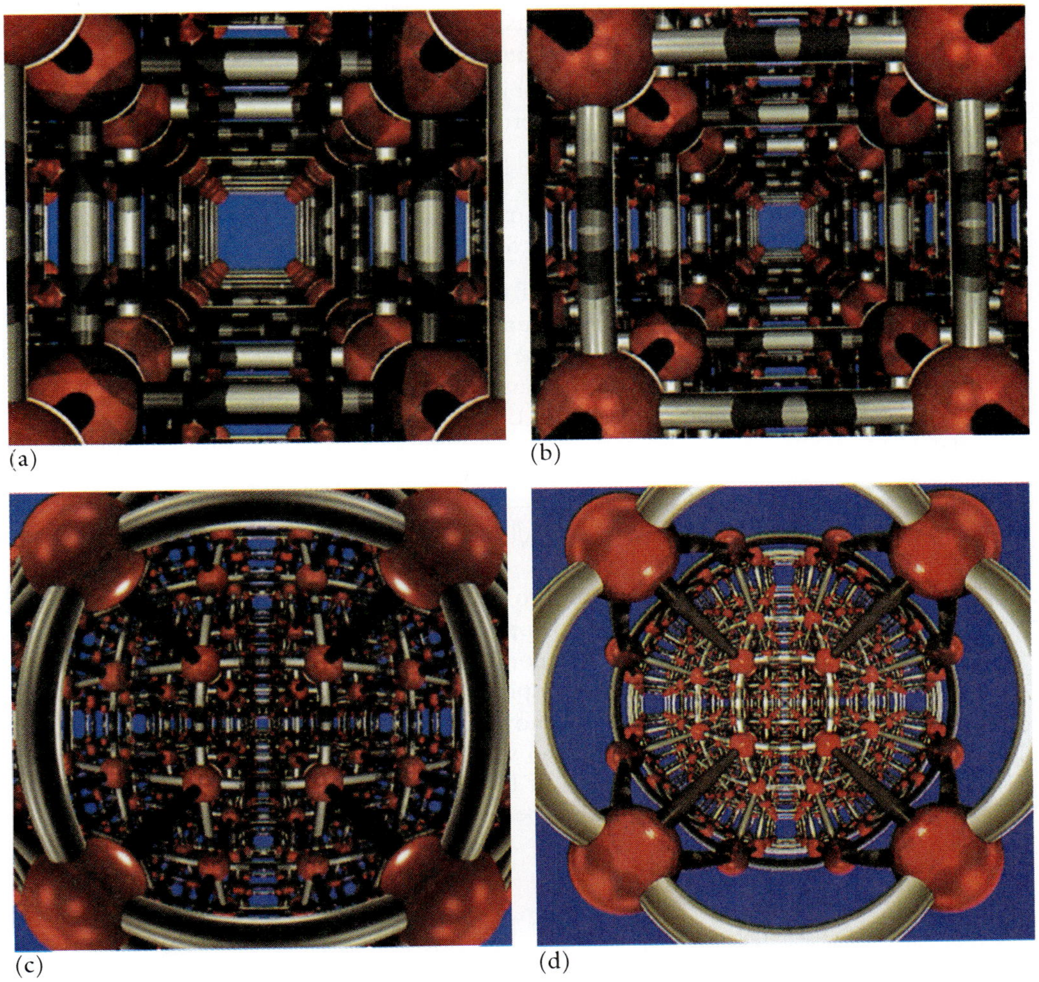

This series of four computer-generated images shows the changing appearance of a network of balls and rods as it moves toward you at different speeds. *(a)* At rest, the normal view. *(b)* At 50% of light speed, the array appears to contract. *(c)* At 95% of light speed, the lattice has curved rods. *(d)* At 99% of light speed, the network is severely distorted.

So What About the Train and the Flashlight?

Now that we understand a little about how relativity works, we can go back and unravel the paradox we discussed earlier in this chapter—the problem of how both an observer on the ground and an observer on the train could see light from a flashlight moving at the same speed.

Velocity is defined to be distance traveled divided by the time required for the travel to take place. Since both length and time appear to be different for different observers, it should come as no surprise that the rule that tells us how to add velocities (such as the velocity of the light and the train) might be more complicated than we would expect. The simple intuition that tells us that we should add the velocity of the train to the velocity of the ball, like our notions of time and space, is valid at small velocities but breaks down for objects moving near the speed of light. For those objects, a more complex addition has to be done, and when it is, we find that both observers see the light moving at a velocity of *c*.

Mass and Relativity

Perhaps the most far-reaching consequence of Einstein's theory of relativity was the discovery that mass, like time and distance, is relative to one's frame of reference. So far we have been faced with two strange ideas:

1. Clocks run fastest for stationary objects; moving clocks slow down. As the speed of light is approached, time slows down and approaches zero.
2. Distances are greatest for stationary objects; moving objects shrink in the direction of motion. As the speed of light is approached, distances shrink and approach zero.

Einstein showed that a third consequence followed from his principle:

3. Mass is lowest for stationary objects; moving objects become more massive. As an object's velocity approaches the speed of light, its mass approaches infinity.

Einstein showed that if the speed of light is a constant in all reference frames—which must follow from the central assumption of the theory of relativity—then an object's mass depends on its velocity. The faster an object travels, the greater its mass and the harder it is to deflect from its course. If a ground-based observer measures an object's stationary or "rest" mass, m_{GG}, then the apparent mass, m_{MG}, of that object moving at velocity v is

$$m_{MG} = \frac{m_{GG}}{\sqrt{[1-(v/c)^2]}}$$

Once again the Lorentz factor comes into play. As we observe an object approach the speed of light, its mass appears to us to approach infinity.

This property of mass leads to the common misperception that relativity predicts that nothing can travel faster than the speed of light. In fact, the only thing we can conclude is that nothing that is now moving at less than the speed of light can be accelerated to or past that speed. It also says that, should there exist objects already moving faster than light, they could not be decelerated to speeds of less than c, and that the only objects that travel at the speed of light (such as photons) are those that have zero rest mass.

Mass and Energy

Time, distance, and mass—all quantities that we can easily measure in our homes or laboratories—actually depend on our frame of reference. But not everything in nature is so variable. The central tenet of relativity is that natural laws must apply to every frame of reference. Light speed is constant in all reference frames in accord with Maxwell's equations. Similarly, the first law of thermodynamics—the idea that total amount of energy in any closed system is constant—must hold, no matter what the frame of reference. Yet here, Einstein's description of the universe seems to run into a problem. He claims that the observed mass depends on your frame of reference. But, in that case, kinetic energy—defined as mass times velocity squared—could not follow the conservation of energy law. In Einstein's treatment, faster frames of reference seem to possess more energy than slower ones. Where does the extra energy come from?

Conservation of energy appeared to be violated because we missed one key form of energy in our equations: mass itself. In fact, Einstein was able to show that the amount of energy contained in any mass turns out to be the mass times a constant.

- ▶ **In words:** All objects contain a rest energy (in addition to any kinetic or potential energy), which is equal to the object's rest mass times the speed of light squared.
- ▶ **In equation form:**

$$\text{rest energy} = \text{rest mass} \times (\text{speed of light})^2$$

- ▶ **In symbols:**

$$E = mc^2$$

This familiar equation has become an icon of our nuclear age, for it defines a new form of energy. It says that mass can be converted to energy, and vice versa. Furthermore, the amounts of energy involved are prodigious (because the constant, the speed of light squared, is so large). A handful of nuclear fuel can power a city; a fist-sized chunk of nuclear explosive can destroy it.

Until Einstein traced the implications of special relativity, the nature of mass and its vast potential for producing energy was hidden from us. Now nearly a quarter of all electrical power in the United States is produced in nuclear reactors that confirm the predictions of Einstein's theory every day of our lives (see Chapter 12).

General Relativity

Special relativity is a fascinating and fairly accessible intellectual exercise, requiring little more than an open mind and a lot of basic algebra. General relativity, which deals with all reference frames including accelerating ones, is much more challenging in its full rigor. While the details are tricky, you can get a pretty good feeling for Einstein's general theory by thinking about the nature of forces.

The Nature of Forces

Begin by imagining yourself in a completely sealed room that is accelerating at exactly one "*g*"—Earth's gravitational acceleration. Could you devise any experiment that would reveal one way or the other if you were on Earth or accelerating in deep space?

If you dropped this book on Earth, the force of gravity would cause it to fall to your feet (Figure 7-6*a*). If you dropped the book in the accelerating spaceship, however, Newton's first law tells us that it will keep moving with whatever speed it had when it was released. The floor of the ship, still accelerating, will therefore come up to meet it (Figure 7-6*b*). To you, standing in the ship, it appears that the book falls, just as it does if you are standing on Earth.

(*a*) On Earth

(*b*) In an accelerating spaceship

• **Figure 7-6** *(a)* If you drop a book on Earth, the force of gravity causes it to accelerate downward and fall at your feet. *(b)* If you dropped the same book in an accelerating spaceship, the floor of the ship will accelerate upward: the book will appear to fall at your feet.

From an external frame of reference, of course, these two situations would involve very different descriptions. In the one case of the book falls due to the force of gravity; in the other the spaceship accelerates up to meet the free-floating book. But no experiment you could devise *in your reference frame* could distinguish between acceleration in deep space and the force of Earth's gravitational field.

In some deep and profound way, therefore, gravitational forces and acceleration are equivalent. Newton saw this connection in a way, for his laws of motion equate force with an accelerating mass. But Einstein went a step further by recognizing that what we call gravity versus what we call acceleration is a purely arbitrary decision, based on our choice of reference frame. Whether we think of ourselves as stationary on a planet with gravity, or accelerating on spaceship Earth, makes no difference in the passage of events.

Although this connection between gravity and acceleration may seem a bit abstract, you already have had experiences that should tell you it is true. Have you ever been in an elevator and felt momentarily heavier when it starts up or momentarily lighter when it starts down? If so, you know that the feeling we call "weight" can indeed be affected by acceleration.

The actual working out of the consequences of this notion of the equivalence of acceleration and gravity is complicated, but a simple analogy can help you visualize the difference between Einstein's and Newton's views of the universe. In the Newtonian universe,

• **Figure 7-7** Newtonian and Einsteinian universes treat the motion of rolling balls in different ways. In the Newtonian scheme *(a)*, a ball travels in uniform motion unless acted upon by a force; motion occurs along curved paths in a flat universe. In the Einsteinian universe *(b)*, a ball's mass distorts the universe; it moves in a straight line across a curved surface.

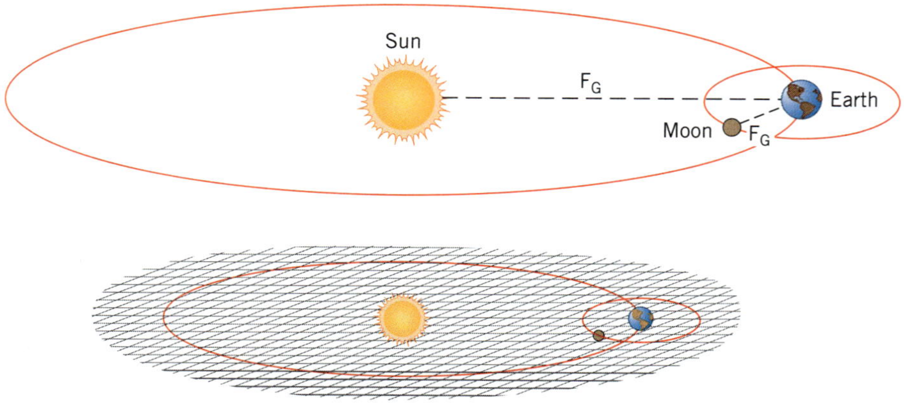

(*a*) Newtonian universe: gravitational forces in a "flat" universe

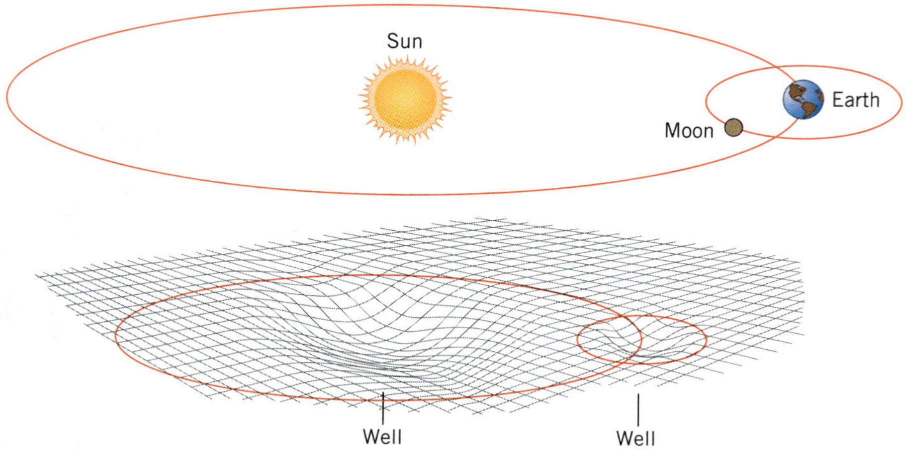

(*b*) Einstein's universe: motion in a curved universe.

forces and motions can be described by a ball rolling on a perfectly flat surface with neatly inscribed grid lines (Figure 7-7*a*). The ball rolls on and on, following a line exactly, unless an external force is applied. If, for example, a large mass rests on the surface, the rolling ball will change its direction and speed—it will accelerate in response to the force of gravity. Thus, for Newton, motion occurs along curving paths in a flat universe.

The description of that same event in general relativity is very different. In this case, as shown in Figure 7-7*b*, we would say that the heavy object distorts the surface. Peaks and depressions on the surface influence the ball's path, deflecting it as it rolls across the surface. For Einstein, the ball moves in a straight line across a curved universe.

Imtek Imagineering/Masterfile

A computer-generated image of a gravity field reveals mass as gravity wells on an otherwise flat grid.

Given these differing views, Newton and Einstein would give very different descriptions of physical events. Newton would say, for example, that the Moon orbits Earth because of an attractive gravitational force between the two bodies (Figure 7-6*a*). Einstein, on the other hand, would say that space has been warped in the vicinity of the Earth–Moon system, and this warping of space governs the Moon's motion (Figure 7-6*b*). In the relativistic view, space deforms around the Sun, and planets follow the curvature of space like marbles rolling around in the bottom of a curved bowl.

We now have two very different ways of thinking about the universe. In the Newtonian universe, forces cause objects to accelerate. Space and time are separate dimensions that are experienced in very different ways. This view more closely matches our everyday experience of how the world seems to be. In Einstein's universe, objects move according to distortions in space, while the distinction between space and time depends on your frame of reference.

You will notice that both Newton and Einstein treat gravity as a force that is always attractive. There's no room for a repulsive force—an "antigravity"—in these theories. In Chapter 15 we discuss some new developments in cosmology that may change this aspect of gravitation. The discovery of what is called "dark energy" indicates that there is another kind of force in the universe—one that, on the scale of galaxies, can be repulsive and play the role of antigravity.

Courtesy NASA, Richard Ellis (Caltech) and Jean-Paul Kneib (Observatoire Midi-Pyrenees, France)

A gravitational lens. A distant massive object bends the light from even more distant objects beyond, causing multiple images.

Predictions of General Relativity

The mathematical models of Newton and Einstein are not just two equivalent descriptions of the universe. They lead to slightly different quantitative predictions of events. In three specific instances, the predictions of general relativity have been confirmed.

1. **The Gravitational Bending of Light**
   One consequence of Einstein's theory is that light can be bent as it travels along the warped space near strong gravitational centers such as the Sun. Einstein predicted the exact amount of deflection that would occur near the Sun, and his prediction was confirmed by precise measurements of star positions during a solar eclipse in 1919. Today these measurements are made with much more precision by measuring the deflection of radio waves emitted by distant galaxies called quasars (see Chapter 18).

> **Stop and Think!** Given what you know about electromagnetic waves, do you think general relativity should predict that other waves—radio, for example—should be bent as they come around the Sun?

2. **Planetary Orbits**
   In Newton's solar system, the planets adopt elliptical orbits, with long and short axes that rotate slightly because of the perturbing influence of other planets. Einstein's calculations make nearly the same prediction, but his axes advance slightly more than Newton's from orbit to orbit. In Einstein's theory, for example, the innermost planet, Mercury, was predicted to advance by 43 seconds of arc per century due to relativistic effects—a small perturbation superimposed on much larger effects due to the other planets. Einstein's prediction almost exactly matches the observed shift in Mercury's orbit.
3. **The Gravitational Redshift**
   The theory of relativity predicts that as a photon (a particle of electromagnetic radiation) moves up in gravitational field, it must lose energy in the process. The speed of light is constant, so this energy loss is manifest as a slight decrease in frequency (a slight increase in wavelength). Thus lights on Earth's surface will appear slightly redder than they do on Earth if they are observed from space. By the same token, a light shining from space to Earth will be slightly shifted to the blue end of the spectrum. Careful measurements of laser light frequencies have amply confirmed this prediction of relativity.

These three instances are regarded as the "classical" tests of general relativity. For the greater part of the twentieth century they were all the experimental evidence that scientists had for general relativity. Over the last several decades, however, we have gotten better at making very precise measurements, so that even tiny differences between Newtonian gravity and general relativity can be probed. One particularly interesting example can be seen in an experiment known as Gravity Probe B.

Scientists have known for some time that general relativity predicts tiny, but strange, deviations in the spin of a gyroscope orbiting Earth. One of these effects comes from the motion of the gyroscope through space–time that has been warped by Earth's mass; the other effects are due to the fact that Earth's rotation tends to drag the surrounding space–time with it.

In the 1960s, two scientists at Stanford University—theorist Leonard Schiff and experimentalist Francis Everitt—began to think about designing an experiment to test Einstein's predictions. The result of decades of work by scores of physicists and engineers was launched into orbit by NASA in 2004.

The heart of the experiment is four ping-pong ball–sized spheres that spin and act as gyroscopes. Made of niobium-covered quartz, they have been called both "the world's roundest objects" and "the world's most uniformly dense objects." (The spheres have to be both round and uniform to allow scientists to measure the tiny changes in their direction of motion predicted by general relativity.) If one of the spheres were blown up to Earth's size, for example, the highest "mountain" would be only several feet tall; the quartz in them is so uniform that they have been used to help establish new international density standards. Gravity Probe B stopped taking data in the fall of 2005, when the liquid helium used to keep the gyroscopes cold began to run out.

Who Can Understand Relativity?

Einstein's theory of relativity was extraordinary, but when first introduced it was difficult to grasp in part because it relied on some complex mathematics that were unfamiliar to many scientists at the time. Furthermore, while the theory made specific predictions about the physical world, most of those predictions were exceedingly difficult to test. Soon after the theory's publication it became conventional wisdom that only a handful of geniuses in the world could understand it.

Einstein did make one very specific prediction, however, that could be tested. His proposal that the strong gravitational field of the Sun would bend the light coming from a distant star was different from other theories. The total eclipse of the Sun in 1919 gave scientists the chance to test Einstein's prediction. Sure enough, the apparent position of stars near the Sun's disk was shifted by exactly the predicted amount.

Around the world, front-page newspaper headlines trumpeted Einstein's success. He became an instant international celebrity, and his theory of relativity became a part of scientific folklore. Attempts to explain the revolutionary theory to a wide audience began almost immediately.

Few scientists may have grasped the main ideas of general relativity in 1915, when the full theory was first unveiled, but that certainly is not true today. The basics of special relativity are taught to tens of thousands of college freshmen every year, while hundreds of students in astronomy and physics explore general relativity in its full mathematical splendor.

If this subject intrigues you, you might want to read some more, watch TV specials or videos about relativity, or even sign up for one of those courses!

Thinking More About | Relativity

Was Newton Wrong?

The theory of relativity describes a universe about which Isaac Newton never dreamed. Time dilation, contraction of moving objects, and mass as energy play no role in his laws of motion. Curved space–time is alien to the Newtonian view. Does that mean that Newton was wrong? Not at all.

In fact, all of Einstein's equations reduce exactly to Newton's laws of motion, at speeds significantly less than the speed of light. This feature was shown specifically for time dilation in the "Science by the Numbers" section in this chapter. Newton's laws, which have worked so well in describing our everyday world, fail only when dealing with extremely high velocities or extremely large masses. Thus Newton's laws represent an extremely important special case of Einstein's more general theory.

Science often progresses in this way, with one theory encompassing previous valid ideas. Newton, for example, merged discoveries by Galileo of Earth-based motions and Kepler's laws of planetary motion into his unified theory of gravity. And someday Einstein's theory of relativity may be incorporated into an even grander view of the universe.

Summary

Every observer sees the world from a different *frame of reference.* Descriptions of actual physical events are different for different observers, but the *theory of relativity* states that all observers must see the universe operating according to the same laws. Because the speed of light is built into Maxwell's equations, this principle requires that all observers must see the same speed of light in their frames of reference.

Special relativity deals with observers who are not accelerating with respect to each other, while general relativity deals with observers in any frame of reference whatsoever. In special relativity, simple arguments lead to the conclusion that moving clocks appear to tick more slowly than stationary ones—a phenomenon known as *time dilation.* Furthermore, moving objects appear to get shorter in the direction of motion—the phenomenon of *length contraction.* Finally, moving objects become more massive than stationary ones, and an equivalence exists between mass and energy, as expressed by the famous equation, $E = mc^2$.

General relativity begins with the observation that the force of gravity is connected to acceleration, and describes a universe in which heavy masses warp the fabric of space–time and affect the motion of other objects. There are three classic tests of general relativity—the bending of light rays passing near the Sun, the changing orientation of the orbit of Mercury, and the redshift of light passing through a gravitational field.

Key Terms

frame of reference
theory of relativity
special relativity
general relativity
time dilation
length contraction

Key Equations

Time dilation: $t_{MG} = \dfrac{t_{GG}}{\sqrt{[1-(v/c)^2]}}$

Length contraction: $L_{MG} = L_{GG} \times \sqrt{[1-(v/c)^2]}$

Mass effect: $m_{MG} = \dfrac{m_{GG}}{\sqrt{[1-(v/c)^2]}}$

Rest mass: $E = mc^2$

Review Questions

1. What is a frame of reference? Give examples of frames of reference you have been in today.
2. What is the central idea of Einstein's theory of relativity?
3. What is the difference between special and general relativity?
4. What is time dilation? How fast does something have to be moving for time dilation to be appreciable?
5. What is the Lorentz factor?
6. According to an observer on the ground, how does the length of a moving object compare to the length of an identical object on the ground? How does the mass compare?
7. What is the relation between the mass of an object and its energy?
8. How can we say that gravitational forces and acceleration are equivalent?
9. Explain three tests of general relativity. Are these the only tests possible?
10. According to Einstein's theory, which of the following factors depend on the frame of reference and which are constant? mass, distance, velocity of light, time, length.

Discussion Questions

1. Imagine arriving by spaceship at the solar system for the first time. Identify three different frames of reference that you might choose to describe Earth.
2. Did Einstein disprove Newton's laws of motion? Explain your answer.
3. In Chapter 2 we talked about the idea that Newton's work was profoundly in tune with the time in which he lived. In what sense might you say that relativity is in tune with the twentieth century?
4. The twentieth century has been called the age of relativism, where each person has his or her own ethical system and no set of values is absolute. Do you agree? Does the theory of relativity imply that no values are absolute?
5. Is is possible for matter to travel faster than the speed of light?
6. What are the variables in $E = mc^2$?

Problems

1. You are traveling 80 km/h in your car when you throw a ball 50 km/h. What is the ball's apparent speed to a person standing by the road when the ball is thrown (a) straight ahead, (b) sideways, and (c) backward?

2. Calculate the Lorentz factor for objects traveling at 1%, 50%, and 99.9% of the speed of light.

3. What is the apparent mass of a 1-kg object that has been accelerated to 99% of light speed?

4. If a moving clock appears to be ticking half as fast as normal, at what percent of light speed is it traveling?

5. Draw a picture illustrating how a spaceship passing the Earth might look at 1%, 90%, and 99.9% of light speed.

Investigations

1. Read a biography of Albert Einstein. What were his major scientific contributions? For what work did he receive a Nobel Prize?

2. Take a bathroom scale into an elevator in a tall building, stand on it, and record your weight under acceleration and deceleration. Why does the scale reading change?

3. Read the novel *Einstein's Dreams* by Alan Lightman. Each of the chapters explores different time–space relationships. Which chapters teach you something about Einstein's theory of relativity?

4. Investigate the influence of Einstein's theory of relativity on twentieth-century art and philosophy.

5. $E = mc^2$ is a cultural icon. Can you think of any other scientific theories or equations that are as recognizable?

8

The Atom

Why are there so many different materials in the world?

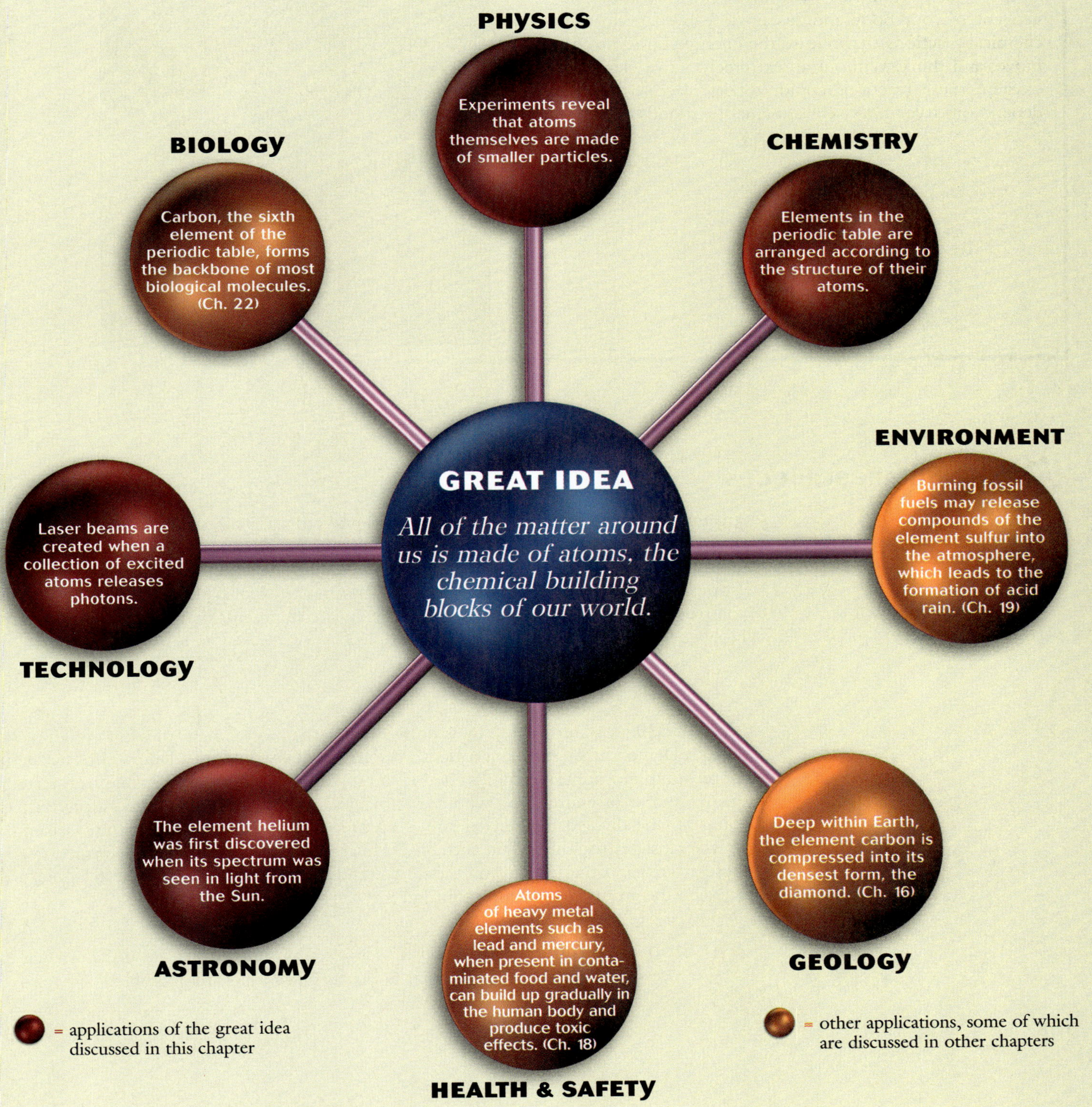

Science Through the Day | A Deep Breath

It's a beautiful day. As you drive down the road, into the open countryside, you open the window and take a deep breath of air. It's so relaxing to get away from school and work.

Breathing is so instinctive that we seldom stop to think about why we need oxygen. Oxygen is a chemical element, one of about a hundred basic building blocks that make up all the objects around us. With every breath you take, oxygen enters your body and sustains life by participating in chemical reactions that release the energy you use to grow, move, and think. Without an extremely active element like oxygen, these reactions couldn't take place. So our lives depend on oxygen, as well as many other kinds of atoms.

Peter Cade/Stone/Getty Images

The Smallest Pieces

Imagine that you took a page from this book and cut it in half, then cut the half in half, then cut half of the half in half, and so on. Two outcomes are possible. On the one hand, if paper is smooth and continuous then there would be no end to this process, no smallest piece of paper that couldn't be cut further. On the other hand, you might find that you reach a point where one more cut results in two fragments that are no longer paper. How could you tell if paper has a smallest piece?

The Greek Atom

In about 530 B.C., a group of Greek philosophers, the most famous of whom was a man named Democritus, gave this question some serious thought. Democritus argued (purely on philosophical grounds) that if you took the world's sharpest knife and started slicing chunks of matter, you would eventually come to a smallest piece—a piece that could not be divided further (Figure 8-1). He called this smallest piece the "atom," which translates roughly as "uncuttable." He argued that all material was formed from these atoms, and that the atoms are eternal and unchanging, but that the relationship between the atoms is constantly shifting.

Stop and Think! What would happen to Democritus's argument if the dividing process never reached a smallest unit? Is such an outcome logically possible?

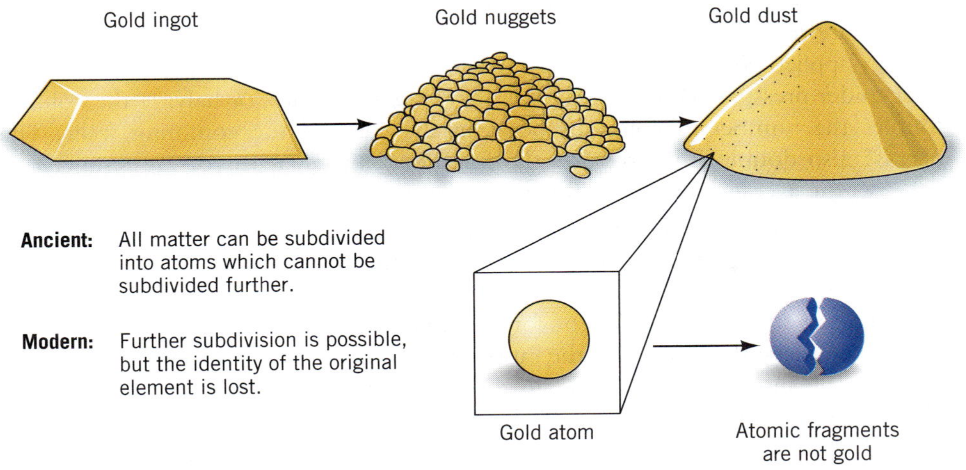

• **Figure 8-1** Repeatedly dividing a bar of gold, just like cutting paper repeatedly, produces smaller and smaller groups of atoms, until you come to a single gold atom. Dividing that atom into two parts produces fragments that no longer have the properties of gold.

Elements

Modern atomic theory is generally attributed to an English meteorologist, John Dalton (1766–1844). In 1808, Dalton published a book called *New System of Chemical Philosophy*, in which he argued that the new knowledge being gained by chemists about materials provided evidence, in and of itself, that matter was composed of atoms. Chemists knew that most materials can be broken down into simpler chemicals. If you burn wood, for example, you get carbon dioxide, water, and all sorts of materials in the ash. If you use an electrical current to break down water, you get two gases, hydrogen and oxygen. Dalton and his contemporaries also recognized that a few materials, called **elements,** could not be broken down into other substances. Wood can be heated to get charcoal (essentially pure carbon), for example; but, try as you might, you can't break the carbon down any further.

The hypothesis that we now call *atomism* was simple in concept. Dalton suggested that for each chemical element there was a corresponding species of indivisible objects called **atoms.** He borrowed the name from the Greeks, but very little else. Two or more atoms stuck together form a **molecule**—the same term applies to any cluster of atoms that can be isolated, whether it contains two atoms or a thousand. Molecules make up most of the different kinds of material we see around us. Water, for example, forms from one oxygen atom and two hydrogen atoms (thus, the familiar H_2O). In Dalton's view, atoms were truly indivisible—he thought of them as little bowling balls (Figure 8-2). In Dalton's world, then, indivisible atoms provide the fundamental building blocks of all matter.

• **Figure 8-2** Atoms may be envisioned as solid balls that stack together to form crystals, like fruit at the supermarket. Atomic models are often drawn with spheres, though we now know that atoms are not solid objects.

Mitch Diamond/Alamy Images

Are Atoms Real?

Democritus and other Greek philosophers did not really engage in science—their reasoning lacked the interplay between observation and hypothesis that characterizes the scientific method. In fact, it wasn't until the beginning of the twentieth century that most scientists became convinced that atoms are real.

No matter how persuasively argued, philosophical speculations on the nature of matter and the existence of atoms were just that—speculations. Over the past three centuries, increasingly convincing evidence has mounted for the reality of atoms. Here are some examples of this growing body of evidence.

1. *The behavior of gas:* The Swiss physicist Daniel Bernoulli (1700–1782) realized that if atoms are real, they must have mass and velocity, and thus kinetic energy. He successfully applied Newton's second law of motion to atoms to explain the behavior of gases under pressure. Doubling the number of gas particles, or halving the volume, doubles the number of collisions between the gas and the confining walls. This increase also doubles the pressure, the force per unit area. Increasing temperature increases the average velocity of the gas particles, also increasing pressure.
2. *Chemical combinations:* English scientist John Dalton advanced the atomic theory based on the law of definite proportions—an empirical law that states that for any given compound, elements combine in a specific ratio of weights: water is always 8 parts oxygen to 1 part hydrogen, for example. Furthermore, when two elements combine in more than one way, the ratios of weights for the two compounds will be a small whole number: 12 pounds of carbon can thus combine with either 16 pounds of oxygen or 32 pounds of oxygen. Dalton realized, therefore, that compounds don't generally have arbitrary fractional ratios of elements. The implication is that some units of elements are fundamentally indivisible.
3. *Radioactivity:* The discovery in 1896 of radioactivity, by which individual atoms emit radiation, provided a compelling piece of evidence for the atomic theory (see Chapter 12). Certain phosphors flash when hit by this radiation. In 1903, upon seeing the irregular twinkling caused by this effect, even the most vocal skeptics of the atomic theory had to take pause.
4. *Brownian motion:* Brownian motion is an erratic, jiggling motion observed in tiny dust particles of pollen grains suspended in water. In 1905 Albert Einstein (1879–1955) demonstrated mathematically that such motions must result from a force—the force of random collisions of atoms. Einstein realized that any small object suspended in liquid would be constantly bombarded by moving atoms. At any given moment, there will, purely by chance, be more atoms hitting on one side than the other. The object will be pushed toward the side with fewer collisions. A moment later, however, more atoms will be hitting another surface, and the object will change direction. Over time, Einstein argued, atomic collisions would produce precisely the sort of erratic motion that you see through a microscope.

   Einstein used the mathematics of statistics to make a number of predictions about how fast and how far the suspended grains would move, based on the hypothesis that the motion was due to collisions with real atoms. These were predictions that other scientists could test in a laboratory. French physicist Jean Baptiste Perrin (1870–1942) published the results of his careful experiments on Brownian motion in 1909. His results agreed with Einstein's calculations and thus convinced many scientists of the reality of atoms.

Note that, in spite of the variety of evidence for atoms, to this point all of this evidence was indirect. Matter was observed to behave *as if* it was made of atoms, but atoms themselves had not been directly observed.

5. *X-ray crystallography:* X-ray crystallography, developed in 1912, convinced any remaining skeptics by demonstrating the sizes and regular arrangements of atoms in crystals. X-rays can't bounce off of hypothetical ideas, so these images were further proof that atoms are real physical objects.
6. *Atomic-scale microscopy:* In the early 1980s the first image of an individual atom was produced at the University of Heidelberg in Germany. This image was produced by an instrument called a scanning tunneling microscope, which detects tiny flows of electrons in a microscopic needle placed next to a solid surface. Now, observational studies of individual atoms are undertaken around the world (Figure 8-3).

• **Figure 8-3** This electronic image representing individual atoms was taken with an instrument called a scanning probe microscope. The "mountains" correspond to individual atoms in a crystal.

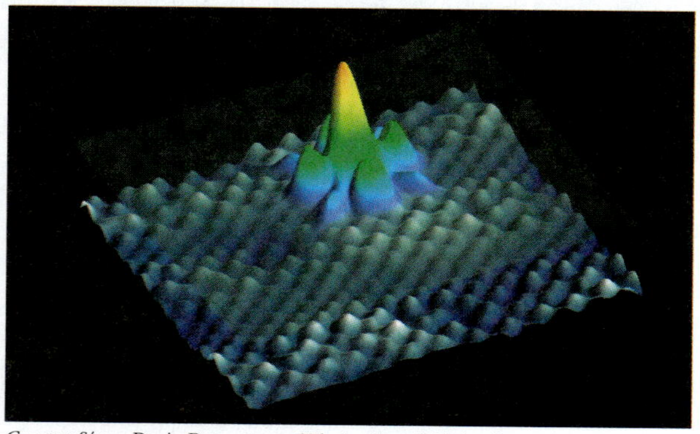

Courtesy Sémus Davis, Department of Physics, Cornell University

Stop and Think! When in the chain of historical events would you have been willing to believe that atoms are real? when Dalton explained the existence of elements? when Einstein explained Brownian motion? when you were shown a picture like the one in Figure 8-3? never? What does it take to make something "real?" And, finally, does it make a difference to science whether atoms are real?

Discovering Chemical Elements

Describing and isolating chemical elements provided a major challenge for chemists of the nineteenth century. In 1800, fewer than 30 elements had been isolated—not enough to establish any systematic trends in their chemical behavior. In the early 1800s, a new process that broke molecules down into atoms was developed. Called *electrolysis* ("splitting by electricity)", it was facilitated by Volta's invention of the battery (see Chapter 5) and allowed many new elements to be separated by means of electrical current. More than two dozen more elements thus were discovered in the first half of the nineteenth century.

Dimitri Mendeleev's invention of the first periodic table of the elements in 1869 (see Chapter 1) capitalized on these discoveries, and it became a powerful tool for predicting more new elements. The original table listed several dozen elements on the basis of their atomic weights (in rows from the upper left) and by groups with distinctive chemical properties (in columns). What Mendeleev could not know was that his table revealed much about the underlying structure of atoms and their electrons.

Today, the periodic table lists more than 110 elements, of which 92 appear in nature and the rest have been produced artificially. Most of the materials we encounter in everyday life are not elements, but compounds of two or more elements bound together. Table salt, plastics, stainless steel, paint, window glass, and soap are all made from a combination of elements.

Nevertheless, we do have experience with a few chemical elements in our everyday lives.

- *Helium:* A light gas that has many uses besides filling party balloons and blimps. In liquid form, helium is used to maintain superconductors at low temperatures (see Chapter 11).
- *Carbon:* Pencil lead, charcoal, and diamonds are all examples of pure carbon. The differences between these materials have to do with the way the atoms of carbon are linked together, as we discuss in Chapter 11.
- *Aluminum:* A lightweight metal used for many purposes. The dull white surface of the metal is actually a combination of aluminum and oxygen, but if you scratch the surface, the shiny material underneath is pure elemental aluminum.
- *Copper:* The reddish metal of pennies and pots. Copper wire provides a cheap and efficient conductor of electricity.
- *Gold:* A soft, yellow, dense, and highly valued metal. For thousands of years the element gold has been coveted as a symbol of wealth. Today it coats critical electrical contacts in spacecraft and other sophisticated electronics.

Although we know of more than 90 different elements in nature, many natural systems are constructed from just a few. Six elements—oxygen, silicon, magnesium, iron, aluminum, and calcium—account for almost 99% of Earth's solid mass. Most of the atoms in your body are hydrogen, carbon, oxygen, or nitrogen, with smaller but important roles played by

Helium-filled blimps.

BENALI REMI/Gamma-Presse, Inc.

phosphorus and sulfur. And most stars are formed almost entirely from the lightest element, hydrogen.

> **Stop and Think!** Look around you. How many different elements do you see? How many different compounds? Is it reasonable that there should be so many more compounds than elements? Why or why not?

The Structure of the Atom

Dalton's idea of the atom as a single indivisible entity was not destined to last. In 1897, English physicist Joseph John Thomson (1856–1940), a teacher of Ernest Rutherford, unambiguously identified a particle called the **electron.** Thomson found that the electron has a negative electrical charge and is much smaller and lighter than even the smallest atom known. Because there was no place from which a particle such as the electron could come, other than inside the atom, Thomson's discovery provided incontrovertible evidence for what people had suspected for a long time. Atoms are not the fundamental building blocks of matter, but rather are made up of things that are smaller and more fundamental still. Table 8-1 summarizes some of the important terms related to atoms.

The Atomic Nucleus

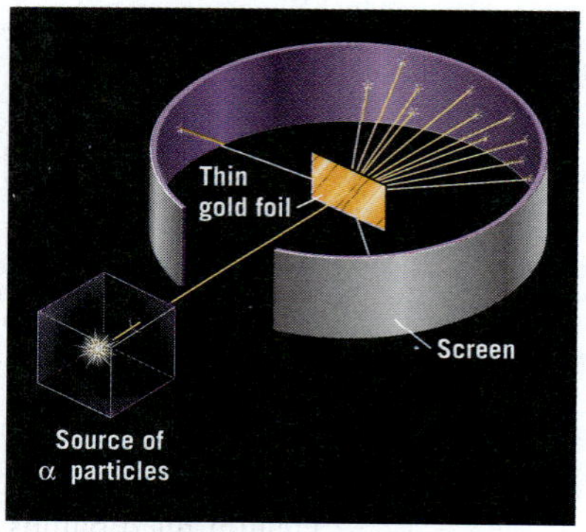

• **Figure 8-4** In Rutherford's experiment, a beam of radioactive particles was scattered by atomic nuclei in a piece of gold foil. A lead shield protected researchers from the radiation.

The most important discovery about the structure of the atom was made by New Zealand–born physicist Ernest Rutherford (1871–1937) and his coworkers in Manchester, England, in 1911. The basic idea of the experiment is sketched in Figure 8-4. The experiment started with a piece of radioactive material—matter that sends out energetic particles (see Chapter 12). For our purposes, you can think of radioactive materials as sources of tiny subatomic "bullets." The particular material that Rutherford used produced bullets that scientists had named *alpha particles,* which are thousands of times heavier than electrons. By arranging the apparatus as shown, Rutherford produced a stream of these subatomic bullets moving toward the right in the figure. In front of this stream, he placed a thin foil of gold.

The experiment was designed to measure something about the way atoms were put together. At the time, people believed that the small, negatively charged electrons were scattered around the entire atom, more or less like raisins in a bun. Rutherford was trying to shoot bullets into the "bun" and see what happened.

Table 8-1 Important Terms Related to Atoms

Element	A chemical substance that cannot be broken down further
Atom	The smallest particle that retains its chemical identity
Molecule	A collection of two or more atoms bound together; the smallest unit of a substances that has the chemical properties of the substance.
Electron	An atomic particle with negative charge and low mass
Nucleus	The small, massive central part of an atom
Proton	Positively charged nuclear particle
Neutron	Electrically neutral nuclear particle
Ion	An electrically charged atom

What the experiment revealed was little short of astonishing. Almost all the subatomic bullets either passed right through the gold foil unaffected or were scattered through very small angles. This result is easy to interpret: it means that most of the heavy alpha particles passed through spaces in between gold atoms, and that those that hit the gold atoms were only moderately deflected by the relatively low-density material in them.

Fewer than one alpha particle in a thousand, however, was scattered through a large angle; some even bounced straight back. After almost two years of puzzling over these extraordinary results, Rutherford concluded that a large part of each atom's mass is located in a very small, compact object at the center—what he called the **nucleus.** About 999 times out of 1000 the alpha particles either missed the atom completely or went through the low-density material in the outer reaches of the atom. About 1 time out of 1000, however, the alpha particle hit the nucleus and was bounced through a large angle.

You can think of the Rutherford experiment in this way. If the atom were a large ball of mist or vapor with a diameter greater than a skyscraper, and the nucleus was a bowling ball at the center of that sphere of mist, then most bullets shot at the atom would go right through. Only those that hit the bowling ball would be bounced through large angles. In this analogy, of course, the bowling ball plays the part of the nucleus, while the mist is the domain of the electrons.

As a result of Rutherford's work, a new picture of the atom emerged, one that is very familiar to us. Rutherford described a small, dense, positively charged nucleus sitting at the atom's center, with light, negatively charged electrons circling it, like planets orbiting the Sun. Indeed, Rutherford's discovery has become an icon of the modern age, adorning everyday objects from postage stamps to bathroom cleaners (Figure 8-5).

• **Figure 8-5** The Nuclear Regulatory Commission uses a highly stylized atomic model as its logo.

Later on, physicists discovered that the nucleus itself is made up primarily of two different kinds of particles (see Chapter 11). One of these carries a positive charge and is called a *proton*. The other, whose existence was not confirmed until 1932, carries no electrical charge and is called a *neutron*.

For each positively charged proton in the nucleus of the atom, there is normally one negatively charged electron "in orbit." Thus the electrical charges of the electrons and the protons cancel out, and every atom is electrically neutral. In some cases, atoms either lose or gain electrons. In this case, they acquire an electrical charge and are called *ions*.

Why the Rutherford Atom Couldn't Work

The picture of the atom that Rutherford developed is intellectually appealing, particularly because it recalls to us the familiar orbits of planets in our solar system. We have already learned enough about the behavior of nature, however, to know that the atom that is described in the text could not possibly exist in nature. Why do we say this?

We learned in Chapter 2 that an object traveling in a circular orbit is constantly being accelerated—it is not in uniform motion because it is continually changing direction. Furthermore, we learned in Chapter 5 that any accelerated electrical charge must give off electromagnetic radiation, as a consequence of Maxwell's equations. Thus, if an atom was of the Rutherford type, the electrons moving in their orbits would constantly be giving off energy in the form of electromagnetic radiation. This energy, according to the first law of thermodynamics, would have to come from somewhere (remember conservation of energy!), so the electrons would gradually spiral in toward the nucleus as they gave up their energy to electromagnetic radiation. Eventually, the electrons would have to fall into the nucleus and the atom would cease to exist in the form we know.

In fact, if you put in the numbers, the life expectancy of the Rutherford atom turns out to be less than a second. Given the fact that many atoms have survived billions of years, since almost the beginning of the universe, this calculation poses a serious problem for the simple orbital model of the atom.

When Matter Meets Light

Almost from its inception, the Rutherford model of the atom encountered difficulties. Some of the problems involved its violations of fundamental physical laws as we have described, whereas others were more mundane—the Rutherford atom simply did not explain all the behavior of atoms that scientists knew about. The first decades of the twentieth century represented a period of tremendous ferment in the sciences as people scrambled to find a new way of describing the nature of atoms.

The Bohr Atom

In 1913, Niels Bohr (1885–1962), a young Danish physicist working in England, produced the first model of the atom that avoided the kinds of objections encountered by Rutherford's model. The **Bohr atom** is very strange: it does not match well with our intuition about the way things "ought to be" in the real world. The only thing in the Bohr atom's favor was that it worked.

Courtesy American Institute of Physics

Niels Bohr (1885–1962) with Aage Bohr, one of his five sons. Both won Nobel prizes in physics.

Bohr's insight began with an educated guess about the distinctive way in which hot hydrogen atoms give off light. Hydrogen gas glows by giving off light in several separate wavelengths, rather than in a continuous range of wavelengths. The young Bohr was deeply immersed in studying this emission of light and the way that atoms interact with light and other forms of electromagnetic radiation. He realized that one way of explaining what he saw in the laboratory was that electrons circling the nucleus, unlike planets circling the Sun, could not maintain their orbits at just any distance from the center. He suggested that there were only certain orbits—he called them "allowed orbits"—located at specified distances from the center of the atom in which an electron could exist for long periods of time *without giving off radiation*. (We prefer to use the terms *electron energy levels* or *electron shells*, rather than *allowed orbits*, when describing the distribution of electrons in atoms, because later work showed the idea of electron orbits is not a good description of the atom.) Bohr's picture of the atom is shown in Figure 8-6. The idea is that the electron can exist at a specific distance r_1 from the nucleus, or at a distance r_2 or r_3, and so on, each distance corresponding to a different electron energy level. As long as the electron remains at one of those distances, its energy is fixed. In the Bohr atomic model, the electron cannot ever, at any time, exist at any place between these allowed distances.

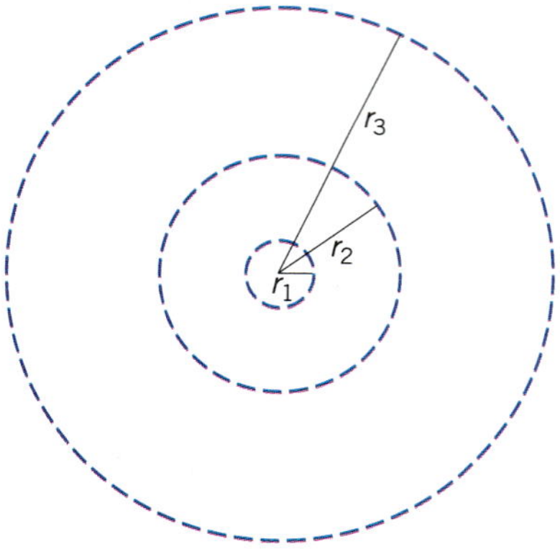

• **Figure 8-6** A schematic diagram of the Bohr atom showing the first three energy levels and respective distances (r_1, r_2, and r_3) from the nucleus.

One way to think about the Bohr atom is to imagine what happens when you climb a flight of steps. You can stand on the first step or you can stand on the second step. It's very hard, however, to imagine what it would be like to stand somewhere between two steps. In just the same way, an electron can be in the first energy level, or in the second energy level, and so on, but it can't be in between these allowed energy levels. In terms of energy, both the steps and the electrons in an atom may be represented by a simple pictorial description (Figure 8-7). Each time you change steps in your home, your gravitational potential energy changes. Similarly, each time an electron changes levels, its energy changes.

An electron in an atom can be in any one of a number of allowed energy levels, each corresponding to a different distance from the nucleus. You would have to exert a force over a distance to move an electron from one allowed energy level to another, just as

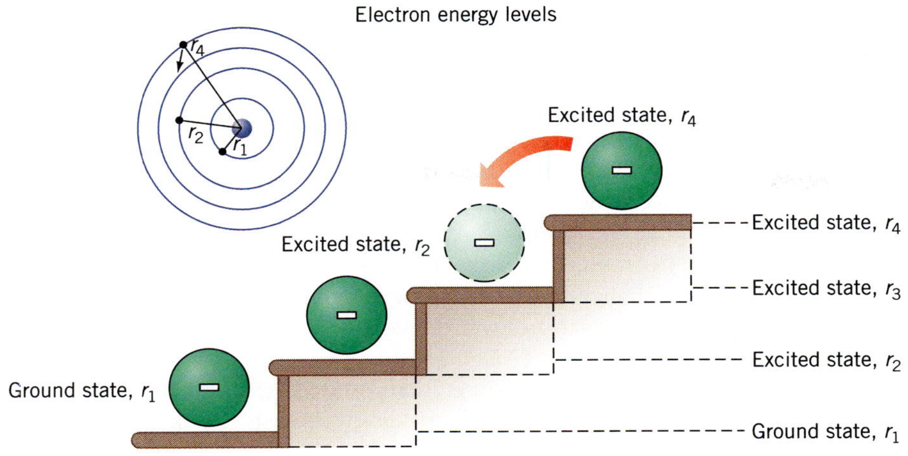

• **Figure 8-7** Stairs provide an analogy to energy changes associated with electrons in the Bohr atom.

your muscles have to exert a force to get you up a flight of stairs. Thus, the allowed energy levels of an atom occur as a series of steps as shown in the figure. An electron in the lowest energy level is said to be in the *ground state,* while all energy levels above the ground state are called *excited states.*

Photons: Particles of Light

One major feature of the Bohr atom is that an electron in a higher energy level can move down into an available lower energy level. This process is analogous to that by which a ball at the top of a flight of stairs can bounce down the stairs under the influence of gravity.

Assume that an electron is in an excited state, as shown in Figure 8-8. The electron can move to the lowest state, but if it does, something must happen to the extra energy. Energy can't just disappear. This realization was Bohr's great insight. The energy that's left over when the electrically charged electron moves from a higher state to a lower state is emitted by the atom in the form of a single packet of electromagnetic radiation—a particle-like bundle of light called a **photon.** Every time an electron jumps from a higher to a lower energy level, a photon moves away at the speed of light.

The concept of a photon raises a perplexing question: Is light—Maxwell's electromagnetic radiation—a wave or a particle? We will explore this puzzle at some length in Chapter 9, once we have learned more about the behavior of atoms.

The interaction of atoms and electromagnetic radiation provides the most compelling evidence for the Bohr atom. If electrons are in excited states, and if they make transitions to lower states, then photons are emitted. If we look at a group of atoms in which these transitions are occurring, we will see light or other electromagnetic radiation. Thus when you look at the flame of a fire or the glowing heating coil of an electric stove in your kitchen, you are actually seeing photons that were emitted by electrons jumping between allowed states in that material's atoms.

Not only does the Bohr atom give us a picture of how matter emits radiation, it provides an explanation for how matter absorbs radiation. Start with an electron in a low-energy state, perhaps its ground state. If a photon arrives that has just the right amount of energy so that it can raise the electron to a higher

• **Figure 8-8** Electrons may jump between the energy levels shown in *(a)* and, in the process, *(b)* absorb or *(c)* emit energy in the form of a photon.

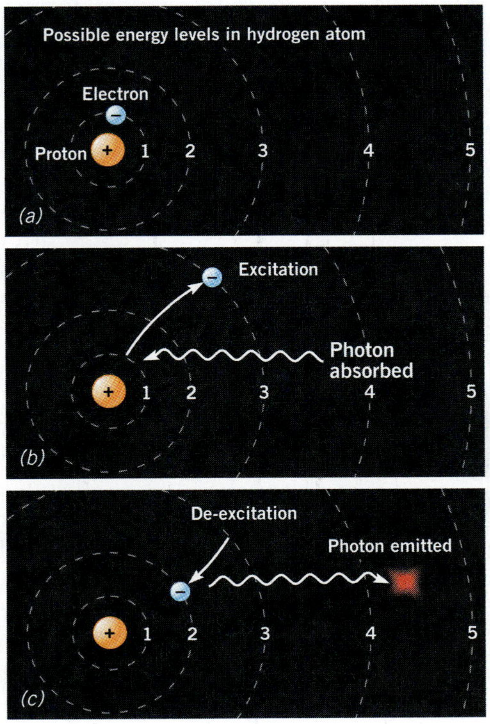

energy (the next step up), the photon can be absorbed and the electron will be pushed up to an excited state. Absorption of light is something like a mirror image of light emission.

Our picture of the interaction of matter and radiation is exceedingly simple, but two key ideas are embedded in it. For one thing, when an electron moves from one allowed state to another, it cannot ever, at any time, be at any place in between. This rule is built into the definition of an allowed energy level. This means that the electron must somehow disappear from its original location and reappear in its final location *without ever having to traverse any of the positions in between.* This process, called a **quantum leap** or **quantum jump,** cannot be visualized, but it is something that seems to be fundamental in nature—an example of the "quantum weirdness" of nature at the atomic scale that we'll discuss in Chapter 9.

The second key idea is that if an electron is in an excited state, it can, in principle, get back down to the ground state in a number of different ways. Look at Figure 8-9. An electron in the upper energy level can move to the ground state by making one large jump and emitting a single photon with large energy. Alternatively, it can move to the ground state by making two smaller jumps, as shown. Each of these jumps emits a photon of somewhat less energy. The energies emitted in the two different jumps will generally be different from each other, but the sum of the two energies will equal that of the single large jump. If we had a large collection of atoms of this kind, we would expect that some electrons would make the large leap while others would make the two smaller ones. Thus, when we look at a collection of these atoms, we would measure three different energies of photons.

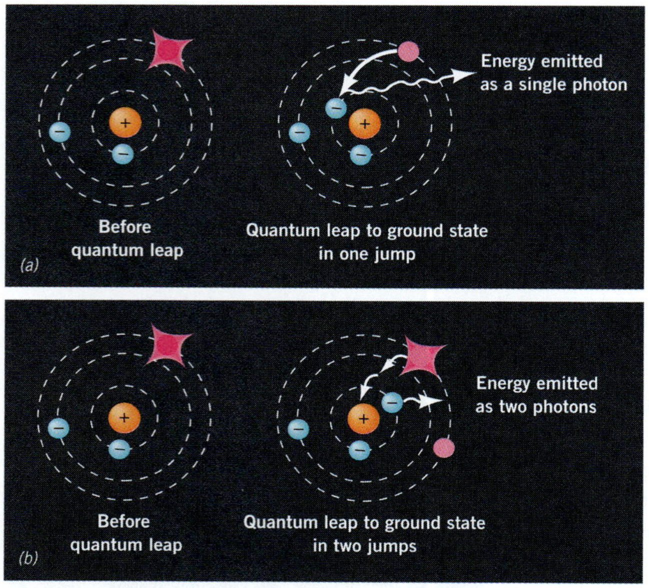

• **Figure 8-9** An electron can jump from a higher to lower energy level in a single quantum leap *(a)* or by multiple quantum leaps *(b)*.

This curious behavior of electron energy levels helps to explain the familiar phenomenon of fluorescence that we introduced in Chapter 6. Recall that the energy of electromagnetic radiation is related to its frequency. In fluorescence, the atom in Figure 8-9 absorbs a higher-energy photon of ultraviolet radiation (which our eyes can't detect). The atom then emits two lower-energy photons, at least one of which is in the visible range. Consequently, by shining ultraviolet "black light" on the fluorescent material, it glows with a bright color.

A key point about the Bohr atom is that energy is required to lift an electron from the ground state to any excited state. This energy has to come from somewhere. We have already mentioned one possibility: that the atom will absorb a photon of just the right frequency to raise the electron to a higher energy level. There are other possibilities, however. If the material is heated, for example, atoms will move fast, gain kinetic energy, and undergo energetic collisions. In these collisions, an atom can absorb energy and then use that energy to move electrons to a higher state. This explains why materials often glow when they are heated.

An Intuitive Leap

Bohr first proposed his model of the atom based on an intuition guided by experiments and ideas about the behavior of things in the subatomic world. In some ways the Bohr model was completely unlike anything we experience in the macroscopic world; indeed, the model seemed to some a little bit "crazy." It took two decades for scientists to develop a theory called *quantum mechanics* that showed why electrons can exist only in Bohr's "allowed orbits" and not in between. We will discuss this justification for the Bohr atom in Chapter 9, but it should be remembered that the justification occurred long after the initial hypothesis. The Bohr atom was accepted by physicists because it worked—it explained what they saw in nature and allowed them to make predictions about the behavior of real matter.

(a) (b) (c)

The elements *(a)* sodium, *(b)* potassium, and *(c)* lithium impart distinctive colors to a flame.

How could Bohr have come up with such a strange picture of the atom? He was undoubtedly guided by some of the early work that would lead to the theory of quantum mechanics (see Chapter 9). In the end, however, this explanation is unsatisfactory. Many people at the time studied the interactions of atoms and light, but only Bohr was able to make the leap of intuition to his description of the atom. This insight, like Newton's realization that gravity might extend to the orbit of the Moon, remains one of the great intuitive achievements of the human mind.

Stop and Think! How are intuitive leaps, such as the one made by Bohr, consistent or not consistent with the scientific method as described in Chapter 1?

Spectroscopy

Whenever energy is added to a system with many atoms in it, electrons in some atoms jump to excited states. As time goes by, these electrons will make quantum leaps down to the ground state, giving off photons or heat energy as they do. If some of those photons are in the range of visible light, the source will appear to glow.

You may not realize it, but you have looked at such collections of atoms all your life. Common mercury vapor street lamps contain bulbs filled with mercury gas. When the gas is heated, electrons are moved up to excited states. When they jump down, they emit photons that give the lamp a bluish-white color. Other types of streetlights, often used at freeway interchanges, use bulbs filled with sodium atoms. When sodium is excited, the most frequently emitted photons lie in the yellow range, so the lamps look yellow.

Yet another place where you can see photons emitted directly by quantum leaps is in Day-Glo colors, the vivid colors often used in sports clothing and advertising. From these examples, you can draw two conclusions: (1) quantum leaps are very much in evidence in your everyday life, and (2) different atoms give off different characteristic photons.

The second of these two facts is extremely important for scientists. If you think about the structure of an atom, the idea that different atoms emit and absorb different characteristic photons shouldn't be too surprising. Electron energy levels depend on the electrical attraction between the nucleus and the electrons, just as the orbits of the planets depend on the gravitational attraction between the planets and the Sun. Different nuclei have different numbers of protons, so electrons circling them are in different energy levels. In fact, the energy between the allowed energy levels within the atom is different in each of the hundred or so different chemical elements. Because the energy and frequency of photons emitted by an atom depend on the differences in energy between these levels, each chemical element emits a distinct set of characteristic photons.

You can think of the collection of characteristic photons emitted by each chemical element as a kind of "fingerprint"—something that is distinctive for that chemical element and none other. This feature opens up a very interesting possibility. The total collection of photons emitted by a given atom is called its **spectrum,** a characteristic fingerprint that can be used to identify chemical elements even when they are very difficult to identify by any other means.

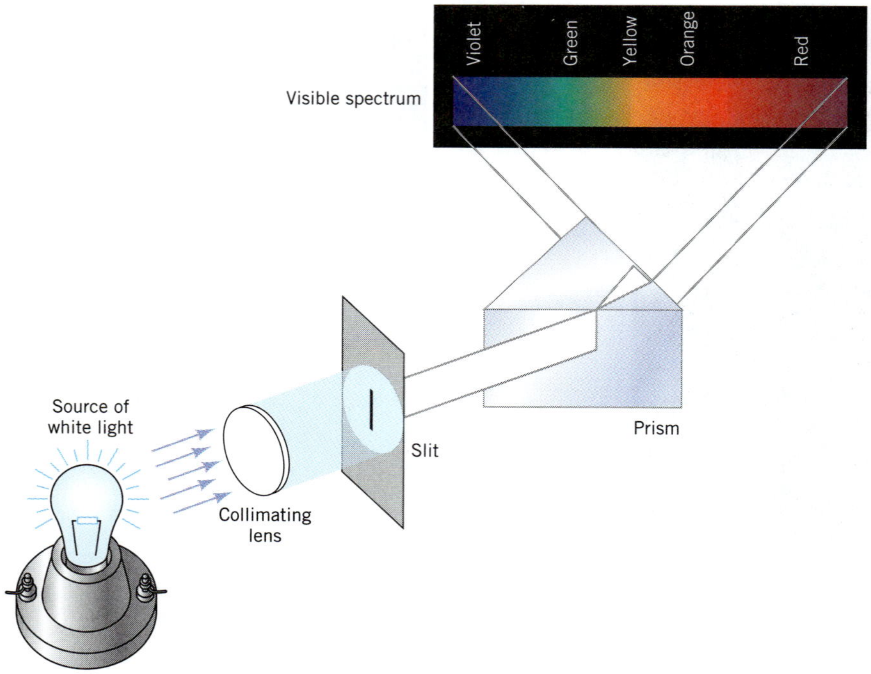

• **Figure 8-10** A glass prism spreads out the colors of the visible spectrum.

In practice, the identification process works like this: Light from the gaseous atoms is spread out by being passed through a prism (Figure 8-10). Each possible quantum jump corresponds to light at a specific wavelength, so each type of atom produces a set of lines, as shown in Figure 8-11. This spectrum is the atomic fingerprint.

The Bohr picture suggests that if an atom gives off light of a specific wavelength and energy, then it will also *absorb* light at that wavelength. The emission and absorption processes, after all, may involve quantum jumps between the same two energy levels but in different directions. Thus if white light shines through a material containing a particular kind of atom, certain wavelengths of light will be absorbed. Observing that light on the other side of the material, you will see certain colors missing. The dark areas corresponding to the absorbed wavelengths are called *absorption lines.* This set of lines is as much an atomic fingerprint as the set of colors that the atoms emit. And although the

• **Figure 8-11** Line spectra, shown here for hydrogen, sodium, and neon, provide distinctive fingerprints for elements and compounds.

Courtesy Bausch & Lomb

use of visible light is very common, these arguments hold for radiation in any part of the electromagnetic spectrum.

Spectroscopy has become a standard tool that is used in almost every branch of science. Astronomers use emission spectra to find the chemical composition of distant stars, and they study absorption lines to determine the chemical composition of interstellar dust and the atmospheres of the outer planets. Spectroscopic analysis is also used in manufacturing to search for impurities on production lines, and by police departments to identify small traces of unknown materials when conducting investigations.

The Science of Life •

Spectra of Life's Chemical Reactions

In a classic set of experiments in the early 1940s, scientists used spectroscopy to work out in detail how chemical reactions governed by large molecules called enzymes (see Chapter 22) proceed in cells. In these experiments, a fluid containing the materials undergoing the chemical reactions was allowed to flow down a tube. The farther down the tube the fluid was, the farther along the reaction was. By measuring spectra at different points along the tube, scientists were able to follow the change in the behavior of electrons as the chemical reactions went along. In this way, part of the enormously complex problem of understanding the chemistry of life was unraveled.

More recently, scientists have begun to develop instruments that can use the principles of spectroscopy to identify pollutants emitted by automobile tailpipes as the cars drive by. If they are successful, we will have a major new tool in our battle against air pollution and acid rain (see Chapter 19). •

Science in the Making •

The Story of Helium

You have probably experienced helium, perhaps to inflate party balloons. Helium gas turns out to be a very interesting material, not only for its properties (it's less dense than air, so it floats up), but because of the history of its discovery.

The word helium refers to *helios,* the Greek word for Sun, because helium was first discovered in spectral lines in the Sun in 1868 by English scientist Joseph Norman Lockyer (1836–1920). Helium is very rare in Earth's atmosphere, and before Lockyer's discovery scientists were not even aware of its existence. Following the discovery, there was a period of about 30 years when astronomers accepted the fact that the element helium existed in the Sun, but were unable to find it on Earth.

This supposition led to a very interesting problem. Could it be that there were chemical elements on the Sun that simply did not exist on our own planet? If so, it would call into question our ability to understand the rest of the universe, for the simple reason that if we don't know what an element is and can't isolate it in our laboratories, then we can never really be sure that we understand its properties. In fact, the existence of helium on Earth wasn't confirmed until 1895, when Lockyer identified its spectrum in a sample of radioactive material. •

Technology •

The Laser

The Bohr atom provides an excellent way of understanding the workings of one of the most important devices in modern science and industry—the laser. The word *laser* is an acronym for *l*ight *a*mplification by *s*timulated *e*mission of *r*adiation. At the core of every laser is a collection of atoms—a crystal of ruby, perhaps, or a gas enclosed in a glass tube. The term *stimulated emission* refers to a process that goes on when light and these atoms

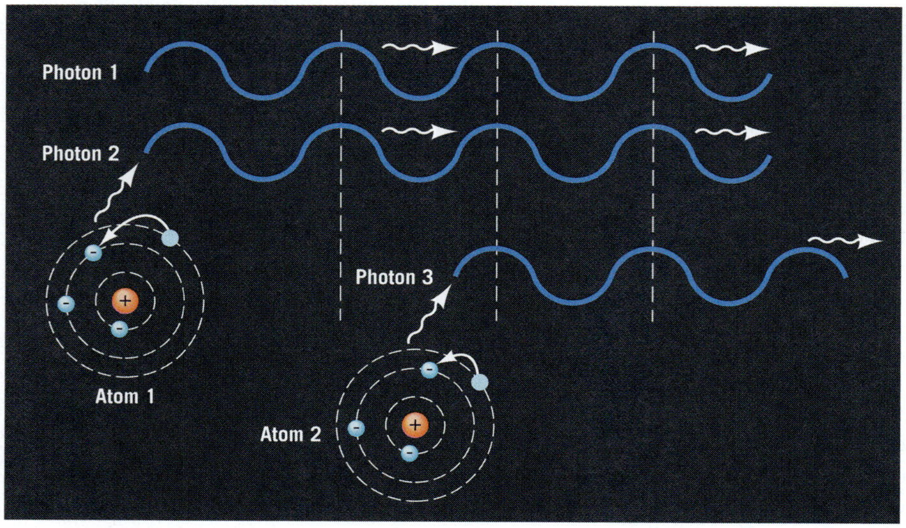

• **Figure 8-12** Lasers produce a beam of light when one photon stimulates the emission of other photons.

interact. If an electron is in an excited state, as shown in Figure 8-12, and one photon of just the right energy passes nearby, the electron may be stimulated to make the jump to a lower energy state, thus releasing a second photon. By "just the right energy" for the first photon, we mean a photon whose energy corresponds to the energy gap between two electron energy levels in the atom.

Furthermore, the stimulated atom emits photons in a special way. Remember that light is a form of electromagnetic radiation that can be described as a wave. In a laser, the crests of all the emitted photon waves line up exactly with the crests of the first photon, and the signal is enhanced by constructive interference. In the language of the physicists, we say that the photons are "coherent." Thus in stimulated emission, you have one photon at the beginning of the process and two coherent photons at the end.

Now suppose that you have a collection of atoms where most of the electrons are in the excited state, as shown in Figure 8-13. If a single photon of the correct frequency enters this system from the left and moves to the right, it will pass the first atom and stimulate the emission of a second photon. You will then have two photons moving to the right. As these photons encounter other atoms, they, too, stimulate emission so that you have four photons. It's not hard to see that light amplification in a laser will happen very quickly, cascading so that soon there is a flood of photons moving to the right through the collection of atoms. Energy added to the system from outside continuously returns atoms to their excited state—a process called *pumping*—so that more and more coherent photons can be produced.

In a laser, the collection of excited atoms is bounded on two sides by mirrors so that photons moving to the right hit the mirror, are reflected, and make another pass through the material, stimulating even more emission of photons as they go. If a photon happens to be lined up exactly perpendicular to the mirrors at the end of the laser, it will continue bouncing back and forth. If its direction is off by even a small angle, however, it will eventually bounce out through the sides of the laser and be lost. Thus only those photons that are exactly aligned will wind up bouncing back and forth between the mirrors, constantly amplifying the signal. Aligned photons will traverse the laser millions of times, building up an enormous cascade of coherent photons in the system.

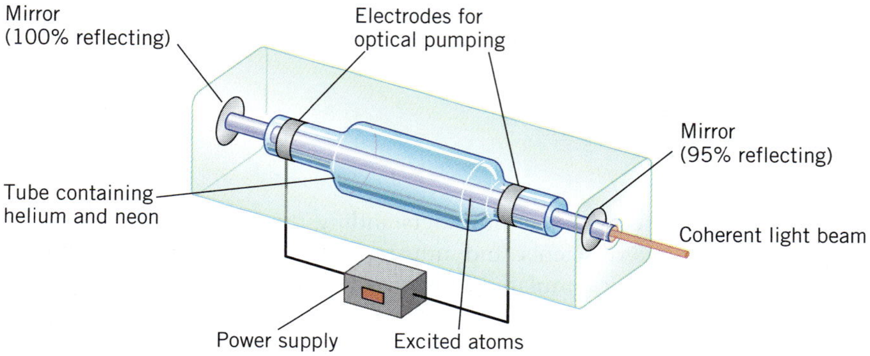

• **Figure 8-13** The action of a laser. Electrons in the laser's atoms are continuously "pumped" into an excited state by an outside energy source, and the beam of photons is released when the electrons return to their ground state.

The mirrors are designed to be partially reflective—perhaps 95% of the photons that hit the mirror are reflected back into the laser. The remaining 5% of photons that leak out form the familiar laser beam, which is made of intense, coherent light.

Laser beams have been applied in thousands of uses in science and industry since their development in the 1960s. Low-power lasers are ideal for optical scanners, such as the ones in supermarket checkout lines, and they make ideal light pointers for lectures and slide shows. The fact that the beam of light travels in a straight line makes the laser invaluable in surveying over long distances—for example, modern subway tunnels are routinely surveyed by using lasers to provide a straight line underground. Lasers are also used to detect movement of seismic faults in order to predict earthquakes (see Chapter 17). In this case, a laser is directed across the fault, so that small motions of the ground are easily measured. Finely focused laser beams have revolutionized delicate procedures such as eye surgery. Much more powerful lasers can transfer large amounts of energy. They are often used as cutting tools in factories, as well as implements for performing some kinds of surgery. The military has also adopted laser technology, in targeting and range finders, and in designs for futuristic energy beam weapons.

From the point of view of science, however, lasers are important because they enable us to make extremely precise measurements of atomic structures and properties. Almost all modern studies of the atom depend in some way on the laser. •

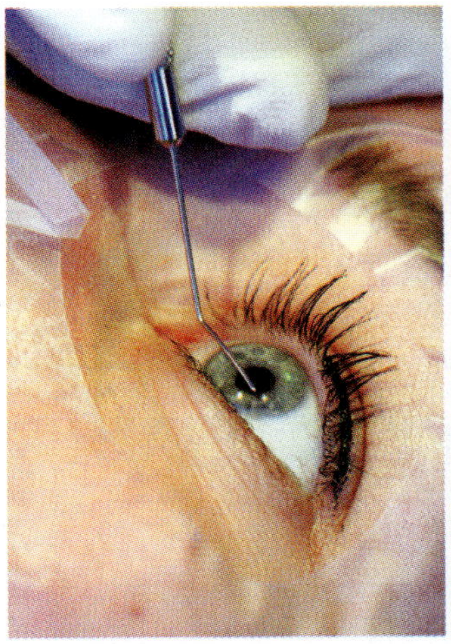

Rolf Vennenbernd/Apa/Landov LLC

Lasers such as this argon laser have many uses. Light generated in the laser is carried by fiber-optic cable for use in surgery on the human eye.

Ray Nelson/Phototake

Lasers are used by astronomers to align and focus telescopes.

The Periodic Table of the Elements

The **periodic table of the elements,** which systematizes all known chemical elements, provides a powerful conceptual framework for understanding the structure and interaction of atoms. Dimitri Mendeleev, the Russian scientist who studied the regularity or periodicity in the known chemical elements (see Chapter 1), related that periodicity to each element's atomic properties. Today, each element is assigned an integer, called the ***atomic number,*** which defines the sequence of elements in the table. The atomic number corresponds to the number of protons in the atom, or, equivalently, if the atom is not charged, to the number of electrons surrounding the nucleus. If you arrange the elements as shown in Figure 8-14, with elements getting progressively heavier as you read from left to right and top to bottom as in a book, then elements in the same vertical column have very similar chemical properties.

Periodic Chemical Properties

The most striking characteristic of the periodic table is the similarity of elements in any given column. In the far left-hand column of the table, for example, are highly reactive elements called ***alkali metals*** (lithium, sodium, potassium, etc.). Each of these soft, silvery elements forms compounds (called *salts*) by combining in a one-to-one ratio with any of the elements in the next to last column (fluorine, chlorine, bromine, etc.). Water dissolves these compounds, which include sodium chloride, or table salt.

The elements in the second column, including beryllium, magnesium, and calcium, are metallic elements called the ***alkaline earth metals*** and they too display similar chemical

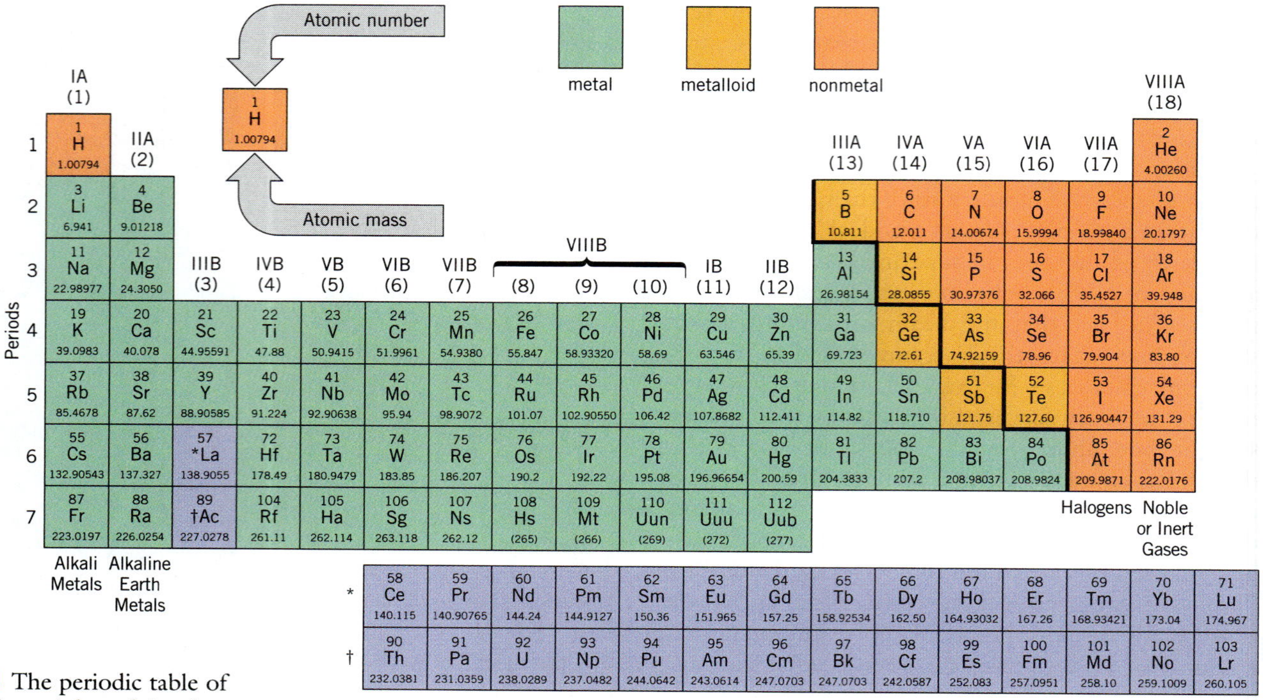

• **Figure 8-14** The periodic table of the elements. The weights of the elements increase from left to right. Each vertical column groups elements with similar chemical properties.

properties among themselves. These elements, for example, combine with oxygen in a one-to-one ratio to form colorless compounds with very high melting temperatures.

Elements in the far right-hand column (helium, neon, argon, and so on), by contrast, are all colorless, odorless gases that are almost impossible to coax into any kind of chemical reaction. These so-called *noble gases* find applications when ordinary gases are too reactive. Helium lifts blimps, because the only other lighter-than-air gas is the dangerous, explosive element hydrogen. Argon fills incandescent lightbulbs, because nitrogen or oxygen would react with the hot filament.

In the late nineteenth century, scientists knew that the periodic table "worked"—it organized the 63 elements known at that time and implied the existence of others—but they had no idea *why* it worked. Their faith in the periodic table was buttressed by the fact that, when Mendeleev first wrote it down, there were holes in the table—places where he predicted elements should go, but for which no element was known. The ensuing search for the missing kinds of atoms produced the elements we now call scandium (in 1876) and germanium (in 1886).

Why the Periodic Table Works: Electron Shells

With the advent of Bohr's atomic model and its modern descendants, we finally have some understanding of why the periodic table works. We now realize that the pattern of elements in the periodic table mirrors the spatial arrangement of electrons around the atom's nucleus—a concentric arrangement of electrons into *shells.*

The atom is largely empty space. When two atoms come near enough to each other to undergo a chemical reaction—a carbon atom and an oxygen atom in a burning piece of coal, for example—electrons in the outermost shells meet each other first. We will see in Chapter 10 that these outermost electrons govern the chemical properties of materials. We have to understand the behavior of these electrons if we want to understand the periodic table.

To do this, we need to know one more curious fact about electrons. Electrons are particles that obey what is called the *Pauli exclusion principle,* which says that no two electrons can occupy the same energy state at the same time. One analogy is to compare electrons to cars in a parking lot. Each car takes up one space, and once a space is filled, no other car can go there. Electrons behave in just the same way. Once an electron fills a particular niche in the atom, no other electron can occupy the same niche. A parking lot can be full long before all the actual space in the lot is taken up with cars, because the driveways and spaces between cars must remain empty. So, too, a given electron shell can be filled with electrons long before all the available space is filled.

In fact, it turns out that there are only two spaces that an electron can fill in the innermost electron shell, which corresponds to the lowest Bohr energy level. One of these spaces corresponds to a situation in which the electron "spins" clockwise on its axis, the other to a situation in which it "spins" counterclockwise on its axis. When we start to catalog all possible chemical elements in the periodic table, we have element one (hydrogen) with a single electron in the innermost shell, and element two (helium) with two electrons in that same shell. After this, if we want to add one more electron, it has to go into the second electron shell because the first electron shell is completely filled. This situation explains why only hydrogen and helium appear in the first row in the periodic table.

Adding a third electron yields lithium, an atom with two electrons in the first shell, and a single electron in the second electron shell. Lithium is the element just below hydrogen in the first column of the periodic table, because both hydrogen and lithium have a lone electron in their outermost shell.

The second electron shell has room for eight electrons, a fact reflected in the eight elements of the periodic table's second row, from lithium with three electrons to neon with 10. Neon appears directly under helium, and we expect these two gases to have similar chemical properties because both have a completely filled outer electron shell.

Thus, a simple counting of the positions available to electrons in the first two electron shells explains why the first row in the periodic table has two elements in it and the second row eight. By similar (but somewhat more complicated) arguments, you can show that the Pauli exclusion principle requires that the next row of the periodic table has 8 elements, the next 18, and so on (Figure 8-15). Thus, with an understanding of the shell-like structure of the atom's electrons, the mysterious regularity that Mendeleev found among the chemical elements becomes an example of nature's laws at work.

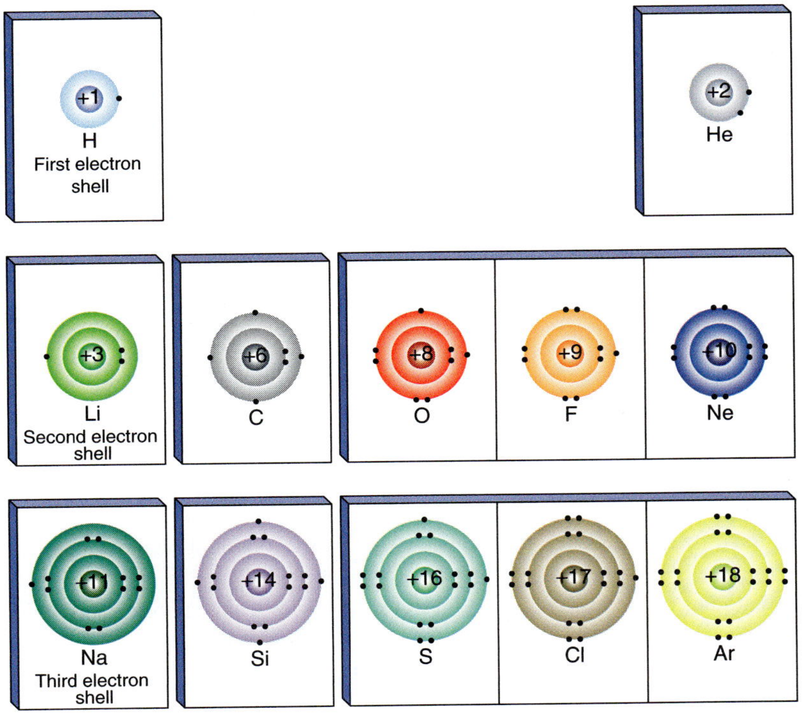

• **Figure 8-15** A representation of electrons in a number of common atoms.

Thinking More About | Atoms

What Do Atoms "Look Like?"

Throughout this book you will find drawings of atoms. In this chapter we drew atoms as electrons in circular shells around a central nucleus. In Chapter 10, atoms appear as little spheres in pictures of molecules like H_2O (water) and crystals like NaCl (table salt). In other chapters atoms are portrayed as fuzzy clouds, or waves, or even collections of dozens of smaller sphere-like particles. So, what do atoms really "look like?"

Strictly speaking, we only "see" something when electromagnetic waves from the visible part of the spectrum enter our eyes. We are accustomed, however, to talking about other ways of "seeing." You cannot see X-rays being absorbed by your teeth, for example, unless some intermediary system—film or electronic—converts the X-rays into a pattern that can be detected in the visible region of the electromagnetic spectrum. Similarly, astronomers often convert radio waves, infrared radiation, and other wavelength data into false-color images of distant objects. Scanning tunneling microscope "pictures" of atoms come from another such transformation. The amount of electrical charge at a particular point on a material's surface is converted into the height of the peak you see in the picture.

Is an X-ray picture of your teeth more real than the microscope picture of the atom? Why or why not?

Summary

About 100 different *elements* are sufficient to form all the solids, liquids, and gases around us. *Atoms,* the building blocks of our chemical world, combine into groups of two or more; these groups are called *molecules.* For thousands of years atoms were discussed purely as hypothetical objects, but studies of Brownian motion early in the twentieth century and recent imaging of individual atoms in new kinds of microscopes have confirmed the existence of these tiny particles.

Each atom contains a massive central *nucleus* made from positively charged protons and electrically neutral neutrons. Surrounding the nucleus are *electrons,* which are negatively charged particles that have only a small fraction of the mass of protons and neutrons. Early models of this kind of atom treated electrons like planets orbiting around the Sun. Those models were flawed, however, because each electron, constantly accelerating, would have to emit electromagnetic radiation continuously. Niels Bohr proposed an alternative model in which electrons exist in various energy levels, much as you can stand on different levels of a flight of stairs.

Electrons in the *Bohr atom* can shift to a higher energy level by absorbing the energy of heat or light. Electrons can also drop into a lower energy level and in the process release heat or a *photon,* an individual electromagnetic wave. These changes in electron energy level are called *quantum leaps* or *quantum jumps. Spectroscopic* studies of the light emitted or absorbed by atoms—the atom's spectrum—reveal the nature of each atom's electron energy levels.

Each atom's electrons are arranged in concentric shells. When two atoms interact, electrons in the outermost shell come into contact. This shell-like electronic structure is reflected in the organization of the *periodic table of elements,* which lists all the elements in rows corresponding to increasing numbers of electrons in each shell, and in columns corresponding to elements with similar numbers of outer shell electrons and thus similar chemical behavior.

Key Terms

element
atom
molecule
electron
nucleus
Bohr atom
photon
quantum leap, or quantum jump
spectrum
spectroscopy
periodic table of the elements

Review Questions

1. Did Democritus use the scientific method to study the existence of atoms?
2. Did Dalton use the scientific method in his studies of the existence of atoms?
3. Review six kinds of observational evidence that were used to support the atomic theory.
4. What three particles make up every atom? What are the major differences among these particles?

5. How does the nucleus differ from electrons?

6. Why is the smallest unit of an element an atom, but the smallest unit of a compound is a molecule?

7. Review the basic elements of Rutherford's experiment. What evidence did Rutherford use to justify his discovery of the nucleus?

8. How does Bohr's model of the atom differ from Rutherford's?

9. What is the relationship between a photon and a quantum leap?

10. How might an emission spectrum and an absorption spectrum of a given element differ in appearance?

11. Cite three examples of everyday objects with vivid emission spectra.

12. How might astronomers on Earth use spectroscopy to determine chemical elements that occur in stars?

13. Describe the basic components of a laser. How does a laser work?

14. In what ways are all the elements in a given column of the periodic table similar? In what ways are they different?

Discussion Questions

1. Which atomic model (i.e., Bohr's or Rutherford's) resembles our solar system of planets orbiting the Sun most closely in structure? How is the degradation of orbiting planets in our solar system like that of the Rutherford atomic model?

2. Why do laser pointers need batteries?

3. Rutherford's experiment involved firing nucleus-sized "bullets" at atoms of gold. Why might he have chosen gold instead of hydrogen?

4. What is a quantum leap? How big is a quantum leap? Advertisers often describe improvements in their products as a "quantum leap." Is this an appropriate use of the term?

5. Based on your knowledge of Newton's laws of motion, the laws of thermodynamics, and the nature of electromagnetic radiation, explain why the Rutherford model of the atom couldn't work and the Bohr model does.

6. When you shine invisible ultraviolet light (black light) on certain objects, they glow with brilliant colors. How might this behavior be explained in terms of the Bohr atom?

7. Why do different lasers have different-colored beams?

8. What does it mean to say the periodic table was useful because it "worked?" How does this relate to the scientific method? Can you think of another invention that "worked" without our having a scientific understanding of the principles that underlied its operation?

9. Why is chlorine used in pools and to bleach clothing? What chemical property does chlorine possess that makes it a good chemical for that purpose? Using the periodic table, what other elements might be used instead of chlorine?

10. Space probes often carry compact spectrometers among their scientific hardware. What kind of spectroscopy might scientists use to determine the surface composition of the cold, outer planets that orbit the Sun? How might they use spectroscopy to determine the atmospheric composition of these planets?

11. In the science fiction series *Star Trek*, there is a weapon called the "photon torpedo." Given what you now know about photons, speculate about how such a weapon might work.

12. If you replaced the tungsten filament of a typical incandescent bulb with an iron filament, would the emission spectrum be the same? Why or why not?

13. If you replaced the argon in a typical incandescent bulb with oxygen, what would happen to the filament? Why?

Problems

1. If the electrons in an atom can occupy any of four different energy levels, how many lines might appear in that atom's spectrum? What if the atom has five different energy levels?

2. Imagine that you have 4 different chemical elements in your chemical laboratory. What is the maximum number of 1:1 chemical compounds that you could form? What if you had 12 different chemical elements?

3. Imagine that you have six different chemical elements. What is the maximum number of 1:1:1 chemical compounds that you could form? What about 1:1:2 compounds? What about 1:2:3 compounds? How do these numbers compare with the number of known chemical elements?

4. Using the periodic table, calculate the result of the following equation: the number of electrons in the outer shell of a hydrogen atom minus the number of electrons in the outer shell of a helium atom plus the number of electrons in the outer shell of a hydrogen atom.

INVESTIGATIONS

1. Investigate the history of the discovery of chemical elements. What technological innovations led to the discovery of several new elements? What was the most recent element to be discovered, and how was it found? How much time did researchers have to study the most recently developed element? How many elements occur in nature, and how many are human-made?

2. Simple handheld spectroscopes are available in many science labs. Look at the spectra of different kinds of lightbulbs: an incandescent bulb, a fluorescent bulb, a halogen bulb, and any other kinds available to you. What differences do you observe in their spectra? Why?

3. Place pieces of transparent materials between a strong light source and the spectrometer described in Investigation 2. Does the spectrum change? Why?

4. Why do colors look different when viewed indoors under fluorescent light, and outdoors in sunlight? How might you devise an experiment to quantify these differences?

5. Investigate the variety of lasers that are currently available. What is the range of wavelengths available? How are different lasers used in medicine? in industry? in science?

6. At your local hardware store, find "full-spectrum" fluorescent or incandescent bulbs. Read the labels describing their emission spectrum. What wavelengths of electromagnetic energy do the bulbs produce? Are they really "full spectrum"?

7. Many television crime shows depict forensic investigators using spectroscopy to detect the residue of bodily fluids at crime scenes. How does spectroscopy detect this residue?

9

Quantum Mechanics

How can the electron behave like both a particle and a wave?

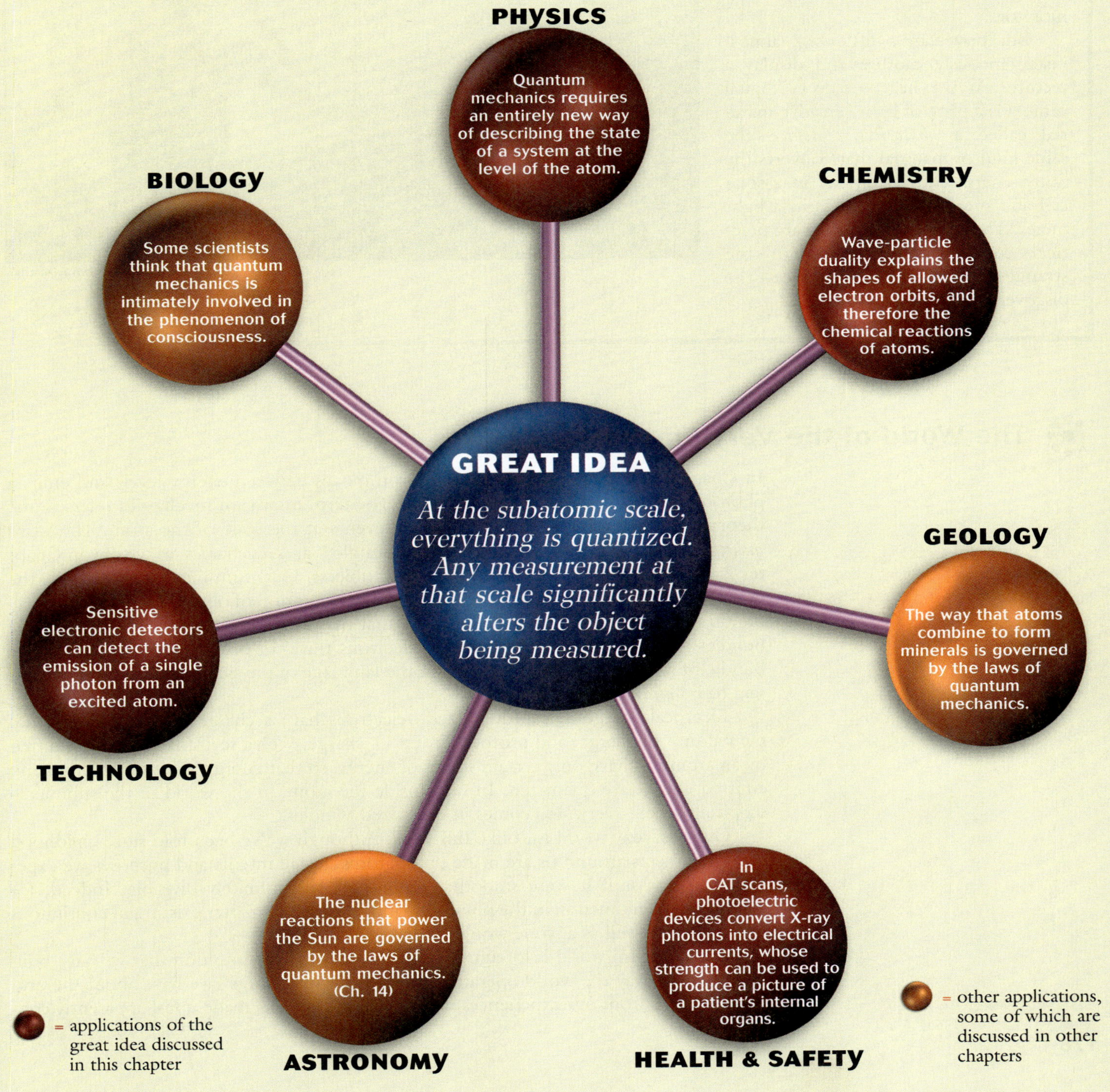

Science Through the Day | Digital Pictures

It's 9:30 A.M. as you pull into the oceanside parking lot. You've made great time and are eager to hit the beach. You see your friends waiting near the entrance. As you shout and wave, a classmate snaps your picture on her new digital camera. Everyone crowds around to see the crisp image on the camera's video monitor.

But how can a little box almost instantaneously capture and display a picture? At the heart of every digital camera is a plate of light-sensitive material called a *photoelectric device*—the same kind of material that converts the Sun's energy into electricity in a solar cell and measures brightness in a light meter. These everyday objects are practical consequences of one of the strangest discoveries in science—the discovery of the quantum world.

Plush Studios/Photodisc/Getty Images, Inc.

The World of the Very Small

In Chapter 8 we saw that when an electron moves between energy levels and emits a photon, it is said to make a *quantum leap*. The term **quantum mechanics** refers to the theory that describes this event and other events at the scale of the atom. The word *quantum* comes from the Latin word for "bundle," and mechanics, as we saw in Chapter 2, is the study of the motion of material objects. Quantum mechanics, then, is the branch of science that is devoted to the study of the motion of objects that come in small bundles, or quanta. We have already seen that material inside the atom comes in little bundles—tiny pieces of matter we call electrons travel in orbits around another little bundle of matter we call the nucleus. In the language of physicists, the atom's matter is said to be *quantized*.

Electrical charge is also quantized—electrons have a charge of exactly −1 fundamental unit of charge, and protons have a +1 charge. We've seen that photons emitted by an atom can have only certain values of energy, so that energy levels in the atom and emitted energy are quantized. In fact, inside the atom, in the world of the submicroscopically small, *everything* comes in quantized bundles.

Our everyday world isn't like this at all. Although we've been told since childhood that the objects around us are made up of atoms, for all intents and purposes we experience matter as if it were smooth, continuous, and infinitely divisible. Indeed, for almost any phenomenon in the physical world, the idea of matter existing in continuous form works as well as anyone would want.

The quantum world is foreign to our senses. All of the intuition that we have built up about the way the world operates—all of the "gut feelings" we have about the universe—comes from our experiences with large-scale objects made up of apparently continuous material. If it should turn out (as it does) that the world of the quantum does not match our intuition, we should not be surprised. We have never dealt with this kind of world, so we have no particular reason, based on observations or experience, to believe that it should behave one way or the other.

This warning may not make you feel much better as you learn just how strange and different the quantum world really is, but it might help you come to intellectual grips with a most fascinating part of our physical universe.

Measurement and Observation in the Quantum World

Every measurement in the physical world incorporates three essential components:

1. A sample—a piece of matter to study
2. A source of energy—light, wave, or heat or kinetic energy that interacts with the sample
3. A detector to observe and measure that interaction

MAI/NASA/Landov LLC

A radar antenna sends out microwaves that interact with flying airplanes, are reflected, and detected on their return. This allows air traffic controllers to keep track of where airplanes are in the sky.

When you look at a piece of matter such as this book, you can see it because light bounces off the book and comes to your eye, a very sophisticated detector (see Chapter 6). When you examine a piece of fruit at the grocery store, you apply energy by squeezing it to detect if it feels too ripe.

Many professions employ sophisticated devices to make their measurements. Air traffic controllers reflect microwaves off airplanes to determine their positions, oceanographers bounce sound waves off deep-ocean sediments to map the seafloor, and dentists pass X-rays through your teeth and gums to look for cavities. In our everyday world we assume that such interactions of matter and energy do not change the objects being measured in any appreciable way. Microwaves don't alter an airplane's flight path, nor do sound waves disturb the topography of the ocean's bottom. And while prolonged exposure to X-rays can be harmful, the dentist's brief exploratory X-ray photograph has no obvious immediate effects on the tooth. Our experience tells us that a measurement can usually be made on a macroscopic object—something large enough to be seen without a microscope—without altering that object, because the energy of the probe is much less than the energy of the object.

The situation is rather different in the quantum world. If you want to "see" an electron, you have to bounce energy off it so that the information can be carried to your detectors. But nothing at your disposal can interact with the electron without simultaneously affecting it. You can bounce a photon off it, but in the process the electron's energy will change. You can bounce another particle off it, but the electron will recoil like a billiard ball. No matter what you try, the energy of the probe is too close to the energy of the thing being measured. The electron cannot fail to be altered by the interaction.

Many everyday analogies illustrate the process of measurement in the quantum world. It's like trying to detect bowling balls by bouncing other bowling balls off them. The act of measurement in the quantum world poses a dilemma analogous to trying to discover if there is a car in a tunnel when the only means of finding out is to send another car into the tunnel and listen for a crash. With this technique you can certainly discover whether the first car is there. You can probably even find out where it is by measuring the time it takes the probe car to crash. What you *cannot* do, however, is assume that the first car is the same after the interaction as it was before. In the same way, nothing in the quantum world can be the same after the interaction associated with a measurement as it was before.

In principle, this argument would apply to any interaction, whether it involves photons and electrons or photons and bowling balls. As we demonstrate in the "Science by the Numbers" section in this chapter, however, the effects of the interaction for large-scale objects are so tiny that they can simply be ignored, while in the case of interactions at the atomic level, they cannot. This fundamental difference between the quantum and macroscopic worlds is what makes quantum mechanics quite different from the classical mechanics of Isaac Newton. Remember that every experiment, be it on planets or fruit or quantum objects, involves interactions of one sort or another. The consequences of small-scale interactions make the quantum world different, not the fact that a measurement is being made.

The Heisenberg Uncertainty Principle

In 1927, a young German physicist, Werner Heisenberg (1901–1976), put the idea of limitations on quantum-scale measurements into precise mathematical form. His work, which was one of the first results to come from the new science of quantum mechanics, is called the *Heisenberg uncertainty principle* in his honor. The central concept of the uncertainty principle is simple:

At the quantum scale, any measurement significantly alters the object being measured.

Suppose, for example, you have a particle such as an electron in an atom and want to know where it is *and* how fast it's moving. The uncertainty principle tells us that it is impossible to measure both the position and the velocity with infinite accuracy at the same time.

The reason for this state of affairs, of course, is that every measurement changes the object being measured. Just as the car in the tunnel could not be the same after the first measurement was made on it, so too will the quantum object change. The result is that as you measure one property such as position more and more exactly, your knowledge of a property such as velocity gets fuzzier and fuzzier.

The uncertainty principle doesn't say that we cannot know a particle's location with great precision. It is possible, at least in principle, for the uncertainty in position to be zero, which would mean that we know the exact location of a quantum particle. In this case, however, the uncertainty in the velocity has to be infinite. Thus, at the point in time when we know exactly where the particle is, we have no idea whatsoever how fast it is moving. By the same token, if we know exactly how fast the quantum particle is moving, we cannot know where it is. It could, quite literally, be in the room with us or in China.

In practice, every quantum measurement involves trade-offs. We accept some fuzziness in the location of the particle and some fuzziness in the knowledge of the velocity, playing the two off against each other to get the best solution to whatever problem it is we're working on. We cannot have precise knowledge of both at the same time, but we can know either one as accurately as we like at any time.

Let's look a little more closely at the differences between the world of our intuition and the quantum world. In the former, we assume that measurement doesn't affect the thing being measured, so that we can have exact, simultaneous knowledge of both the position and velocity of an object such as a car or a baseball. In the quantum world, as Heisenberg taught us, we cannot.

Heisenberg put his notion into a simple mathematical relationship, which is a complete and exact statement of the **uncertainty principle.**

- ▶ **In words:** The error or uncertainty in the measurement of an object's position, times the error or uncertainty in that object's velocity, must be greater than a constant (Planck's constant) divided by the object's mass.
- ▶ **In equation form:**

$$\text{(uncertainty in position)} \times \text{(uncertainty in velocity)} > \frac{h}{\text{mass}}$$

where h is a number known as Planck's constant (see below).

▶ **In symbols:**

$$\Delta x \times \Delta v > \frac{h}{m}$$

This equation is a precise, shorthand way of saying that you can never know both the position and velocity of an object with perfect accuracy. The difference between our everyday world and the world inside the atom hangs on the question of the numerical value of h/m, the numbers on the right side of Heisenberg's equation. In SI units (see Appendix A), Planck's constant, h, has a value of 6.63×10^{-34} joule-seconds.

The important point about the Heisenberg relationship is not the exact value of the number, h/m, but the fact that the number is greater than zero. Look at it this way. If you make more and more precise measurements about the location of a particle, you determine its position more and more exactly, and the uncertainty in position, Δx, must get smaller and smaller. In this situation, it follows that the uncertainty in velocity, Δv, has to get bigger and bigger. In fact, we can use the uncertainty principle to calculate exactly our uncertainty in velocity for a given uncertainty in position, and vice versa.

Science by the Numbers •

Uncertainty in the Newtonian World

The best way to understand why we do not have to worry about the uncertainty principle in our everyday life is to calculate the uncertainty in measurements in two separate situations: large objects and very small objects.

1. **Small Uncertainties with Large Objects.** A moving automobile with a mass of 1000 kilograms is located in an intersection that is 5 meters across. How precisely can you know how fast the car is traveling?

   We can solve this problem by noting that if the car is somewhere in an intersection 5 m across, then the uncertainty in position of the car is about equal to 5 m. Thus we know the car's mass and uncertainty in position, so we can calculate the uncertainty in velocity:

$$\text{(uncertainty in position)} \times \text{(uncertainty in velocity)} > \frac{h}{\text{mass}}$$

First, we must rearrange this equation to solve for uncertainty in velocity:

$$\begin{aligned}\text{(uncertainty in velocity)} &> \frac{(h/\text{mass})}{\text{uncertainty in position}} \\ &> \frac{[(6.63 \times 10^{-34}\,\text{J-s})/1000\,\text{kg}]}{5\,\text{m}} \\ &> \frac{[(6.63 \times 10^{-37}\,\text{J-s})/\text{kg}]}{5\,\text{m}} \\ &> 1.33 \times 10^{-37}\ \text{m/s}\end{aligned}$$

Thus the uncertainty in the velocity of the automobile is greater than 1.33×10^{-37} m/s (note that the unit J-s/kg-m is equivalent to m/s; see Problem 2 at the end of the chapter). This uncertainty is extremely small. Theoretically, we could know the velocity of the car to an accuracy of 37 decimal places! In practice, however, we have no method of measuring velocities with present or foreseeable future technology to an accuracy remotely approaching this. The uncertainty is, for all practical purposes, indistinguishable from zero. Therefore, for objects with significant mass such as automobiles, the effects of the uncertainty principle are totally negligible. The equation confirms our experience that Newtonian mechanics works perfectly well in dealing with everyday objects.

2. **Large Uncertainties with Small Objects.** Contrast the preceding example with the uncertainty in velocity of an electron in an atom, located within an area about 10^{-10} meters on a side. To what accuracy can we measure the velocity of that electron?

The mass of an electron is 9.11×10^{-31}kg. If we take the uncertainty in position to be 10^{-10} m, then according to the uncertainty principle,

$$\text{uncertainty in velocity} > \frac{(h/\text{mass})}{\text{uncertainty in position}}$$

$$> \frac{[(6.63 \times 10^{-34}\,\text{J-s})/(9.11 \times 10^{-31}\,\text{kg})]}{10^{-10}\ \text{m}}$$

$$> 7.3 \times 10^{6}\,\text{m/s}$$

This uncertainty is very large indeed. The mere fact that we know that an electron is somewhere in an atom means that we cannot know its velocity to within a million meters per second.

For ordinary-sized objects such as cars and bowling balls, whose mass is measured in kilograms, the number on the right side of the uncertainty relation is so small that we can treat it as being zero. Only when the masses get very small, as they do for particles such as the electron, does the number on the right get big enough to make a practical difference. •

Stop and Think! How big do you suppose something has to be before we can forget about the effects of the uncertainty principle? as big as a speck of dust? a baseball? a car?

Probabilities

The uncertainty principle has consequences that go far beyond simple statements about measurement. In the quantum world we must radically change the way that we describe events. Consider an everyday example in which the uncertainties are much larger (but easier to picture) than those associated with Heisenberg's equation. Think of a batter hitting a ball during a nighttime baseball game.

Imagine yourself at a big-league ball game under the lights of a great stadium. Cheering fans fill the stands, roving vendors sell their food and drink, and the pitcher and batter play out their classic duel. The pitcher stares the batter down, winds up, and hurls a fastball. But the batter is ready and pounces on the pitch. The ball leaps off the bat with a sharp crack. And then all the lights go out.

Where will the ball be in five seconds? If you were an outfielder, this would be more than a philosophical question. You would need to know where to go to make your catch, even in the dark. In a Newtonian world, you would have no problem in doing this. If you knew the position and velocity of the ball at the instant the lights went out, some simple calculations would tell you exactly where the ball would be at any time in the future.

If you were a quantum outfielder in an atom-sized ball field, on the other hand, you would have a much harder time of it. You couldn't know both the position and velocity of the quantum ball when the lights go out; at best you could put some bounds on them. You might, for example, be able to say something like "It's somewhere inside this 3-foot circle and traveling between 30 and 70 feet per second." This means that when you have to guess where it would be in five seconds, you wouldn't be able to do so with any accuracy. If you were thinking in Newtonian terms, you would have to say that the ball could be 147 feet from the plate (if it were traveling 30 feet per second and located at the back of the 3-foot circle), 353 feet from the plate (if it were traveling 70 feet per second and located at the front of the circle), or anyplace in between. The best you could do would be to predict the likelihood, or **probability,** that the ball would be anywhere in the outfield, and you could present these probabilities on a graph like the one shown in Figure 9-1.

This example shows that the uncertainty principle requires a description of quantum-scale events in terms of probabilities. Just like the baseball in our example of the darkened stadium, there must be uncertainties in the position and velocity for every quantum object when we first start observing it, and hence there will be uncertainties at the end—uncertainties that can be dealt with by reporting probabilities.

This result is extremely important. It tells us that we cannot think of quantum events in the same way that we think of normal events in our everyday world. In particular, we have to rethink what it means to talk about concepts such as regularity, predictability, and causality at the quantum level.

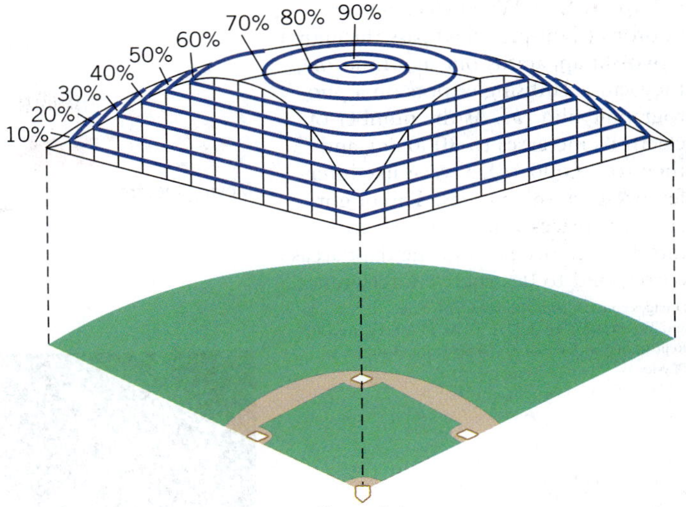

• **Figure 9-1** The position of a "quantum baseball" cannot be precisely determined. Instead, you can predict only the probabilities of the ball being at various distances from home plate, as discussed in the text. The most likely location is at the peak of the curve, but the ball could be anywhere else.

Wave-Particle Duality

Quantum mechanics is sometimes called *wave mechanics* because it turns out that quantum objects sometimes act like particles and sometimes like waves. This dichotomy is known as the problem of wave-particle duality, and it has puzzled some of the best minds in science. To understand it, think about how particles and waves behave in our macroscopic world.

The Double-Slit Test

Energy travels either as a wave or as a particle in our everyday world (see Chapter 6). Particles transfer energy through collisions, while waves transfer energy through collective motion of the media or electromagnetic fields. Every aspect of the everyday world can be neatly divided into particles or waves, and many experiments can be used to determine whether something is a particle or wave. The most famous of these experiments uses a double-slit apparatus, which consists of a barrier that has two slits in it (Figure 9-2). If particles such as baseballs are thrown from the left side, a few will make it through the slits, but most will bounce off. If you were standing on the other side of the barrier, you would expect to see the baseballs coming through more or less in the two places shown, accumulating in two piles behind the barrier. You wouldn't expect to see many particles (baseballs) at the spots between the slits.

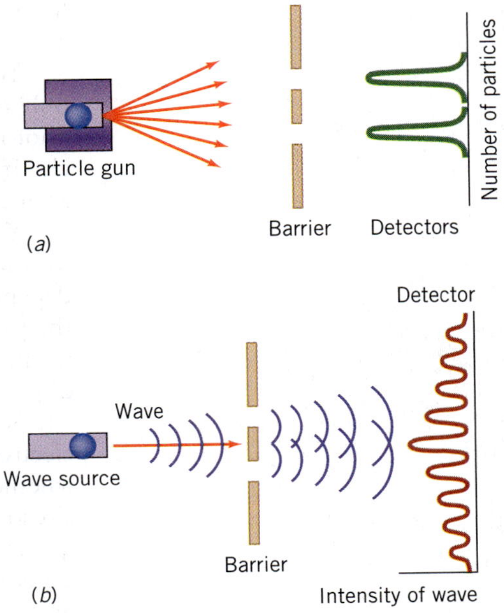

• **Figure 9-2** The two-slit experiment may be used to determine whether something is a wave or a particle. *(a)* A stream of particles striking the barrier will accumulate in the two regions directly behind the slits. *(b)* When waves converge on two narrow slits, however, constructive and destructive interference results in a series of peaks.

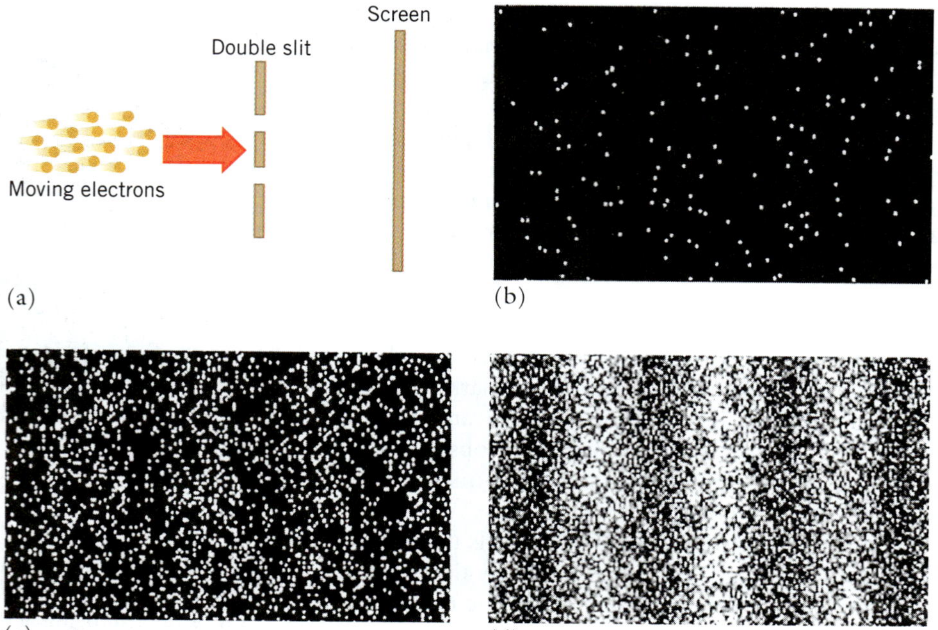

• **Figure 9-3** When electrons or photons (light particles) pass through a two-slit apparatus one at a time *(a)*, they cause 100 single spots on a photographic film *(b)*. As the number of electrons increases to 3000 *(c)*, and then to 70,000 *(d)*, a wave-like interference pattern emerges. The bright areas are places where constructive interference occurs, and the dark areas correspond to destructive interference.

(Images courtesy Akira Tonomura, J. Endo, T. Matsuda and T. Kawasaki, *Am J. Phys.* 57(2): 117, February 1989. Reproduced with permission of American Institute of Physics.)

If, however, waves of water were coming from the left side, you would expect to see the results of constructive and destructive interference (see Chapter 6). Rather than the two piles of baseballs, we would see perhaps half a dozen regions of high waves beyond the barrier, interspersed with regions of still water.

Now, let's use the same arrangement to see whether light behaves as a particle or a wave. In Chapter 8 we learned that light is emitted in discrete bundles of energy called *photons*. On the one hand, photons behave like particles in the sense that they can be localized in space. You can set up experiments in which a photon is emitted at one point, then received somewhere else after an appropriate lapse of time, just as a baseball is "emitted" by a pitcher and "received" later by a catcher (Figure 9-2*a*). If, on the other hand, you shine light—a flood of photons—on the two-slit apparatus, you will definitely get an interference pattern on the right (Figure 9-2*b*). In that experiment, photons act like waves. The big question: How can photons sometimes act like waves and sometimes act like particles?

You can make the problem even more puzzling by setting up the apparatus so that only one photon at a time comes through the slits. If you do this, you find that each photon arrives at a specific point at the screen—behavior you would expect of a particle. If you allow photons to accumulate over long periods of time, however, they will arrange themselves into an interference pattern characteristic of a wave (Figure 9-3).

You could do a similar series of experiments with any quantum object—electrons, for example, or even atoms. They all exhibit the properties of both particles and waves, depending on what sort of experiment is done. If you perform an experiment that tests the particle properties of these things, they look like particles. If you perform an experiment to test their wave properties, they look like waves. Whether you see quantum objects as particles or waves seems to depend on the experiment that you do.

Some experimenters have gone so far as to try to "trick" quantum particles such as electrons into revealing their true identity by using modern fast electronics to decide whether a particle- or wave-type experiment is being done *after* the quantum object is already on its way into the apparatus. Scientists who do these experiments find that the quantum object seems to "know" what experiment is being done, because the particle experiments always turn up particle properties, while the wave experiments always turn up wave properties.

At the quantum level, the objects that we talk about are neither particles nor waves in the classical sense. In fact, we can't really visualize them at all, because we have never encountered anything like them in our everyday experience. They are a third kind of object, neither particle nor wave, but exhibiting the properties of both. If you persist in thinking about them as if they were baseballs or surf coming onto a beach, you will quickly lose yourself in confusion.

It's a little bit like finding someone who has seen only the colors red and green in her entire life. If she has decided that everything in the world has to be either red or green, she will be totally confused by seeing the color blue. What she has to realize is that the problem is not in nature, but in her assumption that everything has to be either red or green.

In the same way, the problem of wave-particle duality arises from our assumption that everything has to be either a wave or a particle. If we allow ourselves the possibility that quantum objects are things that we have never encountered before, and that they therefore might have unencountered properties, the puzzle vanishes. However, it vanishes only if we agree that we won't try to draw a picture of these objects or pretend that we can actually visualize what they are.

Technology •

The Photoelectric Effect

When photons of sufficient energy strike some materials, their energy can be absorbed by electrons, which are shaken loose from their home atoms. If the material in question is in the form of a thin sheet, then when light strikes one side, electrons are observed coming out of the other. This phenomenon is called the *photoelectric effect,* and it finds applications in numerous everyday devices.

One aspect of the photoelectric effect played a major role in the history of quantum mechanics. The time between the arrival of the light and the appearance of the electrons is extremely short—far too short to be explained by the relatively gentle action of a wave nudging the electrons loose. In fact, it was Albert Einstein who pointed out that the explanation of this rapid response depended on the particle-like nature of the photon. He argued that the interaction between the light and the electron is something like the collision between two billiard balls, with one ball shooting out instantly after the collision. It was this work, which led to our modern concept of the photon, that was the basis of Einstein's Nobel Prize in 1921.

The conversion of light energy into electrical current is used in many familiar devices. In a digital camera, for example, one photoelectric device measures the amount of light available to determine how wide to open the lens and what the shutter speed should be. Then a photoelectric plate collects the photographic image. In telephone systems that use fiber optics—glass fibers that act like pipes for visible light—light signals strike sophisticated semiconductor devices (see Chapter 11) and shake loose electrons. These electrons form a current that ultimately drives the diaphragm in your telephone and produces the sound that you hear. In CAT scans (see "The Science of Life" section that follows), photoelectric devices convert X-ray photons into electrical currents whose strength can be used to produce a picture of a patient's internal organs. As all of these examples show, an understanding of the way objects interact in the quantum world can have enormous practical consequences. •

The Science of Life •

The CAT Scan

Photoelectric detectors play a crucial role in a modern medical technique called the CAT scan. Ordinary X-ray photographs depend on the differences in density (and therefore

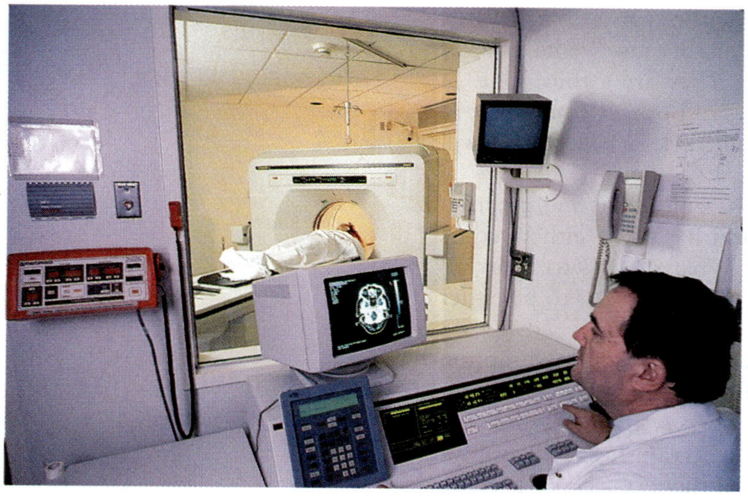

Larry Nulvehill/Photo Researchers

A boy having a CAT scan; a video monitor is in the foreground. A CAT scan of a human skull and brain is shown on the monitor.

in the ability to absorb X-rays) of the various materials in the body. In these photographs, the X-rays make one pass through, in one direction only, to produce pictures. They cannot produce a three-dimensional image of the interior of the body, nor can they produce sharp images of organs whose densities are not significantly different from the densities of their surroundings. These shortcomings are overcome by a different X-ray technique known as *computerized axial tomography (CAT).*

The easiest way to visualize a CAT scan is to imagine dividing the body into slices perpendicular to the backbone, with each slice being a millimeter or so in width. The material in each slice is probed by successive short bursts of X-rays, lasting only a few milliseconds each, that cross the slice in different directions. Each part of the slice is thus traversed by many different X-ray bursts. Each burst of X-rays contains the same number of photons when it starts, and the ones that go all the way through the body (i.e., those not absorbed by material along their path) are measured by a photoelectric device (see the preceding "Technology" section).

Once all the data on a given slice have been obtained, a computer works out the density of each point of the body and produces a detailed cross section along that particular slice. A complete picture of the body (or a specific part of it) can then be built up by combining successive slices. •

Wave-Particle Duality and the Bohr Atom

Treating electrons as waves helps explain why only certain orbits are allowed in atoms (see Chapter 8). Every quantum object displays a simple relationship between its speed (when we think of it as a particle) and its wavelength (when we think of it as a wave). It turns out that for electrons, protons, and other quantum objects, a faster speed always corresponds to a shorter, more energetic wavelength (or a higher frequency).

If you think of an electron as a particle, then you can treat its motion around an atom's nucleus in the same Newtonian way you treat the motion of Earth in orbit around the Sun. That is, for any given distance from the nucleus, the electron must have a precise velocity to stay in a stable orbit. Provided it is moving at such a velocity, it will stay in that orbit just as Earth stays in a stable orbit around the Sun. Any faster and it must adopt a higher orbit; any slower and it will move closer to the nucleus.

• **Figure 9-4** A vibrating string adopts a regular pattern, known as a standing wave. These photos and diagrams illustrate fixed patterns with ½, 1, and 3/2 wavelengths.

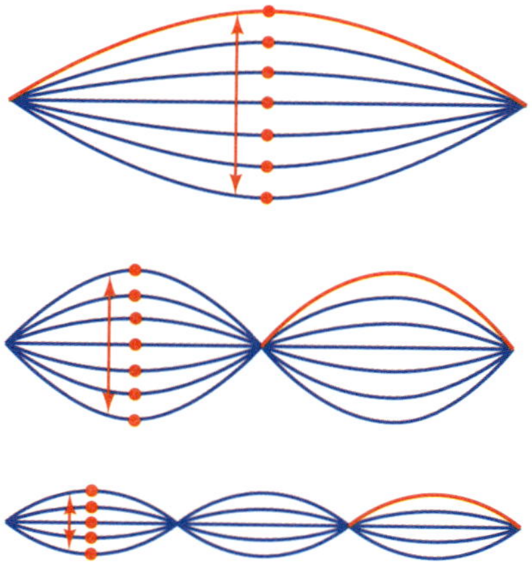

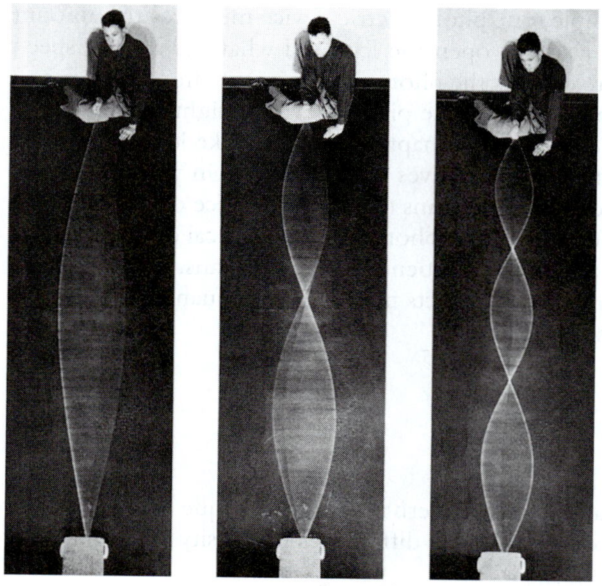

Courtesy Education Development Center

If we choose to think about the electron as a wave, however, a different set of criteria can be used to decide how to put the electron into its orbit. A wave on a straight string (on a guitar, for example) vibrates uniformly only at certain frequencies that depend on the length of the string (Figure 9-4). These frequencies correspond to fitting ½,

1, and 3⁄2 wavelengths on the string in the figure. Now imagine bending the guitar string around into a circular orbit. In this case, you will be able to fit only certain standing waves in the orbit, as shown in Figure 9-5.

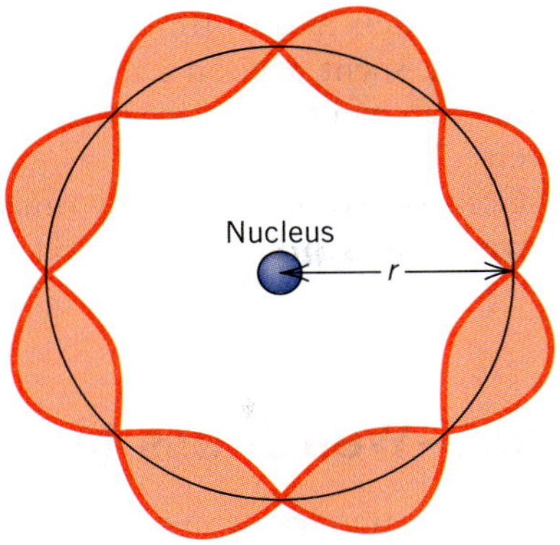

• **Figure 9-5** An electron in orbit about an atom adopts a standing wave like a vibrating string. This illustration shows a standing wave with four wavelengths fitting into the orbit's circumference.

You can now ask a simple question: Are there any orbits for which the wave and particle descriptions are consistent? In other words, are there orbits for which the velocity of the electron (when we think of it as a particle) is appropriate to the orbit, while at the same time the electron wave (when we think of it as a wave) fits onto the orbit, given the relation between wavelength and velocity?

When you do the mathematics, you find that the only orbits that satisfy these twin conditions are the Bohr orbits. That is to say, *the only orbits allowed in the atom are those for which it makes no difference whether we think of the electron as a particle or a wave.* In a sense, then, the wave-particle duality exists in our minds, and not in nature—nature has arranged things so that what we think doesn't matter.

Quantum Weirdness

The fact that quantum objects behave so differently from objects in our everyday experience causes many people to worry that nature has somehow become "weird" at the subatomic level. The description of particles in terms of a wave defies our common sense. Situations in which a photon or an electron seems to "know" how an apparatus will be arranged before the arranging is done seem wrong and unnatural. Many people, scientists and nonscientists alike, find the conclusions of quantum mechanics to be quite unsettling. The American physicist Richard Feynman stressed this point when he said, "I can safely say that nobody understands quantum mechanics. . . . Do not keep saying to yourself, 'But how can it be like that?' . . . Nobody knows how it can be like that."

In spite of this rather disturbing situation, the success of quantum mechanics provides ample evidence that there is a correct way to describe an atomic-scale system. If you ignore this fact, you can get into a lot of trouble. Newtonian notions like position and velocity just aren't appropriate for the quantum world, which must be described from the beginning in terms of waves and probabilities. Quantum mechanics thus becomes a way of predicting how subatomic objects change in time. If you know the state of an electron now, you can use quantum mechanics to predict the state of that electron in the future. This process is identical to the application of Newton's laws of motion in the macroscopic world. The only difference is that in the quantum world, the "state" of the system is a probability.

In the view of most working scientists, quantum mechanics is a marvelous tool that allows us to do all sorts of experiments and build all manner of new and important pieces of equipment. The fact that we can't visualize the quantum world in familiar terms seems a small price to pay for all the benefits we receive.

Science in the Making •

A Famous Interchange

Many people are disturbed by the fact that nature must be described in terms of probabilities at the subatomic level. Many scientists were also disturbed when quantum mechanics was first developed in the early twentieth century. Even Albert Einstein, one of the founders of quantum mechanics, could not accept what it was telling us about the world. He spent a good part of the last half of his life trying to refute it. His most famous statement from this period was, "I cannot believe that God plays dice with the universe."

Confronted one too many times with this aphorism, Einstein's lifelong friend and colleague Neils Bohr is supposed to have replied, "Albert, stop telling God what to do." •

Quantum Entanglement—Weirdness in Action

One of the strangest features of the quantum world goes by the name *quantum entanglement.* It has no real analog in our everyday experience, but here is an example that demonstrates its main characteristic. Suppose you had a set of dice, and each die was perfectly normal—if rolled individually, a die shows each face one-sixth of the time. Now suppose you take one of the dice to New York and the other to Los Angeles and rolled them. Imagine discovering when you did this that whatever showed on the New York die also showed on its partner in Los Angeles. If the New York die came up with a 3, for example, the Los Angeles die would do the same. This strange connection between the two die would be inexplicable in our ordinary world but would simply be an example of entanglement in the quantum world.

Here's a simple example: suppose an atom emits two photons at the same time. The two-photon system is then described by a wave function. Now let the two photons travel in opposite directions, travel so far that there is no possibility that a signal traveling at the speed of light could pass between them in the time that it takes to make a measurement. In our ordinary world—if we were throwing baseballs, for example—we would expect that a measurement on one baseball would have no effect on the other once the two have separated. In the quantum world, however, the wave functions of the two photons never really become separated. They remain *entangled* with each other, so that if you measure one photon you know exactly what state the other one is in. Don't try to picture how measuring one photon can change the other, even when the two have no way of communicating with each other. You can't. This is just another example of Feynman's dictum.

But entanglement is more than just weird—it may also turn out to be the basis of important new technologies. In a process known as *quantum teleportation,* physicists have discovered that if they allow a third photon to interact with one member of an entangled pair, they can re-create that third photon's properties from measurements of the other member of the pair. Like the fictional "transporters" in *Star Trek,* in which people disappeared from one spot and were re-created somewhere else, quantum teleportation destroys the third photon at one place and re-creates it at another.

Stop and Think! Is the photon created by quantum teleportation the same photon that was destroyed? If it has all the properties of the original photon, how could you tell the two apart?

Science in the Making

In 1997, a group in Vienna headed by physicist Anton Zeilinger sent the first picture through the use of quantum teleported photons. Zeilinger explained to his team that since this would be a historic event, they would have to be careful in their choice of subject. In fact, he told them, he had two criteria: first, the image had to be peaceful, and second, it had to be Austrian. Their choice: the so-called Venus of Willendorf, a prehistoric statue of a fertility goddess discovered in an Austrian village. •

Thinking More About | Quantum Mechanics

Uncertainty and Human Beings

The ultimate Newtonian view of the universe was the concept of the Divine Calculator (see Chapter 2). This mythical being, given the position and velocity of every particle in the universe, could predict every future state of those particles. The difficulty with this concept, of course, is that if the future of the universe is laid out with clockwork precision, it allows no room for human action. No one can make a choice about what he or she will do, because that choice is already determined and exists (in the mind of God or the Divine Calculator) before it is made.

Quantum mechanics gives us one way to get out of this particular bind. Heisenberg tells us that, although we might be able to predict the future if we knew the position and velocity of every particle exactly, we can never actually get those two numbers. The Divine Calculator in a quantum world is doomed to wait forever for the input data with which to start the calculation.

One area where the uncertainty principle is starting to play a somewhat unexpected role is in the old philosophical argument about the connection between the mind and the brain. The brain is a physical object, an incredibly complex organ that processes information in the form of nerve impulses. (A more detailed description of the workings of the brain is given in Chapter 11.) The problem: What is the connection between the physical reality of the brain—the atoms and structures that compose it—and the consciousness that we all experience?

Many scientists and philosophers have argued that the brain is no more than a physical structure. These thinkers have run into a problem, however, because if the brain is purely a physical object, its future states should be predictable. Recently, scientists (most notably Roger Penrose of Cambridge University) have argued that quantum mechanics can introduce a kind of unpredictability that squares better with our perceptions of our own minds.

Think about how the workings of the brain might be unpredictable at the quantum level. Why might that uncertainty make it difficult (or even impossible) to make precise predictions of the future state of the brain?

Summary

Matter and energy at the atomic scale come in discrete packets called quanta. The rules of ***quantum mechanics,*** the laws that allow us to describe and predict events in the quantum world, are disturbingly different from Newton's laws of motion.

At the quantum scale, unlike our everyday experience, any measurement of the position or velocity of a particle causes the particle to change in unpredictable ways. The mere act of measurement alters the thing being measured. Werner Heisenberg quantified this situation in the Heisenberg ***uncertainty principle,*** which states that the uncertainty in the position of a particle multiplied by the uncertainty in its velocity must be greater than a small positive number. Unlike the Newtonian world, you can never know the exact position and velocity of a quantum particle.

These uncertainties preclude us from describing atomic-scale particles in the classical way. Instead, quantum descriptions are given in terms of the ***probability*** that an object will be in one state or another. Furthermore, quantum objects are not simply particles or waves, a dichotomy familiar to us in the macroscopic world. They represent something completely different from our experience, incorporating properties of both particles and waves.

Key Terms

quantum mechanics

uncertainty principle

probability

Key Equations

$$\text{(uncertainty in position)} \times \text{(uncertainty in velocity)} > \frac{h}{\text{mass}}$$

Review Questions

1. What does quantum mechanics mean?
2. Give three examples of properties that are quantized at the scale of an electron.
3. What are the three essential parts of every physical measurement?
4. In what way is a measurement at the quantum scale of an electron different from a measurement at large scales of everyday objects?

5. There was once a humorous poster showing a picture of a bed with the caption, "Heisenberg may have slept here." In what way is this an inaccurate representation of Heisenberg's uncertainty principle?

6. Under what circumstances can you know the position of an electron with great accuracy?

7. Why is quantum mechanics sometimes called wave mechanics?

8. Give an everyday example of wave-particle duality.

9. Explain how the photoelectric effect works. Does it depend on the wave or the particle nature of light?

10. How does wave-particle duality explain the Bohr orbits of electrons in atoms?

11. Why did Albert Einstein use playing dice as an analogy for quantum mechanics?

Discussion Questions

1. Identify the sample, the source of energy, and the detector in the following "experiments":

a. measuring the color of a distant star
b. determining the sweetness of a piece of fruit
c. testing the electrical resistance of a piece of wire
d. determining the length of an iron bar
e. measuring the temperature of a room

2. What experiment allows researchers to determine if something is a wave or a particle? How do electrons behave in this experiment?

3. Why is probability necessary to be able to describe subatomic events?

4. Sketch a possible probability diagram for the final resting position of a golf ball on a driving range. Assume that the golf tee is the starting point and that an average drive is 250 feet.

5. In Chapter 2 we discussed the fact that chaotic systems are, for all practical purposes, unpredictable. How does this sort of unpredictability differ from that associated with quantum mechanics?

6. Present an argument in terms of the wave nature of the electron that shows why electrons in Bohr orbits cannot emit radiation and spiral in toward the nucleus, as they might be expected to do on the basis of Maxwell's equations. [Hint: See "Why the Rutherford Atom Couldn't Work" in Chapter 8.]

7. How are electrons, atoms, and light (i.e., photons) similar in behavior?

8. If you threw baseballs through a large two-slit apparatus, would you produce a diffraction pattern? Why or why not? What type of object would you need to produce a diffraction pattern?

Problems

1. A bowling ball (mass 5.0 kg) is thrown down a bowling alley with a speed between 10.0 and 10.1 m/s. How accurately can we determine its position?

2. In the "Science by the Numbers" section in this chapter, we converted the unit J-s/kg-m to the unit of velocity (m/s) without comment. Demonstrate the equivalence of these two units.

3. An atom of gold (mass 3.27×10^{-25} kg) travels at a speed between 20.0 and 20.1 m/s. How accurately can we determine its position? Is this accuracy in position attainable? How does it compare to the size of a nucleus?

4. If the particle in problem 3 was an electron rather than an atom, would our accuracy in determining its position increase or decrease? What if we used an atom of plutonium?

Investigations

1. Look up the doctrine of predestination in an encyclopedia. Does it have a logical connection to the notion of the Divine Calculator? Which came first historically?

2. Werner Heisenberg was a central, and ultimately controversial, figure in German science of the 1930s and 1940s. Read a biography of Heisenberg. Discuss how his early work in quantum mechanics influenced his prominent scientific role in Nazi Germany.

3. What changes in artistic movements were taking place during the period around 1900 (just before the discoveries of quantum mechanics) and in the mid-twentieth century? Are there any connections between the artistic and scientific movements of those times?

4. Some people interpret the Heisenberg uncertainty principle to mean that you can never really know anything for certain. Would you agree or disagree?

5. Who is Schrodinger? What was his role in the development of quantum mechanics?

6. Many people claim that obscure ancient texts such as the "Tao Te Ching" presage and parallel quantum physics. Are they correct?

10

Atoms in Combination: The Chemical Bond

How does blood clot?

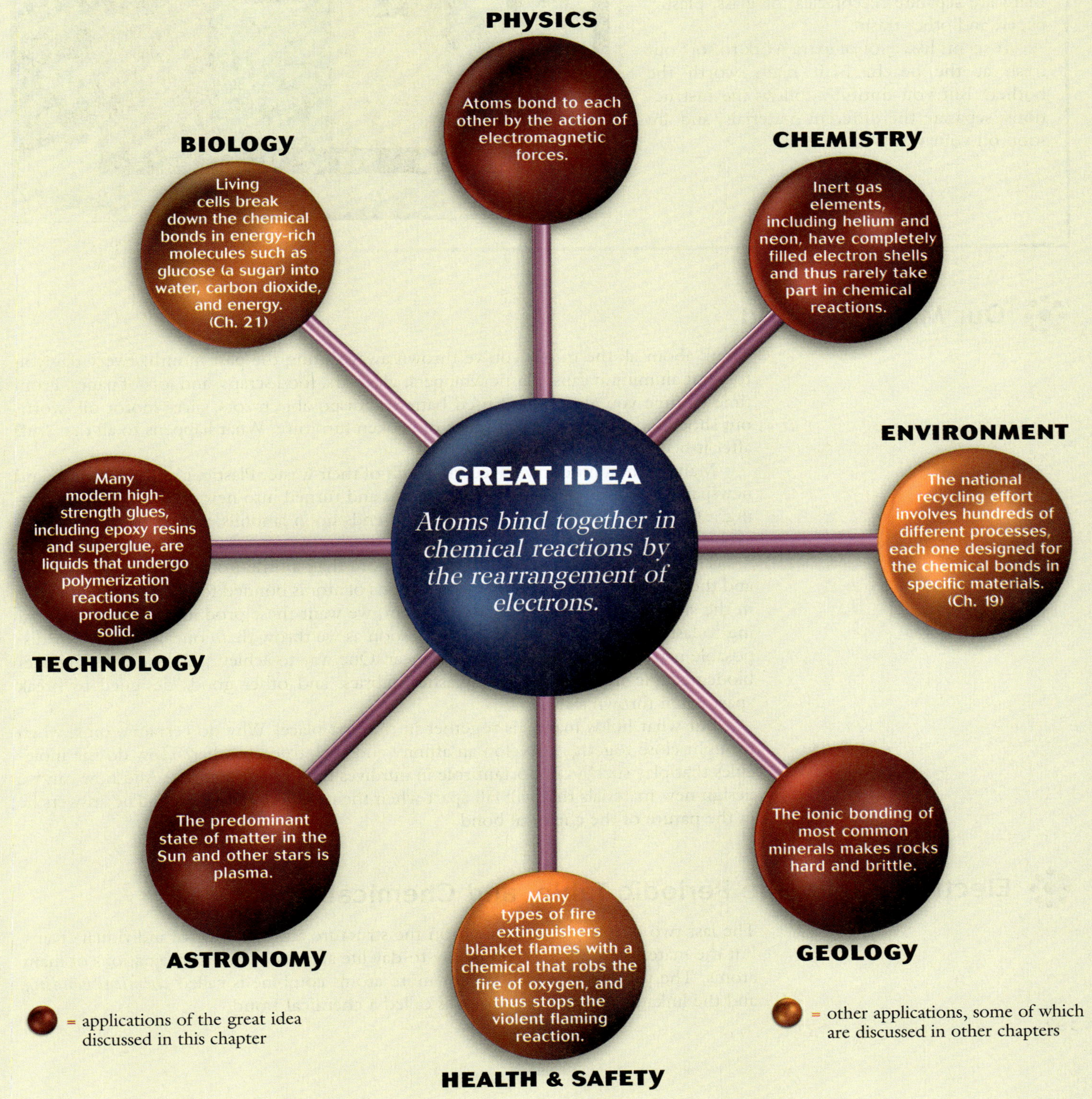

Science Through the Day | Throwing Things Away

On your way to pick the perfect spot on the beach, you and your friends divide up a heavy load of food and drinks. Your backpack is too full already, so you decide to discard a couple of old empty soft drink bottles, plastic wrappers, and an old newspaper to make more room. You walk over to the beach house where there are separate receptacles for glass, plastic, paper, and other trash.

It seems like a lot of extra work to sort out trash at the beach. Is it really worth the bother? But you dutifully follow the instructions, separate the different materials, and are soon on your way.

Emma Lee/Life File/PhotoDisc, Inc./Getty Images

Our Material World

Think about all the things you've thrown away during the past month. Every day you toss out aluminum cans, plastic wrappers, glass jars, food scraps, and lots of paper. From time to time you also discard used batteries, disposable razors, dirty motor oil, worn-out shoes and clothes, even old tires or broken furniture. What happens to all that stuff after it becomes trash?

Many communities try to recycle much of their waste. Plastic, glass, aluminum, and newspaper, for example, can be reprocessed and turned into new products and packaging. Old oil can be refined, but most trash ends up in landfills, where, we hope, it will eventually break down into soil.

The situation that faces our society is more than a little ironic. Everything you use and then throw away is made from collections of atoms bonded together. While they are in the store and for as long as we use them, we want these products and their packaging to last and keep looking new. But as soon as we throw them out, we'd like our disposable materials to fall apart and disappear. One way to achieve this end is to engineer biodegradable materials—paper, plastics, fabrics, and other goods designed to break apart when thrown away.

But what holds materials together in the first place? Why do certain atoms, when brought close together, develop an affinity and stick to each other? How do the molecules that play such an important role in our lives retain their identity? And how can we design new materials that will fall apart when their useful lives are over? The answers lie in the nature of the chemical bond.

Electron Shells, the Periodic Table, and Chemical Bonds

The last two chapters have focused on the structure and behavior of individual atoms, but the materials we depend on in day-to-day life are made from combinations of many atoms. The process by which two or more atoms combine is called *chemical bonding*, and the linkage between two atoms is called a **chemical bond.**

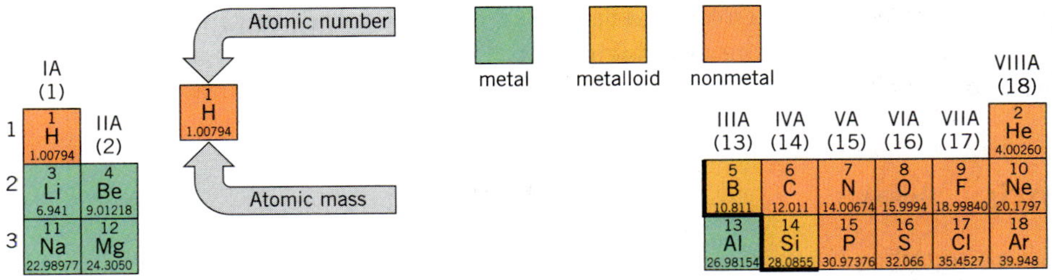

• **Figure 10-1** The first three rows (elements 1 to 18) of the periodic table showing element names, atomic numbers, and principal valences.

Think about how two atoms might interact. You know that the atom is mostly empty space, with a tiny, dense nucleus surrounded by negatively charged electrons. If two atoms approach each other, their outer electrons encounter each other first. Whatever holds two atoms together thus involves primarily those outer electrons. In fact, the outer electrons play such an important role in determining how atoms combine that they are given the special name of *valence electrons* (see Chapter 8). Chemical bonding often involves an exchange or sharing of valence electrons, and the number of electrons in an atom's outermost shell is called its *valence*. Chemists often express the importance of the number of outer electrons by saying that valence represents the combining power of a given atom.

The periodic table of the elements (Figure 10-1) provides the key to understanding the varied strategies of chemical bonding. Different electron shells hold different numbers of electrons, which gives rise to the distinctive structure of the periodic table. It turns out that by far the most stable arrangement of electrons—the electron configuration of lowest energy—has completely filled electron shells. A glance at the periodic table tells us that atoms with a total of 2, 10, 18, or 36 electrons (all the atoms that appear in the table's extreme right-hand column) have filled shells and very stable configurations. Atoms with this many electrons in their outermost shells are *inert gases* (also called *noble gases*), which do not combine readily with other materials. Indeed, helium, neon, and argon, with atomic numbers 2, 10, and 18, respectively, have completely filled electron shells, and are thus the only common elements that do not ordinarily react with other elements.

Every object in nature tries to reach a state of lowest energy, and atoms are no exception. Atoms that do not have the magic number of electrons (2, 10, 18, etc.) are more likely to react with other atoms to produce a state of lower energy. You are familiar with this kind of process in many other natural systems. If you put a ball on top of a hill, for example, it will tend to roll down to the bottom, creating a system of lower gravitational potential energy. Similarly, a compass needle tends to align itself spontaneously with Earth's magnetic field, thereby lowering its magnetic potential energy. In exactly the same way, when two or more atoms come together the electrons tend to rearrange themselves to minimize the chemical potential energy of the entire system. This situation may require that they exchange or share electrons. As often as not, that process involves rearrangements with a total of 2, 10, 18, or 36 electrons.

Chemical bonds result from any redistribution of electrons that leads to a more stable configuration between two or more atoms—especially configurations with a filled electron shell.

Most atoms adopt one of three simple strategies to achieve a filled shell: they give away electrons, accept electrons, or share electrons.

If the bond formation takes place spontaneously, without outside intervention, energy will be released in the reaction. The burning of wood or paper (once their temperature has been raised high enough) is a good example of this sort of process, and the heat you feel when you put your hands toward a fire derives ultimately from the chemical potential energy that is given off as electrons and atoms are reshuffled. Alternatively, atoms may be pushed into new configurations by adding energy to systems. Much of industrial chemistry, from the smelting of iron to the synthesis of plastics, operates on this principle.

Types of Chemical Bonds

Atoms link together by three principal kinds of chemical bonds—ionic, metallic, and covalent—all of which involve redistributing electrons between atoms. In addition, three types of attractions—polarization, van der Waals interactions, and hydrogen bonding—result from shifts of electrons within their atoms or groups of atoms. Each type of bonding or attraction corresponds to a different way of rearranging electrons, and each produces distinctive properties in the materials it forms.

Ionic Bonds

We've seen that atoms with "magic numbers" of 2, 10, 18, or 36 electrons are particularly stable. By the same token, atoms that differ from these magic numbers by only one electron in their outer orbits are particularly reactive—in effect, they are "anxious" to fill or empty their outer orbits. Such atoms tend to form **ionic bonds,** chemical bonds in which the electrical force between two oppositely charged ions holds the atoms together.

Ionic bonds often form as one atom gives up an electron while another receives it. Sodium (a soft, silvery white metal), for example, has 11 electrons in an electrically neutral atom—2 in the lowest orbit, 8 in the next, and a single electron in its outer shell. Sodium's best bonding strategy, therefore, is to lose one electron. The seventeenth element, chlorine (a yellow-green toxic gas), on the other hand, is one electron shy of a filled shell. Highly corrosive chlorine gas will react with almost anything that can give it an extra electron (Figure 10-2). When you place sodium in contact with chlorine gas, the result is predictable: in a fiery reaction, each sodium atom donates its extra electron to a chlorine atom.

In the process of this vigorous electron exchange, atoms of sodium and chlorine become electrically charged—they become ions. Neutral sodium has 11 positive protons in its nucleus, balanced by 11 negative electrons in orbit. By losing one electron, sodium becomes an ion with 11 protons but only 10 electrons (a magic number). The resulting sodium ion has one unit of positive charge, shown as Na^+ in Figure 10-2. Similarly, neutral chlorine has 17 protons and 17 electrons. The addition of an extra negative electron creates a chloride ion with 17 protons and 18 electrons (also a magic number). The resulting chlorine ion has one unit of negative charge, shown as Cl^- in the figure. The mutual electrical attraction of positive sodium and negative chloride ions is what forms the ionic bonds between sodium and chlorine. The resulting compound, sodium chloride or common table salt, has properties totally different from either sodium or chlorine.

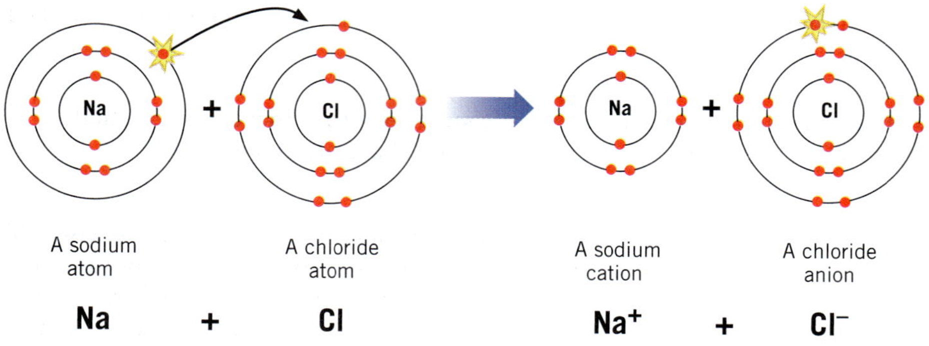

• **Figure 10-2** Sodium, a highly reactive element, readily transfers its single valence electron to chlorine, which is one electron shy of the "magic" number 18. The result is the ionic compound sodium chloride—ordinary table salt. In these diagrams, electrons are represented as dots in shells around a nucleus.

Under normal circumstances, sodium and chlorine ions will lock together into a crystal, a regular arrangement of atoms such as the one shown in Figure 10-3. Alternating sodium and chloride ions form an elegant repeating structure in which each Na^+ is surrounded by six Cl^-, and vice versa.

Ionic bonds may involve more than a single electron transfer. The twelfth element, magnesium, for example, donates two electrons to oxygen, which has eight electrons. In the resulting compound, MgO (magnesium oxide), both atoms have stable filled shells of 10 electrons, and the ions, Mg^{2+} and O^{2-}, form a strong ionic bond. Ionic bonds involving the negative oxygen ion O^{2-} and positive ions, such as aluminum (Al^{3+}), magnesium (Mg^{2+}), silicon (Si^{4+}), and iron (Fe^{2+} or Fe^{3+}), are found in many everyday objects: in most rocks and minerals, in china and glass, and in bones and egg shells.

Compounds with ionic bonds are often very strong along the direction of the bonds, but they can break easily if the bonds are twisted or bent. As a consequence, ionic-bonded materials such as rock, glass, or egg shells are usually quite brittle. These materials are strong in the sense that you can pile lots of weight on them. But once they shatter and ionic bonds are broken, they can't be put back together again.

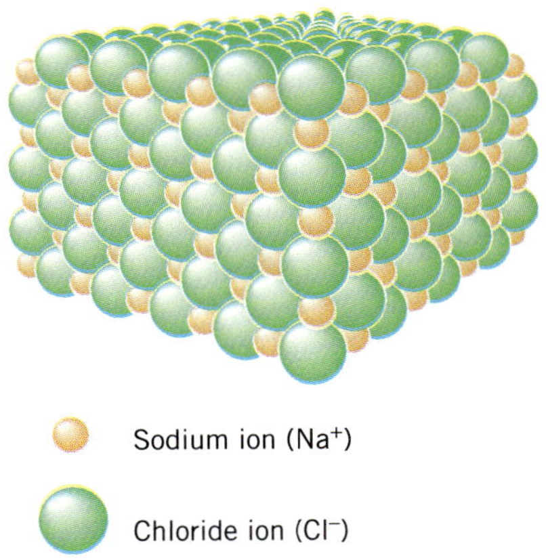

• **Figure 10-3** The atomic structure of a sodium chloride crystal consists of a regular pattern of alternating sodium and chloride ions.

EXAMPLE 10-1

Ionic Bonding of Three Atoms

Magnesium chloride, which plays an important role in some batteries, is an ionic-bonded compound with one part magnesium to two parts chlorine ($MgCl_2$). How are the electrons arranged in this compound?

Reasoning: From the periodic table (see Figure 10-1), magnesium and chlorine are elements 12 and 17, respectively. Magnesium, therefore, has 10 electrons (2 + 8) in inner shells and 2 valence electrons. Chlorine has 10 electrons (2 + 8) in its inner shells and 7 electrons in the outer one, meaning that it is 1 electron short of a filled outer shell (Figure 10-4).

Solution: Magnesium has two electrons to give, and chlorine seeks one electron, to achieve stable filled outer orbits. Thus magnesium gives one electron to each of two chlorine atoms, and the resulting Mg^{2+} ion attracts two Cl^- ions to form $MgCl_2$.

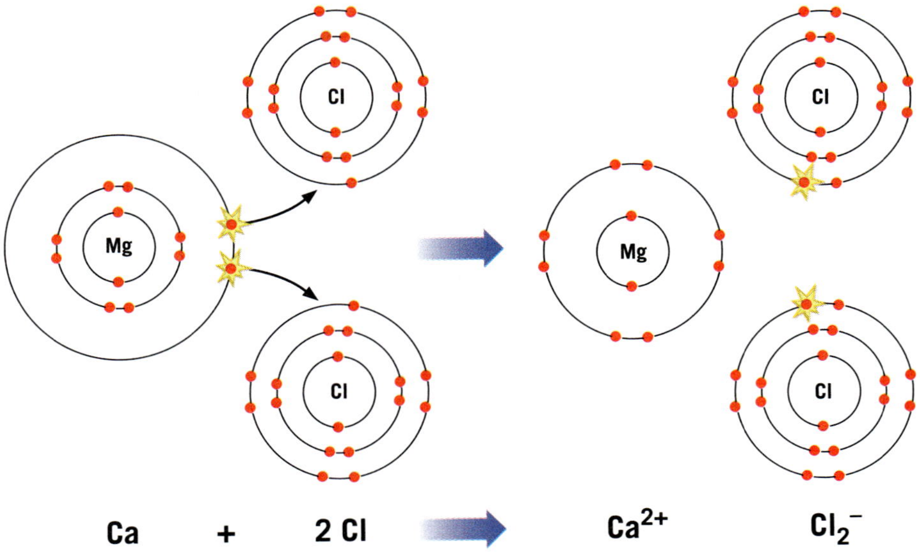

• **Figure 10-4** Magnesium and chlorine neutral-atom electron configurations (left), and their configurations after electrons have been transferred from the magnesium to the chlorine atoms (right).

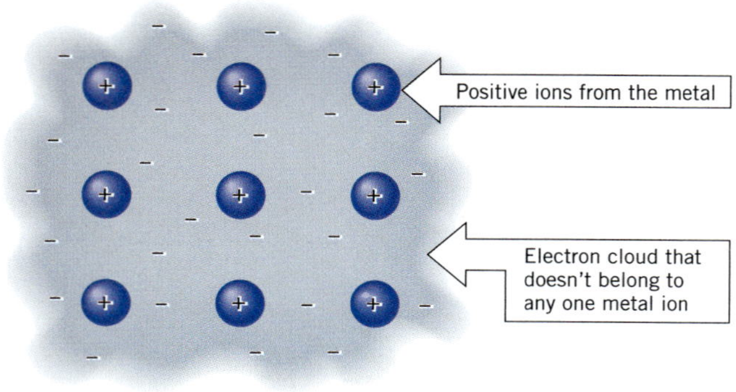

• **Figure 10-5** Metallic bonding, in which a bond is created by the sharing of electrons among several metal atoms.

Metallic Bonds

Atoms in an ionic bond transfer electrons directly—electrons are on "permanent loan" from one atom to another. Atoms in a metal also give up electrons, but they use a very different bonding strategy. In a **metallic bond,** electrons are redistributed so that they are shared by many atoms.

Sodium metal, for example, is made up entirely of individual sodium atoms. All of these atoms begin with 11 electrons, but they release 1 to achieve the more stable 10-electron configuration. The extra electrons move away from their parent atoms to float around the metal, forming a kind of sea of negative charge. In this negative electron sea, the positive sodium ions adopt a regular crystal structure, as shown in Figure 10-5.

You can think of the metallic bond as one in which each atom shares its outer electron with all the other atoms in the system. Picture the free electrons as a kind of loose glue in which the metal atoms are placed. In fact, the idea of a metal as being a collection of marbles (the ions) in a sea of stiff, glue-like liquid provides a useful analogy.

Metals, characterized by their shiny luster and ability to conduct electricity, are formed by almost any element or combination of elements in which large numbers of atoms share electrons to achieve a more stable electron arrangement. Some metals, such as aluminum, iron, and copper, are familiar from everyday experience. But many elements can form into a metallic state when the conditions are right, including some that we normally think of as gases, such as hydrogen or oxygen at very high pressure. In fact, the great majority of chemical elements are known to occur in the metallic state. In addition, two or more elements can combine to form a metal *alloy,* such as brass (a mixture of copper and zinc) or bronze (an alloy of copper and tin). Modern specialty-steel alloys often contain more than half a dozen different elements in carefully controlled proportions.

Iain Baker/Alamy Images

Gold is a soft, malleable metal that can be worked into many shapes, as with these gold Buddhas from Thailand.

The special nature of the metallic bond explains many of the distinctive properties we observe in metals. If you attempt to deform a metal by pushing on the marble-and-glue bonding system, atoms will gradually rearrange themselves and come to some new configuration—the metal is malleable. It's hard to break a metallic bond just by pushing or twisting, because the atoms are able to rearrange themselves. Thus when you hammer on a piece of metal, you leave indentations but do not break it, in sharp contrast to what happens when you hammer on a ceramic plate.

In Chapter 11, we'll examine more closely the electrical properties of materials held together by the metallic bond. We'll see that this particular kind of bond produces materials through which electrons—electrical current—can flow.

Covalent Bonds

In the ionic bond, one atom donates electrons to another on more-or-less permanent loan. In the metallic bond, on the other hand, atoms share some electrons throughout the material. In between these two types of bonds is the extremely important **covalent bond,** in which well-defined clusters of neighboring atoms, called *molecules,* share electrons. These strongly bonded groups may consist of anywhere from two to many millions of atoms.

The simplest covalently bonded molecules contain two atoms of the same element, such as the diatomic gases hydrogen (H_2), nitrogen (N_2), and oxygen (O_2). In the case of hydrogen, for example, each atom has a relatively unstable single electron. Two hydrogen atoms can pool their electrons, however, to create a more stable two-electron arrangement. The two hydrogen atoms must remain close to each other for this sharing to continue, so a chemical bond is formed, as shown in Figure 10-6. Similarly, two oxygen atoms, each with eight electrons, share two pairs of electrons.

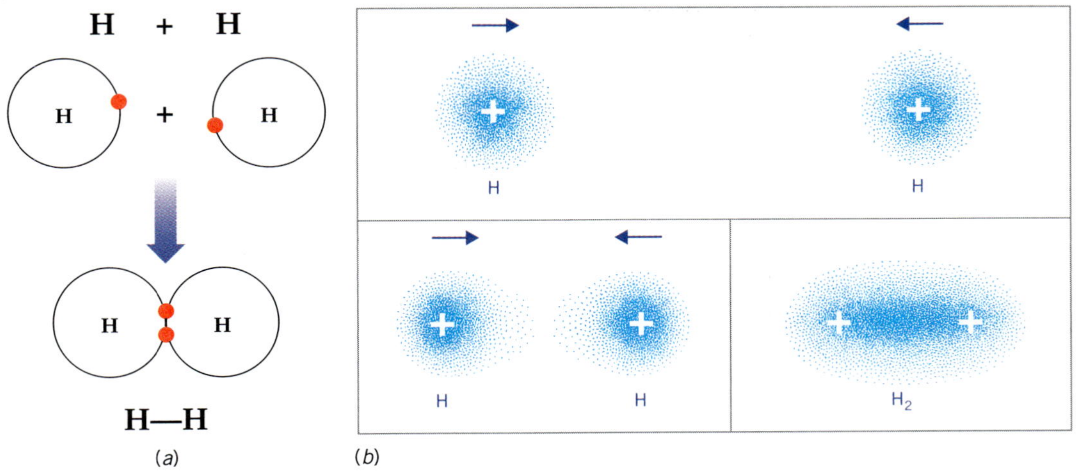

• **Figure 10-6** Two hydrogen atoms become an H_2 molecule by sharing each of their electrons in a covalent bond. This bonding may be represented schematically in a dot diagram *(a)* or by the merging of two atoms with their electron clouds *(b)*.

Hydrogen, oxygen, nitrogen, and other covalently bonded molecules have lower chemical potential energy than isolated atoms because electrons are shared. These molecules are less likely to react chemically than the isolated atoms.

The most fascinating of all covalently bonded elements is carbon, which forms the backbone of all life's essential molecules. Carbon, with two electrons in its inner shell and four in its outer shell, presents a classic case of a half-filled shell. When carbon atoms approach each other, therefore, a real question arises as to whether they ought to accept or donate four electrons to achieve a more stable arrangement. You could imagine, for example, a situation where some carbon atoms give four electrons to their neighbors, while other carbon atoms accept four electrons, to create a compound with strong ionic bonds between C^{4+} and C^{4-}. Alternatively, carbon might become a metal in which every atom releases four electrons into an extremely dense electron sea. But neither of these things happens.

In fact, the strategy that lowers the energy of the carbon–carbon system the most is for the carbon atoms to share their outer electrons. Once bonds between carbon atoms have formed, the atoms have to stay close to each other for the sharing to continue. Thus the bonds generated are just like the bond in the case of hydrogen. The case of carbon is unusual, however, because a single carbon atom can form covalent bonds with up to four other atoms by sharing one of its four valence electrons with each. A *single bond* (shown as C—C) forms when one electron from each atom is shared, while a *double bond* (shown as C=C) results when two electrons from each atom are shared between one another.

By forming bonds among several adjacent carbon atoms, you can make rings, long chains, branching structures, planes, and three-dimensional frameworks of carbon in almost any imaginable shape. There is virtually no limit to the complexity of molecules you can build from such carbon–carbon bonding (Figure 10-7). So important is the study of carbon-based molecules that chemists have given it a special name: *organic chemistry*.

In fact, all the molecules in your body and in every other living thing are held together at least in part by covalent bonds in carbon chains (see Chapter 22). Covalent bonds also drive much of the chemistry in the cells of your body and play a role in holding together the DNA molecules that carry your genetic code. It would not be too much of an exaggeration to say that the covalent bond is the bond of life. Covalent bonds also play a critical role in the silicon-based integrated circuits that run your computer. The element silicon, like carbon, has four electrons in its outer shell.

Stop and Think! Life on Earth is based on the properties of the element carbon. Looking at the first three rows of the periodic table in Figure 10-1, are there any other candidate elements that might form the basis of life elsewhere?

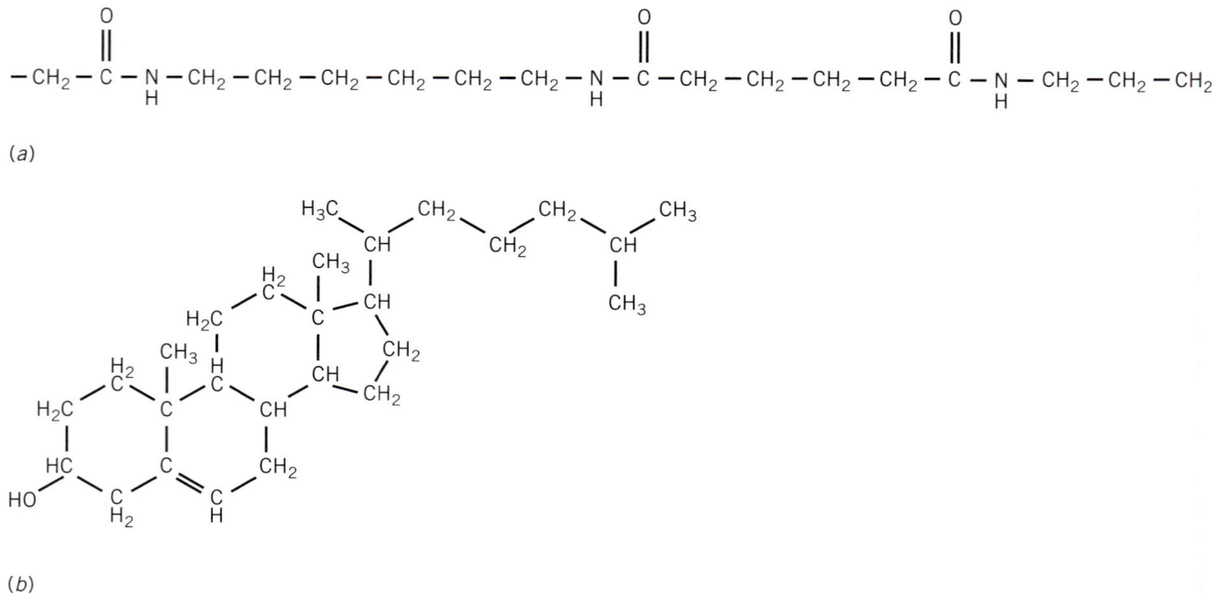

• **Figure 10-7** Carbon-based molecules may adopt almost any shape. The molecules may consist of long, straight chains of carbon atoms that form fibrous materials such as nylon *(a)* or they may incorporate complex rings and branching arrangements that form lumpy molecules such as cholesterol *(b)*.

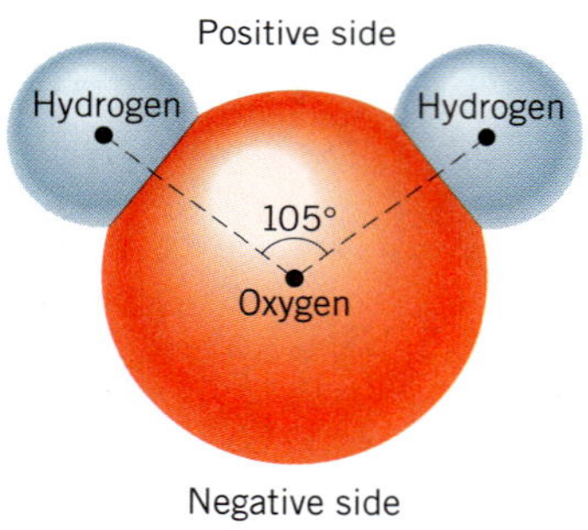

• **Figure 10-8** The water molecule and its polarity.

Polarization and Hydrogen Bonds

Ionic, metallic, and covalent bonds form strong links between individual atoms, but molecules also experience forces that hold one to another. In many molecules, the electrical forces are such that, although the molecule by itself is electrically neutral, one part of the molecule has more positive or negative charge than another. In water, for example, the electrons tend to spend more time around the oxygen atoms than around the hydrogen atoms. This uneven electron distribution has the effect of making the oxygen side of the water molecule more negatively charged, and the two "Mickey Mouse ears" of the hydrogen atom more positively charged (Figure 10-8). Atom clusters of this type, with a positive and negative end, are called ***polar molecules.***

The electrons of an atom or molecule brought near a polar molecule such as water will tend to be pushed away from the negative side and shifted toward the positive side. Consequently, the side of an atom facing the negative end of a polar molecule will become slightly positive. This subtle electron shift, called ***polarization,*** in turn will give rise to an electrical attraction between the negative end of the polar molecule and the positive side of the other molecule. The electron movement thus creates an attraction between the atom and the molecule, even though all the atoms and molecules in this scheme may be electrically neutral. One of the most important consequences of forces due to polarization is the ability of water to dissolve many materials. Water, made up of strongly polar molecules, exerts forces that make it easier for ions such as Na^+ and Cl^- to dissolve.

A process related to the forces of polarization leads to the **hydrogen bond,** a weak bond that may form after a hydrogen atom links to an atom of certain other elements (oxygen or nitrogen, for example) by a covalent bond. Because of the kind of rearrangement of electrical charge described above, a hydrogen atom may become polarized and develop a slight positive charge, which attracts another atom to it. You can think of the hydrogen atom as a kind of bridge in this situation, causing a redistribution of electrons that, in turn, brings larger atoms or molecules together. Individual hydrogen bonds are weak, but in many molecules they occur repeatedly and therefore play a major role in determining the molecule's shape and function. Note that while all hydrogen bonds require hydrogen atoms, not all hydrogen atoms are involved in hydrogen bonds.

Hydrogen bonds are common in virtually all biological substances, from everyday materials such as wood, silk, and candle wax, to the complex structures of every cell in your body. As we shall see in Chapter 23, hydrogen bonds in every living thing link the two sides of the DNA double helix together, although the sides themselves are held together by covalent bonds. Ordinary egg white is made from molecules whose shape is determined by hydrogen bonds, and when you heat the material—when you fry an egg, for example—hydrogen bonds are disrupted and the molecules rearrange themselves so that instead of a clear liquid you have a white gelatinous solid.

Van der Waals Forces

The hydrogen bond exists because atoms or molecules can become polarized as their electrons shift to one side or another and thus create local electrical charges. In the molecules we've discussed so far, that electrical charge is more or less permanently locked into polar molecules in a fixed or static arrangement. Another force between molecules, called the van der Waals force, results from the polarization of electrically neutral atoms or molecules that are not themselves polar.

When two atoms or molecules are brought near each other, every part of one atom or molecule feels an electrical force exerted on it by all parts of the other. For example, an electron in one atom will be repelled by the electrons, but attracted to the nucleus, of an adjacent atom. The net result of these forces exerted on the electron may be a temporary shift of the electron. The same thing happens to every electron in any nearby atom or molecule, and the net result is that every electron is constantly shifting because of the presence of others.

What is remarkable is that this mutual, dynamic deformation sometimes gives rise to a net attractive force. In these van der Waals compounds, even if all the molecules are neutral and nonpolar, the sum of attractive forces wins out over repulsive forces and weak bonds are formed. This weak force that binds two atoms or molecules together is called the **van der Waals force.**

If you take a piece of clay and rub it between your fingers, your fingers pick up a slick coating of the material, even though the clay crumbles easily. The reason for this behavior is that the clay is made up of sheets of atoms. Within each sheet, atoms are held together by strong ionic and covalent bonds. One sheet is held to another, however, by comparatively weak van der Waals forces. This situation is not unlike the way a stack of photocopying paper will stick together on a dry day. Each sheet of paper is strong, but the stack of paper is stuck together by much weaker electrostatic forces. It is easy to pull the stack apart but very difficult to rip the stack in two. When you crumble clay in your fingers, therefore, you are breaking weak van der Waals forces between layers, but preserving the stronger bonds that hold each layer together. The clay stains on your hands are thin sheets of atoms, held together by ionic and covalent bonds, and the crumbling you feel is the breaking of the van der Waals bonds.

Many other examples of van der Waals forces can be seen in everyday life. If you rub talcum powder on your body, for example, you use a layered material not unlike the clay just discussed. Similarly, when you write with a "lead" pencil, van der Waals–bonded layers of graphite (a form of carbon) are transferred from pencil to paper (Figure 10-9). As you draw the pencil across the paper, you break the van der Waals forces and leave behind dark graphite sheets on the paper. Van der Waals forces also link molecules in many everyday liquids and soft solids, from candle wax to Vaseline™ and other petroleum products.

• **Figure 10-9** Graphite, a form of carbon that serves as the "lead" in your pencil, contains layers of carbon atoms strongly linked to each other by covalent bonds (represented by solid lines). These layers are held to each other by much weaker van der Waals bonds (represented by dashed lines).

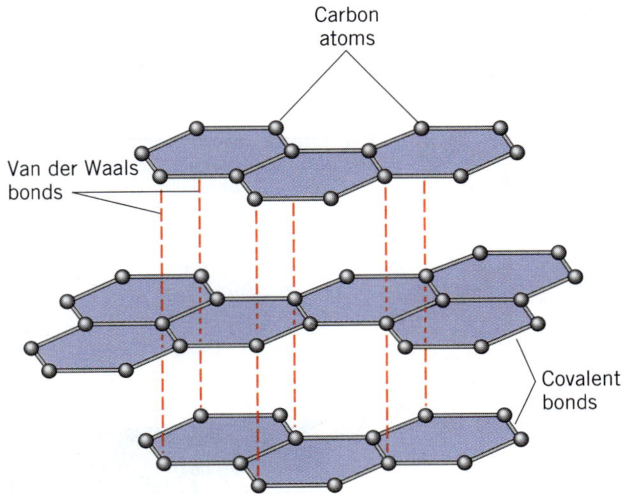

States of Matter

So far, we've been looking at the ways in which the limited number of chemical elements in the periodic table can be linked together by a few different types of chemical bonds or attractive forces. The everyday materials that we use, however, typically incorporate trillions upon trillions of atoms. Countless linkages among vast numbers of atoms collectively produce the remarkable variety of materials in our world. Depending on how these groups of atoms are organized, they may take on many different forms. These different modes of organization, called the **states of matter,** include gases, plasmas, liquids, and solids (Figure 10-10).

Gases

A **gas** is any collection of atoms or molecules that expands to take the shape of and fill the volume available in its container (Figure 10-10*a*). Most common gases, including those that form our atmosphere, are invisible, but the force of a gust of wind is proof that matter is involved. The individual particles that comprise a gas may be isolated atoms such as helium or neon, or small molecules such as nitrogen (N_2) or carbon dioxide (CO_2). If we could magnify an ordinary gas a billion times, we would see these particles randomly flying about, bouncing off each other and anything else they contact. The gas pressure that inflates a basketball or tire is a consequence of these countless collisions.

Plasma

At extreme temperatures like those of the Sun, high-energy collisions between atoms may strip off electrons, creating a **plasma,** in which positive nuclei move about in a sea of electrons. Such a collection of electrically charged objects is something like a gas, but it displays unusual properties not seen in other states of matter. Plasmas, for example, are efficient conductors of electricity and, because they are gas-like, can be confined in a strong magnetic field or "magnetic bottle."

Plasmas are the least familiar state of matter to us, yet more than 99.9% of all the visible mass in the universe exists in this form. Not only are most stars composed of a dense hydrogen- and helium-rich plasma mixture, but several planets, including Earth, have regions of thin plasma in their outer atmospheres. Some gradations exist between gas and plasma. Partially ionized gases in neon lights or fluorescent lightbulbs, for example, have a small fraction of their electrons in a free state. While not a complete plasma, these ionized gases do conduct electricity.

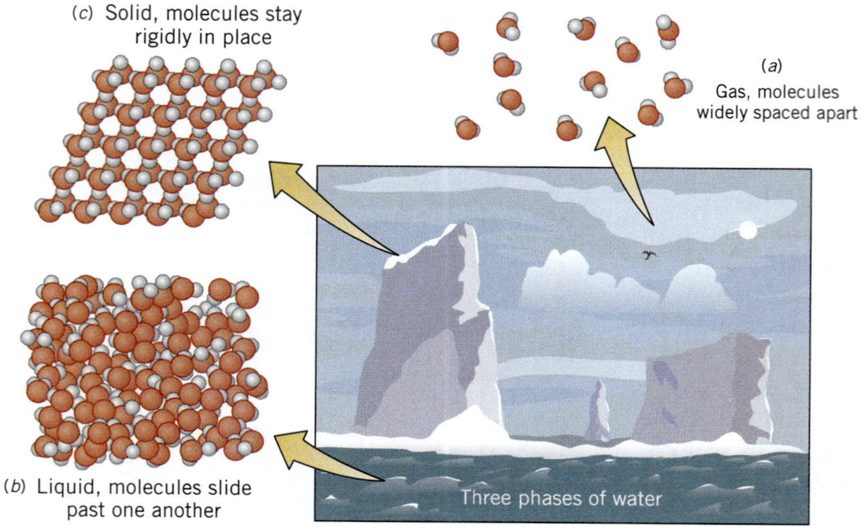

• **Figure 10-10** The different states of matter are distinguished by the arrangements of their atoms (clockwise). In a gas (*a*) atoms or molecules are not bonded to each other, so they expand to fill any available volume. In a liquid (*b*) molecules are bound to each other but they are free to move relative to each other, yielding a material that can change shape but holds its volume. In a solid (*c*) atoms are locked into a rigid pattern that retains its shape and volume.

Liquids

Any collection of atoms or molecules that has no fixed shape but maintains its volume is called a **liquid** (Figure 10-10*b*). Other than water and biological fluids, few liquids occur naturally on Earth. Water, by far the most abundant liquid on Earth's surface, is a dynamic force for geological change (see Chapter 18), and water-based solutions are essential to all life.

At the molecular level, liquids behave something like a container full of sand grains. The grains fill whatever volume they are poured into, freely flowing over each other without ever taking on a fixed shape. Attractive forces between individual atoms or molecules hold the liquid together. At the surface of the liquid, these attractive forces act to prevent atoms or molecules from escaping. In effect, they pull the surface in, giving rise to *surface tension,* the property that causes small quantities of the liquid to form beads or droplets.

Crystals of the mineral quartz, SiO_2, display faceted surfaces that result from the regular repetition of atoms.

Solids

Solids include all materials that possess a more or less fixed shape and volume (Figure 10-10*c*). In all solid materials the chemical bonds are both strong and directional. In detail, however, solids adopt several quite different kinds of atomic structures.

In **crystals,** groups of atoms occur in a regularly repeating sequence, the same atom or atoms appearing over and over again in a predictable way (Figure 10-11*a*). A crystal structure can be described by first determining the size and shape of the tiny box-like unit that repeats, then recording the exact type and position of every atom that appears in the box. In common salt (see Figure 10-3), for example, the box is a tiny cube less than a billionth of a meter on an edge, and each box contains sodium atoms at the cube center and corners, and chlorine atoms at the center of every face. The regular atomic structure of crystals often leads to large single crystals with beautiful flat faces.

Common crystals include grains of sand and salt, computer chips, and gemstones. Most crystalline solids, however, are composed of numerous interlocking crystal grains. The two most important groups of these types of materials in our everyday life are metals and alloys that are characterized by metallic bonds, and most *ceramics,* a broad class of hard, durable solids that includes bricks, concrete, pottery, porcelain, and numerous synthetic abrasives, as well as teeth and bones and most rocks and minerals.

Glasses, in contrast to crystals, are solids with predictable local environments for most atoms, but no long-range order to the atomic structure (Figure 10-11*b*). In most common window and bottle glasses, for example, silicon and oxygen atoms form a strong three-dimensional framework. Most silicon atoms are surrounded by four oxygen atoms, and most oxygen atoms are linked to two silicon atoms. If you were placed on any atom in a glass, chances are you could predict the next-door atoms. Nevertheless, glasses have no regularly stacked boxes of structure. Travel more than two or three atom diameters from any starting point, and there is no way that you could predict whether you'd find a silicon or an oxygen atom.

• **Figure 10-11** The arrangement of atoms in a crystal *(a)* is regular and predictable over distances of thousands of atoms. The arrangement of atoms in a glass *(b)* is regular on a local scale but irregular over a distance of three or four atoms.

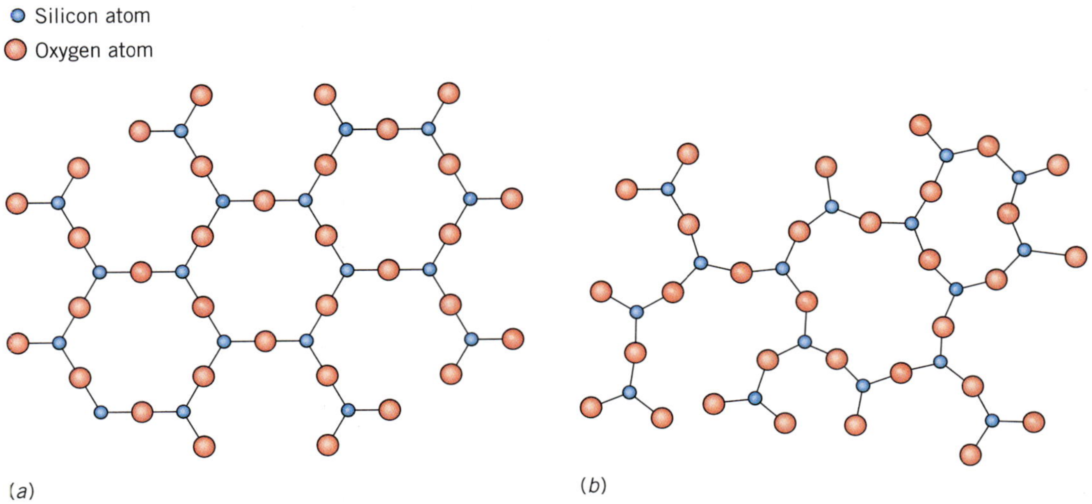

Stop and Think! Glass window panes appear solid but after many, many years some antique glass begins to droop. How would you explain this behavior in terms of the structure of glass?

Polymers are extremely long and large molecules that are formed from numerous smaller molecules, like links forming a chain. The atomic structure of these materials is often one-dimensional, with predictable repeating sequences of atoms along the polymer chain (Figure 10-12). Common polymers include numerous biological materials, such as animal hair, plant cellulose, cotton, and spider's webs.

Polymers include all **plastics,** which are synthetic materials formed primarily from petroleum. They consist of intertwined polymer strands, much like the strands of fiberglass insulation. When heated, these strands slide across each other to adopt new shapes. When cooled, the plastic fiber mass solidifies into whatever shape is available. Though almost unknown a few decades ago, plastics have become our most versatile commercial materials, providing an extraordinary range of uses: films for lightweight packaging, dense castings for durable machine parts, thin strong fibers for clothing, colorful moldings for toys, and many others. (You've probably noticed the small triangular recycling symbol with a number inside on plastic containers. The numbers refer to common types of plastics, which are separated before reprocessing. Table 10.1 lists the most common varieties and their uses.) Plastics serve as paints, inks, glues, sealants, foam products, and insulation. New tough, resilient plastics have revolutionized many sports with products such as high-quality bowling and golf balls, and

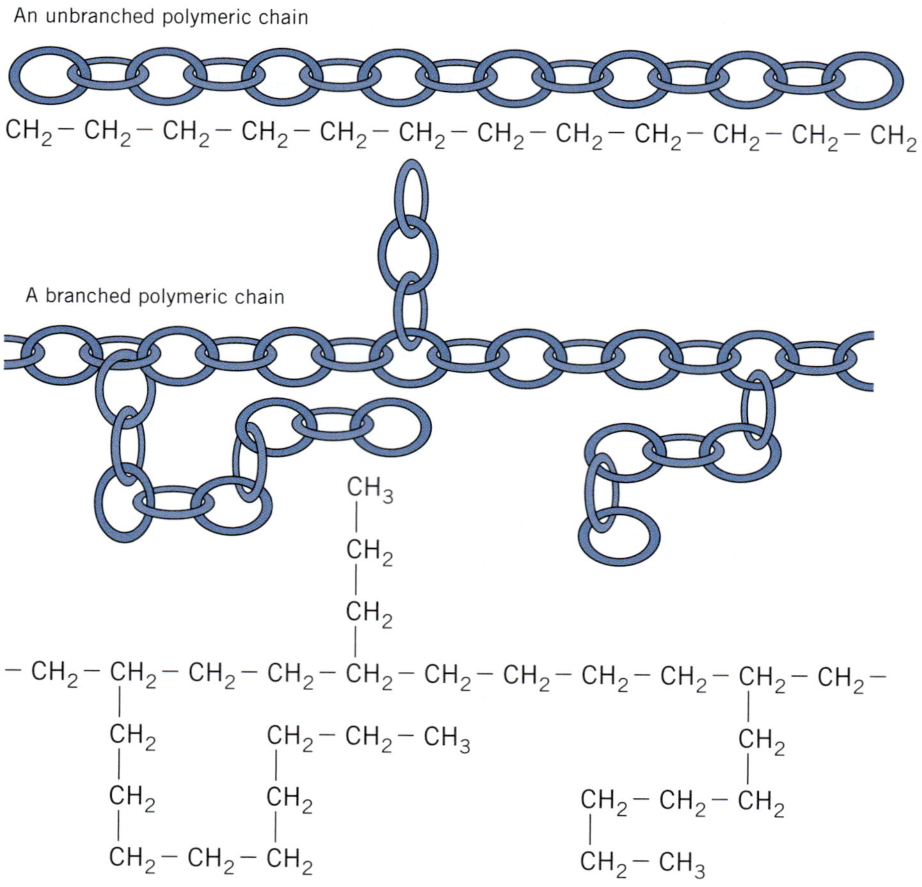

• **Figure 10-12** Branched and unbranched polymers form from small molecules, just as long chains can form from individual links.

Table 10-1 Recycling Plastic

No.	Name	Principal Uses
1	PET	The most common recycled plastic, used for food and beverage containers
2	HDPE	Rigid, narrow-neck containers for detergent and milk; grocery bags
3	PVC	Plastic pipe, outdoor furniture, sturdy containers
4	LDPE	Trash and produce bags, food storage containers
5	PP	Aerosol caps, drinking straws
6	PS	Packing peanuts, cups, and plastic tableware

durable football and ice hockey helmets, not to mention a host of completely new products from Frisbees™ to roller blades.

Technology •

Liquid Crystals and Your Hand Calculator

Almost every material on Earth is easily classified as a solid, a liquid, or a gas, but scientists have synthesized an odd intermediate state of matter called *liquid crystals.* These materials have quickly found their way into many kinds of electronic devices, including the digital display of your pocket calculator. The distinction between a liquid and a crystal is one of atomic-scale order: Atoms are disordered in a liquid, and ordered in a crystal. But what happens in the case of a liquid formed from very long or very flat molecules? Like a box of uncooked spaghetti or a plate of pancakes, in which the individual pieces may shift around but are well-oriented, these molecules may adopt ordered arrangements even in the liquid form.

If the molecules are polar, they may behave like tiny compass needles. Under ordinary circumstances these molecules will occur in random orientations, as in a normal liquid (Figure 10-13*a*). Under the influence of an electrical field, however, the molecules may adopt a partially ordered structure in which the molecules line up side-by-side (Figure 10-13*b*). This change in structure may even change some of the liquid's physical properties—its color or light-reflecting ability, for example. This phenomenon is now widely used in liquid crystal displays in watches and computers, in which electrical impulses align molecules in selected regions of the screen to provide a rapidly changing visual display.

Are liquid crystals found in nature? Every cell membrane is composed of a double layer of elongated molecules, called *lipids* (see Chapter 22). Many scientists now suspect that these "lipid bilayers" originated in the primitive ocean as molecules similar to today's liquid crystals. •

Lawrence Dutton/Stone/Getty Images

Liquid crystal displays are used in most pocket calculators.

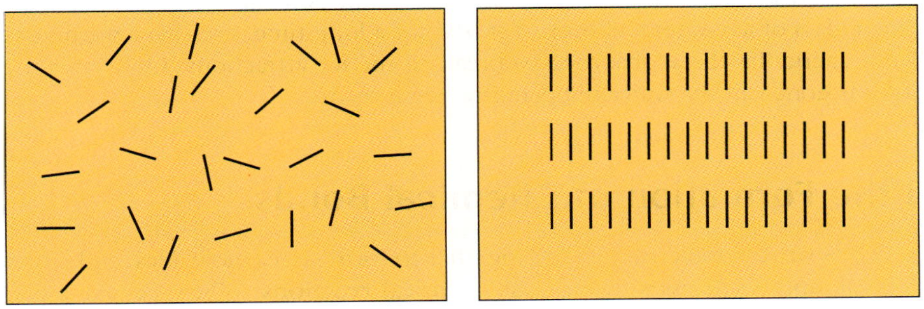

(*a*) (*b*)

• **Figure 10-13** Schematic diagram of a liquid crystal. Under normal circumstances, the elongated molecules are randomly oriented *(a)* but in an electric field the molecules align in an orderly pattern *(b)*.

Science in the Making •

The Discovery of Nylon

Nature's success in making strong, flexible fibers inspired scientists to try the same thing. American chemist Wallace Carothers (1896–1937) began thinking about polymer formation while a graduate student in the 1920s. At the time, no one was sure how natural fibers formed, or what kinds of chemical bonds were involved. Carothers wanted to find out.

The chemical company Du Pont took a gamble by naming Carothers head of its new "fundamental research" group in 1928. No pressure was placed on him to produce commercial results, but within a few years his team had developed the synthetic rubber neoprene, and by the mid-1930s they had devised a variety of extraordinary polymers, including nylon, the first human-made fiber. Carothers also demonstrated conclusively that polymers in nylon are covalently bonded chains of small molecules, each with six carbon atoms.

Du Pont made a fortune out of nylon and related synthetic fibers. Nylon was inexpensive to manufacture and had many advantages over natural fibers. It could be melted and squeezed out of spinnerets to form strands of almost any desired size: threads, rope, surgical sutures, tennis racket strings, and paintbrush bristles, for example. These fibers could be made smooth and straight like fishing line, or rough and wrinkled like wool, to vary the texture of fabrics. Nylon fibers could also be kinked with heat, to provide permanent folds and pleats in clothing. The melted polymer could even be injected into molds to form durable parts such as tubing or zipper teeth.

Sadly, Wallace Carothers did not live to see the impact of his extraordinary discoveries. Suffering from increasingly severe bouts of depression and convinced that he was a failure as a scientist, Carothers took his own life in 1937, just a year before the commercial introduction of nylon. •

Changes of State

Place a tray of liquid water in the freezer and it will turn to solid ice. Heat a pot of water on the stove and it will boil away to a gas. These everyday phenomena are examples of **changes of state,** which are transitions among the solid, liquid, and gas states. *Freezing* and *melting* involve changes between liquids and solids, while *boiling* and *condensation* are changes between liquids and gases. In addition, some solids may transform directly to the gaseous state by *sublimation.*

Temperature induces these transitions by changing the speed at which molecules vibrate. An increase in the temperature of ice to above 0°C (32°F), for example, causes molecular vibrations to increase to the point that individual molecules jiggle loose and the crystal structure starts to break apart. A liquid forms. Then, above 100°C (212°F), individual water molecules move fast enough to break free of the liquid surface and form a gas. These changes require a great deal of energy, because a great many chemical attractions must be broken to change from a solid to a liquid, or from a liquid to a gas. Thus a pot of water may reach boiling temperature fairly quickly, but it takes a long time to break all the attractions between water molecules and boil the water away. By the same token, a glass of ice water will remain at 0°C for a long time, even on a warm day, until enough energy has been absorbed to break all the ice attractions. Only after the last bit of ice is gone can the water temperature begin to rise.

Chemical Reactions and the Formation of Chemical Bonds

Atoms, as well as smaller molecules, come together to form larger molecules, and larger molecules break up, in processes that we call **chemical reactions.** When we take a bite of food, light a match, wash our hands, or drive a car, we initiate chemical reactions.

Earth's chemical reactions include rock formation and rock weathering. Every moment of every day, countless chemical reactions in every cell of our bodies sustain life.

All chemical reactions involve rearrangement of the atoms in elements and compounds, as well as rearrangement of electrons to form chemical bonds. Such reactions can be expressed as a simple equation:

$$\text{reactants} \rightarrow \text{products}$$

All such reactions must balance, so that the total number and kinds of atoms are the same on both sides. For example, oxygen and hydrogen can form water by the reaction:

$$2H_2 + O_2 \rightarrow 2H_2O$$

This reaction is balanced because each side has four hydrogen atoms and two oxygen atoms. In the process of this reaction we can observe both chemical changes (the rearrangement of atoms) and physical changes (the gases hydrogen and oxygen transform into liquid water with different properties).

EXAMPLE 10-2

Balancing Chemical Equations

Your car battery contains plates of lead (Pb) and lead dioxide (PbO_2) immersed in a solution of sulfuric acid (H_2SO_4). After the battery has been discharged, the lead, the lead dioxide, and sulfuric acid have been converted into lead sulfate ($PbSO_4$) and water (H_2O). Write a balanced reaction that models this process.

Reasoning and Solution: The reactants in this process are Pb, PbO_2 and H_2SO_4, while the products are $PbSO_4$ and H_2O. First write the equation in the simplest form, with one of each reactant and product molecule:

$$Pb + PbO_2 + H_2SO_4 \rightarrow PbSO_4 + H_2O$$

This equation, however, is not balanced. Two lead atoms appear on the left side, for example, while only one lead atom is on the right. The only way to make sure that there are as many atoms at the end as at the beginning is to write:

$$Pb + PbO_2 + 2H_2SO_4 \rightarrow 2PbSO_4 + 2H_2O$$

As you can see, on each side of the equation there are now two atoms of lead, two SO4 groups, four hydrogen atoms, and two oxygen atoms. This balanced equation represents the reshuffling of atoms that goes on when your battery discharges. It tells us that two molecules of sulfuric acid will be used for each atom of lead and that two molecules of water and two of lead sulfate will be produced at the end.

Every chemical reaction, no matter how complex, must balance: you must end with the same number of atoms with which you began.

Chemical Reactions and Energy: Rolling Down the Chemical Hill

Before considering the ways that atoms can combine to form molecules, pause for a moment to think about why these reactions take place at all. The fundamental reason, as so often happens with natural phenomena, has to do with energy, as described by the laws of thermodynamics (see Chapters 3 and 4).

Consider, for example, one of the electrons in the neutral sodium atom shown in Figure 10-2. This electron is moving in orbit around the nucleus, so it has kinetic energy. In addition, the electron possesses potential energy because it is a certain distance from the positively charged nucleus. Thus, just by virtue of its position, the electron is capable of doing work (this is the way potential energy was defined in Chapter

3). Finally, the electron has an additional component of potential energy because of the electrical repulsion between it and all of the other electrons in the atom. This is analogous to the small contribution to Earth's potential energy from the other planets. The sum of these three energies—the kinetic energy associated with orbital motion, the potential energy associated with the nucleus, and the potential energy associated with the other electrons—is the total energy of the single electron in its orbit.

The atom's total energy outside the nucleus is the sum of the energies of all of the electrons. For the isolated sodium atom in Figure 10-2, the total energy is the sum of the energy of the 11 electrons; for the chlorine atom, it is the sum of the energies of the 17 electrons. The total energy of the sodium–chlorine system is the sum of the individual energies of the two atoms.

Think about what happens to the energy of the sodium–chlorine system after the ionic bond has formed. The force on each electron is now different than it was before. For one thing, the number of electrons in each atom has changed; for another, the atoms are no longer isolated, so electrons in the sodium can exert forces on electrons in the chlorine and vice versa. Consequently, the orbits of all the electrons will shift a little due to the formation of the bond. This means that each electron will find itself in a slightly different position with regard to the nucleus, will be moving at a slightly different speed, and will experience a slightly different set of forces than it did before. The total energy of each electron will be different after the bond forms, the total energy of each atom will be different, and the total energy of the system will be different.

Whenever two or more atoms come together to form chemical bonds, the total energy of the system will be different after the bonds form than it was before. Two possibilities exist: either the final energy of the two atoms is less than the initial energy, or the final energy is greater than the initial energy.

The reaction that produces sodium chloride from sodium and chlorine is an example of the first kind of reaction, in which the total energy of the electrons in the system is lower after the two atoms have come together. According to the first law of thermodynamics, the total energy must be conserved, and that difference is given off during the reaction in the form of heat, light, and sound (there is an explosion). A chemical reaction that gives off energy in some form is said to be *exothermic.*

Many examples of exothermic reactions occur in everyday life. The energy that moves your car is given off by the explosive chemical combination of gasoline and oxygen in the car's engine. The chemical reactions in the battery that runs your Walkman™ also produce energy, although in this case some of the energy is in the form of kinetic energy of electrons in a wire. At this moment, cells in your body are breaking down molecules of a sugar known as glucose to supply the energy you need to live.

If the final energy of the electrons in a reaction is greater than the initial energy, then you have to supply energy to make the chemical reaction proceed. Such reactions are said to be *endothermic.* The chemical reactions that go on when you are cooking (frying an egg, for example, or baking a cake) are of this type. You can put the ingredients of a cake together and let them sit for as long as you like, but nothing will happen until you turn on the oven and supply energy in the form of heat. When the energy is available, electrons can move around and rearrange their chemical bonds. The result: a cake where before there was only a mixture of flour, sugar, and other materials.

As we saw earlier, you can think of chemical reactions as being analogous to a ball lying on the ground. If the ball happens to be at the top of a hill, it will lower its potential energy by rolling down the hill, giving up the excess energy in the form of frictional heat. If the ball is at the bottom of the hill, you have to do work on it to get it to the top. In the same way, exothermic reactions correspond to systems that "roll down the hill," going to a state of lower energy and giving off excess energy in some form. Endothermic reactions, on the other hand, have to be "pushed up the hill" and hence absorb energy from their surroundings.

Common Chemical Reactions

Many millions of chemical reactions take place in the world around us. Some occur naturally, and some occur as the result of human design or intervention. In your everyday world, however, you are likely to see a few types of chemical reactions over and over again. Let's examine a few of these common reactions in more detail.

Oxidation and Reduction

Perhaps the most distinctive chemical feature of our planet is the abundance of a highly reactive gas, oxygen, in our atmosphere. This trait leads to many of the most familiar chemical reactions in our lives. **Oxidation** includes any chemical reaction in which an atom (such as oxygen or any other atom that will accept electrons) accepts electrons while combining with other elements. The atom that transfers the electrons is said to be *oxidized*. Rusting is a common gradual oxidation reaction in which iron metal combines with oxygen to form a reddish iron oxide, as given by the equation

$$4Fe + 3O_2 \rightarrow 2Fe_2O_3$$

Burning or *combustion* is a much more rapid oxidation, in which oxygen combines with carbon-rich materials to produce carbon dioxide and other byproducts that often pollute.

Hydrocarbons—chemical compounds of carbon and hydrogen—provide the most efficient fuels for combustion, with only carbon dioxide and water (hydrogen oxide) as products. This reaction is

- ▶ **In words:** Hydrocarbon plus oxygen reacts to form carbon dioxide plus water plus energy.
- ▶ **In chemical notation:**

$$C_nH_{2n+2} + \left[\frac{(3n+1)}{2}\right]O_2 \rightarrow nCO_2 + (n+1)H_2O + \text{energy}$$

If you heat or cook with natural gas, then you are using an oxidation reaction to generate energy in your home. The term *natural gas* refers to a compound that chemists call *methane*. A methane molecule consists of a single carbon atom covalently bonded to four hydrogen atoms, as shown in the drawing in Figure 10-14. The oxidation reaction involved in the burning of methane is written

$$CH_4 + 2O_2 \rightarrow CO_2 + 2H_2O$$

The opposite of oxidation is **reduction,** a chemical reaction in which electrons are transferred to an atom from other elements. The atom that receives the electrons is said to be *reduced*. Thousands of years before scientists discovered oxygen, primitive metalworkers had learned how to reduce metal ores by smelting. In the iron-smelting process (typical of the industry carried out at hundreds of North American furnaces 250 years ago), iron makers heated a mixture of ore (iron oxide) and lime (calcium oxide) in an extremely hot charcoal fire. The lime lowered the melting temperature of the entire mixture, which then reacted to produce iron metal and carbon dioxide.

A material that has been oxidized has lost electrons to oxygen or some other atom. A material that has been reduced, on the other hand, has gained electrons. You may find the mnemonic OIL RIG ("oxidation is loss, reduction is gain") useful in keeping the two straight.

Oxidation and reduction are essential to life, and they define the principal difference between plants and animals. As we shall see in Chapter 21, animals take in carbon-based

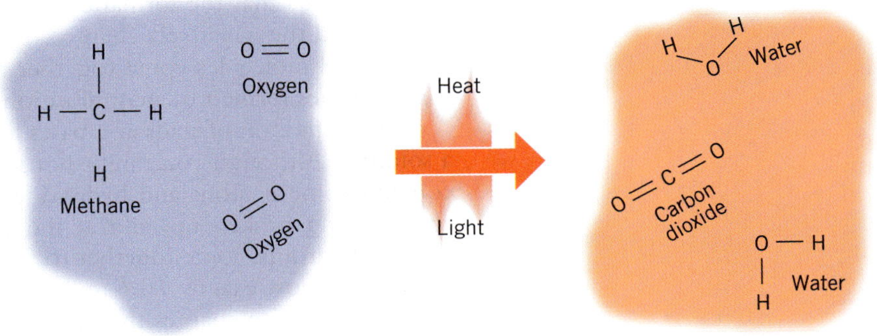

• **Figure 10-14** In pictorial form, an oxidation reaction involves the transfer of electrons to oxygen atoms. When natural gas (CH_4) burns, it combines with two oxygen molecules (O_2) to form a molecule of carbon dioxide (CO_2) and two molecules of water (H_2O).

molecules in their food and allow it to be oxidized in their cells. Carbon dioxide is released as a byproduct. Plants take in carbon dioxide and use the energy in sunlight to reduce it, releasing oxygen as a byproduct.

Precipitation–Solution Reactions

Water and many other liquids have the ability to dissolve solids. You can observe such *solution reactions* when you put salt or sugar into water. You can also watch the opposite process—*precipitation reactions*—occur if you allow ocean water to evaporate. Ocean water contains a rich mixture of elements in solution that precipitate as the water evaporates. The complex sequence of precipitation includes calcium carbonate ($CaCO_3$), calcium sulfate ($CaSO_4$), sodium chloride (NaCl), and dozens of other more exotic compounds. In many locations around the world, including the area around Death Valley in California and the Great Salt Lake in Utah, thick deposits of these so-called evaporite chemicals are mined for sodium, potassium, boron, chlorine, and other elements. The next time you're at the ocean, scoop up a handful of salt water and, as the water evaporates, watch as tiny salt crystals precipitate on your palm.

Acid–Base Reactions

Acids are common substances, used by people for thousands of years. The word has even entered our everyday vocabulary; we may refer to someone with an "acid" wit when we mean a sense of humor that is sharp and corrosive. Acids corrode metals and have a sour taste. For our purposes, we can make a technical definition of an acid as follows: An *acid* is any material that, when put into water, produces positively charged hydrogen ions (i.e., protons) in the solution. Lemon juice, orange juice, and vinegar are examples of common weak acids, while sulfuric acid (used in car batteries) and hydrochloric acid (used in industrial cleaning) are strong acids.

Bases are another class of corrosive materials. They taste bitter and generally feel slippery between your fingers. For our purposes, we can define a *base* as any material that, when put into water, produces negatively charged OH^- ions. This ion, consisting of an oxygen–hydrogen system that has an extra electron, is called the hydroxide ion. Most antacids (e.g., milk of magnesia) are weak bases. Cleaning fluids containing ammonia are the strongest of bases we most often encounter, although still relatively weak. Most common drain cleaners are examples of strong bases.

Although the common definitions of acids and bases involve taste and feel, you shouldn't try these tests yourself. Many acids and bases are extremely dangerous and corrosive—for example, battery acid (H_2SO_4) and lye (NaOH).

When acids and bases are brought together in the same solution, the H^+ and the OH^- ions react together to form water, and we say that the substances neutralize each other. For instance, if we mix hydrochloric acid (HCl) and lye (NaOH), we will find a chemical reaction that can be represented as follows:

$$HCl + NaOH \rightarrow H_2O + NaCl$$

This balanced reaction indicates that molecules of HCl and NaOH recombine to form a molecule of water (H_2O) and one unit of common table salt (NaCl). From this equation it appears that the formation of water removes both the positively charged hydrogen ion and the negatively charged hydroxide ion from solution, and the other parts of the original molecules come together to form a new material. Salt is the general name for molecules formed by neutralization of an acid and a base.

The definition of acids and bases leads to a simple way of measuring the strength of a solution. Although you might not think so at first glance, pure distilled water always contains some protons and hydroxide groups. A small number of water molecules are always being broken up, and at the same time elsewhere in the liquid, protons and hydroxide groups come together to form new molecules of water. In fact, in pure water there are almost exactly 10^{-7} moles of positively charged particles per liter. Acids contain more positive charges than this, while bases contain fewer.

This fact is used to set the scale for measuring acids and bases. Pure water has a *pH* ("*p*ower of *H*ydrogen") of 7. An acid solution that has a larger number of positive charges—a concentration of 10^{-6} moles per liter, for example—will have a lower pH (a pH of 6 in this example). A base that has a lower concentration of positive charges—10^{-10} moles per liter, for example—will have a higher pH (a pH of 10 in this example). Here are some common pH values:

Stomach acid	1.0–3.0
Mean of Adirondack lakes, 1975	4.8
Normal rainwater	5.6
Mean of Adirondack lakes, 1930	6.5
Pure water	7.0
Human blood	7.3–7.5
Household ammonia	11.0

Note in particular the dramatic change in the acidity of lakes in New York's Adirondack Mountains between 1930 and 1975. The cause of this change is acid rain—a phenomenon we will examine in more detail in Chapter 19.

The Science of Life •

Antacids

The first step of digestion, after the food is chewed and swallowed, takes place when acids in the stomach begin to break up the molecules that you have eaten. Occasionally, the stomach's acidity becomes too high, and we take antacids to feel better.

When you take an antacid, you are running a neutralization reaction in your body. Ordinary over-the-counter antacids contain bases such as aluminum hydroxide [$Al(OH)_3$] or sodium bicarbonate ($NaHCO_3$), which react with some of the acid in the stomach. These products do not neutralize all the stomach's hydrochloric acid, only enough of it to alleviate the symptoms.

Polymerization and Depolymerization

The molecular building blocks of most common biological structures are small (see Chapter 22), consisting of a few dozen atoms at most. Yet most biological molecules are huge, with up to millions of atoms in a single unit. How can small building blocks yield large structures characteristic of living things? The answer lies in the process of polymerization.

A polymer is a large molecule that is made by linking smaller, simpler molecules together repeatedly to build up a complex structure (Figure 10-15). The word comes from the Greek *poly* (many) and *meros* (parts). In spider's webs, clotting blood, and a thousand other processes, living systems have mastered the art of combining small molecules into long chains.

Polymerization reactions include all chemical reactions that form very large molecules from small molecules. Synthetic polymers usually begin in liquid form, with small molecules that move freely past their neighbors. Polyethylene, for example, begins as a gas with molecules containing just 6 atoms (2 carbon atoms and 4 hydrogen atoms), while the liquid that makes a common nylon contains molecules with 6 atoms of carbon, 11 of hydrogen, 1 of nitrogen, and 1 of oxygen—a combination that chemists write as $C_6H_{11}NO$. Polymers form from the liquid when the ends of these molecules begin to link up. In the case of nylon, the polymer forms by a *condensation reaction* in which each new polymer bond forms by the release of a water molecule (Figure 10-15*a*). Polyethylene, on the other hand, forms by *addition polymerization,* in which the basic building blocks are simply joined end to end (Figure 10-15*b*).

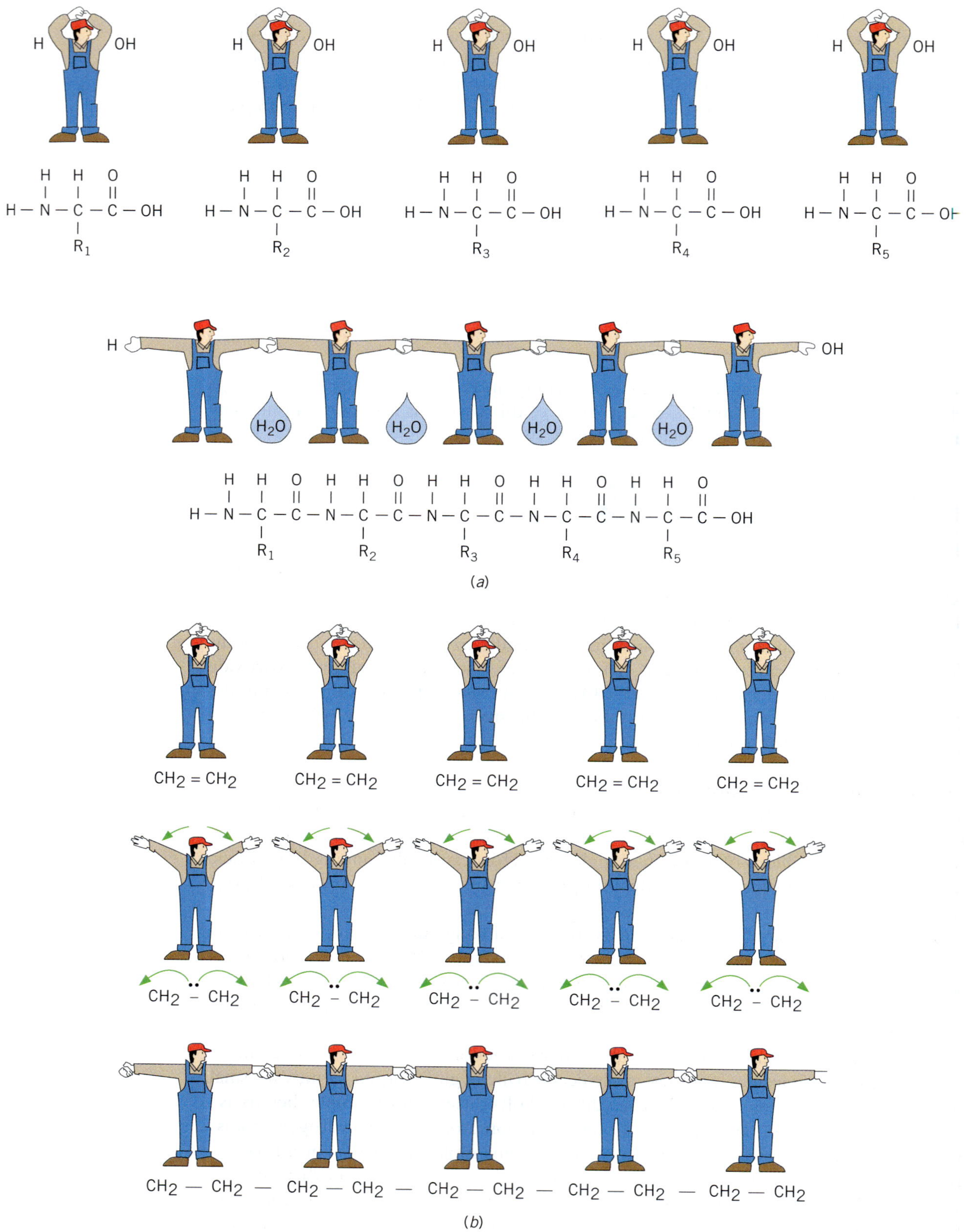

• **Figure 10-15** Polymers may form by condensation *(a)* or addition polymerization reactions *(b)*, with electrons represented as dots.

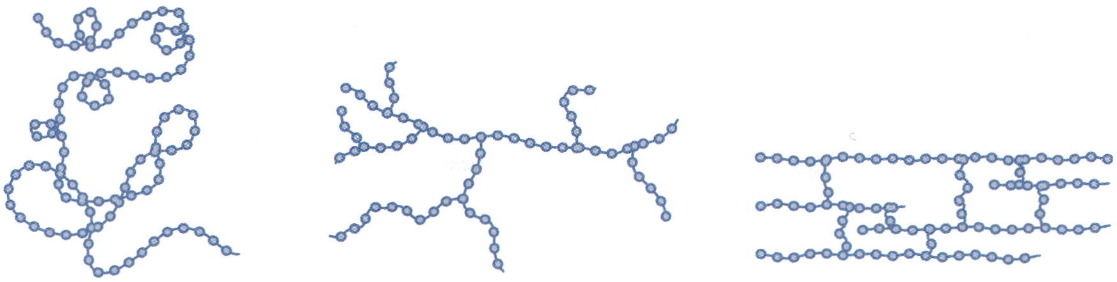

(*a*) Linear polymer (*b*) Branched polymer (*c*) Cross-linked polymer

• **Figure 10-16** Polymers can come in many forms: *(a)* a twisted chain, *(b)* a branched chain, and *(c)* chains that are linked together.

Polymers play an enormous role in our lives. The useful properties of these varied materials are related to the shapes of molecules and the way they come together to form materials (Figure 10-16). In polyethylene, for example, long-chain molecules wrap themselves together into something like a plate of hairy spaghetti. It's hard for water molecules to penetrate into this material, so it is widely used in packaging. The "plastic" on prepackaged fruit or meat at your supermarket may be made from polyethylene. A closely related polymer is polyvinyl chloride (PVC), whose basic building block, vinyl chloride, is just an ethylene molecule in which one of the four hydrogen atoms has been replaced by a chlorine atom. Because the chlorine atom is bigger than hydrogen, the molecules of the polymer are lumpy and cannot pack too closely together. Commercial PVC, widely used in water and sewer pipes, contains other kinds of molecules that move between the polymers, lubricating the system and making the resulting material highly flexible. Credit cards are also made from this material. Other common polymers include polypropylene (artificial turf), polystyrene ("foam" cups and packaging), and Teflon™ (nonstick cookware).

Many polymers are extremely long lasting, a situation that presents a growing problem in an age of diminishing landfills. Nevertheless, most polymers are not permanently stable. Given time, they will decompose into smaller molecules. This breakdown of a polymer into short segments is called *depolymerization*.

Perhaps the most familiar depolymerization reactions occur in your kitchen. Polymers cause the toughness of uncooked meat and the stringiness of many raw vegetables. We cook our food, in part, to break down these polymers. Chemicals such as meat tenderizers and marinades can also contribute to depolymerization and can improve the texture of some foods.

Not all depolymerization is desirable. Museum curators are painfully aware of the breakdown process, which affects leather, paper, textiles, and other historic artifacts made of organic materials. Storage in an environment of low temperature, low humidity, and an inert atmosphere (preferably without oxygen) may slow the depolymerization process, but there is no known way to repolymerize old brittle objects. •

Building Molecules: The Hydrocarbons

As an example of how a wide variety of materials can be made by assembling the same molecular building blocks in different ways, let's start with the methane molecule shown in Figure 10-14 and build a family of molecules known to chemists as *alkanes*. Alkanes are flammable materials (either gases or liquids) that burn readily and are often used as fuels. Most of the components of the gasoline in your car, for example, are members of this family. Alkanes are one example of **hydrocarbons,** molecules made completely from hydrogen and carbon atoms.

You can think of methane as being composed of a carbon atom and three hydrogen atoms (what chemists call the methyl group) plus a fourth hydrogen. We begin by noticing that we can replace the hydrogen in the methane by another methyl group to form

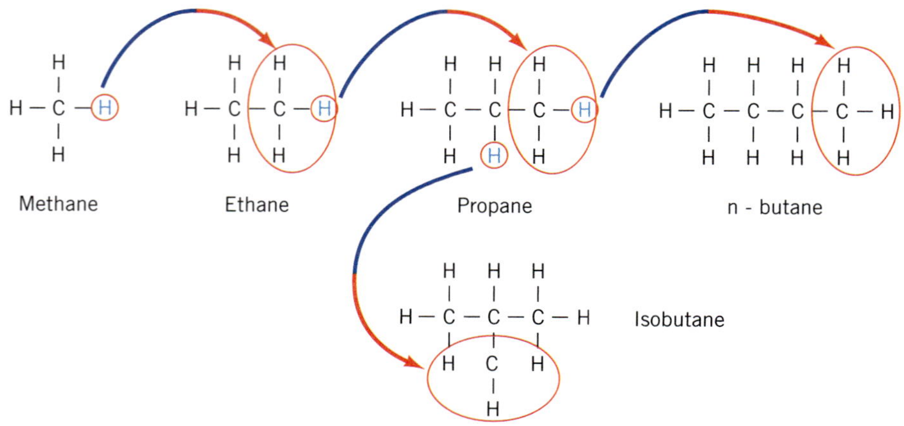

• **Figure 10-17** The alkane series may be built up by adding methyl groups to methane. The first three members of the group are methane (with one carbon atom), ethane (with two carbon atoms), and propane (with three carbon atoms). The next two members are isomers of butane (n-butane and isobutane, each with four carbons).

a molecule with two carbons in it. This larger molecule is ethane, a volatile, flammable gas (Figure 10-17).

You can keep going. Adding a third methyl group produces propane, a three-carbon chain. Propane is widely used as a fuel for portable stoves; you may have used it on your last camping trip. The next step is to substitute another methyl group for hydrogen to form a four-carbon chain, a molecule called butane. But there is an ambiguity here. We could, as shown, add the new group at the end of the chain so that all four carbon atoms form a straight line. This process would give us a form of butane known as n-butane (or "normal" butane). However, we could just as well add the methyl group to the interior carbon atom. In this case, the molecule would be known as isobutane. Isobutane and n-butane have exactly the same numbers of carbon and hydrogen atoms but are actually quite different materials. (To give just one example, the former boils at −11.6°C while the latter boils at −0.5°C.) Molecules that contain the same atoms but have different structures are called *isomers.*

As we continue the building process, moving to molecules with five carbons (pentane), six carbons (hexane), seven carbons (heptane), eight carbons (octane), and beyond, the number of different ways to assemble the atoms grows very fast. Octane, for example, has 18 different isomers; some have long chains, others are branched. As we shall see, these structural differences play an important role in a molecule's usefulness as an automotive fuel.

All other things being equal, the carbon chain length affects whether the alkane is a solid or liquid: the longer the chain, the higher the temperature at which that material can remain a solid. If carbon chains are straight, then alkanes with a half-dozen or so carbons are liquid, but those with more than 10 are soft solids. Good-quality paraffin candle wax, for example, which melts only near a hot flame of a wick, is composed primarily of chains with 20 to 30 carbon atoms. The presence of branches in the chain, however, makes it more difficult for the molecules to pack together efficiently. One consequence of branching is that the melting points are generally lowered compared to those of straight alkanes.

Technology •

Refining Petroleum

Deep underground are vast lakes of a thick, black liquid called petroleum, derived from many kinds of transformed molecules of former life forms. *Petroleum* is an extremely complex mixture of organic chemicals, as much as 98% molecules of hydrogen and carbon (mostly in the form of hydrocarbons), with about 2% of other elements. Engineers must separate this mixture into much purer fractions through the process of *distillation.*

Hydrocarbons with different numbers and arrangements of carbon atoms have very different boiling temperatures. The key to distillation, then, is to boil off and collect different kinds of molecules successively, according to their boiling points. The most *volatile* hydrocarbon—the one with the lowest boiling point—is simple methane (CH_4), or natural gas. At the opposite extreme are very-long-chain hydrocarbons with dozens of carbon atoms, as in the molecules that comprise hard waxes, asphalt, and tar.

Modern chemical plants bristle with tall distillation columns, in which petroleum products are purified.

William Lesch/The Image Bank/Getty Images

Modern chemical plants bristle with tall cylindrical towers that distill petroleum. Engineers pump crude oil into a tower, which is heated from below to create a temperature gradient up the tower (see Figure 10-18). At various levels of the tower, useful petroleum products such as gasoline or heating oil are recovered and sent to other parts of the plant for further processing.

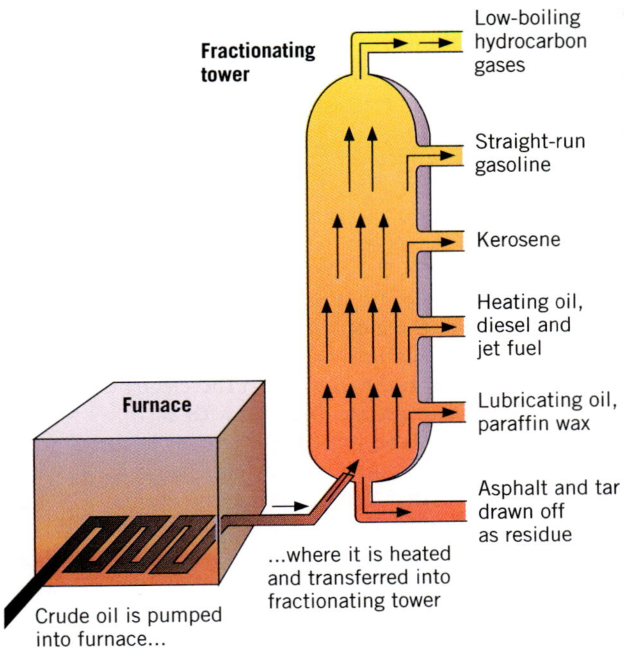

• **Figure 10-18** A distillation column in a chemical plant separates hydrocarbons into fractions useful as gases, gasoline, kerosene, heating oil, lubricating oils and paraffin, asphalt, and tar.

The gasoline you buy at a service station is usually rated in "octanes." The octane rating of a gasoline is based on its ability to stand high compression in a cylinder without igniting. A fuel mixture that ignites while the piston is still moving up and compressing the gas in the cylinder will cause the engine to knock—a highly undesirable quality. In general, the more highly branched a molecule is, the better it will perform without knocking.

A particular isomer of octane that has five carbons in a row and three methyl groups on the sides turns out to have very good antiknock properties. This isomer is called isooctane, and an octane rating of 100 for any fuel mixture means that it is as good as pure isooctane. At the opposite extreme, n-heptane is an isomer with seven carbons in an unbrached chain that produces knocking all the time. An octane rating of zero means the fuel mixture is as bad as pure n-heptane. Thus the octane rating of a fuel is simply a statement that it performs as well as a particular mixture of isooctane and n-heptane. A fuel rated at 95 octane, for example, performs as well as a mixture of 95% isooctane and 5% n-heptane. •

The Science of Life •

The Clotting of Blood

Whenever you get a cut that bleeds, your blood begins a remarkable and complex sequence of chemical reactions called *clotting*. Normal blood, a liquid crowded with cells and chemicals that distribute nutrients and energy throughout your body, flows freely through the circulatory system. When that system is breached and blood escapes, however, the damaged cells release a molecule called *prothrombin*.

Prothrombin itself is inactive, but other blood chemicals convert it into the active chemical *thrombin*. The thrombin reacts to break apart other normally stable chemicals that are always present in blood, and thus produces small molecules that immediately begin to polymerize. The new polymer, called *fibrin*, congeals quickly and forms a tough fiber net that traps blood cells and seals the break in minutes.

Clotting chemical reactions differ depending on the nature of the injury and the presence of foreign matter in the wound. Biologists have discovered more than a dozen separate chemical reactions that may occur during the process. A number of diseases and afflictions may occur if some part of this complex chemical system is not functioning properly. Hemophiliacs lack one of the key clotting chemicals and so may bleed continuously from small cuts. Some lethal snake venoms, on the other hand, work by inducing clotting in a closed circulatory system. •

Science News | Magnetic Overthrow
(SCIENCE NEWS, JAN. 7, 2006, P. 11)

As we shall see in the next chapter, one of the many consequences that can result from the formation of chemical bonds in materials is the production of a permanent magnet. Because electrons are charged and rotate, they act as tiny electromagnets that can, under some circumstances, line up and reinforce each other. The ability to control the alignment of electrons in a solid has enormous potential commercial applications, from data storage technologies to communication.

Traditionally, the only way to change the orientation of a magnet was to subject it to the field of another magnet. Now, however, scientists are starting to develop materials in which magnetic orientation can be controlled by electric currents. The new approach involves what scientists call spin-torque or spin-transfer effects, which work as follows: if electrons in a material line up to form a magnet and a strong electric current passes through a nearby material, the electrons in the current can cause the electrons in the magnet to flip over. In the end, the electrons in the magnet wind up aligning themselves with the electrons in the current. If the electrons in the current are lined up with each other they can twist the electrons in the magnet into their own orientation.

This effect only works at the atomic scale, but scientists have already produced sandwich-like materials in which layers of permanent magnets alternate with layers that conduct electrical current. Because the change of magnetic orientation is very fast, many scientists are starting to think of this kind of device as the memory chip of the future—indeed, prototype memory chips operating on this principle have already been reported. A related effect, in which electrons in the magnet are set spinning rather than being reoriented by the current has the potential of producing a communication system that transmits information 30 times faster than current cell phone technology allows.

Which, if any, of these promising new ideas will have a major impact on industry remains to be seen. Spin-transfer, however, illustrates the wide variety of phenomena that can happen when scientists start rearranging atoms and the way they come together to make materials.

Thinking More About | Atoms in Combination

Life-Cycle Costs

Every month chemists around the world develop thousands of new materials and bring them to market. Some of these materials do a particular job better than those they replace, some do jobs that have never been done before, and some do jobs more cheaply. All of them, however, share one property—when the useful life of the product of which they are a part is over, they will have to be disposed of in a way that is not harmful to the environment. Until very recently, engineers and planners had given little thought to this problem.

Think about the battery in your car, for example. The purchase price covered the cost of mining and processing the lead in its plates, pumping and refining the oil that was made into its plastic case, assembling the final product, and so on. When that battery reaches the end of its useful life, all of these materials have to be dealt with responsibly. For example, if you throw the battery into a ditch somewhere, the lead may wind up in nearby streams and wells.

One way of dealing with this sort of problem, of course, is to recycle materials—pull the lead plates out of the battery, process them, and then use them again. But even in the best system, some materials can't be recycled, either because they have become contaminated with other materials through use, or because we don't have technologies capable of doing the recycling. These materials have to be disposed of in a way that isolates them from the environment. The question becomes, "Who pays?"

Traditionally, in the United States, the person who does the dumping—in effect, the last user—must see to the disposal. In some European countries, however, a new approach is being introduced. Called life-cycle costing, this concept is built around the proposition that once a manufacturer uses a material, he or she owns it forever and is responsible for its disposal. The cost of a product such as a new car, then, has to reflect the fact that someday that car may be abandoned and the manufacturer will have to pay for its disposal.

Life-cycle costing increases the price of commodities, contributing to inflation in the process. What do you think the proper trade-off is in this situation? How much extra cost should be imposed up front compared to eventual costs of disposal?

Summary

Atoms link together by *chemical bonds,* which form when a rearrangement of electrons lowers the potential energy of the electron system, particularly by the filling of outer electron shells. *Ionic bonds* lower chemical potential energy by the transfer of one or more electrons to create atoms with filled shells. The positive and negative ions created in the process bond together through electrostatic forces. In *metals,* on the other hand, isolated electrons in the outermost shell wander freely throughout the material and create *metallic bonds. Covalent bonds* occur when adjacent atoms, or groups of atoms called molecules, share bonding electrons. *Hydrogen bonding* and *van der Waals forces* are special cases involving distortion of electron distributions to create electrical polarity—regions of slightly positive and negative charge that can bind together.

Atoms combine to form several different *states of matter. Gases* are composed of atoms or molecules that can expand to fill any available volume. *Plasmas* are ionized gases in which electrons have been stripped from the atoms. *Liquids* have a fixed volume but no fixed shape. *Solids* have fixed volume and shape. Solids include *crystals,* with a regular and repeating atomic structure; *glasses,* with a nonrepeating structure; and *plastics,* which are composed of intertwined chains of molecules called *polymers.* The various states of matter can undergo *changes of state,* such as freezing, melting, or boiling, with changes in temperature or pressure.

Chemical bonds break and form during *chemical reactions,* which may involve the synthesis or decomposition of chemical elements or compounds. Reactions in which materials lose electrons to atoms such as oxygen are called *oxidation* reactions. In the opposite reaction, called *reduction,* electrons are moved onto atoms.

All life depends on *polymerization* reactions, in which small molecules link together to form long polymer fibers such as natural hair, silk, plant fiber, and skin, and synthetic materials such as polyesters, vinyl, cellophane, and other plastics. *Hydrocarbons,* widely used as fuels, are chainlike molecules made of carbon and hydrogen atoms. High temperatures and certain chemicals can cause the breakdown of polymers, or depolymerization, which is often a key objective in cooking.

Key Terms

chemical bond
ionic bond
metallic bond
metal
covalent bond
hydrogen bond
van der Waals forces
states of matter
gas
plasma
liquid
solid
crystal
glass
polymer
plastic
changes of state
chemical reaction
oxidation
reduction
polymerization
hydrocarbon

Review Questions

1. When is an electron a valence electron? Why are valence electrons especially important in chemical reactions?
2. Describe the ionic bond. Give an example of a material that uses it.
3. Describe the metallic bond. What properties of metal follow from the properties of the bond?
4. Which type of chemical bond is found in an alloy? Give an example of an alloy.
5. Describe the covalent bond. Give an example of a material that uses it.
6. Describe the hydrogen bond. Explain how it affects the properties of water.
7. Describe the van der Waals force. Give an example of a material with van der Waals interactions. What distinctive properties does that material display?
8. Describe three everyday states of matter, including differences among them in volume and shape. In which states do the atoms or molecules have the greatest kinetic energy? the least?
9. How is a plasma like a gas? How is it like a metal? Where are plasmas found in the solar system? Where are they found in modern technologies?
10. How is a glass constructed from its atoms? a plastic? a cystalline solid?
11. Identify common changes of state and give examples of each.
12. In what sense are oxidation and reduction reactions opposites?
13. Are the following substances acid, base, or neutral: sodium bicarbonate (pH = 8.3); sugar solution (pH = 7.0); milk (pH = 6.7); orange juice (pH = 3.6); milk of magnesia (pH = 10.5)?
14. What is polymerization? Give an example.
15. What are the characteristics of alkanes? What are the names and properties of the first five alkanes?
16. What is an isomer? Do all isomers have the same chemical properties?
17. How many isomers of hexane are there? Draw them.

Discussion Questions

1. Identify objects around you that use the three kinds of chemical bonding described in the text.

2. Why do most molecules have covalent bonds?

3. Classify the solid objects around you as ceramics, metals, glasses, and plastics.

4. If the temperature of a solution is decreasing as a chemical reaction is progressing, is the reaction endothermic or exothermic?

5. The chemistry of the planet Mars is quite similar to Earth except that there is almost no water. Which common chemical reactions that occur on Earth would you not expect to see on Mars?

6. Cooks often tenderize meat by soaking it in a liquid such as lemon juice or vinegar for several hours. What chemical reaction do you think is taking place in the meat? How is this reaction analogous to heating in an oven?

7. During icy winter conditions we often throw salt on sidewalks and streets. What occurs when salt comes in contact with ice? What reaction is involved? How do you think the melting point of salt water compares to that of pure water?

8. Explain why melting ice is considered an endothermic process. Are atomic bonds being broken?

9. What are polar molecules? Why is polarization important for bilogical reactions?

10. When iron is rusting, is it gaining or losing electrons?

11. What is the maximum number of electrons that an atom can have in its first orbital? its second and third orbitals?

12. What is the structural difference between liquid water at 0 degrees Celsius and ice at 0 degrees Celsius? What is the structural difference between liquid water at 0 degrees Celsius and liquid water at 100 degrees Celsius?

13. What is an isomer? Do all isomers have the same chemical properties?

14. Why do crystals form? In what substances are crystals more likely to form? Why?

Problems

1. When you burn methane (CH_4), it unites with oxygen (O_2) to form carbon dioxide (CO_2) and water (H_2O). Write an equation to balance the reactants and products of this reaction.

2. Use some other examples of the burning of hydrocarbons (e.g., ethane-C_2H_6 or propane-C_3H_8) to balance reaction equations.

3. Is $CH_4 + O_2 \rightarrow CO_2 + H_2O$ a balanced equation? Why or why not?

Investigations

1. Look around your home and school and list the variety of plastic objects. What strategy might you develop to recycle plastics? Note the numbers surrounded by a triangle on many disposable plastics. What do the numbers mean?

2. What materials were used for the construction of buildings, furniture, and transportation devices in the United States 200 years ago? What modern technologies would be difficult or impossible with just those materials?

3. Why is it that some materials in landfills don't break down into their constituent chemical parts?

4. Dissect a disposable diaper. How many kinds of materials can you identify? What are the key properties of each? What kind of chemical bonding might contribute to the distinctive properties of these materials? Investigate the arguments for and against using disposable diapers.

5. We often refer to drinking water as being "soft" or "hard," based on the kind of impurities present in the water. Which kind do you have in your community? What kind of chemical reaction can take place if water is too hard? How can you prevent that reaction from occurring?

6. Use a pH meter to measure the acidity of various liquids. What is the pH of lemonade? a soft-drink? milk? How do these liquids compare with stomach acids?

7. New plastics are being created from corn and soy beans, and these plastics break down when exposed to air and water. In what ways will the environment benefit from these biodegradable plastics? Should our government mandate the use of materials that biodegrade once their useful life is over?

8. Search the Web to find out how long it takes for common items like a cigarette butt or coffee cup to biodegrade.

11

Materials and Their Properties

How have computers gotten so much faster?

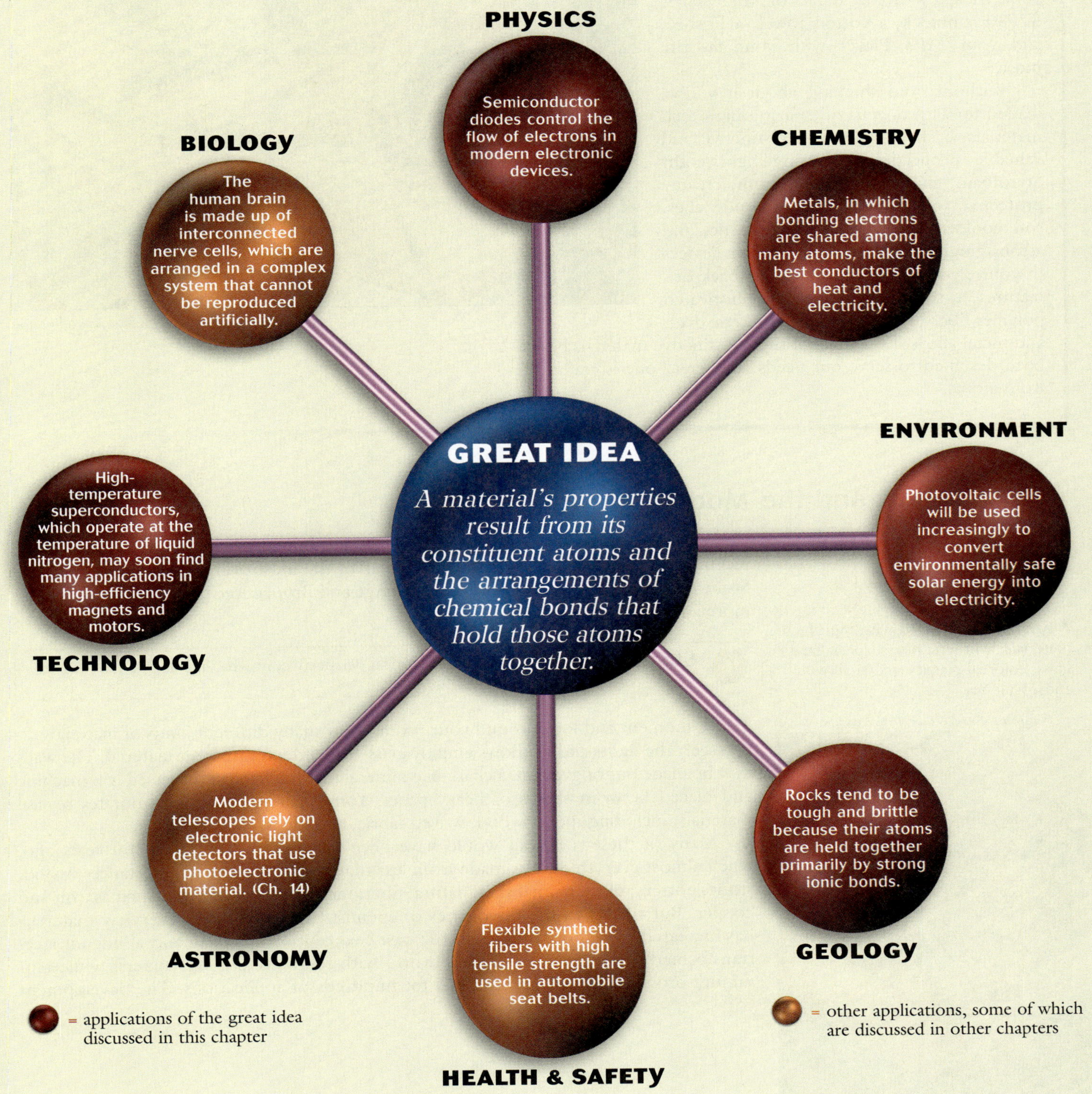

Science Through the Day | Hauling Gear

It's only 10 A.M. but the beach is already starting to get crowded. You and your friends decide to walk a few hundred meters down the beach to a more open stretch.

There's a surprising amount of gear to haul across the beach. You carry a Styrofoam cooler filled with aluminum soda cans, while your backpack holds a pile of sandwiches, SPF30 sunblock, a cotton towel, a Frisbee, and your MP3 Player with your favorite music.

Vera Storman/Getty Images

Without even thinking about it you've loaded up with dozens of amazing high-tech materials, each with its own distinctive and valuable properties: insulating lightweight Styrofoam, shiny strong aluminum, creamy protective lotion, tasty layered sandwiches, soft cool cotton, durable hard plastic, and astonishingly versatile semiconductor devices in your electronic gear. Even your backpack features a score of different sophisticated polymer fibers, plastic zippers, synthetic dyes, and metal alloys. Every one of these distinctive materials has been designed to serve our needs, and every one is crafted from atoms.

Materials and the Modern World

The materials people use, perhaps more than any other facet of a culture, define the technical sophistication of a society. We speak of the most primitive human cultures as Stone Age societies, and we recognize Iron Age and Bronze Age peoples as progressively more advanced.

Stop and Think! Given that historical perspective, in what age are we now living?

A typical room is filled with high-tech materials: synthetic fibers, specialized glass, colorful plastics, metal alloys, and cosmetics.

Patrick Sheandell O'Carroll/PhotoAlto/Getty Images

Take a moment and look around your room. How many different kinds of materials do you see? The lights and windows employ glass—a brittle, transparent material. The walls may be made out of gypsum, a chalk-like mineral that has been compressed in a machine and placed between sheets of heavy paper. Your chair probably incorporates several materials, including metal, wood, woven fabric, and glues.

Many of these materials would have been familiar to Americans 200 years ago, when almost everything was made from less than a dozen common substances: wood, stone, pottery, glass, animal skin, natural fibers, and a few basic metals such as iron and copper. But thanks to the discoveries of chemists, the number of everyday materials has increased by a thousandfold in the past two centuries. Cheap and abundant steel transformed the nineteenth-century world with railroads and skyscrapers, while aluminum provided a lightweight metal for hundreds of applications. The development of rubber, synthetic fibers, and a vast array of other plastics affected every kind of human activity from industry to sports. Brilliant new pigments enlivened art and fashion, while new medications cured many ailments and prolonged lives. And in our electronic age, the discovery of semiconductor and superconductor materials has changed life in the United States in ways that our eighteenth-century ancestors could not have imagined.

Chemists take natural elements and compounds that form earth, air, and water and devise thousands of useful materials. They succeed in part because materials display so many different properties: color, smell, hardness, luster, flexibility, density, solubility in water, texture, melting point, strength—the list goes on and on. Each new material holds the promise of doing some job cheaper or safer or otherwise better than any other.

Based on our understanding of atoms and their chemical bonding (see Chapter 10), we now realize that the properties of every material depend on three essential features:

1. The kind of atoms of which it is made
2. The way those atoms are arranged
3. The way the atoms are bonded to each other

In this chapter, we look at different properties of materials and see how they relate to their atomic architecture. We examine the strength of materials—how well they resist outside forces. We look at the ability of materials to conduct electricity, and we examine whether they are magnetic. And, finally, we describe what are perhaps the most important new materials in modern society, the semiconductor and the microchip.

The Strengths of Materials

Have you ever carried a heavy load of groceries in a thin plastic grocery bag? You can cram a bag full of heavy bottles and cans and lift it by its thin handles without fear of breakage. How can something as light, flexible, and inexpensive as a piece of plastic be so strong?

Strength is the ability of a solid to resist changes in shape. Strength is one of the most immediately obvious material properties, and it bears a direct relationship to chemical bonding. A strong material must be made with strong chemical bonds. By the same token, a weak material, like a defective chain, must have weak links between some of its atoms. While no type of bond or attraction is universally stronger than the other kinds, van der Waals forces are generally the weakest. Any material with van der Waals forces will have one or more particularly soft directions of bonding, and you will probably be able to pull the material apart with your hands. You experience this softness whenever you use baby powder, graphite lubricant, or soap.

By contrast, many strong materials, such as rocks, glass, and ceramics, are held together primarily by ionic bonds. Next time you see a building under construction, look at the way beams and girders link diagonally to form a rigid framework. Chemical bonds in strong materials do the same thing. A three-dimensional network of ionic bonds in these materials holds them together like a framework of steel girders.

The strongest materials we know, however, incorporate long chains and clusters of carbon atoms held together by covalent bonds. The extraordinary strength of natural spider webs, synthetic Kevlar (used to make bulletproof vests), diamonds, and your plastic shopping bag all stem from the strength of covalent bonds to carbon atoms.

Gerard Vandystadt/Photo Researchers

The strength of materials is vital to many activities. Bones and muscles provide a weightlifter's strength.

Different Kinds of Strength

Every material is held together by the bonds between its atoms. When an outside force is applied to a material, the atoms must shift their positions in response. The bonds stretch and compress, and an equal and opposite force is generated inside the material

Suspension bridges feature vertical supports that are extremely strong under compression and massive steel cables that are extremely strong under tension.

to oppose the force that is imposed from the outside, in accordance with Newton's third law of motion. The strength of a material is thus related to the size of the force it can withstand when it is pushed or pulled.

Material strength is not a single property, because there are different ways of placing an object under stress. Scientists and engineers recognize three very different kinds of strength when characterizing materials:

1. Its ability to withstand crushing (*compressive strength*)
2. Its ability to withstand pulling apart (*tensile strength*)
3. Its ability to withstand twisting (*shear strength*)

Your everyday experience will convince you that these three properties are often quite independent. A loose stack of bricks, for example, can withstand crushing pressures—you can pile tons of weight on it without having the stack collapse. But the stack of bricks has little resistance against twisting. Indeed, it can be toppled by a child. A rope, on the other hand, is extremely strong when pulled but has little strength under twisting or crushing.

The point at which a material stops resisting external forces and begins to bend, break, or tear is called its *elastic limit*. We see examples of this phenomenon every day. When you break an egg, crush an aluminum can, snap a rubber band, or fold a piece of paper, you exceed an elastic limit and permanently change the object. When the materials in your body exceed their elastic limit, the consequences can be catastrophic. Our bones may break if put under too much stress, while arteries under pressure that is too high may rupture in an aneurysm.

A material's strength is a result of the type and arrangements of chemical bonds. Think about how you might design a structure using Tinkertoys that would be strong under crushing, pulling apart, or twisting. The strongest arrangement would have lots of short sticks with triangular patterns. Nature's strongest structure, diamond, adopts this strategy; it is exceptionally strong under all three kinds of stress because of its three-dimensional framework of strong carbon–carbon bonds (see Figure 11-1). Glass, ceramics, and most rocks, which also feature rigid frameworks of chemical bonds, are relatively strong. Many plastics like the one in your shopping bag, however, have strong bonds in only one direction and thus are strong when stretched, but have little strength when twisted or crushed. Materials with layered atomic structures, in which planes of atoms are arranged like a stack of paper, are generally strong when squeezed but quite weak

Bruce Hands/Stone/Getty Images

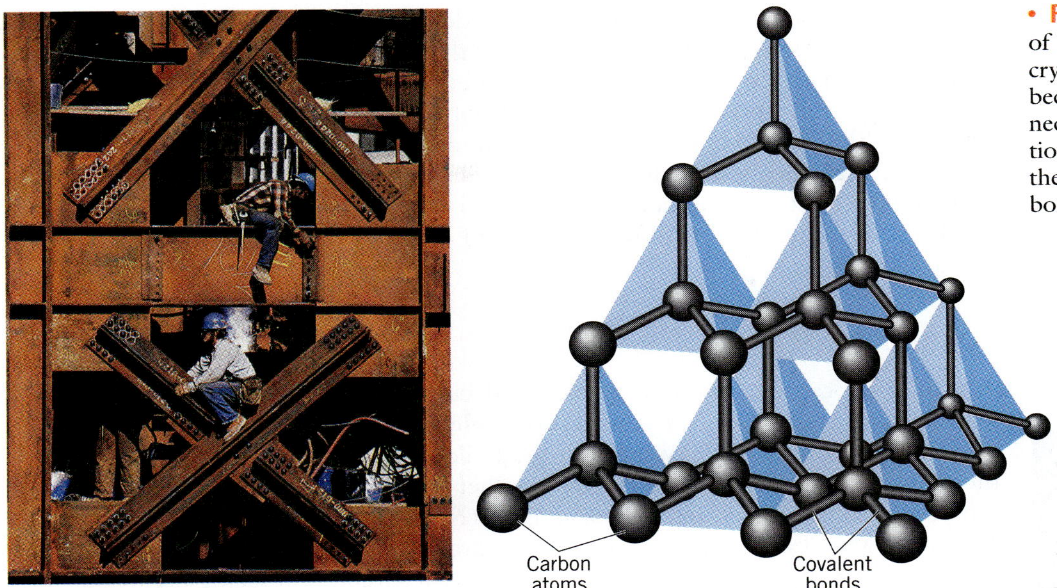

(a)

(b)

• **Figure 11-1** The girder framework of a skyscraper *(a)* and a diamond's crystal structure *(b)* are both strong because of numerous very strong connections. In a building the connections are steel girders; in diamond they are carbon–carbon covalent bonds.

under other stresses. Thus the strength of a material depends on the kind of atoms in it, the way they are arranged, and the kind of chemical bonds that hold the atoms together.

Composite Materials

Composite materials combine the properties of two or more materials. The strength of one of the constituents is used to offset the weakness of another, resulting in a material whose strengths are greater than any of its components. Plywood, one of the most common composite materials, consists of thin wood layers glued together with alternating grain direction. The weakness of a single thin sheet of wood is compensated by the strength of the neighboring sheets. Not only is plywood much stronger than a solid board of the same dimension, but it can also be produced from much smaller trees by slicing thin layers of wood off a rotating log, like removing paper from a roll.

Reinforced concrete is a common composite material in which steel rods (with great tensile strength) are embedded in a concrete mass (with great compressive strength). A similar strategy is used in fiberglass, formed from a cemented mat of glass fibers, and in new carbon-fiber composites that are providing extraordinarily strong and lightweight materials for industry and sports applications.

The modern automobile features a wide variety of composite materials. Windshields of safety glass are layered to resist shattering and reduce sharp edges in a collision. Tires are intricately formed from rubber and steel belting for strength and durability. Car upholstery commonly mingles natural and artificial fibers, and dashboards often employ complexly laminated surfaces. The bodies of many cars are formed from a fiberglass or other molded lightweight composite. And, as we shall see, all of a modern automobile's electronics, from radio to ignition, depend on semiconductor composites of extraordinary complexity.

Hank de Lespinasse/Age Fotostock America, Inc.

In composite materials, such as plywood and reinforced concrete, one material's weakness is compensated by the other's strength.

Electrical Properties of Materials

Of all the properties of materials, none are more critical to our world than those that control the flow of electricity. Glance around you and tally up the number of electrical devices nearby. Chances are your list will quickly grow to several dozen. Almost every aspect of our technological civilization depends on electricity, so scientists have devoted a good deal of attention to materials that are useful in electrical systems. (See Chapter 5 for a review of electricity and magnetism.) If the job at hand is to send electrical energy from a power plant to a distant city, for example, we need a material that will carry the electrical energy without much loss. If, on the other hand, the job is to put a covering over a wall switch so that we will not be endangered by electricity when we turn on a light, we want a material that will not conduct electricity at all. In other words, a large number of different kinds of materials contribute to any electrical device.

Conductors

Dennis MacDonald/PhotoEdit

Electrical wiring consists of a conducting metal core surrounded by an insulating layer of plastic.

Any material capable of carrying electrical current—that is, any material through which electrons can flow freely—is called an **electrical conductor.** Metals, such as the copper that carries electricity through the building in which you are now sitting, are the most common conductors, but many other materials also conduct electricity. Saltwater, for example, contains ions of sodium (Na^+) and chlorine (Cl^-), which are free to move if they become part of an electric circuit. We can find out if a material will conduct electricity by making it part of an electric circuit and seeing if current flows through it.

The arrangement of a material's electrons determines its ability to conduct electricity. In the case of metals, you will recall, some electrons are bonded fairly loosely and shared by many atoms. If you connect a copper wire across the poles of a battery, those electrons are free to move in response to the battery's potential. They flow from the negative pole toward the positive pole of the battery.

As we saw in Chapter 5, the motion of electrons in electrical currents is seldom smooth. Under normal circumstances, electrons moving through a metal will collide continuously with the much heavier ions in that metal. In each of those collisions, electrons lose some of the energy they have gotten from the battery, and that energy is converted to the faster vibration of ions—what we perceive as heat. The property by which materials drain the energy away from a current is called **electrical resistance.** Even very good conductors have some electrical resistance. (The inverse of electrical resistance is *electrical conductance,* or the ease with which electrons flow in a material. Resistance and conductance are thus different ways of describing the same property.)

Insulators

Many materials incorporate chemical bonds in which few electrons are free to move in response to the "push" of an electric field. In rocks, ceramics, and many biological materials such as wood and hair, for example, the electrons are bound tightly to one or more atoms by ionic or covalent bonds (see Chapter 10). It takes considerable energy to pry electrons loose from those atoms—energy that is normally much greater than the energy supplied by a battery or an electrical outlet. These materials will not conduct electricity unless they are subjected to an extremely high voltage, which can pull the electrons loose. If they are made part of an electric circuit, no electricity will flow through them. We call these materials **electrical insulators.**

The primary use of insulators in electric circuits is to channel the flow of electrons and to keep people from touching wires that are carrying current. The shields on your light switches and household power outlets and the casings for most car batteries, for example, are made from plastic, a reasonably good insulating material that has the added advantages of low cost and flexibility. Similarly, electrical workers use protective rubber boots and gloves when working on dangerous power lines. In the case of high-power lines, glass or ceramic components are used to isolate the current because of their superior insulating ability.

Semiconductors

Many materials in nature are neither good conductors nor perfect insulators. We call such materials **semiconductors.** As the name implies, a semiconductor will carry electricity but will not carry it very well. Typically, the resistance of silicon is a million times higher than the resistance of a conductor such as copper. Nevertheless, silicon is not an insulator, because some of its electrons do flow in an electric circuit. Why should this be?

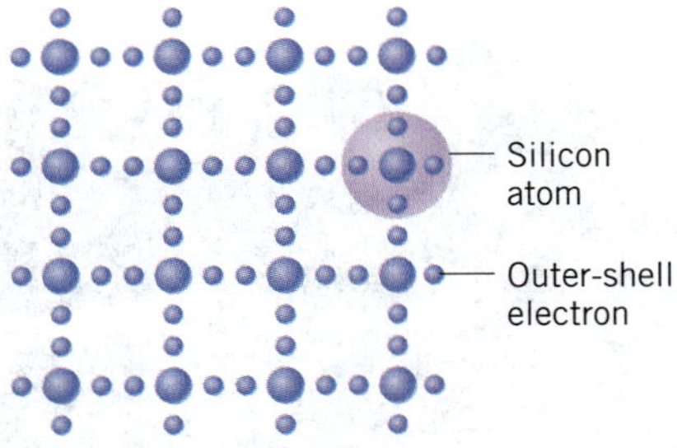

• **Figure 11-2** A normal silicon crystal displays a regular pattern of silicon atoms. Some of its electrons are shaken loose by atomic vibrations, and these electrons are free to move around and conduct electricity.

In a silicon crystal (Figure 11-2), all the electrons are taken up in the covalent bonds that hold each silicon atom to its neighbors. At room temperature, the silicon atoms vibrate and a few of the covalent bonding electrons are shaken loose—think of them as picking up a little of the vibrational energy of the atoms. These *conduction electrons* are free to move around the crystal. If the silicon is made part of an electric circuit, a modest number of conduction electrons are free to move through the solid.

When a conduction electron is shaken loose, it leaves behind a defect in the silicon crystal—the absence of an electron. This missing electron is called a *hole*. Just as electrons move in response to electrical charges, so too can holes (see Figure 11-3).

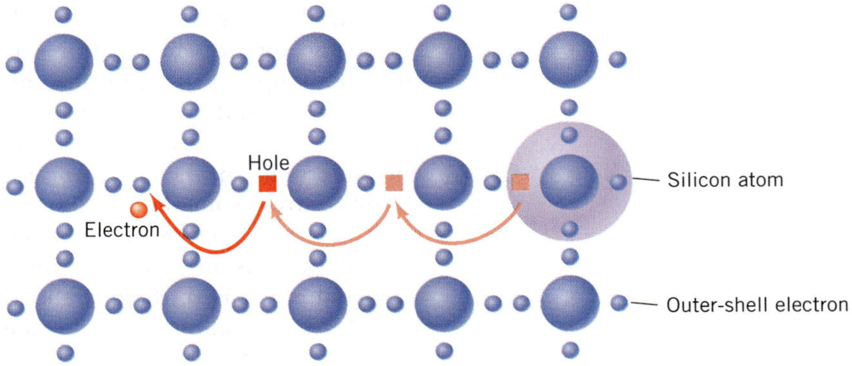

• **Figure 11-3** A hole in a semiconductor is produced when an electron is missing. Holes can move, just like electrons. As an electron moves to fill a hole, it creates another hole where it used to be.

The motion of holes in semiconductors is something like what you see in a traffic jam on a crowded expressway. A space will open up between two cars, after which one car moves up to fill the space, then another car moves up to fill that space, and so on. You could describe this sequence of events as the successive motion of cars. But you could just as easily (in fact, from a mathematical point of view *more* easily) say that the space between cars—the hole—moves backward down the line. In the same way, you can either describe the effects of the successive jumping of electrons from one atom to another, or talk about the hole moving through the material. Although there are relatively few semiconducting materials in nature, they have played an enormous role in the microelectronics industry, as we shall see later.

Superconductors

Some materials cooled to within a few degrees of absolute zero exhibit a property known as **superconductivity**—the complete absence of any electrical resistance. Below some very cold critical temperature, electrons in these materials are able to move without surrendering any of their energy to the atoms. This phenomenon, discovered in Holland in 1911, was not understood until the 1950s. Today, superconducting technologies provide the basis for a multibillion-dollar-a-year industry worldwide. The principal reason for this success is that once a material becomes superconducting and is kept cool, current will flow in it forever. This behavior means that if you take a loop of superconducting wire and hook it up to a battery to get the current flowing, the current will continue to flow even if you take the battery away.

In Chapter 5, we learned that current flowing in a loop creates a magnetic field. If we make an electromagnet out of superconducting material and keep it cold, the magnetic field will be maintained at no energy cost except for the refrigeration. Indeed, superconductors provide strong magnetic fields much more cheaply than any conventional

Joseph Sohm/Photo Researchers

As cars in a traffic jam move slowly forward, "holes" in the traffic can be described as moving backward.

copper-wire electromagnet because they don't heat up from electrical resistance. Superconducting magnets are used extensively in many applications where very high magnetic fields are essential—for example, in particle accelerators (see Chapter 12) and in magnetic resonance imaging systems for medical diagnosis. Perhaps they will eventually be used in everyday transportation.

How is it that a superconducting material can allow electrons to pass through without losing energy? The answer in at least some cases has to do with the kind of electron–ion interactions that occur. At very low temperatures, heavy ions in a material don't vibrate very much and can be thought of as being fixed in more or less one place. As a fast-moving electron passes between two positive ions, the ions are attracted to the electron and start to move toward it. By the time the ions respond, however, the electron is long gone. Nevertheless, when the ions move close together, they create a region in the material with a more positive electrical charge than normal. This region attracts a second electron and pulls it in. Thus the two electrons can move through the superconducting material something like the way two bike racers move down a track, with one running interference for the other.

At the very low temperatures at which a material becomes superconducting, electrons hook up in pairs, and the pairs start to interlock like links of a complex, tangled matrix. While individual electrons are very light, the whole collection of interlocked electrons in a superconductor is quite massive. If one electron in a superconductor encounters an ion, the electron can't be easily deflected. In fact, to change the velocity of any electron, something you would have to do to get energy from it, you would have to change the velocity of *all* the electrons. Because this can't be done, no energy is given up in such collisions, and electrons simply move through the material together. If the temperature is raised, though, the ions vibrate more vigorously and are no longer able to perform the delicate minuet required to produce the electron pairs. Thus above the critical temperature, superconductivity breaks down.

The Ongoing Process of Science •

Searching for New Superconductors

Until the mid-1980s, all superconducting materials had to be cooled in liquid helium, an expensive and cumbersome refrigerant that boils at a few degrees above absolute zero, because none of these materials was capable of sustaining superconductivity above about 20 kelvins. Acting on a hunch, scientists Karl Alex Müller and George Bednorz of IBM's Zurich, Switzerland, research laboratory began a search for new superconductors. Traditional superconductors are metallic, but Bednorz and Müller decided instead to focus on oxides—chemical compounds, such as most rocks and ceramics, in which oxygen participates in ionic bonds. It was an odd choice, for oxides make the best electrical insulators, although a few unusual oxides do conduct electricity.

Working with little encouragement from their peers and no formal authorization from their employers, the scientists spent many months mixing chemicals, baking them in an oven, and testing for superconductivity. The breakthrough came on January 27, 1986, when a small black wafer of baked chemicals was found to become superconducting at greater than 30 degrees above absolute zero—a temperature that shattered the old record and ushered in the era of "high-temperature"(though still extremely cold) superconductors. Their compound of copper, oxygen, and other elements seemed to defy all conventional wisdom, and it began a frantic race to study and improve the novel material.

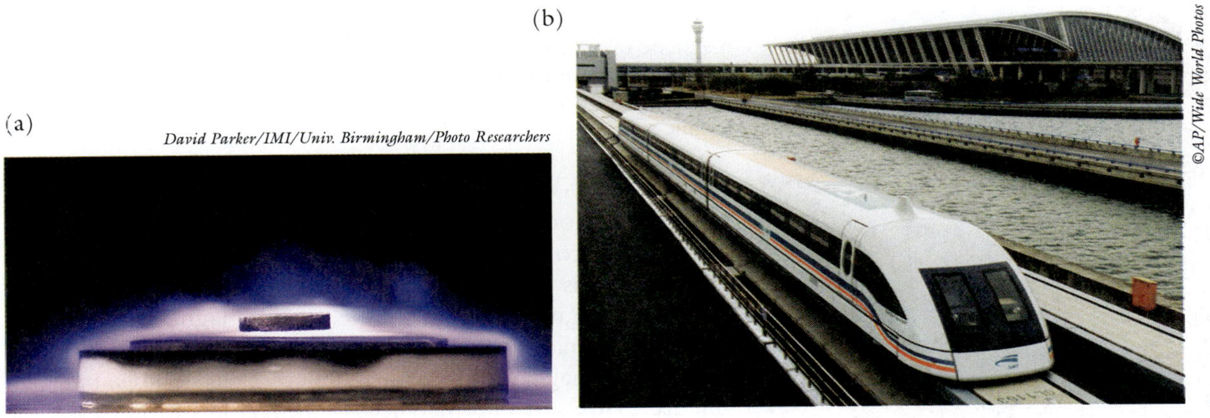

• **Figure 11-4** *(a)* A magnet floats "magically" above a black disk made from a new "high-temperature" superconductor. The clouds in the background form above the cold liquid-nitrogen refrigerant. *(b)* This technology has been used in Japan to float high-speed trains above their tracks.

Today, many scientists are attempting to synthesize new oxides closely related to those first described by Bednorz and Müller, while others struggle to devise practical applications for these new materials. Some recently developed compounds superconduct at temperatures as high as 160 degrees above absolute zero (see Figure 11-4).

High-temperature superconductors have taken superconductivity from the domain of a few specialists and brought it into classrooms around the world. As a new generation of scientists grows up with these new superconductors, new questions will be asked and exciting new ideas and inventions are sure to be found. Within the next generation we may have electric motors that rotate a million revolutions per minute on superconducting bearings, superconducting electrical storage facilities that reduce our energy bills, and magnetically levitated trains that travel at jet speeds between cities. •

Magnetic Properties of Materials

The magnets that lie at the heart of most electric motors and generators, though critical to almost everything we do, are not much evident in our everyday lives. Similarly, we are usually unaware of the magnets that drive our stereo speakers, telephones, and other audio systems. Even refrigerator magnets and compass needles are so common that we take them for granted. But why do some common materials such as iron display strong magnetism, while other substances seem to be unaffected by magnetic fields?

In Chapter 5, we learned that one of the fundamental laws of nature is that every magnetic field is due, ultimately, to the presence of electrical currents. In particular, electrons spinning around an atom can be thought of as a small electrical current, so each electron in an atom acts like a little electromagnet. An atom can be thought of as being composed of many small electromagnets, each with different strength and pointing in a different direction. The total magnetic field of the atom arises by adding together the magnetic fields of all the tiny electron electromagnets.

It turns out that many atoms have magnetic fields that closely approximate the dipole type (originally shown in Figure 5-4); thus each atom in the material can be thought of as a tiny dipole magnet (Figure 11-5). The magnetic field of a solid material like a piece of lodestone arises from the combination of all these tiny magnetic fields.

It's somewhat harder to understand why most materials do not have magnetic fields. In Figure 11-6*a*, we show the orientation of atomic magnets in a typical material. They point in random directions, so at a place outside the material their effects tend to cancel.

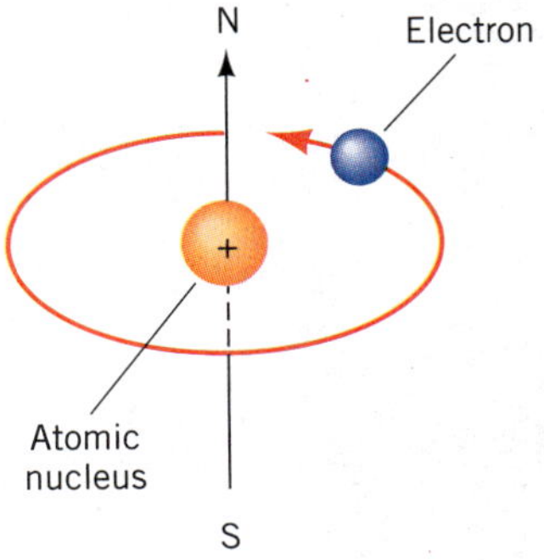

• **Figure 11-5** The dipole magnetic field of atoms takes the same form as that of larger magnets.

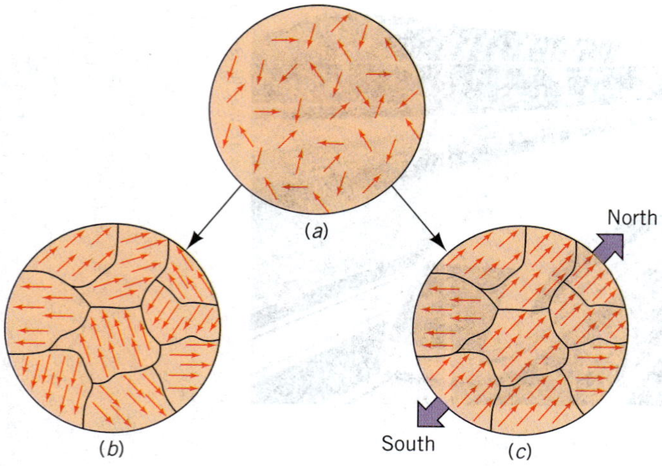

• **Figure 11-6** Different magnetic behavior in materials. *(a)* Nonmagnetic materials have random orientations of atomic spins. *(b)* Ferromagnetic materials with randomly oriented domains are not magnetic. *(c)* A permanent magnet has more uniformly oriented atomic spins.

An observer looking at the material will measure no magnetic field, and a compass placed outside the material will not be deflected. This ordinary situation explains how materials made up of tiny magnets can, as a whole, be nonmagnetic.

In a few materials, including iron, cobalt, and nickel metals, the atomic magnets line up—an effect called *ferromagnetism* (Figure 11-6*b*). In a normal piece of iron, atoms within a specific domain will all be lined up pointing in the same direction, but the orientation of domains is random. Someone standing outside this material will not measure a magnetic field, because the small magnetic fields in different domains cancel each other. In special cases, as when iron cools from very high temperature in the presence of a strong magnetic field, all of the neighboring domains may line up and thus reinforce each other. Only when most of the magnetic domains line up (as shown in Figure 11-6*c*) do you get a material that exhibits an external magnet field—the arrangement that occurs in permanent magnets.

Microchips and the Information Revolution

Every material has hundreds of different physical properties. We have already seen how strength, electrical conductivity, and magnetism all result from the properties of individual atoms and how those atoms bond together. We could continue in this vein for many more chapters, examining optical properties, elastic properties, thermal properties, and so on. But such a treatment would miss another key idea about materials:

New materials often lead to new technologies that change society.

Of all the countless new materials discovered in the last century, none has transformed our lives more than silicon-based semiconductors. From personal computers to auto ignitions, Ipods to sophisticated military weaponry, microelectronics are a hallmark of our age. Indeed, semiconductors have fundamentally changed the way we manipulate a society's most precious resource—information. The key to this revolution is our ability to fashion complex crystals atom by atom from silicon, a material that is produced from ordinary beach sand.

Doped Semiconductors

The element silicon by itself is not a very useful substance in electric circuits. What makes silicon useful, and what has driven our modern microelectronic technology, is a process known as doping. **Doping** is the addition of a minor impurity to an element or compound. The idea behind silicon doping is simple. When silicon is melted before being made into circuit elements, a small amount of some other material is added to it. One common additive is phosphorus, an element that has five valence (bonding) electrons, as opposed to the four valence electrons of silicon.

When the silicon crystallizes to form the structure shown in Figure 11-7*a*, the phosphorus is taken into the crystalline structure. However, of the five valence electrons in each phosphorus atom, only four are needed to make bonds to silicon atoms in the crys-

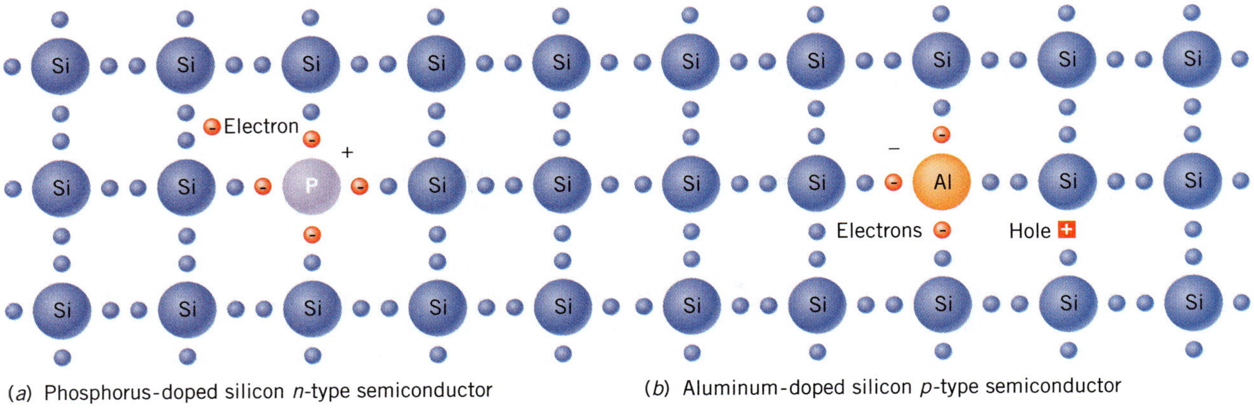

• **Figure 11-7** *(a)* Phosphorus-doped silicon *n*-type semiconductors and *(b)* aluminum-doped silicon *p*-type semiconductors are formed from silicon crystals with a few impurity atoms.

tal. The fifth electron is not locked in at all. In this situation, it does not take long for the extra electron to be shaken loose and wander off into the body of the crystal. This action has two important consequences: (1) there are conduction electrons in the material, and (2) the phosphorus ion that has been left behind has a positive charge. A semiconductor doped with phosphorus is said to be an ***n-type semiconductor***, because the moving charge is a negative electron.

Alternatively, silicon can be doped with an element such as aluminum, which has only three valence electrons (Figure 11-7*b*). In this case, when the aluminum is doped into the crystal structure, there will be one less valence electron compared to the silicon atoms it replaced in the crystal. This "missing" electron—a hole—creates a material that can now more easily carry an electrical current. The hole need not stay with the aluminum atom but is free to move around within the semiconductor as described earlier. Once it does so, the aluminum atom, which has now acquired an extra electron, will have a negative charge. This type of material is called a ***p-type semiconductor***, because a hole—a missing negative electron—acts as a positive charge.

Diodes

You can understand the basic workings of a microchip by conducting an experiment in your mind. Imagine taking a piece of *n*-type semiconductor and placing it against a piece of *p*-type semiconductor. As soon as the two types of material are in contact, how will electrons move?

Near the contact, negatively charged electrons will diffuse from the *n*-type semiconductor over into the *p*-type, while positively charged holes will diffuse back the other way. Thus, on one side of the boundary there will be a region where negative aluminum ions—ions locked into the crystal structure by the doping process—acquire an extra electron. Conversely, on the other side of the boundary is an array of positive phosphorus ions, each of which has lost an electron but which are nonetheless locked into the crystal.

A semiconducting device like this—formed from one *p* and one *n* region—is called a **diode** (see Figure 11-8). Once a diode is constructed, a permanent electrical field tends to push electrons across the boundary in only one direction, from the *n*-type side to the *p*-type side. As electrons are pushed "with the grain" in the diode, from negative to positive, the current flows through normally. When the current is reversed, however, the electrons are blocked from going through by the presence of the built-in electrical field. Thus the diode acts as a one-way gate, allowing the electrical current through in only one direction.

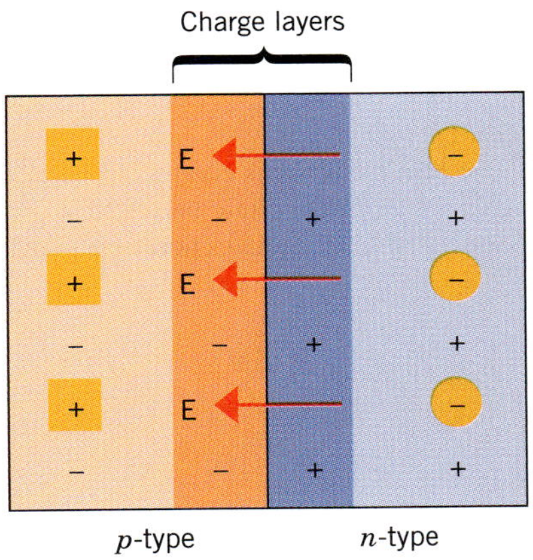

• **Figure 11-8** The semiconductor diode consists of an *n*-type region and a *p*-type region. Electrons in this diode can flow easily from the negative to the positive region. This distribution of electric charge creates a field, labeled *E*, that blocks electrons from flowing the opposite way. The result is a one-way valve for electrons.

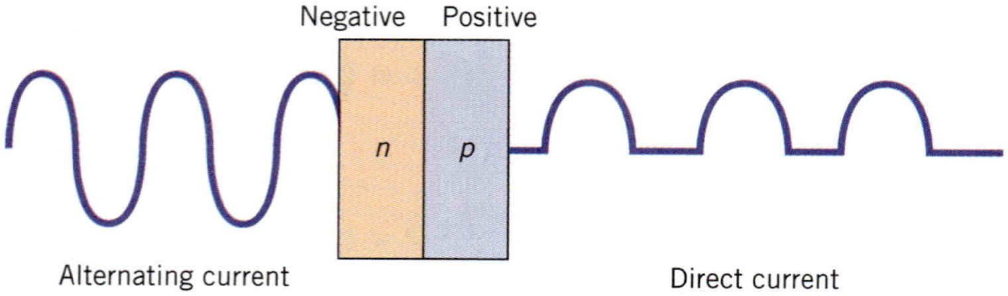

• **Figure 11-9** A diode converts alternating current to direct current in most electronic devices. Half of the alternating current passes through the diode, but the other half is blocked.

The semiconductor diode has many uses in technology. One use, for example, can be found in almost any electronic device that is plugged into a wall outlet. As we saw in Chapter 5, electricity is sent to homes in the form of alternating current, or AC. However, it turns out that most home electronics such as televisions and stereos require direct current, or DC. A semiconductor diode can be used to convert the alternating current into direct current by blocking off half of it. In fact, if you examine the insides of almost any electronic gear, the power cord leads directly to a diode and other components that convert pulsing AC into steady DC, as shown in Figure 11-9.

Technology •

Photovoltaic Cells and Solar Energy

Semiconducting diodes may play an important role in the energy future of the United States, through the use of a device called the photovoltaic cell. A *photovoltaic cell* is nothing more than a large semiconductor diode. A thin layer of *n*-type material overlays a thicker layer of *p*-type. Sunlight striking the top *n*-type layer shakes electrons loose from the crystal structure. These electrons are then accelerated through the *n-p* boundary and pushed out into an external circuit. Thus, while the Sun is shining, the photovoltaic cell acts in the same way as a battery. It provides a constant push for electrons and moves them through an external circuit. If large numbers of photovoltaic cells are put together, they can generate enormous amounts of current.

Photovoltaic cells enjoy many uses today. Your hand calculator, for example, may very well contain a photovoltaic cell that recharges the batteries (it's the small dark band just above the buttons). Photovoltaic cells are also used in regions where it's hard to bring in traditional electricity—to pump water in remote sites, for example, or to provide electricity in backcountry areas of national parks.

Another use of photovoltaics is in cameras. In products from TV cameras to the sensitive detectors that astronomers attach to their telescopes, light strikes a semiconductor rather than film. Using processes slightly more complex than those described for a photovoltaic cell, light striking each part of the semiconductor is converted into an electrical current, with the strengths of the currents from each part depending on the amount

Masterfile

The Sun's energy is converted to electricity by photovoltaic panels at a Southern California generating plant.

of light that falls there. The strength of those currents is then used to reconstruct the visual image. •

The Transistor

The device that drives the entire information age, and perhaps more than any other has been responsible for the transformation of our modern society, is the **transistor**. Invented just two days before Christmas 1947 by Bell Laboratory scientists John Bardeen, Walter Brattain, and William Shockley, the early transistor was simply a sandwich of *n*- and *p*-type semiconductors.

In one kind of transistor, two *p*-type semiconductors form the "bread" of a sandwich, while the *n*-type semiconductor is the "meat." Another kind of transistor uses the *npn* configuration. Both kinds of transistors (Figure 11-10) control the flow of electrons. Electrical leads connect to each of the three semiconductor regions of the transistor. An electrical current goes into the region called the *emitter;* the thin slice of semiconductor in the middle is called the *base;* and the third semiconductor section is the *collector.*

Thus the transistor has two built-in electrical fields, one at each *p-n* junction. The idea of the transistor is that a small amount of electrical charge run into or out of the base can change these electrical fields—in effect, opening and closing the gates of the transistor. The best way to think of the transistor is to make an analogy to a pipe that carries water. The electrical current that flows from emitter to collector is like water that flows through the pipe, and the base is like a valve in the pipe. A small amount of energy applied to turning the valve can have an enormous effect on the flow of water. In just the same way, a small amount of charge run onto the base can have an enormous effect on the current that runs through the transistor.

In your cell phone, for example, weak electrical currents are created when your voice sets up vibrations in a small crystal. This weak current can be fed into the base of a transistor, and can thus be impressed on the much larger current that is flowing from the emitter to the collector. A device that takes a small current and converts it into a large one is called an *amplifier* (see Figure 11-11). The amplifier in your cell phone takes the weak current created by your voice and converts it into the much larger current that runs the speakers.

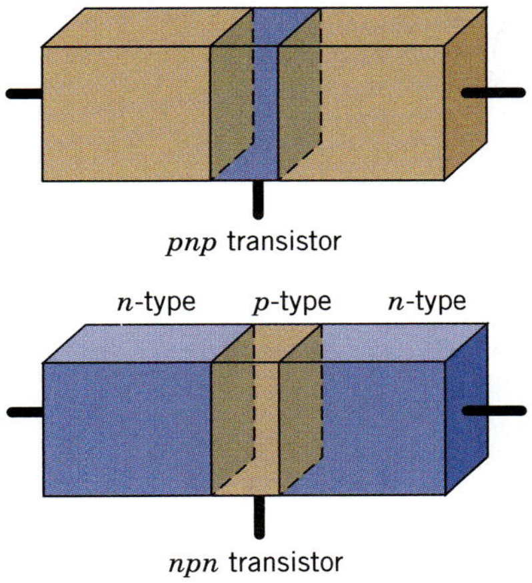

• **Figure 11-10** A *pnp* and an *npn* transistor.

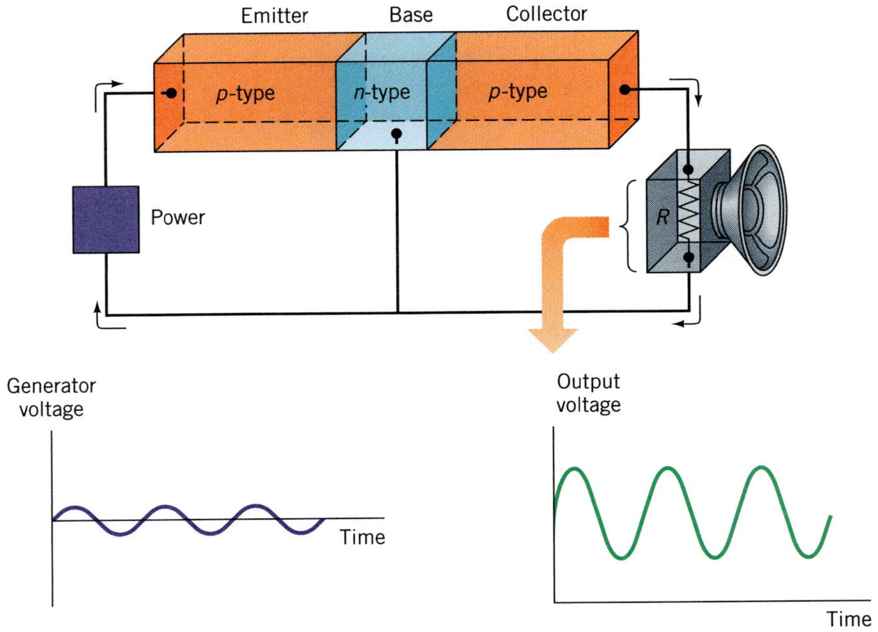

• **Figure 11-11** A transistor acting as an amplifier. A small amount of energy, supplied by a power source such as a CD player, goes to the base of the transistor, where it is amplified as discussed in the text.

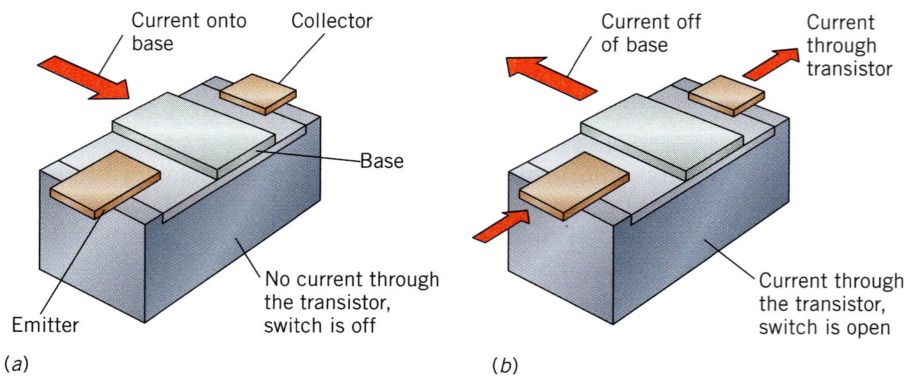

• **Figure 11-12** A transistor acting as a switch. A small current causes the transistor to switch from off (*a*) to on (*b*).

As important as the transistor's amplifying properties are, probably its most important use has been as a switch. If you run enough negative charge onto the base, it can repel any electrons that are trying to get through. Thus moving an electrical charge onto the base will shut off the flow of current through the transistor, whereas running the electrical charge off the base will turn the current back on. In this manner the transistor acts as an electron switch, and it can be used to process information in computers—arguably the most important device developed in the twentieth century (see Figure 11-12).

Field Effect Transistor

Although the transistor shown in Figure 11-10 is the easiest to visualize, the transistors in your laptop computers and cell phones are likely to be slightly more complicated in design. As shown, this type of transistor might have two *n* type semiconductors sandwiching a *p* type, but with a small metal plate, known as a gate, next to the middle segment of the device. The gate is separated from the semiconductor by a small insulating layer. This arrangement is known as a *field effect transistor.*

Here's how it works: if there is no electrical charge on the gate, then the device looks like two back-to-back diodes. As we have seen, free electrons from the *n*-type regions will diffuse into the central p type region and fill the holes, thereby setting up voltages that block the flow of electrical current. If, however, we introduce a small positive charge on the gate, electrons will be attracted into the *p*-type region and current will be able to flow through the device. Again, this type of transistor can be used as an amplifier, since the bigger the positive charge on the gate the bigger the current through the transistor. It can also be used as a switch.

Because the thin insulating layer separating the gate from the semiconductor is often made from a metal oxide, this type of device of sometime referred to as a MOSFET (metal oxide-semiconductor field effect transistor).

Nelson Morris/Photo Researchers

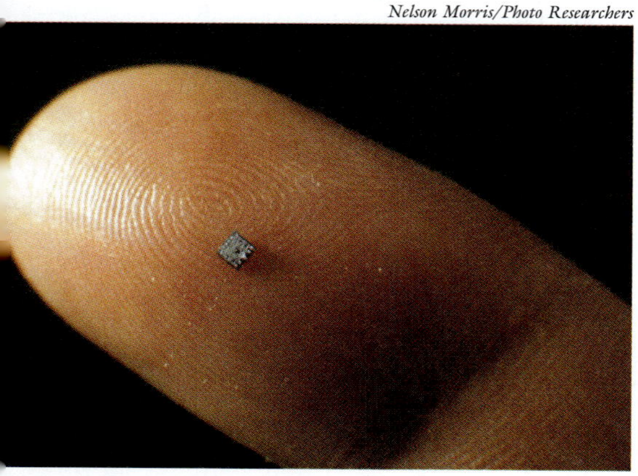

• **Figure 11-13** A microchip incorporates many transistors built into a tiny piece of silicon, as shown here. Fifty years ago, it would have taken several rooms to house the computing power in this single microchip.

Microchips

Individual diodes and transistors still play a vital role in modern electronics, but these devices have been largely replaced by much more complex arrays of *p*- and *n*-type semiconductors, called **microchips** (see Figure 11-13). Microchips may incorporate hundreds or thousands of transistors in one *integrated circuit,* specially designed to perform a specific function. An integrated circuit microchip lies at the heart of your pocket calculator or microwave oven control, for example. Similarly, arrays of integrated circuits store and manipulate data in your personal computer, and they regulate the ignition in all modern automobiles.

The first transistors were bulky things, about the size of a golf ball, but today a single microchip the size of a grain of rice can integrate hundreds of thousands of these devices. California's Silicon Valley has become a well-known center for the design and

PhotoDisc, In./Getty Images

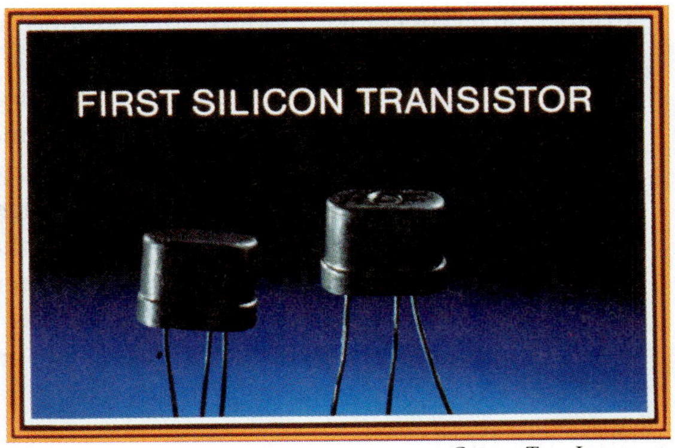

Courtesy Texas Instruments

PhotoDisc, Inc./Getty Images

Semiconductors are used extensively in electronic devices, such as a photovoltaic array (far left), the transistor (center), and the microchip.

manufacture of these tiny integrated circuits. Production of thousands of transistors on a single silicon chip requires exquisite control of atoms. One technique is to put a thin wafer of silicon into a large heated vacuum chamber. Around the edges of the chamber is an array of small ovens, each of which holds a different element, such as aluminum or phosphorus. The side ovens are heated in carefully controlled sequence and opened to allow small amounts of other elements—the dopants—to be vaporized and enter the chamber along with silicon.

If you want to make a *p*-type semiconductor, for example, you could mix a small amount of phosphorus with the silicon in the chamber and let it deposit onto the silicon plate at the bottom. Typically, a device called a *mask* is put over the silicon chip so that the *p*-type semiconductor is deposited only in designated parts of the chip. Then the vapor is cleared from the chamber, a new mask is put on, and another layer of material is laid down. In this way, a complex three-dimensional structure can be built up at a microscopic scale. In the end, each microchip has many different transistors in it, connected exactly as designed by engineers.

Technology •

Jim Trefil Gives His Car a Tune-Up

As a student, I acquired the first of a long string of Volkswagen Beetles. Now let me tell you, my friends, *that* was a sweet car! There were never any problems with the cooling system, for the simple reason that there wasn't any—the engine was cooled by the air flowing by. And almost any repair could be made by someone with reasonable mechanical ability and a set of tools. While in graduate school, I spent many happy hours under my car, adjusting this or that.

But I never work on my cars any more. When I look under the hood, all I see is a complex array of computers and microchips—nothing a person can get a wrench around. Yet the car I drive today, provided everything is working, is much more user friendly than my old Volkswagen. The flow of gasoline to the cylinders, for example, is regulated by a small onboard computer rather than by a clumsy mechanical carburetor.

This personal story about cars turns out to be a pretty good allegory for the way in which the science of materials has developed in the twentieth century. In the beginning, industry turned out big, relatively simple things that were easy to understand and work with—iron wheels for railroads, steel springs for car suspensions, wooden chairs and tables for the home. Today, industry turns out items that perform the same jobs better but that are made from new kinds of materials such as plastics, composites, and semiconductors. Instead of manipulating large chunks of material, we now control the way atoms fit together. Like modern cars, modern materials do their job well, but they cannot be made (or, usually, repaired) by a simple craftsperson working with simple tools.

So while the materials we use are becoming better at what they do and easier for us to use, it becomes harder and harder for us to understand what those materials are. I might have been able to fix my Volkswagen myself, but there is no way I can look under the hood and shift atoms around in my modern car's microchip. In a sense, the improved performance of modern materials has been bought at the price of our ability to understand them. To a large extent, the emphasis of modern materials science has shifted away from manipulating large blocks of stuff, which are readily available to our senses, to manipulating atoms in ever-more-complex ways. And, of course, we can't see or taste or feel atoms. •

Information

The single most important use of semiconducting devices is in the storage and manipulation of information. In fact, the modern revolution in information technology—the development of arrays of interconnected computers, global telecommunications networks, vast data banks of personal statistics, digital recording, and the credit card—is a direct consequence of materials science.

While it may appear strange to say so, almost all the things we normally consider as conveying information—the printed or spoken word, pictures, or music, for example—can be analyzed in terms of their information content and manipulated by the microchips we've just discussed. The term *information,* like many words, has a precise meaning when it is used in the sciences, a meaning that is somewhat different from colloquial usage. In its scientific context, information is measured in a unit that is called the *b*inary dig*it,* or **bit.**

You can think of the bit as the two possible answers to any simple question: yes or no, on or off, up or down. A single transistor being used as a switch, for example, can convey one bit of information—it is either on or off. Any form of communication contains a certain number of bits of information. As we shall see shortly, the computer is simply a device that stores and manipulates this kind of information.

One way of thinking about information in bits is to imagine a row of lightbulbs. Each bulb can be on or off, so each bulb conveys one bit of information. You could imagine making a code—all lights on is the letter "a", all lights on except the first is the letter "b", and so on. In this way, each on-and-off arrangement of the lights would be a different letter. You could then send a message by flashing different patterns.

If you had only one lightbulb, you could convey only two possibilities—on or off. This would be one bit of information, and would correspond to trying to write a message using only the letters "a" and "b". (You could, for example, have a code where "on" meant "a", and "off" meant "b"). If you had two lightbulbs, you would have four different configurations—on-on, on-off, off-on, and off-off—and therefore could convey four different possibilities. With two lightbulbs, in other words, you could add "c" and "d" to your list. In fact, you can work out that the number of different arrangements of the on-off signals increases as the number of bulbs in your array grows. The rate of growth is summarized in the following table:

Number of bulbs	Number of configurations
1	2
2	4
3	8
4	16
5	32
6	64
7	128
8	256

Given this table, how many lightbulbs would you need to send any message in the English language? One way to approach this problem is to think about something most of us take for granted—the design of typefaces. There are hundreds of different typefaces, and new ones are being designed all the time. The type in this book, for example, is set in a typeface called Galliard. People who design these typefaces reckon that they need 228 characters to represent a complete message in English. This number includes letters (lowercase and capital), numbers, fractions, punctuation marks, commercial symbols like the $ sign, and what are called "peculiars"—* and %, for example. From the above table, then, we see that in order to have a full representation of the English language, we would need a bank of eight lightbulbs.

Another way of saying this is that it requires 8 bits of information to specify a letter or symbol in English. In computer science, 8 bits is called a **byte.** From this simple fact we can build up a hierarchy of information content as follows:

A six-letter word requires 6 × 8 = 48 bits of information

A printed page of 500 words requires 500 × 48 = 2,400 bits = 2.4 Kb

A 300-page book requires 300 × 2,400 = 720,000 bits = 720 Kb = 0.72 Mb

A million-volume library requires 1,000,000 × 720,000 = 720 Gb

Where Kb, Mb, and Gb stand for a kilobit (1000 bits), a megabit (a million bits), and a gigabit (a billion bits), respectively.

Stop and Think! Peoples of the world employ many alphabets besides the Latin alphabet used to write English. How does the number of bits required to designate a letter depend on the number of letters in the alphabet?

Science by the Numbers •

Is a Picture Really Worth a Thousand Words?

Pictures and sounds can be analyzed in terms of information content, just like words. Your television screen, for example, works by splitting the picture into small units called pixels. In North America, the picture is split up into 525 segments on the horizontal and vertical axes, giving a total of about 275,000 pixels (in rounded numbers) for one picture on the TV screen. Your eye integrates these dots into a smooth picture. Every color can be thought of as a combination of the three colors—red, green, and blue—and it is usual to specify the intensity of each of these three colors by a number that requires 10 bits of information to be recorded. (In practice, this means that the intensity of each color is specified on a scale of about 1 to 1000.) Thus each pixel requires 30 bits to define its color. Thus the total information content of a picture on a TV screen is

275,000 pixels × 30 bits = about 8 million bits

Thus it requires about 8 megabits, or 1 megabyte, to specify a single frame on a TV picture. We should note that a TV picture typically changes 30 times a second, so the total flow of information on a TV screen may exceed 200 million bits per second.

It thus would appear that a picture is worth not only a thousand words but much more. In fact, if a word contains 48 bits of information, then the picture will be worth 8 million bits per picture divided by 36 bits per word, which equals about 166,000 words per picture.

The old saying, if anything, underestimates the truth! •

Computers

A **computer** is a machine that stores and manipulates information. The information is stored in the computer in microchips, each of which incorporates many thousands of

In less than a quarter of a century, the computer has evolved from a specialized research aid to an essential tool for business and education.

Anderson Ross/Age Fotostock America, Inc.

interconnected transistors that act as switches and carry information. In principle, a machine with a few million transistors could store the text for this entire book. In practice, however, computers do not normally work in this way. They have a *central processing unit (CPU)* in which transistors store and manipulate relatively small amounts of information at any one time. When the information is ready to be stored—for example, when you have finished working on a text in a word processor, or writing a program to perform a calculation—it is removed from the CPU and stored elsewhere. It might, for example, be stored in the form of magnetically oriented particles on a floppy disk or a hard drive. In these cases, a bit of information is no longer a switch that is on or off, but a bit of magnetic material that has been oriented either "north pole up" or "north pole down."

The ability to store information in this way is extremely important in modern society. As just one example, think about the last time you made an airline reservation. You went online and got into communication with the airline's computer. Stored in strings of bits within that computer are the flights, the seating assignments, the ticket arrangements, and often the address and phone number of every passenger who will be flying on the particular day when you want to fly. When you change your reservation, make a new one, or perform some other manipulation, the information is taken out of storage, brought to the central processing unit, manipulated by changing the exact sequence of bits, and then put back into storage. This process—the storage and manipulation of vast amounts of data—forms the very fabric of our modern society.

Human-like machines, such as this Cylon from the TV series *Battlestar Galactica*, are far in the future.

Photofest

You've probably noticed that the speed and information capacity of computers has increased astonishingly over the past few decades. Just look at the improvements in the images and action of video games. This tendency for ever-faster computers was first noted in 1965 by Gordon Moore, the founder of Intel. He pointed to a trend that the number of transistors that can be packed into every square inch of a microchip (a measure of computing power) tends to double about every two years. (Since Moore's time, this number has fallen to 18 months!) "Moore's Law" has held up remarkably for 40 years, though it can't continue indefinitely. The average size of a single transistor is now only a few thousand atoms across, and a semiconductor device can't be much smaller than that!

These advances are primarily the result of many improvements in materials and their processing at the atomic scale—a field called *nanotechnology*. New fine-grained magnetic materials have greatly increased the capacity of information storage devices such as hard disks, while improved semiconductor processing techniques continue to reduce the size of individual *n*- and *p*-type semiconductor domains. The result is smaller, more powerful computers—one of many ways that advances in material science play a direct role in our lives.

The Science of Life •

The Computer and the Brain

When computers first came into public awareness, there was a general sense that we were building a machine that would in some way duplicate the human brain. Concepts such as *artificial intelligence* were sold (some would say oversold) on the basis of the idea that they would soon be able to perform all those functions that we normally think of as being distinctly human. In fact, this scenario has not come to pass. The reason has to do with the difference between the basic unit of the computer, which is the transistor, and the basic unit of the brain, which is the nerve cell.

The transmission of electrical signals between the brain's neurons is fundamentally different from that between elements in ordinary electric circuits (see Chapter 5). This difference in signal transmission alone, however, does not make a brain so different from a computer. A computer normally performs a sequential series of operations—that is, a group of transistors takes two numbers, adds them together, feeds that answer to another group of transistors that performs another manipulation, and so on. Some computers are now being designed and built that have some parallel capacity at the same time—machines in which, for example, addition and other manipulations are done in parallel rather than one after the other. Nevertheless, the natural configuration of computers is to have each transistor hooked to, at most, a couple of others.

A nerve cell in the brain, however, operates in quite a different manner. Each of the brain's trillions of nerve cells connects to a thousand or more different neighboring nerve cells. Whether a nerve cell decides to fire—whether the signal moves out along the axon—depends in a complex way on the integration of all the signals that come into that cell from thousands of other cells.

This complex arrangement means that the brain is a system that is highly interconnected, more interconnected than any other system known in nature. In fact, if the brain has trillions of cells and each cell has a thousand connections, there will be on the order of 1,000,000,000,000,000 connections among brain cells. Building a computer of this size and level of connectedness is at present totally beyond the capability of technology. •

Science News | In Pixels and in Health

(Science News, Jan. 21, 2006, p. 40)

When we think about medical research, we normally picture a lab full of test tubes and flasks. In fact, there is a term—*in vitro* ("in glass")—that is used to describe this kind of laboratory work. The advent of fast computers, however, is generating a new kind of medical research, in which the systems of the body are modeled on a computer rather than studies in a laboratory. With a bow toward history, scientists often refer to this new approach as *in silico* ("in silicon").

The basic tool for this new approach is a computer strategy known as agent-based modeling. In this type of model, the programmer decides what the properties of individual players ("agents") are and how they interact with each other. The program is then run to see what the outcomes are. Unlike ordinary computer modeling, where equations are used to determine outcomes, in agent-based modeling the emphasis is on the rules of interaction, and the programmer often has no idea how the system will evolve until the results are in.

For example, in a recent experiment at the University of Michigan the agents in the program were tuberculosis bacteria and cells in the human immune system. Each agent is programmed with its appropriate behavior and turned loose. It turns out that the system in the machines winds up mimicking many aspects of the behavior of the real cells, including the formation of pockets of cells called granulomas that are often seen in the lungs of patients with the disease.

In another study done at MIT the agents were brain tumor cells, which in real life can either proliferate or migrate (metastasize). It was found that in the model the choice between these two behaviors depended on the presence or absence of a particular chemical, a fact that suggests possible lines of treatment strategies.

In the end, of course, medical advances will ultimately have to be tested both *in vitro* and in real patients. Nevertheless, the *in silico* experiments may well provide useful guides as to how, exactly, those experiments ought to be done.

Thinking More About | Properties of Materials

Thinking Machines

One of the most intriguing questions about the ever-increasing abilities of complex computers is whether a computer can be built that would in some way mimic, or even replace, the human brain. Computers have been built that can add faster or remember more than any single human being, but these specific abilities by themselves do not seem to be crucial in developing a machine that thinks. The real question is whether a machine will be designed that is, by general consensus, regarded as "alive" or "conscious."

British mathematician Alan Turing proposed a test to address this question. The so-called Turing test operates this way: A group of human beings sit in a room and interact with something through some kind of computer terminal. They might, for example, type questions into a keyboard and read answers on a screen. Alternatively, they could talk into a microphone and hear answers played back to them by some kind of voice synthesizer. These people are allowed to ask the hidden "thing" any questions they like. At the end of the experiment, they have to decide whether they are talking to a machine or to a human being. If they can't tell the difference, the machine is said to have passed the Turing test.

As of this date, no machine has passed the test (there have been occasional contests in Silicon Valley in which machines were put through their paces). But what if a machine did actually pass? Would that mean we have invented a truly intelligent machine? John Searle, a philosopher at the University of California at Berkeley, has recently challenged the whole idea of the Turing test as a way of telling if a machine can think by proposing a paradox he calls the "Chinese room."

The Chinese room works like this: An English-speaking person sits in a room and receives typed questions from a Chinese-speaking person in the adjacent room. The English-speaking person does not understand Chinese but has a large manual of instructions. The manual might say, for example, that if a certain group of Chinese characters are received, then a second group of Chinese characters should be sent out. The English-speaking person could, at least in principle, pass the Turing test if the instructions were sufficiently detailed and complex. Obviously, however, the English speaker has no idea of what he or she is doing with the information that comes in or goes out. Thus, argues Searle, the mere fact that a machine passes the Turing test tells you nothing about whether it is aware of what it is doing.

Do you think a machine that can pass the Turing test must be aware of itself? Do you see any way around Searle's argument for the Chinese room? What moral and ethical problems might arise if human beings could indeed make a machine that everyone agreed has consciousness?

Summary

All materials, from building supplies and fabrics to electronic components and food, have properties that arise from the kinds of constituent atoms and the ways those atoms are bonded together. The high *strength* of materials such as stone and synthetic fibers relies on interconnected networks of ionic or covalent bonds, while many soft and pliable materials such as wax and graphite incorporate weak van der Waals forces. *Composite materials,* such as plywood, fiberglass, and reinforced concrete, merge the special strengths of two or more materials.

The electrical properties of materials also depend on the kinds of constituent atoms and the bonds they form. For example, *electrical resistance*—a material's resistance to the flow of an electrical current—depends on the mobility of bonding electrons. Metals, which are characterized by loosely bonded outer electrons, make excellent *electrical conductors,* while most materials with tightly held electrons in ionic and covalent bonds are good *electrical insulators.* Materials such as silicon that conduct electricity, but not very well, are called *semiconductors.* At very low temperatures, some compounds lose all resistance to electron flow and become *superconductors.*

Magnetic properties also arise from the collective behavior of atoms. While most materials are nonmagnetic, ferromagnets have domains in which electron spins are aligned to each other.

New materials play important roles in modern technology. Semiconductors, in particular, are vital to the modern electronics industry. Semiconductor material, usually silicon, is modified by *doping* with small amounts of another element. Phosphorous doping adds a few mobile electrons to produce an *n*-type semiconductor, while aluminum doping provides positive holes in *p*-type semiconductors. Devices formed by juxtaposing *n*- and *p*-type semiconductors act as switches and valves for electricity. A *diode* joins single pieces of *n*- and *p*-type material, for example, to act as a one-way valve for current flow. *Transistors,* which incorporate a *pnp* or *npn* semiconductor sandwich, act as amplifiers or switches for current. *Microchips* can combine up to thousands of *n* and *p* regions in a single integrated circuit.

Semiconductor technology has revolutionized the storage and use of information. Any information can be reduced to a series of simple "yes–no" questions, or *bits.* Eight-bit words, called *bytes,* are the basic information unit of most modern *computers.*

Key Terms

strength
composite materials
electrical conductor
electrical resistance
electrical insulator
semiconductor
superconductivity
doping
diode
transistor
microchip
bit
byte
computer

Review Questions

1. What factors determine the strength of a material?
2. What kinds of chemical bonds are strongest? Why are these bonds so strong?
3. Define three different kinds of strengths. Give examples of materials that are strong in each of these modes. What kind of chemical bonding occurs in each of these materials?
4. Diamonds and graphite are both made from carbon atoms. Why is graphite so much weaker?
5. What is the difference between a composite material and a compound? Give an example of each.
6. Identify the materials that serve as an electrical insulator and an electrical conductor in an electrical device that you use every day.
7. What is unusual about superconductors? Under what conditions do materials exhibit superconductivity?
8. What is a semiconductor? Give an example.
9. Explain how holes can move in a semiconductor.
10. If all atoms have electrons that are in motion about an atom, why aren't all materials magnetic?
11. What is a ferromagnet?
12. What is a semiconductor diode? How do diodes convert AC into DC?
13. What is a transistor? What are the base, emitter, and collector, respectively?
14. How are diodes and transistors similar, and how are they different?
15. What is an integrated circuit? How might one be made?
16. Give an example of a bit of information. What is the difference between a bit and a byte?

Discussion Questions

1. How do the principles of physics and chemistry both come into play when developing new materials?
2. From the point of view of atomic architecture, how does a material like concrete, which is strong under compression, differ from a material like steel, which is strong under tension?
3. How do conductors and insulators differ in their atomic structure?
4. Identify five different materials that were invented in the twentieth century and that you use in your daily life.
5. Identify 10 objects in your home that use semiconductors. What other kinds of materials with special electrical properties are found in all of these 10 objects?
6. If water in a pipe is analogous to electricity in a wire, what is analogous to a diode? a transistor? What electrical device is analogous to a water storage tank?
7. Why are both insulators and conductors needed in all electrical devices?
8. What is the relationship between heat production and resistance?
9. Would a silicon semiconductor doped with boron be *n* or *p* type? How about one doped with arsenic? [*Hint:* Look at the periodic table.]
10. Have you seen solar photovoltaic cells in your town? Why do you suppose they were placed where you saw them?
11. Do electrons flow from the positive terminal to the negative terminal of a battery or vice versa? Why?
12. What determines a material's ability to conduct electricity?

Problems

1. There is an effort in the world today to convert television into so-called high-definition TV (HDTV). In HDTV, the picture is split up into as many as 1100 by 1100 (as opposed to 525 by 525) pixels. What is the information content of an HDTV picture? What is the information content that must be transmitted each second in an HDTV broadcast?
2. Construct a set of yes–or–no questions to specify any letter of the alphabet, both upper- and lowercase, and all digits from zero to nine.
3. Construct a set of yes–or–no questions to specify any planet in our solar system.
4. Estimate the total amount of information contained in the printed words in this book. Estimate the information content of the illustrations in this book.
5. What is the information content in any given minute of a LCD monitor at a resolution of 800×600 with the picture changing 85 times a second? What about a screen resolution of 1024×768 with changes 75 times a second?
6. The Kangxi dictionary compiled in China in 1710 during the Qing dynasty encompasses 46,964 characters. How many bits would it take to specify a specific Kangxi character? Compare this to the number required in languages that have alphabets.

INVESTIGATIONS

1. Why does a magnet become demagnetized when you repeatedly hit it with a hammer? In what other ways can you destroy a permanent magnet? Why aren't "permanent magnets" permanent?

2. Shortly after the discovery of high-temperature superconductivity, many newspapers and TV shows ran features on how these new materials would change society. What is the highest temperature at which superconductivity has been demonstrated? In what ways might superconductivity change society? Historically, what other new materials have caused significant changes in human societies? Have all these changes been productive and positive?

3. Every year, one or two promising new materials capture public attention. Scan recent issues of *Science News* and identify one such material. Who made it? How might it be used?

4. Research the status of magnetically levitated trains, like the one now operating in Japan. How does it operate? How fast might it go? How soon might such a train operate in North America?

5. Read the book or watch the 1951 movie *The Man in the White Suit*. What unique material properties are described, and how is the new technology received by society?

6. A class of new materials called fullerenes, including the substance known as buckyballs, were invented in 1985. Investigate these materials and their possible uses.

7. Visit a sports equipment store. Learn about the new materials that are used in tennis rackets, football helmets, and sports clothing.

8. Write a short story in which a new material with unique properties plays a central role.

9. What kinds of materials do surgeons use to replace broken hip bones? What are the advantages of this material?

10. Plastic surgeons have used silicone-filled implants for breast enlargement and other cosmetic procedures. Intensive research is now under way to understand the effects of silicone on the human body, due to claims of adverse reactions to these implants. Investigate the nature of silicone and summarize some of the contradictory results of recent research. Based on your investigation, do you think such implants should be banned?

11. Investigate the use of new materials in sports medicine such as Gore-Tex tendons. What are the ethical implications of using new materials to create athletes who are stronger due to superhuman replacement parts?

12. Superman's costume was bulletproof. What qualities would the material that made up his costume need to resist the impact of a bullet? What materials are used in modern bulletproof vests and body armor? Under what conditions (i.e., torsion, compression, tension) are they strongest?

13. If you could create a new super-material, what would it be used for? What atomic structure would be necessary to give the material the qualities that you desire? How might this material change society? Would all the changes be productive?

14. Why does Major League Baseball disallow the use of metallic bats? How could a baseball be changed to offset the use of aluminum bats? How could the materials in a baseball be changed to allow more home runs?

12

The Nucleus of the Atom

How do scientists determine the age of the oldest human fossils?

Science Through the Day | Radioactivity Around Us

It's great to be lying on the beach, lulled by the sound of the surf, soaking up the sun. Away from the pressures of school and work, time seems to stand still.

In such a relaxing setting it's hard to imagine that hundreds of energetic radioactive particles are tearing through your body every minute. Some of those speeding particles will damage your cells, breaking apart bonds in the molecules that control critical functions of metabolism and cell division.

But don't lose a moment worrying about this ubiquitous background radioactivity. Since the dawn of life, low levels of radioactivity in rocks, sand, soils, and the oceans have bathed every living thing. This radioactivity, a natural part of every environment on Earth, reveals much about the inner structure of the atom.

Angelo Cavalli/iconica/Getty Images

Empty Space, Explosive Energy

Imagine that you are holding a basketball, while 25 kilometers (about 15 miles) away a few grains of sand whiz around. And imagine that all of the vast intervening space—enough to house a fair-sized city—is absolutely empty. In some respects, that's what an atom is like, though on a much smaller scale, of course. The basketball is the nucleus, and the grains of sand represent the electrons (remember, though, that electrons display characteristics of both particles and waves). The atom, with a diameter 100,000 times that of its nucleus, is almost all empty space.

Previous chapters explored the properties of atoms in terms of their electrons. Chemical reactions, the way a material handles electricity, and even the very shape and strength of objects depend on the way that electrons in different atoms interact with each other. In terms of our analogy, all of the properties of the atoms that we have studied so far result from actions that are taking place 25 kilometers from the location of the basketball-sized nucleus. The incredible emptiness of the atom is a key to understanding two important facts about the relation of the atom to its nucleus.

1. *What goes on in the nucleus of an atom has almost nothing to do with the atom's chemistry, and vice versa.* The chemical bonding of an atom's electrons has virtually no effect on what happens to the nucleus. In most situations you can regard the electrons and the central nucleus as two separate and independent systems.
2. *The energies available in the nucleus are much greater than those available among electrons.* The particles inside the nucleus are tightly locked in. It takes a great deal more energy to pull them out than it does to remove an electron from an atom.

The enormous energy we can get from the nucleus follows from the equivalence of mass and energy (which we will discuss in more detail in Chapter 13). This relationship is defined in Einstein's most famous equation.

- **In words:** Mass is a form of energy. When mass is converted into energy, the amount of energy produced is enormous—equal to the mass of the object multiplied by the speed of light squared.
- **In equation form:**

$$\text{Energy} = \text{mass} \times (\text{speed of light})^2$$

- **In symbols:**

$$E = mc^2$$

Remember that the constant c, the speed of light, is a very large number (3×10^8 meters per second) and that this large number is squared in Einstein's equation to give an even larger number. Thus, even a very small mass is equivalent to a very large energy, as shown in the following "Science by the Numbers" section.

Einstein's equation tells us that a given amount of mass can be converted into a specific amount of energy in any form, and vice versa. This statement is true for any process involving energy. When hydrogen and oxygen combine to form water, for example, the mass of the water molecule is a tiny bit less than the sum of the masses of the original atoms. This missing mass has been converted to binding energy in the molecule. Similarly, when an archer draws a bow, the mass of the bow increases by a tiny amount because of the increased elastic potential energy in the bent material.

Bruno Morandi/Age Fotostock America, Inc.

When a bow is drawn, its mass has increased by a tiny amount.

The change in mass of objects in everyday events such as these is so small that it is customarily ignored, and we speak of the various forms of energy without thinking about their mass equivalents. In nuclear reactions, however, we cannot ignore the mass effects. A nuclear reactor, for example, can transform fully 20% of the mass of a proton into energy in each reaction by a process we will soon discuss. Thus nuclear reactions can convert significant amounts of mass into energy, while chemical reactions, which involve only relatively small changes in electrical potential energy, involve only infinitesimal changes in mass. This difference explains why an atomic bomb, which derives its destructive force from nuclear reactions, is so much more powerful than conventional explosives, such as dynamite, and conventional weapons, which depend on chemical reactions in materials such as TNT.

Science by the Numbers •

Mass and Energy

On the average, each person in the United States uses about 10,000 kilowatt-hours (kwh) of energy each year, a rate of about one kilowatt-hour each hour. In effect, each individual uses the energy equivalent of a toaster going full blast all the time. How much mass would have to be converted completely to energy to produce your year's supply of energy?

In Appendix A, we find that one kilowatt-hour of energy is the same as 3.6 million joules, so every year each of us uses:

$$\begin{aligned}\text{annual energy use} &= (10{,}000 \text{ kwh}) \times (3.6 \times 10^6 \text{ joule/kwh}) \\ &= 36{,}000 \times 10^6 \text{ joule} \\ &= 3.6 \times 10^{10} \text{ joule}\end{aligned}$$

In order to calculate the mass that is equivalent to this large amount of energy, we need to put this energy into the Einstein equation, which we can rewrite as:

$$\text{mass} = \frac{\text{energy}}{(\text{speed of light})^2}$$

Written in this form, the number we seek (the mass) is expressed in terms of two numbers we already know. The speed of light, c, is 3×10^8 m/s, so we find that:

$$\begin{aligned}
\text{mass} &= \frac{(3.6 \times 10^{10} \text{ joule})}{(3 \times 10^{8} \text{ m/s})^2} \\
&= \frac{(3.6 \times 10^{10} \text{ joule})}{(9 \times 10^{16} \text{ m}^2/\text{s}^2)} \\
&= 4.0 \times 10^{-7} \text{ joule-second}^2/\text{meter}^2 \\
&= 4.0 \times 10^{-7} \text{ kilogram}
\end{aligned}$$

In the last step we have to remember that a joule is defined as a kilogram-meter^2/second^2, so the units "joule-second^2/meter^2" in this answer are exactly the same as kilograms (see Appendix B). Our year's energy budget could be satisfied by a mass that weighs less than a millionth of a kilogram, or about the mass of a small sand grain, if you could unlock that energy! •

The Organization of the Nucleus

As we saw in Chapter 10, Ernest Rutherford discovered the atomic nucleus by observing how fast-moving particles scatter off gold atoms. In later experiments with even faster atomic "bullets," scientists found that atomic nuclei sometimes break into smaller fragments. Thus, like the atom itself, the nucleus is made up of smaller pieces, most importantly the proton and the neutron. Approximately equal in mass, the proton and neutron can be thought of as the primary building blocks of the nucleus.

The **proton** (from Latin for "the first one)" has a positive electrical charge of +1 and was the first of the nuclear constituents to be discovered and identified.

Stop and Think! Why might electrically charged particles be easier to identify than electrically neutral ones?

The number of protons determines the electrical charge of the nucleus. An atom in its electrically neutral state will have as many negative electrons in orbit as protons in the nucleus. Thus the number of protons in the nucleus determines the chemical identity of an atom.

When people began studying nuclei, however, they quickly found that the mass of a nucleus is significantly greater than the sum of the mass of its protons. In fact, for most atoms the nucleus is more than twice as heavy as its protons. What accounts for this observation of "missing mass"? Scientists concluded that atoms must contain some kind of particle other than the proton or electron, but what is it?

We can identify at least three characteristics of this missing particle. First, it must be relatively massive to account for the observed mass of atoms. Second, it must reside in the nucleus of the atom, in close proximity to the protons. And third, it must be electrically neutral; otherwise it would be easy to identify in an electric field. We now realize that this extra mass is supplied by a particle in the nucleus with no electrical charge called the **neutron** (for "the neutral one"). The neutron has approximately the same mass as the proton. Thus a nucleus with equal numbers of protons and neutrons will have twice the mass of the protons alone.

The mass of a proton or a neutron is about 2000 times the mass of the electron. Therefore, almost all of the mass of the atom is contained within the protons and neutrons in its nucleus. You can think of things this way: electrons give an atom its size, but the nucleus gives an atom its mass.

Element Names and Atomic Numbers

The most important fact in describing any atom is the number of protons in the nucleus—the **atomic number.** This number defines which *element* you are dealing with.

All atoms of gold (atomic number 79) have exactly 79 protons, for example. In fact, the name "gold" is simply a convenient shorthand for "atoms with 79 protons." Every element has its own atomic number: all hydrogen atoms have just 1 proton, carbon atoms must have 6 protons, and so on. The periodic table of the elements that we discussed in Chapter 7 can be thought of as a chart in which the number of protons in the atomic nucleus increases as we read from left to right and top to bottom.

Protons define the chemical behavior of an atom. The fixed number of positively charged protons dictates the arrangement of the atom's electrons and thus its chemical properties.

Isotopes and the Mass Number

Each element has a fixed number of protons, but the number of neutrons may vary from atom to atom. In other words, two atoms with the same number of protons may have different numbers of neutrons. Such atoms are said to be **isotopes** of each other, and they have different masses. The total number of protons and neutrons is called the **mass number.**

Every element exists in several different isotopes, each with a different number of neutrons. The most common isotope of carbon, for example, has 6 neutrons, so it has a mass number of 12 (6 protons + 6 neutrons); it is usually written ^{12}C or carbon-12 and is called carbon twelve. Other isotopes of the carbon nucleus, such as carbon-13 with 7 neutrons, and carbon-14 with 8 neutrons, are heavier than carbon-12, but they have the same electron arrangements and, therefore, the same chemical behavior. A neutral carbon atom, whether carbon-12, carbon-13, or carbon-14, must have 6 electrons in orbit to balance the required 6 protons.

The complete set of all the isotopes—every known combination of protons and neutrons—is often illustrated on a graph that plots number of protons versus number of neutrons (see Figure 12-1). Several features are evident from this graph. First, every chemical element has many known isotopes, in some cases, dozens of them. Close to 2000 isotopes have been documented, compared to the hundred or so different elements. This plot also reveals that the number of protons is not generally the same as the number of neutrons. While many light elements, up to about calcium (with 20 protons), often have nearly equal numbers of protons and neutrons, heavier elements tend to have more neutrons than protons. This fact plays a key role in the phenomenon of radioactivity, as we shall see.

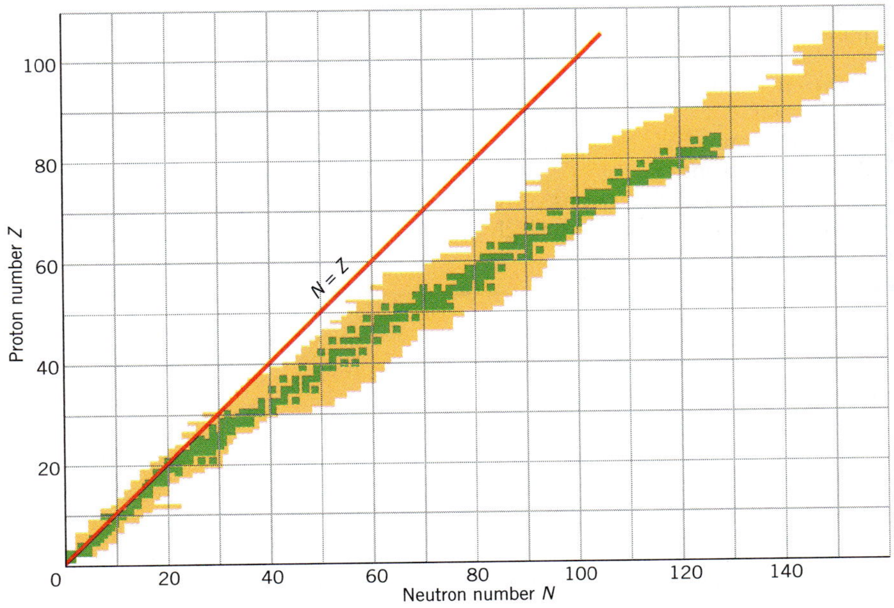

Figure 12-1 A chart of the isotopes. Stable isotopes appear in green, and radioactive isotopes are in beige. Each of the approximately 2000 known isotopes has a different combination of protons (Z on the vertical scale) and neutrons (N on the horizontal scale). Isotopes of the light elements (toward the bottom left of the chart) have similar numbers of protons and neutrons and thus lie close to the diagonal $N = Z$ line at 45 degrees. Heavier isotopes (on the upper right part of the chart) tend to have more neutrons than protons and thus lie well below this line.

EXAMPLE 12-1

Inside the Atom

We find an atom with 9 protons and 8 neutrons in its nucleus and 10 electrons in orbit.

1. What element is it?
2. What is its mass number?
3. What is its electrical charge?
4. How is it possible that the numbers of protons and electrons are different?

Reasoning: We can find the first three answers by looking at the periodic table, but we will refer back to Chapter 10 and the discussion of stable electron states for the last answer.

Solution:

1. The element name depends on the number of protons, which is 9. A glance at the periodic table reveals that element number 9 is fluorine.
2. Next, we calculate the mass number, which is the sum of protons and neutrons: 9 + 8 = 17. This isotope is fluorine-17.
3. The electrical charge equals the number of protons (positive charges) in the nucleus minus the number of electrons (negative charges) surrounding the nucleus: 9 – 10 = –1. The ion is thus F^{-1}.
4. The number of positive charges (9 protons) differs from the number of negative charges (10 electrons) because this atom is an ion. Atoms with 10 electrons are particularly stable (see Chapter 11), so fluorine usually occurs as a –1 ion in nature.

EXAMPLE 12-2

A Heavy Element

How many protons, neutrons, and electrons are contained in the atom ^{56}Fe when it has a charge of +2?

Reasoning: Once again we can look at the periodic table for the first two answers, but we will have to do a simple calculation for the last answer. Remember, the number of protons is the same as the atomic number; the number of neutrons is the mass number minus the number of protons; and we compare the number of protons and the +2 charge to determine the number of electrons.

Solution: From the periodic table, the element Fe (iron) is element number 26, so it has 26 protons.

The number of neutrons is the mass number, 56, minus the number of protons: 56 – 26 = 30 neutrons.

The number of electrons surrounding the nucleus is equal to the number of protons minus the charge on the ion, which in this case is +2. Thus there are 26 – 2 = 24 electrons in orbit.

The Strong Force

In Chapter 5 we learned that one of the fundamental laws of electricity is that like charges repel each other. If you think about the structure of the nucleus for a moment, you will realize that the nucleus is made up of a large number of positively charged objects (the protons) in close proximity to each other. Why doesn't the electrical repulsion between the protons push them apart and disrupt the nucleus completely?

The nucleus can be stable only if there is an attractive force capable of balancing or overcoming the electrical repulsion at the incredibly small scale of the nucleus. Much of the effort of physicists in the twentieth century has gone into understanding the nature of this force that holds the nucleus together. Whatever the force is, it must be vastly stronger than gravity or electromagnetism, the only two forces we've encountered up to this point. For this reason it is called the **strong force.** The strong force must operate only over the very short distances characteristic of the size of the nucleus, because our everyday experience tells us that the strong force doesn't act on large objects. Both with respect to its magnitude and its range, the strong force is somehow confined to the nucleus. In this respect, the strong force is unlike electricity or magnetism.

The strong force has another distinctive feature. If you weigh a dozen apples and a dozen oranges, their total weight is simply the sum of the individual pieces of fruit. But this is not true of protons and neutrons in the nucleus. The mass of the nucleus is always slightly less than the sum of the masses of the protons and neutrons. When protons and neutrons come together, some of their mass is converted into the energy that binds them together. We know this must be true, because it requires energy to pull most nuclei apart. This so-called binding energy varies from one nucleus to another. The iron nucleus is the most tightly bound of all the nuclei. This fact will become important in Chapter 14, when we discuss the death of stars.

Radioactivity

The vast majority of atomic nuclei in objects around you—more than 99.999% of the atoms in our everyday surroundings—are stable. In all probability, the nuclei in those atoms will never change to the end of time. But some kinds of atomic nuclei are not stable. Uranium-238, for example, which is the most common isotope of the rather common element uranium, has 92 protons and 146 neutrons in its nucleus. If you put a block of uranium-238 on a table in front of you and watched for a while, you would find that a few of the uranium nuclei in that block would disintegrate spontaneously. One moment there would be a normal uranium atom in the block, and the next moment there would be fragments of smaller atoms and no uranium. At the same time, fast-moving particles would speed away from the uranium block into the surrounding environment. This spontaneous release of energetic particles is called **radioactivity** or **radioactive decay.** The emitted particles themselves are referred to as radiation. The term *radiation* used in this sense is somewhat different from the electromagnetic radiation that we introduced in Chapter 6. In this case, radiation refers to whatever comes out from the spontaneous decay of nuclei, be it electromagnetic waves or actual particles with mass.

Tom Raymond/Stone/Getty Images

Safety officers in protective clothing use a Geiger counter to examine waste for radioactivity.

Stop and Think! What might the world be like if most atoms were radioactive?

What's Radioactive?

Almost all of the atoms around you are stable, but most everyday elements have at least a few isotopes that are radioactive. Carbon, for example, is stable in its most common isotopes, carbon-12 and carbon-13; but carbon-14, which constitutes about a trillionth of the carbon atoms in living things, is radioactive. A few elements such as uranium, radium, and thorium have no stable isotopes at all. Even though most of our surroundings are composed of stable isotopes, a quick glance at the chart of isotopes (Figure 12-1) reveals that most of the 2000 or so known natural and laboratory-produced isotopes are unstable and undergo radioactive decay of one kind or another.

Courtesy College Physicians of America

The Curie family, with Marie Sklodowska, Pierre, and their daughter, Irene. Both parents received the Nobel Prize in chemistry in 1911 for isolating radium and polonium. Their daughter received the 1935 prize with her husband, Frederic Joliot-Curie.

Science in the Making •

Becquerel and Curie

The nature of radioactivity was discovered in 1896 by Antoine Henri Becquerel (1852–1908), who studied chemicals that incorporate uranium and other radioactive elements. He placed some of these samples in a drawer of his desk along with an unexposed photographic plate and a metal coin. When he developed the photographic plate some time later, the silhouette of the coin was clearly visible. From this photograph he concluded that some as-yet-unknown form of radiation had traveled from the sample to the plate. The coin seemed to have absorbed the radiation and blocked it off, but the radiation that got through delivered enough energy to the plate to cause the chemical reactions that normally go into photographic development. Becquerel knew that whatever had exposed the plate must have originated in the minerals and traveled at least as far as the plate.

Becquerel's discovery was followed by an extraordinarily exciting time for chemists, who began an intensive effort to isolate and study the elements from which the radiation originated. The leader in the field we now call radiochemistry was also one of the best known scientists of the modern era, Marie Sklodowska Curie (1867–1934). Born in Poland and married to Pierre Curie, a distinguished French scientist, she conducted her pioneering research in France, often under extremely difficult conditions because many of her colleagues were unwilling to accept a woman scientist. She worked with tons of exotic uranium-bearing minerals from mines in Bohemia, and she isolated minute quantities of previously unknown elements such as radium and polonium. One of her crowning achievements was the isolation of 22 milligrams of pure radium chloride, which became an international standard for measuring radiation levels. She also pioneered the use of X-rays for medical diagnosis during World War I. For her work she became the first scientist to be awarded two Nobel prizes, one in physics and one in chemistry. She also was one of the first scientists to die from prolonged exposure to radiation, whose harmful effects were not known at that time. Her fate, unfortunately, was shared by many of the pioneers in nuclear physics. •

The Kinds of Radioactive Decay

Physicists who studied radioactive rocks and minerals soon discovered three different kinds of radioactive decay, each of which changes the nucleus in its own characteristic way, and each of which plays an important role in modern science and technology. These three kinds of radioactivity were dubbed alpha, beta, and gamma radiation to emphasize that they were unknown and mysterious when first discovered.

Figure 12-2 The Rutherford experiment led to the identification of the alpha particle, which is the same as a helium nucleus.

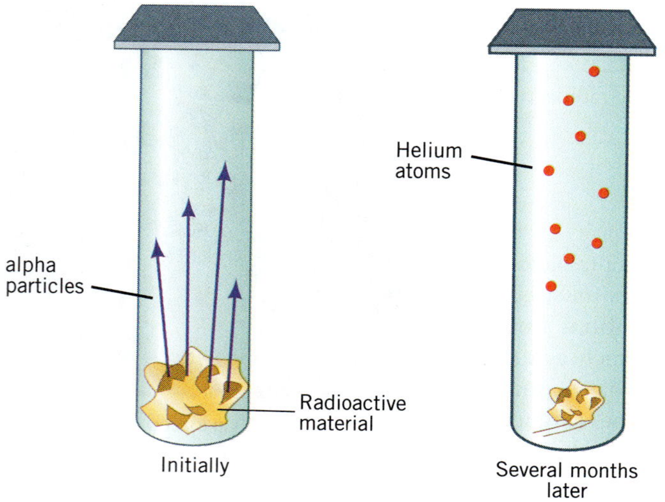

1. Alpha Decay

Some radioactive decays involve the emission of a relatively large and massive particle composed of two protons and two neutrons. Such a particle is exactly the same as the nucleus of a helium-4 atom. It is called an alpha particle, and the process by which it is emitted is called **alpha decay.** (An alpha particle is often represented in equations and diagrams by the Greek letter α.)

The nature of alpha decay was discovered by Ernest Rutherford, the discoverer of the nucleus, in the first decade of the twentieth century. His simple and clever experiment, sketched in Figure 12-2, began with a small amount of radioactive material known to emit alpha particles in a sealed tube. After a number of months, careful chemical analysis revealed the presence of a small amount of helium in the tube, helium that hadn't been present when the tube was sealed. From this observation, Rutherford concluded that alpha particles must be associated with the helium atom. Today we would say that Rutherford observed the emission of the helium nucleus in radioactive decay, followed by the acquisition of two electrons to form an atom of helium gas.

Rutherford received the Nobel Prize in chemistry for his chemical studies and his work in sorting out radioactivity. He is one of the few people in the world who made his most important contributions to science—in this case the discovery of the nucleus—*after* he received the Nobel Prize.

When the nucleus emits an alpha particle, it loses two protons and two neutrons. This means that the daughter nucleus will have two fewer protons than the original. If the original nucleus is uranium-238 with 92 protons, for example, the daughter nucleus will have only 90 protons, which means that it is a *completely different chemical element* called thorium. The total mass of the new atom will be 234, so alpha decay causes uranium-238 to transform to thorium-234. The thorium nucleus with 90 protons can accommodate only 90 electrons in its neutral state. This means that, soon after the decay, two of the original complement of electrons will wander away, leaving the daughter nucleus with its allotment of 90. The process of alpha decay reduces the mass and changes the chemical identity of the decaying nucleus.

Radioactivity is nature's "philosopher's stone." According to medieval alchemists, the philosopher's stone was supposed to turn lead into gold. The alchemists never found their stone because almost all of their work involved what we today would call chemical reactions; that is, they were trying to change one element into another by manipulating electrons. Given what we now know about the structure of atoms, we realize that they were approaching the problem from the wrong end. If you really want to change one chemical element into another, you have to manipulate the nucleus, precisely what happens in the process of radioactivity.

When the alpha particle leaves the parent nucleus, it typically travels at very high speed (often at an appreciable fraction of the speed of light) so it carries a lot of kinetic energy. This energy, like all nuclear energy, comes from the conversion of mass: the mass of the daughter nucleus and the alpha particle, added together, is somewhat less than the mass of the parent uranium nucleus. If the alpha particle is emitted by an atom that is part of a solid body, then it will undergo a series of collisions as it moves from the parent nucleus into the wider world. In each collision it will share some of its kinetic energy with other atoms. The net effect of the decay is that the kinetic energy of the alpha particle is eventually converted into heat, and the material warms up. About half of Earth's interior heat comes from exactly this kind of energy transfer. As we shall see in Chapter 17, this heat is ultimately responsible for many of Earth's major surface features.

2. Beta Decay

The second kind of radioactive decay, called **beta decay,** involves the emission of an electron. (Beta decay and the electron it produces are often denoted by the Greek letter β.) The simplest kind of beta decay that can be observed is for a single neutron. If you put a collection of neutrons on the table in front of you, they would start to disintegrate, with about half of them disappearing in the first 10 minutes or so. The most obvious products of this decay are a proton and an electron. Both particles carry an electrical charge and are therefore very easy to detect. This production of one positive and one negative particle from a neutral one does not change the total electrical charge of the entire system.

In the 1930s, when beta decay of the neutron was first seen in a laboratory, the experimental equipment available at the time easily detected and measured the energies of the electron and proton. Scientists looking carefully at beta decay were troubled to find that the process appeared to violate the law of conservation of energy, as well as some other important conservation laws in physics. When they added up the mass and kinetic energies of the electron and proton after the decay, the total amounted to less than the mass tied up in the energy of the original neutron. If only the electron and proton were given off, the conservation law of energy, as well as other important laws of nature, would be violated.

Rather than face this possibility, physicists at the time followed the lead of Wolfgang Pauli (see Chapter 8) and postulated that another particle had to be emitted in the decay, a particle that they could not detect at the time, but that carried away the missing energy and other properties. It wasn't until 1956 that physicists were able to detect this missing particle—the *neutrino,* or "little neutral one"—in the laboratory. This particle has no electrical charge, travels close to the speed of light, and, if modern theories are correct, carries a very tiny mass. Today, at giant particle accelerators (see Chapter 13), neutrinos are routinely produced and used as probes in other experiments.

When beta decay takes place inside a nucleus, one of the neutrons in the nucleus converts into a proton, an electron, and a neutrino. The lightweight electron and the neutrino speed out of the nucleus, while the proton remains. The electron that comes off in beta decay is not one of the electrons that was originally circling the nucleus in a Bohr electron shell. The electrons emitted from the nucleus come out so fast that they are long gone from the atom before any of the electrons in shells have time to react. The new atom has a net positive charge, however, and eventually may acquire a stray electron from the environment.

The net effect of beta decay is that the daughter nucleus has approximately the same mass as the parent (it has the same total number of protons and neutrons), but has one more proton and one less neutron. It is therefore a different element than it was before. Carbon-14, for example, undergoes beta decay to become an atom of nitrogen-14. If you were to place a small pile of carbon-14 powder—it would look like black soot—in a sealed jar and come back in 20,000 years, most of the powder would have disappeared and the jar would be filled with colorless, odorless nitrogen gas. Beta decay, therefore, is a transformation in which the chemical identity of the atom is changed, but its mass is virtually the same before and after. (Remember: the electron and neutrino that are emitted are extremely lightweight and make almost no difference in the atom's total mass.)

What force in nature could cause an uncharged particle such as the neutron to fly apart? The force is certainly not gravitational attraction between masses, nor is it the electromagnetic force that causes oppositely charged particles to fly away from each other. And beta decay seems to be quite different from the strong force that holds protons together in the nucleus. In fact, beta decay is an example of the operation of the fourth fundamental force in nature, the *weak force.*

3. Gamma Radiation

The third kind of radioactivity, called **gamma radiation,** is different in character from alpha and beta decay. (Gamma decay and gamma radiation are often denoted by the Greek letter γ.) A "gamma ray" is simply a generic term for a very energetic photon—electromagnetic radiation. In Chapter 6 we saw that all electromagnetic radiation comes from the acceleration of charged particles, and that is what happens in gamma radioactivity.

When an electron in an atom shifts from a higher energy level to a lower one, we know that a photon will be emitted, typically in the range of visible or ultraviolet light. In just the same way, the particles in a nucleus can shift between different energy levels. These shifts, or nuclear quantum leaps, involve energy differences thousands or millions of times greater than those of an atom's electrons. When particles in a nucleus undergo shifts from higher to lower energy levels, some of the emitted gamma radiation is in the range of X-rays, while others are even more energetic.

A nucleus emits gamma rays any time its protons and neutrons reshuffle. Neither the protons nor the neutrons change their identity, so the daughter atom has the same mass, the same isotope number, and the same chemical identity as the parent. Nevertheless, this process produces highly energetic radiation.

Table 12-1 Types of Radioactive Decay

Type of Decay	Particle Emitted	Net Change
alpha	alpha particle	new element with two less protons, two less neutrons
beta	electron	new element with one more proton, one less neutron
gamma	photon	same element, less energy

Moving Down the Chart of the Isotopes

The three kinds of radioactivity, summarized in Table 12-1, affect the nuclei of isotopes. Gamma radiation changes the energy of the nucleus without altering the number of protons and neutrons—the isotope doesn't change into a different element. Alpha and beta radiation result in a new element by changing the numbers of protons and neutrons. Think about how alpha and beta radiation might be represented on the chart of the isotopes (Figure 12-1). Alpha decay removes two protons and two neutrons, so we shift diagonally down and to the left two squares on the chart. Alpha decay thus provides a way to move from heavier to lighter elements.

Beta decay, on the other hand, results in one less neutron and one more proton. On the chart of the isotopes we move diagonally up to the left by one square. Beta decay provides a way to reduce the ratio of neutrons to protons, which is generally greater for heavier elements. Combinations of beta and alpha decays, therefore, provide a means to move from heavier radioactive isotopes to lighter stable isotopes.

Radiation and Health

Why is nuclear radiation so dangerous? Alpha, beta, and gamma radiation all carry a great deal of energy—enough energy to damage the molecules that are essential to the workings of the cells that make up your body (Figure 12-3). The most common type of damage is *ionization,* the stripping away of one or more of an atom's electrons. An ionized atom cannot bond in its normal way, and any structures that depend on that atom—a cell wall or a piece of genetic material, for example—will be damaged. Prolonged exposure to ionizing radiation can so disrupt an organism's cells that it will die.

It takes a great deal of radiation to cause sickness or death. Only in unusual circumstances, such as the aftermath of nuclear weapons used on the Japanese cities of Hiroshima and Nagasaki at the end of World War II, or the nuclear reactor accident at Chernobyl in Ukraine in 1986, do people die shortly after exposure. There are, however, possible long-term effects of exposure to lower levels of radiation. While such exposure will not cause immediate death, it may affect a body's ability to replace old cells and can increase the risk of cancer. Radiation may also damage the genetic material that carries the coded information required to reproduce. Birth defects may not appear until decades after exposure to radiation.

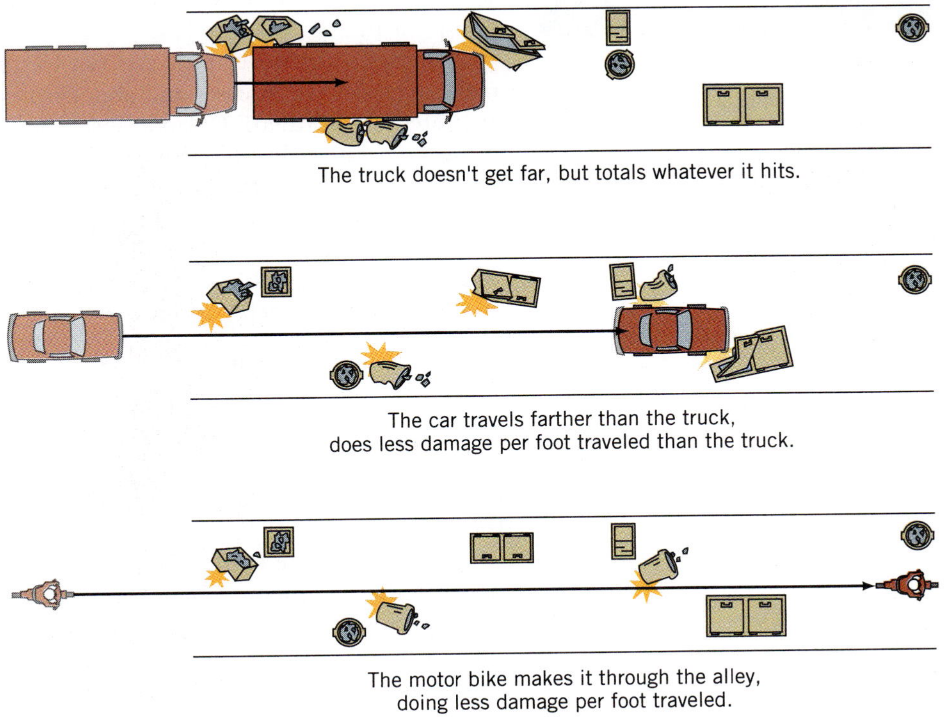

Figure 12-3 The damage to atoms and molecules from different kinds of radiation can be compared to the damage to objects in an alleyway caused by different types of vehicles. The truck resembles an alpha particle, the car resembles a beta particle, and the motorcycle resembles a gamma ray. Although you might conclude that the gamma ray does the least amount of damage, its high energy and ability to penetrate deeply makes it especially dangerous in large quantities.

No one can escape high-energy radiation entirely. Radioactive decay of uranium and other elements in rocks and soils, as well as cosmic radiation from space, bombard us all the time. Radioactive elements even occur in our bones and tissues. Certain kinds of radiation—medical X-rays, for example, and radioactive isotopic tracers for diagnosis—have saved countless lives. Human beings have always lived in a radioactive environment. Nevertheless, it is wise to minimize exposure to unnecessary sources.

The Science of Life •

Robert Hazen's Broken Wrist

I once had an experience that gave me a whole new perspective on radioactivity. Years ago while playing beach volleyball I dove for a ball and bent back my wrist. It hurt a lot, but it was early in the season, so I taped up the wrist and kept on playing. After a couple of weeks it didn't hurt too much, so I forgot about the injury.

Years later, when the wrist started hurting again, I saw a doctor, who said, "Your wrist has been broken for a long time. When did it happen?" Because the break was so old, my doctor had to find out whether the broken bone surfaces were still able to mend. They sent me to a specialized hospital facility where I was given a shot of a fluid containing a radioactive phosphorus compound—a compound that concentrates on active growth surfaces of bone. After a few minutes this radioactive material circulated through my body, with some of the phosphorus compound concentrating on unset regions of my wrist bones. Radioactive molecules constantly emitted particles that moved through my skin to the outside; as I lay on a table, my broken wrist glowed on the overhead monitor. The process produced a clear picture of the fracture, so my doctor was able to reset the bones. My wrist has healed, and I'm back to playing volleyball.

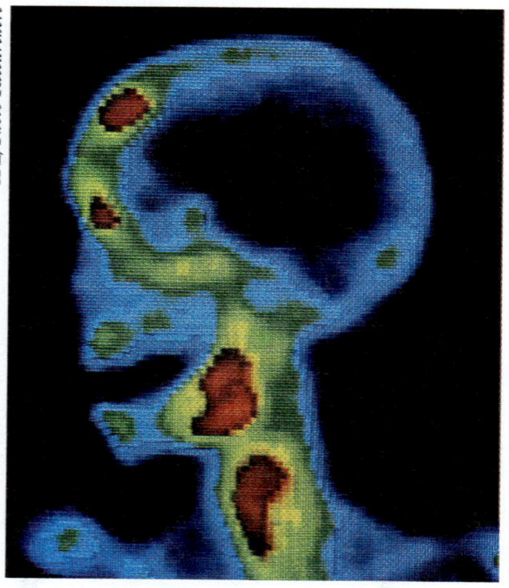
SPL/Photo Researchers

Figure 12-4 Radioactive tracers at work. The patient has been given a radioactive tracer that concentrates in the bone and emits radiation that can be measured on a film. The dark spot in the front part of the skull indicates the presence of a bone cancer.

Today numerous different radioactive materials are useful in medicine and industry because all radioactive isotopes are also chemical elements. The chemistry of atoms is governed by their electrons, while the radioactive properties of a material are totally unrelated to the chemical properties. This means that a radioactive isotope of a particular chemical will undergo the same chemical reactions as a stable isotope of that same element. If a radioactive isotope of iodine or phosphorus is injected into your bloodstream, for example, it will collect at the same places in your body as stable iodine or phosphorus.

Medical scientists can use this fact to study the functions of the human body and to make diagnoses of diseases and abnormalities (Figure 12-4). Iodine, for example, concentrates in the thyroid gland. Instruments outside the body can study the thyroid gland's operation by following the path of iodine isotopes that are injected into the bloodstream. Radioactive or nuclear tracers are also used extensively in the earth sciences, in industry, and in other scientific and technological applications to follow the exact chemical progressions of different elements. Small amounts of radioactive material will produce measurable signals as they move through a system, allowing scientists and engineers to trace their pathways. •

Half-Life

A single nucleus of an unstable isotope left to itself will eventually decay in a spontaneous event. That is, the original nucleus will persist up until a specific time, then radioactive decay will occur, and from that point on you will see only the fragments of the decay.

Watching a single nucleus undergo decay is like watching one kernel in a batch of popcorn. Each kernel will pop at a specific time, but all the kernels don't pop at the same time. Even though you can't predict when any one kernel will pop, you can predict the time during which the popping will go on. A collection of radioactive nuclei behaves in an analogous way. Some nuclei decay almost as soon as you start watching; others persist for much longer times. The percentage of nuclei that decay in each second after you start watching remains more or less the same.

Physicists use the term **half-life** to describe the average time it takes for half of a batch of radioactive isotopes to undergo decay. If you have 100 nuclei at the beginning of your observation and it takes 20 minutes for 50 of them to undergo radioactive decay, for example, then the half-life of that nucleus is 20 minutes. If you were to watch that sample for another 20 minutes, however, not all the nuclei would have decayed. You would find that you had about 25 nuclei at the end, then at the end of another 20 minutes you would most likely have 12 or 13, and so on (Figure 12-5).

Saying that a nucleus has a half-life of an hour does *not* mean that all the nuclei will sit there for an hour, at which point they will all decay. The nuclei, like the popcorn kernels in our example, decay at different times. The half-life is simply an indication of how long on average it will be before an individual nucleus decays.

Radioactive nuclei display a wide range of half-lives. Some nuclei, such as uranium-222, are so unstable that they persist only a tiny fraction of a second. Others, such as uranium-238, have half-lives that range into the billions of years, comparable to Earth's age. Between these two extremes you can find a radioactive isotope that has almost any half-life you wish.

We do not yet understand enough about the nucleus to be able to predict half-lives. On the other hand, the half-life is a fairly easy number to measure and therefore can be determined experimentally for any nucleus. The fine print on most charts of the isotopes (expanded versions of Figure 12-1) usually includes the half-life for each radioactive isotope.

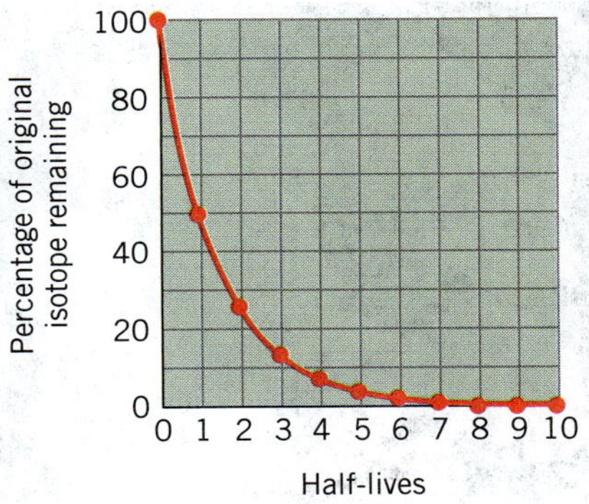

Figure 12-5 The graph shows the number of radioactive nuclei left in a sample as the number of half-lives increases.

Radiometric Dating

The phenomenon of radioactive decay has provided scientists who study Earth and human history with one of their most important methods of determining the age of materials. This remarkable technique, which depends on measurements of the half-life of radioactive materials, is called **radiometric dating.**

The best-known radiometric dating scheme involves the isotope carbon-14. Every living organism takes in carbon during its lifetime. At this moment, your body is taking the carbon in your food and converting it to tissue, and the same is true of all other animals. Plants are taking in carbon dioxide from the air and doing the same thing. Most of this carbon, about 99%, is in the form of carbon-12, while perhaps 1% is carbon-13. But a certain small percentage, no more than one carbon atom in every trillion, is in the form of carbon-14, a radioactive isotope of carbon with a half-life of about 5700 years.

As long as an organism is alive, the carbon-14 in its tissues is constantly renewed in the same small proportion that is found in the general environment. All of the isotopes of carbon behave the same way chemically, so the proportions of carbon isotopes in the living tissue will be nearly the same everywhere, for all living things. When an organism dies, however, it stops taking in carbon of any form. From the time of death, therefore, the carbon-14 in the tissues is no longer replenished. Like a ticking clock, carbon-14 disappears atom by atom to form an ever-smaller percentage of the total carbon. We determine the approximate age of a bone, piece of wood, cloth, or other object by carefully measuring the fraction of carbon-14 that remains and comparing it to the amount of carbon-14 that we assume was in that material when it was alive. If the material happens to be a piece of wood taken out of an Egyptian tomb, for example, we have a pretty good estimate of how old the artifact is and, by inference, when the tomb was built.

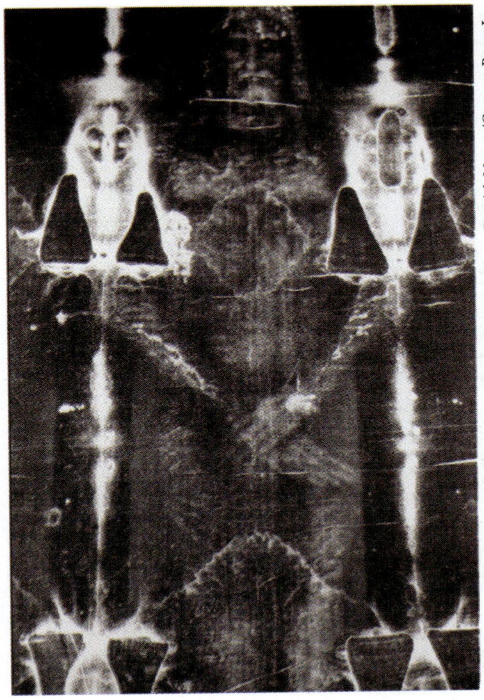

Patrick Mesner/Gamma-Presse, Inc.

The Shroud of Turin, with its ghostly image of a man, was dated by carbon-14 techniques to centuries after the death of Jesus.

Carbon-14 dating often appears in the news when a reputedly ancient artifact is shown to be from more recent times. In a highly publicized experiment, the Shroud of Turin, a fascinating cloth artifact reputed to be involved in the burial of Jesus, was shown by carbon-14 techniques to date from the thirteenth or fourteenth century A.D.

John Reader/Science Photo Library/Photo Researchers

The oldest human fossils are too ancient to be dated by carbon-14 methods. An alternative technique, called potassium-argon dating, is employed for dating the rocks in which these skulls, which are up to 3.7 million years old, were found.

Stop and Think! In Chapter 2 we described the monument known as Stonehenge and gave an age for it. This age came from the carbon dating technique we've just described. Because the monument we see today is made of stone (which has no carbon), how do you suppose this dating was done?

Carbon-14 dating has been instrumental in mapping human history over the last several thousand years. When an object is more than about 50,000 years old, however, the amount of carbon-14 left in it is so small that this dating scheme cannot be used. To date rocks and minerals that are millions of years old, scientists must rely on similar techniques that use radioactive isotopes of much greater half-life. Among the most widely used radiometric clocks in geology are those based on the decay of potassium-40 (half-life of 1.25 billion years), uranium-238 (half-life of 4.5 billion years), and rubidium-87 (half-life of 49 billion years). In these cases, we measure the total number of atoms of a given element, together with the relative percentage of a given isotope, to determine how many radioactive nuclei were present at the beginning. Most of the ages that we will discuss in the chapters on the earth sciences and evolution are ultimately derived from these radiometric dating techniques.

Science by the Numbers •

Dating a Frozen Mammoth

Russian paleontologists occasionally discover beautifully preserved mammoths frozen in Siberian ice. Carbon isotope analyses from these mammoths often show that only about one-fourth of the original carbon-14 is still present in the mammoth tissues and hair. If the half-life of carbon-14 is 5700 years, how old is the mammoth?

To solve this problem it's necessary to determine how many half-lives have passed, with the predictable decay rate of carbon-14 serving as a clock. In this case, only one-fourth of the original carbon-14 isotopes remain ($^1/_4 = {}^1/_2 \times {}^1/_2$), so the carbon-14 isotopes have passed through two half-lives. After 5700 years about half of the original carbon-14 isotopes will remain. Similarly, after another 5700 years only one-half of those remaining carbon-14 isotopes (or one-fourth of the original amount) will remain. The age of the mammoth remains is thus two half-lives, or about 11,400 years. •

Decay Chains

When a parent nucleus decays, the daughter nucleus will not necessarily be stable. In fact, in the great majority of cases, the daughter nucleus is as unstable as the parent. The original parent will decay into the daughter, the daughter will decay into a second daughter, on and on, perhaps for dozens of different radioactive events. Even if you start with a pure collection of atoms of the same isotope of the same chemical element, nuclear decay will guarantee that eventually you'll have many different chemical species in the sample. A series of decays of this sort is called a *decay chain*. The sequence of decays continues until a stable isotope appears. Given enough time, all of the atoms of the original element will eventually decay into that stable isotope.

To get a sense of a decay chain, consider the example we used at the beginning of this chapter—uranium-238, with a half-life of approximately 4.5 billion years. Uranium-238 decays by alpha emission into thorium-234, another radioactive isotope. In the process uranium-238 loses 2 protons and 2 neutrons. Thorium-234 undergoes beta decay (half-life of 24.1 days) into protactinium-234 (half-life of about seven hours), which in turn undergoes beta decay to uranium-234. Each of these beta decays results in the conversion of a neutron into a proton and an electron. After three radioactive decays we are back to uranium, albeit a lighter isotope with a 247,000-year half-life.

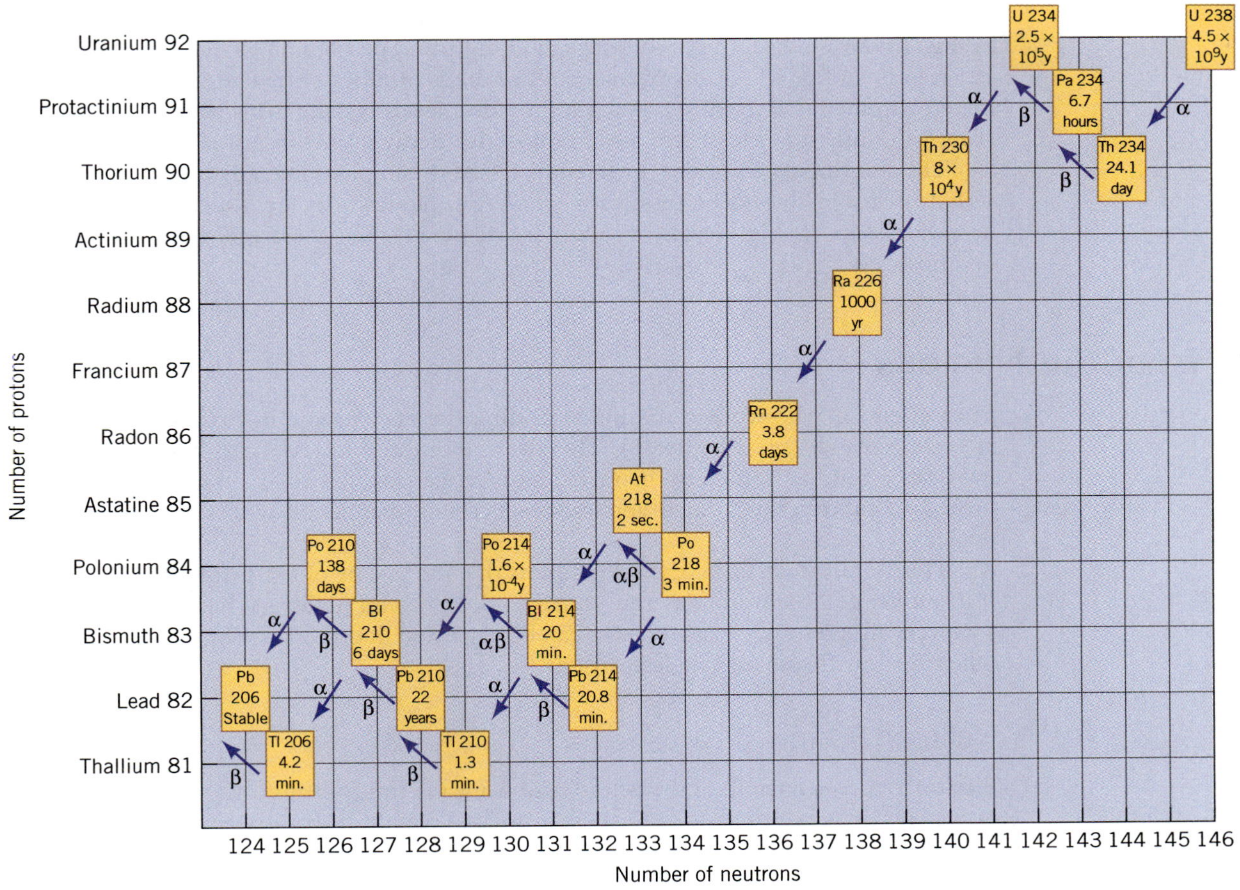

Figure 12-6 The uranium-238 decay chain. The nuclei in the chain decay by both alpha and beta emission until they reach lead-208, a stable isotope. Some isotopes may undergo either alpha or beta decay, as indicated by splits in the chain. Nevertheless, all paths eventually arrive at lead-208 after 14 decay events.

The rest of the uranium decay chain is shown in Figure 12-6. It follows a long path through eight different elements before it winds up as stable lead-206. Given enough time, all of Earth's uranium-238 will eventually be converted into lead. Since Earth is only about 4.5 billion years old, however, there's only been time for about half of the original uranium to decay, so at the moment (and for the foreseeable future) we can expect to have all the members of the uranium decay chain in existence on Earth.

Indoor Radon

The uranium-238 decay chain is not an abstract concept, of interest only to theoretical physicists. In fact, the health concern over indoor radon pollution is a direct consequence of the uranium decay chain. Uranium is a fairly common element—about two grams out of every ton of rocks at Earth's surface are uranium. The first steps in the uranium-238 decay chain produce thorium, radium, and other elements that remain sealed in ordinary rocks and soils. The principal health concern arises from the production of radon-222, about halfway along the path to stable lead. Radon is a colorless, odorless, inert gas that does not chemically bond to its host rock.

As radon is formed, it seeps out of its mineral host and moves into the atmosphere, where it undergoes alpha decay (half-life of about four days) into polonium-218 and a dangerous sequence of short-lived, highly radioactive isotopes. Historically, radon atoms were quickly dispersed by winds and weather, and they posed no serious threat to human health. In our modern age of well-insulated, tightly sealed buildings, however, radon gas can seep in and build up, occasionally to hundreds of times normal levels, in poorly ventilated basements. Exposure to such high radon levels is dangerous because each radon atom will undergo at least five more radioactive decay events in just a few days.

The solution to the radon problem is relatively simple. First, any basement or other sealed-off room should be tested for radon. Simple test kits are available at your local hardware store. If high levels of radon are detected, then the area's ventilation should be improved.

Energy from the Nucleus

Most scientists who worked on understanding the nucleus and its decays were involved in basic research (see Chapter 1). They were interested in acquiring knowledge for its own sake. But, as frequently happens, knowledge pursued for its own sake is quickly turned to practical use. Such applications certainly happened with the science of the nucleus.

The atomic nucleus holds vast amounts of energy. One of the defining achievements of the twentieth century was the understanding of and ability to harness that energy. Two very different nuclear processes can be exploited in our search for energy: processes called nuclear fission and nuclear fusion.

Nuclear Fission

Fission means splitting, and nuclear fission means the splitting of a nucleus. In most cases, energy is required to tear apart a nucleus. Some heavy isotopes, however, have nuclei that can be split apart into products that have less mass than the original. From such nuclei, energy can be obtained from the mass difference.

The most common nucleus from which energy is obtained by fission is uranium-235, an isotope of uranium that constitutes about 7 of every 1000 uranium atoms in the world. If a neutron hits uranium-235, the nucleus splits into two roughly equal-sized large pieces and a number of smaller fragments. Among these fragments will be two or three more neutrons. If these neutrons go on to hit other uranium-235 nuclei, the process will be repeated and a *chain reaction* will begin, with each split nucleus producing the neutrons that will cause more splittings. By this basic process, large amounts of energy can be obtained from uranium.

The device that allows us to extract energy from nuclear fission is called a **nuclear reactor** (Figure 12-7). The uranium in a reactor contains mostly uranium-238, but it has been processed so it contains much more uranium-235 than it would if it were found in nature. This uranium is stacked in long fuel rods, about the thickness of a lead pencil, surrounded by a metallic protector. Typical reactors will incorporate many thousands of fuel rods. Between the fuel rods is a fluid called a moderator, usually water, whose function is to slow down neutrons that leave the rods.

The nuclear reactor works like this: A neutron strikes a uranium-235 nucleus in

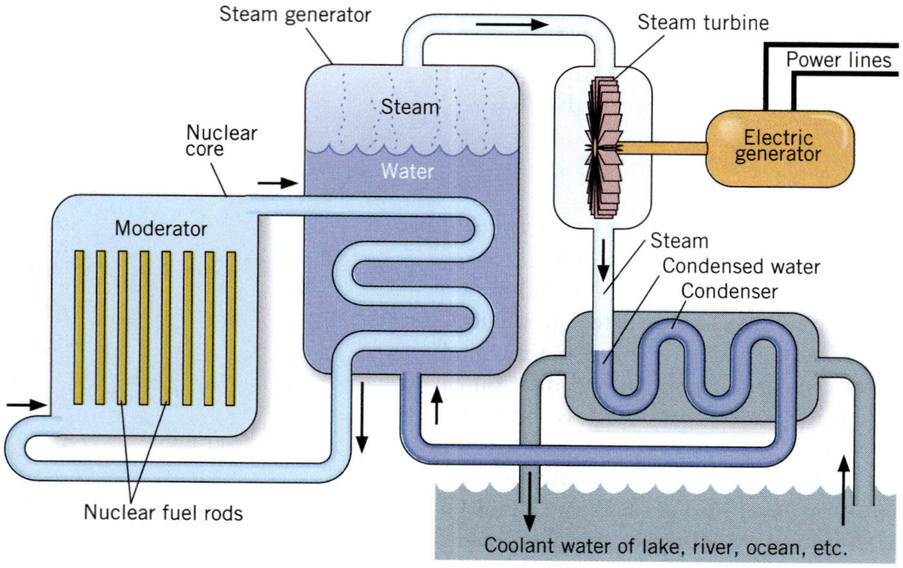

Figure 12-7 A nuclear reactor, shown here schematically, produces heat that converts water to steam. The steam powers a turbine, just as in a conventional coal-burning plant.

one fuel rod, causing that nucleus to split apart. These fragments include several fast-moving neutrons. Fast neutrons are very inefficient at producing fission, but as the neutrons move through the moderator they are slowed down. In this way, they can initiate other fission events in other uranium atoms. A chain reaction in a reactor proceeds as neutrons cascade from one fuel rod to another. In the process, the energy released by the conversion of matter goes into heating the fuel rods and the water. The hot water is pumped to another location in the nuclear plant, where it is used to produce steam.

The steam is used to run a generator to produce electricity as described in Chapter 5 (see Figure 5-10). In fact, the only significant difference between a nuclear reactor and a coal-fired generating plant is the way in which steam is made. In the nuclear reactor, the energy to produce steam comes from the conversion of mass in uranium nuclei; in the coal-fired plant, it comes from the burning of coal.

Nuclear reactors must keep a tremendous amount of nuclear potential energy under control while confining dangerously radioactive material. Modern reactors are thus designed with numerous safety features. The water that is in contact with the uranium, for example, is sealed in a self-contained system and does not touch the rest of the reactor. Another built-in safety feature is that nuclear reactors cannot function without the presence of the moderator. If there should be an accident in which the water was evaporated from the reactor vessel, the chain reaction would shut off. Thus a reactor cannot explode and is *not* analogous to the explosion of an atomic bomb.

Breck P. Kent/Animals Animals/Earth Scenes

One of the reactors at the nuclear power plant at Three Mile Island, near Harrisburg, Pennsylvania, had to shut down after suffering a partial meltdown. Safety measures insured that no radioactive material was released into the environment.

The most serious accident that can occur at a nuclear reactor involves processes in which the flow of water to the fuel rods is interrupted. When this happens, the enormous heat stored in the central part of the reactor can cause the fuel rods to melt. Such an event is called a *meltdown*. In 1979, a nuclear reactor at Three Mile Island in Pennsylvania suffered a partial meltdown but caused only a slight release of radiation—only about 1% of the allowed daily dosage. In 1986, a less carefully designed reactor at Chernobyl, Ukraine, underwent a meltdown accompanied by large releases of radioactivity.

Fusion

Fusion refers to a process in which two atoms of hydrogen combine together, or fuse, to form an atom of helium. In the process, some of the mass of the hydrogen is converted into energy. Under special circumstances it is possible to push two nuclei together and make them fuse in a way that produces energy. When elements with low atomic numbers fuse under these special circumstances, the mass of the final nucleus is less than the mass of its constituent parts. In these cases, it's possible to extract energy from the fusion reaction by conversion of that "missing" mass.

The most common fusion reaction combines four hydrogen nuclei to form a helium nucleus (Figure 12-8). (Remember that an ordinary hydrogen nucleus is a single proton, with no neutron. Thus we use the terms *hydrogen nucleus* and *proton* interchangeably.) This nuclear reaction powers the Sun and other stars and thus is ultimately responsible for all life on Earth.

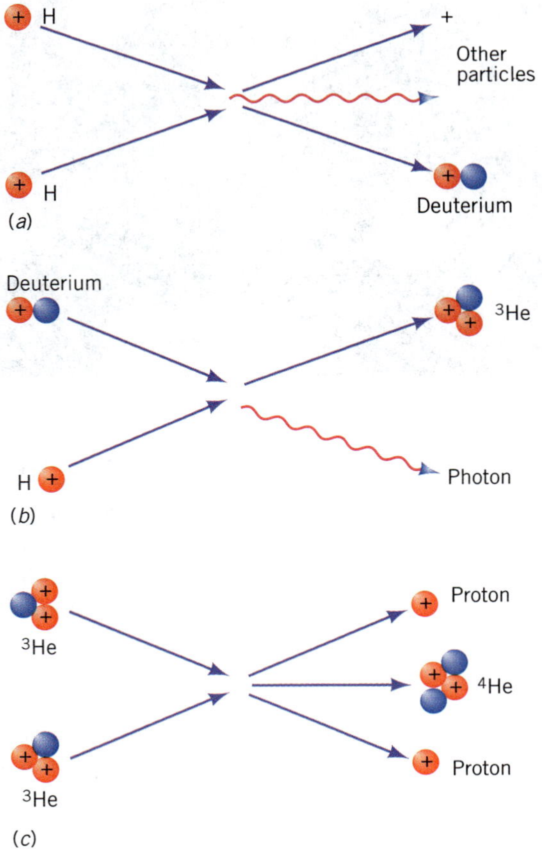

Figure 12-8 A fusion reaction releases energy as nuclei combine. Hydrogen nuclei enter into a multistep process whose end product is a helium nucleus. The red balls are protons, the blue ones are neutrons.

Courtesy Princeton University Physics Laboratory

The Princeton Tokomak is a ring-shaped magnetic chamber. Hydrogen plasma is confined in this ring during attempts to achieve nuclear fusion reactions.

You cannot just put hydrogen in a container and expect it to form helium, however. Two positively charged protons must collide with tremendous force in order to overcome their electrostatic repulsion and allow the strong force to kick in (remember, the strong force operates only over extremely short distances). In the Sun, high pressures and temperatures in the star's interior trigger the fusion reaction. The sunlight falling outside your window is generated by the conversion of 600 million tons of hydrogen into helium each second. The helium nucleus has a mass about half a percent less than the original hydrogen nuclei. The "missing" mass is converted to the energy that eventually radiates out into space.

Since the 1950s many attempts have been made to harness nuclear fusion reactions to produce energy for human use. The problem has always been that it is very difficult to get protons to collide with enough energy to overcome the electrical repulsion between them and initiate the nuclear reaction.

One promising but technically difficult method is to confine protons in a very strong magnetic field while heating them with high-powered radio waves. Alternatively, powerful lasers can be used to heat pellets of liquid hydrogen. This rapid heating produces shock waves in the liquid, and these shock waves raise the temperature and pressure to the point where fusion is initiated.

A number of rather expensive programs are now under way in the United States, Europe, and Japan, where researchers are investigating ways to produce commercially feasible nuclear fusion reactors, perhaps sometime in the twenty-first century. The development is slow and costly, but if researchers are successful, the energy crisis will be over forever, because there is enough hydrogen in the oceans to power fusion reactions virtually forever.

©AP/Wide World Photos

The National Ignition Facility attempts to initiate a fusion reaction in hydrogen-rich pellets that are simultaneously irradiated by dozens of high-powered lasers.

Technology •

Nuclear Weapons

Whenever humans have discovered a new source of energy, that source has quickly been turned into weapons. Nuclear energy, the most concentrated energy source known, is no exception. The earliest atomic bombs, developed in the United States as part of World War II's Manhattan Project, relied on fission reactions in concentrated uranium-235 or plutonium-239. The problem faced by the designers of the atomic bomb was the requirement of a certain number of uranium-235 atoms to sustain a chain reaction to the point where large amounts of energy could be released. This quantity of uranium-235, called the *critical mass,* is about 60 kilograms—a chunk of uranium about the size of a grapefruit.

At the instant of an atom bomb explosion, a critical mass of the radioactive isotope is compressed into a small volume by a conventional chemical explosive. A chain reaction of fission reactions releases a flood of neutrons, which splits much of the nuclear material and releases a destructive wave of heat, light, and other forms of radiation. The first atomic bombs carried the explosive power of many thousands of tons of chemical explosive.

Shortly after World War II, the United States and the Soviet Union developed the hydrogen bomb, which relies on nuclear fusion. In a hydrogen bomb, several atom bomb "triggers" surround a compound rich in the heavy hydrogen isotopes, hydrogen-2 and hydrogen-3 (known as deuterium and tritium, respectively). When the atomic fission bombs are set off, they trigger much more intense fusion reactions in the heavy hydrogen. Unlike atom bombs, which are limited by the critical mass of nuclear explosive, hydrogen bombs have no intrinsic limit to their size. The largest nuclear warheads, which could fit in a closet, carry payloads equivalent to many millions of tons (megatons) of conventional explosive. •

Science in the Making •

Superheavy Elements

Uranium, with 92 protons, is the heaviest element commonly found in nature, but ever since the mid-twentieth century scientists have been able to build heavier ones in the laboratory. If you look at the periodic table of the elements in Chapter 8, all of the elements past uranium are seen only in specialized experiments. The technique used is to bombard a heavy nucleus like lead with other nuclei and hope that, occasionally, enough protons and neutrons will stick together to form the nucleus of a still heavier atom. Although these heavier atoms will be unstable and decay quickly, they can last long enough to be identified by their spectra.

A group at the Lawrence-Berkeley Laboratory in California recently ran an experiment in which a lead target was bombarded with krypton ions. In the debris of the collisions, they saw evidence for elements 116 and 118. Even though the atoms lived only 1.2 milliseconds and 200 microseconds, respectively, they were the heaviest and most complex nuclei ever seen. •

Science News | Thermonuclear Squeeze

(Science News, Jan. 21, 2006, p. 38)

As the discussion of inertial confinement shows, one way to achieve the pressures and temperatures needed to produce fusion is to bring matter to a high state of compression. In a recent set of experiments at Purdue University, a group of scientists believe that they have uncovered another way to produce fusion. If they are correct, their work could lead to cheap fusion and an end to the energy crisis.

Their technique is simple to describe. The process starts with a chilled vat of fluid that is irradiated by ultrasound. In this situation, clusters of bubbles are created in the fluid when an outside agent such as a beam of neutrons passes through. In essence, the bubbles form in the troughs of the ultrasound waves but are then crushed by the high-pressure wave crests. This crushing process, the researchers claim, raises the density of the fluid to the point where fusion can take place. They point to a measured flux of neutrons coming from the tank as proof of their claim.

Because the advent of fusion in the original experiments was deduced from measurements of neutrons, and neutrons are also used to create the bubbles, there was a good deal of skepticism from other scientists about the results. More recently, the experiments have been run using alpha particles to initiate the bubbles.

Actually, this situation is a good example of the process of science we discussed in Chapter 1. Some of the objections are standard, having to do with the details of the measurements and the interpretation of the results. At the moment, however, the main reason that the scientific community is withholding judgment on this experiment is simple: no one else has yet been able to duplicate it. Until that happens, bubble-induced fusion will remain a tantalizing hope for the future, but nothing more.

Thinking More About | The Nucleus

Nuclear Waste

When power is generated in a nuclear reactor, many more nuclear changes take place than those associated with the chain reaction itself. Fast-moving debris from the fission of uranium-235 strike other nuclei in the system—both the ordinary uranium-238 that makes up most of the fuel rods, and the nuclei in the concrete and metal that make up the reactor. In these collisions, the original nuclei may undergo fission or absorb neutrons to become isotopes of other elements. Many of these newly produced isotopes are radioactive. The result is that even when all of the uranium-235 has been used to generate energy, a lot of radioactive material remains in the reactor. This sort of material is called *high-level nuclear waste.* (The production of nuclear weapons is another source of this kind of waste.) The half-lives of some of the materials in the waste can run to hundreds of thousands of years. How can we dispose of this waste in a way that keeps it away from living things?

The management of nuclear waste begins with storage. Power companies usually store spent fuel rods at a reactor site for tens of years to allow the short-lived isotopes to decay. At the end of this period, long-lived isotopes that are left behind must be isolated from the environment. Scientists have developed techniques for incorporating these nuclei into stable solids, either minerals or glass. The idea is that the electrons in radioactive isotopes form the same kind of bonds as stable isotopes, so that with a judicious choice of materials, radioactive nuclei will be locked into a solid mass for long periods of time.

Plans now call for nuclear waste disposal by the incorporation of radioactive atoms into stable glass that is surrounded by successive layers of steel and concrete. These stable containers are to be buried deep under Earth's surface in stable rock formations. Ultimately, if a long sequence of public hearings, construction permits, and other hurdles are passed, the U.S. Department of Energy hopes to confine much of the nation's nuclear waste at the Yucca Mountain repository in a remote desert region of Nevada. The hope is that long-lived wastes can be sequestered from the environment until after they are no longer dangerous to human beings.

The Yucca Mountain project continues to be a controversial subject. Supporters of the site argue that a single, remote, long-term site is vastly preferable to the present 131 temporary repositories now located in 39 different states. Such scattered sites are difficult to monitor and protect from terrorist threats. Opponents of Yucca Mountain counter that hauling thousands of tons of nuclear waste on interstate highways poses a far greater danger to the public than the present sites. Some geologists, furthermore, fear that Yucca Mountain may be subject to occasional earthquakes and volcanic activity, and that its location, less than 100 miles from Las Vegas, is not sufficiently remote.

What should we do with our increasing quantities of nuclear waste? What responsibility do we have to future generations to ensure that the waste we bury stays where we put it? Should the existence of nuclear waste restrain us in our development of nuclear energy? Should we, as some scientists argue, keep nuclear waste materials at the surface and use them for applications such as medical tracers and fuel for reactors?

Summary

The nucleus is a tiny collection of massive particles, including positively charged *protons* and electrically neutral *neutrons.* The nucleus plays a role independent of the orbiting electrons that control chemical reactions, and the energies associated with nuclear reactions are much greater. The number of protons—the *atomic number*—determines the nuclear charge and therefore the type of element; each element in the periodic table has a different number of protons. The number of neutrons plus protons—the *mass number*—determines the mass of the *isotope.* Nuclear particles are held together by the *strong force,* which operates only over extremely short distances.

While most of the atoms in objects around us have stable, unchanging nuclei, many isotopes are unstable—they spontaneously change through *radioactive decay.* In *alpha decay,* a nucleus loses two protons and two neutrons. In *beta decay,* a neutron spontaneously transforms into a proton, an electron, and a neutrino. A third kind of radioactivity, involving the emission of energetic electromagnetic radiation, is called *gamma radiation.* The rate of radioactive decay is measured by the *half-life,* which is the time it takes for half of a collection of isotopes to decay. Radioactive half-lives provide the key for *radiometric dating* techniques based on carbon-14 and other isotopes. Unstable isotopes are also used as radioactive tracers in medicine and other areas of science. Indoor radon pollution and nuclear waste are two problems that arise from the existence of radioactive decay.

There are two forms of nuclear energy. *Fission* reactions, as controlled in *nuclear reactors,* produce energy when heavy radioactive nuclei split apart into fragments that together weigh less than the original isotopes. *Fusion* reactions, on the other hand, combine light elements to make heavier ones, as in the conversion of hydrogen into a smaller mass of helium in the Sun. In each case, the lost nuclear mass is converted into energy.

Key Terms

proton
neutron
atomic number
isotope
mass number
strong force
radioactivity or radioactive decay
alpha decay
beta decay
gamma radiation
half-life
radiometric dating
fission
nuclear reactor
fusion

Review Questions

1. Compare the size of a nucleus to the size of an atom.
2. Which has more mass, electrons or protons?
3. What fact about atomic nuclei suggests the existence of the neutron?
4. What is the difference between mass number and atomic number? Is one always greater than the other?
5. What is an isotope?
6. How do you know that the strong force exists?
7. How is the strong force different from gravity and electromagnetism?
8. What happens to atomic nuclei during radioactive decay?
9. Explain the term *half-life*.
10. Explain how radioactivity can be used to date (a) a piece of wood, and (b) a rock.
11. Describe the major achievement of Marie Curie.
12. What is alpha decay? How does it change the nucleus?
13. Why does beta decay not change the total electrical charge of an atom?
14. What led physicists to hypothesize the existence of the neutrino?
15. How does gamma radiation differ from alpha and beta radiation?
16. How can we obtain energy from nuclear fission?
17. What is a chain reaction?
18. How does a nuclear reactor work?
19. How do fusion reactions produce energy?
20. What is a critical mass?
21. How are radioactive tracers useful in medicine? Give an example.
22. What is nuclear waste? Why is it a serious problem for society?

Discussion Questions

1. What was the hypothesis behind Rutherford's experiment on alpha decay? What did he prove?
2. What are the potential benefits and risks in using nuclear tracers in medical diagnosis?
3. *Critical mass* is a term that is widely used outside of nuclear science. What is its everyday meaning, and how does that relate to its scientific meaning?
4. Why is carbon-14 used in radiometric dating of organic material rather than another isotope or element?
5. How is the principle of conservation of energy seen in (a) fission reactions and (b) fusion reactions?
6. Discuss the pros and cons of nuclear power.
7. Can nuclear radiation escape from nuclear power plants? If so, how?
8. Suppose you are a scientist from the future who has discovered the ruins of the Empire State Building. How would you go about estimating the date when it was built?
9. Why must uranium be enriched in order to be used in a nuclear power plant? What is changed in the process of enrichment?
10. Does the interaction of electrons in chemical bonding affect the nucleus?
11. What isotope would you use to date the pyramids at Giza? a mummy found inside? Why?
12. What is a decay chain and why is it important?

Problems

1. Use the periodic table to identify the element, atomic number, mass number, and electrical charge of the following combinations:
   a. 7 protons, 7 neutrons, 10 electrons
   b. 8 protons, 8 neutrons, 8 electrons
   c. 17 protons, 18 neutrons, 18 electrons
   d. 11 protons, 11 neutrons, 10 electrons
2. Use the periodic table to determine how many protons and neutrons are in each of the following atoms:
   a. C-13
   b. Zn-66
   c. Ag-108
   d. Au-102
3. What are the common names of the elements in problems 1 and 2?
4. The average atomic weight of cobalt atoms (atomic number 27) is actually slightly greater than the average atomic weight of nickel atoms (atomic number 28). How could this situation arise?
5. Imagine that a collection of 1 million atoms of uranium-238 was sealed in a box at Earth's formation 4.5 billion years ago. Use the uranium-238 decay chain (Figure 12-6) to predict some of the things you would find if you opened the box today
6. Isotope X has a half-life of 10 days. A sample is known to have contained about 5 million atoms of isotope X when it was put together but is now observed to have only about 100,000 atoms of isotope X. Estimate how long ago the sample was assembled. Explain the relevance of this problem to the technique of radiometric dating.
7. Why hasn't all the uranium-238 in Earth decayed into lead? Calculate when this milestone will occur. Will anyone now living be around to experience it?

INVESTIGATIONS

1. Read a historical account of the Manhattan Project. What was the principal technical problem in obtaining the nuclear fuel? Why did chemistry play a major role? What techniques are now used to obtain nuclear fuel?

2. What is the current status of U.S. progress toward developing a depository for nuclear waste? How do your representatives in Congress vote on matters relating to this issue?

3. What sorts of isotopes are used for diagnostics in your local hospital? Where are supplies of those radioisotopes purchased? What are the half-lives of the isotopes, and how often are supplies replaced? What is the hospital's policy regarding the disposal of radioactive waste?

4. How much of the electricity in your area comes from nuclear reactors? What fuel do they use? Where are the used fuel rods taken when they are replaced? If the facility offers public tours, visit the reactor and observe the kinds of safety procedures that are used.

5. Obtain a radon test kit from your local hardware store and use it in the basement of two different buildings. How do the values compare? Is either at a dangerous level? If the values differ, what might be the reason?

6. Only about 90 elements occur naturally on Earth, but scientists are able to produce more elements in the laboratory. Investigate the discovery and characteristics of one of these human-made elements.

7. Read an account of the so-called cold fusion episode. At what point in this history were conventional scientific procedures bypassed? Ultimately, do you think that the scientific method worked or failed?

8. Soon the U.S. government will take over responsibility for the nuclear wastes of the 50 states. What options do we have for waste storage? Do you think all the waste should be stored in one place? Should we try to separate and use the radioactive isotopes? What are the factors—social, political, and economic—that will help determine what happens to this nuclear waste?

9. Investigate the Three Mile Island nuclear power accident and compare it to the Chernobyl accident. What design flaws caused the Chernobyl accident to be deadly and the Three Mile Island accident to be relatively benign?

10. What are the half-lives of common isotopes (e.g., carbon-14, uranium-238, uranium-235)?

11. What countries generate the majority of their electric power using nuclear energy? Do these countries have higher rates of cancer or other diseases? Why isn't the United States generating more electricity from nuclear energy?

12. Do you think that nuclear power is a productive idea, or a danger to the environment? Try to find as much information as possible to support the opposing viewpoint (i.e., if you think nuclear power is dangerous, find all relevant scientific publications that suggests its relative safety, and vice versa).

13

The Ultimate Structure of Matter

How can antimatter be used to probe the human brain?

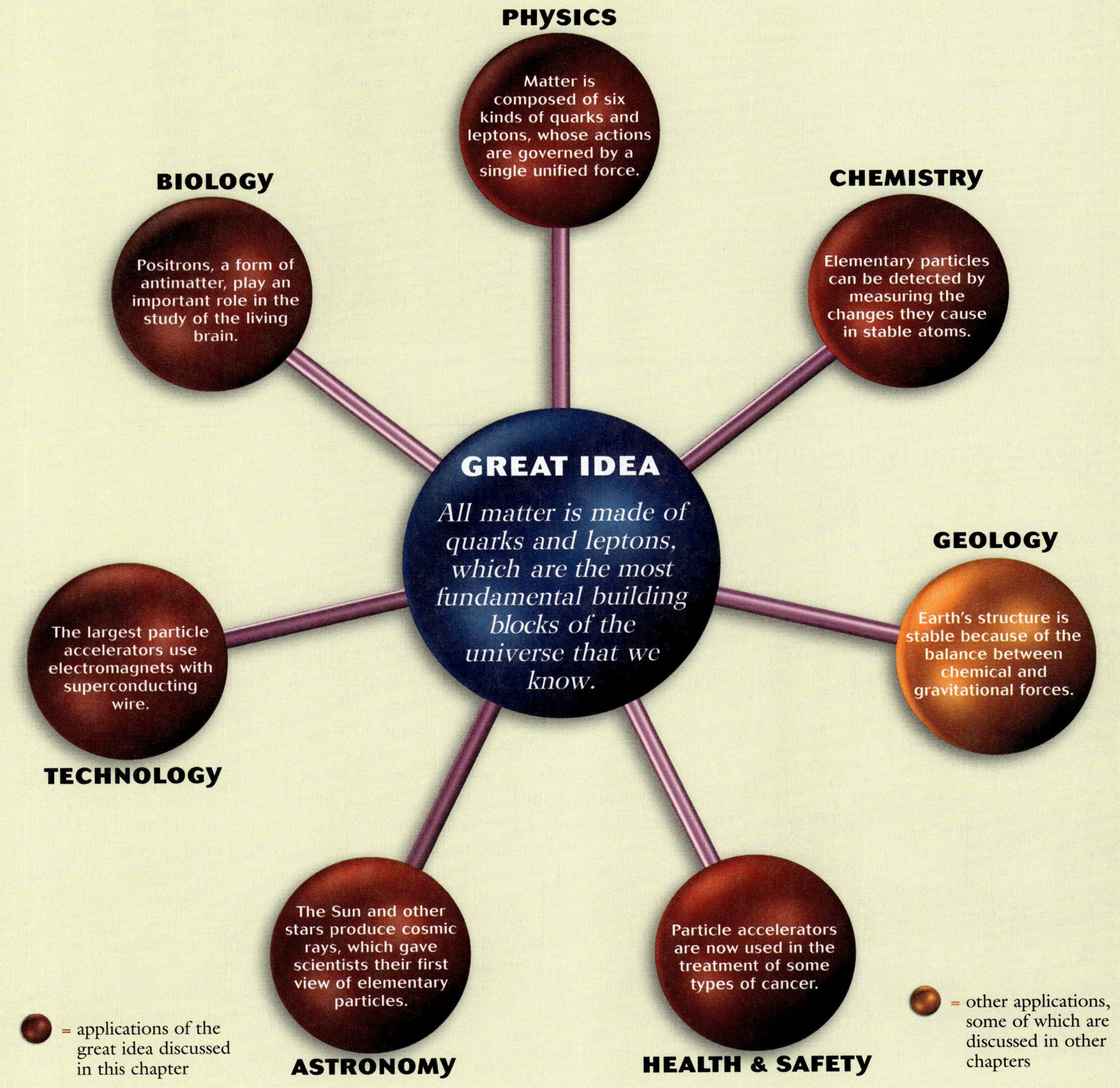

Science Through the Day | Looking at Sand

As you lie on the beach you let a handful of sand sift through your fingers. Look at a single tiny grain, and think about its microscopic structure. Imagine that you could magnify that grain a thousandfold, a millionfold, even more. What would you see?

At a thousand magnification the rounded grain would appear rough and irregular, but no hint of its atomic structure could be seen. At a million magnification individual atoms, each about a ten-billionth of a meter across, would begin to be visible. And at a trillion magnification the atomic nuclei would appear as tiny points, surrounded by almost nothing.

But is that it? Or is there even more to the submicroscopic structure of the atom? What are the ultimate building blocks of matter?

Peter Cade/Getty Images

Of What Is the Universe Made?

In a library, letters form words and words form books. Letters can thus be thought of as the fundamental unit of the library.

James Stachan/Stone/Getty Images

The Library

The next time you head over to the library, wander through the stacks and think about what constitutes the fundamental building blocks of the library. Your first reaction might be to say that books are fundamental building blocks—row after row, shelf after shelf, of bound volumes. But a library is not just a collection of books; the volumes are arranged with an order to them. You could describe the set of rules that dictates how books are arranged in libraries—the Dewey decimal system or the Library of Congress classification scheme, for example. Thus a complete description of a library at this most superficial level includes two things: books as the fundamental building blocks and rules about how the books are organized.

Inside a book, the various volumes are not as different from each other as they might seem at first. They are all made of an even more fundamental unit—the word. You could argue that the word is the fundamental building block of the library; and, as was the case for cataloged books, we require a set of rules, called grammar, that tells us how to put words together to make books. Words and grammar, then, take you down to a more basic level in your probe of a library's reality.

You probably wouldn't be content very long with the notion of the word as the fundamental building block, because all of the thousands of words are different combinations of a small number of more fundamental things—letters. Only 26 letters (at least in the English alphabet) provide the building blocks for all the thousands of words on all the pages in all the books of the library. Furthermore, we need a set of rules (spelling) that tells us how to put letters together into words. The discovery of letters and spelling would constitute perhaps the ultimate description of a library and its organization.

So the library can be described in this way: We use spelling to tell us how to put letters together into words. Then grammar tells us how to put words together into books. Finally, we use organizing rules to tell us how to put books together into a library.

And this, as we shall see, is how scientists attempt to describe the entire physical universe.

Reductionism

How many different kinds of material can you see when you look up from this book? You may see a wall made of cinder block, a window made of glass, a ceiling made of fiberglass panels. Outside the window you may see grass, trees, blue sky, and clouds. We encounter thousands of different kinds of materials every day. They all look different—what possible common ground could there be between a cinder block and a blade of grass? They all look different, but are they really?

For at least two millennia, people who have thought about the physical universe have asked this question. Is the universe just what we see, or is there some underlying structure, some basic stuff, from which it's all made? You could even say that herein lies one of the most fundamental scientific questions.

The quest for the "ultimate building blocks" of the universe is referred to by philosophers as *reductionism*. Reductionism is an attempt to reduce the seeming complexity of nature by first looking for underlying simplicity, and then trying to understand how that simplicity gives rise to the observed complexity. This pursuit is a continuation of an old intellectual belief that the appearances of the world do not tell its true nature, but that its true nature can be discovered by the application of thought and, in the case of science, experiment and observation.

The Greek philosopher Thales (625?–546 B.C.) suggested that all materials are made of water. This supposition was based on the observation that, in everyday experience, water appears as a solid (ice), a liquid, and a gas (water vapor). Thus, alone among the common substances, water seemed to exhibit all the states of matter (see Chapter 10). To Thales, this observation suggested that water was in some sense fundamental. We no longer accept the idea that water is the fundamental constituent of matter, but we do believe that we can find other fundamental constituents.

The Building Blocks of Matter

To many people, the library analogy presents a profoundly satisfying way of describing complex systems. Some would even argue that everything you could possibly want to know about the library is contained in letters and their organizing principles. In just the same way, scientists want to describe the complex universe by identifying the most fundamental building blocks and deduce the rules by which they are put together.

At first, you might say the most fundamental building block of the universe is the atom. All the myriad solids, liquids, and gases are made of just 100 or so different kinds of chemical elements. The complexity of materials that appears to the senses results from the many combinations of these relatively few kinds of atoms. The rules of chemistry tell us how atoms bind together to make all of the materials we see.

Early in the twentieth century, scientists learned that atoms are not really fundamental but are made up of smaller, more fundamental bits—nuclei and electrons. These particles arrange themselves according to their own set of rules, with massive neutrons and protons in the positively charged nucleus, and negatively charged electrons in shells around the nucleus. A picture of the universe with only three fundamental building blocks—protons, neutrons, and electrons—is very simple and appealing. Protons and

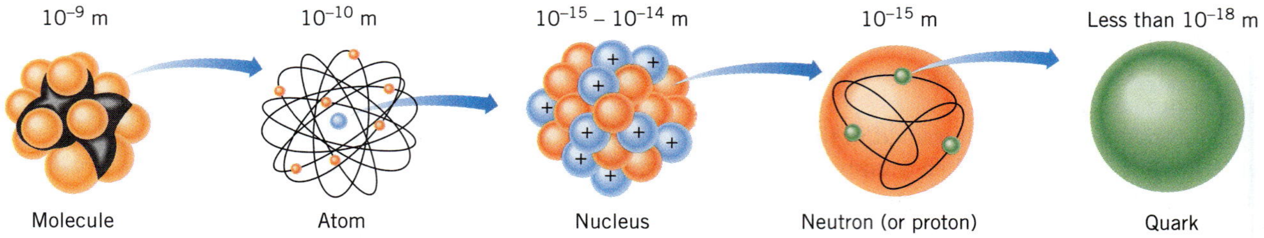

• **Figure 13-1** The modern picture of the fundamental building blocks of the universe. Molecules are made from atoms, which contain nuclei, which are made from elementary particles, which in turn are made from quarks. In some modern theories, the quarks are thought to be made from still more elementary objects called strings.

neutrons together form nuclei, and electrons surround the nucleus to form atoms. Electrons combine and interact with each other to form all the materials we know about.

But just as words and grammar gave us a false level of simplicity in the analogy of the library, this simple picture of the universe didn't stand up to more detailed experiments and observations. As we have hinted, the nucleus contains much more than just protons and neutrons, although this fact did not become clear to physicists until the post–World War II era. If we are going to follow the reductionist line in dealing with the universe, we have to start thinking about what makes up the nucleus. By common usage, the particles that make up the nucleus, together with particles such as the electron, were called *elementary particles* to reflect the belief that they comprised the basic building blocks of the universe (Figure 13-1). The study of these particles and their properties is the domain of a field known as **high-energy physics,** or **elementary-particle physics.**

Discovering Elementary Particles

Nowhere in nature is the equivalence of mass and energy more obvious than in the interactions of elementary particles. Imagine that you have a source of protons traveling at very high velocities, approaching the speed of light. This source might be astronomical in nature, or it might be a machine that accelerates particles. Once the proton has been accelerated, it has a very high kinetic energy. If this high-energy proton collides with a nucleus, the nucleus can be split apart. In this process, some kinetic energy of the original proton can be converted into mass according to the equation $E = mc^2$. When this happens, new kinds of particles that are neither protons nor neutrons can be created.

Cosmic Rays

During the 1930s and 1940s, physicists used a natural source of high-energy particles, so-called **cosmic rays,** to study the structure of matter. Cosmic rays are particles (mostly protons) that rain down continuously on Earth's atmosphere after being emitted by stars in our galaxy and in other galaxies.

Space is full of cosmic rays. When they hit the atmosphere, they collide with molecules of oxygen or nitrogen and produce sprays of very fast-moving secondary particles. These secondary particles, in turn, can make further collisions and produce even more particles, building up a cascade in the atmosphere. It is not uncommon for a single incoming particle to produce billions of secondary particles by the time the cascade reaches Earth's surface. Indeed, on average, several of these rays pass through your body every minute of your life.

Physicists in the 1930s and 1940s set up their apparatus on high mountaintops and observed what happened when fast-moving primary cosmic rays or slightly slower-moving secondary particles collided with nuclei. A typical apparatus incorporated a gas-filled chamber several centimeters across (Figure 13-2). Midway in the chamber was located a thin sheet of target material—lead, for example. Cosmic rays occasionally collided with one of the nuclei in the piece of lead, producing a spray of secondary particles. By studying particles in that spray, physicists hoped to understand what was going on inside the nucleus.

By the early 1940s, when the international effort in physics research shut down temporarily because of World War II, physicists working with these cosmic ray experiments had discovered particles in addition to the proton, neutron, and electron. And when the research effort started up again after the war, these discoveries multiplied as more and more particles were found in the debris of nuclear collisions, both by cosmic ray physicists and by those working at the new particle accelerators we will discuss shortly.

The net result of these discoveries was that the nucleus could no longer be considered as a simple bag of protons and neutrons. Instead, we had to think of the nucleus as a very dynamic place. All kinds of newly discovered elementary particles in addition to protons and neutrons were found there. These exotic particles are created in the interactions inside the nucleus, and they give up their energy (and, indeed, their very existence) in subsequent interactions to make other kinds of particles. This constant dance of the elementary particles inside the nucleus has been well documented since these early explorations.

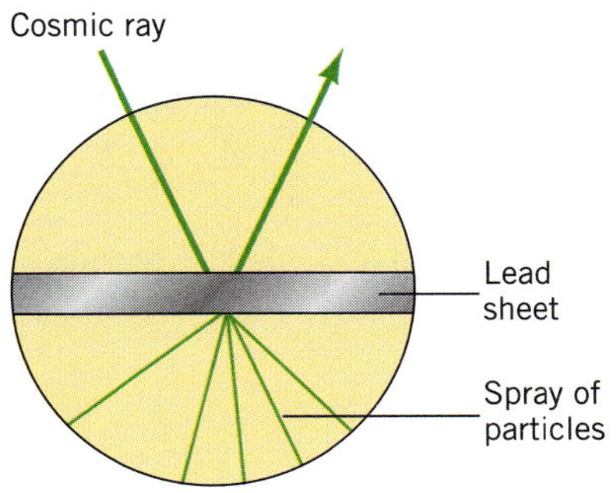

• **Figure 13-2** In a typical cosmic ray experiment, cosmic rays hit a lead nucleus, producing a spray of particles.

Technology •

Detecting Elementary Particles

If elementary particles are smaller even than an individual nucleus, how do we know they're there? Experimental physicists have raised detection of elementary particles to a fine art over the years. Nevertheless, the basic technique used in any detection process is the same: the particle in question interacts with matter in some way, and we measure the changes in matter that are the effects of that interaction.

If an elementary particle has an electrical charge, it may tear electrons loose as it goes by an atom. Thus a charged elementary particle moving through material such as a photographic emulsion will leave a string of ions in its wake, much as a speedboat going across a lake leaves a trail of troubled water.

A more modern detection method is to allow the particles to pass though a grid of thin conducting wires (usually made of gold). As a particle passes a wire, it exerts a force on the electrons in the metal, creating a small pulse of current. By measuring the time that this pulse arrives at the end of the wire, and by putting together such information from many wires, a computer can reconstruct the particle's path with high precision.

Uncharged particles such as neutrons are much more difficult to detect because they do not leave a string of ions in their path. Typically, the passage of an uncharged particle cannot be detected directly; instead, we wait until it collides with something. If that collision produces charged particles, then we can detect them by the techniques just outlined and can work backward and deduce the property of the uncharged particle. •

Particle Accelerators: The Essential Tool

For a time, physicists had to sit around and wait for nature to supply high-energy particles (in the form of cosmic rays) so that they could study the fundamental structure of matter. The arrival of cosmic rays could not be controlled, and it could be very time consuming waiting for one to hit. Physicists quickly realized that they had to build machines that could produce streams of "artificial cosmic rays"—**particle accelerators** that scientists could turn on and off at will and that would take the place of the sporadic cosmic rays in

Ernest O. Lawrence posed in the 1930s with his invention, the cyclotron, which was the first particle accelerator.

Courtesy Lawrence Berkeley Laboratory

experiments. At the beginning of the 1930s at the University of California at Berkeley, Ernest O. Lawrence began producing a new kind of accelerator called a *cyclotron,* an invention for which he won the 1939 Nobel Prize in physics.

The cyclotron works by applying an electrical force to groups of charged particles, usually electrons or protons, that are forced to move in circles by large magnets. At one point in their path, they encounter intense radio waves producing a large acceleration according to Newton's second law. (Force = mass × acceleration: see Chapter 2.) The radio waves are encountered over and over again, and the particles are accelerated almost to the speed of light. Once they have acquired this much kinetic energy, they are allowed to collide with other particles. Those collisions provide the interactions that scientists wish to study.

Lawrence's first cyclotron was no more than a dozen centimeters (about 5 inches) across and produced energies that were pretty puny by today's standards. A modern particle accelerator is a huge, high-tech structure capable of producing energies as high as all but the most energetic cosmic rays. Called a **synchrotron,** its main working part is a large ring of magnets that keep the accelerated particles moving in a circular track.

One aspect of Maxwell's equations that we didn't explore in detail in Chapter 5 is that magnetic fields exert a force on moving charged particles. That force tends to make charged particles move in a circular track. As a particle in a synchrotron moves around the circle, the large electromagnets are adjusted to keep its track within a small chamber (typically several centimeters on a side) in which a near-perfect vacuum has been produced. This chamber, in turn, is bent into the large circle that marks the particle's orbit. Each time the particles come around to a certain point, an electric field boosts their energy. As the velocity increases, the field strength in the magnets is also increased to compensate, so that the particles continue around the circular track. Eventually, the particles reach the desired speed, and they are brought out into an experimental area where they undergo collisions.

As the energy required to stay at the frontier of particle physics increases, so too does the size of accelerators. The highest-energy accelerator in the world today is at the Fermi National Accelerator Laboratory (Fermilab) outside of Chicago, Illinois. There, protons move around a ring almost 2 kilometers (about a mile) in diameter and achieve energies of a trillion volts. In 2007, the title "World's Largest Accelerator" will pass to the European Center for Nuclear Research (CERN) in Geneva, Switzerland. There, a large international consortium (including the United States) is building a machine called the Large Hadron Collider (LHC). Located in an underground tunnel 18 miles (27 km) around, this machine will produce proton beams of over 7 trillion volts. One interesting aspect of this machine is that the protons circling in it will pass the border between Switzerland and France twice on each circuit.

The four-story-high Fermilab CDF particle detector. Particle detectors have gone from being small, desktop pieces of apparatus to huge high-technology instruments like the one shown.

CERN/Science Photo Library/Photo Researchers

The **linear accelerator** provides an alternative strategy for making high-velocity particles. This device relies on a long, straight vacuum tube into which electrons are injected. The electronics are arranged so that an electromagnetic wave travels down the tube, and electrons ride this wave more or less the way a surfer rides a wave on the ocean. The largest linear accelerator

(a)

Courtesy Fermi National Accelerator Laboratory

Bill W. Marsh/Photo Researchers

(b)

(c)

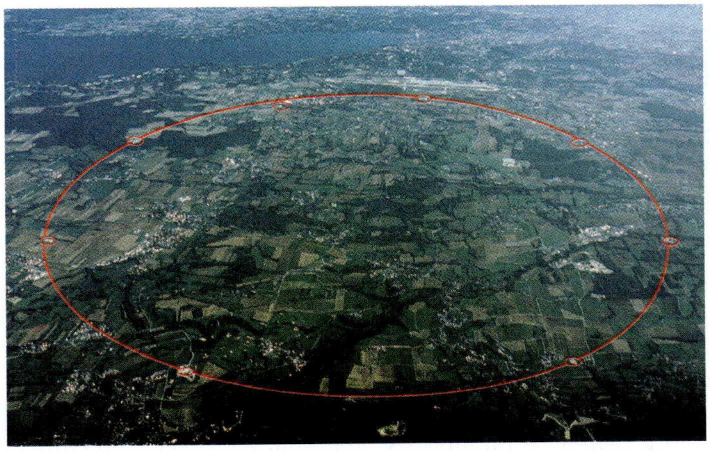

Courtesy CERN

Giant particle accelerators like these are the main working tool of particle physicists. We show Fermilab (*a*), the Stanford Linear Accelerator Center (*b*), and the new large Hadron Collider outside of Geneva, Switzerland (*c*).

in the world, at the Stanford Linear Accelerator Center in California, is about 3 kilometers (almost 2 miles) long.

The Science of Life •

Accelerators in Medicine

The ability to build machines that accelerate charged particles has had an important effect in many areas of medicine, most notably in the treatment of cancer. Often the goal of this treatment is to destroy malignant cells in tumors, and subjecting those cells to high-energy X-rays or gamma rays is a particularly effective way of doing this for some cancers.

To produce a beam of gamma rays for cancer therapy, a small accelerator produces an intense beam of high-speed electrons. These electrons are then directed into a block of heavy metal such as copper, where they are stopped abruptly. As we learned in Chapter 5, electrically charged objects that are accelerated (or, in this case, decelerated) emit electromagnetic waves. In the case of electrons accelerated to an appreciable fraction of the speed of light and suddenly stopped, those waves will be in the form of gamma rays. The direction of the electron beam is arranged so that the gamma rays pass through the tumor, killing cells as they pass through.

A form of cancer therapy still under development involves using beams of accelerated protons, which are allowed to hit a metal target and produce another kind of elementary particle called a pi-meson. When beams of pi-mesons enter tissue, the distance they travel depends on their energy. Thus the accelerator can be set so that the particle beam stops in the tumor itself, delivering large amounts of energy to a relatively small region. •

The Elementary Particle Zoo

At the beginning of the 1960s, the first generation of modern particle accelerators began to produce copious results, and the list of elementary particles known to reside inside the nucleus began to grow rapidly. The list now numbers in the hundreds. A few important groups of particles are summarized in the following sections and in Table 13-1.

Leptons

Leptons are elementary particles that do not participate in the strong force that holds the nucleus together, and they are not part of the nuclear maelstrom. We have encountered two leptons so far—the *electron,* which is normally found in orbit around the nucleus rather than in the nucleus itself, and the *neutrino,* a light neutral particle that hardly interacts with matter at all. Since the 1940s, physicists have discovered four additional kinds of leptons, for a total of six. If you keep in mind that the electron and the neutrino are typical leptons, you will have a pretty good idea of what they're like. The six leptons seem to be arranged in pairs—in each pair there are a particle like the electron, which has a mass, and a specific kind of neutrino.

Hadrons

All of the different kinds of particles that exist inside the nucleus are referred to collectively as **hadrons,** or "strongly interacting ones." The array of these particles is truly spectacular. Hadrons include particles that are stable like the proton, particles that undergo radioactive decay in a matter of minutes like the neutron (which undergoes beta decay), and still other particles that undergo radioactive decay in 10^{-24} seconds. The latter kind of particles do not live long enough even to travel across a single nucleus! Some hadrons carry an electrical charge, while others are neutral. But all of these particles are subject to the strong force, and all participate in holding the nucleus together; thus they help in making the physical universe possible.

Antimatter

For every particle that we see in the universe, it is possible to produce an antiparticle. Every particle of **antimatter** has the same mass as its matter twin, but the particles have opposite charge and opposite magnetic characteristics. The antiparticle of the electron, for example, is a positively charged particle known as the *positron.* It has the same mass as the electron but a positive electrical charge. Antinuclei, composed of antiprotons and antineutrons and orbited by positrons, can form antiatoms.

When a particle collides with its antiparticle, both masses are converted completely to energy in a process called *annihilation,* the most efficient and violent process that we

Table 13-1 Summary of Elementary Particles

Type	Definition	Examples
leptons	do not take part in holding together the nucleus	electron, neutrino
hadrons	participate in holding nucleus together	proton, neutron, roughly 200 others
antiparticles	particles with same mass, but opposite charge and other properties	positron

know in the universe. The original particles disappear, and this means that energy appears as a spray of rapidly moving particles and electromagnetic radiation. This fact has long been adopted by science fiction writers in their descriptions of futuristic weapons and power sources. (The starship *Enterprise* on *Star Trek,* for example, has matter and antimatter pods as its power source.)

Although antimatter is fairly rare in the universe, it is routinely produced in particle accelerators. High-energy protons or electrons strike nuclear targets, and the energy of the particles is converted to equal numbers of other particles and antiparticles. Thus the existence of antimatter is verified daily in laboratories.

Science in the Making •

The Discovery of Antimatter

In 1932, Carl Anderson, a young physicist at the California Institute of Technology, was performing a rather straightforward cosmic ray experiment of the type described in the text. Cosmic rays entered a type of detector called a cloud chamber. In Anderson's cloud chamber, a cosmic ray particle would move through a moisture-laden gas, leaving behind a string of ions. By pulling out a piston at the bottom of the chamber, the gas pressure was lowered, and the liquid (usually alcohol) that had been in gaseous form condensed out into droplets. The ions acted as nuclei for the condensation of these droplets, so that the path of the particle was marked by a string of droplets in the chamber.

The key innovation in Anderson's experiment was the positioning of the cloud chamber between the poles of powerful magnets. These magnets caused electrically charged cosmic rays to move in curved tracks, with the amount of curving dependent on the particle's mass, speed, and charge. Furthermore, the tracks of positively and negatively charged particles curved in opposite directions under the influence of the magnetic field.

Soon after he switched on his apparatus, Anderson saw tracks of particles whose mass seemed to be identical to that of the electron, but whose tracks curved in the opposite direction from those of electrons being detected (Figure 13-3). This feature, he concluded, had to be the result of a "positive electron," a phrase he contracted to positron. Although no one realized it at the time, Anderson was the first human being to see antimatter. •

• **Figure 13-3** Carl Anderson identified the positron (the antiparticle of the electron) from the distinctively curved path left in a bubble chamber. In Anderson's original photograph *(a)* the positron path curves upward and to the left. In a more recent photograph *(b)* an electron (e^-) and a positron (e^+) curve opposite directions in a magnetic field.

Courtesy California Institute of Technology

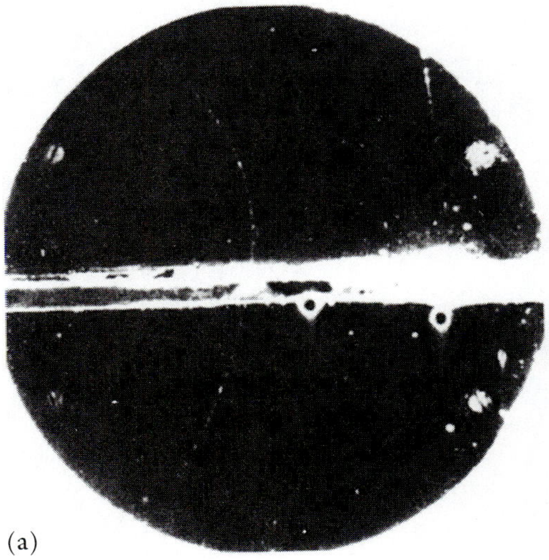

(a)

Courtesy Lawrence Berkeley Laboratory

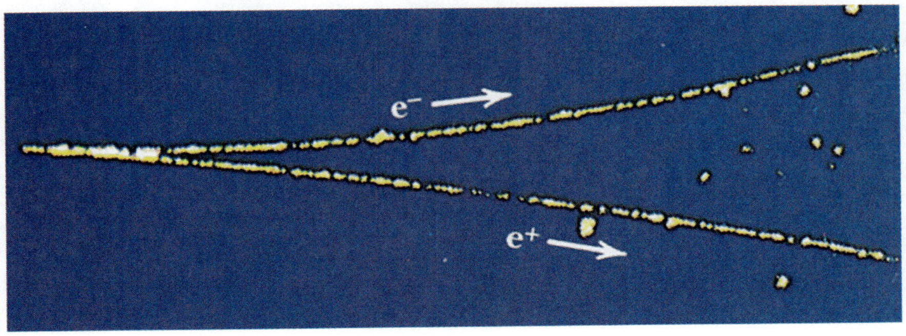

(b)

Stop and Think! How might Anderson have interpreted his results if he had seen tracks of particles curving the same direction as electrons, but curving a different amount? (*Hint:* Remember Newton's second law of motion.)

The Ongoing Process of Science •

How Does the Brain Work?

The study of elementary particles often seems quite abstract, but situations do arise where elementary particles play a very important role in understanding the real world. The fascinating technology of positron emission tomography (PET), for example, helps scientists probe the mysterious workings of the brain. In this medical technique, molecules such as glucose (see Chapter 22) that have been made using an unstable isotope of an element like oxygen (an isotope produced in nuclear reactors) are injected into a patient's bloodstream. Organs in the body, including the brain, take up these molecules. They will go to the parts of the brain that need it; the parts that require extra energy at the time (see Figure 13-4). Alternatively, they may be molecules shaped in such a way that they attach to specified spots on the cells in the brain (see Chapter 21).

The isotopes are chosen for this technique because they emit a positron, the antiparticle of an electron, when they decay. These positrons quickly annihilate with nearby electrons, emitting energetic gamma rays in the process. These gamma rays are relatively easy to detect from outside the body. A PET scan works like this: After the material is injected into the bloodstream, the patient is asked to do something—talk, read, do mathematical problems, or just relax. Each of these activities uses a different region of the brain. Scientists watching the emission of positrons can see those regions of the brain "light up" as they are used. In this way, scientists use antimatter to study the normal working of the human brain without disturbing the patient, as well as to detect and study abnormalities that can perhaps be treated. •

• **Figure 13-4** Positron emission tomography, commonly called the PET scan, reveals activity in the human brain. *(Left):* A patient undergoing a PET scan. *(Right):* A scan of a normal brain is seen at the top of the figure. The bright spots are places where large amounts of glucose (a simple sugar used by most cells for energy) are being used by the brain. The bottom half of the figure shows a scan of a person suffering from Alzheimer's disease.

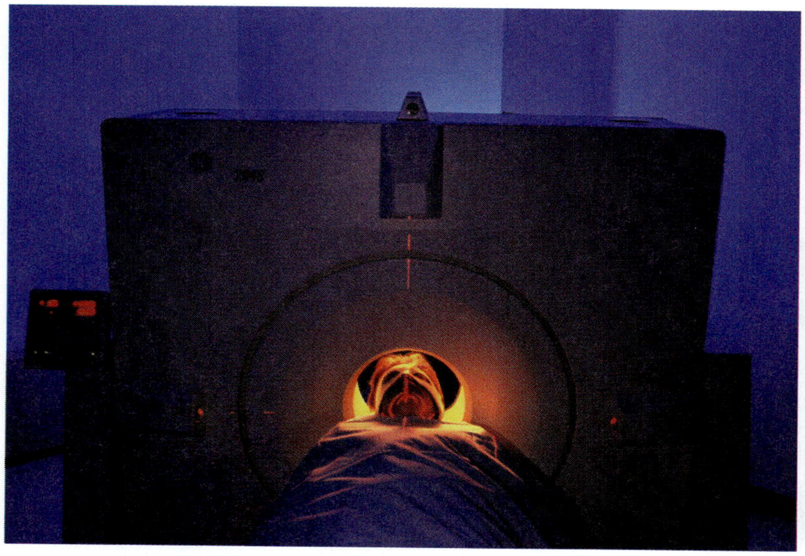

Hank Morgan/Photo Researchers

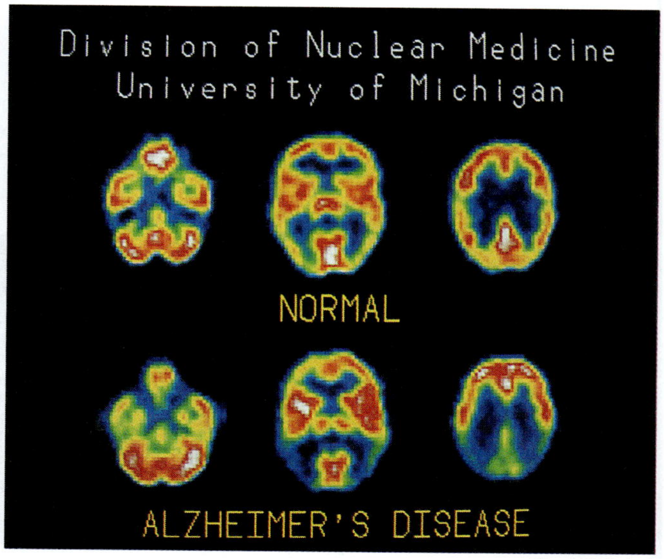

Visuals Unlimited

Quarks

When chemists understood that the chemical elements could be arranged in the periodic table, it wasn't long before they realized what caused this regularity. Different chemical elements were not "elementary," as Dalton had suggested, but were structures made up of things more elementary still. The same thing is true of the hundreds of elementary hadrons, or nuclear particles. They are not themselves elementary but are made up of units more elementary still—units that are given the name **quark** (pronounced "quork)". First suggested in the late 1960s, quarks have come to be accepted by physicists as *the* fundamental building blocks of hadrons. Even though they never have been (and probably cannot be) seen in the laboratory, the concept of quarks has brought order and predictability to the complex zoo of elementary particles. (It is important to remember that only hadrons, not leptons, are made from quarks.)

Quarks are different from other elementary particles in a number of ways. Unlike any other known particle, they have fractional electrical charge, equal to $\pm\frac{1}{3}$ or $\pm\frac{2}{3}$, the charge on the electron or proton. In this model of matter, quarks and antiquarks in pairs or triplets make up all the hadrons, but once they are locked into these particles, no amount of experimental machination will ever pry them loose. Quarks existed as free particles only briefly in the very first stages of the universe (see Chapter 15).

In spite of these strange properties, the quark picture of matter is a very appealing one. Why? Because instead of dealing with numerous hadrons, only six kinds of quarks (and six antiquarks) occur in the universe. The quarks, like many things in elementary-particle physics, have been given fanciful names: *up, down, strange, charm, top,* and *bottom* (see Table 13-2). We have seen elementary particles that contain all of these six. (Experimental confirmation of the top quark was announced in May 1994.)

Table 13-2 Quark Properties

Name of Quark	Symbol	Electrical Charge*
down	d	$-\frac{1}{3}$
up	u	$+\frac{2}{3}$
charm	s	$-\frac{1}{3}$
strange	c	$+\frac{2}{3}$
bottom	b	$-\frac{1}{3}$
top	t	$+\frac{2}{3}$

* Quarks with the same charge differ from each other in mass and other properties.

From these six simple particles, all of the hadrons that we know about—all those hundreds of particles that whiz around inside the nucleus—can be made. The proton, for example, is the combination of two up quarks and one down quark, while the neutron is the combination of two down quarks and one up quark. In this scheme, the charge on the proton, equal to the sum of the charges on its three quarks, is:

$$\frac{2}{3}+\frac{2}{3}+\left(-\frac{1}{3}\right)=+1$$

while the charge on the neutron is:

$$\frac{2}{3}+\left(-\frac{1}{3}\right)+\left(-\frac{1}{3}\right)=0$$

In the more exotic particles, pairs of quarks circle each other in orbit, like some impossible star system.

Quarks and Leptons

The quark model gives us a picture of the universe that restores the kind of simplicity that was brought by both Dalton's atoms and Rutherford's nucleus. All of the elementary particles in the nucleus are made from various combinations of six kinds of quarks. These elementary particles are then put together to make the nuclei of atoms. The six different leptons—primarily the electrons—are stationed outside the nucleus to make the complete atoms, and different atoms interact with each other to produce what we see in the universe. In this scheme, the quarks and leptons are the letters of the universe; they are the basic stuff from which everything else is made. The fact that there are six leptons and six quarks has not escaped the notice of physicists. This phenomenon is built into almost all theories of elementary particles. The question of *why* nature should be arranged this way remains unanswered.

Quark Confinement

It would be nice to be able to study individual quarks in the laboratory, and physicists have conducted extensive searches for them. Yet there has been no generally accepted experimental isolation of a quark, and many particle theorists suspect that quarks can never be pried loose from the particles in which they exist. In these theories, once a quark is taken up into a particle, it is "confined" in that particle forever.

Here's an analogy that may help you think about quark confinement. Suppose you cut a rubber band and then try to isolate just one end of it. (Think of the rubber band as being a particle and the very end of it as being the quark.) You could grab hold of the rubber band and pull it, perhaps even break it. You would then have two shorter rubber bands, but you would never have the end of a rubber band by itself. No matter how many times you broke the rubber band apart, you would get the same result. There just is no such thing as an "end" not attached to something else.

Elementary particles seem to be the same. You can hit them as hard as you like in an attempt to shake the quarks loose, but every time you start to pull out a quark, you've also supplied enough energy to the system to make more quarks and antiquarks, and those new particles will immediately be taken up into ordinary particles. If you hit one particle hard enough, you will wind up with lots of other elementary particles, the things that correspond to the short pieces of the rubber band in our analogy.

The Four Fundamental Forces

In our excursion into the library, finding the letters of the alphabet wasn't enough to explain what we saw. We had to know the rules of spelling and grammar by which letters are converted into words and then books. In the same way, if we are going to understand the fundamental nature of the universe, we have to understand not only the quarks and leptons, but also the forces that arrange them and make them behave the way they do.

One useful analogy is to think of the quarks and leptons as the bricks of the universe. The universe appears to be built of these two different kinds of bricks that are arranged in different ways to make everything we see. But you cannot build a house using bricks alone. There has to be something like mortar to hold the bricks together. The "mortar" of the universe—the things that hold the elementary particles together and organize the physical universe into the structures we know—are the forces. At the moment, we know of only four fundamental forces in nature. Two of these, *gravity* (Chapter 2) and *electromagnetism* (Chapter 5), were known to nineteenth-century physicists and are part of our everyday experience. They are forces with infinite range—that is, objects such as stars and planets can exert these forces on each other even though they are very far apart.

The other two forces are less familiar to us because they operate in the realm of the nucleus and the elementary particle. They have a range comparable to the size of the nucleus (or smaller) and hence play no role in our everyday experience. The *strong force* holds the nucleus together, while the *weak force* is responsible for processes such as beta decay (see Chapter 12) that tear nuclei and elementary particles apart.

Each of the four fundamental forces is different from the others in strength and range (see Table 13-3). The important point about the four forces is that whenever anything happens in the universe, whenever an object changes its motion, it happens because one or more of these forces is acting.

Table 13-3 The Four Forces

Force	Relative Strength*	Range	Gauge Particle
gravity	10^{-39}	infinite	graviton
electromagnetic	$\frac{1}{137}$	infinite	photon
strong force	1	10^{-13} cm	gluon
weak force	10^{-5}	10^{-15} cm	W and Z

* Relative to the strong force.

Force as an Exchange

We know that forces cause matter to accelerate—nothing happens without a force. We have talked about the gravitational force, the electromagnetic force, the strong force, and the weak force. Each has its own distinctive effects on nature. We have not, however, asked how these forces work.

The modern understanding of forces may be thought of schematically as illustrated in Figure 13-5. Every force between two particles corresponds to the exchange of a third kind of particle, called a *gauge particle* for historical reasons. That is, a first particle (an electron, for example) interacts with a second particle (say another electron) by the exchange of a gauge particle. The gauge particles produce the fundamental forces, such as electricity, that hold everything together.

In Chapter 2 we used the analogy of someone standing on skates throwing baseballs to explain Newton's third law of motion. Suppose a person on skates throws a baseball, and another person standing on skates catches the baseball some distance away. The person who threw the baseball would recoil, as we discussed. The person who subsequently caught the baseball would also recoil. We could describe the situation this way: Two people stand still before anything happens. After some time, the two people are moving away from each other. From Newton's first law, we conclude that a repulsive force had acted between those two people. Yet it's very clear in this analogy that that repulsive force is intimately connected with (a physicist would say "mediated by") the exchange of the baseball.

In just the same way, we believe that every fundamental force is mediated by the exchange of some kind of gauge particle (Figure 13-6). For example, the electrical force is mediated by the exchange of *photons.* That is, the magnet holding notes onto your refrigerator is exchanging huge numbers of photons with atoms inside the refrigerator metal to generate the magnetic force.

In the same way, the gravitational force is thought to be mediated by particles called *gravitons.* Right now you are exchanging large numbers of gravitons with Earth, an exchange that prevents you from floating up into space. The four fundamental forces and the gauge particles that are exchanged to generate each of them are listed in Table 13-3.

The two familiar forces of gravity and electromagnetism act over long distances because they are mediated by massless, uncharged particles (of which the familiar photon is one). The weak interaction, on the other hand, has a short range because it is mediated by the exchange of very massive particles—the W and Z *particles*—that have masses about 80 times that of the proton. Like the photon, the W and Z are particles that can be seen in the laboratory—they were first discovered in 1983 and are now routinely produced at accelerators around the world.

The situation with the strong force is a bit more complicated. The force that holds quarks together is mediated by particles called *gluons* (they "glue" the hadrons together). These particles are supposed to be massless, like the photon, but, like the quarks, they are confined to the interior of particles.

• **Figure 13-5** The exchange of a ball between two skaters provides an analogy for the exchange of a gauge particle. Skater *A,* who throws the ball, recoils, and skater *B* recoils when the ball reaches her. Thus both skaters change their state of motion, and, by Newton's first law, we say that a force acts between them.

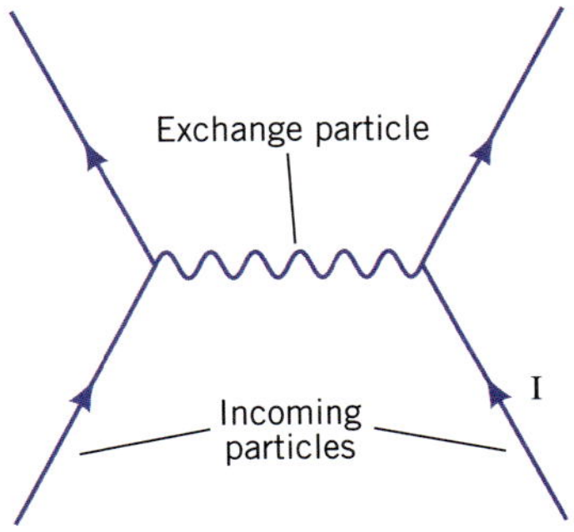

• **Figure 13-6** Exchange diagrams, introduced by physicist Richard Feynman, provide a model for particle interactions and the fundamental forces. Two incoming particles (such as two electrons) exchange a gauge particle (a photon) and thus are deflected by the force.

Unified Field Theories

Although a universe with six kinds of quarks, six kinds of leptons, and four kinds of forces may seem to be a relatively simple one, physicists have discovered an even greater underlying simplicity. The four fundamental forces turn out not to be as different from each other as their properties might at first suggest. The current thinking is that all four of these "fundamental" forces may simply be different aspects of a single underlying force.

Scientists suggest that the four forces appear to be different because we are observing them at a time when the universe has been around for a long time and is at a relatively low temperature. The situation is somewhat analogous to freezing water. When

Courtesy American Institute of Physics

Richard Feynman (1918–1988).

water freezes it can adopt many apparently different forms—powdered white snow, solid ice blocks, delicate hoarfrost on tree branches, or a slippery layer on the sidewalk. You might interpret these forms of frozen H_2O as very different things, and in some respects they are distinct. But heat them up, and they are all simply water.

Similarly, the four forces look different at the relatively low temperatures of our present existence, but heat matter up to trillions of degrees and the different forces are not really different at all. Theories in which fundamental forces are seen as different aspects of one force are called **unified field theories.**

The first unified field theory in history was Isaac Newton's synthesis of earthly gravity and the circular motions observed in the heavens. To medieval scientists, earthly and heavenly motions seemed as different as the strong and electromagnetic forces do to us. Nevertheless, they were unified in Newton's theory of universal gravitation. In the same way, scientists today are working to unify the four fundamental forces.

The general idea of these theories is that if the temperature can be raised high enough—that is, if enough energy can be pumped into an elementary particle—the underlying unity of the forces will become clear. At a few laboratories around the world, it is possible to take protons and antiprotons (or electrons and positrons), accelerate them to extremely high energies, and let them collide. (As we have noted, proton–antiproton collisions involve the process of annihilation between particle and antiparticle.) When these collisions occur, for a brief moment the temperature in the volume of space about the size of a proton is raised to temperatures that have not been seen in the universe since it was less than a second old. In the resulting maelstrom, particles are produced that can be accounted for only if the electromagnetic and weak forces become unified.

In 1983, experiments at the European Center for Nuclear Research and the Stanford Linear Accelerator Center demonstrated that this kind of unification does occur. When protons and antiprotons (at the former laboratory) or electrons and positrons (at the latter) were accelerated and allowed to collide head-on, W and Z particles were seen in the debris of the collisions. Not only were the reactions seen, but the properties of the resulting particles and their rates of production were exactly those predicted by the first unified field theories.

The expectations of today's physicists regarding the unification of forces can be illustrated in a simple flow diagram (Figure 13-7). Scientists have already seen the unification of the electromagnetic and weak force in their laboratories. The resulting force, which physicists call the *electroweak force,* will be studied in great detail by the next generation of particle accelerators. At much higher energies, energies that will probably never be attained in Earth-based laboratories, we expect the strong force to unify with the electroweak. The theories that make this prediction constitute the *standard model*—the best model we have today of the elementary particles. Physicists have accumulated a fair amount of experimental evidence supporting the standard model.

• **Figure 13-7** The four forces become unified at extremely high temperatures, equivalent to those at the beginning of the universe. At 10^{-43} second after the moment of creation, the universe had already cooled sufficiently for gravity to have separated from the other three forces. The strong force separated at 10^{-33} second, while the weak and electromagnetic forces separated at 10^{-10} second.

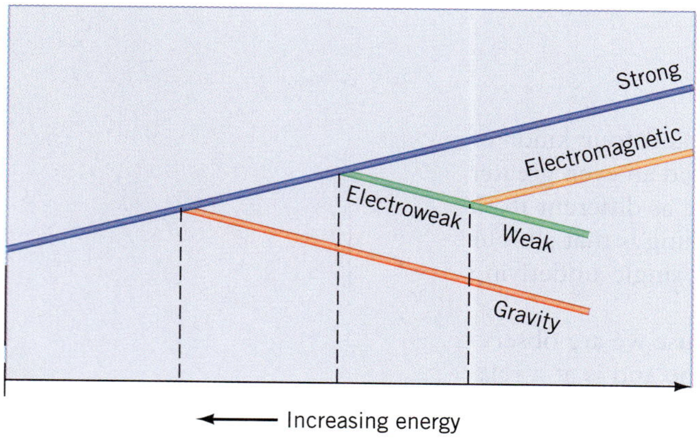

Finally, at still higher energies, we hope to see the force of gravity unify with the strong electroweak force. No theory yet describes this unification successfully, and attempts to develop a successful model are very much a frontier issue. Scientists have, only half in jest, started to refer to theories that combine all four forces as TOEs—*theories of everything.*

The unification of the four forces has no obvious effect on our everyday world because it requires such exotic high-energy conditions to see it happen. Nevertheless, the unification of forces played a crucial role in the formation of the universe. Much of our understanding of what the universe is and how it came to be in its present state (Chapter 15) revolves around the various kinds of unification of the forces of nature.

String Theories

The best candidates for TOE these days are called **string theories.** Basically, they picture the smallest building blocks of matter as tiny vibrating strings. Just as different kinds of vibrations in a violin string produce different frequencies of sound, and therefore have different energies, different vibrations of these fundamental strings produce particles of different mass. Both quarks and leptons are thought to be different aspects of vibrating strings.

One unusual aspect of these theories is that the strings are not like ordinary strings that exist in a three-dimensional world. In order to make the theories mathematically consistent, it turns out that these particular strings have to vibrate in 11 or more dimensions (don't try to picture this—it's not possible). One way to think about the question of how our ordinary four-dimensional world (three space dimensions plus time) could arise from a world in which the fundamental materials have many more dimensions is to consider a simple analogy. If you look at an ordinary garden hose close up, you see it as a three-dimensional object. There is the length of the hose, which is basically a two-dimensional line, and there is the roundness of the hose, which can be thought of as a third dimension. If you look at the same hose from far away, however, you don't see that third dimension—all you see are the two dimensions that describe the length of the hose. In just the same way, scientists argue, when we look at an 11-dimensional world from the human viewpoint, all the dimensions but 4 are basically invisible, and we have to get down inside the elementary particles before we see them.

String theories turn out to be very difficult to work out because of the technical mathematics involved, and they have not yet been developed to the point where they can make predictions that can be tested by experiment. Nevertheless, they may be our best hope at the moment for filling in the next step in the reductionist dream.

Science News | Smashing Success

(Science News, Feb. 4, 2006, p. 68)

The particle accelerator remains our primary tool for investigating the fundamental structure of matter, and the machine called the Tevatron, located at the Fermi National Accelerator Laboratory outside of Chicago, remains the world's highest energy machine. (The name comes from the fact that the machine accelerates protons to one Terravolt, or one million million volts). In the Tevatron, protons are accelerated in one ring while antiprotons are accelerated in another. Bunches of both kinds of particles are accelerated to almost the speed of light in each ring and are then allowed to collide. In these incredibly high-energy impacts, scientists seek to discover the secrets of the material universe.

A common problem in such experiments is that the antiproton beam tends to spread out as it travels around the ring, and this makes collisions less likely when the beams cross paths. This is a serious issue because the events that scientists want to study are rare, so anything that lowers the collision rate makes experiments that much harder to do.

Now workers at Fermilab have successfully tested a clever technique that has already increased the collision rate in their beams by 50% and is expected to double it in the near future. Their technique is simple to describe. In a separate machine, electrons are accelerated to exactly the same speed as the antiprotons in the main ring. The speeding electrons are then injected into the antiproton bunches. The two kinds of particles start colliding with each other as they move along, and because the electrons are much lighter than the antiprotons, energy tends to get transferred to them in these collisions. The net effect is to "cool" the antiprotons, so that engineers can pack more of these particles into each bunch. The more antiprotons there are, the more collisions, and the more collisions the more data.

Because of this new technique (which is already being copied at other accelerators worldwide), scientists hope that the Tevatron may solve many of the outstanding problems in particle physics—problems that have eluded solution for decades.

A final note: During the 1970s, one of the authors (J.T.) worked at Fermilab while the precursor to the Tevatron was being built and was therefore happy to hear that the machine still has a bright future.

Thinking More About | Particle Physics

Basic Research in Particle Theory

One aspect of research in elementary particle physics should be obvious from our description of the current generation of particle accelerators—it is expensive. The cost of the giant machines needed to probe into the heart of matter runs into billions of dollars, and this creates problems. In 1993, for example, the United States Congress terminated a project called the Superconducting Supercollider, a machine even bigger than the Large Hadron Collider (LHC). At the time, the machine was under construction south of Dallas and had a price tag of over $10 billion.

Are projects of this magnitude justified? Some people argue that with all the problems in the world—hunger, poverty, terrorism—it makes no sense to spend large amounts of money on machines that will produce no immediate benefit, or whose benefits may be far off.

On the other hand, others point out that in the past, money spent on apparently useless basic research has resulted in huge benefits to humanity. The development of the theory of electromagnetism in the nineteenth century and quantum mechanics in the twentieth, for example, have both changed the human condition for the better. It's hard to put a price tag on something like the ability to generate electricity or to process information in a computer. Basic research has always paid off big in the past, they argue, so we should support it now.

How much money do you think the federal government should spend on research like this, whose benefits may be a generation in the future? What percentage of your tax dollars would you be willing to allocate to this task?

Summary

High-energy physics, or *elementary-particle physics,* deals with bits of matter that we cannot see, and forces and energies that we can barely imagine. Nevertheless, the study of the subatomic world holds the key to understanding the structure and organization of the universe.

All matter is made up of atoms, which are made up of even smaller particles—electrons and the nucleus—but these are not the most fundamental building blocks of the universe. Physicists originally examined collisions between energetic *cosmic rays* and nuclei to study elementary particles. They now employ *particle accelerators,* including *synchrotrons* and *linear accelerators,* to collide charged particles at near-light speeds. These scientists have discovered hundreds of subatomic particles.

One class of particles, the *leptons* (including the electron and neutrino) are not subject to the strong force and thus do not participate in holding the nucleus together. Nuclear particles called *hadrons* (including the proton and neutron), according to present theories, are made from *quarks*—odd particles that have fractional electrical charge and cannot exist alone in nature. Together, leptons and quarks are the most fundamental building blocks of matter that we know. Each of these particles has an *antimatter* particle, such as the positron, the positively charged antiparticle of the electron.

The four known forces—gravity, electromagnetism, the strong force, and the weak force—cause particle interactions that lead to all of the organized structures we see in the universe. Particle interactions are mediated by the exchange of gauge particles, with a different gauge particle for each of the different forces. Two masses, for example, will exchange gravitons (the gauge particle of gravity) as they attract each other, and two charged particles will exchange photons, much the same way that two skaters will be "repelled" by each other if a mass is thrown (exchanged) from one to the other.

While the four known forces appear to us to be quite different from each other, scientists speculate that early in the universe, when temperatures were extremely high, the four forces were unified into a single force. At the forefront of modern physics research is the search for a *unified field theory* that describes this single force. *String theories,* the most prominent type of unified field theory, envision quarks as made of fundamental units called strings.

Key Terms

high-energy physics, or elementary-particle physics
cosmic rays
particle accelerator
synchrotron
linear accelerator
leptons
hadrons
antimatter
quarks
unified field theory
string theories

Review Questions

1. How is the search for elementary particles an example of reductionism? Why is reductionism appealing?
2. What are the building blocks of a library? Why is there more than one correct answer?
3. What is a synchrotron? (Is there a synchrotron at a laboratory near you?)
4. How do scientists detect the presence of subatomic particles?
5. Why are leptons, such as electrons and neutrinos, said to be weakly interacting particles?
6. Why are there so many different kinds of hadrons but only a few kinds of leptons? Are hadrons or leptons more elementary?
7. What is antimatter, and how do we know it exists?
8. How do quarks differ from other elementary particles? Is there any way to prove that quarks exist?
9. Describe how quarks and leptons are put together to make all the matter we see.
10. Explain what it means for quarks to be confined.
11. List the four fundamental forces from strongest to weakest.
12. What particle is exchanged to generate each of the four fundamental forces?
13. What is a unified field theory? Give an example.
14. What is a PET scan? How does it employ elementary particles?
15. Why is "big science" needed in the study of elementary particles?

Discussion Questions

1. Identify what might be considered the "fundamental units" and rules of organization of (a) a large city, (b) the human body, and (c) a family. How many levels of organization can you identify? (Remember, not all questions have only one correct answer.)
2. Which particle–antiparticle interaction releases more energy: an electron–positron annihilation or a proton–antiproton annihilation? How does the law of conservation of energy come into play?
3. How old is the search for the basic bulding blocks of nature? How do the ideas from antiquity foreshadow modern particle physics? How are they different from modern ideas?
4. Why is a universe made up of only six types of quarks more appealing to physicists than one built from hundreds of hadrons?
5. Describe Carl Anderson's experiment and the observations that led him to conclude that he had discovered a particle with the same mass as the electron, but with a positive electrical charge?
6. In theory, when were the four fundamental forces unified? What does it mean to say that all four fundamental forces were unified?
7. How might you detect the presence of a charged elementary particle?
8. How will we know when we have identified the truly fundamental building blocks?
9. Why are unified field theories called Theories of Everything (TOEs)?

Problems

1. What is the electrical charge of an antiproton? an antineutron? Why?
2. What is the electrical charge of a positron? How does this particle differ from a proton?
3. A hadron called the lambda particle is made from two down quarks and one strange quark. What is the charge of the lambda particle?
4. A particle called the pi-meson is made from an up quark and an antidown quark. What is the charge of this particle?

Investigations

1. Read Michael Riorden's book, *The Hunting of the Quark*. How does the discovery of quarks illustrate the scientific method? What experimental evidence convinced scientists of the existence of quarks?
2. Locate the nearest PET-scan facility and arrange a visit. Where do the physicians obtain the special form of glucose used in the procedure? What kind of educational training would you need to operate such a facility?
3. Watch an episode of *Star Trek* and discuss the use of matter and antimatter in the propulsion system of the *Enterprise*. Can you find any other uses of antimatter in science fiction stories?
4. What does it mean that the fundamental building blocks of the universe are things we can never isolate and study? Does that mean they aren't real? You might want to think about the question of the reality of atoms (see Chapter 8) for a historical precedent to this situation.
5. Investigate the philosophies of Thales and Democritus. What questions did they seek to answer? Has modern science answered the questions that they posed?
6. What does the term *Gestalt* mean? Investigate the philosophical arguments against reductionism in science. How might these arguments be answered by a modern scientist or modern philosopher? How has reductionism benefited humankind?
7. In what ways has modern physics improved our ability to study and understand our behavior and our brains? Investigate the underlying physics of fMRI, MRI, EEP, and PET technologies.

14

The Stars

How much longer can the Sun sustain life on Earth?

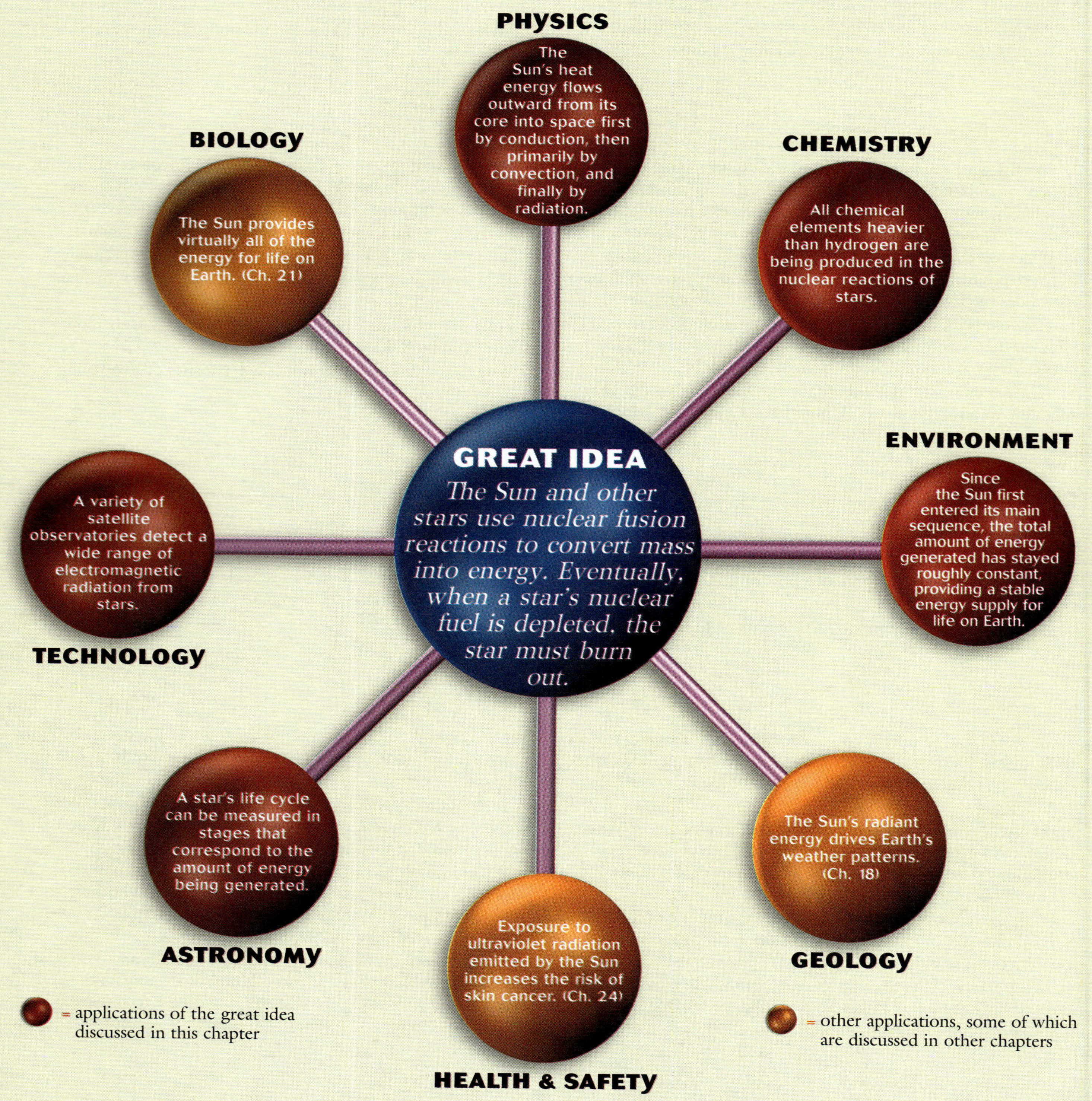

Science Through the Day | Sunshine

The glaring Sun blazes down with midday brilliance. You make sure to use sunblock before stretching out on the beach towel. It's hot, but that's the way it's supposed to be at the beach. And the cooling ocean is just a few steps away.

What is the Sun—this distant glowing object that gives our planet light and warmth? Is the Sun unique? Has it always graced Earth's sky? Will it ever stop shining?

Ben Hall/The Image Bank/Getty Images

The Nature of Stars

Astronomy, the study of objects in the heavens, is perhaps the oldest science. When you examine the night sky, the most striking feature is the thousands of visible stars. Each **star** is an immense fusion reactor in space—a large ball of gas, consisting mostly of hydrogen and helium, which are the two most abundant elements in the universe. Every star is held together by gravity, and every star radiates energy that is generated via nuclear fusion. The Sun, the nearest star to Earth, is just one of countless trillions of stars in our universe.

You have already learned enough about the way the universe works to understand some of the implications of your nighttime view of the stars. The fact that you can see the stars, for example, means that they are emitting electromagnetic radiation in the form of photons (see Chapter 6). Every star you see sends this radiant energy into space—energy that provides the essential data for all astronomers. Your eye intercepts a tiny fraction of that energy and converts it into the image you see, but similar amounts of energy radiate out in every direction from the star.

The laws of nature, including the laws of thermodynamics that describe the behavior of energy, apply everywhere in the universe. If a star sends radiant energy out into space, then the star must have a source of that energy. Furthermore, because every star is a finite object, it must have a finite store of energy. This simple observation leads to perhaps one of the most profound insights about the universe.

All stars have a beginning and an ending.

In other words, the magnificent display that we see in the nighttime sky is a temporary phenomenon. It has lasted from the time that stars first formed until the present, a span of about 13 billion years. However, the view we see in the heavens will not last

Thousands of stars are visible in the night sky.

Jim Ballard/Stone/Getty Images

forever. Each star will eventually run out of energy. Before we look at the life cycle of stars, it's worth examining the kinds of data that astronomers use to understand the history and dynamic processes of stars.

Measuring the Stars with Telescopes and Satellites

Our primary source of data on distant stars is electromagnetic radiation—energy in the form of photons streaming through space at 3×10^8 meters per second. The art and science of astronomy lies in the collection, analysis, and interpretation of these data. Most astronomers spend their lives measuring four aspects of photons from space:

1. Their wavelength, which is measured by spectroscopy
2. Their intensity, which is measured by a device like a light meter
3. Their direction, which is measured by recording two angles—one up from the horizon (called the altitude), and the other around from north (called the azimuth)
4. The variations of these wavelengths, intensities, and positions with time

These data, in turn, enable astronomers to understand many aspects of stars, including their distribution in space, their physical characteristics such as mass and composition, and their histories and future behavior. For example, astronomers find that many stars possess spectra that are virtually identical to that of the Sun. The fact that the intensity of light from these stars is many orders of magnitude weaker than the Sun indicates that they are very far away.

Telescopes

To collect and analyze radio waves, microwaves, light, and other radiation, astronomers have devised a variety of **telescopes,** which are devices that focus and concentrate radiation from distant objects.

The first telescopes could examine only visible light, and when most people use the word "telescope" today, they mean an instrument for gathering and concentrating this form of radiation. The classic reflecting telescope (see Figure 14-1*a*) has a large mirror that reflects and focuses light to produce an image of the object being studied. (See Chapter 6 for a review of the reflection and refraction of light.)

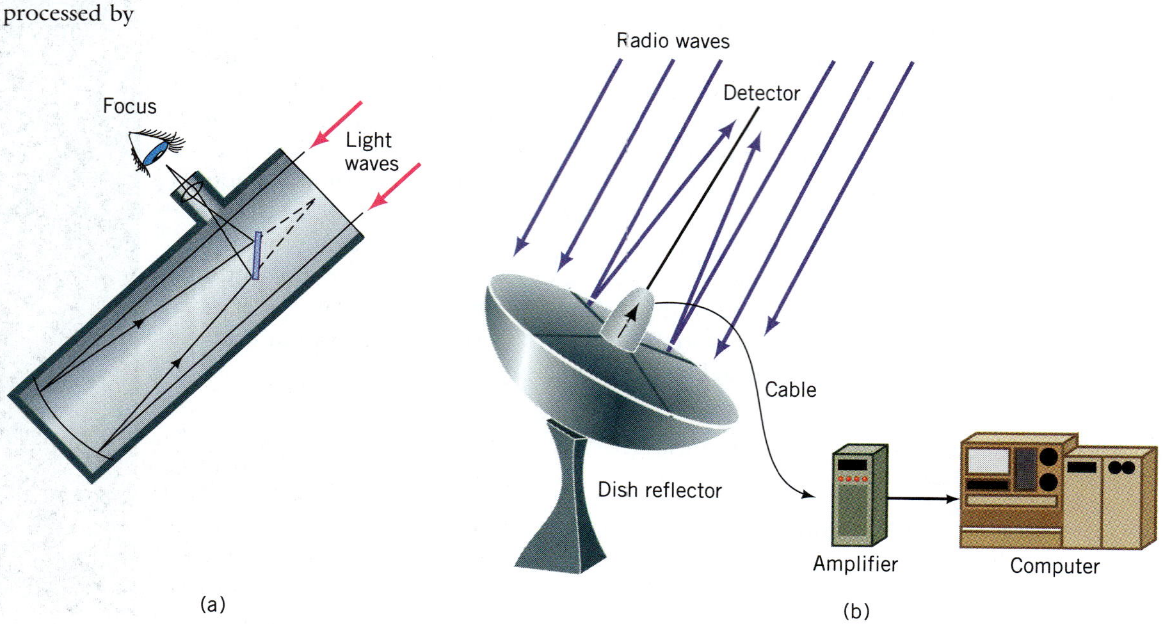

• **Figure 14-1** Schematic diagrams of telescopes. In an optical telescope *(a),* light strikes a curved mirror and is focused on a light-sensitive detector such as the eye or a piece of film. In a radio telescope *(b),* radio waves from space strike a curved metal dish that focuses the waves onto an antenna. Signals are amplified and processed by computer.

Many modern light-gathering telescopes are built differently. Instead of having a solid block of glass for a mirror, they have an array of small, independently controlled, lightweight mirrors that, taken together, produce an image. The Keck telescope on Mauna Kea in Hawaii, the biggest of these new-age instruments with a collection of more than a dozen mirrors, together forming a reflective surface about 10 meters (30 feet) in diameter, was put into operation in 1992. Other factors being equal, the larger the telescope, the more useful it will be, because it will be able to collect more photons and thus detect fainter objects.

David Nunuk/Photo Researchers

The Keck Telescopes in Hawaii are the world's largest.

In the 1930s, astronomers built radio receivers that did for radio waves what the reflecting telescope did for light waves (see Figure 14-1*b*). For the first time, they could look at another kind of electromagnetic radiation. Today, large radio telescope facilities can be found all around the world.

Orbiting Observatories

Except for visible light and radio waves, Earth's atmosphere is largely opaque to the electromagnetic spectrum. Most infrared and all ultraviolet radiation, short-wavelength microwaves, X-rays, and gamma rays entering the top of the atmosphere are absorbed long before they can reach instruments at the surface. The use of satellite observatories during the last half of the twentieth century has ushered in a golden age of astronomy. In this period, we have been able to put instruments into orbit far above the atmosphere and, for the first time, record and analyze the entire flood of electromagnetic radiation coming to us from the cosmos. *NASA* (the *National Aeronautic and Space Administration*) is in the process of creating a fleet of observatories high above atmosphere that will allow astronomers to probe every part of the electromagnetic spectrum. A description of some components of this "Great Observatories" program follows.

- *Hubble Space Telescope (HST)*. Launched in 1990, HST is a reflecting telescope with a 2.4-meter mirror designed to give unparalleled resolution in the visible and ultraviolet wavelengths. Despite a troubled beginning, the HST has proven to be one of the greatest scientific instruments in history. The HST was designed so that astronauts in the Space Shuttle could visit it periodically and install updated equipment, most recently in 2002. Thus, although the telescope has been in orbit for over a decade, it continues to be the premier astronomical instrument in the world. Some HST accomplishments are photographs of the comet Shoemaker-Levy hitting Jupiter in 1994, detection of the most distant supernovae and most distant quasars (1997), and accurate determination of the Hubble constant (2001).
- *Spitzer Infrared Space Telescope*. Launched in 2003, this orbiting observatory surveys the infrared radiation coming to Earth from objects in space. Because everything radiates in the infrared, the telescope has to be cooled in a bath of liquid helium to keep it from

The Very Large Array in Socorro, New Mexico, features a Y-shaped arrangement of linked radio telescopes. The effect of many small telescopes is equivalent to one very large telescope.

Larry Mulvehill/Photo Researchers

The Hubble Space Telescope.

Courtesy NASA

"seeing" itself. This telescope sees the cool objects in the universe—clouds of dust around new stars, for example.

- *Chandra X-Ray Observatory.* Launched in 1999, the Chandra produces high-resolution X-ray images of objects in the sky. Its orbit carries it high above the belts of charged particles that surround Earth, giving it a clear view of the X-ray sky. It is named for the Indian-American astrophysicist Subramanian Chandrasekar, the first scientist to understand the final stages in the lives of stars like the Sun.

The Anatomy of Stars

Astronomical observations reveal that stars are much more than uniform balls of gas. They have a complex and dynamic interior structure that is constantly changing and evolving. The Sun is the only star that is near Earth, and thus it's the only star for which we have the kind of detailed knowledge that allows us to talk about how the various parts function. In this sense, the Sun is not only the giver of life on our planet, but also the giver of knowledge.

The Structure of the Sun

Based on comparisons with literally millions of other more distant stars, the Sun appears to be a rather ordinary star. While we can't peer into the Sun's center, theorists have learned to apply the principles of nuclear reactions to model processes deep inside stars. At its center is the stellar core, comprising about 10% of the Sun's total volume. This core is the Sun's furnace, where nuclear reactions rage, and energy generated in the core streams out from the center. Deep within the Sun, this energy transfer takes place largely through collisions of high-energy particles—gamma rays and X-rays, for example—that are generated by the core's nuclear reactions. About four-fifths of the way out, however, the energy-transfer mechanism changes, and the hydrogen-rich material in the Sun begins to undergo large-scale convection. This outer region, comprising the turbulent upper 200,000 kilometers (about 125,000 miles) of the Sun, is called the *convection zone.* Thus energy is brought from the core to the surface in a stepwise process, first by collisions, then by convection.

The surface of the Sun, showing hot material following magnetic field lines.

Courtesy NASA

The only part of the Sun that we actually see is a thin outer layer. We can observe perhaps 150 kilometers (about 100 miles) into the Sun; any deeper and the stellar material becomes too dense to be transparent. The outer part of the Sun, the part that actually emits most of the light we see, is called the *photosphere.* The Sun does not have a sharp outer boundary, but gradually becomes thinner and thinner farther away

• **Figure 14-2** The Sun's chromosphere and corona become visible during a total eclipse. This halo of incandescent plasma is normally blotted out by light from the Sun's main disk.

from the surface. These gaseous layers are not usually visible from Earth. During a total eclipse of the Sun, however, when the Moon passes in front of the Sun, the Sun's spectacular halo, called the *chromosphere* and the *corona,* may become visible for a few minutes (Figure 14-2).

The Sun constantly emits a stream of particles—mainly ions (electrically charged atoms) of hydrogen and helium—into space around it. This stream of particles, called the **solar wind,** blows by Earth and the other planets all the time. Because the particles are charged, they affect the magnetic fields of the planets, compressing the fields on the "upstream" side and dragging them out on the "downstream" side (Figure 14-3). The interaction of the solar wind with the outer reaches of Earth's atmosphere also gives rise to the aurora borealis, or northern lights.

The flow of energy from the Sun is a complex affair. Beginning with the conversion of mass in fusion reactions, the energy slowly percolates outward, first in collisions and later in great convection cells under the solar surface. It takes a few tens of thousands of years for the energy to work its way to the photosphere, but only eight minutes for photons to cover the distance between the Sun and Earth.

Once the sunlight reaches our planet, a tiny fraction of it is converted by the process of photosynthesis in plants into chemical energy stored in large molecules (see Chapter 21). This is the primary source of energy for most living things on the planet. Another fraction of the energy in sunlight heats the air at the equator and, as we shall see in Chapter 18, drives Earth's weather patterns.

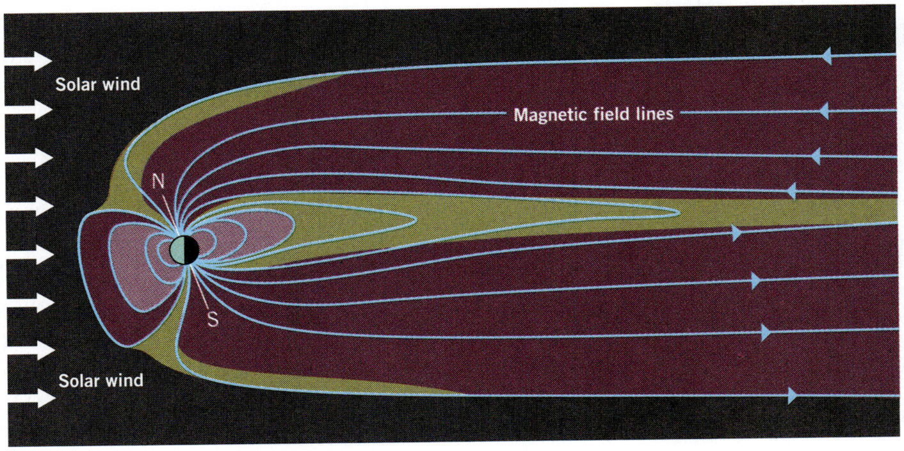

• **Figure 14-3** Earth's magnetic field is swept out into a long tail by the solar wind.

George Lepp/Stone/Getty Images

Northern lights result from interactions of the solar wind with Earth's magnetic field.

The Science of Life •

Why Is the Visible Spectrum Visible?

In Chapter 5 we saw that, of all the possible waves in the electromagnetic spectrum, the human eye can detect only the small interval of wavelengths between red and violet. One reason why the human eye is made this way was discussed in Chapter 5—Earth's atmosphere is transparent to these wavelengths, so it is possible for the waves to travel long distances through the air. But there is another aspect to the development of the human eye that has to do not with Earth, but with the Sun. Because of the fusion reactions at its core, the temperature of the outer part of the Sun is quite high, about 5500°C (for reference, gold melts at about 1065°C). Every object above absolute zero radiates electromagnetic waves, and both the total amount of energy and the wavelengths of the radiation depend on the body's temperature.

In Figure 14-4, we show the amount of energy that the Sun radiates at each wavelength, with the visible spectrum represented by the vertical lines. We see that the Sun's peak output of energy is in the middle of the visible spectrum. Thus the wavelengths between red and violet are visible for two reasons—the air is transparent to them, and the Sun, our main source of light, emits the greatest proportion of its energy in that form.

Science fiction writers often use this fact when they portray imaginary beings from other planets. Those from planets around cooler stars than the Sun may be given large eyes so they can absorb more of the scarcer photons. For the reasons we have cited, however, humans don't require such large optical collectors. •

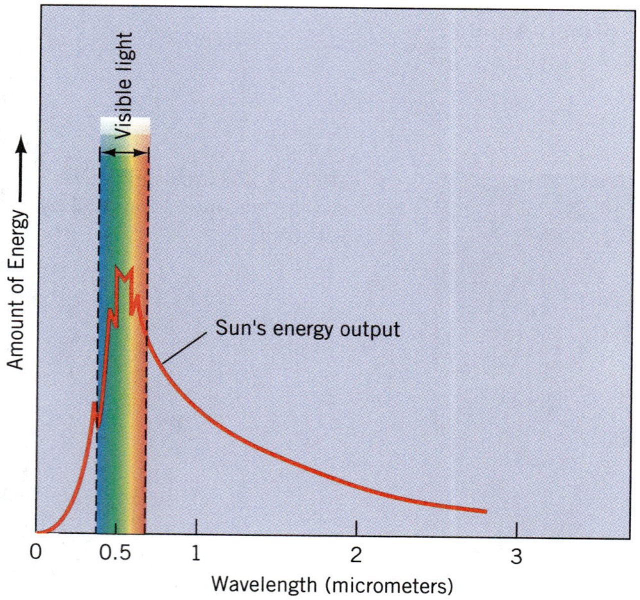

• **Figure 14-4** The Sun's peak output of energy is in the middle of the visible spectrum, with lesser amounts of energy emission at different wavelengths.

The Sun's Energy Source: Fusion

Once people came to understand conservation of energy—that energy has to come from somewhere, and that the total amount of energy in a closed system is constant—two key questions about the stars arose naturally: What is their energy source? How can they continue to burn, emitting huge amounts of energy into space, yet remain seemingly unchanged for such long periods of time?

In the nineteenth century, several scholars attempted to explain the Sun's energy source. One astronomer, for example, calculated how long the Sun could burn if it were composed entirely of the best fuel available at that time—anthracite coal. (The answer turns out to be about 10,000 years.) The Sun's energy source also figured in the famous debate at the end of the nineteenth century regarding Earth's age (see Chapter 3).

Today, we understand that the Sun is indeed using a fuel but that fuel is hydrogen, which is consumed through nuclear fusion reactions (see Chapter 12). Stars are made primarily of the element hydrogen, the most common material in the universe. As a star forms, gravity pulls the hydrogen into a dense ball that heats up. Electrons are torn from the hydrogen and other atoms, creating a plasma made up primarily of protons (the nucleus of the hydrogen atom) and electrons.

Normally, protons would repel each other (see Chapter 5). As matter accumulates in the new star, however, the protons move faster as the temperature increases. Eventually, they acquire enough energy to overcome the electrical repulsion between them. They start to fuse.

The nuclear fusion process in the Sun's core does not take place all at once, with four particles suddenly coming together to make a helium-4 nucleus. Instead, it takes place in three steps.

$$\text{Step 1: } P + P \rightarrow D + e^+ + \text{neutrino} + \text{energy}$$

Two protons *(P)* come together to form a deuterium nucleus (*D*, the isotope hydrogen-2, made up of one proton and one neutron), a positron (e^+, the antiparticle of the electron as described in Chapter 13), and a neutrino.

$$\text{Step 2: } D + P \rightarrow {}^3\text{He} + \text{photon} + \text{energy}$$

Another proton collides with the deuterium produced in the first step to form the isotope helium-3, which has two protons and one neutron in its nucleus. A photon in the form of an energetic gamma ray is also produced.

$$\text{Step 3: } {}^3\text{He} + {}^3\text{He} \rightarrow {}^4\text{He} + 2 \text{ protons} + \text{photon} + \text{energy}$$

Two helium-3 nuclei collide to form helium-4, two protons, and a photon (another gamma ray).

This three-step fusion process is called *hydrogen burning* (though these nuclear reactions *are not* the same as the chemical reactions that we commonly call burning). The net effect of this process is that four protons are converted into a helium-4 nucleus with a few extra particles thrown in. As we saw in Chapter 12, the sum of the masses of all the particles produced in this reaction amounts to *less* than the mass of the original four protons. The lost mass has been converted into energy—the nuclear energy that powers the Sun and eventually radiates out into space.

How long could the Sun consume hydrogen at its present rate? If you simply add up all the hydrogen in the Sun and ask how long it could last, the answer turns out to be something like 75 billion years. Actually, no star ever consumes all of its hydrogen in this way. The hydrogen burning process is generally confined to a small region in the center of the star called the core. The best current estimate of the total lifetime of our Sun is about 11 billion years—that is, our star is almost halfway through its hydrogen-burning phase.

Stop and Think! Why do you suppose fusion proceeds in a stepwise manner, rather than having four protons come together all at once?

The Ongoing Process of Science •

The Solar Neutrino Problem

Our explanation of the Sun's energy source is a theory—a very plausible one—that is subject to experimental verification. In fact, a great deal of observational evidence

©AP/Wide World Photos

Scientists inspect the Super Kamiokande neutrino detector in Japan.

supports the notion that hydrogen-burning reactions account for the Sun's energy. One crucial piece of evidence, however, seemed to indicate that we might not have known as much about the interior of the Sun as we'd like to think. Beginning in the early 1970s, a large experiment located a mile underground in a gold mine in Lead, South Dakota, has been returning results that were puzzling, to say the least.

The idea behind this experiment is that, as we have just seen, nuclear fusion reactions in the Sun's core produce neutrinos. Most of these neutrinos escape from the Sun without being absorbed or changed, and arrive at Earth unchanged. Most of them will pass through Earth as well, but occasionally one will interact with an atom in the apparatus of this experiment, so that it can be detected. Thus the experiment provides us with a "telescope" that can "see" right down to the center of the Sun. If we believe we know what reactions are going on there, we should be able to predict how many neutrinos should be seen.

When these measurements were taken, scientists saw only about one-third to one-half of the number of neutrinos they had expected to see. Other experiments of this type, run in Europe, the former Soviet Union, and Japan, bore out this result. Explaining the missing one-half to two-thirds of the expected neutrinos was known as the "solar neutrino problem."

One possible explanation of the solar neutrino problem was tied to the nature of elementary particles such as neutrinos, and the fact that there are three different kinds of neutrinos. According to this idea, the predicted number of ordinary neutrinos (or electron neutrinos) is produced in the Sun, but while they're in transit to Earth, some of them are converted into the two other kinds of neutrinos (the ones associated with the mu and tau particles). Such transitions between neutrino types are possible in some versions of modern unified field theories. In this way, by the time the neutrino stream reaches Earth, only a fraction of the original particles would be ordinary neutrinos capable of interacting with ordinary atoms in an experimental apparatus.

In 2001, results from a new observatory located in an old nickel mine in Sudbury, Ontario, Canada, gave a spectacular confirmation of this idea, and solved the solar neutrino problem once and for all. This detector contains 8000 tons of pure water, and, at its core, another 1000 tons of what is called "heavy water"—water in which one hydrogen atom contains an extra neutron in its nucleus. That extra neutron can undergo interactions only with electron neutrinos, while all three kinds of neutrinos can scatter from ordinary water. Thus, by comparing reaction rates in the two parts of the detector, scientists were able to show that, by the time they reach Earth, roughly two-thirds of the neutrinos that leave the Sun have been converted into something other than electron neutrinos. •

Technology •

Dyson Spheres, an Ultimate Technology

Sometimes it's fun to speculate about how an extremely advanced technological civilization would use the energy from a star. One approach to the question is to note that most of the energy generated by stars is radiated into space and, from the point of view of planet dwellers, wasted. Physicist Freeman Dyson has suggested that one way to avoid this energy loss would be to dismantle a large planet and convert its material into a sphere surrounding a star—a hypothetical structure now called a Dyson sphere. A Dyson sphere would not only intercept and utilize all of a star's energy, it also could support a tremendous population. Such an immense structure would have an internal surface area comparable to more than 500 million Earth-like planets, and it would be uniformly heated in eternal daylight.

A star enclosed in a Dyson sphere would radiate its energy in the visible and higher energies, as usual, but all that energy would be absorbed by the sphere, which would then be warmed and radiate the energy into space as infrared radiation. •

The Variety of Stars

Knowing how one star, our own Sun, works should help us understand the variety of other stars we see. When you look at the stars in the night sky, one of the first things you notice is that they don't all look the same. For example, some stars appear reddish, while others are almost blue. Your everyday experience with flames provides a simple explanation: different stars must be at different temperatures. Very hot flames, such as a gas burner, emit a greater percentage of high-energy blue photons; cooler fires feature lower-energy orange and red photons.

Stars also differ in their brightness; some appear as brilliant points of light, while others are barely visible. Differences in brightness arise from two factors—distance and energy output. Brightness varies in part because the stars are different distances from Earth. An unusually bright star located far away will appear dim to us, while an average star located nearby might appear relatively bright. The brightness of a star is also related to the amount of energy it is producing. Astronomers often refer to the total energy emitted by a star as its *luminosity.* These differences in a star's appearance are taken into account by distinguishing between a star's *apparent brightness,* which is the brightness it appears to have when viewed from Earth, and its *absolute brightness,* which is the brightness it would have if viewed from a standard distance.

Much of the differences in the stars' appearances arise from the many varieties of stars themselves. Some stars shine a thousand times brighter than the Sun, while others are a thousand times dimmer. Some stars contain 40 times more mass than the Sun, while others have much less. As we shall see, we can bring order to this tremendous diversity of stars by recognizing that the behavior of every star depends primarily on just two factors: its total mass, and its age.

The Astronomical Distance Scale

When we look at the sky, we see a two-dimensional display—all stars look equally distant. Before characterizing the different varieties of stars, we need to add the third dimension, to determine their distances. Only then can we relate apparent brightness (what we see from Earth) to absolute brightness (the luminosity or energy output of the star). Astronomers customarily measure these great distances in **light-years,** which is the distance light travels in one year, or about 10 trillion kilometers (about 6.2 trillion miles).

In practice, no single method can be used to find the distance to every star. Just as you might use a ruler, a tape measure, and a surveyor's tape to measure successively larger distances, astronomers measure distances to stars with a series of "yardsticks," each appropriate to a particular distance scale.

For short distances (up to a few hundred light-years), several different methods involving simple geometry can be used. For nearby stars, the angle of sight to the star measured at opposite ends of Earth's orbit (Figure 14-5) can be used to work out the distance. For centuries, navigators on Earth's surface have used a similar method, called *triangulation,* to determine the position of ships.

For greater distances, a standard type of star called a *Cepheid variable* is used. These stars, the first of which was discovered in the constellation of Cepheus, show a regular behavior of steady brightening and dimming over a period of weeks or months. Henrietta Leavitt (1868–1921) of Harvard College Observatory showed that the absolute magnitude of these stars is related to the time it takes for them to go through the dimming–brightening–dimming sequence. Thus we can watch a Cepheid variable for a while and deduce how much energy it is pouring into space. This measurement, together with knowledge of how much energy we actually receive, tells us how far away it is.

• **Figure 14-5** The triangulation of stellar distances. By measuring the angle of sight to a given star from two points of known separation, we can determine the star's distance from us.

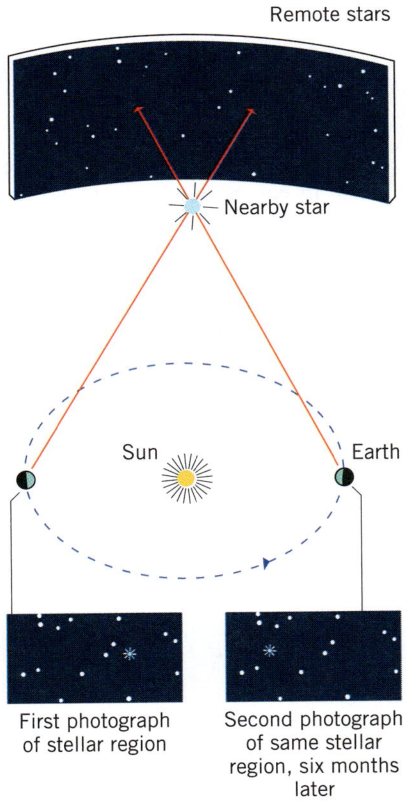

Courtesy Harvard College Observatory

Annie Jump Cannon *(left)* and Henrietta Swan Leavitt *(right)* contributed important studies of the spectroscopy of stars at the Harvard College Observatory.

The method of Cepheid variables can be used to measure distances of many millions of light-years. As we shall see in Chapter 15, it was a crucial ingredient in the birth of modern cosmology.

The Cepheid variable scale is an example of what astronomers call a "standard candle." The idea is that if you know how much energy an object is giving off, and compare that with how much energy you are actually receiving, you can figure out how far away from you the object is. The development of other kinds of standard candles is a major thrust of modern research.

The Hertzsprung-Russell Diagram

Early in this century, two astronomers, Ejnar Hertzsprung of Denmark and Henry N. Russell of the United States, independently discovered a way to find order among the diversity of stars. The product of their work, called the *Hertzsprung-Russell (H-R) diagram,* is a simple graphical technique widely used in astronomy. It works like this: On a graph's vertical axis, astronomers plot the amount of energy given off by a star, as measured by estimating the star's distance and brightness. On the graph's horizontal axis, they plot the star's surface temperature, as determined by its color, or spectrum (see Chapter 6). Each star has its own characteristic combination of energy and temperature, and so it appears as a single point on the Hertzsprung-Russell diagram. The Sun, for example, is one of the points highlighted in Figure 14-6.

When stars are plotted this way, the majority (the ones like the Sun) fall on a band that stretches from the upper left to the lower right in the diagram. That is, most stars conform to a trend from very hot stars emitting lots of energy, down to relatively cool stars emitting less energy. Objects in this grouping are called **main-sequence stars.** All of these stars are in the hydrogen-burning phase of their lives, and their energy is produced in the fusion reactions that we described earlier in this chapter.

Two additional clumpings of stars appear in the H-R diagram. One clumping, in the upper-right corner, corresponds to stars that emit a lot of energy but whose surfaces are very cool. These stars must be very large—many times the size of our Sun—so that the low temperature (and thus the low-energy emission of each square foot of surface area)

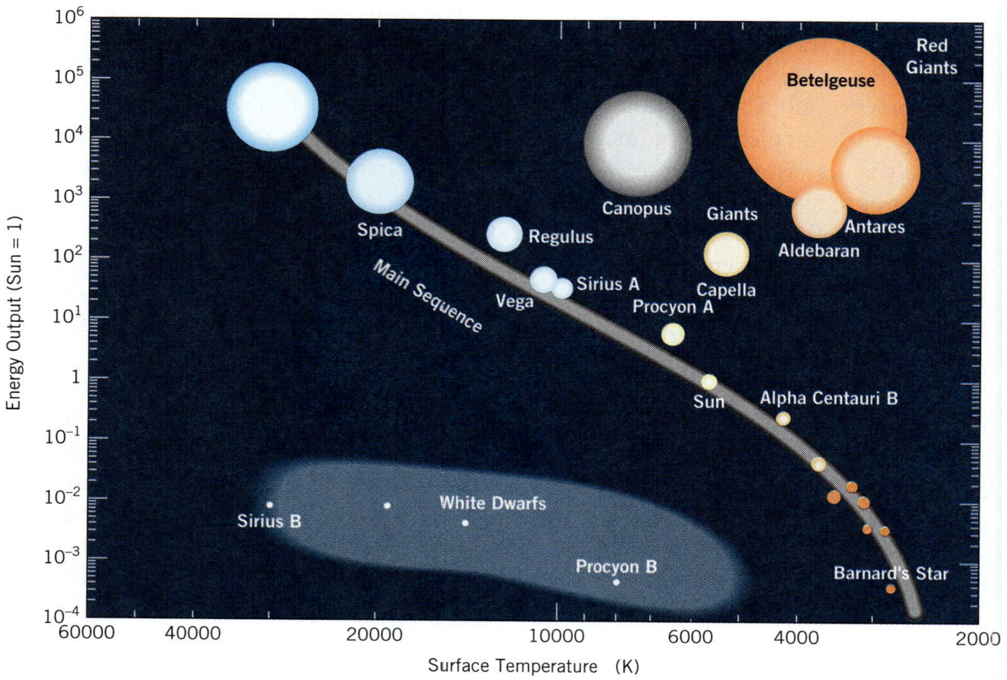

• **Figure 14-6** A Hertzsprung-Russell diagram plots a star's temperature versus its energy output. Stars in the hydrogen-burning stage, including the Sun, lie along the main sequence, while red giants and white dwarfs represent subsequent stages of stellar life.

is compensated by the large surface area. Stars of this type are called **red giants,** and they often do appear somewhat reddish in the sky.

Another grouping of stars appears in the lower-left corner of the H-R diagram. These stars, called **white dwarfs,** have very low emission of energy but very high surface temperatures. Consequently, white dwarf stars must be very small—typically about the size of Earth. Both red giants and white dwarfs play crucial roles in the life cycles of stars, as we shall see shortly.

The Life Cycles of Stars

Every star passes through a cycle that includes formation from dust and gas, a period of nuclear fusion, and an end to nuclear reactions. As we shall see, the duration and violence of that cycle depend almost entirely on the initial mass of the star.

The Birth of Stars

All stars are born in the depths of space, in clouds of gases and other debris. The modern theory of star and planet formation was first put forward by the French mathematician and physicist Pierre Simon Laplace (1749–1827). His was a simple idea that takes into account many of the distinctive characteristics of our solar system, which contains both the Sun and planets (see Chapter 16). According to the model, called the ***nebular hypothesis,*** long ago (about 4.5 billion years ago based on radiometric dating) a large cloud of dust and gas collected in the region now occupied by the solar system. Such dust and gas clouds, called **nebulae,** are common throughout our galaxy, the Milky Way. They typically contain more than 99% hydrogen and helium, with lesser amounts of all the other naturally occurring elements.

Courtesy NASA

The Eagle Nebula, a birthplace of stars.

Under the influence of gravity, a nebula slowly, inexorably, collapses on itself. This collapse causes the cloud to spin faster and faster. The rapid spin means that some of the material in the outer parts of the nebula begins to spin out into a flat disk. This common consequence of fast rotation is familiar to anyone who has watched a pizza maker create a flat disk of dough by spinning a mass overhead. You can imagine a nebula at this stage of its formation as a large pancake with a big lump in the middle. The big lump represents material that eventually will become a star, and the material in the thin flattened disk eventually will become the planets and the rest of the solar system (Figure 14-7). As a new star begins to form, and as more and more mass pours into it from the surrounding region of the nebula, the pressure and temperature at the center of the proto-star begins to climb.

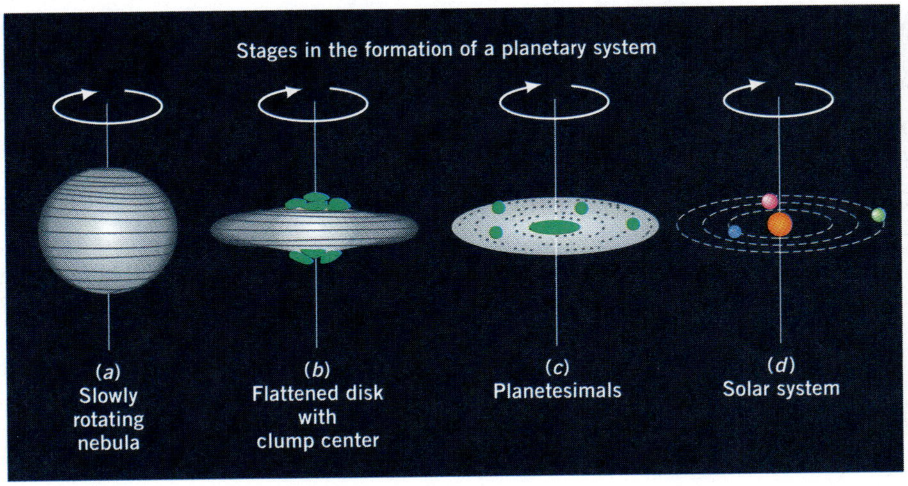

• **Figure 14-7** As the nebula that formed the Solar System collapsed, it began to rotate and flatten into a disk. The stages in solar system formation include *(a)* a slowly rotating nebula, *(b)* a flattened disk with massive center, *(c)* planets in the process of birth represented as mass concentrations in the nebula, and *(d)* the solar system.

Once this central mass achieves a critical size, the pressure and temperature deep inside will become high enough to initiate nuclear fusion reactions. At that moment, a star is born.

The Main Sequence and the Death of Stars

Every star begins as an immense ball of hydrogen and helium, formed by the gravitational collapse of a nebula. The ultimate fate of any given star, however, depends on the total mass of hydrogen and helium. The Hertzsprung-Russell diagram provides the key to understanding the very different fates of stars.

Stars Much Less Massive Than the Sun

All stars begin their lives in the hydrogen burning stage—the stage represented by main-sequence stars on the Hertzsprung-Russell diagram. If a star is much less massive than the Sun—perhaps only 10% of the Sun's mass—it will be just barely large enough to begin hydrogen burning in a slow and fitful way. Such a small star, called a *brown dwarf,* shines faintly compared to the Sun, with surface temperatures of only a few thousand degrees. Nuclear fusion proceeds relatively slowly, so such a star will continue to glow steadily for a hundred billion years without any significant change in size, temperature, or energy output.

Stars About the Mass of the Sun

The Sun and other stars of similar mass enjoy a more central position on the Herzsprung-Russell main sequence (Figure 14-8, position 1). The greater mass of the Sun, relative to brown dwarf stars, means that core temperatures and pressures are much higher and hydrogen burning proceeds at a much faster rate. Consequently, the Sun has a higher surface temperature, and it completes its hydrogen-burning phase much more quickly—in a matter of a few billion years.

• **Figure 14-8** The life cycle of the Sun on a Hertzsprung-Russell diagram. The Sun started hydrogen burning in its core more than 4.5 billion years ago on the main sequence (at point 1), and it will remain near that point on the diagram for several billion years more. As the hydrogen in the core is consumed, however, a short period of helium burning (point 2) will move the Sun's position on the diagram rapidly upward toward the red giant stage (point 3). Once the helium is consumed, the nuclear fusion reactions will cease and gravitational collapse will cause the Sun to heat up (point 4). Eventually, the Sun will cool to a white dwarf (point 5).

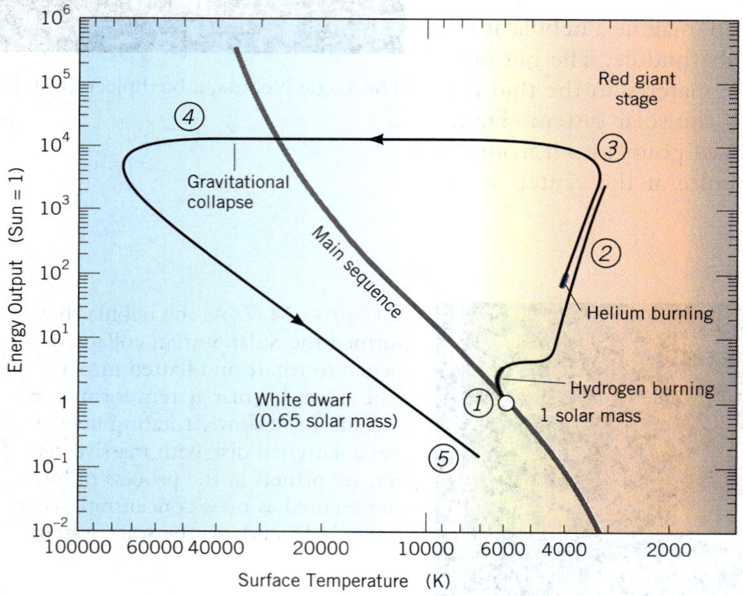

One way to look at the life of a star like the Sun is to think of it as a continual battle against the force of gravity. From the moment when the Sun's original gas cloud started to contract, the force of gravity acted on every particle, forcing it inward and trying to make the entire structure collapse on itself. When the nuclear fires ignited in the core of the Sun 4.5 billion years ago, gravity was held at bay. The increase in temperature in the center raised the pressure in the star's interior and balanced the inward pull of gravity. But in the long view of things, this balance can be only a temporary state of affairs. The Sun can stave off the inward tug of gravity only as long as it has hydrogen to consume. When hydrogen fuel in the core is depleted, the amount of energy generated in the core will decrease, and gravity will begin to take over. The Sun will begin to contract and heat up.

This dramatic situation will have two effects. First, the temperature in the region immediately surrounding the core will begin to rise. Any remaining hydrogen in that region, which had not been consumed because it had been at too low a temperature, will begin to undergo nuclear fusion reactions. Thus a hydrogen-burning shell will begin to form around the extinguished core. The second effect is that the temperature in the core will rise until helium, the "ash" of hydrogen burning, will begin to undergo nuclear fusion reactions. The net reaction will be

$$^{4}He + {}^{4}He + {}^{4}He \rightarrow {}^{12}C + \text{energy}$$

a process called *helium burning,* in which the helium in the core undergoes nuclear fusion reactions to make carbon. The Sun will then resemble an onion, with a helium-burning core surrounded by a layer where hydrogen is being fused. At this stage the Sun will begin to move off of the main sequence (Figure 14-8, position 2).

This notion that the "ashes" of one nuclear fusion process serve as fuel for the next fusion process is central to an understanding of what goes on in stars. In stars like the Sun, the temperature never gets high enough to initiate fusion of the carbon, so helium burning is the final energy-producing stage. In more massive stars, this process of successive nuclear fusion cycles can go on for quite a while, as we shall see.

The Sun will maintain more or less its present size and temperature for billions of years more. Since it first entered the main sequence 4.5 billion years ago, for example, the amount of energy generated by the Sun has increased by only about 30%. This long-term stability has important implications for the development of life on this planet. But in its final stages, our star will undergo dramatic changes. When the core consumes all of its nuclear fuel, the hydrogen-burning shells surrounding the central region will be pulled in. This temporary collapse will increase the amount of energy generated by fusion, and the increased energy will cause the surface of the Sun to balloon out. At its maximum expansion, the dying Sun will extend out past the orbit of Venus. Because the solar wind will also increase during this period, however, the Sun's mass will drop and the planets will move outward. In the end, only Mercury will be swallowed up. During this phase of its life, the Sun will emit almost 10,000 times more energy than it does today, but it will do so through a much larger surface. Consequently, that surface will appear to be very cool—red hot to our eyes. In fact, our Sun will become a red giant, and the helium in the Sun's core will undergo nuclear fusion reactions to produce an inner core primarily of carbon (Figure 14-8, position 3).

As carbon accumulates in the core, a slow collapse will ensue until some other force intervenes. In the case of the Sun, that force will come from the Pauli principle—the principle (see Chapter 8) that tells us that no two electrons can occupy the same state. As the core starts to collapse, its electrons will be compressed into a smaller and smaller volume. For a time the Sun will continue to emit prodigious amounts of energy through a shrinking surface that reaches temperatures in excess of 70,000 degrees (Figure 14-8, position 4). Ultimately, the electrons will reach the point (what we called the "full parking lot" in Chapter 8) where they can no longer be pushed together. At this point, the Pauli principle will take over, and the collapse will stop for the simple reason that the electrons can't be pushed together any closer than they already are. A permanent outward force will be exerted on every element in the star—an outward force that will cancel the inward force of gravity.

When the Sun reaches this stage, it will be rather small—probably about the size of Earth (though still hundreds of thousands of times more massive than Earth)—and it will no longer be generating energy through nuclear reactions. It will be very hot and will take a long time to cool off. During this phase, the temperature of each part of the Sun's surface will be very high, but, because the Sun will be so small, the total amount of radiation coming from it will not be very large. It will be, in other words, a white dwarf (Figure 14-8, position 5). Most of the carbon that is the end product of helium burning will remain locked in the white dwarf and will not be returned to the cosmos.

Stars up to five or six times the mass of the Sun will follow approximately the same path on the H-R diagram (Figure 14-8). Such stars will have different lifetimes; one of the paradoxes of astronomy is that larger stars—those with the most hydrogen fuel—have the shortest lifetimes. This paradox arises because the largest stars have to burn hydrogen at a prodigious rate in order to overcome the intense force of gravity. Thus a star four times as massive as the Sun will complete its cycle in a relatively short time—less than a billion years—compared to the Sun's 11-billion-year span. But all of these stars will have essentially the same life history: main sequence → red giant → white dwarf.

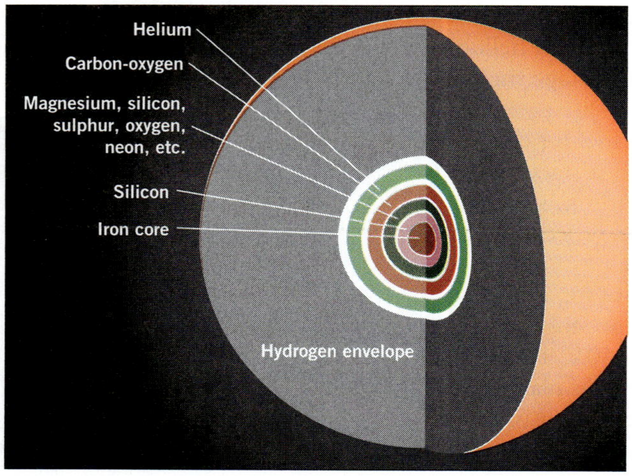

• **Figure 14-9** The interior of a large star displays concentric shells of fusion reactions, yielding progressively heavier elements toward the core.

Very Large Stars

Stars more than 10 times as massive as the Sun end their lives quite differently, in explosions of unimaginable power. For these stars, the pressure exerted by gravity is high enough so that the helium in the core not only burns to carbon, but the carbon can also undergo fusion reactions to produce oxygen, magnesium, silicon, and other larger nuclei. For such a star, the successive collapses and burnings will produce a layered, onion-like structure such as that shown in Figure 14-9.

In fact, in the largest stars this chain of nuclear burning goes on until iron, the element with 26 protons, is produced. As we noted in Chapter 12, iron is the most tightly bound nucleus. The addition of energy is required to break the iron nucleus apart (nuclear fission) and to add more protons and neutrons to it (nuclear fusion). Thus it is impossible to extract energy from iron by any kind of nuclear reaction.

The cores of large stars will eventually fill up with iron "ash," and, no matter how high the pressure and temperature get, iron simply will not burn to produce a countervailing force to gravity. In fact, the iron core builds up until the force of gravity becomes so great that even the pressure of the electrons pushing for elbow room cannot prevent collapse. At the incredible pressures and temperatures at the center of the star, the electrons actually combine with protons inside the iron nuclei, forming neutrons, a process that is the exact opposite of radioactive beta decay (see Chapter 12). Within a second or so all of the protons in the iron nuclei are turned into neutrons, and all of the electrons disappear. At this point, the core of the star begins a catastrophic collapse. The collapse will go on until another force appears on the scene to counteract gravity. In this case, the force is provided by the degeneracy pressure of the neutrons, which, like electrons, are subject to the Pauli exclusion principle.

The core collapses so fast that it falls inward beyond the point where the degeneracy pressure of the neutrons can balance gravity. Like an acrobat jumping on a trampoline, the star's falling matter first bounces inward and then rebounds as the neutrons exert a counter pressure. Meanwhile, the outer gaseous envelope of the star has suddenly lost its support and begins a free-fall toward the interior of the star. When the collapsing envelope of dense gas meets the rebounding core of neutrons, intense shock waves are set up in the star, and the entire outer part of the star literally explodes. From a distance the star suddenly appears to brighten in the sky, usually in a matter of a day or so. We call this dramatic event a **supernova.**

During the explosion, intense shock waves tear back and forth across the exploding star, raising the temperature enough to form all of the chemical elements in the periodic table. In a complex set of collisions, some of the nuclei up to iron that have been created by the successive fusion reactions soak up neutrons and undergo beta decay (see Chapter 12) to form nuclei up to uranium and beyond. All elements beyond iron are created in the short-lived maelstrom of the supernova explosion.

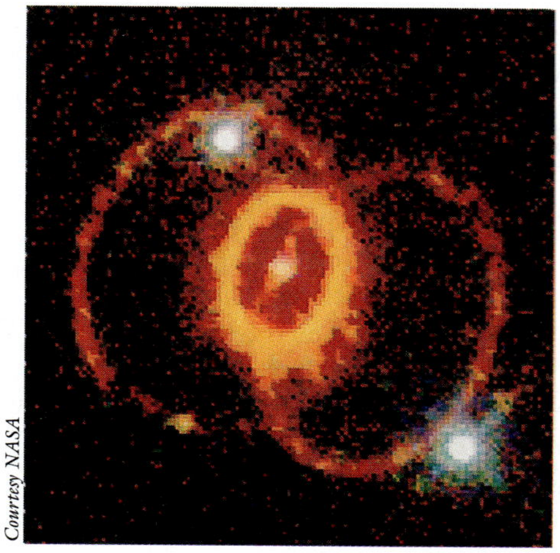

Courtesy NASA

The striking NASA Hubble Space Telescope picture shows three rings of glowing gas encircling the site of supernova 1987A, a star that exploded in February 1987.

Supernovas probably happen about every 30 years in our own Milky Way galaxy. We don't see most of these events because of intervening dust, but we do see them in neighboring galaxies. On February 23, 1987, for example, a supernova was seen in the Large Magellanic Cloud, a small galaxy-like structure near the Milky Way galaxy. Although the supernova was 170,000 light-years from Earth, it caused a great stir in science because it was the first supernova to be observed with modern observatories, including satellites. It was seen by large neutrino detectors and many ordinary telescopes on Earth, and by X-ray and gamma-ray observatories above the atmosphere. Because it was the first supernova observed in 1987, it was given the name "1987A." Perhaps the biggest surprise to come out of the experience was that there were so few surprises. The intricate theories of nuclear reactions that take place in those incredibly complex few hours when a star explodes were largely confirmed.

Neutron Stars and Pulsars

For a while after a star explodes, the supernova is surrounded by a cloud of ejected material. This expanding cloud dissipates into interstellar space, leaving behind the core of neutrons that was created in the collapse. A star that is being held up by degeneracy pressure of neutrons, called a **neutron star,** is in essence a giant nucleus—incredibly dense and very small. A typical neutron star might be 10 miles across, small enough to fit within the city limits of even a moderate metropolis. Several significant changes occur when a large star shrinks down into something the size of a city. For one thing, the rate of rotation of the star goes up substantially. Just as an ice skater increases her spin when she pulls in her arms, a star rotates faster and faster as it contracts. In fact, some neutron stars in our galaxy rotate 1000 times a second. Compare this to the sedate motion of the Sun, which rotates once every 26 days.

Jocelyn Bell Burnell detected the first pulsars in 1967.

Neutron stars do not give off much light, and they would probably have gone undetected if some of them didn't exhibit unusual behavior in the radio part of the spectrum. The reason for this behavior can be understood if you follow the collapse that leads to the neutron star. As the star collapses, the strength of its magnetic field increases. If a normal star has a dipole field (see Chapter 5), for example, then during the collapse the field lines are dragged in with the material of the star so that the field becomes much more concentrated and intense. Some neutron stars in our galaxy possess fields as much as a trillion times that of the magnetic field at Earth's surface.

These two effects—a strong magnetic field and rapid rotation—may combine to produce a special kind of neutron star, which astronomers call a **pulsar.** Fast-moving particles speed out along the intense magnetic field lines of the rotating neutron star, and these accelerating particles give off electromagnetic radiation, as shown in Figure 14-10. Most of this radiation is in the radio range, so the neutron star's signal is seen primarily with radio telescopes.

One way of thinking about a pulsar is to imagine it as being somewhat like a searchlight in the sky. Radio waves are continuously emitted along an axis that goes between the north and south magnetic poles of the neutron star, and this line describes a circle in space as the neutron star rotates. If you are standing in the line you will see a burst of radio waves every time the north or south pole of the pulsar is pointing toward you,

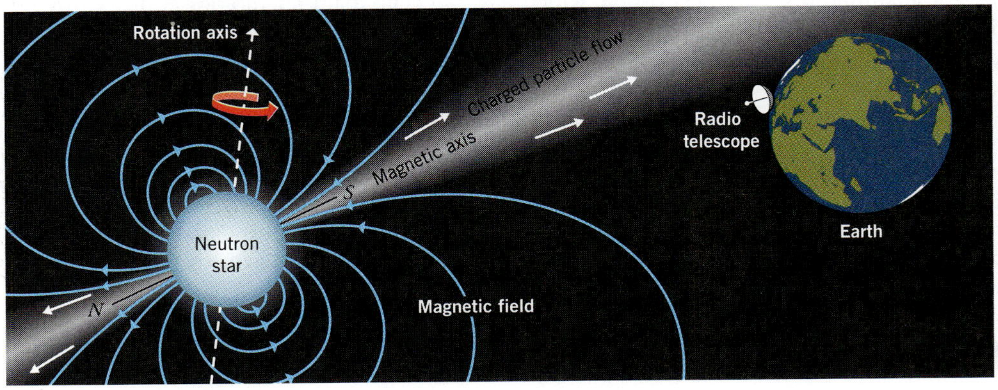

• **Figure 14-10** A schematic diagram of a pulsar reveals its two key attributes—rapid rotation and an intense magnetic field. This combination of traits produces a pulsing, lighthouse-like pattern of energetic radiation.

and nothing when it's not. You will, in other words, see a series of pulses of radio waves. The signature of a pulsar in the sky is a series of regularly spaced pulses, typically some tens to thousands per second. The pulsar represents one possible end state of a supernova. All pulsars are neutron stars, although all neutron stars are probably not seen as pulsars by earthbound astronomers.

We know of several pulsars that are the remnants of previous supernovas. One of the first pulsars discovered lies at the core of the Crab Nebula, a supernova seen from Earth in A.D. 1054. Likewise, Supernova 1987A is also expected to reveal a pulsar when all the dust clears.

Our current theories of stellar evolution say that stars more than 10 times as massive as the Sun will go through the supernova process we've just described, and eject large amounts of heavy elements into space.

Black Holes

Occasionally, a large star may die in a way that does not lead to the formation of a pulsar. If a star is large enough—perhaps 50 or more times as massive as the Sun—there may be processes, as yet only imperfectly understood, by which even the degeneracy pressure of neutrons is overcome and the star collapses. The result is the ultimate triumph of gravity, a **black hole.** A black hole is an object so dense, a mass so concentrated, that nothing, not even light, can escape from its surface.

We do not know how often black holes are formed. Astronomers recognize many black holes, one of which occurs in our galaxy. We can't see that object, a supermassive black hole at the center of the Milky Way Galaxy, but it causes nearby stars to careen wildly in tight orbits, some of which take only a dozen years to complete.

The search for other nearby black holes concentrates on double star systems in which one star has evolved into a black hole. Such a "stellar black hole" would be smaller than the galactic black hole described above. The idea is that even though we can't see these black holes themselves, we can see their effects on partner stars. We can also search for effects of material falling into the black hole. The enormous gravitational energy released in the process is partially converted into X-rays and gamma rays, which can be detected by orbiting observatories.

Science News | Gauging Star Birth

(SCIENCE NEWS, JAN. 7, 2006, P. 6)

Tracing the life and death of stars in our own Milky Way Galaxy is not an easy task because much of the radiation that we would see from both the birth and death of stars is absorbed by dust and other material in the galactic plane. This absorption is particularly strong in the spiral arms where stars are being created. The availability of gamma ray observatories above the atmosphere is starting to change this situation, since the galactic material does not absorb this type of radiation significantly. Thus, if we can find a way of relating the emission of gamma rays to the birth process, we can begin to create a kind of census of stars in our own immediate neighborhood.

A group of researchers from the Max Planck Institute in Germany, using the European Space Agency's INTEGRAL gamma ray satellite, has recently begun looking at radiation emitted in the decay of aluminum-26. This isotope, which has a half-life of about 750,000 years, is created in the supernovae that mark the death of very massive stars. Because these stars have a very short lifetime, aluminum-26 tends to be concentrated in star forming regions of the galaxy.

The group found that, on average, two massive stars per century go through the supernova process in our galaxy. Using this information and established theories about the relative abundances of large and small stars, they were able to come up with an estimate of star birth. On average, they conclude, about seven new stars form each year, with a total mass about four times that of the sun.

The main technological breakthrough that allowed them to take this data is that the instrumentation on the satellite is sensitive enough to see the small changes in radiation frequency caused by the movement of stars that results from the rotation of the galaxy. This allowed them to pinpoint the sources of the aluminum-26 and show that star death (and presumably star birth) is taking place all over the Milky Way.

Thinking More About | Stars

Generation of the Chemical Elements

Think about the remarkable range of elements you can buy at your local shopping center. The hardware store stocks aluminum siding, copper wire, and iron nails. The drugstore sells iodine for cuts, zinc and calcium compounds as dietary supplements, and perhaps bottles of oxygen for patients with breathing difficulties. The jeweler displays rings and necklaces of silver, gold, and platinum set with diamonds, a form of carbon. And your local electronics dealer offers an amazing assortment of audio and video equipment made possible by integrated circuits of silicon, perhaps doped with small amounts of aluminum or phosphorus.

It may come as a surprise to you that almost everything you see about you was made in a supernova. Your body, for example, is made primarily from elements that formed in some distant exploding star more than 4.5 billion years ago. We say this because, as we shall see in Chapter 15, the universe began its life with only light elements—hydrogen, helium, and small amounts of lithium. These elements formed the first stars and were processed in the first stellar nuclear fires. In stars like the Sun, elements heavier than helium may be made, but they remain in that star and never return to the cosmos.

In large stars, however, all the elements up to uranium (the element with 92 protons) and beyond are made and spewed back into the interstellar medium in the titanic explosions we call supernovas. These heavy elements enrich the surrounding galaxy, and when new stars are formed these elements are incorporated into them. The Sun, which formed fairly late in the history of our own galaxy, thus incorporated many heavy elements that had been made in previous supernovas.

You can think of the history of our galaxy as successive and cumulative enrichments by nuclear processing in large, short-lived stars. These stars, with lifetimes as short as tens of millions of years, take the original hydrogen in the galaxy and convert it into heavier elements. Thus we expect that older, smaller stars that have been shining since the early history of the universe will have fewer heavy elements than relatively young stars like the Sun, a prediction that is borne out by astronomical observations.

Think about what this means as you look around you. All the objects in your life—this book, your clothes, even your skin and bones—are made of atoms that formed in the hearts of giant stars long ago.

Summary

Astronomy is the study of objects in the heavens. Astronomers have discovered much about the nature and origins of *stars.* We study stars with *telescopes,* instruments that gather and focus electromagnetic radiation. Earth-based telescopes detect visible and radio waves, while orbiting observatories detect all other regions of the electromagnetic spectrum. The most powerful telescopes can detect stars that are hundreds of millions of *light-years* away.

Extreme temperatures and pressures deep inside a star cause its hydrogen core to undergo nuclear fusion reactions, burning to create helium and heat energy. Ignition of these nuclear fires creates an outward flow of particles, called the *solar wind.* The fusion reaction proceeds in three steps, in which (1) two protons come together to form deuterium, (2) a proton and a deuterium nucleus come together to form helium-3, and (3) two helium-3 nuclei fuse to make helium-4. This energy creates the pressure that balances the force of gravity that pulls the star inward.

Stars such as our own Sun form from giant clouds of interstellar dust called *nebulae*—clouds that gradually collapse under the force of gravity. This collapse subjects the star's atoms, primarily hydrogen, to tremendous temperatures and pressures. The life of a star is a continuous struggle against this gravitational force.

Stars that are burning hydrogen to produce energy are said to be *main-sequence stars.* Larger stars burn hotter and emit more energy, while smaller stars are cooler and radiate less energy. Main-sequence stars are found in a simple band-like pattern on a Hertzsprung-Russell diagram, which graphs a star's energy output versus its temperature.

When a star like the Sun consumes most of its core hydrogen, a helium-rich central region remains. The star once again begins to collapse under gravity, and internal temperatures rise again. Hydrogen burning begins in shells outside the core, while the core's helium may also combine in nuclear fusion reactions to form carbon. These new nuclear processes may cause a star like the Sun to expand briefly and become a *red giant,* a star whose relatively cool outer layers glow red. Eventually, however, nuclear fuel must be exhausted. Gravity will dominate and the carbon-rich star will collapse to a very small, very hot *white dwarf.*

Stars much larger than the Sun may evolve beyond hydrogen and helium burning. If temperatures and pressures are high enough, carbon can undergo additional nuclear reactions to form elements as heavy as iron, the ultimate nuclear ash. Once iron is formed, however, there can be no more energy produced by these reactions and burning will cease. The sudden extinguishing of a star causes a catastrophic gravitational collapse and rebound—a *supernova*—in which the star literally explodes and spews all the chemical elements into the heavens. A dense, spinning *neutron star* or *pulsar* may be the only remnant of the original star. The largest stars may collapse into a *black hole,* an object so massive that not even light can escape its gravitational pull.

Key Terms

astronomy
star
telescope
solar wind
light-year
main-sequence star
red giant
white dwarf
nebulae
supernova
neutron star
pulsar
black hole

Review Questions

1. What is a star?
2. What is the nature of the energy emitted by stars?
3. What conditions are present in stars that cause hydrogen to form helium? What is this process called?
4. What are the major layers of the Sun?
5. What two properties of stars do scientists plot on a Hertzsprung-Russell diagram? Why do they choose these properties?
6. In what ways is the Sun a typical star?
7. What are the effects of the solar wind on Earth?
8. What are four aspects of photons that astronomers measure?
9. Describe two kinds of telescopes. How are they similar?
10. What causes stars to vary in brightness? in color?
11. What are the advantages of placing a telescope in orbit?
12. What is a "standard candle" in astronomy?
13. Describe two ways to determine the distance to another star.
14. How are stars formed?
15. Why must the Sun eventually burn out? What changes will the Sun undergo before it burns out?
16. Why don't larger stars burn longer than smaller stars?
17. Why won't the Sun become a supernova or a black hole?
18. How are supernovas and neutron stars related to each other?
19. How are neutron stars and pulsars related to each other?
20. If iron is the ultimate nuclear ash, where do elements heavier than iron come from?
21. Why is it difficult to detect a black hole from Earth?

Discussion Questions

1. Why do we see stars only at night? Do they shine during the day?
2. How might you determine the age of a star from an Earth-based telescope? What measurements might you make?
3. How long does it take for the energy produced in the Sun's core to reach the photosphere? How long does it take a photon at the edge of the photosphere to reach Earth?
4. In what part of the electromagnetic spectrum does the Sun produce most of its energy? How have animals, including humans, evolved to take advantage of this?
5. How can we talk about the evolution of stars over billions of years when human beings have been observing stars for only a few thousand years?
6. How does the principle of conservation of energy apply to a supernova?
7. Most stars we see are on the main sequence. Stars spend most of their lives consuming their initial stock of hydrogen. Is there a connection between these two statements? If so, what is it?
8. What are stars made of?
9. What is the Sun's source of energy?
10. What are the roles of gravity, temperature, and pressure in the formation and death of a star?
11. What are the effects of solar winds on Earth?

Problems

1. How far away is Alpha Centauri, the nearest star? How long would it take to get there at a speed of 2000 miles per hour (the speed of a fast jet plane?)
2. How much more light-gathering ability does the Keck telescope with its 10-meter diameter mirror array have than the 2.5-meter Hubble Space Telescope? [*Hint:* Light-gathering ability is proportional to the area of the mirror.]

INVESTIGATIONS

1. Locate some stars in the sky and find out their apparent magnitude. (You might want to start with some familiar stars such as those in the Big Dipper.)

2. The Crab Nebula formed from a supernova event that was sighted on Earth almost 1000 years ago. It must have been visible as a brilliant object for several days. What cultures left a record of this astronomical event? How did they explain what they saw?

3. Astronomers often debate the relative merits of Earth-based versus orbiting telescopes. What are some of the arguments on both sides of this issue?

4. You can set up an analog to the astronomical distance scale by using two "yardsticks"—a ruler and a tape measure, for example—to measure distances. Measure the dimensions of your classroom this way. How would you make sure that distances on each yardstick were the same? Does this exercise suggest a way for astronomers to check the consistency of their distance scale?

5. The nineteenth-century American poet Walt Whitman (1819–1892) wrote the following poem about astronomy:

When I Heard the Learn'd Astronomer

When I heard the learn'd astronomer,
When the proofs, the figures,
were ranged in columns before me,
When I was shown the charts and diagrams,
to add, divide, and measure them,
When I sitting heard the astronomer where he
lectured with much applause in the lecture-room,
How soon unaccountable I became tired and sick,
Till rising and gliding out I wander'd off by myself,
In the mystical moist night air, and from time to time,
Look'd up in perfect silence at the stars.

Although Whitman was unimpressed by the facts and figures of the "learn'd astronomer," astronomers of the past century have changed the way we think about our place in the universe. In this respect, how does science complement poetry? How do poetry and astronomy differ as ways of understanding why we are here? How would you answer the poet today?

6. Investigate the effects of light pollution in your area. Is it a major problem for amateur astronomers?

7. Where is the largest terrestrial telescope located?

8. Find out when the next meteor shower or solar eclipse in your area is due. Grab a blanket and some friends and enjoy one of nature's finest exhibitions.

9. Find the constellation that is associated with your astrological sign. Determine the distances to each. Why is the constellation only an illusion and not really the outline of a bull, a crab, or a fish?

15

Cosmology

Will the universe end?

= applications of the great idea discussed in this chapter

= other applications, some of which are discussed in other chapters

Science Through the Day | A Glowing Charcoal Fire

While you were lying down, soaking up the Sun's rays, a couple of your friends started a charcoal fire on a small grill. If you observe closely, you may notice that the color of the coals in the fire changes, depending on how hot the fire is. They are ordinarily red, but in a roaring blaze they can glow blue-white. Then, as the fire starts to go out, the coals glow a dull orange and eventually stop glowing altogether.

But even when the coals aren't glowing, they are giving off energy in the form of infrared radiation, which you can feel if you put your hand out to the fire. Even the next day, you might still be able to feel the radiation given off by the cooling embers.

Believe it or not, a phenomenon like this campfire experience led twentieth-century scientists to a completely new understanding of the structure and history of the universe in which we live.

Stephen Simpson/Taxi/Getty Images

Galaxies

On any given night, as we look into the sky with modest-sized telescopes, we can see that the hazy band of the **Milky Way** is composed of countless millions of stars. Those stars appear as tiny pin-pricks of light. But there are lots of other less distinct objects that appear as fuzzy masses, too distant to resolve. And those cloud-like objects, called *nebulae,* were the subject of intense debate in the early twentieth century.

The Nebula Debate

Some astronomers thought nebulae were nearby dust clouds that are illuminated by other stars. In that case, they would be fairly close by and have no resolvable structures, even in the most powerful telescope. Other astronomers suggested that nebulae were much more distant clusters of stars. They're composed of lots of individual stars but are much too far away for those stars to be resolved.

This controversy came into sharp focus on April 26, 1920, when rival American astronomers Harlow Shapley and Heber D. Curtis engaged in a public debate at the National Academy of Sciences. The younger Shapely had come into prominence by discovering that the Milky Way is much larger than previously thought—more than 100,000 light-years across. Given that immense size, he couldn't imagine that much more distant objects existed. It's ironic that Shapley, who dramatically increased the size of the known universe, just couldn't accept how much larger the universe really is.

The Hale Observatoreis/Courtesy AIP Emilio Segre Visual Archives/American Institute of Physics

Edwin Hubble (1889–1953) at the 100-inch telescope of California's Mount Wilson Observatory.

Curtis, on the other hand, argued that nebulae are much more distant collections of stars like our own. He saw the distinctive shapes of nebulae with spiral arms and central bulges, and concluded that a cloud wasn't likely to adopt that shape.

The more senior Curtis is said to have been the more eloquent of the two, and some attendees found him to have been more persuasive. But in science, debaters don't settle controversies. The scientific method demands that independently verifiable measurements and observations are the ultimate arbiter of any scientific question. The fact of the matter is that no one could make such observations with the tools available before 1920.

Edwin Hubble and the Discovery of Galaxies

As so often happens in science, improved instruments were the key to discovery. In this case a larger telescope, quite literally, resolved the issue. In 1900, the world's largest telescopes were reflectors with mirrors in the range of 50 or 60 inches in diameter—not large enough to reveal nebular structure. So it was that the Carnegie Institution of Washington decided to build a mammoth new telescope with an unprecedented 100-inch diameter mirror on Mount Wilson, near Los Angeles, California. At the time, Mount Wilson was a lonely outpost on the outskirts of a small city. Today it has been engulfed by the Los Angeles metropolitan area, but in those days it afforded astronomers a chance to look at the sky through clear, unpolluted air.

In 1919, the young American astronomer Edwin Hubble (1889–1953), fresh from distinguished service in World War I, went to work at Mount Wilson and used this magnificent instrument to tackle the mystery of the nebula. Because his new telescope allowed him to see individual Cepheid variable stars in some nebulae, which no one had been able to do before, Hubble was able to measure the distance to them. (Recall from Chapter 14 that Cepheid variable stars can be used as standard candles.) It turned out that the Cepheid variable stars were extremely faint, so the distance to the nearest one, located in the Andromeda nebula, was some 2 million light-years, far outside the bounds of the Milky Way. Thus, with a single observation, Hubble established one of the most important facts about the universe we live in: it is made up of billions of galaxies, of which the Milky Way is but one.

We now know that each of these countless **galaxies** is an immense collection of millions to hundreds of billions of stars, together with gas, dust, and other materials, that is held together by the forces of mutual gravitational attraction. In making these discoveries, Hubble set the tone for a century of progress in the new branch of science called **cosmology,** which is devoted to the study of the structure and history of the entire universe.

• **Figure 15-1** A map of the Milky Way galaxy, showing the nucleus and spiral arms.

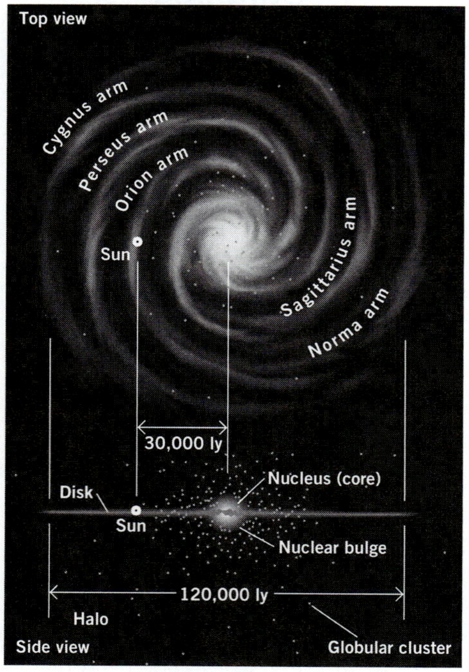

Kinds of Galaxies

The Milky Way is a rather typical galaxy. As shown in Figure 15-1, it is a flattened disk about 100,000 light-years across. A central bulge known as the nucleus holds most of our galaxy's hundreds of billions of stars. Bright regions in the disk, known as spiral arms, mark areas where new stars are being formed. About 75% of the brighter galaxies in the sky are of this spiral type (Figures 15-1 and 15-2).

> **Stop and Think!** What is the connection between the flat, spiral shape of our galaxy and the appearance of the Milky Way in the night sky?

Other galaxies, known as ellipticals, resemble nothing so much as cosmic footballs. The brightest elliptical galaxies tend to have more stars than spiral galaxies do and comprise about 20% of bright galaxies. In addition to the relatively large and bright elliptical and spiral galaxies, the universe is littered with small collections of stars known as irregular and dwarf galaxies. Even though these galaxies are faint and therefore difficult to detect, many of them have been identified. Astronomers thus think that these are probably the most common galaxies in the universe.

The total number of galaxies in the universe has been estimated by taking long exposure photographs of small regions in the sky with no stars—regions that would appear as black voids in smaller telescopes. The results of these so-called deep-field images are astonishing (Figure 15-3). The more we look, the more galaxies we see—perhaps 100 billion galaxies, each with countless stars.

Courtesy NASA

• **Figure 15-2** A typical spiral galaxy, with a bright core and spiral arms where new stars are forming.

Larger elliptical and spiral galaxies and smaller irregular and dwarf galaxies can be thought of as quiet, homey galaxies, where the process of star formation and death goes on in a stately, orderly way. But a small number of galaxies—perhaps 10,000 among the billions known—are quite different and are referred to collectively as active galaxies. The most spectacular of these unusual objects are the *quasars* (for quasi-stellar radio sources). Quasars are wild, explosive, violent objects, where as-yet-unknown processes pour vast amounts of energy into space each second from an active center no larger than our solar system. Astronomers suggest that the only way to generate this kind of energy is for the center of a quasar to be occupied by an enormous black hole (with masses, in some cases, millions of times greater than that of the Sun) and for the energy to be generated by huge amounts of mass falling into this center. Because they are so bright, quasars are the most distant objects we can see in the universe.

Celestial Image Co./Photo Researchers

A typical elliptical galaxy. This one is known as M84 and is located in the constellation Virgo.

Courtesy NASA

• **Figure 15-3** This deep-field image of galaxies depicts a tiny patch apparently "empty" sky. Several hours of exposure by the powerful Hubble Space Telescope reveals more than 100 galaxies—evidence that the universe holds tens of billions of galaxies, each with hundreds of billions of stars.

The Redshift and Hubble's Law

Hubble's recognition of galaxies other than our own Milky Way wasn't the end of his discoveries. When he looked at the light from nearby galaxies, he noticed that the distinctive colors emitted by different elements seemed to be shifted toward the red (long-wavelength) end of the spectrum, compared to light emitted by atoms on Earth. Hubble interpreted this **redshift** as an example of the Doppler effect (see Chapter 6), the same phenomenon that causes the sound of a car whizzing past to change its pitch. Hubble's observation meant that distant galaxies are moving away from Earth. Furthermore, Hubble noticed that the more distant a galaxy, the faster it moves away from us (Figures 15-4 and 15-5).

On the basis of measurements of a few dozen nearby galaxies, Hubble suggested that a simple relationship exists between the distance of an object from Earth and that object's speed away from Earth. Comparing two galaxies—one twice as far away from

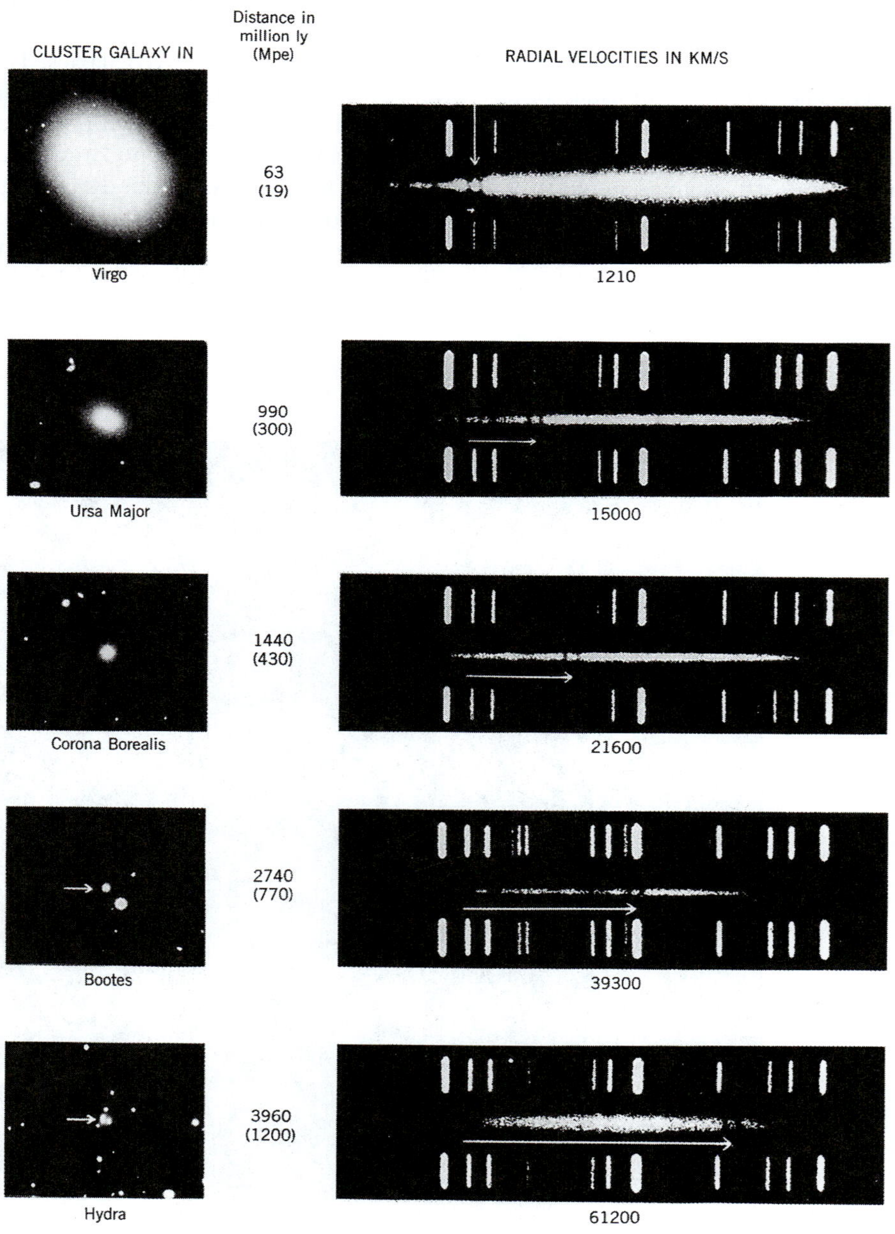

Courtesy California Institute of Technology

• **Figure 15-4** Photographs of galaxies as seen through a telescope (on the left), with spectra of those galaxies (on the right). The distance to each galaxy in megaparsecs is also given. Double dark lines in the spectra, characteristic of the calcium atom, are shifted farther to the right (toward the red) the farther away the galaxy is. Thus more distant galaxies are traveling away from us at higher velocities. This phenomenon was used by Edwin Hubble to derive his law.

Earth as the other—the farther galaxy moves away from us twice as fast. This statement, which has been amply confirmed by measurements in the subsequent half-century, is now called **Hubble's law.** Hubble's law says:

- ▶ **In words:** The farther away a galaxy is, the faster it recedes.
- ▶ **In equation form:**

galaxy's velocity = (Hubble's constant) × (galaxy's distance)

- ▶ **In symbols:**

$$v = H \times d$$

Hubble's law tells us that we can determine the distance to galaxies by measuring the redshift of the light we receive, whether or not we can make out individual stars in them. Most astronomers now accept a value of close to 70 kilometers per second per megaparsec (a megaparsec, or Mpc, is a distance of a million parsecs or 3.3 million light-years). In this view of the cosmos, the redshift becomes the final "ruler" in the astronomical distance scale (see Chapter 14).

One way of interpreting Hubble's constant is to notice that if a galaxy were to travel from the location of the Milky Way to its present position with a velocity v, then the time it would take to make the trip would be distance divided by speed:

$$t = \frac{d}{v}$$

Substituting for v from Hubble's law:

$$T = \frac{d}{(H \times d)} = \frac{1}{H}$$

Thus, the Hubble constant provides a rough estimate of the time that the expansion has been going on and, hence, of the age of the universe. A Hubble constant of 70 km/s/Mpc corresponds to an age of the universe of about 14 billion years.

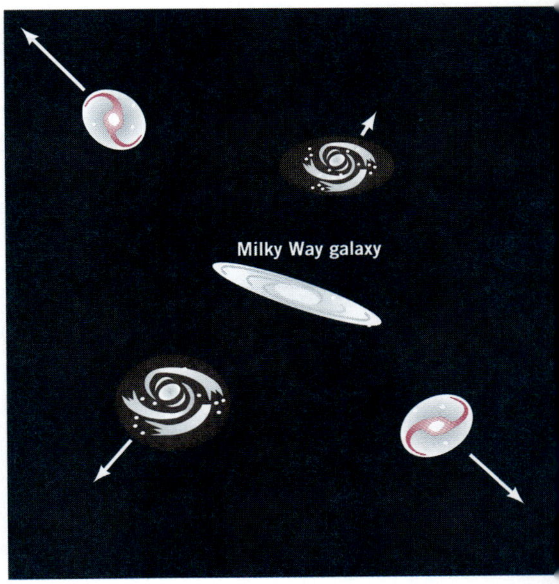

• **Figure 15-5** Illustration of Hubble expansion. The more distant a galaxy is from Earth, the faster it moves away from us.

EXAMPLE 15-1

The Distance to a Receding Galaxy

Astronomers discover a new galaxy and determine from its redshift that it is moving away from us at approximately 100,000 km/s (about one-third the speed of light). Approximately how far away is this galaxy?

Reasoning: According to Hubble's law, a galaxy's distance equals its velocity divided by the Hubble constant.

Solution:

$$\text{distance (in Mpc)} = \frac{\text{velocity (in km/s)}}{[\text{Hubble's constant (in km/s/Mpc)}]} = \frac{(100{,}000 \text{ km/s})}{(70 \text{ km/s/Mpc})} = \frac{100{,}000}{70 \text{ Mpc}} = 1429 \text{ Mpc}$$

Remember, a megaparsec equals about 3.3 million light-years, so this galaxy is almost 5 billion light-years away. The light that we observe from such a distant galaxy began its trip about the time that our solar system was born.

Table 15-1 Some of Hubble's Data

Distance to Galaxy (in megaparsecs)	Velocity (in km/s)
1.0	620
1.4	500
1.7	960
2.0	850
2.0	1090

Science by the Numbers •

Analyzing Hubble's Data

In his original sample, Hubble observed 46 galaxies but was able to determine distances to only 24. Some of his data are given in Table 15-1.

How does one go about analyzing data like these? One common way is to make a graph. In this case, the vertical axis is the velocity of recession of the galaxy, and the horizontal axis is the distance to the galaxy. In Figure 15-6*a* we show the data as originally plotted by Hubble, while Figure 15-6*b* presents a more recent compilation of many galaxies.

Looking at the original data (Figure 15-6*a*), the general trend of Hubble's law is obvious—the farther you go to the right (i.e., the farther away the galaxies are), the higher the points (i.e., the faster the galaxies are moving away). You also notice, however, that the points do not fall on a straight line but are scattered. Confronted with this sort of situation, you can do one of two things. You can assume that the scattering is due to experimental error and that more accurate experiments will verify that the points fall on a straight line; or you can assume that the scatter is a real phenomenon and try to explain it. Hubble took the first alternative, so the only problem left was to find the line about which experimental error was scattering his data.

The way this is usually done is to find the line for which the sum of the distances between the line and each data point is smaller than for any other line. In effect, you find the line that comes closest to all the data points. The slope of this line, which measures how fast the velocity increases for a given change in distance, is the best estimate of Hubble's constant. •

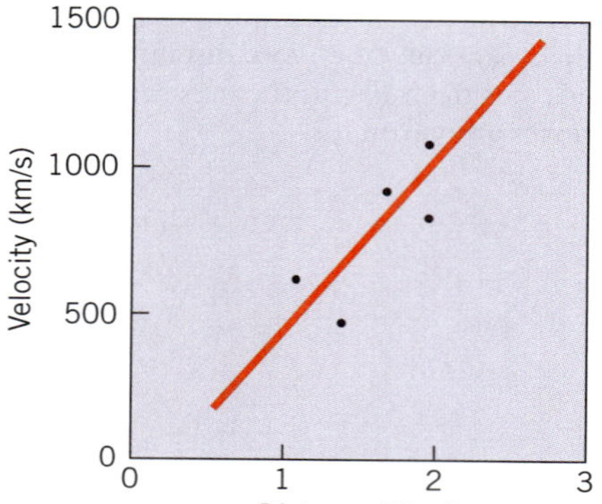

(*a*)

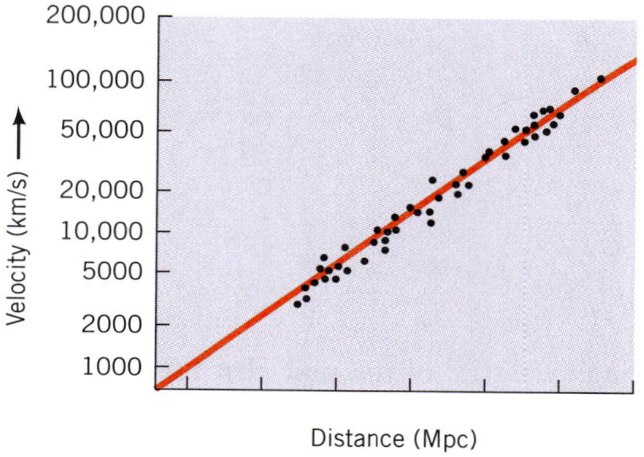

(*b*)

• **Figure 15-6** *(a)* Hubble's original distance versus velocity relationship. *(b)* Modern graphs of distance versus velocity record data from hundreds or thousands of galaxies.

The Big Bang

Hubble's law reveals an extraordinary aspect of our universe: it is expanding. Nearby galaxies are moving away from us, and far-away galaxies are moving away even faster. The whole thing is blowing up like a balloon. This startling fact leads us, in turn, to perhaps the most amazing discovery of all. If you look at our universe expanding today and imagine moving backward in time (think of running a videotape in reverse), you can see that at some point in the past the universe must have started out as a very small object. In other words:

The universe began at a specific time in the past, and it has been expanding ever since.

This picture of the universe—that it began as an infinitely hot, dense concentration of energy and has been expanding ever since—is called the **big bang theory.** This theory constitutes our best idea of what the early universe was like.

Think how different the big bang theory of the universe is from the theories of the Greeks or the medieval scholars, or even the great scientists of the nineteenth century whose work we have studied. To them, Earth went in stately orbit around the Sun, and the Sun moved among the stars, but the collection of stars you can see at night with your naked eye or with a telescope was all that there was. Suddenly, with Hubble's work, the universe grew immeasurably. Our own collection of stars, our own galaxy, is just one of perhaps 100 billion known galaxies in a universe in which galaxies are flying away from each other at incredible speeds. It is a vision of a universe that began at some time in the distant past and will, presumably, end at some time in the future.

The Large-Scale Structure of the Universe

The Milky Way is part of a group of galaxies known as the Local Group, made up of ourselves, the Andromeda galaxy, and perhaps a dozen small "suburban" galaxies. The Andromeda galaxy is visible with the naked eye from Earth—you can see it from a dark spot on a clear summer night as a fuzzy patch of light in the northeast. The Local Group, in turn, is part of the Local Supercluster, a collection of galaxies about 100 million light-years across.

We now know that literally billions of galaxies populate the universe, each a collection of billions of stars. Like the Milky Way, most galaxies seem to be clumped together into *groups* and *clusters,* many of which, in turn, are grouped into larger collections called *superclusters* of thousands of galaxies.

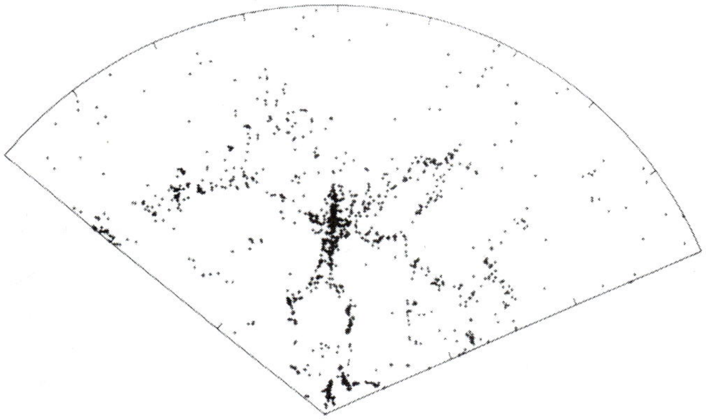

Courtesy C. Park and J. r. Groth, Princeton University

• **Figure 15-7** The large-scale structure of the universe. This figure shows a thin slice of the universe, with each galaxy represented as a point (the Milky Way lies at the lower point in this figure, at the apex of the triangle). Matter is concentrated in superclusters, with large, relatively empty areas called voids between them.

In the 1980s, astronomers began to make "redshift surveys" of the sky, in which they observe distant galaxies and measure their redshifts so we know how far the galaxies are. In this way, it is possible to construct a full, three-dimensional picture of the distribution of matter in the cosmos. With the results from these observations, originally led by the team of Margaret Geller and John Huchra at the Harvard-Smithsonian Astrophysical Observatory, astronomers have put together a picture of the universe that is very different from what you might expect. Instead of finding galaxies scattered more or less at random through space, they find that galaxies are collected into large structures that run for billions of light-years across the sky. In fact, you can get an excellent picture of the structure of the universe by imagining the distribution of galaxies as something like a big pile of soapsuds. The result will give you a structure in which large empty spaces are surrounded by soap film. In exactly the same way, matter in the universe seems to be concentrated in superclusters on the surfaces of large empty areas called voids (Figure 15-7). Attempting to understand the reason for this very complex structure in the universe remains one of the major tasks of modern cosmology.

Some Useful Analogies

The big bang picture of the universe is so important that we should spend some time thinking about it. Many analogies can be used to help us picture what the expanding universe is like, and we'll look at two. Be forewarned, however: none of these analogies is perfect. If you pursue any of them far enough they fail, because none of them captures the entirety and complexity of the universe in which we live. And yet each of the analogies can help us understand aspects of that universe.

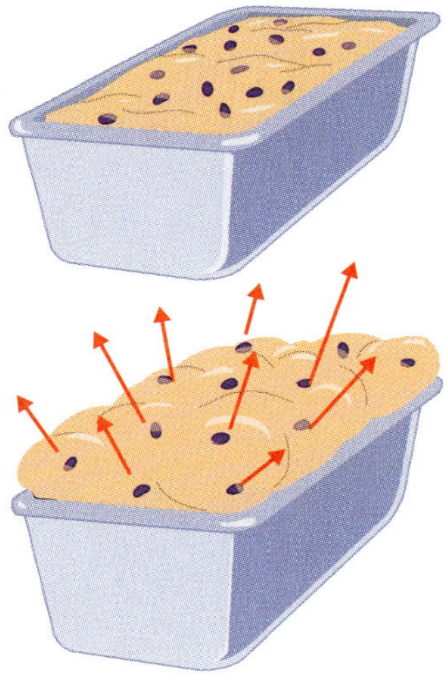

• **Figure 15-8** The raisin-bread dough analogy of the expanding universe. As the dough expands, all raisins move apart from each other. The farther apart two raisins are, the faster the distance between those two raisins increases.

1. The Raisin-Bread Dough Analogy

One standard way of thinking about the big bang is to imagine the universe as being analogous to a huge vat of rising bread dough in a bakery (Figure 15-8). If raisins scattered through the dough represent galaxies, and if you're standing on one of those raisins, then you would look around you and see other raisins moving away from you. You could watch as a nearby raisin moves away because the dough between you and it is expanding. A nearby raisin wouldn't be moving very fast because there isn't much expanding dough between you and that raisin, while more distant raisins would be moving faster because there is more dough between them and you.

Stop and Think! How fast would a raisin that is three times farther away from you than a nearby raisin move away?

The raisin-bread dough analogy is very useful because it makes it easy to visualize how everything could seem to be moving away from us, with objects that are farther away moving faster. If you stand on any raisin in the dough, all the other raisins look as though they're moving away from you. This analogy thus explains why Earth seems to be the center of the universe. It also explains why this fact isn't significant—every point appears to be at the center of the universe.

But the expanding dough analogy fails to address one of the most commonly asked questions about the Hubble expansion: What is outside the expansion? A mass of bread dough, after all, has a middle and an outer surface; some raisins are nearer the center than others. But we believe that the universe has no surface, no outside and inside, and no unique central position. In this regard, the surface of an expanding balloon provides a better analogy.

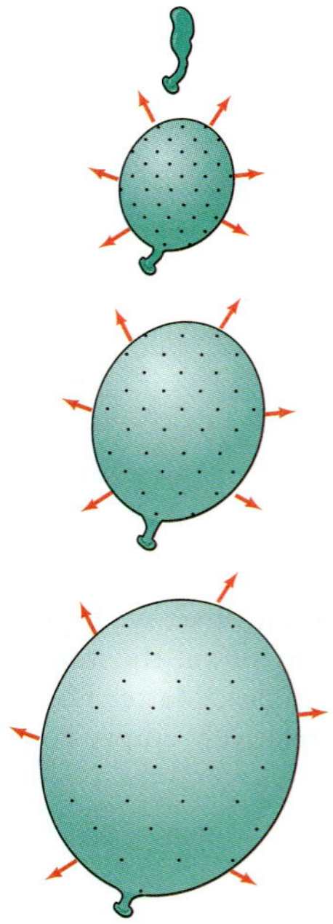

• **Figure 15-9** The expanding-balloon analogy of the universe. All points on the surface of the expanding balloon move away from each other. The farther apart the points, the faster they move apart.

2. The Expanding-Balloon Analogy

Imagine that you live on the surface of a balloon in a two-dimensional universe. You would be absolutely flat, living on a flat-surface universe (similar to the way we are three-dimensional, living in a three-dimensional universe). Evenly spaced points cover the balloon's surface, and one of these points is your home. As the inflating balloon expands, you observe that every other point moves away from you—the farther away the point, the faster away it moves (Figure 15-9).

Where is the edge of the balloon? What are the "inside" and "outside" of the balloon in two dimensions? The answers, at least from the perspective of a two-dimensional being on the balloon's surface, are that every point appears to be at the center, and the universe has no edges, no inside, and no outside. The two-dimensional being experiences one continuous, never-ending surface. We live in a universe of higher dimensionality, but the principle is the same: our universe has no center and no inside versus outside.

The balloon analogy is also useful because it can help us visualize another question that is often asked about the expanding universe: What is it expanding *into*? If you think about being on the balloon, you realize that you could start out in any direction and keep traveling. You might come back to where you started, but you would never come to an end. There would never be an "into." The surface of a balloon is an example of a system that is bounded (in two dimensions) but that has no boundaries.

Evidence for the Big Bang

In Chapter 1 we pointed out that every scientific theory must be tested and have experimental or observational evidence backing it up. The big bang theory provides a comprehensive picture of what our universe might be like, but are there sufficient observational data to support it? In fact, three pieces of evidence make the big bang idea extremely compelling to scientists.

1. The Universal Expansion

Edwin Hubble's observation of universal expansion provided the first strong evidence for the big bang theory. If the universe began from a compact source and has been expanding, then you would expect to see the expansion going on today. The fact that we do see such an expansion is taken as evidence for a big bang event in the past. It is not, however, conclusive evidence. Many other theories of the universe have incorporated an expansion but not a specific beginning in time. During the 1940s, for example, scientists proposed a *steady-state universe*. Galaxies in this model move away from each other, but new galaxies are constantly being formed in the spaces that are being vacated. Thus the steady-state model describes a universe that is constantly expanding and forming new galaxies, but with no trace of a beginning.

Because of the possibility of this kind of theory, the universal expansion, in and of itself, does not compel us to accept the big bang theory.

2. The Cosmic Microwave Background

In 1964, Arno Penzias and Robert W. Wilson, two scientists working at Bell Laboratories in New Jersey, used a primitive radio receiver to scan the skies for radio signals. Their motivation was a simple one. They worked during the early days of satellite broadcasting, and they were measuring microwave radiation to document the kinds of background signals that might interfere with radio transmission. They found that whichever way they pointed their receiver, they heard a faint hiss in their apparatus. There seemed to be microwave radiation falling on Earth from all directions. We now call this radiation the **cosmic microwave background radiation.**

At first they suspected that this background noise might be an artifact—a fault in their electronics, or even interference caused by droppings from a pair of pigeons that had nested inside their funnel-shaped microwave antenna. However, a thorough testing and cleaning made no difference in the odd results. A constant influx of microwave radiation of wavelength 7.35 centimeters flooded Earth from every direction in space. And so the scientists asked: Where is this radiation coming from?

In order to understand the answer to their question, you need to remember that every object in the universe that is above the temperature of absolute zero emits some sort of radiation (see Chapter 6). As we saw in the Science Through the Day that opened this chapter, a coal on a fire may glow white hot and emit the complete spectrum of visible electromagnetic radiation. As the fire cools it will give out light that is first concentrated in the yellow, then orange, and eventually dull red range. Even after it no longer glows with visible light, you can tell that the coal is giving off radiation by holding out your hand to it and sensing the infrared or heat radiation that still pours from the dying embers. As the coal cools still more, it will give off wavelengths of longer and longer radiation.

One way to think about the cosmic microwave background, then, is to imagine that you are inside a cooling coal on a fire. No matter which way you look, you'll see radiation coming toward you, and that radiation will shift from white to orange to red light and eventually all the way down to microwaves as the coal cools.

In 1964, a group of theorists at Princeton University (not far from Bell Laboratories) pointed out that if the universe had indeed begun at some time in the past, then today it would still be giving off electromagnetic radiation in the microwave range. In fact, the best calculations at the time indicated that the radiation would be characteristic of an object at a few degrees above absolute zero. When Penzias and Wilson got in contact with these theorists, the reason they couldn't get rid of the microwave signal became obvious. Not only was it a real signal, it was evidence for the big bang itself. For their discovery, Penzias and Wilson shared the Nobel Prize in physics in 1978—not a bad outcome for a measurement designed to do something else entirely!

We said before that it is possible to imagine theories, such as the steady-state theory, in which the universe is expanding but has no beginning. However, it is difficult to imagine a universe that does not have a beginning but that produces the kind of microwave background we're talking about. Thus Penzias and Wilson's discovery put an end to the steady-state theory.

In 1989, the Cosmic Background Explorer satellite (see Chapter 14) measured the microwave background to extreme levels of accuracy. The purpose of this measurement was to see, in great detail, whether the predictions of the big bang theory about the nature of the cosmic microwave background radiation were correct.

These data established beyond any doubt that we live in a universe where the average temperature is 2.7 kelvins (K). This finding reaffirmed the validity of the big bang theory in the minds of scientists.

3. The Abundance of Light Elements

The third important piece of evidence for the big bang theory comes from studies of the abundances of light nuclei in the universe. For a short period in the early history of the universe, as we'll see at the end of this chapter, atomic nuclei could form from elementary particles. Cosmologists believe that the only nuclei that could have formed in the big bang are isotopes of hydrogen, helium, and lithium (the first three elements, with one, two, and three protons in their nuclei, respectively). All elements heavier than lithium were formed later in stars, as discussed in Chapter 14.

The conditions necessary for the formation of light elements were twofold. First, matter had to be packed together densely enough to allow enough collisions to produce a fusion reaction. Second, the temperature had to be high enough for those reactions to happen, but not so high that nuclei created by fusion would be broken up in subsequent collisions. In an expanding universe, the density of matter will decrease rapidly because of the expansion, and each type of nuclei can form only in a very narrow range of conditions. Calculations based on density and collision frequency, together with known nuclear reaction rates, make rather specific predictions about how much of each isotope could have been made before matter spread too thinly. Thus the cosmic abundances of elements such as deuterium (the hydrogen isotope with one proton and one neutron in its nucleus), helium-3 (the helium isotope with two protons and one neutron), and helium-4 (with two protons and two neutrons) comprise another test of our theories about the origins of the universe.

In fact, studies of the abundances of these isotopes find that they agree quite well with the predictions made in this way. The prediction for the primordial abundance of helium-4 in the universe, for example, is that it cannot have exceeded 25%. Observations of helium abundance are quite close to this prediction. If the abundance of helium differed by more than a few percent from this value, the theory would be in serious trouble.

The Evolution of the Universe

Our vision of an expanding universe leads us to peer back in time, to the early history of matter and energy. What can we say about the changes that must have taken place during the past 14 billion years?

Some General Characteristics of an Expanding Universe

Have you ever pumped up a bicycle tire with a hand pump? If you have, you may have noticed that after you've run the pump for a while, the barrel gets very hot. All matter heats up when it is compressed.

The universe is no exception to this rule. A universe that is more compressed and denser than the one in which we live would also be hotter on average. In such a universe, the cosmic radiation background would correspond to a temperature much higher than 2.7 K (where it is today), and the wavelength of the background radiation would be shorter than 7.35 cm.

When the universe was younger, it must have been much hotter and denser than it is today. This cardinal principle guides our understanding of how the universe evolved. In fact, the big bang theory we have been discussing is often called the "hot big bang" to emphasize the fact that the universe began in a very hot, dense state and has been expanding and cooling ever since.

In Chapter 10 we saw that changes of temperature may correspond to changes of state in matter. If you cool water, for example, it eventually turns into ice at the freezing point. In just the same way, modern theories claim, as the universe cooled from its hot origins it went through changes of state very much like the freezing of water. We will refer to these dramatic changes in the fabric of the universe as *freezings*, even though they are not actually changes from a liquid to a solid state.

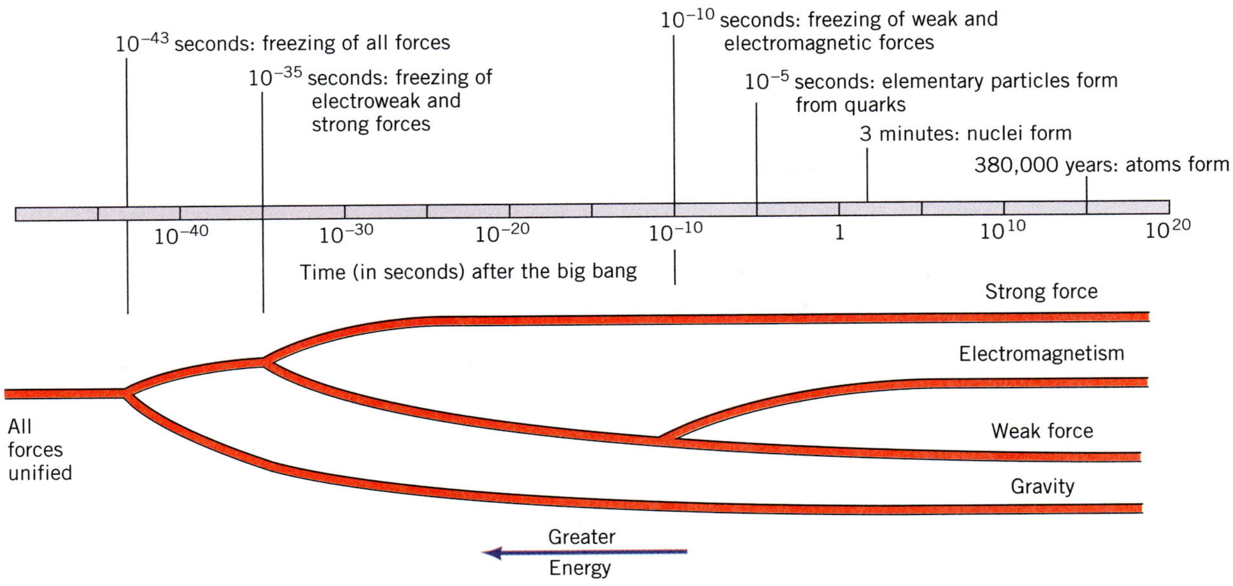

• **Figure 15-10** The sequence of "freezings" in the universe since the big bang. The earliest freezings involve the splitting of forces, while later freezings involve forms of matter.

The universe began as an infinitely hot, dense concentration of energy that immediately began to expand and cool. This cooling led to a succession of so-called freezings that dominated the history of the universe. Six distinct episodes occurred, and each had its own unique effect on the universe that we live in. Between each pair of freezings was a relatively long period of steady and rather uneventful expansion. Once we understand these crucial transitions in the history of the universe, we will have come a long way toward understanding why the universe is the way it is.

Let's look at the transitions in order, from the earliest to the most recent, as summarized in Figure 15-10. The first set of freezings involves the unification of forces we discussed in Chapter 13, and the last set involves the coming together of particles to form more complex structures such as nuclei and atoms.

10^{-43} Second: The Freezing of All Forces

An understanding of the state of the universe at the very beginning is currently beyond the frontiers of scientific knowledge. The first freezing involved the unification of forces that we discussed in Chapter 13. Cosmologists calculate that the first freezing after the beginning of the universe took place at about 10^{-43} second. (This is really a small number: 0.0000000000000000000000000000000000000000001 second!) Before this time, there was only a single unified force. At 10^{-43} second, gravity split off from the strong-electroweak force, so there were two fundamental forces acting in nature.

We cannot reproduce the unimaginably high temperatures that existed at this freezing in our laboratories, and we do not have successful theories that describe the unification of gravity with the other forces. Thus this earliest freezing remains both the theoretical frontier and the limit of our knowledge about the universe at the present time.

10^{-35} Second: The Freezing of the Electroweak and Strong Forces

Unified field theories that describe the behavior of all matter and forces (see Chapter 13) tell us that before the universe was 10^{-35} second old, the strong force was unified with the electroweak force. At 10^{-35} second, the strong force split off from the electroweak force. That is, before this time there were only two fundamental forces acting in the universe (the strong-electroweak force and the force of gravity), but after this time, there were three. It was at this time that cosmologists believe that some of the incredible energy of the early universe was transformed into matter.

Two important events are associated with the freezing at 10^{-35} seconds. They are:

1. The Elimination of Antimatter

With the freezing of the electroweak and strong forces, fundamental particles of matter and antimatter also appeared for the first time. Today, antimatter (see Chapter 13) is fairly rare in the universe. It wasn't until the twentieth century that scientists were able to identify antimatter, and we presently have compelling evidence that no large collections of antimatter exist anywhere in the universe. For example, spaceships have landed on the Moon, Mars, and Venus, and if any of those bodies had been made of antimatter, those spaceships would have been annihilated in a massive burst of gamma rays. As they were not destroyed, we conclude that none of those planets are made of antimatter.

By the same token, the solar wind, composed of ordinary matter, is constantly streaming outward from the Sun to the farthest reaches of the solar system. If any objects in the solar system were made of antimatter, the protons in the solar wind would be annihilating with materials in that body, and we would see evidence of it. The entire solar system, therefore, is made of ordinary matter. By the same type of argument, scientists have been able to show that our entire galaxy is made of ordinary matter and that no clusters of galaxies anywhere in the observable universe are made of antimatter.

The question, then, is this: If antimatter is indeed simply a mirror image of ordinary matter, and if antimatter appears in our theories on an equal footing with ordinary matter, as it does, then why is there so little antimatter in the universe?

Unified field theories give us an explanation of this striking feature of the cosmos. In experiments, we find one instance of a particle that decays preferentially into matter over antimatter—a particle whose decay products more often contain more matter than antimatter. This particle is called the K^0_L ("K-zero-long"), one of the many heavy particles such as protons and neutrons that were discovered in the latter part of the twentieth century.

If you take the theories that are successful in explaining this laboratory phenomenon and extrapolate them to the very early universe, you find that there were about 100,000,001 protons made for every 100,000,000 antiprotons. In the maelstrom that followed the big bang, the 100,000,000 antiprotons were annihilated with 100,000,000 protons, leaving only a sea of intense radiation to mark their presence. From the collection of leftover protons, all the matter in the universe (including Earth and its environs) was made. This discovery allowed physicists to explain the puzzling absence of antimatter in the universe and in the 1980s led to a burst of interest in the evolution of the early universe.

2. Inflation

According to the most widely accepted versions of the unified field theories, the freezing at 10^{-35} second was accompanied by an incredibly rapid (but short-lived) increase in the rate of expansion of the universe. This short period of rapid expansion is called *inflation,* and theories that incorporate this phenomenon are called *inflationary theories.*

One way to think about inflation is to remember that changes in volume are often associated with changes of state. Water, for example, expands when it freezes, which explains why water pipes may burst open when the water in them freezes in very cold weather. In the same way, scientists argue, the universe underwent a period of very rapid expansion during the period when the strong force froze out from the electroweak. Roughly speaking, at this time the universe went from being much smaller than a single proton to being about the size of a grapefruit (Figure 15-11).

Inflation explains another puzzling feature of the universe. We have repeatedly observed that the cosmic microwave background (which is an index of the temperature of the universe) is remarkably uniform. The temperatures associated with microwaves

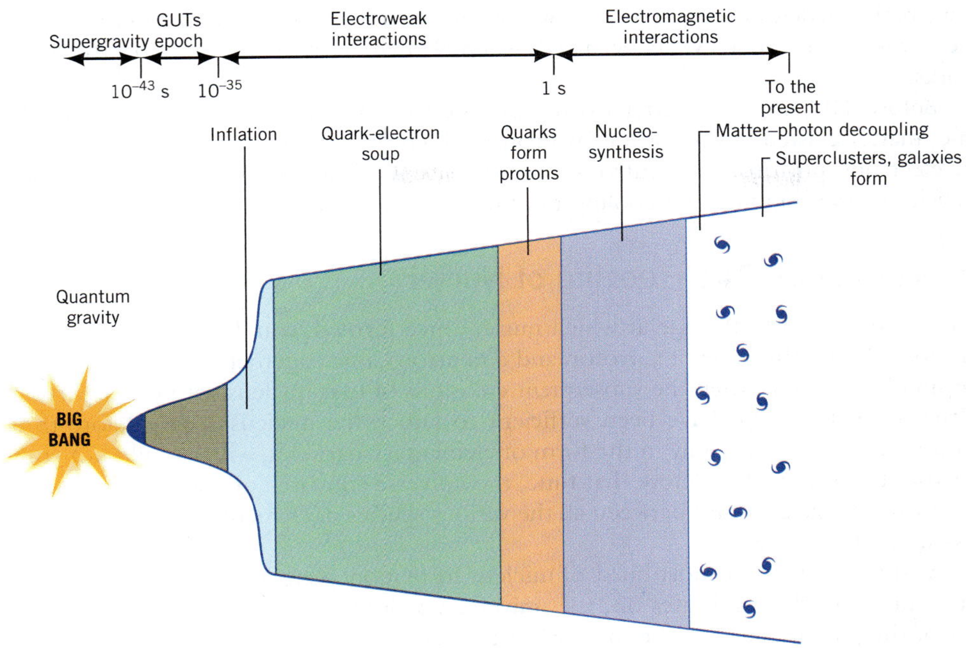

• **Figure 15-11** The evolution of the universe through the succession of freezings discussed in the text. Note the rapid expansion associated with the inflationary period.

coming from one region of the sky differ from those coming from another region by no more than 1 part in 1000. But calculations based on a uniform rate of expansion say that different parts of the universe would not have been close enough together to establish a common temperature.

In the inflationary theory, the resolution of this problem is simple. Before 10^{-35} second, all parts of the universe were in contact with each other because the universe was much smaller than you would have guessed based on a uniform rate of expansion. There was time to establish equilibrium before inflation took over and increased the size of the universe. The temperature equilibrium, established early, was preserved through the inflationary era and is seen today in the uniformity of the microwave background.

Thus the coming together of the theories of elementary particle physics and the study of cosmology has produced solutions to long-standing problems and questions about the universe.

10^{-10} Second: The Freezing of the Weak and Electromagnetic Forces

At 10^{-10} second (that's one ten-billionth of a second), the weak and the electromagnetic forces were unified. In other words, before 10^{-10} second, only three fundamental forces were operating in the universe: the strong, gravitational, and electroweak forces. After 10^{-10} second, the full complement of four fundamental forces was present.

The time of 10^{-10} second also marks another milestone in our discussion of the evolution of the universe. The modern particle accelerators of high-energy physics can just barely reproduce the incredible concentration of energy associated with that event. This means that from this point forward it is possible to have direct experimental checks of the theories that describe the evolution of the universe.

10^{-5} Second: The Freezing of Elementary Particles

Up to this point, matter in the universe had been in its most fundamental form—quarks and leptons (see Chapter 13). The remaining freezings involve the coming together of those basic particles to create matter we see around us. At 10^{-5} second (10 microseconds), the first of these events occurred, when elementary particles were formed out of quarks.

Before 10^{-5} second, matter existed as independent quarks and leptons; after this time, matter existed in the form of hadrons and leptons—that is, the ordinary particles like electrons, protons, and neutrons that we see today. The universe composed of these particles kept expanding and cooling until nuclei and atoms formed.

Three Minutes: The Freezing of Nuclei

Three minutes marks the age at which nuclei, once formed, could remain stable in the universe. Before this time, if a proton and a neutron came together to form deuterium, the simplest nucleus, then the subsequent collisions of that nucleus with other particles in the universe, would have been sufficient to knock the nucleus apart. Before three minutes, matter existed only in the form of elementary particles, which could not come together to form nuclei. Before that time, the universe consisted of a sea of high-energy radiation whizzing around between all the various species of elementary particles we discussed in Chapter 13.

At three minutes, a short burst of nucleus formation occurred, as we discussed earlier. Thus from three minutes on, the universe was littered with nuclei, which formed part of the plasma that was the material of the early universe. Remember, though, that only nuclei of the light elements—hydrogen, helium, and lithium—were made at this time.

Before One Million Years: The Freezing of Atoms

The most recent transition occurred gradually between the time the universe was a few hundred thousand and a million years old. At this time, the background temperature of the hot, dense universe was so great that electrons could not bond to nuclei to form atoms. Even if an atom formed by chance, its subsequent collisions were sufficiently violent that the atom could not stay together. Thus all of the universe's matter was in the form of plasma, a hot fluid mixture of electrons and simple nuclei.

This freezing marks an extremely important point in the history of the universe, because it is a point at which radiation such as light was no longer locked into the material of the universe. You know from experience that light can travel long distances through the atmosphere (which is made of atoms). But light cannot travel freely through plasma, which quickly absorbs light and other forms of radiation. Thus when atoms formed, the universe became transparent and radiation was released. It is this radiation, cooled and stretched out, that we now see as the cosmic microwave background.

The formation of atoms marks an important milestone for another reason. Before this event, if clumps of matter happened to begin forming (under the influence of gravity, for example), they would absorb radiation and be blown apart. This means that there must have been a "window of opportunity" for the formation of galaxies. If galaxies are made of ordinary matter, they couldn't have started to come together out of the primordial gas cloud until atoms started to form. By that time, however, the Hubble expansion had spread matter out so thinly that the ordinary workings of the force of gravity would not have been able to make a universe of galaxies, clusters, and superclusters. This puzzle was known as the "galaxy problem."

Another way of stating this problem is to compare the clumpiness of matter in the universe to the smoothness of the cosmic background radiation. The background radiation seems to be pretty much the same no matter which way you look in the universe. This uniformity argues that the universe had a smooth, regular beginning. How can this statement be reconciled with the lumpy structure we see when we look at the distribution of matter?

Dark Matter and Ripples at the Beginning of Time

As complicated and complete as this history of the early universe may seem, significant gaps in our understanding of the evolution of the universe remain. Some of these gaps were closed with the development of unified field theories and the inflationary scheme of the universe. The problem of explaining the existence of galaxies, clusters, and superclusters, however, remained.

It now appears that all the impressive luminous objects in the sky constitute only about 5% of the mass in the universe. Some of the rest of the matter (by some estimates about 25% of the total mass) exists in a mysterious form called **dark matter,** which we cannot see but whose graviational effects we can measure.

The easiest place to see evidence for dark matter is in galaxies such as our own Milky Way. Far out from the stars and spiral arms that we normally associate with galaxies, we can still see a diffuse cloud of hydrogen gas. This gas gives off radio waves, so we can detect its presence and its motion. In particular, we can tell how fast it is rotating. When we do these sorts of measurements, a rather startling fact emerges. In Chapter 2 we saw that Kepler's laws implied that any object orbiting around a central body under the influence of gravity will travel slower the farther out it is. The distant planet Jupiter, for example, moves more slowly in orbit around the Sun than does Earth. Similarly, you would expect that when hydrogen molecules are far enough away from the center of a galaxy, these more distant atoms would move more slowly than those closer in. Even though we can see these hydrogen atoms out to distances three times and more the distance from the center of the Milky Way to the end of the spiral arms, no one has ever seen the predicted slowing down.

The only way to explain this phenomenon is to say that those hydrogen atoms are still in the middle of the gravitational influence of the galaxy. This means that luminous matter—the bright stars and spiral arms—is not the only thing that is exerting a gravitational force. Something else, something that makes up about 95% of the mass of the galaxy and that extends far beyond the stars, exerts a gravitational force and affects the motion of the hydrogen we observe. Studies of many galaxies show the same effect, and scientists are now convinced that more than 90% of the mass of galaxies is made of something other than ordinary matter. Scientists also find evidence that dark matter exists in between galaxies, in clusters, and in other places in the universe.

Dark matter is strange, indeed. It does not interact through the electromagnetic force. If it did, it would absorb or emit photons and it wouldn't be "dark" in the sense we're using the term here. Yet, because we know that it exerts a gravitational attraction, we can conclude that this unseen "stuff" must be a form of matter—matter that interacts with ordinary matter only through the gravitational force. Detecting dark matter, and finding out what it is, remains a very active research field today.

The existence of dark matter might help us solve the galaxy problem, because dark matter could have formed into clumps *before atoms formed.* In the first several hundred thousand years after the big bang, photons blew apart collections of luminous matter that were trying to form galaxies, but light would not have affected the clumping of dark matter. Therefore, when atoms formed and luminous matter could clump together, it found itself in a universe in which large clusterings of dark matter already existed. The luminous matter would simply have fallen into these clusters and would not have had to form under the influence of its own gravitational attraction. Thus, if dark matter exists, and if dark matter formed clumps early in the history of the universe, the problem of structure is solved.

In 1992, important new results from the COBE satellite supported the notion of dark matter. Examining the microwave background in great detail, astronomers found evidence that some regions in the sky emit microwave background at a slightly higher temperature than the surrounding regions. These so-called ripples at the beginning of time

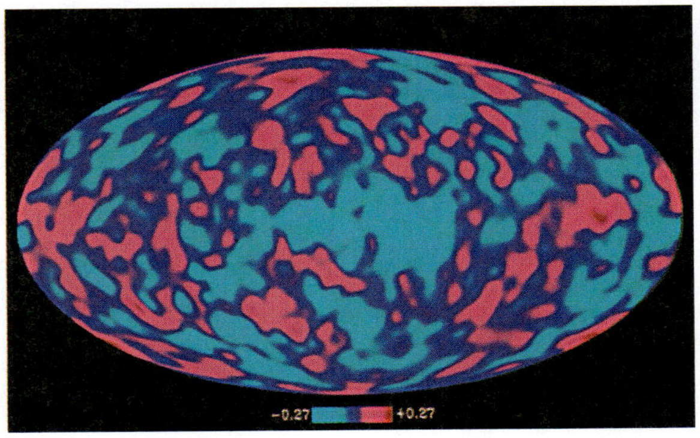

Courtesy NASA

The Cosmic Background Explorer (COBE) satellite produced this map of microwave radiation from the entire sky. Blue indicates regions that are 0.01% cooler than average, whereas red indicates 0.01% warmer regions. This map indicates that the early universe was not perfectly uniform, a situation that led to the present "clumpiness" of the universe.

Courtesy NASA/WMAP Science Team

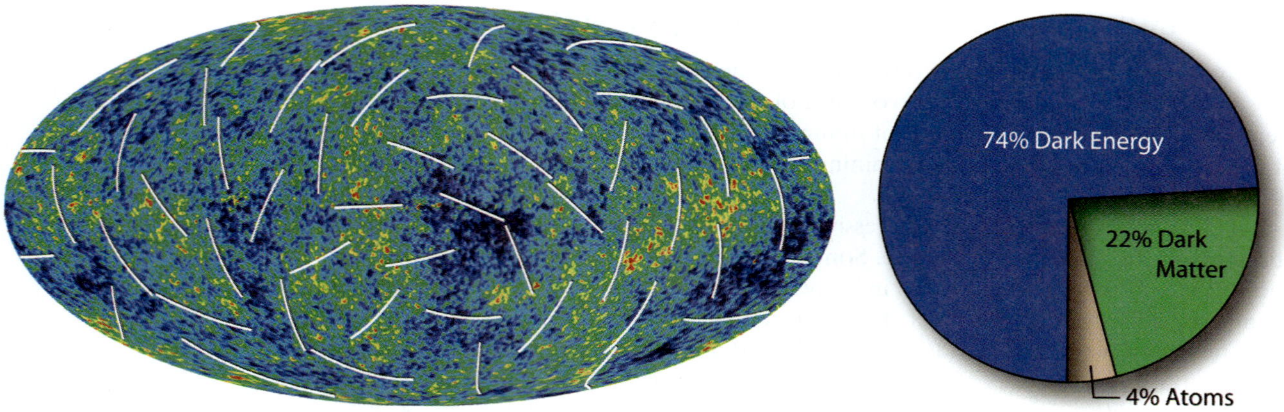

(Left) A detailed map of the cosmic microwave background from the Wilkinson Microwave Anistotropy Probe. *(Right)* The composition of the universe, with ordinary matter being only a small fraction of the whole.

were not very large—they correspond to temperature increases of the tiniest fraction of a degree. Nevertheless, they could have been emitted only from regions that were denser and slightly hotter than their neighbors. These ripples appear to mark the beginning of the collection of luminous matter immediately after the formation of atoms.

In June 2001, the Wilkinson Microwave Anisotropy Probe (WMAP) was launched by NASA to make detailed maps of the small temperature differences in the cosmic microwave background radiation. From the study of the WMAP data, astronomers have been able to produce the best estimate of the age of the universe (13.7 billion years) as well as provide corroborating evidence for the existence of dark energy. In 2007, the European Space Agency hopes to launch a third-generation cosmic microwave radiation satellite, called the Planck Surveyor, which will provide even more detailed measurements.

This particular area of study will continue to be important in the coming years, and you're sure to see information about it in the media.

The End of the Universe

When most people think about the Hubble expansion, they wonder if the universe will continue to expand forever, or if it will someday fall back in on itself. In the case of eternal expansion, astronomers say that the universe is open; in the case of eventual collapse, they say that the universe is closed. Finally, in the intermediate case between the two, where universal expansion slows down, but never quite stops, the universe is said to be flat. Can we tell which kind of universe we live in?

Scientists have approached this question by noting that the force pulling back on distant galaxies is the gravitational attraction associated with the mass of the universe. If there is enough mass, the outward motion of the galaxy will be slowed down and reversed. If there isn't enough mass, the expansion will be slowed but never stopped. The luminous matter of the universe—stars, nebulae, and dust clouds—is not nearly enough to "close" the universe. Even counting dark matter brings us only up to about 20 to 30% of that value. Just from counting mass, then, we would conclude that we live in an open universe.

In 1999, astronomers announced a surprising result that casts new light on this question. Using a new standard candle called a Type Ia supernova, they have measured the distances to the most distant galaxies. Using the fact that light from those galaxies has been traveling toward us for billions of years, they can compare the rate of expansion of the universe as it was long ago to what it is today. The surprising result is that the expansion of the universe isn't slowing down at all—it's speeding up! In fact, more detailed measurements indicate that the universal expansion has had a very strange history. For the first five billion years or so, the expansion slowed down, but then it began to increase.

This behavior can be understood if we realize that there are actually two forces acting between galaxies—ordinary gravity, which tends to slow down the expansion, and a kind of outward pressure, pushing the galaxies apart. This newly discovered force has been dubbed **dark energy** by cosmologist Michael Turner of the University of Chicago. We do not yet know what it is—in fact, most cosmologists consider discovering the nature of dark energy to be the most important question in their field—but we can see its effects. Whatever it is, we know that it supplies the remaining 70% of the universe's mass.

The history of the Hubble expansion, then, can be understood as follows: in the early stages of the universe, matter was close together and the force of gravity predominated. As a result, the expansion slowed. After about 5 billion years, however, the increasing distance between galaxies had weakened the force of gravity to the point that the repulsive force of dark energy took over and expansion accelerated. Today, we live in the age of dark energy.

The future of the universe depends on the nature of dark energy. If its effects die away in the future, then it is possible that the expansion will once again slow down as gravity takes over again. If it stays as it is, then we can expect today's mildly accelerated expansion to continue. There is, however, another possibility. If the repulsive force of dark energy is an intrinsic property of space-time, as some theories suggest, then that force will grow in the future. Some theorists have suggested that it will grow so much that eventually it will not only push galaxies apart, but will even tear up planets and atoms. They call this future the "Big Rip."

Although there's a lot of uncertainty about the nature of dark energy, with its discovery, scientists seem to have completed the roster of the kinds of materials that make up the universe. Perhaps the most humbling thing about this new vision is that the matter with which we are familiar—the stuff of our everyday existence—seems to make up a very small percent of the total picture.

Science News | Blasts from the Past

(Science News, Feb. 11, 2006, p. 88)

If you want to see far into the past, you have to look at events a long way away. If an event happened billions of years ago and the light has been traveling toward us since then, we are, in fact, looking into the past when we see that event today. The longtime goal of cosmologists has been to be able to see back into those misty times just after atoms formed, when the coming construction of galaxies was just beginning. The problem, of course, is that the farther away something is, the fainter it looks to us. This means that the farther we look back, the brighter our "candle" has to be. This is why cosmologists look at very bright objects like quasars and supernovae when they want to talk about the early evolution of the Big Bang.

Recently, a group of astronomers centered at the University of North Carolina at Chapel Hill have started to look at even brighter events called gamma ray bursts. As the name implies, these are events which announce their presence by an intense burst of gamma rays—a burst which usually lasts a few minutes. Typically, these gamma rays are detected by satellites, since they are absorbed in Earth's atmosphere. The bursts are followed, however, by an "afterglow" lasting several hours. This afterglow consists of radiation in the visible to radio regions so that, once ground based astronomers have been alerted to the beginning of a burst, they can train terrestrial telescopes on the spot and make measurements on the afterglow.

We don't know precisely what causes the bursts, although many astronomers believe they result from the collapse of huge stars into large black holes. Whatever their cause, however, their brightness has led some astronomers to predict that within a few years we will be able to use them to see beyond the most distant known quasars and supernovae.

To give an idea of how powerful this new tool might be, a Japanese team measured the redshift of light during the afterglow of a recent burst discovered by the Chapel Hill group. They concluded that, for the first time, we had seen an event in a galaxy that had formed less than a billion years after the big bang. Thus, gamma ray bursts may well prove to be the tool that allows scientists to see as far back into the past as it is possible to see.

Thinking More About | Cosmology

The History of the Universe

The story of the big bang that we have just recounted has one clear feature: there were no human beings around to observe any of the events we've just described. In 1999, creationists on the Kansas Board of Education used this fact as a reason to ban questions about the big bang from statewide high school scientific achievement tests. Let's think for a moment about the kind of evidence we require to establish the existence of events in the past.

How do you know there was an event called the American Civil War? No one alive today actually took part in the Civil War, yet no one suggests that we should doubt its existence. The reason is that there is all sorts of evidence in the form of texts, artifacts, documents, and even recorded stories told by survivors before they died. The weight of this evidence is so overwhelming that the existence of the war is universally accepted.

But what about events farther back in time—the Crusades, for example, or the Thirty Years War? The evidence here is weaker than that for the Civil War. What about events that occurred before the invention of writing—the arrival of the first humans in North America, for example? Here the evidence is exclusively in the form of archeological data. And what about geological events where the evidence is in the rocks themselves?

The evidence for the big bang has been outlined in this chapter. How does it compare to the evidence for other events in the past? How much evidence is required to establish the existence of such events? Why do you suppose so few scientists agree with the decision of the Kansas School Board?

Summary

Early in the twentieth century, Edwin Hubble made two extraordinary discoveries about the structure and behavior of the universe, the science we call *cosmology*. First, he demonstrated that our home, the collection of stars known as the *Milky Way*, is just one of countless *galaxies* in the universe, each containing billions of stars. By measuring the *redshift* of galaxies, he also discovered that these distant objects are moving away from each other. According to *Hubble's law*, the farther the galaxy, the faster it is moving away. This relative motion implies that the universe is expanding.

One theory that accounts for universal expansion is the *big bang*—the idea that the universe began at a specific moment in time and has been expanding ever since. Evidence from the *cosmic microwave background radiation* and the relative abundances of light elements, in addition to expansion, support the big bang theory.

At the moment of creation, all forces and matter were unified in one unimaginably hot and dense volume. As the universe expanded, however, a series of six "freezings" led to the universe we see today. Freezings at 10^{-43} second, 10^{-35} second, and 10^{-10} second caused a single unified force to split into the four forces we observe today: the gravitational, strong, electromagnetic, and weak forces. At that early stage of the universe, when all matter and energy were contained in a volume no larger than a grapefruit, matter was in its most elementary form of quarks and leptons.

At 10^{-5} second, the quarks bonded together to form heavy nuclear particles such as protons and neutrons. Subsequent freezings saw these particles first fuse to nuclei at three minutes and ultimately join with electrons to form atoms at 380,000 years. Stars, which formed from those atoms, then could begin the processes that provided all the other chemical elements. The search for *dark matter*—mass that we cannot see with our telescopes—is a research frontier that may help us determine whether the universe will continue expanding forever. Recent data tells us that the expansion of the universe is accelerating, an effect that scientists attribute to something called *dark energy*.

Key Terms

Milky Way
galaxy
cosmology
redshift
Hubble's law
big bang theory
cosmic microwave background radiation
dark matter
dark energy

Review Questions

1. What is cosmology? How does cosmology differ from astronomy?
2. What is a galaxy? How does a galaxy differ from a star?
3. How are galaxies distributed in the universe?
4. How did Edwin Hubble discover that there are galaxies in the universe other than the Milky Way?
5. Name the different types of galaxies and their distinguishing characteristics.

6. Describe Hubble's law. How did Hubble discover it?

7. What kinds of evidence support the big bang theory?

8. How is the redshift related to the Doppler effect? What does the redshift say about the universe?

9. Make a table with ages of the universe in the left column (10^{-43} seconds, 10^{-35} seconds, 10^{-10} seconds, 10^{-5} seconds, 3 minutes, 380,000 years) and the major events in the history of the universe in the right column.

10. What is the significance of the discovery by Penzias and Wilson of cosmic microwave background radiation?

11. What are "ripples at the beginning of time," and why are they important?

12. What is dark matter, and what evidence exists for it?

Discussion Questions

1. Why does Earth seem to be at the center of the Hubble expansion?

2. Is the universe getting hotter or colder as it expands? In what way will the cosmic background radiation change as the universe changes temperature?

3. Why was the steady-state theory of the universe abandoned? How does this episode fit into the discussion of the scientific method in Chapter 1?

4. What were the conditions of the early universe that allowed for the creation of light elements? Why is there an abundance of lighter elements in the universe?

5. Louis Pasteur once said that "chance favors only the mind that is prepared." Apply this saying to the discoveries of Edwin Hubble, and of Penzias and Wilson.

6. Some advances in our knowledge have been made possible through better equipment, such as Hubble's discoveries using the 100-inch Hooker telescope at Mount Wilson. What other major discoveries in cosmology have relied on improvements in existing apparatus?

7. What is the ultimate fate of a closed universe? an open universe? a flat universe?

Problems

1. Assuming a Hubble constant of 70 km/s/Mpc, what is the approximate velocity of a galaxy 100 Mpc away? 2500 Mpc away? 50,000 Mpc away?

2. If a galaxy is 500 Mpc away, how fast is it receding from us?

3. An observer on one of the raisins in our bread-dough analogy measures distances and velocities of neighboring raisins. The data look like the following:

Distance (cm)	Velocity (cm/hr)
0.9	1.02
1.9	2.00
3.4	2.90
5.1	4.05
7.0	5.90
9.4	7.10

Plot these data on a graph and use the plot to estimate a "Hubble constant" for the raisins.

4. From the data in Problem 3, estimate the time that has elapsed since the dough started rising. Estimate the largest and smallest values of this number consistent with the data.

5. Some theories say that in the inflationary period, the scale of the universe increased by a factor of 10^{50}. Suppose your height were to increase by a factor of 10^{50}. How tall would you be? Express your answer in light-years and compare it to the size of the observable universe.

6. Suppose a proton (diameter about 10^{-13} cm) were to inflate by a factor of 10^{50}. How big would it be? Convert the answer to light-years and compare it to the size of the observable universe.

7. How fast is a galaxy 10 billion light-years from Earth moving away from us? What fraction of the speed of light is this?

8. The average temperature of the universe is 2.7 K. What is that temperature in degrees Farenheit? How far above absolute zero is that?

9. If you allow the thickness of a dollar bill to represent one light-year, how high would a stack of dollar bills have to be to represent the distance to the Sun? to the nearest galaxy? temperature?

INVESTIGATIONS

1. The Milky Way is a band of stars that, seen from Earth in the summer months, stretches all the way across the sky. Given what you know about galaxies, why do you suppose that our own galaxy appears this way to us? Who was the first natural philosopher to figure this out?

2. Will the constellation of Andromeda be above the horizon tonight? If so, go out and try to spot the Andromeda galaxy.

3. Look up the "Great Attractor." How does the existence of such an object fit in with the concept of the Hubble expansion? How would you modify the raisin-bread dough analogy to put in the Great Attractor?

4. Investigate the cosmologies of other societies. How do they think the universe began? Do they predict how it will end?

5. What agencies or organizations fund cosmological research? What was the role of the Carnegie Institution of Washington in Edwin Hubble's research?

6. Investigate the difference between cosmology and cosmogony.

7. The computer and the Hubble telescope were major advancements in technology. What new advances in technology may prove useful for astronomy and comsmology?

16

Earth and Other Planets

Is Earth the only planet with life?

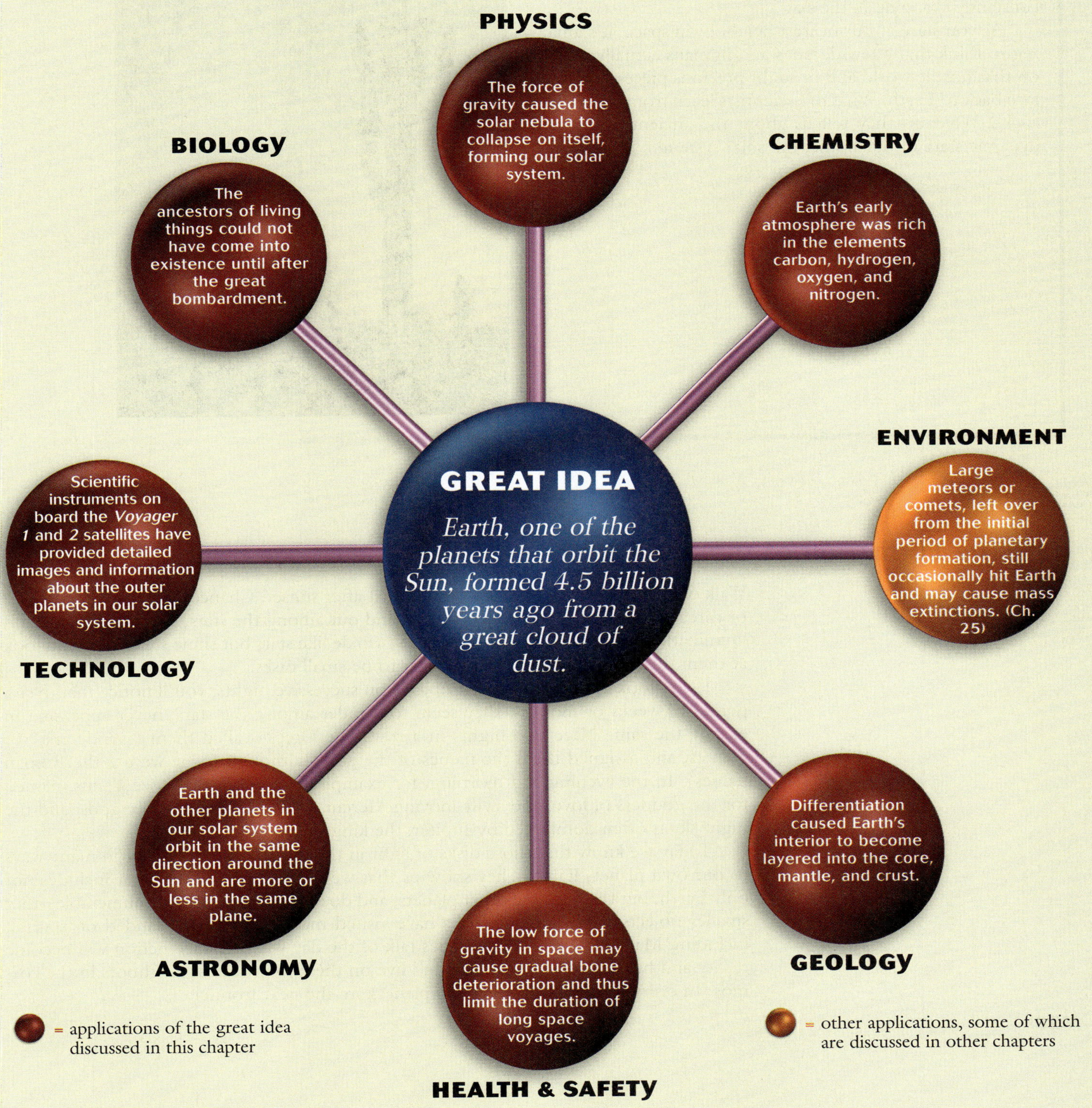

Science Through the Day | The Sun and the Moon

It's shortly after noon; the Sun is blazing overhead. As you scan the horizon you see a perfect half Moon rising in the East. The rough, cratered surface stands out even in daylight. But you recall that just a few days ago you saw the Moon as a thin crescent in the evening sky. And a couple of weeks before that, the night's full Moon was so bright you could almost read by it. The Moon, like other objects in our solar system, is constantly changing in the sky.

As you stare at our nearest neighbor in space, it's amazing to think that a few decades ago humans actually walked on that hostile world and brought precious pieces of its surface back to Earth. What did scientists learn from those alien rocks? What do they tell us about the ancient origin and dynamic state of our home, the solar system?

Purestock/SUPERSTOCK

The Formation of the Solar System

Walk outside and look at the sky tonight just after sunset. Chances are you will find two or three particularly bright objects that stand out among the stars, even in the haze and illumination of a city. They don't seem to twinkle like stars but shine steadily. If you look at them through binoculars, they appear to be small disks.

If you look at the same bright objects on successive nights, you'll notice that over a period of weeks or months, they seem to wander among the stars, never appearing in exactly the same place two nights in a row. The Greeks called them "wanderers," or planets, and assigned them the names of the gods (although today we use the Roman names). In the evening and morning, for example, you are likely to see Venus, named for the goddess of love, and swift-moving Mercury, the messenger of the gods; and the night sky is often dominated by Jupiter, the king of the gods.

Today we know that those disks of light in the sky are objects similar in many ways to our own planet, Earth. They show us that we are part of a system that includes not only Earth, but the Sun, the other planets, and dozens of moons, and innumerable other smaller objects as well. Our probes have visited most of them and landed on several, including Mars and Venus. Visionaries talk of the day when science fiction will become reality and human beings will work and live on these, our nearest neighbors in the cosmos. In every sense of the word, the planets are the next frontier.

Clues to the Origin of the Solar System

• **Figure 16-1** The solar system.

The Copernican revolution radically altered human perceptions of our place in the universe (see Chapter 2). Rather than occupying what was assumed by many to be the center of creation, Earth became just one of a number of planets orbiting the Sun. The **solar system,** which includes many worlds—the Sun, the planets, and their dozens of moons, plus all other objects gravitationally bound to the Sun—displays several distinctive characteristics. Describing these features and explaining in detail how they came to be remains one of the main challenges faced by planetary scientists today. Indeed, the study of these many other worlds helps us to understand the origin and evolution of our own planet.

How can we deduce the origin and present state of the solar system? Until recently, all our observations of the Sun and planets had been made from Earth's surface. We see points of light moving in the sky, but how can that information be translated into a vivid picture of a dynamic system?

Humans have studied the solar system for thousands of years, making observations and proposing models. Ancient scholars recorded the changing positions of the brightest planets, such as Venus and Jupiter. Application of the telescope by Galileo and many subsequent astronomers (see Chapter 2) led to the discovery of numerous new, faint objects, including several moons and other small bodies. More recently, orbiting space probes and flyby missions have returned closeup photographic images of several planets, while spacecraft have landed on Venus and Mars. Our present understanding of the solar system, therefore, represents the cumulative effect of centuries of observation.

As astronomers gathered data on the solar system, they noticed several striking regularities regarding the orbits of planets and the distribution of mass—patterns that provide clues to understanding the evolution of our home (Figure 16-1).

Clue #1: Planetary Orbits

Think about what Newton's laws tell us regarding satellites orbiting a central body. A satellite can go in any direction: east to west or west to east, around the equator or over the poles. There are no constraints regarding the orientation of the orbit, and planets could orbit any which way around the Sun. Yet in our solar system we see three very curious features:

1. All planets, and most of their moons, orbit in the same direction around the Sun, and this direction is the same as that of the rotation of the Sun.
2. All orbits of planets and their larger moons are in more or less the same plane. The solar system resembles a bunch of marbles rolling around on a single flat dish.
3. Almost all planets and moons rotate on their axes in the same direction as the planets orbit the Sun.

> **Stop and Think!** If you had only the preceding information, what scenarios for the origin of the solar system would you construct?

Clue #2: The Distribution of Mass

You could imagine a solar system in which mass is evenly distributed, with all planets more or less the same size and same chemical composition. But our solar system is not that way at all (Figure 16-2). Instead:

• **Figure 16-2** Most of the mass in the solar system is in the Sun, and most of the rest is in the Jovian planets. (Distances in this figure are not to scale.)

- Virtually all of the material of the solar system is contained within the Sun, with only a small fraction in the planets and other objects in orbit.
- There are two distinct kinds of planets. Near the Sun, in the "inner" solar system, are planets like Earth—relatively small, rocky, high-density worlds. These are called the **terrestrial planets** and include **Mercury, Venus, Earth, Mars,** and (although it isn't really a planet) **Earth's Moon.** Farther out from the Sun, in the "outer" solar system, are huge worlds made primarily of hydrogen and helium. We call them "gas giants," or **Jovian planets,** and they are **Jupiter, Saturn, Uranus,** and **Neptune. Pluto,** the outermost of the traditional nine planets, is something of an anomaly, being small and icy. The planets of the solar system and some of their characteristics are listed in Table 16-1.
- Interspersed with the planets are a large number of other kinds of objects. All the planets except the innermost, Mercury and Venus, are orbited by one or more

Table 16-1 The Planets and Their Characteristics

	Mercury	Venus	Earth	Mars	Jupiter	Saturn	Uranus	Neptune	Pluto
Diameter (km)	4,880	12,104	12,756	6,787	142,800	120,000	51,800	49,500	6,000
Mass (Earth=1)	0.0558	0.815	1.0	0.108	317.8	95.2	14.4	17.2	0.003
Density (gm/cm3) (water=1)	5.44	5.20	5.52	3.93	1.30	0.69	1.28	1.64	2.06
Number of moons	0	0	1	2	61	30	21	11	3
Length of day (Earth hours)	1416	5832	24	24.6	9.8	10.2	17.2	16.1	154
Period of one revolution around Sun (Earth years)	0.24	0.62	1.00	1.88	11.86	29.50	84.00	164.90	247.70
Average distance from Sun (millions of km)	58	108	150	228	778	1427	2870	4497	5900

moons. While some moons are little more than boulders a few kilometers across, others are much larger, and Saturn's largest moon Titan is about the same size as Mercury. Saturn and the other Jovian planets also have dramatic rings composed of millions of tiny moons. Small, rocky **asteroids** that circle the Sun like miniature planets are found primarily in orbits between Mars and Jupiter, in what is called the **asteroid belt,** although some have orbits that cross Earth's. Starting at about the orbit of Pluto and extending far beyond we find a collection of rocky objects in a huge disk known as the Kuiper belt. Finally, in a gigantic sphere surrounding the entire system, we find a swarm of icy **comets** with compositions something like a "dirty snowball." Occasionally, one is jostled loose from its orbit and becomes part of the realm of the planets, creating a spectacular display in the sky.

These regularities in the distribution of the solar system's mass, combined with data on planetary orbits, add support to the nebular hypothesis—our best model of how the solar system was formed.

The Nebular Hypothesis

In Chapter 14 we examined the modern theory of star formation—the *nebular hypothesis,* which was first put forward by the French mathematician and physicist Pierre Simon Laplace (1749–1827). His model of star formation also helps to explain many of the distinctive characteristics of the solar system—the rotation of the Sun, the orbits of the planets, and the distribution of mass into one large central object and lots of much smaller orbiting bodies. According to the nebular hypothesis, long ago (about 4.5 billion years ago based on radiometric dating) a large cloud of dust and gas collected in the region now occupied by the solar system. Such dust and gas clouds, called **nebulae,** are common throughout our galaxy, the Milky Way. They typically contain more than 99% hydrogen and helium, with lesser amounts of all the other naturally occurring elements.

Under the influence of gravity, the nebula slowly, inexorably, started to collapse on itself. As was the case for the formation of stars from a nebula, the collapse caused the cloud to spin faster and faster. The rapid spin had several consequences. For one thing, it meant that some of the material in the outer parts of the cloud began to spin out into a flat disk. As we saw in the previous chapter, the solar system at this stage of its formation can be thought of as a large pancake with a big lump in the middle. The big lump represents the material that will eventually become the Sun and the material in the thin, flattened disk will eventually become the planets and the rest of the solar system (Figure 16-3).

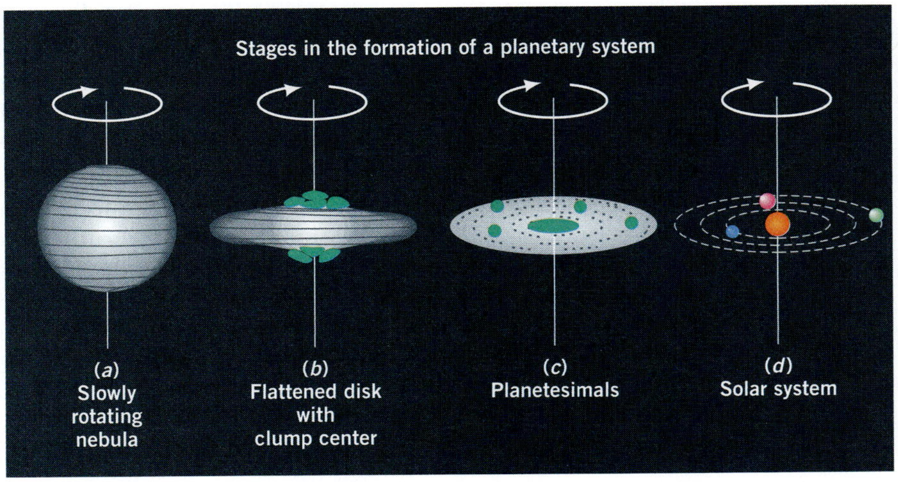

• **Figure 16-3** As the nebula that formed the solar system collapsed, it began to rotate and flatten into a disk. The stages in solar system formation include *(a)* a slowly rotating nebula, *(b)*, a flattened disk with massive center, *(c)* planets in the process of birth represented as mass concentrations in the nebula, and *(d)* the solar system.

Courtesy NASA

The inner planets, like Mars, are small and rocky.

The flattening of the nebula into a disk explains another feature of the solar system. The planets had to form in this rotating disk of material, and hence their eventual orbits had to lie close to the disk's plane. The fact that all planetary orbits lie near the same plane, then, is a simple consequence of the solar system's rapid rotation as the nebular cloud began to contract.

In any clump of matter like the spinning disk, by chance, matter is more densely collected in some regions than elsewhere. These regions exert a stronger gravitational force than their neighbors, so that nearby matter tends to gravitate to them. Once the nearby matter has come in, the concentration of matter at that point is even greater, and it will pull even more material into it. As material accumulates, solid grains start to stick together.

This ultimate consequence of gravitational force leads to the rapid breakup of the disk into small objects called *planetesimals*, which range in size from boulders to masses several kilometers across. Once this has happened, the process of gravitational attraction goes on at a grander scale. Planetesimals collide with each other; larger objects capture smaller ones and continue growing.

About the time that this process was going on in the early solar system, the material at the center—more than 99% of the nebula's original mass—began to turn into a star. Light energy began to radiate out from the Sun, and temperature differences began to develop in the disk. Those parts nearest the Sun warmed up, while those farther out warmed only a little. As a result, the inner and outer solar systems developed differently. In the warm inner system, compounds such as water, methane, and carbon dioxide were in gaseous form, while farther out they were frozen into solids.

Thus, everyday physical processes having to do with phases of matter and the response to temperature—processes as familiar as boiling water and making ice—explain one of the crucial facts about the solar system. The terrestrial planets, including Mercury, Venus, Earth, and Mars, were formed from those materials that could remain solid at high temperatures. Consequently, they are small, rocky worlds.

Farther out in the solar system we find the Jovian planets, including Jupiter, Saturn, Uranus, and Neptune. The compositions of those planets are essentially the same as the material concentrated in the original nebula; that is, they contain large amounts of hydrogen and helium. These planets formed from material that condensed and accumulated under the condition of lower temperatures so far from the Sun. Consequently, these outer Jovian planets have a markedly different chemical composition from the inner terrestrial planets of the solar system.

In passing, we should note that the Jovian planets probably had their own complement of high-density materials. Scientists suspect that beneath the thousands of kilometers of helium, hydrogen, and other condensed gases on these planets is concealed a core like a small terrestrial planet, whose composition is much like that of Earth and its neighbors. But this rocky matter represents only a small fraction of these planets' total mass.

NASA Media Services

Gas giant planets, like Jupiter, are large and are composed mainly of hydrogen and helium. Note the Great Red Spot—a storm that has raged on Jupiter for centuries.

Some astronomers argue that the largest planets, Jupiter and Saturn, formed by a process more like that of a small star than through the accretion of planetesimals. The details of the structure and formation of the Jovian planets remain a rich ground for debate in the sciences.

Just as any construction site has a pile of leftover materials lying around when the building is finished, so too does the solar system have its "scrap pile." These leftovers take the form of the rocky asteroids and icy comets that still orbit the Sun. They represent the matter that never got taken up into planets.

The Science of Life •

Gravity and Bones

The planets of our solar system vary greatly in mass, from tiny Pluto with only 1/500th the mass of Earth, to Jupiter, which is 317 times more massive than our own planet. Consequently, the force of gravity at the surface of each planet is different; you would weigh a small fraction of what you do now on the surface of Pluto, but many times your present weight on Jupiter. (The connection between mass and weight is reviewed in Chapter 2.)

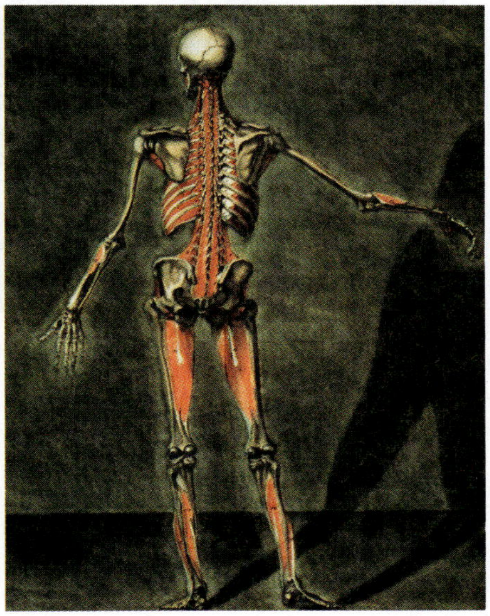

Private Collection/Bridgeman Art Library/NY

Bones respond to the absence of gravitational stress.

In humans, bones in the skeleton support our weight. Bone is not a rigid a material like concrete; rather, it must be flexible in response to its environment. It constantly rebuilds itself, replacing the calcium-rich minerals that form the solid structure. In fact, you can think of what goes on in bones as being analogous to the remodeling of a house. First, the old material is removed (a process called resorption), then new material is added. If a bone is subject to unusual stress (or lack of it), it will change gradually in response, adding or subtracting mass.

On the surface of the Moon, for example, you would weigh one-sixth of your Earth weight. Your bones would start to remodel themselves in response to the lower force of gravity, unless you kept them under stress by an extended program of vigorous exercise. Astronauts spending a few weeks or months in the weightless environment of space have experienced significant bone loss that, fortunately, is eventually made up after they return to Earth. Scientists are less certain, however, of the extremely long-term effects of low gravity on bone loss. What might happen during the long months of a space flight to Mars, for example? Studies on astronauts now may well determine whether such ambitious interplanetary flights take place in the foreseeable future. •

Stop and Think! What advantages to a living thing do you suppose arise from the features of bones we've just discussed? Why do you suppose bones aren't built like bridges, which are designed to carry the heaviest load possible?

The Formation of Earth

The collapse of the solar nebula into the Sun and planets began the solar system's evolution. Following the formation of planets, each object evolved in its own distinctive way. For Earth and the other terrestrial planets, this history had to do with the churning, colliding, roiling cloud of planetesimals. Once planetesimals were formed, the formation of planets followed quickly. As planetesimals moved in their orbits, they collected smaller planetesimals through the process of gravitational attraction. Then these larger planetesimals collided and coalesced into the beginnings of a planet. As the process of accumulation went on, the growing planet gradually swept up all the debris that lay near its orbit.

An artist's impression of Earth's surface during the great bombardment.

Steve Munsinger/Photo Researchers

If you had been standing on the surface of the newly forming planet Earth during this stage, you would have seen a spectacular display. A constant rain of debris left over from the initial period of planetary formation fell to the surface, steadily adding mass to the planet. During this period, called the **great bombardment,** the large amounts of kinetic energy carried by the shower of stones were converted into heat, which was added to the newly forming planet. By

Courtesy NASA

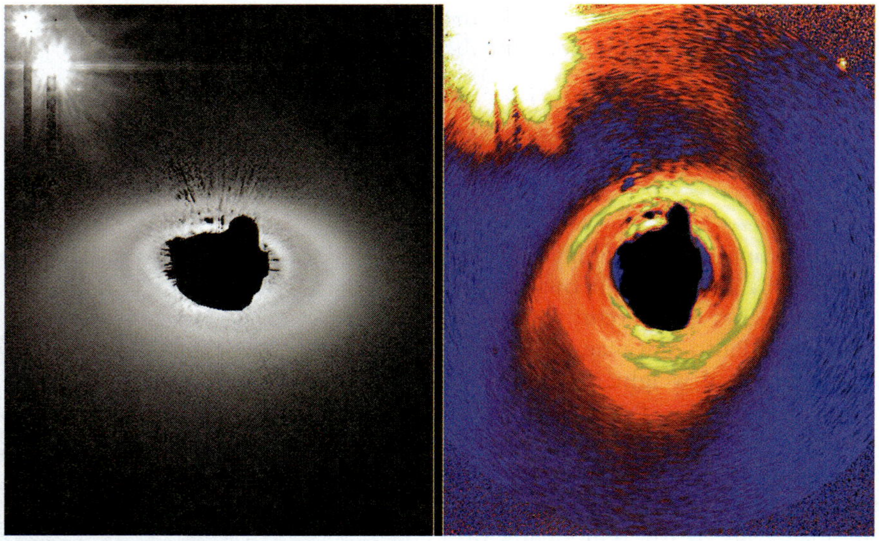

These Hubble Space Telescope pictures show a disk around a young star.

some accounts, much of the planetary surface would have glowed bright red from this accumulating heat and each large impact would have been accompanied by a spectacular splash of molten rock. Although in the case of Earth the addition of material has slowed considerably since the beginning, it has not stopped. Every time you see a **meteor** (often called a shooting star), for example, you are seeing an object roughly the size of a grain of sand being added to our planet. Scientists estimate that Earth's mass grows by about 20 metric tons (20,000 kg, or 2×10^7 g) per day by accretion of material falling from space.

When the nebular hypothesis was first proposed in the eighteenth century, there seemed little chance that any direct observational evidence could be found to support it. In 1992 astronomers using the Hubble Space Telescope (see Chapter 14) detected thick masses of dust encircling newborn stars in a region of space called the Orion nebula. Subsequent observations have confirmed the existence of numerous disks around young stars. It appears that in these cases we are seeing distant solar systems in the process of being born—observations that give us a measure of confidence in our model of how planets come into existence.

Science by the Numbers •

Earth's Growth

Earth's mass is approximately 6×10^{27} grams. If 2×10^7 grams are added per day, how long would it take to double Earth's mass?

Reasoning and Solution: First, we have to calculate how many grams are added to Earth each year by multiplying the daily added mass by the number of days in a year. Earth's total mass, divided by the mass added each year, gives us the time it would take to double the present mass.

First we determine the yearly mass added to Earth.

$$\begin{aligned}\text{mass added per year} &= (365 \text{ days/year}) \times (2 \times 10^7 \text{ g/day}) \\ &= 730 \times 10^7 \text{ g/year} \\ &= 7.3 \times 10^9 \text{ g/year}\end{aligned}$$

Then, divide Earth's total mass by the mass added every year.

$$\begin{aligned}\text{number of years} &= \frac{(6 \times 10^{27} \text{ g})}{(7.3 \times 10^9 \text{ g/year})} \\ &= 0.82 \times 10^{18} \text{ years} \\ &= 8.2 \times 10^{17} \text{ years}\end{aligned}$$

This number is the time (in years) that would be required to double Earth's mass at its present rate of growth. This immense time, nearly a billion-billion years, is vastly greater than the lifetime of our planet, which is a paltry 4.5 billion years. From this calculation we see that the total amount of mass now being added to Earth is trivial, so that most of the planet's mass must have accumulated in the beginning. •

Differentiation

Each time another planetesimal hit the young Earth, all of its kinetic and potential energy was converted into heat. That heat diffused through the planet. Earth's surface glowed red hot and the deep interior reached temperatures of thousands of degrees. Eventually, Earth either melted completely or else was heated to high enough temperatures so that it was very soft all the way through. Heavy, dense materials (like iron and nickel) sank under the force of gravity toward the center of the planet, while lighter, less-dense materials floated to the top. The result of this process, called **differentiation,** is that the present-day terrestrial planets have a distinctively layered structure. (Earth's structure is shown in Figure 16-4.)

In a sense, what happened to these planets long ago isn't too different from what happens to a mixture of oil and water that is shaken up and then allowed to stand. Eventually, the lighter oil will float to the top and the heavier water will sink to the bottom under the influence of gravity. Earth also separated into layers of different density when it underwent differentiation.

At Earth's center, with a radius of about 3400 kilometers (2000 miles), is the **core,** made primarily of iron and nickel metal. Temperatures at Earth's center are believed to exceed 5000°C, but pressures are so high—about 3.5 billion grams per square centimeter (almost 50 million pounds per square inch)—that the iron-nickel inner core is solid. A little farther out the pressures are somewhat lower, so that the outer region of the iron-nickel core is actually a liquid.

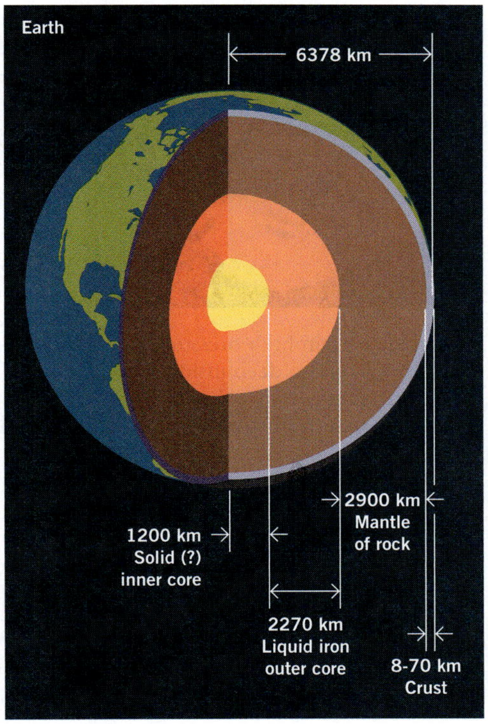

• **Figure 16-4** The layered Earth. The principal layers, which differ in chemical composition and physical properties, are the core, the mantle, the crust, and the atmosphere (not shown). When looked at in detail, each of these layers is itself composed of smaller layers.

The metal core is overlain by a thick layer, the **mantle,** which is rich in the elements oxygen, silicon, magnesium, and iron. Metallic bonding predominates in the core, but the mantle features minerals with primarily ionic bonds between negatively charged oxygen ions and positively charged silicon, magnesium, and other ions. Mantle rocks are similar in composition to some familiar surface rocks, but the atoms in these high pressure materials are packed together in much denser forms.

At Earth's very outer layer is the **crust,** which is made up of the lightest materials. The crust's thickness ranges from less than 10 kilometers (about 6 miles) in parts of the oceans to as much as 70 kilometers (about 45 miles) beneath parts of the continents. The crust is the only layer of the solid Earth with which human beings have had contact, and it remains the source of almost all the rocks and minerals that we use in our lives.

You might wonder how scientists could describe parts of Earth's interior that no human being has ever seen. In the next chapter we introduce seismology, a branch of science that has provided (among other things) our present picture of Earth's interior.

Technology •

Producing World-Record High Pressures

The force of gravity, pulling inward on all of Earth's layers, results in immense internal pressures, exceeding 3 million times the atmospheric pressure at Earth's center. What changes affect rocks and minerals at these extreme conditions? High-pressure researchers, who have learned to sustain laboratory pressures greater than those at Earth's center, are providing surprising answers.

Of all the materials from Earth's deep interior, none holds more fascination than diamond, the high-pressure form of carbon. This magnificent gemstone is also the hardest known substance and the most efficient abrasive for machining the tough metal parts of modern industrial machines. Until the mid-1950s, diamonds were available only from a few natural sources, but in 1954 scientists at General Electric discovered how to manufacture diamonds by duplicating the extreme temperatures and pressures that exist hundreds of kilometers beneath Earth's surface. The researchers squeezed carbon

Courtesy Van Valte

Researchers attain high pressures, equivalent to those deep inside Earth and other planets, using the diamond anvil cell. Looking through such diamond cells you can observe pressurized samples such as this high-pressure ice crystal that was formed at room temperature by squeezing water.

between the jaws of a massive metal vise and heated their sample with a powerful electrical current. Early experiments yielded only a fraction of a carat of diamond, but large factories now produce dozens of tons of diamonds annually, an output exceeding the total amount of diamonds mined since biblical times.

Earth taught us how diamonds are made, and now scientists use diamonds to learn how Earth was made. The highest sustained laboratory pressures available today are obtained by clamping together two tiny pointed anvils of diamond. Samples squeezed between the diamond-anvil faces are subjected to pressures of several million kilograms per square centimeter, greater than at Earth's center. At such extreme conditions, rocks and minerals compress to new, dense forms occupying less than half their original volumes. Dramatic changes in chemical bonding are also observed, with many ionically and covalently bonded compounds transforming to metals at high pressure. •

The Formation of the Moon

The origin of the Moon, the only large body in orbit around Earth, poses one of the oldest puzzles in planetary science. The Moon is one of the largest bodies in the solar system—larger than the planets Mercury and Pluto, and almost as large as Mars. The Moon's density and chemical composition, subjects of intense study by the astronauts of the *Apollo* lunar missions, are quite different from Earth as a whole, though they are remarkably similar to those of Earth's mantle. The problem of the Moon's origin can be stated simply: How could such a large body have arisen in the same region of space as Earth, when its composition is so different?

The current theory is called the "big splash" (Figure 16-5). In this theory, Earth underwent differentiation as described earlier, but while it was still in a formative state an object about the size of Mars struck it. This collision blew a huge quantity of mantle rocks out into orbit around Earth. The Moon then formed from this material, which explains the Moon's unusual composition, density, and large size.

As for Earth, the theories predict that as a result of the collision, large-scale melting occurred so the surface reformed without any crater. When the planet cooled off, no trace of the mammoth impact was left.

Breck P. Kent/Animals Animals/Earth Scenes

The 1200-meter-wide Meteor Crater in Arizona formed from a collision about 20,000 years ago. The meteorite was approximately the size of a small car.

EXAMPLE 16-1

The Density of the Moon

Scientists can measure the mass of the Moon by observing satellites in orbit or by measuring tides on Earth. This mass is approximately 7.4×10^{22} kg. They can also measure the radius of the Moon by observing its apparent size in the sky. Its radius is approximately 1.7×10^6 km. What is the average density of Earth's nearest neighbor?

Reasoning: The density of an object is defined to be its mass divided by its volume. The first step, then, is to find the volume of the Moon. Once we have this, the density will be given by:

$$\text{density} = \frac{\text{mass of Moon}}{\text{volume of Moon}}$$

The volume of a sphere of radius R is given by:

$$\text{volume of sphere} = 4/3 \times \pi \times \text{radius}^3$$

Solution: The volume of the Moon is then:

$$\begin{aligned}\text{volume} &= 4/3 \times 3.14 \times (1.7 \times 10^6)^3 \\ &= 2 \times 10^{19}\ \text{m}^3\end{aligned}$$

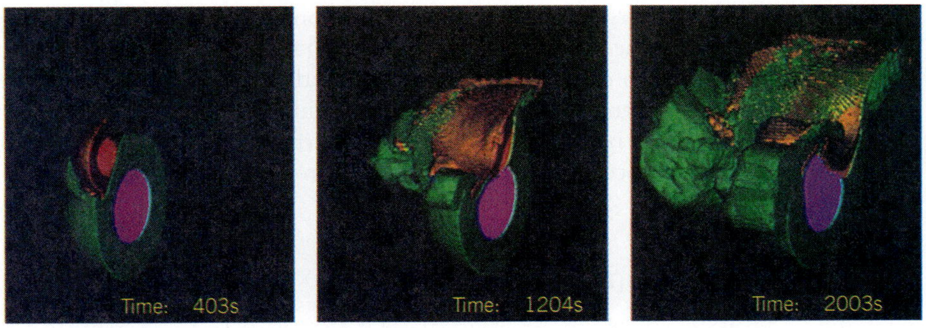

(a) (b) (c)

• **Figure 16-5** The "big splash" theory of the Moon's formation points to a gigantic impact of a Mars-sized body with Earth *(a)*. A large quantity of material from Earth's mantle was blasted into orbit *(b)* and eventually coalesced into the Moon *(c)*.

So that the density is:

$$\text{density} = \frac{7.4 \times 10^{22}\ \text{kg}}{2 \times 10^{19}\ \text{m}^3}$$

$$= 3700\ \text{kg/m}^3$$

For reference, the density of water is 1000 kg/m^3 and Earth's average density is about 5500 kg/m^3. Thus, the overall density of the Moon is considerably less than that of Earth. In fact, it is about the same as the comparatively light material in Earth's mantle, a fact that plays an important role in our theories of the Moon's formation.

Planetary Idiosyncrasies

The natural processes that occurred during Earth's formation affected the other planets as well. Mercury, Mars, and the Moon, for example, display surface cratering that suggests that large chunks of rock bombarded all of these planets late in their formation. Earth undoubtedly looked like this over 4 billion years ago, but all evidence of those early craters has been weathered away. On Mercury and the Moon, which have no atmosphere, no weathering has affected the craters and so they are still there.

The early bombardment may also have affected other characteristics of the terrestrial planets. The direction of rotation of Venus, for example, is opposite that of Earth. (Planets revolve around the Sun, but rotate about their axes.) Earth's axis of rotation, furthermore, is tilted at 23 degrees to the plane of its orbit, while Uranus has its axis of rotation close to the plane of its orbit, a full 90 degrees from an upright orientation. Current thinking is that these differences resulted from the more or less random collisions with large objects, perhaps hundreds of kilometers in diameter, which marked the end of the main phase of planetary formation. You might expect that the details of these late-stage collisions were different for each planet. Thus the nebular hypothesis not only explains how it is that the planets all have their orbits in the same plane and move in the same direction around the Sun, but also allows us to explain why the rotations of individual planets can be so different.

The Science of Life •

When Could Life Begin?

This scenario for Earth's formation also has important implications for the origins of life on our planet. During the period of the great bombardment, Earth was constantly being hit by huge objects—chunks of rock the size of a state or even a country. At the very least, the tremendous energy released by such collisions would be enough to vaporize any oceans that had formed. Each collision would, quite literally, sterilize the planet. Even if life had come into existence during this period, it would have been wiped out by the impacts. Thus the ancestors of modern living things could not have gotten their start until the end of the bombardment, which occurred between 4.2 and 3.8 billion years ago. This fact will become very important when we discuss the origins of life in Chapter 25. •

The Evolution of Planetary Atmospheres

Earth didn't always have the kind of atmosphere it has today. In fact, scientists now suggest that originally it had no atmosphere at all, and that once an atmosphere formed, its chemical composition gradually evolved to its present form. The question of how Earth's atmosphere arose and changed is extremely important, because this history is inseparable from understanding the origin and evolution of life on our planet.

Early Earth may have collected some gases by gravitational attraction. During the early formation of the Sun, large amounts of material and radiation were thrown off. This flood of materials would have blown off any atmosphere Earth had accumulated. Thus, for all intents and purposes, Earth's early atmosphere was an airless ball of hot (or even molten) rock.

During the period of cooling that followed the great bombardment and melting, large amounts of water vapor, carbon dioxide, and other gases would have been released from deep within Earth's solid interior. Countless volcanoes and fissures, all belching steam and other materials, would have blown their gases into the newly forming atmosphere. In other words, the gases that formed the ancestor of today's atmosphere were probably originally locked into the rocks near Earth's surface when the original atmosphere was swept away. Subsequently, a process called *outgassing* released a completely new atmosphere.

Outgassing, which was violent and rapid early in Earth's history, has not ended today. We tend to think of volcanic eruptions as involving the flow of red-hot lava, but if you remember pictures of eruptions, you probably recall large clouds of smoke and steam that accompany the glowing lava flows. Even today, more than 4.5 billion years after the planet's formation, volcanoes release large amounts of gases from Earth's interior.

One estimate is that the principal result of outgassing in the early Earth was the production of an atmosphere composed primarily of nitrogen (N_2), carbon dioxide (CO_2), hydrogen (H_2), and water (H_2O), though scientists are engaged in a spirited debate on the subject of the exact atmospheric composition. Presumably, the same sort of process was occurring on the other terrestrial planets. For a time, Earth's atmosphere was probably too hot for water to condense from a gas to a liquid, but eventually the atmospheric temperature dropped and torrential rains began to fill the ocean basins.

Once a planet has acquired an atmosphere by outgassing, there are several ways that its atmosphere can evolve and change. The simplest is *gravitational escape*. The molecules in an atmosphere heated by the Sun may move sufficiently fast so that appreciable fractions of them can actually escape the gravitational pull of their planet. The Moon, Mercury, and Mars are examples of bodies that had denser atmospheres early in their history, but lost much of these gases through gravitational escape long ago. Most of the light elements such as hydrogen and helium were presumably lost in the same way from Earth, but the heavier gases such as carbon dioxide and water vapor remained because they were too heavy to escape Earth's gravitational force.

A second cause of atmospheric change that operates only on Earth is the effect of living things. To the best of our knowledge, no life exists anywhere else in the solar system (although some scientists argue that simple forms of life might survive beneath the surface of Mars or Jupiter's moon, Europa). By the time Earth was 2 billion years old, photosynthetic organisms had evolved to use the Sun's energy to power the chemical reactions essential for life. In photosynthesis, carbon dioxide and water are taken into the structures of living things, and oxygen is given off as a waste product (see Chapter 21). As life flourished on the planet, the amount of free oxygen increased as well, until today it comprises about 20% of the atmosphere.

We tend to think of oxygen as a benign and beautiful substance, but from a chemical point of view it's really rather nasty stuff. As we saw in Chapter 8, oxygen reacts violently with many materials (think of fire burning or the explosion of hydrogen or gasoline). In fact, the production of oxygen by living things on early Earth can be thought of as the first global pollution event. Thus, life forms both affect and are affected by the atmosphere of the planet on which they reside. In fact, many scientists now suggest that you can tell whether a planet has life on it simply by looking at its atmosphere.

Exploring the Solar System

We live in a time of intense exploration of our planetary neighbors. Dozens of missions by NASA and agencies in other countries have led to remarkable discoveries of new objects and unexpected features in our solar system. Let's look at just a few of these efforts.

The Inner Solar System

Space probes have visited all of our nearest neighbors—the terrestrial planets Mercury, Venus, and Mars. Mercury and Venus, the two planets closest to the Sun, are too hot to sustain life. Thus, of the terrestrial planets, the exploration of Mars continues to generate the greatest interest. Of all our planetary neighbors, Mars is the body most likely to harbor life.

In the 1990s the *Pathfinder* mission and the *Mars Global Surveyor* collected unmistakable evidence that there was once liquid water on the Martian surface—perhaps even a large ocean. The Mars *Odyssey* mission (2001–2002) and the *Spirit* and *Opportunity* rovers (2004–2005) provided new striking evidence that a substantial quantity of water remains locked in the Martian crust. In fact, the current thinking is that early in its history, before it lost its atmosphere to gravitational escape, Mars would have looked much like Earth. And, so the reasoning goes, since life seems to have developed quickly on Earth, it may well have done the same on Mars. Even if the cooling and loss of atmosphere wiped out that early life, we should be able to find evidence for it in the form of fossils.

Courtesy NASA/JPL

The surface of Mars might have been covered by an ocean at one time.

Current plans call for several Mars orbiter and lander missions during the next decade, with both life detection and sample return missions to be launched toward Mars sometime after 2010. NASA planners are working closely with the Centers for Disease Control to ensure that these samples neither contaminate nor are contaminated by microbes from Earth. A high-security containment structure will be constructed to house the Mars samples when they return.

The Outer Solar System

A number of space probes sent out from Earth since the 1970s have visited most of the outer planets and provided a new view of the outer solar system. The distances to the giant outer planets are immense. The closest gas giant, Jupiter, orbits at five times the Earth–Sun distance, over 800 million kilometers away. Saturn is twice that far, while Uranus and Neptune are several billion kilometers away. This far out in the system, the Sun looks like a small marble in the sky, and its warming effects are feeble indeed.

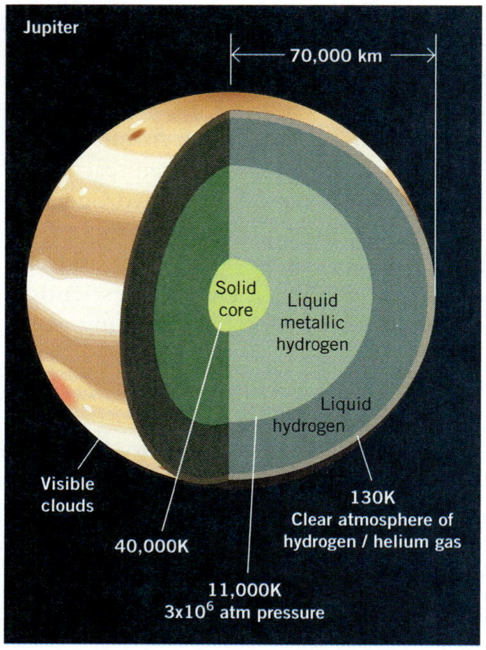

• **Figure 16-6** A theoretical view of the interior of Jupiter, one of the Jovian planets. Most of the planet's volume is highly compressed hydrogen and helium.

Compounds that are normally gases on Earth, such as carbon dioxide, nitrogen, and methane, are found in liquid or even solid form under the intense pressures that exist in the interiors of the Jovian planets.

The structure of the outer giant planets is layered, like that of the terrestrial planets, but they do not have a well-defined solid surface like Earth and the Moon. Moving down from space into the body of Jupiter or Saturn would be a strange experience. You would move through progressively denser and denser layers of clouds and then pass imperceptibly into a layer where the gases change into liquids because of the high pressure. In fact, landing on Jupiter would be more like landing on a giant ice cream sundae than landing on Earth or the Moon. In Figure 16-6, we show a typical structure for one of the Jovian planets.

During the mid-1990s, astronomers got two unique opportunities to study the atmosphere of Jupiter. One of these was fortuitous. From July 16 to 22, 1994, a string of objects known collectively as Comet Shoemaker-Levy collided with Jupiter. For days, most of the telescopes on Earth were trained on Jupiter as one impact after another roiled its upper layer of swirling gases. The collisions were more powerful than thousands of hydrogen bombs. The effect of these collisions was to bring gases that normally lie hundreds of miles deep up to the top of the atmosphere where scientists could see them. Shoemaker-Levy gave astronomers a chance to test their ideas about what was beneath the visible part of the Jovian atmosphere, as well as theories about how the atmosphere would cause the ripples created by the impacts to damp out. The net effect of the impacts, other than providing a spectacular show, was to allow astronomers to fine-tune their notions about the composition of the Jovian atmosphere.

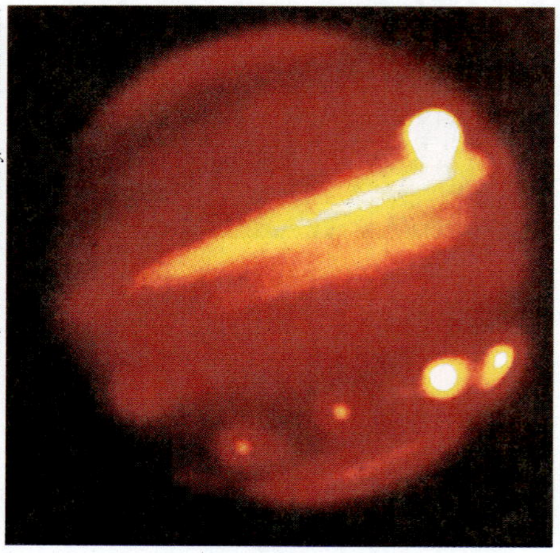

NASA/Science Photo Library/Photo Researchers

This infrared image of Jupiter shows the many impact sites, or splashes, due to fragments of Comet Shoemaker-Levy 9 in July 1994.

In December 1995, the spacecraft *Galileo* arrived in orbit around Jupiter to begin a study of the planet. *Galileo* was launched on October 18, 1989. Its orbit took it around the Sun and Earth for an extra boost from gravity. When it arrived at Jupiter, the satellite launched a small probe into the Jovian atmosphere. Its descent slowed by a parachute system, the probe sank into the atmosphere, sending back information about the material through which it was passing. After 57 minutes of operation, the probe (as expected) was destroyed, but during its brief lifetime it gave scientists a library of new information about the atmosphere of the largest planet. After that, *Galileo* spent several years in orbit around Jupiter, sending back a treasure trove of information about that planet and its moons. On September 21, 2003, the aging spacecraft was deliberately plunged into the atmosphere of Jupiter to guard against possible future contamination of Europa.

Then, in June 2004, NASA's *Cassini* became the first spacecraft to enter orbit around Saturn, where it continues to return spectacular images and masses of data on the beautiful ringed planet. *Cassini* has also returned a wealth of data on many of Saturn's numerous moons.

Moons and Rings of the Outer Planets

Astronomers have found dozens of moons circling Jupiter, Saturn, Uranus, and Neptune. These bodies range from small rocks to planet-sized objects. Each of these moons is its own world, with its own history and formed by its own unique collection of physical processes. Each can be thought of as a small laboratory that sheds some light on the formation of terrestrial planets, but three are of special interest.

Io

The moon Io, which circles close to Jupiter, is the only moon in the solar system known to have active volcanoes. Scientists think that Jupiter's powerful gravitational forces flex and twist the moon to produce the energy to drive those volcanoes.

Europa

Jupiter's second moon has become one of the most studied objects in the solar system, because the *Galileo* spacecraft results suggest the possibility that conditions there may be appropriate for the development of life. The *Voyager* spacecraft photographs of Europa showed a smooth surface made of water ice. The relative absence of craters means that the surface must have formed recently, which would be puzzling in a moon in the frigid outer depths of the solar system.

Stop and Think! Why should the absence of craters indicate a young surface on Europa?

When *Galileo* arrived at Jupiter, it sent back closeup photographs of the surface of Europa that looked more like the Arctic ice pack than a perpetually frozen world. Giant blocks of ice seemed to be jumbled together, welded together at their boundaries by what looked like ridges of freshly frozen material. Scientists began to speculate that under Europa's icy surface, heated by the same kind of gravitational twisting that powers Io's volcanoes, there might actually be liquid water—an entire ocean, in fact. Later measurements showed that Europa has a magnetic field that could arise from a salty ocean in its interior, and pictures of craters were produced that look as if they had been filled in by a slushy fluid after impact. Right now, the consensus is that Europa might have the only nonterrestrial ocean in the solar system, although results from the *Cassini* spacecraft suggest that Saturn's moon Enceladus might have a similar structure.

Since life on Earth developed in the oceans, the possibility exists that life (in microbial form, at least) might have arisen on Europa. NASA is busy planning a major exploration effort for this moon, with the possibility of sending robot probes to melt their way through the ice to explore this new and totally unexpected environment.

Titan

Saturn's moon Titan, one of the largest moons in the solar system (it is about the same size as the planet Mercury), may well be something of a laboratory for early Earth. It may have frigid lakes of methane (CH_4) and ethane (C_2H_6) on its surface, and, from the beginning of the solar system, simple chemical reactions in its atmosphere have probably produced a layer of organic materials there. Thus, Titan may have something to tell us about how organic materials accumulate and about how cellular life developed on our own planet. On January 14, 2005, the *Huygens* probe left its mother spacecraft, *Cassini*, and descended to Titan's surface. During its two-and-a-half hour descent, *Huygens* relayed information about the conditions of Titan's atmosphere and cloud-shrouded surface. Current thinking is that complex organic molecules—the building blocks of life—may litter Titan's surface.

Rings

In addition to these numerous moons, each of the four Jovian planets has a system of rings that are formed from countless small particles of ice and rock. Saturn features the most spectacular of these ring systems—an array of dozens of fine bands, separated by larger objects called shepherd satellites.

Courtesy NASA

Saturn with its rings and moons.

Courtesy NASA

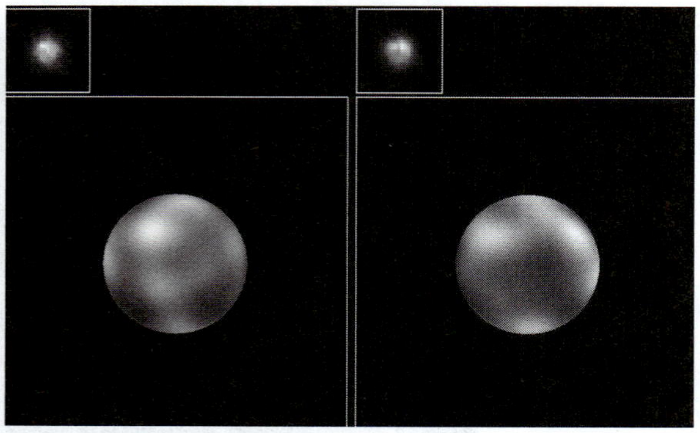

The surface of Pluto as seen by the Hubble Space Telescope.

Pluto and the Kuiper Belt

The outermost planet, **Pluto,** remains something of a mystery. It can be studied through telescopes but has yet to be visited by a space probe. Pluto is a small planet, only about 0.3% of Earth's mass, and is circled by a large moon called Charon that is only slightly smaller than the planet, plus two smaller moons. Its orbit is highly elliptical and, for a period of its orbital "year" (about 250 Earth years), is inside the orbit of Neptune. In fact the strange properties of Pluto have played a role in giving scientists a much more expansive view of the solar system than they had before. Extending outward from the orbit of Pluto is a disc shaped collection of comets and rocky objects left over from the formation of the solar system. This disc is known as the *Kuiper belt,* after the Dutch astronomer Gerard Kuiper who first suggested its existence. In recent years, as we discuss in the *Science News* at the end of this chapter, many other large objects have been found in this region, and we expect many more to be found in the future. Thus, we now see Pluto not as the last of the planets, but as the beginning of the Kuiper belt. In 2005, the International Astronomical Union confirmed this view by naming Pluto and objects farther out (see *Science News*, page 339) as part of a new type of planet called a "dwarf planet".

Science in the Making •

The Discovery of Pluto

Five of the planets—Mercury, Venus, Mars, Jupiter, and Saturn—are easily visible to the naked eye and have been known from ancient times. The other three, most-distant planets—Uranus, Neptune, and Pluto—were discovered after the invention of the telescope. A more recent discovery of a planet occurred on February 18, 1930, by 23-year-old Clyde Tombaugh, who had been brought up on a Kansas farm. Employed as a technician at Lowell Observatory in Flagstaff, Arizona, Tombaugh uncovered convincing evidence for the existence of a new planet.

As a teenager, Tombaugh had built a small telescope, using parts from an old cream separator to make its stand. He drew sketches of the surface of Mars and sent them to Lowell Observatory, which was then engaged in observations of the red planet. The sketches, made with a small amateur's instrument, corresponded so well to what astronomers at Lowell were seeing through their state-of-the-art telescope that Tombaugh received a job offer by return mail.

At Lowell, he began a systematic search for what was then called Planet X. The founder of the observatory, American astronomer Percival Lowell, had predicted the existence of such a planet based on some rather questionable data on variations in the orbit of Neptune. Tombaugh's task was straightforward, if tiring. He would take photographs of each section of the sky, then a second photograph of the same section a few days later. The two photographs were then put into a machine that would show first one photograph, then the other, in an eyepiece. As the photographs were "blinked," any object that had moved between the time of the two photographs would appear to jump back and forth, while stars would remain stationary.

The main problem is that the plane of the solar system is littered with asteroids, each of which could show up as a moving light on such photos. The key point wasn't that Tombaugh found something out there that moved—there were plenty of such objects. The point was to find a point of light that moved by as much as Kepler's laws tell us that a planet out beyond Neptune would move in a few days. That is exactly what Tombaugh found on that day in February, some 10 months into his search.

The discovery photos for Pluto reveal the shift of one point of light between January 23, 1930 *(left),* and January 29, 1930 *(right)*. The white arrows point to Pluto.

Courtesy Lowell Observatory

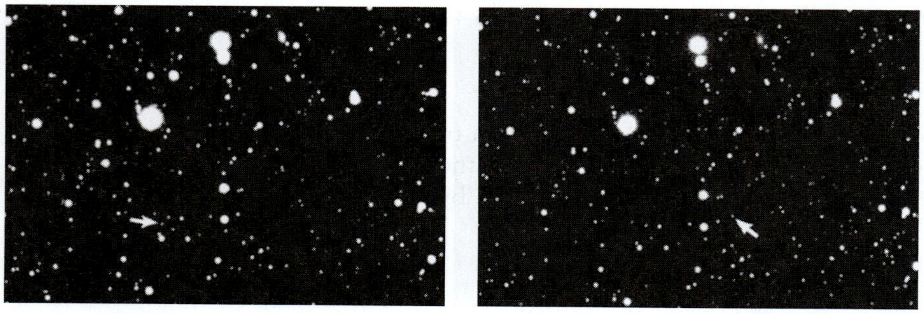

After becoming one of only three human beings to have discovered a new planet, Tombaugh went back to college. Much to his surprise, he was not allowed to take introductory astronomy. "They cheated me out of four hours!" he said.

And his old telescope? When one of the authors (J.T.) asked him before his death a few years ago whether he was going to donate it to the Smithsonian Institution, the 83-year-old astronomer replied, "They want it, but they can't have it. I'm not through using it yet!" •

Science in the Making •

The *Voyager* Satellites

On August 20, 1977, a rocket blasted off from Cape Canaveral in Florida, to set a small space probe on its course. Sixteen days later, another rocket did the same. These two probes, called *Voyager 1* and *2,* respectively, spent the next 15 years moving past the planets of the outer solar system, providing scientists with their first closeup look at the Jovian planets and their moons.

Each spacecraft had 10 scientific instruments on board, each designed to measure a different aspect of the deep-space environment. The ones that had the greatest public impact were the cameras that took pictures of moons, rings, and planets, but measurements were also made of magnetic fields, cosmic ray abundances, and infrared and ultraviolet radiation. Taken together, the *Voyager* probes produced a good deal of the detailed information about the outer solar system contained in this chapter.

One interesting feature of spaceflights like this is that by the time a spacecraft has been in flight for a while, all of its instrumentation has become obsolete. Between its encounters with Jupiter and Neptune, for example, the computers on *Voyager 2* were reprogrammed to make significant changes in the way they analyzed and transmitted data. As a result, the rate of transmission during the Neptune flyby in 1989 was not significantly different from that of the Jupiter encounter in 1979, despite the greater distance and lower light levels at Neptune.

Among their discoveries, the *Voyagers* found ring systems around all the Jovian planets, recorded a volcanic eruption on Io, tripled the number of known moons around Uranus, and clocked record winds on the surface of Neptune. Today, both *Voyagers,* together with a couple of earlier space probes called *Pioneers,* have moved out of the solar system and into interstellar space. *Voyager 2* is expected to keep returning data until its plutonium power supply runs down, sometime around 2020. By that time, it may have reached the place where the Sun's magnetic field blends into the magnetic field of our galaxy, thereby becoming the first human-made object to have broken free from all the dominant influences of the Sun. •

Asteroids, Comets, and Meteors

As the solar system formed, not all the material in the planetary disk was taken up into the bodies of the planets and moons. Even after hundreds of millions of years of accumulation and bombardment, a lot of debris was still floating around out there and remains even today. This debris comes in two main forms, asteroids and comets, which in a sense mimic the compositional differences of the inner and outer planets.

Asteroids

Asteroids are small rocky bodies in orbit around the Sun, like miniature versions of the inner terrestrial planets. Most asteroids are found in a broad, circular asteroid belt between Mars and Jupiter—material thought to be a collection of planetesimals that never managed to collect into a stable planet. The most likely explanation is that the nearby planet Jupiter had a disrupting gravitational effect. In addition, many asteroids possess orbits that cross Earth's orbit, and they produce occasional large impacts on our planet.

©Lynette Cook

A comet develops a tail as it approaches the Sun.

Comets

Comets can best be thought of as "dirty snowballs." Unlike asteroids, they consist of chunks, sometimes many miles in diameter, of material such as water ice and methane ice in which a certain amount of solid, rocky material or dirt is embedded. Also, unlike asteroids, most of the comets in the solar system circle the Sun outside the orbit of Pluto. Two main reservoirs of comets are found in the solar system. One of these is a large spherical array called the *Oort cloud* (named after Dutch astronomer Jan Oort, 1900–1992, who first postulated its existence), located far from the solar system. The other is part of the Kuiper Belt.

Occasionally, when the orbit of a comet is disturbed, the comet will be deflected so that it falls toward the Sun. When this happens, the increasing temperature of the inner solar system begins to boil off materials, and we see a large "tail," blown away from the Sun by the solar wind, that reflects light to us.

Sometimes a comet will be captured and fall into a regular orbit around the Sun. The most famous of these periodic comets is Halley's Comet (see Chapter 2), which returns to the vicinity of Earth about every 76 years. Halley's return in 1910 was quite spectacular, because the comet passed near Earth when it was at its highest temperature and therefore had its largest and most spectacular tail. The return in 1986 was much less spectacular because the comet was on the far side of the Sun when it was at its brightest. The next predicted return in 2061, unfortunately, will probably be just as unspectacular.

Astronomers have actually detected many objects in the inner Kuiper belt with the Hubble Space Telescope. These objects are several hundred miles across. Current thinking is that over the course of time, collisions in the Kuiper belt have gradually removed most of the original comets from it, leaving these objects as the last occupants.

Stop and Think! How do you suppose astronomers knew that the Oort cloud and Kuiper belt existed before objects in the latter could actually be seen?

Two recent space probes have greatly increased our understanding of comets. On February 7, 1999, NASA launched the *Stardust* comet sample return mission, the first mission to return extraterrestrial material from outside the Moon. During its seven-year mission, the spacecraft passed through the tail of comet Wild 2 (pronounced "Vilt 2" after the name of its Swiss discoverer), collected microscopic dust particles, and returned a sample capsule to Earth on January 15, 2006. Ongoing analyses of the thousands of captured particles are expected to reveal details about the kind of dust and gas that formed Earth and the other planets 4.5 billion years ago.

NASA's complementary *Deep Impact* mission was launched January 5, 2005. During a close encounter with comet Tempel 1 on July 3–4, 2005, a 370-kg (816-pound) impactor was released to collide with the comet at 10 kilometers per second. The resulting collison produced a plume of dust and gas that revealed much about the composition and consistency of the comet. Data from *Deep Impact* suggest that comets are soft and porous, less dense than water and more the consistency of powdery snow than soil or rock.

The Science of Life •

Comets and Life on Earth

In addition to providing us with one of the first historical tests of the law of universal gravitation, comets may have had an important effect on the evolution of life on Earth. Many scientists suspect that the impacts of comets or asteroids may have drastically altered Earth's climate and produced mass extinctions, or killings, at various times in Earth's history (see Chapter 25). Most Earth scientists, for example, now believe that

Table 16-2 Major Meteor Showers

Name	Date for Maximum	Extreme Limits	Hourly Rate of Meteors
Quadrantid	January 3	January 1–4	30
Aquarid	May 4	May 2–6	5
Perseid	August 12	July 29–August 17	40
Orionid	October 22	October 18–26	13
Taurid	November 1	September 15–December 15	5
Leonid	November 17	November 14–20	6
Geminid	December 14	December 7–15	55

the dinosaurs and other life-forms that thrived 65 million years ago were driven to extinction following the impact of a large comet or asteroid that hit Earth at a site near Mexico's Yucatan Peninsula.

Meteoroids, Meteors, and Meteorites

Meteoroids are small pieces of ancient space debris in orbit around the Sun. Occasionally one of these bits, perhaps the size of a sand grain, will fall into Earth's atmosphere where it becomes briefly visible as a meteor. Most meteors burn up completely to microscopic particles of ash that slowly, imperceptibly, rain down on Earth. The meteors' bright streaks of light record the path of this burning. Occasionally, if the object is big enough so that only the outer surface burns, a piece of rock may actually reach Earth's surface. Any such rock that has fallen to Earth from space is called a **meteorite**.

Meteor showers are spectacular, regularly occurring events in the night sky. During a shower, every minute or so you can see brilliant streaks in the sky, each one caused by the collision of Earth with swarms of small debris that travel around the orbits of comets. Some of these swarms may be comets that were broken up by the gravitational pull of one of the planets. Table 16-2 lists some of the most spectacular meteor showers.

Meteorites are extremely important in the study of the solar system because they represent the material from which the system was originally made. They are analyzed intensely by scientists, both to get a notion of how and when Earth was made, and to learn what kinds of materials human beings will find when they leave Earth to explore the rest of the solar system. •

Science in the Making •

Discovering New Planetary Systems

In 1994, Alexander Wolszczan at Penn State University announced the discovery of the first planetary system outside of our own. Since that time more than 200 *extrasolar planets* have been discovered, and more are announced every month.

All of these planets are much too faint and distant to be seen directly in today's telescopes, but two clever observational approaches have led to most of these discoveries. Most of these distant planets are identified using the Doppler effect (see Chapter 6). As a planet orbits a star, its gravitational pull causes the star to wobble slightly. By monitoring a star over many nights—sometimes for more than a decade—this regular wobble is revealed by alternating periods of redshift and blueshift of starlight (Figure 16-7).

• **Figure 16-7** Periodic changes in the redshift or blueshift of light may reveal the presence of a planet. This graph illustrates such a red-blueshift versus time or a nearby star. These data indicate a planet that orbits the star every 4.4 days.

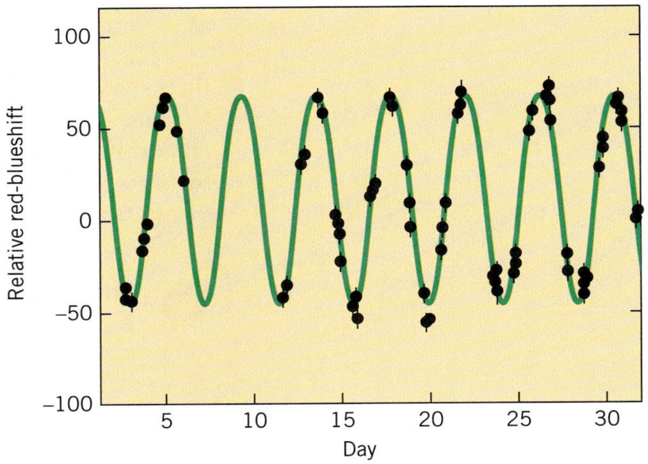

Artist's conception of the transit of a planet in front of a star in a distant solar system.

Paul and Lindamarie Ambrose/Getty Images, Inc.

Alternatively, if an extrasolar planet orbits in a plane viewed edge on, then from time to time the planet will pass in front of the larger star. This transit of the planet slightly reduces the light reaching us—a reduction that can be measured with a sensitive light meter.

Keep watching the news for more reports of new extrasolar planets. •

The Ongoing Process of Science •

How Are Extrasolar Planets Formed?

When scientists had only our solar system to observe, it was fairly easy to devise a theory that explained all of the observed facts. However, with the rapidly growing inventory of extrasolar planets, scientists can test their theories against data obtained from other solar systems. Not surprisingly, these new data are raising problems with the nebular hypothesis outlined in the text.

In the nebular hypothesis, you would expect large planets to be located far from a star, in the region where materials could stay solid. Surprisingly, a number of the new planets don't seem to follow this pattern. Many large planets orbit close to their respective stars. These planets have been dubbed "hot Jupiters" by astronomers, because they are Jupiter-sized objects in their star's warm zone.

The best theories we have to date suggest that these planets were formed far from their stars, in the "cold Jupiter" region, and then, slowed down by clouds of dust that for some reason weren't present in the early solar system, they spiraled into their present orbits. One piece of evidence for this picture: photographs of distant stars that seem to be in the process of formation often show thick dust clouds around the plane of rotation. •

Stop and Think! Given the way new planets are detected, can you think of a reason why "hot Jupiters" would be the easiest ones to discover?

Science News | Outer Limits: Solar System at the Fringe

(SCIENCE NEWS, JAN. 14, 2006, P. 26)

As was explained in the text, our view of the planet Pluto has been undergoing a slow transformation in recent years. Instead of viewing it as the outermost planet (and an oddball at that) we are now starting to see it instead as the nearest member of the Kuiper Belt. As such, it serves as a reminder that the solar system stretches far beyond the traditional planets.

This view has been strengthened recently by a series of discoveries of objects orbiting the Sun far beyond Pluto itself. We have been detecting objects in the Kuiper Belt for a decade—indeed, astronomers had documented over a thousand bodies in the pancake shaped disk. In 2005, the first Kuiper Belt object larger than Pluto was seen. Located 97 AU from the Sun, this object, informally named Xena after the television princess, is 1.5 times as large as Pluto and has been proposed as a candidate for the tenth planet. An object almost as big as Pluto, tentatively named Buffy, has also been seen with an orbit around 58 AU. This menagerie of strange new discoveries was rounded out with the discovery of yet another object almost as big as Pluto that spins faster than any large object in the solar system. Given the prosaic name of 2003EL61, it orbits at about 52 AU.

Photofest

The most distant of these recently discovered objects (it was first seen in 2004) is called Sedna. Its orbit takes it from 76 to 126 AU, which may make it the first known member of the Oort cloud.

Photofest

You may wonder why these objects weren't discovered earlier, since most of them are plainly visible in ordinary astronomical telescopes. The answer is that their orbits are highly tilted with respect to the orbits in the inner solar system. Xena's orbit, for example, tilts at 44 degrees. As a result, the objects spend most of their time in places where, until recently, astronomers have not thought to look.

But, as often happens in science, a discovery like this uncovers as many questions as it answers. In this case, once the new objects were found, astronomers began to ask how the Kuiper Belt could have formed. At the moment, there are no clear answers to this question, but watch the science sections of your newspapers for new ideas in this area.

Thinking More About | Planets

Human Space Exploration

Since before astronaut Neil Armstrong became the first human to walk on the surface of the Moon in 1969, the scientific community has debated the question of how the exploration of the solar system should be carried out. The question is this: Should future missions to the planets carry people, or should they carry only machines?

Those who advocate exploration by machines point to the enormous technical difficulties involved in providing a safe habitat for human beings in the harsh environment of space. Why, they ask, should we make the enormous, expensive effort to put a human being on the surface of Mars, for example, when just as much can be learned by sending instrument packages and robots controlled from Earth?

On the other side of the issue, scientists advocating space exploration by astronauts argue that no machine has the flexibility and ingenuity of a human being. They note that no matter how well designed a machine might be, when it is millions of miles from Earth things can go wrong, and only a trained astronaut can salvage the mission. They point out that even a mammoth project like the Hubble Space Telescope needed astronauts to replace flawed optical systems. Besides, they argue, if one goal of the space program is to establish human colonies on other bodies in the solar system, you can't do that with machines.

What do we hope to learn from our studies of the solar system? Is colonization of the rest of the solar system the real long-term goal of the space program? How much extra effort (and taxpayers' dollars) is it worth expending to put people instead of machines on the surface of Mars?

Summary

Earth formed along with the Sun and other planets in our *solar system* from a *nebula*—a large gas and dust cloud rich in hydrogen and helium—approximately 4.5 billion years ago. As that cloud began to contract as a result of gravitational forces, it also began to rotate and flatten out into the disk that now defines the planetary orbits. More than 99% of the original nebula's mass concentrated at the center, which became the Sun.

Gradually, the matter in the flat disk began to form clumps under the influence of its own local gravitational forces. The largest of these masses swept up more and more debris as they orbited the early Sun, and they began to define a string of planets. *Terrestrial planets,* those nearest the Sun, were subjected to high temperatures and strong solar winds, so that most gases such as hydrogen, helium, and water vapors were swept out into space. Thus the inner four planets, including *Mercury, Venus, Earth,* and *Mars,* are dense, rocky places with a relatively low content of gaseous elements.

Earth's formation was probably typical of these planets. After most of Earth's mass had been collected together, additional rocks and boulders showered down in the *great bombardment,* adding matter and heat energy to the planet. Dense iron and nickel separated from lighter materials by the process of *differentiation* and sank to the center to form a metallic *core.* Most of Earth's mass concentrated in the thick *mantle,* while the lightest elements formed a thin *crust.* The *Moon,* Earth's only large satellite, may have formed when a planet-sized body hit Earth early in its history.

The solar system's outer *Jovian planets,* including *Jupiter, Saturn, Uranus,* and *Neptune,* are quite different from the inner planets. Lying beyond the strong effects of solar heat and wind, they accumulated large amounts of gases such as hydrogen, helium, ammonia, and water. These outer planets are thus giant balls of ice, with thick atmospheres and great frigid oceans of nitrogen, methane, and other compounds that are gases on Earth. Beyond the Jovian planets lies *Pluto,* a rocky body that is the smallest planet. All of the planets except Mercury and Venus, the two closest to the Sun, have *moons* in orbit.

Interspersed with the planets and their moons are many other kinds of objects. Small, rocky *asteroids,* most of which are concentrated in an *asteroid belt* between Mars and Jupiter, circle the Sun like miniature planets. Far outside the solar system, swarms of "dirty snowballs" called *comets* are concentrated in the Oort cloud. If a comet's distant orbit is disturbed, it may fall toward the Sun and create a spectacular display in the night sky. When a piece of interplanetary debris hits Earth's atmosphere, it creates a *meteor,* sometimes called a shooting star, which burns up with a fiery trail. Occasionally, a meteor fragment will hit Earth and become a *meteorite.*

Key Terms

solar system
terrestrial planets (Mercury, Venus, Earth, Earth's Moon, Mars)
Jovian planets (Jupiter, Saturn, Uranus, Neptune)
Pluto
moons
asteroids
asteroid belt
comet
nebula
great bombardment
meteor
differentiation
core
mantle
crust
meteorite

Review Questions

1. Identify three distinctive characteristics of the orbits of planets and moons in the solar system.
2. Identify two distinctive characteristics of the distribution of mass in the solar system.
3. Briefly describe two classes of planets found in the solar system.
4. State the nebular hypothesis. How does it explain the orbits of the planets?
5. What are planetesimals, and what role do they play in the formation of planets?
6. What is differentiation? How has this process affected Earth?
7. Describe the layered structure of Earth's interior.
8. How does the high pressure in the core affect chemical bonds?
9. What is Earth's mantle? Of what elements is it made?
10. Describe the "big splash" theory of the Moon's origin.
11. Explain the importance of outgassing to Earth's history. Is it still going on today?
12. Explain the role of gravity in the evolution of a planet's atmosphere.
13. What is an asteroid? Where are most asteroids found?
14. What is the difference between a meteor and a meteorite?
15. What are comets made of? Where are most comets found?
16. How could asteroids and comets affect life on Earth?
17. Which planets have moons?
18. If Titan is almost as large as the planet Mercury, why is it considered a moon and not a planet?

Discussion Questions

1. What distinctive characteristics of Earth make it suitable for life? How has life altered the chemistry of Earth's atmosphere?
2. What is the difference between rotation and revolution? Why is the rotation of Venus different from that of Earth?
3. The temperature of Earth's core is estimated to be > 5,000 degrees Celsius. Is the core temperature of a planet like Jupiter hotter or colder? Why? Does the distance from the Sun affect the core temperature?
4. Why do Mercury and our Moon lack an atmosphere?
5. What sources of data might help us determine more about how Earth's Moon formed?
6. How does Clyde Tombaugh's work fit into the scientific method?
7. Why was the formation of planets like Jupiter and Saturn more like the development of the Sun than like the development of the terrestrial planets?
8. Why do you suppose scientists worry about material from Earth contaminating the Mars sample when it is brought back?
9. Could material from Earth contaminate Mars? What effect might such contamination have on future missions to the planet?
10. Jupiter is known as a gas giant planet. What are the most common gases in Jupiter's composition?
11. Why do our bones lose minerals and density as we travel in space?

Problems

1. Given the diameters of the planets in Table 16-1, what are the relative volumes of Earth, Mercury, Saturn, and Jupiter? From the same table, what are the relative masses? Which planets are most similar? Why?
2. From the values of mass in Problem 1, calculate the densities (mass divided by volume) for Earth, Mercury, Saturn, and Jupiter. Why do you think they are different? Which planets are most similar? Why?
3. How many asteroids 100 kilometers in diameter would be required to make a planet about the size of Earth? Neglect the effects of compression in the planet's interior.
4. If the average thickness of Earth's crust is 30 kilometers, what fraction of the solid Earth's total volume is in the crust? What fraction is in the mantle? and the core?
5. If Earth had the diameter of Jupiter, and the speed of rotation was the same, how fast would an object on the equator be traveling? Is that faster or slow than an object on the equator currently moves?

Investigations

1. Investigate the history of unmanned planetary probes. What are the names, dates, and target planets of these probes? What countries sponsored them? What kinds of data did they return?
2. What planetary missions are now planned or under way? When will they begin to return data? What kinds of data are going to be gathered?
3. Read a history of the *Apollo* missions to the Moon. What theories about the Moon's origins prevailed before these missions? What new data changed theories about the origin of the Moon?
4. Investigate the discovery of the planet Uranus by William Herschel. What other astronomical contributions did members of the Herschel family make?
5. How would you respond to an argument that went as follows: No one was present when Earth was formed, so how can scientists talk about the details of the formation process?
6. Listen to *The Planets,* a suite for orchestra by the British composer Gustav Holst. In what ways do the musical descriptions of each planet reflect the physical characteristics of that planet? What other sources of inspiration, besides scientific data, did Holst use in creating these pieces? Which planets did he omit and why?
7. There are many more meteor showers than the ones listed in Table 16-2. Find out which ones may be coming in the next month or two and plan a meteor-watching party.
8. Scientists are attempting to document the paths of asteroids with Earth-crossing orbits. Investigate this research and comment on the probability that a large asteroid might hit Earth. Should we increase funding for asteroid monitoring?
9. What is the average cost of a Space Shuttle mission? Is this a productive manner in which to spend tax dollars? What advancements have come from these types of missions?
10. We currently use the Roman names for our planets—what are the Greek equivalents? Investigate the names that other cultures have used for the planets in our solar system.
11. Research the intended path of an unmanned planetary probe. Why do the probes circle the Sun and Earth a number of times before venturing out into deep space?
12. How many satellites are orbiting Earth? What are the purposes of most of these devices? What equipment do you use in your daily life that depends on satellites?
13. How does the GPS (Global Positioning System) work? How accurate is it? Who owns this technology?

17

Plate Tectonics

Can we predict destructive earthquakes?

Science Through the Day | Windblown Sand

Early afternoon at the beach: A cooling breeze has picked up off the water. The steady flow of air is wonderfully refreshing, though occasional gusts of wind kick up sand and grit. Some of that sand blows onto your beach towel and into your hair.

The wind constantly moves soil at Earth's surface, slowly altering the landscape. Shifting sand may seem a trivial phenomenon, but such gradual tiny daily changes add up to extraordinary transformations of the land over countless millions of years. Similar gradual movements of matter deep within our planet accomplish even more remarkable changes. Earth's seemingly permanent continents and oceans are also in constant motion. The continent of North America is about a meter farther from Europe than it was when you were born, the result of forces deep within Earth's interior.

Earth's surface is always changing. No feature of our planet—no desert or broad plain, no mountain or ocean—is permanent. Every feature is constantly evolving into something different.

Adelman-Cohen/Taxi/Getty Images

The Dynamic Earth

Think about the last time that you passed a new construction site after a rain shower. You could probably see little valleys freshly carved by water running over the bare earth, and shallow pools where fine-grained material collected in layers—features that are small-scale examples of the erosion of soil by rain. If the earthmovers had dug a deep pit, you might have noticed different layers of earth and rock freshly exposed—layers that represent sediments deposited by water long ago.

These sorts of small-scale changes in Earth's surface are mirrored by much more dramatic large-scale changes. When Mount St. Helens, a volcano in Washington State, erupted in 1980, the entire side of a mountain was blown away and many square kilometers of forest were flattened. Large earthquakes in our lifetime will change the course of rivers and destroy villages and towns.

But how do we know that Earth's surface is changing at larger scales? We rarely observe significant changes in the landscape, but you can make a simple estimate that will convince you that Earth must be a very dynamic planet. Mountains appear to be as permanent as anything could be, yet, as we see in the following section, it's easy to convince yourself that mountains must wear away in times much shorter than Earth's 4.5-billion-year age. We'll also see that continents are not as permanent as they appear to be.

Science by the Numbers •

How Long Could a Mountain Last?

Although there is no such thing as a "typical" mountain, for the purposes of this rough estimate let's think of a mountain as a rectangular mass about 2 km high, 4 km long, and 4 km wide (that's about 1.2 miles by 2.5 miles by 2.5 miles). The volume of this midsized mountain is

$$\begin{aligned}\text{volume} &= \text{length} \times \text{height} \times \text{width}\\ &= 2\ \text{km} \times 4\ \text{km} \times 4\ \text{km}\\ &= 32\ \text{km}^3\end{aligned}$$

Expressed in cubic meters, that is

$$2000\ \text{m} \times 4000\ \text{m} \times 4000\ \text{m} = 3.2 \times 10^{10}\ \text{m}^3$$

Think about a stream running down a mountainside. You know that such a stream carries a certain amount of sand, silt, and dirt with it. You can see this because the stream has a sandy bottom, and you can watch it depositing sand in little eddies and still water along its side. You might also see gravel and boulders in the stream—evidence that, from time to time, heavy rains cause much more violent movement of material down the mountainside. That material had to be worn off of materials higher up on the mountain, so the existence of the stream means that the mountain is constantly being eroded away.

Masterfile

Pike's Peak near Colorado Springs, Colorado, may be approximated as 2 × 4 × 4 km rectangular block of rock.

You can estimate how long a mountain might survive against erosion by a stream. Suppose, for example, that four principal streams run off the sides of the mountain, and that each stream carries an average of one-tenth of a cubic meter of earth per day off the mountain. (The actual amount would vary from day to day depending on the kind of rock, the amount of water flowing downhill, and other factors.) One-tenth of a cubic meter per day is not very much material. It's like a pile of sand, dirt, and gravel about 50 centimeters (a foot and a half) on a side—a pile that could fit under an ordinary kitchen chair. If you think about the amount of material you might collect if you put your hand down into a stream for a while, you'll see that the number is reasonable. Over a period of a year, the four streams might thus remove

$$4\ \text{streams} \times 0.1\ \text{meter}^3/\text{stream-day} \times 365\ \text{days/year} = 146\ \text{meter}^3/\text{year}$$

Every year, therefore, close to 150 cubic meters of material—about six dumptrucks full—could be removed from a mountain by normal erosional processes of streams.

If the mountain streams remove about 150 cubic meters each year, then the lifetime of the mountain can't be much longer than the volume of the mountain divided by the volume lost each year:

$$\frac{3.2 \times 10^{10}\ \text{m}^3}{(150\ \text{m}^3/\text{year})} = 0.0213 \times 10^{10}\ \text{years}$$

$$= 213{,}000{,}000\ \text{years}$$

Steep slopes and angular peaks characterize young mountains such as the 65-million-year-old Rocky Mountains in Alberta, Canada *(a)* photographed from Mount Rae. The 400-million-year-old Great Smoky Mountains in North Carolina *(b)* display the rounded character of older mountains.

(a) (b)

Michael Wickees/The Image Works

David Muench/Stone/Getty Images

This estimate, though very rough and not directly applicable to any specific mountain, tells us that under normal circumstances mountains can't last more than a few hundred million years. All mountains must disappear and be eroded away to low, rounded hills in times much shorter than Earth's 4.5-billion-year age. •

The Case of the Disappearing Mountains

We must conclude that if the erosion of mountains takes a few hundred million years, then any mountain that existed when Earth first formed 4.5 billion years ago would have been worn away long ago, and Earth's surface by now should be smooth and featureless. The only way that mountains could still exist on Earth is for mountains to be continuously formed.

Everyday observations of erosion and some very simple arithmetic thus lead us to a startling conclusion: tremendous forces must be acting on Earth, creating new mountain chains as the old ones are worn down. Earth's surface cannot be static. Although mountains seem to human beings to symbolize eternal solidity, they are transitory. Geologists who map the distribution and ages of rocks have shown that the Appalachian Mountains were formed a few hundred million years ago, and the Rocky Mountains only about 60 million years ago.

Newton's laws of motion (Chapter 2) tell us that nothing happens unless a force acts. What forces could create entire mountain ranges? Until recently, this question remained one of the greatest puzzles in geology.

Volcanoes and Earthquakes—Evidence of Earth's Inner Forces

Krafft/Hoa-Qui/Photo Researchers

Mount St. Helens in Washington erupted in a violent explosion on July 22, 1980.

Most geological processes such as mountain building and erosion are slow by human standards and take thousands or millions of years to produce noticeable change. But volcanoes and earthquakes may transform a landscape in an instant, thus revealing the tremendous energy stored in our dynamic planet.

Volcanic eruptions provide the most spectacular process by which new mountains are formed. In a typical **volcano,** subsurface molten rock called *magma,* concentrated in Earth's upper mantle or lower crust, breaks through to the surface, as shown in Figure 17-1. This breakthrough may be sudden, giving rise to the kind of dramatic events seen when Mount St. Helens exploded in 1980, or it may be relatively slow, with a stately surface flow of molten rock, known as *lava.* In both cases, however, magma eventually breaches the surface and hardens into new rock.

An **earthquake** occurs when rock suddenly breaks along a more-or-less flat surface, called a *fault.* Have you ever stretched a thick, strong elastic band, only to have it snap back painfully against your hand? You gradually added elastic potential energy to the band, and that energy was suddenly released—converted to violent kinetic energy. The same thing happens in an earthquake when stressed rock suddenly snaps.

When a brittle rock breaks, tremendous amounts of potential energy are released. The two sides of a fault can't fly apart like an elastic material can, so the energy is transmitted in the form of a sound wave or seismic wave (see Chapter 6). These waves, traveling at speeds of several kilometers per second, cause the ground to rise and fall like the

• Figure 17-1 A cross section of a volcano reveals a magma chamber, which stores molten rock, and a system of pipes, cracks, and vents that lead to the surface. The terms in the orange area refer to the kinds of rock formations resulting from cooled magma. Xenoliths are the original rocks encased in this cooled magma.

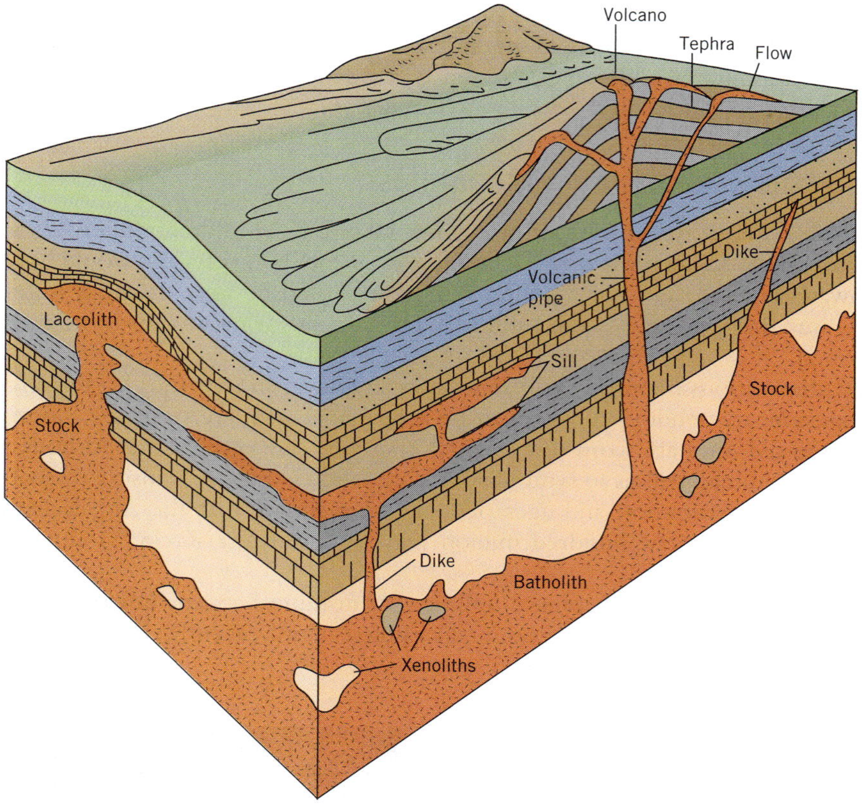

The tsunami that caused great damage and loss of life in 2004 was caused by an underwater earthquake.

surface of the ocean. Normally "solid" ground sways and pitches in a motion that can cause severe damage to buildings and other structures.

If an earthquake occurs under or near a large body of water, violent motions of the ground can transfer energy into great ocean waves that can travel thousands of miles and devastate low-lying coastal areas. Such waves are often referred to as "tidal waves," though they aren't caused by tides. A more correct term is *tsunamis,* a Japanese word for harbor or bay waves. The devastating tsunami of December 26, 2004, which killed hundreds of thousands of people in Sri Lanka, Thailand, Indonesia, Malaysia, and other countries bordering the Indian Ocean, was triggered by a strong earthquake off the west coast of North Sumatra. Most of the death and destruction was caused by powerful waves that raced miles inland across the shallow, populous coastal areas.

Fortunately, such destructive earthquakes and tsunamis are relatively rare, but smaller earthquakes, barely noticeable to the average person, occur every day by the thousands. Earthquakes were traditionally rated on the *Richter scale,* named after Charles Richter, the U.S. geologist who devised it. Technically, the Richter scale refers to the amount of ground motion that would be measured by an instrument a fixed distance from the center of the earthquake. The scale is such that each increase of 1 unit corresponds to 10 times more ground motion. Thus an earthquake that measures 7 will have 100 times more ground motion than one that measures 5, and so on. Today, a similar magnitude scale, based on energy release, is used.

Earthquakes that measure around 5 on the magnitude scale will be felt by most people but will do little damage in areas with well-constructed buildings. An earthquake between 6 and 7 will do considerable damage to buildings, and a magnitude-8 earthquake will level large areas. The earthquake that occurred in the San Francisco Bay area in October 1989 measured 7.1 and was dubbed the "Pretty Big One" by Californians who are waiting for what they call the "Big One." The powerful December 2004 earthquake that triggered the Indian Ocean tsunami measured 8.9 on the magnitude scale.

No earthquakes greater than 9 on the magnitude scale have ever been recorded, probably because no rocks can store that much energy before they rupture.

The puzzle remains, however: Where does all the energy that powers volcanoes and earthquakes come from?

The Movement of the Continents

Geologists have faced other mysteries as well. Think about a large map of the world. In your mind, move North and South America eastward toward Eurasia and Africa. Have you ever noticed how the two coastlines seem to fit together (Figure 17-2)?

English statesman and natural philosopher Francis Bacon (1561–1626) pointed out this fact in 1620. It wasn't until the beginning of the twentieth century, however, that anyone took the parallel coastlines seriously enough to ask about the origin of this pattern. In 1912, a German meteorologist named Alfred Wegener (1880–1930) proposed that Earth's continents are in motion. The reason that the Americas fit so well into the coastline of Europe and Africa, he suggested, is that they were once joined and have since been torn apart.

Wegener's theory, called *continental drift,* was eventually dismissed by most Earth scientists. He amassed some geological evidence to back it up, such as the matching locations of distinctive rock formations on opposite sides of the Atlantic Ocean. But most of this evidence was fragmentary and unconvincing to other scientists; indeed, some of Wegener's arguments later turned out to be wrong. More importantly, he failed to provide any reasonable mechanism by which continents could move. For most of the

• **Figure 17-2** A map of the world's continents reveals the similar shapes of coastlines on the two sides of the Atlantic Ocean.

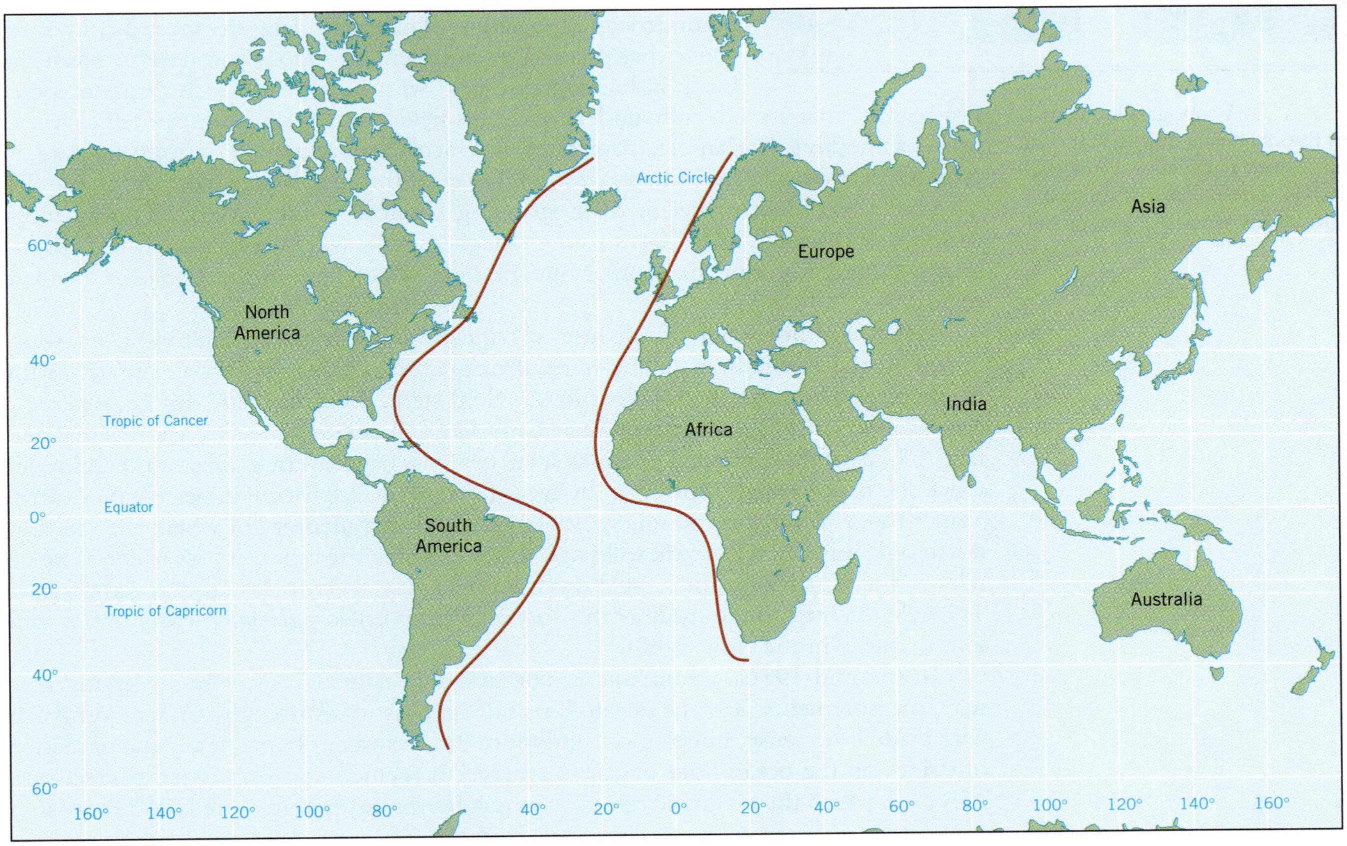

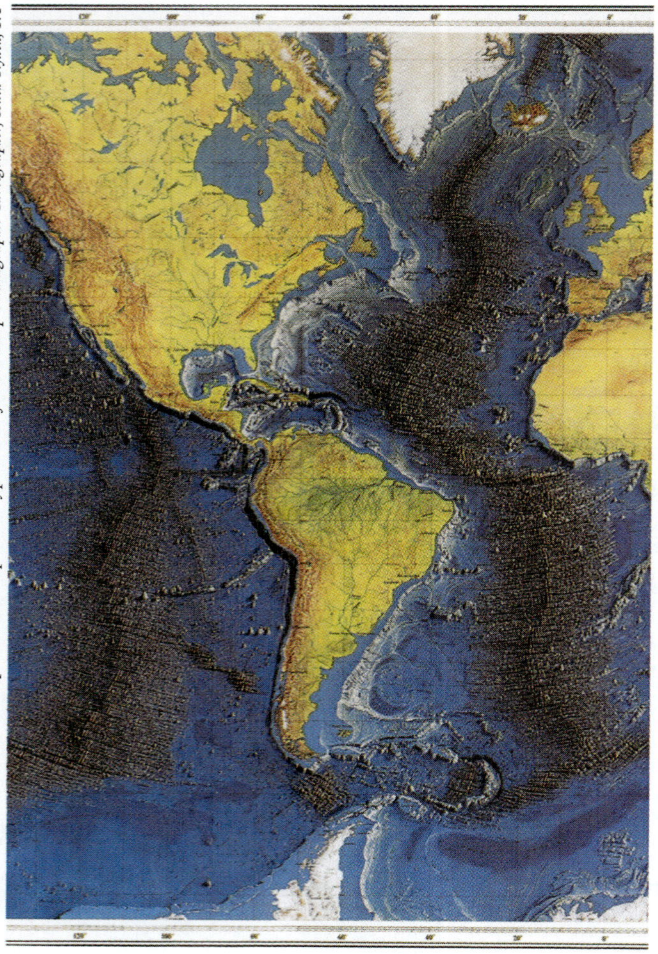

Marie Tharp 1977/2003. Reproduced by permission of Marie Tharp Oceanographic Cartographer, South Nyack, NY

• **Figure 17-3** A topographic map of ocean floors reveals dramatic mountain chains, deep flat planes, canyons, and trenches. These features suggest that ocean basins are active geological regions.

twentieth century, continental drift was regarded as a far-fetched exercise in theory, and few geologists paid much attention to it. Beginning about 1960, however, geologists and oceanographers obtained new evidence to support one aspect of Wegener's notion—the idea that the continents are not fixed.

The discovery that continents do indeed move required the merging of very different kinds of newly acquired geological evidence—topographic profiles of the oceans' floors, maps of rock magnetism, and data on rock ages.

1. Ocean Floors

When the contours of ocean floors were mapped in the years following World War II, oceanographers discovered remarkable, unsuspected features. Most scientists thought that the deep ocean bottoms were simply flat plains, passively collecting the sediments that gradually eroded off the ancient continents. Instead they found steep-walled canyons and lofty mountains, indicating that the seafloor is as dynamic and changing as the continents themselves (Figure 17-3). The longest mountain range on Earth, for example, is not on a continent, but in the middle of the Atlantic Ocean. Called the *Mid-Atlantic Ridge,* this feature extends from Iceland in the North Atlantic to the South Sandwich Islands in the South Atlantic. These ridges are sites of continuous geological activity, including numerous earthquakes, volcanoes, and lava flows. Similar ridges, also called rises, were found on the floors of all Earth's oceans. In fact, oceanographers have now mapped more than 85,000 km of ocean ridges.

2. Magnetic Reversals

To understand the nature of magnetic data, the second kind of evidence that pointed to continental motion, you have to recall that Earth has a magnetic field with north and south magnetic poles. For reasons that are not fully understood, this field changes direction sporadically over time—something like an electromagnet in which the direction of current in the coils changes occasionally (see Chapter 5). Well over 300 reversals of Earth's magnetic field have been recorded in ancient rocks spanning about 200 million years. During recent episodes of reversed fields, Earth's north magnetic pole was located somewhere in what is now Antarctica, and the south magnetic pole somewhere in the Canada-Greenland region.

When lava flows out of a fissure, it contains small crystals of natural iron oxides, including the naturally magnetic mineral magnetite. These bits of iron ore act as tiny magnets, and because the rock is still in a fluid state, their magnetic dipoles are free to turn around and align themselves in a north-south direction parallel to Earth's magnetic field. Think of these mineral grains as small compass needles embedded in the fluid rock. Once the rock hardens, however, the bits of magnetite are frozen in place—they can no longer move. Thus the volcanic rock carries within it a memory of where the magnetic north pole was when the rock solidified. If we examine the tiny compass needles, we can tell whether Earth's magnetic field was oriented as it is today or whether it was reversed. The field devoted to the study of this sort of effect is called *paleomagnetism,* and it came into maturity in the early 1960s.

In the mid-1950s, an oceanic exploration ship named *Pioneer* began taking magnetic measurements near the ocean floor off the coast of Washington State. At first the data made little sense, but as more and more profiles were obtained, a puzzling pattern of stripes on the ocean floor began to emerge. It seemed that there were parallel strips of rock in which the magnetic direction in neighboring strips alternated. (We show some

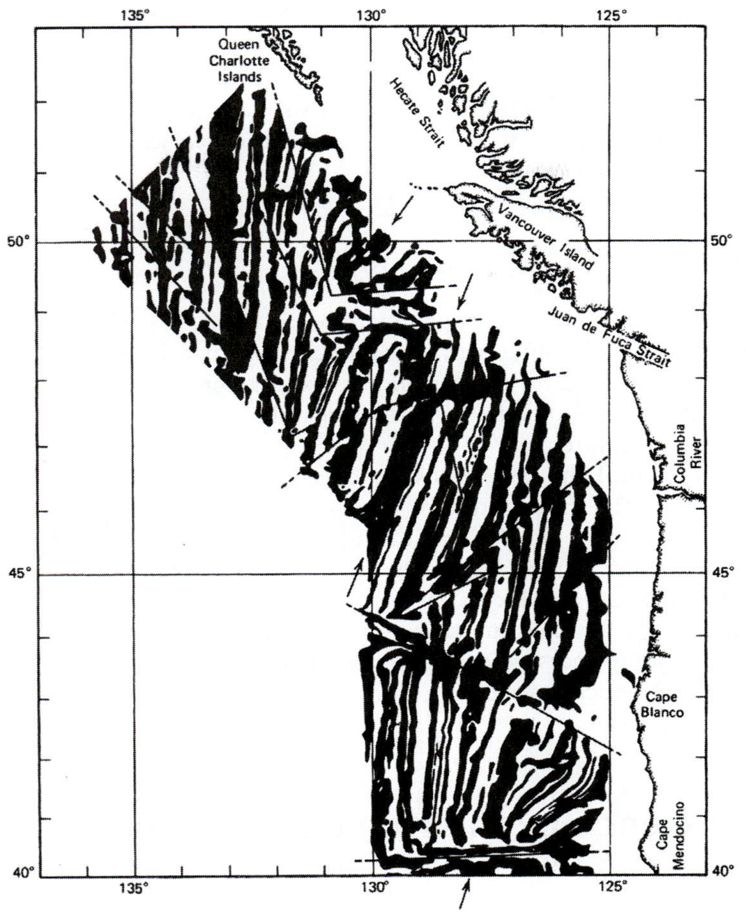

• **Figure 17-4** Measurements in the late 1950s and early 1960s revealed magnetic stripes running nearly parallel to the Vancouver province and Washington State coastlines.

of the original data in Figure 17-4.) Through the mid-1960s, Earth scientists collected more and more data of this type, and it soon became clear that the Mid-Atlantic Ridge, the East Pacific Rise, and many other places on ocean floors show the same pattern of alternating magnetic stripes.

How could these magnetic stripes be explained? In an environment in which the orientations of north and south magnetic poles were switching back and forth over time, the only way to get the observed striping is shown in Figure 17-5. The seafloor must be getting wider, a process called *seafloor spreading,* as new molten rock comes from deep within Earth and erupts through fissures on the ocean bottom. Over time, this new rock will be pushed aside as the continents move apart and as more magma comes up to take its place. The "compass needles" in this newer rock will point to the location of the magnetic north pole when they reach the surface. Each new batch of magma will solidify and lock in the current magnetic orientation, despite any further reversals. Each time Earth's magnetic field reverses, the dipole direction of the planet's magnetic field changes and gets locked into the newly formed rock. Thus, over long periods of time, we would expect to see alternating bands of magnetic orientation—exactly the kind of zebra-striped pattern of alternating north and south compass orientations shown in Figure 17-4.

• **Figure 17-5** Magnetic stripes that parallel ocean ridges must form as new magma wells up from the fissure and pushes out to the sides. In this cross-sectional view, older rocks lie farther from the ridge. (The "lithosphere" includes the uppermost mantle and all of the crust.)

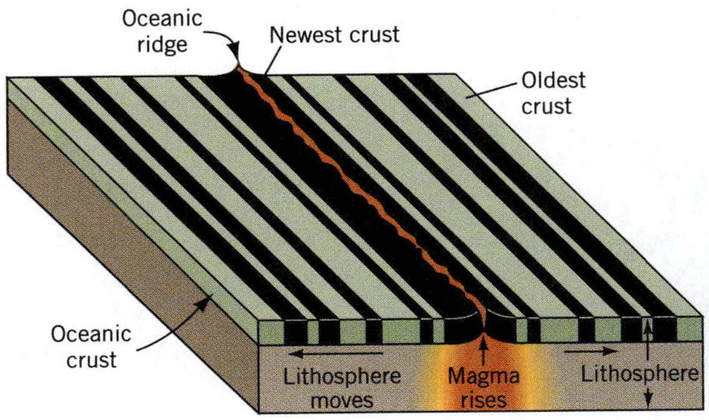

3. Rock Ages

The conclusions from magnetic data were reinforced by studies of the age of volcanic rocks in the oceanic crust. Volcanic rocks contain radioactive isotopes that can be used for dating (see Chapter 12). Rocks near the Mid-Atlantic Ridge and other similar features were found to be quite young, a few million years old or less. Rocks collected successively farther away from the ridge proved to be successively older.

> **Stop and Think!** Given what you know about the scientific method, why do you suppose scientists accept the movement of continents as a fact today, but didn't accept it in Wegener's time?

New Support for the Theory

The new data on the topography of ocean floors, as well as the magnetic properties and ages of its rocks, suggested to many scientists that the width of the Atlantic Ocean must be increasing yearly as the seafloor spreads. Eurasia and North America, it appears, are moving apart. Could the hypothesis that this distance is increasing be tested by an experimental measurement?

Up until the late 1980s no one was able to measure the motion of continents directly. The breakthrough came from an unexpected source—radio astronomy. Astronomers in North America and Europe trained radio telescopes on distant quasars (see Chapter 15). By measuring the times of arrival of the crests of the same radio wave, astronomers were able to get very accurate measurements of the distance between their telescopes. By repeating these sorts of experiments over a period of a few years, they were able to measure exactly the separation of the continents. Their work shows that North America is separating from Europe at the rate of about 5 centimeters (about 2 inches) a year.

• **Figure 17-6** Once the motion of continents was determined, scientists could predict how Earth's surface might have looked in the past. More than 200 million years ago, the present-day continents were joined together as the ancient continent Pangaea.

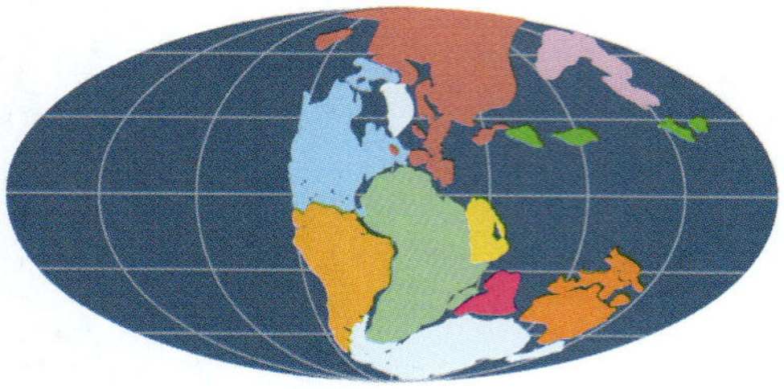

240 million years ago

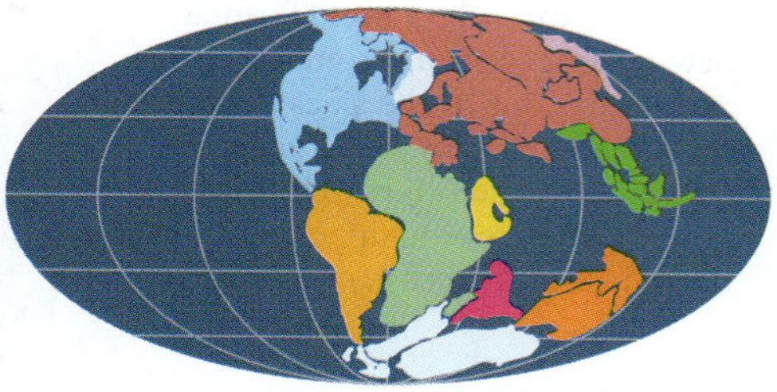

120 million years ago

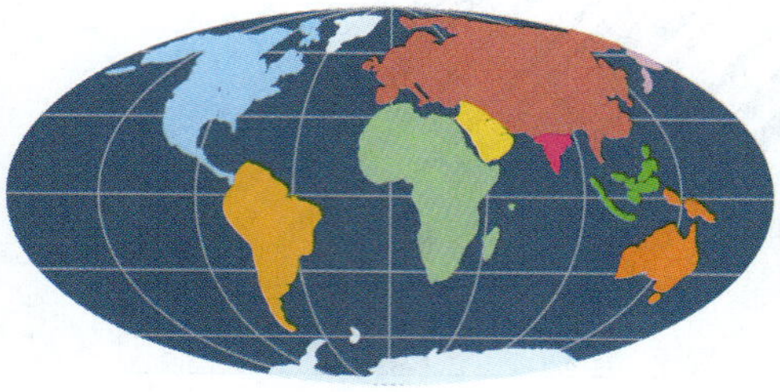

Present

Science by the Numbers •

The Age of the Atlantic Ocean

If continents are constantly moving at speeds up to several centimeters per year, what would a map of Earth's surface have looked like millions of years ago? We can make an educated guess by using present rates of movement and "reversing the tape," so to speak. We know, for example, that the floor of the Atlantic Ocean is spreading at about 5 cm per year. Assuming that the rate of spreading has remained more or less constant, how old is the Atlantic Ocean?

To calculate the answer, we need to apply the familiar equation for travel time:

$$\text{time of travel} = \frac{\text{distance}}{\text{speed}}$$

(You use the same relationship every time you estimate the driving time for a vacation.) The speed in this equation is the spreading rate, 5 cm per year, and the present width of the Atlantic is approximately 7000 km, or 7×10^8 cm. The Atlantic Ocean began to open, therefore, at

$$\text{time} = \frac{7 \times 10^8 \text{ cm}}{(5 \text{cm/yr})}$$
$$= 1.4 \times 10^8 \text{ years}$$
$$= 140 \text{ million years}$$

By this calculation, 140 million years ago Europe and the Americas must have been joined together because there was no Atlantic Ocean! In fact, by retracing the wandering paths of continents, earth scientists have discovered that 200 million years ago what we now call the continents of North America, South America, Eurasia, and Africa were locked together in one giant continent called *Pangaea* (Figure 17-6). A map of that ancient Earth would be all but unrecognizable, with a huge landmass on one side of the globe and a giant ocean on the other.

By the same token, 100 million years from now Earth's continents will have moved thousands of kilometers and appear completely different from today's arrangement. •

Plate Tectonics: A Unifying View of Earth

The compelling model of the dynamic Earth that has emerged from studies of paleomagnetism, rock dating, and much other data is called **plate tectonics.** "Tectonics" is related to the word "architect" and carries the connotation of building or putting things together. Plate tectonics develops a picture of the world that explains many of Earth's large-scale surface features and related phenomena.

The central idea of the plate tectonics theory is that Earth's surface is broken up into about a dozen large pieces (as well as a number of smaller ones) called **tectonic plates** (Figure 17-7). Each plate is a rigid, moving sheet of rock up to 100 km (60 miles) thick, composed of the crust and part of the upper mantle. Oceanic plates have an average 8- to 10-km thickness of dense rock known as *basalt* on top of the mantle rock. Continental plates have an average 35-km thickness of lower-density rock, such as *granite,* capping the basalt.

The tectonic plate boundaries are not the same as those of the continents and oceans. Some plates have continents on all or part of their surface, while some are covered only by oceanic crust. Most of the North American continent, for example, rests on the 8000-km-wide North American Plate, which extends from the middle of the Atlantic Ocean to the Pacific Plate on the West Coast.

About one quarter of Earth's surface is covered by continent; the rest is ocean. On timescales of millions of years, the plates shift about on the planet's surface, carrying the continents with them like passengers on a raft. Thus it's not the motion of the continents themselves that is fundamental to understanding Earth's dynamics, but the constant motion of the underlying plates. Continental motion (what Wegener called continental drift) is just one manifestation of that plate motion.

• **Figure 17-7** Earth's major plates with their directions of motion shown by arrows.

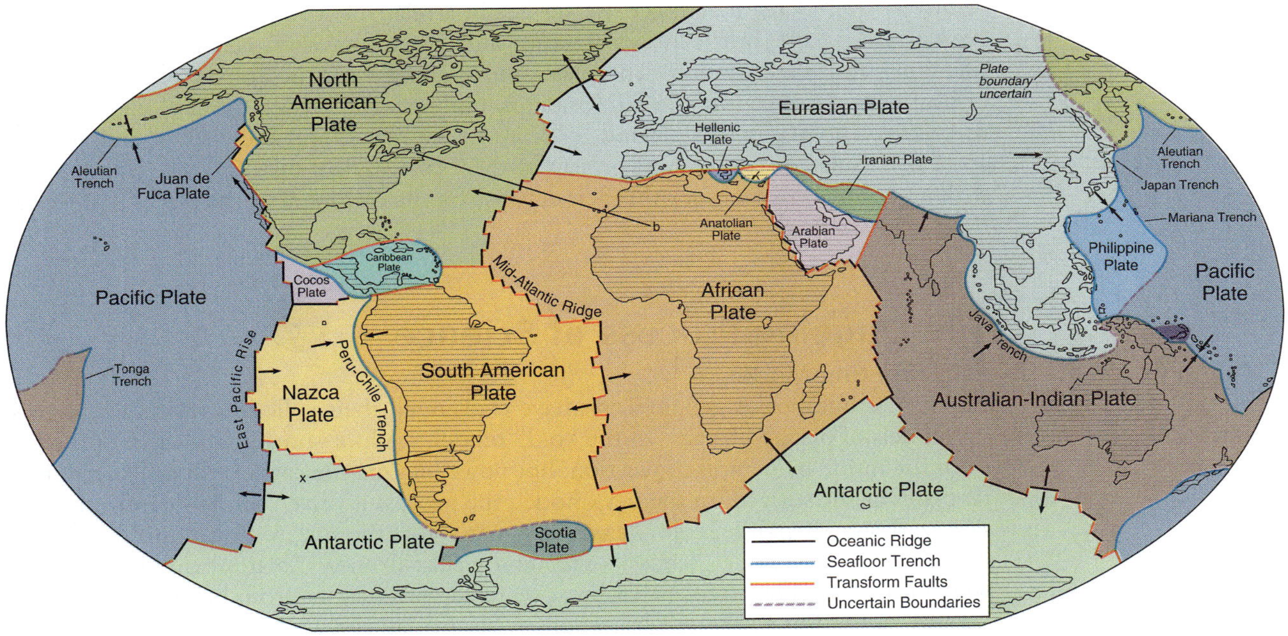

The Convecting Mantle

Nothing happens without a force. What force could possibly be large enough to move not only the continents, but also the plates of which they are a part? Many geophysicists accept the theory that continents move as a result of the force generated by **mantle convection** deep within Earth—motions driven by our planet's internal heat energy.

Two sources of energy contribute to Earth's interior heat. Some of this heat energy is left over from the gravitational potential energy released during the great bombardment and differentiation of the mantle and core as Earth formed (see Chapter 16). The decay of uranium and other radioactive elements (see Chapter 12), which are fairly common throughout Earth's core and mantle, provides a second important source of heat energy. These elements decay over time and produce energetic, fast-moving decay products—particles that collide with atoms and molecules in surrounding rocks and give up their energy as heat. Deep inside Earth, all this heat energy softens rocks to the point that they can flow slowly like hot taffy.

In Chapter 4 we saw that heat energy, once generated, must move spontaneously toward cooler regions. The heat generated in Earth's interior, for example, must eventually be radiated into space. If Earth were somewhat smaller, or if only small amounts of heat were generated, the energy could be carried to the surface entirely by conduction—the movement of heat by atomic collisions. This process operates in the Moon and Mars, for example. In the case of Earth, however, there is too much internal heat to be carried by conduction alone. Rocks in the mantle have been heated to the point where they are able to flow, and immense convection cells are set up deep within Earth's mantle. According to this model, mantle rocks behave like water in a boiling pot.

There are, of course, very important differences between Earth's mantle and a boiling pot—in particular, the timescales. Solid rock cannot flow significantly on timescales comparable to human lifetimes. But give soft, hot rocks a few hundred million years and they can move large distances. Earth scientists now estimate that Earth's convection cells go through a full cycle—with hot rocks rising from the lower mantle, cooling near the surface, and falling back to be replaced by other, warmer rocks—on a timescale of about 200 million years. In effect, Earth behaves something like a giant spherical stove, with burners on the inside and circulating rocks bringing the heat to the surface.

At the very top, these partially molten, circulating mantle rocks encounter the comparatively thin plates that cover the surface in a relatively cool, brittle layer. Along the oceanic ridges the brittle plates fracture and basaltic lava erupts, initiating seafloor spreading and plate motion. The plates move along with the convection cells underneath them, more or less as a film of oil on boiling water would move along on top of the water. The plates shift around, bash into each other, join each other, and are split apart in a constant dance. And on top of these plates, floating along like a thin scum, with no control whatsoever over their destiny, are the continents—the places that we call the "solid Earth."

The Ongoing Process of Science •

A Competing Model

Recently, a number of geophysicists have challenged their colleagues with a new twist on models of plate tectonics. In the "old" model, seafloor spreading is driven primarily from the inside by mantle convection; hot upwelling mantle rocks push apart thin, brittle plates at the surface. In the new model, the process is driven primarily from the outside, with gravity pulling cold, dense plate material at the surface down into the mantle. According to this model, seafloor spreading results from two plates being pulled apart, which leaves a gaping trench that must be filled with magma from below. Both models are now being put to the test by geophysicists around the world.

Stop and Think! How might you test the two competing models described above? Could both be correct?

The theory of plate tectonics caused a revolution in the earth sciences. For the first time, evidence from many different earth science disciplines had been brought together to form a single, coherent picture of our planet. This theory includes the oceans, the landmasses, the planet's deep interior, and the interconnections among all these systems. There was a time when geologists of different specialties—women and men who studied the ocean currents or ancient fossils, ore deposits, or the planet's deep interior—had little to say to each other. That situation is no longer true. All of these different disciplines now share a common way of looking at Earth and thus are able to give each other ideas and gain breadth and depth from interactions with each other. It may be that your college or university no longer has a department of geology but instead has a department called earth sciences or environmental sciences. These changes in name are more than just bureaucratic shufflings. They represent a very real change in the way scientists view and study planet Earth. •

Science in the Making •

Reactions to Plate Tectonics

At first, geologists confronted by the observations of magnetic stripes on the ocean floors, rock ages, and other seemingly odd data tried to find an explanation that did not require new seafloor to be created. All geologists had been taught a "fixed Earth" model in their college courses, and that was the standard picture of our planet they used in their work. Most of these scientists were not prepared to accept this radical new idea, that the continents might actually move, without a fight.

Some experts questioned the statistical significance of the magnetic data, and they wondered whether the distinctive striped patterns weren't the result of some as-yet-unknown effect (such as small electrical currents running around the ocean floor). Others simply tried to ignore the whole thing. But as geologists and oceanographers collected more data—as new measurements of magnetic patterns and more precise rock ages were obtained—the evidence for seafloor spreading simply became overwhelming.

In a very short time, less than a decade from the time the first puzzling data from the *Pioneer* expedition came in, geologists had for the most part accepted a theory that radically changed many of the central principles of their discipline. This dramatic change in perspective brings us back to a point we made in Chapter 1. Good scientists will eventually accept the implications of their observations, regardless of whether those implications violate preconceived concepts. A scientist can't look at data without some preconceived notions. Few scientists, for example, took the original continental drift arguments of Wegener seriously because, in part, no obvious mechanism could cause entire continents to move.

We should note in passing that, although Wegener's theory contained one feature of modern theories, namely, moving continents, continental drift was not plate tectonics. Wegener predicted, for example, that the average elevation of continents would increase with time—a prediction not confirmed by careful measurements. But as more and more data supported the more convincing plate tectonics model, the majority of earth scientists readily changed their notions as the data demanded it.

The fact that the fixed Earth—one of the most revered and widely accepted geological theories—could be abandoned in the space of a few years when confronted by powerful contrary evidence indicates that the scientific method works. It also shows that many of the arguments one hears from the proponents of pseudosciences such as UFOs, astrology, creation science, and the like—arguments to the effect that the scientific community routinely closes its mind to new ideas and will not accept them—are simply wrong.

Courtesy NASA

A satellite photograph of a portion of Africa's Great Rift Valley. The narrow body of water defines a divergent plate boundary where new plate material is being created and plates are moving out to either side.

Scientific theories, unlike the untestable claims of pseudoscience, are subject to repeated scrutiny and can be falsified. When confronted with overwhelming evidence, scientists are, indeed, prepared to accept new ideas and abandon the old "conventional wisdom." •

Plate Boundaries

The boundaries between Earth's tectonic plates are active sites that determine much of the geological character of the surface. Three main types of boundaries separate Earth's tectonic plates: divergent plate boundaries, convergent plate boundaries, and transform plate boundaries.

1. Divergent Plate Boundaries

We saw one aspect of plate motion when we talked about seafloor spreading at the Mid-Atlantic Ridge, where new plate material is formed. We can now understand how such a spreading feature arises. In Figure 17-8, we show what happens when plates happen to lie above a zone where magma comes to the surface. Not only does the volcanic action form a chain of mountains, but the motion of the magma also pushes the two adjoining plates farther and farther away from each other. The newly erupted molten material cools to rock and becomes new plate material. As the brittle tectonic plates crack and separate, shallow earthquakes of relatively low energy occur. This mechanism drives the seafloor spreading that gave us our first indication of the nature of continental motion. Such a spreading zone of crustal formation is called a **divergent plate boundary.**

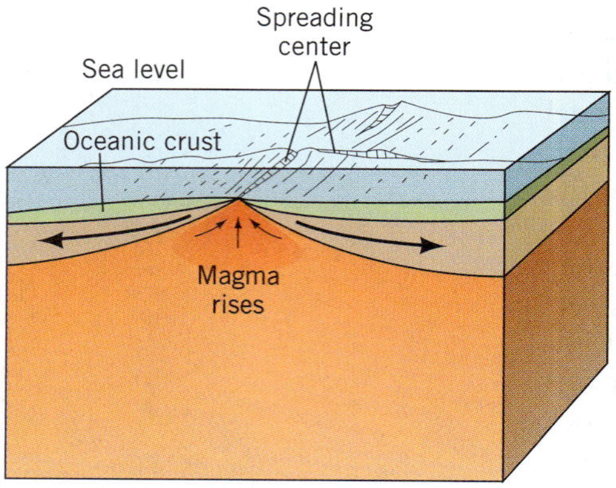

• **Figure 17-8** A divergent plate boundary defines a line along which new plate material is formed from volcanic rock.

When a divergent plate boundary occurs on the ocean floor, the seafloor spreads, basalt lava erupts from the newly created fissures, the two plates are pushed apart, and any continents that might be located on other portions of those plates are pushed apart as well. Eurasia and North America, for example, are separating right now at the rate of about 5 cm per year; consequently, the Atlantic Ocean is getting wider. Note that old spreading centers, such as the Mid-Atlantic Ridge, are always located in the middle of an ocean.

New spreading centers, on the other hand, may begin anywhere, even in the middle of a continent. If a continent happens to be sitting above what will eventually become a divergent plate boundary, then the continent itself will be literally torn apart. The Great East African Rift Valley, which extends south from Ethiopia, along the east coastal interior of central Africa to the coast of Mozambique, and north into Israel and Syria, is a modern-day example of this motion. Millions of years in the future, an ocean may separate the western part of Africa from the eastern part. In fact, at the point where the Great Rift Valley crosses the African coast, this sea is already beginning to form. Look at the Dead Sea, Red Sea, and Gulf of Aqaba and you will see this rift in progress.

The San Andreas Fault in California marks the transform boundary between the North American Plate and the Pacific Plate.

James Balog/Stone/Getty Images, Inc.

2. Convergent Plate Boundaries

Earth is not getting any larger. If new material pushes tectonic plates apart at places such as the oceanic ridges, then old plate material must be pushed together and taken into Earth's interior somewhere else. A place where two plates are coming together is called a **convergent plate boundary.**

At most convergent plate boundaries, one plate sinks beneath another to form a **subduction zone.** The plate that is subducted, or "taken beneath," in this way sinks down to rejoin the mantle material from which it came.

Earth scientists observe three broadly different kinds of surface features associated with convergent plate boundaries, all shown in Figure 17-9. First, if no continents are on the leading edge of either of the two converging plates, the result will be a *deep ocean trench.* As one plate penetrates into Earth's interior, it can bend and buckle the adjacent plate to produce a deep furrow in the ocean floor. Melting of the subducting slab at depths of 100 or 200 km can generate magma. The hot magma slowly rises toward the surface and, if the magma penetrates the overlying ocean crust, continuing eruptions of lava will build a chain of volcanic islands adjacent to the trench. The Marianas Trench, the deepest point in the world's oceans (11 km or about 7 mi deep, 2 km deeper than Mount Everest is high) near the volcanic coastline of the Philippines, is an example of just such a subduction zone and volcanic terrain.

If continents ride on top of both converging plates, they will collide. Continental material will be compressed together like crumpled cloth and pushed up to form a high, jagged mountain chain. The Himalayas, for example, which began to form about 30 million years ago, are still growing taller at about 1 cm per year as the once-separate Indian subcontinent collides with Asia. Similarly, the Ural Mountains mark the point at which Europe and Asia were welded together, and the Alps mark the point at which the Italian peninsula was joined to Europe. All of these geological processes involve the production of midcontinent mountain chains.

Finally, if a continent rests at the leading edge of only one of the two colliding plates, the denser oceanic plate will subduct beneath the continent. Just as in the case where two oceanic plates converge, a deep trench may form a short distance offshore, while the continental material may be crumpled into a coastal mountain range. In addition, the subducting tectonic slab may partially melt and thus provide magma that rises to form a chain of volcanic mountains parallel to the coast. The Andes Mountains of South America and the Cascade Mountains of the northwestern United States are spectacular examples of this phenomenon.

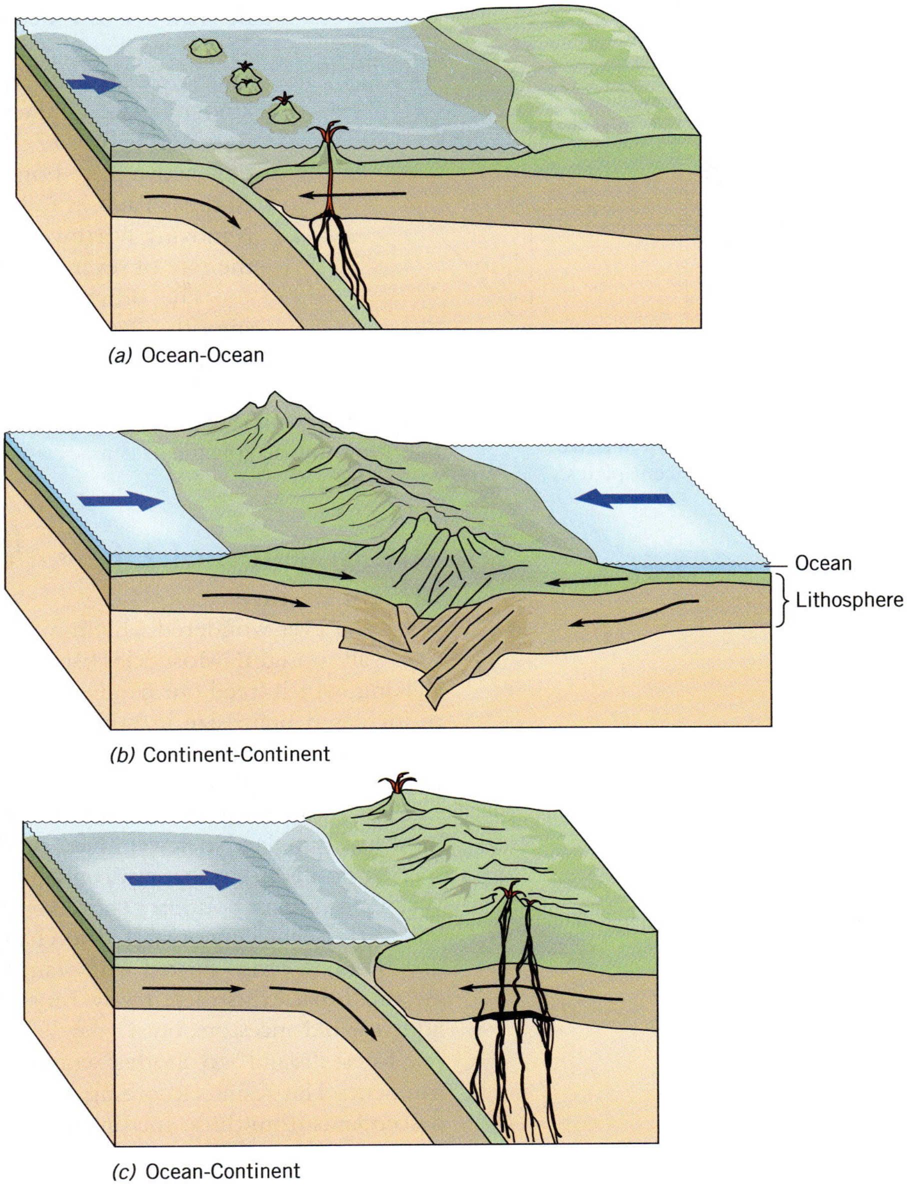

• **Figure 17-9** Convergent plate boundaries may display a variety of surface features, depending on the distribution of continental material. *(a)* When neither tectonic plate carries continental material at the convergent boundary, then a subduction zone is formed. A deep-ocean trench and chain of island volcanoes are often created in this case. *(b)* When both tectonic plates carry continental material at the boundary, the continental materials buckle and fold to form nonvolcanic mountains. *(c)* When only one tectonic plate carries continental material at the boundary, the oceanic plate will subduct beneath the continent. A deep trench may form offshore and a coastal mountain range will form on land.

Roughly speaking, Earth's oceanic plate material renews itself about every 200 million years. The process of seafloor spreading and subduction is constantly replacing the ocean crust, while the lower-density continental plate material experiences no subduction. This process explains why, whereas some rocks on ancient continents formed billions of years ago and are still preserved there, no rocks on the ocean floor are older than about 200 million years.

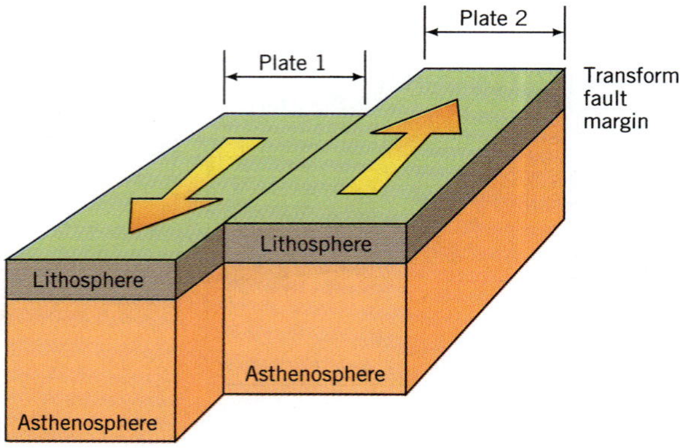

• **Figure 17-10** A transform plate boundary, showing the relative motions of the adjacent plates.

3. Transform Plate Boundaries

The third kind of boundary between plates occurs when one plate scrapes past the other, with no new plate material being produced. This kind of plate contact is called a **transform plate boundary** and is shown in Figure 17-10. The most famous transform boundary (and the only active plate boundary in the continental United States) is the San Andreas Fault in California. At the San Andreas Fault, the Pacific Plate is moving northwestward with respect to the North American Plate at the rate of several centimeters a year.

The process by which two plates slide past each other is not smooth. Over time, the motion of plates compresses and strains rocks at the boundary. Friction normally prevents the stressed rocks from moving, but periodically the rocks simply break, moving as much as several meters in one sudden burst. When they do so, an earthquake occurs. No mountain building or volcanism is associated with transform boundaries.

The Science of Life •

Upright Posture

Have you ever wondered why human beings are among the very few animals on Earth that walk upright? Most scientists today suspect that it was the adaptation of upright walking, which freed our hands, that led eventually to the use of tools and development of increased brain size in humans. Richard Leakey, a well-known anthropologist, has suggested that our upright posture might have resulted indirectly from movements of Earth's tectonic plates.

His argument goes like this: 30 million years ago, most of eastern Africa was covered by a lush jungle. No fewer than 20 different species of apes, including our ancestral species, flourished in that environment and were especially well adapted to living in trees. When a divergent boundary started to pull the continent apart along the East African Rift Valley, the environment started to change. The forest began to disappear, to be replaced first by open plains dotted with stands of trees, and finally, 3 million years ago, by the savannah that exists there today. Most of the apes became extinct long before our 3-million-year-old ancestors, but Leakey argues that walking upright and being able to get from one forest "island" to another would have been a distinct advantage in that sort of environment. The result, according to Leakey, is that today there are only three kinds of descendants from those apes in Africa—gorillas, chimpanzees, and human beings. •

The Geological History of North America

The epic movements of tectonic plates provided geologists with a new way of thinking about the history of Earth's surface. Earth scientists now use our understanding of plate tectonics to tell us something about the formation of our own continent. The oldest parts of the North American continent are in northeastern Canada and Greenland. Here we find large geological formations of rocks several billion years old that form the core of the continent (see Appendix C for the geological timescale). Over long periods of time, land was added to this continent by tectonic activity. Most of the western part of the United States, for example, is made up of small chunks of land called *terranes*—masses of rock several hundred kilometers across. Originally, these terranes were large islands in the Pacific Ocean, but they were carried toward the North American continent by plate activity and added to the mainland as tectonic plates converged. The hills near Wichita, Kansas, for example, are old mountains that once marked the addition of a large South American terrane onto what then comprised North America. (The idea that Wichita might have once had oceanfront property is one of the strange discoveries that comes out of plate tectonics.)

The Appalachian Mountains, which may at one time have rivaled the Himalayas in majesty, were formed over a period from about 450 to 300 million years ago when the continents that are now Eurasia and Africa rammed into the continent that is now North America. A series of long folds and fractures—structures that formed the present-day Appalachian Mountains—appeared in the surface rocks. This process explains, for example, why roads in the mountainous regions of the eastern part of the United States tend to run from southwest to northeast. They follow the mountain valleys that were created by erosion of these folded rocks. Thick wedges of sediments eroded off the mountains, forming the Coastal Plains of eastern North America and contributing to the sediments of the Great Plains.

The dramatic geological features of the western United States record a great variety of mountain-forming events. The Rocky Mountains rose approximately 60 million years ago from a broad warping and subsequent folding and fracturing of continental material. The Colorado Plateau, comprising parts of the states of Colorado, Arizona, and New Mexico, experienced a more gentle uplift, as rivers incised features such as the Grand Canyon. The Sierra Nevada range formed more recently when molten rock pushed up a huge block of sediments. These processes of uplift and erosion continue to this day in many places around the world.

Another Look at Volcanoes and Earthquakes

Plate tectonics provides us with a dynamic picture of our planet. Plates continually move over the hot, partially molten rocks in the mantle. They smash together, rip apart, and scrape by each other. In the process, tall mountain chains are uplifted and worn down, and wide ocean basins are opened and closed as continents come together and split apart. Nothing on Earth is permanent, because heat continuously flows from the hot interior to the cooler surface, and mantle convection provides the primary mechanism for that heat transfer. The scale of these ongoing processes is vast, nearly outside our ability to comprehend, but we are occasionally reminded of the power of geological processes.

For thousands of years humans have realized that Earth's most violent events—volcanoes and earthquakes—do not occur randomly. Earthquakes are common in California and Alaska, but extremely rare in Kansas or Florida. Volcanoes are commonplace in Hawaii and the Pacific Northwest but never appear in New York or Texas. Why should this be? Plate tectonics provides an answer.

Plates and Volcanism

The global distribution of volcanoes may be understood in terms of the principles of plate tectonics. Volcanoes are common in three geological situations: along divergent plate boundaries, near convergent plate boundaries, or above places called "hot spots."

1. Divergent Plate Boundaries
The formation of new crust along volcanic spreading ridges of divergent plate boundaries is the principal way that new crustal rocks are formed. New basaltic plate material forms at the rate of a few centmeters per year along about 85,000 km of oceanic ridges around the world.

2. Convergent Plate Boundaries
Volcanoes are also common near subduction zones, except where two continental tectonic plates collide. As water-rich crustal material plunges into the mantle, it becomes hotter and may partially melt. This magma, which is highly mobile fluid rock, rises to the surface to form chains of volcanoes, typically about 200 km inland from the line of subduction. The "Ring of Fire," a dramatic string of volcanoes that borders much of the Pacific Ocean, is a direct consequence of plate subduction (Figure 17-11).

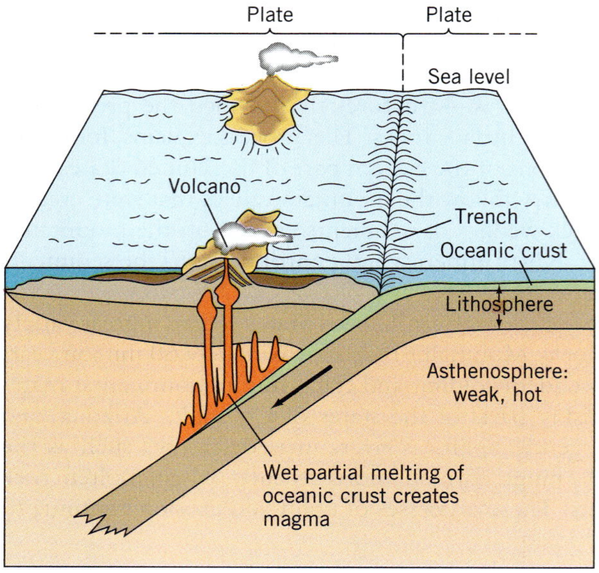

• **Figure 17-11** Volcanoes form above a subduction zone when heated plate material partially melts. The hot magma rises through the overlying crust to form a chain of volcanic islands.

The volcanoes that form the Cascade Mountain chain along the northwestern coast of the United States (including Mount Rainier and Mount St. Helens) are striking examples of the processes associated with subduction of an oceanic plate beneath a continent. Frequent dramatic eruptions of similar volcanoes in Central America, Japan, and the Philippines point to other places where subduction and volcanism occur in tandem.

3. Hot Spots

Finally, **hot spots** are a dramatic type of volcanism indirectly associated with plate tectonics. Earth scientists recognize dozens of hot spots around the world, including Hawaii, Yellowstone Park, Iceland, and others where large isolated chimney-like columns of rising hot rock, also known as mantle plumes, rise to the surface more or less like bubbles coming to the surface in water being heated on a stove. These plumes may originate in the lower mantle or even at the core–mantle boundary. On a geological timescale, sources of hot spots are relatively stationary, so if a tectonic plate slowly moves over the fixed hot spot, the result will be a chain of volcanoes like the Hawaiian Islands that are built through a series of basaltic lava eruptions (Figure 17-12). These islands were created one at a time as the Pacific Plate moved above the localized hot spot. The present-day volcano Kilauea on the "big island" of Hawaii, the site of most of the island chain's active volcanism, is directly over a hot spot. The volcanic islands to the northwest are progressively older, as well as smaller owing to erosion, revealing that the motion of the Pacific Plate is also toward the northwest. In fact, a series of eroded submarine peaks that were islands millions of years ago stretches hundreds of kilometers farther to the northwest. In several million years, the most northwesterly of the present Hawaiian Islands will have been eroded beneath the waves, but new volcanic activity has already

• **Figure 17-12** The Hawaiian Islands stretch along a northwest-southeast line that reveals the northwesterly motion of the Pacific Plate over a fixed hot spot. As the Pacific Plate moves, new volcanic islands are created to the southeast, while older islands erode away. The island of Kauai, currently the oldest, is between 3 and 5.5 million years old, while Hawaii, the youngest island, is less than 0.8 million years old.

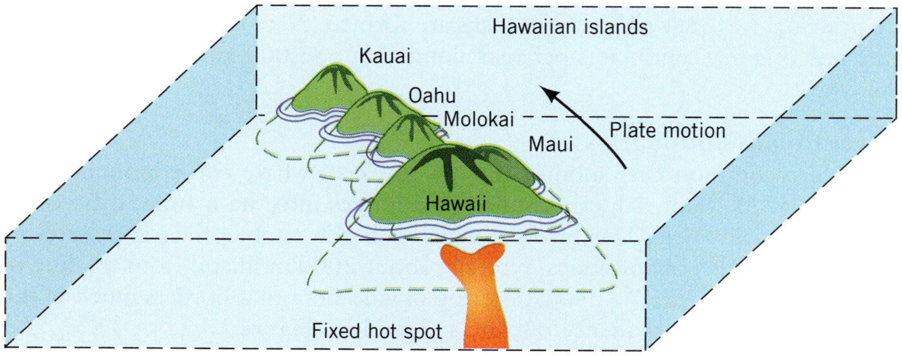

begun on the ocean floor southeast of Kilauea, promising a new island that has already been given the name "Loihi" by islanders.

Earthquakes

Stress builds up in brittle rock for several reasons. Heated rock expands and cooling rock contracts—changes that cause a solid formation to warp and distort. Rock may also become stressed in response to changes in pressure, as overlying mountains wear away or new layers of sediment weigh down. And, of course, stress builds up to extreme levels as two tectonic plates attempt to move past each other at a transform plate boundary.

Earthquakes may be felt near any plate boundary. Minor shallow earthquakes occur near divergent plate boundaries as two oceanic plates move apart. Stronger earthquakes, including "deep-focus" earthquakes originating more than 100 km down, occur near subduction zones. Many of the most destructive shocks in Japan are of this type. In the United States, earthquakes at the transform plate boundary along the San Andreas Fault receive the most attention because of the fault's unusual activity, length, and proximity to major population centers. There are, however, occasional earthquakes in the middle of plates—in Missouri, for example. Such events may arise from gradual warping of the wide, brittle North American Plate, though the origins of these earthquakes are still not fully understood.

Seismology: Exploring Earth's Interior with Earthquakes

Scientists who study earthquakes have discovered that these violent events provide the best means for exploring the deep interior of our planet. Geologists can't get their hands on much more than the outer 10 km or so of rock layers. Everything we know about Earth's interior deeper than a few kilometers has to be obtained by indirect means. The science of **seismology,** the study and measurement of sound vibrations within Earth, is dedicated to deducing our planet's inner structure.

The basic idea of seismology is simple. When an earthquake or explosion occurs, waves of vibrational energy (see Chapter 5) move out through the rocks. Some of these waves travel through Earth's center, others move along the surface, and still others bounce off layers deep within the planet.

So-called seismic waves come in two principal types. *Compressional* or *longitudinal waves* are like sound—the molecules in the rock move back and forth in the same direction as the wave. *Shear waves,* on the other hand, are *transverse waves,* like water waves in which the molecules move up and down perpendicular to the direction of wave motion. These kinds of waves travel through rock at different velocities depending, among other things, on the rock type, its temperature, and the pressure. After a major earthquake, scientists at laboratories around the world record the intensity and time of arrival of the various kinds of waves, both those that pass along the surface and those that pass through Earth's interior (Figure 17-13). By comparing the arrival behavior of waves from the same

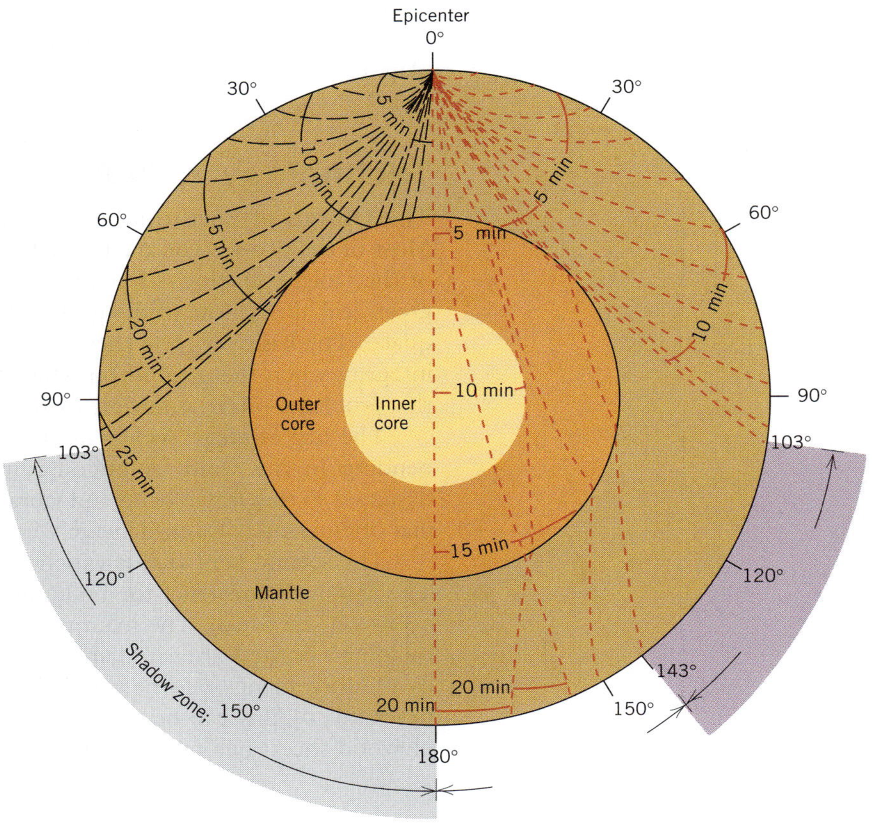

• **Figure 17-13** Seismic waves passing through Earth can take a variety of paths. The speeds of *P* or compressional waves (shown in red) and *S* or shear waves (in black) will be different depending on the type of rock, its temperature, and the pressure. *S* waves, furthermore, cannot travel through the liquid outer core.

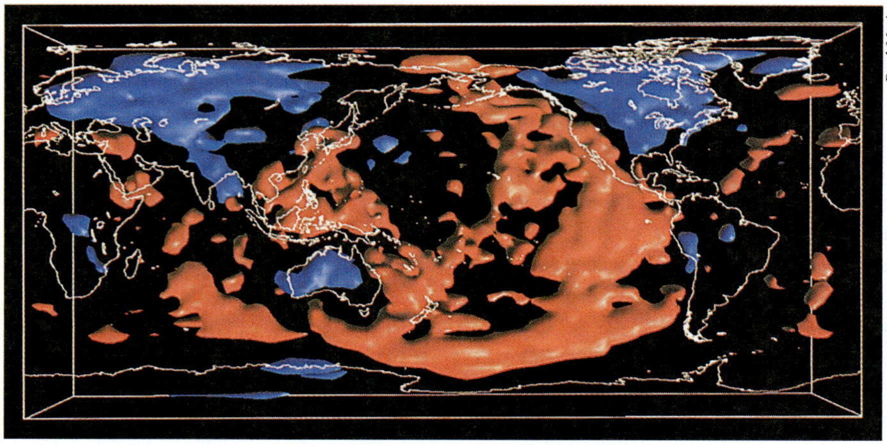

Paul Morin

• **Figure 17-14** A seismic tomograph provides a picture of Earth's deep interior, based on millions of individual measurements of seismic wave velocities. This image reveals hot rocks (red) around the Pacific Ocean rim, and cooler rocks (blue) under the continents.

earthquake at many different sites on Earth's surface, a computer can construct a picture of the material through which those waves passed.

The Ongoing Process of Science •

Seismic Tomography

The picture of Earth we give in Chapter 16, in which we talk about the solid and liquid core, the layered mantle, and the thin brittle crust, comes from studies of seismic waves. Now, as more and more seismic data are collected, and ever-faster computers permit new ways to process those data, a new branch of Earth science called *seismic tomography* is enabling geophysicists to obtain astonishing three-dimensional pictures of Earth's deep interior (Figure 17-14). We are now able to document the basic movements of cold subducting slabs, hot upwelling mantle plumes, and the convection cells that characterize plate tectonics. •

Technology •

The Design of Earthquake-Resistant Buildings

Most of the people who die in earthquakes die because of falling buildings, not because of the violent shaking. Over the past few decades, structural engineers have learned a great deal about how to design buildings so that they do not collapse during an earthquake. The basic problem they face is how to construct a building that will maintain its integrity when the ground on which it sits moves. There are two general solutions to this problem—make it flexible or make it rigid.

The first strategy, widely used in designing tall buildings, is best typified by a tree bending in the wind. A building with a specially reinforced steel skeleton can be designed so that it will bend and vibrate as the ground shakes, but come back to its original orientation without damage when the quake stops.

The second approach is widely used in individual houses and apartment buildings. The idea is to construct the building so that it tosses about on the moving surface like a ship on the ocean. The main preoccupation of the engineers is to guarantee that the building's corners are maintained at 90 degrees, no matter how much it moves around, by reinforcement of corners and rigid connections to the foundation and roof. Sometimes this rigidity can be obtained simply by covering all the walls of the building with plywood sheets before the outer siding is installed. •

Science News | Rome At Risk

(Science News, Feb. 25, 2006, p. 115)

Rome is one of the world's great cities, but it is at risk from the kinds of geological processes we have discussed in this chapter. In particular, the city has been subjected to at least 20 large earthquakes in the last 2000 years, a fact that makes an assessment of the damage a modern earthquake could do quite important.

The city is built on sediments that fill the basin of the Tiber river—you can picture the area as a rocky bowl filled with loosely packed material. When seismic waves move through loose sediment, the soil can shift and settle and even, in some cases, temporarily liquefy. When "solid" ground becomes fluid, there can be significant damage to structures built on it.

The last major earthquake in the Rome region took place in 1915, before any seismic instruments were in place. To predict how the soil in the Tiber basin will respond to the next earthquake, scientists have to use computer models. A group at San Diego State University recently created such a model, and the results of the computer runs are striking.

Using data from over 1000 boreholes taken around the city, the San Diego group looked at what might happen in two likely earthquake situations—a 5.3 magnitude quake centered in the Alban Hills (some 25 km southeast of the city) and a 7.0 magnitude event in the Appenines (some 90 kilometers east). They found that the greatest ground motion occurred around the edge of the basin, where seismic waves reflected off of the surrounding rocks and reinforced each other. They also found that the seismic waves echoed back and forth through the sediments, producing ground motions that lasted over 60 seconds.

The main use of these sorts of simulations of Rome will be to allow scientists to identify the ancient monuments most at risk in an earthquake. This information, in turn, will be used to guide the use of scarce preservation funds to reinforce the structures most at risk.

Thinking More About | Plate Tectonics

Earthquake Prediction

One of the most important roles scientists can play in modern society is to provide warnings of natural disasters such as earthquakes, volcanic eruptions, and large storms. In the fall of 1999, for example, early warnings allowed thousands of Florida residents to escape the path of Hurricane Andrew. The storm caused billions of dollars of property damage, but surprisingly little loss of life. Similarly, volcanic eruptions, which are usually preceded by numerous small earthquakes, also can be forecast with some certainty. The successful prediction of Mount Pinatubo's 1991 eruption in the Philippines gave thousands of people living on the flanks of the long-dormant volcano time to flee.

Earthquake prediction is another story, however. Earthquakes occur because of the predictable and measurable gradual buildup of stresses in Earth's crust. But the sudden failure of rock is not so predictable. You are familiar with this situation if you've ever gradually bent a pencil to the breaking point. It's easy to predict that a bent pencil will eventually break, but it's very hard to say exactly at what point the failure will occur. Much of the scientific effort related to earthquake prediction centers on the careful documentation of stress buildup in earthquake-prone areas. But these measurements alone tell us little about the exact time when failure will occur.

In their efforts to predict earthquakes, many scientists search for "precursor events"—measurable phenomena that precede a quake. A lot of anecdotal evidence suggests that such events may indeed occur. Folklore has it that some domesticated animals become highly agitated before a strong earthquake or that changes are seen in the flow of well water or hot springs. Recognition of such changes enabled Chinese scientists to save many lives prior to a major 1975 earthquake. Similarly, scientists have noticed changes in the regularity of geysers and have recorded swarms of minor quakes just prior to some big earthquakes. Nevertheless, no reliable methods for predicting earthquakes have yet been devised. At best, we can reliably predict the probability that a large earthquake might occur in a given area during a period of a few decades.

Ironically, if we do develop a way to predict the timing of earthquakes precisely, a whole new series of problems could arise. Suppose you could predict with 80% certainty that there will be a major earthquake in the Los Angeles Basin sometime in the next 30 days. Would you then announce it? What would happen in the Los Angeles Basin if you made such an announcement? What would happen if you made the announcement and the earthquake never occurred? What would happen if you didn't make the announcement and the earthquake did occur? These are not easy subjects to deal with.

Summary

Earth's surface constantly changes. Mountains are created and worn away, while entire continents slowly shift, opening up oceans and closing them again. *Plate tectonics,* a relatively new theory that explains how a few thin, rigid *tectonic plates* of crustal and upper mantle material are moved across Earth's surface by *mantle convection,* provides a global context for these changes. According to this theory, plates move over a partially molten underlying sections of Earth's mantle, like rafts on the ocean, in response to convection of hot mantle rocks.

Three different kinds of observations—the geological features of ocean floors, parallel stripes of magnetic rocks situated symmetrically about volcanic ridges on the ocean floor, and the ages of these rocks—provided direct evidence that new crust is being created at *divergent plate boundaries.* Meanwhile, old crust returns to the mantle in *subduction zones,* where plates converge. *Convergent plate boundaries* in the ocean create deep trenches and associated volcanic islands. When an oceanic plate subducts beneath a plate carrying a continent, an offshore trench and chain of continental volcanoes parallel to shore result. The collision of two plates that carry continents at their margins produces mountain ranges of crumpled continental rocks. *Transform plate boundaries* occur where two plates scrape past each other.

Most *volcanoes* form near plate boundaries, either along the volcanic ridges of diverging plates or above subducting plates. Other volcanoes such as the Hawaiian Islands form above *hot spots* originating in Earth's mantle. *Earthquakes* occur when stressed rock ruptures. Earthquakes may be felt at all plate boundaries. The only plate boundary in the United States, California's San Andreas Fault, is a transform boundary in which one block of crust moves horizontally past the opposing block. The science of *seismology,* which documents the passage of earthquake-generated waves through Earth, is providing new insights into the dynamic processes that drive plate tectonics.

Key Terms

volcano
earthquake
plate tectonics
tectonic plates
mantle convection
divergent plate boundary
convergent plate boundary
subduction zone
transform plate boundary
hot spots
seismology

Review Questions

1. What evidence suggests that mountain ranges are not permanent features on Earth's surface?

2. What evidence suggests that Europe, Africa, and North and South America were once joined?

3. What evidence pointed to the process of seafloor spreading, or diverging plates?

4. Describe the three kinds of plate boundaries.

5. Describe the three different kinds of surface features that might occur at a convergent boundary.

6. Explain how mountains might form as a result of plate motions.

7. Identify a mountain range in North America that formed as a result of plate motions.

8. Why does a ring of volcanoes and earthquakes surround much of the Pacific Ocean?

9. What North American mountain range may have been the tallest in the world approximately 300 million years ago?

10. How do we know that tectonic plates move?

11. What is the Richter scale? Where might you read about it?

12. How do the ages of rocks on the ocean floor help support the theory of seafloor spreading?

Discussion Questions

1. Where are the tallest and longest mountain chains on Earth? How were they formed?

2. What plate do you live on? How many adjacent plates are there? What kinds of boundaries do you find to the north, south, east, and west? In which direction are these plates moving?

3. Why are all three types of plate boundaries essential if plate tectonics is to work? What is occurring at each type of boundary?

4. The continent of Antarctica has rocks with plant and animal fossils that suggest the Antarctic climate was once temperate. Explain at least two different ways in which these warm-climate fossils might have ended up in what is now a polar region. How might you test your hypotheses?

5. Volcanic islands, including the Azores, Canaries, and Iceland, lay scattered across the Atlantic Ocean. If you were to date the rocks on these and other Atlantic islands, what pattern do you predict you would find?

6. Geologists estimate that as much as 80% of Earth's surface is covered by volcanic rocks. Is this estimate reasonable? What role might plate tectonics have played in producing these rocks?

7. Geology has been called an integrated science, because it calls on several scientific disciplines to help explain features and processes of Earth. Explain how geologists have used other sciences to answer the following questions:

a. How old is a piece of rock?
b. How is heat transferred from Earth's deep interior to the surface?
c. How does Earth's magnetic field change over time?
d. What is the structure of Earth's interior?
e. What is the topography of the seafloor?

8. What was Pangaea? How does plate tectonics explain what happened to it? Could Earth's continents form into a single, Pangaea-like mass again? Why or why not? If they could, can you estimate how long it would take for them to do so?

9. At some convergent plate boundaries, deep ocean trenches lie a short distance from tall mountains. Why are these two contrasting features related to each other?

10. Popular media sometimes describe the California coast as poised to "slide into the ocean." Based on your understanding of plate tectonics, is this a plausible occurrence? Why or why not?

11. Is it possible to outrun an earthquake in a car? Why or why not? How can solid rock travel faster than a car? How is the energy of the earthquake transmitted through solid rock?

12. What role does elasticity and the storage of potential energy play in the development of an earthquake?

13. With respect to the previous question, why will an earthquake of magnitude-15 probably never happen?

Problems

1. If the African Rift Valley opens up at the rate of 5 cm per year, how long will it be before a body of water 1000 km wide divides the African continent?

2. Estimate the probable lifetime of your favorite mountain. [*Hint:* First get its dimensions from a map, then estimate its volume.]

3. Mount Everest is now approximately 8850 m tall, and it has been growing taller at a rate of about 2 cm per year. Estimate the approximate age of the mountain.

4. Estimate how much wider the Atlantic ocean will be in the year 3000?

5. Make a bar graph of the thickness of Earth's core, mantle, and crust. Make a graph of the densities of the core, mantle, and crust. What do these graphs portray about the interior of our planet?

6. How much more energy does a magnitude-8 earthquake have than a magnitude-7? How much less energy does a magnitude-4

Investigations

1. Examine original sources related to Wegener's continental drift theory. Why was this theory rejected by the majority of earth scientists in the 1920s? Compare and contrast the major features of the continental drift theory with plate tectonics theory.

2. How did ancient civilizations explain the occurrence of earthquakes and volcanoes?

3. Does plate tectonics operate on any other planet or moon in our solar system? Why or why not?

4. In your library, examine newspaper reports of major volcanoes and earthquakes during the past 20 years (each student could take one year). Plot these events on a world map. Do you see any obvious geographic patterns? How do the locations of these events relate to the plate boundaries shown in Figure 17-7?

5. Recent satellite images reveal Jupiter's moon Io to be the most volcanically active object in the solar system. What is the nature of these volcanoes? What provides their energy?

6. A few years ago someone predicted an earthquake on the New Madrid Fault in Missouri, the site of a destructive shock in 1812. He was widely believed and schoolchildren were trained in what to do in case of an earthquake. The earthquake did not take place and still has not occurred. What evidence did the amateur scientist use to make his case? How would you analyze that evidence?

7. Scientists have recently discovered astonishing deep-ocean communities of life-forms associated with plate boundaries. Investigate the nature and distribution of these deep ecosystems. Why are they found close to these boundaries and not elsewhere? What energy source do they utilize to survive?

8. Investigate the history of climbers on Mount Everest. Who was the first Westerner to make the ascent? How many people have climbed Everest? How many people have died while attempting to climb her? What is the name of Earth's second highest mountain?

9. What major cities in the United States are affected by earthquakes? What type of early warning systems are in place to help protect inhabitants of these cities? Would you buy a piece of property a few miles from the San Andreus Fault? Why, or why not?

10. How many volcanoes are there in the United States? How many are active?

11. Where is the safest place on Earth to live? safest in the United States? Research the various natural phenomena that affect ecosystems worldwide (e.g., earthquakes, tornadoes, hurricanes) and decide where you would like to live. What are the probabilities of these phenomena affecting your life? Which has killed more people in the last 100 years: hurricanes or volcanic eruptions?

18

Earth's Many Cycles

Will we ever run out of fresh water?

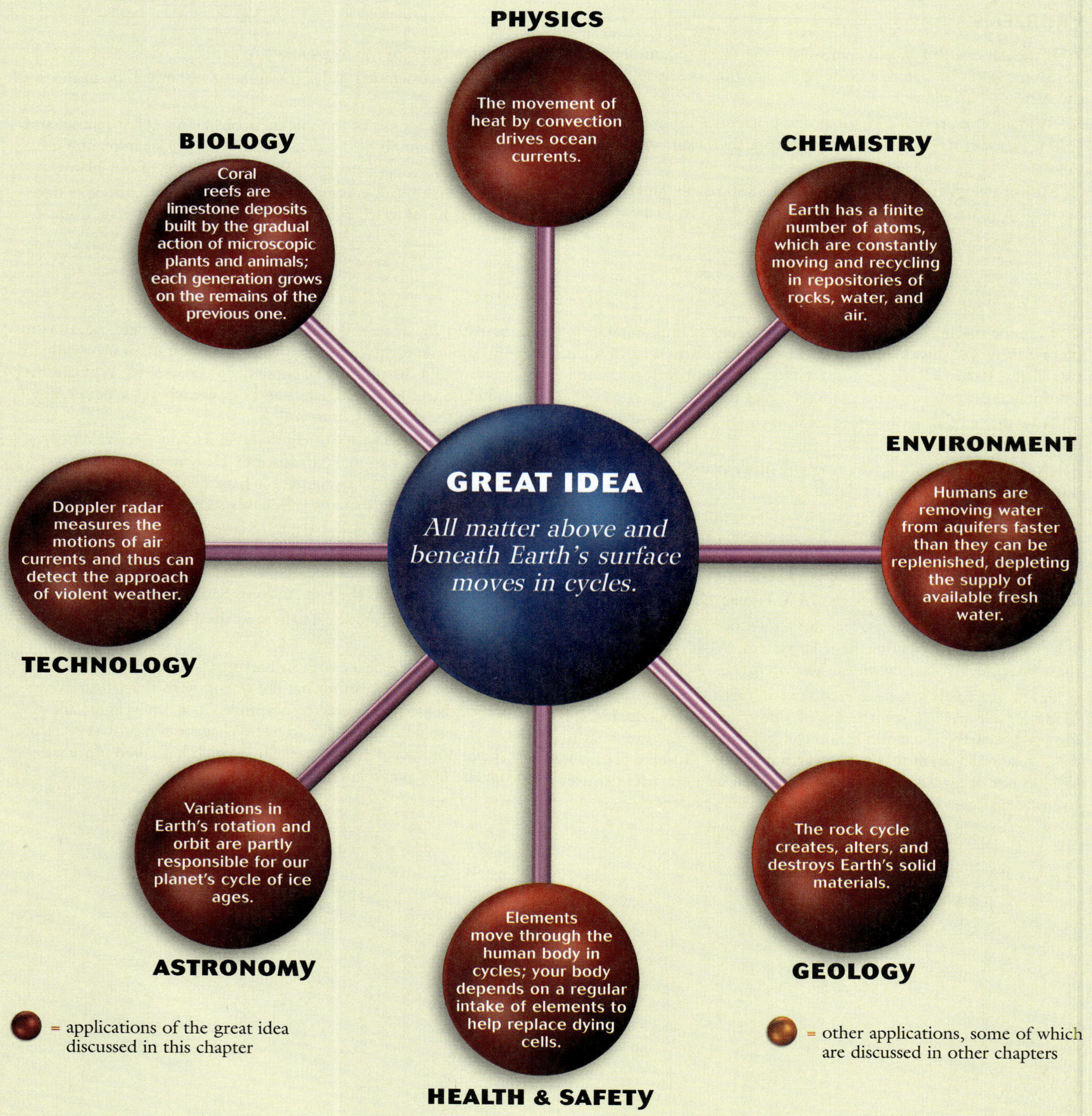

Science Through the Day | A Seaward Breeze

The beautiful day continues, bright and clear. As the Sun gradually arcs overhead into the western sky, the afternoon shadows begin to lengthen and the cool wind picks up off the water. By 2 P.M. there's a steady seaward breeze blowing close to 20 miles per hour.

Day after summer day it's the same story at the shore: refreshing offshore breezes pick up during the day, while warm onshore breezes blow in the evening. This familiar atmospheric behavior is just one of Earth's countless cycles.

Dennis Flaherty/The Image Bank/Getty Images

Cycles Small and Large

Every place we go, every day of our lives, we experience Earth's cycles. A day may start out clear and sunny, with mild temperatures and gentle breezes. But, suddenly, the wind picks up as a line of dark clouds presses in from the west. With the wind comes the first threatening rumble of thunder, flashes of distant lightning, and spurts of rain. A heavy downpour and powerful gusts of wind follow, as thunder booms and lightning illuminates the gray sky around us. Trees sway, windows rattle, and limbs come crashing down at the height of the storm.

Within an hour skies are sunny again, though the temperature is noticeably cooler. The air has a fresh, clean smell, and the sky seems more deeply blue than before. In the span of a few hours we have experienced one of Earth's many cycles—the atmospheric cycle called weather.

Day and night, summer and winter, life and death—these and many other cyclical changes characterize our dynamic planet. As the author of the *Book of Ecclesiastes* wrote 3000 years ago:

> *One generation passeth away, and another generation cometh: but the earth abideth forever;*
> *The sun also ariseth, and the sun goeth down, and hasteth to the place where he arose;*
> *The wind goeth toward the south, and turneth about unto the north; it whirleth about continually, and the wind returneth again according to his circuits;*

All the rivers run into the sea; yet the sea is not full; unto the place from whence the rivers come, thither they return again…

The thing that hath been, it is that which shall be; and that which is done is that which shall be done: and there is no new thing under the sun.

Recycling

Think about the last time that you drank a can of soda. What did you do with the aluminum can when you were through? You may have taken the time to place the can in a recycling bin. Alternatively, you may have tossed it into a trash container, or even by the side of the road. What difference does it make? Where do the aluminum atoms end up?

The atoms that make up Earth, with the exception of a few radioactive isotopes (Chapter 12), will last virtually forever. A single aluminum atom, for example, will appear in many different guises during its lifetime. It may form part of a swirling lava flow in which it is tightly bonded to oxygen atoms. It may then be incorporated with those oxygen atoms into a solid rock. As the rock weathers away, the atom may wind up in soil and become concentrated with other aluminum atoms, where it is mined. Giant smelters separate the aluminum atom—a process that consumes prodigious amounts of energy—to produce the aluminum metal that made your soda can. Once discarded, the atom may be recycled into new cans, or it may go back to the soil where it once again bonds to oxygen.

Stop and Think! One of the main points in Chapter 3 is that energy flows into and out of the Earth system. Does matter flow in the same way through Earth? Explain.

Earth has a vast, though finite, number of aluminum atoms that take part in the aluminum cycle. The advantage to recycling aluminum is that we save all the energy that went into finding concentrated aluminum sources and breaking aluminum-to-oxygen bonds. But no matter what you do with your can, the aluminum atoms still are part of our planet.

The Nature of Earth's Cycles

The history of an aluminum atom is just one example of the many paths within the three great cycles of Earth materials: the oceans, the atmosphere, and rocks. Two central ideas frame our understanding of the movement of matter in our changing planet:

Earth materials move in cycles.

and

A change in one cycle affects the others.

The story of the aluminum atom suggests a useful two-step strategy for analyzing any of the many cycles by which each type of Earth material moves. The first step is to make an inventory of all the different **reservoirs** in which that substance is found. Earth's water, for example, is found in oceans, lakes, rivers, ice caps, and several other reservoirs. The second step is to identify the varied ways that the material is transferred from one reservoir to another. In the case of water, for example, movement may occur by precipitation, evaporation, or gravity.

Each of Earth's cycles illustrates a central theme: our planet's atoms are constantly moving and recycling. Water moves from rivers to oceans to glaciers and to clouds as it takes part in Earth's dynamic hydrologic cycle. Above Earth's surface, the gases of the atmosphere flow in the great cycles of weather, the seasons, and global climate. And the solid surface of Earth slowly alters, erodes away, and forms again in the stately rock cycle.

Many of Earth's cycles are driven by the tendency of heat to spread out—to flow from hot to cold in what we described as the second law of thermodynamics (see Chapter 4). Earth has two primary sources of heat energy: the Sun, and its own geothermal processes, each of which drives its own thermal cycle. More heat energy from the Sun falls at the equator than at the poles, and heat transfer by convection moves gases in the atmosphere and water in the oceans in the great cycles that control weather and climate. Similarly, heat energy in Earth's core and mantle drives the convection cycles that move the tectonic plates.

Thus Earth's cycles reflect the most basic properties of matter and energy. These cycles may be studied at many levels, from an atomic scale for an individual element such as aluminum, to the global cycles involved in plate tectonics. We find it especially useful to consider Earth in terms of the three most familiar cycles around us: the cycles of water, air, and rock.

The Hydrologic Cycle

Water plays a vital role in the unique chemistry of Earth's outer layers. Water saturates the air, falls to the ground as precipitation, moves through a complex system of rivers and streams, and is stored for long periods in underground reservoirs, oceans, and ice. Water shapes the surface of our planet, and it provided the medium in which life began. The combination of processes by which water moves from repository to repository above, below, and on Earth's surface is called the **hydrologic cycle**.

Reservoirs of Water

The total amount of water near Earth's surface has stayed roughly the same from very early times. Water first reached the surface during the outgassing of the young, volcano-covered Earth (see Chapter 16). When the planet's surface temperature finally fell below 100°C, this water condensed into liquid form and began to fill the ocean basins. Relatively minor processes still add and remove small amounts of water from Earth. High in the atmosphere, ultraviolet rays from the Sun break up water molecules, freeing hydrogen atoms, which because of their low mass may escape into space. At the same time, at converging and diverging plate boundaries and other sites of volcanism, small amounts of new water are emitted from Earth's deep interior. These losses and gains are in rough equilibrium, and in any case both are rather small—by one estimate, no more than one or two Olympic-sized swimming pools of water per year. Thus, for all intents and purposes, we can treat Earth as if it has had a fixed amount of water at its surface for billions of years. The water that we have now is all there is.

Earth boasts several major water repositories, as summarized in Table 18-1. In addition to oceans, lakes, and rivers, significant amounts of water are locked into Earth's polar ice caps and glaciers, bodies of ice that form in regions where snowfall exceeds melting. **Ice caps** are layers of ice that form at Earth's north and south polar regions. **Glaciers** are large bodies of ice that slowly flow down a slope or valley under the influence of gravity. Approximately 96% of glaciers (by volume) occur in Antarctica and Greenland, while the rest are widely scattered in mountainous areas. All of these places where water occurs tap into the same central supply. During its lifetime, a given molecule of water will cycle through many different reservoirs, over and over again.

A vast part of the hydrologic cycle remains unseen. Some of the water that falls on the continents does not immediately return

Table 18-1 Reservoirs of Water

Reservoir	Percent of Earth's Supply
Oceans	96.0
Lakes, rivers, and streams	0.009
Ice caps and glaciers	3.0
Groundwater	1.0
Clouds	0.001
Living things	0.0001

to the ocean; rather, it seeps into the soil to become **groundwater.** There, it goes into large *aquifers*—reservoirs that are, in effect, underground storage tanks of water. By some estimates, more than 98% of the world's fresh water is stored as groundwater. Water typically percolates into the ground and fills the tiny spaces between grains of sandstone and other porous rock layers. Impermeable materials, such as clay, which keeps the water from seeping away, often bound these layers of water-saturated rock.

Movements of Water Between Reservoirs

Earth's water is in constant motion both within and between reservoirs—a process that may gradually change the distribution of water near Earth's surface. The hydrologic cycle with which most of us are familiar involves the short-term back-and-forth transfer of water molecules between the oceans and the land. Water evaporates off the surface of the oceans, forms into clouds, falls as rain on the land, and then returns to the oceans via rivers and streams. Most terrestrial life depends on this simple cycle (Figure 18-1).

Much of the movement of Earth's water occurs within the oceans, which are far from static. Each ocean basin has great **currents,** which are like rivers of moving water within the larger ocean (see Figure 18-2). These currents play a vital role in redistributing heat across the surface of the planet, and thus in determining climate. Some surface currents carry warm water from the equator, where a large amount of heat energy from the Sun is absorbed, toward the cooler poles. At the same time, other surface currents carry cold water from the poles back to the equator to be heated and cycled again. These great gyres as they are called have a profound effect on the weather of the land they flow past. In the North Atlantic, for example, the Gulf Stream current starts in the Caribbean and flows past the eastern coast of the United States. It comes near England, making the British Isles much warmer than you might expect them to be based on their latitude.

• **Figure 18-1** A diagram of the hydrologic cycle showing the transfer of water molecules between oceans and land. The numbers in parentheses show the volume of water that cycles through the continental United States in millions of cubic meters each day.

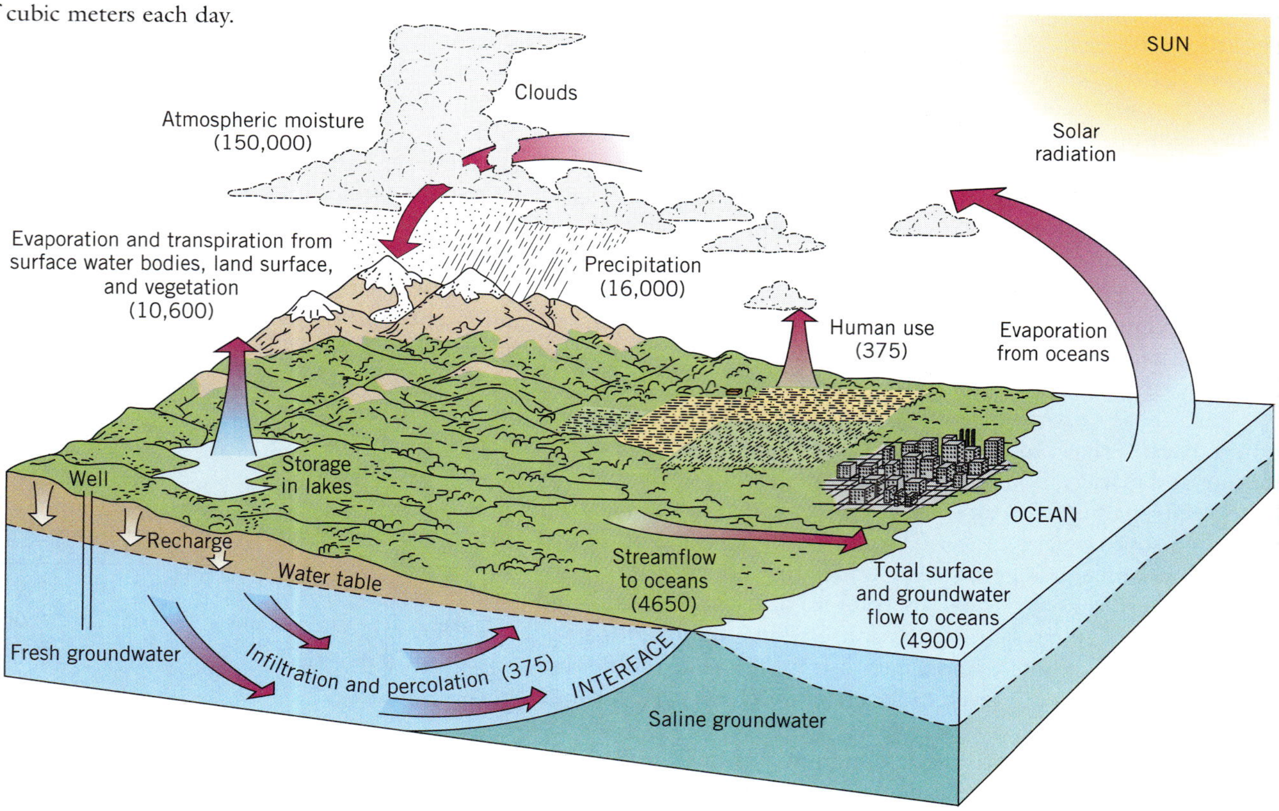

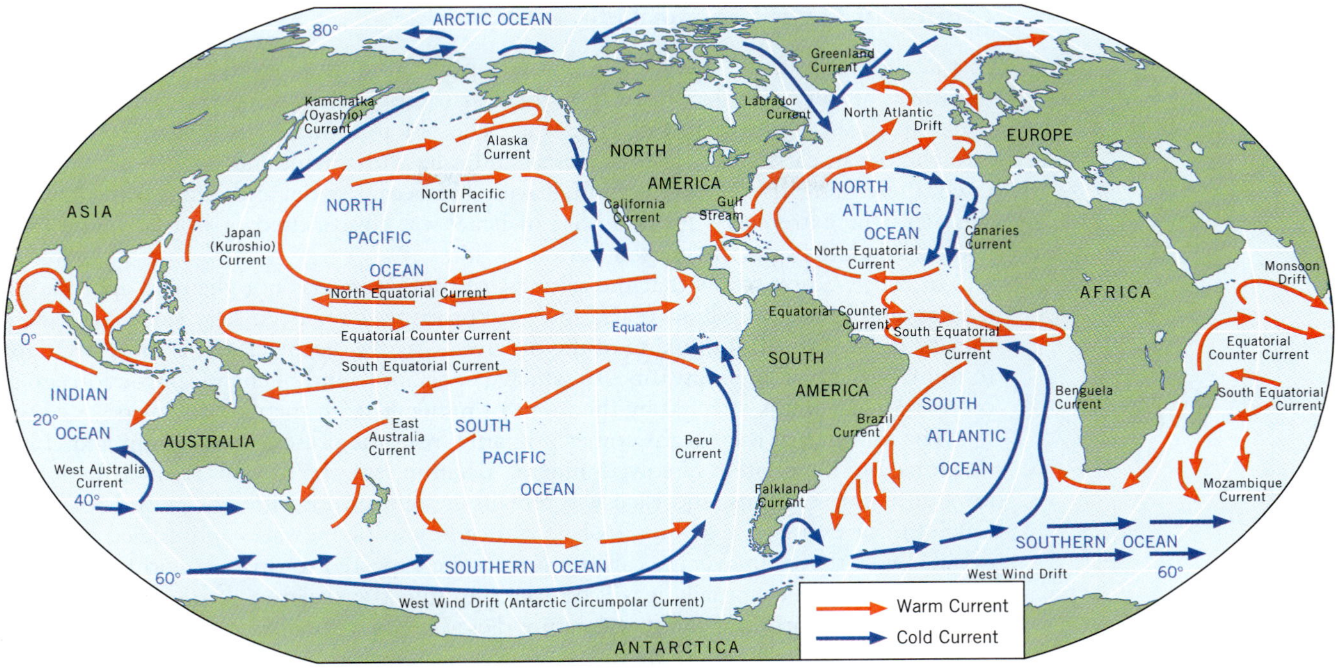

• **Figure 18-2** Ocean currents play a major role in redistributing Earth's heat.

which is farther north than Maine. A much colder current, on the other hand, flows along the western coast of Europe back to the tropics to complete the cycle.

In addition to this rather rapid circulation of water at the surface, we find deeper three-dimensional circulation of water in the ocean. When the effects of surface currents and wind along a coast act in such a way as to push surface water away from the land, colder water from the depths comes up to create an area of upwelling. The waters along the coast of California display this phenomenon, which helps explain why the ocean there is so cold. On a larger scale, water from the Arctic and Antarctic, which is both cold and salty because so much fresh water is removed to form ice, sinks to the bottom of the sea and rolls sluggishly toward the equator. This dense, cold water forms the slow, deep flow that characterizes much of the bottom currents in the world's ocean basins.

Humans also participate in the water cycle by tapping into deep aquifers when they drill wells to supply water for cities and agriculture. One problem with using aquifers as a water supply is that it may take many thousands of years to fill them, but only a few years to drain them. For example, when farmers in the central United States take water from the Ogallala aquifer, one of North America's great underground reservoirs, they are in effect mining the water. Underground water is not a renewable resource except over very long timescales.

The Science of Life •

Sobering Facts About Water

Although Earth's supply of water is vast, about 96% is salty and most of the remaining fresh water is locked into ice caps and glaciers. Thus less than 1% of Earth's water is readily available for human use.

Modern society places tremendous demands on this limited resource. Agriculture, industry, and personal needs result in an average daily water consumption of more than 2000 gallons per person in North America. As supplies of groundwater are reduced and pollution contaminates other reservoirs, shortages of fresh water may become a serious concern in the future. •

Chemical Cycles in the Oceans

Just as the water in the oceans is in constant physical motion, so too are the chemicals that make it salty. Scholars once thought that the oceans were passive receptacles for materials washed into them from the land. The old argument went that rivers flowing into the ocean carried dissolved minerals and salts with them, and when water evaporated, these minerals were left behind, leaving the oceans saltier and saltier with time. In this view, the extremely salty Dead Sea in Israel was always cited as a place where salts had accumulated over the longest period of time.

In fact, we now know that the saltiness of the oceans has not changed appreciably over several hundred million years, and they probably have been salty since soon after they formed. Instead of thinking of the oceans as passive receptacles, it is more accurate to think of them as large test tubes in which a constant round of chemical reactions goes on that affects and is affected by the input of minerals from the world's rivers.

The saltiness of the oceans comes primarily from the presence of sodium and chloride ions, but many other dissolved minerals occur in seawater as well. Each element follows different reactions, and each will remain in solution for different periods of time. Calcium, for example, may be dissolved out of limestone by water and carried into the ocean. Once there, an average calcium ion can be expected to float around for about 8 million years, but eventually it will be taken up into the skeleton of some sea creature and sink to the bottom when that creature dies. There it may once more be formed into limestone, lifted up by tectonic forces, and eventually carried back to the sea through erosion or dissolution.

The average length of time that an atom will stay in ocean water before it is removed by some chemical reaction is called the *residence time* (see Table 18-2). Sodium (one of the atoms that gives seawater its distinctive taste) enters the ocean after dissolving out of various kinds of rocks. A sodium ion will stay in suspension on average for about 260 million years before it is incorporated again into various kinds of clay and mud on the ocean bottom. Once so incorporated, it can go through the same cycle of uplift and erosion as limestone.

Chloride ions, on the other hand, tend to stay in the ocean almost forever, though these atoms may leave the ocean for short periods of time in tiny droplets, or aerosols, of ocean spray. Only when a body of salt water is evaporated, forming dry salt deposits like those surrounding the Great Salt Lake in Utah, is chlorine removed from its water environment for any appreciable length of time. But even these deposits, slowly buried and compressed, could eventually (in perhaps a few hundred million years) rise to the surface as salt domes, where they would weather away, returning the salt once again to the sea.

Thus chemical cycles in the ocean can be simply pictured. Earth's many rivers continuously transport various elements into the sea. Each of these elements resides for a certain amount of time in the ocean and then is removed by chemical reactions. The supply of every kind of atom is being constantly renewed, and the oceans may never be any less salty than they are today.

Table 18-2 Some Typical Residence Times for Elements in the Ocean

Element	Concentration (parts per million)	Residence Times (millions of years)
Sodium	10,800	260
Calcium	413	8
Chlorine	19,400	infinite
Gold	0.00005	0.042
Potassium	387	11
Copper	0.003	0.05

The Science of Life •

Element Residence Times

Your body, like the oceans, constantly recycles atoms. Some of your body's cells, such as the lining of the intestines, are replaced every few days. You need fresh supplies of carbon, oxygen, and nitrogen every day to help replace these cells. Red blood cells last much longer—120 days on average—but you need a regular intake of iron to produce these important cells. Failure to digest enough iron can lead to anemia, a condition characterized by fatigue due to insufficient red blood cells.

Atoms in your bones and tendons last much longer—a decade or more, on average—but even those atoms are constantly being replaced. Gradual loss of calcium in bone, for example, is of special concern in older people who may not consume enough replacement calcium. Osteoporosis, a disease in which bones become weak and brittle, may result from this calcium deficiency. A similar loss of bone calcium affects astronauts who spend more than a few days in the weightless environment of space.

Some harmful elements, including lead, mercury, and other so-called heavy metals, do not easily recycle once taken into the body, because we have no effective biological process to remove them. Their average residence times, in other words, are much longer than a human lifetime. Concentrations of these atoms can thus build up over time and can result in sickness or even death. You may hear about local efforts to test drinking water for high concentrations of lead that are sometimes found in old plumbing systems. •

Science by the Numbers •

The Ocean's Gold

We've just said that every element can be found in seawater. How much gold is there in a cubic kilometer of seawater?

According to Table 18-2, gold is present in the ocean at a concentration of 0.00005 parts per million (ppm). A concentration of 1 ppm corresponds to 1 milligram (mg) of a solid dissolved in a liter (l) of water. A liter is a volume measurement equal to a thousandth of a cubic meter (10^{-3} m^3). The total amount of gold in a cubic meter of seawater, therefore, is 0.00005 milligrams per liter times 1000 liters per meter cubed:

$$(0.00005\ \text{mg/l}) \times (1000\ \text{l/m}^3) = 0.05\ \text{mg/m}^3$$

A gram contains 1000 milligrams, so

$$(0.05\ \text{mg/m}^3) \times (1\ \text{g}/1000\ \text{mg}) = 0.00005\ \text{g/m}^3$$

A cubic kilometer contains (1000 m) × (1000 m) × (1000 m) = 10^9 m^3, so the total amount of gold in a cubic kilometer of seawater is

$$(10^9\ \text{m}^3) \times (0.00005\ \text{g/m}^3) = 5 \times 10^4\ \text{gm}$$

Every cubic kilometer of ocean water holds about 50,000 grams (about 100 pounds) of gold. At $550 an ounce, that much gold is worth close to a million dollars.

The total amount of gold dissolved in the world's oceans is vast, but no economical way to extract these riches is known. The equipment and energy required to process that much water would cost far more than the value of any gold recovered. •

Ice Ages

From time to time, much of Earth's water supply becomes locked into glaciers that advance across land from the poles—a period called an **ice age**. We are now in the middle of an ice age, a period of several million years during which glaciers have repeatedly advanced and retreated. Within the present ice age we are living in an *interglacial period*,

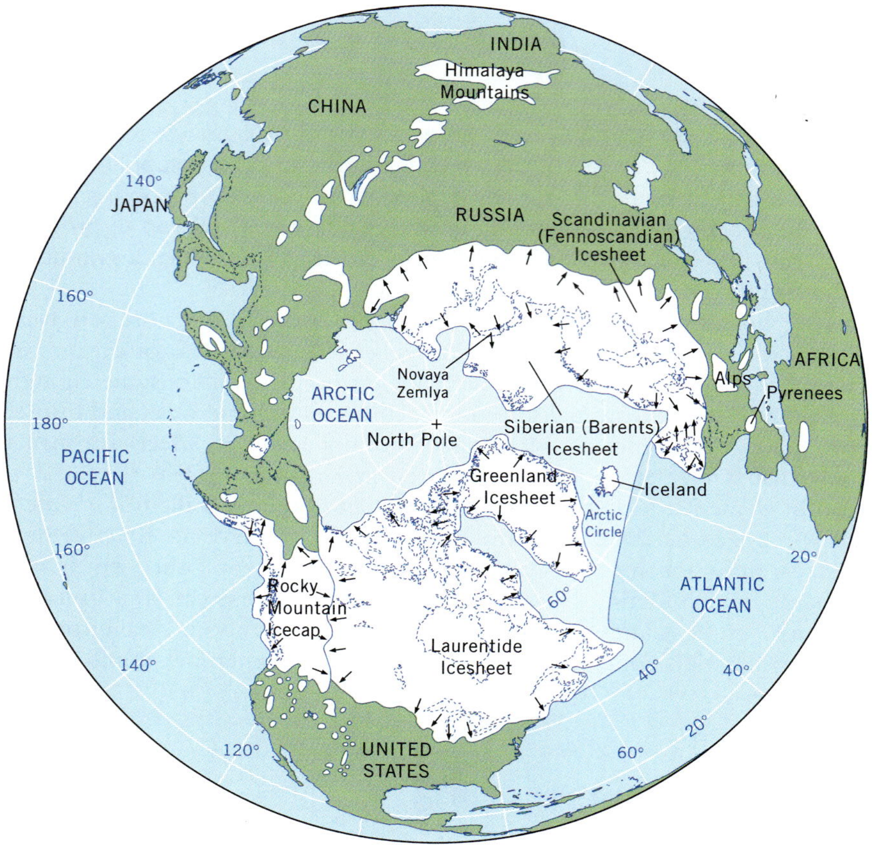

• **Figure 18-3** The extent of the most recent North American glaciation, approximately 20,000 years ago, looking down on the North Pole. Arrows indicate the direction of the glaciers' advances.

which is occurring between two major advances of glaciers. About 20,000 years ago massive glaciers spread down from eastern and central Canada, covering a good deal of northern North America, and then receded to Greenland about 10,000 years ago, as illustrated in Figure 18-3. Glaciers have come and gone many times, and periods of cyclic glaciation like the one in which we now live have occurred relatively often during the past 2 million years of Earth history.

The total amount of Earth's water is fixed, so as ice caps and glaciers grow, the amount of water available to fill the ocean basins decreases and the sea level drops. During the most recent advance of glaciers some 20,000 years ago, for example, as much as 5% of Earth's water was locked into ice. Sea level dropped to the point that the East Coast of what is now the United States was about 250 km farther east than it is today. A land bridge joining western North America and eastern Asia made it possible to walk from Alaska to Siberia. This land bridge provided a route that was taken by the ancestors of many Native Americans when they moved into the Americas from Siberia.

Milankovitch Cycles

The main causes of periodic glaciation were first explained by Milutin Milankovitch, a Serbian civil engineer, in the early part of the twentieth century. His theory was simple: The relationship between Earth and Sun is affected by a number of variations in Earth's rotation and orbit. These variations cause slight changes in the amount of solar radiation absorbed by Earth, as shown in Figure 18-4.

The easiest of the orbital effects to understand is the precession of Earth's axis of rotation. If you have ever watched a child's top spinning, you know that sometimes as the top spins rapidly around its axis, the axis itself describes a lazy circle in space. This circular motion is called a *precession*. In the same way that a top may precess every sec-

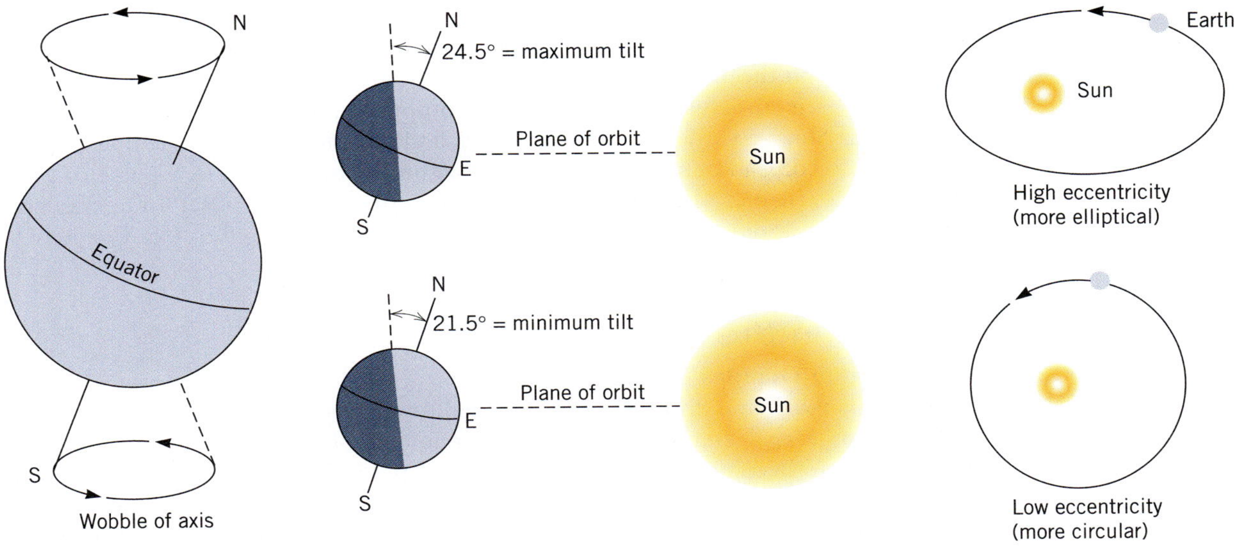

(*a*) Precession of the equinoxes (period = 23,000 years)

(*b*) Tilt of the axis (period = 41,000 years)

(*c*) Eccentricity (dominant period =100,000 years)

• **Figure 18-4** The precession of Earth's axis *(a)*. Small changes in the tilt of the axis *(b)*, and changes in the shape of the orbit induced by the other planets *(c)*, contribute to recurring ice ages.

ond or two, Earth's axis, which is tilted at an angle of 23 degrees, precesses once every 23,000 years. While precession occurs, the axis of Earth's elliptical orbit also moves around the Sun due to the gravitational effects of the other planets. The net effect of these two motions is that when Earth is farthest from the Sun, during the summer, Earth's axis tilts the Northern Hemisphere toward the Sun for half of a 23,000-year cycle. The axis gradually shifts so that the Southern Hemisphere is tilted toward the Sun for the other half of the cycle. Today Earth's axis is oriented such that the Northern Hemisphere is tilted away from the Sun during the winter months (the period in which Earth is actually closest to the Sun). About 11,500 years from now, however, the situation will be reversed, and the Northern Hemisphere will be tilted toward the Sun during the same period.

Stop and Think! Why are winter months in the Northern Hemisphere colder than summer months, even though Earth is closer to the Sun during the winter?

Other orbital effects involve a slow change in the angle of the axis of rotation (it rocks back and forth by about a degree every 41,000 years), as well as a small change in the shape of Earth's orbit caused by other planets (about a 100,000-year cycle). Milankovitch proposed that the global climate varies in cycles (now called *Milankovitch cycles*) when all three of these effects reinforce each other. If we find ourselves in a period of decreasing solar energy absorption and increased precipitation, more snow will fall in the winter and it will stay on the ground longer in the summer. Snow and ice reflect sunlight, so this extra snow and ice further cool Earth's surface and more snow falls and stays on the ground even longer. Thus a decline in absorption of sunlight may trigger a sequence of events that can lead eventually to glacial advance. By the same token, a period of increased absorption of sunlight will result in warmer periods during which glaciers will tend to retreat.

Several other factors play a role in controlling the extent and distribution of glaciers. Large glaciers can form only on landmasses, which gradually shift because of tectonic motion. The locations of mountain chains also play a significant role by altering wind and precipitation patterns. Recent evidence also suggests that the amount of volcanic dust and gases in the atmosphere can cause short-term changes in global temperatures. Finally, some scientists suspect that the energy output of the Sun is cyclical and that variations in the Sun's energy output impose a cyclical variation in Earth's temperature.

For the record, most scientists think that we are heading into a new phase of glacial advance within the next 10,000 years. This cooling trend may be offset for a time, however, by global warming that results from an enhanced greenhouse effect (see Chapter 19).

Science in the Making •

Milankovitch Decides on His Life's Work

Milutin Milankovitch didn't seem to be headed toward a career in the sciences. Trained in Vienna as a civil engineer, he designed reinforced-concrete structures in central Europe prior to becoming a professor of mathematics in his native Belgrade just before World War I. Swept up in the nationalistic movements that were then (as now) prominent in the Balkans, he became friendly with some poets who specialized in writing patriotic verse. One evening, drinking coffee to celebrate a new book of verse, Milankovitch and his friends came to the attention of a banker at a neighboring table. The banker was so taken with the poems that he bought 10 copies on the spot.

With new money in their pockets, the friends celebrated with wine. After the first bottle, Milankovitch says in his journal, "I looked back on my earlier achievements and found them narrow and limited." By the third bottle, he had decided to "grasp the entire universe and spread light to its farthest corners."

He then methodically set apart a few hours each day to study and interpret climate records. Even during World War I, when he served as an engineer on the Serbian general staff and became a prisoner of war, he kept at it. A member of the Hungarian Academy of Sciences arranged for him to have a desk at the Academy after he gave his word of honor that he would not try to escape, and a good deal of the work described in the text was done under those conditions. The final work, published in 1920, was quickly recognized and accepted by the scientific community. •

The Atmospheric Cycle

Earth's atmosphere and oceans play the most important role in redistributing heat across the surface of the planet. The atmosphere also has chemical cycles involving oxygen and carbon, but those cycles are intimately bound up with the presence of living things on Earth, and we will wait to discuss them until we look at Earth's ecosystems (Chapter 19). The circulation of gases near Earth's surface—both the short-term variations of weather, and the longer patterns of climate—is called the **atmospheric cycle**.

Air Masses: Reservoirs of the Atmosphere

At first glance it might seem odd to speak of an atmospheric cycle. After all, the atmosphere appears to be one continuous mass of air rather than several different reservoirs. However, at any one time the atmosphere can be divided into many separate "air masses," each of which has more or less uniform properties. Each air mass can be thought of as a separate reservoir of air, and adjacent air masses differ in physical properties. Adjacent air masses may occupy different regions close to the ground, such as a low-pressure system in the Midwest and an adjacent high-pressure system off the New England coast. On the other hand, adjacent air masses may represent different atmospheric layers high above the surface.

In order to understand the properties of air masses, we need to define two closely related terms—weather and climate. **Weather** is the state of the atmosphere at a given time and place. At any given place, the weather is influenced by many factors and may be highly variable from day to day, not to mention from season to season. **Climate**, on the other hand, is a long-term average of weather for a given region. A regional climate may be hot or cold, wet or dry, though the weather on any given day might be quite different. Climate may remain unchanged for centuries, or it may shift quite dramatically, often for reasons that are as yet uncertain.

Weather

Five variables define the state of the atmosphere: temperature, air pressure, humidity, cloudiness, and prevailing winds. Your local weather report typically covers all of these variables.

1. The *temperature* reported in daily weather predictions refers to temperature at ground level. Temperature varies strongly with altitude above the ground. In fact, the major layers of the atmosphere—regions such as the stratosphere and troposphere—are defined by these temperature variations.
2. The second variable that defines the state of the atmosphere is *pressure*, which decreases significantly with altitude, because air is compressed by its own weight. At a height of 5.5 km, air pressure is only half of its value at sea level, whereas in the deepest South African gold mines air pressure approaches twice that of the surface. Pressure also varies laterally, because air masses tend to move and rotate with respect to each other. Air piles up in some places to form a high-pressure system, while it stretches out in other places to form a low-pressure system. Air in low-pressure systems tends to rise, which causes cooling and increased clouds; conversely, high-pressure systems tend to feature warmer, dry air. Significant air pressure differences, which can arise at boundaries between layers high in the atmosphere, cause high-speed air currents called the **jet stream** (Figure 18-5). The jet stream moves west-to-east across the United States; it causes flights from New York to Los Angeles to average almost an hour longer than flights from Los Angeles to New York.
3. The third atmospheric variable is *humidity*, which is a measure of the atmosphere's highly variable water content. The bulk composition of the atmosphere is remarkably uniform; nitrogen and oxygen make up 99% of dry atmosphere. The atmosphere also always contains some water vapor, though the amount is highly variable, depending

National Oceanic and Atmospheric Administration/ DLR-FRG/Roger Ressmeyer/Corbis Images

A satellite photo of a low-pressure system that is centered over Ireland and moving toward the European continent. Notice the counterclockwise rotation of the air.

• **Figure 18-5** The jet stream is a fast-moving, high-altitude air current above North America. *(a)* The jet stream often follows a relatively straight path, with minor undulations. *(b)* Strongly developed undulations may pull a mass of cold arctic air to the south.

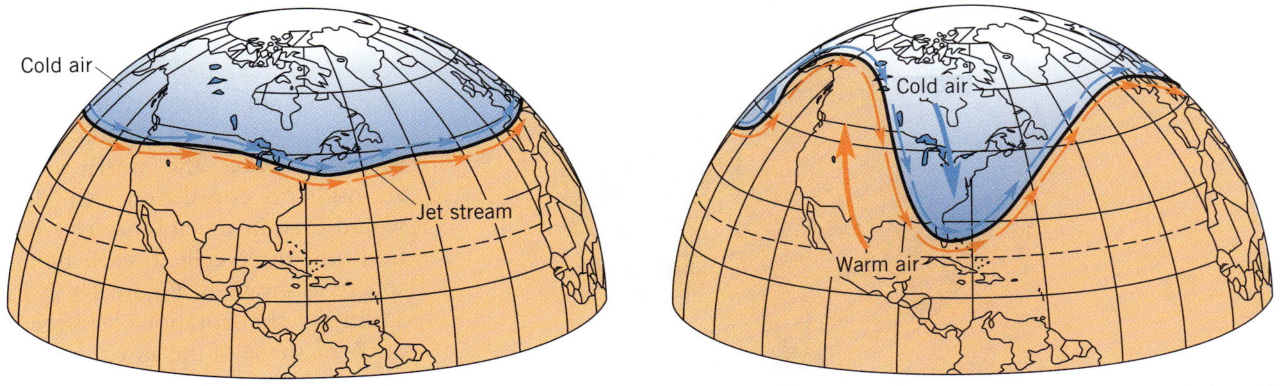

on the temperature and relative humidity. Air on a cold, dry winter day might hold less than 0.1% water by volume, whereas air on a hot, humid summer day may contain several percent water by volume.

4. *Cloudiness,* the fourth weather variable, is closely tied to humidity. Clouds are a concentration of tiny water droplets or ice crystals. These substances scatter light, so clouds appear white. Clouds form when air becomes saturated with water—a process that often occurs when a mass of air rises and cools. Clouds often dramatically outline the contact between two adjacent air masses. A band of clouds may mark a front, where two air masses at different temperatures collide near ground level. Dramatic anvil-shaped thunderhead clouds often form when a warmer air mass collides with a cooler air mass. The warmer air mass is less dense, and so it rides up over the cooler air. This increase in elevation cools the warm, wet air, causing clouds and rain. Large gradients in temperature and pressure generate strong winds and violent lightning. Similarly, clouds and rain often form on the windward side of mountain ranges as an air mass is forced to rise up the mountain flanks. The side of the island away from the wind is usually much drier. Some mountainous areas of Hawaii receive more than 100 inches of rain per year on the eastern side, while experiencing near-arid conditions a few kilometers away on the western slopes.
5. The fifth atmospheric variable is the direction and strength of *winds.* Winds are a consequence of atmospheric convection—a process that helps to redistribute heat. Ocean breezes on a tranquil summer day illustrate how winds can occur. During a sunny day, the land heats up more than water, so warmer air rises from the land and cooler air flows in from the water, producing a refreshing sea breeze. In the evening, as the land cools, the pattern reverses; warmer air over the water rises and the breeze comes from the land.

The General Circulation of the Atmosphere

The atmosphere circulates in vast rivers of air that cover the globe from the equator to the poles. These prevailing winds arise in much the same way as local winds, though on a much larger scale. As in local winds, this circulation is powered by the energy of the Sun. Air in the tropics is heated and rises. If Earth did not rotate, we would expect to have a situation like the one shown in Figure 18-6. Warm air would rise at the equator, cool off, and sink at the poles. This pattern of flow is the familiar convection cell we saw in Chapter 4. Such a pattern arises whenever a fluid is heated nonuniformly in a gravitational field.

If Earth did not rotate, prevailing winds in the Northern Hemisphere would flow from north to south. In fact, they do nothing of the kind. The weather patterns in much of the Northern Hemisphere, including North America, move, in general, from west to east—we live in a region of what meteorologists call *prevailing westerlies.* This behavior of Earth's atmosphere results from the fact that Earth rotates. The rotation breaks the north-south atmospheric convection cell that would exist in the absence of rotation into three cells in each hemisphere as shown in Figure 18-7. In addition, the rotation "stretches out" the shape of the air circulation pattern in each cell. In the cell nearest the equator, the winds at

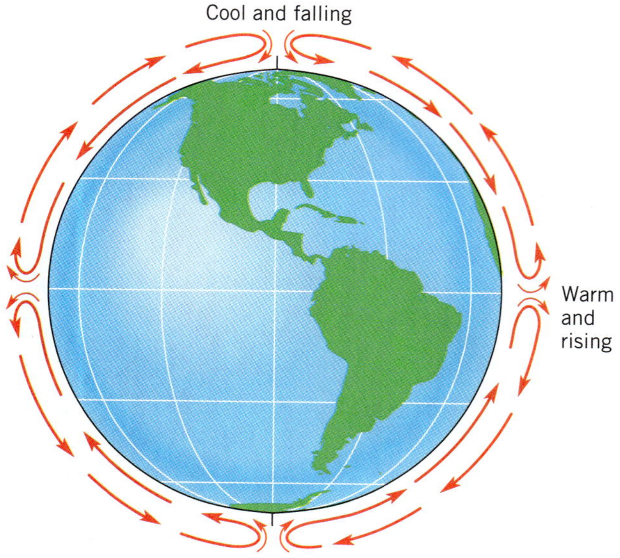

• **Figure 18-6** If Earth did not rotate, the circulation of the atmosphere would take place in convection cells that create high-altitude winds from equator to pole, and low-altitude winds from pole to equator.

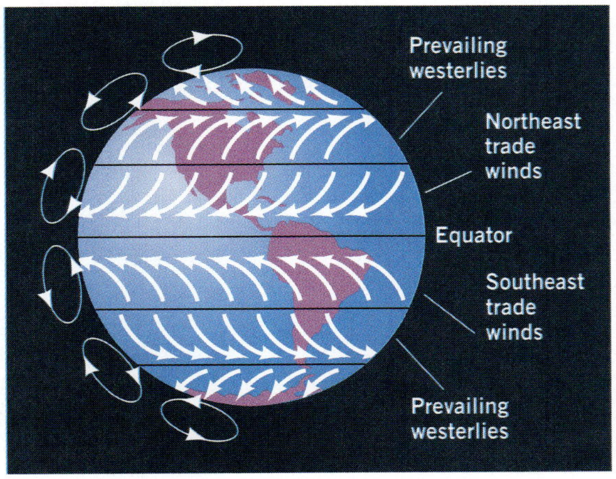

• **Figure 18-7** Atmospheric convection on the rotating Earth, showing the principal air circulation cells. Compare this diagram with the opening photograph in Chapter 16.

the surface tend to blow from east to west—the so-called *trade winds* that drove sailing ships from Europe to North America. In temperate zones, the effect is to cause the winds to blow from west to east, creating regions in which weather patterns also usually move from west to east. Finally, in the Arctic and Antarctic, the winds blow once again from east to west.

Similar patterns of atmospheric motion can be seen on all the planets in the solar system that have atmospheres. In some cases, like the planet Jupiter, the rapid rotation of the planet and the atmospheric dynamics cause more than three convection cells. Jupiter, in fact, has no fewer than 11.

Common Storms and Weather Patterns

Many kinds of severe weather conditions affect our world. *Tropical storms* are severe storms that start as low-pressure areas over warm ocean water. They draw energy from the warm water, growing and rotating in great *cyclonic* patterns hundreds of kilometers in diameter. Tropical storms that begin in the Atlantic Ocean off the coast of Africa or in the Caribbean Sea and affect North America are called *hurricanes;* those that begin in the North Pacific were once called *typhoons,* though they are often now called hurricanes by weather forecasters. Until recently, these violent weather systems frequently hit unprotected coastlines with little warning. Today, weather satellites spot and track tropical storms long before they approach land. In 2005, when hurricane Katrina approached the New Orleans area, residents received several days warning and many were able to get out of the way of the storm.

Tornadoes, much smaller-scale phenomena than hurricanes, are rotating air funnels some tens to hundreds of meters across. Tornadoes descend from storm clouds to the ground, causing intense damage along the path where the funnel touches the ground. The largest tornadoes, with air speeds in excess of 500 km (about 300 miles) per hour, are the most violent weather phenomenon known.

El Niño, a weather cycle that recurs every four to seven years, affects weather from the Pacific Basin to the Atlantic Coast. The name means Christ Child and comes from the fact that the phenomenon, when it happens, usually begins around Christmastime. El Niño can cause severe storms and flooding all along the western coast of the Americas, and drought from Australia to India. El Niño is an example of a coupling between two of Earth's cycles—in this case, the atmospheric and water cycles. It requires both winds and ocean currents to work. Here's what happens: Normally, the winds off the coast of Peru blow westward. They move the warm ocean water westward, like water sloshing in a bathtub, to the western Pacific. As the surface water moves west, the colder, nutrient-rich water from the deep ocean wells up and supports marine life and fish-eating birds. Because the eastern Pacific is cooler, the atmosphere cools and descends there, forming a zone of high pressure and dry weather off the coast of South America. Meanwhile, the western Pacific is warmer, so air warms and rises above it in a rainy, low-pressure zone.

Every four to seven years, however, this pattern changes, signifying the beginning of an El Niño event. Warm surface water sloshes to the east, the water temperature in the eastern Pacific increases by a few degrees, and the normal atmospheric patterns switch places. Westerly winds replace the normally easterly flowing trade winds. This wind reversal reinforces the movement of warm water eastward to the coast of South America, where air warms and rises, creating rainy conditions. The marine life and birds are no longer supported by the nutrients of the cold, deep water. The western Pacific becomes relatively cool and dry. Eventually, the water sloshes back and the whole cycle repeats itself. Historical records tell us that this cycle has been repeating in the Pacific Basin since the 1600s and may have been going on since the last ice age.

Climate

Climate, as opposed to weather, seldom changes much on the scale of human lifetimes. In spite of many uncertainties about climate change, several factors that strongly influence regional climate are now well documented. Large bodies of water and ocean currents, such as the Gulf Stream, can greatly change a region's climate by transferring heat. Oceans and large lakes can also add moisture to an air mass. Northwest New York State, for example, receives heavy rains and snows as Canadian air masses pass over the Great Lakes. Mountain ranges disrupt the movement of air masses, and can efficiently remove moisture from an air mass. We have seen how tall mountains on Hawaii affect rainfall; nearby locations on opposite sides of a volcanic mountain can have radically different rainfalls.

These effects of oceans and mountains on climate reveal that movements of tectonic plates play a major long-term role in Earth's climate. As plates move, bodies of water open and close and mountain ranges are formed. In addition, the presence of continents near one or both poles strongly influences the severity of ice ages, because thick accumulations of ice require a solid base. Thus, Earth's atmospheric cycle is strongly influenced by other global cycles.

The Ongoing Process of Science •

How Steady Is Earth's Climate?

Through most of recorded history, Earth's climate has been pretty much as we know it today, but recorded history covers only 4000 years—a blink of an eye in geological time—and detailed records of weather have been kept for only a few centuries. Until recently, scientists assumed that climate change always happened slowly in response to factors such as the tectonic movement of the continents. However, since the early 1990s thinking on this subject has started to change. It turns out that Earth's climate can change more drastically, and more quickly, than anyone had realized.

Key evidence came from deep-sea cores drilled in the floor of the North Atlantic Ocean. During times corresponding to the last ice age, scientists found layers of rocks in these cores, spaced between 7000 and 11,000 years apart, that are identical to rocks found in northern Canada. The first clue as to what these layers might mean came from geophysicist Douglas MacAyael at the University of Chicago. His explanation was based on the behavior of the ice sheets that covered North America and the rock underneath them. Over most of northeastern Canada, the underlying rock is hard and strong. In Hudson Bay, however, the rock is softer. MacAyael's calculations showed that when the ice over Hudson Bay piled up several miles deep, the soft underlying rock would fracture and, when mixed with melted water, turn into a layer about the consistency of toothpaste. When this happened, the ice sheet would slide out to sea and huge armadas of glaciers would sail out into the North Atlantic. In this scheme, the mysterious Canadian rocks were simply material incorporated into the icebergs that dropped to the ocean floor whenever the iceberg melted.

However, from the point of view of climate stability, the important thing about these events is that they are accompanied by huge swings in temperature—the data seem to indicate that the average temperatures changed by 5°C (9°F) in a matter of 10 years or so. For reference, this change would be roughly like moving the climate of Florida to Boston. The most likely explanation is that the fresh water added to the North Atlantic by melting ice temporarily shut down the ocean currents that distribute heat around the globe, and that these currents stayed "off" until the water had been mixed and become salty again.

Since the discovery of the first of these sudden climate swings during the last ice age, scientists have found evidence for many more. Today, scientists are trying to understand how sudden changes in climate can be caused not only by glaciers, but also by changes in the brightness of the Sun and a host of other effects. It appears that our comfortable view of a stable Earth won't survive long as we unravel the history of the climate. •

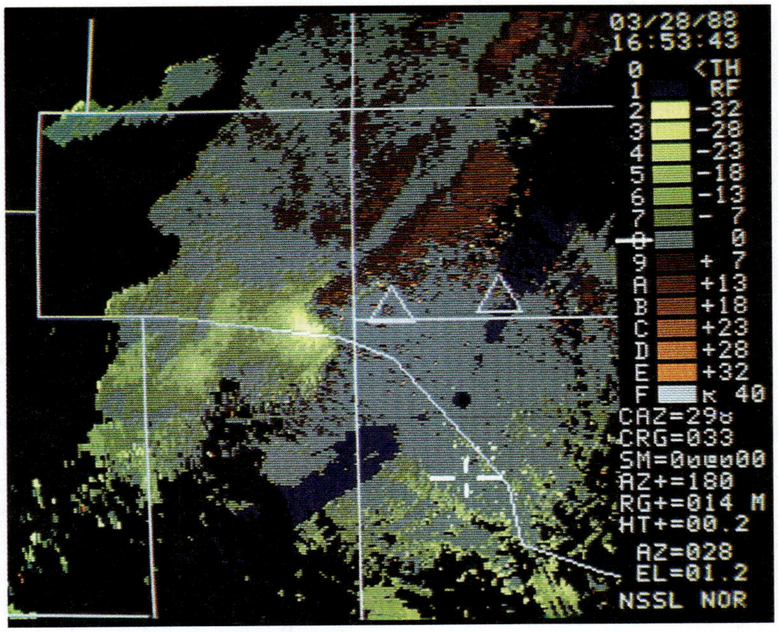

P. Degginger/Bruce Coleman, Inc.

A computerized radar weather map shows areas of cloud cover and precipitation.

Understanding Climate

While the daily weather is often dominated by the position of the jet stream and the creation of high- and low-pressure zones, the long-term climate depends on more lasting features of Earth's surface. These factors include the distribution of heat due to the stabilizing temperature of oceans, and the presence of mountains, which force air masses up over them. The climate is also extremely sensitive to the amount of sunlight that falls on the atmosphere and the amount of heat that is radiated back to space.

At the moment, our best attempts at predicting long-term climate depend on complex computer models of the atmosphere called *global circulation models (GCMs)*. In a typical GCM, a computer splits the world's surface into squares several hundred kilometers on a side and slices the atmosphere into about 10 vertical compartments. In each of these boxes the laws of motion and thermodynamics are used to calculate the amount of heat that flows in and out, how much water vapor comes out of the air, and so on. The computer balances the inflow and outflow from all of the boxes in the atmosphere and projects forward in time to try to predict long-term climate trends. Our current models are still rather crude (they have a great deal of difficulty accounting for the effects of clouds, for example), but they represent the best attempts to date to understand what affects Earth's climate. These models also play a critical role in discussing various types of ecological changes such as global warming (see Chapter 19).

Technology •

Doppler Radar

Radar has been a vital tool for weather forecasters for decades, and you may see radar maps of local weather conditions on TV every night. The way radar works is simple. Microwaves are sent out from a central antenna. When they encounter objects such as raindrops, snowflakes, or ice in the air, the waves are reflected back. Each kind of material produces a distinct pattern of reflected waves because its density is different from that of the surrounding air. These reflection patterns are used to assemble a map of local storm activity.

Ordinary radar, however, cannot detect winds, even winds of high velocity. The reason is that the densities of moving air and stationary air are usually not very different, and the two produce the same reflection pattern. But in many situations it's important to detect air currents. Near airports, for example, sudden downdrafts create violent air turbulence called *wind shear*, an extremely dangerous condition that we need to be able to detect.

Doppler radar is designed to detect motions of the air. It works like this: Reflected waves are analyzed not only for their intensity, as in ordinary radar, but for their frequency as well. From the difference between the emitted and reflected frequencies, a simple analysis of the Doppler effect yields the velocity of the object from which the wave was reflected. In this way, high winds and atmospheric turbulence can be detected at a safe distance. As you might expect, Doppler radar requires powerful computers and is much more expensive than ordinary radar, but the increased safety is well worth the expense. •

The Rock Cycle

When Earth formed there were no rocks. About 4.5 billion years ago, the great bombardment, the process that built Earth from the solar nebula, released prodigious amounts of energy as swarms of meteorites crashed into the growing planet, converting gravitational potential energy into heat. That heat produced a molten ball orbiting the Sun. There was no land, no oceans, and no atmosphere. Only when the bombardment subsided and Earth began to cool did rocks appear. First, as the temperature dropped below the melting point of surface rocks, the outer crust of Earth gradually solidified like the first layer of ice on a pond in winter. Then, when surface temperatures dropped below the boiling point of water, the first rains must have fallen. Together, these two events began the **rock cycle,** a cycle of internal and external Earth processes by which rock is created, destroyed, and altered.

Rock *formations,* which are bodies of rocks that form as a continuous unit, may be thought of as the "reservoirs" of the rock cycle. The atoms that make up the solid Earth spend most of their lives cycling among igneous, sedimentary, and metamorphic rocks—three principal types of rocks that differ in the processes by which they are formed.

Igneous Rocks

Igneous rocks, which solidify from a hot liquid and thus were the first to appear on Earth's ancient surface, come in two principal types. **Volcanic** or **extrusive rocks** solidify on the surface in what are by far the most spectacular of all rock-forming events, volcanic eruptions. Red-hot fountains and flows of lava ooze down the slopes of the growing volcanic cone. The most common variety of volcanic rock is *basalt,* a dark, even-textured rock rich in oxides of silicon, magnesium, iron, calcium, and aluminum. Basalt makes up most of the rock in Hawaii, as well as most of the new material formed at midocean ridges. Other volcanoes feature rocks richer in silicon; if these magmas mix with a significant amount of water or other volatile (easily boiled) substance, the volcanic rock can become the frothy rock called *pumice.*

Igneous rocks. *(a)* Devil's Tower in Wyoming represents the neck of a would-be volcano that may have never quite reached the surface. The surrounding sediments have subsequently eroded away. *(b)* Granite from a quarry in Barre, Vermont, solidified from magma deep underground.

(a)

Francois Gohier/Photo Researchers

(b)

Chromosohm/John Sohm/Photo Researchers

Igneous rocks that harden underground are called **intrusive rocks.** Dark-colored basalt often exploits underground cracks near volcanoes to form layers or sheets of igneous rock. The Palisades on the Hudson River near New York City formed in this way. Lighter in color and density, *granite* is perhaps the most common intrusive rock in Earth's crust. Hard, durable granite, with its attractive pink or gray colors and speckled array of light and dark minerals, makes an ideal ornamental building stone. New England is particularly famous for its many fine granite quarries.

Igneous rocks are still being formed on Earth—for example, when new plate material is formed at diverging boundaries (see Chapter 17) or in active volcanoes. In other places, such as the Yellowstone Park region, hot springs and geysers reveal hidden sources of underground heat and may indicate places where intrusive igneous rocks are forming today.

Sedimentary Rocks

When the first rains began to fall on the first igneous rocks, the process of *weathering* began. Small grains washed off the recently hardened volcanic rocks, flowed down through streams and rivers into the seas, and were deposited on the seafloors when the fast-moving waters of the rivers met the slower currents of the oceans. Weathering also occurred as water dissolved rocks and by the mechanical action of water freezing in cracks. Over time, layers of sediment accumulated, especially at the mouths of rivers near the shores of Earth's new oceans. As more and more sediment collected, these layers became thicker and thicker. In many places on Earth right now—the Mississippi River Delta that extends into the Gulf of Mexico, for example—layers of sediment may reach several kilometers in thickness.

Jonathan A. Meyers/Photo Researchers

A spectacular example of sedimentary rocks in Utah. The different colored bands correspond to layers of different kinds of materials that were deposited on the floor of a long-vanished ocean. The surrounding sediments have been eroded away to provide material for new sedimentary rocks downstream.

As the first sediments were buried deeper, temperature and pressure on them increased. In addition, water flowed through the layers of sediments, dissolving and redepositing glue-like chemicals—something like the crusty deposits that can build up on an ordinary faucet when water drips continuously. The net result of all of these processes—pressure, heat, and the effects of mineral-laden water—was to weld the bits of sediment together into new layered rocks. This kind of rock, appropriately called **sedimentary rock,** is made up of grains of material worn off previous rocks. Other common sedimentary rocks, including salt deposits, may form from layers of chemical precipitates.

While uniform sedimentary rocks can form at the base of a single mountain or cliff, the collection of grains often comes together from many different places. The grains in a single fragment of sedimentary rock being formed in the Mississippi delta, for example, may have come from a cliff in Minnesota, a valley in Pennsylvania, and a mountain in Texas. Similarly, sediments deposited near the mouth of the Colorado River carry bits of history from much of the North American West. Deltas inevitably contain particles from all rocks in their rivers' drainage area.

As you travel across the United States, you will encounter many common varieties of sedimentary rock. They're easy to spot in road cuts and outcrops because of their characteristic layered appearance, like the pages of a book or a many-layered cake. *Sandstone* forms mostly from sand-sized grains of quartz (silicon dioxide or SiO_2), the most common mineral at the beach, and from other hard mineral and rock fragments. Sandstone often formed from ancient beaches, deserts, or stream beds—places where concentrations of sand are found today. Sandstone usually feels rough to your touch, and you can just barely see the individual grains that have been cemented together.

Shale and *mudstone* form from sediments that are much finer grained than sand. These rocks commonly accumulate beneath the calm waters of lakes or in the deep-ocean basins—places often teeming with life. There organisms, both large and small, die and are buried in muddy ooze, where they may eventually form into fossils that provide us with much information about the evolution of life on Earth (see Chapter 25).

Limestone, another distinctive type of sedimentary rock, forms from the calcium carbonate ($CaCO_3$) skeletons of sea animals, or by chemical precipitation directly from ocean water. Some limestone grows from a gradual rain of microscopic debris or broken shells, while others represent a coral reef that spread across the floor of a shallow sea. Like shale and mudstone, limestone commonly bears fossils.

Given what we know about plate tectonics and about the constant movement of materials around Earth's surface, it should come as no surprise that just because sedimentary rocks originally formed at the bottom of the ocean, they have not necessarily stayed there since their formation. Indeed, it's not at all unusual to see sedimentary rocks in mountain passes thousands of meters above the ocean, or in the middle of continents thousands of kilometers from the nearest open water. Spectacular limestone formations form cliffs above Chattanooga, Tennessee, mountains near El Paso, Texas, and the heart of the Canadian Rockies, all far removed from the ocean.

One of the best places to get an appreciation of sedimentary rocks is at the beach. If you pick up a handful of sand, you'll notice that each grain is different. Some are dark colored, some are light. Some have sharp, angular edges, some are smooth and worn down. Each of these grains of sand once was part of a rock in a drainage system of the rivers that feed into the ocean. As the rock weathered away, each grain was chipped off and carried to the sea by wind and water. Eventually, the grains of sand you hold in your hand will be formed into solid rock and subjected to the forces of plate tectonics. That sandstone may some day be uplifted to an altitude far above sea level, where the grain may be weathered again and start the whole cycle all over. Each grain of sand in your hand, then, may have made the trip from rock to beach to sandstone many times in its life.

The story of the grain of sand provides a good model for the way materials move about Earth's surface. The atoms of rocks, just like those of the air, water, or your body, are always shifting around, but it is always the same matter—the same atoms—recycling.

The Science of Life •

Coral Reefs

Coral reefs are the abodes of countless billions of creatures that build their homes, bit by bit, from calcium carbonate. Reefs thrive in shallow, clear, ocean water with temperatures above 18°C (about 64°F). *The Pelican Island* by British poet James Montgomery (1771–1854) captures the extraordinary phenomenon of entire oceanic islands rising from this biological process:

I saw the living pile ascend,
The mausoleum of its architects,
Still dying upwards as their labours closed;
Slime the material, but the slime was turn'd
To adamant, by their petrific touch;
Frail were their frames, ephemeral their lives,
Their masonry imperishable. . . .
Atom by atom, thus their burthen grew,
Even like an infant in the womb, till Time
Deliver'd ocean of that monstrous birth,
—A coral island, stretching east and west.

Massive limestone reefs like the one in Montgomery's poem once thrived in ancient shallow seas of New York, Illinois, Montana, Texas, and many other places where limestone ridges or mountains now stand. •

Art Wolfe/Stone/Getty Images

Coral reefs form around this island in the Pacific.

Metamorphic Rocks

It may happen that sedimentary rocks are buried deep within our planet, where they are subjected to intense pressure and heat. There they will be turned into yet another kind of rock, transformed by Earth's extreme conditions into **metamorphic rock.** If a shale or mudstone formation is buried like this it may eventually turn into a brittle, hard *slate,* the kind of rock from which roofing shingles and school blackboards used to be made. Even higher temperatures and pressure can transform slate into spectacularly banded rocks, called *schists* and *gneisses,* which often boast fine crystals of garnets and other high-pressure minerals. Roadcuts and outcrops of these metamorphic rocks can look like an intensely folded cloth or a giant cross section of swirled marble cake. Sandstone, when exposed to high temperature and pressure, also metamorphoses, recrystallizing to a durable rock in which the original sand grains fuse into a solid mass known as *quartzite.*

The Grand Teton Mountains in Wyoming feature intensely folded metamorphic rocks. These rocks have been altered by high pressure and temperature deep within Earth's crust, and then uplifted and eroded into mountains.

Marli Miller/Visuals Unlimited

The Story of Marble

Of all the metamorphic rocks, none tells a more astonishing tale than *marble,* a rock of extraordinary beauty. If you ever travel the roads of Vermont, chances are you will pass an outcrop or roadcut of distinctive greenish-white cast, a rock with intricate bands and swirls. These marbles take a high polish and have been prized for centuries by sculptors and architects. But no works of humans can match the epic process that formed the stone.

Most marbles began as limestone, which are rocks that originate primarily from the skeletal remains of sea life. Over the ages, limestone in the area we now call Vermont was buried deeper and deeper, crushed under the weight of many kilometers' thickness of sand, shale, and more limestone in an ancient sea. But no ocean or sea can last forever on our dynamic planet. An ancient collision of the Eurasian and North American plates compressed and deformed this ocean basin, crumpling the layered rock into tight folds and subjecting the sedimentary pile to intense temperatures and pressures. The buckled and contorted formations were uplifted to high elevations when the Appalachian Mountains formed several hundred million years ago. During the intense pressures and high temperatures associated with the converging tectonic plates, the limestone was metamorphosed to the marble that we use today. Many millions of years of erosion and uplift have exposed these ancient rocks, which are gradually weathering

Walker Bros. Creations/Photo Researchers

The Lincoln Memorial is one of many famous monuments carved from marble, a metamorphosed limestone.

away to begin the cycle again. And humans, in a futile quest for immortality, quarry the marble for their monuments and tombstones and other transient reminders of Earth's incessant change.

Igneous, sedimentary, and metamorphic rocks all participate in the rock cycle. Igneous rocks, once formed, can be weathered to form sedimentary rocks, or they can undergo metamorphism. Layers of sedimentary rocks also can be transformed into metamorphic rocks. All three kinds of rocks can be subducted into Earth's interior, partially melted, and reformed as new igneous rocks. Thus the rock cycle never ceases.

Science in the Making •

Hutton and the Discovery of "Deep Time"

Near the town of Jedburgh in Scotland is a curious cliff that reveals vertical layers of rock overlain by horizontal layers. How could such a sequence have occurred? In the last decades of the eighteenth century, Scottish scientist James Hutton (1726–1797), a man who is often called "the father of modern geology," studied this remarkable cliff and realized that he was seeing the result of an incredibly long period of geological turmoil.

Knowing what you now know about sedimentary rocks, you will realize when you look at this cliff that you are seeing the end product of a long chain of events (Figure 18-8). First, a series of sedimentary rocks was laid down in the usual horizontal fashion, one flat layer on top of another. Then some tectonic activity disrupted those layers, breaking and folding them until they were tilted nearly vertically. Then, after still more tectonic activity, the rocks found themselves at the bottom of an ocean and another layer of sedimentary rocks formed on top of them. Finally, an episode of uplift and erosion has brought the rocks to our view.

Hutton realized that geological forces must have been operating for very long times indeed. Each step of the formation process—gradual sedimentation, burial, folding, uplift, more sedimentation, and so on—would require countless generations, based on observations of ongoing geological processes. In the words of nature writer John McPhee, Hutton had discovered "deep time." In order for a formation like the one at Jedburgh to exist, Earth had to exist not for thousands of years or even hundreds of thousands of years, but for many millions of years.

Today, we know that Earth's age is calculated in billions of years, and the existence of structures like the one at Jedburgh is not surprising. At the time of its interpretation by James Hutton, however, the rocks at Jedburgh provided a totally new insight into the inconceivable antiquity of our planet.

©C.E. Ford 2004

James Hutton recognized the immense spans of time required to form this spectacular outcrop at Siccar Point, near Jedburgh in Scotland.

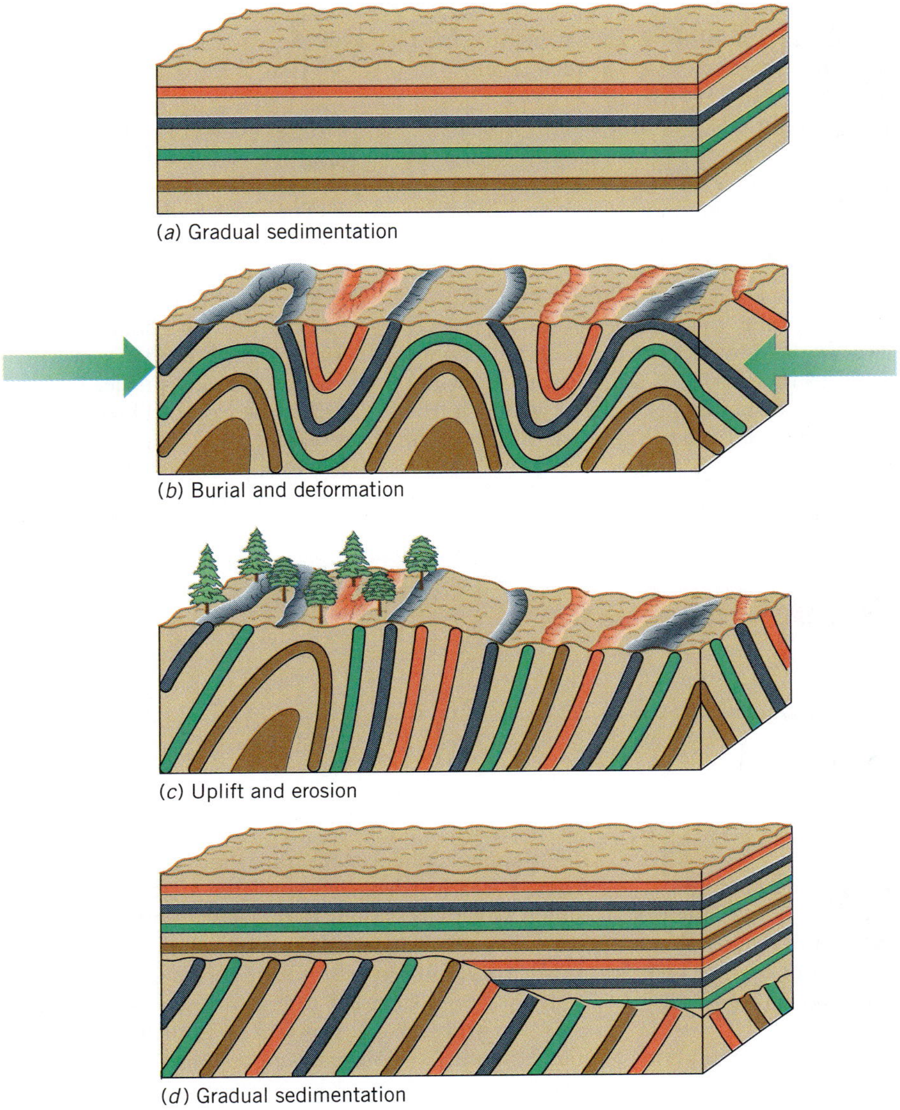

• **Figure 18-8** This series of diagrams shows several stages in the history of the Jedburgh outcrop. *(a)* Layers of sediment were gradually deposited in water. *(b)* Those sediments, deeply buried, were compressed and tilted during tectonic activity. *(c)* Uplift brought the tilted sediments to the surface, where they were partly eroded. *(d)* The rocks subsided, and a new cycle of sedimentation began.

In the words of Hutton himself, the testimony of the rocks offered "no vestige of a beginning, no prospect of an end." •

The Interdependence of Earth's Cycles

We have described the hydrologic, atmospheric, and rock cycles as if they were completely independent of each other, as if they operated alone in splendid isolation. In fact, each cycle affects and is affected by the others.

The amount of rainfall in a given location affects the rate of erosion and thus the amount of sediment being deposited in deltas—and therefore the amount of sedimentary rock being formed. In this way, the atmospheric and water cycles affect the rock cycle. In the same way, the breakdown of rock is essential to the formation of soils in which plants grow. The presence of plants, in turn, affects the absorption of sunlight at Earth's surface and thus the energy balance that controls the movement of the winds and ocean currents. And, over hundreds of millions of years, the global cycle of plate tectonics, which controls the distribution of Earth's mountains and oceans, influences all other cycles. Thus, although Earth's cycles operate on very different timescales, they constantly influence each other.

Science News | Krakatoa Stifled Sea-Level Rise for Decades

(SCIENCE NEWS, FEB. 18, 2006, P. 110)

In 1883, in one of the greatest volcanic eruptions in history, the Indonesian volcano Krakatoa sent huge amounts of ash and other particulate material high into the air. Because of the strength of the eruption, a large quantity of this material was lofted above the lower levels of the atmosphere, where it could be washed out easily by storms and rain. As a result, many of the particles stayed in the air for more than two years before they finally settled out.

Scientists at the Lawrence Livermore Laboratory in California have recently shown that this eruption, part of what we have called the rock cycle, had a long lasting effect on the behavior of the oceans, part of what we have called the hydrological cycle. This event, therefore, provides one more confirmation of our pictures of the operation of Earth as a set of interlocking cycles.

The mechanism in this case is easy to describe: the particles in the air reflected a small fraction of the sunlight coming to the Earth. As a result, the surface of the planet cooled and the waters in the upper surface of the world's oceans contracted. This contraction, in turn, led to a slight drop in sea level. According to the computer models used by the Livermore group, the effect of the eruption was such that the oceans would not have returned to their pre-Krakatoa levels until the 1950s.

The models also suggest that the effect of global warming was to raise sea levels about 1.7 cm. between 1955 and 1998, and that the eruption of Mount Pinetubo in the Philippines (a much smaller eruption than Krakatoa) had a correspondingly smaller effect on sea levels. In the case of Pinetubo, the researchers say that the effects of the 1991 eruption lasted barely a decade and have now played themselves out.

Thinking More About | Cycles

Beach Erosion

Something about the shore appeals to people. Beachfront property is considered to be highly desirable, and over the past half-century America's prosperity has resulted in large-scale development of the Atlantic, Pacific, and Gulf of Mexico coastlines. As a result, Americans are becoming very aware of the effects of natural cycles on property values.

Beaches, like all other systems in nature, are not static but change in response to environmental forces. The action of waves transports sand grains from one place and deposits them somewhere else. Large waves tend to move sand away from a beach and deposit it in offshore bars, while smaller waves tend to move the sand back toward the beach. Thus a seasonal movement of sand occurs on many beaches—offshore in the winter (when storms send in large waves) and onshore during the summer. In addition, waves normally strike a beach at a slight angle, a phenomenon that moves sand along the beachfront. Large storms may completely destroy beaches and dunes, which are rebuilt farther inland over time. Thus every beach is a dynamic, shifting system. Left to itself, a beach will move around in response to the forces of wave and storm.

If the beach were left to itself, this cycle of change would cause no problems. If, however, waterfront properties worth many millions of dollars have been developed on or near the beach, such movements have enormous economic consequences for homeowners. Should governments use public funds to try to protect such homes? Should the government provide low-cost insurance to indemnify the owners for loss? Should insurance be issued to allow people to rebuild beachfront homes after a storm?

SUMMARY

Matter that forms Earth's outer layers follows many cycles, driven by the energy of the Sun and Earth's inner heat energy. Each cycle can be analyzed in terms of *reservoirs* that hold matter and by the movement of matter between reservoirs.

The *hydrologic cycle* traces the path of water as it evaporates from the oceans, falls back to Earth as rain, and forms lakes, rivers, *ice caps, glaciers,* and *groundwater* reservoirs. During unusually cold climatic periods, more water falls as snow, creating a white reflective blanket that further reduces the amount of absorbed solar radiation. This situation, if prolonged, can lead to an *ice age,* during which ocean levels drop significantly and great sheets of ice cover the land at high and middle latitudes. Temperatures in these latitudes may be moderated, however, by ocean *currents* that are important in redistributing temperatures at Earth's surface.

The *atmospheric cycle* of the *weather* redistributes solar energy from the warmer equatorial regions to higher latitudes through the development of global convection cells of air. The prevailing westerly flow of weather across North America marks one of these large cells, while the *jet stream* delineates the boundary between this flow and the contrary cell to our north. *Climate,* in contrast to weather, varies much more slowly in response to ocean circulation, the Sun's energy output, the positions of continents and mountain ranges, and other relatively fixed conditions.

The solid materials of Earth's crust are subject to the *rock cycle*. The first solids to form on the cooling planet were *igneous rocks*, which are formed from hot, molten material. *Volcanic* or *extrusive* igneous rocks solidify on the surface, while *intrusive* igneous rocks cool underground. The first igneous rocks were subjected to weathering by wind and rain, which eventually produced layers of sediment and the first *sedimentary rocks*. Sandstone, shale, limestone, and other sedimentary rocks were deposited in ocean basins, layer upon layer, in sequences often many kilometers thick. Igneous and sedimentary rocks were subsequently buried and transformed by Earth's internal temperature and pressure to form *metamorphic rocks*. Each of the three major rock types—igneous, sedimentary, and metamorphic—can be converted into the others by the ongoing processes of the rock cycle.

Key Terms

reservoirs
hydrologic cycle
ice caps
glaciers
groundwater
current
ice age
atmospheric cycle
weather
climate
jet stream
rock cycle
igneous rock
volcanic or extrusive rock
intrusive rock
sedimentary rock
metamorphic rock

Review Questions

1. What happens to matter during a cyclical process?

2. What form of energy drives the hydrologic cycle, the movement of tectonic plates, and weather patterns?

3. What are two steps in the analysis of a cycle of Earth material?

4. What are the principal repositories of water on Earth?

5. Identify three ways that water moves between repositories.

6. How does water move within the oceans? How does it move within glaciers?

7. By what processes does the amount of water on Earth change from year to year? What is the magnitude of this change from year to year?

8. What are the differences between ice caps and glaciers?

9. What factors might cause glaciers to advance from polar areas to more temperate zones?

10. How do ocean currents affect local climate?

11. Why do we call groundwater in most areas a "nonrenewable resource?"

12. What is the difference between weather and climate? Describe the weather and climate of your area.

13. In what ways are air masses like reservoirs of the atmosphere?

14. What are the five variables that describe the weather?

15. Why does air pressure vary from place to place?

16. What is the prevailing direction of the jet stream? How does it influence your weather?

17. How does the atmosphere distribute heat across Earth's surface?

18. If land heats up more quickly than water, what does this tell you about their relative heat capacities?

19. Why were igneous rocks Earth's first rocks?

20. What are three main kinds of rocks? How do they form?

21. If you were driving past a large roadcut through rock, what features might you observe to tell you its origin?

Discussion Questions

1. In the case of the cycle of an aluminum atom, what are some of the reservoirs of aluminum?

2. Describe three places where you might find volcanic rocks forming today. Describe three places where you could watch sedimentary rocks forming today. Where would you have to go to watch metamorphic rocks form?

3. The thickness of polar ice caps depends critically on the location of continents; much thicker ice can accumulate on land than in water. Where is the only polar continent now?

4. Why does temperature vary with latitude and altitude?

5. How do oceans redistribute Earth's heat? How does the atmosphere accomplish this? Do rocks redistribute heat? Which global cycle is most efficient in transferring heat? Why?

6. Why are there offshore breezes at night and onshore breezes during the day? What does this suggest about the relative heat capacities of land versus the oceans?

7. On the Jovian planets, the amount of heat coming from the interior of the planet is about equal to the amount that falls as sunlight. Should this affect the way the atmosphere circulates on these planets? Why or why not?

8. Why is draining an aquifer akin to mining water? How is the water in an aquifer replaced? How long does this process take?

9. How would our weather patterns be affected if Earth stopped rotating?

10. What is the jet stream? Why is it important?

11. What is the gulfstream? What countries are directly affected by the path that it takes?

Problems

1. How much calcium is in a 100 cubic kilometers of seawater? [*Hint:* Refer to Table 18-2.]

2. If copper is worth $8 per kilogram, what is the value of the copper in 10 cubic kilometers of seawater?

3. An impressive limestone deposit in north-central Montana is 2500 meters thick. If limestone grows at an average rate of 1.25 millimeter per year, how long did it take to form this limestone deposit?

4. Record the temperature, atmospheric pressure, and cloudiness at both noon and midnight in your area for a period of at least 15 days. (You can find these data on the Internet.)

a. Graph the temperature versus pressure. Is there a systematic trend? Why?

b. Is there a relationship between atmospheric pressure and cloudiness? Why?

c. Is there a correlation between cloudiness and the difference between temperatures at noon and midnight? Why?

d. Try graphing your data again with a different type of graph (e.g., bar, line, pie). Did your original choice of graph affect how easily you could interpret the data and results?

Investigations

1. Look at some weather maps in your local newspaper over a period of several weeks and see if observing weather patterns to the west of your location is a good predictor of your weather. Why should this be so?

2. Where does water come from at your college? Is the water processed or treated in any way? How long might that source of water last? What alternatives exist if that supply is depleted?

3. The three kinds of rocks—igneous, sedimentary, and metamorphic—are described in this chapter as being quite distinct, yet some earth scientists have engaged in an intense debate about the origins of certain rocks, such as granites, that formed at high temperature deep within Earth. Some scientists claim that these rocks are igneous, while others say they are metamorphic. How could such a debate arise, and how could it be resolved? [*Hint:* Think about making taffy.]

4. Investigate the biological cycle of calcium in your body. Where in your body is calcium used? How often is it replaced? How much calcium do you need to consume each day? What are the best food sources of this element?

5. What are the "doldrums" and how do they form? What role have they played in poetry and literature?

6. Many movies have been made about weather disasters—hurricanes, tornadoes, blizzards, and so on. Watch such a movie and comment on the accuracy of the science portrayed.

7. Investigate all the possible sources for global warming. What do we know about the Sun's energy output? Is it stable? Does the core of Earth supply any energy to the surface?

8. How many ice ages have there been? How many periods of increasing temperature are associated with interglacial periods?

9. The next time you walk past a large building, see if you can tell the different types of stone that were used in the construction.

10. Why would a sculptor use a metamorphic rock like marble for a detailed sculpture rather than an igneous rock like granite?

11. The next time you are at the seashore, see if you can spot a stone jetty. Why are these constructed? What effect does the construction of a jetty have on beach erosion? What kind of stone was used?

19

Ecology, Ecosystems, and the Environment

Are human activities affecting the global environment?

Science Through the Day | Life under the Sand

You and a friend decide to take a walk down the beach, away from the crowd. Along a deserted stretch you watch as dozens of small shorebirds scurry back and forth, poking their long pointed bills into the wet sand. They seem to be searching for food. A closer look reveals tiny air holes in the sand—the telltale signs of tiny crustaceans. Farther down the beach, the sand is littered with small shiny shells; a golfball-sized crab scurries by, and smelly strands of seaweed wash up onto the shore.

Atlantide S.N.C./Age Fotostock America, Inc.

But those life-forms are only the most obvious members of the oceanside community. If you could take a small sample of beach sand and examine it under a microscope, you would observe countless bacteria and other tiny organisms that thrive in the tidal environment. The beach turns out to be a richly varied community of organisms. In much the same way, a full understanding of our living planet will come if you view it not as a series of isolated individuals but as one vast interconnected community.

Ecology and Ecosystems

Think about the wonderful communities of living things that you've seen in your travels—deep woods and flowering meadows, shallow ponds and ocean beaches, dry deserts and stagnant swamps. Perhaps you've been lucky enough to hike in high-mountain tundra or go snorkeling at a coral reef. Each of these places boasts a collection of interdependent living organisms in a distinctive physical environment.

Stop and Think! What characteristics do all the living communities that we have just listed have in common?

The word **ecology,** derived from the Greek word for household or housekeeping, is the branch of science that focuses on natural living systems in the broadest sense. An **ecosystem** includes all the different kinds of living things that live in a given area, together with their physical surroundings. In every ecosystem, some organisms, such as plants, act as producers; they obtain atoms and energy from their physical surroundings and convert them into the essential carbon-based molecules of life. These biomolecules then sustain other organisms, such as animals, which act as *consumers* in ecosystems. In addition, still other life-forms, including bacteria and fungi, act as *decomposers* that renew the raw materials of life. Together, these diverse organisms form an interdependent *community*.

An ecosystem can be as small as a single community of organisms on and near a bush in a tropical forest. It can be an aquarium in your living room, or a lake, including all the fish, insects, plants, and microrganisms in it. Or an ecosystem can be a mountain meadow, a salt marsh, a continent, even an entire planet. No matter what size ecosystem we talk about, however, the emphasis of ecology is to look at the system—its matter and its energy—as a whole, rather than as a group of independent parts.

Every living organism, from single cells to complex animals and plants, relies on its ecosystem to sustain life. Indeed, the continuance of life on Earth is not a property of isolated individual organisms or even of species, but rather of ecosystems. One key to understanding living organisms, therefore, is to examine the ecosystems in which they survive.

Much can be learned from looking at living things as part of integrated natural systems, but this realization is relatively recent. Throughout the nineteenth century, for example, biologists were concerned with cataloging living things and paid little attention to how they were affected by (and, in turn, how they affected) their environment. Only within the last few decades have many of the insights discussed in this chapter come to be recognized as different aspects of the study of ecology.

Characteristics of Ecosystems

Ecosystems are richly varied. They occur on virtually every body of water and parcel of land on Earth, from the deepest ocean trench to the highest mountain range. Yet, in spite of this diversity, all ecosystems share a few basic characteristics. As you read about these characteristics, think about how they apply to an ecosystem near your home.

Georgette Douwma/The Image Bank/Getty Images

Complex coral reef ecosystems are extremely sensitive to changes in local conditions, such as salinity and water temperature. Large areas of coral near the coasts of North and South America are endangered by human activity.

1. Every Ecosystem Consists of Both Living and Nonliving Parts

Nonliving or *abiotic* parts form the chemical and physical **environment** of the ecosystem—the water, soil, atmosphere, and so forth. Local climate, including average temperature, rainfall, winds, and Sun exposure, are important physical properties of land ecosystems, whereas water temperature, pressure, salinity, and acidity help to characterize ecosystems in oceans, lakes, and other bodies of water.

Living organisms form the *biotic* part of an ecosystem; they form an *ecological community,* which may be defined as all the individuals in an area that interact with each other to maintain life. In a forest ecosystem, for example, an ecological community will include trees, shrubs, insects, birds, snakes, and squirrels, as well as fungi, bacteria, and a host of other microscopic organisms in the soil.

2. Energy Flows Through Ecosystems

The most important interactions of organisms in an ecological community are by way of a *food chain* or *food web,* which indicates who feeds on whom. Each species in a food web obtains energy and chemicals from other organisms; in turn, each species provides energy and chemicals for other organisms. Insects eat plants, birds eat insects, bacteria and fungi in the soil decompose birds and other organisms when they die, and plants obtain vital nutrients from the soil. Food webs for ecological communities may be extremely complex.

The flow of energy between *trophic levels* (see Chapter 3) is an important unifying characteristic of all ecosystems. The first trophic level of photosynthetic plants, which use only the Sun's energy, provides energy for herbivores in the second trophic level. Herbivores, in turn, pass some of their energy to carnivores of the third trophic level and so on. Decomposers, including bacteria and fungi, obtain energy from all other trophic levels. In each energy transfer from one trophic level to another, most of the available energy cannot be recovered in a useful form; it eventually radiates into space as waste heat (see Chapter 4). In fact, only about 10% of the energy available at one trophic level normally finds its way to the next. Thus as energy flows through an ecosystem it must be replaced continuously.

3. Matter Is Recycled by Ecosystems

Atoms continuously cycle from one part of Earth to another. Perhaps the easiest way to understand the cycling of atoms through Earth's biosphere is to follow the *carbon cycle.* This cycle can be illustrated by looking at the possible path of a single atom of carbon that leaves your lungs the next time you breathe out a molecule of carbon dioxide. This carbon atom enters the atmosphere, where many different things can happen to it (Figure

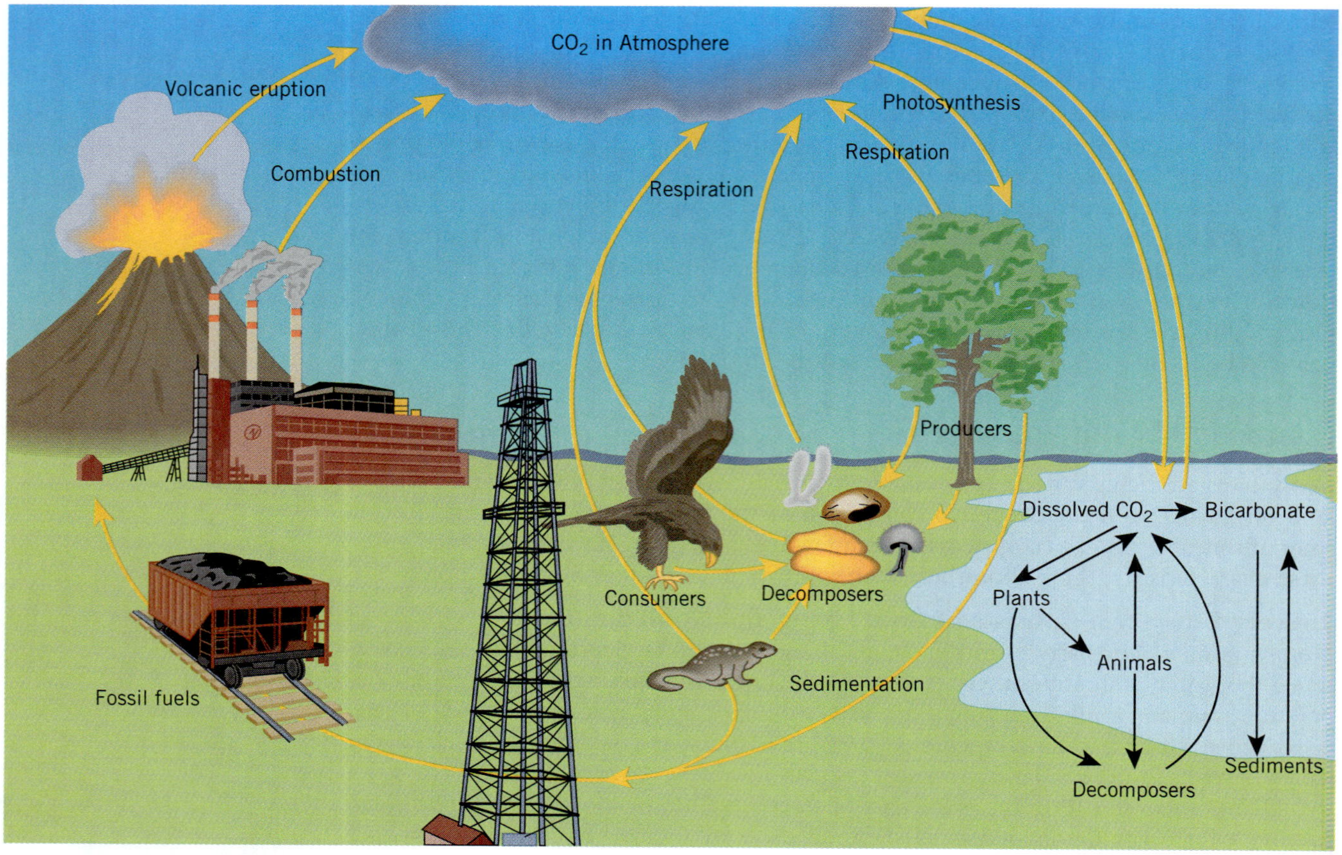

• **Figure 19-1** The carbon cycle. Carbon atoms cycle through both living (biotic) and nonliving (abiotic) parts of Earth's ecosystem. They are found in carbon dioxide in the air, then taken into plants to become part of their structure. If a plant is eaten, the carbon may be returned to the air through respiration or become part of an animal's tissue. When the animal dies, the carbon dioxide returns to the air. Carbon atoms may also be locked into sedimentary rocks such as shale and limestone.

19-1). It can, for example, be taken up by a plant during photosynthesis and then be incorporated into the tissues of a tree or a blade of grass. The plant can then be eaten so that the carbon atom becomes part of the tissue of a herbivore. Alternatively, the carbon can simply return to the atmosphere if the plant dies and rots without being eaten.

If the carbon atom is taken into the tissue of a herbivore, then it may show up on your dinner plate one day and be taken into your body as part of some food you eat. It might even be incorporated into your own body to stay there until you die, or to move through the chemical cycles described in Chapter 21. In either case, the carbon atom, in time, will enter the atmosphere again.

Another possible track for a carbon atom is shown in Figure 19-1. It can enter the ocean by being added to a mollusk shell or the skeleton of a microscopic organism. Upon the death of the organism, these hard parts sink to the ocean bottom, where, in the form of calcium carbonate, they are turned into limestone. In this case, the carbon atom can remain locked up for hundreds of millions of years until the limestone is weathered and the carbon is released into the atmosphere.

A single atom of carbon, in other words, may have gone through many different chemical reactions during the 4.5-billion-year life of the planet and will continue to do so as long as Earth has living things on it. The one thing it will not do, however, is leave the planet. A similar story can be told for an atom of nitrogen or phosphorus or any other chemical element.

Stop and Think! Some toxic chemicals, such as the heavy metal mercury and the pesticide DDT, may gradually concentrate to harmful levels in living things, because cells have no mechanisms to remove them. These dangerous substances are observed to be most concentrated in species at the top of the food chain—a phenomenon known as *bioconcentration* or *biological magnification*. Based on the characteristics of ecosystems, why should this phenomenon occur?

4. Every Organism Occupies an Ecological Niche
The **ecological niche,** a central concept in ecology, refers to a particular mode of survival—a particular way of obtaining matter and energy—within an ecosystem. In a forest ecosystem there may be a niche that can be filled by one or more kinds of warm-blooded, insect-eating, nocturnal animals—bats, for example. Mushrooms growing in shaded wooded areas may fill another niche. Each plant or animal in an ecosystem fills an ecological niche, and different organisms compete for dominance in their preferred ecological niche.

5. Stable Ecosystems Achieve a Balance Among Their Populations
This balance, called *homeostasis,* reflects the fact that matter and energy are limited resources that must be shared among all individuals of an ecosystem. An ecosystem in homeostasis will exhibit some variations in population sizes, as food supplies and other factors vary from season to season and year to year. But the overall distribution of species is usually relatively constant. A one-acre sunny meadow, for example, will boast a large but limited amount of grasses, flowering plants, and other vegetation. Year in and year out, those plants support a limited population of insects, which in turn will feed perhaps a few dozen birds.

6. Ecosystems Are Not Permanent, but Change over Time
While ecosystems may appear to be stable, in fact we know that they change over time. On the longest timescales, the effects of plate tectonics will change the climate in a given area, converting a desert into a fertile plain, for example. On shorter timescales, the advance and retreat of glaciers can have a similar effect, as can changes in patterns of precipitation. Even on very short timescales, the introduction of a new species, by humans or by other natural processes, can profoundly change the pattern of life in a given area. As the science of ecology progresses, understanding and predicting these sorts of changes is becoming a major research goal.

The Law of Unintended Consequences

The complex interweaving of living things in their environment leads to a central insight in the science of ecology, an idea called the **law of unintended consequences.**

It is virtually impossible to change one aspect of a complex system without affecting other parts of the system, often in as-yet unpredictable ways.

Whenever we alter something in an ecosystem other changes will follow, and we have to consider what those changes might be. Examples of this "law" appear in the news almost daily: building levees on the Mississippi River has caused unintended intensification of flooding; extracting petroleum and water from underground reservoirs has caused unintended land subsidence; building jetties into the ocean has resulted in unintended erosion of beaches. Each of these systems is interdependent, so the whole responds to every stimulus.

As often happens when scientists and engineers encounter complex systems for the first time, a good deal of observation and trial and error has to take place before an understanding of the system begins to emerge. Unfortunately, during that period of study serious mistakes can be made (see the discussion of Lake Victoria in the following section). Eventually, however, people learn how to proceed and begin to undertake large-scale projects with some confidence. At the moment, for example, the largest reconstruction project ever attempted is being undertaken in the Everglades of South Florida. The Everglades Restoration Plan is designed to restore the Everglades by changing the flow of water in the entire southern part of the state. As the plan proceeds, you can be sure that everyone—engineers and environmentalists alike—will have the law of unintended consequences firmly in mind.

The Lake Victoria Disaster

Millions of people who live on the shores of Lake Victoria, the largest freshwater lake in Africa, know firsthand about the law of unintended consequences. What was once a rich fishing ground and source of most of their protein has been radically altered by the introduction of a single new species—the Nile perch.

About 35 years ago, sport fishermen, seeking a greater challenge for the growing tourist market, introduced this large, aggressive predator into the lake. The perch thrived and rapidly ate up populations of smaller fish that not only provided an essential part of the local diet but also controlled populations of algae and parasite-bearing snails. Unchecked, live algae spread over the lake's surface, while dead algae sank, decayed, and consumed oxygen in deeper water where fish used to live. Snails have also multiplied and become a serious health hazard because they carry parasites that can affect humans.

Native fishermen now rely on Nile perch, which weigh up to several hundred pounds each, rather than smaller fish, but this change carries its own ecological consequences. Unlike the small fish that were sun dried, Nile perch must be roasted over fires. Lake Victoria's shoreline, each year stripped of more trees for this purpose, is suffering extensive soil erosion and further unanticipated changes to the lake's ecosystem. A single new species has thus drastically altered a vast ecosystem.

Stop and Think! The ecologist Garrett Hardin has stated as a principle of ecology that "We can never do merely one thing." What do you think he meant by this?

Science in the Making •

Island Biogeography

Because ecosystems are so complex, it's sometimes difficult to draw unambiguous conclusions from field studies. In 1963, however, American ecologists Robert MacArthur and Edward O. Wilson looked at the populations on islands, small ecosystems separated from the rest of the terrestrial world by water. From their study, they were able to frame a hypothesis: Whenever a new species migrates to an island that already has a thriving and stable ecosystem, it will flourish only if another species becomes extinct. According to this so-called equilibrium hypothesis, only a fixed number of species exist in any ecosystem, and if a new species invades, one of the old species will be driven to extinction.

New species migrate to islands like this, reestablishing ecosystems.

Thomas Schmitt/The Image Bank/Getty Images

The hypothesis was supported a few years later by Wilson and Daniel Simberloff in a classic ecological experiment. They first surveyed all the insects and crustaceans on a series of small mangrove islands off the coast of southern Florida. They then removed all living animals on the islands by draping large plastic sheets over them and fumigating. Over a period of years, they watched the islands undergo the process of repopulation as new animals migrated from the mainland or from other islands. As expected, the total number of species on each island at the end was about the same as it had been at the beginning. Perhaps less expected, however, was the fact that the kinds of animals on the repopulated islands were often quite different from those that had been there before. New species that happened to be carried to an island on the tides were able to establish themselves in particular ecological niches, which were then unavailable to competitors that arrived later.

In 1995, nature began a similar experiment on its own. A violent hurricane propelled a large raft of fallen trees along with 15 green iguanas—spiny lizards up to four feet in length—from the Caribbean island of Guadeloupe to the island of Anguilla, 200 miles away. A new colony of green iguanas has begun to breed on Anguilla, and it soon will be competing for resources with the native species of brown iguanas. Ecologists are keeping close tabs on this dramatic example of changing island ecology. •

Threats to the Global Ecosystem and Environment

The resources of our global ecosystem are vast but limited, and we often don't know enough about them to predict accurately how they will respond to change. These two inescapable facts, coupled with the growing pressure of human populations for energy and material goods, have led to a number of large-scale environmental problems. We are going to look at four of those problems—the disposal of solid waste, the degradation of the ozone layer, acid rain, and the greenhouse effect. All of these problems are serious, but their solutions entail different levels of national and international commitment. Taken together, they provide a sense of how ecosystems respond to human activities, as well as the difficulties that will have to be solved in order for our industrial society to keep functioning.

The Problem of Urban Landfills

The fact that nothing is ever really thrown away has become very much a concern in urban America (Figure 19-2). The problem is that garbage (so-called solid waste) is generated at an enormous rate in American cities today. New York City alone adds 17,000 tons of solid waste to its landfill every day.

To make matters worse, the nature of modern landfills is such that the normal process of breakdown and decay in the carbon and nitrogen cycles is slowed enormously. In a landfill, solid waste is dumped on the ground and compacted, then covered with a layer of dirt, then another layer of compacted waste, then another layer of dirt, and so on. Material in such a landfill is cut off from air and water, and the bacteria that normally operate to decompose the waste cannot thrive. Archaeologists digging into landfills have discovered, for example, that newspapers from the 1950s are still readable after having been buried for a half century! This situation means that, unlike an ordinary garden compost pile, in which materials are quickly broken down by the action of bacteria, the landfill is really more like a burial site than a location for recycling.

Two approaches respond to the problem of solid waste. One strategy is recycling; every aluminum can that is recycled is one that won't be taking up space in a landfill. The other approach is the creation in rural areas of large depositories that are designed to accept waste shipped from distant locations. Cities pay more to ship and dump trash in facilities like this, but the costs are relatively modest compared to building new landfills close to home.

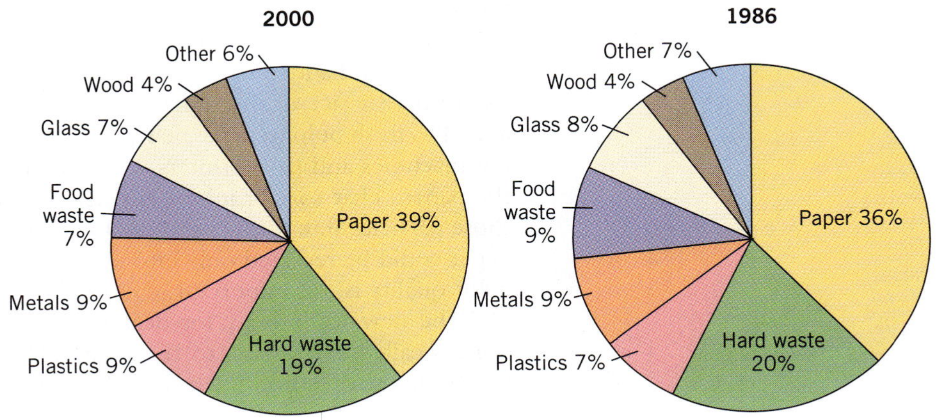

• **Figure 19-2** The percentage of different kinds of trash in urban landfills in 1986 (right) and percentages for 2000 (left).

Science by the Numbers •

Trash

How much solid waste is produced in the United States every year? Engineers estimate that the average American each year is responsible for about 40 tons (80,000 pounds) of trash, including everything from disposable containers, newspapers, and mail-order catalogs to old automobiles and appliances, as well as the industrial wastes necessary to manufacture the things we buy. What is the total volume of this waste? Compacted trash typically weighs about 80 pounds per cubic foot—somewhat denser than water but less dense than rock (of course, it takes up much more volume before it's compacted). Forty tons, therefore, is equivalent to a volume of

$$\frac{80{,}000 \text{ pounds}}{80 \text{ pounds per cubic foot}} = 1000 \text{ cubic feet}$$

That's enough compacted trash to fill two large dump trucks for every man, woman, and child in the United States every year. Thus 250 million Americans produce a total annual volume of trash of

$$250{,}000{,}000 \text{ people} \times 1000 \text{ cubic feet/person} = 2.5 \times 10^{11} \text{ cubic feet}$$

That's almost two cubic miles of trash every year, enough to build a solid 500-foot-wide wall across the Grand Canyon at its widest and deepest point. •

Technology •

The Science in Recycling

Because land that can be used for dumps near big cities is growing ever more scarce, and because the environmental cost of using materials once and then throwing them away is growing steadily, governments have recently begun to pay more attention to recycling. Every recycled plastic milk jug or sheet of paper means less material in landfills, as well as less petroleum taken from the ground or less energy used to convert wood pulp to paper.

But recycling is not as easy as it sounds. A great deal of science and engineering has to be done before even the simplest materials can be reused. In addition, the processes that have to take place to recover one kind of material are, in general, different from those needed to recover another. The recycling of different kinds of plastics (see Chapter 10), for example, requires different kinds of chemical reactions, and processes that work for plastic soft-drink bottles will not necessarily work for ketchup containers. As a result, each kind of material that is to be recycled poses its own unique problems to an engineer.

Take white paper, for example. The average office worker generates about 250 pounds of high-grade paper waste per year, and many offices around the country have paper recycling programs. The first step in this process is simple: the paper is ground up into a pulp and added to water to make a slurry. Ink particles from typewriters and pens rise to the surface of the slurry and can be skimmed off, leaving a material that can be added to fresh pulp to make new paper. As we pointed out in Chapter 5, however, copying machines and laser printers work by melting bits of carbon mixed with resins onto the paper. That sort of ink makes heavier particles when the paper is ground up, and those particles sink to the bottom along with the paper fibers. Until quite recently, such paper could be recycled only into products such as cardboard or tissue paper, for which color quality is not important.

The new technology for dealing with this problem involves the addition of substances called surfactants to the pulp. The molecules in these substances bind to the heavier ink particles on one end and to bubbles of gas on the other. Once the molecules are attached to the ink, various gases are bubbled through the slurry. The surfactants and their load of ink rise to the surface with the bubbles and are skimmed off, leaving clean paper fibers for reuse.

A national recycling effort will involve hundreds of different processes such as this, each geared to a specific material, but each doing its part to make a coherent whole. •

The Ozone Problem

In Chapter 14 we pointed out that, although the Sun gives off most of its radiation in visible light, a certain amount of that radiation comes in the form of ultraviolet light from the higher-energy part of the spectrum. Ultraviolet radiation can be very damaging to living organisms; indeed, it is routinely used to sterilize equipment in hospitals. If Earth's surface were not shielded in some way from the Sun's ultraviolet rays, life on land would be very different, if not impossible.

Ozone, a molecule made up of three oxygen atoms instead of the usual two, absorbs ultraviolet radiation. If enough ozone molecules exist in the atmosphere, they will absorb most of the ultraviolet radiation from the Sun and keep it from reaching the ground. In fact, a protective shield of ozone formed high in Earth's atmosphere several hundred million years ago, and it was only after this shield formed that life moved onto land.

The Ozone Layer

Scientists detect ozone in the atmosphere by using several techniques. One is simply to fly specialized aircraft into the region where ozone is common and collect samples. For the past decade or so, this kind of sampling has been done routinely by organizations such as the National Oceanic and Atmospheric Administration (usually called "Noah" after its acronym NOAA) and its counterparts in other countries. Another way to detect ozone is to measure characteristic spectral lines given off by the ozone molecule (see Chapter 8). These measurements can be made from satellites, from aircraft, or by ground-based observers. In general, all these techniques are now used to give us a picture of the health of the ozone layer.

Measurements reveal that ozone is a trace gas that constitutes less than one molecule in a million in Earth's upper atmosphere. Although ozone is found at every altitude (you are breathing a small amount even as you read this), most of the ozone is found some 30 kilometers (about 20 miles) up in a region called the stratosphere (Figure 19-3). In this region, concentrations of ozone are significantly higher than they are in other parts of the atmosphere, although even here the amounts are very small. This region of enhanced ozone concentration is called the **ozone layer.** Most of the absorption of ultraviolet radiation goes on in this layer, but it should not be thought of as anything analogous to a cloud bank in the sky.

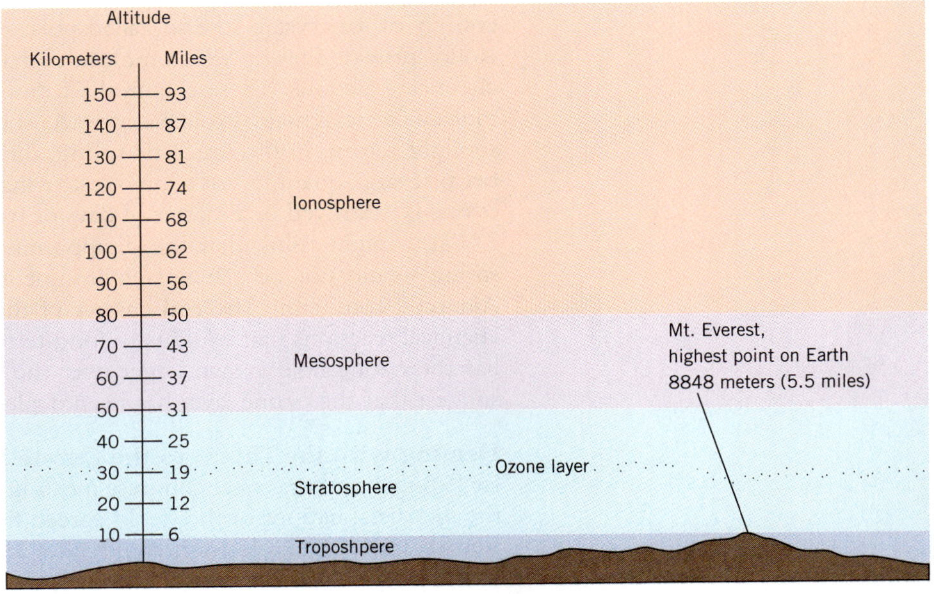

• **Figure 19-3** The ozone layer. Although ozone is found everywhere in the atmosphere, even at ground level, it is concentrated in a layer some 20 miles above Earth's surface. The labels on the left are the standard terms scientists use to describe different levels of the atmosphere.

The Ozone Hole

In 1985, British scientists working in Antarctica noticed that during the Antarctic spring (roughly the months of September through November) the amount of ozone in the ozone layer over Antarctica dropped significantly. Later studies from satellites and ground-based experiments confirmed these results. During this period of the year, the concentration of ozone falls by different amounts in different years. The region over the Antarctic where this phenomenon occurred was dubbed the **ozone hole** (see Figure 19-4). The ozone hole is not a place where the atmosphere has disappeared but a volume of the atmosphere in which the concentration of the trace gas ozone has declined significantly. Scientists became concerned about the appearance of the ozone hole, because the ozone layer worldwide is so vital to the existence of life on our planet.

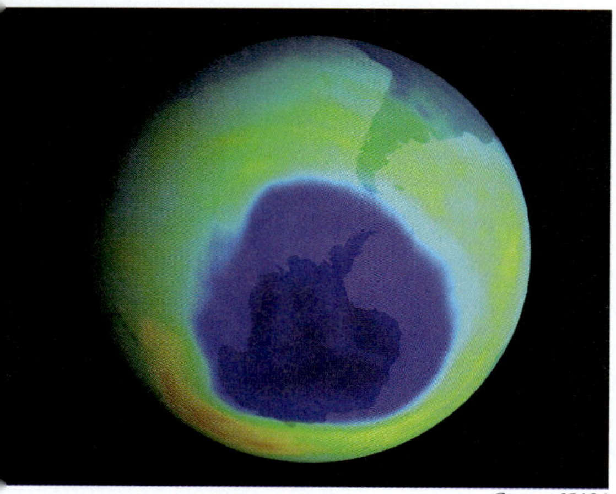

Courtesy NASA

• **Figure 19-4** The dark area marks a region of lower ozone concentration over Antarctica.

In the 1950s, scientists introduced a new class of chemicals, called *chlorofluorocarbons* or *CFCs,* that were a boon to industry. Chlorofluorocarbons are very stable and nontoxic gases; they last a long time and do not break down readily when they are released into the atmosphere. Inexpensive CFCs were ideal for increasingly popular aerosol spray products, and they were valued replacements for rather nasty chemicals such as ammonia that had been used in refrigerators and air-conditioners. Thus CFCs played a key role in the great air-conditioning boom that made the southern part of the United States comfortably habitable during the summer.

In the mid-1970s, before the ozone hole was discovered, a group of researchers realized that CFCs might cause destruction of ozone in the atmosphere. Once the annual appearance of the ozone hole was firmly established in the 1980s, concerns over the role of CFCs increased. In a classic example of the law of unintended consequences, seemingly benign CFCs turned out to present a very real danger to Earth's ozone layer. Over periods of time that range into the decades, molecules of CFCs work their way into the upper regions of the atmosphere, where they can be broken apart by high-energy ultraviolet radiation from the Sun. The chlorine atoms that are freed in this way act as a catalyst in a reaction that can be written as follows:

- **In words:** (ozone plus chlorine plus sunlight) become (ordinary oxygen plus chlorine)
- **In symbols:**

$$2O_3 + Cl + \text{sunlight} \rightarrow 3O_2 + Cl$$

Although this reaction proceeds very slowly, each chlorine atom liberated from a CFC can, over time, destroy millions of ozone molecules before it is safely locked into another chemical species in the atmosphere.

Over most of Earth's surface, the effect of the chlorine atoms is not striking because new ozone molecules are being created all the time. In the Antarctic, however, a number of unusual circumstances come together to create the ozone hole. For one thing, during the months immediately preceding the hole, no sunlight falls in the Antarctic region of Earth. This period of darkness leads to the appearance of high clouds made entirely of ice crystals, the so-called polar stratospheric clouds. Crystals of ice in these clouds provide sites on which molecules that contain chlorine atoms undergo a series of chemical reactions. These chemical reactions proceed up to the final step before ozone molecules are actually broken down. As soon as high energy in the form of ultraviolet sunlight returns in the Antarctic spring, the destruction of ozone proceeds very quickly because large quantities of ozone-destroying chlorine atoms are released all at once. The ozone is destroyed in a matter of days or weeks, and the ozone hole results.

You might think that the disappearance of the ozone shielding in the Antarctic spring would not be a major environmental problem. After all, life is sparse on the Antarctic continent. The real danger of the ozone hole, however, is that it points to chemical reactions that could have long-term effects on the entire ozone layer. Not only has the ozone hole grown larger over the past decade, but also recent measurements suggest that the ozone layer has been depleted by a few percent worldwide.

Dealing with the Threat to the Ozone Layer

In 1986, an international congress meeting in Montreal produced a treaty by which all the industrial nations of the world agreed first to limit, then to eliminate, their production of CFCs. This decision triggered a lot of activity in major chemical companies, where people started looking to find replacement substances. In 1992, the reduction of

CFCs was proceeding so quickly that the target date for elimination of most CFCs was set at 1996. Government mandates prohibited use of Freon in automobile air-conditioning systems by 1994 and called for its complete elimination by 1996. Current calculations suggest that these restrictions are having the desired effect and that the ozone layer will return to normal sometime early in the twenty-first century.

The ozone hole is an example of a serious environmental concern but one that has a relatively straightforward solution. Scientists have established the cause of the problem. The effects of the ozone hole, though serious, are not totally devastating to life on Earth, and the cost of solving the problem is relatively low. The problem of ozone depletion appears to be well on its way to being solved.

Acid Rain and Urban Air Pollution

Burning—the chemical reaction of oxidation—inevitably introduces chemical compounds into the atmosphere. For example, carbon dioxide and water vapor, the common products of hydrocarbon combustion (see Chapter 11), are always released. But burning produces three other significant sources of pollution: nitrogen oxides, sulfur compounds, and hydrocarbons.

1. *Nitrogen oxides.* Whenever the temperature of the air is raised above about 500°C, nitrogen in the air combines with oxygen to form what are called NO_x compounds (pronounced "nox"): nitrogen monoxide (NO), nitrogen dioxide (NO_2), and others. The "x" subscript indicates that these compounds contain different numbers of oxygen atoms.
2. *Sulfur compounds.* Petroleum- and coal-based fossil fuels usually contain small amounts of sulfur, either as a contaminant or as an integral part of their structure. The result is that chemical combinations of sulfur and oxygen, particularly sulfur dioxide (SO_2), are released into the atmosphere as well.
3. *Hydrocarbons.* The long-chain molecules that make up hydrocarbons are seldom burned perfectly in any real-world situation. As a result, a third class of pollutants, bits and pieces of unreacted hydrocarbon molecular chains, enters the atmosphere.

The Effects of Air Pollution and Acid Rain

The emission of NO_x compounds, sulfur dioxide, and hydrocarbons gives rise to a number of serious environmental problems. One of these, which has immediate consequences for urban residents, is **air pollution.** Sunlight hitting nitrogen compounds and hydrocarbons in the air triggers a set of chemical reactions that, in the end, produce ozone. And whereas ozone in the stratosphere is essential to life on Earth, ozone at ground level is a caustic, stinging gas that can cause extensive damage to the human respiratory system. This "bad ozone" is a major product of modern urban air pollution associated with photochemical *smog*—the brownish stuff that you often see over major cities during the summer.

Urban air pollution is a serious problem, but it can sometimes seem to be an immediate and transitory one. If the air quality in a city declines, then people can be alerted about it immediately as part of the weather forecast. Just like the weather, the intensity of air pollution varies on a daily basis, and it can change swiftly with the arrival of a thunderstorm or stiff winds.

However, long-term problems are associated with the presence of nitrogen and sulfur compounds in the air; these problems may not have an immediate effect on the place where the emissions occur. When these compounds are in the air, they interact with water, sunlight, and other atmospheric chemicals to form tiny droplets of nitric

A comparison of Los Angeles during a clear day (top) and on a smoggy day (bottom).

Corbis Digital Stock

PhotoDisc/Age Fotostock America, Inc.

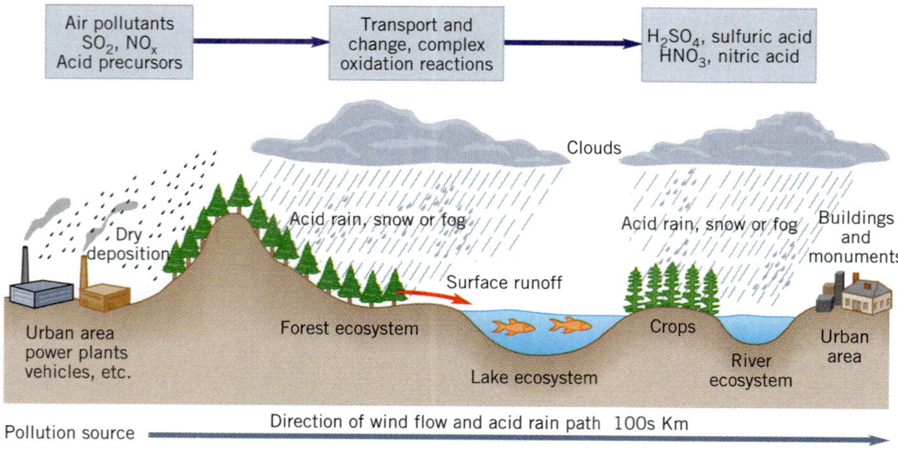

• **Figure 19-5** The formation of acid rain and its effect on ecosystems. Pollutants from urban and industrial areas can travel great distances, affecting lakes and forests hundreds of miles away.

and sulfuric acid. (The latter is the type of acid normally used in automobile batteries.) When it rains, these droplets of acid wash out and they become, in effect, a rain of dilute acid rather than water. This phenomenon is known as **acid rain** (Figure 19-5). (In fact, rain is normally slightly acid because carbon dioxide dissolves in raindrops to make a weak solution of carbonic acid. The term ***acid rain*** refers to the considerable extra acidity produced by human activities.)

You can see one effect of this sort of acid rain in cities. Many of the great historical monuments in European cities, for example, are made from limestone, which is particularly susceptible to the effect of acid. Over the years, the acid rain simply dissolves the fabric of the building (Figure 19-6).

In the mid-twentieth century, the local effects of acid rain and other kinds of pollution in the United States were dealt with by the construction of tall smokestacks, particularly in the industrial parts of the Midwest. The effect was to put the pollutants high enough in the atmosphere to be taken away by the prevailing winds. But, in keeping with our dictum, "you can't throw anything away," that approach didn't really solve the problem. It merely displaced it. The nitrogen and sulfur compounds emitted in Midwestern smokestacks fell as acid rain on the forests of New England.

Acid rain may not be the only cause of damage to forests and lakes. Other agents, such as local climate changes, may be responsible in some cases. As in other ecosystems, scientists cannot be sure of every cause and effect. Nevertheless, in a society that is more and more concerned with preserving nature, the added stress on forests and lakes due to acid rain receives a great deal of attention.

Dealing with Acid Rain

The response of governments to urban air pollution has centered on reducing the levels of emissions associated with the burning of fossil fuels. In California, for example, strict new regulations on average automobile emissions are encouraging the production

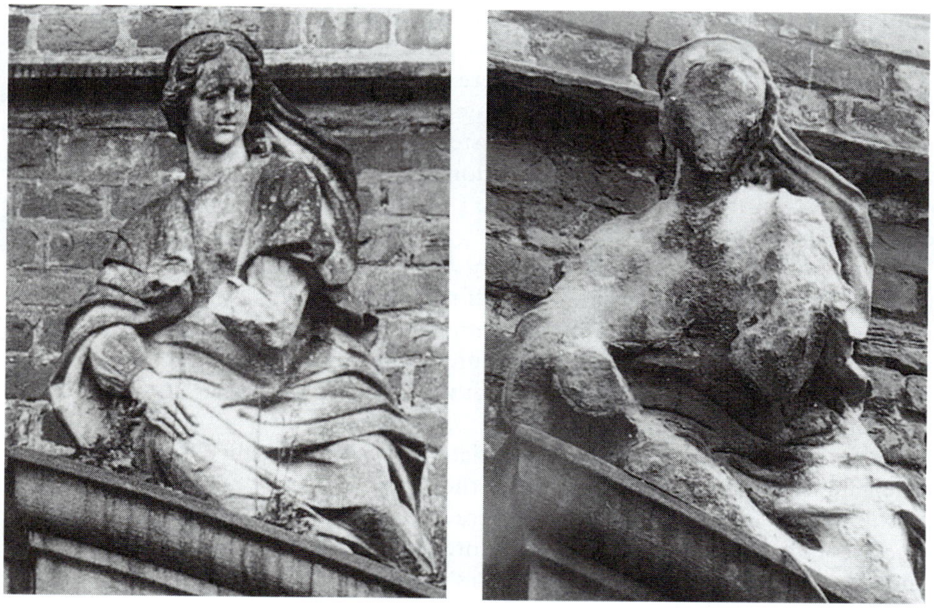

Courtesy Westfalisches Amt fur Denkmalpflege

• **Figure 19-6** The effects of acid rain. Over a period of 60 years, this sandstone statue on a castle in Germany has been completely destroyed.

of hybrid gasoline/electric cars (see Chapter 3). Because of the size of the California automobile market, it is expected that this requirement will lead to the rapid development and reduced cost of hybrid cars nationwide. In addition, in many states large facilities such as power plants, which emit huge amounts of pollutants, are required to use coal with low sulfur content or to install complex engineering devices known as scrubbers, whose job it is to remove the sulfur compounds from the smokestack before they become part of the atmosphere.

Acid rain and air pollution are examples of moderate environmental problems. We understand in a general way what the problems are, what at least some of the consequences of pollution are, and what has to be done to prevent the pollution. The costs of dealing with these problems, however, are considerably higher than the costs of reversing the depletion of the ozone layer. Political and economic questions become very important. How much are we willing to pay for clean air? This is not an easy question, nor is it a question answerable by science alone.

The Greenhouse Effect

The temperature at Earth's surface is determined primarily by the extent to which gases in the atmosphere absorb outgoing infrared radiation (see Chapter 6). The atmosphere is largely transparent to the Sun's incoming visible and ultraviolet radiation that warms the surface, but it is somewhat opaque to the infrared (heat) energy that radiates out into space (Figure 19-7). If it were not for the trapping of heat by the atmosphere, the average temperature of Earth's surface (i.e., the average day–night, winter–summer temperature) would be about –20°C. Thus, like a greenhouse, the atmosphere raises Earth's temperature from an inhospitable –20°C to its present more temperate temperature distribution. This natural temperature increase associated with atmospheric trapping of heat is the so-called **greenhouse effect.**

In today's news, "greenhouse effect" usually refers to possible increases in global temperatures—both a change in average global temperature and a change in the tem-

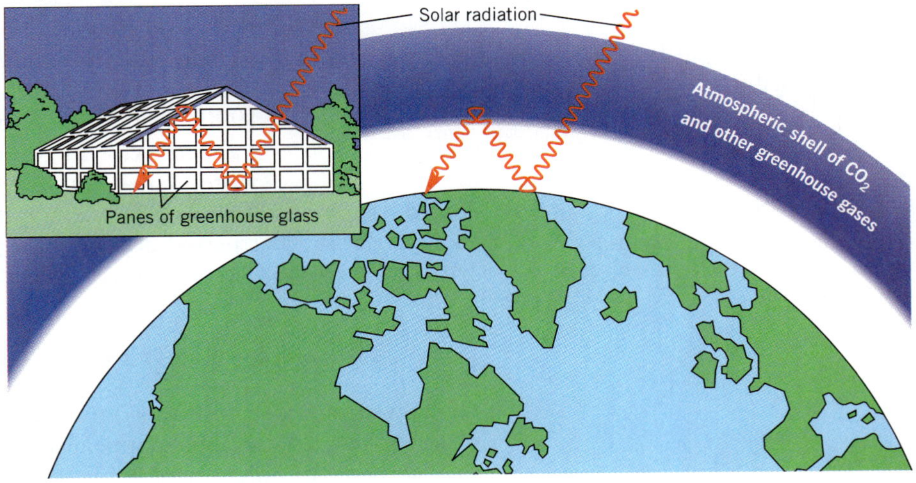

• **Figure 19-7** The greenhouse effect. Just as the Sun's energy passes through the glass of a greenhouse and becomes trapped inside as heat, the atmosphere acts as a greenhouse to warm up Earth's surface.

Smokestacks equipped with an electrostatic precipitator create an electric field that attracts ash and soot and collects them before they can pollute the atmosphere *(a)*. When the precipitator is turned off *(b)*, thick clouds rise from the stacks.

(a)

(b)

Courtesy Environmental Elements Corp.

perature contrast between equator and poles. Three points of general agreement frame debates about global warming.

1. All scientists agree that carbon dioxide absorbs infrared radiation and acts as a greenhouse gas. Our neighboring planet, Venus, which has a thick carbon dioxide atmosphere and surface temperature exceeding 400°C (see Chapter 16), demonstrates this effect most dramatically. In fact, many atmospheric gases contribute to Earth's less severe greenhouse effect and CO_2 accounts for only about 10% of the total infrared absorption. Water vapor, especially in clouds, is the dominant greenhouse gas, while the trace gases methane and CFCs, which make up less than a few millionths of the atmosphere, are molecule-for-molecule the most efficient infrared absorbers.
2. All scientists agree that the burning of fossil fuels by human beings has increased the amount of carbon dioxide in Earth's atmosphere. This dramatic trend is illustrated in Figure 19-8, which is a graph of the amount of carbon dioxide in Earth's atmosphere as measured at a high mountaintop observatory in Hawaii during the past several decades. The small wiggles in the graph correspond to annual cycles by which carbon dioxide is taken into leaves in the spring and then returned to the atmosphere in the fall.
3. And scientists agree that the average global temperature has increased significantly during the past several decades, with the 1990s being the warmest decade on record and 20 of the 25 warmest years in recorded history occurring since 1980. Furthermore, 2004 and 2005 were among the four warmest years on record—at least a full degree warmer than the 30-year average. Several individual months during that period also set historic records, so there can be little doubt that Earth has become warmer in recent years.

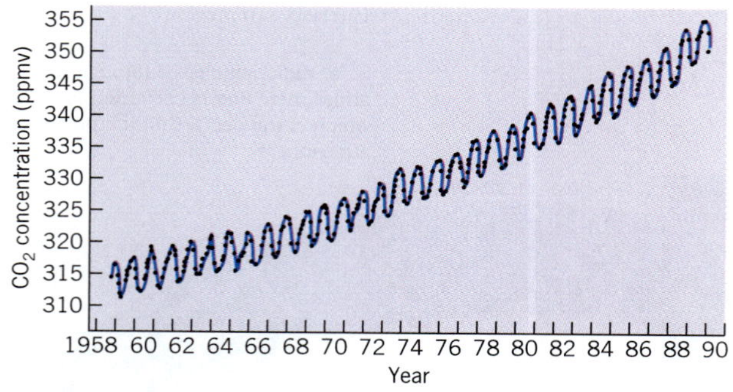

• **Figure 19-8** Measurements of atmospheric CO_2 concentrations reveal an annual cycle, as well as a gradual increase.

Debates About Global Climate Change

Global warming debates focus on whether increased CO_2 is entirely responsible for the observed increase in global temperature. The reasons for these uncertainties stem from the fact that our only way of predicting the behavior of Earth's atmosphere is through global circulation models (see Chapter 17). These models, which break the atmosphere into unrealistic uniform chunks several hundred kilometers on a side, are at best imperfect ways of predicting changes in climate. For example, such a coarse-grained look at the atmosphere cannot possibly hope to deal with effects of clouds that typically are only a few miles on a side. Clouds reflect more incident sunlight into space and thus play a critical role in climate. If the effect of increased carbon dioxide is to increase atmospheric temperature slightly, one consequence might be increased evaporation of water from the ocean and, hence, increased formation of clouds and rainfall on some parts of the globe. Thus, some scientists argue, the clouds produce an automatic feedback that counteracts some of the effects of carbon dioxide.

The world's oceans are another important effect that is difficult to incorporate in global circulation models. A constant interplay takes place between water and atmosphere at an ocean's surface, and carbon dioxide moves into and out of the oceans all the time. In fact, the amount of carbon dioxide locked in the oceans and their sediments is much greater than that stored in the atmosphere. Even small changes in the way that oceans interact with atmospheric carbon dioxide can thus have huge effects on the world's climate. In addition, as we saw in Chapter 17, ocean currents are instrumental in spreading heat around Earth's surface. Small changes in those currents could have enormous effects on Earth's climate, causing some regions to become warmer, while other regions experience a lowering of average temperatures.

It's also conceivable that at least some of the recent observed temperature rise might be due to a relatively short-term increase in solar energy output. Such solar variations

Archivo Iconografico S.A./Corbis Images

During a period known as the "Little Ice Age" Earth's temperature was lower than it is now, and canals like this one in Holland froze over all winter.

have occurred in the recent past, for example, during a short period of global cooling—the "Little Ice Age" from about 1645 to 1715. During that interval the Sun is estimated to have been about 1% cooler, so it's essential to get better and longer-term measurements of the Sun's energy output.

It has become standard practice in the climate change debate to make all calculations and predictions about Earth's temperature for the case in which atmospheric carbon dioxide doubles. A group called the Intergovernmental Panel on Climate Change (IPCC) relies on the participation of thousands of scientists around the world and issues reports every five years Their most recent report suggests that Earth's temperature will increase between 2°C and 6°C over the next century, with a "best guess" of about 4°C.

The range of possible consequences of greenhouse warming in North America is also the subject of debate. As a general rule, for every 0.5°C of greenhouse warming, a global line of a given temperature will move about 100 miles northward. Thus, for 2°C warming, temperatures in Washington, D.C., will become comparable to those in Atlanta, and temperatures in Minneapolis will be comparable to those in St. Louis. The effects on Earth's biosphere and ecosystems might be large or small depending on the magnitude and rate of warming. The total warming in the Northern Hemisphere after the last ice age, for example, was about 5°C and took place over a period of several thousand years. We know from studies of pollen deposited in the bottom of lakes that this warming, though large, was sufficiently gradual that plant populations were able to adapt and migrate north with the retreat of the glaciers. More recently, studies of the northern Atlantic Ocean have indicated that there have been periods in which the temperature in that region has changed by 5°C over a much shorter period, perhaps as little as a few decades. No known ecological disasters appear to be associated with these events. The predictions of consequences of greenhouse warming, should it occur, thus are also surrounded with a great deal of uncertainty.

Whatever the consequences, a growing international consensus holds that global warming is real and should be a matter of concern. One of the first strong international statements was produced in 1995 following a gathering of 1000 experts from around the world. In a report produced by the United Nations Intergovernmental Panel on Climate Change, they endorsed the conclusion that warming is occurring. These studies led to a proposed international agreement on the reduction of carbon dioxide emissions called the Kyoto Protocol. You may have read about the U.S. refusal to sign that accord—a complex political issue that's confused by controversial ways of calculating each country's net contribution of greenhouse gases to the environment.

From the point of view of government policy, the central question remains: What will be the social and economic consequences? Unfortunately, it is extraordinarily difficult to answer this question with the scientific knowledge we now have. Global warming could cause dramatic changes in coastal flooding, agricultural production, distribution of infectious diseases, rainfall, number and intensity of hurricanes, and other factors that influence the well-being of societies. But how much will it cost in social and economic terms to wean ourselves from fossil fuels? Any effort to reduce drastically the consumption of fossil fuels will cost consumers money, and they might require significant changes in lifestyles as well. Just think about all the ways we use carbon-based fuels. They're the basic energy source for automobiles, jet planes, ships, and most of our electric power plants. Thus, finding ways out of this dilemma is not easy.

The Ongoing Process of Science •

Dealing with the Greenhouse Effect

The greenhouse effect may be both the most difficult and the most potentially alarming of the many environmental problems that face the global ecosystem. On the one hand, it is the most difficult to model because the effect of adding carbon dioxide to the atmosphere is uncertain, and the cost of doing something about it is very high. The idea that you can take the world economy, which runs almost entirely on fossil fuels, and change it over to other sources of energy in a very short period of time is unrealistic. In the past, it has taken many decades to make similar changes in a society's energy use and consumption. Figure 19-9, for example, shows the transitions from wood to coal and from coal to oil and gas in the U.S. economy. As you can see, it takes 30 to 50 years for a new fuel to work its way into the economy. If the more disastrous predictions of greenhouse warming are true, in about 50 years the warming will already have occurred, and it will be too late to do anything about it.

In addition, the best scientific estimates now indicate that if warming occurs, it will not cause severe environmental changes for several decades, far beyond the planning horizon of corporations, governments, and other major institutions in any society. The question comes down to something like this: Are you willing to change your driving habits now because a possibility exists that global warming will adversely affect the lifestyles of your grandchildren? Human beings find it difficult to suffer real hardship in the present to prevent an uncertain event from happening in the future. •

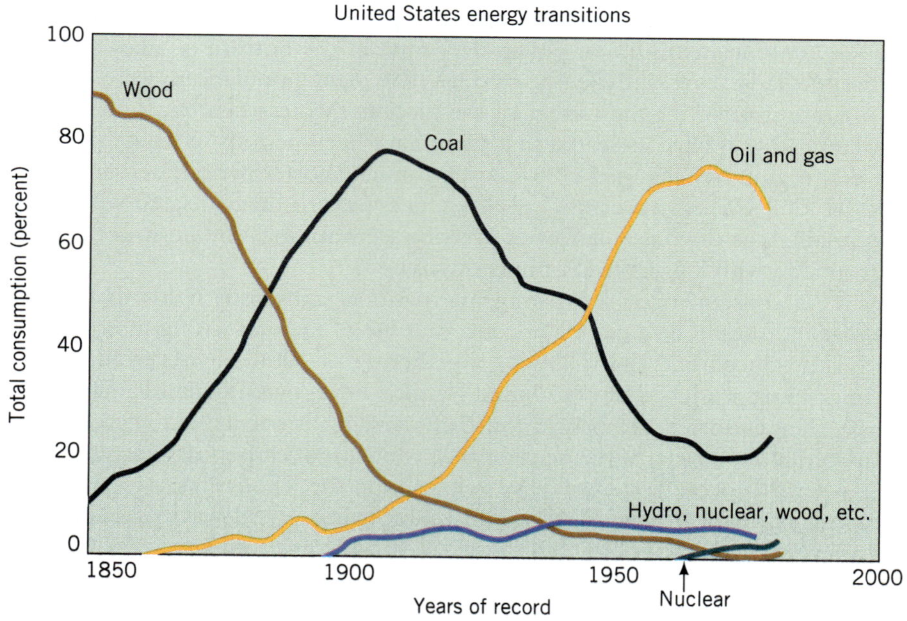

• **Figure 19-9** U.S. energy transitions. In the past, it has taken 30 to 50 years to make the transition from one type of fuel to another. We could expect a transition to solar energy (as an example) to take about this long.

Science News | Global Warming May Already be a Killer

(Science News, Feb. 18, 2006, p. 109)

Ecosystems are dynamic things, and when the environment in which they find themselves changes, the ecosystems change too. In some cases, this means that species of plants or animals that had been part of the ecosystem in the past must either move elsewhere or go extinct. The current warming trend on our planet is changing the environment in many ecosystems worldwide, and scientists are starting to document the resulting changes. In some cases, it is possible not only to document these changes, but to gain some insight into the exact mechanism by which they occur.

It has been known for some time that amphibians, and particularly frogs, are among the species most sensitive to climate change. Now, scientists in Costa Rica have proposed a detailed mechanism for the disappearance of tropical frogs in areas that had, up to this time, been considered pristine preserves.

For some time, scientists have known that a particular fungus, called *Batrachozchytrium dendrobatidis,* had been found in the remains of dead frogs in the Costa Rican cloud forests. The team analyzed records of air and sea surface temperatures and compared it to data on frog disappearances. They reasoned that during periods of warmth, more clouds would form over the mountaintops where the frogs live, a fact that would make the days somewhat cooler and the nights somewhat warmer. Thus, warmer periods would correspond to mountaintop temperatures that remained within the narrow band that the fungus needs for optimal growth. The hypothesis: during warm periods, the fungus flourishes and, as a consequence, infects more frogs.

Of course, finding a correlation between two phenomena—the growth of the fungus and the death of the frogs in this case—does not establish causality. Like all scientific hypotheses, the idea that the growth of the fungus caused the death of the frogs will have to be tested by future research. It could be, however, that in this particular case, we may be coming close to understanding the exact mechanism behind the looming extinction of these particular species of frogs. Whether similar mechanisms can be found to explain the decline of other species in other ecosystems remains to be seen.

Thinking More About | Global Warming

How Certain Do You Have to Be?

As we've seen, the problem of global warming is a complex one. Uncertainties remain about what the effects of the continued use of fossil fuels will be, and whatever those effects are, they are unlikely to be made manifest for decades. Nevertheless, decisions will be made over the next decade that will, at least potentially, have enormous consequences for future generations. In this situation, even doing nothing—pursuing business as usual—is a decision.

On the one hand, if the lower-level predictions of the GCM turn out to be correct—if Earth warms only a degree or so—the consequences will be relatively mild, and it would probably make sense not to take drastic measures to curtail greenhouse gases. On the other hand, if the higher-end predictions turn out to be true, the consequences could be severe and far reaching, and include effects like increased droughts in many areas of the world and the flooding of low-lying coastal areas.

The problem, of course, is that we have to act now, and incur real costs, to prevent something that will happen far in the future. How much sacrifice should people be willing to make today to reduce risks in the future? What sorts of sacrifices are you willing to make? Would you give up driving your car a couple of days a week? Would you buy a lower-performing but more efficient vehicle, or lower the thermostat in your house during the winter? Would you pay more for heating and electricity?

On the other hand, are you willing to ignore the risks of global climate change and rising sea levels? Unfortunately, this is a problem for which there are no easy answers.

Summary

Ecology is the branch of science that studies interdependent groups of living things, called *ecosystems.* Each ecosystem is characterized by its physical *environment* and its community of living organisms. In every ecosystem many different organisms, each competing for matter and energy, occupy their own *ecological niches.* Photosynthetic plants in the first trophic level use energy from the Sun; these plants provide the energy for animals in higher trophic levels. In this way, energy flows through an ecosystem. Matter, on the other hand, is constantly recycled as atoms are used over and over again.

While these principles seem simple, the actual behavior of ecosystems is extremely complex and unpredictable. It's virtually impossible to change one aspect of such a complex interdependent network without affecting something else, often inadvertently—a phenomenon often called the *law of unintended consequences.*

Human actions are causing changes in Earth's global environment—changes that may affect ecosystems. The use of chlorofluorocarbons (CFCs) during the past several decades, for example, is having a pronounced effect on ***ozone,*** a molecule of three oxygen atoms found as a trace gas in the ***ozone layer*** of the upper atmosphere. Ozone provides important protection on Earth from the Sun's harmful ultraviolet radiation, but chlorine atoms from CFCs hasten the breakdown of ozone molecules, thus creating a growing ***ozone hole.***

Burning coal and other fossil fuels releases sulfur and nitrogen compounds into the atmosphere—chemicals that contribute to ***air pollution*** and ***acid rain.*** Dealing with acid rain will require cleaning up emissions from automobiles and power-generating plants.

Carbon dioxide, a necessary product of all combustion of carbon-based fuels, adds to the atmosphere's store of infrared-absorbing gases and thus contributes to the ***greenhouse effect.*** At present, scientists are not able to predict the consequences of these global changes with much certainty.

Key Terms

ecology
ecosystem
environment
ecological niche
law of unintended consequences
ozone
ozone layer
ozone hole
air pollution
acid rain
greenhouse effect

Review Questions

1. Give an example of an ecosystem near your home.

2. What is an ecological niche? Give an example.

3. Describe six characteristics shared by all ecosystems.

4. What is a trophic level? In which trophic level are you?

5. What is bioconcentration? Which trophic levels are most affected?

6. State the law of unintended consequences. Give an example of the law in operation.

7. How does carbon cycle through Earth's ecosystem? What other elements undergo a similar kind of cycle?

8. How does energy move in ecosystems?

9. Why doesn't trash decompose in a modern landfill?

10. What is the ozone layer? Where is it located? Why is it important to life on Earth?

11. What is the ozone hole? How have governments responded to the discovery of the ozone hole?

12. Why is ozone in the stratosphere considered beneficial whereas ozone at ground level is not?

13. What is acid rain? What steps would have to be taken to solve the acid rain problem?

14. Why is the greenhouse effect a current area of scientific concern when Earth has had carbon dioxide, methane, and water vapor for several billion years?

15. Why are predictions of global warming so uncertain?

16. What steps would have to be taken to reduce the severity of the greenhouse effect?

Discussion Questions

1. Would you expect the number of species present on an island to depend on the size of the island or the number of available niches/habitats? Why or why not? Is size important?

2. What does it mean to state that "energy flows through an ecosystem? Does energy only "flow" through the living components of an ecosystem?

3. What environmental changes might result from a global warming of 2°C? What countries might be most affected? Will increased agricultural production, via longer growing seasons, offset rising oceans?

4. Do you think Wilson and Simberloff's experiment was ethical? Why or why not? Was there any other way to get this information?

5. One of the problems of understanding the workings of ecosystems is that it is not possible to hold everything constant and change only one variable. Why is this true? What effects might this have on the interpretation of observations or experiments?

6. How did you affect your environment today? How did it affect you?

7. What would the political, social, and economic consequences be in your community if serious steps were taken to reduce acid rain or air pollution?

8. Suppose that the United States decided today to undergo a conversion from fossil fuels to solar energy. How long do you think it would take to make a complete transition? What are some of the changes that would have to be made? Who would benefit, and who would be hurt by such a change?

9. Of what ecosystem is the squirrel on your lawn or the bird flying across your campus a part? Are there any threats to the well-being of that ecosystem?

10. Where do electric cars obtain their energy? Is it true that they do not generate pollution because they have batteries?

11. Suppose that scientists concluded that an appreciable fraction of any measured global warming was due to warming of the Sun or an increase in the amount of geothermal energy reaching the surface of Earth. What would the policy implications of such a finding be?

12. What are the nonliving components of an ecosystem or environment? How do the nonliving components limit the living components?

13. What is homeostasis? How does the law of unintended consequences relate to homeostasis in an ecosystem?

14. What is the most efficient greenhouse gas? What does cow flatulence have to do with global warming?

15. What is a micro-climate? How does the presence of micro-climates enhance an ecosyetem in terms of biodiversity?

Problems

1. If a global warming of 4°C takes place, what kind of weather might your town experience? [*Hint:* Find a town to the south of you that has that sort of weather now.]

2. If the average American produces 1000 cubic feet of compacted trash each year, how long would it take to fill Yankee Stadium with one person's trash? the Grand Caynon?

Investigations

1. Do commercial jet airliners fly through the ozone layer? What effects might this have?

2. How are solid wastes such as plastics handled in your community? Does that method represent a long-term or short-term solution to the problem? What other options are available to your community?

3. Write a short story chronicling the passage of a nitrogen or phosphorus atom through 10 different stages.

4. What is an environmental impact statement? Are there any projects in your area that have required environmental impact statements? Where should they be required?

5. Identify an environmental law or court ruling that has been enacted in the last year. What impact will this law have? Who benefits from the decision? Will anyone lose his or her job as a result?

6. What happens to your garbage? Is there a recycling program in your town? What materials can be recycled?

7. Read about the "pea-soup fogs" that used to plague London. What caused them? How many people could be killed in one?

8. When the space shuttle is launched, it punches a large hole in the ozone layer. Investigate how long that hole remains and determine if this is a cause for concern.

9. What chemicals are used in recycling paper? different types of plastics? Are the chemicals that are used in the recycling of various products more harmful to the environment than the original waste material? What happens to these chemicals?

10. What is a "superfund" site? How many of these sites are the remains of industrial reclamation and recycling centers?

11. What is the Kyoto Protocol? How does it affect a country like China or India compared to the United States?

12. Watch the film *Darwin's Nightmare*. How does the law of unintended consequences come into play?

20
Strategies of Life

What is life?

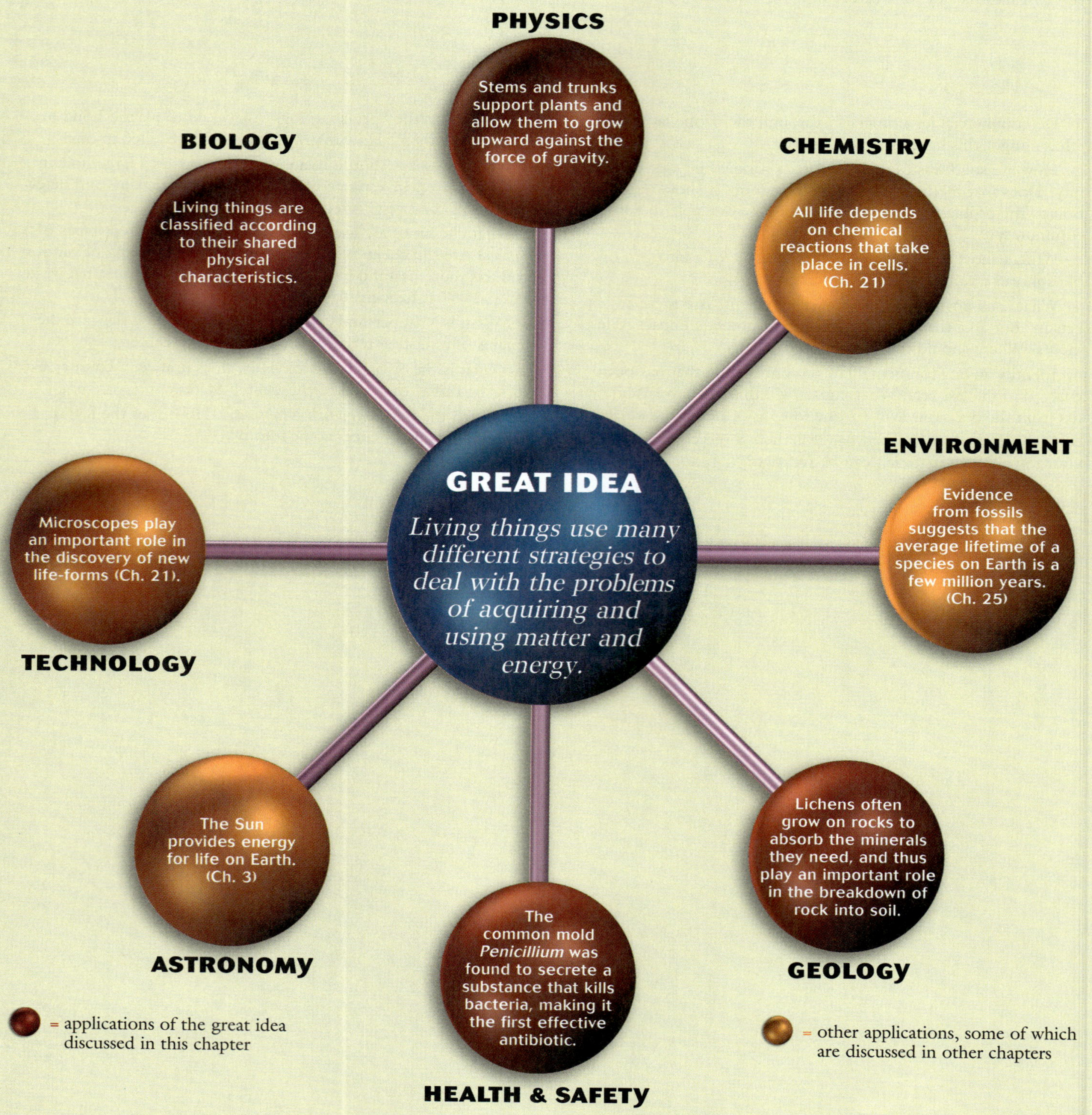

Science Through the Day | The Diversity of Life

Look at how many different living objects you can find at the beach. You've already seen birds, seaweed, crustaceans, a variety of shells, and a crab near the water's edge. Higher up the beach you notice an abundance of dune grasses and small weeds, along with countless flies, ants, and other insects. A rocky tidal pool holds starfish, sea urchins, and myriad tiny swimming creatures. Schools of fish roil the surface of the water close to shore, while a few jellyfish (fortunately not the stinging kind) also inhabit the shallow water. You even remember seeing a majestic whale spouting far offshore during an earlier trip to this very beach.

There's not a place on Earth's surface where you won't find living things. The frigid Arctic seas teem with life, while the frozen wastes of Antarctica yield up hardy lichens and single-celled organisms. Living things may be found in the deepest, darkest parts of the ocean and in the most dry and forbidding deserts. In fact, you could argue that what makes Earth different from every other place we know in the solar system (and perhaps even every other place in the galaxy) is the existence of varied and abundant life.

David Nunuk/Photo Researchers

The Organization of Living Things

Biology is the branch of science devoted to the study of living things, by far the most complex systems that scientists study. Every single cell is astonishingly complex—vastly more intricate than the most advanced machines—and each human being contains tens of trillions of cells. Yet, despite this complexity, living things operate according to the same laws of nature as everything else we've studied. The laws of motion, energy conservation, the laws of electricity and magnetism, and the chemical bonding of atoms, for example, all operate in and govern the behavior of all living things. We have underscored this point by using examples from biology to illustrate all of the preceding chapters.

Ways of Thinking About Living Things

An ant provides a useful way to begin thinking about the study of living things. We can study the ant in many ways. We can, for example, examine it as an individual organism, in which case we ask questions such as "How big is it?" "How much food does it consume?" "Where does it get its energy?" We could take a more reductionist or microscopic view and consider the individual ant as a collection of specialized organs. In this case we might ask about how the ant moves oxygen from the air to its cells, or how its hard outer covering protects it and supports its weight. Penetrating still deeper, we could look at the ant as a collection of cells and ask how a single one of those cells operates. Questions such as "How does this cell carry out its chemical functions?" and "What are the pieces from

David Maitland/Getty Images, Inc.

L. West/Photo Researchers

Hans Christian Heap/Getty Images, Inc.

An ant can be studied at many scales, from individual microscopic molecules and cells to the structure of individual organs and appendages, to the behavior of a solitary ant, to the complex interactions of an ant colony.

which this cell is made?" would then be appropriate. Finally, we could look inside the cell and think about its ultimate constituents—the atoms and molecules that combine and react chemically to make the cell what it is. Here we would ask, "What are the molecules that operate in a cell?" and "How do they interact as chemicals?"

We could also choose to look at the big picture. Instead of probing ever-smaller parts of the ant, we could choose to view the ant as part of larger and larger structures. The single ant, for example, is part of the social organization of an ant colony, which in turn forms part of an ecosystem of living and nonliving things—a sand dune or a field or a patch of forest. This small community, in turn, represents part of the great global system that encompasses all living things on the planet.

Learning about a single living thing such as an ant thus can take place on many levels. Different branches of biology deal with these levels, which we will discuss in the following chapters. The important point to remember, however, is that all of these ways of viewing the ant are important. Each approach complements, and is complemented by, the others.

In spite of this range of approaches, a profound change has occurred in the life sciences during the last half of the twentieth century. Traditional biology concerned itself largely with discovering, understanding, and cataloging organisms and their interactions. Beginning in the nineteenth century, however, chemists began increasingly to study the cells and molecules found in living systems. This work culminated in the 1950s, when scientists discovered the singular role played by the molecule deoxyribonucleic acid (DNA) in determining what traits living organisms inherit from their parents (see Chapter 23). This discovery opened up an entire new world in the life sciences. As a result, during the past few decades the study of living things has undergone a fundamental realignment. Today the great majority of biologists are studying living systems at the level of molecules rather than at the level of the organism. Why this should be so will become clear in the following chapters.

What Is Life?

We all have a sense of what it means to be alive. We recognize some living things by their use of energy to grow and repair themselves, their response to external stimuli, and their ability to reproduce. But the more we learn about the world around us, the harder it becomes to provide a precise definition of life. Some objects, such as the mule, are clearly alive but are unable to reproduce. Certain seeds may lie dormant for centuries without any sign of life, but then suddenly awaken. Furthermore, as technology advances, machines take on more and more of the qualities we usually associate with life. As a result of these sorts of problems, most scientists prefer not to try to define what life is in the abstract, but rather to describe the collective properties of living systems at some level, as we will do.

Other medical, legal, and ethical questions relating to the definition of life concern when life begins and when it ends. How should our society define human life? Is it possible that we could develop machines that are in some way alive? These are ethical questions that must take scientific knowledge into account, but their ultimate answers lie outside the realm of scientific inquiry.

The Characteristics of Life

The diversity of living things is truly staggering. You have only to think of whales, palm trees, mold, and mosquitoes to recognize this fact. Yet biologists have found that beneath this diversity many characteristics link all life together. In fact, the general principles that govern all living things will occupy us for most of the rest of this book. We list them here, however, to make the point that, despite their seeming diversity, living things are really not that different from one another.

1. *All living things maintain a high degree of order and complexity.* Objects can be ranked according to their *complexity*, which is related to the number of different parts that are organized to make the whole. In this sense, a jet airplane is more complex than a wristwatch, which is more complex than a pencil. Even the simplest living thing is vastly more complex than any object ever constructed by humans.
2. *All living things are part of larger systems of matter and energy.* Living things and their surroundings form complex ecosystems (see Chapter 19). Matter continuously recycles in a given system, while energy flows through it. All organisms need energy to continue living. Plants use photosynthesis, by which the Sun's radiant energy is used to produce energy-rich molecules from water and carbon dioxide. Animals and fungi, on the other hand, obtain energy-rich molecules from plants and other animals.
3. *All life depends on chemical reactions that take place in cells.* As we shall see in Chapters 21 and 22, most living things share a basic set of molecular building blocks and chemical reactions. By the same token, specific chemical reactions are what make one living thing different from

Stephen Dalton/Photo Researchers

The chameleon gets its energy like all animals—by eating other living things.

UNEP-Say Boon Foo/The Image Works

All organisms, from single-celled microbes to these complex hummingbirds, grow and develop.

another—what makes you different from a kumquat. Cells, the chemical factories of life, are the highly organized building blocks of life. Many organisms such as bacteria and blue-green algae are single-celled, whereas larger organisms such as human beings may incorporate trillions of interdependent cells.

4. *All life requires liquid water.* Liquid water possesses several unusual properties, including its ability as a solvent (see Chapter 10) and its high heat capacity (see Chapter 4), which make it an essential medium in the cells of all living things.
5. *Organisms grow and develop.* All organisms change in form and function at different stages in their lifetimes. In this chapter we will survey some of the varied ways that organisms accomplish these changes.
6. *Living things regulate their use of energy and respond to their environments.* During periods of extreme cold or dryness, for example, many plants will lie dormant and animals will become sluggish. During warmer or wetter periods, on the other hand, plants may flower and animals may enter their reproductive cycle. You experience this kind of change all the time. When your body temperature increases significantly, you sweat, and heat is removed from the body as the sweat evaporates from your skin. When you get cold, you shiver and the extra heat generated by your muscles warms you up.
7. *All living things share the same genetic code, which is passed from parent to offspring by reproduction.* The chemical reactions in a cell are governed by a code written in the language of the molecule DNA (see Chapter 23). Just as all books in English are written with the same alphabet, so too the heredity information that passes traits from parents to offspring uses a single genetic language. Sometimes the process of reproduction can be as simple as the splitting of a single cell into two offspring, and other times as complex as human sexual reproduction. In all cases, though, life consists of a chain of parents and offspring moving through time.
8. *All living things are descended from a common ancestor.* In Chapter 25 we will review the long chain of evidence that led Charles Darwin and others to recognize the evolution of life. We will see that the many similarities among living things arise from their common ancestry.

Science in the Making •

Measuring Plant Growth

We can see the similarity between biology and the other sciences by looking at how the scientific method was used to answer an old question. All animals derive their nourishment from the food they eat, but where do plants get theirs? Throughout most of recorded history, people thought that plant nourishment must come from the soil—that plants "eat" soil in the same way that animals eat meat or fruit.

Jan Baptiste Van Helmont (1579–1644), a Flemish physician and the discoverer of carbon dioxide, reported an experiment that changed this view. He planted a willow tree weighing five pounds in a pot containing 200 pounds of soil and watered it for five years as it grew. At the end of that time, he weighed the tree and found that its weight had increased to 169 pounds while the amount of soil in the pot had decreased by at most a few ounces. He concluded that all the material used to construct the fabric of the willow tree came from the water.

Subsequent experiments showed that he was wrong; much of the tissue in plants comes from carbon dioxide in the air. The point of the Van Helmont story, however, is that in science a good quantitative experiment, even one with an incorrect conclusion, can clear the way for progress. In this case, Van Helmont's proof that plants did not take their fabric from the soil led eventually to our present understanding of the role of plants in removing carbon dioxide from the atmosphere and producing oxygen. •

Classifying Living Things

In Chapter 1 we saw that science begins with observation. People must start their exploration of a new area by looking to see what's there. Astronomers watched the skies for thousands of years and named many celestial objects before Newton could explain the motion of the solar system. Alchemists mixed chemicals and observed countless chemical reactions long before modern ideas of the atom or chemical bonding were developed. Similarly, humans spent thousands of years observing and naming living things before they could begin to recognize order in the variety of organisms they encountered. **Taxonomy,** the field devoted to cataloging living things, describing them, and giving them names, plays a central role in science, because our search for patterns in the universe depends on recognizing similarities and differences.

Classification provides us with more than just a way of describing our world. It helps us fit new objects and phenomena into an existing framework. Classification enables a biologist who finds a new organism to group it with similar organisms and thereby to make a number of intelligent conjectures about that organism—about its diet, for example, or its mating habits. The same holds true of classification schemes for nonliving objects. Astronomers who classify stars, for example, know by systematic comparisons that a Sun-like star will have a lifetime of about 10 billion years and will eventually become a white dwarf (Chapter 15).

Cataloging Life

Biologists, confronted by the amazing variety of living things, realized that they had to find some systematic way of cataloging life's diversity. Indeed, the earliest attempts to classify life must extend back to the origins of language itself. In ancient times, the Greek philosopher Aristotle (384–322 B.C.) tackled this problem in his extensive biological writings. He noted, for example, that whales and dolphins, though fish-like, are actually mammals.

The most successful attempt to devise a systematic classification scheme was begun by Swedish naturalist Carolus Linnaeus (1707–1778). His work was based on observation. When you look at living things, it becomes obvious that some characteristics are shared while others are not. A human being, for example, is more like a squirrel than like a blade of grass; a sparrow is more like a fish than like algae in a pond. The purpose of the **Linnaean classification** was to group all living things according to their shared characteristics so that each organism is as close as possible to those other organisms that it resembles and as far as possible from those it does not (Figure 20-1).

The basic unit of the classification scheme is the **species,** which we define today as an interbreeding population of individual organisms that produces fertile offspring. Linnaeus, who worked at a time when European scientific institutions were being flooded with new types of plants from around the world, realized that simply describing species would not be enough. Instead, he introduced a system in which all species can be placed into a *hierarchy*—a sequence of categories that places all species into a larger framework based on similarities and differences among organisms.

Linnaeus's original goal was to organize the entire structure of nature, and to this end he published classification schemes for three "kingdoms" of plants, animals, and minerals. As you might expect in the first attempt to achieve such an ambitious goal, there were some errors in his work. (For example, he mistakenly classified the rhinoc-

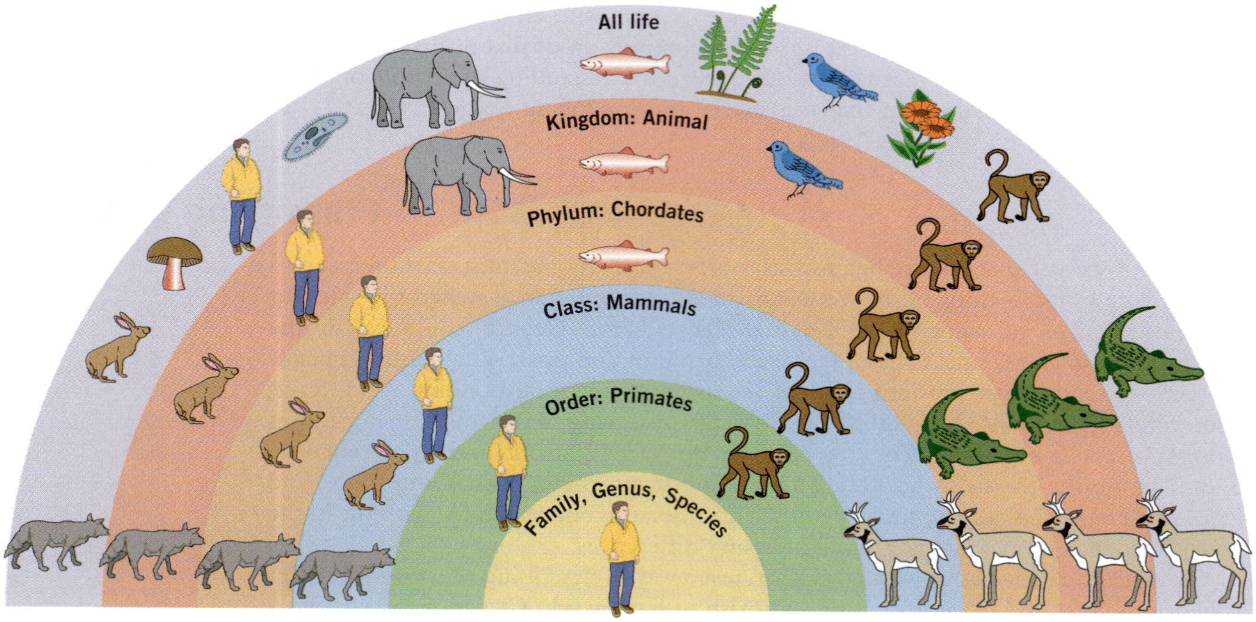

• **Figure 20-1** The Linnaean classification scheme recognizes the relationship of each living thing to every other. We can arrange species into groups that are more and more closely related. Although human beings are not treated differently from other organisms in this classification system, we are naturally more familiar with our own species than with any other.

eros as a rodent.) But Linnaeus's work showed that it is possible to define relationships among different species.

The task of classifying living things is something like the problem of pinpointing one particular building in the entire world—a problem you face every time you mail a letter. You might start by specifying the continent on which the building stands, then the country, then the state or province, the town, the street, and finally the street number. Each step in this list of designations represents a separation, a splitting off. Houses on different continents are more distant than those on the same continent, houses in different towns more distant than those in the same town, and so on. Eventually, you get to an exact designation—a street address in a given town—that specifies the building uniquely.

The modern biological classification scheme uses the same kind of hierarchical scheme, with narrower and narrower divisions. However, instead of political and geographical distinctions such as city or country, the Linnaean scheme uses divisions based on the biological similarities of different species—similarities that point to common evolutionary pathways (see Chapter 25).

The main categories that biologists use, going from broadest to narrowest, are *kingdom, phylum, class, order, family, genus,* and *species.* (A useful mnemonic to help you remember this sequence is the sentence "King Phillip Came Over For Good Spaghetti.") As the number of known species has grown to more than a million, additional divisions such as suborder (a subdivision of an order) and superfamily (a few closely related families) have been added to the Linnaean scheme. You can think of this classification as being represented by a series of ever-smaller circles, with the specifications of kingdom, phylum, class, order, family, genus, and species serving to guide you to ever-smaller groupings. At the end, you come to a single kind of organism sitting in a circle all its own. Each step in this narrowing process involves a judgment about which organisms are like each other and which organisms are not.

This narrowing leads ultimately to the familiar two-part scientific names of organisms. When you go to a zoo or read a biology textbook, you will probably notice that

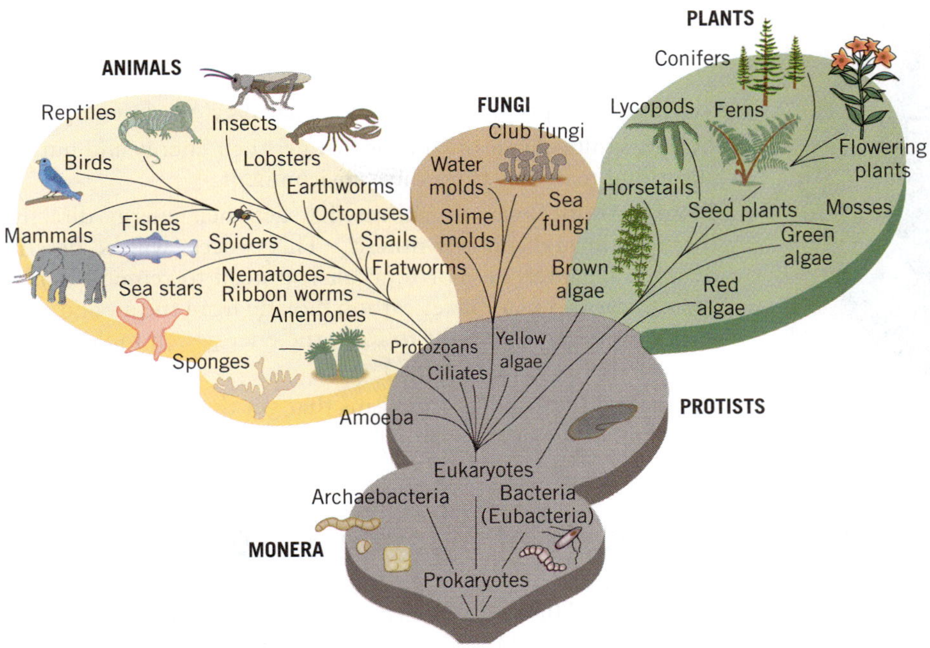

• **Figure 20-2** The five kingdoms of the biological classification system are illustrated by this diagram, which also suggests the progression from simple monera to more complex life-forms.

the scientific names of plants and animals are given in terms of two Latin words—*Homo sapiens* or *Tyrannosaurus rex,* for example—that indicate the genus and species. (By convention, the two words are italicized and the genus is capitalized.) This *binomial nomenclature* is an important legacy of Linnaeus's work.

Biologists have traditionally considered the **kingdom** to be the broadest classification, corresponding to the coarsest division of living things. Until the 1960s, most biologists recognized only two kingdoms—plants and animals. In subsequent decades most biologists classified living things into five kingdoms (Figure 20-2), though, as we shall see, this view is also changing as new data come to light. In the five-kingdom scheme, two of the kingdoms consist primarily of single-celled organisms.

1. *Monera.* Single-celled organisms without an internal structure called the *cell nucleus* (see Chapter 21). Monera are the most primitive living things.
2. *Protista.* Mainly single-celled organisms with a cell nucleus, but also a few multicellular organisms that have a particularly simple structure.

Monera—single-celled organisms without a nucleus—come in a variety of shapes. These microscope photographs show bacteria in the shape of *(a)* spheres, *(b)* rods, and *(c)* spirals.

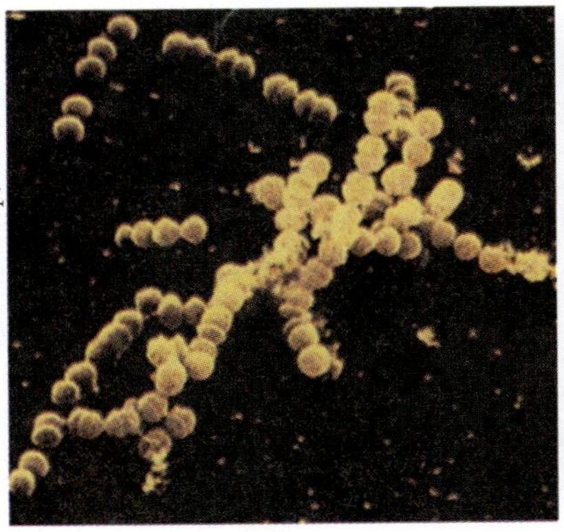
David M. Phillips/Visuals Unlimited

(a)

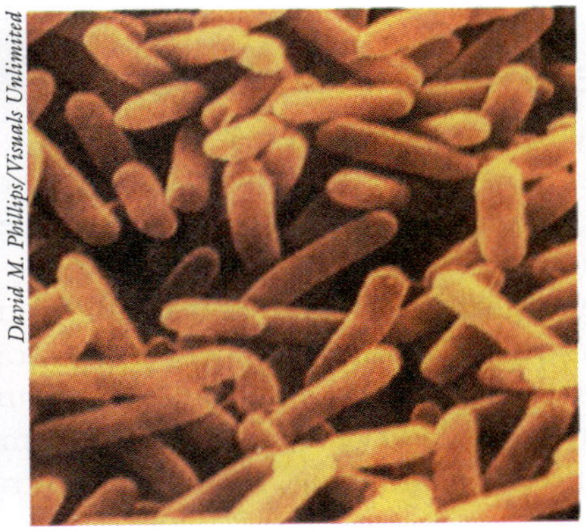
David M. Phillips/Visuals Unlimited

(b)

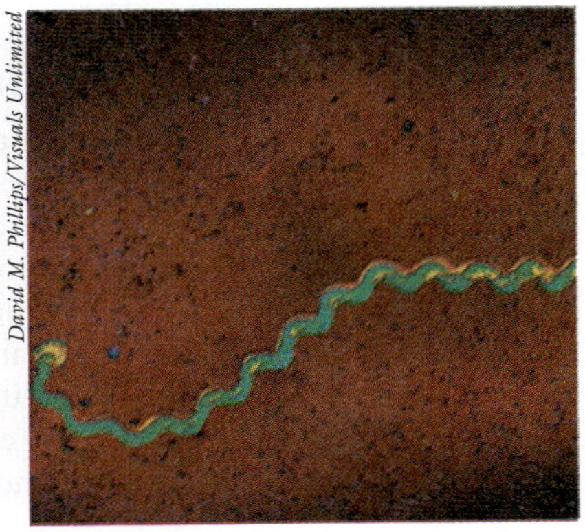
David M. Phillips/Visuals Unlimited

(c)

Eric Grave/Science Source/Photo Researchers

Some protista (single-celled organisms with a nucleus) develop beautiful microscopic shells. This shell of foraminifera houses amoeba-like cells.

The remaining three kingdoms in this classification scheme include *multicellular* organisms, in which several different kinds of interdependent cells combine in a single species. Members of these kingdoms are distinguished primarily by the way that they obtain energy.

3. **Fungi.** Multicellular organisms that get their energy and nutrients by absorbing materials from their environment.
4. **Plants.** Multicellular organisms that get their energy directly from the Sun through photosynthesis. (This process will be described in detail in Chapter 21. For now, all you need to remember is that in *photosynthesis,* a plant takes carbon dioxide from the air and combines it with water and sunlight to form the energy-rich molecules known as sugars, plus some oxygen.)
5. **Animals.** Multicellular organisms that get their energy and nutrients by eating other organisms.

The Ongoing Process of Science •

A Different Division of Life

In the late 1970s, University of Illinois biologist Carl Woese employed the techniques of molecular genetics (see Chapter 24) to discover a large group of extremely simple one-celled organisms that have dramatically altered our view of life's diversity. These microbes, collectively known as *Archaea,* often thrive in extreme environments, including acidic springs, arctic ice, deep-ocean hydrothermal vents, and in solid rock kilometers below the surface. Genetic studies reveal that these cells have remarkably distinctive and varied chemical processes that set them apart from all other cellular life. The profound differences reflected in the unique genetic makeup of *Archaea* led Woese to propose a dramatically new division of life into three distinct **domains** of life.

According to this new and now widely accepted view, *Archaea* and *Bacteria* are separate domains of single-celled life without nuclei (i.e., these domains split the old kingdom of monera in two). Even though these organisms can look quite similar to each other, they differ in many of their internal chemical mechanisms. The third domain in Woese's new scheme, *Eucaryea,* encompasses *all* life based on cells with nuclei, including the multicellular kingdoms of plants, animals, fungi, and the single-celled protista. This new three-domain classification scheme reflects the fact that fungi, plants, and animals are chemically and genetically extremely similar to each other, at least compared to *Archaea* and *Bacteria.* •

Stop and Think! Does it matter how many kingdoms or domains biologists recognize? How might the proposed change to three domains, two of which are microbes, affect our view of life on Earth?

Science by the Numbers •

How Many Species Are There?

Biologists are now engaged in a lively debate on one of the most fundamental questions you can ask about the world: How many species inhabit our planet? Estimates range from 3 million to 30 million species.

For large animals, such as the birds and mammals that command human attention, the situation isn't too bad. All experts agree, for example, that Earth is populated by about 9000 species of birds and 4000 of mammals, and only a few new ones are discovered each decade. For other kinds of organisms, however, we are still in a state of relative ignorance. For one thing, there is no central database where information on new species is summarized, so we can't even make a firm statement about the total number of species that have been discovered, much less about ones that haven't been. At the moment, the number of known species—species that have been examined and recorded by scientists somewhere—is estimated to be between 1.5 million and 1.8 million. The distribution of these species is shown in Figure 20-3.

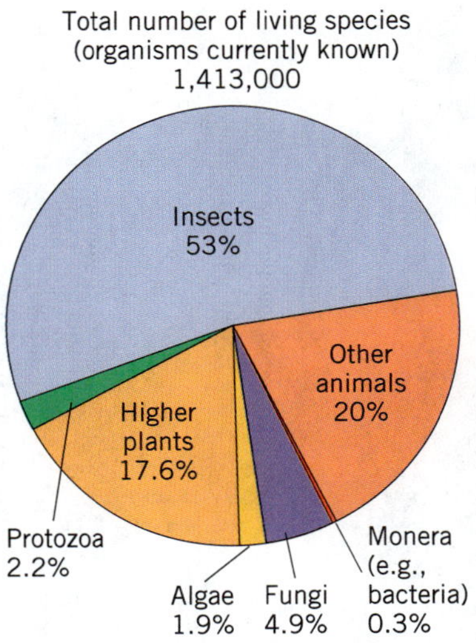

• **Figure 20-3** A pie graph of species distribution among different kinds of living things reveals that insects account for more than half of all known species.

Scientists have developed a number of methods for using current data to make estimates about the total number of species on Earth. If we make a graph of the total number of known species as a function of time, for example, we should get a curve like the one in Figure 20-4. As time goes by and more species become known, the curve should flatten. If we assume that the discovery curve for insects, for example, will follow this same pattern, then by making a guess as to where we are on the curve, we can estimate what the final level will be. Using this notion, estimates of the total number of insect species of from 5 million to 7 million are obtained.

Another estimation technique is to do an exhaustive survey of organisms in a small geographic area, determine the ratio of known to unknown species in that area, and assume that this ratio applies worldwide. A study in the Indonesian rain forest, for example, focused on a particular type of insect of which 1065 species were known. A new exhaustive survey came up with 625 additional species, for a total of 1690 species. Thus the ratio of previously unknown to previously known species is:

$$\frac{\text{previously known species}}{\text{previously unknown species}} = \frac{1065}{625} = 1.7$$

If we assume that this number applies to all insects worldwide (and that's a very big if) and accept that there are about 900,000 known species of insects, the total number of insect species in the world would then be about

$$\begin{aligned}\text{total species} &= 1.7 \times \text{known species}\\ &= 1.7 \times 900{,}000 \text{ species}\\ &= 1{,}530{,}000 \text{ species}\end{aligned}$$

Other studies of this type, making longer strings of assumptions about how to apply local numbers to the global system, have produced estimates for the number of insect species as high as 30 million. We will have to know a lot more about the kinds of species that actually exist before we can be comfortable with these sorts of estimates. •

• **Figure 20-4** The total number of species of a given kind of living thing can be estimated by a graph that plots the number of known species versus time. As fewer and fewer species remain to be discovered, the plot should eventually flatten out to indicate the approximate number of species.

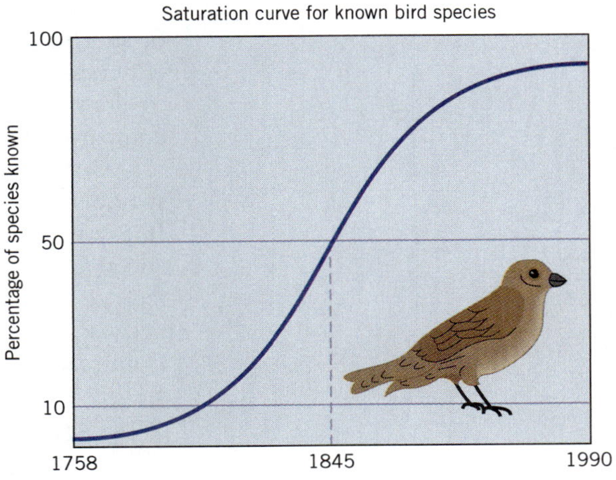

Classifying Human Beings

Human beings are one member of the kingdom of animals. With that decided, we can go on to work out the rest of our address in the classification scheme. Among animals, there is one phylum called *chordates,* whose members have a thickened set of nerves down their back. Most chordates (and most of the organisms that come to mind when we hear the word "animal") have the nerve encased in bone. These animals form the subphylum **vertebrates**—animals with backbones. Because human beings have backbones, we belong to this subphylum, as do amphibians, fish, reptiles, and birds.

Primates, such as this bonnet macaque from India, are characterized by grasping fingers and toes, eyes at the front of the head, a large brain, and fingernails instead of claws.

Among vertebrates, one class is made up of individuals that maintain the same body temperature regardless of the temperature of the environment, that have hair, and whose females nurse their young. Humans belong to this class, which is called **mammals,** as do wolves, rabbits, whales, and antelopes.

Among mammals, we belong to the order **primates,** which have grasping fingers and toes, eyes at the front of the head, a large brain, and fingernails instead of claws. Monkeys and apes are also members of this order. Human beings are members of the *hominid* family (primates who walk erect) and the genus *Homo* (hominids who satisfy still more detailed anatomical criteria having to do with factors such as face shape, tooth shape and size, and brain size).

At this point in the process of zeroing in on our own species we encounter an anomaly. Most animals have several close cousins, which are members of the same genus but different species, but this situation is not true of humans. The grizzly bear *(Ursus horribilis)* and the polar bear *(Ursus maritimus),* for example, are two species within the genus *Ursus* (bear). In the genus *Homo,* though, there is only one living species: *Homo sapiens* (us). In the past, there were other members of the family hominid and the genus *Homo* on Earth (we discuss some of them in Chapter 25), but at present we have no near relatives. All of those who might have been our near relatives are now extinct, perhaps by our own doing.

In any case, all humans can interbreed, so we are all part of a single species, ***Homo sapiens,*** and we all inhabit the same smallest circle in the classification scheme.

Implications of Linnaean Classification

As we have presented it here, and as Linnaeus originally conceived it in the eighteenth century, biological classification concerns itself solely with segregating living things according to their degree of physical similarity to each other. No attempt is made to explain why living things can be grouped in this way.

Today, however, most scientists would argue that there are compelling reasons why a classification scheme like the one we have outlined should exist. For one thing, scientists no longer have to be content with describing organisms purely in terms of their physical structure. In Chapter 23, for example, we will see that the information carried in the DNA molecules found in all organisms provides an alternative way of describing the organisms. One way of talking about how closely two organisms are related to each other, therefore, is to discuss how closely their DNA molecules resemble each other. The closeness of the relationship between two living things—the property that tells us where to draw the circles in Figure 20-1—can thus be determined in a quantitative way by comparing DNA and other specific molecules.

More important, the fact that living things can be grouped in successive layers strongly suggests that Linnaeus and his followers had discovered a kind of family tree. If, as we shall argue in Chapter 25, all living things descended from the same primordial ancestor, then the Linnaean groupings follow naturally. The amount of similarity or difference between two organisms depends on the amount of time and rate of change because the two shared a common ancestor. In addition, each classification group results from real events in the past when species split off from each other.

Stop and Think! How does the classification of living things reflect the scientific method?

Survival: A New Look at the Life Around You

A single-celled organism is one of the most remarkably complex structures known to science. Even the smallest cell features hundreds of interacting chemical processes that must be exquisitely balanced and regulated. Nevertheless, the survival strategies of single-celled organisms are relatively simple.

The first order of business for a cell is to absorb all the material it needs to maintain itself from its environment. In some simple cells, called *heterotrophs,* the cell must consume a variety of biomolecules including amino acids, lipids, and carbohydrates to survive (see Chapter 22). Other more chemically complex cells, called *autotrophs,* are able to manufacture these essential building blocks from simple molecules like H_2O, CO_2, and NH_3. Inside the cell, these materials are used in the chemical reactions needed to keep the cell alive and for it to reproduce. Waste products generated by these reactions leave the cell the same way that materials came in: they pass through the cell boundary and out into the surrounding environment. For most of Earth's history, all life consisted of such single cells.

With the advent of multicellular life, however, strategies became more complicated. Molecules that provided the cell's chemical energy could no longer simply move into individual cells from the environment (most cells in a multicellular organism, after all, are shielded from the environment by other cells). Instead, those molecules must be carried from distant parts of the organism to the cells where they are to be used. Similarly, waste products must be carried away from individual cells to the environment.

Some very primitive multicellular organisms (sponges, for example) are merely collections of cells that could just as well survive on their own. In higher organisms, however, specialized cells group together into organs and organ systems to take care of jobs such as moving energy-rich materials to cells and removing wastes. In humans, for example, the organ we call the heart and those we call blood vessels form an organ system known as the circulatory system, whose task it is to circulate the blood.

One way to think about living things, then, is to identify tasks that all organisms must perform and then ask what processes have evolved that allow a particular organism to perform those tasks. Every multicellular organism, for example, must obtain and distribute molecules that supply energy and build the fabric of the organism, and every organism must reproduce itself.

Let's look at the marvelous diversity of living things with an eye toward seeing what strategies they have evolved to deal with these two basic tasks of life.

Strategies of Fungi

Fungi, a group that includes such diverse organisms as molds, mushrooms, and yeast, were once classified as plants, but they are so different from true plants that they are now given their own kingdom. Some types of fungi (yeast, for example) are single-celled, but most of the ones with which we are familiar, such as mushrooms, are multicellular. Fungi grow by sending out filaments, which are slender, thread-like stalks sometimes no more than one or two cells across, and absorbing food directly through these stalks. In this way, the fungi play an important role in nature by breaking down dead organic material. For example, fungi often grow like shelves out of the sides of fallen trees in a forest.

The structure of fungi is fairly simple, consisting of little more than a mass of filaments. Because of this structure, complex systems to move materials around aren't necessary. No cell is far from the material on which the fungus lives; hence that material can be absorbed directly.

Fungi have developed a variety of reproductive strategies. First, they can reproduce by having their filaments break off and grow. More often, they produce spores, which are usually asexual reproductive organs through which a fungus can produce offspring

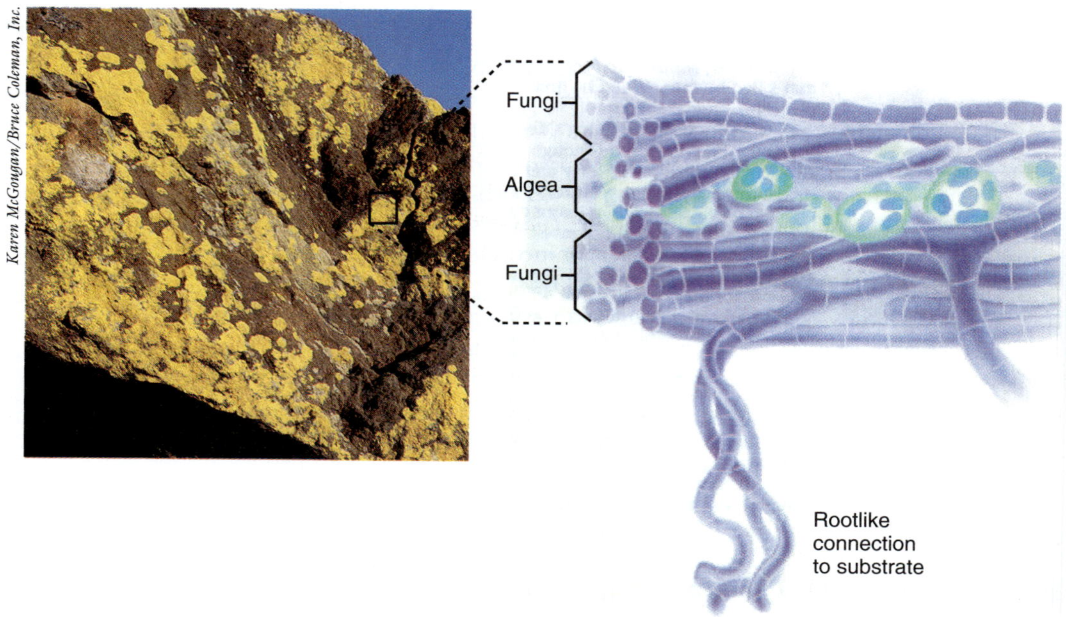

• **Figure 20-5** Lichens, which grow on solid rock, sustain life through a complex cooperative effort by fungi and algae.

without interacting with any other fungus. Spores can travel long distances through air and water, but once growth starts, fungi are as immobile as plants. Spores can also be produced by "mating," which is accomplished by the fusion of two cells in the filaments from different plants. Spores are often held in small containers that grow on top of stalks; in effect, they get a "running start" by being above the ground when the container breaks. The fuzzy appearance of mold on the old food in your refrigerator often comes from the spore containers on top of the stalks.

One of the most remarkable lifestyles displayed by fungi is observed in organisms called *lichens,* which are often seen as crusty coatings on rocks, and which play an important role in the breakdown of rock into soil. Each lichen is actually a combination of two interdependent species, a fungus and a single-celled organism that can use the Sun's energy in photosynthesis. Lichens typically absorb most of the minerals they need from the air and rainfall, and hence can grow in inhospitable places such as mountaintops and deserts (Figure 20-5).

Science in the Making •

The Discovery of Penicillin

When you get an infection, or even just a bad cut, your doctor will very likely prescribe an *antibiotic,* a medicine capable of destroying foreign bacteria that otherwise would flourish in your body. It's hard for us, living in an age where antibiotics are common, to realize that a half-century ago bacterial diseases such as pneumonia and minor cuts that became infected were major killers.

The discovery in 1928 of penicillin, the best known of the modern antibiotics, was the result of a botched experiment in the London laboratory of bacteriologist Alexander Fleming (later Sir Alexander). He was growing cultures of *Staphylococcus* (a common infectious bacterium) in dishes when he noticed that one of his experimental dishes had been contaminated by a common mold called *Penicillium,* and that the bacteria didn't grow in that dish.

Other scientists had probably seen the same thing but had just thrown the contaminated plates away and continued with their experiments. Fleming, however, realized that the mold must have been secreting a substance that killed bacteria. When he finally isolated that substance, he named it *penicillin,* after the mold.

For a period after Fleming's discovery, penicillin could not be made in large quantities or in pure enough form to have much medical effect. In 1938, however, Howard Florey and Ernst Chain at Oxford University succeeded in producing relatively pure forms of the substance. Under the pressure of World War II, a major development program had the drug in mass production by 1943. It saved countless lives on the battlefields of that war and is now one of an array of substances used to maintain human health around the world. Fleming, Florey, and Chain shared the Nobel Prize for medicine in 1945.

The action of penicillin is a good illustration of how molecules function in living systems. The outside cell covering or cell membrane of the bacteria responsible for many infectious diseases is built from molecules that have short tails. Each bacterium cell also contains specialized molecules that link the tails together to create the *cell membrane.* Penicillin locks onto these specialized molecules and prevents them from attaching to the tails of the covering molecules, thus preventing the cell membrane from growing. Human cells don't use the same specialized molecules to build cell membranes, so the drug doesn't have this effect on us (although it can trigger allergic reactions in some people). •

Strategies of Plants

Plants and algae, through the process of photosynthesis (see Chapter 21), take energy from the Sun and lock it up in the form of chemical energy in their tissues and cells. At the same time, they remove carbon dioxide and water from the air and produce oxygen as a waste product, including the oxygen you are breathing right now.

Biologists have not been able to agree about how to assign plants to various phyla, classes, orders, and so forth, or even on how to draw the boundaries of the plant kingdom. Algae, for example, are single-celled organisms (or simple multicellular ones) that carry out between 50 and 90% of Earth's photosynthesis. *Blue-green algae,* or *cyanobacteria,* are single-celled organisms and are normally classified as monera; but other kinds of algae, including primitive multicellular organisms such as seaweeds and kelp (including green, red, and brown algae), are called plants in some schemes and protista in others.

For our purposes, we will define plants to be multicellular organisms that perform photosynthesis. Plants are found primarily on land, and the main divisions between them have to do with the way they reproduce and how they acquire and circulate water.

The Simplest Plants

The most primitive terrestrial plants are in the phylum of bryophytes, whose most familiar members are mosses and liverworts. These plants don't have roots, as more advanced plants do, but absorb water directly through their aboveground structures. For this reason, mosses are found in moist environments. They are anchored to the ground by filaments, as are fungi. Unlike fungi, however, bryophytes use the Sun's energy to produce their own food by photosynthesis.

Like all other plants, mosses and liverworts reproduce both sexually (involving sperm and egg) and asexually (involving spores). A generation produced sexually from the union of sperm and egg produces its offspring by means of spores. Then that asexually produced generation reproduces sexually, the two pathways alternating down through the generations.

As we shall see in Chapter 25, life on Earth began in the oceans and migrated to land only about 400 million years ago. This history is evident in today's bryophytes in that they are not equipped to get moisture directly out of the soil and they cannot reproduce in a dry environment.

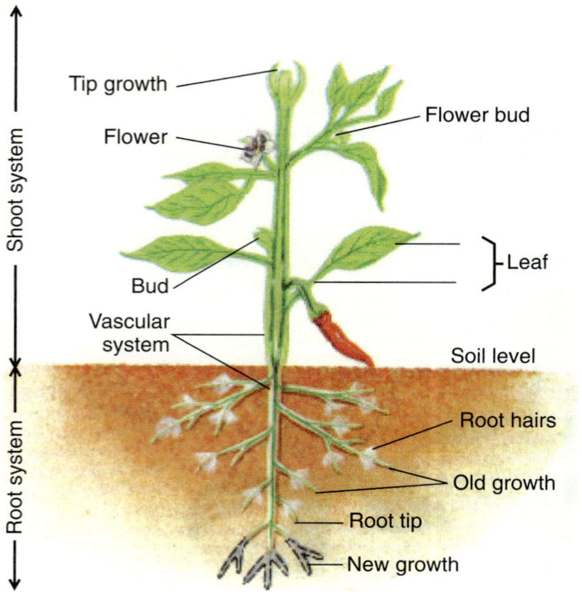

• **Figure 20-6** The basic design of all vascular plants includes a root system below ground and a system of stems and leaves above ground.

Vascular Plants

By far the greatest number of plants that play a role in our everyday life are in the phylum of **vascular plants** (Figure 20-6). These plants have an internal "plumbing" system consisting of roots, stems, and leaves capable of carrying fluids from one part of the plant to another. They also have ways of controlling water loss and protecting the sperm and egg so that they can survive outside of water. The development of internal plumbing not only adapted plants to life in the dry terrestrial environment, but it also began the process of providing internal structures to overcome the downward pull of gravity—both abilities crucial for land plants.

The most primitive vascular plants, a group whose most familiar members are in the class called *ferns,* still reproduce by producing sperm that must swim through water to fertilize eggs and generate spores. You can see the small yellow spore containers on the underside of the leaves of ferns. In this way they differ from the more advanced vascular plants, which, as we shall see, reproduce by means of seeds.

Although seedless vascular plants such as ferns play a relatively minor role on Earth today, they were the main form of plant life 300 million years ago. Huge forests of ferns and related trees blanketed the land, where they used photosynthesis to store the Sun's energy in plant tissues. When these plants died, they were buried and, over millions of years, turned into coal. Thus you could say that the Industrial Revolution, which dramatically altered the structure of Western society in the nineteenth century, depended on seedless vascular plants, as does much of modern technological civilization.

The most common classes of vascular plants today are the **gymnosperms** (plants that produce seeds without flowers; e.g., fir trees) and the **angiosperms** (plants that produce seeds and flowers). The distinguishing feature of these plants, which have dominated the plant kingdom for the last 250 million years, is that they reproduce by means of seeds. All seeds contain a fertilized egg and some nutrient, both wrapped in a protective coating. Like spores, seeds are capable of lying dormant for long periods and hence can wait through times of cold or drought before they sprout. One way that seed-producing plants have become fully adapted to life on land is that the sperm part of these plants, familiar to us as pollen grains, typically moves through the air or is carried by insects. Thus, though seed plants may need water to grow, they do not need to be near standing water in order to reproduce.

The name "gymnosperm" means "naked seed" and refers to the fact that the seeds grow unprotected from the elements. The most familiar gymnosperms are evergreen trees, or conifers, such as the pine. On these trees, some cones produce pollen, which is dispersed by the wind. When pollen grains land on cones that contain unfertilized eggs, fertilization takes place. The seed, which as mentioned consists of a fertilized egg plus some stored nutrients, develops on the cone that originally held the egg, and, when conditions are right, is released and carried by the wind to a new location. Typically, hundreds or even thousands of seeds have to be released to get one new seedling.

Angiosperms, which have been around for at least 100 million years and have dominated Earth's plant life for the last 65 million years, comprise the great bulk of known species of modern plants. These plants reproduce through the complex structure of their flowers. In a flower, the pollen grains containing the sperm grow on stalks known as stamens (Figure 20-7). Wind or insects carry the grains either to another part of the same flower or to other flowers. Once in its new location, each pollen grain grows a tube and enters the ovary, where the eggs are found. After fertilization, a seed forms within the

• **Figure 20-7** Flowers produce sperm and eggs for sexual reproduction. *(a)* Pollinators such as bees and butterflies transport pollen from one flower to the next. *(b)* The structures of a flower are represented schematically.

ovary, and the ovary itself develops into fruit. When you cut into an apple or a peach, you can see the seeds and ovary quite clearly. When the fruit is ripe, it detaches itself from the plant. Many adaptations allow seeds to be carried long distances, from winged seeds (like those of some trees) to small seeds on berries that are eaten and passed through the digestive tracts of animals.

Although angiosperms can reproduce through fertilization, they also reproduce by sending out runners or shoots. Grass on a lawn, for example, reproduces this way if it is prevented from producing seeds by constant mowing. In the first case, reproduction is sexual (because a sperm and an egg come together); in the second case, it is asexual.

Strategies of Animals

Animals are multicellular organisms that must get their nourishment by capturing and consuming molecules produced by other life-forms. The variety of organisms in this kingdom is truly staggering, ranging from sponges to tiny worms to eagles to students. Although the mass of all the plants on Earth far exceeds that of all the animals, the animal kingdom, with over 1.3 million known species, takes the prize for diversity. Depending on how lines are drawn, the kingdom can include more than 30 phyla. This diversity is summarized in Figure 20-8.

It's not easy to make generalizations about animals because of the great variety in this kingdom. However, the essential tasks of reproducing and acquiring energy and nutrients can help us get an overview. As you read the following, remember that respiration in animals is the reverse of photosynthesis in plants. In photosynthesis, a plant takes in carbon dioxide and gives off oxygen as a waste product. Animals, on the other hand, use lungs or gills to breathe in the oxygen that is used in the body's chemical reactions, and then they exhale carbon dioxide as a waste product.

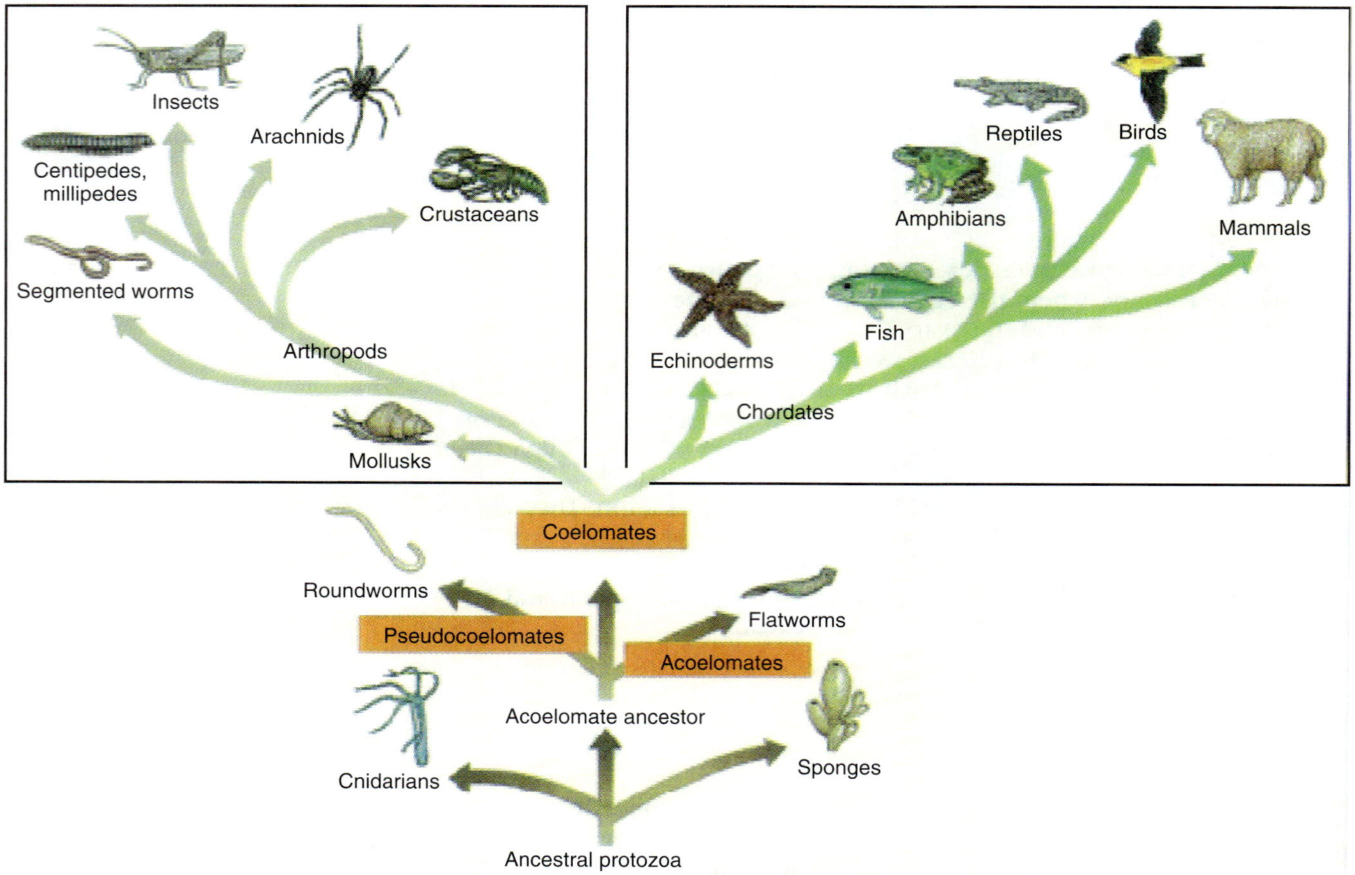

• **Figure 20-8** The family tree of animals, showing some of the major phyla.

Invertebrates

When we think about animals, we usually visualize large organisms that fall under the subphylum of vertebrates, such as eagles, sharks, or elephants. Most animal species, however, are **invertebrates**—organisms without backbones that make up the 30 or so other animal phyla. The simplest invertebrates, such as sponges, exhibit characteristics somewhere between those of an aggregate of individual cells and those of true multicellular organisms. If a sponge is passed through a sieve, the individual cells not only survive, but also eventually reorganize themselves into a sponge. Corals, too, are colonies of countless separate minute organisms; break up the collection and each individual can function on its own.

Most of the phyla of the animal kingdom consist of worms, mollusks, and various microscopic organisms. Some of these animals have become incredibly specialized; one phylum of worms, for example, is represented by more than 70 species, each of which is found as a parasite in the noses, sinuses, and lungs of vertebrates. Sea cucumbers, jellyfish, earthworms, mollusks, snails, and tapeworms are all examples of the diverse invertebrate forms to be found in the animal kingdom.

Arthropods are by far the most successful phylum in the animal kingdom, in terms of both number of species and total mass. Arthropods include familiar forms such as spiders, insects (including beetles, ants, butterflies, and many other kinds of "bugs"), and crustacea (e.g., crabs, shrimp, and lobsters), all of which are animals with segmented bodies and jointed limbs. The more than 900,000 recognized species of insects account

(a) Juan Carlos Muños/Age Fotostock America, Inc.

(b) Robert Lubeck/Animals Animals/Earth Scenes

Most known animal species are arthropods, with segmented bodies and jointed limbs. They include *(a)* spiders, with eight legs and often several pairs of eyes; and *(b)* insects, with six legs and three segments.

for at least 70% of all known animal species. There are more species of beetles than of any other type of animal and more individual ants than individuals of any other type. These facts prompted a famous comment by evolutionary theorist J. B .S. Haldane (1892–1964) who, when asked what his studies of biology had taught him about God, replied, "He has an inordinate fondness for beetles."

One of the problems that all land-dwelling organisms have to deal with is finding a way to support their structures against the pull of gravity. Arthropods solve this problem with a hard external covering known as an exoskeleton. This strategy is different from that of the vertebrates, whose weight is supported by an internal skeleton and whose outer coatings are usually soft. You can see this same difference in strategy illustrated architecturally in the contrast between old buildings held up by massive stone walls, and modern skyscrapers, whose weight is held up by a steel skeleton and whose outer skin may be nothing more substantial than thin sheets of glass.

Stop and Think! Can you think of any other strategies that living things could use to maintain their structures?

The hard exoskeleton provides an evolutionary advantage to arthropods: it is a "coat of armor" that protects the animal from predators. Because the exoskeleton cannot grow, arthropods usually shed their exoskeletons periodically, a process known as molting. A typical insect (Figure 20-9) has a body divided into three segments. Three pairs of legs originate from the central segment, or thorax, while a pair of antennae for sensing the environment adorns the head. Many insects also have one or two pairs of wings. Insects have a heart but no lungs; they bring oxygen into their bodies through a set of tubes.

• **Figure 20-9** The generic insect.

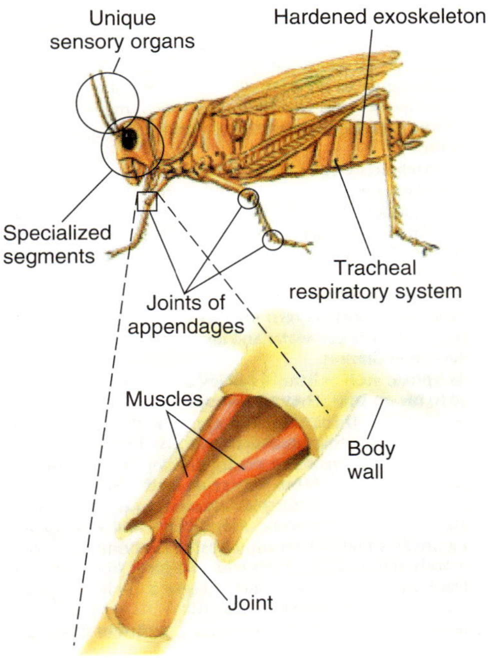

Vertebrates

Familiar vertebrate animals such as rabbits, birds, frogs, or fish have spinal cords encased in a backbone. The easiest way to understand the connection between the several branches of the vertebrate family tree is to think of each new branching up to reptiles as another step in the transition from water-dwelling animals to those fully adapted to life on land. As we shall see in Chapter 25, this line of thought follows the actual evolution of modern vertebrates, whose ancestors developed in the ocean and later made the move to a terrestrial environment.

The earliest fish, which became common about 400 million years ago, had no jaws; they fed by moving water through their mouths and filtering materials out. Lampreys (which look like eels without jaws) are modern descendants of these primitive fish. Over the following 100 million years, jaws evolved, and the advantage of speed over heavy protection led to a loss of bone. Modern fish such as sharks and stingrays, for example, have no bone at all, but skeletons made from cartilage, which is a structural material less rigid than bone. Modern fish absorb oxygen from water that flows through their gills.

Bony fish are a class of vertebrates that includes salmon, perch, trout, and most other organisms we think of when we hear the word "fish." Their skeletons are, as the name implies, made from bone. Oddly enough, the ancestors of these fish developed in fresh water and had both lungs and gills. In modern fish, these lungs have evolved into the swim bladder, an internal sac the fish can inflate to control its ability to float, while the gills function to supply oxygen. A few species of lungfish survive today. These fish live in stagnant water and gulp air occasionally to supplement what they can extract from the oxygen-poor water in which they live. Lungfish can also live out of water for short periods, allowing them to move from one pool to another during droughts.

The first vertebrates clearly adapted to live at least part of their lives on land were the class *amphibians,* whose modern descendants include frogs, toads, and salamanders. Most amphibians spend part of their life cycle in water, part on land. Frogs hatch in water as tadpoles, complete with gills and fins, and then develop into land-living adults with lungs and legs. They have a three-chambered heart and a circulatory system in which blood is pumped to the lungs to obtain oxygen, then returned and sent out into the body. Frogs also can absorb oxygen directly through their skin. Amphibians mark a halfway stage between water and land, in terms of both their anatomy and their place in evolution.

The class *reptiles,* including lizards, turtles, and snakes, include the first animals fully adapted to life on land. Reptiles are covered with hard scales, cutting down the loss of water through the skin. Eggs are fertilized within the body of the female, instead of relying on chance unions of egg and sperm in water, as with fish and amphibians. The young develop in eggs surrounded by a shell that can retain water and thus survive on land. Like amphibians, reptiles have a three-chambered heart, but with divisions in the chambers that allow oxygen to be used more efficiently. Amphibians and reptiles are so-called *cold-blooded* animals—that is, they must absorb heat from their environment to maintain body temperature. It should be noted, however, that a "cold-blooded" lizard lying in the sun may achieve a body temperature much higher than typical "warm-blooded" animals.

• **Figure 20-10** The mammalian family tree.

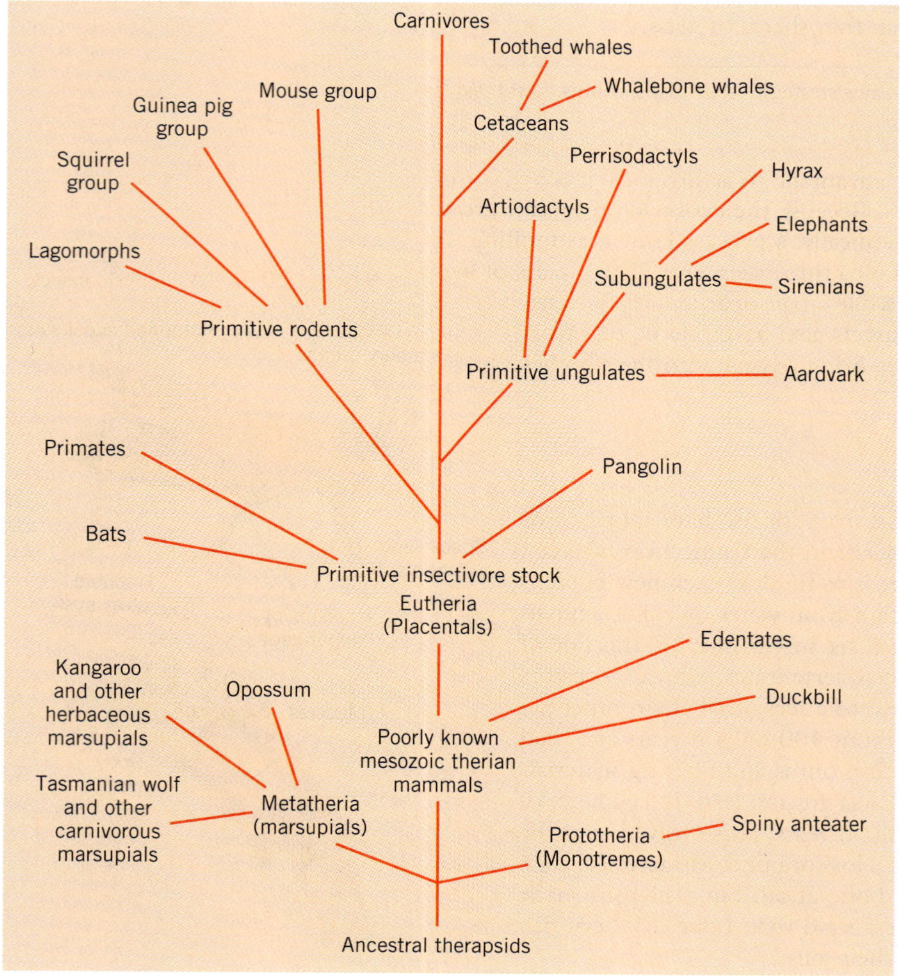

Birds are now widely thought to be modern descendants of reptiles, probably direct descendants of dinosaurs. Their anatomy differs from that of reptiles because of their adaptation to flight. In birds, the scales of the reptiles have evolved into feathers. Birds require high levels of energy to sustain flight, so their respiratory and circulatory systems are more complex than those in reptiles and amphibians. They have a four-chambered heart, as do humans. One side of the heart pumps blood to the lungs to take in oxygen, and the other side pumps this oxygen-rich blood around the body. This feature allows the bird to use the energy in its food with maximal efficiency, so that it is *warm-blooded,* maintaining a relatively constant body temperature in any environment.

Taxonomists recognize 18 living orders of the class *mammals* in the world today (Figure 20-10). Like birds, mammals maintain a constant body temperature by burning food. In almost all cases, the development of the fertilized egg takes place entirely inside the body of the mother, so that the young are born live. Once born, the young are nourished by milk from special glands in the female. Other adaptations to the terrestrial environment include hair to aid in temperature regulation, specialized teeth for breaking up food, legs located under the body, and, perhaps most important, an enlarged brain.

Science News | Life Underfoot

(SCIENCE NEWS, JAN. 14, 2006, P. 21)

When we think about life on our planet, we usually think about large organisms—trees, elephants, birds. We tend to ignore the fact that most of the life on this planet isn't multicellular at all, but rather is in the form of microbes. Indeed, some scientists have suggested that the total mass of microbial life on Earth far exceeds that of the more complex multicelled organisms like humans.

Despite this fact, there has been surprisingly little research on some aspects of the microbial world. In a partial attempt to rectify this situation, scientists at the University of Colorado and Duke University have recently completed an extensive survey of soil microbes in a variety of ecosystems. They collected samples from 96 sites in North and South America, being sure to collect from many different locations—tundra, rain forests, hardwood and conifer forests, desert, and grasslands, to name a few. They then used DNA fingerprinting techniques (which we introduce in Chapter 24) to assess the diversity of microbes in each sample.

Their results were not what you might have expected. We normally think of rain forests as being characterized by a wild proliferation of life, but in fact the soil there is fairly sparse as far as microbes are concerned. The Arizona desert, on the other hand, seems to have much greater biodiversity at the microbial level. Thus, the distribution of microbial diversity seems to be just the opposite of that of larger organisms.

In fact, the researchers found that the factor that has the most influence on microbial diversity is the pH of the soil. Acidic soils, like those in the Amazon, do not seem to be attractive to microbes, while they seem to thrive in more neutral desert soils. This result leads to a simple picture of the distribution of microbes. It seems that microbes can be found anywhere in the world but that they are most abundant in places where the soil pH is to their liking.

Thinking More About | Life's Strategies

Eating Through the Phyla

Human beings consume an amazing variety of foods. One way to make the diversity of life more real to you is to think about the variety of kingdoms and phyla your meals come from. Consider, for example, a slice of mushroom pizza. The crust derives from wheat, a vascular plant. The mushrooms, of course, are fungi. The cheese comes from milk produced by a cow, a vertebrate animal, and the milk is converted into cheese through the action of a single-celled member of the kingdom monera. The remains of these organisms are still in the cheese when you eat it, so with one bite of pizza you are consuming representatives of four kingdoms. If you could imagine adding a dash of seaweed or kelp, which are protista (at least in some classification schemes), you could get all five kingdoms in one bite.

Biologist Harold Morowitz, in his book *Entropy and the Magic Flute* (Oxford University Press, 1993), points out that traditional Japanese cuisine incorporates more phyla than any other. It includes such delicacies as seaweeds (protista) and sea cucumbers (animals in the same phylum as starfish), as well as the usual crustaceans (arthropods), shellfish, and various bony fish. But even a Western meal such as seafood pasta accompanied by a salad with oil and vinegar dressing contains a wide variety of phyla. It has vascular plants (lettuce, tomato, and olive oil), a phylum of monera (which ferments the vinegar), clams and squid (phylum mollusca), and bony fish (vertebrates), not to mention flour (from angiosperms) and perhaps eggs (from vertebrates) in the pasta.

How many phyla combine to make your favorite meal?

Joel Glenn/Cole Group/PhotoDisc, Inc./Getty Images

A slice of mushroom pizza incorporates foods from many phyla.

Summary

Biology, the study of living systems, began with efforts to describe the great variety of organisms on Earth. *Taxonomy,* the grouping of living things by their distinctive characteristics, has been aided by the *Linnaean classification* scheme, which groups organisms according to similarities in structure. Scientists now recognize five *kingdoms,* including *fungi,* which eat dead organic matter; *plants,* which make their own food by photosynthesis; and *animals,* which eat other organisms. Alternatively, all living organisms have been divided into three *domains* based on their genetic characteristics. A given *species* is placed in groups making up a series of increasingly specialized labels. The categories are, from most general to most specific, phylum, class, order, family, genus, and species.

The species, defined to be an interbreeding population of individuals that produces fertile offspring, is the basic unit of classification. *Homo sapiens* (the human species) is in the phylum chordata, the subphylum *vertebrates,* the class *mammals,* the order *primates,* the family hominids, and genus and species *Homo sapiens.* The fact that living things can be grouped in this way provides evidence that they all descended from a common ancestor.

Every multicellular organism must develop ways to obtain and distribute molecules for energy and structure, and to reproduce itself. Different life-forms have evolved different ways to deal with these problems. Fungi absorb materials through slender filaments and reproduce through the production of spores. *Vascular plants,* the most abundant plants, use thin tubes to distribute water to their leaves. The two largest groups of vascular plants are *gymnosperms,* which have exposed seeds, and *angiosperms,* which have flowers. The most abundant animals are *invertebrates,* which are dominated by *arthropods* such as insects and spiders.

Key Terms

biology
taxonomy
Linnaean classification
species
kingdom
fungi
plants
animals
domains
vertebrates
mammals
primates
Homo sapiens
vascular plants
gymnosperms
angiosperms
invertebrates
arthropods

Review Questions

1. How can you tell if an object is alive?
2. What is complexity?
3. Identify eight characteristics of all living things.
4. List the levels in the modern system of biological classification. At each level, identify the name of the group that includes humans.
5. What are some distinctive characteristics of the five kingdoms of living things?
6. Why do some biologists think there are more than five kingdoms?
7. Why do some biologists think there are fewer than five kingdoms?
8. How do the energy-gathering strategies of fungi, plants, and animals differ?
9. Name two tasks that all living things carry out.
10. What are bryophytes? Give some examples.
11. What characteristics distinguish vascular plants from others? Give examples of different kinds of vascular plants.
12. What are the differences between gymnosperms and angiosperms?
13. Why are angiosperms the most successful group of plants?
14. What are the four main structures of flowering plants? What is the function of each structure?
15. What are arthropods? How do they support their weight?
16. List the major groups of vertebrates and their distinguishing characteristics. Give an example of an animal from each group.
17. How are reptiles better adapted for life on land than amphibians?
18. What classes of animals are warm-blooded? What are the advantages of being warm-blooded?

Discussion Questions

1. In what ways is the Linnaean classification scheme like a postal address? In what ways is it different?
2. How does the fact that living things can be classified in ever more specialized groups support the idea that they all descended from a common ancestor?
3. What is the range of estimates of the number of species on Earth? Why is the number so uncertain?
4. Given the definition of a species, how many different species of dogs are in the United States? How many species of humans are in the United States?
5. What are some of the reasons that two scientists might disagree on the Linnaean classification of a new kind of worm? Is the Linnaean system an "exact" science, with only one possible correct answer?
6. Why are biologists more confident of the total number of bird species than of insect species? Do you think we know a greater percentage of butterfly species or of worm species? Why?
7. Is your Christmas/holiday tree a gynosperm or an angiosperm? What evolutionary advantages do gynosperms and angiosperms possess that seedless vascular plants (e.g., ferns) do not?

8. Speculate on why vascular plants are more widely distributed than bryophytes.

9. Why are arthropods the most successful phylum in the animal kingdom?

10. If two different looking animals breed and produce fertile offspring, are they the same species? Why is appearance not a productive way to classify organisms? (*Hint:* Does a great dane look like a chihuahua?)

11. In what ways might changes in the nature of land plants have affected the evolution of land animals?

12. Where are Earth's main coal deposits? What does this tell you about the location of forests hundreds of millions of years ago?

13. What are the properties of water that make it necessary for life?

14. What is the binomial nomenclature for a human being?

15. What structures have plants and animals developed in order to support their weight? Is there a maximum size for a plant or animal?

16. Are insects or worms animals? Why or Why not?

Investigations

1. Think about courses at your university other than those in biology. In what ways does classification play a role in chemistry? in psychology? in English? Is there any field of study that does not use classification in one way or another?

2. Examine recent issues of scientific journals and find an article that describes a new species of animal or plant. How was this new species classified?

3. In the eighteenth and nineteenth centuries, many well-educated amateur naturalists made significant contributions to the study of plants, animals, and fossils. Statesman Thomas Jefferson, artist John James Audubon, and explorers Lewis and Clark are among the famous Americans who described unusual plants and animals. Read a biography of an amateur naturalist and discuss how his or her work contributed to the science of biology.

4. Investigate the research of Carl Woese of the University of Illinois. How did his discoveries alter thinking about the classification of living things?

5. Take a walk around your campus and see how many of the four major plant groupings—bryophytes, seedless vascular plants, gymnosperms, and flowering plants—you can identify. On most campuses you should be able to find all four, and even in the middle of a city you should be able to find two or three.

6. Go to your favorite supermarket and try to count how many different phyla of plants and animals are for sale. What is the average number of phyla per aisle? Does this number vary much from one store to another?

7. Many medicines were derived originally from plants. List some of them. Are any of the plants that produced those medicines now endangered?

8. Many single-celled organisms appear as tiny round objects about a millionth of a meter in diameter. Investigate the procedures a biologist might use to classify such an organism.

9. When an individual makes the statement that species loss (i.e., the loss of biodiversity) is greater now than at any time in the history of Earth, what assumptions are they making? What information would we need to evaluate that comment? Are they violating the rule of parsimony (i.e., Occam's razor)?

10. Why can some types of plants live without soil? Where do they get their nutrients? What are these plants called?

11. Investigate the role of cyanobacteria in the evolution and development of plants. What structures in modern plants are evolved forms of cyanobacteria?

21

The Living Cell

What is the smallest living thing?

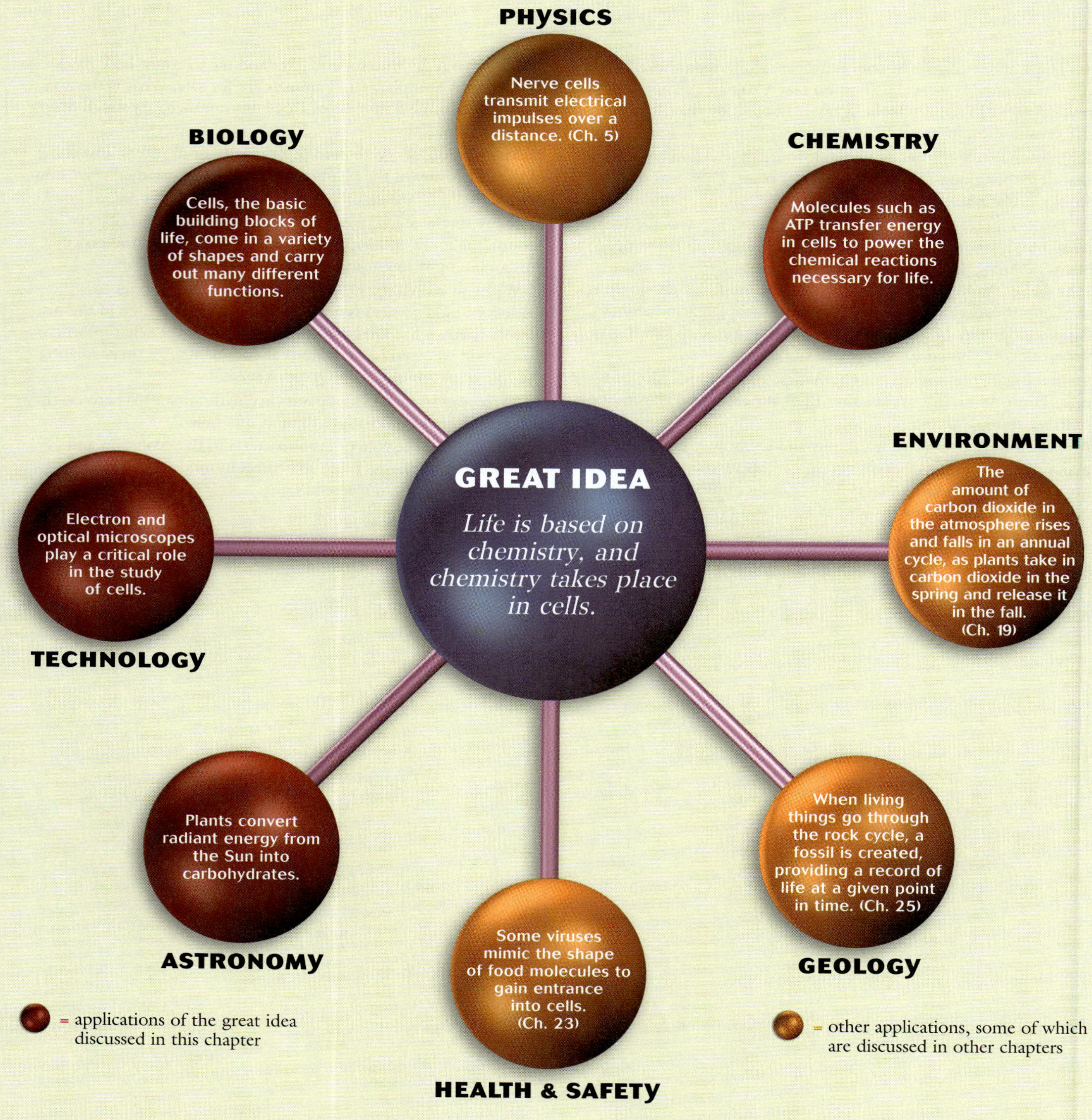

Science Through the Day | Sunburn!

It's late afternoon at the beach when you notice that the tops of your feet are bright red. You've got sunburn. Hours earlier you used sunblock but you missed those areas. Now they hurt!

Past experience tells you what will happen. For the next couple of days the tops of your feet will be tender and painful, especially when you get into a hot shower. Then the outer layers of skin will peel off. But within a week or so new skin will grow and your feet will be back to normal.

The human body is amazing. When injured, parts of the body like sunburned skin may die, but the skin is quickly regenerated. How is that possible? The answer lies in the behavior of cells—the fundamental building blocks of life.

Peter Cade/Stone/Getty Images

The Nature and Variety of Cells

For centuries, scientists have tried to answer questions about nature's fundamental building blocks. In this context, dealing with living things is particularly complex. Although all living things are made out of atoms and molecules, as we saw in the previous chapter, living things are more than just collections of atoms. An entity must do many things such as reproduce and take in matter and energy for us to say that it is alive. These functions cannot be performed by a random collection of atoms; rather, they result from the collective behavior of large numbers of atoms organized into some kind of system. For our purposes, the **cell** can be considered to be the smallest identifiable unit capable of carrying on the basic tasks that we associate with living things.

An enormous number of different kinds of cells can be found in nature. Cells come in a wide range of sizes and shapes, and perform all sorts of functions. While typical animal cells are about one-hundredth of a millimeter (a thousandth of an inch) in diameter, they can range in size from bacteria only a few hundred-thousandths of a centimeter across (much too small to see in most light microscopes and smaller than some large molecules) to the yolk portion of an ostrich egg that is much larger than most species of animals. Most cells are too small to be seen with the unaided eye but are easily studied with a microscope.

Cells also come in a wide variety of shapes. Plant cells are often rectangular or polygonal, while egg cells are usually spherical. Bacteria may be rod-shaped or spiral in form, muscle cells are extremely elongated, nerve cells sport a complex array of branching fibers, and a sperm cell has a tail-like flagellum that helps it swim. The recognition of common characteristics in this extraordinary collection represents one of the great advances in biology.

These differences in shape reflect the differences in the functions that the cells perform. Elongated muscle cells exert forces when they contract. Branching nerve cells (see Chapter 5) transmit impulses to many other cells. To fulfill their functions, cells constantly require raw materials and energy to live and reproduce. Living things use two very different strategies to satisfy these needs. Some cells (such as bacteria and protista) operate as separate entities, ensuring their survival by reproducing in vast numbers. Multicellular organisms such as plants and animals, on the other hand, employ cells collectively. In these more complex life-forms, different groups of cells serve very different functions, with each group depending on others in a complex web of interdependence.

Stop and Think! The fact that cells require energy implies that they do work. What kind of work do cells do?

Science in the Making •

The Discovery of Cells

An essential and distinctive feature of all cells is a membrane that isolates and protects the interior from the outer environment. In 1663, Robert Hooke (1635–1703), a brilliant and contentious contemporary of Isaac Newton, used one of the first microscopes to observe honeycomb structures in a thin slice of cork. It was Hooke who first called the tiny, box-like units "cells."

Within the next few years, Dutch merchant and self-taught scientist Anton van Leeuwenhoek (1632–1723) employed superb microscopes of his own design and construction to discover a rich variety of cells, including those in blood, saliva, semen, and the intestines. On October 9, 1676, van Leeuwenhoek sent a letter to the president of the Royal Society in London. He wrote, "In the year 1675 I discovered living creatures in Rain water, which had stood for a few days in a new earthen pot...," and he went on to describe a series of "animacules" that were visible through his microscope. •

The Cell Theory

In spite of van Leeuwenhoek's colorful descriptions, it was not until the nineteenth century that scientists finally accepted the idea that animals and plants are essentially aggregates of cells. In 1838, the German botanist Matthais Schleiden proposed that all plants are made of cells. In the following year his countryman, zoologist Theodor Schwann, extended this idea to animals and proposed what is now known as the *cell theory.* Three tenets of the Schwann's cell theory are:

1. All living things are composed of cells.
2. The cell is the fundamental unit of life.
3. All cells arise from previous cells.

The cell is like an oil refinery.

Corbis Digital Stock

Thus, biologists recognized that only cells can produce other cells and that these tiny objects represent the indivisible units of life—a discovery as fundamental as the discovery of atoms in chemistry and quanta in physics. The cell theory initiated the field of cell biology, which remains one of the central efforts in biology.

Observing Cells: The Microscope

Advances in understanding how cells work have relied in large part on the development of microscopes. Early microscopes were rather primitive affairs; consequently, scientists were unable to see many details of cell structure. Indeed, until the middle part of the twentieth century, science textbooks often spoke of something called "protoplasm." This substance was supposed to be a kind of uniform, molasses-like fluid that filled cells. Today, with much better microscopes we know that cells are very complex indeed. Advanced cells are full of specialized structures, as complicated in their own way as larger life-forms such as human beings. In fact, in the next chapter we'll see that the molecules of life play a crucial role in the complex workings of the cell, with each performing a separate vital function. Today, we refer to the fluid that takes up the spaces between all this complexity as *cytoplasm*.

Early microscopes and their modern high-tech descendants all operate on the same basic principle shown in Figure 21-1*a*. Ordinary visible light passes through a specimen, which is often placed between two transparent layers of glass or plastic. The light transmits through a series of lenses so that a magnified image is presented in the eyepiece. This kind of apparatus is called an *optical microscope,* and today these instruments can magnify more than 1000 times and resolve details less than a ten-thousandth of a centimeter across—enough to make an ordinary cell look as big as a quarter. In many modern optical microscopes, a miniature video camera in the eyepiece allows the image to be displayed on a television screen.

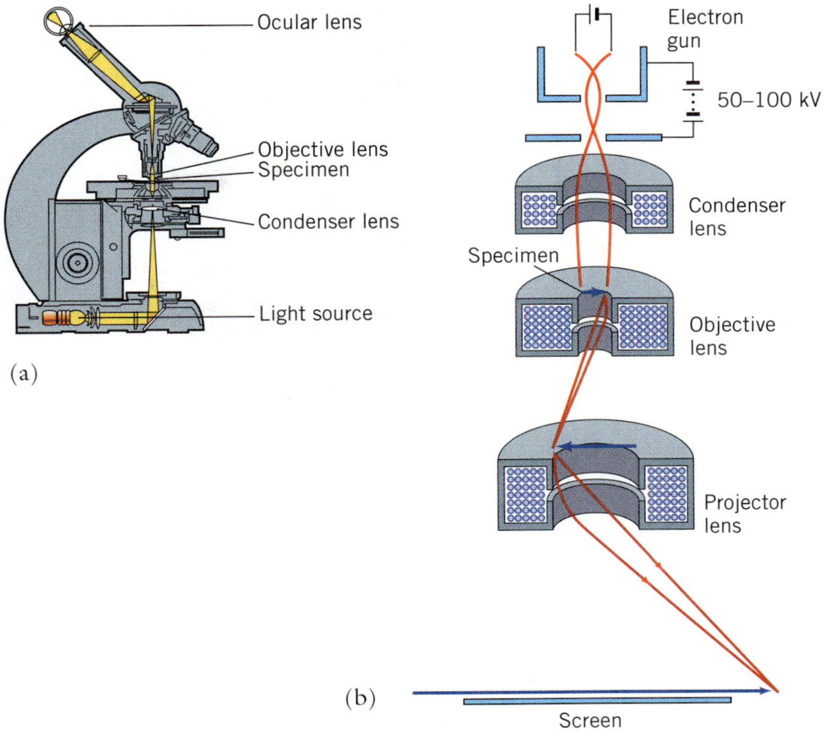

• **Figure 21-1** Light microscope *(a)* and electron microscope *(b)*. In the light microscope, waves of ordinary visible light travel through a series of lenses to form an image. The electron microscope uses the wave-like nature of electrons (see Chapter 8) to accomplish the same purpose.

Special dyes that are taken up by only one part of a specimen are often used to increase contrast in the image, and hence to make internal structures clearer. For example, we shall see that parts of cells called *chromosomes* play an important role in reproduction. These features were first seen as colored structures in cells that had been stained, a fact that is reflected in their name.

The ability of a microscope to differentiate objects that are close to each other is called its resolving power. The resolving power of all microscopes is limited by the wavelength of the light used: objects about the size of one wavelength appear blurred. Light microscopes, for example, typically employ light waves with wavelengths on the order of a ten-thousandth of a centimeter; thus objects about that size or smaller will appear as undifferentiated blurs in even the most perfectly designed instrument. This limitation means that many of the smaller structures in the cell cannot be seen with this sort of microscope.

A scientist operates an electron microscope.

Will & Demi McIntyre/Photo Researchers

In the 1930s, German scientist Ernst Ruska, working at a university in Berlin, introduced the *electron microscope,* a major new advance in microscopes that uses electrons instead of light to illuminate objects. In Chapter 9, we discussed the notion that quantum objects such as the electron can be thought of as tiny particles, but also as energetic waves. The electron's wavelength depends on its energy—the greater the energy, the shorter the wavelength—and typical electron wavelengths in modern instruments are comparable to the size of a single atom. In a situation such as that shown in Figure 21-1*b*, where an electron beam is shot at a target, we are in effect examining the target with very short wavelengths and thus achieving resolving powers up to 100,000 times that of optical microscopes. Modern electron microscopes are often used to resolve atomic-scale features.

The electron microscope works this way: An electrical current heats a tungsten filament in a strong electric field—typically about 100,000 volts—to produce an

• **Figure 21-2** Electron microscope photograph of a fruit fly with a wing mutation.

electron beam. Electrons leave the negatively charged tungsten wire and accelerate toward the positive end of a tube. This beam of electron "waves" is focused by specially designed ring-shaped electromagnets, the analogs of glass lenses in a conventional microscope. The focused beam strikes the sample, and the electrons then hit a detector that converts the beam into an image, as shown in Figure 21-2.

Modern electron microscopes are very expensive; it's not unusual for one to cost more than $500,000. Nevertheless, electron microscopes are an invaluable tool in all areas of science and industry that require examination of objects at extremely high magnification—particularly in the study of cells.

How Does a Cell Work?

As the fundamental unit of life, the cell must perform all of the varied tasks that we associate with living things (see Chapter 20). The cell must obtain atoms and energy from its environment, grow, respond to changes in environmental conditions, and reproduce. As we shall see, each of those tasks is accomplished by remarkable cellular mechanisms. But before examining those complex processes, it's useful to imagine the cell in a different way—as a factory that produces and distributes chemicals.

Have you ever driven by an oil refinery or other kind of chemical plant? It's a place of bewildering complexity, laced with a maze of pipes and towers, bustling with diverse activity as energy and materials constantly flow in and out.

As complex and diverse as chemical plants might seem, they all share a few basic features. Every chemical plant must have walls, a control room, and facilities to provide and distribute energy. There must be loading docks to bring in supplies and remove trash, conveyor belts or pipes to move materials from one place to another, and storage rooms to keep a stock of critical items at the ready. And at the heart of every plant must be pieces of machinery that control chemical reactions and manufacture the desired chemical products.

A chemical plant is, in fact, a lot like a living cell.

• **Figure 21-3** All cells possess a lipid bilayer membrane, which is studded with protein receptors. The membrane separates the inside of the cell from the outside.

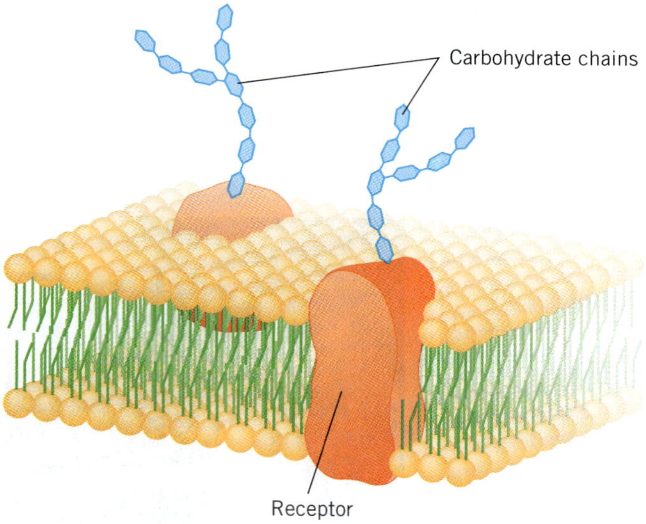

Cell Membranes

Every cell must be isolated from its environment—just like a chemical factory, there must be an "inside" that is distinct from an "outside." In addition, complex cells also require different parts of the cell to be separated from each other by inner partitions. Both of these requirements are satisfied by **cell membranes.** The simplest cells have only one external membrane (Figure 21-3), whereas more complex cells have many internal membranes in addition to the outer envelope. The basic molecular structure of cell membranes is a flexible double layer of elongated molecules called lipids (see Chapter 22).

If a cell membrane were totally impermeable, life would not be possible. In order to be alive, a cell must take in raw materials from its surroundings and pass wastes and other chemicals into the environment, just like the loading docks and pipelines that run to and from a chemical plant. Materials are transported across cell membranes in many ways. The simplest is the movement of small individual molecules across the cell membrane. You may see this process at work in your local supermarket, where produce managers often spray fresh vegetables with water. They don't do this for decoration—they put water on the carrots, lettuce, and other vegetables so that it will move through the membranes into the cells, making up for water that has evaporated out. In this way, vegetables maintain a fresher appearance for longer periods of time.

Cell membranes also incorporate various kinds of channels and molecular-sized openings, which allow specific materials to go back and forth. When nerve signals move through the human body, as we saw in Chapter 5, sodium and potassium ions move back and forth across nerve cell membranes to create the signal. The various kinds of channels that exist in different kinds of cells allow different kinds of atoms and molecules to pass through.

One important means of bringing material through a cell membrane, however, depends on the notion that the chemistry of life is controlled by the size and shape of molecules (see Chapter 22). Interspersed here and there in a cell membrane are large molecular structures, called **receptors.** Receptor molecules each have a specific geometrical shape, and each receptor will bind to a specific type of molecule in the environment. When that molecule is present, it is attracted to the receptor's binding site. Thus receptors can be thought of as the cell's "door guard" looking over prospective molecular entrants and picking out only those nutrients whose shape is exactly right.

When a receptor "recognizes" a particular molecule, the molecule and receptor are attracted to each other, through hydrogen bonds for example, and they fit together. A sequence of events such as that sketched in Figure 21-4 thus takes place. The receptor binds to the particle in question and holds it while the cell membrane deforms. Once the particle is inside, as shown, the membrane may nip off, enclosing the particle in its own special wrapping, and the cell membrane reforms behind it. The tiny container, called a *vesicle,* then becomes the vehicle by which the particle moves around inside the cell. A similar process that works in reverse is used when molecules from inside the cell are moved out. Once in a while a receptor can be fooled. As we'll see in Chapter 23, some tiny disease-causing objects called viruses gain entrance into cells by mimicking the shape of particular molecules and thus triggering the receptor mechanism.

The outer covering of plant cells contains an additional structure in addition to the kind of flexible membranes we have described. Plant cells may also be connected to each other by a **cell wall,** which is a solid framework made of strong polymers, such as

• **Figure 21-4** The action of receptors in a cell. *(a)* A food particle (in green) approaches a receptor. *(b)* The receptor bonds to the particle and draws it close to the cell membrane. *(c)* The particle is taken inside the cell and surrounded by lipids to form a vesicle.

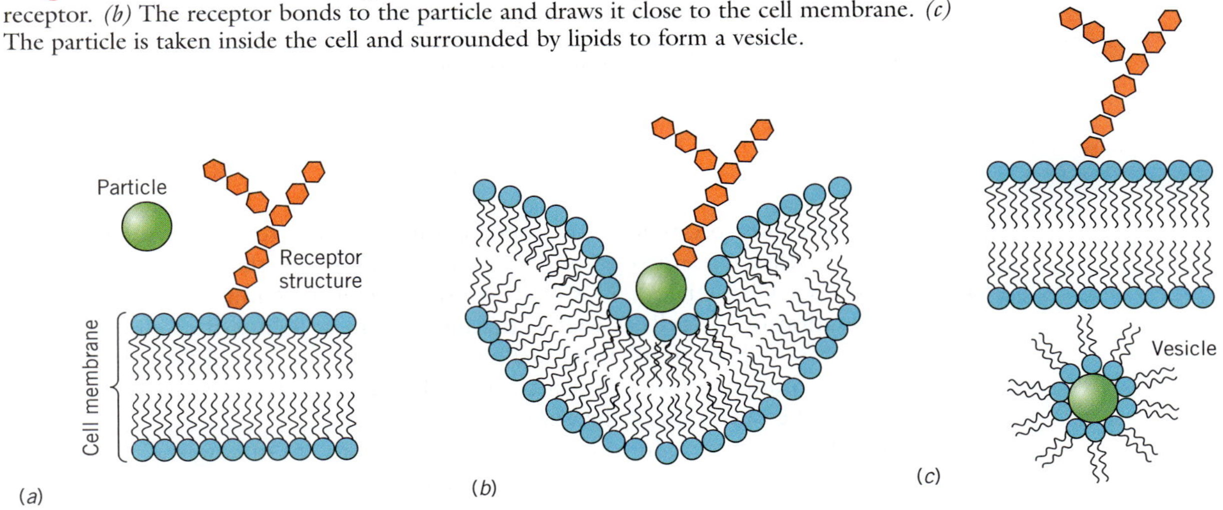

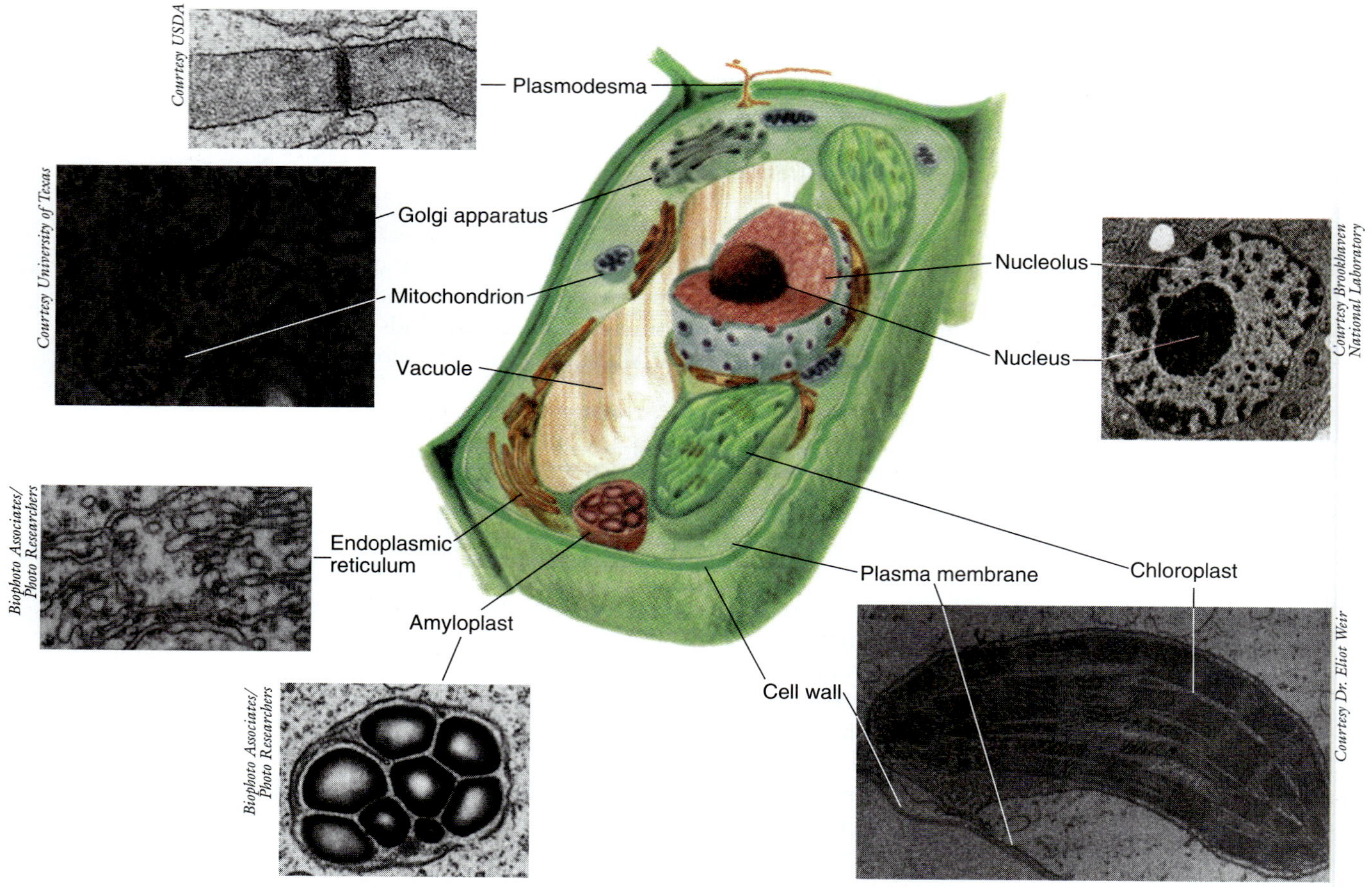

(a)

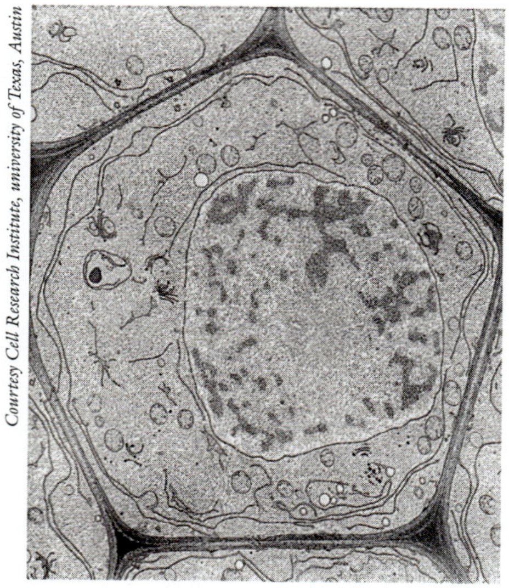

(b)

• **Figure 21-5** A typical plant cell. *(a)* A generalized drawing with electron micrographs of some key organelles (see Table 21-2). *(b)* Photograph of a cell of maize rust. The dark boundary is the cell wall, made from cellulose. The nucleus takes up almost half the area of the central part of the cell.

cellulose (see Chapter 22). Cell walls, which often account for about a third of a living plant's mass, give tree trunks and leaves the strength to grow upright against the force of gravity. In fact, it was cell walls (as opposed to cells per se) that Robert Hooke saw when he looked at his piece of cork in 1663 (see Figure 21-5).

Stop and Think! From a thermodynamic point of view, are cells open or closed systems? Explain.

The Nucleus

In most cells, the most prominent and important interior structure is the **nucleus.** The nucleus forms a relatively large enclosed structure that contains the cell's genetic material—its DNA (see Chapter 23). This DNA contains the instructions for the day-to-day chemical operation of the cell, as well as the mechanism by which the cell reproduces itself. If we think of the cell as being analogous to a large chemical factory, then the nucleus can be thought of as the front office. There, the blueprints are stored and instructions for the operation of the entire system go out.

Not all cells have nuclei. In some cells, the DNA is present in a tight coil but is not separated from the rest of the material in the interior. Presumably, these sorts of primi-

Table 21-1 Some Terms Related to Different Kinds of Cells and Single-Celled Organisms

Archaea	One of Carl Woese's three domains of life; all Archaea are prokaryotes, and all are also members of the kingdom monera.
Bacteria	One of Carl Woese's three domains of life; all Bacteria are prokaryotes, and all are also members of the kingdom monera. Note that "bacteria" (not capitalized) is also sometimes used as a general term for microbes.
Eucarya	One of Carl Woese's three domains of life; Eucarya include all of the single-celled kingdom of protista. as well as the three multicelled kingdoms: fungi, plants, and animals.
Eukaryote	A cell with a nucleus; all organisms in Woese's domain Eucarya are made of one or more eukaryotic cells.
Microbes	A general name for all microscopic single-celled organisms. Microbiology is the field of science devoted to the study of microbes.
Monera	The kingdom containing all cells without nuclei; monera is synonymous with prokaryotes, and it includes all single-celled organisms in the domains Bacteria and Archaea.
Protista	The kingdom containing single-celled organisms with nuclei; all protista are eukaryotes.
Prokaryote	A cell without a nucleus; all organisms in the kingdom monera, and in the domains Bacteria and Archaea, are prokaryotic cells.

tive cells, called *prokaryotes* ("before the nucleus"), evolved first. The kingdom monera (see Chapter 20), including bacteria and their relatives, includes all cells that do not have a nucleus. The more advanced single-celled organisms, the *eukaryotes* ("true nucleus"), as well as all multicellular organisms (including human beings), are made from cells that do contain nuclei. The kingdom protista includes single-celled eukaryotic organisms. Virtually all of the organisms with which we are familiar are made up of eukaryotic cells (Figure 21-5). By now, you've probably noticed that there are quite a few words that relate to different kinds of cells and single-celled organisms. Table 21-1 summarizes this sometimes confusing vocabulary.

One interesting feature of the nucleus—a feature that may contain a good deal of information about the evolution of higher life-forms—can be found in its confining membranes. The nucleus has not one, but two membranes, as shown in Figure 21-6. The standard explanation of the double membrane in the nucleus is that it is a vestige of an earlier stage of development. The idea is that at some point in the past, a large cell engulfed a small one, much as modern cell membranes use receptors to engulf molecules. Over time, a symbiotic relationship developed between those first two cells. Each cell was able to do better in a partnership than it could do alone. The double-membrane nucleus is interpreted as having an inner membrane, descended from the original membrane of the swallowed cell, and an outer membrane, descended from the vesicle that formed when the first cell was enveloped.

Other structures in the cell also have a double membrane (see the following section), suggesting that, while cells are indeed the basic unit of life, individual cells in complex organisms may be more like colonies of smaller cells than a single cell.

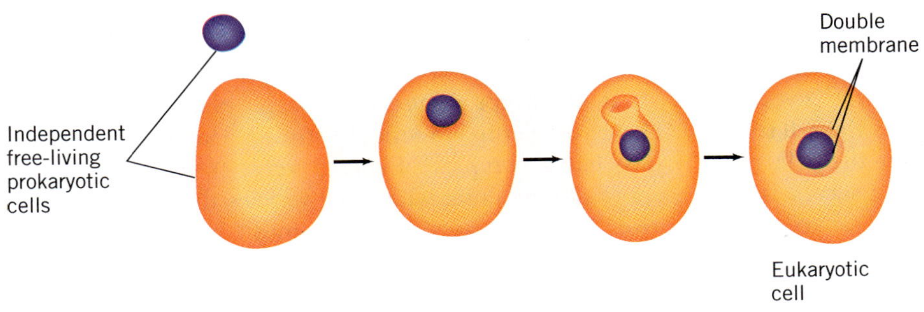

• **Figure 21-6** The nucleus has a double membrane, perhaps because it evolved from an earlier stage in which a large cell engulfed a small one, as shown.

21-2 Some Organelles and Their Functions (See Figures 21-5 and 21-7)

Organelle	Primary Function
Nucleus	Stores DNA and controls the cell's chemistry
Endoplasmic reticulum	Contributes to protein and lipid synthesis
Mitochondria	Release energy from food by metabolism
Chloroplasts	Site of photosynthesis (in plants only)
Ribosomes	Site of protein synthesis
Nucleoli	Manufacture the subunits of ribosomes
Golgi apparatus	Processes proteins previously synthesized at the ribosomes
Lysosomes	Contain digestive enzymes for breakdown of wastes
Vesicles	Small containers for chemical raw materials
Cytoskeleton	Provides cell structure and internal transport of vesicles
Vacuoles	Waste and water storage
Amyloplasts	Storage of starch (in plants only)
Plasmodesmata	Water conduits between plant cells

The Energy Organelles: Chloroplasts and Mitochondria

Eukaryotic cells have many inner structures similar to the nucleus. Each of these structures carries out a special chemical function in the cell. Any specialized structure in the cell, including the nucleus, is called an **organelle.** Important organelles are shown in Figures 21-5 and 21-7, and a listing of some of their primary functions is given in Table 21-2.

Every chemical factory requires energy, and living cells gather energy in two very different ways. Plants rely on the Sun for their energy, while animals ultimately depend on the chemical energy stored in plants.

Chloroplasts are the main energy transformation organelles in plant cells. As the name suggests, they are the places where molecules of *chlorophyll* are found. Chlorophyll absorbs the energy from sunlight and uses that energy to transform atmospheric carbon dioxide and water into energy-rich sugar molecules such as glucose. Chloroplasts have a double cell membrane, which suggests that they once may have been independent cells.

Mitochondria, sausage-shaped organelles, are places where molecules derived from the sugar glucose react with oxygen to produce the cell's energy. Mitochondria are, in effect, the furnaces where fuels are oxidized. A typical eukaryotic cell will have anywhere from a few hundred to a few thousand mitochondria.

Like the nucleus, chloroplasts and mitochondria have double cell membranes and even their own complement of DNA. Most scientists have concluded, therefore, that chloroplasts and mitochondria were originally independent cells in the early history of life on Earth.

Cytoskeleton

The *cytoskeleton* gives the cell its shape, keeps things anchored in place, and, in some cases, allows the cell to move. The cytoskeleton is a series of strong filaments that extend throughout the cell, more or less like a complex of spider webs. Inside the cell, the cytoskeleton serves as the transport system along which the vesicles that carry material from one place to another move. In some cases, cells can move by shortening and lengthening filaments inside the cell, or by causing structures related to the cytoskeleton that extend outside the cell to move like little oars.

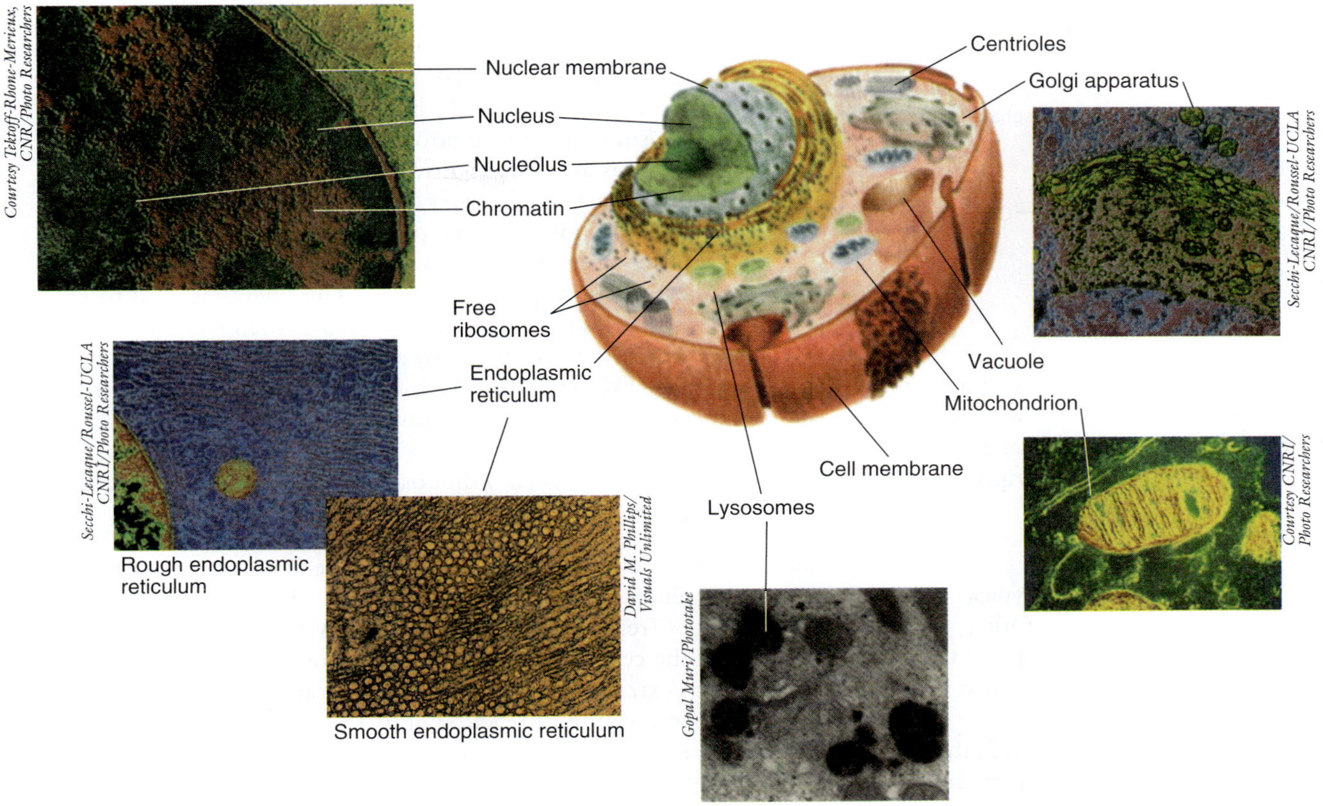

• **Figure 21-7** A typical animal cell showing the nucleus, mitochondria, and various other organelles (see Table 21-1).

Metabolism: Energy and Life

The cell's process of deriving energy from its surroundings is called **metabolism.** Cells need a means to transfer that energy from one place to another, to power the varied pieces of chemical machinery necessary for life.

The Cell's Energy Currency

Several molecules are used to store and distribute energy in all living cells. One way to think about this suite of molecules is to think about the money in your wallet. You may have some cash, but you also probably have credit cards, and perhaps even a check or two. Each of these items provides a way of moving money around, and each is appropriate for different situations. You pay cash for small purchases, make larger purchases with a credit card, and pay some of your bills by check. In the same way, a cell has different molecules that store different amounts of energy, each of which is appropriate to a particular use.

The most common of these energy carriers is *adenosine triphosphate (ATP)*—a molecule that provides energy for countless chemical processes in all living cells. A sketch of this molecule is given in Figure 21-8. The structure of ATP illustrates an important characteristic of life's molecular building blocks: they tend to be built from a few simple building blocks. ATP contains three phosphate groups (collections of phosphorus and oxygen atoms) at the end of the molecule (these three phosphates are what give ATP the "tri" part of its name). The other parts of the molecule consist of a sugar molecule called ribose, which is also a building block of the RNA structure (see Chapter 23), and the base adenine, which is part of both DNA and RNA.

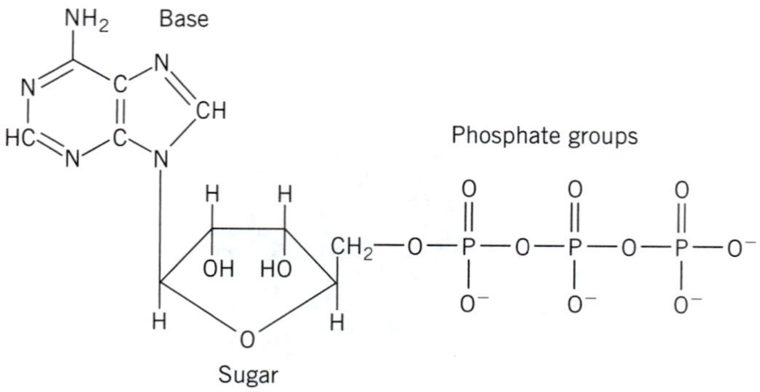

• **Figure 21-8** Sketch of ATP, the energy "money" of cells. Note that it is built from a sugar (ribose), a base (adenine), and three phosphate groups.

A considerable amount of energy is required to put phosphate groups onto the ends of the tail of an ATP molecule. In the language of Chapter 10, putting the last phosphate group on the ATP tail is an endothermic process. If the phosphate group is subsequently removed in another chemical reaction, that energy is available to drive other chemical reactions. Thus the ATP molecule can carry energy in the form of phosphorus–oxygen bonds from one part of the cell to another.

In one place in a cell—in the mitochondria, for example—chemical reactions produce energy. This energy is used to produce molecules of ATP. These molecules then move out of the place where they are made to a place where energy is needed. At this point, ATP acts something like a tiny battery: an ATP molecule attaches to part of the cell's chemical machinery, a phosphate group is removed, and the stored chemical potential energy becomes available to drive the desired chemical reactions. The triphosphate (three phosphates) then becomes a diphosphate (two phosphates) ADP:

$$\text{ATP} \rightarrow \text{ADP} + \text{PO}_4 + \text{energy}$$

ATP is the molecule that serves as the cell's "cash" in the cell's energy system. A typical cell will have several million ATP molecules doing their job at any given time. Other, more complex molecules (represented by the letters FADH and NADH) correspond to the "credit cards" in the cell's energy system. They store up energy and can be cashed in on short notice when extra energy is required. One way of thinking about the role of ATP is to say that when a chemical reaction adds the last phosphate group to ATP, the molecule picks up the equivalent of a pocketful of money. That money can be spent later for almost any purpose.

Photosynthesis

Photosynthesis, the mechanism by which plants convert the energy of sunlight into energy stored in carbohydrates, provides the chemical energy for almost all species (Figure 21-9). In plants, this complex process operates as follows: A large molecule, usually chlorophyll, absorbs sunlight. After a series of chemical reactions, this energy is ultimately stored in a set of molecules that includes ATP. Once the energy has been captured in this way, it is used in another complex series of reactions to produce essential molecules called carbohydrates. The most important carbohydrate molecule is glucose, an energy-rich sugar that also provides the module from which all of a plant's cellulose and starch polymers are made (see Chapter 22). The end result is the conversion of the energy in the electromagnetic radiation from the Sun into chemical energy stored in the bonds holding the carbohydrate molecules together.

The shorthand way of thinking about photosynthesis is to say:

- ▶ **In words:** Energy plus carbon dioxide plus water react to produce carbohydrate plus oxygen.
- ▶ **In equation form:**

$$\text{energy} + CO_2 + H_2O \rightarrow \text{carbohydrate} + O_2$$

• **Figure 21-9** The process of photosynthesis. Chloroplasts in the leaf absorb energy from the Sun. That energy is then used to convert carbon dioxide from the atmosphere and water into carbohydrates, such as glucose.

The rate at which plants produce oxygen and carbohydrates is usually limited by the amount of carbon dioxide in the air.

The most familiar molecule involved in photosynthesis, chlorophyll, occurs in various forms that can absorb red and blue light. The energy that falls as sunlight on a leaf is white light, roughly equal mixtures of all colors of the visible spectrum (see Chapter 6). The leaf absorbs red and blue components of light from the Sun, while green light is reflected—a situation that explains why leaves appear green. In addition to chlorophyll, a number of secondary molecules are involved in photosynthesis. These molecules tend to absorb blue light, so they appear to be red and orange. A normal leaf contains much more chlorophyll than secondary molecules, so the color of the secondary molecules is masked. In the fall, however, when the leaf dies and chlorophyll is no longer produced, its underlying color can be seen. We say that the leaves "change color" although, in fact, the brilliant fall colors were there all the time.

Vicky Kasala/PhotoDisc, Inc./Getty Images

Hans Strand/Stone/Getty Images

Plants are green because of the presence of chlorophyll.

Glycolysis: The First Step in Energy Generation in the Cell

The primary source of energy for living things comes from the oxidation of carbohydrates such as glucose. These sorts of reactions, called **respiration**, are taking place in all of your cells at this very moment. Your lungs breathe in oxygen produced by plants, while blood in your circulatory system transports that oxygen to every cell in your body. At the same time carbon dioxide, which is the end product of the breakdown of carbohydrates that you ingest in your food, is removed by the circulatory system to the lungs and breathed out as waste.

Respiration retrieves the energy stored in glucose in a complex series of cellular chemical reactions. Chemical bonds of the glucose molecule store chemical potential energy. The more glucose bonds that are broken—that is, the smaller the pieces of the final molecules—the more energy the cell will have transferred.

The first step in the extraction of energy from glucose is called **glycolysis** (the "lysis," or splitting, of glucose). This rather complex process takes place in nine separate steps, each of which is governed by a specific molecule called an enzyme (see Chapter 22). At the end of the process, a single molecule of glucose, which contains six linked carbon atoms, is split into two smaller molecules called pyruvic acids, each containing three carbon atoms. In addition, the reaction makes two molecules of ATP and two molecules of other energy carriers. In most cells, the energy stored in these other carriers is converted into two or three more molecules of ATP before they leave the mitochondria. Thus each glucose molecule can ultimately yield six to eight molecules of ATP through the process of glycolysis.

After glucose has been split by glycolysis, energy can be generated in two separate and distinct ways: respiration and fermentation. Respiration requires the presence of oxygen and is therefore said to be *aerobic*. The primary function of your lungs and circulatory system is to maintain this aerobic respiration. Fermentation, on the other hand, can occur in the absence of oxygen and is said to be *anaerobic*.

Fermentation: A Way to Keep Glycolysis Going

Pyruvic acid molecules still hold a great deal of chemical potential energy. In the absence of oxygen, however, that energy cannot be liberated to run cellular metabolism. In this situation, a process called **fermentation** can be used to provide energy to keep glycolysis going. As long as there is a supply of glucose, the cell can go on generating energy, albeit somewhat inefficiently. In some cases, as in single-celled yeast, the end product of fermentation is ethanol—ordinary beverage alcohol. This sort of fermentation provides the basis for the production of wine and other alcoholic drinks.

Microscopic organisms undergo fermentation—a process that is critical to the production of cheese, bread, and wine.

Charles Schiller/FoodPix/Jupiter Images Corp

When cells have to use glucose in the absence of oxygen, only a fraction of the available energy is used, and a great deal of energy is left stored in other molecules. Yeast is a good example. You know that alcohol, which is produced by yeast during the process of fermentation, contains a great deal of energy—it can, after all, be burned as a fuel. The chemical energy in alcohol is left behind by the yeast cells that made it—energy that the cells could not use because they were not able to metabolize it.

A somewhat different kind of fermentation takes place in cells of animals. The energy in pyruvic acid is normally tapped by the process of respiration (see the following section). In the absence of oxygen, however, our muscles can use fermentation to keep glycolysis going (often taking glucose from materials stored in the muscles themselves). The end product of this sort of fermentation is lactic acid, a three-carbon molecule that then accumulates in the muscle. When we undergo strenuous exercise, if our

Tim Davis/Photo Researchers

The process of respiration expels water vapor, which appears as condensation on a cold day.

bodies are not prepared to deliver all the oxygen that is needed, the cells will eventually fall back on this simpler process.

The fact that some of our cells can operate both with and without oxygen—the fact that they have this reserve process to fall back on—is taken by some scientists to indicate that cells evolved fermentation reactions first and only later developed the ability to burn oxygen. You can think of the body's use of fermentation as analogous to writing a term paper with a pencil when a power outage makes a computer unavailable. It's not the most efficient way to work, but it gets the job done.

The Final Stages of Respiration

In human cells, the energy-rich products of glycolysis react in the mitochondria, and all the available energy that was stored in the glucose is retrieved. The end effect of these chemical reactions is that oxygen and the pyruvic acids take part in a complex series of reactions to produce carbon dioxide, water, and a large amount of energy stored in ATP molecules.

In cells where oxygen is available, pyruvic acids (three-carbon molecules) are first broken down into two-carbon groups and then enter a complex series of chemical reactions called the *Krebs cycle*. In the course of this cycle, the original glucose is broken down and its carbon is converted into carbon dioxide, some energy is released to ATP molecules, and the rest of the energy is stored in some of the other energy-carrying molecules. In the final stage of respiration, the energy in these other carriers is used to produce even more ATP molecules.

The exact number of ATP molecules produced from a single glucose molecule depends on details of the structure of the mitochondrial membranes and varies slightly from one cell to another. As a general rule, however, the metabolism of a single glucose molecule ultimately produces 36 to 38 molecules of ATP, which can then be used by the cell to run all the rest of its chemical machinery. Compare this production to the 6 to 8 ATP molecules produced by glycolysis alone.

Thus aerobic reactions yield significantly more energy per molecule of glucose than anaerobic ones yield. It can be argued that the large amounts of energy needed to maintain a multicellular organism would not have been available to organisms that had not developed respiration. The outcome of this line of thought is that before a significant amount of oxygen became available in the atmosphere, complex life-forms could not have developed. We will discuss the development of complex organisms in Chapter 25.

Stop and Think! Where did you get the energy that keeps you alive today?

Cell Division

A key principle of the cell theory is that all cells arise from previous cells, but how does this process occur? Individual cells do not last forever. As you read this text, cells are dying and being replaced throughout your body. In order for this sort of replacement to occur, cells must be able to reproduce. Microscopic observations of living cells have revealed that cells divide and reproduce by two separate processes, called mitosis and meiosis.

Mitosis

In the great majority of cell divisions in living organisms, a single cell splits, so that two cells appear where once there was only one. It is by means of this process of cell division, called **mitosis,** that organisms grow and maintain themselves. When you get a cut or sunburn, this process quickly replaces damaged cells. Mitosis involves the reproduction of individual cells but is not involved in sexual reproduction in higher plants and animals.

In Chapter 23, we will discover that DNA governs the chemical workings of any cell. DNA in eukaryotes is contained within the cell nucleus in structures called *chromosomes*. When chromosomes were first discovered in the nineteenth century, there was an intense debate about their function. Today, we understand that each chromosome is a long strand of the DNA double helix, with the strand wrapped around a series of protein cores like tape around a spool.

Chromosomes come in pairs, but there is no connection between the number of chromosomes and the complexity of an organism. Humans have 46 chromosomes (23 pairs), but the number of pairs varies from one species to another. Mosquitoes, for example, have 6 while dogs have 78.

The process of mitosis is shown schematically in Figure 21-10. Assume for simplicity that we begin with a cell that has just two pairs of chromosomes, one shown larger than the other in Figure 21-10*a*. Each individual chromosome of the pair, furthermore, differs slightly from the other because (as we shall see in the discussion of meiosis, below) one comes from the male parent and the other from the female parent. Individual chromosomes in a pair are thus illustrated in red and green. These differences in size and color will help you follow the path of each chromosome through cell division.

The first step in mitosis is the copying of the chromosomes (a process we will describe in more detail in the next chapter). As shown in Figure 21-10*b*, a cell that is about to divide has twice the normal number of chromosomes, neatly paired off like socks that have been sorted after going through the laundry.

After duplication of the chromosomes, the nuclear membrane dissolves and a series of fibers called *spindle fibers* develop (Figure 21-10*c*). The matched chromosome pairs are pulled apart and migrate to opposite ends of the cell. After this separation, the nuclear membranes reform and the cell splits down the middle (Figure 21-10*d*). The result is two cells, each of which carries a set of chromosomes that are identical to the original. Powerful microscopes can capture photographs of these stages of mitosis in progress (Figure 21-11).

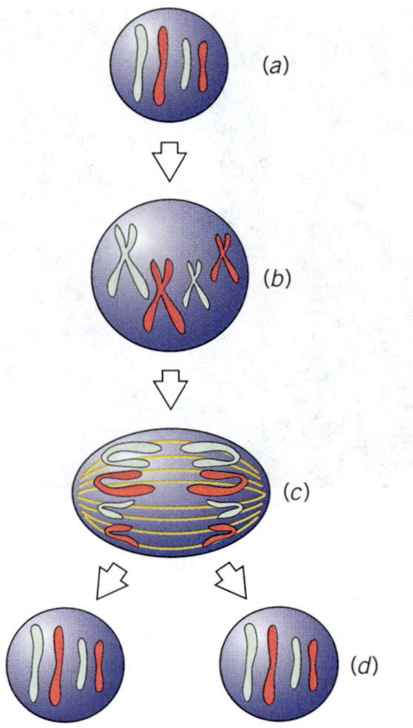

• **Figure 21-10** Mitosis, shown schematically for a cell with two pairs of chromosomes, one larger and one smaller *(a)*. In each pair, red and green individual chromosomes are from different parents. *(b)* Chromosomes duplicate, resulting in two identical sets of two pairs. *(c)* Matched pairs of chromosomes are pulled along spindles to opposite ends of the cell. *(d)* A new membrane forms and separates the parent cell into two identical daughter cells.

• **Figure 21-11** Mitosis, shown in actual photographs of a dividing cell. *(a)* Chromosomes are duplicated and thicken. *(b)* They align along the center of the cell. *(c)* They are sorted into two groups. *(d)* The matched pairs migrate to opposite poles of the cell. Finally, the cell divides, and each daughter has a full complement of chromosomes.

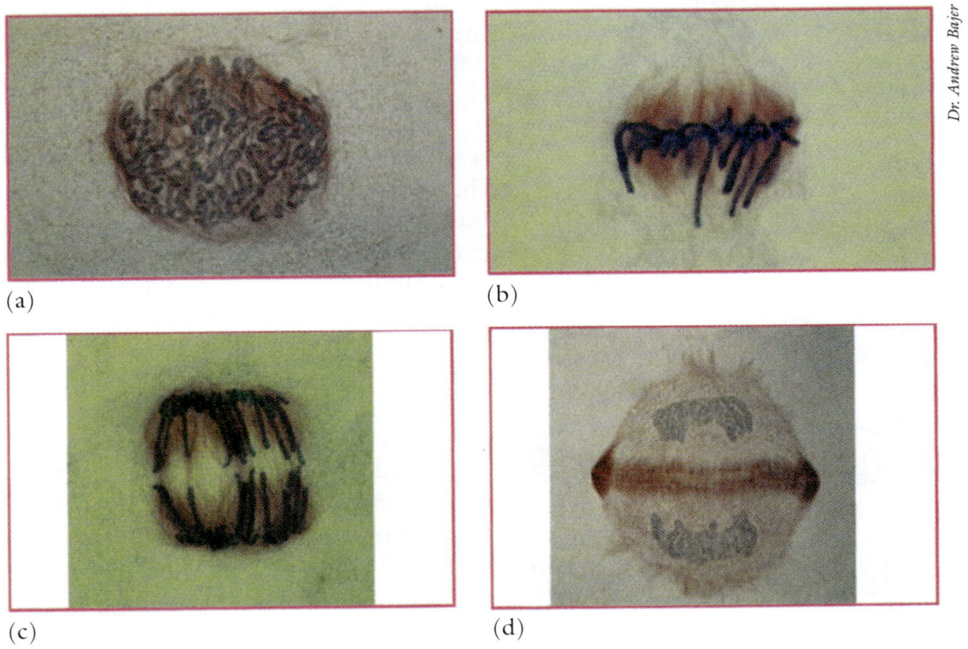

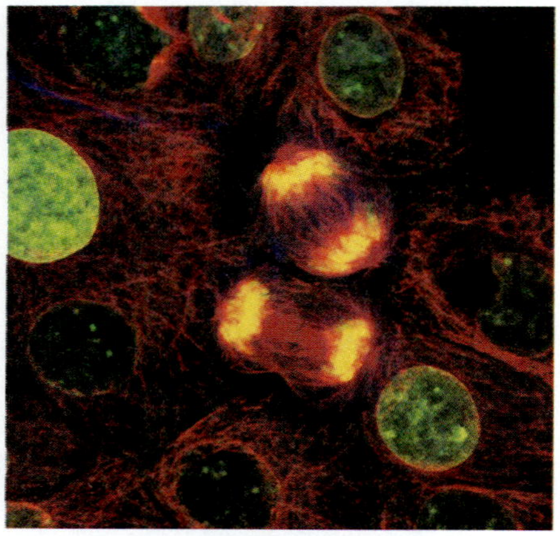

David Becker/Stone/Getty Images

A human cell dividing. Genetic material shows as dark pink in this false-color photomicrograph.

Some cells in your body divide often; the cells in the lining of the small intestine, for example, are replaced every few days. Other cells, such as those of the nervous system, don't divide at all after maturity.

Meiosis

A remarkable, specialized kind of cell division called **meiosis** takes place in a few cells in organisms that reproduce sexually. In this process a single cell with a full complement of chromosomes splits to form four daughter cells, or *gametes,* each of which has half the number of chromosomes found in most normal cells. The central function of meiosis is to generate the sperm and eggs (or ova) that will later combine in sexual reproduction to produce a new member of the species. Recall that in mitosis, two daughter cells are genetically identical to the original cell, but in meiosis each gamete has its own unique new combination of genetic material.

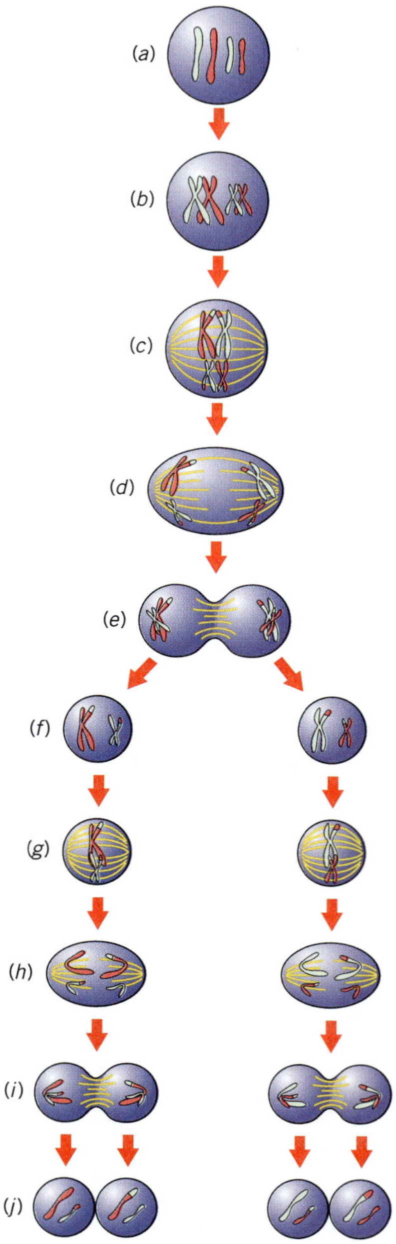

• **Figure 21-12** Meiosis, shown schematically (see text). As in mitosis, the chromosomes are duplicated and paired. The pairs separate and the cell divides for the first time. The chromosome pairs then separate and each daughter divides again, producing a total of four cells, each with half the normal complement of DNA.

Key steps of meiosis are illustrated in Figure 21-12. As in Figure 21-10, we begin with a cell that has two pairs of chromosomes, one shown larger than the other and with distinctively colored individual chromosomes (Figure 21-12*a*). The first step of meiosis is the same as for mitosis—the chromosomes are copied so that the cell has twice the usual amount of DNA—two larger identical green chromosomes, two smaller identical red chromosomes, and so on—in "X"-shaped pairs (compare Figures 21-10*b* and 21-12*b*). But from this point, meiosis differs from mitosis in several important and striking ways.

By an extraordinary mechanism, two X-shaped pairs of chromosomes (one all-red and one all-green) cross over each other and can exchange short lengths of genetic material, thus generating chromosomes with a new mix of genetic material from both parents (Figure 21-13; this effect is illustrated as mixed red and green in Figure 21-12*c*). Note that at this point the cell has eight chromosomes, some of which differ from any of the four original red or green chromosomes.

The remaining steps of meiosis consist of a sequence of changes that sort out these eight chromosomes into smaller groups. First, the four X-shaped pairs of chromosomes segregate along spindle fibers so that each of two daughter cells has two X-shaped pairs of chromosomes—one longer and one shorter (Figure 21-12*d–f*). Then the X-shaped pairs of chromosomes in each daughter cell are pulled apart along more spindle fibers and these cells split again, producing a total of four gametes (Figure 21-12*g–j*). Each of these four sex cells has two individual chromosomes, or half the normal complement. These chromosomes eventually are incorporated into sperm or egg.

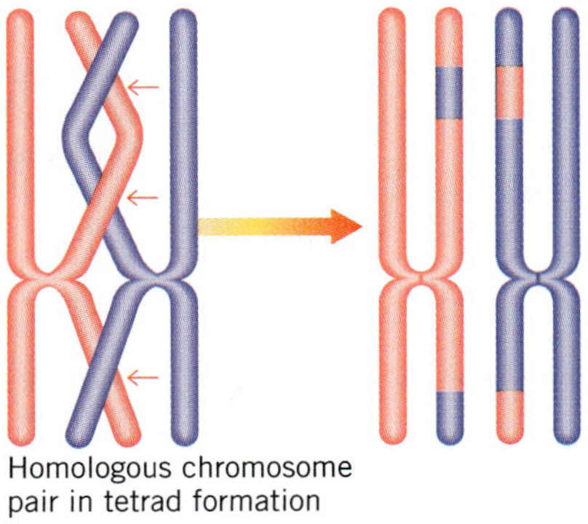

• **Figure 21-13** Crossing over between pairs of chromosomes results in the shuffling of genetic material to yield chromosomes with a new genetic makeup.

At first glance this elaborate process of meiosis may seem to be an extravagant and unnecessary way to divide cells. However, as we shall see in Chapter 25, the ability of sexually reproducing organisms constantly to vary their genetic makeup can provide a tremendous advantage in the struggle to survive.

Thinking More About | Cells

Biochemical Evidence for Evolution

The most striking thing about the energy metabolism of cells is that every single living thing on Earth, from the lowest bit of pond scum to the cells in our own bodies, uses part or all of the same chemical reaction cycles to obtain energy. In other words, they share a common biochemical background.

Most cells get energy from glucose by the process of glycolysis. Cells in advanced organisms—those in your own body, for example—can get more energy by adding more oxidation steps to the process of glycolysis. Some cells cannot do this, and therefore obtain less energy from each glucose molecule. This difference turns out to be a universal feature of living things; that is, when you examine life's chemical reactions, you find that more specialized cells tend to use more chemical processes, but those specialized reactions are built up from chemical reactions present in more primitive cells.

You can think of the situation in cells as something like the way a complex chemical factory might develop. Long ago the factory may have made just one kind of chemical, perhaps white powdered lime for your lawn. As the factory grew and expanded, many new chemicals were produced—fertilizers and insecticides, for example. But the lime-making operation was still intact, ready to be used any time. We could, in fact, deduce the history of the factory by taking it apart and seeing how various chemical operations have been added on.

Scientists suspect that cells, the chemical factories of life, behave the same way. Biochemical evidence demonstrates that older, simpler chemical reactions lie at the heart of the more complex operations of today's cells. Some biologists argue that this fact implies that all life descended from a common ancestor. How could you make such an argument based on what you know of respiration and fermentation? What do you think the more-primitive ancestors must have been like? Do you think the ancestors must have been in an environment that was rich in oxygen? Why or why not?

Summary

Cells, complex chemical systems with the ability to duplicate themselves, are the fundamental units of life. All cells are bounded by a *cell membrane* consisting of a double layer of elongated molecules. Most plants also have a *cell wall* made of cellulose and other strong polymers. Nutrients move into and wastes pass out of the cell through the cell membrane at *receptors,* which bind to specific molecules because of their distinctive shapes.

Cells possess a complex internal structure with many different kinds of chemical machinery. All but the most primitive cells have a *nucleus,* a structure surrounded by a double cell membrane that contains DNA. Other discrete structures, or *organelles,* in the cell perform various specialized functions.

Every cell must have a chemical mechanism for obtaining and distributing energy—the process of *metabolism.* Plants absorb light from the Sun and convert this radiant energy into chemical energy in *chloroplasts* by the process of *photosynthesis.* Animals must eat food with chemical potential energy, primarily carbohydrates such as glucose originally derived from plants. The first step in getting energy from glucose is *glycolysis,* a series of chemical reactions that take place in *mitochondria,* by which the glucose molecule is split into pyruvic acids. In the process of *fermentation,* pyruvic acids are broken down into molecules such as ethanol and lactic acid and the energy is used to keep fermentation going. In the process of *respiration,* pyruvic acid molecules are broken down to carbon dioxide and water, liberating much more energy in the process.

Most cells divide by the process of *mitosis,* in which chromosomes are first duplicated, then separated. The cell then divides, producing two daughters, each of which has the same complement of DNA as the original cell. In *meiosis,* which produces sperm and ova for sexual reproduction, chromosome duplication is followed by two divisions that result in a set of four cells, each of which has half the normal complement of DNA.

Key Terms

cell
cell membrane
receptor
cell wall
nucleus
organelle
chloroplasts
mitochondria
metabolism
photosynthesis
respiration
glycolysis
fermentation
mitosis
meiosis

Review Questions

1. What is a cell?
2. How big are the largest and smallest cells?
3. Give an example of how the shape of a particular type of cell is well suited to its function.
4. State three tenets of the cell theory.
5. What is the difference between a light microscope and an electron microscope? What are the smallest things that can be seen with each?
6. How do materials move across cell membranes?
7. How is the cell membrane analogous to the walls of a factory?
8. What is the function of receptors in the cell membrane?
9. How do cell walls differ from cell membranes?
10. What is the difference between a prokaryote and a eukaryote? Give examples of each.
11. What are the differences between chloroplasts and mitochondria? How are they similar?
12. What does the double membrane of the nucleus tell us about the evolution of eukaryotes?
13. What is ATP? What role does it play in the energy balance of a cell?
14. In what ways are chloroplasts and mitochondria similar? How do they differ?
15. Why do leaves appear green? What happens when they change color?
16. What are the products of photosynthesis? What molecules are involved in making photosynthesis happen in plants?
17. What is fermentation? How does it provide energy for living cells?
18. What is respiration? How does it provide energy for living cells?
19. Compare the energy released by the conversion of glucose in respiration versus fermentation.
20. In what ways are mitosis and meiosis similar? How do they differ?

Discussion Questions

1. How do organelles relate to cells? What organelles have a double cellular membrane?
2. What does it mean to say that almost all life on Earth depends on photosynthesis?
3. What sources of energy other than the Sun might some organisms use?
4. In what ways do the cells of plants and animals differ? In what ways are they the same?
5. List all the ways you can think of in which cells are analogous to chemical factories.
6. Why is it necessary for a cell's membrane to be semipermeable? How do receptors improve the transport of substances across the cell's membrane?
7. Does a larger organism need more chromosomes? Why or why not?
8. Explain how the development of the electron microscope improved our knowledge of cell structure and function. What other technological advances have furthered our understanding of biological processes?

Investigations

1. Examine a drop of your own blood in a light microscope. What kinds of cells do you see?
2. Locate an electron microscope on your campus or at a nearby laboratory. Arrange a visit to watch the microscope in action. All analytical equipment has three major components: hardware to produce and control a source of energy (in this case the electron beam), hardware to mount and manipulate the specimen, and hardware to detect the interaction of the sample with the energy. Sketch the microscope and control panels and indicate which parts are associated with which of these three components.
3. Many everyday products, including vinegar, Swiss cheese, and bread dough, rely on the process of fermentation. Investigate some of these varied products and the microorganisms that enable their manufacture.
4. We often hear of "aerobic" exercises. Is there any connection between these exercises and aerobic processes in cells?

5. Look at water from a local pond or lake under a microscope. If you were van Leeuwenhoek, seeing this for the first time, how would you describe it?

6. Investigate the relative division rates of the body's different kinds of cells. Which cell types divide most rapidly? Which divide most slowly? Why are there such different rates?

7. Investigate what diseases are associated with cells that divide too rapidly or too slowly.

8. Visit a local vineyard and learn about the various forms of yeast and fermentation that are used to make wine. Why does sparkling wine and Champagne have carbonation? Where does the carbonation come from?

9. What forms of energy are used when someone lifts a barbell to momentary muscular failure? What are the byproducts of this activity? Are they different from the byproducts produced by a marathoner's muscles as the marathoner's race is completed?

10. Organelles perform various functions within each cell. Investigate the various fuctions that different types of cells perform within the human body.

11. Investigate how many different types of muscle cells are found within the human body. How are muscle cells different from neurons?

22
Molecules of Life

What constitutes a healthy diet?

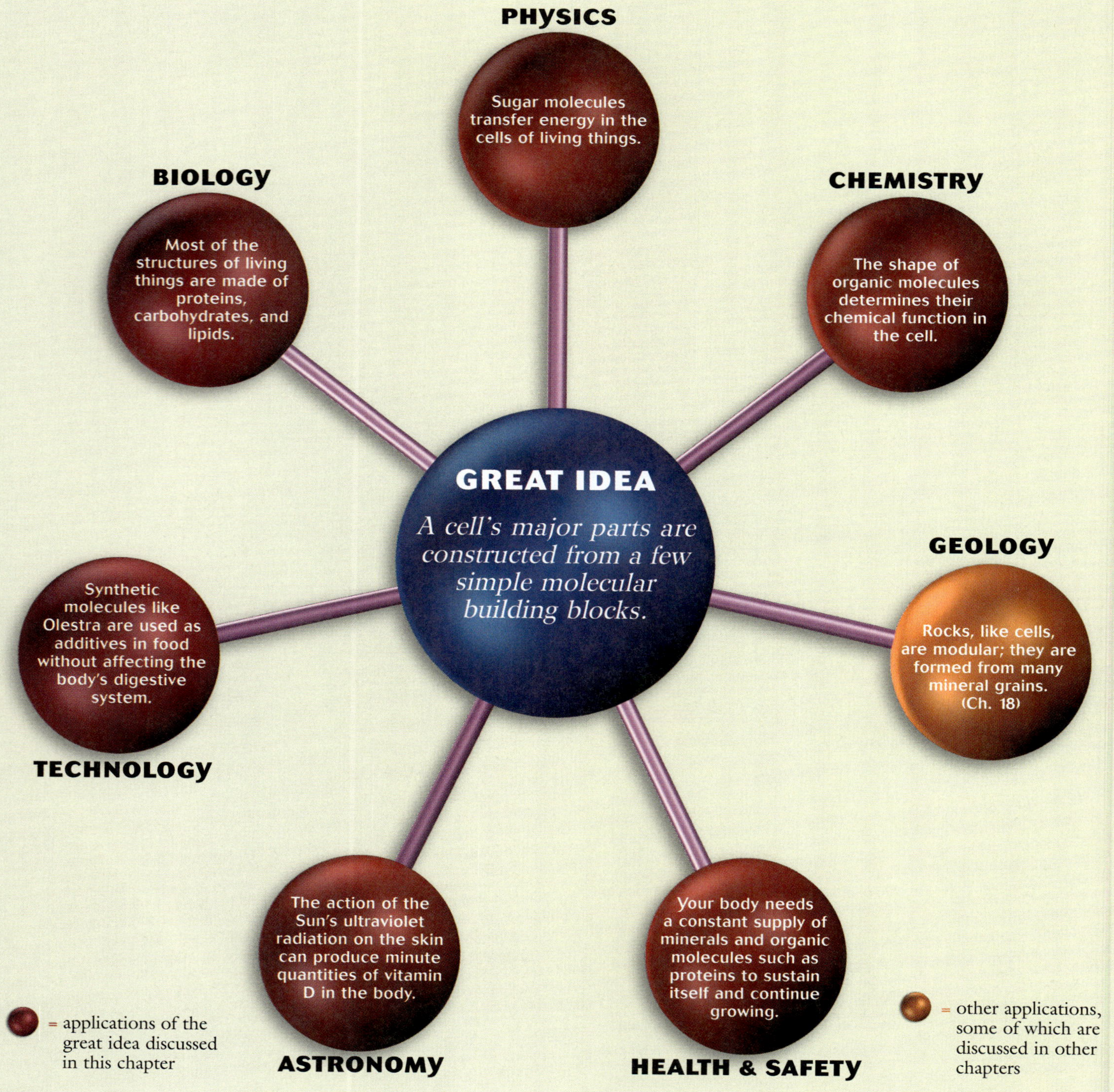

Science Through the Day | An Afternoon Snack

A granola bar makes a tasty, energy-rich, mid-afternoon snack. You lie back on your beach towel, take a bite and start to think about food. Why do we get hungry? What chemicals make up food? Why do some foods taste better than others?

Take a close look at the colorful granola bar wrapper and find the "Nutrition Facts" printed on the back. At the top of the list is "Calories"—a measure of food energy. Our bodies require energy to do work, just like every other physical system. That's why we get hungry.

The nutrition facts also include information on specific kinds of molecules, notably fat, carbohydrates and protein. These molecules are fundamental building blocks of every living thing and so are an essential part of our diets. We need a steady supply of these molecules because we are, quite literally, what we eat. Food tastes good because our tastebuds are fine-tuned to these critical molecules.

Jonathan A. Meyers/Photo Researchers

Organic Molecules

Next time you're outside, look closely at a tree. The trunk and limbs divide over and over again, a branching that is mirrored by the hidden root system. The tree has countless almost identical leaves on every limb, as well as myriad seeds in their season. Repeating the same basic patterns over and over again results in the complex structure of the tree.

Structures in your city or town reveal the same kind of patterns. Buildings feature stacks of identical bricks, row after row of identical windows, and numerous identical shingles, slates, or other roofing materials. The sidewalk is made of slab after slab of concrete, while street lamps, signs, fence posts, and telephone poles also repeat over and over again.

Indeed, almost any complex structure found in nature or designed by humans is modular, composed of a few simple pieces that combine to form larger objects. Molecules of water form the ocean, mineral grains form rocks, and countless identical hydrogen atoms form stars. The chemicals of life are no different. A few basic molecules combine to create the wonderful complexity of life around us.

Four Basic Characteristics

Wood. Leather. Hair. Cotton. Skin. All of these materials originated in living systems on our planet. And like all other materials found in living things, they share some basic chemical characteristics.

Table 22-1 Atoms in the Human Body

Element	Percent
Hydrogen	61.2
Oxygen	23.5
Carbon	11.7
Nitrogen	1.1
Calcium (mostly in bones)	2.0
Phosphorus	0.2
Sulfur	0.1
All others	0.2

1. Most Molecules in Living Systems Are Based on the Chemistry of Carbon

In Chapter 10, we saw that carbon atoms possess the ability to form long chains, branches, and rings. In fact, chemists usually refer to molecules containing carbon as **organic molecules**, whether or not they are part of a living system. The branch of science devoted to the study of such carbon-based molecules and their reactions is called *organic chemistry.*

2. Life's Molecules Form from Very Few Different Elements

In terms of the percentages of atoms, just four elements—hydrogen, oxygen, carbon, and nitrogen—comprise 97.5% of our bodies' weight. Calcium in bones accounts for 2%, while phosphorus, sulfur, and all the other elements make up the remaining 0.5% (see Table 22-1). These elements combine to form the molecules that control chemical reactions in all living things.

3. The Molecules of Life Are Modular, Composed of Simple Building Blocks

Large and complicated molecules could be put together in two contrasting ways. One way would be to build each one from scratch, so that no piece of one molecule would be part of another. Another very different way would be to make the molecules modular, that is, to build them from a succession of simpler, widely available parts so that each large molecule differs from another only in the arrangement of those parts. Nature, for the most part, displays modularity in the molecules of living systems.

Modern buildings illustrate the versatility of modular construction. All kinds of buildings, from a humble cottage to a soaring skyscraper, can be built from a few basic parts—bricks, beams, windows, doors, stairs, and so on. The skyscraper and the cottage differ from each other both in the amount of material in them and in the arrangement of those materials, but they contain many of the same basic modules. This kind of modular construction is extremely efficient. It takes a great deal of work, time, and money to custom-design every door, window, and other component of your home. You might end up with a better-designed structure but at a very high price. By building your home with widely available parts, you save money and still end up with a very satisfactory dwelling.

Similarly, though life's molecules come in an extraordinary variety of shapes and functions, they are made from collections of just a few smaller molecules. This modularity does not mean that the final products are simple, just as there's nothing particularly simple about a skyscraper. It merely means that if we wish to understand how large molecules behave, we first have to talk about the simple pieces from which they are built.

4. Shape Helps to Determine the Behavior of Organic Molecules—In Other Words, Molecular Geometry Controls the Chemistry of Life

The connection between geometry and the behavior of organic molecules can be understood if you remember one important thing about chemical bonds. All chemical bonds result from the shifting of electrons among specific pairs or groups of atoms. This bonding property is particularly true of atoms that tend to form ionic, covalent, and hydrogen bonds (see Chapter 10).

A very large and complex molecule may have millions of atoms arranged in a complicated shape. If this large molecule is to take part in chemical reactions—if it is to bind to another molecule, for example—then that binding must take place through the actions of the valence electrons of atoms near the outsides of the two molecules. Specific atoms in each molecule must be able to get near enough to each other so that their electrons can form the bond. Consequently, the geometrical shape of a molecule plays a crucial role, because it determines whether atoms that can form bonds in each molecule will be able to get close enough together for the bonds actually to form.

In principle, an infinite number of molecules could be constructed according to these four rules. In fact, when we examine natural systems, we find that only four general classes of molecules govern most of life's main chemical functions. We'll discuss three of these classes—proteins, carbohydrates, and lipids—in this chapter (the fourth important group of molecules, nucleic acids, are introduced in Chapter 23 on the genetic code). Throughout this discussion, you should keep in mind that all of these molecules conform to the four rules: they are carbon-based, they form from just a few elements, they are modular in structure, and their behavior depends on shape.

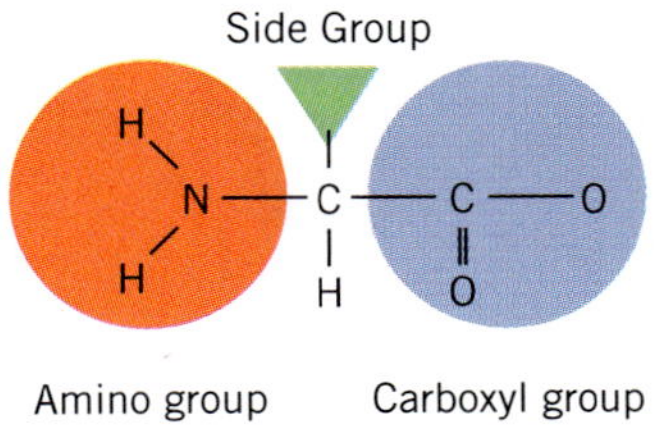

• **Figure 22-1** An amino acid, showing the amino (NH_2) and carboxylic acid (COOH) groups and the side group. The side group varies from one type of amino acid to another and gives that particular amino acid the chemical properties that distinguish it from any other.

Chemical Shorthand

If we kept showing all of the atoms and bonds, as we do for an amino acid in Figure 22-1, diagrams of molecules would get very cluttered as the molecules become more complex. Consequently, chemists have adopted several standard shorthand ways of representing organic molecules. Many molecules can be represented by the following rules:

1. *No hydrogen atoms or bonds to hydrogen atoms are shown in the diagram.*
2. *Carbon atoms are not shown explicitly.*

As an example of how this notation works, look at the following diagram. Both of these drawings show molecules of benzene (a volatile liquid sometimes used as a motor fuel). On the left, all the atoms are shown, and you can see that each carbon atom forms four bonds to its neighboring atoms. On the right, the carbon atoms are not shown, but we know they are located at the points where the bonds come together. Similarly, the hydrogen atoms are not shown, but we see that each carbon atom has only three bonds shown. We infer the existence of the hydrogen atom by the "missing" bond.

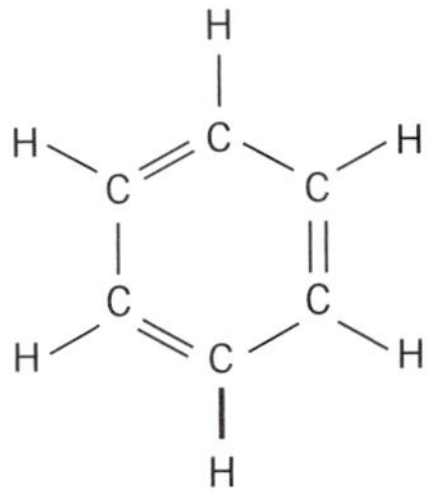

All atoms and bonds are shown.

Only carbon–carbon bonds are shown. Carbon atoms, hydrogen atoms, and carbon–hydrogen bonds are implied.

Science in the Making •

The Synthesis of Urea

In the early 1800s, scientists were not convinced that molecules in living systems are formed according to the same chemical rules that govern those in nonliving systems. Such molecules, after all, had not been produced in the laboratory. In 1828, a German chemist by the name of Friedrich Wöhler (1800–1882) performed a series of experiments that were crucial in establishing the ordinariness of organic molecules.

Like many scientists at that time, Wöhler had a breadth of experience that is unusual today. Before he began his career as a chemistry teacher, for example, he became a medical doctor and qualified in the specialty of gynecology. He was also interested in the practical aspects of chemistry, and he collected minerals from the time he was a child. He described his crucial experiments this way: "I found that whenever one tried to combine cyanic acid (a common laboratory chemical) and ammonia, a white crystalline solid appeared that behaved like neither cyanic acid nor ammonia."

After extensive testing, Wöhler found that the white crystals were identical to urea, a substance routinely found in the kidneys and (as the name suggests) urine. In other words, the appearance of that "white crystalline solid" showed that it is possible to take ordinary chemicals off the shelf and produce a substance found in living systems. He had demonstrated that the same chemical processes typical of abiotic materials might form organic molecules.

With humor uncharacteristic of most academicians, Wöhler announced his findings in a letter as follows: "I can no longer, as it were, hold back my chemical urine: and I have to let out that I can make urea without needing a kidney, whether of man or dog." •

Proteins: The Workhorses of Life

The molecules we call proteins play many key roles in living systems. Some proteins form building materials from which large structures are formed. Your hair, your fingernails, the tendons that hold your muscles in place, and much of the connective tissue that holds your body together, for example, are made primarily of protein molecules. Proteins also serve as the *receptors* that regulate the movement of materials across cell walls, and thus control what goes into and out of each cell in your body (see Chapter 21). Proteins play many specialized roles in our bodies—for example, as hormones that regulate bodily functions and as antibodies that protect against infection and disease. In addition, proteins serve as enzymes, molecules that control the rate of complex chemical reactions in living things (see the following section).

A spider's silk, fingernails, and hair are everyday examples of structural proteins.

Nuridsany et Perennou/Photo Researchers

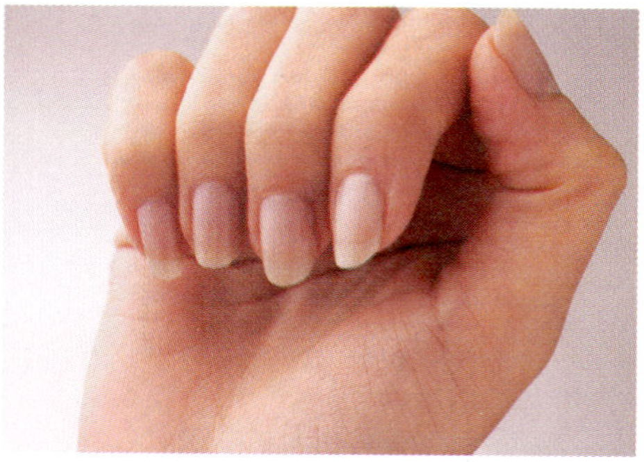

Laurent/Lamy/Photo Researchers

Donna Day/Stone/Getty Images, Inc.

Because of these and many other functions, proteins are vital components of your diet, as you have probably heard. You must regularly take in proteins to supply your body with building materials to effect repairs and growth.

Amino Acids: The Building Blocks of Proteins

Proteins are modular just like all complex biological molecules. They are made up of strings of basic building blocks called **amino acids.** A typical amino acid molecule is sketched in Figure 22-1. All biological amino acids incorporate a characteristic backbone of atoms. One end terminates in a *carboxylic acid group* (COOH), a combination of carbon, oxygen, and hydrogen. On the other end is an *amino group* (NH_2), a nitrogen bonded to two hydrogen atoms. (These two groups give this category of molecules their name.) Between these two ends a carbon atom completes the backbone.

Branching off the central carbon atom is another atom or cluster of atoms, the "side group" that makes each kind of amino acids unique and interesting. Hundreds of different amino acids can be made in the laboratory, each with its different characteristic side group. A few common amino acids are sketched in Figure 22-2 to give you a sense of the kind of diversity that is possible within this basic structure.

Two amino acids can bond together in a very simple way. A hydrogen atom (H) from the amino end will connect to the hydroxyl (OH) group of the carboxylic acid end of another amino acid to form a molecule of water (H_2O). This water molecule moves off (you can think of this process as "squeezing out" the water), leaving the two amino acids bonded together in what is called a *peptide bond*. This process is identical to the *condensation polymerization* reaction that is often used to manufacture plastics and other polymers (see Chapter 10). Indeed, chemists often refer to a bonded chain of amino acids as a *polypeptide*.

Once two amino acids have joined together with a peptide bond, more amino acids can be hooked onto either end by the same process to form a long string of amino acids. A **protein** is a large molecule formed by linking amino acids together in this way. There are many different amino acids to choose from, and different proteins correspond to a different ordering (as well as a different total number) of the amino acids in the string.

One of the great surprises that came out of the study of biochemistry in the early part of the twentieth century was that although chemists can synthesize hundreds of different amino acids, only a small number of amino acids actually appear in the proteins

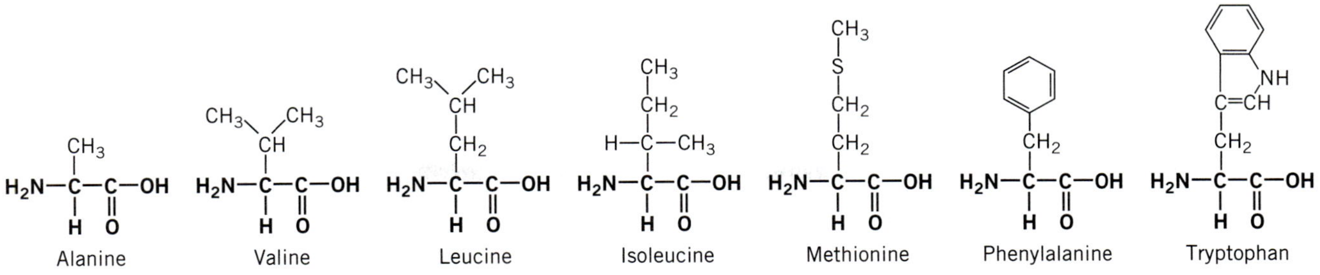

• **Figure 22-2** Several amino acids. Each has a distinctive side group (blue type) that branches off the central carbon atom.

of living systems on Earth. Only 20 different amino acids are produced in cells, although some of these are modified once the amino acid string is put together. The mystery of why only 20 amino acids are found in living things has a possible explanation in terms of the theory of evolution, which we explore in Chapter 25. Note, however, that even with only 20 basic building blocks, an almost infinite variety of different strings or proteins can be formed (see the following "Science by the Numbers" section).

The Structure of Proteins

Proteins are extremely complex molecules, sometimes consisting of many thousands of amino acids and millions of atoms. One of the great triumphs of modern science has been to determine the exact atomic structures of many of these large molecules. To accomplish this feat, biochemists first have to isolate quantities of pure protein, form delicate single crystals in which the large molecules line up in a regular array, and examine the crystals by X-ray techniques that reveal the distribution of atoms in space.

A protein's structure is usually described in four stages, each representing an increasing order of complexity (Figure 22-3).

1. Primary Structure

The exact sequence of amino acids that go into a given protein is called its *primary structure*. Every distinct protein has a different primary structure—that is, it has a different sequence of amino acids along its string.

2. Secondary Structure

Depending on the arrangements of amino acids in the primary structure, hydrogen bonds can form that give the final protein a specific shape. Some proteins, for example, take the form of a long helix or long spring. Others fold back on themselves repeatedly to form rough spheres. Shapes taken by the string of amino acids that makes up the primary structure of a protein are called its *secondary structure*.

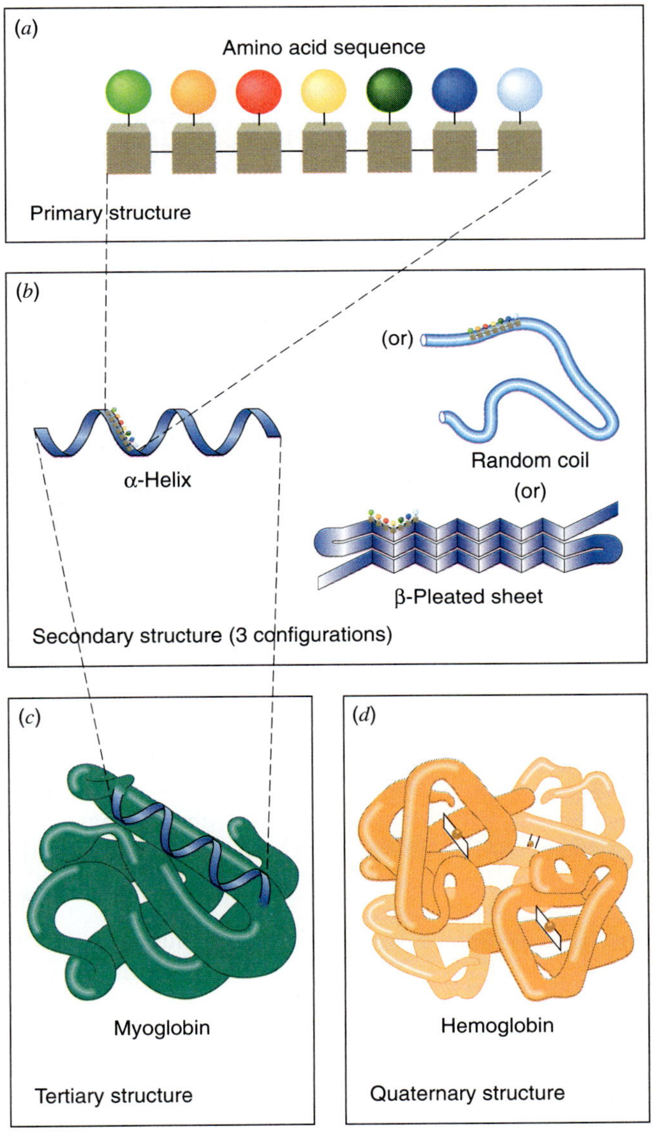

• **Figure 22-3** The structure of a protein can be described in four steps. Primary structure *(a)* is the sequence of amino acids. Secondary structure *(b)* is the way the sequence kinks or bends. Tertiary structure *(c)* is the shape of the completely folded protein. Quaternary structure *(d)* is the clustering of several proteins to form the active structure, in this case, hemoglobin, which carries oxygen in your bloodstream.

When you cook an egg, you can see the effect of secondary structure. The proteins in egg white are wrapped up into tiny spheres scattered throughout the fluid. This is why normal egg white is transparent. When you cook the egg white, you break the hydrogen bonds that keep the protein wrapped up and allow the molecules to unfold. The tough mat they form when they interlock gives the cooked egg white its characteristic texture and appearance.

3. Tertiary Structure

As parts of the amino acid chain fold back on itself, atoms in the side groups can come into contact with each other. As a result, additional cross-linking chemical bonds form between side groups in amino acids in different parts of the chain. One common link occurs between sulfur atoms in different side groups. The distinctive shape of human insulin, for example, arises because of bonds that form between sulfur atoms in the amino acid cystine.

As a result of these links, a protein will twist around, kink up, and fold itself into a complex shape, much as a string will fold itself into a complex shape if it's dropped on a table. This complex folding is the *tertiary structure* of the protein.

4. Quaternary Structure

Finally, two or more long chains, each with its own secondary and tertiary structure, may come together to form a single larger unit. This joining of separate protein chains determines the *quaternary structure* of the protein.

Predicting the exact shape that will be assumed by a given sequence of amino acids remains one of the great goals of modern biochemistry, a goal that we are still far from reaching. But whether or not we can predict the ultimate shape of a protein, the fact remains that each different sequence of amino acids will produce a large molecule with a different three-dimensional shape. This fact will become important when we consider the role of proteins in the cell's chemistry.

Science by the Numbers •

How Many Proteins Can You Make?

At first, it may seem that with only 20 different amino acids available to build proteins in living systems, the number of different kinds of proteins you could make would be rather limited. Let's do some calculations to see why this isn't the case.

Suppose we start by asking a simple question: How many different proteins, each 10 amino acids long, can we make from amino acids found in living systems? (Once you've seen the answer to this question, you'll be able to figure out for yourself how to calculate the answer for a protein with any number of amino acids.)

One way of thinking about this question is to imagine that each protein consists of 10 amino acids on a string and each amino acid can be selected from one of 20 different boxes. We could choose the first amino acid of the string from any one of 20 boxes. For each of these 20 choices for the amino acid in the first position, there are 20 choices we could make for the amino acid in the second position. Thus we could choose amino acids to fill the first two vacancies on the string in $20 \times 20 = 400$ different ways.

Following this logic, the number of ways to arrange 10 amino acids in a string is

$$20 \times 20 \times 20 \times 20 \times 20 \times 20 \times 20 \times 20 \times 20 \times 20 = 1.028 \times 10^{13}$$

Thus we could make about 10 trillion different proteins that contain 10 amino acids. This number is huge—100 million times larger than the number of proteins used in the human body. And, of course, this is just the number of different proteins you could make containing exactly 10 amino acids. Typical proteins in living systems contain many more amino acids, usually hundreds to thousands of them. The bottom line of this calculation is that, although only 20 different amino acids appear in living systems, this number still allows for a tremendous diversity of proteins. •

Proteins as Enzymes

One of the key roles that proteins play in living systems is to act as enzymes in chemical reactions in cells. An **enzyme** is a molecule with a specific shape and structure that facilitates bonding between two other molecules, but that is not permanently altered or used up in that overall reaction. Because of the presence of the enzyme, the chemical reaction takes place at a much faster rate than it otherwise would.

Enzymes play a role in every cell's chemical reactions similar to a broker or an agent in a business deal. The broker brings together a buyer and seller, but does no buying or selling. The buyer and seller eventually might find each other without the help of the broker, but the deal goes through much quicker if the broker is there. In the same way, a molecule that plays the role of an enzyme possesses a shape and structure that may bring together two other molecules in a cell and facilitate their forming a bond, or it may tear a molecule apart without itself being included in the chemical reaction. Because of the enzyme, the reaction takes place relatively quickly.

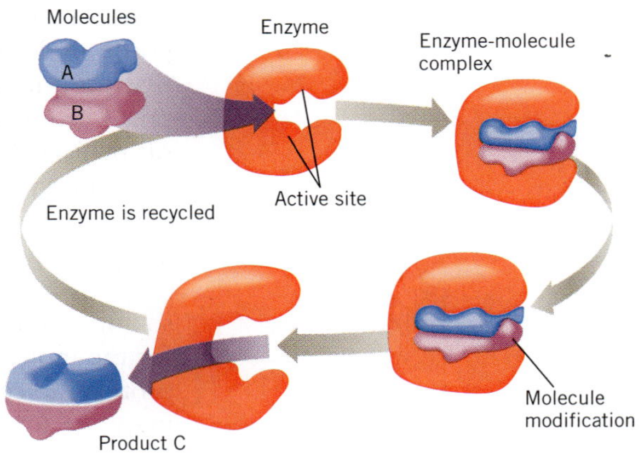

• **Figure 22-4** An enzyme in action joins two molecules (designated A and B) and produces a product (C). The product is released, and the enzyme is free to repeat the process.

Enzymes illustrate the primary importance of geometrical shape in determining how chemical reactions take place among large molecules. You can easily visualize the workings of an enzyme (see Figure 22-4). Each large molecule has places on it, atoms or small groups of atoms, where chemical bonding can take place. Think of these locations as sticky spots somewhere on a large, convoluted molecular shape. In order for two or more molecules to interact, their respective sticky spots have to come into contact. More precisely, the atoms whose electrons will eventually form the bonds must be brought close enough together for the electrons to interact. This proximity is unlikely to happen at random.

Imagine each molecule as a large pile of string that is dumped in the corner of a room, and think of the spots that could form chemical bonds as patches of glue located at random places along the string. If you took two such pieces of string and tossed them together in the corner, the chances are very slight that any of the sticky spots would come near each other. If, on the other hand, you picked up the strings and arranged them so that the sticky spots were next to each other, you could make sure that they formed a bond. In this "chemical reaction," you are playing the role of the enzyme. You cause bonds to form that probably wouldn't form without you, but you do not become a part of the bond.

Enzymes perform an analogous function in organic reactions. Typically, an enzyme is a large molecule that has particular spots on its surface into which reacting molecules will just fit. The enzyme attracts first one of the molecules and then the other. In some enzymes, two specific molecules attach themselves in only one way, so it is guaranteed that their "sticky spots" will be near each other. The chemical bonds that hold them

(a) (b)

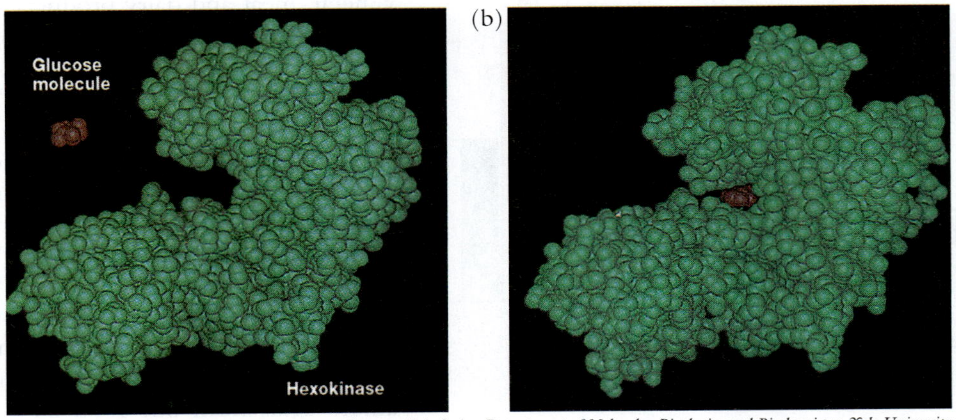

Courtesy T.A. Steitz, Department of Molecular Biophysics and Biochemistry, Yale University

A computer-generated image of an enzyme in action. A glucose molecule approaches the enzyme hexokinase (*a*). When the two molecules combine, the shape and function of the enzyme change (*b*).

together will form. Once the bonds have formed, the overall shape of the resulting composite molecule suddenly becomes different from that of either of the two molecules that went into it. Consequently, the new large molecule no longer fits into the appropriate grooves and alleys of the enzyme, and it spontaneously breaks free and wanders off by itself. This separation leaves the enzyme free to mediate the same reaction again, each time with two new pieces. Another kind of enzyme, like those in your stomach, performs the opposite function, breaking apart large molecules into smaller units over and over again.

If you think about the way an enzyme works, you'll realize why molecular shape is so important. The ridges and grooves on the surface of an enzyme serve as resting places for the molecules that interact on the enzyme's surface. Tens of thousands of different protein molecules, each of which adopts a different shape and therefore provides a resting place for different interacting molecules, are ideally suited to function in this way. For precisely this reason, proteins participate in most of the chemical reactions in living organisms.

Enzymes mediate the reactions of complex molecules in living systems. Thus the molecules that act as enzymes in living systems play a crucial role in determining the properties of those systems.

Stop and Think! The relationship between an enzyme and the molecules that it reacts with is sometimes compared to a "lock and key" mechanism. What do you think is meant by this statement, and in what ways does it apply to enzymes?

The Science of Life •

Proteins and Diet

Because proteins play such an important role in living systems, the cells in your body need a constant supply of all 20 amino acids. In adults, 12 of the 20 amino acids are synthesized in the body. The other 8, the so-called *essential amino acids,* have to be taken into the body in the proteins and other foods that we eat. Because amino acids, unlike fat, cannot be stored for long periods by the body, the essential amino acids have to be present in every meal in roughly the proportion in which they occur in the body's own proteins.

Foods vary widely in their total protein content, from about 1% in bananas and carrots to almost 30% in peanuts and some cheese. Foods that supply amino acids in roughly the same proportion as those in human proteins are called *high-quality proteins,* while those that supply too little of one or more amino acid are called *low-quality proteins.* In general, meat and dairy products supply high-quality proteins, while plant products supply low-quality proteins.

In Figure 22-5, we make this point by comparing the amount of each of the eight essential amino acids found in eggs (the food whose amino acids most closely match human protein proportions) and cornmeal. You should note, however, that it is not necessary for each food we eat, in and of itself, to supply all essential amino acids. It's possible to plan meals so that amino acids from one food make up

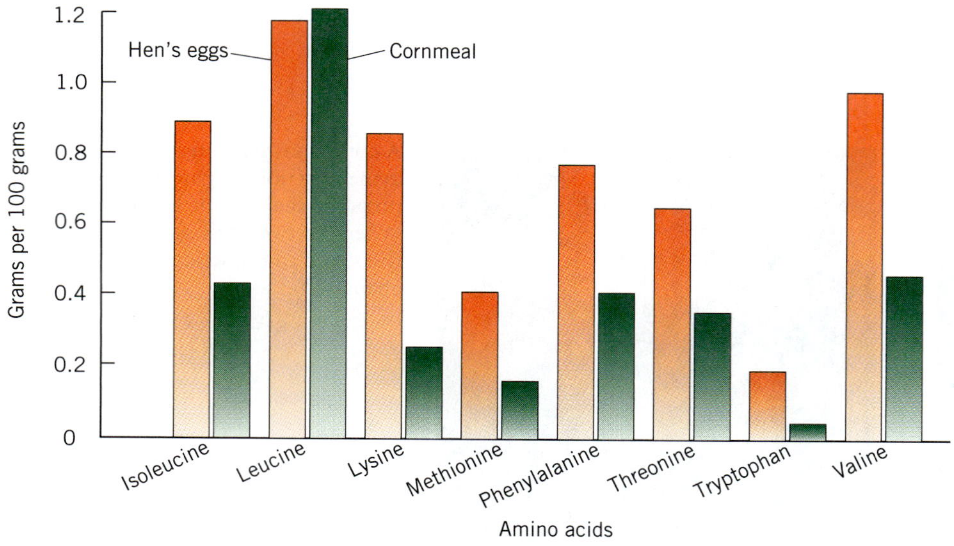

• **Figure 22-5** Proportions of essential amino acids in egg and cornmeal. The amino acid proportions for egg are close to those in the human body, whereas the cornmeal contains too little of the amino acids lysine, methionine, and tryptophan.

for deficiencies of that amino acid in the other. Many traditional meals have this property. Milk, for example, provides the lysine that breakfast cereal lacks. The American staple, the peanut butter and jelly sandwich, provides the same kind of matching proteins. In fact, many traditional foods from around the world do pretty well in supplying complementary sources of amino acids. Some examples: corn tortillas and beans (Mexico), rice and tofu (Japan), and rice and ground nuts (West Africa). Because of the fact that plants provide low-quality protein, however, individuals on vegetarian diets must plan their food intake carefully to compensate for possible protein deficiencies.

By the way, have you ever wondered why we cook meats and other foods? High temperatures quickly depolymerize proteins (see Chapter 10), thus transforming long polymer chains into individual amino acid molecules. This chemical reaction breaks down tough protein fibers so foods are more tender and easily digested. At the same time, any potentially harmful bacteria are killed when their proteins are destroyed. •

How Drugs Work

Many of the drugs we take produce their effect because of the shape of their molecules. Some drugs, for example, alter our body chemistry by blocking the action of enzymes. You can understand how such a drug might work by looking at Figure 22-4. The efficiency of the enzyme depends on the fact that the shape of its surface matches the shape of the molecules involved in the reaction. A drug molecule that attached itself to one of those crucial sites on the enzyme would block that site, preventing one of the molecules involved in the original reaction from occupying it. As a result, the enzyme would not be able to facilitate the reaction as it normally does, and the chemical balance of the cell would be changed. When you take an aspirin, for example, you are blocking the action of an enzyme that facilitates the production of molecules called prostaglandins. These molecules, among other things, affect the transmission of nerve signals.

Other drugs work in similar ways on other cellular processes. We saw in Chapter 21, for example, that part of the process of moving materials in and out of a cell across the cell membrane involves the fit between the molecules being moved and the specialized proteins, called receptors, in the membrane. A drug that attaches to the receptor or to the material that is being brought in or out of the cell will block this match and alter the traffic in and out of the cell. Similarly, in Chapter 5, we noted that nerve impulses are transmitted from one nerve cell to the next by special molecules called neurotransmitters. These molecules are shaped so that they fit into specific sites on the "downstream" nerve cell. Many drugs, including alcohol and Valium, gain their effect because they have the right shape to bind to the synapses and alter their operation.

As our understanding of the geometry of organic molecules has increased, scientists are increasingly able to produce molecules with the right shape from scratch. Products made in this way have been nicknamed "designer drugs" (you'll learn more about them in Chapter 24). One such drug, called captopril, has been in use since 1975. This drug blocks the action of an enzyme that produces molecules that contribute to hypertension, and so is used to control that condition. Designer drugs for treating psoriasis, glaucoma, AIDS, and some forms of cancer and arthritis are in advanced stages of testing and may be on the market soon.

Carbohydrates

Carbohydrates, the second important class of modular molecules found in all living things, are made up of carbon, hydrogen, and oxygen. They play a central role in the way that living things acquire and use energy, and they form many of the solid structures of living things. You use carbohydrates every day in many of the foods you eat, the fuels you burn, the clothes you wear, and even the paper of this book.

Walter Bibikow/Getty Images

The fibers that hold these plants up are made from glucose.

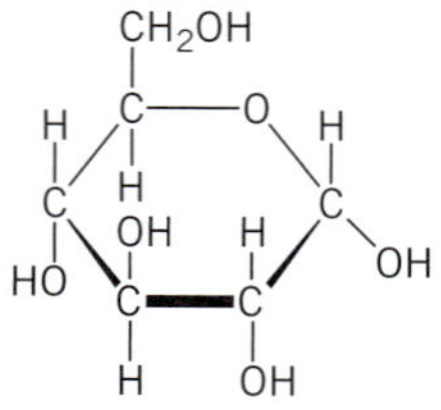

Glucose

• **Figure 22-6** The structure of glucose.

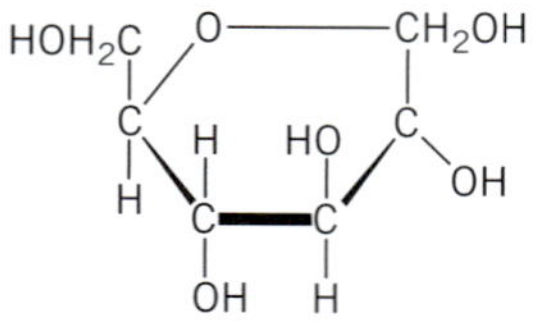

Fructose

• **Figure 22-7** The structure of fructose. It has the same number and kinds of atoms as glucose but is a different arrangement.

The simplest carbohydrates are **sugars,** molecules that usually contain five, six, or seven carbon atoms arranged in a ring-like structure. *Glucose,* an important sugar in the energy cycle of living things, is sketched in Figure 22-6. Glucose figures prominently in the energy metabolism of every living cell; it supplies the energy that we use to move and grow.

The general chemical formula for sugar is $C_nH_{2n}O_n$ or $C_n(H_2O)_n$. Glucose, for example, has the formula $C_6H_{12}O_6$. As often happens with organic molecules, other forms of the molecule have the same chemical composition but have the component arranged differently. In Figure 22-7, for example, we show the sugar fructose. As the name implies, this sugar is commonly found in fruit. It has the same number of carbon, hydrogen, and oxygen atoms as glucose, but the atoms are arranged slightly differently, and this different arrangement gives fructose a different chemical behavior.

Chemists call individual sugar molecules *monosaccharides,* meaning "one sugar." (The same root word is used when an overly sentimental story is described as "saccharine.") The carbohydrates that we eat, however, are usually formed from two or more sugar molecules. Ordinary table sugar, for example, is made from two sugars, glucose and fructose, linked together by covalent bonds.

When many sugars are strung together in a chain, the resulting molecule is called a *polysaccharide* ("many sugars"). The two most familiar polysaccharides are starch and cellulose. Both of these kinds of molecules are made from long chains of glucose molecules. They differ from each other only in the details of the way the glucose molecules bind to each other (Figure 22-8).

Starches, a common component of the human diet, are a large family of molecules in which the glucose constituents link together at certain points along the ring. Starches are found in many plants, such as potatoes and corn. Animals also form a glucose polymer, called *glycogen* or *animal starch,* which is stored in the liver and in muscle tissues. Humans break down starch molecules with an enzyme in the digestive system, thus releasing individual glucose molecules, which provide the fundamental energy fuel used by cells.

Cellulose, a long, stringy polymer that provides the main structural element in plants, from stems and leaves to the trunks of trees, also forms from glucose molecules. Because the glucose molecules are linked in a different way, however, human beings cannot digest cellulose. We do not manufacture an enzyme that can separate individual glucose molecules from the cellulose polymer. Consequently, humans don't go out and graze on the lawn at lunchtime, though people on diets often eat celery and other "roughage" or "fiber." On the other hand, cellulose can be digested and broken down by many bacteria. Cows, for example, have bacteria in their stomachs that perform this function for them, as do wood-eating termites.

Stop and Think! Why do long-distance runners often load up on carbohydrates before a race?

The wood fibers in the paper on this page are made from glucose molecules bonded into cellulose, basically the same chemical as in the stalk of a celery stick. The same glucose molecules, bonded in a different way, form the flour in the spaghetti you ate the last time you had a pasta dinner. An amazing diversity can be built into organic molecules through modular construction.

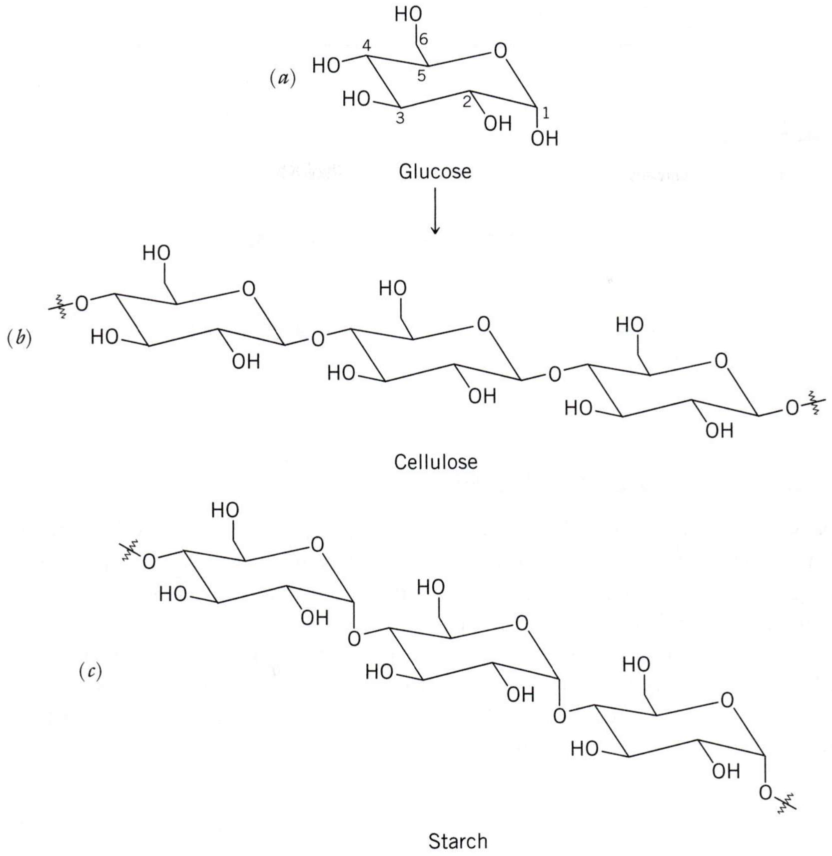

• **Figure 22-8** An individual glucose molecule *(a)* has six carbon atoms as numbered. These molecules can be linked into polymers such as cellulose *(b)* and starch *(c)*, which differ in the way that glucose molecules are linked together.

Lipids

Lipids encompass a grab bag of vital organic molecules that go into making up every living thing. **Lipids** include a variety of molecules that will not dissolve in water, including fats in food, waxes in candles, greases for lubrication, and a wide variety of oils. If you think of drops of oil or bits of fat floating around on top of a pot of soup, you have a pretty good picture of what large clumps of lipid molecules are like.

At the molecular level, lipids play two important roles in living things. First, they form cell membranes that separate living material from its environment, as well as separate one part of a cell from other parts. They are also used to store energy. In fact, in the human body excess weight is usually carried in the form of fat, which is a different kind of lipid from those in cell membranes. Lipids are extremely efficient storehouses for energy. A typical gram of fat, for example, contains twice as many calories as a gram of either protein or carbohydrate.

Like proteins and carbohydrates, numerous lipid molecules can come together to form large modular structures in every cell. An important class of these molecules, called *phospholipids,* are long and thin with a carbon backbone, as shown in Figure 22-9. In phospholipids, a phosphate group (one phosphorus and four oxygen atoms) is incorporated into one end of the molecule. The oxygen atoms in this group tend to be negatively charged, so that this end of the molecule is attracted to water (we say it is hydrophilic). The other end of the molecule, however, is repelled by water (we say it is hydrophobic). These particular types of lipids play an extremely important role in living systems because, as we shall see, they are the materials from which cell membranes are made.

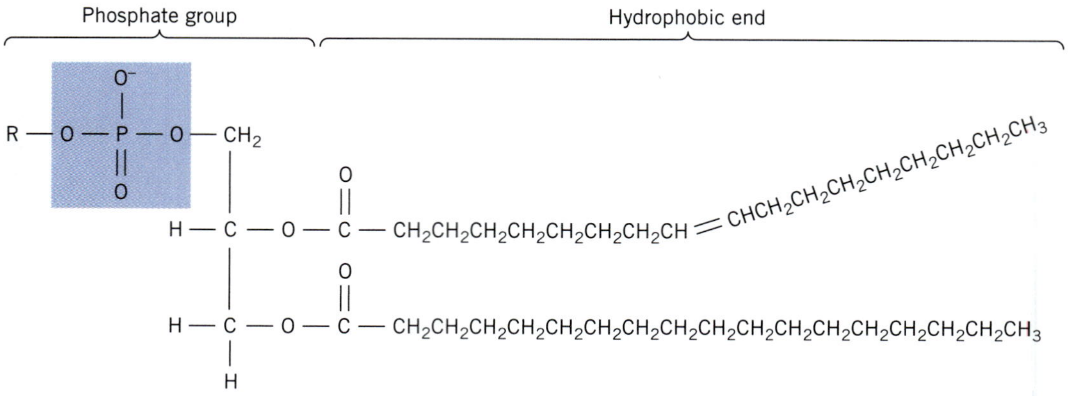

• **Figure 22-9** A phospholipid molecule, showing the negatively charged phosphate group at one end, and ordinary hydrocarbon chains at the other. The end with the phosphate group is attracted to water, and the hydrocarbon end is repelled by it. Different collections of molecules in the group labeled "R" correspond to different kinds of phospholipids.

Saturated and Unsaturated Fats

Every carbon atom in a lipid chain forms exactly four bonds to neighboring atoms (see Chapter 10). In a straight chain, each carbon atom bonds to two adjacent carbon atoms along the chain and two hydrogen atoms on the sides. Carbon atoms of this type are *saturated*—fully bonded to four other atoms.

In some lipids, adjacent carbon atoms will have only three neighbors, including two carbon and one hydrogen atoms. An angled "double bond" will thus form between the two carbon atoms (see Figure 22-10). A chain with one double bond is *monounsaturated,* while two or more double bonds yield a *polyunsaturated* lipid.

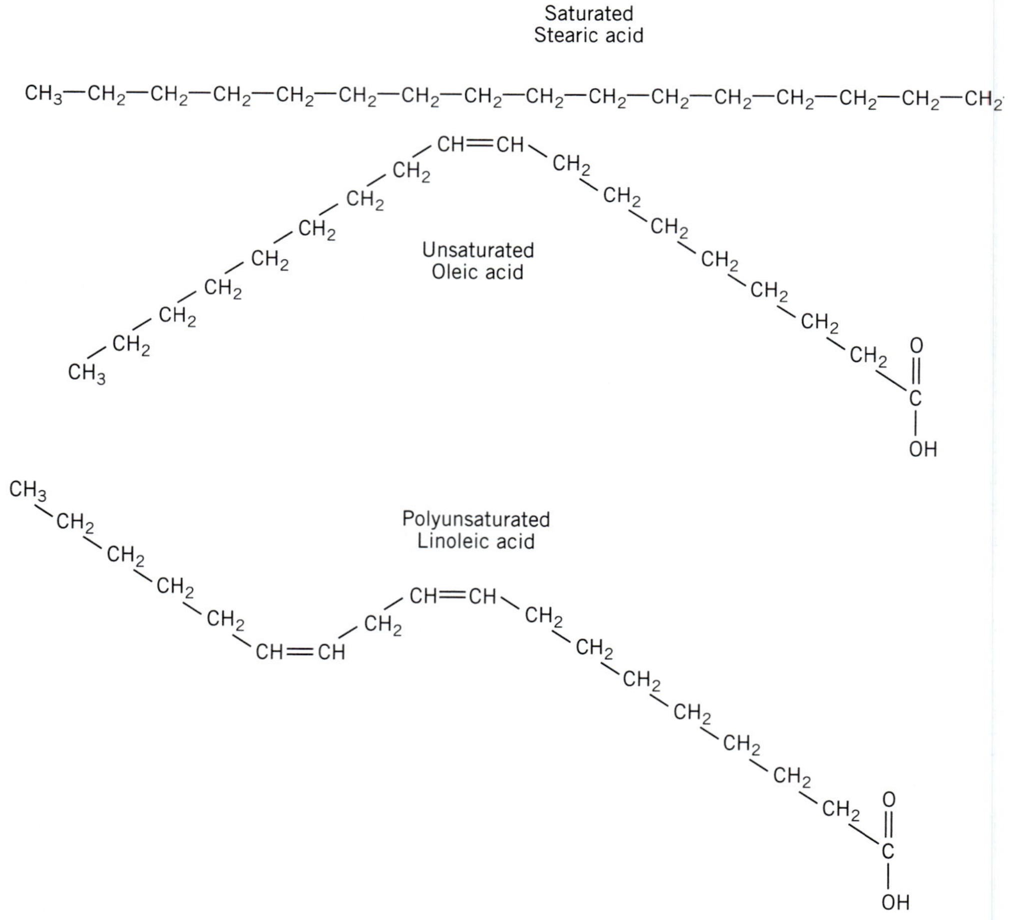

• **Figure 22-10** Lipid molecules with saturated, unsaturated, and polyunsaturated forms, showing the resulting kinks.

Saturated fats in the diet provide the raw materials from which the body can synthesize *cholesterol,* an essential component of all cell membranes. Unfortunately, high levels of cholesterol in the blood can also lead to fatty deposits that clog arteries. For these reasons, many food producers emphasize their use of cholesterol-free foods, rich in polyunsaturated fats. Advertising often suggests that unsaturated foods are "good for you."

Be warned, however. Many of these polyunsaturated products require a further processing step, called *hydrogenation,* to give them a pleasing texture and consistency. Popular chocolate candies, for example, must be made from fats and oils that soften near body temperature. Hydrogenation—the addition of hydrogen atoms back into the carbon chains—eliminates carbon–carbon double bonds. Each added hydrogen atom pulls one of the carbon bonds apart and thus partially saturates the lipid chains. Many popular cooking oils that begin with highly unsaturated lipids are "partially hydrogenated for freshness and consistency" at the manufacturing plant, a process that undoes the good of the unsaturated bonds.

John Barr/Getty Images News and Sport Services

Potato chips made with "no-fat fat."

Technology •

Nonfattening Fats

For most of human history, energy-rich fat was a rare delicacy, something enjoyed only occasionally by most people. Consequently, we acquired a taste for fat that remains with us today in our more affluent situation. A taste for fat combined with widespread availability has led to a serious problem with excess weight in the United States.

Until recently, there was little that people could do to keep their weight down except to reduce their food intake and exercise regularly. Now, however, new abilities in molecular technology have added a third option—we can eat foods that taste like fat, but that cannot be digested, and hence supply the body with no energy.

The first "no-fat fat" was approved for use in 1995 under the trade name Olestra. One ordinary fat found in foods consists of three long-chain molecules connected to a small alcohol molecule. The whole thing looks something like a capital Y, with the alcohol molecule at the center. In the intestines, specialized molecules from the digestive system attach to the alcohol and break off the "legs," which are then broken down further by other molecules. Olestra is shaped very similarly, except that it has eight chains attached to the alcohol instead of three. Because of the extra chains, the molecules from the digestive system can't get at the alcohol and the Olestra passes undigested through the human body. It tastes like fat but adds no calories. Manufacturing specialized molecules like this to use in the human diet will be a growth industry in the future. •

Cell Membranes

The most important single function of lipids in our bodies is the formation of *cell membranes,* the structure that separates the inside of every cell from its environment. Phospholipids, with their hydrophobic and hydrophilic ends, perform this function because when placed in water, these molecules typically adopt a double-layered structure

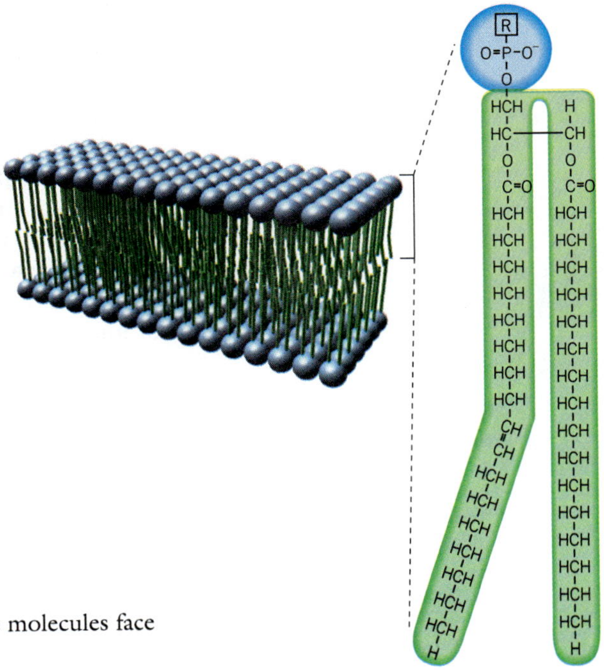

• **Figure 22-11** The structure of a lipid bilayer. The hydrophobic ends of the molecules face each other, while the hydrophilic ends are in the surrounding water.

like the one shown in Figure 22-11. The hydrophobic ends of the molecule line up facing each other, while the hydrophilic ends face to the outside. In this way, water is kept away from the hydrophobic ends and nearer the hydrophilic ends. A double-layered structure of molecules like this functions very well as a membrane of a cell. It is flexible and can change its shape, but it also provides a tough barrier. Special protein receptors are required in order for anything to elbow its way through the bimolecular layer.

The structure of the lipid bilayers that make cell membranes is remarkably similar to liquid crystals (see Chapter 10). Like molecules in a liquid crystal, the lipid molecules are ordered in their orientation and spacing, but they are somewhat disordered in their exact positions side-to-side. This loose structure provides an important measure of flexibility to cell membranes.

One way to visualize the cell membrane is to think of a technique that's often used in moderate climates to protect swimming pools from freezing in the winter. Instead of draining water from the pool, an expensive and time-consuming operation, owners simply throw a large number of Styrofoam balls into the pool. These balls float next to each other. They cover the water, constantly touching, but also constantly jostling and moving around. They lift up and down when waves move across the water, but the covering retains its integrity. In the same way, cell membranes are made up of molecules stacked or arranged next to each other. These molecules can change shape and move around according to the dictates of their environment, but they retain their integrity and do not rupture. Thus they perform the function of separating a cell from its environment.

Minerals and Vitamins

Though most of our body is made and operates with proteins, carbohydrates, lipids, and nucleic acids (see Chapter 23), other chemicals are also vital to life. These essential chemicals include the familiar minerals and vitamins that must form part of our diet.

Minerals

Minerals, in a nutritional context, include all chemical elements in our food other than carbon, hydrogen, nitrogen, and oxygen. The most abundant mineral in our bodies is calcium, which is concentrated in bones and teeth and comprises almost 2% of our total weight. Even though bones appear to be solid, permanent structures, your calcium is constantly being replenished. In many women over 30 the rate of calcium uptake may lag behind calcium loss, which is a major cause of bone disease and injury.

Cellular fluids require small amounts of the elements potassium, chlorine, sodium, and magnesium to maintain proper body acidity and control electrical charges in nerve processes. A grab bag of minor or trace elements, from iodine in the thyroid gland to iron in the blood, are also involved in the body's chemistry.

Every few years the National Research Council publishes a list of Recommended Dietary Allowances (RDA, sometimes referred to as Recommended Daily Allowances) for minerals (see Table 22-2). These values are gradually being replaced by new Dietary Reference Intakes (DRI), which differ from earlier values. Calcium DRIs, for example, are significantly greater for most men and women than the earlier recommendations, while phosphorus DRIs are significantly less.

Vitamins

Biologists have discovered a host of complex organic molecules that, in small quantities, play an essential role in good health. These chemicals, though unrelated to each other in any chemical or physiological sense, are known collectively as **vitamins**. They are gen-

Table 22-2 Selected Recommended Dietary Allowances (RDAs and DRIs) for Minerals[a]

		Weight		Height		Ca	P	Fe	Mg	Zn	I	Se
Gender	Age	kg	lb	cm	ft'in"	(mg)	(mg)	(mg)	(mg)	(mg)	(μg)[b]	(μg)[b]
Both	0–0.5	6	13	60	2′	210	100	6	30	5	40	10
	0.5–1	9	20	71	2′4″	270	275	10	75	5	50	15
	1–3	13	29	90	2′11″	500	460	10	80	10	70	20
Men	15–18	66	145	176	5′9″	1300	1250	12	410	15	150	50
	19–24	72	160	177	5′10″	1000	700	10	420	15	150	70
	25–50	79	174	176	5′10″	1000	700	10	420	15	150	70
	51+	77	170	173	5′8″	1200	700	10	420	15	150	70
Women	15–18	55	120	163	5′4″	1300	1250	15	360	12	150	50
	19–24	58	128	164	5′5″	1000	700	15	310	12	150	55
	25–50	63	138	163	5′4″	1000	700	15	320	12	150	55
	51+	65	143	160	5′3″	1200	700	10	320	12	150	55
– Pregnant						1000	700	30	320	15	175	65
– Lactating (First 6 months)						1000	700	15	320	19	200	75
– Lactating (Second 6 months)						1000	700	15	320	16	200	75

[a] Condensed version of Recommendations by the Food and Nutrition Board of the National Research Council. For up-to-date information visit their web site: http://www4.nationalacademies.org/IOM/IOMHome.nsf/Pages/Food + and + Nutrition + Board.
[b] 1μg (one microgram) = 10^{-6} g = 10^{-3} mg.

erally designated by a letter, such as vitamin A. For historical reasons, a number of different vitamins were grouped together under vitamin B and have been given a series of numbers such as B_1 (thiamine) and B_2 (riboflavin).

With one exception, vitamins are not made in the body and must be taken in with our food. The exception, vitamin D, can be produced in the body through the action of ultraviolet radiation on the skin. However, in most parts of the world exposure to sunlight is normally too low to produce enough vitamin D. Thus, as a practical matter, all vitamins must be taken in as part of the diet.

The vitamins in the B category, along with vitamin C, are *water-soluble vitamins.* As the name implies, these vitamins dissolve in water and hence are not retained by the body. The supply of water-soluble vitamins must be renewed daily. Vitamins A, D, E, and K, however, are *fat-soluble vitamins.* They can be stored in the body (in the liver, for example). In some cases, taking in too much of a fat-soluble vitamin can have unwanted or even harmful consequences. Too much vitamin D, for example, can lead to calcium deposits forming in the heart and kidneys, and too much vitamin A can be seriously toxic. (Too much beta-carotene, a precursor of vitamin A, can even turn your skin orange, but only temporarily.)

Vitamins serve a wide variety of functions in the body. Many of them assist enzymes in mediating the body's chemical reactions. In fact, most vitamins were discovered through the study of diseases that are caused by a chemical deficiency. The disease scurvy, for example, causes degeneration of tissues when the body fails to obtain enough vitamin C, a chemical abundant in citrus fruits. Scurvy was particularly common among sailors on long ocean voyages until the connection between diet and disease was made. Subsequently, sailors on British naval vessels were fed a regular diet of limes (hence the nickname "limeys"). Similarly, the bone disease rickets results from a deficiency of vitamin D. The modern diet with vitamin-enriched foods and vitamin supplements can virtually eliminate these deficiency diseases. As with minerals, the National Research Council publishes DRIs for vitamins. The DRIs for some vitamins are shown in Table 22-3.

Citrus fruits are an important source of vitamin C in our diets.

PhotoDisc, Inc./Getty Images

Table 22-3 Selected Recommended Dietary Allowances (RDAs and DRIs) for Vitamins[a]

		Weight		Height		Fat-Soluble Vitamins			Water-Soluble Vitamins						
Gender	Age	kg	lb	cm	ft′in″	A (RE[b])	D (µg[c])	E (mg α-TE[d])	Folacin (µg[c])	Niacin (mg NE[e])	Riboflavin (mg)	Thiamine (mg)	B_6 (mg)	B_{12} (µg[c])	C (mg)
Both	0–0.5	6	13	60	2′	375	5	3	25	5	0.4	0.3	0.3	0.3	30
	0.5–1	9	20	71	2′4″	375	5	4	35	6	0.5	0.4	0.6	0.5	35
	1–3	13	29	90	2′11″	400	5	6	50	9	0.8	0.7	1.0	0.7	40
Men	15–18	66	145	176	5′9″	1000	5	10	200	20	1.8	1.5	2.0	2.0	60[f]
	19–24	72	160	177	5′10″	1000	5	10	200	19	1.7	1.5	2.0	2.0	60
	25–50	79	174	176	5′10″	1000	5	10	200	19	1.7	1.5	2.0	2.0	60
	51+	77	170	173	5′8″	1000	10	10	200	15	1.4	1.2	2.0	2.0	60
Women	15–18	55	120	163	5′4″	800	5	8	180	15	1.3	1.1	1.5	2.0	60
	19–24	58	128	164	5′5″	800	5	8	180	15	1.3	1.1	1.6	2.0	60
	25–50	63	138	163	5′4″	800	5	8	180	15	1.3	1.1	1.6	2.0	60
	51+	65	143	160	5′3″	800	10	8	80	13	1.2	1.0	1.6	2.0	60
– Pregnant						800	5	10	400	17	1.6	1.5	2.2	2.2	70
– Lactating (First 6 months)						1300	5	12	280	20	1.8	1.6	2.1	2.6	95
– Lactating (Second 6 months)						1300	5	11	260	20	1.7	1.6	2.1	2.6	90

[a] Published in 1989; vitamin D values revised in 1997. For up-to-date information visit their web site: http://www4.nationalacademies.org/IOM/IOMHome.nsf/Pages/Food+and+Nutrition+Board.
[b] RE represents the number of retinol equivalents.
[c] 1µg (one microgram) = 10^{-6} g = 10^{-3} mg.
[d] α-TE represents the number of α-tocopherol equivalents.
[e] NE represents the number of niacin equivalents.
[f] These represent recommended RDAs for nonsmokers. The RDAs of vitamin C for smokers are 67% greater than those for nonsmokers.

Science News | Low-Fat Diet Falls Short

(Science News, Feb. 11 , 2006, p. 85)

The Woman's Health Initiative (WHI) is one of the largest studies ever undertaken in the area of public health. In 2004, for example, it was a WHI study that alerted women to the fact that hormone replacement therapy increased their risk of breast cancer, triggering a massive change in the types of medications women were taking. In 2006, however, WHI produced one of the most confusing reports ever published as a result of a study on the effects of low-fat diets.

The study included nearly 50,000 women, aged 50 to 79, who were followed over a period of eight years. About 40% of the volunteers were asked to switch to a low-fat diet, while the others ate as normal. Researchers saw the women on the low-fat diet four times a year to document their eating habits (and, in the process, encourage them to stay on their diet). Under these circumstances, most people expected to see dramatic decreases in the health risk of the "low-fat" women. Contrary to expectations, however, the results of the study showed no decrease in the incidence of heart disease or other difficulties for this group, although there was a slight decrease in the incidence of breast cancer.

When the report was published, the attention of the scientific community immediately turned to trying to understand the results. Some of these comments centered on the methodology—the difficulty in putting confidence in self-reported diets, for example, or the fact that, over time, the fat consumption of the "low-fat" group increased until, at the end, only an 8% difference separated the two groups. More importantly, however, it was pointed out that the study says nothing about the effects of a low-fat diet undertaken earlier in life. It may be, for example, that starting to watch fat intake at 50 can't compensate for a life of cheeseburgers and fries.

In the end, this study illustrates some of the difficulties involved in doing large-scale studies on human health.

Thinking More About | The Molecules of Life

Dietary Fads

The realization that the functioning of the body depends on the foods we eat is an old one, and is bolstered by the understanding that the cell's basic structures are built from molecules brought in through the digestive system. This understanding, coupled with the current preoccupation with health and fitness in the United States, leads occasionally to fads in which one food or another is touted as a new cure-all. It's hard to get enough information to analyze a fad while it's in full swing, but studies of fads after the fact can teach us a lot about them. The rise and fall of oat bran is a particularly enlightening case.

In the mid-1980s, people began to understand that high levels of cholesterol in the blood were correlated to the incidence of heart disease. Studies available at the time indicated that the inclusion of fiber in the diet, particularly oat bran, helped lower blood cholesterol levels. Oat bran became a fad food, and for a time it was virtually impossible for stores to keep it in stock.

Then, in 1990, newspaper headlines blared that a study in the prestigious *New England Journal of Medicine* (vol. 322: 147 [1990]) showed that oat bran did not, in fact, lower cholesterol levels. The oat bran industry, running at $54 million a year, collapsed. Processing plants closed and people lost their jobs.

Was this a reasonable response to the *New England Journal* paper? Let's look at the study that was reported and try to find out. The study took 20 people, all healthy hospital employees of ages 23 to 49 with low cholesterol levels, and tested them on diets with high-fiber oat bran and low-fiber foods for six-week periods. The result? The mean cholesterol levels of the subjects was 172 ± 28 milligrams per deciliter on the low-fiber diet, and 172 ± 25 on oat bran. (Physicians usually start to worry when your cholesterol level gets to the neighborhood of 220.) This inconclusive result, based on 20 healthy people, provided the basis for the headlines.

Does this study tell you anything about what would happen if someone with high cholesterol went on an oat bran diet? How representative of the entire population are 20 healthy hospital employees in Boston? Given the spread of cholesterol levels in the group, could the actual levels have gone down (or up) without the researchers being able to detect it?

Summary

Organic molecules share the following characteristics: (1) they are based on carbon, (2) they usually form from only a few elements, (3) they are generally modular structures (that is, no matter how large or complex they are, they are formed from a few simple building blocks), and (4) their chemical function is largely determined by their geometrical shape. Three important types of biological molecules are proteins, carbohydrates, and lipids.

Proteins form from chains of *amino acids* to make many of the body's physical structures, such as hair and muscle. Proteins in cells also function as *enzymes,* which are molecules that increase reaction rates between other molecules but are, themselves, unaffected by the reaction. Proteins thus mediate many of life's chemical reactions.

Carbohydrates are modular molecules built from *sugars,* which are relatively simple molecules built from carbon, oxygen, and hydrogen. Carbohydrates provide an essential source of energy for all animals, and they provide much of the solid structure in the cellulose of plants.

Lipids, including fats and oils, are molecules that will not dissolve in water. If the carbon atoms form single bonds, the lipid is said to be saturated, whereas molecules on which adjacent carbon atoms form double bonds are said to be unsaturated. All cell membranes are constructed from bilayers of lipids, which are terminated by one end that attracts water and the other end that repels water.

In addition to the major nutrients proteins, carbohydrates, and lipids, humans also require small amounts of other chemicals—*minerals* and *vitamins*—that perform specialized chemical functions in the body. The National Research Council publishes Dietary Reference Intakes for both minerals and vitamins.

Key Terms

organic molecules
amino acids
protein
enzymes
carbohydrates
sugars
lipids
minerals
vitamins

Review Questions

1. What is the difference between an organic and inorganic molecule? Give an example of each.
2. What is an enzyme? How does it work?
3. What is a protein? Why are proteins sometimes referred to as polypeptides?
4. What are some of the biological functions of proteins?
5. What is an amino acid? What groups of atoms are common to all amino acids?
6. How is a protein constructed from amino acids?
7. How are drugs able to affect chemical reactions in living things?

8. What are the basic building blocks of carbohydrates?

9. What is the difference between cellulose and starch at the molecular level? Give examples of each substance.

10. What is the relationship between cellulose and fiber?

11. What roles do lipids play in the human body?

12. How does the structure of cell membranes enable them to carry out their functions?

13. What is the difference between saturated and unsaturated fats? Give examples of each.

14. Why are minerals an important part of a balanced diet? Give some examples of minerals and describe their functions.

15. What are vitamins? Which are water soluble? Which are fat soluble?

16. What is a DRI? How does it differ from an RDA?

Discussion Questions

1. There are several different forms of vegetarianism. Some people simply avoid red meat, but will eat fish and chicken. Others avoid all meat, but will consume milk and eggs. Still others avoid all animal products. What precautions would people in each group have to take to assure that they had the proper supply of amino acids?

2. What is organic chemistry? Why is it called that?

3. Look at a typical menu at your campus food service. Does it provide a balanced source of nutrition? If not, how would you change it to do so?

4. Regulations require that drugs meet certain advertising standards. If a drug is claimed to stop hair loss or promote weight gain, for example, there has to be evidence that the drug actually works. Should vitamin and mineral supplements have to meet the same standard? Why or why not?

5. Almost any table salt you buy in a store has iodine added to it. Why do you suppose this is done?

6. What does it mean to say that the chemistry of life is based on geometry?

7. Should people be cautious before eating manufactured foods like Olestra? Why or why not?

8. Why is the shape of an enzyme important?

9. Why can horses and cattle survive by eating grass or hay, and humans cannot?

10. What category of organic molecules is wood made from? How do termites digest wood?

Problems

1. How many different proteins can be formed from exactly 15 amino acids? from 20 amino acids?

2. Plot the values in Problem 1 on a graph of number of amino acids versus the number of different proteins. Is the plot a straight line? Why or why not?

Investigations

1. Read the nutritional information on a box of standard cereal and on one that claims to be "natural." Which actually supplies more of the RDA of minerals and vitamins?

2. Make a detailed record of one week's intake of food, vitamins, and other supplements. Consult nutrition charts and determine the percentage by weight of protein, carbohydrate, fats, and other substances that you consumed. What percentage of the fat you consumed was saturated? What changes in your diet could reduce the total percentage of fat consumed and lower the ratio of saturated to unsaturated fat?

3. Read about a vitamin-deficiency disease. How was it discovered and how was it cured?

4. Investigate dietary sources of vitamin C, and review how the body uses this vitamin. Is there a difference between the vitamin C in freshly squeezed orange juice and in a vitamin C tablet? Some years ago the Nobel Prize–winning chemist Linus Pauling advocated vitamin C as a defense against cancer. How did he justify these claims? What was the response of the medical community?

5. Visit a health food store in your community. Read the percentages of the RDA of various vitamin/mineral supplements. Given what you know about the storage of vitamins and minerals, are these pills safe?

6. How would you design an experiment to study the effectiveness of oat bran in reducing cholesterol?

7. Investigate the relationship between health and cholesterol levels. Is it possible for your cholesterol level to be too low?

8. Investigate how many amino acids must be supplied by the diet of various organisms for them to survive. How many amino acids do humans need to consume? How many are manufactured in our body?

9. Many animals manufacture vitamin C in their bodies. Which common animals do not?

10. Some athletes consume massive amounts of protein. Investigate exercise science journals and find the optimum amount of complete protein that a 150-pound endurance athlete should consume. Now compare that to how many grams per day a 200-pound strength athlete should consume.

11. Investigate why many endurance athletes "carb-load" before a race. How does the term *hitting-the-wall* relate to stored energy? How long can an elite endurance athlete run before he or she runs out of stored energy.

23

Classical and Modern Genetics

Why do offspring resemble their parents?

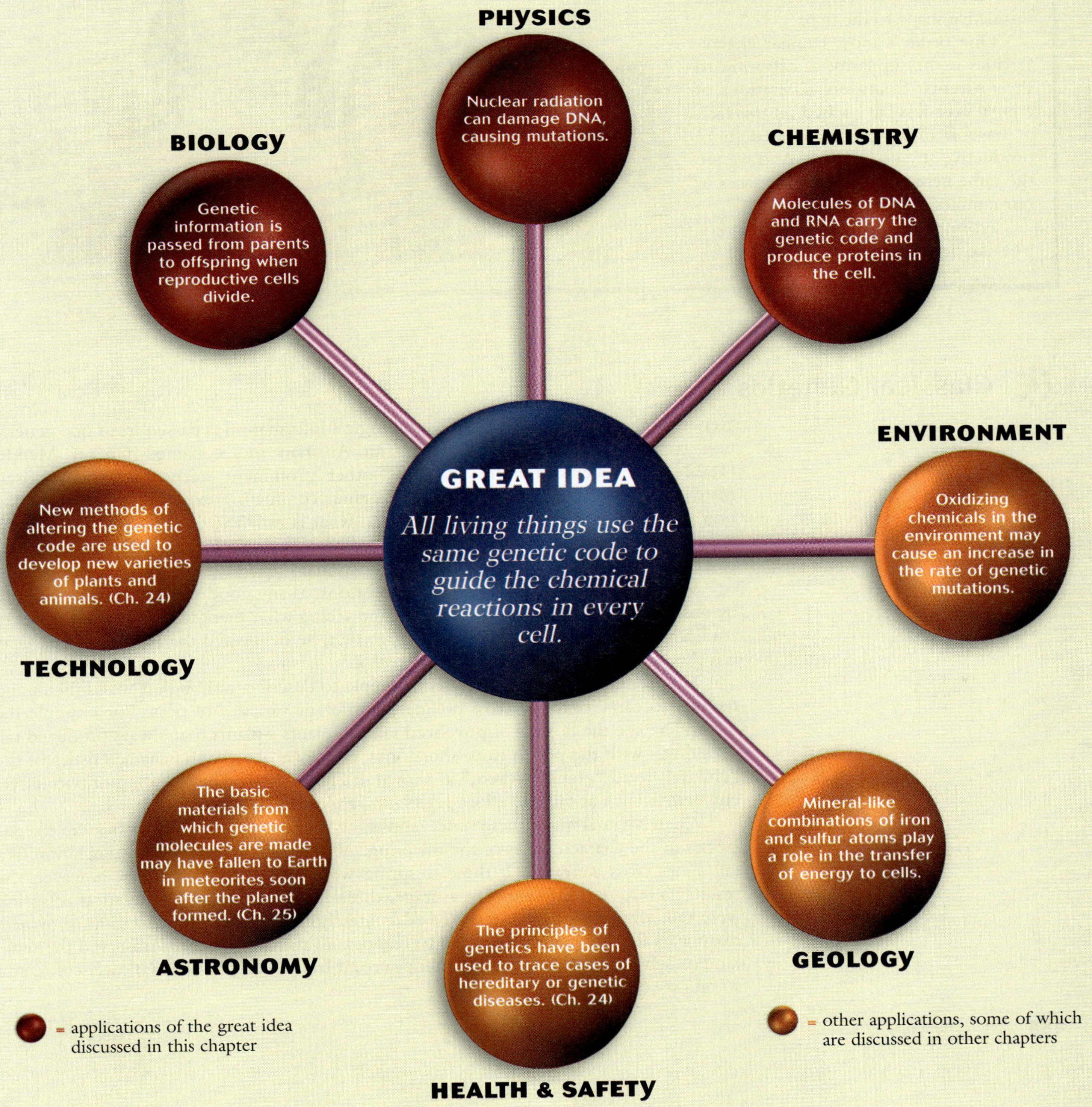

Science Through the Day | A Family Resemblance

It's just about time to head back home after a great day in the sun. You'll have company during the drive, because a friend has asked you to give her brother a ride back to campus. You've never met him before, but there's no mistaking the family relationship: the same wavy brown hair, the same wide-set eyes, the same distinctive shape to the nose.

One of life's most familiar characteristics is the similarity of offspring to their parents. Countless generations of animal breeders have relied on this fact, as have farmers who developed more productive strains of crops. And we see the same hereditary links in the faces of our families and friends.

From penguins to potatoes to people, like begets like.

Peter Griffith/Masterfile

Classical Genetics

Genetics, the study of ways in which biological information is passed from one generation to the next, was pioneered by an Austrian monk named Gregor Mendel (1822–1884). Perhaps more than any other prominent scientist, Mendel closely matches the popular image of the lonely genius conducting exacting research in isolation. Working at the monastery in Brno, in what is now the Czech Republic, Mendel began to ask the kinds of questions we have been posing: Why do offspring resemble parents? And why do offspring differ from parents?

Mendel attempted to answer these questions, as any good scientist should—that is, by observing nature, doing experiments, and seeing what there was to see. In a series of studies with pea plants in his monastery garden, he delineated the basic laws that govern the inheritance of physical characteristics.

The technique that Mendel used is simple to describe, although it was difficult and tedious to carry out. He cross-pollinated different varieties of peas. For example, he would fertilize the flowers of **purebred** tall pea plants—plants that always produced tall offspring—with the pollen from short ones, and then observe the characteristics of the "children" and "grandchildren," as shown in Figure 23-1. The offspring of two different strains, such as tall and short pea plants, are called **hybrids.**

When Mendel made these observations, he found that there were remarkable regularities in the characteristics of the offspring. All offspring from the first generation of a tall–short cross were tall. If these offspring were bred with each other, however, the results were quite different. On average, three-fourths of second-generation offspring were tall, while one-fourth reverted to being short. Thus, in hybridization, shortness disappears for one generation, only to reappear in the next. Mendel observed the same kind of behavior in half-a-dozen other pea plant traits: seed pod shape, flower color, and so on.

Mendel invented the "unit of inheritance," what we now call the **gene**, to explain his findings. He had no idea what a gene might be, or even whether it had a real physical existence. Today, as we shall see shortly, the gene can be identified as part of a long molecule of DNA. For Mendel, however, the existence of DNA was unknown, and he deduced the presence of genes purely from mathematical analysis of how traits of his plants were inherited.

Stop and Think! In what ways were Mendel's experiments with peas similar to Galileo's experiments with falling bodies?

In the simplest version of Mendelian or **classical genetics**, we assume that every offspring receives two genes for every characteristic—one from the father and one from the mother. In the experiment with pea plants, for example, every offspring in every generation received a gene for height (either tall or short) from its mother (the plant that provided an egg) and another gene for height from its father (the plant that provided the pollen). Mendel concluded that pairs of genes determined every characteristic he observed, and that the offspring may receive a different gene from the father than from the mother. So, if two genes are present, which characteristic is actually seen in the offspring? In the language of modern geneticists, we phrase the question by asking, Which gene is "expressed"?

Returning to our example of the pea plants, we recall that Mendel produced plants with both a gene for tallness and a gene for shortness in the first generation. The fact that all of these first-generation plants were tall means that, in all cases, the gene for tallness was expressed. Mendel stated this fact by saying that the gene for tallness is **dominant**. By this he meant that if an offspring receives a "tall gene" from one parent and a "short gene" from the other, that offspring will be tall. In this situation, the short gene is said to be **recessive**. The gene is present in the offspring, but it does not determine the offspring's physical characteristics; it is not expressed. That gene, however, can be passed along to subsequent generations. You should note that, in spite of the name, "dominant" is not the same as "good" or "strong" in the world of genes. Many fatal genetic diseases are passed from generation to generation by dominant genes.

Mendel's experiment can be understood in very simple terms. In the first generation, every hybrid receives a tall gene and a short gene. Because the tall gene is dominant, all of the first generation of hybrid plants will be tall. In the next generation, there are four possible gene combinations, as shown in Table 23-1. Each plant in the second generation can receive either a tall or a short gene from each of its parents. On average, the distribution of genes will be random so that we can argue as follows: In roughly one-fourth of the cases, the offspring will receive a tall gene from its mother and a tall gene from its father. In another one-fourth of the cases, the offspring will receive a short gene from its mother and a short gene from its father. In the remain-

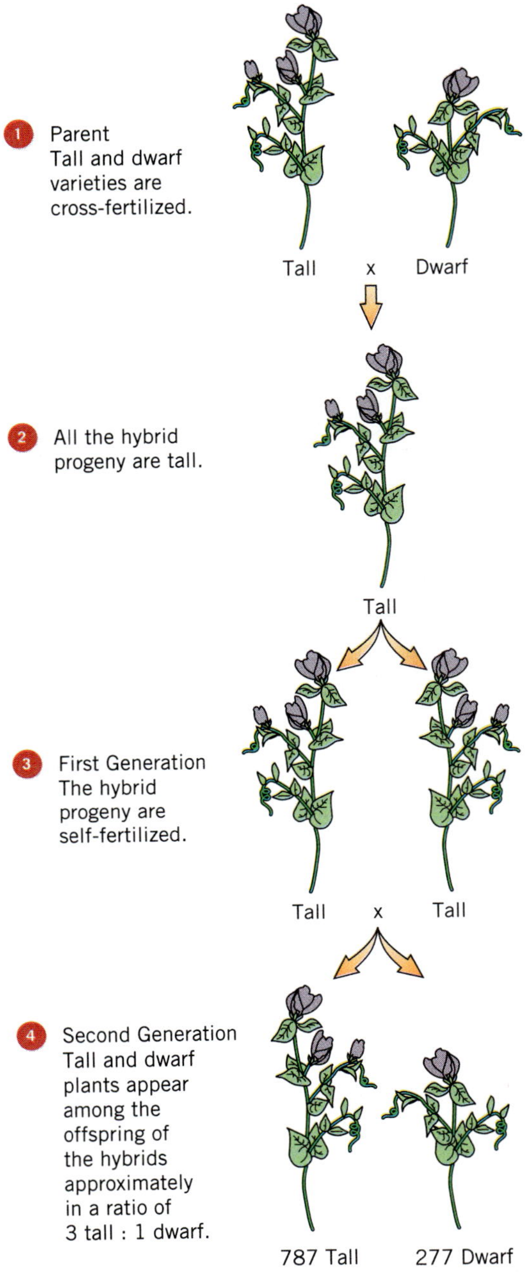

• **Figure 23-1** The parents, first, and second generations of tall versus short pea plants. On average, the second generation shows a 3:1 ratio of dominant traits. Three-fourths of the plants, for example, will be tall and one-fourth short.

Table 23-1 Tall (T) versus Short (t) Hybrids

		Father's Genes	
		Tall	Short
Mother's genes:	Tall	TT	Tt
	Short	tT	tt

ing half of these cases, the offspring will receive a tall gene from its father and a short gene from its mother, or vice versa.

Consequently, in the second generation approximately three out of every four offspring will have at least one gene for tallness, and only one in four will have two genes for shortness. Given the fact that tallness is a dominant characteristic, this distribution means that three of four offspring in the second generation will be tall, while only one will be short. This situation is precisely what Mendel observed.

Table 23-2 SsPp Matrix with Resulting 9:3:3:1 Distribution

	SP	Sp	sP	sp
SP	SSPP	SSPp	SsPP	SsPp
Sp	SSpP	SSpp	SspP	Sspp
sP	sSPP	sSPp	ssPP	sspP
sp	sSpP	sSpp	sspP	sspp

1 SSPP 2 SSPp 2 SsPP

4 SsPp 1 SSpp 2 Sspp

1 ssPP 2 ssPp 1 sspp

Smooth + Purple = 9

Smooth + white = 3

wrinkled + Purple = 3

wrinkled + white = 1

EXAMPLE 23-1

Breeding Peas

You are given two purebred pea plants. One plant has smooth pea pods and purple flowers (dominant traits). The other plant has wrinkled pea pods and white flowers (recessive traits). These characteristics are expressed independently of each other. What distribution of characteristics would you expect in the first generation of plants bred from these two parent plants? What distribution of traits would you see in the second generation?

Reasoning: Every plant in the first generation of offspring receives dominant genes for a smooth pea pod (S) and purple flower (P) from one parent, and recessive genes for a wrinkled pod (s) and white flower (p) from the other. Every plant in the first generation, therefore, has exactly the same gene combination, abbreviated SsPp. All of these plants will appear with smooth pods and purple flowers because S and P are dominant.

The second generation, however, will display a mixture of traits. The easiest way to predict the distribution of these traits is to set up a matrix, similar to the one shown in Table 23-1. In this case, however, we must deal with four different genes in each parent (SsPp), so the matrix must be 4 × 4, as shown in Table 23-2.

This table shows that there are 16 different possible combinations of the four genes. On average, 9 out of every 16 plants will appear with smooth pods and purple flowers—both dominant genes will be expressed. In addition, 3 of 16 on average will display wrinkled pods but purple flowers, and 3 of 16 will have white flowers but smooth pods. Finally, only 1 in 16 of the second generation will display both recessive traits: white flowers and wrinkled pea pods.

Mendel's observation of this characteristic 9:3:3:1 distribution of second-generation traits for two different genes was instrumental in his development of the genetic theory.

The Rules of Classical Genetics

Mendel's research can be summarized by three rules that frame classical genetics.

- *Rule 1.* Physical characteristics or traits are passed from parents to offspring by some unknown mechanism (we call it a gene).
- *Rule 2.* Each offspring has two genes for each trait, one gene from each parent.
- *Rule 3.* Some genes are dominant and some are recessive. When present together, the trait of a dominant gene will be expressed in preference to the trait of a recessive gene.

The rules of classical genetics were deduced during the early twentieth century. Careful records were kept on many kinds of organisms, from humans to cattle to agricultural plants, and large lists of dominant and recessive genes were compiled. In human beings, for example, dark hair and eye color are dominant over light, the ability to roll your tongue is dominant over inability, and hairy toe knuckles are dominant over hairless.

Many varieties of tomatoes have been bred selectively to achieve desired qualities, such as color, size, or taste.

Carson Baldwin, Jr./Animals Animals/Earth Scenes

Qualitative versus Quantitative Genetics

In one sense, the qualitative aspects of Mendelian genetics have been understood for many centuries. Early human societies knew, for example, that if you saved the largest potatoes and planted them in the spring, the resulting crop would be better than if you just planted potatoes at random. They also knew that if you had a bull that gained weight rapidly and produced lots of meat, you should breed that bull to as many cows as possible so some of the offspring would share the characteristics of the father.

But Mendel's careful statistical analysis of pea plant traits carried genetics beyond the qualitative level. By discovering the distinctive 3:1 and 9:3:3:1 ratios of traits in second-generation plants, Mendel was able to propose a predictive model of genetics—a model that recognized the equal importance of both parents, and the distinction between dominant and recessive traits. When Mendel's rather obscure publications were "discovered" at about the turn of the century, they provided a model that allowed breeders to approach their work in a far more controlled and directed manner.

The traits of prize bulls and racehorses, for example, are carefully documented, as are the pedigrees of their offspring. The success of plant and animal breeders in controlling the flow of genes from one generation to the next is attested to by the appearance of cattle such as Black Angus (which are little more than a rectangular block of beef on very short legs) and the many varieties of vegetables and fruits that stock supermarket shelves.

Of equal importance, the laws of Mendelian genetics can now be used to trace cases of hereditary or genetic disease, such as the many cases of families with cystic fibrosis, a disease that affects approximately one in every 2000 Caucasian children in North America. Individuals with cystic fibrosis suffer from thick mucus deposits that obstruct the lungs, as well as other abnormalities of the body's chemistry. When both parents carry the recessive gene for cystic fibrosis, their children have about a one-in-four chance of acquiring the disease.

Although we have chosen examples in which one physical characteristic is correlated to one gene, most cases of inheritance are not this simple. Human height and skin color, for example, are affected by the action of several genes, and nutrition as well as genetics can influence height. Thus, while the principles of classical genetics have widespread validity, the way that they work out in practice may be quite complex.

DNA and the Birth of Molecular Genetics

The key to understanding Mendel's genetic principles is **molecular genetics**, which is the study of the mechanism that passes genetic information from parents to offspring at the molecular level. In Chapter 22 we saw that cellular functions, the basic mechanisms of all life, depend on chemical interactions between molecules. Chromosomes, the distinctive elongated structures that appear to divide just prior to cell division, became an obvious focus for genetic study. Could these structures carry information and pass it from one generation to the next? Studies of cell division by meiosis pointed strongly in that direction. Recall that meiosis produces gametes—sex cells with half the usual number of chromosomes. Gametes from two parents are subsequently joined during sexual reproduction to yield a full complement of chromosomes.

By the mid-twentieth century, biochemists analyzed chromosomes and showed that they are made primarily of DNA, deoxyribonucleic acid. The discovery of the nature and function of nucleic acids has fundamentally transformed the study of biological systems in the past three decades. **Nucleic acids,** so called because they were originally found in the nucleus of cells, include **DNA** and **RNA,** the molecules that carry and interpret the genetic code. These chemicals govern both the inheritance of physical traits by offspring and the basic chemical operation of the cell. These extraordinary molecules conform to the twin principles of modularity and geometry that are followed by all other organic materials (see Chapter 22).

Nucleotides: The Building Blocks of Nucleic Acids

Proteins (chains of amino acids) and carbohydrates (clusters of sugar molecules) can form large structures from a single kind of building block. Nucleic acids, on the other hand, are

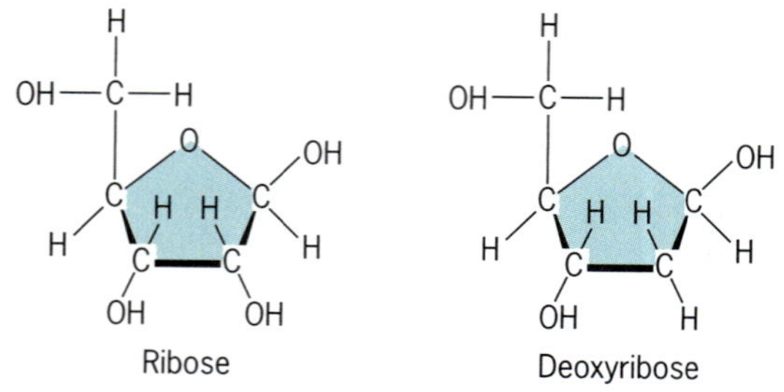

• **Figure 23-2** Ribose and deoxyribose are 5-carbon sugars that differ in the number of oxygen atoms.

assembled from subunits that are themselves made from three different kinds of smaller molecules. The assemblage of three molecules is called a *nucleotide*, and nucleic acids are made by putting nucleotides together in a long chain.

The first of the smaller molecules that go into an individual nucleotide is a sugar. The sugar in DNA is *deoxyribose* (thus giving DNA its complicated name, *d*eoxyribo*n*ucleic *a*cid), while in RNA (*r*ibo*n*ucleic *a*cid) the sugar is *ribose*. Ribose is a common sugar containing five carbon atoms. Deoxyribose, as the name implies, is like ribose but is missing one oxygen atom (Figure 23-2).

The second small molecule of the nucleotide is the phosphate ion, which includes one phosphorus atom surrounded by four atoms of oxygen.

Finally, each nucleotide incorporates one of four different kinds of molecules in DNA that are called *bases*. The four different base molecules are often abbreviated by a single letter—A for adenine, G for guanine, C for cytosine, and T for thymine.

Each nucleotide combines the three basic building blocks: a sugar, a phosphate, and a base (Figure 23-3). These three molecules bond together, with the sugar molecule in the middle. Think of a nucleotide as something like a prefabricated wall in a house. Both DNA and RNA are made by linking nucleotides together in a specific way.

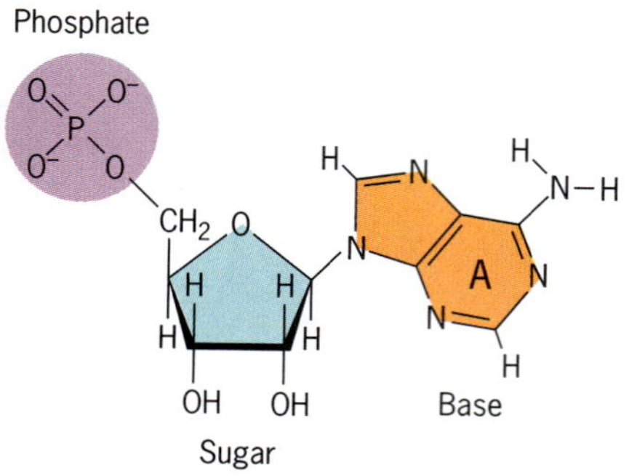

• **Figure 23-3** A nucleotide, formed by a sugar, base, and phosphate group.

DNA Structure

We can start putting DNA together by assembling a long strand of nucleotides. In this strand, the alternating phosphate and sugar molecules form a long chain, and the base molecules hang off the side. The whole thing looks like a half-ladder that has been sawn vertically through the rungs.

DNA consists of two such strands of nucleotides joined together to form a complete "ladder." The bases sticking out to the side provide the natural points for joining the two single strands. As you can see from Figure 23-4, however, the distinctive shapes of the four bases ensure that only certain pairs of bases can form hydrogen bonds. Adenine, for example, can form bonds with thymine but not with any of the other bases or with itself. Similarly, cytosine can form a bond with guanine but not with itself, thymine, or adenine.

As a consequence, there are only four possible rungs that can exist in a DNA ladder. They are:

AT
TA
CG
GC

With the bonding of these base pairs, the complete DNA molecule is formed into a ladder-like double strand. Because of the details of the shape of the bases, each rung is twisted slightly with respect to the one before it. The net result is that this ladder comes to resemble a spiral staircase—a helical shape that gives DNA its common nickname, the **double helix.**

RNA Structure

RNA is built in a manner similar to DNA with three important differences. First, RNA is only half the ladder; that is, it consists of only one string of nucleotides put together. Second, the sugar in the RNA nucleotide is ribose instead of deoxyribose. And third, the base thymine is replaced by a different base, uracil, abbreviated U. The shape of uracil is such that, like thymine, it will bond to the base adenine. As we shall see, the ability of uracil to bond to adenine plays an important role in regulating chemical reactions in the cell. Several different kinds of RNA operate in the cell at any given time. All of them, however, have the same basic structure.

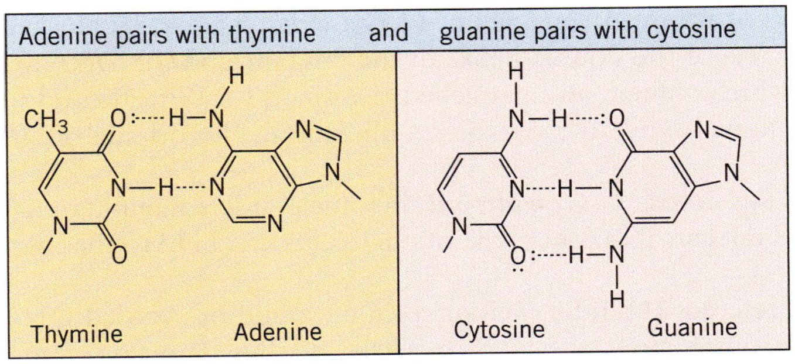

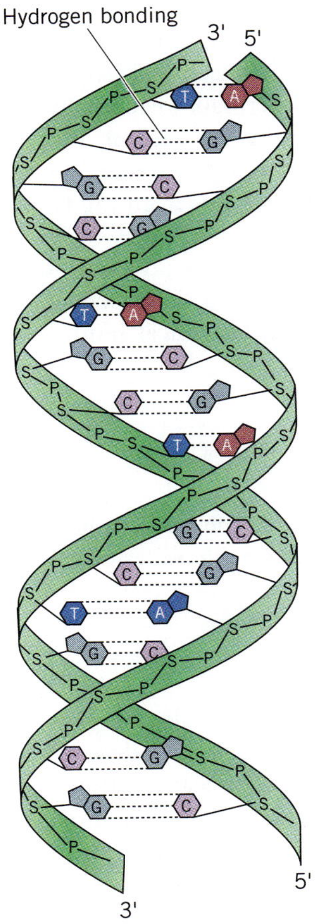

• **Figure 23-4** The structure of DNA. AT and CG base-pair linkages are shown above the DNA strand. The dotted lines are hydrogen bonds.

• **Figure 23-5** DNA replication. A DNA double helix may be split, thus exposing bases on both strands. Two new identical double helices may then be formed from the original.

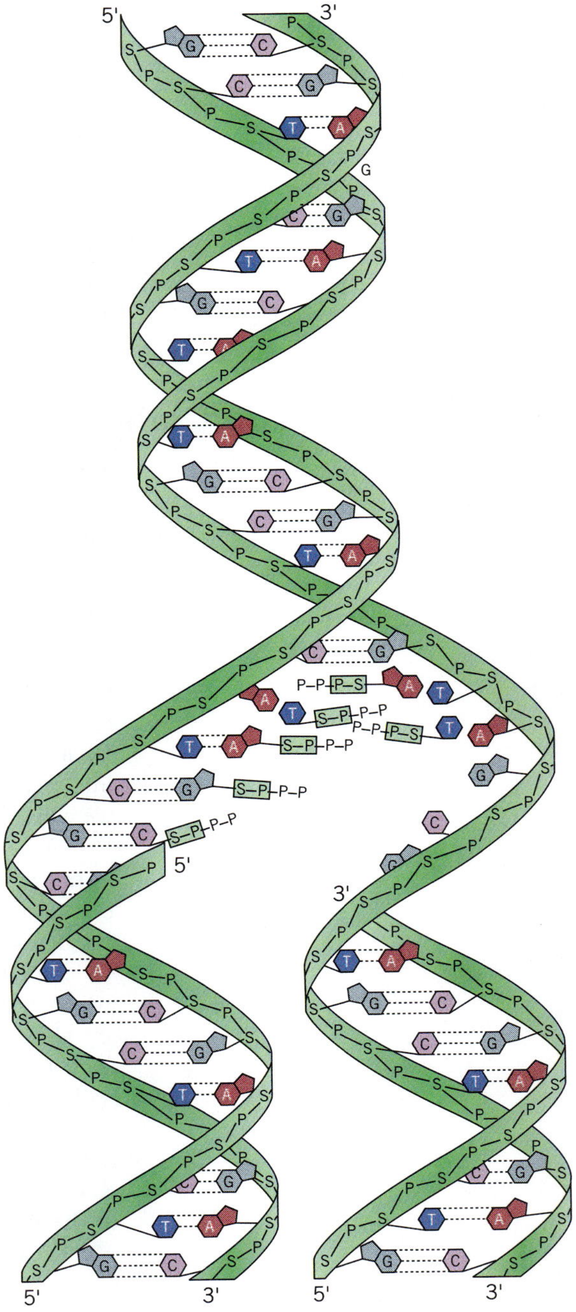

The Replication of DNA

In Chapter 21, we described the processes by which cells divide. Prior to both mitosis and meiosis, DNA in the chromosomes is copied. Thus DNA replication is one of the first steps in passing genetic information from one generation to the next.

DNA replication is possible because the geometry of the base pairs allows only certain kinds of bindings; that is, adenine (A) binds only to thymine (T), and cytosine (C) binds only to guanine (G). No other pairings are allowed. When a cell is about to divide, special enzymes move along the DNA double helix, breaking the hydrogen bonds that link the bases—in effect, breaking the "rungs of the ladder," as shown in Figure 23-5. As a result, the two split arms of the DNA ladder have exposed bases.

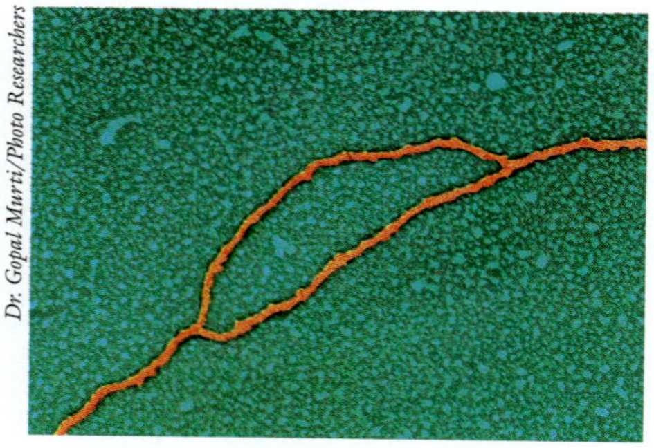

Electron microscope image of the DNA in a dividing human cancer cell.

Consider, just for the sake of argument, an adenine (A) base that is no longer locked into its partner on the other side of the double helix. In the fluid around the DNA are many nucleotides, some of which contain an unattached thymine (T). With the aid of another enzyme, this thymine will bind to the exposed adenine in the original DNA strand.

In the same way, an exposed cytosine (C) will bind to a nucleotide containing guanine (G) from the fluid in the nucleus. No other type of nucleotide can bind to that particular site.

The net result of these preferential bindings along a single strand of exposed DNA is that the missing strand is reconstructed, base by base. The same thing happens in mirror image to the other half of the exposed DNA strand. Thus, once the DNA is unraveled, each strand replicates its missing partner. The end product is two double-stranded DNA molecules, each of which is identical to the original molecule.

When a cell divides by means of mitosis, the genetic information contained in the DNA of one cell is passed on to its daughters. Thus each daughter cell will have chromosomes identical to those of the parent. In meiosis, on the other hand, each daughter cell has only one chromosome from each pair of chromosomes in the original. When a sperm and an egg come together during fertilization, the resulting cell once again has a full set of chromosomes, but now one chromosome in each pair comes from the father, the other from the mother.

The simple chemistry of the base pairs provides a mechanism for reproducing DNA. This feature of DNA molecular structure accounts for one of the striking facts about life—offspring do share many traits of their parents. Ultimately, chemical binding of base pairs results in the inheritance of parental traits.

The Genetic Code

DNA carries all our genetic information; this molecule is, in effect, the book of life. But how is the book read? How are the almost endless strings of DNA nucleotides translated into flesh and blood? That is the role of RNA.

Transcription of DNA

In addition to replicating itself so that cell division can take place, DNA also supplies the information that runs the chemistry within each individual cell. This process depends on the fact that all cells are governed by protein enzymes that run chemical reactions (see Chapter 22). Thus the question of how cell chemistry is regulated boils down to how the information in DNA can be used to produce proteins. If we understand this step, then we will understand how DNA governs the chemical functioning of every cell in our body.

DNA is a very large molecule. In eukaryotic cells it is found outside the nucleus only in mitochondria and chloroplasts. Thus the first question we have to ask is how information in the DNA gets out into the cell at large. The answer to this question involves a process called *transcription,* which uses the other nucleic acid, RNA.

When it is time to fabricate a new protein to act as an enzyme in a cell, other enzymes "unzip" a section of DNA as shown in Figure 23-6. Nucleotides of RNA that are always floating in the nuclear material are then hooked, with the aid of enzymes, onto the appropriate bases by a process exactly analogous to that which occurs in the replication of DNA. Each of the exposed bases on the "unzipped" strand of DNA binds to its appropriate nucleotide—A to U, C to G, and so forth. (Remember that in RNA, the base uracil, U, substitutes for the thymine in DNA.) In this way, a short strand of RNA is created that carries information from the original exposed strand of DNA. Think of the RNA as being the "negative" of the true picture, which is the DNA.

Because it is relatively short and not connected to anything else, the RNA strand can move out through tiny pores in the wall of the nucleus and into the cell at large.

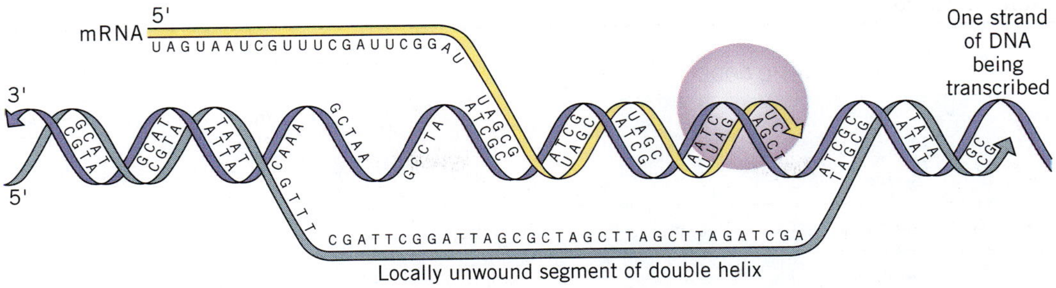

• **Figure 23-6** Transcription of DNA occurs when a segment of DNA is split and a single-stranded messenger RNA segment forms. The mRNA carries the same information that was on the original DNA segment.

Thus the function of this kind of RNA is to carry the information that was contained in the central DNA molecule out into the region of the cell where chemical reactions are going on. Because it carries a message, this kind of RNA (one of three important types in every cell) is called **messenger RNA**, or **mRNA** for short.

The Synthesis of Proteins

The exact sequence of base pairs on messenger RNA carries a coded message that contains chemical instructions. Once the mRNA arrives at the place in the cell where proteins are to be synthesized, it encounters a second type of RNA—a molecule called **transfer RNA,** or **tRNA** for short. The job of tRNA is to read that coded message. Transfer RNA, whose shape is shown in Figures 23-7 and 23-8, has a shape at one end that attracts 1 of the 20 amino acids found in living things (see Chapter 22). At the other end is a small loop of molecules with three exposed bases on it. One of four different bases can be found in each of the places on the top loop, so there are 64 (4 × 4 × 4) different kinds of tRNA molecules. Of these, 61 tRNA molecules attach to a specific amino acid at its other end, while the remaining 3 act as "stop" signs, which end the construction of a protein.

Ken Eward/Photo Researchers

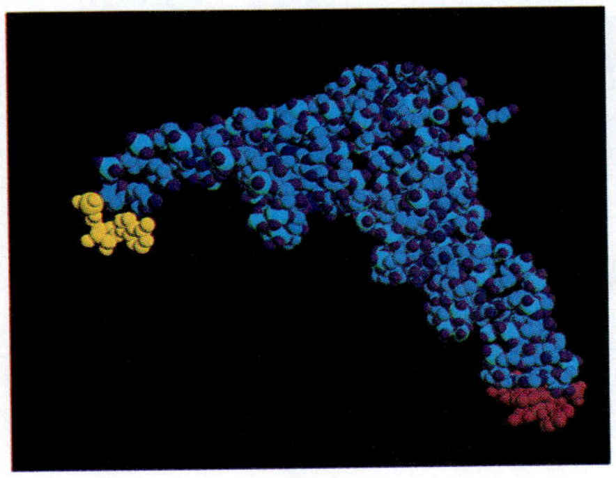

• **Figure 23-7** Computer-generated model of tRNA. The triplet of bases is shown in red, the spot that binds to the amino acid (in this case, serine) is shown in yellow.

The sequence of bases along the mRNA is, as we have seen, a transcription of the information contained in the sequence of bases along the original DNA. Messenger RNA in effect carries a coded message, spelled out in four letters: A, U, C, and G. Each group of three exposed bases on the mRNA chain is like a word—a sequence of three letters that will bind to one, and only one, of the sets of bases on 1 of the 64 tRNA molecules. If a segment along the mRNA reads A-U-U, for example, then the tRNA molecule that has U-U-A as its unpaired bases will bond to that particular spot. Thus, after time, the mRNA and tRNA will form a sequence as shown in Figure 23-8.

The set of three bases on the mRNA, called a *codon,* determines which of the possible tRNA molecules will attach at that point. Each codon on the mRNA determines a single amino acid, and the string of codons determines the sequence of amino acids—what we have called the primary structure of the protein that is being assembled. This connection between the codons and the amino acid they select is called the *genetic code,* as detailed in Table 23-3. All living things share this code.

As the tRNA molecules attach themselves along the mRNA, a string of amino acids in a specific order—a protein—is assembled as shown in

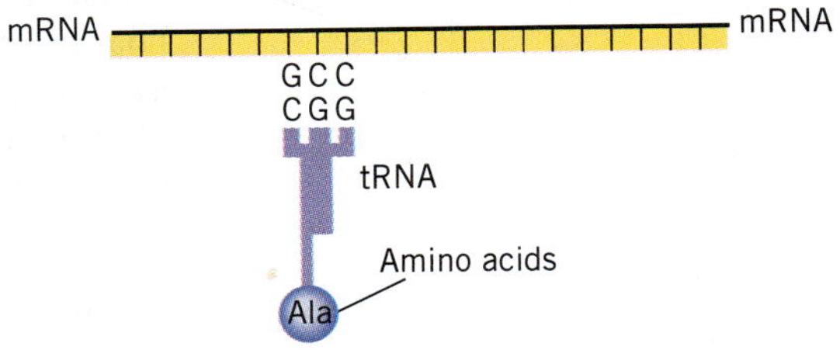

• **Figure 23-8** The interaction of mRNA and tRNA. One end of a tRNA molecule is attached to bases in the mRNA, and the other end to a specific amino acid. Enzymes hook the amino acids together to form a protein molecule.

Table 23-3 The Genetic Code

THE GENETIC CODE

1st letter	U	C	A	G	3rd letter
U	Phenylalanine	Serine	Tyrosine	Cysteine	U
U	Phenylalanine	Serine	Tyrosine	Cysteine	C
U	Leucine	Serine	stop	stop	A
U	Leucine	Serine	stop	Tryptophan	G
C	Leucine	Proline	Histidine	Arginine	U
C	Leucine	Proline	Histidine	Arginine	C
C	Leucine	Proline	Glutamine	Arginine	A
C	Leucine	Proline	Glutamine	Arginine	G
A	Isoleucine	Threonine	Asparagine	Serine	U
A	Isoleucine	Threonine	Asparagine	Serine	C
A	Isoleucine	Threonine	Lysine	Arginine	A
A	(start) Methionine	Threonine	Lysine	Arginine	G
G	Valine	Alanine	Aspartic acid	Glycine	U
G	Valine	Alanine	Aspartic acid	Glycine	C
G	Valine	Alanine	Glutamic acid	Glycine	A
G	Valine	Alanine	Glutamic acid	Glycine	G

(2nd letter across the top)

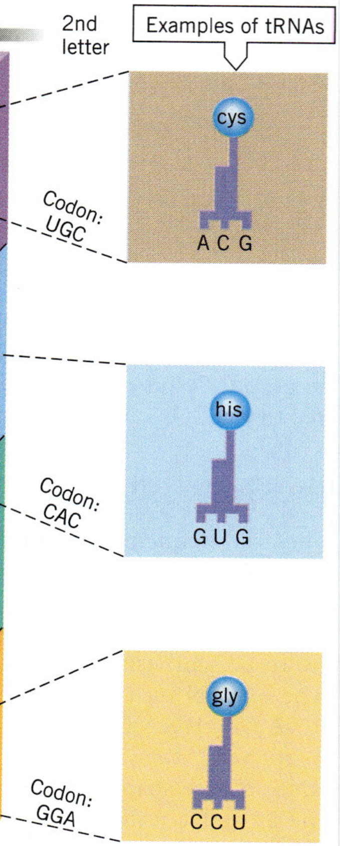

Figure 23-9. Once its amino acid has been incorporated into the protein, a tRNA molecule moves away to be replenished with another amino acid and used again.

The protein synthesis actually takes place on ribosomes, which are large, irregularly shaped organelles made of proteins and yet another kind of RNA, called *ribosomal RNA*, or *rRNA*. As shown in Figure 23-9, the process of synthesis is somewhat more complex than the simple discussion we have given here. Ribosomes align the messenger RNA and transfer RNA during protein assembly. Thus three different kinds of RNA—transfer, messenger, and ribosomal—are involved in the synthesis of a single protein.

As a net effect of this rather complex molecular manufacturing process, the information encoded in the DNA molecule has been expressed as a particular sequence of amino acids that determines the identity of the appropriate protein enzyme. Thus a specific stretch of DNA located on one chromosome produces the enzyme that runs a particular chemical reaction in the cell. This stretch of DNA is what we have called a gene. That chemical might control skin color, hair texture, or any of the other traits that we recognize.

One of the central rules of modern biology, often referred to as the "central dogma of molecular biology," is:

One gene codes for one protein.

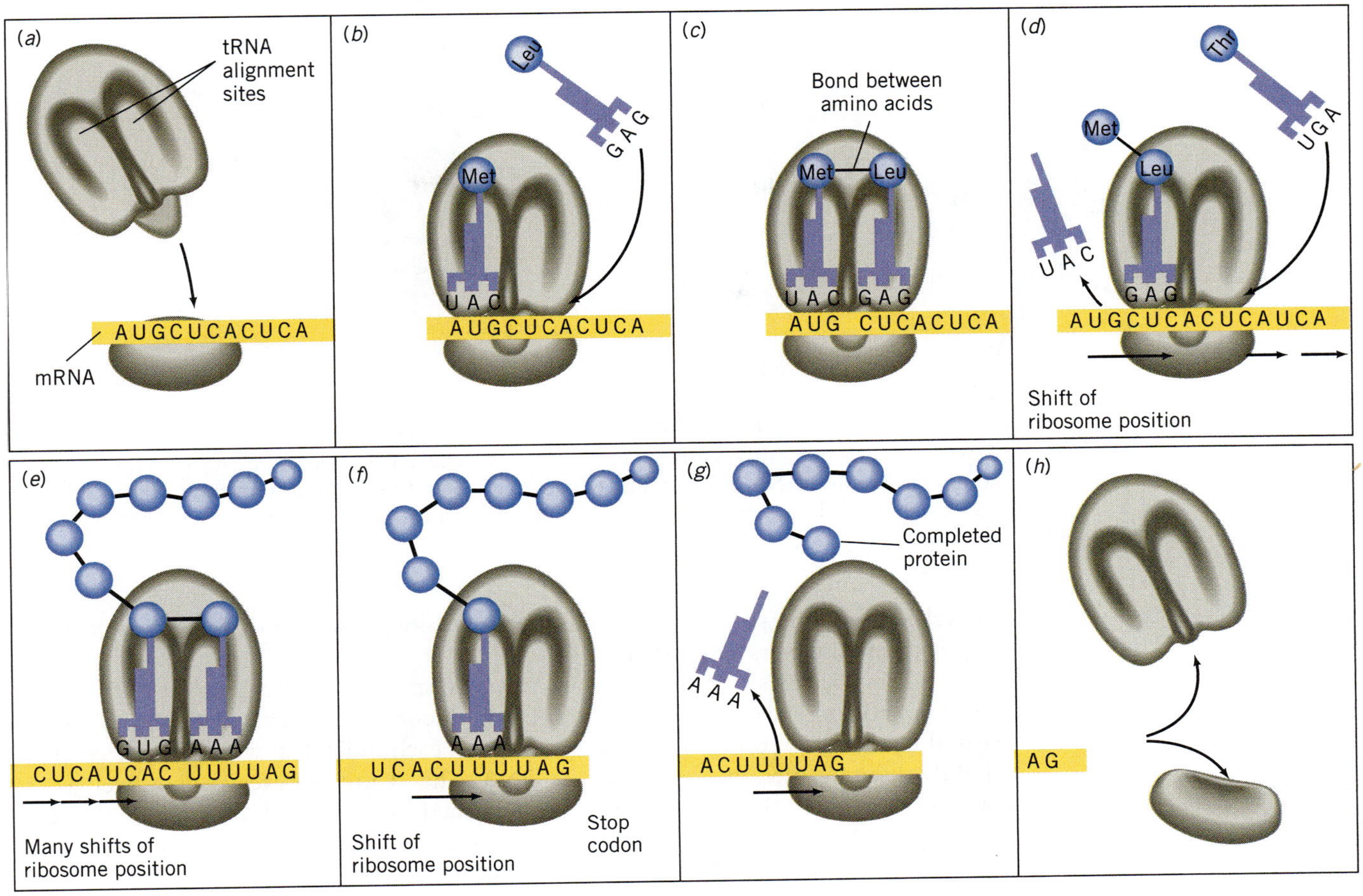

• **Figure 23-9** The formation of a protein requires three kinds of RNA. *(a)* A strand of messenger RNA fits into a groove in a ribosome (an organelle formed from proteins and ribosomal RNA). *(b)* The ribosome attracts the appropriate transfer RNA, which carries with it an amino acid (shown in blue). *(c)* A second tRNA attaches to the ribosome, and the two adjacent amino acids are linked *(d–f)*. The ribosome begins to shift along the mRNA, attracting new tRNA molecules and adding amino acids to the chain. Once the amino acids and tRNA are disconnected, the tRNA floats off to find another amino acid *(g–h)*. The completed protein is assembled and released by the ribosome, and all the components are available to start the process over again.

That is, one stretch of DNA will code for one mRNA molecule, which will code for the sequence of amino acids in one protein, which will drive one chemical reaction in the cell (Figure 23-10). It was once believed that all genetic processes follow this rule. Today we understand that, while genes in prokaryotes are usually found on one continuous stretch of DNA, in eukaryotes like human beings the geometry of genes is often more complicated. A gene on human DNA does not consist of a single continuous stretch of DNA; rather the coding sections of the DNA of a single gene are often separated from each other by stretches of noncoding DNA. The parts of the DNA that code for the protein are called *exons,* while the noncoding sections that are interspersed between them are called *introns.* The cellular machinery that transcribes the gene is able to cut out the introns and assemble the protein only from exons. In the assembly process, however, the exons can be put together in different ways, so that a single gene can code for more than one protein. In humans, for example, a single stretch of DNA may contribute to three or more different proteins.

But the great truth of modern biology is this: more than a century ago, Mendel postulated the existence of a gene without knowing what it was. Today molecular biologists

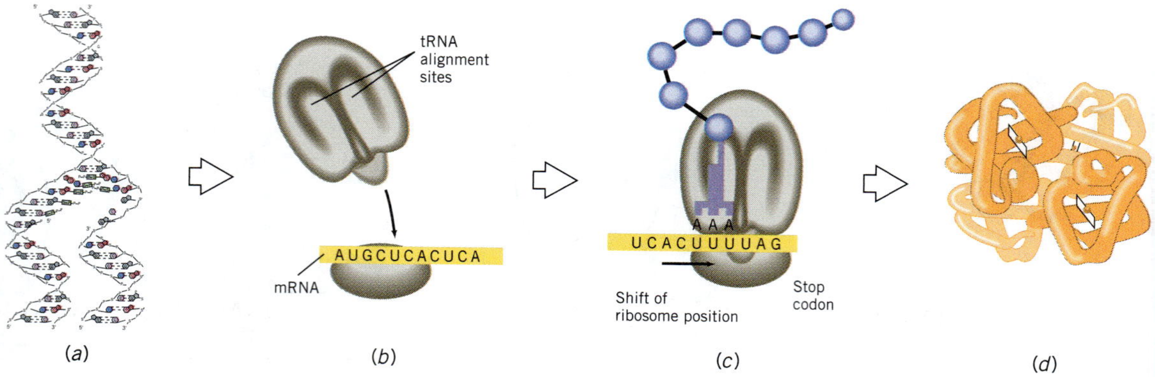

• **Figure 23-10** A schematic diagram of protein production from DNA. *(a)* One stretch of DNA codes for one mRNA molecule. *(b)* One messenger RNA molecule attaches to a ribosome. *(c)* Transfer RNA molecules match an amino acid to each codon on the messenger RNA. *(d)* Amino acids link together to make one protein, which will drive one chemical reaction in the cell.

can tell you exactly where many specific genes lie along a stretch of DNA, as well as the sequence of base pairs along them.

All living systems employ the genetic mechanism we have just described. The transfer of genetic information by DNA and the production of proteins by RNA is a process shared by every cell on Earth. Each species, and each individual within a species, has a slightly different message written on its DNA. The identity of every cell, as well as the organism of which the cell is a part, is determined by the chemical reactions that take place there. The enzymes determine the chemical reactions, and the enzymes are coded for in the DNA. Thus DNA is truly the molecule that contains the code of life.

What is perhaps most remarkable about this process is that all living things use essentially the same code to translate between the messages carried in the genes of DNA, the messages carried in RNA, and the string of amino acids in proteins. This relationship explains why biologists speak of "the genetic code" when they refer specifically to the relationship between a triplet of base pairs on the mRNA and the corresponding amino acid in the protein. The basic "word" of the molecular world, then, is the triplet of bases along DNA—the codon. Each codon eventually codes to one amino acid in a string of proteins.

The fact that all living organisms, from single-celled yeast to human beings, use precisely the same biochemical apparatus and precisely the same technique for making proteins and running their chemistry is one of the great unifying ideas in the science of biology. Indeed, one of the great principles of science is:

All living things on Earth use the same genetic code.

This finding in no way limits the tremendous variety and diversity one can find in living things. Just as many different books can be written using the 26 letters of the English alphabet, so too can many different life-forms be constructed using the four "letters" in the genetic code.

Mutations and DNA Repair

If DNA were copied faithfully from one generation to the next, no living thing could be much different from its ancestors. But mistakes do happen, and many agents in nature can alter and even damage the DNA molecule. Numerous chemicals (particularly those that cause oxidation reactions in cells), nuclear radiation, X-rays, and ultraviolet light (which also produces oxidizing chemicals) are all examples of such agents.

If the DNA of a parent's egg or sperm is altered, then the alteration will be faithfully copied by the process we have just described. The offspring will inherit the change, just as they inherit all other genetic information from the parents. Such a change in the DNA of the parent is called a **mutation**. As we shall see in Chapter 25, mutations have played a very important role in the development of life on Earth.

Recently, scientists have begun to realize that DNA is damaged at a far higher rate than had previously been thought. Careful chemical analyses indicate that damage to DNA in humans goes on at the rate of about 10,000 "hits" per cell per day. Fortunately, the body has developed repair mechanisms that take care of almost all of this damage as soon as it happens. The study of DNA repair, and the hope that it may help us deal with diseases such as cancer, represents a major frontier in science today and will be discussed more fully in Chapter 24.

Why Are Genes Expressed?

Every cell in your body except the reproductive cells contains an identical set of chromosomes—the exact same set of DNA molecules—yet your cells are not all alike. In fact, chemical reactions that are critical to one set of cells—those that produce insulin in your pancreas, for example—play no role whatsoever elsewhere. The genetic coding for making insulin is contained in every cell in your body but turned on only in a few. How do the cells in the pancreas "know" that they are supposed to activate the particular gene for insulin, while the cells in the brain know they are not supposed to?

The mystery of DNA's operation runs even deeper than this. It now appears that only about 5% of all DNA in human beings is actually taken up by the genes. The other 95% used to be called "junk DNA" because nobody understood why it was there. Scientists are increasingly coming to believe, however, that at least some of the rest of the DNA contains instructions for turning genes on and off. The study of gene control is a frontier field, and we understand very little about how it works. We do know, however, that genes are activated at certain times in the growth of plants or animals, and the triggers for this activation appear to be enzymes or other chemical agents.

Many scientists also believe that the failure of these instructions leads to diseases such as cancer. If a cell is dividing and the mechanism that tells it when it's time to stop is faulty, the cell may continue to multiply and produce a tumor. Damage to the control mechanisms in a cell thus may be much more serious than damage to the genes themselves.

Viruses

If you have ever had influenza ("the flu") or a common cold, you've experienced the consequences of viruses. Viruses aren't alive in the sense that bacteria and other single-celled organisms are. Unlike the life-forms we discussed in Chapter 20, viruses do not metabolize and are not capable of reproduction on their own. Rather, they rely on the genetic mechanisms of cells to reproduce.

A **virus** consists of nothing more than a short length of RNA or DNA wrapped in a protein coating (Figure 23-11). The protein is shaped so that it fits cell receptors and is taken into a cell. Once inside the cell, a variety of events may occur, depending on the exact nature of the virus. The viral DNA may replicate itself, producing its own mRNA, or viral RNA may serve directly as messenger RNA. Thus the virus takes over the cell's machinery, using the cell's enzymes and tRNA to produce more viruses like itself, eventually killing the cell.

Note that a "computer virus" operates in the same way. This kind of virus is a set of instructions taken into a computer that highjacks all the computer's machinery to its own ends.

• **Figure 23-11** Viruses can have a wide variety of shapes and sizes. This diagram of a bacterial virus shows the protein coat containing DNA at the head. The tail fibers at the bottom attach the virus to the cell wall. DNA is then injected into the cell through the cylindrical core.

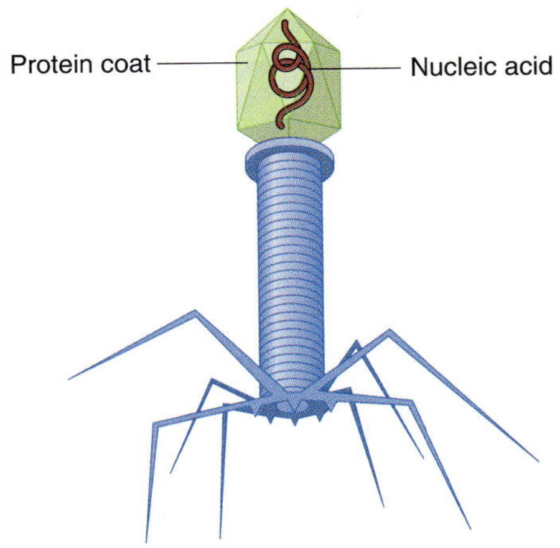

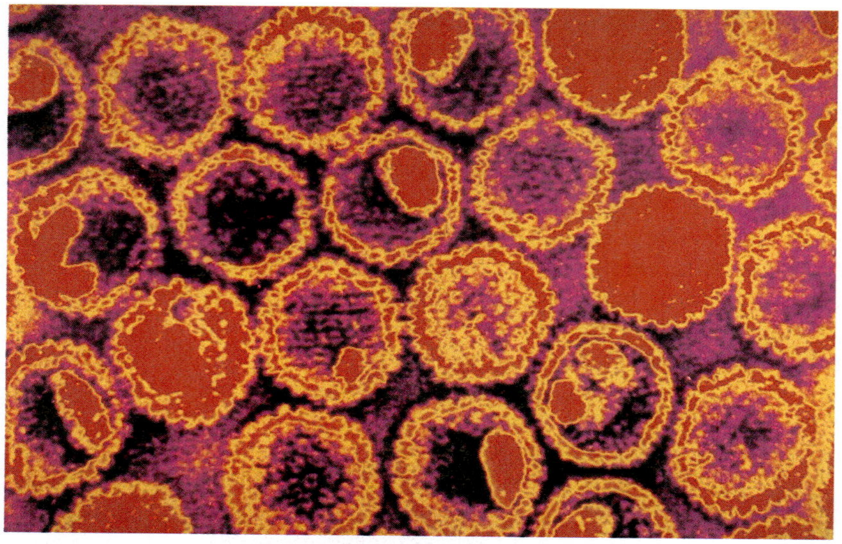

An electron microscope photograph of herpes viruses reveals the regular protein coating that surrounds a strand of DNA.

Alternatively, as in the HIV (human immunodeficiency virus) that causes AIDS, the virus contains an RNA sequence that can be transcribed back into DNA, along with some enzymes that insert the DNA into the cell's own DNA. Once that stretch of DNA is inserted, it acts just like any other gene and co-opts the cell into making more viruses. No matter what the mechanisms, however, the result is the same: the cell eventually dies.

HIV turns out to be an unusually complex virus (Figure 23-12). It has two coats of proteins: the outer coat contains molecules that fit receptors in cells in the human immune systems known as T cells, while the inner coat encloses the RNA that will be translated into DNA by attached enzymes. The net effect of the virus's action is to destroy cells that are essential to the operation of the immune system, making the infected person vulnerable to many deadly diseases. We will discuss methods that have been developed for managing AIDS in the next chapter.

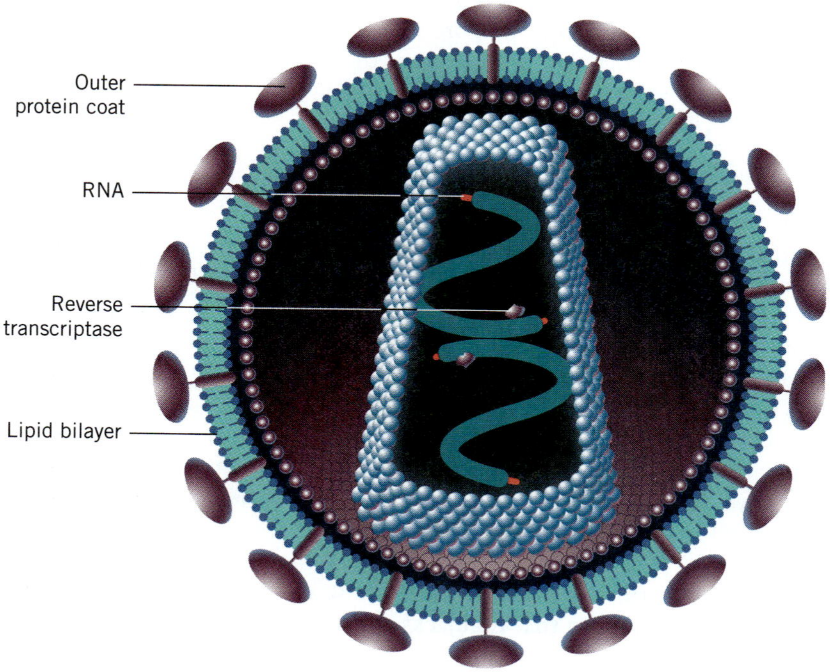

• **Figure 23-12** A diagram of the HIV virus. The reverse transcriptase is the enzyme in the virus that translates a strand of RNA into DNA.

Viral Epidemics

There is an old joke about someone who goes to a doctor with a cold and is told to take a shower and stay outside in the cold with wet hair and without a coat.

"But if I do that, I'll get pneumonia," the patient protests.

"Of course," says the doctor, "but I can cure pneumonia."

The medical profession has enjoyed a great deal of success in dealing with diseases such as pneumonia that are caused by invading bacteria. Antibiotics often work by blocking particular enzymes in the bacteria. Because these enzymes don't operate in human cells, antibiotics can destroy the bacteria without harming the human whose body they are invading.

On the other hand, viruses with their simple structure of a protein coat surrounding a piece of genetic material, are able to co-opt most of the host cell's machinery while antibiotics do not affect them. This difference is why viral diseases such as the common cold cannot be treated as effectively with commonly available drugs as bacterial infections. The most effective countermeasure for viral diseases has been vaccination, which stimulates the human immune system to produce antibodies that neutralize the virus. These antibodies are molecules that have a precise shape that binds to the virus and prevents them from attaching to cells. Poliomyelitis, smallpox, and yellow fever have all been dealt with in this way.

The human body produces immune system cells, called phagocytes, that destroy viruses, bacteria, and other foreign substances. This photo shows a phagocyte stalking a small bacterium.

Viruses not only hide inside cells, many of them also have the ability to change very rapidly, producing new forms as quickly as we find vaccines against them. The copying of DNA in cell division is subject to the cell's "proofreading" mechanisms so that daughter cells are the same as the parents. However, some viruses like HIV have no such proofreading, and consequently they mutate at a rate up to a million times faster than normal eukaryotic cells. The influenza virus adopts a different strategy. If two influenza viruses invade the same host, they have the ability to swap sections of their nucleic acids, producing a new strain in the process. This rapid rate of mutation in influenza viruses is the main reason that Americans are urged to get new flu shots each year. The new vaccine attempts to counteract whatever virus has developed since last year's shot.

As news about AIDS and possible epidemics of SARS, bird flu, and other diseases should remind us, viral diseases remain a very real threat to the human race. Several features of modern life make human beings particularly susceptible to viral attack. For one thing, we now tend to live together in cities, providing a large host population for new viruses. We also travel a great deal so that a virus that develops in one part of the world will quickly spread. Finally, humans are coming into more contact with isolated wilderness areas and therefore into contact with whatever viruses are already living on hosts in those areas. One example is the virus responsible for AIDS, which is believed to have arisen from a virus affecting monkeys in remote African forests. A hunter cutting his finger while skinning an infected monkey, for instance, could have introduced the virus to the human population.

Stop and Think! How much attention do you think governments and scientists should pay to the dangers of new viral diseases? Do you think an international medical center should be established to monitor the appearance of new diseases? What good would such an early warning system do?

The Human Genome

In the summer of 2000, one of the most ambitious scientific projects in history was completed. Called the **Human Genome Project,** its goal was nothing less than a complete description of all the of base pairs in human DNA—all three *billion* pairs on all 23 chromosomes.

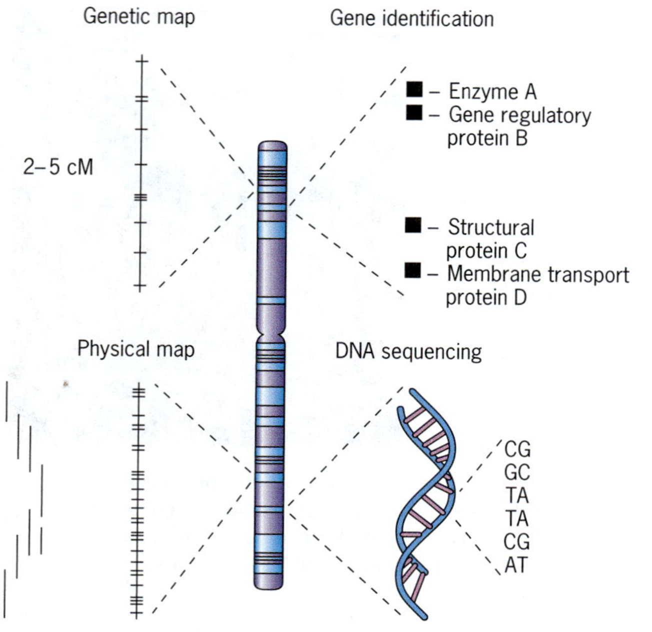

• **Figure 23-13** Two important goals of the Human Genome Project are DNA mapping and DNA sequencing. A genetic map shows the location and sequence of genes along a chromosome. It can be used to identify the genes for a specific trait. Scientists working on the Human Genome Project created physical maps that describe the chemical characteristics of the DNA molecule at any given point. The physical maps were used for DNA sequencing, which determined the exact sequence of base pairs along a DNA molecule.

In human beings, as in other eukaryotes, the DNA does not occur as one long, continuous molecule but is cut up into bundles called chromosomes. In a chromosome, a stretch of DNA is wrapped around a core of protein molecules. A human being receives 23 different chromosomes from each parent, and each gene has a specific location on a specific chromosome.

Different organisms have different numbers of chromosomes. Humans have a total of 23 pairs, for example, while goldfish have 47 pairs and cabbages have 9. There is no connection between the number of chromosomes and the complexity of the organism. It is best to think of chromosomes as the "packaging" into which the DNA is put.

The first job in analyzing human DNA is a process called **mapping** (Figure 23-13). In this process, the locations of genes on specific chromosomes are determined. This is particularly important in medicine, since many diseases arise from mutations on specific genes. As we shall see in the next chapter, for example, a common form of cystic fibrosis results from a mutation on a specific gene on chromosome 7. In recent years, scientists have been able to pinpoint the causes of diseases like sickle-cell anemia and some forms of arthritis on specific chomosomes.

The genetic map, like a good road atlas, tells us the general location of the most interesting places in our tour of the human genome. Genes are like villages and towns in our atlas, but these maps alone tell us little about the details of those places. We also need directories to each village and town if we are to really understand how the genome works. **DNA sequencing** is the process of determining, base pair by base pair, the exact order of bases along a DNA molecule. The net result of a sequencing operation is a string of letters (ATTGCGCATT..., and so on), a sequence that tells us how the DNA is put together in that particular stretch (Figure 23-13). The entire sequence of base pairs in an organism's DNA is called the *genome* of that organism. For reference, the relationships among DNA, genes, chromosomes, and genomes are summarized in Table 23-4.

Many people are surprised to learn that a key goal of the Human Genome Project is to determine the complete genomes of many other species, including the mouse, the fruit fly, yeast, and numerous microbes. These life-forms, so crucial to ongoing genetic research, have many of the same genes and thus reveal many of the same genetic mechanisms that occur in humans. One result of this sort of knowledge is that a gene sequence can be used to deduce the sequence of amino acids in a protein; this information, in turn, may give some insight into the function of that protein in the organism.

Keep watching the news for announcements of the latest progress in this mammoth undertaking.

Table 23-4 Relationships among DNA, Genes, Chromosomes, and Genomes

Unit	What it is
DNA	The molecule that caries genetic information. It is in the shape of a double helix
Gene	A stretch of DNA that carries the code for making one or more proteins
Chromosome	A specific length of an organism's DNA wrapped around a protein core
Genome	The sum total of all the base pairs in an organism's DNA

Science in the Making •

Connecting Genes and DNA

In 1911, an undergraduate student and a professor were talking at Columbia University. The professor was Thomas Hunt Morgan, who was studying the genetics of fruit flies in his laboratory. Like Mendel's pea plants, fruit flies are ideal organisms for this sort of work, since they produce new generations in a matter of weeks. (Morgan, incidentally, was the great-grandson of Francis Scott Key, the man who wrote "The Star Spangled Banner"). The student was Alfred Sturtevant, a young man who went on to have a distinguished scientific career.

The two were discussing the fact that in their experiments, certain characteristics of the flies seemed to be inherited in groups—if one appeared in an offspring, the others were likely to appear as well. They were also finding, however, that occasionally this linkage was broken and that the frequency of the breaking of the link varied from one pair of genes to the next.

During the conversation, Sturtevant realized that if the genes were laid out in a linear array on the chromosomes, then the process of gene exchange that occurs during meiosis would be more likely to separate genes that lay far apart from each other than genes that are close together. In fact, the process of gene exchange would be like cutting up a highway map. Nearby towns would tend to be on the same piece of paper when the cutting was finished, while distant towns would be separated more often. Using this insight and the data on how often linkages were broken, Sturtevant came into the lab the next day with the first genetic map of a chromosome.

Work in the Columbia "fly room" thus led to one of the most important basic tenets of modern genetics—that genes are laid out in a linear sequence on chromosomes. During the coming decades, with support from the Carnegie Institution, this lab remained at the center of genetic research. Morgan received the Nobel Prize in 1933 and, in a telling gesture, shared the prize money with Sturtevant and another former student in order to help the two men pay their children's college tuition bills. •

Science by the Numbers •

The Human Book of Life

In Chapter 10 we saw that information can be quantified in units of the "bit"—a simple statement about "yes or no" or "on or off." We can use this notion to calculate the amount of information in the human genome.

Each site along the DNA molecule can be occupied by one of four bases. This information can be represented by two bits. We could, for example, set up a code as follows:

A: on on

T: on off

C: off on

G: off off

Using this code, we could go down the molecule specifying two bits of information at each nucleotide, and this would tell us the sequence. For example, the sequence AGT would be rendered:

on on; off off; on off

The human genome contains about 3 billion bases, so the total information content is:

$$3{,}000{,}000{,}000 \text{ bases} \times 2 \text{ bits/base} = 6{,}000{,}000{,}000 \text{ bits}$$

Let's compare this information content to that of a familiar object—this textbook. A textbook transmits information by letters, numbers, and other symbols, each of which can be represented by eight bits (see Chapter 10). An average page of this book contains about 3000 characters, for an information content of

$$3000 \text{ characters/page} \times 8 \text{ bits/character} = 24{,}000 \text{ bits/page}$$

The number of pages required to carry the entire human genome equals the number of bits per genome, divided by the number of bits per page:

$$\frac{(6{,}000{,}000{,}000 \text{ bits/genome})}{(24{,}000 \text{ bits/page})} = 250{,}000 \text{ pages}$$

It would take almost 400 volumes the size of this book to record the entire blueprint for a human being. It's amazing to think that all of that information is contained in every one of your cells. •

Marty Katz

J. Craig Venter

Technology •

New Ways to Sequence

When the Human Genome Project was starting, scientists estimated that it would take decades and cost billions of dollars. Even well into the project, the official estimate was that it wouldn't be completed until 2005 and would cost $3 billion (about $1 per base pair).

This situation was changed drastically when molecular biologist J. Craig Venter, who was then head of Celera Corporation, developed a new way of combining computers with automatic DNA sequencing machines. As a result of his work, the Genome Project finished in 2000, five years ahead of schedule, with the cost of sequencing being only about 10 cents per base pair.

Venter's novel technique is called shotgun, and here's how it works: Long stretches of DNA are broken up into many small pieces. These pieces are fed into an army of sequencing machines, each of which "reads" only a short segment—a few hundred base pairs of the original. By identifying overlapping segments from among the thousands of short DNA strands, powerful computers are able to reconstruct the entire DNA sequence.

It is important to realize that in this technique, the contributions of computers are just as important as those of the sequencers. This is why scientists often speak of the Genome Project as an example of the *bioinformatics* revolution.

Today, Celera's sequencing system continues to operate 24 hours a day, and each day they sequence a million base pairs and use $4000 to $5000 worth of electricity in the process. •

Science News | Shades of Flesh Tone

(Science News, Dec. 17, 2005, p. 388)

The fact that all living things share the same genetic code sometimes crops up in unexpected places. For example, scientists at the Penn State College of Medicine recently came to interesting insights about human skin color by studying the stripes on zebra fish.

These small fish, a favorite subject for laboratory study, normally have black stripes running the length of their bodies, but there is a mutation in which the stripes are honey colored. It had been known for some time that the lighter colored fish had fewer pigment particles, and the researchers set out to see if they could identify the gene responsible for this condition. Their work eventually turned up a mutation in a gene called *slc24a5*. Fish with a specific mutation had lighter colored stripes.

The scientists wondered whether there might not be a similar gene operating in humans. A quick look in to the data banks of the Human Genome Project turned up a similar gene, called *SLC24A5* on human chromosome 15. Further work on the data banks showed that this gene has slightly different form in people of African descent than it has in people descended from Europeans. The team then took DNA samples from 308 people of mixed African and European origins, and found that the European form of the gene tended to be found in the genome of people with lighter skin.

Having established the importance of this gene in determining human skin color, the researchers quickly found that it cannot be the only gene involved. Asian genomes in the data banks, for example, typically display the African form of the gene even though the individuals involved have light skin. This finding means that other genes, as yet unidentified, must play a role in skin color along with *SLC24A5*.

Because skin color is connected to the complex social category we call race, this research must be interpreted carefully. In the words of Francis Collins, director of the National Human Genome Research Institute, "To say that this is the gene for race is a fundamental misconception of that complex term."

Thinking More About | Genetics

The Ethics of Genes

Advances in genetic research are dramatically altering our understanding of human health and behavior. Scientists now can detect many characteristics of an individual, including the presence of life-threatening diseases, before birth. Every year we learn more about genetic characteristics, and thus are better able to foresee aspects of a child's future. But with this knowledge comes an ethical challenge that will face every American in the coming decades. What should we do with genetic information?

Eventually we may be able to test every fetus for a variety of incurable genetic diseases. Should those tests be mandated? Should parents be informed of their future child's fate? Should the prospect of an incurable disease provide grounds for abortion? It has also been suggested (though not proven in detail) that alcoholism and other behavioral disorders may be related, at least in part, to genetic factors. Suppose a person was found to carry a particular gene or combination of genes that were thought to predispose individuals toward alcoholism? To whom should that information be conveyed? To the individual? To his or her doctor? His or her employer? His or her insurance company?

Taking these issues a step further, it may soon be possible to alter an individual's DNA in utero, perhaps even in the first weeks of pregnancy. Many people would probably agree to genetic manipulation if it could cure their child of a fatal disease, but where does society draw the line? Would you allow such a procedure to improve genetically defective eyesight, or perhaps prevent crippling arthritis in later years? Would you be willing to enhance your child's IQ, or make her more athletic? What about changing his height or hair color? As with many other aspects of science and technology, we must come to grips with the question of whether it is ethical to do something simply because we are able to do it.

SUMMARY

Genetics, the study of the way in which biological information is carried from one generation to the next, is a field as old as the selective breeding of animals and the selection of seeds for crops. Gregor Mendel attempted to quantify aspects of this process by cross-pollinating *purebred* varieties of pea plants to produce *hybrids.* He discovered that all first-generation hybrids appeared the same, with the traits of just one parent plant, but the second generation displayed characteristics of both parents. Typically, three-fourths of the members of the second generation display one trait, one-fourth the other. Mendel explained his observations by developing laws of *classical genetics:* (1) traits are passed from parent to offspring by "units of inheritance" (we call them *genes*); (2) each parent contributes one gene for each trait; and (3) some genes are *dominant* and will be expressed, while others are *recessive* and will appear only if no dominant gene is present.

Modern *molecular genetics* seeks to understand the molecular basis for Mendel's observations. The key to understanding genetics lies in the unique structure of the *nucleic acids,* including *DNA,* with its *double helix,* ladder-like sequence of base pairs, and the closely related single-stranded *RNA.* The four different DNA bases, A, T, C, and G, which always come in the pairs AT or CG, act like letters of a coded message—the message of life. Because of its structure, DNA can replicate itself and store the information needed to make proteins.

Every cell has a set of chromosomes with the complete DNA blueprint in its nucleus. The process of copying DNA before cell division is called replication, and involves the splitting of the two sides of the DNA double helix, exposing the complementary base pairs. Each exposed base binds to its complement, and so two complete DNA strands form where before there was only one.

The coded DNA message is read by RNA, a process called transcription. *Messenger RNA,* a single-stranded molecule, copies the sequence for one gene and carries it out of the nucleus to the part of the cell where proteins are made. *Transfer RNA* matches sequences of three base pairs to corresponding amino acids; thus an RNA sequence translates into a string of amino acids—a protein. The correspondence between base-pair sequences and amino acids is called the *genetic code,* which is shared by every living organism.

While the DNA message is resilient to most damage, errors in the coded sequence can occur and cause *mutations. Viruses,* on the other hand, cause sickness by usurping a cell's chemical factories with foreign genetic instructions.

Segments of DNA are wrapped around a protein core to form *chromosomes.* The complete description of an organism's genetic code is called its *genome.* Scientists determine a *genome* by first *mapping* the positions of every gene on every chromosome and then *sequencing* the exact order of base pairs on every gene. The *Human Genome Project* has produced the 3-billion-base-pair sequence of the human genome, as well as genomes for many other organisms.

Key Terms

genetics
purebred
hybrid
gene
classical genetics
dominant
recessive
molecular genetics
nucleic acids
DNA
RNA
double helix
messenger RNA (mRNA)
transfer RNA (tRNA)
genetic code
mutation
virus
genome
Human Genome Project
mapping
DNA sequencing

Review Questions

1. How did Mendel define the gene? How do we define it today?

2. Why was it important for Mendel to begin with purebred plants for each trait he was studying?

3. What is the difference between a dominant and a recessive gene?

4. What is a nucleotide?

5. Name the four bases that occur in DNA. What pairs can they form?

6. Describe the construction of the double-helix structure of DNA.

7. How does RNA differ from DNA?

8. What are the main steps in the process of DNA replication?

9. How is the information of DNA copied onto mRNA?

10. What is the function of mRNA?

11. How does tRNA determine the primary structure of proteins?

12. What is a codon? What is the genetic code?

13. Why do genetic mutations occur? What agents cause them?

14. What is a virus? Why are they so difficult to control?

15. What is the difference between mapping and sequencing DNA?

Discussion Questions

1. Could a recessive trait skip more than one generation? How could this happen?

2. What is a hybrid? How is gene expression affected in the production of a hybrid?

3. Why is DNA sequencing more time-consuming than DNA mapping?

4. How does cell chemistry, and therefore all life, depend on the production of proteins? What role do genes, RNA, and DNA play in the production of proteins?

5. State some of the arguments for and against the use of genetic engineering.

6. Inbreeding, or the mating of closely related individuals, tends to perpetuate both good and harmful traits. Why should this be so?

7. If every cell in your body has exactly the same DNA, how can the cells perform such different functions?

8. Why do most biologists say that viruses are not alive? *(Hint:* Respiration and metabolism.)

9. Exposure to environmental chemicals or radiation may cause damage to children, even though those children have not even been conceived at the time of the exposure. Give a molecular explanation of how such harm could occur. What role should information on DNA repair play in such discussions?

10. How many types of RNA are there in a cell? Why is more than one type necessary in the production of a DNA sequence?

11. Why do many cultures have a taboo and/or laws against marrying your close relatives? Why is incest a genetically unproductive practice?

12. Why do offspring resemble their parents? Attempt to include nucleotides, genes, chromosomes, RNA, DNA, mitosis, and meiosis in your answer.

Problems

1. The *Encyclopedia Britannica* has about 1500 words per page, 1000 pages per volume, and 30 volumes. How many sets of the *Encyclopedia Britannica* would it take to transmit the same amount of information as is contained in human DNA? [*Hint:* Remember, the average word has five characters and a single character has eight bits of information.]

2. Suppose a particular breed of rat can be either white or brown and have either clear or pink eyes. Suppose further that if purebred white rats are crossed with purebred brown rats, all the offspring are brown; and that if true-breeding clear-eyed rats and true-breeding pink-eyed rats are crossed, all the offspring have pink eyes. What will be the distribution of hair and eye color in the second generation if we start by crossing true-breeding brown pink-eyed rats with true-breeding white clear-eyed rats?

3. Scientists frequently use fruit flies, which breed every 10 days, to do genetics experiments. How long would it take to repeat one of Mendel's experiments on peas using fruit flies? What if we used elephants? [*Hint:* Elephants have roughly one offspring every two years and take 13 to 20 years to reach maturity.]

INVESTIGATIONS

1. Prepare a report on a genetic disease. What progress has been made in mapping the defective gene? sequencing the gene? What kinds of medical treatments are now available?

2. Read *The Double Helix* by James Watson, codiscoverer with Francis Crick of the DNA structure. What data did they use to unravel the structure? What were the key steps in solving the double-helix structure?

3. Investigate the role that Rosalind Franklin played in the history of DNA and the discovery of the double-helix structure. Was she properly recognized for her efforts? Why didn't she win the Nobel Prize for her discoveries?

4. Some psychological disorders are now believed to be caused by defects in the body's chemistry. Read about one such disease, and summarize the argument between those who believe that psychological problems all have a molecular basis and those who believe that they are all due to the environment in which the individual has lived.

5. Make a family tree for your own family, recording characteristics such as eye and hair color, height, causes of death, and so on. Can you apply Mendel's rules to this tree?

6. A number of obscure viral diseases have arisen over the past few decades. Look up Korean hemorrhagic fever, dengue fever, Lassa fever, or the Ebola and Marburg viruses. What symptoms do these diseases or viruses produce? What danger do they pose to the larger human population?

7. Mendel used mathematical analyses to deduce the presence of genes despite that fact that he couldn't see them directly. What other great discoveries relied on the use of mathematics to prove the existence of something that was impossible to directly observe?

8. Investigate the "Nature vs. Nurture" debate. Why do most scientists now state that it is usually nature and nuture, and not one or the other?

9. What is bioinformatics? Does your college or university have a bioinformatics department? What are you studying if you pursue a degree in bioinformatics or biotechnology?

10. Investigate the history of thoroughbred (i.e., racehorse) or canine (i.e., dog) pedigrees. Why are these valuable resources? What does it mean to own a "purebreed" dog? What does it mean to own a thoroughbred horse?

24

The New Science of Life

Can we cure cancer?

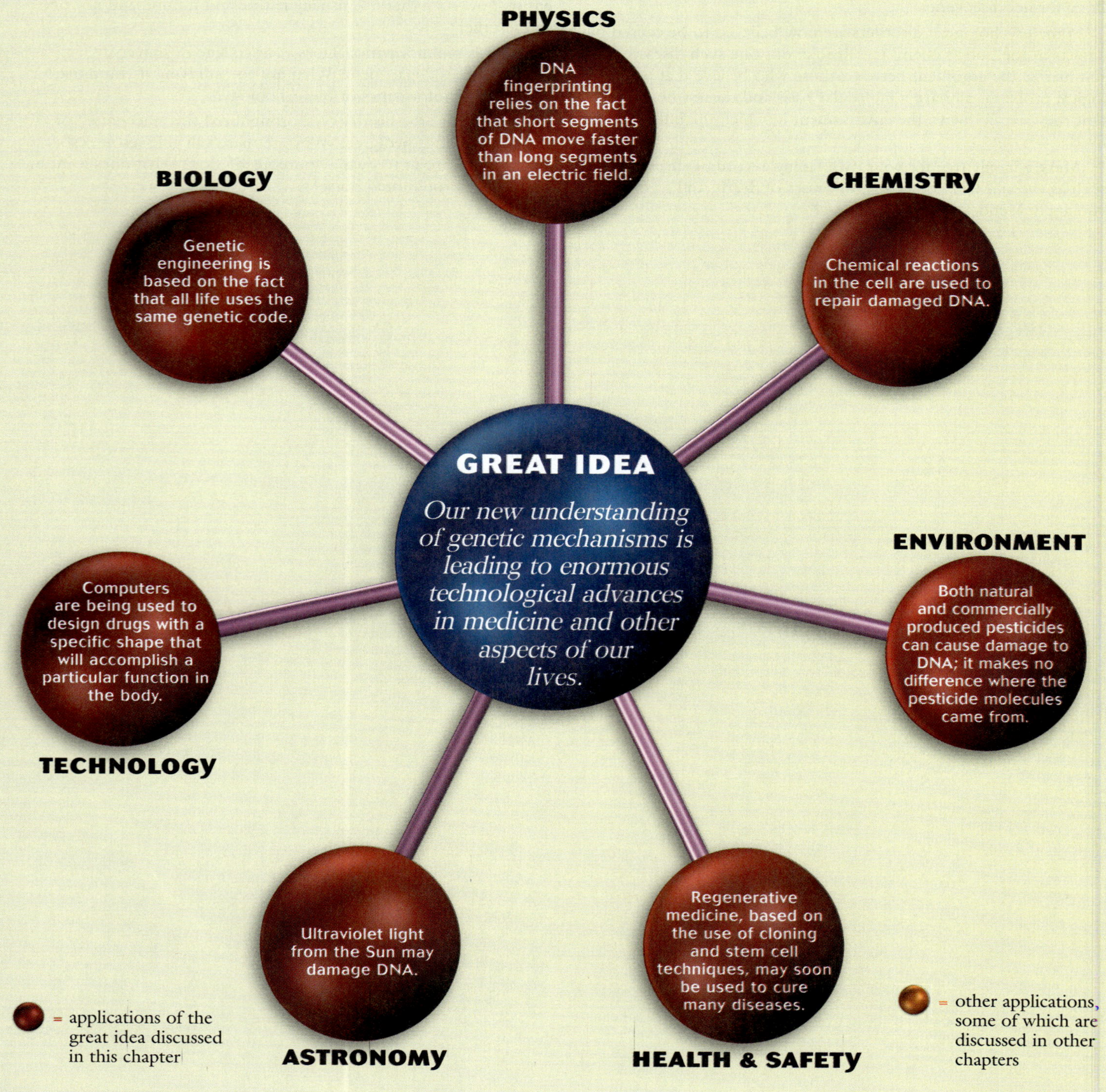

Science Through the Day | A Break in the Case

You head down the highway, listening to your favorite music station, when the program is interrupted for a news flash. New DNA evidence has led police to the arrest of a suspect in a highly publicized murder. A few skin cells under the victim's fingernails, analyzed at an FBI crime lab, cracked the case.

It seems as if DNA and genetic technologies are in the news every day. Paternity testing, cloning, tests for genetic diseases, DNA fingerprinting, stem cells, gene therapy, genetically modified foods—our world has been transformed by our understanding of the genetic code. What are these remarkable new technologies? How will they affect our lives and the lives of our children?

Greg Pease/Taxi/Getty Images

The Technology of Genes

Fundamental new insights into the workings of nature often trigger dramatic changes in the human condition. The discovery of the nature of electricity and magnetism, for example, led to the electrification of entire continents. The discovery of the basic laws of quantum mechanics eventually led to the modern information revolution. Now, our new understanding of the genetic mechanisms of all living things is leading to changes every bit as profound and pervasive. In fact, this revolution has already begun, although its consequences are not always immediately visible to the general public. At research centers and hospitals around the world the new molecular understanding of life is being put to work to cure disease and to better the human condition. In this chapter we present a few areas of current effort to give you a sense of what will soon become possible. Remember, though, that these advances are just the tip of the iceberg with respect to technologies of the new science of life.

Genetic Engineering

Genetic engineering is a procedure by which foreign genes are inserted into an organism, or existing genes are altered, to modify the function of living things. The basic technique of genetic engineering is very simple. Certain proteins, called *restriction enzymes,* have the ability to cut a DNA molecule (as shown in Figure 24-1) so that the DNA has several unattached bases at the cut end. Think of these exposed bases as something like pieces of Velcro at the ends of the DNA strands.

If another strand of DNA is cut in the same way, and if the exposed base pairs on that second strand are complementary to the base pairs on the original strand, then

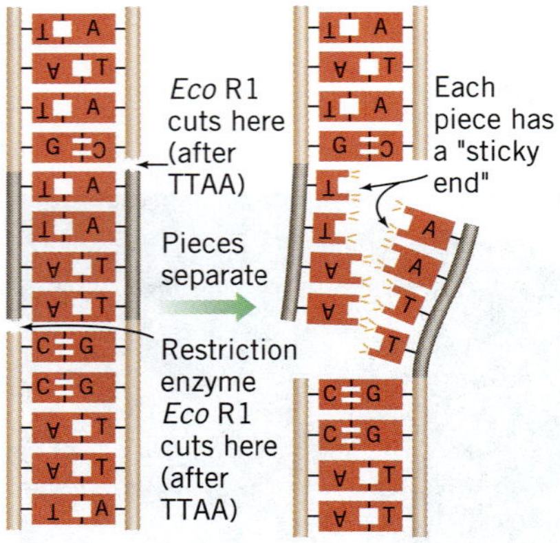

• **Figure 24-1** Restriction enzymes act something like a pair of scissors that break a DNA chain at specific sequences. Biologists can use this procedure to insert or remove segments of DNA.

when the two strands are put together the bases will bind and the strands will stick together. This procedure allows researchers to take a stretch of DNA, cut it, and splice in another stretch of DNA that has the appropriate base pairs on its ends (Figure 24-2). The new DNA will contain an extra stretch of genetic information in it.

If the new stretch of DNA is a gene, then the same mechanism that drives the chemistry in every cell on Earth can start expressing that gene in its new environment. For example, more than 100 copies of the gene that makes human insulin have been spliced together into a loop of DNA called a *plasmid*. Biologists introduced that plasmid into the single-celled bacterium, *E. coli* (so-called because it is common in the human colon), and the genetically modified *E. coli* copies the plasmid along with its own DNA when it divides. A vat full of genetically engineered *E. coli* thus produces large quantities of human insulin that is almost indistinguishable from insulin produced in your own pancreas. In fact, most of the insulin used to treat diabetes is now made this way. This genetically based process is a great improvement over the old method, which involved tedious extraction of pig insulin from the pancreases of slaughtered animals—insulin that precipitated an adverse immune response in some patients.

The story of genetically engineered insulin is only a small part of the growing list of changes that are possible with genetic engineering. In the United States, the biggest use of this technology is not in medicine but in agriculture. Today, over a third of the corn, three-quarters of the soybeans, and a quarter of the cotton grown on American farms are genetically engineered. One important use of the technology is in pest control. Genes that contain the natural insecticide Bt, derived from a common bacterium, are inserted into the DNA of crop plants. Because of the presence of this gene, when insects such as the European corn borer start to feed, they are quickly killed. Beside the obvious advantage of allowing the plant to remain healthy, this process may also benefit the environment, because genetically engineered plants require much less in the way of pesticide application. In 2000, more than 40 million hectares (150,000 square miles) were planted in genetically modified corn worldwide, a strategy that is estimated to have prevented over a billion dollars' worth of crop damage.

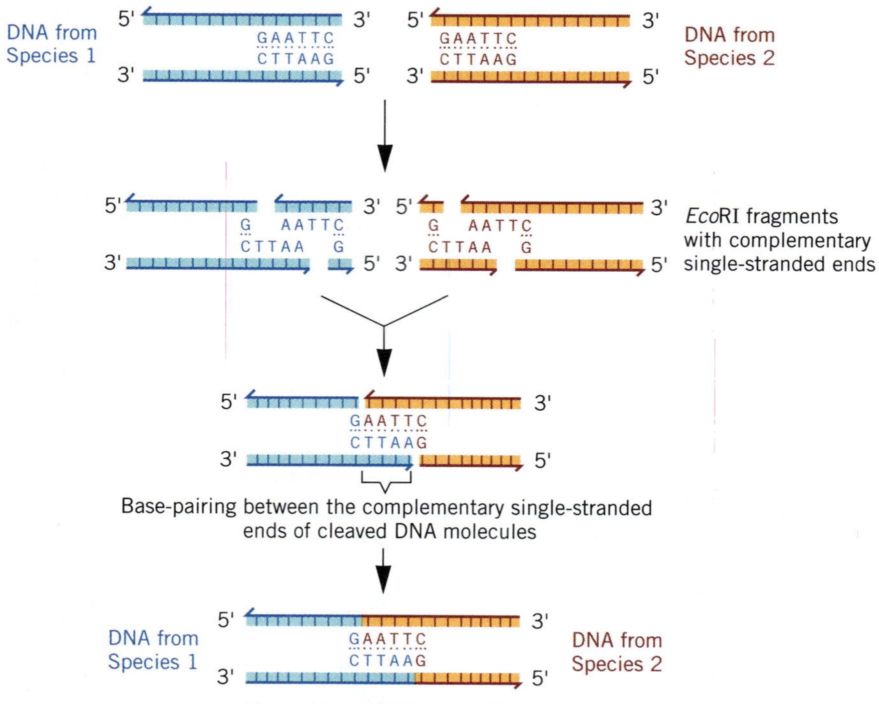

• **Figure 24-2** The process of genetic engineering. Two strands of DNA are cut by restriction enzymes. Each cut is carefully made so that the exposed bases of each strand are complementary. The two strands are joined together to form one DNA molecule.

Another use of genetic engineering involves dealing with the other great enemy of agriculture—weeds. In conventional agriculture, weeds are controlled by cultivation (turning soil over between rows of crop plants) and the spraying of herbicides. Both of these practices have the potential of damaging the environment, either through erosion or runoff. It is possible to engineer crop plants to be resistant to specific kinds of herbicides—a common technique involves so-called Roundup ready plants (Roundup is a popular commercial herbicide). These crops can be planted in unplowed fields, which can then be sprayed to eliminate weeds. This so-called no-plow agriculture is gaining wide acceptance as a way of preventing soil erosion.

Other applications of genetic engineering in agriculture include strawberries that are highly resistant to frost, plants that are unaffected by specific diseases, colored varieties of cotton, and crops that manufacture natural insect repellents. Genetic engineering of animals has led to varieties that grow faster or have other agricultural advantages, and researchers have recently patented varieties of mice especially "designed" for medical research. There's even a patent for genetically engineered petroleum-eating bacteria to clean up oil slicks from tanker accidents.

Underlying all of this technology is the central fact that all life is based on the same genetic code—the translation of DNA sequences in a gene to amino acid sequences in a protein. The exact same geometrical shapes and chemical properties of the four base molecules occur in every living thing. That scientists can routinely switch genes from plants to animals and back again is simply another demonstration of the chemical unity of all life.

In the end, what's new about genetic engineering is that, unlike the selective breeders of the past, modern biologists can usually control exactly what gene is being added to or deleted from the organism being developed.

Stop and Think! What harmful effects might result if a gene to prevent frost damage in strawberries were to get into other plants?

A number of groups around the world are attempting to ban or restrict the introduction of genetically modified foods. This opposition is largely motivated by the fear that there may be unknown environmental and health consequences to the introduction of these kinds of foods. In the United States, genetically modified organisms (GMOs) are controlled by three agencies. The Department of Agriculture is concerned with whether the crop is safe to grow, the Food and Drug Administration with whether it is safe to eat, and the Environmental Protection Agency with whether it is safe for the environment. The criterion used by the FDA is "reasonable expectation of no harm," with the primary test being whether the GMO is as safe as things that have been in the food supply for generations.

Historically, the concern has been that GMOs might contain unexpected allergens—that someone allergic to shellfish, for example, might encounter the protein responsible for that seafood allergy in an apple. The screening of GMOs, then, begins with excluding products that contain any one of a long list of allergens, as well as molecules that might have properties of known allergens. As more experience with GMOs accumulates, fears about unexpected health effects seem to be subsiding.

Today, different countries around the world have adopted different policies toward GMOs. In general, they are either banned or rigidly controlled in Europe, allowed in North America, and eagerly embraced in many Third World countries. Roughly speaking, using the current generation of genetically engineered crops increases productivity by about 10%, enough to be significant in countries with large populations to feed.

We have not even begun to imagine the changes that can take place through the use of this technology. The social issues involved in genetic engineering are profound. In 1974, scientists working in the field of genetic engineering voluntarily undertook a moratorium on further research until thought could be given to the question of how to keep potentially dangerous organisms from escaping into the environment. In most

Chris Knapton/Science Photo Library/Photo Researchers

Courtesy R.L. Brinster

Genetic engineering has produced a variety of modified organisms, including *(a)* pest-resistant crops and *(b)* genetically identical mice for medical research.

cases, such as the *E. coli* used in insulin production, the host bacteria are so specialized and so dependent on their laboratory culture that they could not survive in the wild. In this age of terrorism, however, there is another threat—the deliberate release of genetically engineered pathogens into the environment, an activity known as *bioterrorism*. Bioterrorism is an important concern of agencies such as the Department of Homeland Security.

Technology •

The PCR Process

Development of a simple technique sometimes opens the door for all sorts of new applications. In biotechnology, the process called *polymerase chain reaction (PCR)* has played this role. In essence, PCR is a way of making copies of select strands of DNA so that, starting with a very small sample (a few cells, for example), investigators can produce as much of the desired DNA as they need. As we shall see below, the PCR technique is often used to amplify DNA prior to DNA fingerprinting.

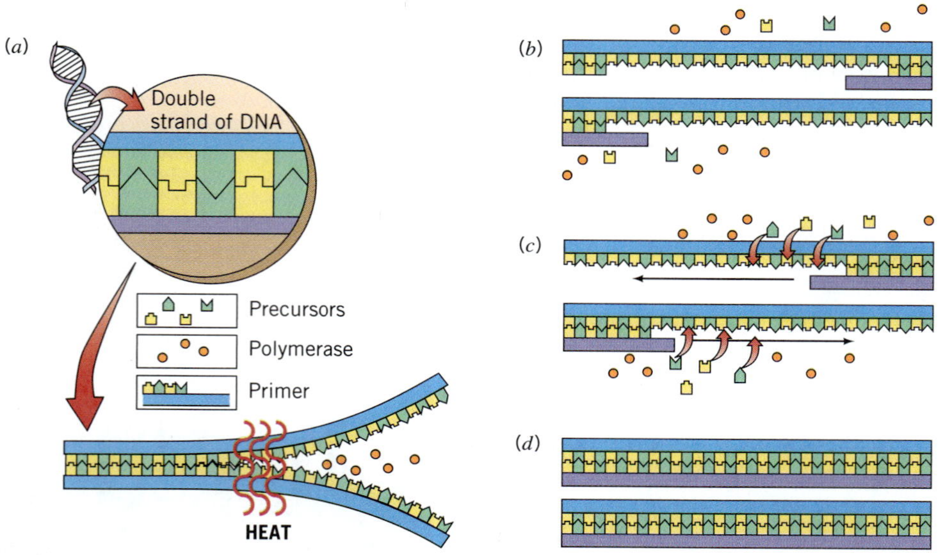

• **Figure 24-3** The polymerase chain reaction (PCR) copies a sequence of DNA. *(a)* A strand of DNA is mixed in solution with DNA precursors (nucleotides), a primer that targets a specific piece of DNA, and an enzyme (polymerase) that helps to assemble DNA. The mix is heated to about 90 degrees to separate DNA strands. *(b)* When cooled to about 60°C, primers attach to the DNA strands. *(c)* At 70°C, nucleotides begin to attach to the DNA strands. *(d)* At the end you have two copies of the desired DNA.

The process is illustrated in Figure 24-3. A sample that contains the DNA to be copied is mixed in solution with three ingredients: DNA nucleotides (the building blocks or precursors of DNA), a short stretch of DNA known as the "primer" (which is designed to identify the desired section of DNA to be copied), and an enzyme called DNA polymerase that helps to assemble DNA strands. First, the mixture is heated to about 90°C to separate the DNA into two strands (Figure 24-3*a*). Once the strands are separated, the solution is cooled to 60°C, at which temperature primers attach to the desired portion of the DNA (Figure 24-3*b*). In the third step the solution is heated to 70°C, which enables polymerase to attach nucleotides onto the DNA strands (Figure 24-3*c*). Eventually, we have two identical DNA strands in place of the original (Figure 24-3*d*). This process, repeated many times, can create as many copies of the original DNA strand as needed. •

Science by the Numbers •

PCR Multiplication

How many times would you have to go through the heating and cooling cycle in the PCR process to multiply the original supply of DNA by a billion?

Each time you go through the cycle, you double the number of DNA molecules. This means that the number of molecules will grow as indicated in the following table

Number of Repeats	Number of Molecules
1	2
2	4
3	8
.	.
.	.
10	1028

Roughly speaking, then, when you go through the cycle 10 times, you multiply the number of DNA molecules by 1000. This means that if you go through the cycle 20 times, you will multiply the number of molecules by approximately:

$$1000 \times 1000 = 1{,}000{,}000 = 1 \text{ million}$$

and if you do the cycle 30 times you will have:

$$1000 \times 1000 \times 1000 = 1{,}000{,}000{,}000 = 1 \text{ billion}$$

It is this property of the PCR process that allows technicians to have enough DNA to identify individuals from a tiny drop of blood or tissue. •

DNA Fingerprinting

Photofest

Evidence from modern biotechnology plays an important role in the television series *CSI*.

The analysis of DNA in human tissue, a technique called **DNA fingerprinting,** is becoming increasingly important in the judicial system in the United States. Except for identical twins, no two human beings in the world have the same DNA. Thus analysis of blood, skin, or semen samples from the scene of a crime can be used to identify criminals in much the same way that fingerprints do, and this process can also help to identify victims of airplane crashes and natural disasters.

In principle, one could sequence an individual's entire genome in order to make an unambiguous identification. In practice, this is both expensive and not necessary. The DNA fingerprinting techniques in common use depend on the fact that there are stretches of DNA where a certain sequence of nonsense bases repeats itself over and over. The number of repeats in these sections is essentially random, so by comparing the number of repeats in two samples of DNA at several different locations, it is possible to tell whether they come from the same individual.

The original DNA fingerprinting technique, accepted by U.S. courts in the 1990s, was accurate but cumbersome. It used relatively long repeating sections, known as variable number tandem repeat *(VNTR)* sequences, in which up to 80 nonsense phrases would appear in a row. Enzymes cut the DNA at places where there is a specific sequence of bases, so segments containing different VNTRs will be of different lengths. These DNA segments are placed in a gelatin-like material, then subjected to an electrical field. The smaller segments move through the gel faster, so that after a certain time, the different strands of DNA will have moved different distances. The DNA is then tagged with a radioactive tracer. The end result of this process is that the information in each person's DNA is reduced to something like a bar code. It has been found that five segments of DNA containing VNTR are enough to establish identification.

In the early years of the twenty-first century, DNA fingerprinting technology underwent a significant change. Instead of using the VNTR technique, which is accurate but slow, scientists found that they could use other segments of DNA to establish identification more easily and quickly. The new technique is based on stretches of DNA known as *short tandem repeats,* or STR, which are stretches of DNA where a nonsense phrase is repeated a small number of times—typically from 2 to 25. The PCR technique is used to copy a given sample many times, and the primer molecules (see the "Technology" section) are built to fluoresce (give off light) when a laser beam shines on them.

The products of the PCR process are then fed through a small, liquid-filled tube. An electric field causes segments of different lengths to separate from each other, a laser is shone on the molecules, and the light they give off is measured. The result is a curve like the one shown in Figure 24-4, in which each peak corresponds to a certain number of repeats of a specific type. These curves are then compared to standard curves obtained from known DNA sequences.

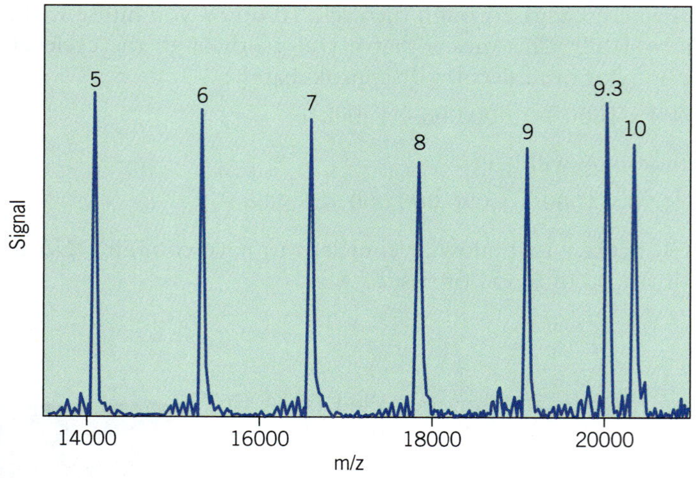

• **Figure 24-4** DNA finger printing using the STRS method. Each spike in the curve corresponds to different lengths of DNA.

The Federal Bureau of Investigations (FBI) databases have established the standard for STR analysis in America. While there are hundreds of STR systems known in the human genome, it has been found that 13 different STR sites, spread across many chromosomes, are sufficient to produce an identification. The probability of two people having the same DNA sequence in all 13 sites is so low that it is unlikely that any two people in the United States would have identical STR profiles.

Stem Cells, Cloning, and Regenerative Medicine

As we saw in Chapter 23, every cell in the human body (except for sperm and ova) contains exactly the same DNA. The DNA, which first comes together in the fertilized egg, is copied trillions of times during the period in which the human grows from an embryo to an adult, and every daughter cell receives a copy of that original genetic material.

Yet even though all cells have the same DNA, all cells do not carry out the same functions in the body. In an adult, blood cells cannot produce skin, nor can skin cells produce muscle tissue. This is because early on in the development process, cells start to become specialized through a process by which genes in DNA are "switched off." Thus, although every cell contains the same 30,000 genes, in adult cells different combinations of those genes are turned off, so that in each adult cell only a small fraction of the genes actually produce protein enzymes to use in chemical reactions.

Once a cell has become specialized in this way, the DNA copying process can only produce more cells of the same type. Yet early in the process of development there must be cells in which all of the genes are still capable of functioning. Such cells are said to be *pluripotent,* because they have the potential of developing into any kind of cell in the body. Cells that have this potential are called **stem cells.**

• **Figure 24-5** Early stages of embryonic development.

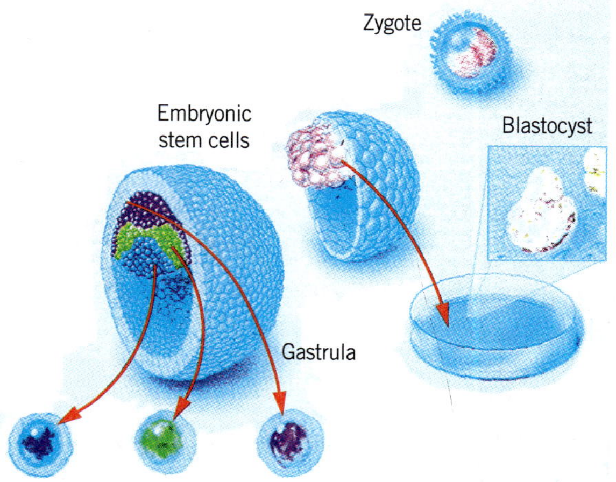

When a single fertilized egg begins to divide, all of the genes in the resulting cells remain potentially active. A few days after fertilization, as shown in Figure 24-5, the embryo (at this point called a *blastocyst*) is a simple structure, consisting of a spherical outer cell wall and an inner cell mass. The outer cells will develop into the placenta when the embryo implants itself in the walls of the uterus during pregnancy, while the cells in the inner cell mass will develop into the fetus and, eventually, into an adult human being. The cells in this inner cell mass, then, will produce all of the cells in the human body and therefore qualify as stem cells. Because they are found in the embryo, they are called *embryonic stem cells.*

Two weeks later, the embryo has reached a stage (known as a *gastrula*) in which the cells are no longer pluripotent. By this time the inner cell mass has evolved into three distinctive layers, as shown. Each of these layers will eventually produce different types of tissues in the adult. For example, cells from one layer will form organs such as the liver and lungs, those from another layer bone and blood vessels, and those from the third layer skin and neurons. This division of cells into specialized types is called *differentiation.*

The pattern of differentiation continues throughout the growth process. Even in adulthood, however, many cells in the body can produce a limited number of different kinds of tissue. Many different kinds of skin cells, for example, are derived from a single progenitor. Cells that have this limited ability are called *somatic stem cells,* or sometimes, *adult stem cells.* They form a kind of biological resupply system for the body, supplying new cells as old ones wear out.

Scientists have known about stem cells for a long time, but it wasn't until 1998 that a group under the direction of James Thomson at the University of Wisconsin managed to produce a line of cells that, while reproducing, never differentiated. Up to this time, when scientists tried to get stem cells to reproduce in the laboratory, some process (which we do not yet understand and is still under intense study) would cause them to turn into specialized tissue such as muscle. By finding just the right chemical environment for his stem cells, Thomson was able to keep the genes in his cells from being switched off. As the stem cells divided, they retained their pluripoitency from one generation to the next. A collection of cells like this is called a *stem cell line.*

The medical potential of stem cells is enormous. Scientists immediately realized that if they could learn to coax stem cells into turning into different kinds of tissue, they could deal with diseases that are now untreatable. You could imagine, for example, generating new muscle to repair damaged hearts, new neurons to relieve the symptoms of Parkinson's disease, and new pancreatic cells to treat diabetes. Thus, worldwide attention was paid to this new development.

But the new development also raised serious moral and ethical issues in the minds of many. These issues center around two points. First, in order to obtain embryonic stem cells (the ones that seem to hold the greatest promise), it is necessary to destroy a blastocyst. In the United States, this means that the discussion of stem cells immediately became entangled in the abortion debate, one of the most difficult and insoluble public issues. A second concern has to do with the fear of many people that by manipulating stem cells we are, in essence, "playing God"—something that many people argue we ought to avoid. We will return to this difficult debate in the Thinking More About section at the end of this chapter.

Science in the Making •

Cloning Dolly the Sheep

In 1997, headlines around the world announced the birth of Dolly the sheep. She was the first cloned mammal in history and was treated accordingly in the popular media. The birth of Dolly was the product of research by Ian Wilmut at the Roslyn Institute in Scotland. The end result was a sheep whose DNA was identical to that of another adult sheep—in effect, Dolly was a one of a pair of "twins" whose "sibling" had not been born from the same mother.

Here is how **cloning** is done: the nucleus, with its cargo of DNA, is removed from the egg of an adult female. This procedure can be carried out with a microscopic pipette. In Wilmut's work, the egg came from a Scottish Blackface ewe. A cell from another adult sheep (a Finn Dorest ewe in this case) was then fused with this egg by applying a small electrical shock. The egg, which now had a full complement of DNA, began to divide, and each daughter cell had a full complement of Finn Dorset DNA, as it would have in a normal development process. At the appropriate time, the developing embryo

Roslin Institute/Phototake

Dr. Ian Wilmut, the scientist who carried out the first successful cloning of a mammal and whose work led to Dolly.

Time Life Pictures/Getty Images News and Sport Services

Dolly, the first cloned mammal, was the subject of great media attention.

was implanted into the uterus of yet another adult sheep and allowed to come to maturity.

The key point in this process is that, although we do not know how to "turn on" the genes that were "switched off" in the development process that led to the adult Finn Dorset DNA, the egg seems to be able to do it. The DNA in the daughter cells of that first processed egg is exactly the same as the DNA that would have resulted from a normal fertilization, which means that all the genes are "switched on." How this process is done remains a subject of intense research.

Dolly lived in a media spotlight until her death in 2002. She gave birth to a lamb in 1998 (through the normal procedure). Since her birth, many other mammals have been cloned—mice, rats, pigs, cows, horses, and even monkeys. In 2004 a strange sect called the Raelians claimed that they had cloned a human being, but no evidence for this claim has been brought forth.

The birth of Dolly conjured up visions of armies of identical cloned human beings being produced. People imagined clones of Michael Jordan making up a "dream team" in basketball, or, on the darker side, clones being raised to produce organs for transplant.

A moment's thought should convince you that neither of these nightmare scenarios is likely to happen. It may be that Michael's Jordan's physical attributes contributed to his skills, but it took years of dedicated work to mold those skills into a champion athlete. As one commentator put it, a Michael Jordan clone would be as likely to be a tall violinist as a basketball player.

As for the use of clones as sacrificial organ donors, it is necessary to remember that a cloned human, should one ever exist, would just be an adult whose DNA is identical to that of another adult. We have millennia of experience with people like that—we call them twins. And just as no one would imagine forcing one twin to donate an organ to another, we wouldn't allow that to happen to clones either.

Dolly is a result of what is called *reproductive cloning*—that is, the act of cloning was carried out with the intention of producing another adult. As we shall see in a moment, there is another way in which cloning can be used. Called *therapeutic cloning*, this process stops short of implanting an embryo and is carried out for medical purposes and to improve human health and well-being.

The real issues arise, however, when the ability to produce stem cell lines is combined with the process of cloning discussed in the "Science in the Making" section above. If the DNA inserted into an egg is that of a given individual, then all of the cells in the blastocyst will have that individual's DNA, and any stem cell lines that are derived from that blastocyst will have that DNA as well. This means that any tissue derived from those stem cells and implanted in the donor will be genetically identical to that donor's cells, and will not be rejected by his or her immune system. This is an important consideration, because one of the great medical hurdles in transplant operations is that when a new organ such as a kidney or heart is implanted into a patient, that patient's immune system sees it as a foreign object and tries to destroy it. This rejection means that transplant patients must be given drugs that suppress their immune systems, a process that has to continue for the rest of the patient's life.

A photograph showing a foreign gene being introduced into an animal cell.

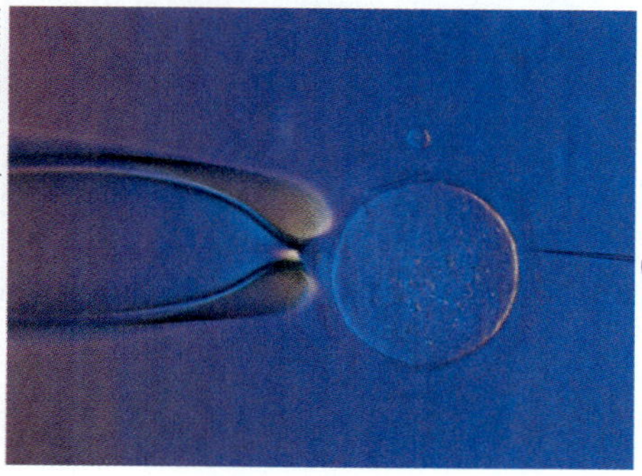

M. Baret/Photo Researchers

The expectation is that tissues grown from stem cells derived from that patient's own DNA will not be rejected by his or her immune system. This possibility means that sometime in the future it might be possible to grow tissues, and perhaps even entire organs, that can be transplanted surgically to replace parts that have become diseased or just worn out. The new field of research has been given the name *regenerative medicine*.

Many researchers are now trying to use cloning techniques to create human embryos that survive long enough in the laboratory to produce stem cell lines. Development of stem cell lines from embryonic stem cells in this way is called therapeutic cloning, since the goal of the work is not to produce a new human being but to use the cells to treat humans that are already alive. Obviously, the same moral and ethical objections raised against stem cell research apply to this new technique.

Different countries have responded in different ways to this challenge, so that at present the world is a kind of patchwork of different regulations. In the United States, for example, President George W. Bush ordered that research on stem cells lines developed before 2002 could be supported by the federal government, but not research on cell lines developed after that (there is at present no restriction on private funding for research on other lines). In 2004, the voters in the state of California passed a three billion dollar referendum that established an Institute for Regenerative Medicine to carry out this kind of research, while in 2006 the legislature of the state of Maryland passed a proposal to do the same in that state.

On the international scene, the response has been just as varied. Some countries, such as Ireland, Norway, and Denmark, ban both reproductive and therapeutic cloning as well as research on human embryonic stem cells. Others, such as Germany, Austria, France, and the Netherlands, ban both reproductive and therapeutic cloning but not stem cell research. Still others, such as Great Britain, Belgium, Sweden, Spain, South Korea, Japan, and Singapore, allow and even encourage work on therapeutic (but not reproductive) cloning.

Although there is no relation, in principle, between cloning and stem cells, the fact remains that at present the only way to obtain stem cells with a given individual's DNA is through the creation of an embryo. This limitation is why the political debate on this issue is so intense. There is one possible way around this difficulty. Some scientists have argued that it might be possible that some of the somatic stem cells in the body, or even fully differentiated normal cells, could be reprogrammed in such a way that they returned to their earlier state of pluripotency. In effect, this process, called ***dedifferentiation,*** would turn back the clock in the cell's DNA. If this could be done, we could have the benefits of embryonic stem cells without encountering the moral difficulties of sacrificing embryos.

We know that some animals have cells that are able to dedifferentiate. An amphibian like the newt, for example, can regrow lost limbs by reprogramming its normal cells into stem cells at the site of the injury. Mammalian cells are not normally able to do this, but there is some indication that they might be manipulated into doing so. In experiments with mice in 2004, for example, a group at Scripps Research Institute was able to turn mouse muscle cells into bone and fat cells by producing a partial dedifferentiation. How far this process can be pushed in the future is not clear at this time. •

Stop and Think! If scientists are successful in using therapeutic cloning techniques to grow new organs for implanting, how will people in the future have to answer the question "How old are you?"

The New Face of Medicine

Computer-Assisted Drug Design

Every medicine is made of one or more molecules. When you take an aspirin or Tylenol, you are ingesting molecules that play a particular role in your body. Some headache remedies, for example, alter your brain's chemistry by changing the molecules that go back and forth between neurons. Medicines work like any other molecules in living systems. Because of their shape and chemical characteristics, they are able to lock onto other specific molecules, thus altering your cellular chemistry.

Until very recently, the search for new medicines followed a standard course. Scientists in research laboratories (most commonly in pharmaceutical companies) would search in nature to find molecules that were useful against a specific condition. The search was hit or miss, and often scientists would develop drugs that they knew worked, even if they had no idea why they worked.

The new molecular understanding of living systems is changing all that. If we know the chemistry behind a certain condition, then we know the molecules that are involved and their shapes. It becomes possible to use that knowledge to design drugs "from scratch," rather than searching for them at random.

A simple analogy can be used to understand this new approach to pharmaceuticals. Think about a bottle. A bottle is designed to hold fluids, and it does so by having a small open neck and a large holding area. You can stop the bottle from taking in fluids by placing a cork in the narrow opening. In this analogy, the cork plays the role of the medicine or drug, and the bottle the role of a molecule operating inside your cell. By finding a cork that fits a particular bottle, you can alter the functioning of that bottle. In the same way, by finding a "molecular cork" that fits a particular "molecular bottle" in the human body, you can alter the body's chemistry.

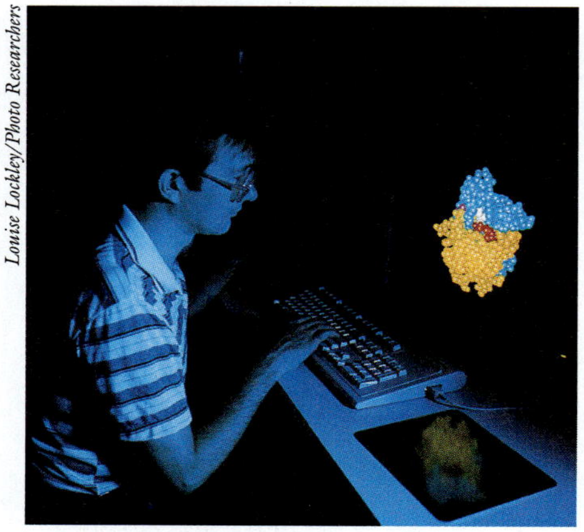

Louise Lockley/Photo Researchers

A scientist examines a computer image of a molecule to evaluate its usefulness as a medicine. Quick procedures are common in computer-aided drug design.

In terms of this analogy, the traditional search for drugs can be thought of as rummaging through a large pile of corks in hope of finding one that will fit a particular bottle. The rain forest, for example, with its enormous biological diversity, can be thought of as a very large pile of corks through which one can rummage to find the one cork that fits a particular bottle.

There is, however, another way of achieving the same objective. You can look at the bottle and measure its neck, then manufacture a cork that will fit it exactly. This new approach, which must rely heavily on the use of computers, is called *computer-assisted drug design (CADD)*. The idea of designing drugs to order is a fairly old one. In fact, the first such drug was put on the market in 1973. However, with the flood of new molecular knowledge, this field of technology is expanding rapidly.

The basic design strategy is very simple and can be illustrated by talking about a molecule called a *protease inhibitor*, which was designed by several pharmaceutical companies to combat the human immunodeficiency virus, HIV, which is the cause of AIDS. AIDS was the first major disease to come on the scene after scientists learned how to understand the basic molecular processes of life. Protease inhibitors are the result of the long scientific study of the HIV virus.

At one stage in the life cycle of HIV it inserts DNA produced from the virus's RNA into the DNA of the cell, at which point the cell starts manufacturing material for new viruses. Several proteins serve as enzymes for this insertion process, and some of these proteins have to be cut into pieces before they can play their role in making more viruses. A molecule known as a protease does this cutting. It is shaped something like a large convoluted doughnut. The proteins to be cut are pulled into the "hole" of the doughnut, where the actual cutting takes place when the "doughnut" constricts. If the proteins can't be pulled into the doughnut they can't be cut, and if they can't be cut, the virus can't reproduce.

Starting with this understanding, scientists designed a molecule that would plug the hole, blocking access for the viral proteins. Protease inhibitors were one of the first sets of drugs designed with new computer visualization techniques. In 1996, these drugs got their first clinical trials, and today they have turned AIDS from a disease that inevitably led to death to one that can be managed, if not cured.

Protease inhibitors represent a technological milestone. More drugs like them will be designed in the future. In fact, it is not too much to expect that someday the main business of pharmaceutical companies will not be modifying molecules found in nature, but designing molecules to do specific jobs in the body, based on the knowledge of how those molecules work in the body.

Stop and Think! Do you think computer-assisted drug design, when it becomes commonplace, will weaken arguments for preserving the rain forest based on potential new supplies of medicines?

Cancer—A Different Kind of Genetic Disease

Cancer, a disease that strikes more than a million Americans every year, occurs when a group of cells in the body reproduce without restraint. It is not a single disease, but rather a large collection of diseases that affect different organs in the human body in different ways.

The human body's trillions of cells have to maintain an exquisite balance. Complex chemical communication between cells ensures that the mechanism of cell division (see Chapter 21) operates only when new cells are needed and is turned off when that is not the case. Cancer occurs when these regulatory processes fail—when genetic defects cause a cell to divide again and again in a runaway fashion to form a tumor.

Normal cells recognize several different kinds of damage. Have there been mistakes in DNA duplication during cell division? If so, then fix the mistake or kill the cell. Has the DNA been duplicated fully and only once? If not, fix the mistake or kill the cell. Are the chromosomes correctly segregated? Is the cell correctly oriented to partition the chromosomes? At each transition the cell stops to check whether everything is okay. Every step of mitosis—the cycle of DNA duplication and partitioning—has to be accomplished with the extraordinary fidelity that life demands. If not, kill the cell.

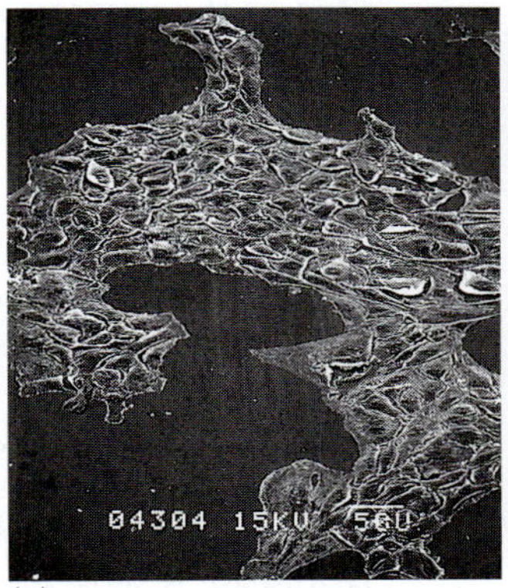

(a)

(b)

Michael Atkinson

Scanning electron micrographs showing the features of normal *(a)* and cancerous *(b)* rat kidney cells growing in culture. The normal cells adhere to the surface of the culture dish, forming monolayers of flat cells. The cancerous cells overgrow each other, forming clumps. Magnification: *(a)* 200X; *(b)* 280X.

Cancer occurs when this fundamental guardianship fails. In cancer, the cell cycle continues unchecked, often despite profound damage to the DNA and to the chromosomes. And by ignoring chromosomal damage, additional harmful changes accumulate in the cell. The result is a terribly damaged cell that just keeps duplicating itself over and over again, making more copies of the defective cell.

Normally, no single DNA mutation is sufficient to turn a normal cell into a cancer cell. Rather, a handful of genetic abnormalities—perhaps five or six separate damaged genes in one single cell—are required. Many of these DNA changes are acquired or at least accelerated by exposure to mutagenic chemicals or radiation that damage DNA. In other cases, if some condition exists that causes cells to multiply more often than normal—a condition produced in the lungs by constant exposure to the chemicals in cigarette smoke, for example—the chances of a copying accident evading the cell's protection mechanisms increases. In these cases, it is usually possible to identify the cause of the cancer, as smoking has been identified as the major cause of lung cancer.

The situation is considerably worse for some individuals who are born with genetic defects. In the United States, about a tenth of cancer patients diagnosed each year have inherited an abnormality in one of their genes. Because these individuals already carry what is called the "first genetic hit" on the road to cancer in *all* of their cells, the probability that any single cell will accumulate the additional hits needed to make a tumor is much higher than normal. In fact, people with an inherited cancer gene can carry lifetime risks of developing cancer that may be greater than 80%. The search for these cancer-related genes is one of the hottest areas of cancer research.

The growing recognition of a genetic basis for many cancers points to new approaches for its cure. Today the treatment of cancer, while often successful, usually involves heroic measures such as surgery, radiation therapy, and the use of deadly chemicals to remove or kill these rogue cells. But some day that therapy will be tailored to the specific genetic fingerprint of each person's cancer. Missing proteins will be synthesized and supplied; damaged genes will be repaired or bypassed. As we discover and identify a growing list of inherited and acquired cancer susceptibility genes, we'll be able to determine the best preventative treatments for individuals at risk.

One hope for the future involves a technique known as gene therapy, discussed later in this chapter. Try to imagine what it would be like to walk into a doctor's office, be diagnosed with cancer, and be given a virus-laden injection or a nose spray as your only treatment. Today this seems like a fairy tale, but if the work of molecular biologists in developing gene therapy is successful, having cancer in the future may be no worse than having an ear infection at the end of the twentieth century.

Science by the Numbers •

Double-Blind Clinical Trials

One of the great problems medical researchers face in testing new medical procedures such as gene therapy is proving that the therapies actually work. It's often difficult for scientists to be certain that the treatment they prescribe is the cause of any improvement seen in the patient. To see why, imagine that you had a new medicine that you claimed cured the common cold. Suppose that you tried the medicine on some people with colds and found that after a few days, all the people who tried the medicine got rid of their colds. Would this prove that your medicine was effective? Of course not. We know that the human immune system also battles the common cold, so if you had just left those people alone and gave them no treatment at all, they'd get better in a few days on their own. The medicine, as likely as not, was irrelevant.

To deal with these kinds of situations, researchers commonly use what is called the *double-blind clinical trial.* It works like this: A group of patients suffering from a particular disease is separated into two sections. Efforts are made to match the two sections in terms of age, gender, previous health history, and so on. One group is given the new treatment while the other group is given a placebo (that is, a sugar pill). For example, if the treatment being tested is a new drug, half the people will be given the new drug while the other half will be given either a placebo or the best conventional treatment. The patients are not told which treatment they are getting, nor do the physicians treating the patients know if a particular patient is getting the new drug. Thus neither the patients themselves nor the physicians who will be judging the efficacy of the treatment know which patients are receiving the drug and which are not. This is why it is called a double-blind trial.

In order for a drug to be judged effective, it has to pass a clinical trial of this type. Unfortunately, new "wonder cures" are often tested without such experimental rigor. For example, a man recently stood up in a conference and claimed that he had found a cure for a particular kind of cancer based on a new-age therapy involving meditation and natural foods. He was asked what evidence he had; his reply was that he had a patient who had a tumor, and when he started the patient on this treatment, the tumor began to shrink in size. He was asked, "How do you know that it was your treatment that caused the tumor to shrink?" His reply: "What else could it have been?"

In fact, tumors left to themselves often grow and shrink in irregular and unpredictable ways. There is no way of knowing, based on this one example, whether the patient's tumor would have regressed on its own, as tumors often do. This particular treatment, like any other, can be validated only by a double-blind trial, with two groups of people in the same medical condition, some of whom are not receiving the treatment. Such rigor is rarely found in the sorts of activities that go by the name of alternative medicine. •

Gene Therapy

Until quite recently, the only thing that physicians could do when faced with a genetic disease was to treat the symptoms. For example, in a disease such as diabetes, which is brought about by a failure of the body to produce the protein called insulin, treatment can run from modifying a patient's diet to injecting genetically engineered insulin on a daily basis. More recently, however, scientists have been exploring the possibility of using gene therapy, a new and potentially revolutionary kind of treatment.

Gene therapy is defined as a procedure for replacing a defective gene with a healthy one. Although still very much in the experimental stages, it holds enormous promise. Gene therapy can be done *in vitro* (that is, the gene can be injected into cells outside of the body, and the cells can then be introduced into the body) or *in vivo* (that is, the genes can be injected into cells in the body). As of this writing, only *in vitro* therapy has been accomplished in clinics, but many groups around the world are trying to develop *in vivo* techniques.

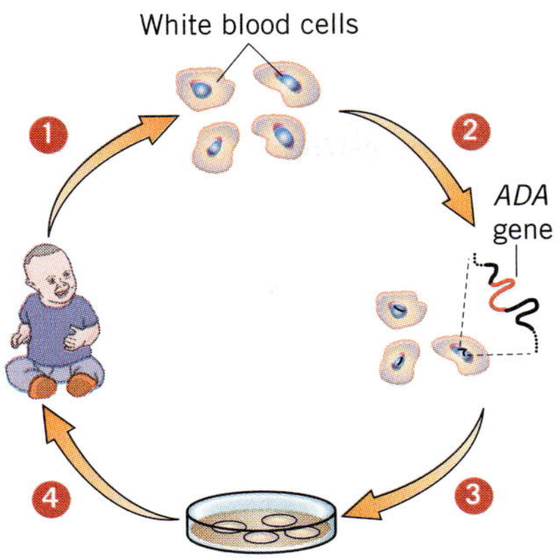

• **Figure 24-6** Gene therapy was first used successfully in the treatment of SCID. (1) White blood cells were removed from the patient. (2) Normal copies of the defective gene were inserted into the blood cells. (3) The cells were placed in a culture (a medium of nutrients) to verify that the DNA would replicate and proteins would form in the cell. (4) The genetically modified cells were returned to the patient's bloodstream. Because white blood cells have a relatively short life span, patients must undergo treatment regularly to maintain a constant supply of normal genes.

The first successful gene therapy took place in the early 1990s at the National Institutes of Health (Figure 24-6). Ashanti de Silva was born with a disease known as severe combined immunodeficiency (SCID). Because of faulty coding in one gene in her DNA, she was unable to produce a protein called adenosine deaminase that is vital for the functioning of the immune system. Because her immune system didn't work, she had to be quarantined and was able to leave home only to visit her doctor. She was always sick and had a life that bore almost no resemblance to that of a normal child.

Courtesy National Institute of Health

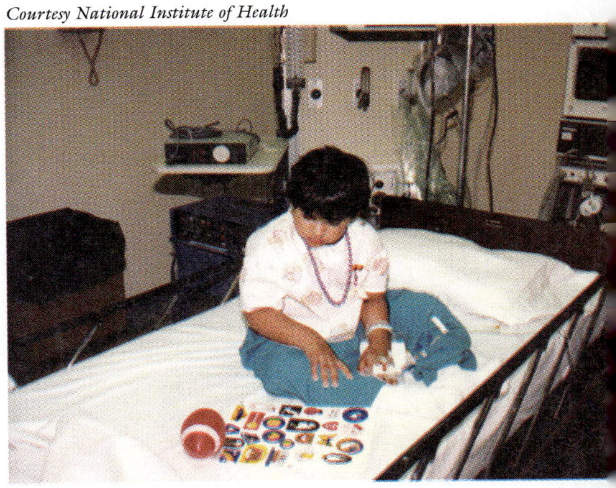

Ashanti de Silva was the first patient to be treated with gene therapy.

Children who are born with this defect are extraordinarily sensitive to any kind of contact with disease. Before the late twentieth century, most SCID babies died within their first year. In the late twentieth century, a few of these children lived into their teens by being kept in complete isolation from the external environment—they were called "bubble babies."

In September 1990, Ashanti de Silva became the first person to undergo a new kind of medical treatment. Doctors removed white blood cells from her veins and, using the new technology of genetic engineering, inserted normal copies of the defective gene. Over a period of months, the corrected cells were returned to her bloodstream, where they could produce the missing protein. The results seemed miraculous. From a sick, reclusive child, she was transformed into a normal, active preteen.

Unfortunately, at this time the preliminary results of most gene therapy trials have not been very encouraging. Doctors have identified many gene defects that cause disease, and have even managed to insert corrected genes in some cells. Even so, in almost every case the new genes don't work—the modified cells cannot make the desired protein. The problem appears to be that the new genes are inserted into a chromosome more or less at random locations; the cell is, in effect, unable to find the gene and transcribe it to messenger RNA.

The ultimate procedure in gene therapy would be to be able to introduce an agent into the body that would seek out the cells that have faulty genes, be taken into those cells, and then to insert healthy genes into the DNA of those cells at the correct location. While this may sound like science fiction, nature has many organisms that can insert genes in target cells: they are called viruses. The hepatitis virus, for example, can be taken into the human body, move to the liver, and be taken into the liver cells. Furthermore, as we saw in Chapter 23, many viruses are capable of inserting genes into existing DNA in a cell. Thus research efforts in gene therapy are beginning to conc trate on the construction of what are called therapeutic viruses.

The idea of a therapeutic virus is that it will carry as its cargo a healthy human rather than a normal viral gene. It will have an outer coating that is shaped so that be recognized by receptors on only certain cells in the body (just as the hepati is recognized only by cells in the liver). A therapeutic virus, when recognized, v taken into the cell and its cargo of healthy genes inserted into an appropriat the cell's DNA.

Constructing a therapeutic virus is a tall order. As of the publication of this edition, research has progressed to the point where viruses can be constructed that can be recognized by specific cells in the human body. These viruses, if injected into the bloodstream, will be recognized only by certain cells. At the moment the main roadblock to gene therapy is the difficulty in having the viruses, once recognized, taken into the cell. It appears that more is involved than a single receptor, and working this mechanism out is a major task for molecular biologists.

DNA Repair in the Cell

The transcription process we described in Chapter 23 shows how a specific sequence of bases along a DNA molecule is translated into the production of a specific protein in the cell. We also pointed out that if for some reason the DNA is damaged so that there is something wrong with the sequence of bases, the protein for which that gene codes will not be produced.

A common misconception about cellular DNA, one that is often encountered in popular writings on environmental problems, holds that the DNA in human cells is extremely fragile and is at the mercy of any kind of influence emanating from the environment. In fact, research that has been going on since the 1980s gives us a very different picture of DNA. It turns out that not all damage to DNA comes from outside the cell. In fact, most "hits" come from inside the cell itself. Cellular metabolism, for example, depends on respiration—a process with byproducts, some of which may be quite harmful. The best-known harmful byproducts of cellular respiration are a class of molecules called oxidants, such as the superoxide ion (O^{-2}). These ions are created copiously inside the cell and, if they make their way to the cell's nucleus, can cause damage to DNA. In addition, we ingest many kinds of molecules in our food, some processed, some natural, and these, too, can cause damage to the cells if they find their way to the cell's nucleus.

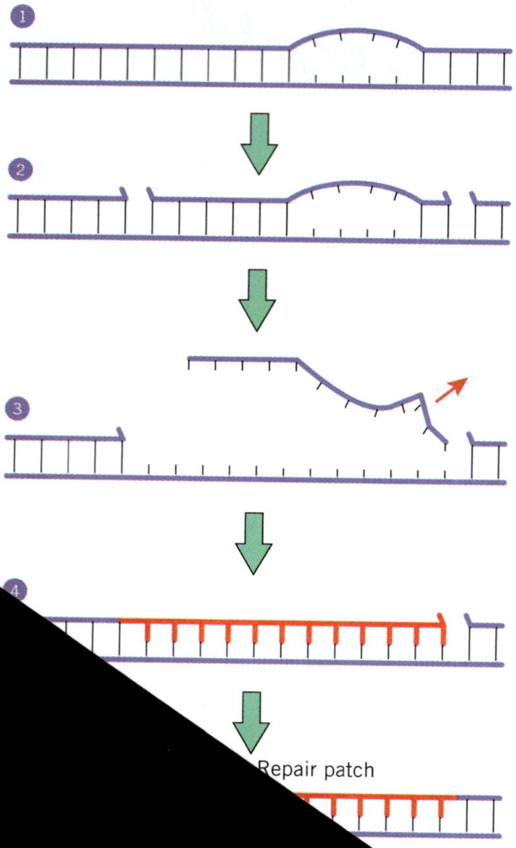

But the story doesn't end with the damage. Cells possess two different types of mechanisms for dealing with mistakes in DNA. Both of these mechanisms depend on sets of enzymes that wrap themselves around the DNA molecules and move up and down the spiral, looking for abnormalities. When abnormalities are found, these molecules call up one of two different kinds of repair mechanisms, depending on the kind of mistake that is found. Thus our picture of DNA in the cell's nucleus has to be a dynamic one, involving constant damage followed by constant repair.

One common kind of mistake in DNA, called a point defect, involves something like a simple misprint—the substitution of one base for another in the double helix. For example, the normal code for a particular spot on the DNA might require the base A, but for some reason we find the base T in that spot. In this case, the double helix will bulge slightly and the patrolling enzymes will detect the bulge. Other enzymes will come to that spot and snip out the offending bit of DNA, allowing the normal replication process to replace the blank spot with the correct base (Figure 24-7).

Other kinds of mistakes also occur. For example, two bases forming one side of the DNA double helix occasionally stick to one base on the other side. (This error may result when ultraviolet sunlight damages cells in the skin.) Alternatively, during the copying process, one strand of DNA can slide down, leaving a loop sticking out to the side. This kind of error is called a "mis-

• **Figure 24-7** DNA repair in the cell. Patrolling enzymes will identify defects in the DNA molecule, as indicated by a bulge in the double helix. Other enzymes will then remove the damaged section of DNA and allow the normal replication process to reconstruct the missing stretch.

match." When these sorts of mistakes are encountered, a second kind of repair mechanism, called mismatch repair, is initiated, and the entire side of the DNA molecule that contains the offending section is removed. As before, the normal processes of DNA replication then reconstruct the missing stretch of DNA.

> **Stop and Think!** Given what you know about the effect of ultraviolet light on DNA, why should you wear sunscreen when you are outdoors?

Richard R. Hansen/Photo Researchers

Pesticides are routinely sprayed on crops to cut down on insect pests, as in this field of snow peas in California.

What is perhaps most amazing about the way DNA operates in our cells is the sheer amount of damage that the molecules receive. As we said in the previous chapter, scientists measuring the chemical debris of the repair process estimate that every cell in your body sustains some 10,000 "hits" per day to its DNA and succeeds in repairing almost all of them.

In fact, the process of DNA repair seems to be very similar to the process of repairing a house that has been damaged by a hurricane. In the case of the house, you would be sure that the roof and walls were repaired and the electricity restored before you started worrying about replacing the carpets. In the same way, in the DNA there seems to be a hierarchy in the repair mechanisms. Highest in the hierarchy is the repair of those genes that are actually expressed in the cell in which damage has occurred. The point is that this repair has to be finished before the cell divides. If it is not, then the process of replication discussed in Chapter 23 will ensure that every descendant of the particular cell will contain the defect. Thus, the life of every cell can be thought of as a race between the repair mechanisms that we just described and the normal process of mitosis.

Michael P. Gadmonski/Photo Researchers

Plants, like this common milkweed, have developed their own pesticides over the millennia.

One important message to learn from the DNA repair story is that molecules cause damage to DNA. If the shape of the molecule is right, it will produce a defect, regardless of where that molecule came from. *It makes no difference whether the molecule is a product of our society or of nature.*

To underscore this point think about pesticides, which are among the most commonly cited causes of DNA damage. Some pesticides are produced commercially, of course, but many occur naturally in plants as a defense mechanism. In fact, it is estimated that only about one-tenth of 1 percent of the pesticides that human beings take in each day are commercially produced, with the rest being a normal part of the plants we eat. Once inside the body, however, it makes no difference where the pesticide molecule came from. About half of both the synthetic and natural pesticides are capable of causing cancer in laboratory animals.

Unraveling the Past: Mitochondrial DNA

One of the most engaging characteristics of science is that advances in one field often have profound and completely unpredictable effects in areas that seem, at first glance, to have no connection with the advance. The new genetic technologies provide a good example of this process, because it turns out that they can shed light on the complex issues of human evolution that we will discuss in the next chapter.

In Chapter 21 we saw that there are many organelles inside the cells of eukaryotes like human beings. One of these, the mitochondria, is believed to represent the result of a symbiotic event in the distant past. These organelles, where carbohydrates are "burned" to provide the cell's energy, retain many characteristics as reminders of their independent past. One of these characteristics is the fact that mitochondria have their own small complement of DNA, completely independent of the DNA found in the nuclei of the cell.

The DNA of mitochondria, usually called mtDNA, consists of about 16,500 base pairs, a relatively small amount. As in bacteria, this DNA is arranged in a single loop (Figure 24-8). It contains 37 genes and has a small noncoding section at one point in

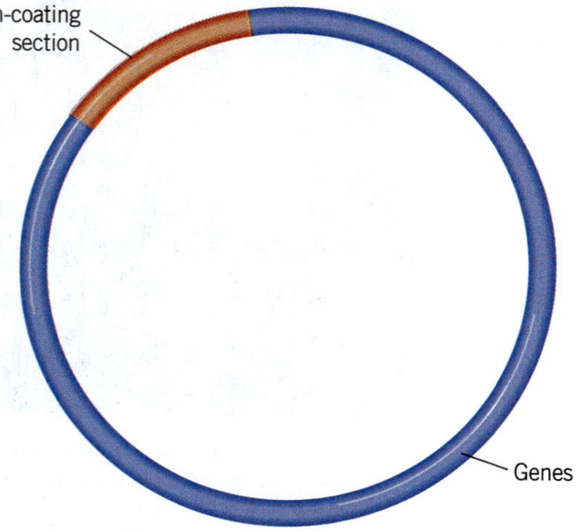

• **Figure 24-8** The DNA in mitochondria is in the form of a loop. A non-coding section of about 1000 base pairs is used in the studies described in the text.

the loop. This section, about 1000 base pairs long, is not used to generate proteins, but acts as a kind of marker to tell you when you have gone all the way around the loop. Think of it as being analogous to the "12" at the top of a clock face. It is the sequence of bases on this stretch of DNA that scientists use to uncover the ancestry of modern humans.

The process of fertilization involves the sperm, which contain only enough mitochondria to allow movement, and the egg, which contains a full complement of the organelles. The sperm's mitochondria are destroyed soon after it enters the egg, so all of the mitochondria in the zygote come from the egg. This means that mtDNA is transmitted from mother to child. Whether you are male or female, in other words, you got all of the mitochondria in your cells from your mother.

In the language of genealogists, mtDNA descends in the maternal line. (As such, it is the mirror image of family names in European cultures, which descend in the male line, since the father's family name has traditionally been taken by all of his children.) You can get an estimate of how long it has been since two individuals shared a common female ancestor by comparing the sequence of their mtDNA—the more differences, the farther back in time that ancestor lived.

Stop and Think! How many differences in mtDNA would you expect to find between two brothers? between a brother and his sister? between two half brothers who had the same mother? the same father?

It is important to realize that, like family names, mtDNA lines can disappear. In the language of genealogists, a family can "daughter out"—have only daughters in one generation so that the family name doesn't get passed down. In the same way, women can "son out"—have only sons, so that their mtDNA does not get passed on. It is important to realize that in both of these cases, the main DNA in the nucleus descends in an unbroken line.

Science by the Numbers •

Daughtering Out

Suppose you had a village with eight people in it—four men and four women, and that there were four family names. Assuming that each couple has two children and the birth of boys and girls is random, what is the shortest amount of time that would have to pass before everyone in the village had the same last name?

In the first generation, you would expect one couple (call it couple A) to have two boys, one couple to have two girls (call it couple D), and the other two couples to have one each (call them couple B and C). After one generation, there would be only three family names—A (with two couples), B, and C (with one each). Couple D will have daughtered out.

If couple C daughters out in the next generation and one of the couples A has two sons, then by the third generation there will be only two names—A (three couples) and B. Thus, after three generations we could easily have a village with only one family name.

In fact, more complex statistical arguments suggest that this is a likely outcome—that after several generations only one family name will survive. In the same way, lines of mtDNA will die out over time.

Using the technique of mtDNA analysis, scientists have argued that all living Europeans are descended from a set of seven women who lived from 40,000 to 10,000 years ago. Some have even claimed to have traced all living humans to a single woman who lived in Africa 200,000 years ago, although there is a good deal of controversy about this claim. The woman, should she exist, has been given the name "Mitochondrial Eve." More recently, similar analysis of the Y chromosome (the chromosome that is carried by males) has been undertaken to trace the descent of males.

One point to ponder: if there actually was a "Chromosomal Adam," he probably didn't live at the same time as "Mitochondrial Eve," and therefore couldn't have known her, much less fathered her children. •

Science News | The Sum of the Parts

(SCIENCE NEWS, DEC. 10, 2005, P. 378)

"Genetic engineering isn't engineering in its true form." These words, spoken by a researcher at a Cambridge, Massachusetts, biotech company, symbolize a new way of approaching applications of our new knowledge about living systems. An engineer building a bridge will usually make plans and build models before construction starts. Genetic engineering, on the other hand, typically involves moving a gene from one organism's DNA to another, seeing what happens, and then repeating the operation (perhaps with modifications) until a useful result is obtained.

Now, however, a new field of research, called *synthetic biology*, is being developed with an eye toward bringing the practices of bioengineers more in line with those of their more traditional counterparts. In laboratories around the world, scientists are learning to put together stretches of ready-made DNA—in effect, creating a set of standardized components—that can be combined in different ways to produce predictable results. Like an engineer putting together a model of a bridge, synthetic biologists can tinker with their standardized bits of DNA to get the effect they want.

For example, a group at the University of California, San Francisco, is working on modifying bacteria so that they can be used to combat certain kinds of tumors. They start by building two receptors into their bacteria—one that responds to the presence of low oxygen levels, the other that responds to the presence of large numbers of bacteria. These sensors would only be triggered when the modified bacteria find themselves inside a tumor that has been infiltrated by bacteria. At this point, another gene in the modified bacterium would turn on and produce rigid rods of protein that protrude out of the bacterial surface. The protein rods stick to the walls of tumor cells, which then engulf the entire bacterium. The next step in the process, which is still under study, is to turn on another gene at this point and have the modified bacterium produce a chemical that will kill the cancer cell.

Many scientists feel that synthetic biology is at the same place now that information technology was in the 1960s. If so, will there be a biological equivalent of the Internet?

Thinking More About | Embryonic Stem Cells

A worldwide debate rages on the ethical implications of embryonic stem cell research. In the United States, this debate is intimately related to the debate over the ethics of abortion. In essence, the question comes down to this: is the creation of a blastocyst for the purpose of producing stem cells morally allowable?

©AP/Wide World Photos

Actor Christopher Reeve was paralyzed after a riding accident. Stem cell research holds the promise of regenerating damaged tissues, including severed nerve cells in people with spinal cord injuries.

The answer to this question depends on what you think the blastocyst is. If, as many people do, you believe that human life begins at conception and that even a single-celled zygote is a human being entitled to the full protection of the law, then the destruction of the blastocyst and the harvesting of stem cells is equivalent to murder. If, on the other hand, you believe that an organism consisting of a few hundred cells is no more equivalent to a human being than a blueprint is equivalent to a building, then there is a powerful moral compulsion to harvest the stem cells in order to relieve the real suffering of real people.

This is an example of a conflict that arises from advances in science but that cannot be answered by the scientific method. A biologist can tell you in great detail what the cellular structure and function of the blastocyst is, but she cannot tell you whether the blastocyst should have legal protection. In the end, that is a question that is decided on moral, religious, ethical, and legal grounds. It is the question of when the embryo becomes a "person" in the legal sense, entitled to full protection of the law. The answer to this question varies from one society to the next and has little to do with science. Many people have wrestled with this question without producing a consensus.

Here are some questions that might help you think about this difficult issue:

- If you believe that life begins at conception and that the blastocyst is a potential human life, how do you justify allowing real human beings to suffer to protect human beings that are only "potential"? If a treatment for Parkinson's disease based on stem cells were developed in a place like South Korea, would you ban Americans from seeking that treatment on moral grounds? Would you put them in jail if they did?
- If you believe that it is morally justifiable or even morally compulsory to harvest stem cells from blastocysts created specifically for that purpose, where do you draw the line? When is the destruction of the embryo not permissible? after it implants in the uterus? after the second trimester of pregnancy? one second before birth? How do you avoid the "slippery slope" and the ultimate devaluing of human life?

These are not simple questions, and, unless scientists find ways to reprogram somatic stem cells, they will remain with us for a long time.

Summary

Our enhanced understanding of genetic mechanisms has led to new advances in *genetic engineering,* which involves the insertion of foreign genes into an organism, or the alteration of existing genes, to create modified life-forms. A variety of genetically engineered plants for improved crops, animals for medical research, and single-celled organisms for drug production are now available. Our ability to manipulate genetic material has also been applied in *DNA fingerprinting,* which is used in many legal cases to establish the identity of individuals from their unique genetic makeup.

Stem cells are cells that can grow into any tissue in an adult organism. Embryonic stem cells can be harvested from the blastocyst, while somatic stem cells, though less versatile, can be obtained from adult tissue. *Cloning* is a procedure for producing a fertilized egg with the DNA of another adult. Therapeutic cloning is the use of this technology for medical purposes, whereas reproductive cloning has as it aim the production of a new organism.

One outcome of modern technology is computer-assisted drug design, in which medicines are designed according to their function at the molecular level. *Cancer,* a suite of diseases that afflict millions of Americans, has its basis in the mutation of DNA. DNA repair mechanisms are known to operate inside the cell. A promising future technology is *gene therapy,* which involves replacing a defective gene with a healthy one.

An unexpected result of modern technology is the ability to trace ancestral lineages through the sequence of mitochondrial DNA.

Key Terms

genetic engineering
DNA fingerprinting
stem cells
cloning
cancer
gene therapy

Review Questions

1. What is genetic engineering?

2. What do restriction enzymes do? How are they used in genetic engineering?

3. Give an example of a genetically engineered product. Why is it appropriate to use the term *engineered* to describe it?

4. What is DNA fingerprinting, and how does it work?

5. What is a genetic disease? Give an example.

6. What is gene therapy? Is it always successful?

7. How are viruses used in gene therapy?

8. What cell function appears to go awry in the case of cancer cells? How can this damage an individual?

9. What is a double-blind clinical trial? Why are such trials important in medical research?

10. How can computers be used to design drugs? What advantages would computer-designed drugs have over other drugs?

11. What is DNA repair, and where does it take place?

12. What is acquired immune deficiency syndrome? How is it transmitted?

13. Why do antibiotics, which kill bacteria, gradually lose their effectiveness? Why do we need new antibiotics?

Discussion Questions

Discussion Questions

1. What genetically engineered products do you currently use or consume? Are they safe? Why or why not?

2. In what ways is DNA fingerprinting like traditional fingerprinting? In what ways do the two differ?

3. What is a stem cell? Why is stem cell research a potentially valuable area for study?

4. In what ways does ultraviolet radiation affect a living cell? How is this damage repaired?

5. Why aren't stories of miracle cures by new drugs sufficient to bring these drugs quickly to market?

6. What difference would it make if the physicians knew which group in a clinical trial had treatment? What difference would it make if the patients knew?

7. What role does protease play in the reproduction of HIV? What does a protease inhibitor do? Do these new drugs cure AIDS?

8. What is a therapeutic virus? What problems are therapeutic viruses designed to overcome? In what ways will this type of virus benefit modern medicine?

9. Why is AIDS so difficult to cure? How does the AIDS virus attack the body?

10. Some people claim that crystals, prayer, or vitamin supplements can cure cancer. How would you test their claims? If you tested it on one person and that person recovered, could you be sure that your "treatment" was a success?

11. How does cellular respiration affect a cell's DNA? How do antioxidants protect our cells?

Problems

1. A pharmaceutical company claims that a new drug cuts in half the time an average patient suffers from a cold. Given a pool of 100 cold sufferers, describe a double-blind experiment that would test this claim.

2. A second company claims that two different drugs, working in combination, are even more effective than the single drug referred to in Problem 1. Given a pool of 200 cold sufferers, how would you test this claim in a double-blind clinical trial?

3. Scientists argue that all living Europeans are descended from seven women who lived over 10,000 years ago. Estimate how many generations of human beings are possible in 10,000 years time.

Investigations

1. Is DNA fingerprinting evidence used in your state or local courts? If so, investigate how such evidence has been used.

2. Find out if one of the more than 200 gene therapy trials is taking place near you (the National Institutes of Health in Bethesda, Maryland, maintains a list of such research projects). What disease is being treated, and what are the results so far?

3. Read Michael Crichton's novel *Jurassic Park,* which describes genetic engineering experiments. Is the scenario realistic? What precautions might the fictional scientists in the novel have taken?

4. Look over the newspapers for the last few months and find an announcement that scientists have discovered the gene behind a particular disease or condition. How does that discovery fit in with the material in this chapter?

5. From time to time a new AIDS drug will receive publicity because of reportedly miraculous results. Should such a drug be made available immediately to AIDS sufferers? Why or why not?

6. Read the prize-winning novel *Arrowsmith* by Sinclair Lewis. How does the novel's hero, Martin Arrowsmith, test his new plague vaccine? Was this a double-blind procedure? What goes wrong with the experiment?

7. Identify a pharmaceutical company that uses computers to design drugs. Investigate one of their recent projects. Obtain promotional literature and clinical trial reports to learn how the drug is used and how it was designed.

8. How long have genetically engineered foods been consumed? What problems have been encountered?

9. What are so-called frankenfoods? What does the acronym GMO stand for? What percentage of common vegetables are currently genetically modified?

10. Investigate the history of insulin production. Has genetic engineering decreased the suffering of animals and humans?

11. There are many countries that ban or regulate genetically modified organisms. What is the policy in the United States? Are our policies based on science? How would you test a genetically modified organism to ensure its safety?

12. What government organizations oversee the use of genetically engineered organisms?

13. Investigate Mitochondrial Eve or Chromosomal Adam. Are we all related?

25

Evolution

How did life emerge on the ancient Earth?

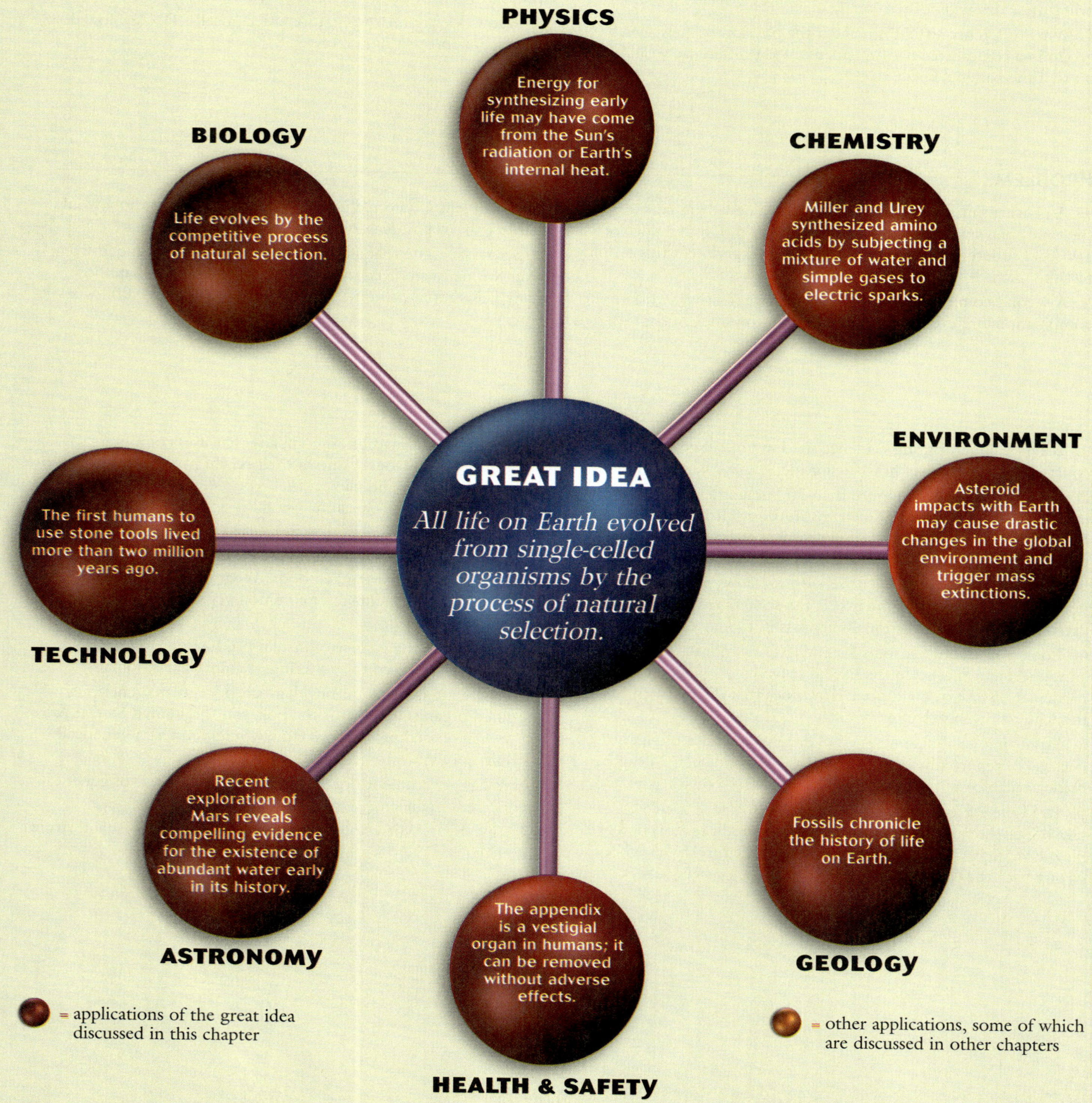

Science Through the Day | Day's End

A wonderful day is almost over. You close your eyes and relive some of the sensations; the sights, the sounds, the smells. But one aspect of the day stands out—how amazingly rich with life our planet is. The green fields and forests that lined the road, the birds and insects (and people) along the shore, the tidal pools crowded with strange, colorful creatures; everywhere you look life abounds.

How could such an incredible array of living things have developed on a once-lifeless planet? How could living things on our planet include such extraordinary variety, from seaweed to a whale? The answer to these questions requires us to think not only about what life is, but also how it got to be the way it is.

Bavaria/Taxi/Getty Images

The Fact of Evolution

Earth started out as a hot, lifeless ball of molten rock (see Chapter 16). The first rocks were formed when the planet cooled, but even then Earth looked nothing like it does today. Water filled the ocean basins, but no fish swam in it and no algae floated on it. All of the countless millions of different life-forms that would someday develop were absent in this early stage.

The transition from a lifeless planet to the modern living world came in two stages. The first stage involved the appearance of the first living cell from lifeless chemical compounds—rock, water, and gases. The laws of chemistry and physics that we have studied governed that process. The second stage was the multiplication, diversification, and transformation of that first living cell into the astonishing variety of life that we observe on Earth now. This ongoing process of change is called **evolution.**

Today, *virtually all scientists accept evolution as a historical fact.* Evolution—the concept that life has changed over vast spans of geological time—is an observational phenomenon that is as well established as the fact that Earth goes around the Sun or that a ball falls when you drop it.

As we shall see later in this chapter, this acceptance of evolution as a fact does not mean that there aren't debates about different *theories* of evolution. For example, scientists debate how fast evolution proceeds and by what mechanisms. But differences in opinion about these details should not be confused with the unambiguous observational *fact* that life has evolved on Earth for billions of years. A tremendous body of scientific literature is devoted to this subject, and we will discuss here only three of the most important pieces of evidence for the process of evolution: the fossil record, the evidence of biochemical similarity, and the occurrence of vestigial organs.

James L. Amos/Photo Researchers

From Proceedings of the National Academy of Sciences, December 27, 2005, vol. 102, no. 52, 18998–19002. Reproduced with permission.

Alfred Pasieka/SPL/Photo Researchers

A wide variety of fossils are found in rocks from every continent. *(a)* A fossil trilobite, an arthropod from 500 million years ago. *(b)* The fossil bird Archaeopteryx from 150 million years ago. *(c)* A fossil relative of the scorpion preserved in amber (hardened tree sap).

The Fossil Record

The most dramatic and compelling evidence for life's changes over geological time comes from **fossils,** the tangible evidence of past life. When a plant or animal dies, the remains are usually lost. A tree will rot, the carcass of an animal will be torn apart by scavengers and dispersed, a crab shell will be broken up by the action of the surf. Occasionally, however, an organism is removed quickly from the environment, typically by being buried in sediments and sealed off from the surface. The hard parts of such an organism may remain underground for a long period of time.

As time goes by, two things may happen. First of all, the material around the organism may go through the rock cycle, as described in Chapter 17, and be turned into rock. Second, minerals in the water flowing through the surrounding area may gradually replace the calcium and other atoms in the buried hard parts, thus creating a fossil. The word "fossil" typically brings to mind a large dinosaur skeleton in a museum, but the term also refers to other records of past life, such as a leaf imprint on mud that changes into rock, or an insect preserved in amber.

The term *fossil record* refers to all of the fossils that have been found, catalogued, and analyzed since human beings first began to study them in a systematic way in the early part of the nineteenth century. The fossil record reveals how different organisms came to be what they are. The fossil record of horses, for example, includes a series of precursor animals beginning with one about the size of a cat some 50 million years ago and changing through many intermediate forms up to modern times. Throughout this sequence of fossil mammals is a gradual transition from a small, quick animal to a large, grazing one.

The fossil record also contains some sequences of gradual changes in species. In order to do this, the fossil record has to be very complete, with many thousands of years of continuous sediments. Such continuity is rare, but in some instances the transitions from one species to another can be documented.

Even so, the major problem with the fossil record is that it is very incomplete. It is estimated that perhaps only one species (*not* one individual) out of every 10,000 early lifeforms is represented in the fossil record. Thus, in interpreting the past, we must always be aware that we are dealing with a very small and select sample of what was actually there. This sample is strongly biased toward organisms that were more likely to have been buried soon after death. Thus, we have a much better record of mollusks and clams, which had hard shells and lived in sediments on the continental shelf, than we do of insects that flew around primeval forests. Nevertheless, the fossil record provided the first substantial body of evidence that backed up the notion that life is constantly changing and evolving.

Stop and Think! From the preceding discussion, it is clear that animals with skeletons and shells will be fossilized more easily than those with soft bodies. What animals alive today are likely to be found as fossils a million years from now? Would future paleontologists get an accurate view of present-day life by examining those fossils?

Three key ideas quickly emerged from studies of fossils. First, the older the rocks, the more their animal and plant fossils differ from modern forms. Mammals in 5-million-year-old rocks are not terribly different from today's fauna, but few species that existed 50 million years ago would be recognizable today, and dinosaurs rather than mammals were dominant 150 million years ago. Similar patterns occur in shells, plants, fish, and all other forms. Often the earlier forms appear to combine characteristics of later organisms. Ancient insects preserved in amber, for example, show some forms that may be intermediate between ants and wasps. Similarly, early mammals have general mammalian characteristics, but not the specialized structures that evolved more recently in flying bats, swimming whales, or hopping rabbits.

Fossils also display general trends in overall complexity of form. All known fossils from before about 570 million years ago are either single-celled organisms or simple invertebrates such as jellyfish. Marine invertebrates with hard parts—mollusks, coral, and crustacea, for example—dominate the record for the next 200 million years or so. Simple land animals and plants appear next, followed by flowering plants and a much greater variety of large land animals. This long-term trend toward increasing complexity of organization is consistent with all theories of evolution.

Finally, the fossil record proves beyond a doubt that most species that have lived on Earth have died out and are now **extinct.** Scientists estimate that for every species on the planet today, perhaps a thousand species have become extinct at some time in the past. In fact, the average lifetime of a species in the fossil record seems to be a few million years. Species, like individuals, are born, live out their life, and die. This fact alone is ample evidence that some natural mechanism must exist to produce new species as the old disappear.

The Biochemical Evidence

We all carry within us evidence for the fact of evolution—a molecular record of our descent from the first primeval cell. The DNA of each living organism represents the sum of all the changes in the DNA that connect that organism back to the DNA in the first forms of life. If we can learn how to "read" the DNA in living organisms, then we should be able to deduce some things about the way those organisms developed.

According to the standard picture of evolution, for example, human beings and the great apes had a common ancestor about 7 or 8 million years ago. Much farther back in time, about 250 million years ago, human beings and reptiles shared a common ancestor. DNA changes slowly under the influence of mutation and natural selection. The fact that we've had less than 10 million years for human DNA and ape DNA to differentiate, compared to 250 million years during which human DNA differentiated from the reptiles, suggests that there ought to be more similarities between human and primate DNA than there are between DNA of humans and reptiles.

DNA strands from two different organisms cannot always be compared directly, but from Chapter 23 we know that the proteins in cells are related to DNA in much the same way as a negative is to a photograph. You can get the same kind of information by comparing sequences of amino acids along proteins as you can by comparing base pairs along the DNA molecule. In a protein called cytochrome C that every living cell uses in its energy metabolism, for example, the difference between humans and chimpanzees (our closest relative) is nonexistent. The cytochrome C molecules from the chimpanzee and human are exactly the same. As you move farther and farther away from human beings in the main classification scheme (see Chapter 20), the differences become greater. In a rattlesnake, for example, there is an 86% overlap in the molecules, whereas in common brewer's yeast only 58% of the molecules are the same. The fact that our DNA is very similar to those organisms with which we shared the most recent ancestors is one of the most important pieces of evidence for evolution. If, for example, each plant and animal was created separately and specially, there would be no reason at all to see this kind of progression.

Evidence from Anatomy: Vestigial Organs

Physical structures within our own bodies provide more compelling evidence for the fact of evolution. We have a number of internal features that serve no useful function whatsoever—**vestigial organs** that are reminders of our mammalian ancestors. Organs that are well adapted to their environment, surprisingly, *do not* provide unambiguous evidence for evolution. The perfection of the human eye, for example, was often claimed in the nineteenth century as proof of God's special creation of human beings. The evidence for evolution comes instead from considering organs that have no use or are even harmful to the organism in which they are found.

Tom Brakefield/The Image Works

The wings of a penguin are vestigial characteristics, because they can no longer be used to fly.

Consider the human appendix, a thin, closed tube connected to the upper part of the large intestine. This three-inch-long organ has no proven function in modern humans, and it actually poses a threat to every one of us. Before the development of surgery, inflammations of the appendix were often fatal. The pressures of natural selection would never lead to the development of a harmful organ in a human being, yet the appendix sits there at the end of everyone's intestines. Unless the appendix has some as-yet-undiscovered function, it is hard to understand how this organ could come to be.

Vestigial organs such as the appendix can be explained by recognizing that they once had a function that they no longer have, and are in the process of disappearing. In a sense, modern human beings are a snapshot in a continuous process in which the appendix perhaps once served as an important part of the digestive system but is no longer needed.

Numerous examples of vestigial characteristics have been identified, and they provide important evidence against the argument that every organ in every creature is part of a grand design. Penguins have vestigial wings now used to swim, some whales have tiny internal vestigial hind legs, and humans have vestigial tailbones and vestigial muscles to wag them. Another striking example of vestigial organs is found in species of cave-dwelling worms that evidently evolved from surface-dwelling worms with eyes. They now have no need of eyes, but they still have vestigial eye sockets *under their skin.*

Chemical Evolution

Chemical evolution, the first step in life's long history, is the process by which rocks, water, and gases chemically combined to become the first living cell. The central question of chemical evolution is how one can start with the simple chemical compounds that were present in the early Earth and wind up with an organized, reproducing cell. This area of research is relatively new and immensely challenging; few clear answers have yet emerged. The first important experiment relating to chemical evolution was performed in 1953 by Stanley Miller (b. 1930) and Harold Urey (1893–1981) at the University of Chicago. The novel apparatus of the **Miller-Urey experiment** is sketched in Figure 25-1.

Miller and Urey argued that Earth's early atmosphere contained simple compounds composed principally of hydrogen, carbon, oxygen, and nitrogen—compounds including water vapor (H_2O), methane (CH_4), hydrogen (H_2), and ammonia (NH_3). Miller and Urey mixed these materials together in a large flask that was half-filled with water. Then, realizing that powerful lightning would have laced the turbulent atmosphere of the early Earth, they caused electrical sparks to jump between electrodes in the flask. After just a few days, they noticed that the liquid in the flask became cloudy and started to turn a dark-brown color. Analysis revealed that this brownish liquid contained a large number of amino acids, carbohydrates, and other basic building blocks of life (see Chapter 22).

Thus, as early as the 1950s, experiments had shown scientists that natural processes in the oceans of the early Earth might generate the modules of life's important molecules. Since that time, it has been found that energy sources such as ultraviolet radiation (from the Sun) and heat (for example, from volcanoes) will also produce key biomolecules. In subsequent experiments at the University of Chicago and other laboratories, scientists have used modified Miller-Urey devices to make all sorts of organic molecules, including lipids and bases, as well as complex substances such as long protein chains and nucleic acids.

Some scientists suggest that this scenario has important implications for the early Earth. For perhaps several hundred million years, the hypothesis goes, the amino acids and other molecules created by the Miller-Urey process were concentrated in the ocean, producing a rich broth, sometimes called the *primordial soup*. Additional organic molecules may have been added to this chemical mixture in the early oceans by other sources, such as meteorites and comets, which are known to carry carbon-based molecules. However the process happened, it seems clear that the enrichment of organic chemicals in Earth's early oceans required nothing beyond normal chemistry. By the 1970s, this small piece of the chemical evolution puzzle was well understood.

Our greatest gap in the evolutionary story comes next. Could the countless molecules floating in random patterns in the ocean have organized themselves into a functioning, reproducing cell? While mechanisms such as condensation polymerization (see Chapter 10) can join simple organic molecules together, sunlight tends to break these bonds apart.

We simply do not know how the first cell formed. However, a number of creative ideas may help close this significant gap in our knowledge. We know, for example, that molecules more than 10 meters or so deep in the primeval ocean would have been shielded from the Sun's ultraviolet radiation. In this environment polymers and other complex molecules might have grown and diversified. If the concentration of organic molecules was high enough, then the sunlight breaking up these molecules would not have been able to overcome their formation rate, and the concentrations might have increased even more.

For example, some scientists have proposed that the first cell may have evolved in a tidal pool. If it turns out that something like a protected tidal pool is necessary for the development of life, then life may be relatively rare in the universe. Our present understanding is that the formation of a terrestrial planet together with a large moon (and, thus, the generation of significant tides) is an unlikely event.

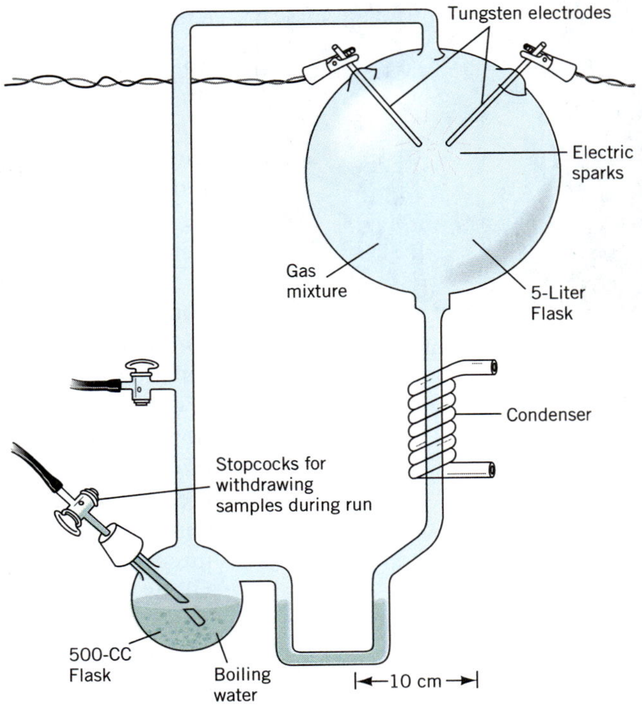

• **Figure 25-1** The Miller-Urey experiment. Several of the chemical compounds thought to have been present on the early Earth were mixed and subjected to electrical discharges. Within a few weeks, amino acids had formed.

> **Stop and Think!** Many science fiction stories, from *Frankenstein* to *Jurrasic Park*, revolve around the ability of humans to synthesize life. How close did Miller and Urey come to synthesizing life? Do you think scientists will ever be able to synthesize living cells beginning with organic molecules?

A major weakness of chemical evolution theories is that they do not tell us about how organic molecules could become isolated from the environment and organized into the larger structures essential for life. How could a cell membrane form, for example? Early optimism that research on the primordial soup would lead quickly to an understanding of life's origins has faded, and scientists now understand that major questions remain. On the other hand, this work has shown clearly that the basic building blocks of life were available very early in Earth's history, perhaps within a few million years after the first oceans formed. This growing understanding has led to alternative hypotheses regarding life's origins.

A colony of living things three miles underwater at a midocean vent in the Atlantic.

Black Smokers

In 1979, biologists diving to the deep-ocean floor in the submersible *Alvin* discovered an unexpected diverse ecosystem surrounding vents of mineral-rich hot water, called *black smokers,* near midocean volcanoes (see Chapter 19). The remarkable bacteria that thrive in these extreme environments obtain their energy from Earth's internal heat, rather than the Sun. These bacteria, among the most primitive life-forms known, may be closer on the evolutionary tree to the first living cell than any organisms living at Earth's surface.

This discovery has led many scientists to wonder if deep, dark, hydrothermal zones on the ocean floor might have been the site of life's origin. These extreme environments are not only rich in the chemical energy needed to drive chemical evolution, but they also abound in mineral surfaces that are known to select, concentrate, and organize organic molecules into polymers and other large structures. Some researchers now speculate that warm, gas-rich water circulating through cracks and fissures near midocean volcanic ridges provided an ideal protected environment for the origin of life. The surface of the early Earth was repeatedly bombarded by large meteorites, was constantly bathed in harmful ultraviolet radiation, and was continuously blasted by intense lightning. Deep-ocean environments were protected from these environmental insults.

Black smokers also provide an ideal chemical environment for organic synthesis, because water at high temperature and pressure has physical properties very different from those that are familiar to us. For one thing, water at these extreme conditions is much less polar and thus may facilitate the synthesis of amino acids, lipids, and other key biological molecules, while promoting their assembly into larger structures by polymerization reactions. One of the authors (RMH) is now engaged in experiments to understand how organic chemical reactions proceed—and how life may have originated—in hot, pressurized water.

RNA Enzymes

Today's cells run most of their chemistry by using protein enzymes, which, in turn, are coded for in DNA. On the other hand, in order to turn the DNA into a "working" protein, other enzymes are necessary. This cycle gets us into a kind of chicken-and-egg controversy. You need DNA to make the proteins, but you need the proteins to make the DNA. How could the first living cell have solved this dilemma?

Scientists have attempted to resolve this problem with a number of intriguing solutions, all of which share one assumption: that the very earliest life-forms had a rather different (and much simpler) chemistry than the ones we see around us today. The problem facing scientists is something like trying to reconstruct the Wright Brothers' first airplane by examining a modern jetliner. Many of the original design features have been replaced by more efficient components. Similarly, the first cell's chemical mechanisms, being rather inefficient, may have been largely replaced when the DNA-RNA-protein system evolved later. Thus we do not see these chemical mechanisms in living systems today, but perhaps we can deduce their properties from studies of biochemistry.

One particularly interesting observation is that some kinds of RNA molecules have been found to act as enzymes for chemical reactions, in addition to their usual role as nucleic acids. This behavior suggests one way that the present system of cell chemistry could have evolved. RNA molecules catalyzed reactions that created proteins, and, over time, the proteins necessary for the development of the more complex (and presumably more efficient) DNA coding system were developed. Alternatively, other scientists have suggested that some kind of clay or other inorganic mineral may have provided sites for chemical reactions, as well as catalytic properties to help those reactions along.

Speculative ideas about black smokers and RNA enzymes are not necessarily exclusive. It may well be that the best place for chemistry involving RNA as an enzyme to occur is a deep-ocean fissure. What is certain is that life's chemical evolution will remain an exciting challenge for scientists.

The Window of Opportunity

Whatever the chemical processes were that led to the first organism capable of reproducing itself, we know that those processes had to take place rapidly. We know that Earth, like all the other planets, went through the period of the great bombardment (see Chapter 16). During this period, large chunks of debris fell onto the planets from space, bringing enormous amounts of energy with them. An impact involving an asteroid several hundred miles across would heat Earth enough to boil the oceans—the planet would literally be sterilized by such an impact. Any life that might have developed would be wiped out. Therefore, the process that led to the ancestors of all present life on Earth could not have begun until after the last big impact. The best estimate for this date is about 4 billion years ago.

On the other hand, recent discoveries have convinced some paleontologists that by at least 3.5 billion years ago life was not only present on Earth but flourishing. In 1996, William Schopf of UCLA and his coworkers reported evidence for colonies of primitive bacteria in rocks that were laid down as sediment in a shallow bay in what is now Australia. When he takes thin slices of these old rocks and looks at them under a microscope (see Chapter 21), he sees the imprints that in size and shape resemble single-celled organisms (see Figure 25-2).

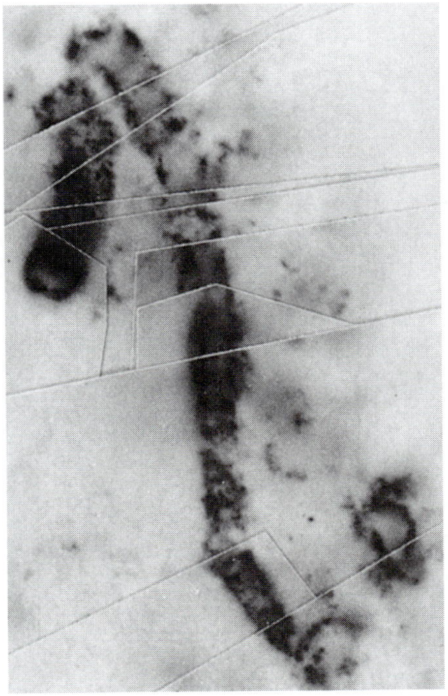

Biolobical Photo Service

• **Figure 25-2** Some paleontologists argue that objects like this are clusters of bacteria that lived about 3.5 billion years ago—the earliest evidence of life on Earth. These bacteria may have been part of a complex ecosystem, so the earliest life must have appeared considerably before this time.

Although Schopf's original claims have been called into question, new evidence on distinctive carbon-based molecules extracted from Australian rocks of similar age support the idea that life was thriving at this ancient time. It would have taken quite a while for life to develop from the first cell to this microbial ecosystem, which means that the first cell must have appeared soon after the last big impact during the great bombardment.

The first cell had to develop during a well-defined window of opportunity. One side of the window is fixed by the time of the last big impact, the other by the appearance of fossils. Our present best estimates are that this window extended roughly from 4.0 to 3.5 billion years ago, and the origin of life may well have occurred early in that interval.

The First Cell

Think about the unique status of the very first cell on Earth. It need not have been particularly efficient in using the chemicals found in its environment—after all, it had no competition. There were no predators and no other life-forms to compete for the abundant stock of organic molecules that enriched the early ocean. Once the first cell formed, it may have multiplied rapidly.

Biologists have suggested that the special characteristics of the first cell may explain one of the great mysteries of modern biochemistry, the fact that living things today contain only 20 different kinds of amino acids (see Chapter 22). The notion is that, perhaps by chance or perhaps because this particular combination gave them a competitive edge, some early cells contained only these amino acids and it was the descendants of these cells that managed to dominate Earth. In this way of thinking, the combination of these 20 amino acids is something of a "frozen accident," one of perhaps many chance events in the formation of life on Earth. Like so many other questions about the origin of life, this one will remain unanswered until we know more about the subject than we do now.

Science by the Numbers •

Cell Division

The first cell was a microscopic organism, but it may not have taken long for that first bit of life to spread great distances around the globe. To get a feel for this process, imagine how long it would take to fill up the Mediterranean Sea starting with a single microscopic cell that divides once a day, assuming all cells survive and continue to divide.

To get an answer, we must estimate the volume of an ordinary bacterium and compare it with the volume of the Mediterranean Sea. In Chapter 21 we learned that a typical bacterium is about a thousandth of a centimeter across, so its volume is approximately

$$(1/1000 \text{ cm})^3 = 10^{-9} \text{ cubic cm}$$

A recent world atlas gives the surface area of the Mediterranean Sea as about 2.5 million square kilometers, with an average depth of 1.4 kilometers, for a total volume of

$$2{,}500{,}000\text{km}^2 \times 1.4\text{km} = 3{,}500{,}000\text{km}^3 = 3.5 \times 10^6\text{km}^3$$

The question thus boils down to how many times you would have to double a 10^{-9} cm^3 bacterium to fill 3.5×10^6 km^3. To make things easier, we convert cubic kilometers to cubic centimeters:

$$1\text{km} = 10^5 \text{ cm}$$

so

$$1 \text{ km}^3 = 10^{15} \text{ cm}^3$$

The total volume of the Mediterranean in cubic centimeters is

$$3.5 \times 10^6\text{km}^3 \times 10^{15}\text{cm}^3/\text{km}^3 = 3.5 \times 10^{21} \text{ cm}^3$$

How many bacteria would it take to fill this volume? We divide the immense volume of the Mediterranean Sea by the tiny volume of a single bacterium:

$$3.5 \times 10^{21}\text{cm}^3/10^{-9} \text{ cm}^3 = 3.5 \times 10^{30} \text{ bacteria}$$

Starting with a single bacterium on the first day, there would be two on the second day, four on the third, eight on the fourth, and so on. After about three weeks there would be more than a million bacteria, taking up only about a thousandth of a cubic centimeter.

Day by day, however, the number would increase geometrically. After two months there would be more than 10^{18} bacteria; after three months 10^{27} individuals, occupying more than 10,000 cubic kilometers. And in just 10 days more—only 100 days after the first cell began to divide—the Mediterranean Sea would be completely filled with bacteria (Figure 25-3).

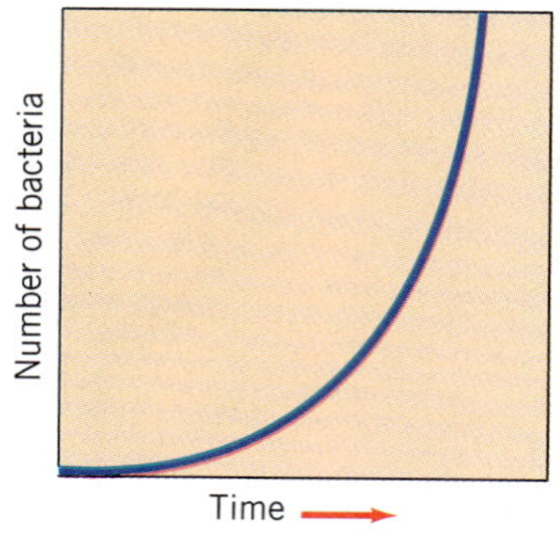

• **Figure 25-3** The number of bacteria grows rapidly, in what scientists call an exponential curve. In a matter of months, a single cell whose descendants divide once a day could easily populate a large ocean.

Naturally, no body of water could be "completely filled" with bacteria. In addition, early life probably did not spread quite this fast, nor was the process so regular and predictable. But the implication is clear. While it may have taken hundreds of millions of years for the first cell to evolve, a large number of descendants of that first cell could have spread throughout the world's oceans relatively quickly. •

The Ongoing Process of Science •

Did Life Also Originate on Mars?

The development of life on Earth would not have been possible without the presence of liquid water on the planet's surface. As we saw in Chapter 16, there was probably liquid water on the surface of Mars during its early history. In fact, some astronomers argue that the entire northern hemisphere of the planet was covered by an ocean and that the wet period of Martian history may have lasted as much as a billion years. After this period, the planet lost most of its atmosphere and hydrosphere to space and became the barren world it is today.

This scenario raises an interesting possibility. Since life on Earth seems to have developed rapidly once the great bombardment came to a halt, could the same thing have happened on Mars? Could life have evolved in those Martian oceans, only to perish when the oceans disappeared? If so, there should be fossil evidence to mark its existence.

In 1996 a team of scientists suggested that they had found such evidence in a meteorite that was blasted off the surface of Mars millions of years ago. The meteorite, labeled ALH84001 (because it was the first meteorite collected in 1984 from Allan Hills region of Antarctica), contains tiny gas bubbles whose chemical composition matches that of the Martian atmosphere. The idea is that millions of years ago a large meteorite on our sister planet blew this rock fragment into space from which, after millions of years of wandering in the void, it fell to Earth. It is one of about two dozen meteorites thought to come from Mars.

In a lively press conference and subsequent *Science* article in August 1996, scientists from the National Aeronautics and Space Administration (NASA) and other laboratories presented several lines of evidence that might point to past life. They observed complex organic molecules laced through the meteorite, magnetic mineral grains typical of those deposited by Earth bacteria, isotopic compositions characteristic of living things, and tiny structures reminiscent of bacteria. Any one of these features, by itself, would be little cause for excitement. Carbon-rich molecules, for example, are well known in meteorites and comets, as are magnetic grains of iron minerals. But some NASA scientists argue that these observations, taken together, "are evidence for primitive life on early Mars."

Over time, other scientists made additional observations that called these initial claims into question. The "fossils," for example, turned out to be layered mineral deposits viewed end on. Nevertheless, the excitement generated by the possibility that Martian life had already been discovered led NASA to initiate a program in *astrobiology*—the search for the origin and distribution of life in the universe. Thanks to the support of NASA's new Astrobiology Institute, hundreds of scientists are studying processes that may have led to life on Earth, Mars, and other worlds. •

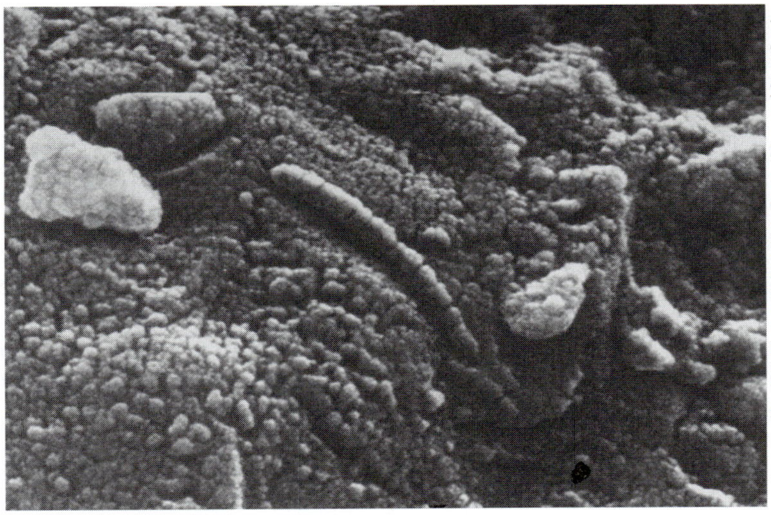

Time Life Pictures/NASA/Getty Images News and Sport Services

This 4.5-billion-year-old rock, labeled meteorite ALH84001, is believed to have once been a part of Mars and has been claimed to contain fossil evidence that primitive life may have existed on Mars more than 3.6 billion years ago. The rock is a portion of a meteorite that was dislodged from Mars by a huge impact about 16 million years ago and that fell to Earth in Antarctica 13,000 years ago.

Stop and Think! Think about the possibility that life exists on planets orbiting the billions of stars in each of the billions of galaxies. Would such an abundance of life affect your view of life on Earth? Should we spend more tax dollars to search for extraterrestrial life?

Natural Selection and the Development of Complex Life

Once we get beyond the time when the first cell formed, our understanding of how life developed becomes much more detailed and precise. This understanding is due in large measure to the work of one man, Charles Darwin (1809–1882). His *Origin of Species*, published in 1859, is arguably one of the most influential books ever written. In it he sets forward a view of the development of living things that, since his time, has been expanded and developed to the point where it is fair to say that it is the single theory that unifies all of biology. A biochemist working on the transport of particular molecules across the cell membrane and a zoologist working on the ecology of a tropical lake will both share the central ideas of Darwin's theory, and hence will have a common vocabulary and a common way of attacking problems. Darwin's theory was influential and controversial because it identified a simple mechanism for evolving complex multicellular life-forms from single-celled life. His entire theory is built around one central concept—natural selection.

Natural Selection

The easiest way to understand what Darwin meant by natural selection is to think first about the process that he called *artificial selection*. Farmers have known for millennia that the way to get bigger fruit, healthier plants, or animals with more meat on them is to carry out a conscious process of breeding. (Think back to Mendel's experiments discussed in Chapter 23.) If you want large potatoes, you should plant the eyes from only the largest potatoes in any given crop. Over long periods of time, this practice will give you a new variety of potato that is significantly different from the one you started with. Because human choice, not nature, drives this process, it is given the name of artificial selection. It explains how you can get animals as different from each other as longhorn and Angus cattle, or Chihuahuas and Great Danes, from the same ancestral stock.

If human beings can introduce such wide-ranging changes in living things, Darwin reasoned, then nature should be able to do the same. The mechanism he proposed, which he called **natural selection,** depends on two basic facts for its operation:

1. *Every population contains genetic diversity.* The individual members of any population possess a range of characteristics. Some are able to run a little faster than others, some have a slightly different color than others, and so forth.
2. *Many more individuals are born than can possibly survive.* Therefore, those characteristics that make it more probable that a given member of the population will live long enough to reproduce will tend to be passed on to a greater percentage of the population's subsequent generations.

Think about a hypothetical example to see how natural selection works. Suppose an island supports a certain number of birds, and suppose that the environment of this island is such that having a color that blends in with the local vegetation makes it easier for those birds to avoid their predators. Just by chance, some members of the bird population will have colors that match the colors of local leaves and trees better than others. As we saw in Chapter 23, the cells' DNA would determine this property in those particular birds.

Better-camouflaged birds will be less likely to be eaten by predators, and, therefore, will be more likely to survive to adulthood and mate. You would expect, then, that the particular genes that give this advantage will be more likely to be passed to the next generation. In effect, natural forces influence the genes that are propagated in the next generation. In this case, the selection is based on the color of the feathers.

If this process goes on for a long period of time, the entire population would eventually begin to share those advantageous genes for feather color. Natural selection works

Contrasting breeds of dogs, including *(a)* Collie, *(b)* Bulldog, and *(c)* Chihuahua, illustrate the changes possible with artificial selection.

(a)

Jeanne White/Photo Researchers

(b)

Jeanne White/Photo Researchers

(c)

this way to modify a gene pool, just as populations of farm animals now share genes for rapid growth and meat production. Nature "selects" those characteristics that will be propagated in any given species. A structure, process, or behavior that helps an organism survive and pass on its genes is called an **adaptation.**

Natural selection, it should be remembered, is neither as controlled nor as rapid as artificial selection. It's always possible that birds that do not carry the selected gene will, in some generations, be more successful at mating than those who do. Over the long haul, however, the selective advantage granted by color will win. Thus Darwin envisioned natural selection as a process that operates over long time periods to produce gradual changes in populations, not a process that can explain short-term variations in a few individual traits. It's important to understand that natural selection relates to changes in populations over time. Each individual in that population retains the DNA it was born with and does not change in response to environmental stresses.

Science in the Making •

The Reception of Darwin's Theory

Charles Darwin formulated the basic outline of his theory of natural selection in 1838, but he waited more than 20 years to publish his findings. This delay was not simple procrastination. He realized that the central precepts of his theory would cause a furor. Eventually, learning that another British naturalist, Alfred Russell Wallace, had developed similar ideas, Darwin hastened to get his *Origin of Species* into print.

Written in accessible prose and published in a widely available edition, his theory evoked intense reactions. Some theologians denounced the book for its denial of a miraculous creation and relatively short Earth history, which they claimed were demanded by a literal reading of the Bible.

Equally disturbing to Darwin was the reaction of many readers who embraced the "theory of evolution" as scientific evidence for God's hand in the progress of nature and thus proof of the human being's moral and spiritual superiority. They seized Darwin's discovery as an example of God's wisdom and beneficence. Some intellectuals of the late nineteenth century even went so far as to cite Darwin in their defense of an economically and socially stratified society—the most "fit" individuals rose to the top of society, they claimed.

Ironically, Darwin never intended his theory to suggest the idea of inevitable "progress" in nature—only inevitable change. Indeed, Darwin didn't use the word "evolution"—a word that connotes improvement—in the first edition of his book, nor did he address the question of human origins in *Origin of Species.* Far from being guided by a divine hand, he saw natural processes as violent and amoral—a constant struggle for survival in which the ability to reproduce fertile offspring was the only measure of success. He observed successful natural strategies that his contemporaries would have viewed as repulsive in any moral sense—species whose females devour their mates, species whose offspring eat each other until just a few survive, and parasites and predators that kill without thought in the frantic quest for energy to survive. To Darwin, human ascendancy seemed an evolutionary accident rather than a divine plan, and he saw no sign of God in the brutal process of natural selection. Nevertheless, in his own concluding words:

There is grandeur in this view of life, with its several powers, having been originally breathed by the Creator into a few forms or into one; and that, whilst this planet has

From Stephan Jay Gould, Wonderful Life, *New York, 1989, W.W. Norton & Company*

The "progression" from chimpanzee to human is often used as an icon of Darwinian evolution. Darwin, however, did not see natural selection as leading inevitably from lower forms to humans.

gone cycling on according to the fixed law of gravity, from so simple a beginning endless forms most beautiful and most wonderful have been, and are being, evolved. •

The Story of Life

As soon as the first cell split into two competing individuals, natural selection began to operate. In that early environment, where the first cells were surrounded by energy-rich molecules and very few neighbors, competition would not have been very intense. Before long, however, genetic mutations would have started to occur and some cells would have been different from others. Some of those differences involved the efficiency with which cells were able to utilize the molecules that they found in their environment. Certain cells, for example, might have been able to get energy more quickly from those molecules (and therefore reproduce faster) than others. Over time, the beneficial mutations would come to be shared throughout the entire population by the process of natural selection.

At this early stage, just as in today's life-forms, the vast majority of mutations and the resultant differences were not beneficial. Random changes in DNA, after all, are not likely to produce organisms that can interact with their environment more efficiently than their fellows. Nonbeneficial mutations died out quickly, and only beneficial mutations remained. This process is a little like our view of movies from the 1930s and 1940s. A great many poor films were made in those days, but we don't watch them anymore. What we remember and preserve are the most successful films, such as *Citizen Kane* and *Casablanca*. In the same way, only the "greatest hits" of all the mutations survived into the future.

Over time, you would expect the descendants of that first cell to spread around Earth's surface and to occupy most of the oceans. Some scholars have suggested that this spread may have taken as little as a few years, given the lack of competition for the environmental resources. (The results we calculated in the "Science by the Numbers" section of this chapter suggest that such a scenario might be reasonable.) In this process of spreading, some cells would wind up in different environments than others. Some, for example, would be in warm tropical waters, while others would be in the chilling Arctic. Some would be in deep oceans, while others would be in shallow water next to the shore. Each of these environments would exert slightly different pressures on the cells. An adaptation that might be very advantageous in the tropics, for example, might not be advantageous near the poles, and vice versa. The driving force of natural selection, coupled with the fact that many different environments existed on our planet, would quickly have produced a number of very different living things. Thus we would expect the appearance of diversity—the process of speciation—to have begun quite early in the history of life.

Our knowledge of this early period of life is limited by the fact that we have very little in the way of hard physical evidence that pertains to it. As you might guess, it is difficult to find fossils of single-celled or microscopic organisms, though scientists have found them. As Figure 25-2 shows, paleontologists have found examples of suspected fossil bacteria, and they have even unearthed a few cases of fossil bacteria caught in the act of dividing.

The best guess as to what went on until about a billion years ago is that the new varieties of single cells spread around the world and differentiated, driven all the while by natural selection and changes in Earth's climate. At some point in this evolutionary process, perhaps about 2.5 billion years ago, the oceans became dominated by cyanobacteria, which are single-celled life-forms that produce oxygen as a byproduct of photosynthesis. To an outside observer, Earth would have looked remarkably sterile. There was no life at all on land, but the margins of the oceans were covered with collections of green scum that was going about the business of taking in carbon dioxide and returning oxygen to the atmosphere.

About a billion years ago, symbiotic relationships were set up between cells that eventually led to the development of eukaryotes. At some point, smaller cells found that they did better living inside their larger neighbors than they could do on their own, and cells whose genetic materials were carried inside a nucleus were born. These cells, like their neighbors and ancestors the prokaryotes, remained as single-celled organisms.

Another important development that occurred early in the history of life was that cells began to clump together into mats or chains to form large colonies. At first, these objects were probably nothing more than clumps of single-celled organisms living next to each other. Later, however, they developed into larger bodies. Indeed, by about 600 million years ago the seas were probably full of large multicellular animals and plants. You can think of some of them as resembling modern jellyfish. The stage was set for one of the most important developments in the history of life, the hard shell.

About 545 million years ago a crucial development took place in living systems. By a process that we don't fully understand, but that may have involved a new enzyme that converted calcium in the ocean water into shell material, some animals began to grow hard shells. This new chemical trick was so advantageous that the seafloor was soon teeming with many different kinds of hard-shelled animals. As always happens when a new evolutionary path develops, there was a great deal of competition and experimentation among living things as they evolved outer shells, body designs, and metabolisms suited for each environment.

From the scientist's point of view, one of the most important aspects of this development was that, for the first time, living things left large numbers of fossils. In fact, for most of the nineteenth and twentieth centuries, before discovery of the fossils that indicated the presence of primitive forms of life, it looked to scientists as if life suddenly exploded at the beginning of this period. This sudden change in life on Earth, therefore, is often referred to as the *Cambrian explosion.* (Geologists refer to the time during which skeletons developed as the Cambrian period, after Cambria, the old Roman name for Wales, where rocks from this period were first studied.)

Following the momentous development of shells, the last half-billion years or so have seen enormous growth in both the complexity and diversity of life. A summary of major developments is given in Table 25-1 (see Appendix B for more details).

Table 25-1 Major Steps in the Evolution of Life

Time (millions of years)	Event
~3500	First cell
~2500	Photosynthetic cells
1000	Eukaryotes
700	Multicellularity
545	Animals with shells
450	Vertebrates and land plants
400	Amphibians
350	Reptiles
250	Largest known mass extinction
140	Appearance of flowering plants
100	Placental mammals
65	Primates; extinction of dinosaurs
7	Hominids
2.5	The genus *Homo*
0.2	*Homo sapiens*

Geological Time

Before the development of radiometric dating in this century (see Chapter 12), scientists knew about the existence of fossils and could see that some fossils were older than others by the sequence of rock layers. Younger layers of fossil-bearing rocks are always deposited on top of older layers of rock. However, they had no way of attaching numbers to any of the changes they observed in the fossil record. Several landmarks that stand out in the process of evolution were used as boundaries in the delineation of past times.

In the nineteenth century, scientists were not aware of bacterial fossils, or even fossils of soft-bodied organisms. To them, fossils seemed to indicate that life suddenly appeared at the beginning of the Cambrian (when fossils of hard-bodied organisms first appeared). The era from the beginning of Earth's existence to 545 million years ago was therefore called the *Proterozoic* ("before life"). Next was the *Paleozoic* ("old life") era from about 545 to 250 million years ago. This era saw a marvelous diversification of life, including the development of fish, amphibians, land plants and animals, and rudimentary forms of reptiles. The third great era (250 to 65 million years ago) was the *Mesozoic* ("middle life"), also known as the age of dinosaurs, when the major vertebrate

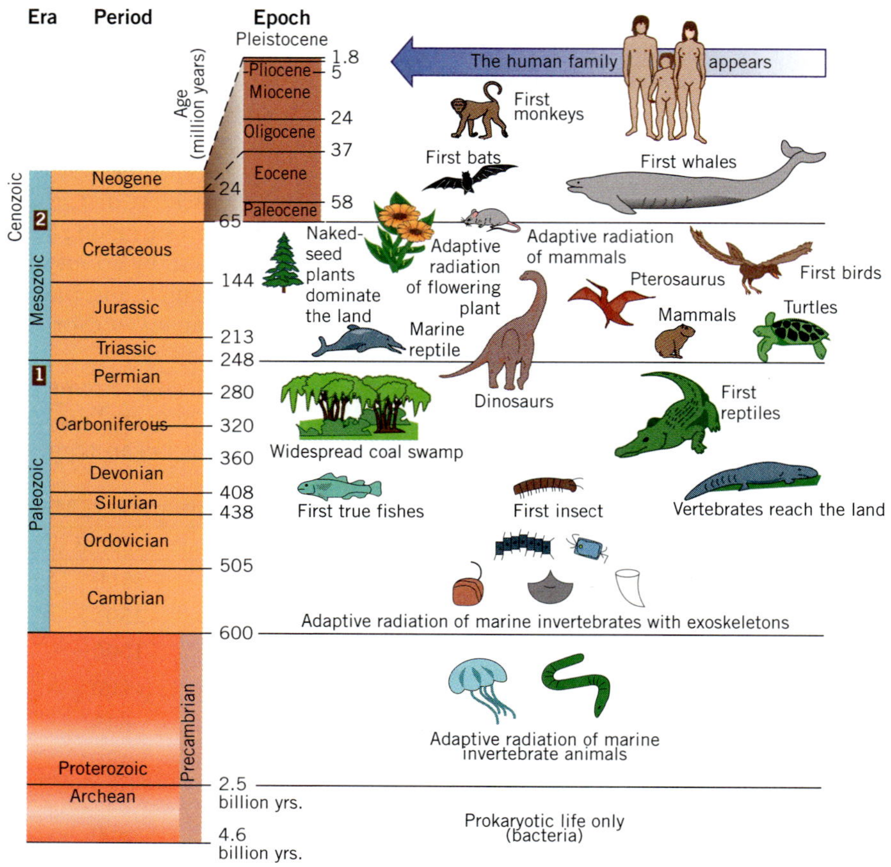

• **Figure 25-4** The geological timescale with representative living things illustrated.

life-forms on Earth were large reptiles. Finally, the *Cenozoic* ("new life") era began with the extinction of the dinosaurs some 65 million years ago and continues to the present day. This is the time when mammals proliferated and began to dominate Earth. The human species arose at the very end of the Cenozoic.

Throughout this long and intricate process of change, the principle of natural selection was always at work, shaping and molding life-forms (Figure 25-4).

The Ongoing Process of Science •

The Evolution of Whales

The power of Darwin's theory of evolution lies in its predictive power. For example, 20 years ago, critics of evolution pointed to the modern whale as an example of a form so specialized that it could not possibly have been produced by Darwinian evolution. An outspoken creationist, Alan Haywood, put it this way: "Darwinists rarely mention the whale because it presents them with one of their most insoluble problems. They believe that somehow a whale must have evolved from an ordinary land-dwelling animal, which took to the sea and lost its legs. . . . A land mammal that was in the process of becoming a whale would fall between two stools—it would not be fitted for life on land or sea, and would have no hope of survival."

Faced with such a challenge, one can test the theory. The theory of evolution predicts that whales with tiny, vestigial hind legs must have once swum in the seas. If Darwin is correct, then somewhere their fossils must lie buried. Furthermore, those strange

Courtesy Philip D. Gingerich, Museum of Paleontology, University of Michigan

• **Figure 25-5** Several types of fossil animals discovered in the past two decades reveal hind limbs and other features intermediate between land animals and whales.

creatures must have arisen during a relatively narrow interval of geological time, bounded by the era before the earliest known marine mammals (about 60 million years ago) and the appearance of streamlined whales of the present era (which appear in the fossil record during the past 30 million years). Armed with these predictions, several paleontologists have plotted expeditions into the field and targeted their search on shallow marine formations from the crucial gap between 35 and 55 million years ago for new evidence in the fossil record.

Sure enough, in the past two decades paleontologists have excavated dozens of these "missing links" in the development of the whale—curious creatures that sport combinations of anatomical features characteristic to both land and sea mammals (Figure 25-5). Moving back in time, one such intermediate form is the 35 million year old *Basilosaurus*—a sleek, powerful, toothed whale. This majestic extinct whale has been known from fossils for more than a century, but a recent discovery of an unusually complete specimen in Egypt for the first time included tiny hind leg bones. That's a feature without obvious function in the whale, but such atrophied legs provide a direct link to four-limbed ancestral land mammals.

And then a more primitive whale, *Rodhocetus,* discovered in 1994 in Pakistani sediments about 46 million years old, has more exaggerated hind legs, not unlike those of a seal. And in that same year paleontologists reported the new genus *Ambulocetus,* the "walking whale." This awkwardly beautiful 52-million-year-old creature represents a true intermediate between land and sea mammals. These and other recent discoveries underscore the predictive power of Darwin's theory. •

Mass Extinctions and the Rate of Evolution

Under normal circumstances, the rate of extinction seems to be such that roughly 10 to 20% of the species represented in the fossil record at any given time will be extinct in a matter of 5 or 6 million years. The fossil record shows, however, that not all extinctions are "normal." **Mass extinctions,** rare catastrophic events in the past, have caused large numbers of species to become extinct suddenly (Figure 25-6).

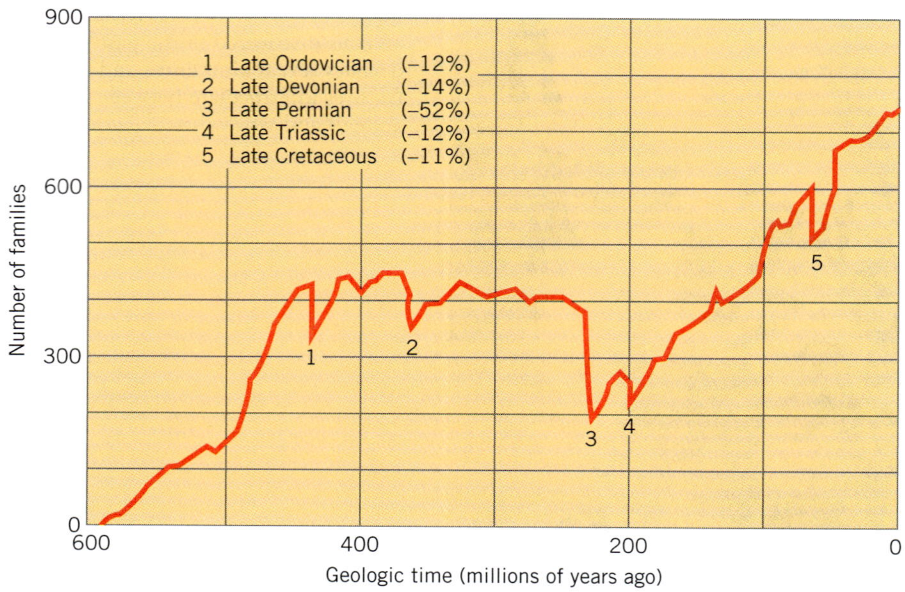

• **Figure 25-6** The diversity of life on Earth has not increased steadily but has gone through a series of sharp changes. This graph of marine animals in the fossil record is indicative of the overall growth in families and of extinctions. The extinction of the dinosaurs is indicated by the event labeled 5.

By "large numbers of species," we mean anywhere from 30 to 90% of the species alive at the time. By "suddenly," we mean a time too short to be resolved by standard geological techniques. The extinction may have taken place over a period of a few tens of thousands of years, or over a couple of days.

The best known of these mass extinctions is the one in which the dinosaurs perished some 65 million years ago at the end of the Cretaceous Period, which was also at the end of the Mesozoic Era. In that extinction, about two-thirds of all living species disappeared. In some cases, as with ocean plankton, this number may have climbed as high as 98%. But the extinction at the end of the Mesozoic was neither the largest nor the most recent mass extinction. About 250 million years ago near the end of the Paleozoic Era, about 80% of existing species disappeared in a single extinction event. A somewhat milder extinction, which wiped out 30% of existing species, appears to have taken place about 11 million years ago. In fact, geologists who study the past history of life in detail recognize five major mass extinction events and perhaps another half-dozen smaller ones.

One of the most interesting explanations for how these mass extinctions could occur was put forward in 1980 by the father-and-son team of Luis Alvarez (a Nobel laureate in physics) and Walter Alvarez (a geologist). Based on evidence they accumulated, they suggested that the impact of a large asteroid killed off the dinosaurs and other life-forms. Such an impact would have raised a dust cloud that blocked out sunlight for several years. This catastrophe would have been such a shock to the world ecosystem that it is a wonder anything survived at all.

Stop and Think! What would happen if an asteroid like the one hypothesized by Luis and Walter Alvarez hit Earth today?

Most scientists today accept that an asteroid hit Earth at the end of the Cretaceous, and they agree that it was responsible for the mass extinction. This conclusion was bolstered in 1992, when a giant crater over 100 miles across dating from that time was discovered buried under the seafloor near the Yucatan Peninsula in Mexico (Figure 25-7). Less certain is the role that other factors played in these events. The world ecosystem was under a great deal of stress at that time because of rapid changes in climate and the recent creation of mountain chains, both of which were altering habitats.

Mass extinctions illustrate an important point about the history of life on our planet. Evolution is not a smooth, gradual progress through time. There are times when sudden changes (such as those in the mass extinctions) are followed by rapid evolution, as new species develop to take the place of those that disappeared. After the extinction of the dinosaurs, for example, the number of species of mammals increased dramatically. Scientists continue to debate about the rate of evolution. The two extremes in the

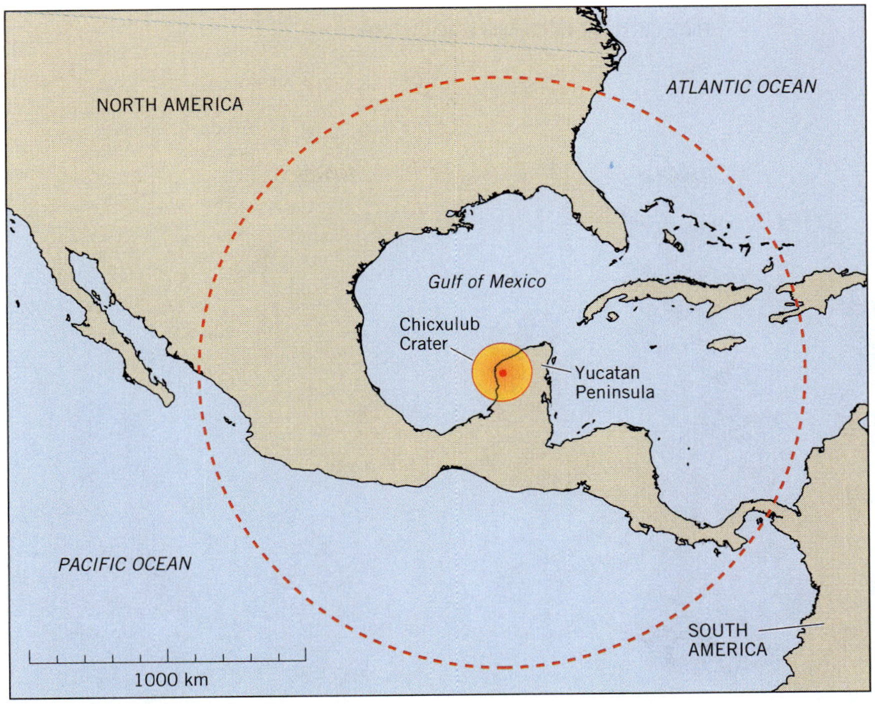

• **Figure 25-7** The location of the giant crater near the Yucatan Peninsula in Mexico. The effects of the asteroid's impact were recorded in rocks as far away as the red dashed circle.

debate have been the *gradualism* hypothesis, which holds that most change occurs as a result of the accumulation of small adaptations; and *punctuated equilibrium,* which holds that changes usually occur in short bursts, separated by long periods of stability. It now appears that both of these extremes, and probably any rate of evolution in between, occurred at some time in Earth's past.

The Evolution of Human Beings

The evolution of our own species, *Homo sapiens,* provides a good illustration of the kind of process that must have occurred for every other species. The most widely accepted hypothesis of human evolution is that our branch of the family tree broke off from the branch that includes orangutans and other primates about 7 to 8 million years ago. A possible human family tree is sketched in Figure 25-8.

Finding fossils of the oldest hominid has always been something of an obsession with paleontologists, but the problem is exceptionally difficult for three principal reasons. First, before modern times hominid populations were concentrated in Africa and were never very large, so fossils would be rare even if a significant fraction of individuals had been fossilized. Second, fossil-bearing sedimentary rocks from the period from 4 to 8 million years ago are rare in Africa, so relatively few individuals could have been fossilized. And third, many of the sedimentary formations that might contain hominid fossils are located in politically unstable regions where collecting is not possible. Nevertheless, slow progress is being made in this area.

As of this writing the oldest hominid fossil, dating back 6 to 7 million years, was found in Chad in Central Africa, where a single skull was discovered in 2002. This fossil possesses a brain case about the size of that found in modern chimpanzees, but with teeth and bone structure like that found in later humans. Scientists named this species *Sahelanthropus tchadensis* (man from the Sahel desert, from Chad).

• **Figure 25-8** A chart of human evolution. The earliest hominid appeared about 6 million years ago. For most of the intervening period, there was more than one kind of "human" on Earth. The disappearance of the Neanderthals 35,000 years ago left *Homo sapiens* as the sole hominid on Earth.

Another ancient hominid, ***Australopithecus ramidus*** ("southern ape, root of humans"), is known from several partial skeletons about 4.5 million years old, as well as additional fossil fragments that date back as far as 5.8 million years. This 4-foot-tall ancestor appears to be midway in form between later hominids and modern great apes. The best-known early human fossils are bones of *Australopithecus afarensis* ("southern ape from the Afar triangle region of Ethiopia"), better known as *Lucy* after the name given by paleontologists to a nearly complete skeleton of the species. The name of this fossil, which was discovered in 1974, arose because the paleontologists celebrated their discovery around a campfire while playing tapes of the Beatles' song "Lucy in the Sky with Diamonds." Radiometric dating reveals that this species lived between about 3 and 4 million years ago. *A. afarensis* is a different species and different genus from our own ***Homo sapiens,*** but it is closer to us than to any other primate.

Lucy and her family walked erect but had brains about the size of a modern chimpanzee's. They were also rather small (the adults probably weighed no more than 60 to 80 pounds and were typically less than 5 feet tall) and may have been covered with hair. Scientists used to think that the development of large brains made human beings special and that the brain's development led to upright walking. In fact, the evolutionary story seems to be the other way around. We walked upright first, which freed the hands for use, and then the large brain developed. Some scientists have suggested that the evolutionary advantage bestowed by hand-eye coordination provided the competitive edge for *Australopithecus,* and that led to the large brain.

Following Lucy, the line of *Australopithecines* developed larger and larger brains, and at various times there were several different species within the genus. From our point of view, however, the most important event happened about 2.5 million years ago, when the first known member of the genus *Homo* appeared. Fossils of *Homo habilus* ("man the toolmaker") were discovered in East Africa in the mid-twentieth century. *Homo habilus* was larger than Lucy and had a larger brain. More importantly, *H. habilus* fossils are found with crude stone tools, so the association of human beings with toolmaking starts with this species. Shortly thereafter, another member of our genus, *Homo erectus* ("man the erect") appeared. *Homo erectus* fossils are found not only in East Africa but in Asia and the Middle East as well. Many of the famous fossil humans you may have heard of—Java Man and Peking Man, for example—were members of this species. *Homo erectus* lived at the same time as some of the later *Australopithecines* and survived until about 500,000 years ago. *Homo erectus* was the first in the line of human ancestors known to use fire.

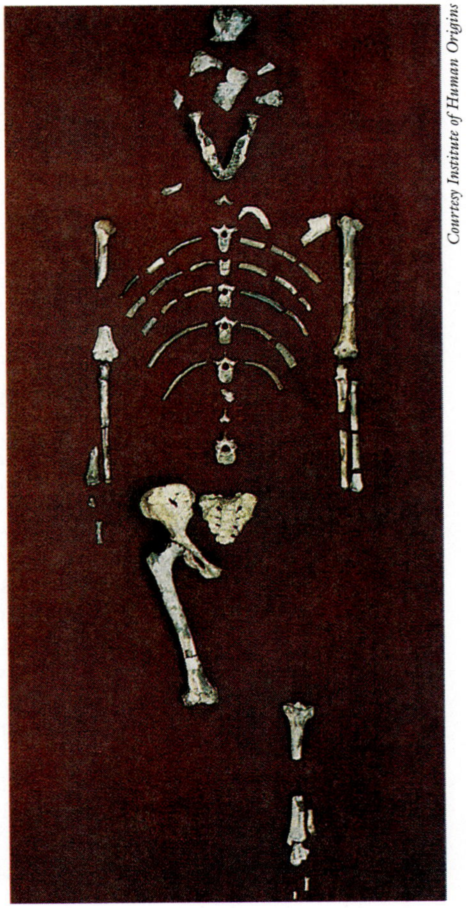

Courtesy Institute of Human Origins

"Lucy," a 40%-complete skeleton of *Australopithecus afarensis,* lived 3.5 million years ago in what is now northern Africa. This skeleton proved that hominids of that period walked erect.

Fossils that we recognize as anatomically modern humans begin to appear in rocks about 200,000 years old. About the same time yet another type of human being appeared on the scene—the so-called **Neanderthal man.** We sometimes use "Neanderthal" to denote something stupid. This use of the word comes from the fact that early studies of Neanderthal fossils concluded that this species walked stooped over, knuckles swinging, and had the thick brow ridge we associate with gorillas. These early suggestions were based on the study of a single skeleton of an old man who had a severe case of arthritis. Modern studies on other fossils reveal that Neanderthals, although far from being identical to modern human beings, were not all that different. They tended to be short, with thick, powerful arms and legs, and a skull that is much more elongated and pulled forward than that of modern *Homo sapiens.* On the other hand, Neanderthals had large brains, on the average 10% larger than those of modern humans. They had a complex social structure, cared for elderly and infirm members of their tribe, and performed burials with ritual—facts that suggest the presence of both a religion and a language. Thus Neanderthal was not too different from its contemporaries among the anatomically modern humans.

Several mysteries and controversies surround Neanderthal. The first puzzle is how closely Neanderthals were related to modern human beings. Were they, as some scientists claim, merely a subspecies of *Homo sapiens?* Scientists who adopt this view classify Neanderthal as *Homo sapiens neanderthalensis.* On the other hand, the traditional view (and the view of many modern scientists) is that Neanderthal, though our nearest relative, was a separate species. People who hold this view classify Neanderthal as *Homo neanderthalensis,* to indicate that it is the same genus but a different species than modern humans. In 1997, scientists succeeded in extracting bits of DNA from Neanderthal fossils. The DNA sequences were markedly different from those in modern humans. The results of this work provide the best evidence to date that *Homo sapiens* and the Neanderthal were separate species.

The second great mystery about the Neanderthals, some would say *the* mystery about Neanderthals, is the question of what happened to them. In Europe, where the fossil record is most complete, it appears that Neanderthals flourished until 35,000 years ago and then disappeared rather suddenly. Their disappearance coincided with the entry into Europe of modern *Homo sapiens.* Several theories have been put forward to explain Neanderthal's disappearance. Some suggest Neanderthals were wiped out by the invading members of our own species in what might be described as a prehistoric instance of genocide. Other scientists have proposed that Neanderthals intermarried with the invaders so that a certain percentage of the genes of modern human beings are Neanderthal in origin. In order for this to be true, Neanderthal, by definition, would have been a subspecies of (as opposed to a separate species from) *Homo sapiens.* Finally, some have suggested that Neanderthal couldn't compete with the more technologically advanced newcomers and simply died out. In this case, Neanderthal was not wiped out by acts of war, but was simply moved away from the desirable settlement locations and eventually disappeared. Such a situation would be an example of the displacement of one species by another, a common phenomenon in the history of life.

The descent of modern human beings raises an important point. In the past, many different beings could be classed as "human"—many members of the hominid family have walked Earth's surface. For whatever reason, none of them survived to this day except ourselves. The processes of natural selection and extinction, in other words, have extensively pruned the branch of the family tree leading to human beings. This fact made it easy for people in the nineteenth century to discount or misinterpret Darwin and to believe that the human race was special and not related to the rest of the web of life that exists on our planet.

Science News | First Steps

(SCIENCE NEWS, JAN. 28, 2006, P. 56)

Given the importance of the fossil record in documenting evolution, you would think that scientists would have studied the fossilization process in detail. In fact, they have not, and the question of how and under what circumstances a dead organism turns into a fossil is only now beginning to be explored in detail.

For example, one group at the City University of New York studied what happens to bird carcasses when they fall into the water. This is an important question because the early evolution of birds depends on fossils that show details of feathers and other delicate parts. The traditional problem is that dead birds float on water because of air sacs within their bodies. Indeed, experiments by the CCNY group show that bird carcasses will remain afloat for weeks, during which time they decompose to the point that they would not produce useful fossils. It took the researchers some time to discover a path to fossilization for dead birds. It turns out that if a carcass is dropped on wet clay soil, the sort of sediment that might be found along a riverbank or lake shore, it takes only a few minutes for the soil to soak the bird's feathers, fastening it to the ground. Even if water is added, the carcass stays mired in the soil and becomes a candidate for fossilization.

The most striking experiment in fossilization began in 1983 at the University of Michigan. A rhinoceros had died at a local zoo and the body was donated to the University. Scientists buried the animal in sandy, well drained-soil and waited to see what would happen. Twice—in the early 1990s and again in 2002—scientists dug up the carcass for examination and then reburied it. So far they have seen many of the soft parts such as the skin disappear, while chemical processes have started to produce a waxy outer coating (often seen in mummies) as well as the beginning of mineralization between the vertebrae. As you read this, that rhino is still buried under the Michigan soil, slowly going through the processes that produced the fossils of so many of its ancestors.

Thinking More About | Evolution

Young-Earth Creationism and Intelligent Design

Opposition to Darwin did not end in the nineteenth century. In the United States today, many vocal opponents to Darwin's theory believe in young-Earth creationism, which is based on a literal interpretation of the Bible. Three central tenets of young-Earth creationism are:

1. Earth and the universe were created relatively recently, no more than about 10,000 years in the past.
2. All life-forms were created by God in a miraculous act, in essentially their modern forms.
3. The present disrupted Earth's surface and the distribution of fossils are primarily the consequence of a great catastrophic flood.

These beliefs differ dramatically from many of the scientific ideas presented in this book. The big bang origin of the universe (Chapter 15), the origin of the solar system (Chapter 16), the immense span of geological history (Chapters 17 and 18), and the chemical origin and evolution of life (this chapter) are all at odds with these religious beliefs. It's not surprising, therefore, that science and creationism have come into conflict. In particular, evidence in favor of evolution requires a very old Earth and a means for transforming one species into another. Darwin's idea of natural selection, particularly as applied to the origin of human beings, is not comforting. In the scientific picture, *Homo sapiens* cannot lay claim to a history that is intrinsically different from other species.

In the early 1980s, the Arkansas State Legislature passed a law requiring that the biblical story of creation be taught alongside the theory of evolution in public schools. Federal courts eventually ruled that this law was an attempt to impose religious beliefs in the public schools, something expressly forbidden by the United States Constitution. It is now against the law to teach creationism as part of any public school science curriculum.

Young-Earth creationists then adopted a different strategy by trying to eliminate evolution from public school curricula. In 1999, for example, the Kansas State Board of Education had a majority of elected members sympathetic to the creationist position. They voted to eliminate any references to the big bang, Earth's origin, historical geology, and biological evolution from statewide standardized science tests. That decision was overturned in 2001, when a new Board was elected, but similar challenges continue to arise in many states and have re-emerged in Kansas.

The latest opposition to teaching evolution is in the guise of the "doctrine of intelligent design," or ID. Proponents of ID argue that life on Earth is so extraordinarily complex that it could not possibly have emerged through any natural process. An intelligent engineer must have done the job (though ID advocates avoid talking about who designed the designers). Unlike young-Earth creationism, ID does make a few testable predictions, albeit negative ones. They predict, for example, that the complex tail-like flagellum that powers many microbes could not have arisen by a natural sequential process. It is possible, in principle, to detail an evolutionary process by which a flagellum arose (and a number of microbiologists are working on that problem), so the claims of ID are falsifiable. The problem with ID is that it has not made one testable prediction that has been shown to be true. Evolution, by contrast, has made countless thousands of confirmed predictions regarding the continuous, progressive tree of life.

JUSTIN LANE/EPA/Landov LLC

In 2005, in a case in federal courts involving the Dover Area High School, the courts ruled that Intelligent Design is not science, and therefore should not be introduced into the public schools.

We maintain that it is reasonable, perhaps even desirable, to discuss different ways of knowing about the origin and evolution of life in classes on the history of ideas, or comparative religions, or even current events. However, we view efforts to eliminate the teaching of evolution or to promote the creationist agenda in a science classroom as misguided and a significant threat to the integrity of public science education. We argue that evolution is an essential unifying concept in biology and thus is a critical aspect of any scientific education. All students should be expected to *understand* the principle of evolution and to be familiar with the extensive observational evidence that scientists have discovered to support it, even if they don't *believe* that evolution actually happened.

To what extent do you think that parents or local school boards should have the right to decide what scientific theories and ideas are presented in schools? To what extent do you think parents ought to have the right to demand that opposing religious views be taught as well? Should the views of creationism, which are primarily based on one particular type of Christianity, be given special consideration?

Summary

Many types of evidence support the fact of *evolution.* A rich record of *fossils* demonstrates that life began simply and increased in complexity over time. The older a rock, the more its fossils are likely to differ from modern forms, because the vast majority of life-forms have become *extinct.* Biochemical evidence also supports the fact of evolution. Not only do all life-forms employ the same biochemical mechanism for translating DNA into proteins, but also many of those proteins are similar in very different species. Comparison of structural details reveals that closely related species, like humans and chimpanzees, have nearly identical proteins, while those of more distantly related animals show more protein differences. *Vestigial organs,* such as the human appendix, provide yet another piece of evidence in the evolution story.

Life on Earth evolved in two stages. The first period of *chemical evolution* was characterized by the gradual buildup of organic chemicals in the primitive oceans. The *Miller-Urey experiment* showed that simple compounds, including water, methane, ammonia, and hydrogen, subjected to electrical sparks or some other energy source, combine to make the building blocks of life—amino acids, lipids, and other molecules. These chemicals may have become concentrated on mineral surfaces, perhaps in deep volcanic zones. Through a sequence of events not yet well understood, a primitive but complex self-replicating chemical system developed. All subsequent life evolved from that first cell.

The first cell, free from competitors, quickly multiplied in the nutrient-filled oceans. As oceans became crowded and competition for resources increased, a new phase of evolution, *natural selection,* began. The theory of natural selection, introduced by Charles Darwin in his 1859 monograph *Origin of Species,* is based on two facts: every species exhibits variations in traits, and some traits enhance an individual's ability to survive and produce offspring. Just as breeders develop new varieties of animals by selecting desirable traits artificially, nature selects traits through the struggle for survival. These new traits are called *adaptations.* In this way, over immense spans of time, new species arise. Geological time is divided into Precambrian, Paleozoic, Mesozoic, and Cenozoic eras, depending on the kinds of fossils found from the period when the rocks formed. While extinction is a continuous process, there have been a number of catastrophic episodes of *mass extinction,* when many species disappeared in a brief time interval. Asteroid impacts may account for some of these events.

Human evolution can be traced back approximately 6 million years to *Australopithecus,* a hominid that walked erect but had a brain about the size of a chimpanzee's. *Homo habilis,* the first member of our genus that appeared about 2 million years ago, was distinguished by a larger brain and the first appearance of stone tools. *Homo erectus,* who learned to use fire, evolved at about the same time but disappeared about half a million years ago. Modern humans of the species *Homo sapiens* are recognized in fossils as old as 200,000 years. The status of the so-called *Neanderthal man* is still under debate: some say Neanderthal is a separate species, now extinct, while others argue that it is merely a subspecies of *Homo sapiens.*

Key Terms

evolution	vestigial organ	natural selection	*Australopithecus*
fossil	chemical evolution	adaptation	*Homo sapiens*
extinct	Miller-Urey experiment	mass extinction	Neanderthal man

Review Questions

1. What is evolution?
2. What types of observational evidence demonstrate that life has changed over time?
3. What types of observational evidence point to the common ancestry of all living organisms?
4. What is the fossil record?
5. What are the major stages in the history of life on Earth?
6. How does the fossil record support the theory of evolution?
7. What is chemical evolution? When did it occur on Earth?
8. How does chemical evolution differ from natural selection?
9. Describe the Miller-Urey experiment. Why are its results important?
10. Why do some scientists argue that the surface of the early Earth was inhospitable to life? What was an alternate site for life's origin?
11. Where is the greatest gap in our knowledge of the evolution of life?
12. What recent evidence is consistent with the idea that life originated in a deep-ocean environment?
13. Why is RNA thought to be an important molecule in the origin of life?
14. Which came first, DNA or protein? How do scientists answer this question at this time?
15. What is natural selection? Give examples of natural selection at work.
16. How does natural selection differ from artificial selection?
17. State the two basic facts that govern the operation of natural selection.
18. What was the Cambrian explosion?
19. What is a mass extinction?
20. What are some possible reasons for mass extinctions?
21. How does the overlap of human DNA with that of other living things support the theory of evolution?
22. When did the first members of the hominid family appear on Earth?
23. Which came first in human evolution, large brains or upright posture? How do scientists know this?
24. Give an example of a theory used to explain the disappearance of Neanderthal.
25. What are the basic tenets of young-Earth creationism? In what ways do these tenets counter scientific principles described in this book?

Discussion Questions

1. Discuss the possible connection between the constant processes of plate tectonics and natural selection. How might a study of fossils and plate motions be used to test Darwin's theory?
2. All scientific theories must be able to make testable predictions. What are some predictions that follow from Darwin's theory of evolution by natural selection?
3. Why do most scientists think all life evolved from a single cell? What evidence do we have to support this hypothesis? What alternative hypotheses can you propose? Are your hypotheses testable?
4. What role may ultraviolet light have played in the early development of complex molecules? What ecosystems are protected from the effects of ultraviolet light?
5. Is the development of intelligent life an inevitable consequence of natural selection? Why or why not?
6. Fossils are usually found in sedimentary rocks. Why aren't they likely to be found in igneous rocks? What biases might this fact introduce into the fossil record?
7. What is evolutionary fitness? What does it mean to be well

adapted to one's environment in terms of evolutionary fitness? What advantages does better adaptation give you in terms of passing along your genes?

8. How fast are species disappearing from Earth right now? What is the main reason for these extinctions? What kinds of species appear to be most vulnerable?

9. What is intelligent design? What are the testable predictions of intelligent design? Is it a scientific theory? Should it be taught in science classrooms?

10. What scientific discoveries would be necessary to validate intelligent design as a scientific theory?

11. Some people have argued that the progress of modern medicine has stopped the workings of natural selection for human beings. What basis might there be for such an argument? Should this argument be taken into account in formulating public policy? Why or why not?

12. Some religious leaders have made the statement that the Devil put fossils on Earth to test our faith in the teachings of the bible. Is this a statement that is subject to falsification? Is it a statement that can be understood using the scientific method?

13. What are the environmental antecedents of life? Why are the Moon and Mars devoid of life?

14. What are the most dramatic examples of artificial selection that you can think of?

Investigations

1. Read the National Academy of Science's pamphlet *Science and Creationism*. Who wrote this pamphlet and why? Does it make a convincing case?

2. Consult your geology department and find out locations of the nearest fossil-bearing rocks. Visit a fossil location and collect a variety of specimens. What kinds of life-forms did you find, and what kind of environment did they live in? How old are these fossils? What living organisms most resemble these fossils? What kinds of rocks were they found in? Where else in the world are fossils of a similar age found?

3. Read accounts of any of the many recent debates to alter public school science curricula by eleminating evolution or by introducing intelligent design. How did members of the school board rationalize their votes? Have there been legal challenges to the ruling?

4. Investigate the concept of social Darwinism. What was this doctrine? When was it in fashion? What policies did it encourage?

5. Read an account of Charles Darwin's visit to the Galapagos Islands while he was on the voyage of the *H.M.S.Beagle*. What did he see there that led him to his ideas about natural selection and evolution? Why did it take Darwin so long to publish his theory?

6. Read an account, such as *The Nemesis Affair* by David Raup, of the development of the hypothesis that an asteroid was responsible for the extinction of the dinosaurs. What role did the chemistry of the element iridium play in this hypothesis? Does the history of this idea support our argument in Chapter 1 that scientists must believe the data that result from their observations?

7. Read an account of the Scopes "Monkey Trial," or see a movie based on it—for example, *Inherit the Wind*. How was the conflict between science and religion portrayed in these writings and movies? What was the final verdict in the trial and what was the penalty, if any? Is such a conflict between science and religion inevitable when it comes to the subject of life's origin and evolution?

8. Investigate mass extinctions. How many mass extinctions have there been? What evidence supports previous extinctions?

9. Is intelligent design just another name for creationism? Investigate the debate. Are there creation myths from other religions that should be taught in school?

10. Before the nineteenth century, most people believed that life was created through spontaneous generation. Investigate the various theories that have been proposed over the course of time to explain the creation of life.

11. Investigate Jean-Baptiste Lamarck. What were his theories about evolution? What were his contributions?

12. Who is Sir Charles Lyell? What were his contributions to the science of evolution?

A

Human Anatomy

Science Through the Day | Waking Up

Think about your body as you woke up this morning. You stretched your muscles, and noticed the first sensations from nerves in your eyes, ears, and skin. As you lay in bed, summoning the energy to get up you may have noticed your heart beating. You took a few deep breaths, swung your legs to the ground, and headed to the shower. After you dressed, enjoyed a hearty breakfast, and made a final trip to the bathroom, you were ready to begin the day. In that short hour before leaving home you engaged in all of the essential activities of life (with the probable exception of reproduction).

From a strictly biological standpoint, there is no reason to single out *Homo sapiens* for special attention. Nevertheless, as members of this species, we have an understandable and justifiable interest in how our own bodies work. In what follows, we give a brief description of the organ systems in our body.

Skeleto-Muscular System

As in all vertebrates, the weight of the human body is supported by an internal **skeleto-muscular system** (Figure A-1). The rigid structure consists of bone, and movement is produced by the action of muscles that are attached to the bone by tendons, as shown. Muscles are made of long cells that can contract when they are stimulated. When you move your arm or leg, the simultaneous contraction of many of these cells produces the movement.

Bones are held together at joints by tough tissues called ligaments. Unlike muscles, ligaments are fairly inelastic and, once torn or injured, can take a long time to heal. Padding between bones is provided by cartilage, which you may know as the "gristle" in the joints of your Thanksgiving turkey.

Two kinds of muscle in the human body have names derived from the way they look under a microscope. The muscles that are under your control (such as the ones in your arms and legs) are called striated muscles; muscles that perform their function automatically (such as those that open and close the iris in your eye) are called smooth muscles. The muscles in the heart are similar to the striated muscles that move the skeleton, but they have a different metabolism that allows them to pump continuously and cannot be controlled voluntarily.

Respiratory and Circulatory Systems

Oxygen, essential for the operation of the chemical reactions that produce energy in our bodies, is distributed by the **respiratory and circulatory systems**. When you breathe in, air is pulled into your lungs and, ultimately, into tiny thin-walled sacs called alveoli (Figure A-1). Blood vessels are in close contact with the walls of the alveoli, so that oxygen from the air diffuses across the thin membranes into the blood. At the same time, carbon dioxide, the result of the burning of energy-rich molecules in the cells, diffuses back from the blood into the lungs. When you breathe out, you exhale the carbon-dioxide-rich air. On the next breath, the whole process starts again.

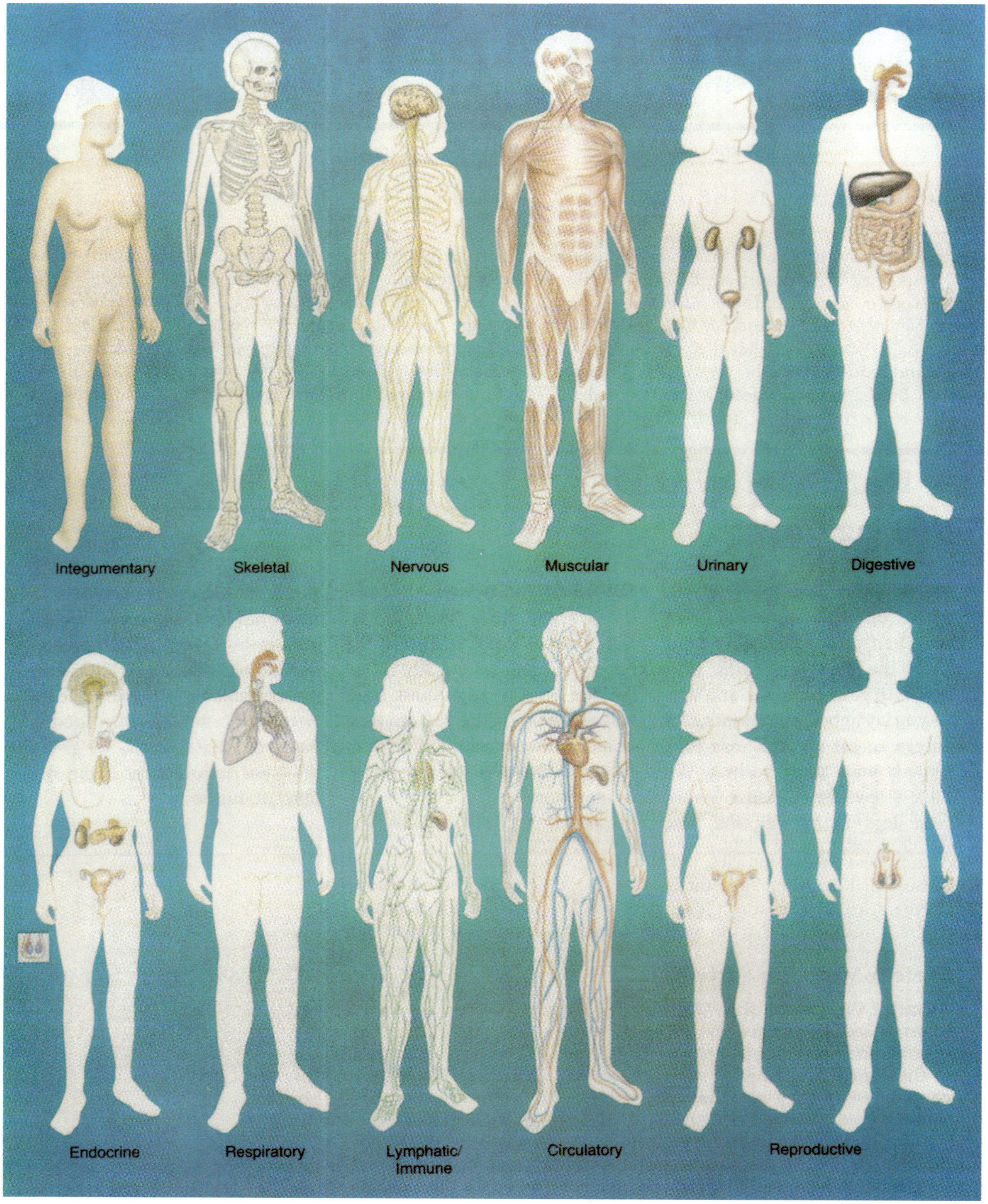

• **Figure A-1** The organ systems of the human body.

The blood with its load of oxygen goes back to the heart (Figure A-2). Like the heart of birds, the mammalian heart has four chambers, each of which carries out a separate function. Oxygenated blood from the lungs enters the left upper chamber, called the left atrium, from which it is pumped into the left lower chamber (left ventricle) and then out into the body through a series of smaller and smaller arteries. Eventually, it enters a network of thin-walled tubes called capillaries, where the oxygen diffuses out into cells and carbon dioxide diffuses back in. The deoxygenated blood is then returned to the right upper chamber of the heart through a series of larger and larger veins. It is then pumped into the right lower chamber and out to the lungs, where the entire process starts again.

Paralleling the blood system is the **lymphatic system**, which also moves fluids through the body. The lymphatic system, consisting of an extensive network of capillaries and veins linked to about 500 lymph nodes in the human body, removes material that fails to be reabsorbed into the capillaries. It also transports fat from the intestines to the bloodstream and supplies the blood with lymphocytes, which are a kind of white blood cell important in the working of the immune system.

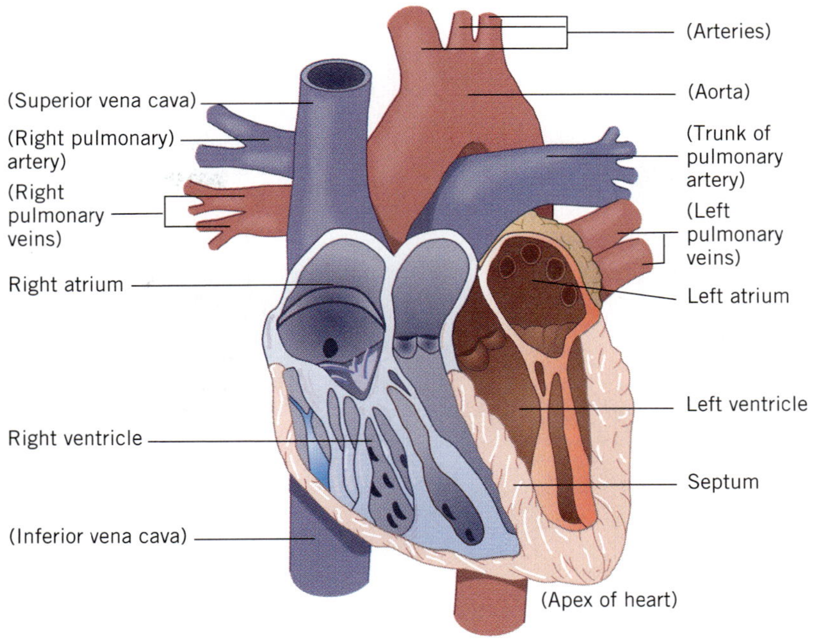

• **Figure A-2** The human heart. Blood is sent by the heart to the lungs to remove carbon dioxide and take on oxygen, returned to the heart, and then pumped out to the rest of the body.

Digestive System

Like all other animals, human beings must derive their energy from ingested food, and hence must have systems that break down food so that its stored energy can be used by cells. In humans, this job is the function of the **digestive system** (Figure A-1).

After being broken up by chewing, food enters the stomach, where strong acids and other chemicals break it down into molecules that can be used by individual cells—a process that is begun by saliva in the mouth. In the small intestine, this process continues as the liver, gall bladder, and pancreas secrete specialized substances that break down the starches, carbohydrates, proteins, and fats in the food to small molecules. These molecules then pass through the walls of the intestine and enter the bloodstream. They are carried to the cells, where their energy is released in chemical reactions analogous to burning. Muscles along the intestinal wall propel the undigested food into the large intestine, where water is removed and feces are formed and, ultimately, voided.

Waste products from the metabolism of the cells are carried by the blood to the kidneys. In a complex series of chemical reactions, the blood is filtered and then materials are selectively reabsorbed. Whatever isn't reabsorbed becomes part of the urine, which, after being collected in the urinary bladder, is voided.

The kidneys also maintain the balance of salt and water in the human body. Their structure is such that they cannot produce urine with a salt concentration of more than 2%. If the waste has a higher concentration of salt, then the kidneys have to take water from elsewhere in the body to dilute it. This limitation explains why drinking sea water (which is roughly 3% salt) always increases your thirst.

Sensing and Control Systems

Human beings become aware of their environment through the action of five senses—sight, hearing, touch, taste, and smell. The eye, arguably our most important sense organ, was discussed in Chapter 6. The ear (Figure A-3) contains a membrane that

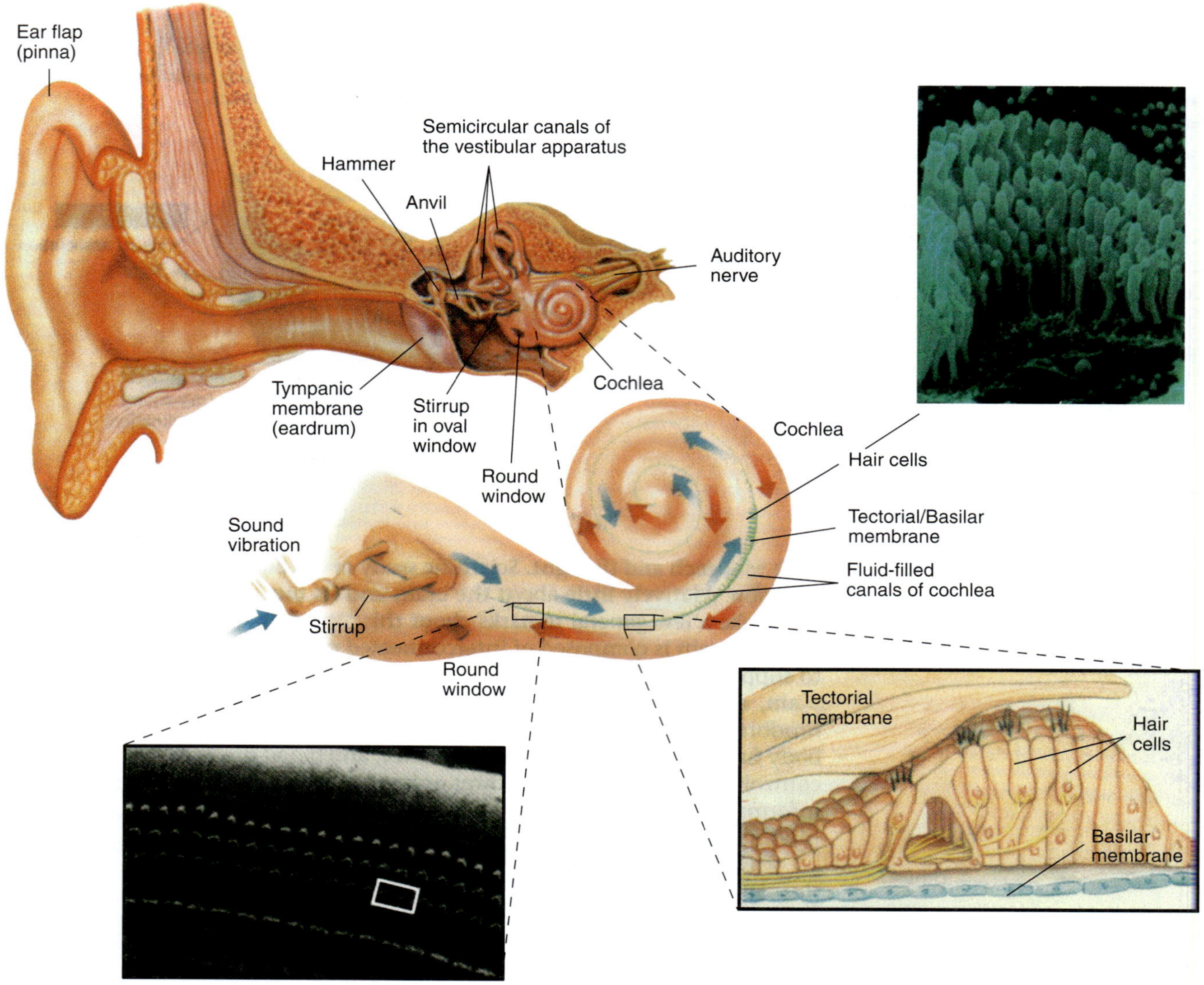

• **Figure A-3** The human ear and its inner structures.

senses the arrival of sound waves and vibrates. This vibration, in turn, is transmitted through three small bones to the inner ear, where it is converted into signals on the auditory nerve.

Smell and taste both involve specialized chemical receptors. Molecules of the material being sensed come into physical contact with the receptors, which then change their shape and generate a nerve signal. Touch is a sense generated by specialized cells in the skin that respond to pressure, and the skin also has specialized sensors for temperature and pain.

Our response to the environment is mediated through the two control systems in our body. The more familiar of these is the *nervous system*, whose main component, the nerve cell, was discussed in Chapter 5. Chains of nerve cells run throughout the human body. Some of these comprise the autonomic nervous system, which controls actions such as the beating of the heart and contractions of the gut. We aren't aware of the effects of the autonomic nervous system—we don't have to think about every breath or heartbeat, for example. The contractions of muscles that are part of ordinary volitional motion are controlled by nerves in the somatic nervous system.

The central organ of the human nervous system is the **brain**, which receives signals from sense organs as well as signals that keep it apprised of the status of internal organs.

The brain constantly sends out signals to the body to keep it functioning, and serves as the seat for all higher functions such as speech and thought. Scientific study of the brain is still in its infancy; we know relatively little about the brain and its functions. Nevertheless, we can make a few general remarks about this remarkable organ.

The brain is composed of interconnected nerve cells, and cells that serve to support and nourish them. It can be split roughly into three parts: hindbrain, midbrain, and forebrain or cerebrum, as shown in Figure A-4. The hindbrain, which is located at the top of the spinal cord, controls basic body functions such as breathing, balance, and blood pressure. The midbrain controls eye movements (in lower animals it is also the place where visual information is processed) and processes auditory signals. The midbrain and hindbrain, respectively, are often referred to as the brain stem.

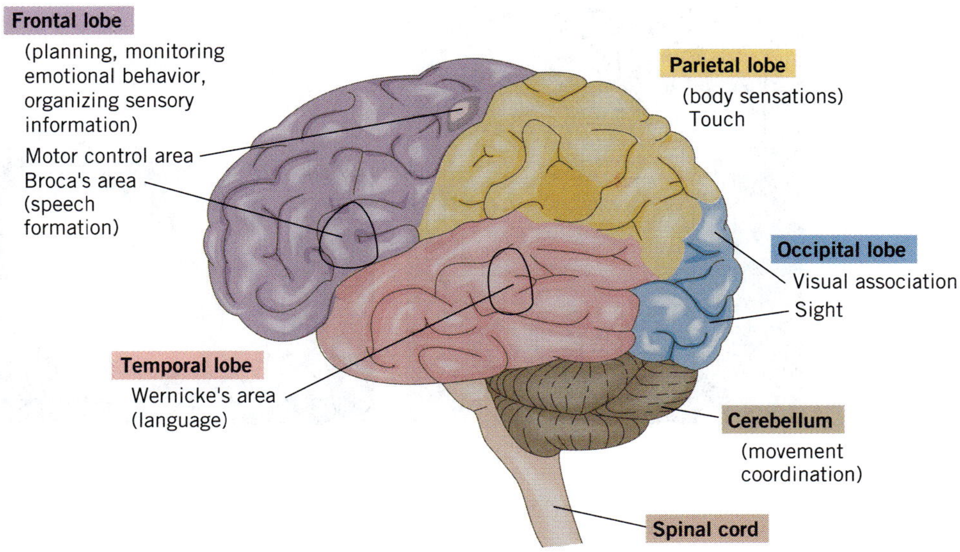

• **Figure A-4** The human brain.

The lowest part of the forebrain controls basic body metabolism and, through the pituitary gland, the body's system of hormones. The part of the brain that you usually see in illustrations—the wrinkled "gray matter"—is the outer layer of the cerebral cortex. All of the activities we normally associate with the higher human faculties—speech, rational thought, and memory, for example—are carried out here. The cerebral cortex also acts as the seat for processing of sensory information and conscious movement.

In addition to the nervous system, the human body has a second control mechanism in the **endocrine system**. The body's several glands secrete specific molecules, called hormones, that travel through the bloodstream. When they encounter cells that have a specialized receptor that fits their particular shape, they are taken into that cell and produce specific chemical effects. The adrenals located on top of the kidneys, for example, secrete substances that raise blood pressure and heart rate and send blood to the skeletal muscles. This surge of adrenalin prepares the body for "fight or flight." The pituitary gland secretes growth hormones that are crucial in human development—if they are not present in sufficient amounts, the individual will not reach full height. Human growth hormone is one substance that can now be produced by genetic engineering. Other hormones control basic metabolism, the maintenance of secondary sexual characteristics, the development of sexual organs in fetuses, and a wide variety of other human bodily functions.

Reproductive System

The human species, like all other higher animals, reproduces sexually. Sexual reproduction requires the joining of two sex cells, or gametes, each with 23 single chromosomes. The female's ova, or egg, and the male's sperm combine following intercourse to form a fertilized egg with 23 pairs of chromosomes.

Male and female reproductive systems are illustrated in Figure A-1. Sperm are formed in vast numbers in the male's testes. Each sperm, less than a thousandth of a centimeter long, has a rounded head that contains chromosomes and the enzymes required to interact with and ultimately penetrate the egg, and a tail that enables it to swim toward the egg. During intercourse, hundreds of millions of sperm are released, though only one can fertilize an egg.

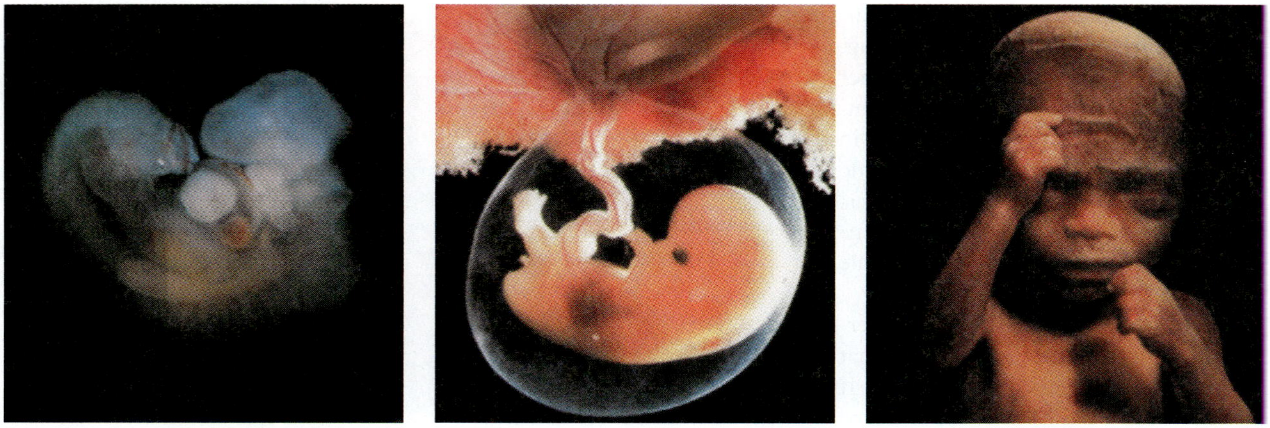

(*a*) (*b*) (*c*)

• **Figure A-5** Stages in the development of the human embryo and fetus. (*a*) At 4 weeks (length 0.7 cm), structures that will become the heart, eyes, and legs are evident. (*b*) At 2.5 months (3 cm), the fetus, floating in the amniotic cavity, is connected to the mother by an umbilical cord. All the major organs are defined. (*c*) At 5.5 months (30 cm), the fetus is identifiably human, with all organs in their permanent positions.

Eggs are produced in the female's ovaries. By the time a girl baby is born, all of her potential egg cells, a total of several hundred thousand, have been formed and are stored in the ovaries. Each month between the ages of about 12 and 45, one of these cells matures and is released into the fallopian tubes, where it may be fertilized.

Shortly after fertilization, the egg begins to divide over and over again to form the embryo, which is the beginning of a new individual. Approximately one week after fertilization, the egg becomes implanted in the wall of the uterus, where the mother provides all necessary nutrients and disposes of wastes as the embryo grows (see Figure A-5). Pregnancy lasts about nine months, during which time the embryo lies in the fluid-filled amniotic sac. This sac ruptures during labor, which precedes childbirth.

B

Units and Numbers

Science Through the Day | The Hardware Store

Walk into any hardware store in the United States and immediately you will notice that the things for sale are measured in many different ways. You buy paint by the gallon, grass seed by the pound, and insulation in terms of how many BTUs will leak through it. In some cases, the units are strange indeed—nails, for example, are ranked by "penny" (abbreviated "d"). A 16d nail is a fairly substantial object, perfect for holding the framework of a house together, whereas a 6d nail might find use tacking up a wall shelf.

But no matter what the material, there is a unit to measure how much is being sold. In the same way, all areas of science have systems of units to measure how much of a given quantity there is. We've encountered some of these units in the text—the newton as a measure of force, for example, and the degree as a measure of temperature. Every quantity used in the sciences has an appropriate unit associated with it.

Systems of Units and Standards

We customarily use certain kinds of units together, in what is called a system of units. In a given system, units are assigned to fundamental quantities such as mass, length, time, and temperature. Someone measuring with that system will use only those units and ignore the units associated with other systems. Once units of mass, length, and time have been specified, a whole series of derived units (for force, for example, or energy) follow from them.

Two systems of units are in common use in the United States. The one encountered most often in everyday life is the English system. This traditional system of units has roots that go back into the Middle Ages. The basic unit of length is the foot (which was defined in terms of the average length of the shoes of men outside a certain church on a certain day), and the basic unit of weight is the pound.

Throughout this book, and throughout most of the world outside the United States, the preferred system of units is the metric system, or, more correctly, the International System (or Systéme Internationale, SI). In this system, the unit of length is the meter (originally defined as a certain fraction of the distance around Earth at the longitude of Paris), and the unit of mass is the kilogram. In both the SI and English systems, the basic unit of time is the second.

Systems of units are one case where governments become intimately involved with science, because the maintenance of standards has traditionally been the task of governments. In the Magna Carta, a document signed in England in 1215 and generally considered to be one of the founding instruments of modern democracy, King John agreed that "There shall be a standard measure of wine, corn, and ale throughout the kingdom," and to establish measures of length (for cloth merchants) and weights. Since that time, governments have maintained standards for use in industry and commerce. When you buy a pound of meat in a supermarket, for example, you know that you are getting full weight for your money because the scale is certified by a state agency, which ultimately relies on international standards of weight maintained by a treaty between all nations.

Originally, the standards were kept in sealed vaults at the International Bureau of Weights and Measures near Paris, with secondary copies at places such as the National

Institute of Standards and Technology (formerly National Bureau of Standards) in the United States. The meter, for example, was defined as the distance between two marks on a particular bar of metal; the kilogram as the mass of a particular block of iridium-platinum alloy; the second as a certain fraction of the length of the day.

Today, however, only the kilogram is still defined in this way. Since 1967, the second has been defined as the time it takes for 9,192,631,770 crests of the light emitted by a certain quantum jump in a cesium atom to pass by a given point. In 1960, the meter was defined as the length of 1,650,763.73 wavelengths of the radiation from a particular quantum jump in the krypton atom. In 1983, the meter was redefined to be the distance that light travels in a vacuum: 1/299,792,458 per second. In all these cases, the old standards have been replaced by numbers relating to atoms—standards that any reasonably equipped laboratory can maintain for itself. Atomic standards have the additional advantage of being truly universal—every cesium or krypton atom in the universe is equivalent to any other. Only mass is still defined in the old way, in relation to a specific block of material kept in a vault, and scientists are working hard to replace that standard by one based on the mass of individual atoms.

The International System of Units

Within the SI system, units are based on multiples of 10. Thus the centimeter is one-hundredth the length of a meter, the millimeter one-thousandth, and so on. In the same way, a kilometer is 1000 meters, a kilogram is 1000 grams, and so on. This organization differs from that of the English system, in which a foot equals 12 inches, and 3 feet make a yard. A list of metric prefixes follows.

Metric Prefixes

If the prefix is:	Multiply the basic unit by:
giga-	billion (thousand million)
mega-	million
kilo-	thousand
hecto-	hundred
deka-	ten
If the prefix is:	**Divide the basic unit by:**
deci-	ten
centi-	hundred
milli-	thousand
micro-	million
nano-	billion

Units of Length, Mass, and Temperature

Next we give the conversion factors between SI and English units of length and mass.

Length and Mass Conversion from SI to English Units

To get:	Multiply:	By:
inches	meters	39.4
feet	meters	3.281
miles	kilometers	1.609
pounds	newtons	0.2248*

*Recall that the weight of a 1-kilogram mass is 9.806 newtons.

Thus, for example, a distance of 5 miles can be converted to kilometers by multiplying by the factor 1.609:

$$5 \text{ miles} \times 1.609 = 8.05 \text{ kilometers}$$

Length and Mass Conversion from English to SI Units

To get:	Multiply:	By:
meters	inches	0.0254
meters	feet	0.3048
kilometers	miles	0.6214
newtons	pounds	4.448

To convert from Celsius to Fahrenheit degrees, use the following formula:

$$T(\text{in °F}) = 1.8 \times T(\text{in °C}) + 32$$

To find temperatures in the Kelvin scale, simply add 273.15 to the temperature on the Celsius scale.

Units of Force, Energy, and Power

Once the basic units of mass, length, time, and temperature have been defined, the units of other quantities such as force and energy follow. Recall the energy units that we have defined in the text:

joule: a force of 1 newton acting through 1 meter
foot-pound: a force of 1 pound acting through 1 foot
calorie: energy required to raise the temperature of 1 kilogram of water by 1 degree Celsius
British Thermal Unit, or BTU: energy required to raise the temperature of 1 pound of water by 1 degree Fahrenheit
kilowatt-hour: 1000 joules per second for 1 hour

Power units are:

watt: 1 joule per second
horsepower: 550 foot-pounds per second

Conversion factors between SI and English units for energy and power follow.

Energy and Power Conversion from SI to English Units

To get:	Multiply:	By:
BTUs	joules	0.00095
calories	joules	0.2390
kilowatt-hours	joules	2.78×10^{-7}
foot-pounds	joules	0.7375
horsepower	watts	0.00134

Energy and Power Conversion from English to SI Units

To get:	Multiply:	By:
joules	BTUs	1055
joules	calories	4.184
joules	kilowatt-hours	3.6 million
joules	foot-pounds	1.356
watts	horsepower	745.7

Powers of 10

Powers of ten notation allows us to write very large or very small numbers conveniently, in a compact way. Any number can be written by the following three rules:

1. Every number is written as a number between 1 and 10 followed by 10 raised to a power, or an exponent.
2. If the power of 10 is positive, it means "move the decimal point this many places to the right."
3. If the power of 10 is negative, it means "move the decimal point this many places to the left."

Thus, using this notation, five trillion is written 5×10^{12}, instead of 5,000,000,000,000. Similarly, five-trillionths is written 5×10^{-12}, instead of 0.000000000005.

Multiplying or dividing numbers with powers of 10 requires special care. If you are multiplying two numbers, such as 2.5×10^3 and 4.3×10^5, you multiply 2.5 and 4.3, but you add the two exponents:

$$\begin{aligned}(2.5 \times 10^3) \times (4.3 \times 10^5) &= (2.5 \times 4.3) \times 10^{3+5} \\ &= 10.75 \times 10^8 \\ &= 1.075 \times 10^9\end{aligned}$$

When dividing two numbers, such as 4.3×10^5 divided by 2.5×10^3, you divide 4.3 by 2.5, but you subtract the denominator exponent from the numerator exponent:

$$\begin{aligned}\frac{4.3 \times 10^5}{2.5 \times 10^3} &= \frac{4.3}{2.5} \times 10^{5-3} \\ &= 1.72 \times 10^2 \\ &= 172\end{aligned}$$

Conversion to Metric Units

The reasons that the United States still uses English units long after most of the rest of the world has converted to SI have to do with nonscientific factors such as the geographical isolation of the country, the size of our economy (the world's largest), and, perhaps most importantly, the expense of making the conversion. Think, for example, of what it would cost to change all of the road signs on the Interstate Highway System so that the distances read in kilometers instead of miles.

To understand the debate over conversion, you have to realize one important point about units. There is no such thing as a "right" or "scientific" system of units. Units can only be convenient or inconvenient. Thus U.S. manufacturers who sell significant quantities of goods in foreign markets long ago converted to metric standards to make those sales easier. Builders, on the other hand, whose market is largely restricted to the United States, have not.

By the same token, very few scientists use SI units exclusively in their work. United States engineers use English units almost exclusively—indeed, when the federal government was considering a tax on energy use in 1993, it was referred to as a "BTU tax," not as a "joule tax." Hospital and medical professionals routinely use the so-called "cgs" system, in which the unit of length is the centimeter and the unit of mass is the gram. Next time you have blood drawn, take a look at the needle. It will be calibrated in "cc"—cubic centimeters. Even scientists doing basic research sometimes choose non-SI units for convenience. Astronomers, for example, talk about light-years, or parsecs instead of meters. Nuclear physicists measure distances in "fermis"—roughly the distance across a proton.

Stop and Think! Given this wide range of units actually in use, how much emphasis should the U.S. government give to metric conversion? How much money should the government be willing to spend on the conversion process: how many new signs as opposed to how many repaired potholes on the road?

C

The Geological Time Scale

Science Through the Day | In Time

As you drive through the countryside, you may come across an abandoned farmhouse, its windows boarded up, its roof open to the elements, its only inhabitants animals and insects. The surrounding fields, once cultivated, may have been overtaken by the prairie grasses that were there long before the farmhouse was built. Within a very short time span, perhaps as short as 25 years, that farmhouse may be razed and a subdivision built on the same site. Over a longer time span, the same site may have been at the bottom of a prehistoric ocean, then lifted to the top of a mountain, and finally eroded to the level at which the farmhouse was built. All things change over time.

All things also affect others as they change. In the following pages, we show you the geological time scale, a chronological arrangement of geological time units as approved in 2002 by the International Commission on Stratigraphy (these numbers thus differ slightly from those used in earlier geologic time scales). In addition, we show you the major steps in evolution that were made possible, in part, by the conditions that existed at every step of that time scale.

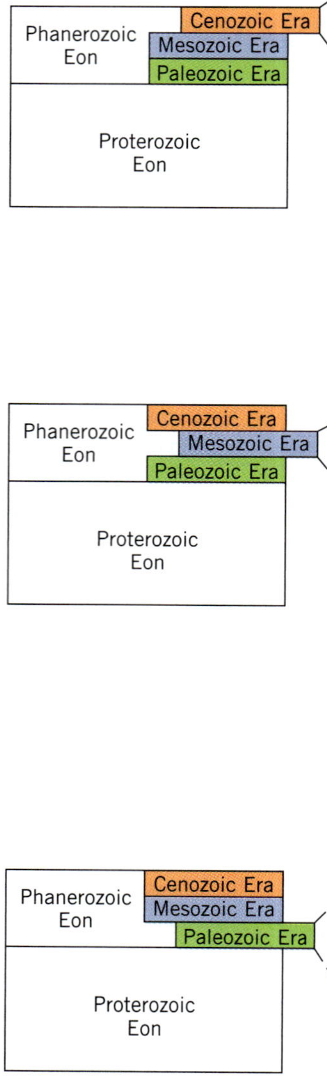

Millions of years ago	PERIOD	EPOCH	PLANT EVOLUTION
	Quaternary	Holocene Pleistocene	
1.8	**Tertiary**	Pliocene Miocene Oligocene Eocene Paleocene	Decline of forests, spread of grasslands Explosive radiation of flowering plants
65	**Cretaceous**		First flowering plants
142	**Jurassic**		Forests of gymnosperms and ferns over most of Earth
205	**Triassic**		Gymnosperms dominant
250	**Permian**		Widespread extinction Decline of nonseed plants Conifers diversify
292	**Carboniferous** Pennsylvanian Mississippian		Gymnosperms diversify Widespread forests of giant club moss trees, horsetails and tree fern — create vast coal deposits
354	**Devonian**		First seed plants Development of vascular plants: club mosses and ferns
417	**Silurian**		First vascular plants
440	**Ordovician**		First mosses
495	**Cambrian**		Algae dominant
545			

Millions of years ago

ANIMAL EVOLUTION	MAJOR GEOLOGICAL EVENTS
Appearance of *Homo sapiens* First use of fire Appearance of *Homo erectus*	Worldwide glaciations Linking of North America and South America
Appearance of hominids Appearance of first apes All modern genera of mammals present In seas, bony fish abound Rise of mammals First placental mammals	Opening of Red Sea Formation of Himalayan Mountains Collision of India with Asia Separation of Australia and Antarctica Opening of Norwegian Sea and Baffin Bay
Dinosaurs extinct Modern birds	Formation of Alps Formation of Rocky Mountains
First birds Age of dinosaurs	
Explosive radiation of dinosaurs First dinosaurs First mammals Complex arthropods dominant in seas First beetles	Opening of Atlantic Ocean
Widespread extinction Appearance of mammal-like reptiles Increase of reptiles and insects Decline of amphibians	Final assembly of Pangaea
Early reptiles First winged insects Increase of amphibians	Formation of coal deposits
Amphibians diversify into many forms First land vertebrates—amphibians	
Golden Age of fishes First land invertebrates—land scorpions	
First vertebrates—fishes Increase of marine invertebrates	
Trilobites dominant Explosive evolution of marine life	

Time	Eon*
Precambrian	Proterozoic
	Archean
	Hadean

* No further subdivisions into eras or periods are in common use.

Millions of years ago	EVOLUTION OF LIFE	MAJOR GEOLOGICAL EVENTS
	Earliest known multicellular animals	
1,000	Algal groups diversify	Formation of early super-continent
1,500		
2,000	Earliest known algal-like fossils	
2,500		
3,000	Earliest single-celled fossil organisms	
3,500	Trace organics of possible biological origin	Oldest Earth rocks
4,000		Oldest Moon rocks Heavy meteorite bombardment
4,500		Formation of Earth
4,600		

D

Selected Physical Constants and Astronomical Data

Avogadro's number
$6.022 \times 10^{23}/\text{mol}$
Charge on electron
$1.602 \times 10^{-19}\text{C}$
Electron mass
$m_e = 9.10939 \times 10^{-31}$ kg
Gravitational constant
$G = 6.674 \times 10^{-11}\ \text{N} \cdot \text{m}^2/\text{kg}^2$
Planck's constant
$h = 6.62608 \times 10^{-34}\ \text{J} \cdot \text{s}$
Proton mass
$m_p = 1.6726 \times 10^{-27}$ kg
$= 1836.1\ m_e$
Speed of light in a vacuum
$c = 2.9979 \times 10^8$ m/s

Astronomical unit
$\text{AU} = 1.4959789 \times 10^{11}$ meters
Hubble's constant
$H \sim 20$ km/s/Mly
Light-year
$\text{ly} = 9.46053 \times 10^{15}$ meters
$= 6.324 \times 10^4$ AU
Mass of Sun
$M_{\text{sun}} = 1.989 \times 10^{30}$ kg
Radius of Sun
$R_{\text{sun}} = 6.96 \times 10^5$ km
Mass of Moon
$M_{\text{moon}} = 7.348 \times 10^{22}$ kg
Radius of Moon
$R_{\text{moon}} = 1.738 \times 10^3$ km

E

Properties of the Planets

Planet	Length of Day	Distance from Sun (millions of km)	Length of Year (Earth year)	Average Radius (km)	Radius (Earth radii)	Mass (kg)	Mass (Earth masses)
Mercury	58.65 days	57.9	0.24	2,439	0.38	3.30×10^{23}	0.0562
Venus	243.01 days (retrograde)	108.2	0.615	6,052	0.95	4.87×10^{24}	0.815
Earth	23 h 56 min 4.1 s	149.6	1.000	6,378	1.00	5.974×10^{24}	1.000
Mars	24 h 37 min 22.6 s	227.9	1.881	3,397	0.53	6.42×10^{23}	0.1074
Jupiter	9 h 50.5 min	778.4	11.86	71,492	11.19	1.899×10^{27}	317.9
Saturn	10 h 14 min	1424	29.46	60,268	9.45	5.68×10^{26}	95.1
Uranus	17 h 14 min (retrograde)	2872	84.01	25,559	4.01	8.66×10^{26}	14.56
Neptune	16 h 3 min	4499	164.8	25,269	3.96	1.03×10^{26}	17.24
Pluto	6.39 days (retrograde)	5943	248.6	1,140	0.18	1.1×10^{22}	0.0018

F

The Chemical Elements

Table of Atomic Weights

Elements by Name/Symbol, Atomic Number, and Atomic Weight
(Atomic weights are given to four significant figures for elements below atomic number 104.)

Name	Symbol	Atomic Number	Atomic Weight
Actinium	Ac	89	227.0
Aluminum	Al	13	26.98
Americium	Am	95	243.1
Antimony	Sb	51	121.8
Argon	Ar	18	39.95
Arsenic	As	33	74.92
Astatine	At	85	210.0
Barium	Ba	56	137.3
Berkelium	Bk	97	247.1
Beryllium	Be	4	9.012
Bismuth	Bi	83	209.0
Bohrium	Bh	107	(264)
Boron	B	5	10.81
Bromine	Br	35	79.90
Cadmium	Cd	48	112.4
Calcium	Ca	20	40.08
Californium	Cf	98	252.1
Carbon	C	6	12.01
Cerium	Ce	58	140.1
Cesium	Cs	55	132.9
Chlorine	Cl	17	35.45
Chromium	Cr	24	52.00
Cobalt	Co	27	58.93
Copper	Cu	29	63.55
Curium	Cm	96	247.1
Darmstadtium	Ds	110	281
Dubnium	Db	105	(262)
Dysprosium	Dy	66	162.5
Einsteinium	Es	99	252.1
Erbium	Er	68	167.3
Europium	Eu	63	152.0
Fermium	Fm	100	257.1
Flourine	F	9	19.00
Francium	Fr	87	223.0
Gadolinium	Gd	64	157.2
Gallium	Ga	31	69.72
Germanium	Ge	32	72.59
Gold	Au	79	197.0
Hafnium	Hf	72	178.5
Hassium	Hs	108	(269)
Helium	He	2	4.003
Holmium	Ho	67	164.9
Hydrogen	H	1	1.008
Indium	In	49	114.8
Iodine	I	53	126.9
Iridium	Ir	77	192.2
Iron	Fe	26	55.85
Krypton	Kr	36	83.80
Lanthanum	La	57	138.9
Lawrencium	Lr	103	260.1
Lead	Pb	82	207.2
Lithium	Li	3	6.941
Lutetium	Lu	71	175.0
Magnesium	Mg	12	24.30
Manganese	Mn	25	54.94
Meitnerium	Mt	109	(268)
Mendelevium	Md	101	256.1
Mercury	Hg	80	200.6
Molybdenum	Mo	42	95.94
Neodymium	Nd	60	144.2
Neon	Ne	10	20.18
Neptunium	Np	93	237.0
Nickel	Ni	28	58.69
Niobium	Nb	41	92.91
Nitrogen	N	7	14.01
Nobelium	No	102	259.1
Osmium	Os	76	190.2
Oxygen	O	8	16.00
Palladium	Pd	46	106.4
Phosphorus	P	15	30.97

(table continues)

Table of Atomic Weights (Continued)

Name	Symbol	Atomic Number	Atomic Weight	Name	Symbol	Atomic Number	Atomic Weight
Platinum	Pt	78	195.1	Strontium	Sr	38	87.62
Plutonium	Pu	94	239.1	Sulfur	S	16	32.07
Polonium	Po	84	210.0	Tantalum	Ta	73	180.9
Potassium	K	19	39.10	Technetium	Tc	43	98.91
Praseodymium	Pr	59	140.9	Tellurium	Te	52	127.6
Promethium	Pm	61	144.9	Terbium	Tb	65	158.9
Protactinium	Pa	91	231.0	Thallium	Tl	81	204.4
Radium	Ra	88	226.0	Thorium	Th	90	232.0
Radon	Rn	86	222.0	Thulium	Tm	69	168.9
Rhenium	Re	75	186.2	Tin	Sn	50	118.7
Rhodium	Rh	45	102.9	Titanium	Ti	22	47.88
Roentgenium	Rg	111	(272)	Tungsten	W	74	183.8
Rubidium	Rb	37	85.47	Ununbium	Uub	112	(285)
Ruthenium	Ru	44	101.1	Ununquadium	Uuq	114	(289)
Rutherfordium	Rf	104	(261)	Ununtrium	Unt	113	284
Samarium	Sm	62	150.4	Uranium	U	92	238.0
Scandium	Sc	21	44.96	Vanadium	V	23	50.94
Seaborgium	Sg	106	(266)	Xenon	Xe	54	131.3
Selenium	Se	34	78.96	Ytterbium	Yb	70	173.0
Silicon	Si	14	28.09	Yttrium	Y	39	88.91
Silver	Ag	47	107.9	Zinc	Zn	30	65.39
Sodium	Na	11	22.99	Zirconium	Zr	40	91.22

[a] Names of elements 112–114 are temporary; official names and symbols must be approved by the International Union of Pure and Applied Chemistry.

AAAS (pronounced "triple-A S") See *American Association for the Advancement of Science.*
abiotic Nonliving. (Ch. 19)
absolute magnitude The brightness a star appears to have when it is viewed from a standard distance. (Ch. 14)
absolute zero The temperature, zero kelvins, at which no energy can be extracted from atoms; the coldest attainable temperature, which is equal to –273.16°C or –459.67°F. (Ch. 4)
absorption One of three possible responses of an electromagnetic wave encountering matter, in which light energy is converted into some other form, usually heat energy. See also *transmission* and *refraction.* (Ch. 6)
absorption line A dark line in an absorption spectrum that corresponds to the absorbed wavelength of light. (Ch. 8)
absorption spectrum The characteristic set of dark lines used to identify a chemical element or molecule from the photons absorbed by the material's atoms or molecules. (Ch. 8)
AC See *alternating current.*
acceleration The amount of change in velocity divided by the time it takes the change to occur. Acceleration can involve changes of speed, changes in direction, or both. (Ch. 2)
acid Any material that when put into water produces positively charged hydrogen ions (i.e., protons) in the solution; for example, lemon juice and hydrochloric acid. (Ch. 10)
acid rain A phenomenon that occurs when nitrogen and sulfur compounds in the air interact with water to form tiny droplets of nitric and sulfuric acid, which makes raindrops more acidic than normal. (Ch. 19)
acquired immune deficiency syndrome (AIDS) A disease caused by a virus known as the human immunodeficiency virus (HIV), which is transmitted by exchange of bodily fluids, most commonly in sexual contacts and the sharing of needles among drug abusers. (Ch. 24)
adaptation A structure, process, or behavior that helps an organism survive and pass its genes on to the next generation. (Ch. 25)
addition polymerization The formation of a polymer in which the basic building blocks are simply joined end to end; for example, polyethylene. (Ch. 10)
adenosine triphosphate (ATP) An energy-carrying molecule, found in a cell, that contains three phosphate groups, the sugar ribose, and the base adenine. (Ch. 21)
aerobic A process that requires the presence of oxygen; for example, respiration. (Ch. 21)
AIDS See *acquired immune deficiency syndrome.*
air pollution A serious environmental problem, with immediate consequences for urban residents, from the emission of NO_x compounds, sulfur dioxide, and hydrocarbons into the atmosphere. (Ch. 19)
algae Single-celled organisms (or simple multicelled ones) that carry out between 50% and 90% of Earth's photosynthesis. (Ch. 20)
alkali metals Elements that are highly reactive, such as lithium, sodium, and potassium; listed in the far lefthand column of the periodic table of elements. These elements possess one valence electron. (Ch. 8)
alkaline earth metals Elements that combine with oxygen in a one-to-one ratio and form colorless solid compounds with high melting temperatures. Listed in the second column in the periodic table of elements: beryllium, magnesium, calcium, and others. These elements possess two valence electrons. (Ch. 8)
alkane A family of molecules based on the methane molecule, which burn readily and are used as fuels. (Ch. 10)
alloy The combination of two or more chemical elements in the metallic state; for example, brass (a mixture of copper and zinc) or bronze (an alloy of copper and tin). (Ch. 10)
alpha decay The loss by an atom's nucleus of a large and massive particle composed of two protons and two neutrons. (Ch. 12)
alpha particle A subatomic radioactive particle, made of two protons and two neutrons, used by Ernest Rutherford in a well-known experiment in which the nucleus was discovered. (Ch. 8)
alternating current (AC) A type of electrical current, commonly used in household appliances and cars, in which charges alternate their direction of motion. (Ch. 5)
AM See *amplitude modulation.*
American Association for the Advancement of Science (AAAS) One of the largest scientific societies, representing all branches of the physical, biological, and social sciences. AAAS is a strong force in establishing science policy and promoting science education. (Ch. 1)
amino acid The building block of protein, incorporating a carboxyl group (COOH) at one end, an amino group (NH_2) at the other end, and a side group (which varies from one amino acid to the next). Ch. 21
amino group A group of atoms of nitrogen and hydrogen (NH_2) that forms one end of an amino acid. See *carboxyl group.* (Ch. 22)
amp See *ampere.*
ampere A unit of measurement for the amount of electrical current (number of charges) flowing in a wire or elsewhere per unit of time. (Ch. 5)
amphibians The first vertebrates adapted to live part of their lives on land; modern descendants include frogs, toads, and salamanders. (Ch. 20)

amplifier A device that takes a small current and converts it into a large one to do work. (Ch. 11)

amplitude modulation (AM) A process by which information is transmitted by varying the amplitude of a radio wave signal being transmitted. After transmission, the signal is converted to sound by the radio receiver. (Ch. 6)

amplitude The height of a wave crest above the undisturbed level of the medium. (Ch. 6)

anaerobic A process that can occur in the absence of oxygen; for example, fermentation. (Ch. 21)

angiosperm The class of vascular plants that flower. (Ch. 20)

animals Multicelled organisms that get their energy by eating other organisms; one of five kingdoms in the modern Linnaean classification. (Ch. 20)

annihilation A process that occurs when a particle collides with its antiparticle, completely converting both masses to energy. (Ch. 13)

antibiotic A medicine capable of destroying foreign bacteria in an organism. (Ch. 20)

antimatter Particles that have the same mass as their matter twins, but with an opposite charge, magnetic characteristics, and other properties. (Ch. 13)

apparent magnitude The brightness a star appears to have when it is viewed from Earth. (Ch. 14)

applied research The type of research performed by scientists with specific and practical goals in mind. This research is often translated into practical systems by large-scale research and development projects. (Ch. 1)

aquifer An underground body of stored water, often a layer of water-saturated rock bounded by impermeable materials. (Ch. 18)

arthropods All invertebrate animals with segmented bodies and jointed limbs. The most successful phylum in the animal kingdom in terms of numbers of species and total mass; includes insects, spiders, and crustacea. (Ch. 20)

artificial intelligence A field of research based on the idea that computers eventually will be able to perform all functions of thought that we normally think of as being distinctly human. (Ch. 11)

artificial selection The process of conscious breeding for specific characteristics in plants and animals. (Ch. 25)

asteroid belt A collection of small rocky planetesimals, located in a circular orbit between Mars and Jupiter, debris of material that never managed to collect into a single planet. (Ch. 15)

asteroids Small rocky objects, concentrated mostly in an asteroid belt between Mars and Jupiter, that circle the Sun like miniature planets. (Ch. 15)

astrobiology The scientific search for the origin and distribution of life in the universe. (Ch. 25)

astronomy The study of objects in the heavens. (Ch. 14)

atmospheric cycle The circulation of gases near Earth's surface, which includes the short-term variations of weather and the long-term variations of climate. (Ch. 18)

atom Fundamental building blocks for all matter; the smallest representative sample of an element. It consists of a positively charged nucleus surrounded by negatively charged electrons. (Ch. 8)

atomic number The number of protons in the nucleus, which determines the nuclear charge, and therefore the chemical identity of the atom. (Ch. 12)

atomism The hypothesis that for each chemical element there is a corresponding species of indivisible objects called atoms. (Ch. 8)

ATP See *adenosine triphosphate.*

Australopithecus The first hominid, a primate closer to humans than any other; lived approximately 4.5 to 1.5 million years ago, walked erect, and had a brain about the size of that of a modern chimpanzee. (Ch. 25)

autotroph A complex organism that is able to manufacture the essential building blocks of life from simple molecules. (Ch. 20)

axon The longest filament connecting one nerve cell to another, along which nerve signals move. (Ch. 5)

basalt A dense, dark, even-textured volcanic rock forming the oceanic plates; rich in oxides of silicon, magnesium, iron, calcium, and aluminum. (Ch. 17)

base A class of corrosive materials that when put into water produce negatively charged hydroxide ions; usually tastes bitter and feels slippery. (Ch. 10)

base load The steady day-to-day demand in the mass market of electricity. (Ch. 3)

base pair One of four possible bonding combinations of the bases adenine, thymine, guanine, and cytosine on the DNA molecule: AT, TA, GC, and CG. (Ch. 23)

basic research The type of research performed by scientists who are interested simply in finding out how the world works, in knowledge for its own sake. (Ch. 1)

battery A device that converts stored chemical energy into kinetic energy of charged particles (usually electrons) running through an outside wire. (Ch. 5)

beta decay A kind of radioactive decay in which a particle such as the neutron spontaneously transforms into a collection of particles that includes an electron. (Ch. 12)

big bang theory The idea that the universe began at a specific point in time and has been cooling and expanding ever since. (Ch. 15)

binomial nomenclature The two-part scientific name assigned to every organism that begins with the genus name and ends with the species name. (Ch. 20)

bioinformatics revolution The increased use of computers in biological experiments and scientific study. A term often used in reference to the Human Genome Project. (Ch. 23)

biology The branch of science devoted to the study of living systems. (Ch. 20)

biodiversity The number of different species that coexist at a given place. (Ch. 1)

biotic Living. (Ch. 19)

bird Modern descendant of reptiles with an anatomical adaptation to flight and feathers evolved from scales. (Ch. 20)

bit Binary digit: a unit of measurement for information equal to "yes-no" or "on-off." (Ch. 11)

black hole Formed at the death of a very large star, an object so dense, with a mass so concentrated, that nothing—not even light—can escape from its surface. (Ch. 14)

blue-green algae Also known as *cyanobacteria*. Single-celled organisms that are classified as monera, even though they carry on photosynthesis. (Ch. 20)

blueshift The result of the Doppler effect on light waves, when the source of light moves toward the observer: light-wave crests bunch up and have a higher frequency. (Ch. 6)

Bohr atom A model of the atom, developed by Niels Bohr in 1913, in which electrons exist only in allowed energy levels. In these energy levels, the electrons maintain fixed energy for long periods of time, without giving off radiation. (Ch. 8)

boiling A change of state from liquid to gas caused by an increase in temperature or decrease in pressure of the liquid, which speeds up the vibration of individual molecules of the liquid, allowing them to break free and form a gas. (Ch. 10)

bony fish A class of vertebrates that includes salmon, perch, and other fish with bone skeletons. (Ch. 20)

brain The central organ of the human nervous system, which receives signals from sense organs, as well as signals that keep it apprised of the status of internal organs. It sends out signals to keep the body functioning, and serves as the seat for all higher functions, such as thought and speech. (App. A)

Brownian motion A phenomenon that describes the rapid, random movements caused by atomic collisions of very small objects suspended in a liquid. (Ch. 8)

bryophyte The phylum of primitive terrestrial plants, including mosses, that can use photosynthesis, are anchored to the ground by rhizoids, and absorb water directly through aboveground structures. (Ch. 20)

byte In a computer, a group of eight switches storing eight bits of information; the basic information unit of most modern computers. (Ch. 11)

c The speed of light and other electromagnetic radiation; a constant whose value is 300,000 kilometers per second (about 186,000 miles per second), equal to the product of the wavelength and frequency of an electromagnetic wave. (Ch. 6)

calorie A common unit of energy defined as the amount of heat required to raise 1 gram of room-temperature water 1 degree Celsius in temperature. (Ch. 4)

Cambrian explosion The sudden change in life on Earth, well-documented in the fossil record, when hard-bodied organisms first appeared about 545 million years ago. (Ch. 25)

Cambrian period The geological period, beginning about 545 million years ago, during which animals first began to develop shells and skeletons. (Ch. 25)

cancer A type of disease characterized by the uncontrolled growth of cells in the body. (Ch. 24)

carbohydrate A class of modular molecules made from carbon, hydrogen, and oxygen that form the solid structure of living things and play a central role in how living things acquire oxygen. (Ch. 22)

carbon cycle The cycle a carbon molecule may undergo in an ecosystem. For example, it may start in the atmosphere, be taken in by a producer, then a eaten by a consumer. When the consumer dies, it is broken down by a decomposer, at which point the carbon molecule is released back into the atmosphere. (Ch. 19)

carboxyl group A group of atoms of carbon, hydrogen, and oxygen (COOH) that forms one end of an amino acid string. See *amino group*. (Ch. 22)

carnivore Animals that get their energy by eating organisms in the second trophic level. (Ch. 3)

CAT See *computerized axial tomography*.

cell A complex chemical system with the ability to duplicate itself; the fundamental unit of life. (Ch. 21)

cell membrane A structure, formed from bilayers of lipids, that separates the inside of a cell from the outside, or separates one part of a cell from another. (Ch. 21)

cell theory The theory that holds that all living things are made up of cells, the cell is the fundamental unit of life, and all cells arise from previous cells. (Ch. 21)

cell wall A solid framework made from cellulose molecules and other strong polymers, by which plant cells are separated from one another. (Ch. 21)

cellulose A long, stringy polymer that is the main structural element in plants but cannot be digested by humans. (Ch. 22)

Celsius scale A temperature scale that measures 0 and 100 degrees as the freezing and boiling points of water, respectively. (Ch. 4)

Cenozoic Era The fourth era, which began 65 million years ago and continues to the present day, also known as "new life." The time when mammals proliferated and began to dominate Earth. (Ch. 25)

central processing unit (CPU) The part of a computer in which transistors store and manipulate relatively small amounts of information at any one time. (Ch. 11)

Cepheid variable A type of star with a regular behavior of steady brightening and dimming, which is related to the star's luminosity. Cepheid variables are used to calculate distances to many millions of light-years. (Ch. 14)

ceramics A broad class of hard, durable solids, ranging from rocks and minerals to bones. (Ch. 10)

CFCs See *chlorofluorocarbons*.

chain reaction The process in a nuclear reactor in which nuclei undergoing fission produce neutrons that will cause more splitting, resulting in the release of large amounts of energy. (Ch. 12)

change of state Transition between the solid, liquid, and gas states caused by changes in temperature and pressure. The processes involved are freezing and melting (for solids and liquids), boiling and condensation (for liquids and gases), and sublimation (for solids and gases). (Ch. 10)

chaos A field of study modeling systems in nature that can be described in Newtonian terms but whose futures are, for all practical purposes, unpredictable; for example, the turbulent flow of water or the beating of a human heart. (Ch. 2)

chemical bond The attraction that results from the redistribution of electrons between two or more atoms, leading to a more stable configuration—particularly by filling the outer electron shells—and that holds the two atoms together. The principal kinds of chemical bonds are ionic, covalent, and metallic. (Ch. 10)

chemical evolution An area of research concerned with the process by which simple chemical compounds present in Earth's early atmosphere became an organized, reproducing cell. (Ch. 25)

chemical potential energy The type of energy that is stored in the chemical bonds between atoms, such as the energy in flashlight batteries. (Ch. 3)

chemical reaction The process by which atoms or smaller molecules come together to form large molecules, or by which larger molecules are broken down into smaller ones; involves the rearrangement of atoms in elements and compounds, as well as the rearrangement of electrons to form chemical bonds. (Ch. 10)

chlorofluorocarbons (CFCs) A class of stable and generally nonreactive chemicals widely used in refrigerators and air-conditioners until the late 1980s. See *ozone hole*. (Ch. 19)

chlorophyll A molecule, found in the chloroplasts of plant cells, that absorbs energy from sunlight and uses the energy to transform atmospheric carbon dioxide and water into energy-rich sugar molecules such as glucose and oxygen (as a byproduct). (Ch. 21)

chloroplasts The main energy transformation organelles in plant cells; places where the molecules of chlorophyll are found and photosynthesis occurs. (Ch. 21)

cholesterol An essential component of the cell membrane synthesized by the body from saturated fats in the diet; in high levels, can cause fatty deposits that clog arteries. (Ch. 22)

chordate A phylum of animals with a thickened set of nerves down their backs; includes the subphylum vertebrates. (Ch. 20)

chromosomes A long strand of the DNA double helix, with the strand wrapped around a series of protein cores. (Ch. 21)

chromosphere One of the Sun's outer layers, visible for a few minutes as a spectacular halo during a total eclipse of the Sun. (Ch. 14)

circulatory system The system that distributes blood through the body; includes the blood vessels and the heart. (App. A)

class The third broadest classification in the Linnaean classification system; humans are in the class of mammals. (Ch. 20)

classical genetics The laws developed from the observations of Gregor Mendel: (1) traits are passed from parent to offspring by genes, (2) each parent contributes one gene for each trait, and (3) genes are either dominant or recessive. (Ch. 23)

climate The average weather conditions of a place or area over a period of years. (Ch. 18)

cloning The process of engineering a new individual entirely from the genetic material in a cell from another individual. A clone is genetically identical to the cell donor. (Ch. 24)

closed ecosystem An ecosystem through which energy will flow but material will cycle. (Ch. 19)

closed system A type of system in which matter and energy are not freely exchanged with the surroundings; an isolated system. (Ch. 3)

closed universe A universe in which the expansion will someday reverse because the universe holds enough matter to exert a strong enough gravitational force to reverse the motion of receding galaxies. (Ch. 15)

cloud A concentration of tiny water droplets or ice crystals, which form when the air becomes saturated with water. (Ch. 18)

cloudiness A weather variable caused by the formation of clouds as air masses rise and fall and the air is saturated with water. (Ch.18)

cluster A collection of galaxies. (Ch. 15)

COBE See *Cosmic Background Explorer.*

codon The set of three bases on mRNA that determines which of the possible tRNA molecules will attach at that point, and which amino acid will appear in a protein. (Ch. 23)

cold-blooded Animals, such as amphibians and reptiles, that must absorb heat from their environment to maintain body temperature. (Ch. 20)

combustion A rapid combination with oxygen, producing heat and flame (Ch. 10)

comet An object, usually found outside the orbit of Pluto, composed of chunks of materials such as water ice and methane ice embedded with dirt. A comet may fall toward the Sun, if its distant orbit is disturbed, and create a spectacular display in the night sky. (Ch. 16)

compass A needle-shaped magnet designed to point at the poles of Earth's magnetic field. (Ch. 5)

complexity A new branch of science that studies systems in which many agents act on, and are affected by, other agents. Ecosystems, stock markets, and the human brain are examples of complex systems. (Ch. 20)

composite material A combination of two or more substances in which the strength of one of the constituents is used to offset the weakness of another, resulting in a new material whose strengths are greater than any of its components; for example, plywood and reinforced concrete. (Ch. 11)

compressional wave One of two principal types of seismic waves, in which the molecules in rock move back and forth in the same direction as the wave; a longitudinal wave. (Ch. 17)

compressive strength A material's ability to withstand crushing. (Ch. 11)

computer A machine that stores and manipulates information. (Ch. 11)

computer-assisted drug design An approach to developing new drugs that relies on computers to predict the shapes, and therefore the behavior, of molecules. (Ch. 24)

computerized axial tomography (CAT) A scan that uses high-energy photons to produce a three-dimensional picture of the interior of the body and that uses a computer to quantify the density of each point of the body where the photons make contact. (Ch. 9)

community Organisms that interact to sustain life, including producers, consumers, and decomposers. (Ch. 19)

condensation A change of state from gas to liquid caused by a decrease in temperature or pressure of the gas, which slows down the vibration of individual molecules of the gas, allowing them to form a liquid. (Ch. 10)

condensation polymerization A chemical reaction often used to manufacture plastics and other polymers, and which, in the body, occurs during the formation of a peptide bond. (Ch. 10)

condensation reaction The formation of a polymer in which each new polymer bond releases a water molecule as the ends of the original polymer molecules link up. (Ch. 10)

conduction The movement of heat by collisions between vibrating atoms or molecules; one of three mechanisms by which heat moves. (Ch. 4)

conduction electron An electron in a material that is able to move in an electrical field. (Ch. 11)

conductor A material capable of carrying an electrical current; any material through which electrons can flow freely. (Ch. 11)

cone A light-absorbing cell in the eye, which is sensitive to red, blue, or green light, enabling color vision. Compare to *rod*. (Ch. 6)

conservation law Any statement that says that a quantity in nature does not change. (Ch. 3)

constructive interference A situation in which two waves act together to reinforce or maximize the wave height at the point of intersection. (Ch. 6)

consumers Organisms, such as animals, that sustain life from the carbon-based molecules created by producer organisms in an ecosystem. (Ch. 19)

continental drift A theory that states that Earth's continents are in motion and are, therefore, not fixed. Continental drift is part of the modern theory of plate tectonics. (Ch. 17)

convection The transfer of heat by the physical motion of masses of fluid. Dense, cooler fluids (liquids and gases) descend in bulk and displace rising warmer fluids, which are less dense. One of three mechanisms by which heat moves. (Ch. 4)

convection cell A region in a fluid in which heat is continuously being transferred by a bulk motion of heated fluid from a heat source to the surface of the fluid, where heat is released. The cooled fluid then sinks and the cycle repeats. (Ch. 4)

convection zone The outer region of the Sun, comprising the upper 200,000 km (about 125,000 mi) where the dominant energy transfer mechanism changes from collision to convection. (Ch. 14)

convergent plate boundary A place where two tectonic plates are coming together. (Ch. 17)

core (*a*) In geology, the heaviest elements of Earth's mass, primarily iron and nickel, concentrated at the center with a radius of about 3400 km (2000 mi). (*b*) In astronomy, a small region in the center of a star where hydrogen burning is generally confined. (Ch. 14, Ch. 17)

corona One of the Sun's outer layers, visible for a few minutes as a spectacular halo during a total eclipse of the Sun. (Ch. 14)

Cosmic Background Explorer (COBE) An orbiting observatory that measures the presence of microwave radiation present as background noise in every direction of the sky. (Ch. 14)

cosmic microwave background radiation Microwave radiation, characteristic of a body at about 3 K, falling to Earth from all directions. This radiation is evidence for the big bang. (Ch. 15)

cosmic rays Particles (mostly protons) that rain down continuously on Earth's atmosphere after being emitted by stars in our galaxy and in others. (Ch. 13)

cosmology The branch of science that is devoted to the study of the structure and history of the entire universe. (Ch. 15)

coulomb (pronounced "*koo*-loam") The unit for measuring the magnitude of an electrical charge. (Ch. 5)

Coulomb's law An empirically derived rule that states that the magnitude of the electrostatic force between any two objects is proportional to the charges of the two objects, and inversely proportional to the square of the distance between them. (Ch. 5)

covalent bond A chemical bond in which neighboring molecules share electrons in a strongly bonded group of at least two atoms. (Ch. 10)

CPU See *central processing unit*.

critical mass The minimum number of uranium-235 atoms needed to sustain a nuclear chain reaction to the point where large amounts of energy can be released. (Ch. 12)

crust A thin layer at Earth's surface formed from the lightest elements, ranging in thickness from 10 km (6 mi) in parts of the ocean to 70 km (45 mi) beneath parts of the continents. (Ch. 16)

crystal A group of atoms that occur in a regularly repeating sequence. Crystal structure is described by first determining the size and shape of the repeating boxlike group of atoms and then recording the exact type and position of every atom that appears in the box. (Ch. 10)

current A river of moving water on an ocean's surface, found in each of the ocean basins. (Ch. 18)

cyclone A great rotational pattern in the atmosphere, hundreds of kilometers in diameter, that can draw energy from warm oceanic waters and create low-pressure tropical storms. (Ch. 18)

cyclotron The first of the particle accelerators, for which Ernest Lawrence won the 1939 Nobel prize in physics. (Ch. 13)

cytoplasm The fluid that takes up the spaces between the organelles of a cell. (Ch. 21)

cytoskeleton A series of protein filaments that extend throughout the cell, giving the cell a shape and, in some cases, allowing it to move. (Ch. 21)

dark matter Material that exists in forms that do not interact with electromagnetic radiation and that may constitute 90% of the matter of the universe. (Ch. 15)

DC See *direct current.*

decay chain A series of decays, or radioactive events, ending with a stable isotope. (Ch. 12)

decomposers Organisms, such as bacteria and fungi, that renew the raw materials of life in an ecosystem. (Ch. 19)

deep-ocean trench A surface feature associated with convergent plate boundaries in which no continents are on the leading edge of either of the two converging plates and one plate penetrates deep into Earth. (Ch. 17)

dendrite One of a thousand projections on each nerve cell in the brain through which nerve signals move; each is connected to different neighboring nerve cells in the brain. (Ch. 5)

deoxyribonucleic acid (DNA) A strand of nucleotides with alternating phosphate and sugar molecules in a long chain, and with base molecules adenine, guanine, cytosine, and thymine at the side. The nucleotide strand bonds with a second nucleotide strand to make a molecule with a ladderlike double helix shape. DNA stores the genetic information in a cell. (Ch. 23)

deoxyribose The five-carbon sugar lacking one oxygen atom in deoxyribonucleic acid (DNA). (Ch. 23)

depolymerization The breakdown of a polymer into short segments. (Ch. 10)

destructive interference A situation in which two waves intersect in a way that decreases or cancels out the wave height at the point of intersection. (Ch. 6)

diatomic The simplest molecules, containing two atoms of the same element, such as the diatomic gases hydrogen (H_2), nitrogen (N_2), and oxygen (O_2). (Ch. 10)

differentiation The process by which heavy, dense materials (such as iron and nickel) sank under the force of gravity toward the molten center of the planet, while lighter, less dense materials floated to the top, resulting in the layered structure of the present-day Earth. (Ch. 16)

diffuse scattering A process by which light waves are absorbed and reemitted in all directions by a medium such as clouds or snow. (Ch. 6)

diffusion The transfer of molecules from regions of high concentration by ordinary random thermal motion. (Ch. 21)

digestive system The parts of the body that are responsible for breaking down food so that its stored energy can be used by cells; includes the stomach, small intestine, liver, pancreas, and gall bladder. (App. A)

diode An electronic device that allows electrical current to flow in only one direction. (Ch. 11)

dipole field The magnetic field that arises from the two poles of a magnet. (Ch. 5)

direct current (DC) A type of electrical current in which the electrons flow in one direction only; for example, in the chemical reaction of a battery. (Ch. 5)

distillation A process by which engineers separate the complex mixture of petroleum's organic chemicals into much purer fractions. (Ch. 10)

divergent plate boundary A spreading zone of crustal formation; a place where neighboring plates move away from each other. (Ch. 17)

Divine Calculator An eighteenth-century idea, proposed by Pierre Simon Laplace, which stated that if the position and velocity of every atom in the universe is known, with infinite computational power, the future position and velocity of every atom in the universe could be predicted. (Ch. 2)

DNA See *deoxyribonucleic acid.*

DNA fingerprinting A procedure by which DNA in human tissue is used to match the tissue to an individual. This technique is becoming increasingly important in the judicial system in the United States. (Ch. 24)

DNA mapping The process of finding the location of genes on chromosomes. (Ch. 23)

DNA sequencing The process of determining, base pair by base pair, the exact order of bases along a specific stretch of a DNA molecule. (Ch. 23)

domain Region in magnetic material where neighboring atoms line up with each other to give a strong magnetic field. (Ch. 11)

dominant A genetic characteristic that always appears, or is expressed. (Ch. 23)

doping The addition of a minor impurity to a semiconductor. (Ch. 11)

Doppler effect The change in frequency or wavelength of a wave detected by an observer because the source of the wave is moving. (Ch. 6)

double-blind clinical trial A procedure for testing the effectiveness of new medical treatments. A group of patients is separated into two sections; half the people will be given the new treatment while the other half will be given a placebo. (Ch. 24)

double bond The type of covalent bond formed when two electrons are shared by two atoms. (Ch. 10)

double helix The twisted double strand of nucleotides that forms the structure of the DNA molecule. (Ch. 23)

ear A sense organ that includes a membrane that vibrates at the arrival of sound waves. (App. A)

earthquake Disturbance caused when stressed rock on Earth suddenly snaps, converting potential energy into released kinetic energy. (Ch. 17)

ecological niche The habitat, functional role(s), requirements for environmental resources, and tolerance ranges within an ecosystem. (Ch. 19)

ecology The branch of science that studies interactions among organisms as well as the interactions of organisms and their environment. (Ch. 19)

ecosystem Interdependent collections of living things; includes the plants and animals that live in a given area together with their physical surroundings. (See *open ecosystem* and *closed ecosystem*.) (Ch. 19)

efficiency The amount of work you get from an engine, divided by the amount of energy you put in; a quantification of the loss of useful energy. (Ch. 4)

El Niño A weather cycle in the Pacific basin that recurs every four to seven years and can cause severe storms and flooding all along the western coast of the Americas, as well as drought from Australia to India. (Ch. 18)

elastic limit The point at which a material stops resisting external forces and begins to deform permanently. (Ch. 11)

elastic potential energy The type of energy that is stored in a flexed muscle, a coiled spring, and a stretched rubber band. (Ch. 3)

electric circuit An unbroken path of material that carries electricity and consists of three parts: a source of energy, a closed path, and a device to use the energy. (Ch. 5)

electrical current A flow of charged particles, measured in amperes. (Ch. 5)

electrical field The force that would be exerted on a positive charge at a position near a charged object. Every charged object is surrounded by an electric field. (Ch. 5)

electric generator A source of energy producing an alternating current in an electric circuit through the use of electromagnetic induction. (Ch. 5)

electric motor A device that operates by supplying current to an electromagnet to make the magnet move and generate mechanical power. Many motors employ permanent magnets and rotating loops of wire inside the poles of this magnet. (Ch. 5)

electrical charge An excess or deficit of electrons on an object. (Ch. 5)

electrical conductivity The ease with which a material allows electrons to flow. The inverse of electrical resistance. (Ch. 11)

electrical conductor Any material capable of carrying electrical current. (Ch. 11)

electrical insulator Material that will not conduct electricity. (Ch. 11)

electrical potential energy The type of energy that is found in a battery or between two wires at different voltages; energy associated with the position of a charge in an electric field. (Ch. 3)

electrical resistance The quantity, measured in ohms, that represents how hard it is to push electrons through a material. High-resistance wires are used when electron energy is to be converted into heat energy. Low-resistance wires are used when energy is to be transmitted from one place to another with minimum loss. (Ch. 5)

electricity A force, more powerful than gravity, that moves objects both toward and away from each other, depending upon the charge. (Ch. 5)

electroweak force A force resulting from the unification of the electromagnetic and weak forces. (Ch. 13)

electromagnet A device that produces a magnetic field from a moving electrical charge. (Ch. 5)

electromagnetic force A term used to refer to the unified nature of electricity and magnetism. (Ch. 5)

electromagnetic induction A process by which a changing magnetic field produces an electrical current in a conductor, even though there is no other source of power available. (Ch. 5)

electromagnetic radiation See *electromagnetic wave.*

electromagnetic spectrum The entire array of waves, varying in frequency and wavelength, but all resulting from an accelerating electrical charge; includes radio waves, microwaves, infrared, visible light, ultraviolet, X-rays, gamma rays, and others. (Ch. 6)

electromagnetic wave A form of radiant energy that reacts with matter by being transmitted, absorbed, or scattered. A self-propagating wave made up of electric and magnetic fields fluctuating together. A wave created when electrical charges accelerate, but requiring no medium for transfer. Electromagnetic radiation. (Ch. 6)

electron Tiny, negatively charged particles that surround a positively charged nucleus of an atom. (Ch. 5)

electron microscope An instrument, introduced in the 1930s, that was a major new advance in microscopes because it used electrons instead of light to illuminate objects and had resolving power up to 100,000 times that of the optical microscope. (Ch. 21)

electron shell A specific energy level in an atom that can be filled with a predetermined number of electrons. (Ch. 8)

electrostatic The type of electrical charge that doesn't move once it has been placed on an object, and the forces exerted by such a charge. (Ch. 5)

electroweak force The force resulting from the unification of the electromagnetic and weak force. (Ch. 13)

element A material made from a single type of atom, which cannot be broken down any further. (Ch. 8)

elementary-particle physics The study of particles that are believed to comprise the basic building blocks of the universe; for example, the particles that make up the nucleus, and particles such as electrons. Also known as high-energy physics. (Ch. 13)

elementary particles Particles that make up the nucleus, together with particles such as the electron; the basic building blocks of the universe. (Ch. 13)

ELF radiation Extremely low-frequency waves associated with the movement of electrons to produce the alternating current in household wires. (Ch. 6)

embryonic stem cell A cell that is totipotent and able to develop into any of the specialized cells that will later appear in the adult organism. (Ch. 24)

emission spectrum The characteristic set of lines used to identify a chemical element or molecule from the total collection of photons emitted during quantum leaps. (Ch. 8)

emitter The region in a transistor that first receives an electrical current. (Ch. 11)

endocrine system A group of glands that secrete hormones that are taken by the bloodstream to produce specific chemical effects; part of the body's control system. See *nervous system*. (App. A)

endoplasmic reticulum One of the cellular organelles that contribute to protein and lipid synthesis. (Ch. 21)

endothermic A chemical reaction in which the final energy of the electrons in the reaction is greater than the initial energy; energy must be supplied to make the reaction proceed. (Ch. 10)

energy The ability to do work; the capacity to exert a force over a distance. A system's energy can be measured in joules or foot-pounds. (Ch. 3)

entropy The thermodynamic quantity that describes the degree of randomness of a system. The greater the disorder or randomness, the higher the statistical probability of the state, and the higher the entropy. (Ch. 4)

environment The nonliving chemical and physical parts of an ecosystem, including the water, soil, and atmosphere. (Ch. 19)

enzyme A molecule that facilitates reactions between two other molecules, but which is not itself altered or taken up in the overall reaction. (Ch. 22)

essential amino acid One of the 8 amino acids that cannot be synthesized by the body and have to be consumed. (Ch. 22)

eukaryote An advanced single-celled organism and all multicelled organisms that are made from cells containing a nucleus. (Ch. 21)

evolution An ongoing process of change. There are various theories of evolution that differ in regard to how fast it proceeds and by what mechanisms. (Ch. 25)

excited state All energy levels of an atom above the ground state. (Ch. 8)

exothermic A chemical reaction in which the final energy of the electrons is less than the initial energy, and therefore energy is given off in some form. (Ch. 10)

experiment The manipulation of some aspect of nature to observe the outcome. (Ch. 1)

experimentalist A scientist who manipulates nature with controlled experiments. (Ch. 1)

extinct Species that have lived on Earth and have died out. Scientists estimate that for every species on the planet today, 999 species have become extinct. (Ch. 25)

extinction The disappearance of a species on Earth (Ch. 25)

extrasolar planet Any planet that exists outside of Earth's solar system. (Ch. 16)

extrusive rock See *volcanic rock*.

eye The most important of the five sense organs through which human beings become aware of their environment. (Ch. 6)

Fahrenheit scale A temperature scale that measures 32 and 212 degrees as the freezing and boiling points of water, respectively. (Ch. 4)

falsifiability A property of the scientific method that states that every theory and law of nature is subject to change, based on new observations. (Ch. 1)

family A grouping of similar genera in the Linnaean classification system; humans are in the family of hominids. (Ch. 20)

fat-soluble vitamin A vitamin that can be stored in the body, including vitamins A, D, E, and K. (Ch. 22)

fault A fracture in a rock along which movement occurs. (Ch. 17)

fermentation An anaerobic cellular process in which pyruvic acids are broken down and the energy is used by the cell to keep glycolysis going. (Ch. 21)

fern Primitive vascular plants that reproduce by producing sperm that must swim through water to fertilize eggs and generate spores. (Ch. 20)

ferromagnetism The property of a few materials in nature, such as iron, cobalt, and nickel metals, in which the individual atomic magnets are arranged in a nonrandom manner, lined up with each other into small magnetic domains to produce a small magnetic field. (Ch. 11)

field The force—magnetic, gravitational, or electrical—that would be felt at a particular point. For example, forces exerted by one object that would be felt by another object in the same region. (Ch. 5)

field researcher A scientist who works in natural settings to observe nature. (Ch. 1)

first law of thermodynamics The law of the conservation of energy. In an isolated system, the total amount of energy, including heat energy, is conserved. (Ch. 3)

first trophic level All plants that produce energy from photosynthesis. (Ch. 3)

fission A reaction that produces energy when heavy radioactive nuclei split apart into fragments that together have less mass than the original isotopes. (Ch. 12)

flat universe A model of the future of the universe in which the expansion slows and comes to a halt after infinite time has passed. (Ch. 15)

fluorescence A phenomenon in which energy contained in ultraviolet wavelengths is absorbed by the atoms in some materials and partially emitted as visible light, or "black light." (Ch. 6)

FM See *frequency modulation.*

food chain, or food web A complete set of pathways by which animals in an ecosystem obtain their energy and raw materials. (Ch. 3)

foot-pound The amount of work done by a force of one pound acting through one foot; the unit of energy in the English system. (Ch. 3)

force A push or pull that, acting alone, causes a change in acceleration of the object on which it acts. (Ch. 2)

fossil Evidence of past life preserved in rocks; notably when atoms in the hard parts of the buried organism are replaced by minerals in the water flowing through the surrounding area. (Ch. 25)

fossil fuel Carbon-rich deposits of ancient life that burn with a hot flame and have been the most important energy source for 150 years. Examples include coal, oil, and natural gas. (Ch. 3)

fossil record A term that refers to all of the fossils that have been found, catalogued, and studied since human beings first began to study them in a systematic way. (Ch. 25)

frames of reference The physical surroundings from which a person observes and measures the world. (Ch. 7)

freezing A change of state from liquid to solid caused by a decrease in temperature or increase in pressure of the liquid, which slows the vibration of individual molecules and forms the solid structure. (Ch. 10)

frequency The number of wave crests that go by a given point every second. A wave completing one cycle (sending one crest by a point every second) has a frequency of one hertz, 1 Hz. (Ch. 6)

frequency modulation (FM) A process by which information is transmitted by varying the frequency of a signal. After being transmitted, the signal may be converted to sound by circuits in a receiver. (Ch. 6)

fungi One of the five kingdoms in the Linnaean classification, organisms that obtain energy by absorbing materials through filaments and reproduce by production of spores. May be single-celled (e.g., yeasts) or multicellular (e.g, mushrooms). (Ch. 20)

fusion A process in which two nuclei come together to form a third, larger nucleus. When this reaction combines light elements to make heavier ones, the mass of the final nucleus may be less than the mass of its constituent parts. The "missing" nuclear mass can be converted into energy. (Ch. 12)

g A constant numerical value for the specific acceleration that all objects experience at Earth's surface, determined by measuring the actual fall rate of objects in a laboratory. It is equal to $9.8\ m/s^2$, or $32\ feet/s^2$. (Ch. 2)

G See *gravitational constant.*

galaxy A large assembly of stars (between millions and hundreds of billions), together with gas, dust, and other materials, that is held together by the forces of mutual gravitational attraction. (Ch. 15)

gametes Sex cells that are formed when a single cell splits into four daughter cells during the process of cell division called meiosis, each gamete processing half the number of chromosomes that normal cells have. (Ch. 21)

gamma radiation A kind of radioactivity involving the emission of energetic electromagnetic radiation from the nucleus of an atom, with no change to the number of protons or neutrons in the atom. (Ch. 12)

gamma ray The highest-energy wave of the electromagnetic spectrum with wavelengths less than the size of an atom, less than one-trillionth of a meter; normally emitted in very high-energy nuclear particle reactions. (Ch. 6)

Gamma Ray Observatory (GRO) An orbiting observatory that detects the highest-energy end of the electromagnetic spectrum, gamma rays. It was one of the first permanent orbiting observatories launched by NASA's Great Observatories Program for monitoring in all parts of the electromagnetic spectrum. (Ch. 14)

gas Any collection of atoms or molecules that expands to take that shape and fill the volume available in its container. (Ch. 10)

gauge particles Particles whose exchange produces the fundamental forces that hold everything together; corresponds to every force between two particles. (Ch. 13)

GCM See *global circulation models.*

gene A unit of biological inheritance, or a section of a long molecule of DNA. One gene carries the information needed to assemble one protein. (Ch. 23)

gene therapy A promising future technology that involves replacing a defective gene with a healthy one. (Ch. 24)

general relativity The second and more complex of two parts of Einstein's theory of relativity, which applies to any reference frames whether or not those frames are accelerating relative to each other. (Ch. 7)

genetic code The correspondence between base-pair sequences and amino acids. The connection, in all living things, between the codons and the amino acid for which they code. (Ch. 23)

genetic disease A hereditary mutation that can cause sickness or death; for example, hemophilia. (Ch. 23)

genetic engineering A technology in which foreign genes are inserted into an organism, or existing genes altered, to modify the function of living things. (Ch. 24)

genetics The study of ways in which biological information is passed from one generation to the next. (Ch. 23)

genome The sum of all information contained in the DNA for any living thing; the sequence of all the bases in all the chromosomes. (Ch. 23)

genus A grouping of similar species in the Linnaean classification system; humans are in the genus *Homo*. (Ch. 20)

glacier A large body of ice that slowly flows down a slope or valley under the influence of gravity; found primarily in Greenland and Antarctica. (Ch. 18)

glass A solid with predictable local environments for most atoms, but no long-range order to the atomic structure. Compared to crystal, glass lacks the repeating unit of atoms. (Ch. 10)

global circulation models (GCM) Complex computer models of the atmosphere that are the best attempts to date to predict long-term climate and to discuss various types of ecological changes such as global warming. (Ch. 18)

global warming A change in average global temperature and in the temperature gradient between equator and poles that could result from the temperature increase owing to the greenhouse effect (Ch. 19)

glucose An important sugar ($C_6H_{12}O_6$) in the energy cycle of living things, figuring prominently in the energy metabolism of every living cell. (Ch. 22)

gluon A massless particle, confined to the interior of particles, that mediates the force holding quarks together. (Ch. 13)

glycogen A glucose polymer that is formed in animals and stored in the liver and muscle tissues. Also called *animal starch*. (Ch. 22)

glycolysis The first step in the extraction of energy from glucose, which takes place in nine separate steps, each of which is governed by a specific enzyme, and which splits each glucose molecule into two smaller molecules called pyruvic acids. (Ch. 21)

gneiss The metamorphic rock formed from slate under extreme temperature and pressure. (Ch. 18)

Golgi apparatus One of the cellular organelles that takes part in the synthesis of molecules (Ch. 21)

gradualism A hypothesis that holds that most evolutionary change occurs as a result of the accumulation of small adaptations. (Ch. 25)

granite A rock that is lower in density than the mantle rock it caps, and which forms much of the continents. (Ch. 17)

gravitational constant (*G*) A universal constant that expresses the exact numerical relation between the masses of two objects and their separation, on the one hand, and the force between them on the other; equal to 6.67×10^{-11} N-m^2/kg^2. (Ch. 2)

gravitational escape One way that a planet's atmosphere can evolve and change. Molecules in the atmosphere heated by the Sun may move sufficiently fast so that appreciable fractions of them can actually escape the gravitational pull of their planet. (Ch. 16)

gravitational potential energy Energy associated with the position of a mass in a gravitational field. The gravitational potential energy of an object on Earth's surface equals its weight (the force of gravity exerted by the object) times its height above the ground. (Ch. 3)

graviton The gauge particle of gravity. (Ch. 13)

gravity An attractive force that acts on every object in the universe. (Ch. 2)

great bombardment An event following the initial period of planetary formation in which meteorites showered down on planets, adding matter and heat energy. (Ch. 16)

greenhouse effect A global temperature increase caused by the fact that Earth's atmospheric gases trap some of the Sun's infrared (heat) energy before it radiates out into space. (Ch. 19)

GRO See *Gamma Ray Observatory*.

ground state. The lowest energy level of an atom. (Ch. 8)

groundwater Fresh water from the surface, which typically percolates into the ground and fills the tiny spaces between grains of sandstone and other porous rock layers. (Ch. 18)

gymnosperm The class of vascular plants that produce seeds without flowers, such as fir trees. (Ch. 20)

gyre A circulation of water at the surface of the ocean, transporting warm water from the equator toward the cooler poles, and cold water from the poles back to the equator to be heated and cycled again. (Ch. 18)

hadron Particles, including the proton and neutron, that are made from quarks and are subject to the strong force. (Ch. 13)

half-life The rate of radioactive decay measured by the time it takes for half of a collection of isotopes to decay into another element. (Ch. 12)

heat (thermal energy) A measure of the quantity of atomic kinetic energy contained in every object. (Ch. 3)

heat conductor An object that allows heat to flow through it, such as metal. (Ch. 4)

heat insulator An object that impedes the flow of heat, such as wood. (Ch. 4)

heat transfer The process by which heat moves from one place to another, through three different mechanisms: conduction, convection, or radiation. (Ch. 4)

helium burning The final energy-producing stage of a star in which the temperature in the interior becomes so hot that the helium begins to undergo nuclear fusion reactions to make carbon. The net reaction is: $^4He + ^4He + ^4He \rightarrow ^{12}C$. (Ch. 14)

herbivore Animals that get their energy by eating plants of the first trophic level. (Ch. 3)

hertz (Hz) The unit of measurement for the frequency of waves; one wave cycle per second. (Ch. 6)

Hertzsprung-Russell (H-R) diagram A simple graphical technique widely used in astronomy to plot a star's temperature (determined by its spectrum) versus the star's energy output (measured by its energy and brightness). (Ch. 14)

heterotrophs Organisms that must consume the essential building blocks of life from the surrounding environment to survive. (Ch. 20)

hierarchy A system that organizes all species based on shared and differing qualities into categories within a larger framework. (Ch. 20)

high-energy physics See *elementary-particle physics.*

high-grade energy Sources of energy that can be used to produce very high-temperature reservoirs; for example, petroleum and coal. (Ch. 4)

high-level nuclear waste The radioactive materials with long half-lives that remain in the nuclear reactor when uranium-235 has been used to generate energy. (Ch. 12)

high-quality protein Foods that supply amino acids in roughly the same proportion as those in human proteins, such as meat and dairy products. (Ch. 22)

high-temperature reservoir Any hot object from which energy is extracted to do work. Within the cylinder of a gasoline engine is a high-temperature reservoir. (Ch. 4)

HIV See *human immunodeficiency virus.*

hole The absence of an electron; in a silicon crystal, for example, a hole is left behind after the conduction electron is shaken loose. (Ch. 11)

homeostasis A balance among the populations of an ecosystem, resulting from the fact that matter and energy are limited resources that must be shared among all individuals of an ecosystem. (Ch. 19)

hominid The family of the order primate whose members walk erect; includes humans, which are the only hominids that are not extinct. (Ch. 20)

Homo erectus ("man the erect") The species of modern human's genus who first walked erect and learned to use fire; disappeared about 500,000 years ago. (Ch. 25)

Homo habilus ("man the toolmaker") The first member of the genus of modern humans who appeared about 2 million years ago in East Africa; distinguished by a larger brain and stone tools. (Ch. 25)

Homo sapiens The single species that includes all branches of the human race; recognized in fossils as old as 200,000 years. (Ch. 20)

horsepower Unit of power equal to 550 foot-pounds per second in the English system of measurement; commonly used to assess the power of engines and motors. (Ch. 3)

hot spot A dramatic type of volcanism indirectly associated with plate tectonics. Large isolated chimney-like columns of hot rock, or mantle plumes, rising to Earth's surface; for example, Yellowstone National Park, Iceland, and Hawaii. (Ch. 17)

Hubble Space Telescope (HST) An Earth-orbiting reflecting telescope, launched in 1990, with a 2.4-meter mirror designed to give unparalleled resolution in the visible and ultraviolet wavelengths. Manufacturing flaws in the main mirror were corrected by astronauts in late 1993. (Ch. 14)

Hubble's law The law relating the distance to a galaxy, d, and the rate at which it recedes from Earth, V, as measured by the redshift: $V = Hd$, where H is the Hubble constant. (Ch. 15)

Human Genome Project A large-scale scientific project that will result in a complete knowledge of the entire human genome, which includes 46 chromosomes and 3 billion base pairs. (Ch. 23)

human immunodeficiency virus (HIV) A virus that causes the disease AIDS and is transmitted through the exchange of bodily fluids. (Ch. 24)

humidity A measure of the atmosphere's variable water content. (Ch. 18)

hurricane Tropical storms having winds in excess of 120 km/h (75 mi/h) that begin in the Atlantic Ocean off the coast of Africa and affect North America. (Ch. 18)

hybrid An individual whose parents possess different genetic traits. (Ch. 23)

hydrocarbon A chainlike molecule from a chemical compound of carbon and hydrogen, which provides the most efficient fuels for combustion, with only carbon dioxide and water as products. (Ch. 10)

hydrogen bond A bond that may form when polarized hydrogen atoms link to other atoms by a covalent or ionic bond. (Ch. 10)

hydrogen burning A three-step process, generally confined to a small region in the center of a star, in which four protons are converted into a ^{4}He nucleus, two protons, and a photon. (Ch. 14)

hydrogenation The addition of hydrogen atoms into the carbon chains of polyunsaturated products; a process that eliminates the carbon–carbon double bonds. (Ch. 22)

hydrologic cycle The combination of processes by which water moves from repository to repository near Earth's surface. (Ch. 18)

hydrophilic Attracted to water. (Ch. 22)

hydrophobic Repelled by water. (Ch. 22)

hypothesis A tentative guess about how the world works, based on a summary of experimental or observational results and phrased so that it can be tested by experimentation. (Ch. 1)

Hz See *hertz.*

ice age A period of several million years during which glaciers have repeatedly advanced and retreated, causing radical changes in climate and influencing human evolution. (Ch. 18)

ice cap Layers of ice that form at the north and south polar regions of Earth. (Ch. 18)

igneous rock The first rock to form on a cooling planet, solidified from hot, molten material; intrusive or extrusive (volcanic). (Ch. 18)

immune system The system that defends an organism against harmful microorganisms by recognizing the geometric shape of molecules of foreign invaders and destroying them without harming the body's cells. (Ch. 23)

in vitro gene therapy A process where the gene is injected into cells outside of the body and then these cells are introduced into the body. (Ch. 24)

in vivo gene therapy A process where genes are injected into cells inside the body. (Ch. 24)

inertia The tendency of a body to remain in uniform motion; the resistance to change. (Ch. 2)

inflation A short period of rapid expansion of the universe, which, according to the grand unified theories, accompanied the "freezing" at 10^{-35} seconds. (Ch. 15)

inflationary theories Those cosmological theories that incorporate the phenomenon of universal inflation. (Ch. 15)

infrared Astronomical Satellite (IRAS) An orbiting observatory launched in 1983 by the United States, United Kingdom, and Netherlands to view infrared radiation in the universe. IRAS is no longer functioning. (Ch. 14)

infrared energy A form of electromagnetic radiation that travels from a source to an object, where it can be absorbed and converted into the kinetic energy of molecules. (Ch. 4)

infrared radiation Wavelengths of electromagnetic radiation that extend from a millimeter to a micron; felt as heat radiation. (Ch. 6)

insulator A material that will not conduct electricity. (Ch. 11)

integrated circuit A microchip made of hundreds or thousands of transistors specially designed to perform a specific function. (Ch. 11)

Interference When waves from two different sources come together at a single point, they interfere with each other. The observed wave amplitude is the sum of the amplitudes of the interfering waves. (Ch. 6)

interglacial period A period that occurs between two major glacier advances during an ice age. (Ch. 18)

intrusive rock Igneous rock that cools and hardens underground. (Ch. 18)

inversely proportional The relationship between two variables such that if the value of one variable increases, the other variable decreases, and vice versa, by a constant proportion. (Ch. 2)

invertebrates Organisms without backbones. (Ch. 20)

ion An atom that has an electrical charge, from either the loss or gain of an electron. (Ch. 8)

ionic bond A chemical bond in which the electrostatic force between two oppositely charged ions holds the atoms in place, often formed as one atom gives up an electron while another receives it, lowering chemical potential energy when atom shells are filled. (Ch. 10)

ionization Stripping away one or more of an atom's electrons to produce an ion. (Ch. 12)

IRAS See *Infrared Astronomical Satellite.*

isolated system A type of system in which matter and energy are not exchanged with the surroundings; a closed system. (Ch. 3)

isomer A molecule that contains the same atoms as another molecule, but has a different structural arrangement. (Ch. 10)

isotopes Atoms whose nuclei have the same number of protons but a different number of neutrons. (Ch. 12)

jet stream A high-altitude stream of fast-moving winds that marks the boundary between the northern polar cold air mass and the warmer air of the temperate zone. (Ch. 18)

joule The amount of work done when you exert a force of one newton through a distance of one meter. (Ch. 3)

Jovian planets Huge worlds also known as "gas giants" located in the outer solar system and made up primarily of frozen liquids and gases such as hydrogen, helium, ammonia, and water, with atmospheres of nitrogen, methane, and other compounds: Jupiter, Saturn, Uranus, Neptune. (Ch. 16)

kilowatt A commonly used measurement of electrical power equal to 1000 watts and corresponding to the expenditure of 1000 joules per second. (Ch. 3)

kinetic energy The type of energy associated with moving objects; the energy of motion. Kinetic energy is equal to the mass of the moving object times the square of that object's velocity, multiplied by $\frac{1}{2}$. (Ch. 3)

kingdom The broadest classification in the Linnaean classification system, corresponding to the coarsest division of living things. (Ch. 20)

Krebs cycle A complex series of chemical cellular reactions in which the products of glycolysis are broken down completely into carbon dioxide and water, releasing some energy to the ATP molecules and storing some in other energy-carrying molecules. (Ch. 21)

Kuiper Belt A region close to our solar system that contains comets that orbit the Sun; a reservoir of new comets. (Ch. 16)

laser An instrument that uses a collection of atoms, energy, and mirrors to emit photons that have wave crests in exact alignment. The instrument name is the acronym for *l*ight *a*mplification by *s*timulated *e*mission of *r*adiation. (Ch. 8)

lava Molten rock that flows from the surface of a volcano. (Ch. 17)

law of conservation of linear momentum A law that states that the quantity of an object's momentum will not change unless an outside force is applied to the object. Therefore, the object's present momentum will be conserved. (Ch. 2)

law of nature An overarching statement of how the universe works, following repeated and rigorous observation and testing of a theory or group of related theories. (Ch. 1)

law of unintended consequences A phenomenon demonstrating the interdependent nature of ecosystems: it is virtually impossible to change one aspect of an ecosystem without affecting something else, often inadvertently. (Ch. 19)

length contraction The phenomenon in relativity in which moving objects appear to be shorter than stationary ones in the direction of motion. (Ch. 7)

lepton A particle (such as the electron, muon, and neutrino) that participates in the weak and electromagnetic, but not the strong, interaction. (Ch. 13)

lichen (pronounced "*lie*-kin") A combination of a fungus and a single-celled organism that can use the Sun's energy through photosynthesis; important to the processes of weathering rock and creating soil. (Ch. 20)

light A form of electromagnetic wave to which the human eye is sensitive. Light travels at a constant speed and needs no medium for transfer. (Ch. 6)

light-year The distance light travels in one year, 10 trillion kilometers (about 6.2 trillion miles). (Ch. 14)

limestone A sedimentary rock formed from the calcium carbonate ($CaCO_3$) skeletons of sea animals, shells, and coral. (Ch. 18)

linear accelerator A device for making high-velocity particles, which relies on a long, straight vacuum tube into which particles are injected to ride an electromagnetic wave down the tube. (Ch. 13)

linear momentum The product of an object's mass times its velocity. (Ch. 2)

Linnaean classification A systematic attempt by Swedish naturalist Carolus Linnaeus to catalogue the diversity of all living things according to their shared characteristics so that each organism is as close as possible to those things it resembles, and as far apart as possible from those it does not. (Ch. 20)

lipid An organic molecule that is insoluble in water. At the molecular level, lipids form the cell membranes that separate living material from its environment. Lipids are also an extremely efficient storage medium for energy; for example, fat in foods, wax in candles, and grease for lubrication. (Ch. 22)

liquid Any collection of atoms or molecules that has no fixed shape but maintains a fixed volume. (Ch. 10)

liquid crystal A recently synthesized substance, used in digital displays, which is formed from very long molecules that may adopt a very ordered arrangement even in the liquid form. (Ch. 10)

load The location in an electric circuit where the useful work is done, such as the filament in a light-bulb or the heating element of a dryer. (Ch. 5)

longitudinal wave A kind of wave in which the motion of the medium is in the same direction as the wave movement; pressure wave or sound wave. (Ch. 6) Also, one of two principal types of seismic waves in which molecules in the rock move back and forth in the same direction as the wave; a compressional wave. (Ch. 17)

Lorentz factor A number, equal to the square root of $[1 - (v/c)^2]$, that appears in relativistic calculations and is an indication of the magnitude of change in time and scale. (Ch. 7)

low-quality protein Foods, such as that from plants, that lack one or more of the amino acids found in human proteins. (Ch. 22)

low-temperature reservoir The ambient atmosphere into which the waste heat generated by an engine is dumped; for example, from a cylinder in a gasoline engine to the atmosphere. (Ch. 4)

Lucy The name given to a nearly complete skeleton of a female *Australopithecus,* found in Ethiopia in 1974. (Ch. 25)

luminosity The total energy produced by a star. (Ch. 14)

lymphatic system An extensive network of capillaries and veins, parallel to the blood system and linked to about 500 lymph nodes in the human body. (App. A)

lysosome One of the cellular organelles that has digestion and breakdown of wastes as its primary function. (Ch. 21)

magma Subsurface molten rock, concentrated in the upper mantle or lower crust, which can breach the surface and harden into new rock. (Ch. 17)

magnet Materials that exert a magnetic field on other objects. Magnetite or "lodestone" is a common natural magnet. (Ch. 5)

magnetic field A collection of lines that map out the direction that compass needles would point in the vicinity of a magnet. (Ch. 5)

magnetic force The force exerted by magnets on each other. (Ch. 5)

magnetic monopole A hypothetical single isolated north or south magnetic pole, existing in theory but not yet located through experimentation. (Ch. 5)

magnetic potential energy The type of energy stored in a magnetic field. (Ch. 3)

magnetism A fundamental force in the universe. (Ch. 5)

main-sequence star A star that derives energy from the fusion reactions of hydrogen burning; found on the Hertzsprung-Russell (H-R) diagram within a bandlike pattern. (Ch. 14)

mammal One of a group of vertebrates made up of individuals that are warm-blooded, have hair, and whose females nurse their young. Human beings are mammals. (Ch. 20)

mantle The thick layer rich in oxygen, silicon, magnesium, and iron that contains most of Earth's mass; it overlies Earth's metal core. (Ch. 16)

mantle convection A force deep within Earth, driven by internal heat energy, that moves continents and the plates of which they are a part. (Ch. 17)

marble A metamorphic rock that begins as limestone that is subjected to intense pressure and high temperatures.

mass The amount of matter contained in an object, independent of where that object is found. (Ch. 2)

mass extinctions Rare and catastrophic events in the past that have caused large numbers of species to become extinct suddenly. (Ch. 25)

mass number The number of neutrons plus the number of protons, which determines the mass of an isotope. (Ch. 12)

Maxwell's equations Four fundamental laws of electricity and magnetism: (1) Coulomb's law: like charges repel and unlike charges attract; (2) magnetic monopoles do not exist in nature; (3) magnetic phenomena can be produced by electrical effects; and (4) electrical phenomena can be produced by magnetic effects. (Ch. 5)

mechanics The branch of science that deals with the motions of material objects and the forces that act on them; for example, a rolling rock or a thrown ball. (Ch. 2)

meiosis The division process that produces cells with one-half the number of chromosomes in each somatic cell. Each resulting daughter cell has half the normal complement of DNA. See *mitosis.* (Ch. 21)

meltdown The most serious accident that can occur at a nuclear reactor, in which the flow of water to the fuel rods is interrupted and the enormous heat stored in the central part of the reactor causes the fuel rods to melt. (Ch. 12)

melting A change of state from solid to liquid caused by an increase in temperature or decrease in pressure of the solid, which increases the vibration of individual molecules and breaks down the structure of the solid. (Ch. 10)

Mesozoic Era The third era, from 250 to 65 million years ago, known as "middle life," when the dinosaurs existed. (Ch. 25)

messenger RNA (mRNA) The single-stranded molecule that copies the sequence for one gene and carries that DNA information to the region of the cell where proteins are made. (Ch. 23)

metabolism The process by which a cell derives energy from its surroundings. (Ch. 21)

metal An element or combination of elements in which the sharing of a few electrons among all atoms results in more stable electron arrangement; characterized by a shiny luster and ability to conduct electricity. (Ch. 19)

metallic bond A chemical bond in which electrons are redistributed so that they are shared by all the atoms as a whole. (Ch. 10)

metamorphic rock Igneous or sedimentary rock that is buried and transformed by Earth's intense internal temperature and pressure. (Ch. 18)

meteor A piece of interplanetary debris that hits Earth's atmosphere and forms a bright streak of light from friction with atmospheric particles: a "shooting star." (Ch. 16)

meteor showers A set of spectacular, regularly occurring events in the night sky, caused by the collision of Earth with clouds of small debris that travel around the orbits of comets. (Ch. 16)

meteorite The fragment of a meteor that hits Earth. (Ch. 16)

microchip A complex array of *p*- and *n*-type semiconductors, which may incorporate hundreds or thousands of transistors in one integrated circuit. (Ch. 11)

microwave Electromagnetic waves, with wavelengths ranging from approximately 1 meter to 1 millimeter, which are used extensively for line-of-sight communications and cooking. (Ch. 6)

Mid-Atlantic Ridge The longest mountain range on Earth, which is located in the middle of the Atlantic Ocean. (Ch. 17)

Milankovitch cycles Slow cyclical changes in Earth's climate due primarily to orbital effects. (Ch. 18)

Milky Way A collection of hundreds of billions stars that forms the galaxy of which the Sun is a part. (Ch. 15)

Miller-Urey experiment A demonstration of chemical evolution, performed in 1953 by Stanley Miller and Harold Urey, which showed that a combination of gases, believed to be present in the early atmosphere, and a series of electrical sparks, simulating the lightning on the early Earth, will produce amino acids, a basic building block of life. (Ch. 25)

mineral In a nutritional context, all chemical elements in food other than carbon, hydrogen, nitrogen, and oxygen. (Ch. 22)

mitochondria Sausage-shaped organelles that are places where molecules derived from glucose react with oxygen to produce the cell's energy. (Ch. 21)

mitosis The process of cell division producing daughter cells with exactly the same number of chromosomes as in the mother cell. See *meiosis.* (Ch. 21)

molecular genetics The study of how the mechanism that passes genetic information from parents to offspring functions on the basis of molecular chemistry. (Ch. 23)

molecule A cluster of atoms that bond together; the basic constituent of many different kinds of material. (Ch. 8)

monera Single-celled organisms without cell nuclei; the most primitive living things in the Linnaean classification of kingdoms. (Ch. 20)

monosaccharide An individual sugar molecule. (Ch. 22)

monounsaturated A type of lipid that forms when one kinked "double bond" forms between two carbon atoms in a molecule. See *unsaturated.* (Ch. 22)

monsoon Any wind system on a continental scale that seasonally reverses its direction because of seasonal variations in relative temperatures over land and sea. (Ch. 18)

Moon Earth's only satellite, which may have formed when a planet-sized body hit Earth early in its history. (Ch. 16)

mRNA See *messenger RNA.*

mudstone A sedimentary rock formed from sediments that are much finer-grained than sand. (Ch. 18)

mutation A change in the genetic material of a parent that is inherited by the offspring. (Ch. 23)

N See *newton.*

***n*-type semiconductor** A type of electrical conductor formed from doping, that has a slight excess of mobile negatively charged electrons. (Ch. 11)

nanotechnology A new field of engineering that concentrates on extreme miniaturization and often creates new objects, atom by atom. (Ch. 11)

National Academy of Sciences A nationally recognized association of scientists, elected to membership by their peers to provide professional advice for the government on policy issues ranging from environmental risks and natural resource management, to education and funding for science research. (Ch. 1)

National Institutes of Health A federal agency that provides funding for basic and applied research in medicine and biology. (Ch. 1)

National Science Foundation A federal agency that funds American scientific research and education in all areas of science. (Ch. 1)

natural selection The mechanism by which nature can introduce wide-ranging changes in living things over long periods of time by modifying the gene pool of a species. (Ch. 25)

Neanderthal man A type of human with a large brain who lived until 35,000 years ago in groups with a complex social structure; either a separate species of the genus *Homo* or a subspecies of *Homo sapiens.* (Ch. 25)

nebulae Dust and gas clouds, common throughout the Milky Way galaxy, rich in hydrogen and helium. (Ch. 15)

nebular hypothesis A model that explains the formation of the solar system from a large cloud of gas and dust floating in space 4.5 billion years ago. This cloud collapsed upon itself under the influence of gravity and began to spin faster and faster, eventually forming the planets and the rest of the solar system along a flattened disk of matter surrounding a central star. (Ch. 16)

negative charge An excess of electrons on an object. (Ch. 5)

nervous system One of two control systems in the body that mediate responses to the environment. See *endocrine system.* (App. A)

neurotransmitter A group of molecules, produced in nerve cells, that transfer a nerve signal from one nerve cell to another. (Ch. 5)

neutrino A subatomic particle, emitted in the decay of the neutron, that has no electrical charge, travels at the speed of light, and has no rest mass. (Ch. 11)

neutron A type of subatomic particle, located in the nucleus of the atom that carries no electrical charge but has approximately the same mass as the proton; one of two primary building blocks of the nucleus. See *proton.* (Ch. 8)

neutron star A very dense, very small star, usually with a high rate of rotation and a strong magnetic field; the core remains of a supernova, held up by the degeneracy pressure of neutrons. (Ch. 14)

newton (N) A unit of force defined as the force needed to accelerate a mass of 1 kg by 1 m/s^2, or 1 kilogram-meter-per-second-squared. (Ch. 2)

Newton's law of universal gravitation Between any two objects in the universe there is an attractive force (gravity) that is proportional to the masses of the objects and inversely proportional to the square of the distance between them. In other words, the more massive two objects are, the greater the force between them will be, and the farther apart they are, the less the force will be. (Ch. 2)

Newton's laws of motion Three basic principles, expressed as laws, that govern the motion of everything in the universe, from stars and planets to cannonballs and muscles. The *first law* states that a moving object will continue moving in a straight line at a constant speed, and a stationary object will remain at rest, unless acted on by an unbalanced force. The *second law* states that the acceleration produced on a body by a force is proportional to the magnitude of the force and inversely proportional to the mass of the object. The *third law* states that for every action there is an equal and opposite reaction. (Ch. 2)

noble gases Elements listed in the far righthand column of the periodic table of elements, including helium, argon, and neon, which are odorless, colorless, and slow to react. (Ch. 8)

nonrenewable energy Sources of energy that, once used, are not quickly replaced; for example, petroleum and coal. (Ch. 4)

nonrenewable resources Resources such as coal and petroleum, which are forming at a much slower rate than they are being consumed. (Ch. 3)

nuclear reactor A device that controls fission reactions to produce energy when heavy radioactive nuclei split apart. (Ch. 12)

nucleic acid Molecule originally found in the nucleus of cells that carries and interprets the genetic code; includes DNA and RNA (Ch. 23)

nucleotide Molecule that is the basic element from which all DNA and RNA are built; formed from a sugar, a phosphate group, and one of four bases (adenine, guanine, cytosine, and thymine or uracil). (Ch. 23)

nucleus (1) The very small, compact object at the center of an atom; made up primarily of protons and neutrons. (2) A prominent structure in the interior of a cell that contains the cell's genetic material—the DNA—and controls the cell's chemistry. (Ch. 8, Ch. 18)

observation The act of observing nature without manipulating it. (Ch. 1)

ohm A unit of measurement for the electrical resistance of a wire. (Ch. 5)

oil shale A form of fossil fuel in which petroleum is dispersed through solid rock. (Ch. 3)

omnivore Animals that gain energy from plants and from organisms in other trophic levels. (Ch. 3)

Oort cloud A region beyond the orbit of Pluto that contains billions of comets circling the Sun; the reservoir for new comets. (Ch. 16)

open ecosystem An ecosystem in which materials are free to move in and out. (Ch. 19)

open system A type of system within which an object can exchange matter and energy with its surroundings. (Ch. 3)

open universe A model of the future of the universe in which the expansion will continue forever because the universe lacks enough matter to exert a gravitational force to slow receding galaxies. (Ch. 15)

optical microscope An instrument that uses visible light to present a magnified image from a sample through a lens to an eyepiece. (Ch. 21)

order The fourth broadest classification in the Linnaean classification system; humans are in the order of primates. (Ch. 20)

organelle Any specialized structure in the cell, including the nucleus. (Ch. 21)

organic chemistry The branch of science devoted to the study of carbon-based molecules and their reactions. (Ch. 10)

organic molecules Carbon-based molecules that may or may not be part of a living system. (Ch. 22)

osmosis A special case of molecular movement in which materials such as water are transferred across a membrane while at the same time molecules dissolved in the water are blocked. (Ch. 21)

outgassing Release of gases from nongaseous materials; extrusion of gases from the body of a planet after its formation. (Ch. 16)

oxidation A chemical reaction in which an atom such as oxygen accepts electrons while combining with other elements; for example, rusting of iron metal into iron oxide, or animal respiration. (Ch. 10)

oxides Chemical compounds that contain oxygen, such as most common minerals and ceramics. (Ch. 11)

ozone A molecule made up of three oxygen atoms, instead of the usual two, which absorbs ultraviolet radiation. (Ch. 19)

ozone hole A volume of atmosphere above Antarctica during September through November in which the concentration of the trace gas ozone has declined significantly. (Ch. 19)

ozone layer A region of enhanced ozone (O_3) 20 to 30 miles above Earth's surface where most of the absorption of the Sun's ultraviolet radiation occurs. (Ch. 19)

***p*-type semiconductor** A type of electrical conductor, formed from doping, that has a slight deficiency of electrons, resulting in mobile positively charged holes. (Ch. 11)

paleomagnetism The field devoted to the study of remnant magnetism in ancient rock, recording the direction of the magnetic poles at some time in the past. (Ch. 17)

Paleozoic Era The second era, lasting from 545 to 250 million years ago, during which time fish, amphibians, land plants and animals, and rudimentary reptiles developed; term meaning "old life." (Ch. 25)

Pangaea A giant continent consisting of North America, South America, Eurasia, and Africa, which existed 200 million years ago. (Ch. 17)

parallel circuit A circuit in which different loads are situated on different wire loops. (Ch. 5)

parsec A unit of measurement equal to about 3.3 light-years, which roughly corresponds to the average distance between nearest-neighbor stars in our galaxy. (Ch. 14)

particle accelerator A machine such as a synchrotron or linear accelerator that produces particles at near light speeds for use in the study of the fundamental structure of matter. (Ch. 13)

Pauli exclusion principle A statement that says no two electrons can occupy the same state at the same time. (Ch. 8)

PCR See *polymerase chain reaction.*

peak load The especially high demand in the mass market of electricity due to special circumstances, such as a heat wave. (Ch. 3)

peer review A system by which the editor of a scientific journal submits manuscripts considered for publication to a panel of knowledgeable scientists who, in confidence, evaluate the manuscript for mistakes, misstatements, or shoddy procedures. Following the review, if the manuscript is to be published, it is returned to the author with a list of modifications and corrections to be completed. (Ch. 1)

pencillin A substance that kills bacteria; the best-known modern antibiotic. (Ch. 20)

Penicillium A common mold that secretes the substance penicillin, an antibiotic. (Ch. 20)

peptide bond A connection between two atoms that remains after hydrogen (H) at one end of an amino acid and the hydroxyl (OH) from the end of another amino acid combine, releasing a water molecule (H_2O). The process is identical to the condensation polymerization reaction. (Ch. 22)

periodic table of the elements An organizational system, first developed by Dmitri Mendeleev in 1869, now listing more than 110 elements by atomic weight (in rows) and chemical properties (in columns). The pattern of elements in the periodic table reflects the arrangement of electrons in their orbits. (Ch. 8)

petroleum Thick black liquid found deep underground, derived from many kinds of transformed molecules of former life forms. (Ch. 10)

phosphate group One phosphorus atom surrounded by four oxygen atoms. (Ch. 22)

phospholipid The class of molecules that form membranes in cells. Lipids have a long, thin structure with a carbon backbone, and a phosphate group at one end of the molecule. One end of these molecules is hydrophilic, one hydrophobic. (Ch. 22)

photoelectric effect A phenomenon that occurs when photons strike one side of a material and cause electrons of that material to be emitted from the opposite side. This effect is observed in modern cameras, CAT scans, and fiber optics. (Ch. 9)

photon A particle-like unit of light, emitted or absorbed by an atom when an electrically charged electron changes state. The form of a single packet of electromagnetic radiation. (Ch. 8)

photosphere The gaseous layers of the Sun's outer part, which emit most of the light we see. (Ch. 14)

photosynthesis The mechanism by which plants convert the energy of sunlight into energy stored in carbohydrates, the chemical energy of virtually all life on Earth: energy + $CO_2 + H_2O \rightarrow$ carbohydrate + oxygen. (Ch. 21)

photovoltaic cell A semiconductor diode that uses sunlight to produce electrical current. They are also used in hand calculators and in some cameras for power. (Ch. 11)

phylum The second broadest classification in the Linnaean classification system; humans are in the phylum chordata, subphylum vertebrata. (Ch. 20)

Planck's constant (*h*) A constant named after German physicist Max Planck that is the central constant of quantum physics, equal to 6.63×10^{-34} joule-seconds in SI units. (Ch. 9)

planetesimal Small objects, which range in size from boulders to several miles across, formed from the accretion of solid material during the formation of the planets. (Ch. 16)

plants Multicelled organisms that get their energy directly from the Sun through photosynthesis. One of five kingdoms in the Linnaean classification. (Ch. 20)

plasma A state of matter existing under extremely high temperatures in which electrons are stripped from their atoms during high-energy collisions, forming an electron sea surrounding positive nuclei. (Ch. 10)

plasmid A loop of DNA in which genes are linked; it can be introduced into a cell for DNA replication. (Ch. 24)

plastic Synthetic polymers that are formed primarily from petroleum. They consist of intertwined polymer strands, much like the strands of fiberglass insulation. When heated, these strands slide across each other to adopt new shapes. When cooled, the plastic fiber mass solidifies into whatever shape is available. (Ch. 10)

plate A rigid moving sheet of rock up to 100 km (60 mi) thick, composed of the crust and part of the upper mantle. (See *plate tectonics*.) (Ch. 17)

plate tectonics The model of the dynamic Earth that has emerged from studies of paleomagnetism, rock dating, and much other data. A theory that explains how a few thin, rigid tectonic plates of crustal and upper mantle materials are moved across Earth's surface by mantle convection. (Ch. 17)

Pluto A rocky body that is located beyond the Jovian planets and is the smallest of all planets in the solar system. (Ch. 16)

polar molecule Atom clusters with a positive and negative end; exerts electrical force on neighboring atoms. Water is a polar molecule. (Ch. 10)

polarization The subtle electron shift from negative to positive that takes place when the electrons of an atom or a molecule are brought near a polar molecule such as water, resulting in a bond caused by the electrical attraction between the negative end of the polar molecule and the positive side of the other molecule. (Ch. 10)

poles The two opposite ends of a magnet, named north and south, that repel a like magnetic pole and attract an unlike magnetic pole. (Ch. 5)

polymer Extremely long and large molecules that are formed from numerous smaller molecules, like links in a chain, with predictable repeating sequences of atoms along the chain. (Ch. 10)

polymerase chain reaction (PCR) A process of copying select strands of DNA so that as much can be created as is needed for research. (Ch. 24)

polymerization A reaction that includes all chemical reactions that form long strands of polymer fibers by linking small molecules. (Ch. 10)

polypeptide A bonded chain of amino acids. See *peptide bond*. (Ch. 22)

polysaccharide A molecule that is the result of many sugar molecules strung together in a chain; for example, starch and cellulose. (Ch. 22)

polyunsaturated A type of lipid that forms when two or more kinked "double bonds" between carbon atoms are in the molecule. See *unsaturated*. (Ch. 22)

positive charge A deficiency of electrons on an object. (Ch. 5)

positron The positively charged antiparticle of the electron. (Ch. 13)

potential energy The energy a system possesses if it is capable of doing work, but is not doing work now. Types of potential energy include magnetic, elastic, electrical, and chemical. Any type of energy waiting to be released; stored energy. (Ch. 3)

power The rate at which work is done or energy is expended. The amount of work done, divided by the time it takes to do it. Power is measured in watts in the metric system, horsepower in the English. (Ch. 3)

power stroke The downward motion of a piston in a gasoline engine, in which the actual work is done and the energy released by combustion is translated into the motion of the car. (Ch. 4)

precession The circular motion of the spinning axis of Earth in space, which causes the tilt of the Northern Hemisphere to change on a 26,000-year cycle. (Ch. 18)

precipitation A chemical reaction that is the reverse of a solution reaction, producing a solid that separates from very concentrated solutions. (Ch. 10)

prediction A guess about how a particular system will behave, followed by observations to see if the system did behave as expected within a specified range of situations. (Ch. 1)

pressure A force on a surface divided by the area of the surface. (Ch. 18)

prevailing westerly Wind in the temperate zones that blows primarily from west to east, causing weather patterns to move in the same direction. (Ch. 18)

primary structure The simplest of the four stages of the organization of amino acids in a protein molecule. The exact order of amino acids along the protein string. (Ch. 22)

primates An order of mammals that have grasping fingers and toes, eyes at the front of their heads, large brains, and fingernails instead of claws; includes monkeys, apes, and humans. (Ch. 20)

primordial soup A rich broth of amino acids and other molecules thought to have been produced in the early oceans over a period of several hundred million years, recreated by the Miller-Urey process. (Ch. 25)

probability The likelihood that an event will occur or that an object will be in one state or another; how nature is described in the subatomic world. (Ch. 9)

producers Organisms, such as plants, that obtain atoms and energy from physical surroundings to produce carbon-based molecules of life in an ecosystem. (Ch. 19)

prokaryote A type of primitive cell in which the DNA is coiled together, but not separated in the nucleus. Prokaryotes constitute the kingdom monera, including all cells that do not have a nucleus. (Ch. 21)

protease inhibitor A molecule that is designed using new computer visualization techniques to combat HIV as a result of long study of the HIV virus structure and processes. (Ch. 24)

protein An extremely complex molecule, which can consist of thousands of amino acids and millions of atoms formed in a chain structure. Proteins function as enzymes and direct the cell's chemistry. (Ch. 22)

Proterozoic Era The era lasting from the beginning of Earth's existence to 545 million years ago; a term meaning "before life" (Ch. 25)

protista Single-celled organisms with nuclei, and a few multicelled organisms that have a particularly simple structure. One of five kingdoms in the Linnaean classification. (Ch. 20)

proton One of two primary building blocks of the nucleus; with a positive electrical charge of +1 and a mass 1.672643×10^{-24} g approximately equal to that of the neutron. (Ch. 12)

pseudoscience A kind of inquiry falling in the realm of belief or dogma, which includes subjects that cannot be proved or disproved with a reproducible test. The subjects include creationism, extrasensory perception (ESP), unidentified flying objects, astrology, crystal power, and reincarnation. (Ch. 1)

publication A peer-reviewed paper written by a scientist or a group of scientists to communicate the results of their research to a larger audience. A publication will include the technical details of the methodology, so that the research can be reproduced, and a concise statement of the results and conclusions. (Ch. 1)

pulsar A neutron star in which fast-moving particles speed out along the intense magnetic field lines of the rotating star, giving off electromagnetic radiation that we detect as a series of pulses of radio waves. (Ch. 14)

pumice Frothy volcanic rock rich in silicon from magmas that mix with a significant amount of water or other volatile substance. (Ch. 18)

pumping The process in a laser that adds energy to the system from the outside to return atoms continuously to their excited states so that coherent photons can be produced. (Ch. 8)

punctuated equilibrium A hypothesis that holds that evolutionary changes usually occur in short bursts separated by long periods of stability. (Ch. 25)

purebred Bred from members of a single strain. (Ch. 23)

pyruvic acid Three-carbon molecules in a cell that were formed by glycolysis, splitting a glucose molecule into two smaller molecules. (Ch. 21)

quantized Whenever energy or another property of a system can have only certain definite values, and nothing in between those values, it is said to be quantized. (Ch. 9)

quantum leap A process by which an electron changes its energy state without ever possessing an energy intermediate between the original and the final energy state; also known as a quantum jump. (Ch. 8)

quantum mechanics The branch of science that is devoted to the study of the motion of objects that come in small bundles, or quanta, which applies to the subatomic world. (Ch. 9)

quarks (pronounced "quorks") The truly fundamental building blocks of the hadrons. Particles that have fractional electrical charge and cannot exist alone in nature. (Ch. 13)

quartzite A durable rock in which the original sand grains of sandstone, under high temperature and pressure, recrystallize and fuse into a solid mass. (Ch. 18)

quasar Quasi-stellar radio source. Objects in the universe, where as-yet unknown processes pour vast amounts of energy into space each second from an active center no larger than the solar system; the most distant objects known. (Ch. 15)

quaternary structure The joining of separate protein chains, each with its own secondary and tertiary structures. (Ch. 22)

R&D See *research and development.*

radiation The transfer of heat by electromagnetic radiation. The only one of the three mechanisms of heat transfer that does not require atoms or molecules to facilitate the transfer process. (Ch. 4) Also, the particles emitted during the spontaneous decay of nuclei. (Ch. 12)

radio wave Part of the electromagnetic spectrum that ranges from the longest waves—wavelengths longer than Earth's diameter—to waves a few meters long. (Ch. 6)

radioactive decay The process of spontaneous change of unstable isotopes. (Ch. 12)

radioactivity The spontaneous release of energy by certain atoms, such as uranium, as these atoms disintegrate. The emission of one or more kinds of radiation from an isotope with unstable nuclei. (Ch. 12)

radiometric dating A technique based on the radioactive half-lives of carbon-14 and other isotopes that is used to determine the age of materials. (Ch. 12)

radon A colorless, odorless inert gas that can cause an indoor pollution problem when it undergoes radioactive decay. (Ch. 12)

receptor A large structure found in the cell membrane and made of proteins folded into a geometrical shape that will bond chemically only to a specific type of molecule. (Ch. 21)

recessive A characteristic that will appear only if no dominant gene is present. (Ch. 23)

recessive gene A gene that is present in offspring and can be passed along to subsequent generations, but may not determine the offspring's physical characteristics. (Ch. 23)

red giant An extremely large star that emits a lot of energy but whose surface is very cool and therefore appears somewhat reddish in the sky; found in the upper right-hand corner of the H-R diagram. (Ch. 14)

redshift An increase in the wavelength of radiation received from a receding celestial body as a consequence of the Doppler effect. A shift toward the long-wavelength (red) end of the spectrum. (Ch. 14)

redshifted The result of the Doppler effect on light waves, when the source of light moves away from the observer: light-wave crests are farther apart and have a lower frequency. (Ch. 6)

reduction A chemical reaction in which electrons are transferred from an atom to other elements, resulting in a gain in electrons for the material being reduced; for example, smelting of metal ores, and photosynthesis. (Ch. 10)

reductionism The quest for the ultimate building blocks of the universe. An attempt to reduce the seeming complexity of nature by first looking for an underlying simplicity and then trying to understand how that simplicity gives rise to the observed complexity. (Ch. 13)

reflection A process by which light waves are scattered at the same angle as the original wave; for example, from the surface of a mirror. (Ch. 6)

refraction One of three responses of an electromagnetic wave encountering matter, in which electromagnetic waves slow down and change direction in the matter. See also *absorption* and *transmission*. (Ch. 6)

relativity An idea that the laws of nature are the same in all frames of reference, and that every observer must experience the same natural laws. (Ch. 7)

reproducible A criterion for the results of an experiment. In the scientific method, observations and experiments must be reported in such a way that anyone with the proper equipment can verify the results. (Ch. 1)

reproductive cloning An application of cloning technology that produces a new living being. See *cloning*. (Ch. 24)

reptiles The first animals fully adapted to life on land; includes lizards, turtles, and snakes. (Ch. 20)

research and development (R&D) A kind of research aimed at specific problems, usually performed in government and industry laboratories. (Ch. 1)

reservoirs Locations where a substance is to be found. Earth's water, for example, is found in oceans, rivers, ice caps, and several other reservoirs. (Ch. 18)

residence time The average length of time that any given atom will stay in ocean water before it is removed by some chemical reaction. (Ch. 18)

respiration The process by which animals retrieve energy stored in glucose, in a complex series of cellular chemical reactions, which include breathing in oxygen produced by plants, burning carbohydrates ingested for food, and breathing out carbon dioxide. (Ch. 21)

respiratory system The system that takes oxygen from the air and transfers it to the circulatory system; includes the lungs and the alveoli. (App. A)

restriction enzyme Proteins that have the ability to cut a DNA molecule so that the DNA has several unattached bases at the cut end. (Ch. 24)

ribonucleic acid (RNA) A molecule that consists of one string of nucleotides put together around the sugar ribose, and with the bases adenine, guanine, cytosine, and uracil. RNA plays a crucial role in the synthesis of proteins in the cell. (Ch. 23)

ribose The standard sugar containing five-carbon atoms in ribonucleic acid (RNA). (Ch. 23)

ribosomal RNA (rRNA) A constituent of ribosomes; involved in the synthesis of protein. (Ch. 23)

ribosome One of the cellular organelles that is the site of protein synthesis. (Ch. 21)

RNA See *ribonucleic acid.*

rock cycle An ongoing cycle of internal and external Earth processes by which rock is created, destroyed, and altered. (Ch. 18)

rock formations Bodies of rock that form as a continuous unit, possibly combining many different types of rock. (Ch. 18)

rod One type of light-absorbing cell in the eye providing night vision; sensitive to light and dark. Compare to *cone.* (Ch. 6)

Roentgen Satellite (ROSAT) An X-ray satellite launched in 1990 by the United States, United Kingdom, and Germany as the latest in a series of satellites equipped to detect X-rays. (Ch. 14)

ROSAT See *Roentgen Satellite.*

rRNA See *ribosomal RNA.*

sandstone A sedimentary rock formed mostly from sand-sized grains of quartz (silicon dioxide) and other hard mineral and rock fragments. (Ch. 18)

saturated A fully bonded carbon atom in a lipid. In a straight lipid chain, every carbon atom bonds to two adjacent carbon atoms along the chain and two hydrogen atoms on the sides. (Ch. 22)

scattering A process by which electromagnetic waves may be absorbed and rapidly re-emitted; can be diffuse scattering or reflection. (Ch. 6)

schist Metamorphic rock formed from slate under extreme temperature and pressure. (Ch. 18)

scientific method A continuous process used to collect observations, form and test hypotheses, make predictions, and identify patterns in the physical world. (Ch. 1)

second law of thermodynamics Any one of three equivalent statements: (1) heat will not flow spontaneously from a colder to a hotter body; (2) it is impossible to construct a machine that does nothing but convert heat into useful work; and (3) the entropy of an isolated system always increases. (Ch. 4)

second trophic level All herbivores, including cows, rabbits, and many different kinds of insects, that get their energy by eating plants. (Ch. 3)

secondary structure Shapes taken by the string of amino acids that makes up the primary structure of a protein.

sedimentary rock A type of rock that is formed from layers of sediment produced by the weathering of other rock or by chemical precipitation. (Ch. 18)

seismic tomography A branch of Earth science that enables geophysicists to obtain three-dimensional pictures of Earth's interior. (Ch. 17)

seismic wave The form through which an earthquake's energy is transmitted, causing Earth's surface to rise and fall like the surface of the ocean. (Ch. 17)

seismology The study and measurement of vibrations within Earth's interior, dedicated to deducing our planet's inner structure. (Ch. 17)

semiconductor Materials that conduct electricity but do not conduct it very well. Neither a good conductor nor a perfect insulator; for example, silicon. (Ch. 11)

series circuit An electric circuit in which two or more loads are linked along a single loop of wire. (Ch. 5)

shale A sedimentary rock formed from sediments that are much finer grained than sand. (Ch. 18)

shear strength A material's ability to withstand twisting. (Ch. 11)

shear wave One of two principal types of seismic waves, in which molecules move perpendicular to the direction of the wave motion. A transverse wave. (Ch. 17)

single bond The type of covalent bond formed when only one electron is shared. (Ch. 10)

skeleto-muscular system An internal structure that supports the weight and produces movement of the human body. (App. A)

slate A brittle and hard metamorphic rock, formed from shale or mudstone. (Ch. 18)

smog The brownish stuff of modern urban air pollution that you often see over major cities during the summer, caused by a photochemical reaction. (Ch. 19)

solar system The Sun, the planets and their moons, and all other objects gravitationally bound to the Sun. (Ch. 16)

solar wind A stream of charged particles—mainly ions of hydrogen and electrons—emitted constantly by the Sun into the space around it. (Ch. 14)

solid Any material that possesses a fixed shape and volume, with chemical bonds that are both sufficiently strong and directional to preserve a large-scale external form. (Ch. 10)

solution reaction A chemical reaction in which a solid such as salt or sugar is dissolved in a liquid. (Ch. 10)

somatic stem cell A cell in an adult organism that may be made to develop into other specialized cells. (Ch. 24)

sound wave A longitudinal wave created by a vibrating object and transmitted only through the motion of molecules in a solid, gas, or liquid. The energy of the sound wave is associated with the kinetic energy of those molecules. (Ch. 3)

special relativity The first of two parts of Einstein's theory of relativity that deals with reference frames that do not accelerate. (Ch. 7)

species The basic unit of the Linnaean classification; an interbreeding population of individual organisms. (Ch. 20)

specific heat capacity A measure of the ability of a material to absorb heat energy, defined as the quantity of heat required to raise the temperature of one gram of that material by 1°C. Water displays the largest heat capacity of any common substance. (Ch. 4)

spectroscopy The study of emission and absorption spectra of materials in order to discover the chemical makeup of a material; a standard tool used in almost every branch of science. (Ch. 8)

spectrum The characteristic signal from the total collection of photons emitted by a given atom that can be used to identify the chemical elements in a material; the atomic fingerprint. (Ch. 8)

speed The distance an object travels divided by the time it takes to travel that distance. (Ch. 2)

speed of light ***(c)*** The velocity at which all electromagnetic waves travel, regardless of their wavelength or frequency; equal to 300,000 kilometers per second (about 186,000 miles per second). (Ch. 6)

spindle fibers A series of fibers that develop after chromosomes have duplicated and the nuclear membrane has dissolved. (Ch. 21)

spreading The widening of the seafloor, as magma comes from deep within Earth and erupts through fissures on the seafloor. (Ch. 17)

standard model Theories, supported by experimental evidence, that predict the unification of the strong force with the electroweak force. (Ch. 22)

Staphylococcus A common infectious bacteria that can be killed by penicillin and other antibiotics. (Ch. 20)

star Objects such as our Sun that form from giant clouds of interstellar dust and generate energy by nuclear fusion reactions. (Ch. 14)

starch A polysaccharide, with glucose constituents linked together at certain points along the ring. A large family of molecules found in many plants, such as potatoes and corn. (Ch. 22)

states of matter Different modes of organization of atoms or molecules, which result in properties of gases, plasmas, liquids, or solids. (Ch. 10)

static electricity A phenomenon caused by the transfer of electrical charge between objects. Often observed as lightning or as sparks produced when walking across a wool rug on a dry, cold day. (Ch. 5)

steady-state universe A model, no longer believed to be valid, that describes a universe that is constantly expanding and forming new galaxies, but with no trace of a beginning. (Ch. 15)

strength The ability of a solid to resist changes in shape; directly related to chemical bonding. (Ch. 11)

strong force The force responsible for holding the nucleus together; one of the four fundamental forces in nature. This force operates over extremely short distances and between quarks to hold elementary particles together. (Ch. 12)

subduction zone The regions of Earth's deep interior where plates converge and old crust returns to the mantle. (Ch. 17)

sublimation The direct transformation of a solid to a gaseous state, without passing through the liquid state. (Ch. 10)

sugar The simplest of the carbohydrates. Common sugars contain five, six, or seven carbon atoms arranged in a ring-like structure. (Ch. 22)

superclusters Large collections of clusters and groups of thousands of galaxies. (Ch. 15)

superconductivity The ability of some materials to exhibit the complete absence of any electrical resistance, usually when cooled to within a few degrees of absolute zero. (Ch. 11)

supernova A stupendous explosion of a star, which increases its brightness hundreds of millions of times in a few days; results from the implosion of the core of a massive star at the end of its life. (Ch. 14)

synchrotron A particle accelerator in which magnetic fields are increased as particles become more energetic, keeping them moving on the same track. (Ch. 13)

system A part of the universe under study and separated from its surroundings by a real or imaginary boundary. (Ch. 3)

taxonomy The science of cataloging living things, describing them, and giving them names. (Ch. 20)

technology The application of the results of science to specific commercial or industrial goals. (Ch. 1)

tectonic plate One of a dozen sheets of moving rock in various sizes forming Earth's surface. (Ch. 17)

telescope A device that focuses and concentrates radiation from distant objects; used by astronomers to collect and analyze radio waves, microwaves, light, and other radiation. (Ch. 14)

temperature A quantity that reflects how vigorously atoms are moving and colliding in a material. (Ch. 4)

temperature scales Standard scales that can be used to measure and compare the temperatures of two different objects. (Ch. 4)

tensile strength A material's ability to withstand pulling apart. (Ch. 11)

terminal electron transport The final stage of respiration in which energy is used to produce more ATP molecules. (Ch. 21)

terminal velocity The point at which a dropped object stops accelerating and continues to fall at a constant velocity. (Ch. 2)

terrane A mass of rock as much as several hundred kilometers across, found in most of the western part of the United States, which was once a large island in the Pacific Ocean and carried toward the North American continent by plate activity. (Ch. 17)

terrestrial planets The relatively small, rocky, high-density planets located in the inner solar system nearest the Sun: Mercury, Venus, Earth, Earth's Moon, and Mars. (Ch. 16)

tertiary structure The complex folding of a protein, caused by the cross-linking of chemical bonds from side groups in the amino acid chain. (Ch. 22)

theories of everything A term that scientists use to refer to theories that unify all of the four forces. (Ch. 13)

theorist A scientist who uses mathematical models and logical inference to make statements about the universe in order to explain its processes and organisms. (Ch. 1)

theory A description of the world that covers a relatively large number of phenomena and has met many observational and experimental tests. A conclusion based upon observations of nature. (Ch. 1)

theory of relativity The idea that the laws of nature are the same in all frames of reference. Einstein divided his theory into two parts—special relativity and general relativity. (Ch. 7)

therapeutic cloning An application of cloning technology that uses cloning in medical procedure to improve human health. See *cloning*. (Ch. 24)

thermal conductivity The ability of a material to transfer heat energy from one molecule to the next by conduction. When thermal conductivity is low, as in wood or fiberglass insulation, the transfer of heat is slowed down. (Ch. 4)

thermal energy The kinetic energy of atoms and molecules; what we normally call heat. (Ch. 3)

thermodynamics The study of the movement of heat; the science of heat, energy, and work. (Ch. 3)

thermometer A device that measures temperature using a temperature scale and a material that expands and contracts with temperature change, such as mercury. (Ch. 4)

time dilation A phenomenon in special relativity in which moving clocks appear to tick more slowly than stationary ones. (Ch. 7)

tornado The most violent weather phenomenon known. A rotating air funnel some tens to hundreds of meters across, descending from storm clouds to the ground, causing intense damage along the path where the funnel touches the ground. (Ch. 18)

totipotent A state that occurs in an early stage of embryonic cell division where each cell retains the ability to express all of its genes; the cell is not yet specialized. (Ch. 24)

trace element A chemical, such as iodine in the thyroid gland and iron in the blood, that is needed in minor amounts by the body. (Ch. 22)

trace gas A gas that constitutes less than one molecule in a million in Earth's atmosphere; for example, ozone. (Ch. 19)

trade wind Surface winds near the equator of the Atlantic Ocean that blow east to west. (Ch. 18)

transcription A process by which a cell transfers information in DNA to molecules of mRNA. (Ch. 23)

transfer RNA (tRNA) The molecule with special configuration that attracts amino acids at one end, and, at the other end, attaches to a specific codon of mRNA. (Ch. 23)

transform plate boundary The type of boundary between plates that occurs when one plate scrapes past the other, with no new plate material being produced; for example, California's San Andreas Fault. (Ch. 17)

transistor A device that sandwiches *p*- and *n*-type semiconductors in an arrangement that can amplify or redirect an electrical current running through it; a device that played an essential role in the development of modern electronics. (Ch. 11)

transmission One of three responses of an electromagnetic wave encountering matter, in which light energy passes through the matter unaffected. See also *absorption* and *refraction*. (Ch. 6)

transverse wave A kind of wave in which the motion of the wave is perpendicular to the motion of the medium on which the wave moves. (Ch. 6)

triangulation A geometrical method used to measure the distances to the nearest stars up to a few hundred light-years away. The angle of sight to the star is measured at opposite ends of Earth's orbit and the distances are calculated. (Ch. 14)

tRNA See *transfer RNA*.

trophic level All organisms that get their energy from the same source. (Ch. 3)

tropical storm A severe storm that starts as a low-pressure area over warm ocean water and, while drawing energy from the warm water, grows and rotates in great cyclonic patterns hundreds of kilometers in diameter. (Ch. 18)

tsunami A great wave, which can devastate low-lying coastal areas, occurring when the energy of an earthquake under or near a large body of water is transferred through the water. (Ch. 17)

typhoon A tropical storm that begins in the North Pacific Ocean (Ch. 18)

ultraviolet radiation High-frequency wavelengths, shorter than visible light, ranging from 400 nanometers to 100 nanometers. (Ch. 6)

uncertainty principle The idea quantified by Werner Heisenberg in 1927 that at a quantum scale, the location and velocity of an object can never be known at the same time, because quantum-scale measurement affects the object being measured. Specifically, "the error or uncertainty in the measurement of an object's position, times the error or uncertainty in that object's velocity, must be greater than a constant, *h*, divided by the object's mass." (Ch. 9)

unified field theory The general name for any theory in which fundamental forces are seen as different aspects of the same force. (Ch. 13)

uniform motion The motion of an object if it travels in a straight line at a constant speed. All other motions involve acceleration. (Ch. 2)

unsaturated In a lipid chain, a carbon atom bonded with two carbon atoms and one hydrogen atom, and with one kinked "double bond" with one of the adjacent carbon atoms. See *saturated*. (Ch. 22)

vacuole In plants, a cellular organelle that is responsible for waste storage. (Ch. 21)

valence electron An outer electron of an atom that can be exchanged or shared during chemical bonding. (Ch. 10)

valence The combining power of a given atom, determined by the number of electrons in an atom's outermost orbit. (Ch. 10)

van der Waals force A net attractive bond and weak force resulting from the polarization of electrically neutral atoms or molecules. (Ch. 10)

vascular plant The phylum of plants that have internal "plumbing" capable of carrying fluids from one part of the plant to another. (Ch. 20)

vector A quantity that measures rate and direction. Velocity and speed are examples of vectors because they are measured in units of distance and time. (Ch. 2)

velocity The distance an object travels divided by the time it takes to travel that distance, including the direction of travel. The velocity of a falling object is proportional to the length of time that it has been falling. (Ch. 2)

vertebrate A subphylum of chordates in which the nerves along the back are encased in bone. (Ch. 20)

vesicle The vehicle by which a particle moves around inside a cell; a tiny container formed from the cell membrane, and a particle with its receptor. (Ch. 21)

vestigial organ A bodily feature that serves no useful function at present and is compelling evidence for evolution. (Ch. 25)

virus A short length of RNA or DNA wrapped in a protein coating that fits cell receptors and replicates itself using the cell's machinery. (Ch. 23)

visible light Electromagnetic waves with a wavelength that can be interpreted by nerve receptors in the brain; wavelengths range from 700 nanometers for red light to 400 nanometers for violet light. (Ch. 6)

vitamin One of a host of complex organic molecules that, in small quantities, play an essential role in good health; for example, by mediating the body's chemical reactions. May be fat soluble and stored, or water soluble and not retained by the body. (Ch. 22)

volcanic rock Extrusive igneous rock that solidifies on Earth's surface. (Ch. 18)

volcano Places where subsurface molten rock breaks through to Earth's surface to form dramatic short-term changes in the landscape. (Ch. 17)

voltage The pressure produced by the energy source in an electric circuit, measured in volts. (Ch. 5)

***w* particle** A massive particle that, along with the *z* particle, mediates the weak interaction. (Ch. 13)

warm blooded Animals, such as birds and mammals, that have a four-chambered heart and can maintain a constant body temperature in any environment. (Ch. 20)

water-soluble vitamin A vitamin that can dissolve in water and is not retained by the body, including vitamins B and C. (Ch. 22)

watt A unit of measurement that is the expenditure of 1 joule of energy in 1 second. (Ch. 3)

wave A traveling disturbance that carries energy from one place to another without requiring matter to travel across the intervening distance. (Ch. 6)

wave energy The kinetic energy associated with different kinds of waves, such as kinetic energy possessed by large amounts of water in rapid motion, and electromagnetic radiation stored in changing electrical and magnetic fields. (Ch. 3)

wave mechanics Another term for quantum mechanics, indicating the dual (wave and particle) nature of quantum objects. (Ch. 9)

wavelength The distance between adjacent wave crests, the highest points of adjacent waves. (Ch. 6)

weather Daily changes in rainfall, temperature, amount of sunshine, and other variables resulting partly from the general circulation in the atmosphere, and partly from local disturbances and variations. (Ch. 18)

weathering A process in which rock wears away, for example by washing away particles, dissolving rock, or freezing in rock cracks. (Ch. 18)

weight The force of gravity on an object. (Ch. 2)

white dwarf A star that has a very low emission of energy but very high surface temperature; plots on the lower left-hand corner of the H-R diagram. (Ch. 14)

wind A weather variable that is caused by atmospheric convection—a process that redistributes heat. (Ch 18)

wind shear Violent air turbulence created from sudden downdrafts, which can cause an extremely dangerous condition near airports. (Ch. 18)

work The force that is exerted times the distance over which it is exerted; measured in joules in the metric system, in foot-pounds in the English. (Ch. 3)

X-rays High-frequency and high-energy electromagnetic waves that range in wavelength from 100 nanometers to 0.1 nanometer, used in medicine and industry. (Ch. 6)

***z* particle** A massive particle that, along with the *w* particle, mediates the weak interaction. (Ch. 13)

Index

F